R
V.27

D0131308

Contemporary Authors®

NEW REVISION SERIES

SANTA ANA PUBLIC LIBRARY

ISSN 0275-7176

R   O.E.
928
CON
1989
V-27
097.00
(428-2577)

Contemporary Authors®

**A Bio-Bibliographical Guide to
Current Writers in Fiction, General Nonfiction,
Poetry, Journalism, Drama, Motion Pictures,
Television, and Other Fields**

HAL MAY
JAMES G. LESNIAK
Editors

BRYAN RYAN
Associate Editor

THOMAS WILOCH
Senior Writer

NEW REVISION SERIES volume 27

Gale Research Inc. • BOOK TOWER • DETROIT, MICHIGAN 48226

STAFF

Hal May and James G. Lesniak, *Editors, New Revision Series*

Bryan Ryan, *Associate Editor*

Thomas Wiloch, *Senior Writer*

Marilyn K. Basel, Margaret Mazurkiewicz, and Michael E. Mueller, *Senior Assistant Editors*

Marian Gonsior, Sharon Malinowski, and Kenneth R. Shepherd, *Assistant Editors and Writers*

Melissa J. Gaiownik, Cheryl Gottler, Kevin S. Hile, Jani Prescott, Diane Telgen, and Michaela Swart Wilson, *Assistant Editors*

Jean W. Ross and Walter W. Ross, *Interviewers*

Mimi Reisel Gladstein, Joan Goldsworthy, William J. Harris, Anne Janette Johnson, Donna Olendorf, and Susan Salter, *Contributing Editors*

Linda Metzger, *Senior Editor, Contemporary Authors*

Mary Rose Bonk, *Research Supervisor*
Alysa I. Hunton, *Research Coordinator*
Jane Cousins-Clegg, *Assistant Research Coordinator*
Reginald A. Carlton, Andrew Guy Malonis, and Norma Sawaya, *Senior Research Assistants*
Shirley Gates, Clare Kinsman, Sharon McGilvray, and Tracey Head Turbett, *Research Assistants*

Copyright © 1989 by Gale Research Inc.

Library of Congress Catalog Card Number 81-640179
ISBN 0-8103-1981-0
ISSN 0275-7176

No part of this book may be reproduced in any form without permission in writing from the publisher, except by a reviewer who wishes to quote brief passages or entries in connection with a review written for inclusion in a magazine or newspaper. Printed in the United States.

Computerized photocomposition by
Typographics, Incorporated
Kansas City, Missouri

Contents

Indexing note: All *Contemporary Authors New Revision Series* entries are indexed in the *Contemporary Authors* cumulative index, which is bound into the back of even-numbered *Contemporary Authors* original volumes (blue and black cover with orange bands) and available separately as an offprint.

Authors and Media People
Featured in This Volume

Harriet S. Adams (American children's writer who died in 1982)—While running the literary syndicate founded by her father, Edward L. Stratemeyer (see below), Adams helped produce the "Nancy Drew," "Hardy Boys," and other Stratemeyer series under such pseudonyms as Franklin W. Dixon and Carolyn Keene. Entries for Dixon, Keene, and other collective pseudonyms of the Stratemeyer Syndicate also appear in this volume.

Woody Allen (American humorist, filmmaker, playwright, and actor)—Allen has become one of the world's best-recognized cinematic figures, in part because his personal vision pervades every aspect of his work. Among his films are the Academy Award winners "Annie Hall" and "Hannah and Her Sisters."

Martin Amis (British novelist and short story writer)—In such novels as *The Rachel Papers, Dead Babies, Success,* and *Other People: A Mystery Story,* Amis creates a fictional world defined by Swiftian excess and metropolitan satire. (Entry contains interview.)

Amiri Baraka (American playwright, poet, and essayist)—Formerly known as LeRoi Jones, Baraka is a prolific critic of American civilization and was a major figure in the 1960s black arts movement. His works include *The Dead Lecturer* and *Blues People: Negro Music in White America.*

Gwendolyn Brooks (American poet, novelist, and author of books for children)—Brooks was the first black recipient of the Pulitzer Prize, awarded to her in 1950 for the poetry collection *Annie Allen.*

Orson Scott Card (American science fiction and fantasy writer)—With *Ender's Game* and *Speaker for the Dead,* Card became the first author to win both the Hugo and Nebula awards—science fiction's highest honors—in consecutive years. (Entry contains interview.)

John Cheever (American short story writer and novelist who died in 1982)—Considered one of the finest American writers of the century, Cheever wrote of the despair afflicting ordinary lives in stories that earned him a Pulitzer Prize, an American Book Award, and a National Book Critics Circle Award. His daughter, Susan Cheever, also has an entry (with an interview) in this volume.

Samuel R. Delaney (American author of science fiction and criticism)—Delaney, acclaimed for his stylistic innovations within the science fiction genre, explores the American black experience, women's rights, and gay rights in works such as *Babel-17, The Einstein Intersection,* and the "Neveryon" series.

Rita Dove (American poet and short story writer)—Dove is best known for her Pulitzer Prize-winning work *Thomas and Beulah,* a sequence of poems loosely based on her grandparents' lives.

Loren D. Estleman (American novelist)—Although he is widely known for his hard-boiled mysteries set in Detroit, Estleman is also recognized for his westerns, especially *This Old Bill,* which garnered a Pulitzer Prize nomination. (Entry contains interview.)

Stephen Jay Gould (American geology professor and essayist)—Gould explains complex scientific theories in a fashion understandable to the lay reader, most notably in his American Book Award-winning *The Panda's Thumb* and the National Book Critics Circle Award-winning *The Mismeasure of Man.* (Entry contains interview.)

Bob Greene (American journalist)—A nationally syndicated columnist, Greene focuses on stories of human interest in his columns, some of which have been compiled in *American Beat, Good Morning Merry Sunshine,* and *Be True to Your School.* (Entry contains interview.)

Emily Hahn (American biographer, novelist, and author of autobiographies)—A biographer of Chiang Kai-shek and D. H. Lawrence, Hahn is better known for *China to Me,* an account of her life in that country during the Japanese invasion. (Entry contains interview.)

E. D. Hirsch, Jr. (American literary critic)—In his best-selling and highly controversial *Cultural Literacy: What Every American Needs to Know,* Hirsch argues that many Americans are ignorant of the shared terms and concepts of their society, and that this renders them incapable of full participation in society. (Entry contains interview.)

Martin Luther King, Jr. (American civil rights activist who died in 1968)—King received the Nobel Peace Prize in 1964 for encouraging non-violent social action in the struggle for racial justice. An entry for his wife, Coretta Scott King, also appears in this volume.

Brad Leithauser (American poet and novelist)—Leithauser is known as a meticulous poet whose use of formal structure sets him apart from many contemporary writers. His *Hundreds of Fireflies* and *Cats of the Temple* were both nominated for the National Book Critics Circle Award.

Toni Morrison (American novelist)—A gifted storyteller, Morrison is the critically acclaimed and best-selling author of such novels as *Song of Solomon,* which won the National Book Critics Circle Award, and *Beloved,* winner of the Pulitzer Prize.

Gloria Naylor (American novelist)—Recipient of an American Book Award for her first novel, *The Women of Brewster Place,* Naylor is respected for her realistic narratives and imaginative use of language.

Howard Nemerov (American poet, novelist, essayist, and short story writer)—Nemerov has captured numerous honors for his witty, philosophical verse, including a Pulitzer Prize, a National Book Award, and the title Poet Laureate of the United States. (Entry contains interview.)

Sally Quinn (American journalist and novelist)—A best-selling author in both fiction and nonfiction, Quinn provides a personal account of television network news in *We're Going to Make You a Star* and portrays in her novel *Regrets Only* the wheeling and dealing of Washington power brokers. (Entry contains interview.)

Ayn Rand (Russian-born American novelist and philosopher who died in 1982)—A rugged individualist and a believer in rational self-interest, Rand championed the capitalist system in such well-known novels as *The Fountainhead* and *Atlas Shrugged*.

Ntozake Shange (American poet, playwright, novelist, and educator)—Shange is the author of the internationally acclaimed "For Colored Girls Who Have Considered Suicide When the Rainbow Is Enuf," a play nominated for both Grammy and Emmy awards.

Wole Soyinka (Nigerian playwright, novelist, and poet)—Soyinka is a Nobel Prize winner often compared to Shakespeare and the classical Greek dramatists for his powerful portrayal of universal issues.

Edward L. Stratemeyer (American novelist and short story writer who died in 1930)—As founder and head of the literary syndicate bearing his name, Stratemeyer created such well-known juvenile characters as the Bobbsey Twins, Tom Swift, the Hardy Boys, and Nancy Drew.

Alice Walker (American poet, novelist, and short story writer)—Walker's novel *The Color Purple* won the Pulitzer Prize and American Book Award in 1983, and served as the basis for the popular motion picture. (Entry contains interview.)

Irving Wallace (American novelist and author of nonfiction)—Wallace is one of the five most popular living writers in English. Known for the extensive research that goes into his novels, he has also collaborated on nonfiction ventures with wife Sylvia, daughter Amy, and son David Wallechinsky, all of whom have sketches in this volume. (Entry contains interview.)

Jessamyn West (American novelist, short story writer, and author of nonfiction who died in 1984)—A prolific writer in several genres, West is remembered primarily for short stories that plumb rural American life in a sensitive yet unsentimental fashion. Her works include *The Friendly Persuasion* and *Cress Delahanty*.

Preface

The *Contemporary Authors New Revision Series* provides completely updated information on authors listed in earlier volumes of *Contemporary Authors (CA)*. Entries for active individual authors from *any* volume of *CA* may be included in a volume of the *New Revision Series*. The sketches appearing in *New Revision Series* Volume 27, for example, were selected from more than twenty previously published *CA* volumes.

As always, the most recent *Contemporary Authors* cumulative index continues to be the user's guide to the location of an individual author's listing.

Compilation Methods

The editors make every effort to secure information directly from the authors. Copies of all sketches in selected *CA* volumes published several years ago are routinely sent to the listees at their last-known addresses. Authors mark material to be deleted or changed and insert any new personal data, new affiliations, new writings, new work in progress, new sidelights, and new biographical/critical sources. All returns are assessed, more comprehensive research is done, if necessary, and those sketches requiring significant change are completely updated and published in the *New Revision Series*.

If, however, authors fail to reply or are now deceased, biographical dictionaries are checked for new information (a task made easier through the use of Gale's *Biography and Genealogy Master Index* and other Gale biographical indexes), as are bibliographical sources such as *Cumulative Book Index* and *The National Union Catalog*. Using data from such sources, revision editors select and revise nonrespondents' entries that need substantial updating. Sketches not personally reviewed by the biographees are marked with an asterisk (*) to indicate that these listings have been revised from secondary sources believed to be reliable, but they have not been personally reviewed for this edition by the authors sketched.

In addition, reviews and articles in major periodicals, lists of prestigious awards, and, particularly, requests from *CA* users are monitored so that writers on whom new information is in demand can be identified and revised listings prepared promptly.

Format

CA entries provide biographical and bibliographical information in an easy-to-use format. For example, individual paragraphs featuring such rubrics as "Addresses," "Career," and "Awards, Honors" ensure that a reader seeking specific information can quickly focus on the pertinent portion of an entry. In sketch sections headed "Writings," the title of each book, play, and other published or unpublished work appears on a separate line, clearly distinguishing one title from another. This same convenient bibliographical presentation is also featured in the "Biographical/Critical Sources" sections of sketches where individual book and periodical titles are listed on separate lines. *CA* readers can therefore quickly scan these often-lengthy bibliographies to find the titles they need.

Comprehensive Revision

All listings in this volume have been revised and/or augmented in various ways, though the amount and type of change vary with the author. In many instances, sketches are totally rewritten, and the resulting *New Revision Series* entries are often considerably longer than the authors' previous listings. Revised entries include additions of or changes in such information as degrees, mailing addresses, literary agents, career items, career-related and civic activities, memberships, awards, work in progress, and biographical/critical sources. They may also include extensive bibliographical additions and informative new sidelights.

Writers of Special Interest

CA's editors make every effort to include in each *New Revision Series* volume a substantial number of revised entries on active authors and media people of special interest to *CA*'s readers. Since the *New Revision Series* also includes sketches on noteworthy deceased writers, a significant amount of work on the part of *CA*'s editors goes into the revision of entries on important deceased authors. Some of the prominent writers, both living and deceased, whose sketches are contained in this volume are noted in the list on pages vii-viii headed Authors and Media People Featured in This Volume.

Exclusive Interviews

CA provides exclusive, primary information on certain authors in the form of interviews. Prepared specifically for *CA,* the never-before-published conversations presented in the section of the sketch headed "*CA* Interview" give users the opportunity to learn the authors' thoughts, in depth, about their craft. Subjects chosen for interviews are, the editors feel, authors who hold special interest for *CA*'s readers.

Authors and journalists in this volume whose sketches contain exclusive interviews are Martin Amis, Nathaniel Branden, Orson Scott Card, Susan Cheever, Loren D. Estleman, Stephen Jay Gould, Bob Greene, Emily Hahn, E. D. Hirsch, Jr., Kitty Kelley, Robert Jay Lifton, Howard Nemerov, Rosamunde Pilcher, Sally Quinn, Alice Walker, and Irving Wallace.

Contemporary Authors Autobiography Series

Designed to complement the information in *CA* original and revision volumes, the *Contemporary Authors Autobiography Series* provides autobiographical essays written by important current authors. Each volume contains from twenty to thirty specially commissioned autobiographies and is illustrated with numerous personal photographs supplied by the authors. Common topics of discussion for these authors include their motivations for writing, the people and experiences that shaped their careers, the rewards they derive from their work, and their impressions of the current literary scene.

Autobiographies included in the series can be located through both the *CA* cumulative index and the *Contemporary Authors Autobiography Series* cumulative index, which lists not only personal names but also titles of works, geographical names, subjects, and schools of writing.

Contemporary Authors Bibliographical Series

The *Contemporary Authors Bibliographical Series* is a comprehensive survey of writings by and about the most important authors since World War II in the United States and abroad. Each volume concentrates on a specific genre and nationality and features approximately ten major writers. Series entries, which complement the information in other *CA* volumes, consist of three parts: a primary bibliography that lists works written by the author, a secondary bibliography that lists works about the author, and a bibliographical essay that thoroughly analyzes the merits and deficiencies of major critical and scholarly works.

These bibliographies can be located through both the *CA* cumulative index and the *Contemporary Authors Bibliographical Series* cumulative author index. A cumulative critic index, citing critics discussed in the bibliographical essays, also appears in each *Bibliographical Series* volume.

CA Numbering System

Occasionally questions arise about the *CA* numbering system. Despite numbers like "97-100" and "126," the entire *CA* series consists of only 92 physical volumes with the publication of *CA New Revision Series* Volume 27. The following information notes changes in the numbering system, as well as in cover design, to help users better understand the organization of the entire *CA* series.

CA **First Revisions**	• 1-4R through 41-44R (11 books) *Cover:* Brown with black and gold trim. There will be no further *First Revisions* because revised entries are now being handled exclusively through the more efficient *New Revision Series* mentioned below.
CA **Original Volumes**	• 45-48 through 97-100 (14 books) *Cover:* Brown with black and gold trim. • 101 through 126 (26 books) *Cover:* Blue and black with orange bands. The same as previous *CA* original volumes but with a new, simplified numbering system and new cover design.

CA New Revision Series	• *CANR*-1 through *CANR*-27 (27 books) *Cover:* Blue and black with green bands. Includes only sketches requiring extensive change; **sketches are taken from any previously published *CA* volume.**
CA Permanent Series	• *CAP*-1 and *CAP*-2 (2 books) *Cover:* Brown with red and gold trim. There will be no further *Permanent Series* volumes because revised entries are now being handled exclusively through the more efficient *New Revision Series* mentioned above.
CA Autobiography Series	• *CAAS*-1 through *CAAS*-9 (9 books) *Cover:* Blue and black with pink and purple bands. Presents specially commissioned autobiographies by leading contemporary writers to complement the information in *CA* original and revision volumes.
CA Bibliographical Series	• *CABS*-1 through *CABS*-3 (3 books) *Cover:* Blue and black with blue bands. Provides comprehensive bibliographical information on published works by and about major modern authors.

Retaining *CA* Volumes

As new volumes in the series are published, users often ask which *CA* volumes, if any, can be discarded. The Volume Update Chart on page xiii is designed to assist users in keeping their collections as complete as possible. All volumes in the left column of the chart should be retained to have the most complete, up-to-date coverage possible; volumes in the right column can be discarded if the appropriate replacements are held.

Cumulative Index Should Always Be Consulted

The key to locating an individual author's listing is the *CA* cumulative index bound into the back of even-numbered original volumes (and available separately as an offprint). Since the *CA* cumulative index provides access to *all* entries in the *CA* series, the latest cumulative index should always be consulted to find the specific volume containing a listee's original or most recently revised sketch.

Those authors whose entries appear in the *New Revision Series* are listed in the *CA* cumulative index with the designation **CANR-** in front of the specific volume number. For the convenience of those who do not have *New Revision Series* volumes, the cumulative index also notes the specific earlier volumes of *CA* in which the sketch appeared. Below is a sample index citation for an author whose revised entry appears in a *New Revision Series* volume.

> Clavell, James (duMaresq) 1925- CANR-26
> Earlier sketch in CA 25-28R
> See also CLC 6, 25

For the most recent *CA* information on Clavell, users should refer to Volume 26 of the *New Revision Series*, as designated by "CANR-26"; if that volume is unavailable, refer to *CA* 25-28 First Revision, as indicated by "Earlier sketch in CA 25-28R," for his 1977 listing. (And if *CA* 25-28 First Revision is unavailable, refer to *CA* 25-28, published in 1971, for Clavell's original listing.)

Sketches not eligible for inclusion in a *New Revision Series* volume because the biographee or a revision editor has verified that no significant change is required will, of course, be available in previously published *CA* volumes. Users should always consult the most recent *CA* cumulative index to determine the location of these authors' entries.

For the convenience of *CA* users, the *CA* cumulative index also includes references to all entries in these related Gale literary series: *Authors in the News, Black Writers, Children's Literature Review, Concise Dictionary of American Literary Biography, Contemporary Literary Criticism, Dictionary of Literary Biography, Short Story Criticism, Something About the Author, Something About the Author Autobiography Series, Twentieth-Century Literary Criticism,* and *Yesterday's Authors of Books For Children.*

Acknowledgments

The editors wish to thank Judith S. Baughman and Armida Gilbert for their assistance with copyediting.

Suggestions Are Welcome

The editors welcome comments and suggestions from users on any aspect of the *CA* series. If readers would like to suggest authors whose *CA* entries should appear in future volumes of the *New Revision Series,* they are cordially invited to write: The Editors, *Contemporary Authors New Revision Series,* Book Tower, Detroit, MI 48226; or, call toll-free at 1-800-521-0707.

Volume Update Chart

IF YOU HAVE:	YOU MAY DISCARD:
1-4 First Revision (1967)	1 (1962) 2 (1963) 3 (1963) 4 (1963)
5-8 First Revision (1969)	5-6 (1963) 7-8 (1963)
Both 9-12 First Revision (1974) AND *Contemporary Authors Permanent Series,* Volume 1 (1975)	9-10 (1964) 11-12 (1965)
Both 13-16 First Revision (1975) AND *Contemporary Authors Permanent Series,* Volumes 1 and 2 (1975, 1978)	13-14 (1965) 15-16 (1966)
Both 17-20 First Revision (1976) AND *Contemporary Authors Permanent Series,* Volumes 1 and 2 (1975, 1978)	17-18 (1967) 19-20 (1968)
Both 21-24 First Revision (1977) AND *Contemporary Authors Permanent Series,* Volumes 1 and 2 (1975, 1978)	21-22 (1969) 23-24 (1970)
Both 25-28 First Revision (1977) AND *Contemporary Authors Permanent Series,* Volume 2 (1978)	25-28 (1971)
Both 29-32 First Revision (1978) AND *Contemporary Authors Permanent Series,* Volume 2 (1978)	29-32 (1972)
Both 33-36 First Revision (1978) AND *Contemporary Authors Permanent Series,* Volume 2 (1978)	33-36 (1973)
37-40 First Revision (1979)	37-40 (1973)
41-44 First Revision (1979)	41-44 (1974)
45-48 (1974) 49-52 (1975) ↓　　↓ 126　(1989)	NONE: These volumes will not be superseded by corresponding revised volumes. Individual entries from these and all other volumes appearing in the left column of this chart will be revised and included in the *New Revision Series.*
Volumes in the *Contemporary Authors New Revision Series*	NONE: The *New Revision Series* does not replace any single volume of *CA.* All volumes appearing in the left column of this chart must be retained to have information on all authors in the series.

Contemporary Authors

NEW REVISION SERIES

* Indicates that a listing has been revised from secondary sources believed to be reliable but has not been personally reviewed for this edition by the author sketched.

AASENG, Rolf E(dward)   1923-

PERSONAL: Surname is pronounced *Aw*-sing; born November 28, 1923, in McIntosh, Minn.; son of Ingeman and Sunniva (Scheie) Aaseng; married Viola Anderson, March 19, 1948; children: Lenore, Norman, Nathan, Grant, Scott. *Education:* Concordia College, Moorhead, Minn., B.A., 1948; Luther Theological Seminary, St. Paul, Minn., B.Th., 1950; New York Theological Seminary, S.T.M., 1958.

ADDRESSES: Office—Lutheran Theological Seminary, Umpumulo, South Africa.

CAREER: Ordained to ministry, 1951. Evangelical Lutheran Church, Minneapolis, Minn., publicity director, 1949-51; Calvary Lutheran Church, Park Rapids, Minn., pastor, 1951-57; *Lutheran Teacher,* Minneapolis, editor, 1958-60; *Lutheran Standard,* Minneapolis, associate editor, beginning 1960; curriculum editor for American Lutheran Church, 1972-79; currently a teacher at Lutheran Theological Seminary, Umpumulo, South Africa. Lutheran Church Library Association, president, chairman of board of directors, 1966-70; chairman of St. Louis Park Human Rights Commission, 1972-74. *Military service:* U.S. Army, 1943-46.

WRITINGS:

Anyone Can Teach (They Said), Augsburg, 1964.
The Sacred Sixty-Six, Augsburg, 1966.
Blessed to Be a Blessing, American Lutheran Church Women, 1969.
God Is Great, God Is Good, Augsburg, 1971.
Jesus Loves Me, This I Know, Augsburg, 1972.
Sense and Nonsense: A Word for Teens, Baker Book, 1976.
Basic Christian Teaching, Augsburg, 1982.
When Jesus Comes Again: What the Bible Says, Augsburg, 1984.
What's the Score?: Devotions for Sports Lovers, Baker Book, 1987.*

*   *   *

ABBOTT, Manager Henry
   See STRATEMEYER, Edward L.

ADACHI, Barbara (Curtis)   1924-
   (Catherine Anthony)

PERSONAL: Surname rhymes with "apache"; born July 16, 1924, in Harbin, Manchuria, China; daughter of John Libby (a banker) and Alice (Perkins) Curtis; married James Shogo Adachi (a lawyer), June 1, 1949; children: Catherine Anthony Adachi Rocher, Daniel Curtis. *Education:* Smith College, B.A., 1945. *Religion:* Episcopalian.

ADDRESSES: Home—19-3, Akasaka 6-chome, Minato-ku, Tokyo, Japan.

CAREER: Writer and lecturer on Japanese crafts and traditional theater, and advisor on Japanese culture for film projects. *Mainichi Daily News,* Tokyo, Japan, author of regular columns "Hands of Japan" (under pseudonym Catherine Anthony) and "Something Different," 1971-81; *Asahi Evening News,* Tokyo, author of weekly column "Adventures in Food," 1983—. Lecturer on Bunraku at Yale University School of Drama, 1987.

MEMBER: International House (member of board of directors), College Women's Association of Japan, Japan American Society, Asiatic Society of Japan.

AWARDS, HONORS: Smith College Medal, 1986.

WRITINGS:

The Living Treasures of Japan, Kodansha International, 1973.
The Voices and Hands of Bunraku, Kodansha International, 1978.
Backstage at Bunraku, Weatherhill, 1985.

Contributor of articles to numerous periodicals, including *Craft Horizons, Fiber Arts, Wall Street Journal, Imperial,* and *Okura Lantern.*

WORK IN PROGRESS: Essays and reminiscences of life in China, Japan, and the United States.

SIDELIGHTS: Barbara Adachi wrote *CA* about her book *The Voices and Hands of Bunraku:* "Writing about the people of Bunraku, the traditional puppet theater of Japan, was particularly satisfying as I had known the men (and one woman) of the Osaka Bunraku Troupe for a decade. I wanted to write about the fact that even the puppet theater is made up of people, and that the unseen ones—the prop man, the wig master, the head carver, etc.—are vital. The fascinating thing was discovering that each person, whether puppeteer or costume director, head repairer or musician—each one felt the troupe could not get on without him—that's what makes Bunraku so unusual: each member of the troupe gives his all.

''My book came out in Japanese also and was considered unusual because of the personal approach and the inclusion of 'those who are unseen.' Since then, similar approaches have been used in many articles in the vernacular. I'm glad that at last interest in Bunraku on the part of the Japanese is increasing and that the rest of the world is starting to appreciate the fascination and artistry of this almost 400 year old dramatic art.''

*   *   *

ADAMS, Anne H(utchinson)   1935-1980

PERSONAL: Born August 25, 1935, in Hamilton, Miss.; daughter of James Perry and Lois (Wright) Hutchinson; married Charles Floyd Adams, June 27, l959 (divorced); children: Charles Floyd, Jr. *Education:* Attended Mississippi State University, 1952-53; Mississippi State College for Women (now Mississippi University for Women), B.S., 1956; Duke University, M.Ed., 1957; University of Mississippi, Ed.D., 1966; University of Georgia, additional study, 1967-68. *Religion:* Presbyterian.

ADDRESSES: Office—Department of Education, Duke University, Durham, N.C. 27708.

CAREER: Elementary teacher in Atlanta, Ga., 1957-59, Tampa, Fla., 1959-60, Hattiesburg, Miss., 1960-61, and Oxford, Miss., 1961-64; Muscogee County School District, Columbus, Ga., director of elementary education, 1965-67; Leflore County School District, Greeenwood, Miss., director of education, 1967-68; University of Mississippi, Oxford, inservice education specialist, 1968, curriculum and research specialist at Special Education Service Center, 1969; University of Texas at Austin, assistant professor of special education and associate director of training, Exemplary Early Childhood Education Centers for Handicapped Children, 1969-71; Duke University, Durham, N.C., associate professor, 1970-73, professor of education, 1973-80, director of Reading Center, 1971-80, director of Writing Institute and of Leadership Institute on Improvement of Preservice and Inservice Education in Reading and Language Arts, member of advisory board of preschool. Visiting professor at University of Mississippi, 1964, and University of Georgia, 1966. Member of President of the United States Committee on Mental Retardation. Member of national advisory board, J. B. Lippincott Co. Consultant on special education to universities and school systems in a number of states.

MEMBER: International Reading Association, National Education Association, Council for Exceptional Children, American Association for Higher Education, American Association of University Women, American Association of University Professors, Association of College Professors of Reading (president, 1971-73; member of board of directors, 1973-80), Association for Children with Learning Disabilities (member of advisory board of Durham chapter), North Carolina Association of University Professors of Reading (past president), Pi Gamma Mu, Delta Kappa Pi, Delta Kappa Epsilon, Alpha Delta Kappa, Chi Omega.

AWARDS, HONORS: Named Outstanding Young Woman in America, 1967; outstanding professor award from Duke University, 1971-72.

WRITINGS:

(With S. Alan Cohen) *The Random House Reading Program*, Random House, 1969.

Plan Readiness Experience Program (multi-media), Programmed Learning Aids Nations, 1970.

The Reading Clinic, Macmillan, 1970.

Sounds for Me, Leswing Communications, 1971.

Learning Abilities, Macmillan, 1972.

Threshold Learning Abilities for Children with Handicaps, Macmillan, 1972.

(Author of introduction) Richard Greene, *Forgotten Children: Techniques in Teaching the Mentally Retarded*, Leswing Communications, 1972.

Pre-and Post-Instructional Development Audits: An Evaluation Prototype for Early Education, Programmed Learning Aids National, 1972.

Prep Progress Audits: An Evaluation Prototype for Early Education, Programmed Learning Aids National, 1972.

The Clock Struck One, Leswing Communications, 1973.

(Contributor) Philip D. Vairo and Robert J. Knajewski, editors, *Learning and Teaching in the Elementary School*, Scarecrow, 1974.

(With Susanne A. Goldberg) *Practical Mathematics Program*, Benefic, Volume I: *Addition*, 1975, Volume II: *Subtraction*, 1976, Volume IV: *Division*, 1977.

(With Charles R. Coble and Paul B. Hounshell) *Mainstreaming Language Arts and Social Studies*, Goodyear Publishing, 1977.

(With Coble and Houndshell) *Mainstreaming Science and Mathematics*, Goodyear Publishing, 1977.

A Book for Parents and Other Important People, Leswing Communications, 1977.

(With Anne Flowers and Elsa E. Woods) *Reading for Survival in Today's Society*, two volumes, Goodyear Publishing, 1978.

''*SUCCESS IN READING AND WRITING*'' SERIES

Success in Beginning Reading and Writing: The Basal Concept of the Future, Goodyear Publishing, 1977.

(With Judith Connors) . . . *Kindergarten Reading and Writing: The Readiness Concept of the Future*, Goodyear Publishing, 1978.

(With Helen Cappleman) . . . *Reading and Writing, Grade Two*, Goodyear Publishing, 1978.

. . . *Beginning Reading and Writing, Grade Three*, Goodyear Publishing, 1978.

. . . *Reading and Writing, Grade Four*, Goodyear Publishing, 1982.

(With Patricia Horne Sumner and Jean F. Bernholz) . . . *Reading and Writing, Grade Five: The Textbook Concept of the Future*, Goodyear Publishing, 1982.

(With Elisabeth L. Bebensee) . . . *Reading and Writing, Grade Six*, Goodyear Publishing, 1983.

AUDIO-VISUAL MATERIALS

''A Look at You'' (four films and teacher's guide), produced by Educational Communications, 1971.

''Your Self-Image,'' produced by Educational Communications, 1971.

''Are You Listening?,'' produced by Educational Communications, l971.

"Litter, Litter Everywhere," produced by Educational Communications, 1971.

Also author of other materials which include video tapes, audio cassette tapes, transparencies, and spirit duplicator masters.

OTHER

Also author of two skills reinforcement books to accompany *Exploring Lands in the Sea*, published by Leswing Communications, 1971. Contributor of numerous articles to professional journals. Member of advisory boards, *Mini-Page*, Universal Press Syndicate, 1977-80; member of editorial advisory board, *Reading Teacher*, 1978-80. Manuscript consultant to several journals, dictionaries, and books, including *American Educational Research Journal*, *Webster's New World Dictionary*, and *Helping Students Cope with the Language of Every Subject*.

WORK IN PROGRESS: A first grade evaluation program, for Leswing Communications.*

*   *   *

ADAMS, Harriet S(tratemeyer)   1892(?)-1982

PERSONAL: Born December 3, 1892 (some sources say December 6, 1894), in Newark, N.J.; suffered a fatal heart attack while watching "The Wizard of Oz" on television for the first time, March 27, 1982, in Pottersville, N.J.; daughter of Edward L. (a writer of children's books and founder of the Stratemeyer Syndicate) and Magdalene (Van Camp) Stratemeyer; married Russell Vroom Adams (an investment banker), 1915 (died, 1966); children: Russell, Jr. (deceased), Patricia Adams Harr, Camilla Adams McClave, Edward Stratemeyer Adams. *Education:* Graduated from Wellesley College, 1914.

CAREER/WRITINGS: Senior partner in Stratemeyer Syndicate, 1930-82; designer, plotter, editor, reviser, and writer of series books for children under a variety of pseudonyms, including volumes in the "Tom Swift" series (as Victor Appleton), the "Tom Swift Jr." series (as Victor Appleton II), the "Barton Books for Girls" (as May Hollis Barton), the "Hardy Boys" series (as Franklin W. Dixon), the "Bobbsey Twins" series (as Laura Lee Hope), the "Dana Girls" and "Nancy Drew" series (as Carolyn Keene), the "Linda Craig" series (as Ann Sheldon), the "Honey Bunch" series (as Helen Louise Thorndyke), and many others. Also taught Sunday school, founded a woman's club magazine, chaired a college's fundraising work for New Jersey, worked for two years as a Republican county committeewoman, and worked with the Red Cross and Girl Scouts. Endower of Harriet Stratemeyer Adams Professor of Juvenile Literature chair in literature department at Wellesley College.

MEMBER: League of American Pen Women, New Jersey Woman's Press Club, New Jersey Wellesley Club (founder and first president; class treasurer), New York Wellesley Club, Zonta, Business and Professional Women's Club.

AWARDS, HONORS: Certificate of appreciation, New Jersey Congress of Parents and Teachers, 1978; honorary doctorate, Kean College, and Upsala College, both 1978; Annual Alumnae Achievement Award, Wellesley College, 1978; Mother of the Year citation, National Mother's Day Committee, 1979; special Edgar Award, Mystery Writers of America, 1979, for the "Nancy Drew" series; two citations from New Jersey Institute of Technology, for the "Nancy Drew" series and *The*

Nancy Drew Cookbook; certificate of merit from American Red Cross.

SIDELIGHTS: "Sweetness and virtue always triumphed as long as Harriet Stratemeyer Adams had any say in such matters, but now she is gone, and it's all over for Nancy Drew, the Hardy Boys, the Bobbsey Twins and Tom Swift Jr," wrote Louis Cook in the *Detroit Free Press*. Adams and her sister Edna Squier took over the management of the Stratemeyer Syndicate after the death of their father Edward Stratemeyer in 1930, and continued to produce hundreds of juvenile mystery and adventure stories each year. Although Squier took no operative role in the Syndicate after 1942, Adams remained an active partner until her death. "For 52 years," reported *Washington Post* contributor Curt Suplee, ". . . she shaped the imaginations of countless millions of American children through books whose gee-whiz appeal our cynical age cannot stale nor changing customs wither."

"Mrs. Adams was the indefatigable inheritor of a tradition of writing for children in ways that dealt with adventure without danger," Cook continued. Publishing techniques used by the Syndicate had been developed by Edward Stratemeyer. He created detailed outlines of series volumes, mailed them out to independent contract writers, and finally edited the manuscripts with the assistance of a skeleton staff as the writers sent them in. He also required the contract writers to sign pledges not to reveal their authorship, in "the belief that if the general public were to learn that there was no Carolyn Keene, Franklin W. Dixon, Laura Lee Hope et al," disclosed Ernie Kelly in the *Yellowback Library*, "they might become disillusioned with series books and stop buying them."

These pledges form part of the reason that identifying authors who wrote for the Stratemeyer Syndicate is so difficult. Thanks to various biographies and reminiscences, however, readers now know that Syndicate veteran Howard R. Garis wrote many of the original "Tom Swift" books, that his wife Lilian composed numerous volumes under the pseudonym Laura Lee Hope, that Canadian Leslie McFarlane originated the "Hardy Boys," and that Mildred Augustine Wirt Benson, a newspaper reporter from Toledo, Ohio, scripted the early "Nancy Drew" mysteries, all at Stratemeyer's request. Another difficulty lies in the thorough editing and rewriting the manuscripts often received when they reached the Syndicate. Occasionally this amounted to total rewriting; indeed, in the late 1950s and early 1960s, the early volumes of the "Hardy Boys," "Nancy Drew," and the "Bobbsey Twins" series were all extensively revised under Adams's supervision, which may be why she later claimed to have written all the "Nancy Drews."

Adams attempted to carry on her father's system with Garis's assistance, but outside pressures—economic problems during the Depression, paper shortages during World War II—caused the decline of many once-popular series. Before the end of the Second World War, reported Kelly, the Syndicate had "ceased publication of over 20 ongoing series including . . . Tom Swift, Don Sturdy, Bomba, Ted Scott, the X Bar X Boys, Garry Grayson, Ruth Fielding, Betty Gordon, Six Little Bunkers, Bunny Brown, and the Outdoor Girls." "During the same time period," he added, "only two new series were successfully introduced."

Change came in the late 1940s and early '50s, when Adams began to make additions to the Syndicate's cast of characters. She introduced Tom Swift, Jr., son of the original Tom Swift, in 1954, and brought back Kay Tracey and the Dana Girls, two series featuring girl detectives. Over the next twenty years

Adams and Syndicate partner Andrew Svenson launched several new series, but few of them lasted for more than four or five volumes. The rewriting project on the Bobbseys, Hardys, and Nancy Drew was much more successful, modernizing these characters and making them more appealing to the post-war generation. Beginning in the 1970s, Adams capitalized on the popularity of these characters, releasing a flood of spin-off volumes ranging from *The Nancy Drew Cookbook: Clues to Good Cooking* to *The Hardy Boys' Who-Dunnit Mystery Book*. She was working on several series-related ghost stories when she died.

Adams's personal favorite among the series characters was Nancy Drew. Although the manuscripts of Nancy's early adventures were written by Mildred Benson, Adams undoubtedly had the greatest influence on the girl sleuth's later career. She supervised Nancy very carefully, doing much of the background research for her adventures and producing long, complex, heavily-detailed outlines when she could not write the stories personally. According to *People* magazine, she referred to Nancy as "my fictional daughter," adding, "And my fictional daughter always does and says what I tell her to."

Dissatisfied with Grosset & Dunlap's royalty payments and their reluctance to promote Syndicate characters, in 1979 Adams negotiated with Simon & Schuster to produce new Hardy Boys, Nancy Drew, and Bobbsey Twins adventures in paperback. In 1984, after Adams's death, Simon & Schuster bought the Syndicate, and presently controls the rights to all Syndicate characters. For more information see the sketches in this volume for James Duncan Lawrence, Edward L. Stratemeyer, Andrew E. Svenson, and for the following pseudonyms: Victor Appleton, Victor Appleton II, Franklin W. Dixon, Laura Lee Hope, Carolyn Keene, Ann Sheldon, and Helen Louise Thorndyke.

BIOGRAPHICAL/CRITICAL SOURCES:

BOOKS

Authors in the News, Volume 2, Gale, 1976.
Billman, Carol, *The Secret of the Stratemeyer Syndicate: Nancy Drew, the Hardy Boys, and the Million Dollar Fiction Factory*, Ungar, 1986.
Prager, Arthur, *Rascals at Large; or, The Clue in the Old Nostalgia*, Doubleday, 1971.
Winn, Dilys, compiler, *Murder Ink: The Mystery Reader's Companion*, Workman Publishing, 1977.

PERIODICALS

Detroit Free Press, October 10, 1975, March 31, 1982.
Detroit News, February 17, 1980.
Fort Lauderdale News, April 23, 1975.
New York Times, April 4, 1968, March 27, 1977, April 4, 1982.
New York Times Book Review, May 4, 1975.
Publishers Weekly, March 5, 1979, May 7, 1979, May 14, 1979, May 9, 1982, August 17, 1984.
Saturday Review, July 10, 1971.
Time, April 28, 1980, June 30, 1980.
Wall Street Journal, January 15, 1975.
Washington Post, March 30, 1982.
Yellowback Library, July/August, 1983, September/October, 1983, November/December, 1983, January/February, 1986, October, 1988, December, 1988.

OBITUARIES:

PERIODICALS

AB Bookman's Weekly, April 12, 1982.

Chicago Tribune, March 30, 1982.
Detroit Free Press, March 30, 1982.
Newsweek, April 5, 1982.
New York Times, March 29, 1982.
Publishers Weekly, April 9, 1982.
School Library Journal, May, 1982.
Time, April 12, 1982.
Times (London), March 30, 1982.
Washington Post, March 30, 1982.*

—*Sketch by Kenneth R. Shepherd*

*　　*　　*

ADELMANN, Frederick J(oseph) 1915-

PERSONAL: Born February 18, 1915, in Norwood, Mass.; son of Frederick Michael and Helen Margaret (Casey) Adelmann. *Education:* Boston College, A.B., 1937, M.A., 1942; Weston College, Ph.L., 1942, S.T.L., 1948; St. Louis University, Ph.D., 1955. *Politics:* Democrat.

ADDRESSES: Home—140 Commonwealth Ave., Newton, Mass. 02167. *Office*—Department of Philosophy, Boston College, Chestnut Hill, Mass. 02167.

CAREER: Ordained Roman Catholic priest of the Society of Jesus (Jesuit), 1947; Boston College, Chestnut Hill, Mass., instructor in mathematics and physics in Army Specialized Training Program, 1942-44; St. Louis University, St. Louis, Mo., teaching fellow in philosophy, 1950-54; Boston College, assistant professor, 1955-68, associate professor, 1968-70, professor of philosophy, 1970—, chairman of department, 1955-65. Lecturer in philosophy, Weston College, 1960-62.

MEMBER: American Association of University Professors, American Philosophical Association, Jesuit Philosophical Association, Realist Society.

AWARDS, HONORS: L.H.D. from Boston College, 1985.

WRITINGS:

From Dialogue to Epilogue, Nijhoff, 1967.
(With J. M. Bochenski and others) *A Guide to Marxism*, Swallow Press, 1972.

EDITOR

The Quest for the Absolute, Nijhoff, 1968.
Demythologizing Marxism, Nijhoff, 1970.
Authority, Nijhoff, 1974.
Philosophical Investigation in the USSR, Nijhoff, 1975.
Soviet Philosophy Revisited, Boston College, 1977.
Contemporary Chinese Philosophy, Nijhoff, 1982.

*　　*　　*

ADLER, Freda 1934-

PERSONAL: Born November 21, 1934, in Philadelphia, Pa.; daughter of David R. (an industrialist) and Lucia Green (DeWolfson) Schaffer; married Herbert M. Adler (a physician), June 18, 1955 (divorced, 1975); married Gerhard O. W. Mueller (chief of United Nations Crime Section), February 29, 1976; children: (first marriage) Mark, Jill, Nancy. *Education:* University of Pennsylvania, B.A., 1956, M.A., 1968, Ph.D., 1971.

ADDRESSES: Home—30 Waterside Plaza, Apt. 37J, New York, N.Y. 10010. *Office*—School of Criminal Justice, Rutgers University, 53 Washington St., Newark, N.J. 07102.

CAREER: Temple University, Philadelphia, Pa., instructor in psychiatry, 1971, research coordinator at Addiction Science Center, 1971-72; Medical College of Pennsylvania, Philadelphia, assistant professor of psychiatry and research director of Section on Drug and Alcohol Abuse, 1972-74; Rutgers University, Newark, N.J., associate professor, 1974-78, professor of criminal justice, 1978-84, distinguished professor, 1984—. Member of faculty of National College of State Judiciary, 1973—, and of National College of Criminal Defense Lawyers and Public Defenders, 1976; visiting fellow at Yale University, 1976. Member of board of directors of Institute for the Continuous Study of Man, 1974—. Consultant to National Commission on Marijuana and Drug Abuse.

MEMBER: International Association of Penal Law, American Sociological Association, American Society of Criminology (executive counselor, 1971-72, 1974-75), University of Pennsylvania Alumnae Association (member of board of directors, 1974-77).

AWARDS, HONORS: Herbert Bloch Award from American Society of Criminology, 1972; Ancient Order of Chamorri (Guam); Beccaria Medal from Deutsche Kriminologische Gesellschaft, 1979.

WRITINGS:

(Editor with husband, Gerhard O. W. Mueller) *Politics, Crime and the International Scene: An Interamerican Focus,* North-South Center for Technical and Cultural Interchange, 1972.
(With Arthur D. Moffett, Frederick B. Glaser, and others) *The Treatment of Drug Abuse in Pennsylvania,* Governor's Council on Drug and Alcohol Abuse, 1973.
(Contributor) William White, Jr., and Ronald F. Albano, editors, *North American Symposium on Drugs and Drug Abuse,* North American Publishing, 1974.
(With Moffett, Glaser, and others) *A Systems Approach to Drug Treatment,* Dorrance, 1974.
(With Moffett, Glaser, and Diana Horvitz) *Medical Lollipop, Junkie Insulin, or What?: Patient and Staff Views of the Chemotherapy of Addiction,* Dorrance, 1974.
(With Stephanie W. Greenberg) *Crime and Addiction: An Empirical Analysis of the Literature, 1920-1973* (booklet), Governor's Council on Drug and Alcohol Abuse, c. 1974.
(With Herbert M. Adler and Hoag Levins) *Sisters in Crime: The Rise of the New Female Criminal,* McGraw, 1975.
(Editor with Rita James) *The Criminology of Deviant Women,* Houghton, 1978.
(Editor) *The Incidence of Female Criminality in the Contemporary World,* New York University Press, 1981.
Nations Not Obsessed with Crime, Fred B. Rothman, 1983.
(With Mueller) *Outlaws of the Ocean: The Complete Book of Contemporary Crime on the High Seas,* Morrow, 1985.
(Editor with William S. Laufer) *Advances in Criminological Theory* (multi-volume work), Volume 1, Transaction Books, 1987.
Understanding Criminology, McGraw, 1990.

Contributor to criminology, sociology, and psychiatry journals, law and medical journals, and *Washington Post.* Member of editorial board of *Criminology: An Interdisciplinary Journal,* 1971-73; consulting editor of *Journal of Research in Crime and Delinquency,* 1977, and *Journal of Criminal Law and Criminology,* 1982.

SIDELIGHTS: Freda Adler writes: "Several years ago while working for the government as an evaluator of drug and alcohol treatment centers it was part of my task to interview addicts in treatment. One of the important areas of concern was in each individual's arrest record. After studying hundreds of these profiles, I became aware that there was a change in the types of crime in which females were involved. No longer content with shoplifting and prostitution they were turning to crimes such as robbery and burglary. This realization led me to a three-year research study involving visits with inmates, administrators, police officers, judges, etc. These changing female crime patterns and their relationship to women's emancipation became the subject of *Sisters in Crime.* Since that time I have been studying female criminality and lecturing on the topic in many countries, including Mexico, Venezuela, Brazil, Canada, Switzerland, Germany, Finland, Poland, Hungary, Guam, Australia, Ivory Coast, and Saudi Arabia.''

AVOCATIONAL INTERESTS: Horseback riding, skiing, sailing.

* * *

AHERN, Emily M.
  See MARTIN, Emily

* * *

AIRD, Catherine
  See McINTOSH, Kinn Hamilton

* * *

ALBERT, Linda   1939-

PERSONAL: Born November 15, 1939, in New York, N.Y.; daughter of J. Louis (in advertising) and Sadie (Korn) Albert; married Byron G. Eakin, September 24, 1988; children: (previous marriage) Ken, Judith M. Rachel, Steven. *Education:* State University of New York at Cortland, B.A., 1968, M.S., 1972; William Lyon University, Ph.D. (psychology), 1984; graduate study at University of Arizona, 1976-77.

ADDRESSES: Home—5238 Bon Vivant Dr. #74, Tampa, Fla. 33603.

CAREER: Teacher at public schools in Ithaca, N.Y., 1968-72, teacher specialist in diagnosis and remediation of behavioral and learning problems, 1972-81; Family Education Center of Florida, Tampa, director, 1982—. Adjunct professor at Elmira College, 1978-86. Presents workshops. Spokesperson for teacher and parent education; has appeared on local and nationally syndicated television programs. Educational consultant.

MEMBER: North American Society of Adlerian Psychology, National Association for Humanistic Psychology, American Personnel and Guidance Association, Florida Network of Parent Educators.

WRITINGS:

Coping With Kids (Better Homes and Gardens Book Club selection), Dutton, 1982.
Coping With Your Child's Education, Dutton, 1984.
(With Elaine Shimberg) *Coping With Kids and Vacation,* Ballantine, 1986.
Strengthening Stepfamilies, American Guidance Service, 1986.
Quality Parenting, American Guidance Service, 1987.
Cooperative Discipline, American Guidance Service, in press.

Also author, with Elizabeth Einstein, of booklet series, "Stepfamily Living," 1983. Author of "Coping With Kids," a bi-weekly column syndicated by Gannett News Service, 1979—. Contributor of columns and articles to magazines, including *Family Magazine, Working Mother,* and *Parents.*

SIDELIGHTS: Linda Albert told *CA:* "My involvement in publishing and parent education began the day my first child was born. Like most American parents, I was totally untrained and unprepared for parenthood. The births of two additional children reaffirmed my conviction that today's parents lack information on how to cope with kids effectively.

"In 1969, I began working in the Ithaca public schools, primarily as a consultant to teachers and parents dealing with kids' learning and behavior problems. Most parent conferences ended with questions concerning how to handle everyday problems at home: fighting, whining, uncooperative behavior, temper tantrums. Parents were weary of scolding, reminding, and punishing their children, only to have the same misbehaviors recur with distressing frequency. Yet I was in no position to answer the questions of other parents, for similar problems with my own children challenged me.

"In 1974, I began to research all materials and programs currently available to parents on coping with kids' misbehavior. I spent 1976 and 1977 at the University of Arizona's Graduate School, interning in their child guidance and family education program. Since then, I have synthesized parenting education into a workable system for today's confused parents.

"I reach and teach parents in diverse ways. I developed and direct the Family Education Center of Florida. During summers, I teach graduate courses in discipline and in parenting education at Elmira College in New York State. I travel extensively, lecturing to parents and teachers, and appear frequently on radio and television programs.

"My largest audience is reached through my newspaper column, which focuses on the problems parents experience at home and on concerns parents have about schools and the education of their children. More than one hundred of these columns have been expanded and organized into my book, *Coping With Kids.*"

Albert's book discusses such pieces of advice as: solve one problem at a time; don't choose the hardest problem first; expect improvement—not perfection; expect occasional unhappiness; recognize the four basic motivations for misbehavior; learn the language of respect; and plan helpful outside support.

The author's second book, *Coping With Your Child's Education,* is a comprehensive guide to schools and education, explaining the vast changes in educational curriculum and structure that have taken place within the past several decades. Albert looks particularly at which parental attitudes and behaviors are effective in motivating children to succeed in school. The book *Coping With Kids and Vacation* completes the series.

Strengthening Stepfamilies, Albert's multi-media training program for remarried parents, is the first systematically organized set of readings, recordings, and activities designed to help stepfamilies reach their full potential for a rich family life.

Her latest book, *Quality Parenting,* was written with the needs of today's working parents in mind. In it parents learn how to transform the ordinary, everyday moments they spend with their children into special, meaningful times.

BIOGRAPHICAL/CRITICAL SOURCES:

PERIODICALS

St. Petersburg Times, November 21, 1982.

*   *   *

ALEXANDER, Jean   1926-

PERSONAL: Born April 5, 1926, in Forest Grove, Ore.; daughter of Clyde M. (a teacher) and Mildred (Carlyle) Alexander. *Education:* University of Oregon, B.A., 1947; University of Washington, Seattle, M.A., 1955, Ph.D., 1961.

ADDRESSES: Office—Department of English, California State University, Fresno, Calif. 93710.

CAREER: Louisiana State University, Baton Rouge, instructor in English, 1958-61; University of Calgary, Calgary, Alberta, assistant professor, 1961-68, associate professor of English, 1968-77; California State University, Fresno, associate professor of English, 1977—.

MEMBER: International Association for the Study of Anglo-Irish Literature, Canadian Association of University Teachers, Rocky Mountain Modern Language Association.

AWARDS, HONORS: Fulbright fellow in France, 1957-58.

WRITINGS:

(Compiler) *Affidavits of Genius: Edgar Allan Poe and the French Critics, 1847-1924,* Kennikat, 1971.
(Contributor) *Sunshine and the Moon's Delight,* Colin Smythe, 1972.
The Venture of Form in the Novels of Virginia Woolf, Kennikat, 1974.
Let's Get Down to Cases, Anti-Defamation League of B'nai B'rith, 1976.

WORK IN PROGRESS: A novel.

AVOCATIONAL INTERESTS: Writing poetry, swimming, mountain climbing.*

*   *   *

ALEXANDER, Martin   1930-

PERSONAL: Born February 4, 1930, in Newark, N.J.; son of Meyer (a haberdasher) and Sarah (Rubinstein) Alexander; married Renee R. Wulf (a lecturer), August 26, 1951; children: Miriam H., Stanley W. *Education:* Rutgers University, B.S., 1951; University of Wisconsin, M.S., 1953, Ph.D., 1955.

ADDRESSES: Home—301 Winthrop Dr., Ithaca, N.Y., 14850. *Office*—708 Bradfield Hall, Cornell University, Ithaca, N.Y. 14853.

CAREER: Cornell University, Ithaca, N.Y., assistant professor, 1955-59, associate professor, 1959-64, professor of soil microbiology, beginning 1964, Liberty Hyde Bailey Professor, 1977—. Visiting professor, Hebrew University of Jerusalem, 1961-62.

MEMBER: International Cell Research Organization, International Society of Soil Science, American Academy of Microbiology (fellow), American Society for Microbiology, American Society of Agronomy (fellow), American Association for the Advancement of Science (fellow), Phi Beta Kappa.

AWARDS, HONORS: Soil science award from American Society of Agronomy, 1966; Industrial Research-100 award, 1968; Fisher Award, 1980.

WRITINGS:

Introduction to Soil Microbiology, Wiley, 1961, 2nd edition, 1977.
Microbial Ecology, Wiley, 1971.
Microbial Degradation of Pesticides: Final Report, Office of Naval Research, Department of the Navy, 1977.
(Editor) *Biological Nitrogen Fixation: Ecology, Technology and Physiology,* Plenum, 1984.

Contributor of more than two hundred scientific articles and reviews to journals in his field. Consulting editor, *Soil Science,* 1965—; member of five editorial boards, including *Journal of Bacteriology,* 1970—, and *Pesticide Biochemistry and Physiology,* 1971—.

WORK IN PROGRESS: Scientific articles.

*   *   *

ALGER, Horatio, Jr.
    See STRATEMEYER, Edward L.

*   *   *

ALLEN, Betsy
    See HARRISON, Elizabeth Cavanna

*   *   *

ALLEN, Woody 1935-

PERSONAL: Given name, Allen Stewart Konigsberg; born December 1, 1935, in Brooklyn, N.Y.; son of Martin (a waiter and jewelry engraver) and Nettie (Cherry) Konigsberg; married Harlene Rosen, 1954 (divorced, 1960); married Louise Lasser (an actress), February 2, 1966 (divorced); currently living with Mia Farrow (an actress); children: (with Farrow) Satchel. *Education:* Attended New York University and City College (now City College of the City University of New York), 1953. *Politics:* Democrat.

ADDRESSES: Office—Orion Pictures, 9 West 57th St., New York, N.Y. 10019. *Agent*—Jack Rollins, Rollins, Joffe, Morra & Brezner Productions, 130 West 57th St., New York, N.Y. 10019.

CAREER: Comedian, actor, director, and writer for television, films, and the stage. Began writing jokes for columnists and celebrities while in high school; regular staff writer for National Broadcasting Corp., 1952, writing for such personalities as Herb Shriner, Sid Caesar, Art Carney, Kaye Ballard, Buddy Hackett, Carol Channing, Pat Boone, Jack Paar, and Garry Moore. Performer in nightclubs, on television, and on the stage, 1961—.

AWARDS, HONORS: Sylvania Award, 1957, for script of a "Sid Caesar Show"; Academy Awards for best director and best original screenplay from the Academy of Motion Picture Arts and Sciences, National Society of Film Critics award, and New York Film Critics Circle award, all 1977, for "Annie Hall"; British Academy Award and New York Film Critics award, both 1979, for "Manhattan"; Academy Award nomination for best director, 1984, for "Broadway Danny Rose"; Academy Award for best original screenplay, Golden Globe Award for best motion picture comedy or musical, New York

Film Critics award, and Los Angeles Film Critics award, all 1987, for "Hannah and Her Sisters."

WRITINGS:

Getting Even (humor collection), Random House, 1971.
Without Feathers (humor collection), Random House, 1975.
Non-Being and Somethingness (collections from comic strip "Inside Woody Allen"), Random House, 1978.
Side Effects (humor collection), Random House, 1980.

SCREENPLAYS

(And actor) "What's New, Pussycat?," United Artists, 1965.
(With Frank Buxton, Len Maxwell, Louise Lasser, and Mickey Rose, and actor) "What's Up, Tiger Lily?," American International, 1966.
(With Rose, and actor and director) "Take the Money and Run," Palomar, 1969.
(With Rose, and actor and director) "Bananas" (also see below), United Artists, 1971.
(And actor and director) "Everything You Always Wanted to Know about Sex But Were Afraid to Ask" (based on the book by David Ruben), United Artists, 1972.
(And actor) "Play It Again, Sam" (also see below; based on the play), Paramount, 1972.
(With Marshall Brickman, and actor and director) "Sleeper" (also see below), United Artists, 1973.
(And actor and director) "Love and Death" (also see below), United Artists, 1975.
(With Brickman, and actor and director) "Annie Hall" (also see below), United Artists, 1977.
(And director) "Interiors" (also see below), United Artists, 1978.
Four Screenplays: Sleeper, Love and Death, Bananas, Annie Hall, Random House, 1978.
(With Brickman, and actor and director) "Manhattan" (also see below), United Artists, 1979.
(And actor and director) "Stardust Memories" (also see below), United Artists, 1980.
(And actor and director) "A Midsummer Night's Sex Comedy," Warner Brothers, 1982.
Four Films of Woody Allen (includes "Annie Hall," "Manhattan," "Stardust Memories," and "Interiors"), Random House, 1982.
(And actor and director) "Zelig," Orion, 1983.
(And actor and director) "Broadway Danny Rose," Orion, 1984.
(And director) "The Purple Rose of Cairo," Orion, 1985.
Hannah and Her Sisters (produced by Orion, 1986), Random House, 1986.
(And narrator and director) "Radio Days," Orion, 1987.
(And director) "September," Orion, 1987.

PLAYS

(With Herbert Farjeon, Hermoine Gingold, and others) "From A to Z," produced in New York at Plymouth Theatre, April 20, 1960.
Don't Drink the Water (produced in New York at Morosco Theatre, November 17, 1966), Samuel French, 1967.
Play It Again, Sam (produced on Broadway at Broadhurst Theatre, February 12, 1969), Random House, 1969.
Death: A Comedy in One Act, Samuel French, 1975.
God: A Comedy in One Act, Samuel French, 1975.
The Floating Light Bulb (produced in New York at Vivian Beaumont Theatre, April 27, 1981), Random House, 1982.

OTHER

Author of radio production of ''God,'' produced by National Radio Theatre of Chicago, 1978. Featured on recording ''Woody Allen, Stand-up Comic: 1964-1968,'' United Artists Records, 1978.

WORK IN PROGRESS: Another film.

SIDELIGHTS: Woody Allen falls into one of the most rarified categories of artist—the *auteur* filmmaker, one whose vision pervades every aspect of his work. Allen is also one of the world's best-recognized cinematic figures; indeed, he has more ''name value'' as a writer or director than do many of the stars of his pictures. A Woody Allen movie, for his fans and many critics and scholars, has become an eagerly awaited event (and he has usually turned out his films at the rather reliable rate of one per season for nearly two decades). He has won a score of professional honors, all of which he seems to scorn. And yet, for all Allen's artistic success, his movies rarely are ''blockbusters'' in the big-budget Hollywood sense. The director's works, in fact, are independent features, produced on small budgets, given limited release on occasion, and often just earn back their costs in domestic rentals. And that is the way Allen has said he prefers it.

So many myths have been perpetuated about Allen, stemming from rumor, from scenes of his films, and from the author's own writings, that few outside his inner circle can claim to know the real man. One of the most familiar stories about Allen is that he suffers from anhedonia, the inability to experience pleasure. The truth is, Allen did originally want to title ''Anhedonia'' his film that became famous as ''Annie Hall.'' But the truth also is that Allen, though critical of our society at large, has ''a great capacity for joy,'' according to Diane Keaton, who starred in several Allen movies and played a lead role in the director's romantic life for some years. As Keaton relates to *Newsweek*'s Jack Kroll, Allen is ''moved by things and he has a great sense of beauty. He's very sensitive and he has these feelings of guilt and anger and shame.'' In the same article, former co-star and wife Louise Lasser concedes that while Allen is ''one of the unfortunate tormented people,'' he still has ''a sweet side and a silly side and a sexual side.''

Another popular Allen myth holds that the director's onscreen stories are direct retellings of his own life. People point to movies like ''Radio Days'' as examples of Allen's youth, and they see the contemporary romances, especially ''Annie Hall'' and ''Manhattan,'' as testimony to the ''real'' Woody Allen's relationship with women. And then there is ''Stardust Memories,'' a virulent 1980 comedy about a famous film director who despises his fans, a movie that outraged Allen's own fans and critics, primarily because Allen himself played the lead role so convincingly.

Addressing the question of autobiography in his films, Allen tells *New York Times* reporter Caryn James that many of his works contain a ''brush from real life; I'll play characters who are in show business, who live in an apartment like mine, but those are the outer trappings. If I had played the Michael Caine part of Hannah's husband [in 'Hannah and Her Sisters'], people would have been convinced I'd had an affair with my wife's sister, just as in 'Manhattan' they were completely convinced I wanted to marry a 17-year-old girl. I wrote 'Manhattan' [and 'Annie Hall'] with Marshall Brickman, and some of the ideas triggered from life were from *his* life, not even mine, and they

didn't even happen to him. They came from things he observed.''

In a 1980 *New York Times* article, Tony Schwartz outlines another Allen image: that of ''the artist of uncompromising standards, a man with high-minded concern who lives reclusively and isn't interested in fame and adulation, nor in the wealth that has accompanied it.'' But in Allen's own words, to Natalie Gittelson in another *New York Times* piece, ''I'm not holed up in my apartment every night poring over Russian literature and certain Danish philosophers. I'm really hardly a recluse. When a half-dozen *paparazzi* follow me down the street, naturally I don't like that very much. But I do go out all the time—to movies, to shop, to walk around in the street, to those parties I think I'll enjoy.''

The object of all this speculation was born Allen Stewart Konigsberg in pre-World War II Brooklyn, New York, although not, as his ''Annie Hall'' alter ego Alvy Singer suggests, in a house sitting under the roller coaster at Coney Island. In many ways, the growing boy resembled his peers: ''I was out in the streets from 8 o'clock in the morning,'' Allen tells Kroll, ''playing baseball and basketball. At lunchtime I'd race into the house, eat a tuna-fish sandwich by myself and read a comic book—Superman, Batman or Mickey Mouse. I'd run back out on the street and play ball. Then I'd run back in for dinner, read another comic book, run back out again for two hours, come in and watch the St. Louis Cardinals beat the Dodgers on television.''

And, as so many children do, young Allen hated school—but not for the usual reasons. In a *Rolling Stone* interview, the writer recalls the ''equally bad'' experience of attending public school and Hebrew school, in a neighborhood that, though primarily Jewish, was filled with ''teachers [who] were backward and anti-Semitic.'' As Allen continues to William E. Geist, his early writing efforts were thwarted, deemed ''dirty by the backward, ignorant standards of my teachers. My mother was called in to school so often because of that and other problems,'' including ''truancy, bad marks, causing disturbances.''

With that kind of academic background, it's not surprising that Allen shunned higher education as well. He briefly attended New York's City College and entered into an equally brief teenage marriage to childhood sweetheart Harlene Rosen. By this time the young man was also submitting jokes and one-liners, some of which caught the attention of columnists like Earl Wilson. From there it was a quick foray into television, where Allen was among the youngest—and quietest—staff writers for shows starring Sid Caesar, Art Carney, and Jack Paar, among others. During the early 1960s Allen worked as a comedian in nightclubs, where he began to create the persona that would bring him fame—that of the intellectual bumbler, unlucky in love, adversary of nature and small appliances, a perpetual victim of his own urban angst. His comedy was embraced by a generation of city sophisticates, but the persona didn't exactly reflect its creator. ''People always associated me with Greenwich Village and sweaters with holes in them and things like that,'' Allen remarks to Tom Shales in an *Esquire* piece. ''And I've never been that kind of person. Never. I never lived in the Village. I always lived on the Upper East Side of Manhattan.''

In one of his stand-up routines from that era, Allen brags about being discovered by a famous film producer, who found Allen sensual, handsome, exciting—a perfect sex symbol. Pause. The producer was ''a short man with red hair and glasses.''

Actually, Allen was discovered in 1964 by producer Charles Feldman, who offered the comic a screenwriting job on a movie called "What's New, Pussycat?" The story of a man who simply cannot stay faithful to the woman he loves, the movie also marked Allen's acting debut as a neurotic psychiatric patient. In a *Dictionary of Literary Biography* profile, Alan S. Horowitz notes that even in this knockabout farce, the "conflict between security and freedom, and its related problem of freedom versus commitment, recurs in later Allen films."

While "What's New, Pussycat?" "was a great financial success, Allen was not entirely pleased with the finished film," continues Horowitz. The writer "began looking for a project over which he would have more creative control. He acquired the Japanese-made spy film 'Dagi no Kagi' (1964), reedited it, and dubbed in a sound track written and performed by himself, [second wife Louise] Lasser, Frank Buxton, and Len Maxwell, changing the film to a spy spoof about a search for an egg salad recipe." The film, "What's Up, Tiger Lily?," has enjoyed cult status to this day.

The success of Allen's first two films marked the onset of an era, between the late 1960s and the mid-1970s, that saw the comic writing, directing, or starring in (in various combinations) six movies that the pushy fans in "Stardust Memories" would later characterize as "the early, funny ones." Beginning with "Take the Money and Run," the comedies reinforced the Allen persona, a kind of modern version of Charlie Chaplin's Little Tramp. Horowitz points out that in "Take the Money and Run" Allen also introduces "a character type which appears regularly in Allen's [early] films—the inferior woman who never quite equals the protagonist in wit, talent, or intelligence." Allen plays compulsive crook Virgil Starkwell in this mock documentary. Despite Starkwell's shortcomings, says Horowitz, "his wife, the pretty but unintelligent Louise . . . , is deficient when compared to him. This inequality between characters is a flaw in this and later Allen films. The focus is on the relationships between the main characters, but all the characters are written as inferior to the protagonist so that the films' central relationships can never be developed fully; instead these [encounters] merely serve as a background for jokes."

Jokes, of course, are what sell comedies, and "Bananas," Allen's next outing, certainly has its share. Political intrigue spices the tale of products-tester Fielding Mellish, who becomes a soldier in the tiny banana-republic of San Marcos (a country that "leads the world in hernias"), all for the love of an activist, played by Lasser. Through an entirely logical Allenesque series of circumstances, Mellish becomes president of San Marcos and a marked man by U.S. agents as a Communist threat.

"Both 'Bananas' and 'Take the Money and Run' boast sharp bits of parody (of prison movies, TV commercials, courtroom dramas), with Allen kidnapping the cliches and transporting them into wildly inappropriate settings," finds *Film Comment*'s Richard Zoglin. "The laughs provoked by such scenes are two-pronged: the incongruity of seeing familiar actions in absurdly wrong contexts is topped by the fact that no one onscreen notices it. Henri Bergson, the noted French standup, asserted that comedy derives from the sight of people acting like machines. In Allen's world, such machine-like behavior is triggered by over-familiar, routinized modes of action. The underlying message of Allen's comedy is the tyranny of the cliche, which threatens to dehumanize us, to turn us into reflexive automatons. This is not random gag-writing but social comedy of a subtle subversiveness."

Allen the playwright had written and starred in the Broadway production of "Play It Again, Sam," a romantic farce about identity and commitment, with Allen's character, Allan Felix, fantasizing about being as tough and irresistible as Humphrey Bogart. When Felix finds himself increasingly attracted to his best friend's wife, the spirit of the real Bogey appears periodically to explain the mysteries of the female mind. "Play It Again, Sam" enjoyed a prosperous run on the boards and was adapted by Allen for his fifth produced screenplay. As Zoglin sees it, the film is "the most conventionally 'well-made' of his movies, with a neat framing device: Allan watches the closing scene of *Casablanca* at the start of the film, and the scene is replayed in real life at the end. Though more exaggerated and farcical than his later relationship comedies, ['Play It Again, Sam'] is still Allen's smartest comic exploration of the theme of male insecurity."

The same year that brought out "Play It Again, Sam," 1972, brought an unusual departure for Allen: a genuine sex farce. Based—very loosely—on Dr. David Ruben's controversial bestseller, *Everything You Always Wanted to Know about Sex But Were Afraid to Ask*, the like-titled Allen movie takes an anecdotal approach to sexual queries based on some of the book's chapter headings, like "Do Aphrodisiacs Work?" (featuring Allen as a medieval court jester who uses a love potion to get his hands on "the royal tomatoes"—i.e., the queen). Allen's version of "Sex" "comes closest to the savage dissection of sexual absurdity of which Woody Allen seems capable," according to Michael Dempsey in another *Film Comment* piece. "It is a sputtering, misfiring movie with stunning boffos one moment, stony silences the next. Most of the episodes are too short for daffy digressions, yet all but the first ['Do Aphrodisiacs Work?'] and the last ['What Happens During Ejaculation?,' with Allen as a nervous sperm in that great machine known as the human body] collapse from weak construction. It is too bad that Allen didn't or couldn't find one storyline for the film instead of seven playlets. Nevertheless, it gives us some of film's harshest depictions of sex."

Allen's next film, "Sleeper," both prefigured and made fun of the science-fiction epics that would become all the rage a few years after its 1973 premiere. Many critics find this work one of the comic's most cohesive to date. The story of Miles Monroe (Allen), owner of The Happy Carrot health food store, whose disastrous ulcer operation results in his being frozen alive, "Sleeper" recounts what might happen if this urban specimen were to defrost 200 years later, in a world turned upside-down. In 2173 technology has taken over, with robots acting as servants, as Jewish-accented tailors, even as cordial little dogs. The time-traveling Miles, with his memory of a more natural earth, is perceived as a threat by the dictatorial government. Miles joins a rebel force that includes Luna (Diane Keaton), an anthem-spouting free spirit who helps him escape his foes.

"Sleeper" explores themes familiar to Allen works, including the search for cultural identity (Miles has to be cued to his time by being shown artifacts of his own epoch, including a beauty pageant, and a picture of Richard Nixon, whom Miles cannot identify). Sex also plays a role in Miles' identity crisis—after Luna comments that he has gone two hundred years without it, Miles corrects her: "Two hundred and four, if you count my marriage." But in the new age, sex has been replaced by machinery-made stimuli, a concept that Miles sam-ples but ultimately rejects. ''During the conclusion of 'Sleeper' (filmed to replace another ending, months after principal photography was completed), Miles Monroe comes right out with his total disbelief in science and politics, opting for 'sex and death, two things which come once in my life—but at least after death you're not nauseous,''' as Dempsey quotes. Comparing ''Sleeper'' to works like ''Bananas,'' Dempsey continues that often in Allen films ''characters get involved with political causes out of personal insecurity, and use them the way they use culture: for personal oneupmanship.''

While Horowitz describes ''Sleeper'' as ''the last of Allen's slapstick, antic-filled movies,'' the director's next release, ''Love and Death,'' did contain its share of raucous physical gags. But in many ways, ''Love and Death'' represents the turning point of the Allen filmic assembly. At once a spoof of Russian literature and certain Russian films, and a serious look into one Russian's quest to find the meaning of life as he awaits his execution, ''Love and Death'' marks one of the last times Allen would employ his stock-in-trade character, by now a combination of Harold Lloyd's amiable bumbler and Bob Hope's boastful coward.

The movie opens on 18th-century Czarist Russia, where the citizens of a small village are preparing to join in the fight against Emperor Napoleon's invading forces—all except Boris (Allen), a ''militant coward'' in love with his cousin Sonia (Keaton). Pressured into joining the army after Sonia decides to marry the town's herring merchant, Boris, as klutzy as ever, becomes a quite inadvertant war hero (''*You* should have such inadvertant heroism,'' he sniffs to a rival). By this time Sonia is single again, after the herring merchant dies defending her dubious honor. She and Boris marry and each finds happiness—until they devise a plot to kill the visiting Napoleon. The plan backfires, Boris is captured, and is sentenced to die the next morning at six o'clock. ''It was supposed to be five o'clock, but I had a smart lawyer,'' he remarks. ''The film ends with Boris and the Angel of Death frolicking by a lakeside,'' recounts Horowitz.

''Although the story sounds tragic, 'Love and Death' is a comedy,'' Horowitz goes on to say. ''The dead Boris appears at the beginning, joking about death and setting the story in flashback. By letting the audience know what Boris's fate will be, Allen makes the film lighter and more amenable to humor.'' The critic also finds that ''Love and Death'' has ''other literary and theatrical devices which Allen has used in many of his films. Frequently he speaks directly to the audience in absurdist fashion. The film is filled with allusions to Russian literature [specifically, the works of Leo Tolstoy and Feyodor Dostoevsky] and to the films of Ingmar Berman, one of Allen's favorite filmmakers. Finally, Allen's discussion of death leads him to examine the rationale behind death, which brings him to explore the existence and nature of God.''

''Comedians are supposed to shtik to their lasts: Harpo could never speak and Groucho could never be at a loss for words,'' writes Richard Schickel in a 1977 *Time* article. ''What, then, is Woody Allen doing starring in, writing and directing a ruefully romantic comedy that is at least as poignant as it is funny and may be the most autobiographical film ever made by a major comic?'' The film Schickel is referring to is ''Annie Hall.'' The setting is contemporary New York, the characters are witty and self-motivated, and the plot goes back farther than *Pygmalion:* a highly sophisticated man uses education and culture to create the perfect mate out of a simple, small-town woman and then watches in mounting disbelief as the newly

liberated female breaks from his influence and forms a life of her own. Like Schickel, most critics and viewers took ''Annie Hall'' as a retelling of the relationship between Allen, who played comic Alvy Singer, and Keaton, the title character. But with its insights into the way romances blossom and wilt in the 1970s, ''Annie Hall'' was embraced by many as a representative film of its age.

''Annie Hall'' opens with Allen's character telling a metaphoric joke: Two women on vacation in the Catskills are complaining about the food. Such poor quality—and such small portions! That, says Alvy, is a symbol of his romantic life—his relationships are trying affairs, full of strife and heartbreak. And they're over much too quickly. ''Annie and I broke up,'' he continues, ''and I still can't believe it.'' From there flashbacks relate the awkward meeting, first date, declaration of love, and eventual breakup of Alvy and Annie. The movie, declares *Newsweek*'s Janet Maslin, ''is a perverse self-help manual about How to Be Your Own Worst Enemy, and even its most uproarious moments ride an undercurrent of wistfulness.''

Allen himself noted ''Annie Hall'''s biggest departure from his previous works in the interview with Natalie Gittelson: '''Sleeper' and 'Love and Death' were cartoon-style films. I was still struggling to develop a sense of cinema, a better feeling for technique. But even though those films tried for some satirical content, they were still cartoon. I had intended to be very serious in 'Love and Death.' But the serious intent underlying the humor was not very apparent to most audiences. Laughter submerges everything else. That's why I felt that, with 'Annie Hall,' I would have to reduce some of the laughter. I didn't want to destroy the credibility for the sake of the laugh.''

Despite the often somber nature of ''Annie Hall,'' finds Schickel, ''traditionalists need not worry. There are plenty of one-liners about the classic anti-hero's copelessness in sexual and other matters as Allen dips once again into the comic capital that he has been living off for years. It is, however, the best measure of [the movie's] other strengths that even when these gags are very good, they often seem unnecessary and intrusive: mood busters.'' This film ''perfects a sort of humor that can best be described as psychoanalytic slapstick,'' remarks *New Yorker*'s Penelope Gilliatt. ''It has a Geiger-counter ear for urban cliches, and a hatred of Los Angeles which is appealing to all who share it,'' she continues, citing a sequence in which Annie takes up a California lifestyle, which Alvy sees as the final crack in the deepening chasm of their romance. In an extremely brave moment, Alvy deserts New York and flies to Los Angeles ''only to rescue his girl from all this, and heaven knows if he can do it,'' Gilliatt relates. When he meets her at a health food cafe, after stiffly ordering a plate of mashed yeast, he cannot relate this confident, successful woman to the Annie Hall he knew back home. They mutually agree to make their final parting with dialogue that ''deliberately exaggerates the habit of speaking in quotation marks which often seems now to be strangling simplicity,'' in Gilliatt's view.

As Schickel concludes, what gives ''Annie Hall'' its landmark status is the film's ''general believability. [Allen's] central figures and all who cross their paths are recognizable contemporary types. Most of us have even shared a lot of their fantasies. Their world, however cockeyed, is our world. Without abandoning the private demi-demons that have been the basis of his past comic success, Allen has fashioned broad new connections with his audience. Ironically, his most personal film may turn out to have the widest appeal of all.''

''Annie Hall'''s wide appeal was confirmed when the film swept the 1978 Academy Awards, taking best picture, best director for Allen, best original screenplay for Allen and Marshall Brickman, and best actress for Keaton. America's newest *auteur,* however, made headlines as much for his boycotting of the ceremony as for his Oscar triumphs. While Allen had made no secret of his disregard for awards—not to mention that the ceremony is held in the dreaded Los Angeles—his key reason for not attending, he has said, is that the Oscars are held on Monday nights, and on that evening he has a permanent previous commitment—playing clarinet with the New Orleans Funeral and Ragtime Band at a New York City nightclub.

In the *Newsweek* interview with Jack Kroll, Allen explains the inspiration behind his ''Annie Hall'' follow-up this way: ''When you do comedy you're not sitting at the grownups' table, you're sitting at the children's table.'' And so in 1978 the filmmaker moved to the grownups' table with ''Interiors.'' ''It deals with the spiritual turmoil, the floating unrest that can only be traceable to bad choices in life. Also the apotheosis of the artist beyond his real worth. And how a lover can possess the loved one as an object he can control,'' Allen tells Kroll. While these are all themes the writer explored in previous comedies, ''Interiors'' is deadly serious in the manner of Ingmar Bergman, one of Allen's influences.

The shift in mood came as no surprise to the filmmaker. ''The kinds of films I've always liked, right from the start, were serious movies,'' Allen says in a *Saturday Review* interview with David Remnick. Even still, ''it took a lot of convincing to get the studio to let me make *Interiors.* But it came right after *Annie Hall,* so they were flush with some success. Then I did it and it didn't make any money at all.''

''Interiors'' deals with a family in trouble: The parents, Eve and Arthur, are at the breaking point in their marriage. Their three enigmatic daughters, Flyn, Joey, and Renata, ''are like [Anton] Chekhov's *Three Sisters,*'' as *Dictionary of Literary Biography*'s Horowitz sees it. ''Chekhov's women talk about 'going to Moscow' but never go anywhere. Allen's women talk about becoming artists and achieving self-fulfillment, yet manage only to wallow in their own despair. Arthur leaves Eve and marries vivacious and lively Pearl. . . . The family, particularly Eve, cannot accept this, and Eve commits suicide.'' Horowitz echoes many critics in his view that with this work Allen's ''conscious avoidance of laughter gives the film a stilted, unnatural quality, and his dialogue is unrealistic, filled with psychological jargon.'' Other reviewers, getting right to the point, compared ''Interiors'' unfavorably to a soap opera.

The critical and financial failure of ''Interiors'' was put into perspective by Allen, who tells Shales, ''*Interiors* helped *Manhattan.* I don't think I would have been in good shape if, instead of *Annie Hall,* I had made another film like *Sleeper* and then another film like *Bananas* and then another film like *Sleeper.* I don't dislike comedy. . . . But it can be an artistic dead end for a person.'' He further remarks that an artist who consistently turns out hits is ''on a bad treadmill, I feel. You want your films to be successful, but every now and then, when one doesn't work at all, it's a sign of life.''

''Manhattan,'' released in 1979, is the movie many people think is the true follow-up to ''Annie Hall.'' Certainly there

are many similarities. Like ''Annie Hall,'' ''Manhattan'' follows the romantic foibles of New York's intellectual elite. The movie again stars Allen and Keaton as nervous lovers; this time, however, Allen plays a disgruntled television hack yearning to write the Great American Novel, and Keaton portrays an overeducated critic who cranks out movie novelizations on the side. Their romance is doomed, though, by the lovers and ex-spouses who satellite them: Keaton's Mary Wilke has had a long-running affair with a married college professor; Allen's Issac Davis must cope with a 17-year-old girlfriend as well as an ex-wife (bisexual when they married, but who left Issac shortly afterward for another woman) publishing a tell-all account of their relationship called *Marriage, Divorce and Selfhood.*

''The first thing to say is that *Manhattan* is not a comedy at all, though Woody Allen himself has many funny lines,'' according to *Commentary* critic Richard Grenier. ''But no one else in the film has a scrap of wit. . . . One is tempted to think that [Allen,] who has been known to needle sanctimony, now has a list of subjects that he feels it would be particularly unseemly, or perhaps too risky, to use for humorous purposes,'' he adds, citing his belief that he sees ''no laughter at the expense of Meryl Streep, who plays the lesbian ex-wife . . . ; nor is any fun made of her lesbian lover or their relationship.'' Schickel, in another *Time* article, addresses the question of ''Manhattan'''s humor by noting that ''the picture induces howls of laughter in the opening reels, raising expectations that we are again simply going to see the superb comic character whom Allen has been developing since the early '60s. After a while, however, the raucousness dies down. The movie never ceases to be funny, but it starts to be something more. In the end, by administering a series of steadily intensifying shocks of recognition, silence in the theater is almost complete—and there is something awed about it. We are not prepared for the earnestness, integrity and palpable truthfulness that is offered in *Manhattan.*''

In Vincent Canby's opinion, ''Manhattan'' ''moves on from both 'Interiors' and 'Annie Hall,' being more effectively critical and more compassionate than the first and more witty and clear-eyed than the second.'' As Canby goes on to say in a *New York Times* review, the film is ''mostly about Issac's efforts to get some purchase on his life after he initiates a breakup with his illegal, teenage mistress . . . and his attempt to forge a relationship with the deeply troubled Mary Wilke. Unlike all of his friends except the still-learning [teenager] Tracy, Issac believes in monogamy. 'I think people should mate for life,' he says, 'like pigeons and Catholics.'''

''Ironically, Keaton's character has acquired many of the disdainful, snobbish tendencies that made Allen's Alvy Singer seem like a terminal New York chauvinist in 'Annie Hall,''' writes *Washington Post* reviewer Gary Arnold. ''At last acknowledging the pathetic absurdity of that snobbery, Allen now uses his own character to contradict the pretensions of the New York intelligentsia and/or cognoscenti. Not that Issac himself has his own life in order or has cured himself of a literary man's vanities. But he seems to know when to put on the brakes.'' Better late than never in that sense, Arnold continues. ['Manhattan'] has comic integrity in part because Allen is now making jokes at the expense of his own parochialism. There's no opportunity to heap condescending abuse on the phonies and sellouts decorating the Hollywood landscape [as in 'Annie Hall']. The result appears to be a more authentic and magnanimous comic perception of human vanity and foolhardiness.''

Most critics and scholars considered ''Annie Hall'' and ''Manhattan'' Allen's two best films to date. But the movie Allen himself is most proud of, from that period, is the one that offended so many of his fans. ''The best film I ever did, really, was *Stardust Memories*,'' the director tells Shales. ''It was my least popular film. That may automatically mean it was my best film. It was the closest that I came to achieving what I set out to achieve.'' In ''Stardust Memories,'' famous film director Sandy Bates (played by Allen) spends a weekend at an upstate New York resort where a collection of critics and fans pay homage to his work. Along the way he meets a mysterious woman and anticipates a visit from his French mistress (married with children, but no less accessible to Sandy's advances). He also confronts his current girlfriend, a neurotic actress. Beseiged, Sandy contemplates his future while everyone in his life pulls him in opposite directions. Eventually, fantasy and reality become a blur.

Such is the basic plot of ''Stardust Memories'' but, to many who saw it, plot played a secondary role to character and tone. Sparks flew as audiences saw ''themselves'' portrayed as overbearing, even physically grotesque, caricatures. Their questions are obvious, their pleas for autographs and mementoes absurd. They badger Bates about taking risks in his work, always pleading for a return to his comedies, ''the early, funny ones.'' Says one hanger-on, ''with that look of pained disappointment that is an important prop in every critic's bag of sincere expressions, 'Doesn't that man know he has the greatest gift of all? The gift of laughter?''' as a *New York Times* reviewer relates.

Whether meant satirically or sincerely, ''Stardust Memories'' nonetheless bore the wrath of insulted patrons. Critics generally panned the film, citing uneven pacing and overall sourness. One *Washington Post* writer calls the work an example of the ''self-pitying tradition'' of Frederico Fellini's ''8½,'' which ''Stardust Memories'' distinctly resembles. The critic adds that the spectacle of ''the celebrity artist [envisioning] himself as a potential victim of this freak show of admirers and supplicants'' doesn't help Allen's case. ''Allen even shows [Sandy] Bates fantasizing his own murder at the hands of some blandly psychotic fan. There's no satiric distancing to soften or contradict the impression of fundamental distaste. It's never seriously suggested that Bates' perception of his milieu may be a trifle myopic. If anything, he is congratulated for being too much of a realist, for seeing things more clearly and painfully than his public desires.''

Janet Maslin, in a *New York Times* piece, speculates that while Allen may present a wicked view of his fans, ''he isn't any gentler when it comes to Sandy. In the deserted lobby of the Stardust Hotel, . . . Sandy is accosted by an old schoolmate who says he's now a cabdriver. 'You look good,' Sandy lies, and the camera lingers patiently, watching Sandy squirm.'' In his treatment of this alter ego, Maslin says, ''Stardust Memories'' ''becomes most ambitious and most troubled. Sandy has a great deal in common with other characters [the director] has played, most notably Alvy Singer . . . but the character this time seems imbued with an intentional weariness. So many scenes here serve as pale echoes of 'Annie Hall' that the effect is overpoweringly sad.'' ''I caught a lot of flak on that picture,'' Allen admits to Shales. ''Some people came away saying that I had contempt for my audience. This was not true. I never had contempt for my audience; if I had contempt for an audience, I'd be too smart to put it in a picture. I'd grouse about it at home. I've always felt that the audience was at the

least equal to me or more. I've always tried to play *up* to the audience.''

Whether or not Allen was truly influenced by the negative press he received for ''Stardust Memories,'' his next effort, ''A Midsummer Night's Sex Comedy,'' certainly marked a departure in another direction. This film is a pastoral comedy centering on love, adultery, and the spirit world in a turn-of-the-century setting. In this movie Allen again evokes images of Ingmar Bergman, but not the gray-skied Bergman who inspired ''Interiors.'' Rather, ''Midsummer Night's'' recalls the lyrical Bergman who produced ''Smiles of a Summer Night.'' Appraising the story of a crackpot inventor, played by Allen, who brings a group of friends and lovers to a country retreat where couplings and recouplings abound, critics generally agreed that ''Midsummer Night's,'' while a pleasant diversion, is nonetheless a minor work in Allen's career. *New York Times* writer Maslin appreciates the director's willingness to move in unfamiliar circles. But she finds that Allen ''works in such a direct, linear style that the substance of his work is uninterrupted—and consequently small. The material is minor enough, and familiar enough from other Woody Allen films, to have benefited from some of his masterly digressions.''

While ''Midsummer Night's'' didn't garner much critical or popular attention, the film did mark the debut of Mia Farrow in an Allen movie. Farrow, whom Allen had taken up with romantically as well as professionally, would star in several more of the writer's works, the first being 1983's ''Zelig.'' Having as its subject the assimilation of minorities into mainstream American culture, ''Zelig,'' set in the 1920s, used a myriad of modern technological magic to evoke the jumpy, crackling film footage of that era. By shooting black-and-white film and then running it through a gauntlet of edits and scratches, Allen and cinematographer Gordon Willis created authentic-looking action. Willis also succeeded in editing Allen's image into actual old footage, thus showing the character of Leonard Zelig with such notables as Babe Ruth, Calvin Coolidge, and even Adolph Hitler.

These juxtapositions fit into a tall tale of how the title character, played by Allen as a rather nondescript urban Jew, amazingly adopts the looks and characteristics of any distinct individual or group he encounters. Among fat men, for instance, Zelig's weight balloons; among black jazz musicians, Zelig's skin darkens. Eventually, ''The Human Chameleon'' catches the fancy of a fickle Roaring Twenties America, and Leonard finds himself the subject of songs, dances, and movies. Exploited by his ruthless sister, however, Leonard is miserable. Then a psychiatrist, Eudora Fletcher, enters the scene. Fletcher, played by Farrow, is convinced that she can cure Zelig of his tendencies. But his public doesn't want cured the man who inspired the hit tune ''You May Be Six People But I Love You.'' The resulting backlash drives Leonard out of the country—and into the clutches of Germany's emerging Socialist party, in effect an entire nation of conformists, led by Hitler. Fortunately for Leonard, Eudora spots his face among the masses in a newsreel film and embarks on a daring rescue.

Zelig's fate after his liberation seems deliberately unclear. For ''Zelig'' the film ''is a meditation on fame, on the emptiness of it,'' as *Commentary* critic Colin L. Westerbeck, Jr., sees it. The title character ''is a man famous for being famous,'' Westerbeck continues. ''He's Charles Lindbergh, the quintessential twenties figure, someone who becomes the most famous of them all simply by being such a modest, unassuming likable guy.''

''We are familiar with the Soviet practice of removing inconvenient figures from the pages of history, but the insertion into those pages of a person who never existed is a new kind of chicanery,'' notes Robert Hatch in *Nation*. ''Having established Zelig as the most bizarre celebrity of that feverish era between the World Wars, Allen then 'documents' his career by persuading several of our present-day social critics, among them Susan Sontag, Irving Howe, Saul Bellow and Bruno Bettelheim, to appear before the camera and comment on the Zelig phenomenon. Each of them does so in phrases utterly characteristic of his or her platform manner.'' The director's purpose in ''Zelig,'' Hatch continues, ''is to astonish and entertain, but like most celebrated jesters, he puts an edge on his clowning. The extreme malleability of his hero can be read as a warning that we are becoming a people whose personalities are not autonomous but are accretions from role models who come and go like shadows.''

Some critics split over whether the technical brilliance of *Zelig* overrides the movie's message. *New Republic* reviewer Stanley Kauffmann, for instance, praises Allen's ''keen eye for the way people looked, and thought they looked, in the period: the way they glanced at cameras, posed themselves for photographs, or invented 'business' for newsreels.'' But while he finds ''Zelig'' ''a fascinating premise for a film,'' Kauffmann ultimately wonders, ''Where's the film? [Allen] uses wit and insight to describe a character, to prepare him for engagement—and then he quits. He never *employs* Zelig: to any narrative, dramatic, or thematic point.'' John Simon likewise finds ''Zelig'' ''a curious example of a film with too much cleverness for its own good.'' Assessing the film in *National Review,* Simon goes on to say that ''though the kaleidoscopic fortunes of the protagonist are aptly mirrored in the collage-like quality of the movie, the art of assemblage, instead of enhancing the semblance of reality, proves an inadequate way of dissembling: the cunningly joined snippets challenge us to peer behind them and discover the central hollowness.''

London *Times* writer David Robinson, on the other hand, finds no reason not to include ''Zelig'' in the company ''of great comedies, like *Candide* or *Verdoux* or *Viridiana*,'' adding that in all such narratives the ''seemingly transparent simplicity leave you with quite as many questions about the condition of man as do great tragedies. When you recover from the laughter, this pure, perfect, beautiful comedy leaves a trail of reflections about truth and fiction and the difficulty of preserving one's own personality in a society which offers so many off-the-peg models for being which are so much easier to wear.'' And to *Time*'s Schickel, ''Zelig'' is ''the culmination of a long quest by Allen. He is virtually the only celebrity who has continually investigated the values and liabilities of his own status. . . . Acutely satirizing mediaspeak, the film hilariously exposes the vulgarizations and misleading distortions of that language. At the same time, it touchingly demonstrates that celebrity is a kind of victimization, capable of claiming the souls of those who have some skill or talent, no matter how strange or silly, that is marketable.''

''In the long run 'Zelig' is far more touching than side-splitting,'' concludes *Washington Post* critic Gary Arnold. ''One's perception of Zelig's condition deepens as the story unfolds, and the absurdity of it has a benevolent psychological payoff, the revelation that Zelig doesn't so much *cure* his craziness as get it *under control* and make it work for him when the chips are down.''

Embarking on yet another narrative form, Allen brought out ''Broadway Danny Rose'' to follow ''Zelig.'' A Damon Runyonesque showbiz romance, ''Broadway Danny Rose'' again stars the writer/director and his steady leading lady as an unlikely pair of lovers. He is Danny Rose, very-small-time theatrical agent to such showstopping acts as a skating rabbi, a blind xylophonist, a woman who plays the rims of drinking glasses, and a parrot who warbles standards like ''I Gotta Be Me.'' She is Tina Vitale, ex-moll of an unsuccessful gangster, current girlfriend of Lou Canova, an Italian lounge-singer whose career Danny is trying to resuscitate. Lou is married, so he asks Danny to be his ''beard''—stand-in—and accompany Tina to a nightclub opening where Lou is making a comeback. A series of misunderstandings and backstabbings results in Danny and Tina on the run from the mob, discovering their feelings for one another in the process.

''We learn the story in flashbacks, anecdotes told by a tableful of sagging borscht belt comics one night at the Carnegie Deli,'' Katha Pollitt relates in *Nation*. Noting the way Danny stands behind his hopelessly corny acts—'''Smile, Strong, Star,' he urges them to say to their dressing-room mirrors''—she adds that Danny's reward is that ''the minute they get a chance at a real break, they desert him for agents with better connections and fewer scruples.'' ''Broadway Danny Rose'' contains its share of sight gags and one-liners (as in Danny's invocation of a sagacious old uncle's advice: ''You can't ride two horses with one behind'') but Pollitt sees behind them ''a moral contest. Who is right? Tina, with her philosophy of 'go for what you want' and screw the next guy, or Danny, with his uncle's message of 'forgiveness, acceptance, love'?''

Some critics see ''Broadway Danny Rose'' as a throwback to Allen's earlier comedies like ''Sleeper''; others find it gratifying in a way they hadn't expected from such a modern filmmaker. Richard Corliss, for one, thinks the movie ''is free of the Post-Funny School's hip condescension toward mediocrity. In the melancholy perseverance of these 'entertainers,' Danny and Woody find something admirable, even lovable. So should the movie audience,'' says the *Time* reviewer. Acclaim, however, was not unanimous.

Kauffmann, again in *New Republic,* cites his ''chief reservation'' to the work: ''Every Italian-American in the film is shown to be some kind of bum or grotesque.'' (Perhaps in an attempt at balance, he also notes, Allen shows many Jewish characters as equally laughable.) And to Kauffmann, this kind of humor shows ''just mockery and dislike. Instead of Fellini's mischievous embrace, we get an extension of Allen's self-hate.'' But to Vincent Canby, ''Broadway Danny Rose'' represents a distinctive step forward. In his *New York Times* column, Canby remarks that the movie ''is a love letter not only to American comedy stars and to all of those pushy hopefuls who never quite make it to the top in show biz, but also to the kind of comedy that nourished the particular genius of Woody Allen.'' Furthermore, ''never before, perhaps, has [the director] so successfully shaped his humor without letting the sharp edges show. I relish [Allen] when the sharp edges show and when taste approaches poor, but 'Broadway Danny Rose' wouldn't support it. It's a different kind of Woody Allen comedy.''

In an Allen short story, ''The Kugelmass Episode,'' the eponymous hero, having developed a crush on Emma of *Madame Bovary* fame, finds himself through magical means transported into the pages of Flaubert's classic novel where he carries on a lively affair with Emma to the confusion of readers everywhere. This same theme Allen utilizes in ''The Purple Rose of Cairo,'' his fifteenth film. The setting has changed to Depression-era New Jersey, and the story centers on Cecilia, the unhappy wife of a ne'er-do-well. Suffering from a lack of money and a surfeit of harsh treatment from her husband, Cecilia finds her only solace at the local movie house, where an adventure film, ''The Purple Rose of Cairo,'' is playing. Her obsession with the movie becomes apparent as she sits through screening after screening. One day, the film's clean-cut hero, Tom Baxter, stops the action during the movie, peers into the audience, remarks on Cecilia's constant presence and, as the other characters stand slack-jawed and members of the audience faint, steps off the screen and into Cecilia's world.

Finding herself the love interest of a fictional character proves both confusing and exhilarating to Cecilia. ''See Tom try to pay for a restaurant meal with stage money,'' Schickel details in *Time*. ''See his puzzlement when he leaps behind the wheel of a car and it refuses to take off ['They don't start without a key,' Cecilia has to remind him].'' But back in Hollywood, studio executives are panicked. It seems that Tom Baxters have begun to leave their movies all across America. The executives decide that only Gil Shepard, the actor who plays Tom, might convince the make-believe adventurer to return to the ''Purple Rose'' sets, as the movie cannot continue without him.

And so Gil is dispatched to New Jersey, where he meets Cecilia and appears to fall for her as hard as Tom Baxter has. She allows herself to be swept away with Gil's charm, and accepts his invitation to follow him back to Hollywood. Rebuffed, Tom Baxter returns to the ''Purple Rose'' story. But when Cecilia, bags packed, goes to the movie house to meet Gil, he doesn't show up. He has left without her. Evidently he only pretended to love Cecilia in order to get Tom Baxter to return to the big screen. The movie's final image is of Cecilia, sitting in the audience once again, waiting for a movie to bring her out of her misery.

This ''down'' ending proves a point of contention for some critics, who believe that ''The Purple Rose of Cairo'' deserved a happier ending. (In some interviews, Allen maintained that this *was* his happy ending.) *New Yorker*'s Pauline Kael sees the heroine's fate as typical of her creator's character: Allen ''has a naturally melancholic, depressive quality,'' she says. ''It's his view of life; the movie casts a spell, yet at the end it has a bitter tang. It says sweetness doesn't get you anywhere.'' Comparing ''Purple Rose'' to similar movie-within-a-movie themes by Buster Keaton and Charlie Chaplin, Kael finds that ''most of . . . Keaton's comedies ended happily, and when Chaplin wasn't being maudlin so did his. Woody Allen puts a strain on his light, paradoxical story about escapism when he gives it a desolate, 'realistic' ending. The author's voice that emerges from his movies, and from this one in particular, is that of a winner who in his deepest recesses feels like a loser. Happiness and success aren't real to him; painfullness is the only reality he trusts.''

Lloyd Rose, in an *Atlantic* review, is forthrightly critical of the film's wrap-up. The director's very life, he remarks, ''gives lie to the wet ending. It doesn't gibe with what we sense about [Allen] as a person and a star. When [Cecilia, played by Mia Farrow] watches the [movie's 'fictional' version of 'Purple Rose'], her face rapt in the reflected light from the screen, it's an echo of the shot of Allen at the beginning of *Play It Again, Sam*, gazing open-mouthed at the last scene of *Casablanca*. In that film Allen made fun of his character's fantasies of

living like someone in the movies. His hero learned that it's all right to be yourself. . . . But in fact Allen has done spectacularly well being himself. He's not some nerd who dreamed away his life in a movie theater. He didn't stay down in the audience looking wistfully at the screen—he went up there. He did something about his dreams. By any standard he's a winner. What's he doing turning out a movie about settling for what little life allows you?''

Other reviewers find more to praise about ''Purple Rose of Cairo.'' Canby, for one, decides to be ''blunt about it'' in his *New York Times* column when he states that the movie ''is pure enchantment[, a] sweet, lyrically funny, multilayered work that again demonstrates that Woody Allen is our premier film maker.'' To Schickel, the comedy ''is not merely one of the best movies about movies ever made. It is still more unusual, because it comes at its subject the hard way, from the front of the house, instead of from behind the scenes. Its subject is not how movies work but how they work on the audience. Or more accurately, how they once did.'' And Kael declares ''Purple Rose'' to be ''the most purely charming'' of Allen's films to date. ''And though it doesn't have the sexual friskiness and roughhousing of some of his other comedies, and doesn't speak to the audience with the journalistic immediacy of his movies in contemporary settings, it may be the fullest expression yet of his style of humor,'' she adds.

Followers of Allen's work have noted his tendency, since the ''Annie Hall'' period, to write female characters who are strong-willed, highly intelligent, and independent. The filmmaker himself acknowledged this bond when he told Shales in the *Esquire* interview, ''You know, my friends are all women, most of them. . . . I mean, I'm not one of those guys who's at the fights with the guys and playing poker with the guys. They're females, my friends. And Mia kids me about that all the time. She thinks there's nothing I'd rather do than go out to lunch and dish with the gals.''

''Hannah and Her Sisters,'' a 1986 comedy-drama, does much to cement Allen's point of view about his affinity for exploring the characters of women in love. The director returns to the contemporary mode for the first time since ''Stardust Memories'' (''Broadway Danny Rose'' is set in the present, but has a 1950s *mood*, many critics feel) to tell the story of how shifting allegiances and marital strife affect the lives of three grown sisters and their families. Hannah, the eldest, is a Broadway actress married to Elliott, a financial advisor. Elliott, however, has a desperate passion for Lee, the youngest sister, who herself lives with an alienated artist, Frederick. Holly, the middle sister, is a would-be actress or writer, depending on her mood. She ends up in a romance with Mickey, Hannah's first husband and, as played by Allen, a rampant hypochondriac.

''Hannah and Her Sisters'' has ''the narrative scope of a novel,'' according to Canby. ''Beginning with a big, festive family celebration . . . the film covers several years in the lives of its six principal characters, moving effortlessly from the mind of one into another. [Allen's] most surprising achievement is the manner by which he has refracted his own, very pronounced screen personality into the colors of so many fully realized characters that stand at such a far remove from the film maker,'' Canby writes in the *New York Times*.

That ''Hannah and Her Sisters'' again focuses on the pains and pleasures of privileged, if troubled, Manhattanites doesn't stop many critics from labelling it Allen's most accessible film in years. Indeed, the movie's protagonists are surrounded by art and culture (even the sisters' parents are a famous husband-

and-wife team of actors) and refer to them constantly. One who is not so impressed by this trait is John Simon, a *National Review* critic. Referring to a scene in which two characters exchange the lines "Do you like Caravaggio?" "Oh, yes. Who doesn't?," Simon asks, "Is that answer informed, snide, or foolish? Or a bluff to cover up ignorance? Nothing about the speaker . . . provides a clue. A highbrow moviegoer can laugh at the character; a middlebrow, empathize; a lowbrow, gape, awestruck. But the statement has no artistic value." All through the film, he adds, "there are discussions of art, architecture, literature, and music (classical and popular) so trivial as to be meaningless." What's more, Allen shoots New York "so ravishingly that it looks like a cross between Paris and Paradise."

Tom O'Brien, a *Commonweal* writer, voices different criticism, starting with structure: "Allen does not always manage to connect his character's story with the three sisters', and the plot often seems less juncture than fracture. More seriously, it's no accident that Allen here touches on a variety of incest in tracing the sisters' intertangled sex lives, which Allen and other men share on a kind of rotating basis. The plot of *Hannah and Her Sisters* thus simply literalizes the claustrophobic tone of all Woody Allen films. It is noteworthy that everyone in *Hannah* is either an actor, artist, or writer (except one accountant, a heavy); all the men, moreover, are losers or villains except for Allen's character. Such self-serving self-referentiality is not the hallmark of a comprehensive imagination." And Kael, while calling the movie "agreeably skillful," points out that she feels the work overall seems "a little stale, and it suggests the perils of inbreeding. It might be time for Woody Allen to make a film with a whole new set of friends [the cast includes such Allen veterans as Farrow, Dianne Weist and Tony Roberts] or, at least, to take a long break from his sentimentalization of New York City. Maybe he'd shed the element of cultural self-approval in the tone of this movie."

On the other hand, several critics praise "Hannah and Her Sisters" as a full-bodied, uplifting work. Paul Attanasio deems the movie "an encyclopedia of the emotions of ordinary life, not a movie so much as a prayer, if prayers could be so funny and tortured and full of love." In his *Washington Post* piece, Attanasio continues that what the movie "is about, in the end, is both the triumph and liabilities of the imagination. Mickey's hypochondria is, in a way, a metaphor for what's wrong with all these characters; they're always imagining problems, in the culture, in their spouses, in their sisters, in their bodies. In 'Hannah,' happiness is just around the corner, but that's the last place anyone would look for it."

"It is one of the extraordinary aspects of the film that 'Hannah and Her Sisters' is most secure when it's being least self-consciously funny," notes Canby in his *New York Times* column. The director "skates very near the edge of any reality when we see Mickey, who's planning to convert to Catholicism, return to his apartment with a newly purchased crucifix and a portrait of a soulful Christ, as well as a jar of Hellman's mayonnaise and a loaf of Wonder Bread." (Those last two items carry symbolic weight in another Allen film. In "Annie Hall" his Jewish Alvy watches wryly as Protestant Annie orders her pastrami sandwich on white with mayo.)

Newsweek's David Ansen points out that "Hannah and Her Sisters" "marks the first time Allen has cast himself in a supporting role. When Woody is at the center, his movies tend to divide the world into us and them, with the supporting cast playing straight man to his anxious monologues and defensive/

aggressive one-liners—he doesn't interact with his fellow actors so much as bounce off them. Here the story revolves around a family, and Woody is only one of the interesting spokes in the wheel. This may be one reason the movie has a richer texture—the ensemble has freed him from solipsism." Ansen finds another reason to like the film, given the country's surplus of youth-oriented entertainment. "Anyone bemoaning the disappearance of adult matter from the movies need look no farther," he writes. "Here Allen singlehandedly restores glamour and substance to middle age. He juggles these overlapping stories with novelistic finesse, counterpointing hilarity and pathos with almost faultless tact." "With this film," Canby concludes, "it's apparent that [Allen] has become the urban poet of our anxious age—skeptical, guiltily bourgeois, longing for answers to impossible questions, but not yet willing to chuck a universe that can produce the Marx Brothers."

A young, red-haired Jewish boy spends his early adolescence in the Rockaway section of Brooklyn sharing a home with many relatives, playing with his friends, and listening to classic radio shows. Whether or not the story is directly autobiographical, people couldn't help but assume that "Radio Days," Allen's next self-directed screenplay, is pulled from events in its creator's early years. As usual, Allen wasn't telling the press how much of the movie was fact and how much fiction. But he did acknowledge how much radio meant in those lean years preceding World War II. In a *New York Times* article, Avery Corman quotes the filmmaker: "The whole country was tied together by radio. We all experienced the same heroes and comedians and singers. They were giants. They were so huge and now today the whole thing has completely vanished. All those tremendous heroes and mythological characters that we lived with for decades when I was younger are completely forgotten or remembered by so few people. It tells you something. It's very sobering. . . . We think we're such hotshots. We think we have such a hold on the public and then with the passage of time it all gets dissipated. You really learn humility from it."

An anecdotal film with Allen providing a voice-over narration, "Radio Days" follows two narratives: one featuring young Joe and his family, the other tracing the rise of Sally White, a cigarette girl with more spunk than talent but one who nonetheless becomes the toast of radio high-society, thanks to some influential friends and a brace of elocution lessons. The duality of plotlines "splits [the movie] right down the middle, between social history and show-biz anecdotes," Stanley Kauffmann remarks in *New Republic*. "If Allen had stayed with the former and explored it further, the film might have been stronger; most of the latter are familiar or strained."

Simon, of *National Review,* and O'Brien, of *Commonweal,* both of whom disliked "Hannah and Her Sisters," take a similar negative tack with "Radio Days." Simon sees the work as "yet another vehicle for Allen's warring urges, a battlefield on which self-aggrandizement and self-hatred fight it out as symbolic goofballs pelt one another with figurative spitballs." And O'Brien thinks that "Radio Days" "will challenge all those for whom [the filmmaker] can do no wrong." The critic goes on to cite "not enough plot to sustain a single genuine role" as among the movie's faults. And both O'Brien and Simon wonder if an overenthusiastic reception by their fellow reviewers to Allen's works has contributed to what they see as a decline in Allen's talents.

If Simon and O'Brien are among Allen's staunchest critics, Canby is among the director's most vocal supporters. "Never has Mr. Allen been so steadily in control, as 'Radio Days' slides from low blackout sketch to high satire to family drama that's as funny as it is moving,'' he writes in the *New York Times*. Devoting two articles to ''Radio Days,'' Canby also states that the film ''is so densely packed with vivid detail of place, time, music, event and character that it's virtually impossible to take them all in in one sitting.'' Citing those who would label the movie a minor work, Canby notes that his subject's films ''can be seen as part of a rare continuum. Each of us has his favorite Allen movie, but to cite one over another as 'more important,' 'bigger,' 'smaller' or 'less significant' is to miss the joys of the entire body of work that is now taking shape. 'Radio Days' is a joyful addition.''

But even Canby admits that the director's next feature, ''September,'' ''has big problems.'' Probably the most universally panned Allen film to date, the straight drama is notable for the fact that Allen, after seeing a first version of the film, ''went out and filmed it all over again—rethought, rewritten and, because time, tide and actors wait for no man, substantially recast,'' as Eric Lax relates in a *New York Times* report. The director is no stranger to refilming—as Thierry De Navacelle describes in his book *Woody Allen on Location*, ''Radio Days'' was also overhauled after its first edit. But to hear critics and audience receipts tell it, the new version is no more successful. Gloomy and claustrophobic are common adjectives the reviewers use to describe ''September,'' which takes place in one house and centers around infidelity, suicide, and scandal.

New Yorker's Kael, comparing the movie to ''Interiors,'' calls ''September'' ''smoother and easier to take. But it's profoundly derivative and second-rate. When [a character] lifts up a large bouquet of wilting wildflowers and complains that her mother picked them but didn't bother to put them in water, some part of you refuses to believe that Woody Allen thought this up and that it survived the months of writing and shooting and reshooting and editing.'' The conspicuous absence of humor in the film caught the attention of some critics. ''But whether his films are comic or serious or both is something [Allen] wishes people would not concern themselves over,'' says Lax. ''Although he established himself first as a comedian, he is, after all, an artist in the middle of his career whose work is still evolving. For audiences to complain that he's not producing a comedy each time is rather like complaining to Picasso that he should never have stopped using blue.''

While Allen has made himself known in many artistic categories—not just films, but television, theatre, print, and others—the movies are his most familiar and longstanding tradition. And yet the writer-director-actor has said that he doesn't enjoy the physical process of filmmaking, the early hours, the reshooting. ''I wish somebody would come in and tell me I can't make films anymore,'' Allen revealed to Shales in *Esquire*. ''I don't have the discipline not to make them.'' Perhaps audience attendance and critical essays ''have no role in Woody Allen's improvement over the years as a filmmaker and he did it all himself, listening to himself, learning from mistakes,'' writes Shales. ''He is hardly pleased with his progress, however. 'There's never been a film of mine that I've been really satisfied with,' he says, and he never ever sees his films once they've been released because 'I think I would hate them.'''

''At their best,'' Shales states, Allen's films ''are capable of imparting immense emotional and aesthetic gratifications. Although some of his austere touches, like holding a shot of an empty room while characters walk into and out of the frame,

are a trifle arch. There is nevertheless real fluidity to many of his films, and from time to time, they have bordered on joy. Muted joy, of course. How can there be unmitigated joy when the universe is expanding and will all go bang someday?''

BIOGRAPHICAL/CRITICAL SOURCES:

BOOKS

Adler, Bill and Jeff Feinman, *Woody Allen: Clown Prince of American Humor*, Pinnacle, 1975.
Anobile, Richard, editor, *Woody Allen's 'Play It Again, Sam,'* Grosset, 1977.
Brode, Douglas, *Woody Allen: His Films and Career*, Citadel, 1985.
Burton, D., *I Dream of Woody*, Morrow, 1984.
Contemporary Literary Criticism, Volume 16, Gale, 1981.
De Navacelle, Thierry, *Woody Allen on Location*, Morrow, 1987.
Dictionary of Literary Biography, Volume 44: *American Screenwriters, Second Series*, Gale, 1986.
Guthrie, Lee, *Woody Allen: A Biography*, Drake, 1978.
Hample, Stuart, *Non-Being and Somethingness: Selections from the Comic Strip 'Inside Woody Allen,'* Random House, 1978.
Hirsch, F., *Love, Sex, Death, and the Meaning of Life: Woody Allen's Comedy*, McGraw, 1981.
Kael, Pauline, *Reeling*, Little, Brown, 1976.
Lax, Eric, *On Being Funny: Woody Allen and Comedy*, Charterhouse, 1975.
McKnight, Gerald, *Woody Allen: Joking Aside*, WH Allen, 1983.
Palmer, M., *Woody Allen*, Proteus Press, 1980.
Quinlan, David, *The Illustrated Guide to Film Directors*, Barnes & Noble Books, 1985.
Welch, Julie, *Leading Men*, Villard, 1985.
Yacowar, Maurice, *Loser Take All: The Comic Art of Woody Allen*, Ungar, 1979.

PERIODICALS

Atlantic, August, 1971, December, 1982, May, 1985.
Chicago Tribune, April 30, 1977, May 11, 1979, October 3, 1980, April 30, 1981, May 31, 1981, June 1, 1981, August 19, 1983, January 27, 1984, January 29, 1984, March 25, 1985, February 7, 1986, February 4, 1987.
Commentary, July, 1979, June, 1982, November, 1983.
Commonweal, September 24, 1982, September 9, 1983, March 23, 1984, April 19, 1985, March 14, 1986, February 27, 1987.
Dissent, fall, 1985.
Esquire, April, 1987.
Film Comment, March/April, 1974, March/April, 1978, May/June, 1979, May/June, 1986.
Film Quarterly, winter, 1972, March/April, 1987.
Los Angeles Times, June 24, 1982, March 22, 1983, July 29, 1983, March 1, 1985, January 30, 1987, December 18, 1987.
Nation, September 11, 1982, September 17, 1983, March 17, 1984, February 21, 1987.
National Review, June 22, 1979, September 17, 1982, August 5, 1983, May 3, 1985, March 14, 1986, March 27, 1987.
New Republic, August 16, 1982, August 15, 1983, February 20, 1984, April 1, 1985, February 10, 1986, March 9, 1987.
Newsweek, June 23, 1975, May 2, 1977, April 24, 1978, July 19, 1982, July 18, 1983, January 30, 1984, February 25,

1985, February 3, 1986, February 2, 1987, January 4, 1988.

New York, April 25, 1988.

New Yorker, May 15, 1971, June 16, 1975, April 25, 1977, July 26, 1982, July 8, 1983, February 6, 1984, March 25, 1985, February 24, 1986, March 9, 1987, January 25, 1988.

New York Review of Books, June 29, 1978, August 16, 1979, August 13, 1987.

New York Times, June 29, 1975, August 2, 1978, April 29, 1979, September 19, 1980, September 20, 1980, September 28, 1980, October 19, 1980, March 19, 1981, July 16, 1982, July 25, 1982, October 19, 1982, July 15, 1983, July 17, 1983, July 18, 1983, January 27, 1984, January 29, 1984, June 4, 1984, March 1, 1985, February 7, 1986, February 9, 1986, January 25, 1987, January 30, 1987, February 1, 1987, May 14, 1987, November 24, 1987, December 16, 1987, December 18, 1987.

New York Times Book Review, June 1, 1975, October 26, 1980.

New York Times Magazine, January 7, 1973, April 22, 1979, January 19, 1986.

Rolling Stone, April 9, 1987.

Saturday Review, January 6, 1979, May, 1986.

Spectator, December 9, 1978.

Time, April 25, 1977, April 30, 1979, August 2, 1982, July 11, 1983, January 23, 1984, March 4, 1985, February 3, 1986, February 2, 1987, December 21, 1987.

Times (London), June 3, 1981, October 7, 1983, August 17, 1984, July 26, 1985, June 25, 1987.

Washington Post, May 2, 1979, September 25, 1979, October 3, 1980, June 2, 1981, August 7, 1983, January 27, 1984, March 22, 1985, February 7, 1986, January 30, 1987, April 1, 1987, March 11, 1988.

Washington Post Book World, October 17, 1971, June 22, 1975, September 21, 1980.*

—*Sketch by Susan Salter*

*   *   *

ALPER, Benedict S(olomon)   1905-

PERSONAL: Born June 28, 1905, in Revere, Mass.; son of Morris (a merchant) and Fredericka (Klatschken) Alper; married Ethel Machanic, June 14, 1935; children: Fredrika Clara. *Education:* Harvard University, A.B., 1927, additional study, 1932-33.

ADDRESSES: Home—146 Tappan St., Brookline, Mass. 02146. *Office*—Department of Sociology, Boston College, Newton, Mass. 02167.

CAREER: Massachusetts Child Council, Boston, research director, 1934-39; Judge Baker Guidance Center, Boston, research associate, 1939-41; New York State Joint Legislative Committee on Courts, research director, 1941-42; American Parole Association, New York City, field secretary, 1942; Federal Bureau of Prisons, Washington, D.C., chief statistician and special assistant to director, 1942-43, 1945-46; United Nations, New York City, chief of Section of Social Defence, 1946-51; treasurer for food brokerage firm in Brookline, Mass., 1951-65; Boston College, Newton, Mass., visiting professor of criminology, 1965—. Has also taught at New School of Social Research, Rutgers University, United Nations Crime Institute, Victoria University, and Australian Institute of Criminology. *Military service:* U.S. Army, 1943-45; served in North

Africa, Italy, and Trieste; became major; received five battle stars.

AWARDS, HONORS: Rockefeller Foundation grant, 1939.

WRITINGS:

Criminal Youth and the Borstal System, Commonwealth Fund, 1941.

People in the Courts of New York State, Williams Press, 1942.

(With Oliver J. Keller, Jr.) *Halfway Houses: Community-Centered Correction and Treatment,* Heath, 1970.

(With Jerry F. Boren) *Crime: International Agenda,* Heath, 1972.

Prisons Inside-Out: Alternatives in Correctional Reform, Ballinger, 1974.

Beyond the Courtroom: Programs in Community Justice and Conflict Resolution, Lexington Books, 1981.

Also author of reports. Contributor of articles and reviews to social sciences journals, including *Albany Law Review, Harvard Law Review, Federal Probation, Prison Journal, British Journal of Criminology, Journal of Criminology, Journal of Marketing, Journal of Criminal Law and Criminology, Crime and Social Justice, Probation, Harvard International Law Journal, International Law Journal of Criminology and Penology,* and *New Zealand Law Journal.*

WORK IN PROGRESS: Compiling a textbook on criminology.

*   *   *

ALPERN, Andrew   1938-

PERSONAL: Born November 1, 1938, in New York, N.Y.; son of Dwight K. (a college professor, engineer, and mineralogist) and Grace (in public relations; maiden name, Michelman) Alpern. *Education:* Columbia University, B.Arch., 1964.

ADDRESSES: Home—315 Eighth Ave., New York, N.Y. 10001. *Office*—Coopers & Lybrand, 1251 Sixth Ave., New York, N.Y. 10020.

CAREER: Haines Lundberg Waehler (architectural firm), New York City, student trainee, 1959-61, architect, 1962-67; W. T. Grant (department store chain), New York City, project director, 1968-72; Environmental Research and Development, Inc., (planning, design, and real estate firm), New York City, vice-president and director of architecture, 1972-75; independent consulting architect, 1975-77; Hellmuth, Obata & Kassabaum, P.C. (architecture, engineering, and planning firm), New York City, project manager, 1977-78; Coopers & Lybrand (public accounting and consulting firm), New York City, director of real estate and planning, 1978—. Certified by National Council of Architectural Registration Boards, 1967; registered architect in New York, Pennsylvania, California, Washington, D.C., and West Virginia. National arbitrator for American Arbitration Association, beginning 1971. Lecturer at the City College of the City University of New York and Institute for Architecture and Urban Studies. Member of advisory board, Institute of Applied Psychotherapy, 1969-72.

MEMBER: American Institute of Architects, Society of Architectural Historians, National Trust for Historic Preservation, New York State Association of Architects, Architectural League of New York, Metropolitan Association of Urban Designers and Environmental Planners, New York Historical Society, Bronx County Historical Society, Municipal Art Society, Fifth Avenue Association of New York (member of design awards committee), Friends of Cast Iron Architecture.

AWARDS, HONORS: Sc.D. from London College of Applied Science, 1971; named as jury member to Hall of Fame of the Real Estate Board of the State of New York, 1988.

WRITINGS:

Apartments for the Affluent: A Historical Survey of Buildings in New York, McGraw, 1975.
Garret Ellis Winants: 1818-1890, privately printed, 1976.
Alpern's Architectural Aphorisms, McGraw, 1979.
Handbook of Specialty Elements in Architecture, McGraw, 1980.
In the Manor Housed, Metropolis, 1982.
(With Seymour Durst) *Holdouts!*, McGraw, 1983.
Fifth Avenue, Metropolis, 1986.
New York's Fabulous Luxury Apartments, Dover, 1987.

Editorial advisor and consultant to McGraw-Hill periodicals for architects. Regular contributor to *Habitat*. Editor-in-chief of *Legal Briefs for the Construction Industry*, 1978—.

SIDELIGHTS: Andrew Alpern writes *CA:* "The practice of architecture encompasses science, technology, business, and art, and it is a wonderfully challenging and stimulating profession, but writing about architecture and buildings can reach a larger audience than mere construction. And though the written word (and copious illustrative material) the crucial, intimate, and often tempestuous interrelationships between architects, developers, and the world-at-large can be described. Buildings are stone and glass and steel, of course, but far more important, they represent physical manifestations of human needs. Perhaps the most important basic need after food and water, is enough of a shelter to call home."

Concerning the future outlook for architecture and architects, Alpern remarks: "The relentless pressure of economic realities is forcing architects, and indeed our entire society, to reevaluate how we deal with our built environment within the context of our ever-changing needs as human beings and as a society. The days of bulldozing the old to make way for the new every twenty years or so are over. The philosophy that progress means a total rejection of what went before has proven disastrously wrong, both in social terms and in economic ones. At long last America has come around to a recognition of its significant architectural heritage and resource that does not necessarily have to be destroyed when it no longer meets its functional or economic imperatives.

"Architectural preservation has come out of the closet with a vengeance. But has it gone too far? Any city that relentlessly destroys its past destroys its soul and its humanity. But one that is loath to raze any structure that retains a bit of classical molding or a graceful cornice will rapidly doom itself to economic and social obsolescence. What is sorely needed is a rational balance that preserves the best of the old, recognizes the need for continual change and rejuvenation, and that fosters the wisdom of knowing when and how to compromise in a reasonable and realistic way. Extreme positions and blind zealotry may make good newspaper copy, but they cannot yield a truly livable yet economically viable place in which humans can function. It is only through cooperation, careful analysis, and a ready willingness to compromise that the architecture produced by our entire society (guided and aided by our architects) will be the responsive resource it has the capability of being."

ALT, David D. 1933-

PERSONAL: Born September 17, 1933, in St. Louis, Mo.; son of Arthur and Louisa Alt; married second wife, Sandra Dewald, June 17, 1972; children: (first marriage) Konrad, Lisa Alt-Levi; stepdaughters: Debra Bestwick, Diane Bestwick Trethewey, Sarah. *Education:* Washington University, St. Louis, Mo., A.B., 1955; University of Minnesota, M.S., 1958; University of Texas, Ph.D., 1961.

ADDRESSES: Home—505 East Beckwith, Missoula, Mont. 59801. *Office*—Department of Geology, University of Montana, Missoula, Mont. 59801.

CAREER: University of Leeds, Leeds, England, senior research associate, 1961-62; University of Florida, Gainsville, assistant professor of geology, 1962-65; University of Montana, Missoula, assistant professor, 1965-68, associate professor, 1968-72, professor of geology, 1972—.

MEMBER: Geological Society of America.

WRITINGS:

(With Donald W. Hyndman) *Roadside Geology of the Northern Rockies*, Mountain Press, 1972.
(With Hyndman) *Rocks, Ice, and Water: Geology of Watertow Glacier Park*, Mountain Press, 1973.
(With Hyndman) *Roadside Geology of Northern California*, Mountain Press, 1974.
(With Hyndman) *Roadside Geology of Oregon*, Mountain Press, 1978.
Physical Geology: A Process Approach, Wadsworth, 1982.
Profiles in Montana Geology, Montana Bureau of Mines and Geology, 1984.
(With Hyndman) *Roadside Geology of Washington*, Mountain Press, 1984.
(With Hyndman) *Roadside Geology of Montana*, Mountain Press, 1986.
(Editor with Hyndman) Keith Frye, *Roadside Geology of Virginia*, Mountain Press, 1986.
(Editor with Hyndman) Bradford B. Van Diver, *Roadside Geology of New Hampshire-Vermont*, Mountain Press, 1987.
(Editor with Hyndman) Halka Cronic, *Roadside Geology of New Mexico*, Mountain Press, 1987.
(With Hyndman) *Roadside Geology of Idaho*, Mountain Press, 1988.
(Editor with Hyndman, Cathy Connor, and Daniel O'Haire) *Roadside Geology of Alaska*, Mountain Press, 1988.

Also author of column on Montana geology, *Montana* magazine. Contributor to journals.

WORK IN PROGRESS: Research projects relating to the regional geology of the Pacific Northwest and the problems of petrology.

*   *   *

ALYER, Philip A.
See STRATEMEYER, Edward L.

*   *   *

AMBLER, John S(teward) 1932-

PERSONAL: Born January 2, 1932, in Portland, Ore.; son of Herbert (a bank official) and Helen (Gordon) Ambler; married

Joyce Hill (a social worker), June 19, 1959; children: Lorraine, Deborah, Mark. *Education:* Willamette University, B.A., 1953; Stanford University, A.M., 1954; University of Bordeaux, Certificat d'Etudes Politiques, 1955; University of California, Berkeley, Ph.D., 1964. *Politics:* Democrat.

ADDRESSES: Home—2242 Dryden Rd., Houston, Tex. 77030. *Office*—P.O. Box 1892, Rice University, Houston, Tex. 77251.

CAREER: University of California, Berkeley, instructor in political science, 1963-64; Rice University, Houston, Tex., assistant professor, 1964-67, associate professor, 1967-71, professor of political science, 1971—, chairman of department, 1978-82. *Military service:* U.S. Army, 1955-57.

MEMBER: American Political Science Association, Southern Political Science Association.

AWARDS, HONORS: Fulbright scholarship, 1954-55; Social Science Research Council fellowship, 1961-62; Fulbright research scholarship, 1969.

WRITINGS:

The French Army in Politics, 1945-1962, Ohio State University Press, 1966, published as *Soldiers against the State: The French Army in Politics,* Doubleday-Anchor, 1968.
(With others) *Papers in Political Science,* Rice University, 1968.
The Government and Politics of France, Houghton, 1971.
(Editor) *The French Socialist Experiment,* Institute for the Study of Human Issues, 1985.

*   *   *

AMIS, Martin (Louis) 1949-

PERSONAL: Born August 25, 1949, in Oxford, England; son of Kingsley William (the writer) and Hilary (Bardwell) Amis; married Antonia Phillips, 1984; children: two sons. *Education:* Oxford University, B.A. (with honors), 1971.

ADDRESSES: Home—14 Kensington Gardens Sq., London W2, England. *Agent*—Jonathan Cape Ltd., 30 Bedford Sq., London WC1B 3EL, England.

CAREER: Times Literary Supplement, London, England, editorial assistant, 1972-75; *New Statesman,* London, assistant literary editor, beginning 1975; full-time writer, 1980—. Actor in the film "A High Wind in Jamaica," 1965.

AWARDS, HONORS: Somerset Maugham Award, National Book League, 1974, for *The Rachel Papers.*

WRITINGS:

The Rachel Papers (novel), J. Cape, 1973, Knopf, 1974.
Dead Babies (novel), J. Cape, 1975, Knopf, 1976, published as *Dark Secrets,* Panther, 1977.
(With others) *My Oxford,* edited and introduced by Ann Thwaite, Robson Books, 1977, revised edition, 1986.
Success (novel), J. Cape, 1978, Crown, 1987.
(Contributor) Caroline Hobhouse, editor, *Winter's Tales 25,* Macmillan (London), 1979, St. Martin's, 1980.
Other People: A Mystery Story (novel), Viking, 1981.
Invasion of the Space Invaders (autobiographical), with an introduction by Stephen Spielberg, Hutchinson, 1982.
Money: A Suicide Note (novel), J. Cape, 1984, Viking, 1985.
The Moronic Inferno and Other Visits to America (articles, reviews and interviews), J. Cape, 1986, Viking, 1987.
Einstein's Monsters (essay and short stories), Harmony Books, 1987.

Also author of a screenplay, "Saturn 3," 1980. Contributor of short stories to *Encounter, Penthouse, Granta 13, London Review of Books,* and *Literary Review.* Contributor of articles and reviews to periodicals, including *Times Literary Supplement, Observer, New Statesman, New York Times,* and *Sunday Telegraph.*

WORK IN PROGRESS: London Fields, a novel about the nuclear threat.

SIDELIGHTS: The son of English novelist Kingsley Amis, Martin Amis has firmly established a reputation of his own, having created in such novels as *The Rachel Papers, Dead Babies, Success,* and *Other People: A Mystery Story* a recognizable fictional world, one described by Michiko Kakutani of the *New York Times* as "a place defined by Swiftian excess and metropolitan satire, a place where various shabby characters partake of lust and violence in hopes of being allowed a second chance." Blake Morrison of the *Times Literary Supplement* notes that Martin "has certainly not been afraid to borrow either [his father's] favourite phrases ('All fixed,' 'How about you?,' 'I want you . . . Now') or his oldest jokes. But in doing so he has indicated the difference in their approaches. When in *The Rachel Papers* ['Lucky Jim'] Dixon's commonsensical 'nice things are nicer than nasty ones' was altered to 'Surely, nice things are dull, and nasty things are funny,' the revision was a calculated one: Martin Amis was making clear that 'nastiness,' the comedy of the grotesque, was to be his specialty."

Morrison points out that in Amis's first three novels the objects of satire are familiar to readers of contemporary fiction: adolescent sex in *The Rachel Papers,* drugs and communal living in *Dead Babies,* and bisexuality and incest in *Success.* James Wolcott of *Esquire* comments, "Dead babies, frayed underwear, gutter scum; yes, as you read Amis's novels you can feel the grime accumulating beneath your fingernails. And yet, and yet: his work is often fleet, brittle, bright, alert, and profanely funny." Writing in the *Dictionary of Literary Biography,* Marla Levy summarizes, "Amis writes humorously about the sorry state of the human condition. He has a curious way of extracting laughs at the expense of human baseness and poverty. . . . He writes about the breakdown in communication between people and their brutality toward each other." Thus, deception, vengeance, and violence characterize his later novels, and his shorter fiction chides mankind *en masse* for its self-destructive tendencies. Margaret Drabble suggests in the *New York Times Book Review* "that Amis is so horrified by the world he sees in the process of formation that he feels compelled to warn us all about it." Known as much for his style as for his themes, Amis is, notes Charles Champlin in the *Los Angeles Times,* "a writer with what can only be called a furious command of words, a social commentator of lethal invention and savage wit." In matters of style, his books, full of word-play and conscious of themselves as works of fiction, show his admiration for the master novelist Vladimir Nabokov. In fact, reports John Greenya in the *Detroit News,* Amis has been "called by one critic 'the nearest thing to a Nabokov that the punk generation has to show.'"

For Amis, becoming a writer was not, as some have supposed, a matter of "taking over the family business," he told Amanda Smith in a *Publishers Weekly* interview. Exposure to other cultures—Spain and the United States—did more to shape his perceptions and his writings. "Some of the anthropologist's detachment" when commenting on human behavior is evident in Amis's novels and essays, notes Sven Birkerts in the *New*

Republic. A fascination with the grotesque, which, in his books, is often tempered with a measure of dread, developed during a stay in America when he was twelve, Amis reveals in *The Moronic Inferno and Other Visits to America.* His father's temporary professorship at Princeton occasioned this first sampling of American life, but the elder Amis "didn't really take much notice of my efforts to write until I plonked the proof of my first novel on his desk," Martin told Smith.

In 1973, Martin Amis entered the British literary scene with *The Rachel Papers,* a novel that "caused a stir in Britain—and, it may be, a dreadful thrill of excitement at what may by some be regarded as the spectacle of a crusadingly nasty adolescent unburdening himself in print," writes Karl Miller in the *New York Review of Books.* In the *New Leader,* Pearl K. Bell elaborates, "*The Rachel Papers* offers a candid, groin-level view of teen-age sex, circa 1970, in Swinging Britain. Amis' hero, Charles Highway, is no slouch at telling us exactly what-he-did-and-then-she-did. But since he is also a precocious and totally self-absorbed intellectual, this indefatigable swordsman is more interested in what he thought, pretended, felt, and above all what he *wrote* in his journal about his sexual happenings, than he is in the act itself." Assessments of room for improvement in the novel take up limited space in reviews that recognize Amis's uncannily mature comic talent. Clive Jordan, for instance, remarks in *Encounter,* "Martin Amis directs a determined, dead-pan stare at his chosen patch of the lush teenage jungle, teeming with characters who are about as appealing as bacilli on a face flannel, described with the detached, excessively detailed physicality common to satirists down the ages. What holds the attention are not these limited characters, but the author's verbally inventive scrutiny of them." Reviews of *The Rachel Papers* helped Amis to become known in England as a young writer of substantial promise.

Many American readers first became aware of Martin Amis as the British author who charged that his novel *The Rachel Papers* had been plagiarized by Jacob Epstein, an American. Amis alleged in an October 19, 1980, article in the *London Observer* that some fifty sizable chunks of Epstein's first novel, *Wild Oats,* were virtual duplications of wording from *The Rachel Papers,* which had been published seven years earlier. Susan Heller Anderson of the *New York Times* writes that when Amis first made the discovery, he "pondered what action to take. 'My own resentment was largely one of embarrassment,' he said. 'I am no real admirer of my first novel or indeed my second, regarding them as a mixture of clumsy apprenticeship and unwarranted showing off. It shamed me to see sentences exhumed for reinspection ten years on.'" Anderson reports that the *London Observer* article was Amis's only revenge and quotes him as saying: "'I'm not terrifically indignant, but just feel it ought to be made public. . . . The saddest thing about the case is that *Wild Oats* is the work of a genuinely talented writer.'"

Two days after Amis's article appeared, Jacob Epstein verbally admitted that he had indeed copied passages and images from Amis, as well as from other writers. Epstein then explained in the October 26, 1980, issue of the *London Observer* that out of admiration and a desire to learn his craft, he had copied passages from *The Rachel Papers* and from books by Nabokov, Turgenev, and Goethe into several notebooks. "After several rewrites and homogenizations," writes Anderson, "Mr. Epstein . . . assumed he was working with virtually original wording." When Epstein discovered in June of 1979 that several phrases and images in his novel had come verbatim from *The Rachel Papers,* he asked his editor at Little, Brown &

Co. about making revisions. Though this was impossible for the first printing, Epstein did make thirteen deletions for the second American edition and asked that the British publisher work from the revision. The letter to the British publisher, however, went astray.

Embarrassed by the British edition, Amis was infuriated by the revised American edition, because Epstein, who had recognized and regretted his error, only made thirteen deletions. According to an interview quoted by Anderson, Amis replied: "'There aren't thirteen bits, there are fifty odd bits from my book. Looking at his revisions, he had lost track of what he'd taken from me. How do you rewrite a novel and leave word-for-word passages?'"

Reviews of early novels by Amis mention his lineage more often than the highly publicized plagiarism case. Similarities between the two Amis careers invite the comparison, Smith explains. Kingsley Amis won the Somerset Maugham Award in 1955 for his first novel, *Lucky Jim,* and Martin won it in 1974 for *The Rachel Papers.* The younger Amis further "compels the reference," Miller says, by using a voice no less belligerent than his father's. Highway of *The Rachel Papers* "sneers, very much as Lucky Jim did, at pretensiousness. But Highway also sneers prolifically at himself," thereby endearing him to both his father's and his own generation, Miller reports. Furthermore, both writers have maintained a somewhat adversarial relationship with the critics, who have indicted them for expressing excess profanity and misogyny—sentiments later recognized as elements of a broad misanthropy. However, relates Champlin, Martin Amis's performance in later books has been such that mentions of his parentage in reviews have become increasingly parenthetical, and in the late 1980s, reviewers on two continents deem him "one of England's hottest literary properties."

Dead Babies, though not as popular as *The Rachel Papers,* "shows Amis's usual humor and satire but with an especially decadent setting and bizarre violence," notes Levy. Short on suspense but long on the sadness and horror well known to the "post-permissive" generation, the novel castigates "our contemporary practice with drugs and sex, or some features of it," Michael Mason maintains in the *Times Literary Supplement.* Amis's youth of the future, "the heirs of liberation," says Mason, "only respect glamour and violence. That process of degeneration which led from Bob Dylan and Ken Kesey to David Bowie and Charles Manson is complete. The novel's only spokesman for other values . . . turns out to be by far the most evil and brutal member of the group." Hailed as a comic success by some, the novel, says Drabble, is "too extreme" and "not at all funny." Publishers granted its paperback edition a new title, *Dark Secrets,* to make it more appealing. It was generally received in the United States "like a smirk at a funeral," according to Wolcott; however, argues Mason, its formal structure and black humor confirm its author's affinities with the great satirists Menippe and Jonathan Swift.

Amis's next offering, *Success,* is the "first of three fictions, a series of turmoils, in which orphan and double meet," observes Miller in *Doubles: Studies in Literary History.* Terry Service, bereft of his father (a man who murdered his own wife and baby daughter), sets himself against his upper-class foster brother Gregory Riding. As they begin with opposite fortunes, so they end, Gregory having fallen from what seemed to be a charmed position of wealth and sexual opportunity, Terry rising to a higher level of success. "At the crossing-point of their two lives lies the smashed body of Ursula, Gregory's sister, successful at the second attempt in a suicide nurtured in an incestuous childhood with Gregory, and triggered by a more recent relationship with Terry," Neil Hepburn notes in the *Listener*. Both brothers relate this turn of events "in alternating and remarkably distinct voices," Jay Parini writes in the *New York Times Book Review*. Terry's voice is marked by the overuse of a particular four-letter word, a feature that perhaps contributed to the nine-year delay between the book's publication in England and its first American edition, Amis believes. Reviewers generally express disappointment with the book's style, but *Encounter* contributor Tom Paulin sees a method behind the author's "madness": "Amis heaps up verbal triplets and refuses to write well. But in a valueless world style may be a value that he is deliberately rejecting."

To Wolcott, *Success* is "a doomsday reverie, in which Terry represents the brutal, heartless spirit of Urban Apocalypse," while Miller calls it a "comedy of orphan malice and adolescent trauma." The malice these brothers level at women is nearly equal to their hatred of themselves, says Parini. Jonathan Yardley, writing in the *Washington Post,* guesses that Amis means to express his contempt for both young men; Paulin and Hepburn feel that Amis targets the entire contemporary world. Paulin contends, "Central to Amis's vision is a sense of deprivation which annihilates the past and makes the present moment seem an exhausted bundle of vicious, fetid and desperate energies.... The only constants in the dead secular world are 'self-pity, self-disgust, and self-love.' "

Reviewers did not agree about the book's success as a satire. "It may be that Amis is attempting to take the negative way through the hell he depicts, but there is a helpless uncertainty in his treatment of it. Far from subverting or qualifying his demonic competence he tends to recommend it," notes Paulin, who, like Parini and Yardley, feels the book is less successful than other novels by Amis. *Village Voice* contributor Graham Fuller, on the other hand, sees in *Success* an enjoyable "parody of England's class war, with Gregory and Terry symbolizing the spiritual decay of the landed gentry and the greedy self-betterment of the 'yobs,' each appraising the other's position with eloquent disgust or shameless envy." In exposing "his characters' self-absorption and the past transgressions that will maim their futures," Fuller finds Amis without peer among British contemporary satirists.

A profusion of doubles complicates Amis's second orphan delirium, or madman's diary, *Other People: A Mystery Story*. Mary Lamb, an amnesiac, faintly recalls her past as bad girl Amy Hide, who nearly died after being attacked by a sadistic psychopath. Two voices tell her story; its ending suggests a return to the beginning for a second take. Her social worker may be sincere, or may be her abductor, setting her up for more abuse. Numerous ambiguities throughout the book make the mystery hard to solve, say some reviewers, while others, like Miller, feel that "its obscurities may be considered a necessary element." Amis provides the answer to this long riddle in literary allusions too subtle for some readers to decipher, but *Encounter* contributor Alan Brownjohn and others recognize the voice of Amis throughout, musing on his own godlike power to manipulate his characters. When read this way, *Other People* appears to be an analysis of the process of making fiction. Extending the analogy, Charles Nichol declares in the *Saturday Review*, "Not all readers will agree with Martin Amis that writing a novel is necessarily a sado-masochistic process, but the force and brilliance of his speculation are undeniable."

In *Other People*, Brownjohn sees "a familiar Martin Amis world made more hideously surprising through the eyes of this lamb on the way back to the slaughter," a vision of uncertainty and violence that makes it "a most original and memorable fable for the Eighties." Evan Hunter muses in the *New York Times Book Review* that Amis "would seem far too young to have acquired such a dismal view of the world." Others, like Brownjohn, indicate that the novel is "more sorry than cynical" about Mary's fate. For this reason, several critics call the book a notable accomplishment. To confront the fact that one's trusted "savior" might be full of diabolical intent takes remarkable courage, suggests Geoffrey Stokes in a *Village Voice* review. Stokes, who sees *Other People* as a slight departure from the stance Amis established in prior books, claims, "The great virtue of *Other People* is that Amis has harnessed his cleverness, turned it into a vehicle for the compassionate exploration of the world—and of the received ideas that shape it.... Instead of giving the finger to life, he is trying to embrace it."

Amis elicits sympathy for another unlikely character in *Money: A Suicide Note*. Narrator John Self lost his mother when he was seven and later received a bill from his father to cover the cost of his upbringing. Obsessed with money and overcome by his appetites, Self, says John Gross in the *New York Times*, "embodies . . . just about everything your mother told you not to play with." Yardley elaborates in the *Washington Post*, "[Money] is one long drinking bout, interrupted only briefly by a period of relative sobriety; it contains incessant sexual activity, much of it onanistic; it has a generous supply of sordid language . . . ; and it has an unkind word for just about every race, creed or nationality known to exist." According to *Time* reviewer R. Z. Sheppard, Self demonstrates that "a culture geared to profit from the immediate gratification of egos and nerve endings is not a culture at all, but an addiction. As an addict, he discovers that bad habits and ignorance are the bars of self-imprisonment." *Listener* contributor Angela Huth deems *Money* "a grim book; a black study of the humiliations and degradations of an alcoholic, a warning of the corruptibility of money and the emptiness of a life with no culture to fall back on." In any other novel, Self's indecencies might cause offense, says Yardley, but in this case, Amis "has created a central character of consummate vulgarity and irresistible charm."

In Self's defense, Amis told Smith, "I'm very, very fond of all my characters.... The central character, repulsive though he is in many ways, is a sort of very dedicated sufferer. Nothing ever goes too well for him. And all his attempts to drain as much pleasure out of life as he has entails such suffering on his part. This is a book in a way about the cost of pleasure." In the end, when Self's avarice culminates in his ruin, he is penniless, but better off, Amis told Stephanie Mansfield of the *Washington Post*. The book's popularity with readers confirms his belief that everyone finds stories of misfortune more interesting than stories of success.

"It is a measure of Amis's narrative and stylistic gifts that he makes of his deeply unpromising material an exhilaratingly readable long novel," Nigel Andrew states in the London *Times*. However, many reviewers find fault with the drunken Self's repetitive account of his demise, wrought behind the scenes in the American film industry. Labeled tedious by some, "that ack-ack prose" is the novel's strength, claims Melvyn Bragg in *Punch*. Self's language, he feels, "has impact and often a breathless force," and captures the real world of the eighties in a way "which can lift the roof of your brain." In a more balanced view, Yardley concedes that *Money* "is amply endowed with flaws," but they are less in number than its achievements. "It takes great risks, it boils with energy, . . . it even manages . . . to shock. And for all of that it is so unremittingly, savagely hilarious that reading it is quite literally an exhausting experience from which one emerges simultaneously gasping for air and pleading for more." Yardley concludes, "If there is excess here, then there is also excess in John Self and excess in the 20th century he so pornographically and flamboyantly mirrors."

"*Money* really needs to be read twice (at least): the first time for the sheer pleasure of encountering the grotesque and lovable John Self, for the laughs, the plot, the extraordinary urban atmospherics. The second time round . . . you can begin to relish the book's marvellously intricate design," Ian Hamilton observes in the *London Review of Books*. Doubling, for instance, takes many forms in the novel. In addition to literary allusions which Self repeats but doesn't fully comprehend, parodies and double-talk, double takes and alter egos abound. At one point, Self approaches a London-based writer named Martin Amis to rewrite a movie script. "From that point on the writer—the fictional writer—threatens to usurp the novel—the real novel. It is like the Escher drawing of a hand drawing itself," muses Gross. Disciplined and cultured, the character Martin Amis has a female counterpart in New York, a Martina Twain, who befriends Self, introduces him to opera, and encourages him to sample great books. Miller indicates that, on another level, the auto-eroticism and self-examination so frequent in the book require the narrator to see himself objectively with an awareness equal to doubling on a psychological plane. Other notable semblances Miller sees in *Money* are its affinities with the works of Norman Mailer, Mickey Spillane, Saul Bellow, and Nabokov's novel of doubling, *Despair*. Commenting on these complexities, Amis told Michael Billingsworth for the *New York Times Book Review*, "What I've tried to do is create a high style to describe low things," which he described to Smith as "a very solid thread in English literature." In addition, "*Money* owes much of its drive to contemporary American fiction," observes Sheppard, who compares it to Joseph Heller's *Catch-22* and Philip Roth's *Portnoy's Complaint*. Hamilton expects that "*Money* will be thought of for years to come as one of the key books of the decade."

The Moronic Inferno shows the same fascinated disdain for American culture through essays, reviews, and interviews with American writers. Reviewers on both sides of the Atlantic mention the negative slant of these pieces, most of which appeared first in the *Observer*. London *Times* reviewer Fiona MacCarthy suggests, "Amis . . . is answering some devastating inner urge to search out and describe in minute detail the worst side of America, the false, silly, double-thinking land of violence, vulgarity, of grid-lock and decay. He ignores have-a-nice-day America completely. Almost all his cast of characters have absolutely dreadful days. At best, Truman Capote in the grip of a grand hangover. At worst, Sunny von Bulow, so well cared for in her coma." Perhaps anticipating charges of anti-Americanism, Amis claims in the introduction that the cultural ailment diagnosed in *The Moronic Inferno* is not "a peculiarly American condition. It is global and perhaps eternal." His America is "primarily a metaphor . . . for mass, gross, ever-distracting human infamy."

In *Einstein's Monsters*, a collection of short stories centered on the danger of nuclear holocaust, Amis continues his "attack on the apocalyptic folly of the age," as Hepburn once called it. "In addition to high verbal energy and flashes of satiric genius, the stories hum with resentment and loathing of a man who fears for his natural patrimony, the earth, the sky and time itself," Sheppard writes in a *Time* review. Bruce Cook, writing in the *Washington Post Book World*, comments on the author's emotional intensity: "Usually a writer with a cool, commanding manner (utterly unflappable in . . . *The Moronic Inferno*) he comes unglued before us here, attributing his high excitement over the nuclear issue to his impending fatherhood and to a relatively late reading of Jonathan Schell's *The Fate of the Earth*." Speaking to John Blades in the *Chicago Tribune*, Amis said Schell's book helped him identify the previously felt but unnamed concern that distinguishes his generation from all others: "We are at the evolutionary crisis point, it seems to me. We're in a new moral universe. We can unmake the world. Extinction is a possibility." He feels that rabid consumerism and many other "present-day peculiarities have to do with this damaged set of time we have. We don't think into the future. People behave as if there were no future." Meanwhile, maintains Amis in the opening essay, the generation that invented and proliferated the A-bomb (or "Z-bomb," in his view) does not give the matter much thought. "The argument is really with our fathers," Amis told Ruth Pollack Coughlin of the *Detroit News*. "But it's also about our children. And all the unborn children."

In the *Times Literary Supplement*, Adam Mars-Jones observes that the stories in *Einstein's Monsters* attempt to make the threat of apocalypse an emotional reality for its readers. The collection lives up to its ambitions, says Norman Snider in the Toronto *Globe and Mail*: "Like that of the Nazi death camps, the subject of nuclear annihilation is one of such appalling magnitude that it takes the strongest of minds to see it whole, without flinching, and at the same time manage a response that avoids the bathetic. Amis succeeds for the most part, although his tone at times sounds the characteristically strident note of the newly converted." Even so, Snider adds, "most of these stories are of the laughing-out-loud variety, the blackest humor of the eighties. . . . It's not every writer who can peer over the brink of human extinction and make you laugh at the same time."

This comparatively thin Amis book has the taut energy of an athlete's body, says Francis King in a *Spectator* review; yet it also rewards connoisseurs of Amis's characteristic style, which so fills *Einstein's Monsters* that Mars-Jones compares it to "a painting composed entirely of signatures." No Amis book has failed to receive accolades for distinctive style. Phrases such as "the commodious cellerage of her eyes" in *The Rachel Papers* moved Grace Glueck of the *New York Times Book Review* to say "Shakespeare lives"; Christopher Lehmann-Haupt's negative assessment of *Dead Babies* deems its verbal wittiness "elegant"; and Fuller qualifies his few complaints about *Success* with his comment that its "Nabokovian word-play is beautifully wrought." At the same time, Amis has consistently exposed and scorned civilization's decay through unappealing characters that he somehow makes interesting. Says Sheppard, "Amis is quite the scold. His Rabelaisian comic gift cuts savagely at the patchwork of relativism and materialism that passes for modern social fabric." Offers Mansfield, "In fact, were it not for his undisputed command of language, his comedic genius and keen ear for dialogue, Amis might be dismissed as just another clever and, yes, snotty young Brit armed with an arsenal of Chelsea one-liners such as 'Style is sort of everything and nothing, but it's mostly everything.'" Summing up, Coughlin remarks, "It is no wonder that [Amis] has been called 'diabolically talented.'"

CA INTERVIEW

CA interviewed Martin Amis by telephone on October 9, 1987, at the London, England, apartment where he writes.

CA: You started in 1972, just out of Oxford, as an editorial assistant for the Times Literary Supplement *and soon thereafter became a Somerset Maugham Award-winner for your first novel,* The Rachel Papers, *published in 1973. How early did you actually start writing?*

AMIS: I started as soon as I finished at university; that was 1971. And I wrote *The Rachel Papers* in a year, working evenings and weekends.

CA: So you hadn't been writing through the student years?

AMIS: Not really, no. Although I always knew that I wanted to be a writer, it was always in the head rather than on the page.

CA: Was fiction your primary goal from the beginning?

AMIS: Yes.

CA: Do you think the traveling around during your childhood and the spotty pre-Oxford schooling were in some way a spur to the writing?

AMIS: Yes. I think a peripatetic childhood does perhaps help. There's basically the question of new schools; you're always having to make your personality for every new immersion, and that makes you conscious of how you're going down. It often turns you into a bit of a comedian, just to avoid getting beat up.

CA: Charles Michener described something about your style very well when he commented in his Esquire *profile on your "remarkable verbal energy." Is that crackling, fast-moving prose—at its best, I think, in* Money—*the result of a great deal of slow writing and rewriting?*

AMIS: Yes, although when you're labeled as having "style," I think some people imagine that you write quite an ordinary paragraph and then spend a lot of time boiling it up. In fact, your style is quite deeply embedded in your perceptions. The work is really involved in making it euphonious—not jazzing it up, but just smoothing it down.

CA: Do you hear it, then, as you're writing or rewriting?

AMIS: Yes. The way I write—and I'm sure many other writers do this too—is to say the sentence or the phrase in my head until it sounds right, changing it a bit here and there. When it tunes with your inner ear, then it's done; it's ready.

CA: You go from home to your work place six days a week. Would you talk about that separation, and how it figures in your writing physically and psychologically? Do you need the separate place in order to write well?

AMIS: I seem to, and especially since the two children have arrived. The house is never quiet. There are always childish dramas or pleasures going on that you can't a hundred percent absent yourself from, and you do need to be a hundred percent to write. I think solitude and writing are almost synonyms. You could never be a writer unless you not only could tolerate a lot of solitude, but actually you crave solitude. It's a solitary job.

CA: Your characters have wonderful names, names frought with meaning: Charles Highway in The Rachel Papers; *Quentin Villiers, Keith Whitehead, and Giles Coldstream in* Dead Babies; *Mary Lamb in* Other People; *John Self in* Money. *Are the names an early part of the characters' formation in your mind?*

AMIS: Sometimes they are, and sometimes you don't quite get it right for a while. In the first draft of *Money*—and in fact also in the second draft—he was still called John Sleep. Then he was going to be called John Street, but finally I firmly settled on John Self. But I had written the whole thing before I was absolutely sure about it. Other times the name is more or less everything; it determines everything about the character.

CA: One might guess from your writing that you have a love-hate relationship with large cities. How do you feel about them generally, and about London and New York in particular?

AMIS: I like cities as a writer. As a citizen and as a human being, I'm not so happy with them. I think they are very deforming, very unnatural, very frightening concentrations. I think London is perhaps the only one I really understand. I can look at a street in New York and make some sort of guess as to what's going on, but it's all conjecture. London I've grown up in and have some feel for. I think cities are very mysterious and frightening places.

CA: Are you ever tempted to go off to the country to write?

AMIS: No. A lot of my friends are moving out of London, and particularly with children you do feel that it's an unhealthy environment. But it seems to be deeply necessary for me to soak it up. I very much feel it's a part of my fuel.

CA: You have such a lovely countryside there, I think it's easy to become a country person and find it almost horrifying to come back to the cities.

AMIS: I think it's more the other way for me. I get the horrors in the countryside—or I used to. I like it as relief from the city. But the provinces strike me as toytown. If one is interested in the modern action, he has no choice really but to live in the biggest city available.

CA: The question of anti-Americanism seems to come up in almost every interview you give, and I would be remiss not to continue the tradition. Do you still consider yourself innocent of the charge? What are your feelings?

AMIS: I don't think anti-Americanism is an option anymore, particularly in the nuclear context. We're all in this together, and it seems to me an otiose luxury, anti-Americanism. It doesn't make any sense to me, and it doesn't mean anything to me. We're too closely bound by language and history. I feel we're all part of the same thing.

CA: So when you're criticizing America, you're also criticizing England in some larger sense?

AMIS: Yes—or criticizing the planet, really.

CA: Success was published in England in 1978, but we didn't get it here until this year. Most of your books have come to us soon after their original publication in England. Why was Success *different?*

AMIS: It just wasn't accepted by Knopf—I was then with Knopf. It went around and was nearly taken by other publishers, but it wasn't. I don't think there was any particular angle on it; they just didn't like it.

CA: It wasn't a case, then, of all the publishers saying it was "too English" for American readers, as sometimes happens?

AMIS: No. I guess sometimes it's considered good there that a novel is English, and sometimes it's bad. That's all mysterious.

CA: As you've commented, the writer in England is regarded less heroically and publicly than the writer in the United States. Does your mail from readers follow that general trend?

AMIS: No, I think I still get more from here. But it's evening out.

CA: You must often be writing novels, reviews, and journalistic pieces at the same time, with extensive travel sometimes involved in the journalism. How easy is it to mix them?

AMIS: People always imagine that novelists must be very disciplined characters. For me it's discipline *not* to write when it comes to fiction: that's what I want to do when I get up in the morning. Journalism does demand a more military aspect. But they tend to mix pretty well until a novel is nagging to be finished. Then you tend to clear the decks and get on with that and not do journalism for a while. That's what I'm doing now.

CA: The Moronic Inferno, *a collection of previously published essays and reviews, was in part a response to the request that you do a book on this country. Some reviewers didn't feel it was a serious enough response. Would you do it differently, or do a completely new book, given the chance?*

AMIS: It wasn't really written in response to that; it was just that I found I had written enough for a book. But, no; in fact, I couldn't imagine any other way of going about it. To settle down and write a book about America would be a life's work, I think.

CA: Of the writers you deal with in the collection, only Saul Bellow really comes out well. Are there any U.S. writers among the younger ones just getting established whose work you enjoy?

AMIS: The truth is that one doesn't get around to younger writers until they're older writers. Again, it would be a full-time job trying to keep up with the bright new names. Since time is limited, I tend to start investigating writers once they've been around for a while, once they've proved they've got the stamina to go on being interesting. If one followed up every new name in the *New York Times Book Review*, there wouldn't be much time for anything else.

CA: How healthy do you consider the state of current fiction in England?

AMIS: Very healthy, I think. There seems to be no shortage of opposition. *Horrifyingly* healthy from that point of view. There are at least a dozen interesting writers around my age.

CA: What do you feel a book reviewer owes his readers?

AMIS: As a reviewer, I think you're writing for an imaginary literary review called *Consumer Report*, or *Which?* You're telling the readers what they need to bother with. But more generally, I think novelists have a duty to keep on reviewing. I think they have a stake in it if they want to keep standards up. And it's self-interest in that you want to keep the reading public in good shape so that when you're next novel comes out, they understand it. And with a general trend towards stupefaction of one kind or another, I think it's vitally important to keep up your contribution to reviewing.

CA: Has being a reviewer yourself enabled you to accept unfavorable reviews of your books more philosophically than you might otherwise?

AMIS: I don't think so, but I don't get upset—or I don't get upset *yet*. But I think that's a purely temperamental matter. I don't think there's any training for it, rather just your character will decide how much you mind about a bad review. I don't think it's got anything to do with how good you are, either. It's just one of those things.

CA: So many writers have said that one shouldn't pay attention to the good reviews any more than the bad ones.

AMIS: Yes. Actually, one doesn't often find that a bad review or even a good review really goes to what you think is the quick. All writers could write incredibly hostile reviews of the books they've written. They know the real flaws, the real cowardices of their own book, and the reviewer just seems to be flailing away with a blunt instrument. The writer has read the book a hundred times, and the reviewer hasn't.

CA: I've avoided the son-of-famous-father question as long as I can. You've told various interviewers that his greatest gift to you was not encouraging you to be a writer. It has also been noted that he doesn't read everything you write. How close are you and Kingsley Amis now?

AMIS: We're very close. It's a very enjoyable adversarial type of relationship in that we agree a lot more about literature than we do about politics, but we don't agree *that* much about literature. So it's argumentative, but close.

CA: I think you've said previously too that your children have made you and your father closer, because he was so pleased with having grandchildren.

AMIS: I think having children changes your relationship to your parents and deepens it whether you're a writer or not. It strengthens the whole thing. Also you see in horrifying close-up exactly the million little tasks they effected for your benefit when you were tiny.

CA: Many critics have perceived your writing as pessimistic; yet you told Charles Gill for Interview, *"I really regard writing as black fun, not the expression of deep miseries or dissatisfaction." Would you amend that statement since you've turned to the nuclear threat in* Einstein's Monsters, *the essay "Nuke City" in* Esquire, *and a novel-in-progress?*

AMIS: I think the business of writing is all celebratory, no matter how gloomy it sounds to some. It is always a positive thing to write a book. I don't think unadorned pessimism has any place in writing; it's always a complicated pessimism, or a qualified pessimism.

CA: In "Nuke City" you said of the disaster that would result from a nuclear strike on Washington, which could apply of course to any place, "Now is the time to see this, and your head is the place to see it in. The reality won't be seen by anyone." Will this be a theme of the novel you're working on?

AMIS: Yes. The novel is set in 1999. There's plenty of other stuff going on in the book, but there's a background of nuclear crisis. The world isn't blown up. The crisis comes and it passes, but there is a sort of heightened awareness of how the whole thing could go any second.

CA: What's beyond the nuclear novel? Are there new concerns, budding novels, anything completely unlike what you've done before?

AMIS: I don't think I'll be going straight on with the nuclear thing—much to the relief of many of my readers, I'm sure. But I think the nuclear matter and various other planetary matters will be at least in one's imagery from now on—the sense that history is reaching a climax of some kind, that we've got to dig for the planet and that enormous changes are not too far off in the future.

BIOGRAPHICAL/CRITICAL SOURCES:

BOOKS

Amis, Martin, *The Rachel Papers*, J. Cape, 1973, Knopf, 1974.

Amis, Martin, *Success*, J. Cape, 1978, Crown, 1987.

Amis, Martin, *Other People: A Mystery Story*, Viking, 1981.

Amis, Martin, *Invasion of the Space Invaders* (autobiographical), with an introduction by Stephen Spielberg, Hutchinson, 1982.

Amis, Martin, *The Moronic Inferno and Other Visits to America*, J. Cape, 1986, Viking, 1987.

Amis, Martin, *Einstein's Monsters*, Harmony Books, 1987.

Contemporary Literary Criticism, Gale, Volume 4, 1975, Volume 9, 1978, Volume 38, 1987.

Dictionary of Literary Biography, Volume 14: *British Novelists since 1960*, Gale, 1983.

Miller, Karl, *Doubles: Studies in Literary History*, Oxford University Press, 1985.

PERIODICALS

Chicago Tribune, April 21, 1985, February 23, 1986, June 11, 1987, September 1, 1987.

Cosmopolitan, August, 1978.

Detroit News, June 16, 1985, June 14, 1987.

Encounter, February 1974, February, 1976, September, 1978, May, 1981.

Esquire, November, 1980, November, 1986, January, 1987, October, 1987.

Globe and Mail (Toronto), January 26, 1985, September 6, 1986, June 6, 1987.

Interview, June, 1985.

Listener, August 15, 1974, October 30, 1975, April 13, 1978, March 5, 1981, September 27, 1984.

London Magazine, February/March, 1974.

London Review of Books, May 7-20, 1981, September 20-October 3, 1984.

Los Angeles Times, June 28, 1987, September 27, 1987.

Los Angeles Times Book Review, March 31, 1985.

New Leader, May 13, 1974.

New Republic, January 26, 1987.

New Statesman, November 16, 1973, October 17, 1975, March 13, 1981.

Newsweek, May 6, 1974, March 25, 1985.

New Yorker, June 24, 1974, August 10, 1981, June 10, 1985.

New York Magazine, April 29, 1974.

New York Review of Books, July 18, 1974.

New York Times Book Review, May 26, 1974, February 8, 1976, July 26, 1981, March 24, 1985, May 17, 1987, September 6, 1987.

Publishers Weekly, February 8, 1985.

Punch, October 10, 1984.

Saturday Review, June, 1981.

Spectator, November 24, 1973, April 15, 1978, March 21, 1981, October 20, 1984, July 12, 1986, December 6, 1986, May 2, 1987.

Sunday Times (London), March 8, 1981, September 26, 1982.

Time, March 11, 1985, June 22, 1987.

Time Out, March 27, 1981.

Times (London), September 27, 1984, August 14, 1986, April 30, 1987, July 25, 1987.

Times Literary Supplement, October 17, 1975, March 6, 1981, November 26, 1982, October 5, 1984, July 18, 1986, May 1, 1987.

Tribune Books (Chicago), May 29, 1988.

Village Voice, January 26, 1976, June 10-June 16, 1981, February 24, 1987, December 1, 1987.

Wall Street Journal, April 24, 1985.

Washington Post, April 28, 1985, January 7, 1987, September 16, 1987.

Washington Post Book World, March 24, 1985, July 5, 1987.

World Literature Today, spring, 1982.

—Sketch by Marilyn K. Basel

—Interview by Jean W. Ross

*　　　*　　　*

AMOS, Winsom 1921-

PERSONAL: Born May 10, 1921, in Lansing, Mich.; son of Charles and Inez (Kinnebrew) Amos; married Oris Carter (a college professor), April 16, 1954; children: Patsy. *Education:* Ferris State College (now University), B.S., 1951; graduate study at Michigan State University, 1952; Ohio State University, M.A., 1970. *Religion:* Protestant.

ADDRESSES: Home—P.O. Box 416, Yellow Springs, Ohio 45387.

CAREER: Teacher in Martinsville, Va., 1951-53; self-employed collections agent in Martinsville, 1953-55; William B. Muse, Jr., Martinsville, broker's assistant, 1953-55; Defense Construction Supply Center, Columbus, Ohio, supply cataloger, 1955-69, counselor, 1969-70, coordinator, 1970-83. Self-employed public accountant, 1951—. President of Worthington Human Relations Council, 1971-73. *Military service:* U.S. Army, 1942-45; received Bronze Star.

MEMBER: Ohio Adult Education Association.

WRITINGS:

Like a Dream (poems), Harlo, 1971.
Oriole to Black Mood (poems), privately printed, 1973.
Surprise!, Soma Press, 1982.
Youth Poems, Soma Press, 1983.

Contributor to several poetry anthologies, including *Poetry of Our Time, 50 Outstanding American Poets during 1977*, and *On the Threshold of a Dream*. Also contributor of poetry to *Pittsburgh Courier, Lansing State Journal, Columbus Call and Post, Poetry Parade*, and *Journal of Contemporary Poetry*.

SIDELIGHTS: Winsom Amos told *CA:* "I always try to write with tenderness and force. My philosophy is to be successful in your own way, but don't forget from where you came. Don't forget and turn your back."

*   *   *

ANDERSEN, Francis Ian 1925-

PERSONAL: Born July 28, 1925, in Warwick, Australia; son of Emil (a grocer) and Hilda (a seamstress; maiden name, Homes) Andersen; married Lois Garrett (a physician), December 5, 1952; children: John, David, Martin, Nedra, Kathryn. *Education:* University of Queensland, B.Sc. (with honors), 1946; University of Melbourne, M.Sc., 1951, B.A., 1955; Australian College of Theology, Th.L., 1955; University of London, B.D. (with honors), 1956; Johns Hopkins University, M.A., 1958, Ph.D., 1960; Church Divinity School of the Pacific, D.D., 1972. *Religion:* Christian.

ADDRESSES: Home—86 Pullenvale Rd., Pullenvale, Queensland 4069, Australia. *Office*—Studies in Religion, University of Queensland, St. Lucia, Brisbane 4067, Australia.

CAREER: Ordained Anglican minister, 1958, currently mission chaplain of Fellowship of St. John, Diocese of Brisbane, Australia. Ridley College, Australia, vice-principal, 1960-62; Church Divinity School of the Pacific, professor of Old Testament, 1963-73; St. John's College, New Zealand, warden, 1973-74; Australian Institute of Archaeology, Melbourne, research scholar, 1974; Macquarie University, North Ryde, Australia, associate professor of history, 1975-80; University of Queensland, Brisbane, Australia, professor of studies in religion, 1980-89; New College, Berkeley, Australia, professor of Old Testament, 1989—.

WRITINGS:

The Verbless Clause in the Hebrew Pentateuch (monograph), Abingdon, 1970.
(With A. Dean Forbes) *A Synoptic Concordance to Hosea, Amos, Micah*, Biblical Research Associates, 1972.
The Sentence in Biblical Hebrew, Mouton, 1974.
Job, Tyndale Press, 1976.
(With Forbes) *A Linguistic Concordance of Ruth and Jonah: Hebrew Vocabulary and Idiom*, Biblical Research Associates, 1976.
(With Forbes) *Eight Minor Prophets: A Linguistic Concordance*, Biblical Research Associates, 1976.
(With Forbes) *Jeremiah: A Linguistic Concordance*, Volume I: *Grammatical Vocabulary and Proper Nouns*, Volume II: *Nouns and Verbs*, Biblical Research Associates, 1978.
(Translator, contributor and author of introduction, with David Noel Freedman) *Hosea: A New Translation*, Doubleday, 1980.
(Contributor) James A. Charlesworth, editor, *Pseudepigrapha*, Volume I: *Apocalyptic Literature and Testaments*, Doubleday, 1983.
(With Forbes) *Spelling in the Hebrew Bible*, Biblical Institute Press (Rome), 1986.
(Contributor) Peter T. O'Brien and David G. Peterson, editors, *God Who Is Rich in Mercy: Essays Presented to Dr. D. B. Knox*, Baker Book, 1986.

(Contributor) Edgar W. Conrad and Edward G. Newing, editors, *Perspectives on Language and Text: Essays and Poems in Honor of Francis I. Andersen's Sixtieth Birthday, July 28, 1985*, Eisenbrauns (Winona Lake, Indiana), 1987.

Also author of *Anchor Bible: Amos*, 1989. Also co-author with Forbes of *The Computer Bible* (five volumes).

WORK IN PROGRESS: The Vocabulary of the Old Testament, with Forbes, and *Further Studies in Hebrew Spelling*, with Forbes and Freedman.

*   *   *

ANDERSON, Charles 1933- (Chuck Anderson)

PERSONAL: Born March 25, 1933, in Queens, N.Y.; son of Charles A. (an insurance executive) and Margaret (Bassett) Anderson; married Judith Hall, August 31, 1957; children: Donald, Gordon, Edward. *Education:* Bucknell University, B.A., 1956; Adelphi University, M.A., 1970. *Politics:* Independent. *Religion:* Episcopalian.

ADDRESSES: Home—37 Chapel Rd., Brookhaven, N.Y. 11719. *Office*—Longwood High School, Middle Island, N.Y.

CAREER: High school teacher of English in Southfold, N.Y., 1958-60, and Bellport, N.Y., 1960-63; Longwood High School, Middle Island, N.Y., teacher of English and media studies, 1963—. Assistant professor of philosophy, mythology, and English at Suffolk County Community College, 1966—; member of faculty at New School for Social Research, 1970-75; fellow, Center for Understanding Media, New York, N.Y., 1970—; artist-in-residence at St. Mary of Redman School, 1973, Foxfire, Rabun Gap, Ga., 1974, and several public schools in Dubuque, Iowa, 1976. Instructor at Boces II Summer Institute for Gifted and Talented, 1976—. Producer of films "Common Thread," 1977 and "The Mediation Film," 1984.

MEMBER: National Educational Association, New York Teachers Association.

AWARDS, HONORS: National Endowment for the Humanities fellowship, 1984.

WRITINGS—Under name Chuck Anderson:

The Electric Journalist, Praeger, 1973.
Video Power: Grass Roots Television, Praeger, 1975.
Composition: Level IV, Scholastic Inc., 1980.

Also author of educational documentary on hearing handicapped, "To Break the Silence," shown as part of a media exhibit that toured European museums in 1974. Contributor of articles and reviews to *Media and Methods, Radical Software, Long Island Advance, New York Times*, and *East End Independent*.

SIDELIGHTS: Charles Anderson wrote *CA*, "My work has been influenced and inspired by Bucknell University teachers Harry Garvin and Wendell Smith."

*   *   *

ANDERSON, Chuck
See ANDERSON, Charles

ANDERSON, James D(esmond)   1933-

PERSONAL: Born February 9, 1933, in Christiansburg, Va.; son of Walter Willard and Sarah Margaret (Hardin) Anderson; married Winifred Guthrie, June 12, 1955; children: Walter, Mark, Kent. *Education:* Northwestern University, B.A., 1955; Virginia Theological Seminary, M.Div., 1961.

ADDRESSES: Home—3204 Old Dominion Blvd., Alexandria, Va. 22305. *Office*—Cathedral College of the Laity, Washington, D.C. 20016.

CAREER: Ordained priest in Episcopal Church, 1961; associate rector of Episcopal church in Kenosha, Wis., 1961-63; Bethesda-by-the-Sea, Palm Beach, Fla., director of Christian education, 1963-65; St. John's Church, Arlington, Va., priest in charge, 1965-67; Diocese of Washington, Washington, D.C., bishop's assistant for parish development, 1967-81; Cathedral College of the Laity, Washington, D.C., director of field research, 1981—. Lecturer at Princeton Seminary and Episcopal Seminary of the Southwest. Founding member of board of directors of Alban Institute. *Military service:* U.S. Marine Corps, communications officer, 1955-58; became first lieutenant.

MEMBER: International Association of Applied Social Scientists (charter member), Association for Creative Change.

WRITINGS:

(Contributor) James Westerhoff, editor, *A Colloquy on Christian Education,* Pilgrim Press, 1972.
(With Jean M. Haldane and others) *Prescription for Parishes,* Seabury, 1973.
To Come Alive!: A New Proposal for Revitalizing the Local Church, Harper, 1973.
(With Ezra Earl Jones) *The Management of Ministry,* Harper, 1978.
(With others) *Building Effective Ministry,* Harper, 1983.
Ministry of the Laity, Harper, 1986.

WORK IN PROGRESS: Research on information systems in the church, and on the relationship between church membership and personal religious life.

*   *   *

ANDERSON, Robert H(enry)   1918-

PERSONAL: Born July 28, 1918, in Milwaukee, Wis.; son of Robert Dean (a production manager) and Eleanor (Weil) Anderson; married Mary Jane Hopkins (an educational specialist and professional harpist), July 19, 1941 (divorced January, 1979); married Karolyn J. Snyder (an educational consultant), January 24, 1979; children: (first marriage) Dean Robert, Lynn Mary (Mrs. William D. Grant), Scott William, Carol Jane. *Education:* University of Wisconsin, B.A., 1939, M.A., 1942; University of Chicago, Ph.D., 1949. *Politics:* Democrat. *Religion:* Episcopalian.

ADDRESSES: Home—13604 Waterfall Way, Tampa, Fla. 33624. *Office*—P.O. Box 271669, Tampa, Fla. 33688.

CAREER: Junior high school teacher and coach in Oconomowoc, Wis., 1941-43; elementary school principal in River Forest, Ill., 1947-49; superintendent of schools, Park Forest Ill., 1949-54; Harvard University, Graduate School of Education, Cambridge, Mass., lecturer, 1954-59, associate professor, 1959-61, professor of education, 1962-73, director of elementary school internship and apprentice-teaching program, 1954-63, director of Teaching Teams Project in Lex-

ington, Mass., 1957-64; Texas Tech University, Lubbock, dean of College of Education, 1973-83, professor and dean emeritus, 1983—; University of South Florida, Tampa, professor of education, 1984—. Visiting professor, University of Iowa, 1953, University of Wisconsin, 1960, and University of Hawaii, 1962. President, Pedamorphosis, Inc., 1977—. Lecturer and consultant on school organization, administration, and architecture. *Military service:* U.S. Navy Reserve, Supply Corps, 1943-46; became lieutenant.

MEMBER: National Society for the Study of Education, American Association of School Administrators, Association for Supervision and Curriculum Development, National Education Association, American Educational Research Association, National Association of Elementary School Principals, Phi Delta Kappa.

AWARDS, HONORS: M.A., Harvard University, 1959; presidential citation from Illinois Association of School Administrators, 1973.

WRITINGS:

(With J. I. Goodlad) *The Nongraded Elementary School,* Harcourt, 1959, revised edition, 1963.
(With others) *The Healthy Child: His Physical, Psychological, and Social Development,* edited by H. C. Stuart and D. G. Prugh, Harvard University Press, 1960.
Teaching in a World of Change, Harcourt, 1966.
(Editor with H. G. Shane) *As the Twig Is Bent,* Houghton, 1971.
(Editor with M. Hiratsuka and Isao Amagi) *Current Trends in Education,* Dai-ichi Koko (Japan), 1971.
(Editor) *Education in Anticipation of Tomorrow,* Charles A. Jones Publishing, 1973.
Opting for Openness, National Association of Elementary School Principals, 1973.
(With Robert Goldhammer and Robert J. Krajewski) *Clinical Supervision: Special Methods for the Supervision of Teachers,* 2nd edition (Anderson not associated with earlier edition), Holt, 1980.
(With wife, Karolyn J. Snyder) *Managing Productive Schools: Toward an Ecology,* Harcourt, 1986.
(With Snyder) *Coaching Teaching: Clinical Supervision in Action,* Random House, 1988.

CONTRIBUTOR

J. T. Shaplin and H. F. Olds, Jr., editors, *Team Teaching,* Harper, 1964.
Richard I. Miller, editor, *Perspectives on Educational Change,* Appleton, 1967.
D. D. Bushnell and D. Allen, editors, *The Computer in American Education,* Wiley, 1967.
Sidney G. Tickton, editor, *To Improve Learning: An Evaluation of Instructional Technology,* Bowker, 1971.
Louis Rubin, editor, *The In-Service Education of Teachers,* Allyn & Bacon, 1978.

GENERAL EDITOR

Kaoru Yamamoto, editor, *The Child and His Image: Self-Concept in the Early Years,* Houghton, 1972.
Robert D. Hess and Doreen J. Croft, *Teachers of Young Children,* with teacher handbook, Houghton, 1972.
Richard E. Hodges and E. Hugh Rudorf, editors, *Language and Learning to Read: What Teachers Need to Know about Language,* Houghton, 1972.

Kevin Ryan and James M. Cooper, *Kaleidoscope: Readings in Education*, Houghton, 1972.
Ryan and Cooper, *Those Who Can, Teach*, Houghton, 1972.

OTHER

Contributor to four yearbooks of National Society for the Study of Education. Contributor to *Encyclopedia of Educational Research*, Macmillan. Contributor of about seventy articles to journals, including *National Education Association Journal, Educational Leadership, Architectural Record,* and *Journal of Teacher Education.* Editorial advisor, Houghton Mifflin Co., 1968-72. Consulting editor, *Colloquy,* 1967-71; editor, *Texas Tech Journal of Education,* beginning 1974.

SIDELIGHTS: Robert H. Anderson writes that his main interests are in promoting flexible school organization patterns by implementing team teaching, open programs, open-space architecture, and flexible uses of personnel. He has both worked and travelled abroad, assisting American schools overseas as well as foreign ministries of education. Anderson's writings have been translated into Japanese, Italian, Hebrew, Chinese, Spanish, German, and Dutch.

*   *   *

ANDREWS, Michael F(rank) 1916-

PERSONAL: Born March 4, 1916, in Cairnbrook, Pa.; son of Frank (a miner) and Libra (Testa) Andrews; married Helen Wilma Baker (an administrative executive), December 30, 1940; children: Judi (Mrs. Stanley Thomas III), Connee (Mrs. Larry Dolin), Michael C. *Education:* Attended Juniata College, 1935-37; University of Kansas, B.F.A., 1940, M.S., 1948; Ohio State University, Ph.D., 1952.

ADDRESSES: Home—69 Briarwood Rd., Woodland Hills, Asheville, N.C. 28804-1003. *Office*—Department of Synaesthetic Education, Syracuse University, Syracuse, N.Y. 13210.

CAREER: Public school teacher in Lawrence and Hayes, Kan., 1940-42; University of Kansas, Lawrence, instructor in art, 1945-48; Ohio State University, Columbus, instructor in art, 1948-50; University of Southern California, Los Angeles, assistant professor of art education, 1950-52; University of Wisconsin, Madison, assistant professor of art education, 1952-55; Syracuse University, Syracuse, N.Y., professor of art, 1955-70, professor of synaesthetic education and department chairman, 1970-82, professor emeritus, 1983—. Visiting professor at University of Hawaii, summer, 1967. Lecturer at art assemblies, congresses, and other institutions in U.S., Canada, Japan, and Europe. Work as sculptor has been exhibited throughout the country; sculpture and photography exhibited in one-man show at Fine Arts Festival, Cortland, N.Y., 1961. Consultant in art therapy at Marcy State Hospital. *Military service:* U.S. Army Air Forces, 1942-45; became first lieutenant.

MEMBER: International Society for Education through Art, National Art Educators Association (president of Eastern region, 1966-68), National Education Association, Eastern Regional Art Educators Association (president, 1967-69), Kansas Art Teachers Association (president, 1947-49), California Art Teachers Association (vice president, 1951-52), New York State Art Teachers Association.

AWARDS, HONORS: First place in professional division for sculpture at Ohio State Fair, 1949; National Decorative Arts and Ceramic Exhibition honorable mention, 1949; Columbus Art League sculpture award, 1950; Sculpture House award, 1953, for metal sculpture; Wisconsin Salon of Art award, 1954; honorable mention for Hall of Education symbol for New York World's Fair, 1962; Art Teacher of the Year Award, New York State Art Teachers Association, 1978.

WRITINGS:

(With Maud Ellsworth) *Growing with Art,* eight books, Benjamin Sanborn, 1950.
(Editor and contributor) *Aesthetic Form and Education,* Syracuse University Press, 1958.
(Editor) *Creativity and Psychological Health,* Syracuse University Press, 1961.
Creative Printmaking, Prentice-Hall, 1964.
Creative Education: The Liberation of Man, Syracuse University Press, 1965.
Sculpture and Ideas, Prentice-Hall, 1966.
(With Larry Bakke, O. Charles Giordano, and James Ridlon) *Synaesthetic Education,* Syracuse University Press, 1971.
Sensory Learning at Syracuse University, Syracuse University Press, 1981.

OTHER

Also author of sound recordings *Adventure beyond Knowledge* and *The Quest for Self-Actualization,* both for J. Norton. Coauthor of educational film, "People, Purpose, Progress." Consulting editor of *Journal of Creative Behavior,* 1969—.

WORK IN PROGRESS: The Baobab Tree, a children's book; *Taste the Sound of Raindrops.*

SIDELIGHTS: Michael F. Andrews once told *CA:* "In creative writing my concern is not so much to arrive at a product or performance, but to nurture a living experience perceived significantly and completely. Such an enhancing and enlightening experience, like all human experiences, is an episode in a process of viewing my life on a deeper and more personal level of understanding and enjoyment than I could otherwise. My focus is on perceiving, developing holistic sensory awareness, and expressing my immediate synaesthetic experiences in concrete terms as a reflection of myself in my environment."

*   *   *

ANTHONY, Catherine
See ADACHI, Barbara (Curtis)

*   *   *

ANTHONY, James R(aymond) 1922-

PERSONAL: Born February 18, 1922, in Providence, R. I.; son of Howard W. (a bank teller) and Lena (Latham) Anthony; married Louise R. Macnair, May 24, 1952; children: Barbara, Janet, Stephen. *Education:* Columbia University, B. S., 1946, M. A., 1948; Sorbonne, University of Paris, Diplome, 1951; University of Southern California, Ph. D., 1964.

ADDRESSES: Home—800 North Wilson Ave., Tucson, Ariz. *Office*—Department of Music, University of Arizona, Tucson, Ariz. 85721.

CAREER: Montana State University (now University of Montana), Missoula, instructor in music, 1948-50; University of Arizona, Tucson, 1952—, began as assistant professor, currently professor of music. Consultant to National Endowment for the Humanities, 1974—. *Military service:* U. S. Army Air Forces, 1942-45; became staff sergeant; received Air Medal and Distinguished Flying Cross.

MEMBER: International Musicological Society, Societe francaise de musicologie, American Council of Learned Societies, American Musicological Society, College Music Society, Music Teacher's National Association, Music Educators National Council, American Association of University Professors, Arizona State Music Teacher's Association.

WRITINGS:

French Baroque Music from Beaujoyeuix to Rameau, Batsford, 1973, Norton, 1974, revised edition, 1978.
(Editor with D. Akmajian) Michel-Pignolet de Monteclair, *Cantatas for One and Two Voices,* Madison, 1978.
(Editor) Michel-Richard Delalande, *De Profundis,* University of North Carolina Press, 1980.
(Translator into French) *French Baroque Music,* Flammarion (Paris), 1980, Norton, 1981.
Michel-Richard Delelande's "De Profundis": Grand Motet for Soloists, Chorus, Woodwind, Strings, and Continuo, University of North Carolina Press, 1981.

Contributor, with N. Dufourcq, to *New Oxford History of Music,* 1975, and to *Grove's Dictionary of Music and Musicians,* 6th edition, 1977; also contributor to proceedings of professional organizations.*

*   *   *

ANTHONY, Michael   1932-

PERSONAL: Born February 10, 1932, in Mayaro, Trinidad and Tobago; son of Nathaniel (a farmer) and Eva (Jones) Anthony; married Yvette (a typist), February 8, 1958; children: two sons, two daughters. *Education:* "No institution of note attended and no degrees or awards gained." *Politics:* "Uncategorized."

ADDRESSES: Home—99 Long Circular Rd., St. James, Port-of-Spain, Trinidad and Tobago.

CAREER: Held a number of factory jobs after immigrating to England; Reuter News Agency, London, England, sub-editor, 1964-68; lived in Brazil, 1968-70; Texaco Trinidad, Pointe-a-Pierre, Trinidad and Tobago, assistant editor, 1970-72; Ministry of Culture, Port-of-Spain, Trinidad and Tobago, researcher, 1972—.

WRITINGS:

The Games Were Coming (novel), Deutsch, 1963, expanded edition with introduction by Kenneth Ramchand, Heinemann and Deutsch, 1977.
The Year in San Fernando (novel), Deutsch, 1965, revised edition with introduction by Paul Edwards and Kenneth Ramchand, Heinemann, 1970.
Michael Anthony's Tales for Young and Old, Stockwell, 1967.
Green Days by the River (novel), Houghton, 1967.
Cricket in the Road (short stories), Heinemann Educational, 1973.
Sandra Street and Other Stories, Heinemann Educational, 1973.
Glimpses of Trinidad and Tobago with a Glance at the West Indies, Columbus (Trinidad), 1974.
King of the Masquerade, Thomas Nelson, 1974.
Profile Trinidad: A Historical Survey from the Discovery to 1900, Macmillan, 1975.

(Editor with Andrew Carr) *David Frost Introduces Trinidad and Tobago,* Deutsch, 1975.
Folk Tales and Fantasies (short stories), illustrations by Pat Chu Foon, Columbus, 1976.
Streets of Conflict (novel), Deutsch, 1976.
The Making of Port-of-Spain, 1757-1939, Key Caribbean, 1978.
All that Glitters (novel), Deutsch, 1981.
Handbook of Small Business Advertisiing, Addison-Wesley, 1981.
Bright Road to El Dorado (novel), Nelson Caribbean, 1982.
First in Trinidad, Circle Press, 1985.

SIDELIGHTS: Michael Anthony writes apparently simple tales of life on the island of Trinidad that convey deep insights on human relationships. Often told from the viewpoint of a child, these tales also give the reader a taste of Caribbean life. *New York Times* contributor Martin Levin claims, "Mr. Anthony has perfect pitch and an artist's eye for the finer shadings of the native scene he knows so intimately." Writing of Anthony's short story collection *Cricket in the Road* in *Books and Bookmen,* James Brockway finds "an evocative power I have rarely come across, a power drawn not merely from observation, but from observing *the things that matter,* and conveying them in exactly the right words and not a word too many." Discussing Anthony's book *Green Days by the River,* Levin reports that the author "makes his characters appealing without overly romanticizing them, and his ear for dialogue is magnificently accurate." Brockway concludes, "Mr. Anthony reminds us that there are simpler, more essential things in life than getting and spending and he writes about them with a serenity that can only come from strength."

Anthony once said, "I am essentially a novelist and since I hold that the novel tells a story I feel strongly that I should not use the medium to air my philosophies. However, I feel very strongly about the brotherhood of mankind and as a consequence abominate war. One of my main hopes is that human beings will find a way to live together without friction, and my feeling is that the most distressing thing in this world is the inhumanity of man to man on the grounds of race. I feel that if the racial problem is solved man will have found the key to peace on this planet. Although I am not hopeful about any immediate change in the Southern African situation, I think the thousands of people who are trying to solve the problem in the United States must make a great difference to the basic situation there. Yet, though I feel this way, the books I write have nothing (on the surface) to do with race or war."

Anthony also writes that he is extremely interested in space exploration "as I sometimes find the mystery of the Universe too much to bear. I often wonder if space exploration will one day explode our present theories about God, and about the origin and formation of the matter about us. I do consider man's quest for knowledge vital and, in fact, inevitable." He also commented that he would "like to see this world of rich and poor nations, powerful and weak nations, superseded by a world of one strong nation formed out of all. In other words I am advocating World Government. I sometimes think that I am merely being idealistic, but being an optimist I am not surprised."

BIOGRAPHICAL/CRITICAL SOURCES:

BOOKS

Ramchand, Kenneth, *The West Indian Novel and its Background,* Faber, 1970.

PERIODICALS

Books and Bookmen, February, 1974.
London Magazine, April, 1967.
New York Times Book Review, August 6, 1967, April 14, 1968.
Observer, July 26, 1981.
Punch, February 22, 1967.
Spectator, February 21, 1976.
Times Literary Supplement, March 4, 1965, April 13, 1967.
World Literature Today, spring, 1984.*

*   *   *

AOKI, Haruo   1930-

PERSONAL: Born April 1, 1930, in Kunsan, Korea; son of Akira and Yae Aoki; married Mary Ann Schroeder, August 30, 1958 (divorced, 1977); children: Kanna, Akemi, Mieko. *Education:* Hiroshima University, B.A., 1953; University of California, Berkeley, M.A., 1958; University of California, Los Angeles, Ph.D., 1965.

ADDRESSES: Office—Department of Oriental Languages, University of California, Berkeley, Calif. 94720.

CAREER: University of California, Berkeley, assistant professor, 1965-69, associate professor, 1969-72, professor of oriental languages, 1972—.

MEMBER: Linguistic Society of America, American Oriental Society, Linguistic Association of Great Britain, Cercle Linguistique de Copenhagne, Linguistic Society of Japan, Nihon Gengogakkai, Kokugogakkai, Kokugo Kenkyuukai, Keiryoo Kokugo Gakkai.

AWARDS, HONORS: Fulbright fellow, 1953-54.

WRITINGS:

Nez Perce Grammar, University of California Press, 1970.
Horobiyuku-kotoba o Otte (title means "In Pursuit of a Vanishing Language"), Sanseido Press (Tokyo), 1972.
Nez Perce Texts, University of California Press, 1979.
(With others) *Basic Structure in Japanese,* Asian Humanities Press, 1984.
(With Shigeko Okamoto) *Rules for Conversational Rituals in Japanese,* Taishu-kan, 1988.

Associate editor of *Northwestern Anthropological Research Notes,* 1967—, and *Papers in Japanese Linguistics,* 1973—.

*   *   *

APPIGNANESI, Lisa   1946-
(Jessica Ayre)

PERSONAL: Born January 4, 1946, in Lodz, Poland; daughter of Aron (a businessman) and Hana (Lipschyz) Borenstein; married Richard Appignanesi (a writer), January 3, 1967 (divorced, 1982); currently living with John Forrester; children: (first marriage) Joshua; (with Forrester) Katrina Max. *Education:* McGill University, B.A., 1966, M.A., 1967; Sussex University, D.Phil., 1970. *Politics:* "Reflected."

ADDRESSES: Home—69 Whitehall Park, London N 19, England. *Office*—Deputy Director, Institute of Contemporary Arts, The Mall, London SW1Y 5AH, England. *Agent*—Christine Bernard, 7 Well Rd., London NW 3, England.

CAREER: Centre for Community Research, New York, N.Y., staff writer, 1970-71; University of Essex, Colchester, Essex, England, lecturer in literature, 1971-73; New England College, Sussex, England, lecturer in literature, 1973-80. Founding member and editorial director, Writers and Readers Publishing Cooperative, 1975-81; Institute of Contemporary Arts, London, director of seminars, 1981-86, deputy director, 1986—. Independent television producer of programs for Channel 4 and British Broadcasting Corp., 1986—.

WRITINGS:

(With Douglas and Monica Holmes) *Language of Trust,* Science House, 1972.
Femininity and the Creative Imagination, Barnes & Noble, 1973.
Brand New York, Quartet Books, 1982.
Feminism for Beginners, Pantheon Books, 1983.
The Cabaret: The First Hundred Years, Methuen, 1984.
(Editor with Steven Rose) *Science and Beyond,* Basil Blackwell, 1986.
Simone de Beauvoir, Viking, 1988.
(Editor with Hilary Lawson) *Dismantling Truth,* Weidenfeld & Nicholson, 1989.

Also author of fiction under the pseudonym Jessica Ayre. Editor of "ICA Document" series for Institute of Contemporary Arts, 1985-88. Contributor of articles to journals in her field.

WORK IN PROGRESS: Fiction.

BIOGRAPHICAL/CRITICAL SOURCES:

PERIODICALS

New York Times Book Review, April 28, 1985.

*   *   *

APPLETON, Victor
[Collective pseudonym]

WRITINGS:

"DON STURDY" SERIES

Don Sturdy on the Desert of Mystery; or, Autoing in the Land of Caravans, Grosset & Dunlap, 1925.
. . . with the Big Snake Hunters; or, Lost in the Jungles of the Amazon, Grosset & Dunlap, 1925.
. . . in the Tombs of Gold; or, The Old Egyptian's Great Secret, Grosset & Dunlap, 1925.
. . . across the North Pole; or, Cast Away in the Land of Ice, Grosset & Dunlap, 1925.
. . . in the Land of Volcanoes; or, The Trail of the Ten Thousand Smokes, Grosset & Dunlap, 1925.
. . . in the Port of Lost Ships; or, Adrift in the Sargasso Sea, Grosset & Dunlap, 1926.
. . . among the Gorillas; or, Adrift in the Great Jungle, Grosset & Dunlap, 1927.
. . . Captured by Head Hunters; or, Adrift in the Wilds of Borneo, Grosset & Dunlap, 1928.
. . . in Lion Land; or, The Strange Clearing in the Jungle, Grosset & Dunlap, 1929.
. . . in the Land of Giants; or, Captives of the Savage Patagonians, Grosset & Dunlap, 1930.
. . . on the Ocean Bottom; or, The Strange Cruise of the Phantom, Grosset & Dunlap, 1931.
. . . in the Temples of Fear; or, Destined for a Strange Sacrifice, Grosset & Dunlap, 1932.
. . . Lost in Glacier Bay; or, The Mystery of the Moving Totem Poles, Grosset & Dunlap, 1933.

. . . *Trapped in the Flaming Wilderness; or, Unearthing Secrets in Central Asia*, Grosset & Dunlap, 1934.

. . . *with the Harpoon Hunters; or, The Strange Cruise of the Whaling Ship*, Grosset & Dunlap, 1935.

"MOTION PICTURE CHUMS" SERIES

The Motion Picture Chums' First Venture; or, Opening a Photo Playhouse in Fairlands (also see below), Grosset & Dunlap, 1913.

The Motion Picture Chums at Seaside Park; or, The Rival Photo Theatres of the Boardwalk (also see below), Grosset & Dunlap, 1913.

. . . *on Broadway; or, The Mystery of the Missing Cash Box* (also see below), Grosset & Dunlap, 1914.

The Motion Picture Chums' Outdoor Exhibition; or, The Film That Solved a Mystery (also see below), Grosset & Dunlap, 1914.

The Motion Picture Chums' New Idea; or, The First Educational Photo Playhouse (also see below), Grosset & Dunlap, 1914.

. . . *at the Fair; or, The Greatest Film Ever Exhibited* (also see below), Grosset & Dunlap, 1915.

The Motion Picture Chums' War Spectacle; or, The Film That Won the Prize (also see below), Grosset & Dunlap, 1916.

"MOVING PICTURE BOYS" SERIES

The Moving Picture Boys; or, The Perils of a Great City Depicted (also see below), Grosset & Dunlap, 1913.

. . . *in the West; or, Taking Scenes among the Cowboys and Indians* (also see below), Grosset & Dunlap, 1913.

. . . *on the Coast; or, Showing the Perils of the Deep* (also see below), Grosset & Dunlap, 1913.

. . . *in the Jungle; or, Stirring Times among the Wild Animals* (also see below), Grosset & Dunlap, 1913.

. . . *in Earthquake Land; or, Working amid Many Perils* (also see below), Grosset & Dunlap, 1913.

. . . *and the Flood; or, Perilous Days on the Mississippi* (also see below), Grosset & Dunlap, 1914.

. . . *at Panama; or, Stirring Adventures along the Great Canal* (also see below), Grosset & Dunlap, 1915.

. . . *under the Sea; or, The Treasure of the Lost Ship* (also see below), Grosset & Dunlap, 1916.

. . . *on the War Front; or, The Hunt for the Stolen Army Film* (also see below), Grosset & Dunlap, 1918.

. . . *on French Battlefields; or, Taking Pictures for the U.S. Army* (also see below), Grosset & Dunlap, 1919.

The Moving Picture Boys' First Showhouse; or, Opening up for Business in Fairlands (originally published as *The Motion Picture Chums' First Venture; or, Opening a Photo Playhouse in Fairlands*), Grosset & Dunlap, 1921.

. . . *at Seaside Park; or, The Rival Photo Theatres of the Boardwalk* (originally published as *The Motion Picture Chums at Seaside Park; or, The Rival Photo Theatres of the Boardwalk*), Grosset & Dunlap, 1921.

. . . *on Broadway; or, The Mystery of the Missing Cash Box* (originally published as *The Motion Picture Chums on Broadway; or, The Mystery of the Missing Cash Box*), Grosset & Dunlap, 1921.

The Moving Picture Boys' Outdoor Exhibition; or, The Film That Solved a Mystery (originally published as *The Motion Picture Chums' Outdoor Exhibition; or, The Film That Solved a Mystery*), Grosset & Dunlap, 1922.

The Moving Picture Boys' New Idea (originally published as *The Motion Picture Chums' New Idea; or, The First Educational Photo Playhouse*), Grosset & Dunlap, 1922.

"MOVIE BOYS" SERIES

The Movie Boys on Call; or, Filming the Perils of a Great City (originally published as *The Moving Picture Boys; or, The Perils of a Great City Depicted*), Garden City, 1926.

. . . *in the Wild West; or, Stirring Days among the Cowboys and Indians* (originally published as *The Moving Picture Boys in the West; or, Taking Scenes among the Cowboys and Indians*), Garden City, 1926.

. . . *and the Wreckers; or, Facing the Perils of the Deep* (originally published as *The Moving Picture Boys on the Coast; or, Showing the Perils of the Deep*), Garden City, 1926.

. . . *in the Jungle; or, Lively Times among the Wild Beasts* (originally published as *The Moving Picture Boys in the Jungle; or, Stirring Times among the Wild Animals*), Garden City, 1926.

. . . *in Earthquake Land; or, Filming Pictures amid Strange Perils* (originally published as *The Moving Picture Boys in Earthquake Land; or, Working amid Many Perils*), Garden City, 1926.

. . . *and the Flood; or, Perilous Days on the Mighty Mississippi* (originally published as *The Moving Picture Boys and the Flood; or, Perilous Days on the Mississippi*), Garden City, 1926.

. . . *in Peril; or, Strenuous Days along the Panama Canal* (originally published as *The Moving Picture Boys at Panama; or, Stirring Adventures along the Great Canal*), Garden City, 1926.

. . . *under the Sea; or, The Treasure of the Lost Ship* (originally published as *The Moving Picture Boys under the Sea; or, The Treasure of the Lost Ship*), Garden City, 1926.

. . . *under Fire; or, The Search for the Stolen Film* (originally published as *The Moving Picture Boys on the War Front; or, The Hunt for the Stolen Army Film*), Garden City, 1926.

. . . *under Uncle Sam; or, Taking Pictures for the Army* (originally published as *The Moving Picture Boys on French Battlefields; or, Taking Pictures for the U.S. Army*), Garden City, 1926.

The Movie Boys' First Showhouse; or, Fighting for a Foothold in Fairlands (originally published as *The Motion Picture Chums' First Venture; or, Opening a Photo Playhouse in Fairlands*), Garden City, 1926.

. . . *at Seaside Park; or, The Rival Photo Houses of the Boardwalk* (originally published as *The Motion Picture Chums at Seaside Park; or, The Rival Photo Theatres of the Boardwalk*), Garden City, 1926.

. . . *on Broadway; or, The Mystery of the Missing Cash Box* (originally published as *The Motion Picture Chums on Broadway; or, The Mystery of the Missing Cash Box*), Garden City, 1926.

The Movie Boys' Outdoor Exhibition; or, The Film That Solved a Mystery (originally published as *The Motion Picture Chums' Outdoor Exhibition; or, The Film That Solved a Mystery*), Garden City, 1927.

The Movie Boys' New Idea; or, Getting the Best of Their Enemies (originally published as *The Motion Picture Chums' New Idea; or, The First Educational Photo Playhouse*), Garden City, 1927.

. . . *at the Big Fair; or, The Greatest Film Ever Exhibited* (originally published as *The Motion Picture Chums at the Fair; or, The Greatest Film Ever Exhibited*), Garden City, 1927.

The Movie Boys' War Spectacle; or, The Film That Won the Prize (originally published as *The Motion Picture Chums' War Spectacle; or, The Film That Won the Prize*), Garden City, 1927.

"TOM SWIFT" SERIES

Tom Swift and His Motor Cycle; or, Fun and Adventures on the Road, Grosset & Dunlap, 1910.

. . . and His Motor Boat; or, The Rivals of Lake Carlopa, Grosset & Dunlap, 1910.

. . . and His Airship; or, The Stirring Cruise of the Red Cloud, Grosset & Dunlap, 1910.

. . . and His Submarine Boat; or, Under the Ocean for Sunken Treasure, Grosset & Dunlap, 1910.

. . . and His Electric Runabout; or, The Speediest Car on the Road, Grosset & Dunlap, 1910.

. . . and His Wireless Message; or, The Castaways of Earthquake Island, Grosset & Dunlap, 1911.

. . . Among the Diamond Makers; or, The Secret of Phantom Mountain, Grosset & Dunlap, 1911.

. . . in the Caves of Ice; or, The Wreck of the Airship, Grosset & Dunlap, 1911.

. . . and His Sky Racer; or, The Quickest Flight on Record, Grosset & Dunlap, 1911.

. . . and His Electric Rifle; or, Daring Adventures in Elephant Land, Grosset & Dunlap, 1911.

. . . in the City of Gold; or, Marvelous Adventures Underground, Grosset & Dunlap, 1912.

. . . and His Air Glider; or, Seeking the Platinum Treasure, Grosset & Dunlap, 1912.

. . . in Captivity; or, A Daring Escape by Airship, Grosset & Dunlap, 1912.

. . . and His Wizard Camera; or, The Perils of Moving Picture Taking, Grosset & Dunlap, 1912.

. . . and His Great Searchlight; or, On the Border for Uncle Sam, Grosset & Dunlap, 1912.

. . . and His Giant Cannon; or, The Longest Shots on Record, Grosset & Dunlap, 1913.

. . . and His Photo Telephone; or, The Picture That Saved a Fortune, Grosset & Dunlap, 1914.

. . . and His Aerial Warship; or, The Naval Terror of the Seas, Grosset & Dunlap, 1915.

. . . and His Big Tunnel; or, The Hidden City of the Andes, Grosset & Dunlap, 1916.

. . . in the Land of Wonders; or, The Underground Search for the Idol of Gold, Grosset & Dunlap, 1917.

. . . and His War Tank; or, Doing His Bit for Uncle Sam, Grosset & Dunlap, 1918.

. . . and His Air Scout; or, Uncle Sam's Mastery of the Sky, Grosset & Dunlap, 1919.

. . . and His Undersea Search; or, The Treasure on the Floor of the Atlantic, Grosset & Dunlap, 1920.

. . . among the Fire Fighters; or, Battling with Flames from the Air, Grosset & Dunlap, 1921.

. . . and His Electric Locomotive; or, Two Miles a Minute on the Rails, Grosset & Dunlap, 1922.

. . . and His Flying Boat; or, The Castaways of the Giant Iceberg, Grosset & Dunlap, 1923.

. . . and His Great Oil Gusher; or, The Treasure of Goby Farm, Grosset & Dunlap, 1924.

. . . and His Chest of Secrets; or, Tracing the Stolen Inventions, Grosset & Dunlap, 1925.

. . . and His Airline Express; or, From Ocean to Ocean by Daylight, Grosset & Dunlap, 1926.

. . . Circling the Globe; or, The Daring Cruise of the Air Monarch, Grosset & Dunlap, 1927.

. . . and His Talking Pictures; or, The Greatest Invention on Record, Grosset & Dunlap, 1928.

. . . and His House on Wheels; or, A Trip to the Mountain of Mystery, Grosset & Dunlap, 1929.

. . . and His Big Dirigible; or, Adventures over the Forest of Fire, Grosset & Dunlap, 1930.

. . . and His Sky Train; or, Overland through the Clouds, Grosset & Dunlap, 1931.

. . . and His Giant Magnet; or, Bringing up the Lost Submarine, Grosset & Dunlap, 1932.

. . . and His Television Detector; or, Trailing the Secret Plotters, Grosset & Dunlap, 1933.

. . . and His Ocean Airport; or, Foiling the Haargolanders, Grosset & Dunlap, 1934.

. . . and His Planet Stone; or, Discovering the Secret of Another World, Grosset & Dunlap, 1935.

. . . and His Giant Telescope, Whitman, 1939.

. . . and His Magnetic Silencer, Whitman, 1941.

OTHER

(Contributor) Stephen Dunning and Henry B. Maloney, editors, *A Superboy, Supergirl Anthology: Selected Chapters from the Earlier Works of Victor Appleton, Franklin W. Dixon, and Carolyn Keene*, Scholastic Book Services, 1971.

SIDELIGHTS: "Of all the characters created by [Edward] Stratemeyer," states J. Randolph Cox in his introduction to John Dizer's *Tom Swift & Company: "Boys' Books" by Stratemeyer and Others*, "probably none arouses more affection than Tom Swift. His adventures serve as a symbol of American ingenuity and technological progress, one part of that American Dream." Aided and abetted by a large cast of characters—including his father, retired inventor Barton Swift, his chum and accountant Ned Newton, his blushing sweetheart Mary Nestor, his eccentric companion Mr. Wakefield Damon, his faithful black hired hand Eradicate Sampson, his giant servant Koku, and a wide assortment of villains: the red-haired, squinting bully Andy Foger, the shyster lawyers Smeak & Katch, and the unspeakable Hankinshaw—Tom overcame all obstacles and emerged as one of the best-selling series heroes of all time. Estimated sales of the series suggest that children bought well over fifteen million "Tom Swift" volumes in the years between 1910 and 1941. Arthur Prager reports in an *American Heritage* article that in 1926 "a survey of 36,750 school children in thirty-four representative cities revealed that 98 per cent of them were reading Stratemeyer series books, and that most of them liked Tom Swift best."

Although some enthusiasts have seen Thomas Edison and aircraft engineer Glenn Curtiss as prototypes for the hero of this early science fiction series, Prager declares that the author based Tom "nearly 100 per cent [on] Stratemeyer's own idol, Henry Ford. In 1910 Edison was a deaf old man in his sixties, and hardly a figure with whom a teen-ager could identify. Ford, on the other hand, was in his vigorous prime, and in the news almost every day. Boys could . . . marvel at his Model T, introduced in 1908 and not unlike Tom Swift's own 'runabout.'" Like Ford, Prager adds, Tom had a distaste for labor unions, and he eventually formed his own version of Ford's automotive empire—the Swift Construction Company, located on the shores of Lake Carlopa near the town of Shopton, New York, manufactured many of Tom's inventions.

The youthful inventor's scientific ingenuity attracted readers. "Tom, in his private laboratory, casually solved problems that had stumped the world since Newton," states Russel B. Nye in his survey *The Unembarrassed Muse: The Popular Arts in America*. "What he invented was always *almost* plausible, just far enough around the corner to be visionary, not quite far enough to be absurd; many of his inventions, in fact, were only a year or so ahead of their real-life counterparts." "His color television was twenty years ahead of its time," reports Prager. "His electric rifle, first produced in Tom's Shopton laboratory in 1911, anticipated the first Browning machine rifle by five years. Although Tom's rifle fired a charge of electricity instead of a bullet, it was similar to Browning's 1916 rapid-fire repeater," he adds. "Tom's 'wizard camera,' which was constructed in 1912, was eleven years ahead of Victor's original portable motion-picture camera. His electric locomotive was in service two years before the New Jersey Central ran its first diesel electric, and his photo telephone was eleven years ahead of the Bell Laboratories' first successful phototelegraphy process," Prager declares. Even his famous "house on wheels" preceded the first camper-trailer by a year.

Tom's faith in technology's ability to solve all problems made him truly a twentieth-century hero, Nye reports. Money was not important to Tom in the way it had been to Horatio Alger's heroes, the critic adds: "What mattered was Tom's success at breaking through the barriers of the unknown. His books were filled, in their naive way, with the excitement of a conquest of matter and space, the thrill of accomplishing with one's own brain and hands what others had hoped to do." "It was not Rockefeller or Carnegie, Honus Wagner or Eddie Plank who were the implied heroes of the Swift books," Nye continues, "but the Wright brothers, Steinmetz, Tesla, Edison, and the others who were pushing back the frontiers of knowledge and invention." "Whereas Alger's boys faced the problems of an urbanized, acquisitive society, and the Merriwells the ethics of the competitive contest, Tom Swift grasped the technology of the machine age and brought it under control," the critic concludes. "He made scientific discovery exciting and technological advance adventurous, and most of all he made both seem useful and optimistic."

While the Tom Swift books were undeniably popular, some critics see them as lacking in literary qualities. For instance, Selma Lanes, in *Down the Rabbit Hole: Adventures and Misadventures in the Realm of Children's Literature*, calls them "decidedly regressive so far as literary or human content are concerned," and states that "they play subtly upon the restlessness and idealism of older children, perhaps even staving off adolescent depression with their pure fantasies of the power of youth and the glory of the life of action." Prager points out that the series occasionally made disparaging remarks about Jews, foreigners, and blacks, although he adds that "these references were later expunged in revised editions." Editor Neil Barron, writing in *Anatomy of Wonder: A Critical Guide to Science Fiction*, calls the writing in the Tom Swift books wooden, and maintains that they "emphasize rapidity of incident and stereotypical characterization." Other reviewers disagree; although allowing for the defects of series fiction, they see Tom as a cut above the rest. Nye asserts, "The best of the Stratemeyer books was the *Tom Swift* series," and Prager declares that "the books are as much fun to read as they ever were, anachronisms and prejudices notwithstanding; one can always put them in the context of their times."

Though his adventures have been out of print for many years, Tom remains a prime favorite among readers. Prager explains the attraction his exploits hold in his 1971 book *Rascals at Large; or, The Clue in the Old Nostalgia*: "They gave us a taste of power, of the thrill of invention, the dim rattle of a foreign land in the earphones of a homemade radio, the trembling of a joystick in the treacherous updrafts of the Rockies, the excitement of a technological breakthrough in the backyard lab." He continues, "The recent landings on the moon were anticlimactic compared with some of Tom Swift's adventures. After all, the astronauts simply got into their capsule, went to the moon, and came back again. No bullies dropped bolts into the machinery. No unscrupulous inventors tried to steal their mortgaged homes. No one was kidnaped or locked in a burning barn. They were all married. Not one of them was a gallant teen-ager." "Good luck to those brave astronauts," Prager concludes, "but if I had not known Edward Stratemeyer was dead these thirty years I would have sworn he was writing their dialogue. One Great Leap Forward for Mankind indeed. How he would have loved that line."

Victor Appleton was also the pseudonym used for the "Don Sturdy" books, featuring a young man whose adventures took him into all sorts of exotic locales, and various stories about boys who make, produce and show motion pictures. Tom Swift himself has passed into the realm of literary immortality through the "Tom Swifties" jokes that play on the Stratemeyer Syndicate's liberal use of adverbs: for example, "That's the last time I try to feed a lion," Tom said offhandedly. Edward Stratemeyer and Howard R. Garis both worked on the Tom Swift series, although sources differ on the exact amount of their individual involvement. Harriet S. Adams also contributed some of the later volumes in the series. For more information see the sketches in this volume for Harriet S. Adams, Howard R. Garis, and Edward Stratemeyer.

MEDIA ADAPTATIONS: Barry Kirk Productions and Twentieth Century-Fox designed a film based on the "Tom Swift" series that was never produced. Twentieth Century-Fox also planned a musical based on Tom's life, but the project was shelved. Barry Kirk Productions and Levy-Gardner-Laven Productions mapped out a Tom Swift television series that never materialized.

BIOGRAPHICAL/CRITICAL SOURCES:

BOOKS

Barron, Neil, editor, *Anatomy of Wonder: A Critical Guide to Science Fiction*, 2nd edition, Bowker, 1981.

Dictionary of Literary Biography, Volume 42: *American Writers for Children before 1900*, Gale, 1985.

Dizer, John T., Jr., *Tom Swift & Company: "Boys' Books" by Stratemeyer and Others*, McFarland & Co., 1982.

Garis, Roger, *My Father Was Uncle Wiggily*, McGraw-Hill, 1966.

Johnson, Deidre, editor and compiler, *Stratemeyer Pseudonyms and Series Books: An Annotated Checklist of Stratemeyer and Stratemeyer Syndicate Publications*, Greenwood Press, 1982.

Lanes, Selma G., *Down the Rabbit Hole: Adventures and Misadventures in the Realm of Children's Literature*, Atheneum, 1971.

Moskowitz, Sam, *Strange Horizons: The Spectrum of Science Fiction*, Scribner, 1976.

Nye, Russel B., *The Unembarrassed Muse: The Popular Arts in America*, Dial, 1970.

Prager, Arthur, *Rascals at Large; or, The Clue in the Old Nostalgia*, Doubleday, 1971.

PERIODICALS

American Heritage, December, 1976.
Art Journal, fall, 1983.
Children's Literature, Volume 7, 1978.
Hobbies, August, 1985.
New Yorker, March 20, 1954.
Saturday Review, July 10, 1971.
Time, June 30, 1980.

—*Sketch by Kenneth R. Shepherd*

*   *   *

APPLETON, Victor II
[Collective pseudonym]

WRITINGS:

"TOM SWIFT JR. ADVENTURES" SERIES

Tom Swift and His Flying Lab, Grosset & Dunlap, 1954, reprinted, Tempo, 1977.
. . . *and His Jetmarine*, Grosset & Dunlap, 1954, reprinted, Tempo, 1977.
. . . *and His Rocket Ship*, Grosset & Dunlap, 1954, reprinted, Tempo, 1977.
. . . *and His Giant Robot*, Grosset & Dunlap, 1954, reprinted, Tempo, 1977.
. . . *and His Atomic Earth Blaster*, Grosset & Dunlap, 1954.
. . . *and His Outpost in Space*, Grosset & Dunlap, 1955, published as *Tom Swift and His Sky Wheel*, Tempo, 1977.
. . . *and His Diving Seacopter*, Grosset & Dunlap, 1956.
. . . *in the Caves of Nuclear Fire*, Grosset & Dunlap, 1956, reprinted, Tempo, 1977.
. . . *on the Phantom Satellite*, Grosset & Dunlap, 1957.
. . . *and His Ultrasonic Cycloplane*, Grosset & Dunlap, 1957.
. . . *and His Deep-Sea Hydrodome*, Grosset & Dunlap, 1958.
. . . *in the Race to the Moon*, Grosset & Dunlap, 1958.
. . . *and His Space Solartron*, Grosset & Dunlap, 1958.
. . . *and His Electronic Retroscope*, Grosset & Dunlap, 1959, published as *Tom Swift in the Jungle of the Mayas*, Tempo, 1973.
. . . *and His Spectromarine Selector*, Grosset & Dunlap, 1960, published as *Tom Swift and the City of Gold*, Tempo, 1973.
. . . *and the Cosmic Astronauts*, Grosset & Dunlap, 1960.
. . . *and the Visitor from Planet X*, Grosset & Dunlap, 1961.
. . . *and the Electronic Hydrolung*, Grosset & Dunlap, 1961.
. . . *and His Triphibian Atomicar*, Grosset & Dunlap, 1962.
. . . *and His Megascope Space Prober*, Grosset & Dunlap, 1962.
. . . *and the Asteroid Pirates*, Grosset & Dunlap, 1963.
. . . *and His Repelatron Skyway*, Grosset & Dunlap, 1963.
. . . *and His Aquatomic Tracker*, Grosset & Dunlap, 1964.
. . . *and His 3-D Telejector*, Grosset & Dunlap, 1964.
. . . *and His Polar-Ray Dynasphere*, Grosset & Dunlap, 1965.
. . . *and His Sonic Boom Trap*, Grosset & Dunlap, 1965.
. . . *and His Subocean Geotron*, Grosset & Dunlap, 1966.
. . . *and the Mystery Comet*, Grosset & Dunlap, 1966.
. . . *and the Captive Planetoid*, Grosset & Dunlap, 1967.
. . . *and His G-Force Inverter*, Grosset & Dunlap, 1968.
. . . *and His Dyna-4 Capsule*, Grosset & Dunlap, 1969.
. . . *and His Cosmotron Express*, Grosset & Dunlap, 1970.
. . . *and the Galaxy Ghosts*, Grosset & Dunlap, 1971.

NEW "TOM SWIFT" ADVENTURES

Tom Swift: The City in the Stars, Wanderer, 1981.
. . . *Terror on the Moons of Jupiter*, Wanderer, 1981.
. . . *The Alien Probe*, Wanderer, 1981.
. . . *The War in Outer Space*, Wanderer, 1981.
. . . *The Space Fortress*, Wanderer, 1981.
. . . *The Rescue Mission*, Wanderer, 1981.
. . . *Ark Two*, Wanderer, 1982.
. . . *Crater of Mystery*, Wanderer, 1983.
. . . *Gateway to Doom*, Wanderer, 1983.
. . . *The Invisible Force*, Wanderer, 1983.
. . . *Planet of Nightmares*, Wanderer, 1984.
. . . *Chaos on Earth*, Wanderer, in press.

SIDELIGHTS: The last Stratemeyer Syndicate book featuring Tom Swift, hero of one of the best-selling juvenile series of all time, appeared in 1941. In 1954 the Stratemeyer Syndicate attempted to recreate Tom's success with a new series starring his son, Tom Jr. Harriet Adams, head of the Syndicate, explained to the *New Yorker* some of the chief differences between the old and new series: "We use a more up-to-date brand of humor. You won't find any stammerers in the Tom, Jr., series. As far as inventing goes, Tom, Jr., is more prolific. He's invented Tomasite Plastic, to encase nuclear reactors. It absorbs radiation more effectively than lead. And a Damonscope, which is really a photometer with nonabsorptive prisms to detect fluorescence from a distance and record its density on photographic film. And a Swift Spectrograph, which, not to go into too much detail, analyzes anything in a split second."

Readers familiar with the old series may note the loss of many familiar characters. Barton Swift, Mr. Damon, and Eradicate Sampson have all passed away. But several familiar faces remain: Tom Sr., his wife, Mary Nestor, and Ned Newton, now manager of the Swift Construction Company. And many new characters are introduced, including Tom and Mary's daughter Sandra, Ned's daughter Phyllis, Chow Winkler, the cowboy chef, and Tom Jr.'s sidekick Bud Barclay—described by Neal Rubin in the *Detroit Free Press* as "the Ed McMahon of juvenile fiction, the perpetual second banana."

Tom Jr.'s adventures differ from his father's; instead of being primarily adventure stories with a science background, they tend to concentrate on real science. The *New Yorker* states that the Syndicate "consulted with jet experts, rocket experts, TV experts, and physicists" while creating the series. Writers had to have some background in science; Stratemeyer author Jim Lawrence explains to *Yellowback Library* interviewer Geoffrey S. Lapin, "You had to have at least some smattering of science to begin to even wing it in that stuff." The young inventor's exploits filled thirty-three volumes before Grosset & Dunlap stopped publishing the series in 1971.

"But Tom Swift lives," declares Rubin. In 1981, Simon & Schuster began producing new stories of Tom's adventures, which Rubin views with some trepidation: Tom, he says, "has become a man of the '80s. Phyllis, his all-but-mute girlfriend of decades past, has evolved into Anita Thorwald, a brilliant co-worker with a bionic leg. Bud is a computer hacker named Benjamin Walking Eagle." "Tom probably has taken to styling his hair and drinking Perrier," he concludes, "but progress always has its price."

In 1989 Simon & Schuster, who acquired the Stratemeyer Syndicate in 1984, announced plans to bring back Tom Swift Jr.

(in California rather than Shopton, N.Y.) early in 1990. Harriet Adams and Andrew Svenson originally conceived the "Tom Swift Jr." series, and Stratemeyer Syndicate writer Jim Lawrence actually wrote many of the volumes in the years between 1954 and 1967. For more information see the entries in this volume for Harriet S. Adams, James Duncan Lawrence, and Andrew E. Svenson.

MEDIA ADAPTATIONS: "The Tom Swift and Linda Craig Mystery Hour" was produced by Paramount and aired by ABC-TV on July 3, 1983. It starred Willie Aames as Tom and Lori Loughlin as Linda.

BIOGRAPHICAL/CRITICAL SOURCES:

BOOKS

Barron, Neil, editor, *Anatomy of Wonder: A Critical Guide to Science Fiction*, 2nd edition, Bowker, 1981.
Dizer, John T., *Tom Swift & Company: "Boys' Books" by Stratemeyer and Others*, McFarland & Co., 1981.
Johnson, Deidre, editor and compiler, *Stratemeyer Pseudonyms and Series Books: An Annotated Checklist of Stratemeyer and Stratemeyer Syndicate Publications*, Greenwood Press, 1982.
Moskowitz, Sam, *Strange Horizons: The Spectrum of Science Fiction*, Scribner, 1976.
Prager, Arthur, *Rascals at Large; or, The Clue in the Old Nostalgia*, Doubleday, 1971.

PERIODICALS

American Heritage, December, 1976.
Children's Literature, Volume 7, 1978.
Detroit Free Press, November 25, 1984.
New Yorker, March 20, 1954.
Yellowback Library, January/February, 1986.

*   *   *

ARNOLD, Arnold (Ferdinand)   1921-

PERSONAL: Born February 6, 1921, in Germany; brought to U.S., 1931; naturalized in 1942; married Alison Arnold, 1981. *Education:* Studied at St. Martin's School of Art, London, England, 1937-38, Pratt Institute, 1938-39, New York University and Columbia University, 1939-42.

ADDRESSES: Home—422B Finchley Rd., London NW2 2HY, England.

CAREER: Graphic and industrial designer, 1946—. Free-lance designer, New York City, 1946-60; Workshop School, New York City, director, 1949-52; Manuscript Press, Inc., New York City, president, 1963-65; Arnold Arnold Design, Inc., New York City, president, 1963-66. Cyberneticist, writer and consultant in systems analysis and operational research, London, 1976—. Designer of children's play and learning materials and of programs produced by companies in the United States, Great Britain, France, Germany, Australia, and Holland, including CBS Learning Corp., Creative Playthings, Parker Brothers, Inc., Ed-U-Cards, Inc., Chaspec, Inc., Miro Cie., Summit Games, Otto Meier, and Waddington's, Ltd. His posters were exhibited at the New York Museum of Modern Art, 1952, and his work has been the subject of one-man exhibits at the New York Museum of Modern Art, 1953, Philadelphia Art Alliance, 1955, Miami Museum of Fine Art, 1956,

Birmingham (Alabama) Museum of Fine Art, 1956, and the Brussels World's Fair, 1956. His work was also part of the "Good Design U.S.A." exhibit that travelled to twenty-one major museums throughout the United States, 1963-65. Fellow of Boston University; Leverhulme fellow, London. Consultant editor, Rutledge Books, 1962-67. *Military service:* U.S. Army Infantry, 1942-45; served in European theater; received Purple Heart.

WRITINGS:

How to Play with Your Child, Ballantine, 1955.
The Arnold Arnold Book of Toy Soldiers (self-illustrated), Random House, 1963.
The Big Book of Tongue Twisters and Double Talk (self-illustrated), Random House, 1964.
Games, four volumes, McGraw, 1965.
Your Child's Play: How to Help Your Child Reap the Full Benefits of Creative Play, Essandess Special Editions, 1968.
Violence and Your Child, Regnery, 1969.
Pictures and Stories from Forgotten Children's Books, Dover Publications, 1969.
Your Child and You, Regnery, 1970, reprinted, 1987.
The Yes and No Book, Reilly and Lee, 1970.
Career Choices for the '70s, Crowell-Collier Press, 1971.
Teaching Your Child to Learn from Birth to School Age, Prentice-Hall, 1971.
The World Book of Children's Games, World Publications, 1972.
(Editor) *Antique Paper Dolls, 1915-1920*, Dover Publications, 1975.
The Crowell Book of Arts and Crafts for Children, Crowell, 1976.
The World Book of Arts and Crafts for Children, Macmillan, 1976.

Editor of "Look and Do Books" series, Rand McNally, 1964. Also author of thrice-weekly column on education syndicated in more than 120 newspapers in the United States and Great Britain. Contributor to numerous periodicals, including *Life, This Week, Graphics Magazine, Posters, Idea Magazine, Woman's Journal, Educational Computing, Computer Weekly, Far Eastern Technical Review, Guardian*, and the London *Times*.

WORK IN PROGRESS: The Mindbenders: The Myth of Artificial Intelligence; Man Against Man and Nature.

SIDELIGHTS: Arnold Arnold wrote *CA:* "My career has taken some (to me) extraordinary turns. Nonetheless, there seems to be a logic to it, each next step based on what I had learnt and done before. From wanting to be a fine artist I was forced by economic and other circumstances to turn to graphic and industrial design. Disenchanted by the fact that I found myself designing promotional material, packaging and products that I could not endorse, I began looking for a field in which I might design my own products. Toys and learning materials were a neglected field in the early 1950s. The last attempts to redesign them had been made by Maria Montessori fifty years earlier. I also began what turned out to be a major and valuable collection of early children's books, toys, games, books on education and other juvenalia that served as an inspiration and reference to my designing and writing for and about children.

"Succeeding perhaps only because I had moved into a vacuum, I became deeply interested in learning theory, psychology and neurophysiology, including the early work of Piaget, that of Sherrington, and Grey Walter. My writing on play, learning, arts, crafts, and games, and eventually my newspaper column on education were direct outgrowths of this work and led to new and wider interests and involvements. In 1969, one of my publishers asked me to write a book on the development of learning in children and I agreed to give it a try. But first, I felt, I would have to build a model of human learning, based on what was known at that time. This inevitably led to my becoming involved in cybernetics, general systems analysis, and to my current interests and work.

"In 1974, I returned to Britain for personal and professional reasons where, by 1976, I had completed my model of learning. It turned out to be a general systems analytic method that I applied in following years in a growing number of fields—among them, mathematics, game theory, general forecasting, linguistics, and artificial intelligence. In 1985, I began work on *The Mindbenders: The Myth of Artificial Intelligence*, based on my general systems analytic method, using it as a yardstick to assess the similarities and differences between human and 'machine' intelligence. I am also working on a book that redefines game theory in a way that may make it a useful tool for penetrating the so-called 'black-box' of the human psyche. Additionally, I am developing a versatile general systems analytic program, which I have applied to problems that seem to have resisted solution by application of other methods and means."

BIOGRAPHICAL/CRITICAL SOURCES:

PERIODICALS

Los Angeles Times, October 17, 1976.
New York Times, August 23, 1954.
Time, December 14, 1953.
Times Educational Supplement, January 2, 1976.

*   *   *

ASHABRANNER, Brent (Kenneth) 1921-

PERSONAL: Born November 3, 1921, in Shawnee, Okla.; son of Dudley (a pharmacist) and Rose Thelma (Cotton) Ashabranner; married Martha White, August 9, 1941; children: Melissa Lynn, Jennifer Ann. *Education:* Oklahoma State University, B.S., 1948, M.A., 1951; additional study at University of Michigan, 1955, and Boston University and Oxford University, 1959-60.

ADDRESSES: Home and office—15 Spring W., Williamsburg, Va. 23185.

CAREER: Oklahoma State University, Stillwater, instructor in English, 1952-55; Ministry of Education, Technical Cooperation Administration, Addis Ababa, Ethiopia, educational materials adviser, 1955-57; International Cooperation Administration, Tripoli, Libya, chief of Education Materials Development Division, 1957-59; Agency for International Development, Lagos, Nigeria, education program officer, 1960-61; Peace Corps, Washington, D.C., acting director of program in Nigeria, 1961-62, deputy director of program in India, 1962-64, director of program in India, 1964-66, director of Office of Training, 1966-67, deputy director of Peace Corps, 1967-69; Harvard University, Center for Studies in Education and Development, Cambridge, Mass., research associate, 1969-70; Pathfinder Fund, Boston, Mass., director of Near East-South Asia Population Program, 1970-71; director of project

development, World Population International Assistance Division, Planned Parenthood, 1971-72; Ford Foundation, New York, N.Y., associate representative and population program officer, 1972-80, deputy representative to Philippines, 1972-75, deputy representative to Indonesia, 1975-80; full-time writer, 1980—. *Military service:* U.S. Navy, 1942-45.

AWARDS, HONORS: National Civil Service League career service award, 1968; Notable Children's Trade Book in the Field of Social Studies, 1982, and Carter G. Woodson Book Award, National Council for the Social Studies, 1983, both for *Morning Star, Black Sun: The Northern Cheyenne Indians and America's Energy Crisis;* Notable Children's Trade Book in the Field of Social Studies, American Library Association (ALA) Notable Book, and Books for the Teen-Age, New York Public Library, all 1983, all for *The New Americans: Changing Patterns in U.S. Immigration;* Notable Children's Trade Book in the Field of Social Studies, 1984, ALA Best Book for Young Adults, 1984, and Carter G. Woodson Book Award, 1985, all for *To Live in Two Worlds: American Indian Youth Today;* Notable Children's Book in the Field of Social Studies, and ALA Notable Book, both 1984, both for *Gavriel and Jemal: Two Boys of Jerusalem;* ALA Notable Book, 1985, *Boston Horn-Globe* Honor Book, 1986, and Carter G. Woodson Book Award, 1986, all for *Dark Harvest: Migrant Farmworkers in America;* ALA Notable Book, *School Library Journal* Best Book of the Year, both 1986, both for *Children of the Maya: A Guatemalan Indian Odyssey;* Notable Children's Trade Book in the Field of Social Studies, *School Library Journal* Best Book of the Year, ALA Notable Book, and Christopher Award, all 1987, all for *Into a Strange Land: Unaccompanied Refugee Youth in America;* Notable Children's Trade Book in the Field of Social Studies, 1987, for *The Vanishing Border: A Photographic Journey along Our Frontier with Mexico.*

WRITINGS:

(Editor) *The Stakes Are High*, Bantam, 1954.
(Wih Judson Milburn and Cecil B. Williams) *A First Course in College English* (textbook), Houghton, 1962.
A Moment in History: The First Ten Years of the Peace Corps, Doubleday, 1971.

JUVENILES

(With Russell Davis) *The Lion's Whiskers*, Little, Brown, 1959.
(With Davis) *Point Four Assignment*, Little, Brown, 1959.
(With Davis) *Ten Thousand Desert Swords*, Little, Brown, 1960.
(With Davis) *The Choctaw Code*, McGraw, 1961.
(With Davis) *Chief Joseph*, McGraw, 1962.
(With Davis) *Land in the Sun*, Little, Brown, 1963.
(With Davis) *Strangers in Africa*, McGraw, 1963.
Morning Star, Black Sun: The Northern Cheyenne Indians and America's Energy Crisis (Junior Literary Guild selection), Dodd, 1982.
The New Americans: Changing Patterns in U.S. Immigration (Junior Literary Guild selection), Dodd, 1983.
To Live in Two Worlds: American Indian Youth Today (Junior Literary Guild selection), Dodd, 1984.
Gavriel and Jemal: Two Boys of Jerusalem (Junior Literary Guild selection), Dodd, 1984.
Dark Harvest: Migrant Farmworkers in America, Dodd, 1985.
Children of the Maya: A Guatemalan Indian Odyssey, photographs by Paul Conklin, Dodd, 1986.

(With daughter, Melissa Ashabranner) *Into a Strange Land: Unaccompanied Refugee Youth in America* (Junior Literary Guild selection), Dodd, 1987.

The Vanishing Border: A Photographic Journey along Our Frontier with Mexico (Junior Literary Guild selection), Dodd, 1987.

Always to Remember: The Story of the Vietnam Veterans Memorial, photographs by daughter, Jennifer Ashabranner, Dodd, 1988.

OTHER

Contributor of articles and short stories to periodicals.

SIDELIGHTS: In March, 1971, on the tenth anniversary of the inception of the Peace Corps, Brent Ashabranner's book *A Moment in History: The First Ten Years of the Peace Corps* was published. Ashabranner was involved with the organization from the beginning, helping to shape and develop a number of its programs. From 1964 to 1966 he was director of the program in India, which at the time was the largest with over 750 volunteers. Before he left the Peace Corps in 1969, Ashabranner had become the deputy director of the entire agency.

Critics observe that *A Moment in History* contains an honest portrayal of the corps during its first decade. Although he cites the Peace Corps's successes, Ashabranner also outlines examples of the agency's failures and explains the reasons behind them. *Library Journal* contributor R. F. Chapman notes that the book ''is a frank account of the first decade of the Peace Corps,'' calling the author's approach a ''human presentation.'' Similarly, a *New York Times Book Review* writer remarks that Ashabranner is ''particularly good on the Peace Corps' inception and the bureaucratic infighting that accompanied it.''

Although Ashabranner left the Peace Corps in 1969, he continued working abroad for various charitable agencies until 1980, when he began writing full-time. The author's experiences with different cultures led him to write about people who live outside mainstream culture. Ashabranner gears his work toward young adults, frequently writing about ''children in crisis,'' as *Washington Post Book World* writer Michael Dirda describes. For example, in *Children of the Maya: A Guatemalan Indian Odyssey,* the author recounts the everyday village life of young Indian children, often using the children's own memories. The result, comments Dirda, is ''as usual with Ashabranner. . . . His book—powerfully enhanced by [Paul] Conklin's black and white photographs—blends careful reporting with social conscience.''

AVOCATIONAL INTERESTS: Bridge, golf, African art.

BIOGRAPHICAL/CRITICAL SOURCES:

PERIODICALS

Library Journal, August, 1971.
Los Angeles Times, October 17, 1987.
New York Times Book Review, August 5, 1962, April 4, 1971.
Washington Post Book World, June 8, 1986.

*   *   *

ASTRO, Richard 1941-

PERSONAL: Born February 11, 1941, in New York, N.Y.; son of Ralph (a social worker) and Sylvia (Bach) Astro; mar-

ried Betty Ann Lubinski (a personnel director), June 6, 1964. *Education:* Oregon State University, B.A., 1964; University of Colorado, M.A., 1965; University of Washington, Seattle, Ph.D., 1969. *Politics:* Independent.

ADDRESSES: Home—776 Bear Creek Circle, Winter Springs, Fla. 32108. *Office*—Office of the Provost, University of Central Florida, Orlando, Fla. 32816.

CAREER: Oregon State University, Corvallis, instructor, 1966-68, assistant professor, 1968-71, associate professor, 1971-77, professor of English, 1977-86, chairman of department, 1975-86, director of humanities development, 1976-86; University of Central Florida, Orlando, provost, 1986—.

MEMBER: Modern Language Association of America, John Steinbeck Society of America, Rocky Mountain Modern Language Association.

WRITINGS:

(Editor with Tetsumaro Hayashi) *Steinbeck: The Man and His Work,* Oregon State University Press, 1971.
John Steinbeck and Edward F. Ricketts: The Shaping of a Novelist, University of Minnesota Press, 1973.
(Editor with Jackson Benson) *Hemingway in Our Time,* Oregon State University Press, 1974.
Edward F. Ricketts, Boise State University, 1976.
Literature and the Sea, Oregon State University, 1976.
(Editor with Benson) *The Fiction of Bernard Malamud,* Oregon State University Press, 1977.
(Editor with James Nagel) *American Literature: The New England Heritage,* Garland Publishing, 1981.

Contributor to literature journals. Associate editor, *Steinbeck Quarterly.*

WORK IN PROGRESS: Directing a major curriculum development program supported by the National Endowment for the Humanities and the National Oceanic and Atmospheric Administration.

*   *   *

AUGUST, Eugene R(obert) 1935-

PERSONAL: Born October 19, 1935, in Jersey City, N.J.; son of Joseph Lawrence (a printer) and Florence (Brown) August; married Barbara Ann Danko (a teacher), June 18, 1964; children: Robert Eugene, James Eugene. *Education:* Rutgers University, B.A., 1958; University of Connecticut, M.A., 1960; University of Pittsburgh, Ph.D., 1965. *Politics:* Democrat. *Religion:* Roman Catholic.

ADDRESSES: Home—3115 Regent St., Kettering, Ohio 45409. *Office*—Department of English, University of Dayton, Dayton, Ohio 45469.

CAREER: Carnegie-Mellon University, Pittsburgh, Pa., instructor, 1962-64, assistant professor of English, 1964-66; University of Dayton, Dayton, Ohio, assistant professor, 1966-69, associate professor, 1969-76, professor of English, 1976—. Visiting associate professor at University of Hawaii, 1974-75.

MEMBER: International Hopkins Association, Modern Language Association of America, Tennyson Society.

AWARDS, HONORS: Mellon fellowship, 1960-62; Younger Humanist fellowship from National Endowment for the Humanities, 1973-74, for a book-length study of the art of John Stuart Mill.

WRITINGS:

(Contributor) Harry J. Cargas, editor, *The Continuous Flame: Teilhard in the Great Traditions,* B. Herder, 1970.

(Editor) Thomas Carlyle, *The Nigger Question* [and] John Stuart Mill, *The Negro Question,* Appleton, 1971.

John Stuart Mill: A Mind at Large, Scribner, 1975.

(Editor) *Men's Studies: A Selected and Annotated Interdisciplinary Bibliography,* Libraries Unlimited, 1985.

Contributor to *PMLA, Victorian Poetry, James Joyce Quarterly,* and *Hopkins Quarterly.* Member of advisory board, *Victorian Poetry;* assistant editor, *University of Dayton Review.*

*   *   *

AYRE, Jessica
    See APPIGNANESI, Lisa

B

BAKER, John R(andal)   1900-1984

PERSONAL: Born October 23, 1900, in Woodbridge, Suffolk, England; died June 8, 1984, in Oxford, England; son of Julian Alleyn (a rear admiral in the Royal Navy) and Geraldine Eugenie (Alison) Baker; married Inezita Davis, 1923 (divorced, 1937); married Helen Edge, July 6, 1939; children: (first marriage) Venice Ina, Gilbert Samuel. *Education:* New College, Oxford, B.A. (first class honors), 1922, M.A., 1927, D.Phil., 1927, D.Sc., 1938.

ADDRESSES: Home—45 Lakeside, Oxford OX2 8JQ, England. *Agent*—A. P. Watt Ltd., 26-28 Bedford Row, London WC1R 4HL, England.

CAREER: Oxford University, Oxford, England, lecturer in zoology, reader in cytology, 1955-67, reader emeritus, 1967-84, professorial fellow of New College, 1964-67. Participated in scientific expeditions to New Hebrides, 1922-23, 1927, 1933-34.

MEMBER: Royal Society (fellow), Royal Microscopical Society (fellow; president, 1964-65).

AWARDS, HONORS: Oliver Bird Medal from Family Planning Association, 1958, for research on chemical contraception; honorary fellowship of Royal Microscopical Society, 1968.

WRITINGS:

Sex in Man and Animals, Routledge, 1926.
Man and Animals in the New Hebrides, Routledge, 1929.
Cytological Technique, Methuen, 1933, 5th edition, 1966.
(With J. B. S. Haldane) *Biology in Everyday Life,* Allen & Unwin, 1933.
(With Julian Huxley, Bertrand Russell, and others) *Science in the Changing World,* Allen & Unwin, 1933.
The Chemical Control of Conception, Chapman & Hall, 1935.
The Scientific Life (also see below), Allen & Unwin, 1942.
Science and the Planned State (also see below), Allen & Unwin, 1945, Macmillan, 1946.
(With C. E. K. Mees) *The Path of Science,* Wiley, 1946.
Abraham Trembley of Geneva, E. J. Arnold, 1952.
Principles of Biological Microtechnique, Methuen, 1958.
Race, Oxford University Press, 1974, revised edition, Foundation for Human Understanding (Athens, Ga.), 1981.

(Editor) Julian Huxley, *Evolution: The Modern Synthesis,* Allen & Unwin, 3rd edition (Baker was not associated with earlier editions), 1974.
The Freedom of Science: An Original Anthology (includes *The Scientific Life* and *Science and the Planned State*), Ayer, 1975.
Julian Huxley, Scientist and World Citizen, 1887 to 1975: A Biographical Memoir, UNESCO, 1978.
(Editor with Angela Taylor) *Methods of Cultivating Parasites in Vitro,* Academic Press, 1978.
The Biology of Parasitic Protozoa, Edward Arnold, 1982.
Perspectives in Trypanosomiasis Research: Proceedings of the Twenty-first Trypanosomiasis Seminar; London, 24 September 1981, Wiley, 1982.
(Editor with R. Muller) *Advances in Parasitology,* Academic Press, Volume 21, 1982, Volume 22, 1983, Volume 23, 1985, Volume 24, 1985, Volume 25, 1986.
Parasitic Protozoa in British Wild Animals, Institute of Terrestrial Ecology, 1982.

Contributor of about two hundred articles to scientific journals. Editor, *Quarterly Journal of Microscopical Society,* 1946-64.

SIDELIGHTS: John R. Baker wrote of his expeditions to the New Hebrides: "On Espiritu Santo, the largest island of the group, we explored a large area that had not previously been entered by Europeans, and we had the opportunity to study Melanesian life while it was still scarcely affected by external influences. It was here that I first became interested in anthropology. In my opinion the interests of anthropologists tend to be centered too much on man alone. As T. H. Huxley wrote more than a century ago, 'Anthropology is a section of zoology . . . the problems of ethnology are simply those which are presented to the zoologist by every widely distributed animal he studies.' It is particularly important that anthropologists should be well grounded in the principles of zoological taxonomy.

"I hope to foster a less emotional outlook on racial matters. Ethical and political problems are of course involved, but for their solution one needs a solid basis of demonstrable fact. The welfare of mankind as a whole would be best served by dispassionate study of racial differences and resemblances."

Race has been translated into German.

BAKER, Kenneth F(rank) 1908-

PERSONAL: Born June 3, 1908, in Ashton, S.D.; son of Frank (a physician) and May (Boyer) Baker; married Katharine Cummings, June 17, 1944. *Education:* State College of Washington (now Washington State University), B.S., 1930, Ph.D., 1934; additional study at University of Wisconsin, 1934-35, Cornell University, 1947-48, and University of Adelaide, 1961-62.

ADDRESSES: Home—6980 Northwest Cardinal Dr., Corvallis, Ore. 97330. *Office*—Horticultural Crops Research Laboratory, U.S.D.A.-ARS, 3420 Orchard Ave., Corvallis, Ore. 97330.

CAREER: Pineapple Producers Cooperative Association, Experiment Station, Honolulu, Hawaii, associate plant pathologist, 1936-39; University of California, Los Angeles, assistant professor, 1939-42, associate professor, 1942-48, professor of plant pathology, 1948-60, developer of research program on pathology of ornamental plants; University of California, Berkeley, professor of plant pathology, 1961-75, professor emeritus, 1975—; Oregon State University, Corvallis, collaborator with United States Department of Agriculture, 1976—. Visiting professor, Pennsylvania State University, 1969.

MEMBER: International Society of Plant Pathologists, American Phytopathology Society (fellow), Mycological Society of America, Netherlands Phytopathology Society, Australasian Plant Pathology Society, British Mycological Society, Association of Applied Biology (England), British Phytopathological Society.

AWARDS, HONORS: Research awards from California Association of Nurserymen, 1956, California Florists Association, 1966, and Federation of Australian Nurserymen's Associations, 1969; Norman J. Colman Award, American Association of Nurserymen, 1959; Fulbright fellow in Australia, 1961-62; named to Horticultural Hall of Fame, 1966; North Atlantic Treaty Organization (NATO) fellowship, 1972.

WRITINGS:

(Editor) *The U.C. System for Producing Healthy Container-Grown Plants,* Agricultural Experiment Station, University of California, 1957.
A Plant Pathogen Views History, Clark Memorial Library, 1965.
(Editor with W. C. Snyder) *Ecology of Soil-Borne Plant Pathogens,* University of California Press, 1965.
Wildflowers of Western Australia, Rigby (Adelaide), 1971.
(With R. James Cook) *Biological Control of Plant Pathogens,* W. H. Freeman, 1974.
(With Cook) *The Nature and Practice of Biological Control of Plant Pathogens,* American Phytopathology Society, 1983.

Editor, monographs of American Phytopathology Society, 1963-77. Editor, *Annual Review of Phytopathology,* 1963-77.

WORK IN PROGRESS: Scientific papers.

AVOCATIONAL INTERESTS: Music, photography, travel.

BIOGRAPHICAL/CRITICAL SOURCES:

PERIODICALS

Phytopathology, Volume 60, Number 1, 1970.

BANKS, Arthur S. 1926-

PERSONAL: Born May 30, 1926, in Quincy, Mass.; son of Gordan T. (a dealer in rare manuscripts) and Miriam (Goodspeed) Banks. *Education:* Cornell University, A.B., 1951; George Washington University, A.M., 1954, Ph.D., 1967.

ADDRESSES: Home—156 Center Rd., Shirley, Mass. 01464. *Office*—Department of Political Science, State University of New York, Binghamton, N.Y. 13901.

CAREER: George Washington University, Washington, D.C., lecturer, 1958-59, assistant professor of political science and research associate, Sino-Soviet Institute, 1966-68; University of New Hampshire, Durham, instructor in department of government, 1959-60; Indiana University at Bloomington, research associate in International Development Research Center, 1963-65; State University of New York at Binghamton, associate professor of political science and director of Center for Comparative Political Research, 1968-76, professor of political science and senior fellow of Center for Social Analysis, 1976—, chairman of department of political science, 1980—. *Military service:* U.S. Marine Corps, 1943-46.

MEMBER: American Political Science Association, Pi Gamma Mu, Pi Sigma Alpha.

AWARDS, HONORS: National Science Foundation research grant, 1969-71; Mellon and Ford Foundation grants, 1982.

WRITINGS:

(With Robert B. Textor) *A Cross-Polity Survey,* M.I.T. Press, 1963.
Cross-Polity Time-Series Data, M.I.T. Press, 1971.
Cross-National Data Analysis, LRIS, 1974.
(Editor) *Political Handbook of the World,* McGraw, 1975, and annual revisions, 1976-1983, CSA Publications, 1984—.
(Editor) *Economic Handbook of the World,* McGraw, 1981, and annual revision, 1982.

Contributor to political science and social science journals.

*   *   *

BARAKA, Amiri 1934-
(LeRoi Jones)

PERSONAL: Born October 7, 1934, in Newark, N.J.; original name Everett LeRoi Jones; name changed to Bantuized Muslim appelation Imamu (''spiritual leader'') Ameer ('blessed'') Baraka (''prince''); later modified to Amiri Baraka; son of Coyette Leroy (a postman and elevator operator) and Anna Lois (Russ) Jones; married (divorced, August, 1965); married Sylvia Robinson (Bibi Amina Baraka), 1966; children: (first marriage) Kellie Elisabeth, Lisa Victoria Chapman; (second marriage) Obalaji Malik Ali, Ras Jua Al Aziz, Shani Isis, Amiri Seku, Ahi Mwenge. *Education:* Attended Rutgers University for one year; also attended Howard University, Columbia University and New School for Social Research.

ADDRESSES: Office—Department of Africana Studies, State University of New York, Long Island, N.Y. 11794-4340.

CAREER: Founded *Yugen* magazine and Totem Press, 1958; New School for Social Research, New York, N.Y., instructor, 1961-64; State University of New York at Stony Brook, associate professor, 1983-85, professor of Afro-American studies, 1985—. Visiting professor, University of Buffalo, summer, 1964, Columbia University, fall, 1964, and 1966-67, Yale University, 1977-78, George Washington University, 1978-

79, and San Francisco State University. Founder, April, 1964, and director, 1964-66, of Black Arts Repertory Theatre, disbanded, 1966; currently director of Spirit House (also known as Heckalu Community Center), Newark, a black community theatre, and head of advisory group at Treat Elementary School, Newark. Member, Political Prisoners Relief Fund, and African Liberation Day Commission. In 1968 Jones ran for a seat on a Newark community council which would oversee slum rehabilitation, but lost the election. *Military service:* U.S. Air Force, 1954-57; weather-gunner; stationed for two and a half years in Puerto Rico with intervening trips to Europe, Africa, and the Middle East.

MEMBER: Black Academy of Arts and Letters, National Black Political Assembly (secretary general; co-governor), Congress of African People (chairman), United Brothers; All African Games; Pan African Federation.

AWARDS, HONORS: Longview Best Essay of the Year award, 1961, for "Cuba Libre"; John Whitney Foundation fellowship for poetry and fiction, 1962; Obie Award, 1964, for *Dutchman*; Guggenheim fellowship, 1965-66; Yoruba Academy fellow, 1965; second prize, International Art Festival, Dakar, 1966, for "The Slave"; National Endowment for the Arts grant, 1966; Doctorate of Humane Letters, Malcolm X College, Chicago, Ill., 1972; Rockefeller Foundation fellow, 1981; Poetry Award, National Endowment for the Arts, 1981; New Jersey Council for the Arts award, 1982; American Book Award, Before Columbus Foundation, 1984, for *Confirmation: An Anthology of African-American Women*; Drama Award, 1985.

WRITINGS—Under name LeRoi Jones until 1967:

PLAY PRODUCTIONS

"A Good Girl Is Hard to Find," first produced in Montclair, N.J., at Sterington House, August 28, 1958.

"Dante" (an excerpt from the novel *The System of Dante's Hell*; also see below), first produced in New York, at Off-Bowery Theatre, October, 1961; produced again as "The Eighth Ditch," at the New Bowery Theatre, 1964.

"Dutchman" (also see below), first produced Off-Broadway at Village South Theatre, January 12, 1964; produced Off-Broadway at Cherry Lane Theater, March 24, 1964; produced in London, 1967.

"The Baptism" (also see below), first produced Off-Broadway at Writers' Stage Theatre, May 1, 1964, produced in London, 1971.

"The Slave" [and] "The Toilet" (also see below), first produced Off-Broadway at St. Mark's Playhouse, December 16, 1964.

"Jello" (also see below), first produced in New York by Black Arts Repertory Theatre, 1965.

"Experimental Death Unit #1" (also see below), first produced Off-Broadway at St. Mark's Playhouse, March 1, 1965.

"A Black Mass" (also see below), first produced in Newark, at Proctor's Theatre, May, 1966.

"Slave Ship: A Historical Pageant" (also see below), produced in Newark, at Spirit House, March, 1967; first produced in New York City, November 19, 1969.

"Madheart" (also see below), first produced in San Francisco, Calif., at San Francisco State College, May, 1967.

"Arm Yourself, or Harm Yourself!" (also see below), first produced in Newark, at Spirit House, 1967.

"Great Goodness of Life (A Coon Show)" (also see below), first produced in Newark, at Spirit House, November, 1967.

"Home on the Range" (also see below), first produced in Newark, at Spirit House, March, 1968; produced in New York City at a Town Hall rally, March, 1968.

"Resurrection in Life," first produced in Harlem, N.Y., August 24, 1969.

"Junkies Are Full of SHHH..." and "Bloodrites" (also see below), produced Off-Broadway at Henry Street Playhouse, November 21, 1970.

"A Recent Killing," first produced Off-Broadway at the New Federal Theatre, January 26, 1973.

"Columbia the Gem of the Ocean," first produced in Washington, D.C., by Howard University Spirit House Movers, 1973.

"The New Ark's A-Moverin," first produced in Newark, February, 1974.

"Sidnee Poet Heroical, or If in Danger of Suit, The Kid Poet Heroical" (also see below), first produced Off-Broadway at the New Federal Theatre, May 15, 1975.

"S-1" (also see below), first produced in New York at Afro-American Studios, July 23, 1976.

'The Motion of History" (also see below), first produced in New York at New York City Theatre Ensemble, May 27, 1977.

"What Was the Relationship of the Lone Ranger to the Means of Production?" (also see below), first produced in New York at Ladies Fort, May, 1979.

"Dim Cracker Party Convention," first produced in New York at Columbia University, July 1980.

"Boy and Tarzan Appear in a Clearing," first produced Off-Broadway at New Federal Theatre, October, 1981.

"Money," first produced Off-Broadway at La Mama Experimental Theatre Club, January, 1982.

Also author of "Board of Education," "The Kid Poeta Tragical," "The Coronation of the Black Queen," "Insurrection," and "Vomit and the Jungle Bunnies," all unpublished.

PUBLISHED PLAYS

Dutchman [and] *The Slave*, Morrow, 1964.

The Toilet (also see below), Sterling Lord, 1964.

The Baptism: A Comedy in One Act (also see below), Sterling Lord, 1966.

The System of Dante's Hell (contains "Dante"), Grove, 1965.

Dutchman, Faber & Faber, 1967.

Slave Ship, Jihad, 1967.

The Baptism [and] *The Toilet*, Grove, 1967.

Arm Yourself, or Harm Yourself! A One-Act Play, Jihad, 1967.

Four Black Revolutionary Plays: All Praises to the Black Man (contains "Experimental Death Unit # One," "A Black Mass," "Great Goodness of Life," and "Madheart"), Bobbs-Merrill, 1969.

(Contributor) Ed Bullins, editor, *New Plays from the Black Theatre* (contains "The Death of Malcolm X"), Bantam, 1969.

J-E-L-L-O, Third World Press, 1970.

(Contributor) Woodie King and Ron Milner, editors, *Black Drama Anthology* (contains "Bloodrites" and "Junkies Are Full of SHHH..."), New American Library, 1971.

(Contributor) Rochelle Owens, editor, *Spontaneous Combustion: Eight New American Plays* (contains "Ba-Ra-Ka"), Winter House, 1972.

What Was the Relationship of the Lone Ranger to the Means of Production?: A Play in One Act, Anti-Imperialist Cultural Union, 1978.

The Motion of History and Other Plays (contains "Slave Ship" and "S-1"), Morrow, 1978.

The Sidnee Poet Heroical, in Twenty-Nine Scenes, Reed & Cannon, 1979.
Selected Plays and Prose of LeRoi Jones/Amiri Baraka, Morrow, 1979.

Also author of the plays "Home on the Range" and "Police," published in *Drama Review*, summer, 1968, "Rockgroup," published in *Cricket*, December, 1969, and "Black Power Chant," published in *Drama Review*, December, 1972.

SCREENPLAYS

"Dutchman," Gene Persson Enterprises, Ltd., 1967.
"Black Spring," Black Arts Alliance (San Francisco), 1968.
"A Fable" (based on "The Slave"), MFR Productions, 1971.
"Supercoon," Gene Persson Enterprises, Ltd., 1971.

POETRY

April 13 (broadside), Number 133, Penny Poems (New Haven), 1959.
Spring & So Forth (broadside), Number 111, Penny Poems, 1960.
Preface to a Twenty Volume Suicide Note, Totem/Corinth, 1961.
The Dead Lecturer (also see below), Grove, 1964.
Black Art (also see below), Jihad, 1966.
Black Magic (also see below), Morrow, 1967.
A Poem for Black Hearts, Broadside Press, 1967.
Black Magic: Sabotage; Target Study; Black Art; Collected Poetry, 1961-1967, Bobbs-Merrill, 1969.
It's Nation Time, Third World Press, 1970.
Spirit Reach, Jihad, 1972.
Afrikan Revolution: A Poem, Jihad, 1973.
Hard Facts: Excerpts, People's War, 1975, 2nd edition, Revolutionary Communist League, 1975.
Spring Song, Baraka, 1979.
AM/TRAK, Phoenix Bookship, 1979.
Selected Poetry of Amiri Baraka/Leroi Jones (contains "Poetry for the Advanced"), Morrow, 1979.
In the Tradition: For Black Arthur Blythe, Jihad, 1980.
Reggae or Not! Poems, Contact Two, 1982.

ESSAYS

Blues People: Negro Music in White America, Morrow, 1963, published in England as *Negro Music in White America*, MacGibbon & Kee, 1965, reprinted under original title, Greenwood Press, 1980.
Home: Social Essays (contains "Cuba Libre," "The Myth of a 'Negro Literature,'" "Expressive Language," "the legacy of malcolm x, and the coming of the black nation," and "state/meant"), Morrow, 1966.
Black Music, Morrow, 1968, Greenwood Press, 1980.
Raise, Race, Rays, Raze: Essays since 1965, Random House, 1971.
Strategy and Tactics of a Pan-African Nationalist Party, Jihad, 1971.
Kawaida Studies: The New Nationalism, Third World Press, 1972.
Crisis in Boston!, Vita Wa Watu—People's War, 1974.
Daggers and Javelins: Essays, 1974-1979, Morrow, 1984.
(With wife, Amina Baraka) *The Music: Reflections on Jazz and Blues*, Morrow, 1987.

EDITOR

January 1st 1959: Fidel Castro, Totem, 1959.
Four Young Lady Poets, Corinth, 1962.

(And author of introduction) *The Moderns: An Anthology of New Writing in America*, 1963, published as *The Moderns: New Fiction in America*, 1964.
(And co-author) *In-formation*, Totem, 1965.
Gilbert Sorrentino, *Black & White*, Corinth, 1965.
Edward Dorn, *Hands Up!*, Corinth, 1965.
(And contributor) *Afro-American Festival of the Arts Magazine*, Jihad, 1966, published as *Anthology of Our Black Selves*, 1969.
(With Larry Neal and A. B. Spellman) *The Cricket: Black Music in Evolution*, Jihad, 1968, published as *Trippin': A Need for Change*, New Ark, 1969.
(And contributor, with Larry Neal) *Black Fire: An Anthology of Afro-American Writing*, Morrow, 1968.
A Black Value System, Jihad, 1970.
(With Billy Abernathy under pseudonym Fundi) *In Our Terribleness (Some Elements of Meaning in Black Style)*, Bobbs-Merrill, 1970.
(And author of introduction) *African Congress: A Documentary of the First Modern Pan-African Congress*, Morrow, 1972.
(With Diane DiPrima) *The Floating Bear, A Newsletter, No. 1-37, 1961-1969*, McGilvery, 1974.
(Co-editor with Amina Baraka) *Confirmation: An Anthology of Afro-American Women*, Morrow, 1983.

OTHER

The Disguise (broadside), [New Haven], 1961.
Cuba Libre, Fair Play for Cuba Committee (New York City), 1961.
(Contributor) Herbert Hill, editor, *Soon, One Morning*, Knopf, 1963.
The System of Dante's Hell (novel), Grove, 1965.
(Author of introduction) David Henderson, *Felix of the Silent Forest*, Poets Press, 1967.
Striptease, Parallax, 1967.
Tales (short stories), Grove, 1967.
(Author of preface), *Black Boogaloo (Notes on Black Liberation)*, Journal of Black Poetry Press, 1969.
"Focus on Amiri Baraka: Playwright LeRoi Jones Analyzes the 1st National Black Political Convention" (sound recording), Center for Cassette Studies, 1973.
Three Books by Imamu Amiri Baraka (LeRoi Jones), (contains *The System of Dante's Hell*, *Tales*, and *The Dead Lecturer*), Grove, 1975.
The Autobiography of LeRoi Jones/Amiri Baraka, Freundlich, 1983.

Works represented in more than seventy-five anthologies, including *A Broadside Treasury*, *For Malcolm*, *The New Black Poetry*, *Nommo*, and *The Trembling Lamb*. *Blues People*, *The System of Dante's Hell*, and *Tales* have been translated into German; *Blues People* and *The Slave* have been translated into French; *Blues People*, *The Dead Lecturer*, and *Home: Social Essays*, have been translated into Spanish. Editor with Diane Di Prima, *The Floating Bear*, 1961-1963. Contributor to *Evergreen Review*, *Poetry*, *Downbeat*, *Metronome*, *Nation*, *Negro Digest*, *Saturday Review*, and other periodicals.

WORK IN PROGRESS: "Why's/Wise," an epic poem.

SIDELIGHTS: Amiri Baraka (formerly LeRoi Jones) is a major and controversial author. He is one of those mavericks, such as Allen Ginsberg and Norman Mailer, who have produced large bodies of work that are highly critical of American civilization. Perhaps more than Ginsberg or Mailer, Baraka continues to be an irritant to the American literary establishment. Baraka may be the most difficult American author to evaluate dispassionately since the modernist poet Ezra Pound, another important writer whose work still evokes volatile critical response. Like Pound, Baraka has dared to bring radical politics into the world of literature and to deliver his explosive ideas in an inflammatory style.

It is not surprising, then, that critical opinion about Baraka is highly divided. For example, Stanley Kauffmann says in *Dissent* that Baraka is "the luckiest man of our times, a writer who . . . would be less than lightly held if he did not happen to be a Negro at this moment in American history." Kimberly Benston, on the other hand, asserts in *Baraka: The Renegade and the Mask,* "Imamu Amiri Baraka is one of the foremost American artists of our century." Baraka is an author who demands that his audience accept his Afro-American identity as central to his art. Furthermore, he is an avant-garde writer whose variety of forms, including poetry, drama, music criticism, fiction, autobiography, and the essay, makes him difficult to categorize. Moreover, Baraka's stormy history clouds critical objectivity. No armchair artist, he has gone through a series of dramatic stages, from wild Beatnik ranting against the square world in the late 1950s through early 1960s, to black cultural nationalist renouncing the white world in the mid 1960s through mid 1970s, to Marxist-Leninist rejecting monopoly capitalism since the mid 1970s. Beyond Baraka's multifarious talents as a creative writer, his ideas and art— especially, as the primary architect of the Black Arts Movement of the 1960s—have had a profound influence on the direction of subsequent black literature. Therefore, when Arnold Rampersad claims in *American Book Review* that Baraka "stands with [Phillis] Wheatley, [Frederick] Douglass, [Paul Laurence] Dunbar, [Langston] Hughes, [Zora Neale] Hurston, [Richard] Wright and [Ralph] Ellison as one of the eight figures . . . who have significantly affected the course of African-American literary culture," he does not overstate the case.

During his Beat period, when he was known as LeRoi Jones, Baraka lived in New York's Greenwich Village and Lower East Side, where he published important little magazines such as *Yugen* and *Floating Bear* and socialized with such Bohemian figures as Ginsberg, Frank O'Hara, and Gilbert Sorrentino. He was greatly influenced by the white avant-garde: Charles Olson, O'Hara and Ginsberg, in particular, shaped his conception of a poem as being exploratory and open in form. Donald Allen records in *The New American Poetry: 1945-1960* Baraka's Beat-period views on form: "There must not be any preconceived notion or design for what a poem ought to be. 'Who knows what a poem ought to sound like? Until it's thar' says Charles Olson . . . & I follow closely with that. I'm not interested in writing sonnets, sestina or anything . . . only poems."

Baraka's first book, *Preface to a Twenty Volume Suicide Note,* has met with general critical approval. In *The New Poets: American and British Poetry since World War II,* M. L. Rosenthal says that the early Jones/Baraka "has a natural gift for quick, vivid imagery and spontaneous humor, and his poems are filled with sardonic or sensuous or slangily knowledgeable passages." Theodore Hudson, in *From Leroi Jones to Amiri Baraka: The Literary Works,* observes: "All things considered, *Preface* was an auspicious beginning for LeRoi Jones the poet." However, sometimes the positive critical response to the early work comes at the expense of the later poetry. Lloyd Brown represents such a position when he announces in *Amiri Baraka:* "The scurrilities and general lack of control are a major drawback in the later collections, especially the

black nationalist and socialist verse. But, despite the monotony that plagues the style of the first two volumes they remain Baraka's most consistently successful collections of poetry."

At first glance *Preface* looks like a typical product of integrated Bohemia; in fact, it ends: "You are / as any other sad man here / american." Yet there is a "blues feeling" throughout, that is, an infusion of black culture and reference. The reader can hear the "moaning . . . [of] Bessie Smith" in the book's lines, although blackness is not its principal focus. As David Ossman reports in *The Sullen Art: Interviews with Modern American Poets,* Baraka remarked in early 1960: "I'm fully conscious all the time that I am an American Negro, because it's part of my life. But I know also that if I want to say, 'I see a bus full of people,' I don't have to say, 'I am a Negro seeing a bus full of people.' I would deal with it when it has to do directly with the poem, and not as a kind of broad generalization that doesn't have much to do with a lot of young writers today who are Negroes." This view proved to be transitory. With the Civil Rights movement, Martin Luther King, and the black political upsurge of the late 1960s, Baraka's attitude toward race and art changed; he found that being a Negro wasn't some abstract and generalized stance but was integral to his art. Furthermore, with the coming of ethnic consciousness came political consciousness and the slow and painful rejection of Bohemia.

In July 1960 Baraka visited Castro's Cuba. In *The Autobiography of LeRoi Jones/Amiri Baraka,* Baraka refers to this visit as "a turning point in my life." While in Cuba he met forceful and politically committed Third World artists and intellectuals who forced him to reconsider his art and his apolitical stance. They attacked him for being an American; he tried to defend himself in "Cuba Libre," an essay reprinted in *Home: Social Essays,* by saying: "Look, why jump on me? . . . I'm in complete agreement with you. I'm a poet . . . what can I do? I write, that's all, I'm not even interested in politics." The Mexican poet, Jaime Shelley, answered him: "You want to cultivate your soul? In that ugliness you live in, you want to cultivate your soul? Well, we've got millions of starving people to feed, and that moves me enough to make poems out of." Finally, the Cuban revolution impressed Baraka as an alternative to the unanchored rebellion of his Bohemian friends at home. In Cuba the young intellectuals seemed to be doing something concrete to create a better and more humane world. Baraka felt that the Cuban government, unlike that of the United States, was actually being run by young intellectuals and idealists. This trip was the beginning of Baraka's radical political art and his identification with Third World artists.

Although Baraka started publishing in the early 1960s, he did not achieve fame until the 1964 publication of his play *Dutchman,* which won the *Village Voice*'s Obie Award. Werner Sollors notes in *Amiri Baraka/LeRoi Jones: The Quest for a "Populist Modernism"* that Norman Mailer called it "the best play in America." Baraka's most famous work, it has often been reprinted and performed, including a British film version by Anthony Harvey. (The play also provides scenes for Jean-Luc Godard's movie *Masculine-Feminine.*) In *Dutchman* Baraka no longer presents the melancholy hipster world where, as he declared in *Preface,* "Nobody sings anymore," but instead a realm where an angry young man fights for his ethnic identity and his manhood. Lula, the symbolic agent of the white state, sent out to find the latent murderer in the assimilated middle-class Negro Clay, locates and kills him. The play is highly stylized, reflecting the 1960s movement to propel black literature away from naturalism, the principal mode from the 1940s to 1960s, to a more experimental avant-garde art. Moreover, Baraka believed what a character in his play *The Slave* says: "the worst thing that ever happened to the West was the psychological novel." In a 1979 *New York Times Book Review* Darryl Pinckley commends Baraka's skill as a playwright: "He is a highly gifted dramatist. Much of the black protest literature of the 60's now seems diminished in power, even sentimental. But 'Dutchman' immediately seizes the imagination. It is radically economical in structure, striking in the vivacity of its language and rapid shifts of mood."

The Dead Lecturer, Baraka's second book of poetry, is the work of a black man who wants to leave white music and the white world behind. As civil rights activities intensified, Baraka became more and more disappointed with his white friends; in fact, the word "friends" becomes ironic in this second volume. In "Black Dada Nihilismus," for example, he realizes that he must "Choke my friends / in their bedrooms" to escape their influence and vision. To elude Western metaphysical domination Baraka must call up the dark gods of the black soul; he demands violence in himself and his people to escape the white consciousness. He no longer wants to be the Dead Lecturer; he wants life. In this book of poetry he attempts to reject the "quiet verse" of the Beat Generation and claim the black chant of political commitment.

This blackening and politicalization of Baraka's art is formal as well as thematic. The poetic line becomes longer as the verse imitates the chant. In the poem "Rhythm and Blues," Baraka reveals that he does not want to become a martyr for Western art. Richard Howard, writing in the *Nation,* finds the Baraka of *The Dead Lecturer* "much surer of his own voice. . . . These are the agonized poems of a man writing to save his skin, or at least to settle in it, and so urgent is their purpose that not one of them can trouble to be perfect." Howard understands Baraka's pain. In a negative review of *The Dead Lecturer* in *Salmagundi,* Rosenthal makes an important statement which anticipates the far more political art of Baraka's Black Arts and Marxist periods: "No American poet since Pound has come closer to making poetry and politics reciprocal forms of action." Rosenthal perceives that Baraka wants his poems to act on the world; as Baraka wrote to his friend, Black Mountian poet Edward Dorn, in a 1961 letter: "'Moral earnestness' . . . ought [to] be transformed into action. . . . I know we think that to write a poem, and be Aristotle's God is sufficient. But I can't sleep. . . . There is a right and a wrong. And it's up to me, you, all of the so called minds, to find out. It is only knowledge of things that will bring this 'moral earnestness'."

Baraka had joined the Beat Generation because he regarded its members as spiritual outsiders who were against white middle-class America. Yet over the years he became disillusioned with this apolitical avant-garde that refused to take action in the world. Disengagement was no longer enough for Baraka who notes in the essay "Cuba Libre": "The rebels among us have become merely people like myself who grow beards and will not participate in politics. Drugs, juvenile delinquency, complete isolation from the vapid mores of the country, a few current ways out. But name an alternative here." Baraka wanted an alternative to Bohemianism.

During this transitional period Baraka produced two fine works, his only serious efforts in fiction: *The System of Dante's Hell,* a novel, and *Tales,* a collection of short stories. As Sollors points out, the sections of the novel parallel the themes and even passages found in *Preface, Dead Lecturer,* and the early

uncollected poems. Although *System* was published in 1965 it was mostly written in the early 1960s. Baraka commented on the book and the times to Kimberly Benston in an interview published in *Boundary 2:* "I was really writing defensively. I was trying to get away from the influence of people like Creeley and Olson. I was living in New York then and the whole Creeley-Olson influence was beginning to beat me up. I was in a very closed circle—that was about the time I went to Cuba—and I felt the need to break out of the type of form that I was using then. I guess this was not only because of the form itself but because of the content which was not my politics."

Tales, published in 1967, treats the years 1963 through 1967, a time of radical change in Baraka's life, and reflects the themes of the poetry in *Black Magic,* which also appeared in 1967. Both works try to convey a sense of the ethnic self away from the world of white culture. In *Conscientious Sorcerers: The Black Postmodernist Fiction of LeRoi Jones/Baraka, Ishmael Reed and Samuel R. Delany,* Robert Elliot Fox remarks on Baraka's fiction: "However, the essential energy linking these two works—which recount and reevaluate his life up to that time—is a relentless momentum deeper into blackness. These fugitive narratives describe the harried flight of an intensely self-conscious Afro-American artist/intellectual from neo-slavery of blinding, neutralizing whiteness, where the arena of struggle is basically within the mind. In *Tales* Baraka describes the posture and course he wishes to adopt: that of "The straight ahead people, who think when that's what's called for, who don't when they don't have to. Not the Hamlet burden, which is white bullshit, to always be weighing and analyzing, and reflecting." Baraka wants action, and the story "Screamers" casts action in musical terms. For Baraka dance and music are associated with vitality and political action. In this tale blacks riot in the streets because of the wild music of Lynn Hope, a jazz saxophonist: "We screamed at the clear image of ourselves as we should always be. Ecstatic, completed, involved in a secret communal expression. It would be the sweetest revolution, to hucklebuck into the fallen capital, and let the oppressors lindy hop out." In the 1960s Baraka was the pioneer of black experimental fiction, probably the most important since Jean Toomer who had written during the Harlem Renaissance of the 1920s. In the 1970s and 1980s Baraka has been joined by a band of younger experimental black writers, including Ishmael Reed, Clarence Major, and Charles Johnson.

During the early 1960s Baraka composed his major social-aesthetic study of black music in America, *Blues People: Negro Music in White America.* A history, it begins in slavery and ends with contemporary avant-garde jazz (John Coltrane, Ornette Coleman, and Cecil Taylor). Baraka argues that since Emancipation the blues have been an essential feature of black American music and that this form was born from the union of the American and the African experience; as Baraka says, "Undoubtedly, none of the African prisoners broke out into 'St. James Infirmary' the minute the first of them was herded off the ship." *Blues People* gave Baraka an opportunity to meditate on a profound and sophisticated art form created by blacks and to do so during a time when he was trying to find a model for his own art that was not white avant-garde. Although he later retracted his evaluation, he had temporarily rejected black literature as mediocre and middle-brow. In his *Home* essay "The Myth of a 'Negro Literature,'" he declares: "Only in music, and most notably in blues, jazz, and spirituals, *i.e.,* 'Negro Music,' has there been a significantly profound contribution by American Negroes.'' In the *New York Times Book Review,* Jason Berry calls Baraka ''an eloquent jazz critic; his 1963 study, *Blues People: Negro Music in White America* is a classic.'' Furthermore, Clyde Taylor maintains in James B. Gwynne's *Amiri Baraka: The Kaleidoscopic Torch,* ''The connection he nailed down between the many faces of black music, the sociological sets that nurtured them, and their symbiotic evolutions through socio-economic changes, in *Blues People,* is his most durable conception, as well as probably the one most indispensable thing said about black music.''

Although *Blues People* is his only sustained study of Afro-American music, Baraka has published two other collections containing important essays on the subject: *Black Music,* written from a cultural nationalist perspective, and *The Music: Reflections on Jazz and Blues,* written from a Marxist one. In *Black Music* Baraka crystallizes the idea of John Coltrane as the prime model for the new black art: ''Trane is a mature swan whose wing span was a whole world. But he also shows us how to murder the popular song. To do away with weak Western forms. He is a beautiful philosopher.'' Brown asserts: ''As an essayist Baraka's performance is decidedly uneven. The writings on music are always an exception. As historian, musicological analyst, or as a journalist covering a particular performance Baraka always commands attention because of his obvious knowledge of the subject and because of a style that is engaging and persuasive even when the sentiments are questionable and controversial.'' In *The Kaleidoscopic Torch* Joe Weixlmann states: ''Baraka's expertise as an interpreter of Afro-American music is, of course, well-known. Had he never done any belletristic writing or political organizing, he would be remembered as the author of *Blues People . . .* and *Black Music.*''

In 1965, following the assassination of Black Muslim leader Malcolm X, Baraka left Greenwich Village and the Bohemian world and moved uptown to Harlem and a new life as a cultural nationalist. He argued in ''the legacy of malcolm x, and the coming of the black nation'' (collected in *Home*) that ''black People are a race, a culture, a Nation.'' Turning his back on the white world, he established the Black Arts Repertory Theatre/School in Harlem, an influential model that inspired black theaters throughout the country. In 1967, he published his black nationalist collection of poetry, *Black Magic,* which traces his painful exit from the white world and his entry into blackness. Unfortunately, his exorcism of white consciousness and values included a ten-year period of intense hatred of whites and most especially Jews; in ''A POEM SOME PEOPLE WILL HAVE TO UNDERSTAND,'' Baraka expressed his impatience with liberals and Bohemians, and he requests: ''Will the machinegunners please step forward?'' Espousing political action and political art, he declares, ''We want poems that kill.'' After a year in Harlem, he returned home to his birthplace, Newark, New Jersey, where he continued his cultural nationalist activities. In 1967 he changed his name from LeRoi Jones to the Bantuized Muslim appellation Imamu (''spiritual leader,'' later dropped) Ameer (later Amiri, ''blessed'') Baraka (''prince''), as confirmation of his pride in his blackness.

While in Harlem Baraka had become the main theorist of the Black Aesthetic, defined by Houston Baker in *Black American Literature Forum* as ''a distinctive code for the creation and evaluation of black art.'' The aesthetician felt that the black artist must express his American experience in forms that spring from his own unique culture and that his art must be evaluated by standards that grow out of his own culture. Baraka writes in ''Expressive Language,'' an essay in *Home:* ''Words'

meanings, but also the rhythm and syntax that frame and propel their concatenation, seek their culture as the final reference for what they are describing of the world.'' In ''And Shine Swam On,'' an essay in *Black Fire: An Anthology of Afro-American Writing,* Larry Neal provides one of the central statements of the Black Aesthetic: ''The artist and the political activist are one. They are both shapers of the future reality. Both understand and manipulate the collective myths of the race. Both are warriors, priests, lovers and destroyers.'' In his *Home* essay, ''state/meant'' Baraka declares fiercely: ''The Black Artist's role in America is to aid in the destruction of America as he knows it. His role is to report and reflect so precisely the nature of the society, and of himself in that society, that other men will be moved by the exactness of his rendering and, if they are black men, grow strong through this moving, having seen their own strength, and weakness; and if they are white men, tremble, curse, and go mad, because they will be drenched with the filth of their evil.'' In a less rhetorical fashion, Fox presents the goals of the contemporary black artist: ''The radical inversion of Western systems of belief and order [that black artists] engage in can be termed 'mythoclasm,' the drastic demystification of ideological signs that have been turned into false universals. . . . Their praxis as artists involves countering the hegemonic [authoritarian] code inscribed by the master culture with alternatives of discourse and desire (transformational longings).'' Or, as Baraka writes in his essay ''the legacy of malcolm x,'' ''The song title 'A White Man's Heaven Is a Black Man's Hell' describes how complete an image reversal is necessary in the West.''

In *Understanding the New Black Poetry: Black Speech and Black Music as Poetic References,* Stephen Henderson observes, ''[Baraka] is the central figure of the new black poetry awakening''; in an essay collected in *Modern Black Poets,* Arthur P. Davis calls him ''the high priest of this new Black literary renaissance and one who has done most to shape its course.'' Baraka dominated the Black Arts Period of the late 1960s both as a theorist and artist. He was the main artist-intellectual responsible for shifting the emphasis of contemporary black literature from an integrationist art conveying a raceless and classless vision to a literature rooted in the black experience. The Black Arts Era, both in terms of creative and theoretical writing, is the most important one in black literature since the Harlem Renaissance. No post-Black Arts artist thinks of himself or herself as simply being a human being who happens to be black; blackness is central to his or her experience and art. Furthermore, Black Arts had its impact on other ethnic groups and primarily through the person of Baraka. The Native American author Maurice Kenny writes of Baraka in *The Kaleidoscopic Torch:* ''He opened tightly guarded doors for not only Blacks but poor whites as well and, of course, Native Americans, Latinos and Asian-Americans. We'd all still be waiting the invitation from the *New Yorker* without him. He taught us all how to claim it and take it.'' In *The Kaleidoscopic Torch* Clyde Taylor says of Baraka's poems of the Black Arts period: ''There are enough brilliant poems of such variety in *Black Magic* and *In Our Terribleness* to establish the unique identity and claim for respect of several poets. But it is beside the point that Baraka is probably the finest poet, black or white, writing in this country these days.'' However, the response to the poetry was not all favorable. In *With Eye and Ear,* the avant-garde critic and poet Kenneth Rexroth contended: ''In recent years he [Baraka] has succumbed to the temptation to become a professional Race Man of the most irresponsible sort. . . . His loss to literature is more serious than any literary casualty of the Second War.''

The play "Madheart" epitomizes Baraka's writings of the Black Arts period. It is a morality play in which Black Man ritualistically tries to kill White Woman, who symbolizes the power of white consciousness and influences the consciousness of blacks. Until such influence is destroyed, the play contends, the black mind cannot be free. Baraka insists in "the legacy of malcolm x" that "the Black artist . . . is desperately needed to change the images this people identify with, by asserting Black feeling, Black mind, Black judgment." Implicitly, Black Man is a black cultural nationalist artist.

In 1966 Baraka published *Home,* an important book of essays, in which the reader sees Baraka becoming "blacker" and more radical in each essay. The collection includes the famous "Cuba Libre," which documents his trip to Cuba and his awakening to Third-World conceptions of art and political activism. A spiritual autobiography written at its author's fullest powers, *Home* assumes the same importance in Baraka's career as *Advertisements for Myself* does in Mailer's. The poet Sterling D. Plumpp observes in *The Kaleidoscopic Torch* that he regards *Home* as a major work "for its forthrightness and daring courage to call for 'revolutionary changes,' [and moreover it] . . . is unsurpassed for its seminal ideas regarding black art which is excellent and people-centered."

Baraka's years in Greenwich Village had made him a master of avant-garde technique that he utilized in his own work and passed on to younger black artists such as Nikki Giovanni and Don L. Lee. Ironically, avant-garde ideas of form cohered perfectly with the new black artist's need to express his or her own oral traditions; the free verse and the eccentric typography of the white avant-garde were ideal vehicles for black oral expression and experience. Unlike Harlem Renaissance poets—such as Claude McKay, who constantly battled the rigid, archaic form of the English sonnet replete with nineteenth-century diction and conventions to express 1920s black American language and life—the Black Arts poet had the flexibility of contemporary forms, forms committed to orality and polyrhythms. In a 1971 issue of *Black World* Dudley Randall observes: "The younger poets have a teacher of great talent, and while they think they are rejecting white standards, they are learning from LeRoi Jones, a man versed in German philosophy, conscious of literary traditions . . . who uses the structure of Dante's *Divine Comedy* in his *The System of Dante's Hell* and the punctuation, spelling and line divisions of sophisticated contemporary poets." Arnold Rampersad maintains in *American Book Review:* "Among all the major writers who helped to wean younger black writers away from imitation and compulsive traditionalism and toward modernism, Baraka has been almost certainly the most influential. . . . In speaking of his modernizing influence on younger black poets, one does not mean that Baraka taught them to imitate or even to admire the verse of Pound and Eliot, Stevens and Williams, Ginsberg and Kerouac, all of whose poetry he himself attempted to absorb. More than any other black poet, however, he taught younger black poets of the generation past how to respond poetically to their lived experience, rather than to depend as artists on embalmed reputations and outmoded rhetorical strategies derived from a culture often substantially different from their own."

In 1974, dramatically reversing himself, Baraka rejected black nationalism as racist and became a Third World Socialist. He declared, in *The New York Times:* "It is a narrow nationalism that says the white man is the enemy. . . . Nationalism, so-called, when it says 'all non-blacks are our enemies,' is sickness or criminality, in fact, a form of fascism." Since 1974 he has produced a number of Marxist poetry collections and plays, including *Hard Facts,* "Poetry for the Advanced," and "What Was the Relationship of the Lone Ranger to the Means of Production?" He has also published a book of Marxist essays, *Daggers and Javelins.* The goal of his socialist art is the destruction of the capitalist state and the creation of a socialist community. In *The Poetry and Poetics of Amiri Baraka: The Jazz Aesthetic,* William J. Harris records Baraka's assessment of his goals as a Third World Socialist: "I think fundamentally my intentions are similar to those I had when I was a Nationalist. That might seem contradictory, but they were similar in the sense I see art as a weapon, and a weapon of revolution. It's just now that I define revolution in Marxist terms. I once defined revolution in Nationalist terms. But I came to my Marxist view as a result of having struggled as a Nationalist and found certain dead ends theoretically and ideologically, as far as Nationalism was concerned and had to reach out for a communist ideology." His socialist art is addressed to the black community, which has, he believes, the greatest revolutionary potential in America.

Baraka's socialist works have not fared well in the establishment press. In the *New York Times Book Review* Darryl Pinckney comments that Baraka has "sacrificed artistic vitality on the altar of his political faith. . . . his early work is far better than his recent efforts: he now seems content to express his Marxism in the most reductive, shrill propaganda." Henry C. Lacey in his 1981 book on Baraka, *To Raise, Destroy, and Create: The Poetry, Drama, and Fiction of Imamu Amiri Baraka (LeRoi Jones),* ignores the Marxist work entirely; Fox, in his 1987 study, says, "The Marxist work is intellectually determined, whereas the cultural-nationalist pieces are emotionally felt." On the other hand, E. San Juan, an exiled Filipino leftist intellectual, writes in *The Kaleidoscopic Torch* that he finds the "Lone Ranger" "the most significant theatrical achievement of 1978 in the Western hemisphere." Weixlmann sensitively responds in *The Kaleidoscopic Torch* to the tendency to categorize the radical Baraka instead of analyze him: "At the very least, dismissing someone with a label does not make for very satisfactory scholarship. Initially, Baraka's reputation as a writer and thinker derived from a recognition of the talents with which he is so obviously endowed. The assaults on that reputation have, too frequently, derived from concerns which should be extrinsic to informed criticism."

As the critical climate cools, critics will find merit in the recent poetry, especially the long *In the Tradition: For Black Arthur Blythe,* and the epic-in-progress, "Why's/Wise," both accomplished works. Also with the 1984 publication of *The Autobiography* Baraka has joined the great tradition of the black autobiography, which runs from Frederick Douglass to W. E. B. DuBois to Richard Wright to Malcolm X. Like other authors in this tradition, in the act of making sense of his life, Baraka makes sense of American culture. Arnold Rampersad comments on Baraka and his autobiography in *The Kaleidoscopic Torch:* "His change of heart and head is testimony to his honesty, energy, and relentless search for meaning, as demonstrated recently once again with the publication of his brilliant *The Autobiography of LeRoi Jones.*"

In a piece on Miles Davis in *The Music: Reflections on Jazz and Blues,* Baraka quotes the contemporary trombonist, Craig Harris: "Miles is gonna do what Miles wants to do. And everybody else can follow, if they feel like it." Like Davis, Baraka is going his own way; he is an original, and others can follow if they like. He is a black writer who has taken the techniques and notions of the white avant-garde and made them his own; like the great bop musicians before him, he has united avant-garde art with the black voice, creating a singular expressive mode. Baraka has created a major art, not by trying to blend into Western tradition but by trying to be true to himself and his culture. He speaks out of a web of personal and communal experience, minimizing the so-called universal features he shared with the white world and focusing on the black cultural difference—what has made the black experience unique in the West. Out of this experience Baraka fashions his art, his style, his distinctive vision of the world.

Papers by and about Amiri Baraka/LeRoi Jones are housed in the Dr. Martin Sukov Collection at Yale University's Beinecke Rare Book and Manuscript Library; numerous letters to and from the author, and several of Baraka's manuscripts are collected at Indiana University's Lilly Library; the author's letters to Charles Olson are housed at the University of Connecticut's Special Collections Library; other manuscripts and materials are collected at Syracuse University's George Arents Research Library.

BIOGRAPHICAL/CRITICAL SOURCES:

BOOKS

Abramson, Doris E., *Negro Playwrights in the American Theatre: 1925-1959,* Columbia University Press, 1969.

Allen, Donald M., *The New American Poetry: 1945-1960,* Grove, 1960.

Allen, Donald M., and Warren Tallman, editors, *Poetics of the New American Poetry,* Grove, 1973.

Allen, Robert L., *Black Awakening in Capitalist America,* Doubleday, 1970.

Archer, Leonard C., *Black Images in the American Theatre,* Pageant-Poseidon, 1973.

Baraka, Amiri, *Tales,* Grove, 1967.

Baraka, Amiri and Larry Neal, editors, *Black Fire: An Anthology of Afro-American Writing,* Morrow, 1968.

Baraka, Amiri, *Black Magic: Sabotage; Target Study; Black Art; Collected Poetry, 1961-1967,* Bobbs-Merrill, 1969.

Baraka, Amiri, *The Autobiography of LeRoi Jones/Amiri Baraka,* Freundlich Books, 1984.

Benston, Kimberly A., editor, *Baraka: The Renegade and the Mask,* Yale University Press, 1976.

Benston, Kimberly A., *Imamu Amiri Baraka (LeRoi Jones): A Collection of Critical Essays,* Prentice-Hall, 1978.

Bigsby, C. W. E., *Confrontation and Commitment: A Study of Contemporary American Drama, 1959-66,* University of Missouri Press, 1968.

Bigsby, C. W. E., editor, *The Black American Writer, Volume II: Poetry and Drama,* Everett/Edwards, 1970, Penguin, 1971.

Bigsby, C. W. E., *The Second Black Renaissance: Essays in Black Literature.* Greenwood Press, 1980.

Birnebaum, William M., *Something for Everybody Is Not Enough,* Random House, 1972.

Brown, Lloyd W., *Amiri Baraka,* Twayne, 1980.

Cohn, Ruby, *Dialogue in American Drama,* Indiana University Press, 1971.

Concise Dictionary of American Literary Biography, Volume 1: *The New Consciousness,* Gale, 1987.

Contemporary Literary Criticism, Gale, Volume 1, 1973, Volume 2, 1974, Volume 3, 1975, Volume 5, 1976, Volume 10, 1979, Volume 14, 1980, Volume 33, 1985.

Cook, Bruce, *The Beat Generation,* Scribner, 1971.

Cruse, Harold, *The Crisis of the Negro Intellectual,* Morrow, 1967.

Dace, Letitia, *LeRoi Jones (Imamu Amiri Baraka): A Checklist of Works by and about Him,* Nether Press, 1971.

Dace, Letitia and Wallace Dace, *The Theatre Student: Modern Theatre and Drama,* Richards Rosen Press, 1973.

Dictionary of Literary Biography, Gale, Volume 5: *American Poets since World War II,* 1980, Volume 7: *Twentieth-Century American Dramatists,* 1981, Volume 16: *The Beats: Literary Bohemians in Postwar America,* 1983, Volume 38: *Afro-American Writers after 1955: Dramatists and Prose Writers,* 1985.

Dukore, Bernard F., *Drama and Revolution,* Holt, 1971.

Ellison, Ralph, *Shadow and Act,* New American Library, 1966.

Emanuel, James A., and Theodore L. Gross, editors, *Dark Symphony: Negro Literature in America,* Free Press, 1968.

Fox, Robert Elliot, *Conscientious Sorcerers: The Black Postmodernist Fiction of LeRoi Jones/Baraka, Ishmael Reed and Samual R. Delany,* Greenwood Press, 1987.

Frost, David, *The Americans,* Stein & Day, 1970.

Gayle, Addison, editor, *Black Expression: Essays by and about Black Americans in the Creative Arts,* Weybright & Talley, 1969.

Gayle, Addison, *The Way of the New World: The Black Novel in America,* Anchor/Doubleday, 1975.

Gibson, Donald B., *Five Black Writers: Essays on Wright, Ellison, Baldwin, Hughes, LeRoi Jones,* New York University Press, 1970.

Gibson, Donald B., editor, *Modern Black Poets: A Collection of Critical Essays,* Prentice-Hall, 1973.

Gilman, Richard, *Common and Uncommon Masks: Writings on the Theatre 1961-1970,* Random House, 1971.

Gwynne, James B., editor, *Amiri Baraka: The Kaleidoscopic Torch,* Steppingstones Press, 1985.

Hall, Veronica, *Chicorel Theater Index to Plays in Anthologies, Periodicals, Discs and Tapes,* Chicorel Library Publishing, 1970.

Harris, William J., *The Poetry and Poetics of Amiri Baraka: The Jazz Aesthetic,* University of Missouri Press, 1985.

Haskins, James, *Black Theater in America,* Crowell, 1982.

Hatch, James V., *Black Image on the American Stage: A Bibliography of Plays and Musicals, 1770-1970,* Drama Book Specialists, 1970.

Hatch, James V., editor, *Black Theatre, U.S.A.,* Free Press, 1974.

Henderson, Stephen E., *Understanding the New Black Poetry: Black Speech and Black Music as Poetic References,* Morrow, 1973.

Hill, Herbert, *Soon, One Morning,* Knopf, 1963.

Hill, Herbert, editor, *Anger, and Beyond: The Negro Writer in the United States,* Harper, 1966.

Hudson, Theodore, *From LeRoi Jones to Amiri Baraka: The Literary Works,* Duke University Press, 1973.

Hughes, Langston, and Milton Meltzer, *Black Magic: A Pictorial History of the Negro in American Entertainment,* Prentice-Hall, 1967.

Jones, LeRoi, *Preface to a Twenty Volume Suicide Note,* Totem Press/Corinth Books, 1961.

Jones, LeRoi, *The Dead Lecturer,* Grove, 1964.

Jones, LeRoi, *Blues People: Negro Music in White America,* Morrow, 1963.

Jones, LeRoi, *Home: Social Essays,* Morrow, 1966.

Keil, Charles, *Urban Blues,* University of Chicago Press, 1966.

King, Woodie, and Ron Milner, editors, *Black Drama Anthology,* New American Library, 1971.

Klinkowitz, Jerome, *Literary Disruptions: The Making of a Post-Contemporary American Fiction,* 2nd edition, University of Illinois, 1980.

Knight, Arthur and Kit Knight, editors, *The Beat Vision*, Paragon House, 1987.

Kofsky, Frank, *Black Nationalism and the Revolution in Music*, Pathfinder, 1970.

Lacey, Henry C., *To Raise, Destroy, and Create: The Poetry, Drama, and Fiction of Imamu Amiri Baraka (LeRoi Jones)*, The Whitson Publishing Company, 1981.

Lewis, Allan, *American Plays and Playwrights*, Crown, 1965.

Littlejohn, David, *Black on White: A Critical Survey of Writing by American Negroes*, Viking, 1966.

Lumley, Frederick, *New Trends in Twentieth Century Drama*, Oxford University Press, 1967.

Mezu, Okechukwu, editor, *Modern Black Literature*, Black Academy Press, 1971.

O'Brien, John, *Interviews with Black Writers*, Liveright, 1973.

Ossman, David, *The Sullen Art: Interviews with Modern American Poets*, Corinth, 1963.

Pool, Rosy E., editor, *Beyond the Blues*, Hand & Flower Press, 1962.

Popkin, Michael, editor, *Modern Black Writers*, Ungar, 1978.

Rexroth, Kenneth, *With Eye and Ear*, Herder and Herder, 1970.

Ricard, Alain, *Theatre et Nationalisme: Wole Soyinka et LeRoi Jones*, Presence Africaine, 1972.

Rosenthal, M. L., *The New Poets: American and British Poetry since World War II*, Oxford University Press, 1967.

Sollors, Werner, *Amiri Baraka/LeRoi Jones: The Quest for a "Populist Modernism,"* Columbia University Press, 1978.

Stepanchev, Stephen, *American Poetry since 1945*, Harper, 1965.

Weales, Gerald, *The Jumping-Off Place: American Drama in the 1960s*, Macmillan, 1969.

Whitlow, Roger, *Black American Literature: A Critical History*, Nelson Hall, 1973.

Williams, Martin, *The Jazz Tradition*, New American Library, 1971.

Williams, Sherley Anne, *Give Birth to Brightness: A Thematic Study in Neo-Black Literature*, Dial, 1972.

PERIODICALS

America, May 26, 1984.

American Book Review, February, 1980, May-June, 1985.

American Dialog, spring, 1968.

American Imago, Volume 28, summer, 1972.

Antioch Review, fall, 1967.

Atlantic, January, 1966, May, 1966.

Avant Garde, September, 1968.

Best Sellers, August, 1971.

Black American Literature Forum, spring, 1980, spring, 1981, fall, 1982, spring, 1983, winter, 1985.

Black Collegian, March 3, 1973.

Black Dialogue, July-August, 1965.

Black Lines, winter, 1970.

Black Scholar, March, 1971.

Black Theatre, 1968.

Black Times, October, 1974.

Black World, volume 29, number 6, April, 1971, December, 1971, November, 1974, July, 1975.

Book Week, December 24, 1967.

Book World, October 28, 1979.

Boundary, Volume 2, number 6, 1978.

Chicago Defender, January 11, 1965.

Chicago Tribune, October 4, 1968.

Christian Science Monitor, June 21, 1966.

CLA Journal, March, 1971, September, 1971, September, 1972, September, 1973, December, 1977.

Commentary, February, 1965.

Commonweal, June 28, 1968, June 13, 1969.

Comparative Drama, summer, 1984.

Contemporary Literature, Volume 12, 1971.

Cue, June 6, 1964.

Der Spiegel, August 18, 1969.

Detroit Free Press, January 31, 1965.

Detroit News, January 15, 1984, August 12, 1984.

Dissent, spring, 1965.

Downbeat, January 2, 1964, August, 1987.

Drama Review, summer, 1968, winter, 1970.

Ebony, August, 1967, August, 1969, February, 1971.

Educational Theatre Journal, March, 1968, March, 1970, March, 1976.

Esquire, June, 1966.

Essence, September, 1970, May, 1984, September, 1984, May, 1985.

Evergreen Review, November, 1965, December, 1967, June, 1968, February, 1970.

Freedomways, winter, 1968.

Globe & Mail (Toronto), September 19, 1987.

Greenfield Review, fall, 1980.

Guardian, March 23, 1968, March 30, 1968.

Hudson Review, winter, 1964.

International Times, February 2-15, 1968.

Jazz, April, 1966-July, 1967.

Jazz Review, June, 1959.

Jet, January 16, 1975, July 23, 1984.

Journal of Black Poetry, fall, 1968, spring, 1969, summer, 1969, fall, 1969.

Journal of Black Studies, December, 1973.

Journal of Ethnic Studies, spring, 1974.

Journal of Popular Culture, fall, 1969.

Kenyon Review, Volume XXX, number 5, 1968.

Liberator, February, 1965, February, 1966.

Life, August 4, 1967.

Listener, March 14, 1968, September 25, 1969.

Literary Times, May-June, 1967.

Los Angeles Free Press, Volume 5, number 18, May 3-May 9, 1968.

Los Angeles Times Book Review, May 15, 1983, March 29, 1987.

Massachusetts Review, spring, 1973.

Metronome, September, 1961.

Midwest Quarterly, volume 12, July, 1971.

Minnesota Review, spring, 1978.

Minority Voices, spring, 1977.

Modern Drama, February, 1971, summer, 1972, September, 1972, June, 1974.

Ms., September, 1983.

Nation, October 14, 1961, November 14, 1961, March 13, 1964, April 13, 1964, January 4, 1965, March 15, 1965, January 22, 1968, February 2, 1970.

National Guardian, July 4, 1964.

National Observer, June 29, 1964.

National Review, March 23, 1965, December 23, 1983.

Negro American Literature Forum, March, 1966, winter, 1973.

Negro Digest, December, 1963, February, 1964, Volume 13, number 19, August, 1964, March, 1965, April, 1965, March, 1966, April, 1966, June, 1966, April, 1967, April, 1968, January, 1969, April, 1969.

New Leader, March 13, 1967.

New Republic, January 23, 1965, May 28, 1966.

Newsday, August 20, 1969.

New Statesman, July 16, 1965, September 5, 1969.

Newsweek, March 13, 1964, April 13, 1964, November 22, 1965, May 2, 1966, March 6, 1967, December 4, 1967, December 1, 1969, February 19, 1973.

New York, November 5, 1979.

New Yorker, April 4, 1964, December 26, 1964, March 4, 1967, December 30, 1972.

New York Herald Tribune, March 25, 1964, April 2, 1964, December 13, 1964, October 27, 1965.

New York Post, March 16, 1964, March 24, 1964, January 15, 1965, March 18, 1965.

New York Review of Books, January 20, 1966, May 22, 1964, July 2, 1970, October 17, 1974, June 11, 1984, June 14, 1984.

New York Times, April 28, 1966, May 8, 1966, August 10, 1966, September 14, 1966, October 5, 1966, January 20, 1967, February 28, 1967, July 15, 1967, January 5, 1968, January 6, 1968, January 9, 1968, January 10, 1968, February 7, 1968, April 14, 1968, August 16, 1968, November 27, 1968, December 24, 1968, August 26, 1969, November 23, 1969, February 6, 1970, May 11, 1972, June 11, 1972, November 11, 1972, November 14, 1972, November 23, 1972, December 5, 1972, December 27, 1974, December 29, 1974, November 19, 1979, October 15, 1981, January 23, 1984.

New York Times Book Review, January 31, 1965, November 28, 1965, May 8, 1966, February 4, 1968, March 17, 1968, February 14, 1971, June 6, 1971, June 27, 1971, December 5, 1971, March 12, 1972, December 16, 1979, March 11, 1984, July 5, 1987, December 20, 1987.

New York Times Magazine, February 5, 1984.

Observer, May 14, 1967, February 25, 1968, August 31, 1969, December 1, 1985.

Obsidian, spring, 1975.

Partisan Review, Volume 31, summer, 1964.

Poetry, March, 1965, February, 1967.

Progressive Leader, November-December, 1964.

Publishers Weekly, August 8, 1966, January 15, 1968, September 10, 1979.

Ramparts, June 19, 1968.

Realist, May, 1965.

Salmagundi, spring-summer, 1973.

San Francisco Chronicle, August 23, 1964.

San Francisco Review of Books, November, 1984.

Saturday Evening Post, July 13, 1968.

Saturday Review, April 20, 1963, January 11, 1964, January 9, 1965, December 11, 1965, December 9, 1967, October 2, 1971, July 12, 1975.

Southwestern Review, spring, 1982.

Spectator, September 16, 1966, February 16, 1968.

Studies in Black Literature, spring, 1970, Volume 1, number 2, 1970, Volume 3, number 2, 1972, Volume 3, number 3, 1972, Volume 4, number 1, 1973.

Sunday News (New York), January 21, 1973.

Theatre Journal, May, 1982.

Time, December 25, 1964, November 19, 1965, May 6, 1966, January 12, 1968, April 26, 1968, June 28, 1968, June 28, 1971.

Times Literary Supplement, November 25, 1965, September 1, 1966, September 11, 1969, October 9, 1969.

Trace, summer, 1967.

Tribune Books, March 29, 1987.

Village Voice, December 17, 1964, May 6, 1965, May 19, 1965, August 30, 1976, August 1, 1977, December 17-23, 1980, October 2, 1984.

Virginia Quarterly Review, August, 1966.

Washington Post, August 15, 1968, September 12, 1968, November 27, 1968, December 5, 1980, January 23, 1981, June 29, 1987.

Washington Post Book World, December 24, 1967, May 22, 1983.

Woman's Review of Books, summer, 1983.

World Literature Today, spring, 1979, winter, 1981, summer, 1984.

—Sidelights by William J. Harris

*   *   *

BARBOUR, Douglas (Fleming)   1940-

PERSONAL: Born March 21, 1940, in Winnipeg, Manitoba, Canada; son of Harold Douglas (a fundraising executive) and Phyllis (Wilson) Barbour; married M. Sharon Nicoll, May 21, 1966. *Education:* Acadia University, B.A., 1962; Dalhousie University, M.A., 1964; Queen's University, Kingston, Ontario, Ph.D., 1976. *Politics:* "Anarchist (at heart)."

ADDRESSES: Home—Edmonton, Alberta, Canada. *Office*—Department of English, University of Alberta, Edmonton, Alberta, Canada T6G 2E5.

CAREER: Alderwood Collegiate Institute, Toronto, Ontario, teacher of English, 1968-69; University of Alberta, Edmonton, assistant professor, 1969-77, associate professor, 1977-82, professor of English, 1982—. Member of editorial board of Ne West Press and Longspoon Press, 1980—.

MEMBER: Association of Canadian University Teachers, League of Canadian Poets (co-chairman, 1972-74).

WRITINGS:

POETRY

Land Fall, Delta Books, 1971.

A Poem as Long as the Highway, Quarry Press, 1971.

White, Fiddlehead Books, 1972.

Song Book, Talon Books, 1973.

He and She and, Golden Dog Press, 1974.

Visions of My Grandfather, Golden Dog Press, 1977.

Shore Lines, Turnstone Press, 1979.

Vision/Sounding, League of Canadian Poets, 1980.

(With Stephen Scobie) *The Pirates of Pen's Chance*, Coach House Press, 1981.

The Harbingers, Quarry Press, 1984.

Visible Visions: Selected Poems, Ne West Press, 1984.

Canadian Poetry Chronicle, Quarry Press, 1985.

OTHER

(Editor) *The Story So Far Five* (short stories), Coach House Press, 1978.

Worlds Out of Words: The Science Fiction Novels of Samuel R. Delany (criticism), Bran's Head Books, 1978.

(Editor with Scobie) *The Maple Laugh Forever: An Anthology of Canadian Comic Poetry*, Hurtig Press, 1981.

(Editor with Marni Stanley) *Writing Right: New Poetry by Canadian Women*, Longspoon Press, 1982.

(Editor with Phyllis Gollieb) *Tesseracts²* (science fiction anthology), Porcepics, 1987.

Author of "Canadian Poetry Chronicle," in *Dalhousie Review*, 1969-77, *West Coast Review*, 1977-82, and *Quarry*, 1983. Member of editorial board of *Quarry*, 1965-68, *White Pelican*, 1972-76, and *Canadian Forum*, 1978-80.

WORK IN PROGRESS: Poetry.

SIDELIGHTS: Douglas Barbour told *CA:* "I share with those writers I most admire a sense of language as alive, as something which speaks out its own life rather than simply as a tool to be 'used'; the language shaped *by* desire gives shape *to* desire."

*　　　*　　　*

BARKER, A(udrey) L(ilian)　1918-

PERSONAL: Born April 13, 1918, in England; daughter of Harry (an engineer) and Elsie A. (Dutton) Barker. *Education:* Attended county secondary schools in England.

ADDRESSES: Home—103 Harrow Rd., Carshalton, Surrey SM5 3QF, England.

CAREER: British Broadcasting Corp., London, England, secretary and sub-editor, 1949-78; free-lance writer. Member of panel of judges, Katherine Mansfield Prize, 1984, and Macmillan Silver Pen Award, 1986.

MEMBER: Royal Society of Literature (fellow), English PEN (member of executive committee, 1981-85).

AWARDS, HONORS: Atlantic Award in Literature, 1946; Somerset Maugham Award, 1947, for *Innocents: Variations on a Theme;* Cheltenham Festival Literary Award, 1962; South East Arts Creative Book Award, 1981; Macmillan Silver Pen Award, 1988; Society of Authors Traveling Scholarship, 1988.

WRITINGS:

Innocents: Variations on a Theme (short stories), Hogarth, 1947, Scribner, 1948.
Apology for a Hero, Scribner, 1950.
Novelette, with Other Stories, Scribner, 1951.
"Pringle" (television script), British Broadcasting Corp. (BBC-TV), 1958.
The Joy-Ride and After, Hogarth, 1963, Scribner, 1964.
Lost upon the Roundabouts (short stories), Hogarth, 1964.
A Case Examined (novel), Hogarth, 1965.
The Middling: Chapters in the Life of Ellie Toms, Hogarth, 1967.
John Brown's Body, Hogarth, 1969.
Femina Real (short stories), Hogarth, 1971.
A Source of Embarrassment (novel), Hogarth, 1974.
A Heavy Feather (novel), Hogarth, 1978, Braziller, 1979.
Life Stories (autobiographical and fictional), Hogarth, 1981.
Relative Successes (novel), Hogarth, 1984, Salem House, 1986.
No Word of Love (short stories), Hogarth, 1985.
The Gooseboy (novel), Hutchinson, 1987.
(Author of introduction) Elizabeth Taylor, *Hester Lilly,* Virago, in press.
(Contributor) Chris Mirgan, editor, *Dark Fantasies,* Century Hamilton, in press.
(Contributor) Anne Boston, editor, *Wave Me Goodbye: Stories of World War II,* Virago, in press.

SIDELIGHTS: A. L. Barker has often been called a "writer's writer"—a title that reflects her ability if not her popularity. Her work tends to be complex, and she concentrates on the short story; even some of her novels take on an episodic form reminiscent of the short story. *The Middling,* for example, is subtitled *Chapters in the Life of Ellie Toms;* a more recent work, *A Heavy Feather,* "has the sense that what one is reading is not a novel, . . . but rather a collection of short stories," comments Francis King in *Spectator.* In addition, her anthology *Life Stories* "eschew[s] the traditional forms of autobiography," writes *Times Literary Supplement* contributor David Profumo. The critic elaborates, noting that "much of [Barker's] best work has drawn strength from avoiding the artificial neatness that narrative shapeliness imposes on the representation of life." King also sees a distinctive approach in the author's "memoir": "She set about linking together these fables or . . . extended metaphors for her experiences, instead of directly relating the experiences themselves."

Many themes appear throughout Barker's work, including "the isolation of human personality, the impossibility of communication, and the ambivalence of love," lists Kim D. Heine in a *Dictionary of Literary Biography* essay. "Throughout her fiction, Barker explores the world of social and psychological outcasts: the ill, the poor, the lonely." But while her subjects may seem ordinary or common, Barker uses her skill to explore the private nature beyond their surfaces. For example, *John Brown's Body* "carries us characteristically into the private exotic world behind the drab, commonplace exterior," describes a *Times Literary Supplement* reviewer. "Like life itself," writes King of *Relative Successes,* "Miss Barker constantly provides tricks, surprises and sudden, disconcerting illuminations of what previously was dark." Concludes the critic: "The freshness of vision that she brings to the often humiliating circumstances in which her characters entrap themselves is matched by the freshness of her style."

Because of the extreme situations in which her characters exist, King believes that "many of Miss Barker's stories are concerned—as she herself has recognized—with the jarring impact caused by a collision between innocence and experience." But this collision is relieved, notes Heine, by an "ironic detachment [that] renders her work not oppressive but strangely comic. Through caricature and understatement," adds the critic, "Barker infuses her work with humor. She has a penchant for horror and the macabre, which ironically lightens the tone by lifting the weight of unrelieved realism." In her *Spectator* review of *The Gooseboy,* Anita Brookner makes a similar observation: "Not insistent enough to be labelled 'stoical,' [Barker] catches perfectly the downside of events, their very lack of emphasis giving her the tone she needs. She is a quietly excellent and very English writer, who believes in fatalism as others believe in action."

Whatever her theme or subject, Barker is frequently praised for the consistent quality of the several aspects of her writing. In *John Brown's Body,* for instance, a *Times Literary Supplement* critic finds that "without ever sounding pretentiously 'poetic,' Miss Barker succeeds in using startling memorable imagery." Barker also possesses a talent for conciseness that allows her to integrate several elements so that an episode "leaves in the reader's mind an illuminating, utterly recognizable picture of human sadness and absurd resilience," writes Anne Duchene in the *Times Literary Supplement.* Profumo similarly comments on Barker's ability to bring out various images and themes: "Her art is not concerned to juggle histrionically with a plot, to strive for technical developments which cause gasps of astonished admiration, but rather to work quietly and with understatement: she can make loneliness interesting, and invest suburban greyness and domestic trivia with a sense of menace or exoticism—a much more difficult feat." And Philip Howard sees in *The Gooseboy,* Barker's most recent novel, "a pleasure in eccentricity, and class and character cattily observed," he notes in the London *Times.* "A. L. Barker has a strong idiosyncrasy, and a sharp eye for detail. She has original and entertaining notions. . . . Dialogue and plot work through indirections and obliquities.'' As with much of Barker's work, Howard notes that in this novel ''you never guess what is going to happen next.''

Barker wrote *CA*: ''I am by choice and capacity a short story writer. I believe the short story to be one of the two most challenging literary forms: the other—which I am not qualified to attempt—is poetry. Some poets can create a word-perfect, completely integrated short story in a dozen lines.

''The possibilities for the short story have always been enough to occupy me. It is a lifetime's engagement, and as life time dwindles, tantalisingly the scope increases. Technically a form, it now seems to be blessedly formless. A thousand words, or twenty thousand, in Austen's English, or Joyce's, the moment is all, is what I want to catch, with a turn of phrase, a hint, an implication, a repetition. Ideally, the moment should persist, like a flavour, so that the reader after reading, or days or years later, finds the moment complete, for better for worse, and beyond reproach or censure.''

BIOGRAPHICAL/CRITICAL SOURCES:

BOOKS

Barker, A. L., *Life Stories,* Hogarth, 1981.
Dictionary of Literary Biography, Volume 14: *British Novelists since 1960*, Gale, 1982.

PERIODICALS

New Statesman, July 28, 1978, October 2, 1981, August 10, 1984, May 31, 1985.
New Yorker, February 26, 1979.
Saturday Review, April 28, 1979.
Spectator, July 29, 1978, September 26, 1981, August 4, 1984, October 3, 1987.
Times (London), October 1, 1987.
Times Literary Supplement, November 2, 1967, November 13, 1969, August 27, 1971, March 22, 1974, July 21, 1978, September 25, 1981, August 3, 1984, June 21, 1985, October 30, 1987.

*   *   *

BARKER, Eric   1905-1973

PERSONAL: Born July 9, 1905, in Thames Ditton, Surrey, England; came to United States, 1921, naturalized, 1931; died February 8, 1973, in Big Sur, Calif.; son of Edward Wilson and Katherine (Tigg) Barker; married Madelynne Greene (former head of International Dance Theater), 1936 (deceased); children: (previous marriage) Jean Parker Pentico. *Education:* Educated in England.

ADDRESSES: Home—Big Sur, Calif.

CAREER: Writer; gardener.

AWARDS, HONORS: Borestone Mountain Poetry Award, 1956, for *Directions in the Sun;* Silver Medal, Commonwealth Club of California, 1961, for poetry; California Literature Medal Award, 1962, for ''A Ring of Willows''; Shelley Memorial Award, Poetry Society of America, 1963.

WRITINGS:

The Planetary Heart, foreword by Benjamin DeCasseres, introduction by John Cowper Powys, Wings Press, 1942.
Directions in the Sun, foreword by Merle Armitage, Powys, and Robinson Jeffers, Gotham Book Mart, 1956.

In Easy Dark, preface by Henry Miller, privately printed (Big Sur, Calif.), 1958.
A Ring of Willows, New Directions, 1961.
Looking for Water: New and Selected Poems, October House, 1964.
Under Orion, drawings by Francesca Greene, Kayak, 1970.

Also author of *Big Sur and Other Poems* and *Twenty Poems.* Contributor of poems to anthologies. Contributor of poems to numerous periodicals, including *New York Times, Saturday Review, Yale Review, Harper's, Atlantic, American Scholar, Harper's Bazaar, Poetry,* and *Beloit Poetry Journal.*

SIDELIGHTS: The *Washington Post* reports that when Eric Barker was nominated state poet laureate in 1965 by the California Assembly, he declined the honor explaining, ''I remember [poet Robinson] Jeffers saying somewhere, 'Write and be quiet.' Such good advice for a poet.''

AVOCATIONAL INTERESTS: Music and dancing.

BIOGRAPHICAL/CRITICAL SOURCES:

PERIODICALS

Holiday, February, 1959.
Life, July, 1959.
Literary Review, autumn, 1963.
New York Times Book Review, July 23, 1961.
Poetry, November, 1961.
Saturday Review, May 6, 1961.

OBITUARIES:

PERIODICALS

New York Times, February 9, 1973.
Washington Post, February 10, 1973.*

*   *   *

BARNETT, Adam
See FAST, Julius

*   *   *

BARNUM, P. T., Jr.
See STRATEMEYER, Edward L.

*   *   *

BARNUM, Theodore
See STRATEMEYER, Edward L.

*   *   *

BARON, Dennis E(mery)   1944-

PERSONAL: Born May 9, 1944, in New York, N.Y.; son of R. C. Roy (a historian) and Sylvia (a teacher; maiden name, Mayer) Baron; married Iryce White (a teacher), October, 1979; children: Cordelia, Rachel. *Education:* Brandeis University, B.A., 1965; Columbia University, M.A., 1968; University of Michigan, Ph.D., 1971.

ADDRESSES: Home—Urbana, Ill. *Office*—Department of English, University of Illinois, 608 South Wright St., Urbana, Ill. 61801.

CAREER: Eastern Illinois University, Charleston, Ill., assistant professor of English, 1971-73; City College of the City University of New York, New York, N.Y., assistant professor of English, 1973-74; University of Illinois, Urbana, assistant professor, 1975-81, associate professor, 1981-84, professor of English and linguistics, 1984—, director of rhetoric, 1985—. Fulbright lecturer at Universite de Poitiers, France, 1978-79.

MEMBER: American Dialect Society, Modern Language Association of America, National Council of Teachers of English, Linguistic Society of America.

WRITINGS:

Case Grammar and Diachronic English Syntax, Mouton, 1974.
Going Native: The Regeneration of Saxon English (monograph), University of Alabama Press, 1982.
Grammar and Good Taste: Reforming the American Language, Yale University Press, 1982.
Grammar and Gender, Yale University Press, 1986.
English First: The Official Language Question in America, Yale University Press, in press.

Contributor of articles to language and linguistics journals, including *American Speech, English Today, College English, Journal of Literary Semantics, Language Problems and Language Planning, Journal of Popular Culture, Verbatim, Righting Words,* and *Language and Style.* Associate editor of *Publications of the American Dialect Society,* 1982-85, editor, 1985—.

WORK IN PROGRESS: An Eye for an Eye, a mystery novel; *The Old Torn Book; Self-Referentiality in the Poetry of Geoffrey Chaucer; Declining Grammar and Other Essays on the English Vocabulary.*

SIDELIGHTS: Stuart B. Flexner writes in the *New York Times Book Review* that Dennis E. Baron's *Grammar and Good Taste: Reforming the American Language* is a "well-researched, . . . excellent and useful dissertation" on the history of American English. According to Edward B. White in the *Los Angeles Times Book Review,* Baron has written a "sensible and careful book . . . a wonderfully amusing collection of oddities, testimony to the vanity, pedantry and earnestness of those who seek to hold back or make more rational the tides of language." Both reviewers further express that the crucial chapters of *Grammar and Good Taste* are those devoted to the movements for a federal English and other reform efforts present in the United States since the eighteenth century.

Baron told *CA:* "I am interested in a variety of topics dealing with the history of the English language, the question of sexism and language, attitudes toward language use, the movement to make English the official language of the United States, and attempts to change language. My audience is the general educated reader, as well as the language specialist, and I broadcast language commentary twice a month for WILL-Radio, the central Illinois National Public Radio affiliate. My graduate training is in medieval English language and literature, and I have developed a subsidiary interest in detective fiction, trying my hand at writing a mystery novel."

BIOGRAPHICAL/CRITICAL SOURCES:

PERIODICALS

Los Angeles Times Book Review, March 6, 1983.
New York Times Book Review, November 28, 1982.
Psychology Today, August, 1986.
Times Literary Supplement, July 4, 1986.

BARSTOW, Phyllida 1937-
(Phyllida Hart-Davis; Olivia O'Neill, a pseudonym)

PERSONAL: Born September 30, 1937, in London, England; daughter of John (a barrister) and Diana (a farmer) Barstow; married Duff Hart-Davis (an author), April 22, 1961; children: Alice, Guy. *Education:* Attended school at Lawnside, Great Malvern. *Religion:* Church in Wales.

ADDRESSES: Home—Owlpen Farm, Uley, Dursley, Gloucestershire, England. *Agent*—Richard Scott-Simon, 32 College Cross, London N.1, England.

CAREER: Has worked as a journalist for Amalgamated Press, Mirror Group Magazines, *Argosy,* and *Women's Journal.*

WRITINGS:

The Queen Bee, Macdonald & Co., 1977.
Doublecross Country (fiction), Macdonald & Co., 1979.
Night Is for Hunting (fiction), Century, 1981.
Glacier Run (fiction), Century, 1982.
(Under name Phyllida Hart-Davis) *Grace: The Story of a Princess,* Collins, 1983.
The Dolphin Shore (juvenile novel), Century, 1984.
Daughters of the Regiment, Century, 1987.
(Adaptor) Barbara Sneyd, *Riding High: Country Diary of a Young Horsewoman,* Dodd, 1987.
The Nabob's Wife, Century, 1988.

FICTION; UNDER PSEUDONYM OLIVIA O'NEILL

Distant Thunder, Futura, 1978.
Imperial Nights, Hamlyn, 1979.
Dragon Star, Macdonald & Co., 1980.

AVOCATIONAL INTERESTS: History, the countryside, farming, horses, field sports.*

*   *   *

BARTH, Edna 1914-1980
(Edna Weiss)

PERSONAL: Born March 13, 1914, in Marblehead, Mass.; died October 1, 1980, in New York, N.Y.; daughter of Charlton Lyman (a writer) and Elizabeth (Bateman) Smith; married Julius Weiss, August 22, 1938 (divorced, 1965); married George Francis Barth (a writer and lecturer), November 19, 1966; children (first marriage) Elizabeth Weiss Fein, Joel Peter, Paul Jeremy. *Education:* Radcliffe College, B.A., 1936; Simmons College, B.S. (library science), 1937. *Politics:* Independent. *Religion:* Nonsectarian.

ADDRESSES: Home—5 Isle of Wight Rd., East Hampton, N.Y. 11937. *Office*—Lothrop, Lee & Shepard Co., 105 Madison Ave., New York, N.Y. 10016.

CAREER: Jones Library, Amherst, Mass., librarian, 1937-39; New York Public Library, New York City, assistant children's librarian, 1939-41; Hillsboro Center School, Hillsboro, N.H., teacher, 1947-49; McGraw-Hill Book Co., New York City, associate editor of children's books, 1961-63; Thomas Y. Crowell Co., New York City, editor, 1963-66; Lothrop, Lee & Shepard Co., New York City, editor, 1966-68, editor-in-chief, 1968-79; William Morrow & Co., New York City, vice-president, 1971-79.

MEMBER: Children's Book Council (member of board of directors; director, 1970-73), Authors Guild, Authors League of

America, National Organization of Women, Radcliffe Club of New York.

WRITINGS:

UNDER NAME EDNA WEISS; JUVENILES

Sally Saucer, Houghton, 1956.
Truly Elizabeth, Houghton, 1957.
The Rainbow, Nelson, 1960.

UNDER NAME EDNA BARTH; JUVENILES

Lilies, Rabbits, and Painted Eggs: The Story of Easter Symbols, Seabury, 1970.
The Day Luis Was Lost, Little, Brown, 1971.
I'm Nobody, Who Are You?: The Story of Emily Dickinson, Seabury, 1971.
Holly, Reindeer, and Colored Lights: The Story of the Christmas Symbols, Seabury, 1971.
Witches, Pumpkins, and Grinning Ghosts: The Story of the Halloween Symbols, Seabury, 1972.
Hearts, Cupids, and Red Roses, Seabury, 1973.
Jack-O-Lantern, Seabury, 1974.
Turkeys, Pilgrims, and Indian Corn: The Story of the Thanksgiving Symbols, Seabury, 1975.
Cupid and Psyche: A Love Story, Seabury, 1976.
Shamrocks, Harps, and Shillelaghs: The Story of the St. Patrick's Day Symbols, Seabury, 1977.
Balder and the Mistletoe: A Story for the Winter Holidays, Seabury, 1978.
A Christmas Feast: Poems, Sayings, Greetings, and Wishes, Houghton, 1979.

SIDELIGHTS: Edna Barth once told *CA:* "Since childhood I have wanted to be an author and/or editor, but was past forty and the mother of three before realizing either ambition.

"My stories always seem to come from experiences I have had with people within a year or two of the writing. Whether children or adults, they had made a deep impression, and from this impression a story would begin to grow. The settings, too, are always one I have visited or lived in fairly recently."

OBITUARIES:

PERIODICALS

Publishers Weekly, October 17, 1980.*

*   *   *

BATTLE, Lois   1942-

PERSONAL: Born October 6, 1942, in Australia; daughter of John H. (in U.S. Navy) and Doreen (White) Battle. *Education:* University of California, Los Angeles, B.A., 1961.

ADDRESSES: Agent—Jane Rotrosen Agency, 318 East 51st St., New York, N.Y. 10022.

CAREER: Writer. Worked as actress and director, nursery school teacher, probation officer, and dance instructor.

MEMBER: American Federation of Television and Radio Artists, Authors Guild, Authors League of America, Actors' Equity Association, Screen Actors Guild.

WRITINGS:

Season of Change, St. Martin's, 1980.
War Brides, St. Martin's, 1982.
Southern Women, St. Martin's, 1984.

A Habit of the Blood, St. Martin's, 1987.

SIDELIGHTS: Lois Battle writes primarily about the lives of women; and because of the realism that marks her fiction, critics believe that her work transcends the romance genre. For example, a *Publishers Weekly* contributor describes Battle's first novel, *Season of Change*, as a "sentimental but realistic novel about modern widowhood." And in a *Publishers Weekly* critique of *War Brides*, in which Battle focuses on the adjustments that three Australian war brides must make to their new lives in America, a contributor suggests that Battle, "herself the daughter of a war bride, writes easily and realistically" about each of her heroines. Similarly, in the *New York Times Book Review*, Miriam Berkley praises *Southern Women*, a novel about "three generations of Southern women represented by the female line of a prominent Savannah family," for its insightful writing and "absorbing and convincing" characterizations, and concludes that the novel "goes beyond genre fiction." A *Publishers Weekly* reviewer observes that in *Southern Women*, "Battle's fluid style, attention to the small details that summon up a scene and dialogue so realistic it seems to be snatched out of the air make this traditional novel a satisfying pleasure." More recently, in *A Habit of the Blood*, about a young woman who returns to her family's Jamaican estate only to find the world of "tawdry politics and the drug subculture," Battle has written a novel that a *Publishers Weekly* contributor feels "should prove to be her most successful yet."

BIOGRAPHICAL/CRITICAL SOURCES:

PERIODICALS

New York Times Book Review, September 16, 1984.
Publishers Weekly, November 14, 1980, December 11, 1981, March 23, 1984, January 9, 1987.

*   *   *

BAUMGARTNER, Frederic J(oseph)   1945-

PERSONAL: Born September 26, 1945, in Medford, Wis.; son of Michael and Theresa (Stauner) Baumgartner, married Lois Ann Hoffman, January 31, 1970; children: two. *Education:* Mount St. Paul College, B.A., 1967; University of Wisconsin—Madison, M.A., 1969, Ph.D., 1972.

ADDRESSES: Home—1109 Lora Lane, Blacksburg, Va. 24060. *Office*—Department of History, Virginia Polytechnic Institute and State University, Blacksburg, Va. 24061.

CAREER: Georgia College, Milledgeville, assistant professor of history, 1972-76; Virginia Polytechnic Institute and State University, Blacksburg, assistant professor, 1976-80, associate professor, 1980-87, professor of history, 1987—. Member of council, Sixteenth-Century Studies Conference, 1982-85.

MEMBER: American Catholic Historical Association, American Society for Reformation Research, Society for French Historical Studies, Southern Historical Association.

WRITINGS:

Radical Reactionaries: The Political Thought of the French Catholic League, Librairie Droz, 1976.
Change and Continuity in the French Episcopate: The Bishops and the Wars of Religion, Duke University Press, 1986.
Henry II: King of France, Duke University Press, 1988.

Contributor of over fifty articles and reviews to history journals.

WORK IN PROGRESS: Textbook for military history from the fall of Rome to the French Revolution; biography of King Louis XII.

SIDELIGHTS: Frederic J. Baumgartner wrote *CA:* "My research and writing have concentrated on France in the sixteenth century. Most of my work thus far in my career has been concerned with the second half of the century; but in beginning research for a biography of Louis XII, I have turned my attention to the early 1500s. It will help me realize my long-term goal of writing an interpretive history of sixteenth-century France. Central to that project is the question of why France remained Catholic despite the presence of a dynamic and powerful Protestant movement after 1550. Most of my publications have dealt with how French Catholics reacted to its presence, while my current research will help me understand what the condition the French Church was in during the era just before the Reformation began."

BIOGRAPHICAL/CRITICAL SOURCES:

PERIODICALS

American Historical Review, December, 1977.

*   *   *

BECK, Clive 1939-

PERSONAL: Born January 5, 1939, in Australia; son of Lawrence Mackie (a farmer) and Sylvia (Kemble) Beck; married Julianne Galdy (a librarian), January 2, 1965; children: Paul, Nicholas. *Education:* University of Western Australia, B.Ed., 1959; University of Sydney, B.A., 1963; University of New England, Australia, Ph.D., 1967.

ADDRESSES: Home—Toronto, Ontario, Canada. *Office*—Ontario Institute for Studies in Education, 252 Bloor St. W., Toronto, Ontario, Canada.

CAREER: University of New England, Armidale, Australia, lecturer in philosophy of education, 1964-67; Ontario Institute for Studies in Education, Toronto, Ontario, assistant professor, 1967-69, associate professor, 1969-74, professor of philosophy of education, 1974—, head of department, 1969-71, director of Moral Education Project, 1969—, coordinator of graduate studies, 1975—.

MEMBER: Philosophy of Education Society, Philosophy of Education Society of Great Britain, Canadian Society for the Study of Great Britain, Canadian Society for the Study of Education, American Educational Studies Association.

WRITINGS:

(Editor with B. S. Crittenden and E. V. Sullivan) *Moral Education: Interdisciplinary Approaches,* University of Toronto Press, 1970.
Moral Education in the Schools, Ontario Institute for Studies in Education, 1971.
Ethics, McGraw, 1972.
Educational Philosophy and Theory: An Introduction, Little, Brown, 1974.
The Moral Education Project: Curriculum and Pedagogy for Reflective Values Education, Ontario Ministry of Education, 1978.
Reflecting of Values, Ontario Institute for Studies in Education, 1980.
Values and Living, Ontario Institute for Studies in Education, 1983.

BEEZLEY, William H(oward Taft) 1942-

PERSONAL: Born March 22, 1942, in Albuquerque, N.M.; son of Howard C. and Lorene (Sallee) Beezley; married Alda Reil, August 22, 1964 (divorced, 1983); married Cherlye Blue Champion, 1983; children: Paul Richard, John Sallee, Mark Madrid. *Education:* Chico State College (now California State University, Chico), A.B., 1964; University of Nebraska, M.A., 1966, Ph.D., 1969.

ADDRESSES: Home—Raleigh, N.C. *Office*—Department of History, North Carolina State University, Raleigh, N.C. 27607.

CAREER: State University of New York College at Plattsburgh, assistant professor of Latin American history, 1968-72; North Carolina State University, Raleigh, assistant professor, 1972-74, associate professor, 1974-83, professor of Latin American history, 1983—. Visiting professor at University of Texas at Austin, 1982.

MEMBER: Latin American Studies Association, North Carolina High School Athletics Officials Association.

AWARDS, HONORS: American Philosophical Society grant, 1972; National Endowment for the Humanities grant, 1973.

WRITINGS:

Insurgent Governor: Abraham Gonzalez and the Mexican Revolution in Chihuahua, University of Nebraska Press, 1973.
The Wolfpack: Intercollegiate Athletics at North Carolina State University, University Graphics, 1977.
(Contributor) *Essays on the Mexican Revolution: Revisionist Views of the Leaders,* University of Texas Press, 1979.
(Editor with W. Dirk Raat) *Twentieth-Century Mexico,* University of Nebraska Press, 1986.
Judas at the Jockey Club and Other Episodes of Porfirian Mexico, University of Nebraska Press, 1987.
(Editor with Judith Ewell) *The Human Tradition in Latin America,* Scholarly Resources, 1987.

Editor of *Americas,* 1974—.

WORK IN PROGRESS: Locker Rumors: Folklore in the NFL.

AVOCATIONAL INTERESTS: Sports history.

*   *   *

BEILHARZ, Edwin Alanson 1907-1986

PERSONAL: Born June 18, 1907, in Phillipsburg, Kan.; died of cancer, October 6, 1986, in Santa Clara, Calif.; buried at Madronia Cemetery, Saratoga, Calif.; son of William Tobias (a carpenter) and Lavara (Lowe) Beilharz; married Frances Marian Fuller, June 19, 1937; children: Frieda M. Beilharz Rosenberg, Ann Beilharz Pflager, Alan Francis, Claire G. *Education:* Creighton University, A.B., 1931; University of Nebraska, M.A., 1934; University of California, Berkeley, Ph.D., 1951. *Politics:* Democrat. *Religion:* Roman Catholic.

ADDRESSES: Home—16021 Wood Acres Rd., Los Gatos, Calif. 95030. *Office*—Department of History, University of Santa Clara, Santa Clara, Calif. 95053.

CAREER: University of Santa Clara, Santa Clara, Calif., instructor, 1936-41, assistant professor, 1941-45, associate professor, 1945-51, professor of history, 1951-72, professor emeritus, 1972-86, chairman of department, 1941-68, director, Division of Social Studies, 1951-63. Sidney H. Ehrman

University scholar in history, University of California, Berkeley. Secretary-treasurer, Pacific Coast Council of Latin American Studies, 1964. Chairman, committee of survey for Catholic bay area colleges.

MEMBER: American Historical Association, Catholic Historical Association (chairman of program committee, 1965), California Historical Society.

AWARDS, HONORS: Selected as an Outstanding Educator of America by Santa Clara University, 1971; Doctor of Humane Letters, University of Santa Clara, 1972; fellow, University of California, Berkeley.

WRITINGS:

The New Frontiers and the Old, University of Santa Clara, 1961.
Felipe de Neve: First Governor of California, California Historical Society, 1971.
We Were '49ers: Chilean Accounts of the California Gold Rush, Ritchie, 1976.
(With Donald O. DeMers, Jr.) *San Jose: California's First City,* Continental Heritage Press, 1980.
Institutions in Conflict: Freedom through the Ages, Pioneer Press, 1982.

Contributor to history journals. A collection of Beilharz's work is held by the Michel Orradre Library at Santa Clara University.

*   *   *

BELL, Emerson
    See STRATEMEYER, Edward L.

*   *   *

BENOLIEL, Jeanne Quint   1919-
    (Jeanne Quint)

PERSONAL: Surname is accented on third syllable; born December 9, 1919, in National City, Calif.; daughter of John Edwin (a machinist) and Marie Lyda (a registered nurse; maiden name, Wade) Quint; married Wilson Sherrill, September 24, 1949 (annulled, 1953); married Robert William Benoliel (a chemical engineer), February 14, 1970. *Education:* Attended San Diego State College (now University), 1937-38; St. Luke's Hospital School of Nursing, R.N., 1941; further study at University of California, Berkeley, 1943; Oregon State University, B.S., 1948; University of California, Los Angeles, M.S., 1955, additional graduate study, 1959-61; University of California, San Francisco, D.N.Sc., 1969.

ADDRESSES: Home—34722 Fall City-Snoqualmie Rd., Fall City, Wash. 98024. *Office*—School of Nursing, University of Washington, Seattle, Wash. 98195.

CAREER: Registered nurse in California, Oregon, and state of Washington. Staff nurse at San Diego County Hospital, San Diego, Calif., 1941-43, and in hospitals in Astoria, Ore., 1946, and Chula Vista, Calif., 1947; Fresno General Hospital School of Nursing, Fresno, Calif., instructor in medical-surgical nursing, 1948-51, educational director, 1951-53; Metropolitan State Hospital, Norwalk, Calif., staff nurse, 1953-54; San Diego County Hospital, instructor in medical nursing, 1954; University of California, Los Angeles, instructor, 1955-57, assistant professor of surgical nursing, 1957-59, junior research statistician and junior research nurse, 1961-62; University of Cal-

ifornia, San Francisco, assistant research sociologist, 1962-67, associate professor of nursing, 1969-70; University of Washington, Seattle, professor of nursing, 1970-87, Elizabeth Soule Distinguished Professor of Nursing and Health Promotion, 1987—, chairman of department of comparative nursing care systems, 1970-76.

Member of board of California League for Nursing, 1964-68; member of professional advisory board of Foundation of Thanatology, 1969—; member of Western Interstate Commission for Higher Education in Nursing, 1969—; member of research advisory committee of American Nurses' Foundation, 1970-74. Appointed to Washington State Board of Health, 1971-77. Guest lecturer at Tel-Aviv University, 1972. Has participated in and led workshops and conferences; consultant on death-related problems and issues. *Military service:* U.S. Army, Nurse Corps, 1943-46; served in Philippines and New Guinea; became first lieutenant.

MEMBER: American Nurses Association, National League for Nursing (fellow), American Public Health Association, American Association of University Professors, Society for the Study of Social Problems, Association for Humanistic Psychology, Academy of Religion and Mental Health, American Association for the Advancement of Science, Sigma Theta Tau.

AWARDS, HONORS: National Institute of Mental Health grant to study adjustment after mastectomy, 1961-63; National Institutes of Health grants, 1962-67, 1973-88; professional achievement award, Alumni Association of University of California, Los Angeles, 1972; U.S. Department of Health, Education, and Welfare grants, 1973-77; Arnold and Marie Schwartz Award, American Nurses Association, 1976; Linda Richards Award, National League for Nursing, 1981; Helen Nahm Research Lecture Award, University of California, San Francisco, 1983; distinguished service award, National Cancer Society, 1986; McCorkle Lecture Award, Puget Sound Oncology Nursing Society, 1987; distinguished merit award, International Society for Nurses in Cancer Care, 1988.

WRITINGS:

Human Rights Guidelines for Nurses in Clinical and Other Research, American Nurses Association, 1975.
(Editor) *Death Education for the Health Professional,* McGraw, 1982.

UNDER NAME JEANNE QUINT

(Contributor) *Report of Conference on Terminal Illness and Impending Death among the Aged,* Division of Chronic Diseases, U.S. Department of Health, Education, and Welfare, 1966.
The Nurse and the Dying Patient, Macmillan, 1967.
(Contributor) Margaret Harrop and Vera M. Rubenstein, editors, *Nursing Clinics of North America,* Volume II, Saunders, 1967.

CONTRIBUTOR UNDER NAME JEANNE QUINT BENOLIEL

Marjorie Batey, editor, *Communicating Nursing Research: Methodological Issues in Research,* Western Interstate Commission for Higher Education, 1970.
Bernard Schoenberg and others, editors, *Psychosocial Aspects of Terminal Care,* Columbia University Press, 1972.
Eliot Freidson and Judith Lorber, editors, *Medical Men and Their Work,* Aldine-Atherton, 1972.
L. H. Schwartz and J. L. Schwartz, editors, *The Psychodynamics of Patient Care,* Prentice-Hall, 1972.

Loretta Bermosk and Raymond Corsini, editors, *Critical Incidents in Nursing,* Saunders, 1973.

Richard H. Davis and Margaret Neiswender, editors, *Dealing with Death,* Ethel Percy Andrus Gerontology Center, University of Southern California, 1973.

Batey, editor, *Communicating Nursing Research: Collaboration and Competition,* Volume VI, Western Interstate Commission for Higher Education, 1973.

Margaret Dimond and Susan Lynn Jones, editors, *Chronic Illness across the Life Span,* Appleton-Century-Crofts, 1983.

Powhatan J. Wooldridge, Madeline H. Schmitt, James K. Skipper, and Robert C. Leonard, editors, *Behavioral Science and Nursing Theory,* Mosby, 1983.

Doris Christensen and Randi Mortensen, editors, *Kvalitative metoder isygeplejeforskning,* Munksgaard, 1985.

M. Barnard, M. Chard, J. Howe, and P. Phillips, editors, *Comprehensive Pediatric Nursing,* 3rd edition, McGraw, 1986.

R. McCorkle and G. Hongladarom, editors, *Issues and Topics in Cancer Nursing,* Appleton-Century-Crofts, 1986.

H. Wass, F. M. Berardor, and R. A. Neimeryer, editors, *Dying: Facing the Facts,* 2nd edition, Hemisphere Publishing, 1988.

Thelma Schorr and Anne Zimmerman, editors, *Making Choices, Taking Chances: Nurse Leaders Tell Their Stories,* Mosby, 1988.

OTHER

Contributor of about sixty articles and reviews to health care journals, including *Imprint, Nursing Forum, Journal of Thanatology, Patient Care-Management Concepts, International Journal of Nursing Studies,* and *Nursing Research.* Member of editorial boards of *Journal of Thanatology* and *Omega,* both 1970—; manuscript reviewer for *Nursing Research,* 1970—.

WORK IN PROGRESS: Writing on spouse bereavement and adherence to breast self-examination.

SIDELIGHTS: Jeanne Quint Benoliel once told *CA:* "Living close to the reality of death and dying gives zest to living. Facing up to the reality that dignity in living is the essence of dignity in dying was an important learning for me. It didn't happen suddenly but over time and by means of some difficult life experiences. The relationship between caring and human dignity underlies much of my writing."

*   *   *

BERNSTEIN, Jeremy 1929-

PERSONAL: Born December 31, 1929, in Rochester, N.Y.; son of Philip Sidney (a rabbi) and Sophy (Rubin) Bernstein. *Education:* Harvard University, B.A., 1951, M.A., 1953, Ph.D., 1955.

ADDRESSES: Office—Department of Physics, Stevens Institute of Technology, Hoboken, N.J. 07030.

CAREER: Harvard University, Cambridge, Mass., research associate, 1955-57; Princeton University, Institute for Advanced Study, Princeton, N.J., research associate, 1957-60; National Science Foundation and Brookhaven National Laboratory, Brookhaven, N.Y., research associate, 1960-62; New York University, New York City, associate professor of physics, 1962-67; *New Yorker,* New York City, staff writer, 1962—; Stevens Institute of Technology, Hoboken, N.J., faculty member of physics department, 1967—.

MEMBER: American Physical Society, Royal Society of the Arts, American Alpine Club, French Alpine Club.

AWARDS, HONORS: Westinghouse Prize for science writing, 1964; Brandeis creative arts medal, 1979.

WRITINGS:

The Analytical Engine: Computers, Past, Present, and Future, Random House, 1964, 2nd edition, Morrow, 1982.

Ascent: Of the Invention of Mountain Climbing and Its Practice, Random House, 1965.

A Comprehensive World: On Modern Science and Its Origins, Random House, 1967.

Elementary Particles and Their Currents, W. H. Freeman, 1968.

The Elusive Neutrino, Division of Technical Information, U.S. Atomic Energy Commission, 1969.

The Wildest Dreams of Kew: A Profile of Nepal, Simon & Schuster, 1970.

Einstein, Viking, 1973.

Mountain Passages, University of Nebraska Press, 1978.

Experiencing Science: Profiles in Discovery, Basic Books, 1978.

Hans Bethe: Prophet of Energy, Basic Books, 1980.

Science Observed: Essays Out of My Mind, Basic Books, 1982.

Three Degrees above Zero: Bell Labs in the Information Age, Scribner, 1984.

The Life It Brings: One Physicist's Beginnings, Ticknor & Fields, 1987.

Contributor of essays to periodicals, including *American Scholar* and *New York Times Book Review.*

SIDELIGHTS: Jeremy Bernstein is a professional physicist and a principal science writer for the *New Yorker* magazine. Bernstein's duties at the *New Yorker* include reviewing science-related books, writing profiles on modern scientists, and explaining the intricacies of physics and mathematics to the general reader. According to Jonathan Yardley in the *Washington Post Book World,* Bernstein "is best known outside his field as a writer of articles and books that bring complex scientific matters within the layman's grasp. This is no mean feat, for writing about science—especially a science as arcane as physics—is nearly as difficult as writing about music; scarcely anyone does it as well as Bernstein, most particularly as in the profiles of eminent physicists he has published in the *New Yorker* over the past quarter-century." Bernstein, a staff member of the Stevens Institute of Technology, began writing essays in his spare time in the early 1960s. His favorite subject, to quote *Nation* contributor D. D. Guttenplan, is "the nuts and bolts of the scientific process—not just how scientists think and talk but how they solve real-world problems." Yardley addresses Bernstein's achievements: "To be an accomplished scientist is one thing, to be an accomplished journalist is another; to be both borders on the extraordinary."

In his memoir *The Life It Brings: One Physicist's Beginnings,* Bernstein describes his youth as very ordinary. The son of a prominent rabbi, he grew up in Rochester, New York, where he preferred music, sports, and comic books to his studies. "As far as I was concerned," he writes, "mathematics was a series of exercises and puzzles that had no purpose other than to lead to a final examination. That it was a real subject with intellectual content and beauty I had no inkling. In fact, I think that in some profound sense I had no intellectual interests at all." That state of affairs changed when Bernstein enrolled at Harvard University. "I thought I might like to become a journalist," he remembers in a *New York Times Book Review* essay. "This ambition did not last very long, and gradually—under the influence of some great teachers, such as Philipp Frank and Julian Schwinger—I shifted to mathematics and then, in graduate school to theoretical physics. All the while, I was writing—but for nobody in particular. . . . If someone had asked me why I was writing, I don't know what I would have said. It was just something I did." Having earned his Ph.D., Bernstein was appointed to the prestigious Institute for Advanced Study at Princeton University in 1957, and there he worked with some of the country's eminent physicists.

Bernstein recalls that his chosen discipline was so difficult that for ten years he "ate, slept, and breathed physics." Still, he relished the opportunity to study the personalities of his senior colleagues, many of them leaders in the field. "They were fantastic characters;" he notes, "no one could have invented them." In 1960 he wrote his first piece, an essay about his experiences teaching summer school on the island of Corsica. Friends suggested sending it to the *New Yorker,* so he did. Months later, he received a reply. The *New Yorker* wanted to publish the story and anything else he might write "about science as a form of experience." At first the assignment was daunting, but gradually Bernstein began to perceive the possibilities of producing profiles "without compromising myself or the dignity—and, often, the grandeur—of the people I was writing about." From these he moved into essays about nuclear physics, computers, and mathematics, subjects that often required complex explanations. "It is sometimes difficult for a scientist to realize just how much has to be spelled out," he observes, "for we scientists tend to speak in codes. . . . People have told me they find my science writing fairly accessible, and, believe me, despite appearances, this is the end product of a lot of work."

Mountain-climbing is Bernstein's hobby, and it too has provided topics for his pen. *Time* magazine contributor Peter Stoler writes: "As anyone who reads the literature can attest, most mountain climbers cannot write. Fair enough; most writers cannot climb. Jeremy Bernstein is an exception to both rules." The author's books on mountaineering include *Ascent: Of the Invention of Mountain Climbing and Its Practice, Dreams of Kew: A Profile of Nepal,* and *Mountain Passages;* even the titles reflect the international scope of his high mountain treks. "Bernstein is at his best evoking the sounds and sights and terrors of a world that touches the sky," notes Stoler. ". . . No one who reads *Mountain Passages* should have any trouble understanding why mountaineers are so addicted to the ascent." Raymond A. Sokolov likewise contends in the *New York Times Book Review* that Bernstein has mastered two of the most demanding mental and physical activities in the world—physics and mountain climbing. "Jeremy Bernstein is a professional at particle physics and an amateur at mountaineering," Sokolov concludes, "but he writes about both fields for the layman better than anyone else writes about either."

Science writing remains Bernstein's forte, however. As a respected contributor to scientific scholarship himself, he is able to communicate with his fellow practitioners and translate their achievements into understandable prose. In the *New York Times Book Review,* Rosalind Williams claims that if a writer works hard, "the reader doesn't have to, and Mr. Bernstein gives a lucid and fascinating tour of the brave new world of modern physics and high technology. The intelligent layman who knows what a molecule is and is willing to concentrate will have little trouble following him into these mysterious realms." Bernstein, Williams adds, "wants to convey how science is done, to elucidate the process of science more than its gadgets or

even its ideas." *Los Angeles Times Book Review* correspondent David Graber notes that some of the scientists the author writes about, such as Albert Einstein, Robert Oppenheimer, and Hans Bethe, "led exciting quests of discovery, and Bernstein communicates that most successfully. . . . You suddenly realize you have learned a great deal and been thoroughly engrossed the whole time." Perhaps the most telling assessment of Bernstein's accomplishments comes from *Washington Post Book World* contributor Michael Dirda. Bernstein, Dirda concludes, "allows those of us who couldn't dissect a clam, let alone solve a quadratic equation, a sense of that universe, a glimpse of those mountains and canyons."

Bernstein told the *New York Times Book Review:* "I was always honest enough with myself to know I would never be a great physicist—a good one, perhaps, but not a great one. My writing has given me the perspective to deal with this realization without rancor. It has enriched my life, and I have never regretted doing it."

AVOCATIONAL INTERESTS: Mountain climbing, music.

BIOGRAPHICAL/CRITICAL SOURCES:

BOOKS

Bernstein, Jeremy, *The Life It Brings: One Physicist's Beginnings,* Ticknor & Fields, 1987.

PERIODICALS

Chicago Tribune, April 21, 1987.
Los Angeles Times Book Review, April 18, 1982.
Nation, November 17, 1984.
New Republic, June 24, 1978.
Newsweek, October 20, 1980.
New York Times, August 3, 1978.
New York Times Book Review, November 21, 1965, September 23, 1973, August 6, 1978, March 4, 1979, September 28, 1980, February 28, 1982, October 14, 1984, April 5, 1987.
Time, January 22, 1979.
Times Literary Supplement, December 29, 1966, April 9, 1971, November 2, 1973.
Washington Post, August 15, 1978, December 25, 1978.
Washington Post Book World, May 6, 1973, February 14, 1982, March 15, 1987.

—*Sketch by Anne Janette Johnson*

*   *   *

BERRY, D. C.
   See BERRY, David (Chapman)

*   *   *

BERRY, David (Chapman)   1942-
   (D. C. Berry)

PERSONAL: Born July 23, 1942, in Vicksburg, Miss.; son of David C. (an inspector) and Annette (Hays) Berry; children: Davy. *Education:* University of Tennessee, Ph.D., 1973. *Religion:* Episcopalian.

ADDRESSES: Home—P.O. Box 5144, University of Southern Mississippi, Hattiesburg, Miss. 39406. *Office*—Department of English, University of Southern Mississippi, Southern Station, Box 5001, Hattiesburg, Miss. 39406.

CAREER: General Motors Corp., Flint, Mich., member of management staff, 1965-66; University of Southern Mississippi, Hattiesburg, 1973—, currently associate professor of English and poet in residence. *Military service:* U.S. Army Medical Corps, 1966-69; became captain.

WRITINGS:

(Under name D. C. Berry) *Saigon Cemetery* (poems), University of Georgia Press, 1972.
Jawbone, Thunder City Press, 1978.

Contributor of more than three hundred poems to magazines and literary journals, including *Poetry* and *Chicago Review*.

WORK IN PROGRESS: Wishbone, a poetry collection.

*　　*　　*

BLAYLOCK, James P(aul)　1950-

PERSONAL: Born September 20, 1950, in Long Beach, Calif.; son of Loren Calvin (an orthotist) and Daisy (a nurse; maiden name, Teeslink) Blaylock; married Viki Lynn Martin (a secretary), August 12, 1972; children: John Andrew, Daniel Robert. *Education:* California State University, Fullerton, B.A., 1972, M.A., 1974. *Politics:* "Unidentifiable." *Religion:* Protestant.

ADDRESSES: Home—Orange, Calif. *Agent*—Writers House, Inc., 21 West 26th St., New York, N.Y. 10010.

CAREER: Clerk at pet food store in Garden Grove, Calif., 1967-72; construction worker in Placentia, Calif., 1972-80; California State University, Fullerton, part-time instructor of English, 1980—. Part-time instructor at Fullerton Community College, 1976—.

MEMBER: Blake Society (vice-president, 1979—).

AWARDS, HONORS: World Fantasy Award, 1986, for the short story "Paper Dragons."

WRITINGS:

The Elfin Ship (fantasy novel), Ballantine, 1982.
The Disappearing Dwarf (fantasy novel), Ballantine, 1983.
The Digging Leviathan (science fiction novel), Ace Books, 1984.
Homunculus (science fiction novel), Ace Books, 1986.
Land of Dreams (fantasy novel), Ace Books, 1987.
The Last Coin (fantasy novel), Ace Books, 1988.

WORK IN PROGRESS: "A contemporary fantasy novel set in Mendocino County, involving stolen Japanese woodcuts and the ghosts of members of the pre-Raphaelite Brotherhood."

SIDELIGHTS: James P. Blaylock told *CA:* "I write novels largely for the joy of writing novels and because I'm constitutionally fit for it. It's the best of all possible jobs—a truth that some authors try to mask by talking out loud about 'shouldering the burdens of the writer'—which include, one would suppose, lounging around the study all day, drinking your own coffee and tapping out fictions that other people will be compelled not only to pay for, but to read. I've found that life is generally pretty good to the writer, and I hope to be at it for a long, long time. I'll take this opportunity to thank my readers for their kindness; I'll try not to let you down."

BIOGRAPHICAL/CRITICAL SOURCES:

PERIODICALS

Village Voice Literary Supplement, October, 1984.
Washington Post Book World, November 29, 1987.

BLISHEN, Edward　1920-

PERSONAL: Born April 29, 1920, in Whetstone, Middlesex, England; son of William George (a civil servant) and Elizabeth Ann (Pye) Blishen; married Nancy Smith, November 4, 1948; children: Jonathan Edward, Nicholas Martin. *Education:* Educated in England.

ADDRESSES: Home—12 Bartrams Lane, Hadley Wood, Barnet, England. *Agent*—Irene Josephy, 35 Craven St., Strand, London WC2, England.

CAREER: Employed in London, England, and vicinity, as journalist, 1937-41, preparatory schoolmaster, 1946-49, and teacher of English in secondary school, 1950-59; University of York, Heslington, England, part-time lecturer in department of education, 1963-65; free-lance writer, Barnet, England, 1965—. Conductor for thirteen years of British Broadcasting Corp. overseas program directed at young African writers; presenter of "World of Books" program, British Broadcasting Corp., 1973—.

MEMBER: PEN (member of executive committee of English Center, 1962-66), Society of Authors.

AWARDS, HONORS: Carnegie Award, Library Association, 1971, for *The God beneath the Sea;* Society of Authors traveling scholarship, 1979; J. R. Ackerley Prize for autobiography, 1981.

WRITINGS:

Roaring Boys, Thames & Hudson, 1955.
(Editor) *Junior Pears Encyclopaedia,* Pelham Books, 1961, annual revisions, 1962—.
(Editor) *Education Today,* BBC Publications, 1963.
(Editor) *Oxford Book of Poetry for Children,* Oxford University Press, 1963.
Town Story, Anthony Blond, 1964.
(Editor) *Miscellany,* Oxford University Press, six volumes, 1964-69.
(Editor) *Come Reading* (anthology of prose for young readers), M. Joseph, 1968.
Hugh Lofting (monograph), Bodley Head, 1968.
(Editor) *Encyclopaedia of Education,* Anthony Blond, 1969.
This Soft Lot, Thames & Hudson, 1969.
The School that I'd Like, Penguin, 1969.
(With Leon Garfield) *The God beneath the Sea,* Longmans, Green, 1970.
A Cackhanded War, Thames & Hudson, 1972.
(With Garfield) *The Golden Shadow,* Longman, 1973.
Uncommon Entrance, Thames & Hudson, 1974.
(Editor) *The Thorny Paradise,* Kestrel, 1975.
Sorry, Dad, Hamish Hamilton, 1978.
A Nest of Teachers, Hamish Hamilton, 1980.
Shaky Relations, Hamish Hamilton, 1981.
Lizzie Pye, Hamish Hamilton, 1982.
Donkey Work, Hamish Hamilton, 1983.
A Second Skin, Hamish Hamilton, 1984.
The Outside Contributor, Hamish Hamilton, 1986.
The Disturbance Fee, Hamish Hamilton, 1988.

SIDELIGHTS: Edward Blishen told *CA:* "I write in a curious form, a sort of false autobiography, for reasons I don't at all understand. They must spring, I guess, from whatever appetite has driven me to keep a diary since June 10, 1934. I take the facts provided by this diary and convert them into fictions:

needing to rename even my wife, my children, and the town where I've always lived. I have this heretical feeling that life is an astoundingly able storyteller, and that the writer at best trails far behind. Look back over a long diary and you see that you have been living in hundreds of different simultaneous novels and thousands of short stories, some marvellously commonplace and some marvellously subtle, as well as having many other extraordinary shapely scraps of experience. What I like to do has something of the kaleidoscope about it, I think: I shake up the fragments that compose some patch of time and see what pattern is made. I like to set myself cruel deadlines, getting as close as possible to the hopeless ideal that a book should be the product of a single uninterrupted effort.

"I am astonished when people assume that an autobiographer must be self-centered. I have the usual interest in myself, but when it comes to writing, count myself as one character among many, distinguished only by the specially large amount of deadly knowledge I have of him.

"In the end, I love work with words—jeweller's work—and also the toil of making books—laborer's work."

BIOGRAPHICAL/CRITICAL SOURCES:

PERIODICALS

Times (London), July 2, 1981, September 1, 1983, October 25, 1984.
Times Literary Supplement, March 21, 1980, October 15, 1982, January 18, 1985.

*   *   *

BOA, Kenneth 1945-

PERSONAL: Born July 22, 1945, in Kearney, Neb.; son of Kenneth (a bus driver) and Ruthelaine (a driver; maiden name, Kelley) Boa; married Karen Powelson, December 29, 1967; children: Heather Robin. *Education:* Case Institute of Technology (now Case Western Reserve University), B.S., 1967; Dallas Theological Seminary, Th.M., 1972; New York University, Ph.D., 1985; additional study at Oxford University, 1986—. *Religion:* Biblical Christianity.

ADDRESSES: Home—45 Willow Springs Ln., Roswell, Ga. 30075.

CAREER: University of Plano, Plano, Tex., instructor in mathematics, 1969-72; New Life, Inc., Knoxville, Tenn., instructor, writer, and director of publications and research, 1972-75; King's College, Briarcliff Manor, N.J., instructor in biblical studies and college pastor, 1976-79; Walk Thru the Bible Ministries, Atlanta, Ga., writer and teacher, 1979-82; Search Ministries, Lutherville, Md., director of research and writing, 1982—. Part-time consultant and teacher, Effective Communication and Development, Inc., 1984—.

MEMBER: Evangelical Theological Society.

AWARDS, HONORS: C. F. Lincoln Award, 1972; Rollin Thomas Chafer Award, 1972; W. E. Hawkins, Jr. Award in Christian Service, 1972.

WRITINGS:

God, I Don't Understand, Victor, 1975, revised edition, Zondervan, 1988.
Cults, World Religions, and You, Victor, 1977.
The Return of the Star of Bethlehem, Doubleday, 1980, revised edition, Zondervan, 1985.

Talk Thru the Old Testament, Tyndale, 1981.
I'm Glad You Asked, Victor, 1982.
Seeds of Change, Crossway Books, 1982.
Talk Thru the Bible, Thomas Nelson, 1983.
(Editor and author of introduction) *The Open Bible*, Thomas Nelson, 1983.
The Open Bible Companion, Thomas Nelson, 1986.
Visual Survey of the Bible, Thomas Nelson, 1986.
Drawing Near: A Scripture Guide to Prayer and Renewal, Thomas Nelson, 1987.

WORK IN PROGRESS: A comparative study of psychological and theological models of human needs.

SIDELIGHTS: Kenneth Boa writes: "I am interested in showing that biblical Christianity, more specifically, the claims and credentials of Jesus Christ, has relevance for people and their problems today."

AVOCATIONAL INTERESTS: Music, art, films.

*   *   *

BONEHILL, Captain Ralph
See STRATEMEYER, Edward L.

*   *   *

BOOTH, Irwin
See HOCH, Edward D(entinger)

*   *   *

BORDIN, Ruth B(irgitta) 1917-

PERSONAL: Born November 11, 1917, in Litchfield, Minn.; daughter of Emil William (a merchant) and Martha (Linner) Anderson; married Edward Bordin (a psychologist), June 20, 1941; children: Martha (Mrs. Steven A. Hillyard), Charlotte (Mrs. Sung Piau Lin). *Education:* University of Minnesota, B.S., 1938, M.A., 1940. *Politics:* Democrat. *Religion:* Unitarian Universalist.

ADDRESSES: Home—1000 Aberdeen, Ann Arbor, Mich. 48104. *Office*—Bentley Historical Library, University of Michigan, Ann Arbor, Mich. 48109.

CAREER: University of Minnesota, Minneapolis, research assistant, 1945-46; Washington State University, Pullman, research associate, 1946-48; University of Michigan, Ann Arbor, research associate, 1956-57, assistant curator, 1957-60, curator of Michigan Historical Collections, 1960-65, research associate, 1965-67; Eastern Michigan University, Ypsilanti, lecturer in history, 1967-78; University of Michigan, Bentley Historical Library, research affiliate, 1978—.

MEMBER: American Historical Association, Organization of American Historians, Phi Beta Kappa, Mortar Board.

WRITINGS:

(Editor) L. V. McWhorter, *Hear Ye My Chiefs*, Caxton, 1952.
(With Robert M. Warner) *The Manuscript Library*, Scarecrow, 1966.
The University of Michigan: A Pictorial History, University of Michigan Press, 1967.
Woman and Temperance, Temple University Press, 1981.
Frances Willard: A Biography, University of North Carolina Press, 1986.
Washtenaw County: An Illustrated History, Windsor Publications, 1988.

Contributor to *Notable American Women*.

WORK IN PROGRESS: Alice Freeman Palmer: A Career in Higher Education.

SIDELIGHTS: Historical researcher Ruth B. Bordin has written a biography on Woman's Christian Temperance Union (WCTU) leader Frances Willard that rescues from obscurity "the Queen of Temperance," who was once, according to *Business History Review* contributor K. Austin Kerr, "the best-known woman in the English-speaking world after Queen Victoria." Kerr continues, "Ruth Bordin's gracefully written new biography does justice to this extraordinary figure in nineteenth-century history. Based solidly on Willard's published writings and extant manuscripts, many of which were only recently reopened to scholars or discovered, Bordin has crafted an analysis of prize-winning quality that ingeniously guides the reader topically into Willard's personality while clarifying its development over time." In *Frances Willard*, Bordin describes Willard's unusual career, from her decision to involve herself fully in the temperance movement at age thirty-five, to her headship of the WCTU from 1883 to 1898. While Willard shared the WCTU's belief that hard-drinking husbands and fathers threatened the safety of their own families and that alcohol should be banned, she also moved the organization toward concentrating on women's involvement in politics. She thus used her position to promote a wider public role for women, which eventually led to female suffrage.

While critics praise Bordin's coverage of Willard's political life, they often criticize her handling of the reformer's personal side. "Bordin's portrait gives us a superb understanding of Willard's methods and accomplishments as well as a balanced assessment of her influence in the reform context of the period," writes Susan Dye Lee in the *Journal of Southern History*. "For those interested in Willard's inner motives, however, the reader is left with myriad questions. . . . too often Bordin's interpretation lacks a satisfactory explanation of the psychic forces that made Frances Willard the nineteenth century's preeminent woman reformer." *Christian Century* reviewer Alice-Catherine Carls agrees, pointing out that "Bordin meticulously retraces a life full of ups and downs, triumphs and doubts, strengths and weaknesses. And yet her protagonist manages to appear larger than life. For one, Bordin refuses to engage in hazardous speculation about Willard's most intimate secret, her sexuality. . . . Bordin's biography thus remains a puritan, old-fashioned work whose self-imposed limits are frustrating since she has the evidence for a deeper psychological analysis." And *New York Times Book Review* contributor Elisabeth Griffith believes that Bordin has left some of Willard's deepest motives unexamined: "Nor does Ms. Bordin probe Willard's uncomfortable relationship with her distant, undemonstrative, disapproving father, or investigate the possibility that he was once an alcoholic as his son and grandsons became. Indeed, it is ironic that Ms. Bordin never fully examines Willard's attitudes toward alcoholics." Still, Carls adds, "These flaws, however, do not keep the book from being a masterful political biography. . . . We should be grateful to the author for shattering the prejudices that might remain associated with the WCTU." And Griffith concludes that "Ms. Bordin's vivid study adds to the list of recent 'great woman' biographies and allows both for comparisons among them and for revision and re-evaluation of the history of the Gilded Age."

BIOGRAPHICAL/CRITICAL SOURCES:

PERIODICALS

Business History Review, summer, 1987.

Christian Century, October 7, 1987.
Journal of Southern History, November, 1987.
New York Times Book Review, December 14, 1986.

*   *   *

BORTON, John C., Jr. 1938-
(Terry Borton)

PERSONAL: Born August 25, 1938, in Washington, D.C.; married, June 18, 1960; wife's name, Deborah H.; children: Lynn, Mark. *Education:* Amherst College, B.A. (cum laude), 1960; University of California, Berkeley, M.A., 1962, General Teaching Certificate, 1964; Temple University, graduate study, 1964; Harvard University, Ed.D., 1970.

CAREER: Assistant director of school resource volunteers, Berkeley (Calif.) Unified School District, 1962-63; high school teacher of English in Richmond, Calif., 1963-66; Board of Education, Philadelphia, Pa., consultant to Curriculum Office, 1966-67, acting director of Affective Education Project, 1970-71, director of Dual Audio Television Project, beginning 1971. Forum member, White House Conference on Children, 1970. Lecturer, University of Pennsylvania. Consultant to U.S. Office of Education and to Ford, Carnegie, and other foundations.

MEMBER: Phi Delta Kappa.

WRITINGS:

Herman Melville: The Philosophical Implications of Literary Techniques in "Moby Dick" (booklet), Amherst College Press, 1960.

UNDER NAME TERRY BORTON

(With James Morrow) "A Lot of Undoing to Do" (filmscript), Philadelphia Board of Education, 1968.
(With Norman Newberg) *Education for Students Concerns* (curriculum guide), Philadelphia Public Schools, 1969.
Reach, Touch and Teach: Student Concerns and Process Education, McGraw, 1970.
(Contributor) Mario Fantini and Gerald Weinstein, editors, *Toward Humanistic Education: A Curriculum of Affect*, Praeger, 1970.
After the Turn-on, What?, Research Press, 1972.
Find Your Own Way: An Interpersonal Language Arts Program, Harcourt, 1973.
Process Education: The What, So What, Now What Sequence (sound recording), Jeffrey Norton, 1974.

OTHER

Also author of educational films "Prelude," with Morrow and Oliver Nuse, 1966, and "Hard to Hang on To," with Morrow, 1968. Writer of tapes and recordings, including *Poetry, Like It or Not*, and *All's Fair in Love and War*, with Norman Newberg and Joan Newberg, both for Educational Activities, Inc. Contributor to *Harvard Educational Review, Saturday Review, Learning*, and other periodicals.

WORK IN PROGRESS: Development of theory and practice of "concomitant instruction," designed for out-of-classroom use.

AVOCATIONAL INTERESTS: Camping, skiing, travel, sculpture, poetry, carpentry.*

BORTON, Terry
  See BORTON, John C., Jr.

* * *

BOURNE, L(arry) S(tuart) 1939-

PERSONAL: Born December 24, 1939, in London, Ontario, Canada; son of Stuart Howard (a mechanic) and Florence (Adams) Bourne; married Paula O'Neill (an educational researcher), August 14, 1967; children: David Stuart Alexander, Alexandra Lucy Elisabeth. *Education:* University of Western Ontario, B.A. (with honors), 1961; University of Alberta, M.A., 1963; University of Chicago, Ph.D., 1966.

ADDRESSES: Home—26 Anderson Ave., Toronto, Ontario, Canada M5P 1H4. *Office*—Centre for Urban and Community Studies, University of Toronto, 455 Spaldina Ave., Toronto, Ontario, Canada M5S 1A1.

CAREER: University of Toronto, Toronto, Ontario, assistant professor, 1966-69, associate professor, 1969-73, professor of geography, 1973—, Centre for Urban and Community Studies, associate director, 1969-72, director, 1972-84.

MEMBER: Royal Society of Canada (fellow), Canadian Association of Geographers, Canadian Association of University Teachers, Association of American Geographers, Urban Studies Association, Regional Science Association, Land Economics Fraternity, Urban Affairs Association.

AWARDS, HONORS: Award from Association of American Geographers, 1985; award for scholarly distinction from Canadian Association of Geographers, 1985.

WRITINGS:

Private Redevelopment of the Central City, University of Chicago, 1967.
(Editor) *Internal Structure of the City*, Oxford University Press, 1971, 2nd edition, 1982.
(Editor) *Urban Systems Development in Central Canada: Selected Papers*, University of Toronto Press, 1972.
(Editor) *The Form of Cities in Central Canada*, University of Toronto Press, 1973.
(Editor) *Urban Futures for Central Canada*, University of Toronto Press, 1974.
Urban Systems: Strategies for Regulation, Oxford University Press, 1975.
(Editor) *Systems of Cities*, Oxford University Press, 1978.
(Editor) *Urban Housing Markets*, University of Toronto Press, 1979.
Geography of Housing, Edward Arnold, 1981.
(Editor) *Urbanization and Settlement Systems: International Perspectives*, Oxford University Press, 1984.
(Editor) *Progress in Settlement Systems Geography*, Franco Angeli, 1986.
(Editor) *Urban Systems in Transition*, Utrecht, 1986.

* * *

BOVEE, Courtland L(owell) 1944-

PERSONAL: Born October 4, 1944, in Red Bluff, Calif.; son of Courtney Van (an orchardist) and Shirlee Patricia (Safford) Bovee. *Education:* Shasta College, A.A., 1965; University of North Dakota, B.S., 1967; University of Tennessee, M.S., 1968. *Politics:* Independent. *Religion:* Protestant.

ADDRESSES: Home—6458 Lake Shore Dr., San Diego, Calif. 92119. *Office*—Grossmont College, 8800 Grossmont College Dr., El Cajon, Calif. 92020.

CAREER: Grossmont College, El Cajon, Calif., professor of business communications, 1968—. Communications and advertising consultant, 1970—.

MEMBER: American Academy of Advertising, American Business Communication Association.

WRITINGS:

Better Business Writing for Bigger Profits, Exposition, 1970.
Techniques of Writing Business Letters, Memos, and Reports, Banner, 1974.
(With William F. Arens) *Contemporary Advertising*, Irwin, 1982, 3rd edition, 1989.
Business Communication Today, Random House, 1986, 2nd edition, 1989.
(Contributor) *Business Today*, 6th edition (Bovee was not associated with previous editions), Random House, 1989.

* * *

BOWDEN, Henry Warner 1939-

PERSONAL: Born April 1, 1939, in Memphis, Tenn.; son of Warner Hill (a salesman) and Jeannette (Winn) Bowden; married Karin Svensson, June 9, 1962; children: Robin Warner, Annika Hillary. *Education:* Baylor University, B.A., 1961; Princeton University, Ph.D., 1966.

ADDRESSES: Office—Department of Religion, Rutgers University, New Brunswick, N.J. 08903.

CAREER: Rutgers University, New Brunswick, N.J., instructor, 1964-67, assistant professor, 1967-71, associate professor, 1971-79, professor of religion, 1979—.

MEMBER: American Society of Church History (president, 1984), American Catholic Historical Association, American Association of University Professors.

WRITINGS:

Robert Baird, Religion in America: A Critical Abridgment, Harper, 1970.
Church History in the Age of Science: Historiographical Patterns in the United States: 1876-1918, University of North Carolina Press, 1971.
(Contributor) Edwin S. Gaustad, editor, *Dictionary of American Biography*, Greenwood Press, 1977.
(Editor with James P. Ronda) *John Eliot's Indian Dialogues: A Study in Cultural Interaction*, Greenwood Press, 1981.
American Indians and Christian Missions, University of Chicago Press, 1981.
(Editor) *A Century of Church History: The Legacy of Philip Schaff*, University of Southern Illinois Press, 1988.

WORK IN PROGRESS: Twentieth-century historiographical analysis; native American religious traditions and their interaction with patterns of Christianity.

* * *

BOWER, Robert T(urrell) 1919-

PERSONAL: Born June 1, 1919, in Yonkers, N.Y.; son of Ernest Turrell and Katherine (Bunker) Bower; married Betty Blanchard, 1943 (divorced); married Jean Just, 1971; children:

Stephen Cutler. *Education:* Yale University, A.B., 1941; Columbia University, Ph.D., 1954.

ADDRESSES: Home—2729 Dumbarton Ave. N.W., Washington, D.C. 20007.

CAREER: Columbia University, New York, N.Y., research associate, Bureau of Applied Social Research, 1948-50; Bureau of Social Science Research, Washington, D.C., director, 1950-82. Adjunct professor at American University, 1950-56. Senior research scholar, University of Maryland, 1986—. Member of National Council on the Humanities, 1966-72; president of National Council on Public Polls, 1969-73. *Military service:* U.S. Army Air Forces, 1941-45.

MEMBER: World Association for Public Opinion Research (secretary-general, 1967-69), American Association for Public Opinion Research (president, 1969-70), American Sociological Association, Society for International Development, Society for the Study of Social Problems.

WRITINGS:

Communication of Ideas in India: A Survey in Lucknow and Three Indian Villages, three volumes, Bureau of Social Science Research, 1951.
(Contributor) Leo Bogart, editor, *Social Research and the Desegregation of the U.S. Army,* Markhem, 1969.
Information and Attitudes about Drugs in Washington, D.C., Bureau of Social Science Research, 1973.
Television and the Public, Holt, 1973.
(With Priscilla de Gasparis) *Ethics in Social Research: Protecting the Interests of Human Subjects,* Praeger, 1978.
The Changing Television Audience in America, Columbia University Press, 1985.

Contributor to public opinion and other journals.

*   *   *

BOWIE, Jim
    See STRATEMEYER, Edward L.

*   *   *

BOYD, John
    See UPCHURCH, Boyd (Bradfield)

*   *   *

BOYER, Richard Lewis   1943-
    (Rick Boyer)

PERSONAL: Born October 13, 1943, in Evanston, Ill.; son of Paul Frederick (an attorney) and Betty (Hatton) Boyer; married Elaine Edith Smudsky, June 29, 1968 (divorced, 1983); children: Clayton Paul, Thomas Edward. *Education:* Denison University, B.A., 1965; University of Iowa, M.F.A., 1968. *Politics:* Independent. *Religion:* Roman Catholic.

ADDRESSES: Office—Places Rated Partnership, P.O. Box 8040, Asheville, N.C. 22814. *Agent*—Helen Rees, 308 Commonwealth Ave., Boston, Mass. 02116.

CAREER: New Trier High School, Winnetka, Ill., English teacher, 1968-70; Little, Brown & Co. (publishers), Boston, Mass., textbook salesman, 1971-73, acquisitions editor in College Division, 1973-78; Places Rated Partnership, Asheville, N.C., founding partner, 1978—; Western Carolina University, Cullowhee, N.C., assistant professor of English, 1988—.

MEMBER: Mystery Writers of America, International Crime Writers Association.

AWARDS, HONORS: Chicago Geographic Society publication award, 1981, for *Places Rated Almanac;* Edgar Award for best novel, Mystery Writers of America, 1982, for *Billingsgate Shoal.*

WRITINGS:

The Giant Rat of Sumatra (novel), Warner Books, 1976.

UNDER NAME RICK BOYER

Billingsgate Shoal, Houghton, 1982.
The Penny Ferry, Houghton, 1984.
The Daisy Ducks, Houghton, 1986.
Moscow Metal, Houghton, 1987.
The Whale's Footprints, Houghton, 1988.

"PLACES RATED" SERIES; UNDER NAME RICK BOYER

(With David Savagau) *Places Rated Almanac: Your Guide to Finding the Best Places to Live in America,* Rand McNally, 1981, 2nd edition, 1985.
(With Savagau) *Places Rated Retirement Guide,* Rand McNally, 1983.
(With Savagau) *Rand McNally Retirement Places Rated,* Rand McNally, 1987.

SIDELIGHTS: Richard Lewis Boyer writes that he began *The Giant Rat of Sumatra* in 1970. "From the time of its conception, it was to be a serious attempt to continue the Sherlockian saga much as Sir Arthur Conan Doyle would have written it were he still alive." Boyer continues: "After ten years of writing, I have reached my goal to combine writing with a full-time teaching position at a college or university."

*   *   *

BOYER, Rick
    See BOYER, Richard Lewis

*   *   *

BRANDEN, Nathaniel   1930-

PERSONAL: Original name Nathan Blumenthal; surname legally changed to Branden in early 1950s; born April 9, 1930, in Brampton, Ontario, Canada; came to United States, 1949, naturalized, 1965; son of Joseph and Dinah (Copp) Blumenthal; married Barbara Weidman (a writer), January, 1953 (divorced, 1968); married Patrecia Gullison (an actress under the name Patrecia Wynand), November 7, 1969 (died March 31, 1977); married Estelle Devers, December, 1978. *Education:* Attended University of California, Los Angeles, 1949-51; New York University, B.A., 1954, M.A., 1956; California Graduate Institute, Ph.D., 1973. *Politics:* Libertarian. *Religion:* Atheist.

ADDRESSES: Home—1427 Laurel Way, Beverly Hills, Calif. 90210. *Office*—Branden Institute for Self-Esteem, P.O. Box 2609, Beverly Hills, Calif. 90213. *Agent*—Nat Sobel, Sobel Weber Associates, 146 East 19th St., New York, N.Y. 10003.

CAREER: Psychologist, licensed in New Jersey and the District of Columbia; marriage, family, and child counselor, licensed in California; private practice of psychotherapy, 1956—. Nathaniel Branden Institute (center for adult education in philosophy and psychology), New York, N.Y., founder and president, 1958-68; Branden Institute for Self-Esteem (formerly

Biocentric Institute; center for research, teaching, and therapy), Los Angeles, Calif., executive director, 1968—, conductor of workshops and intensives in the areas of self-esteem development, man/woman relationships, and personal transformation, including "Self-Esteem and the Art of Being," 1968—. Lecturer in biology and psychology at University of Southern California, 1969; guest lecturer at universities in United States and Canada.

MEMBER: American Psychological Association, American Association for the Advancement of Science, American Association of Marriage and Family Counselors, American Association of Group Psychotherapy, Academy of Psychologists in Marital Therapy, California State Marriage Counseling Association, California Psychology Association.

WRITINGS:

Who Is Ayn Rand?: An Analysis of the Novels of Ayn Rand (includes biographical essay by former wife, Barbara Branden), Random House, 1962.
(Contributor) Ayn Rand, *The Virtue of Selfishness: A New Concept of Egoism,* New American Library, 1964.
(Contributor) Rand, *Capitalism: The Unknown Ideal,* New American Library, 1966.
The Psychology of Self-Esteem: A New Concept of Man's Psychological Nature (also see below), Nash Publishing, 1970.
The Disowned Self (also see below), Nash Publishing, 1972.
The Psychology of Romantic Love, J. P. Tarcher, 1980.
A Nathaniel Branden Anthology (contains *The Psychology of Self-Esteem, Breaking Free,* and *The Disowned Self*), J. P. Tarcher, 1980.
(With wife, Estelle Devers Branden) *The Romantic Love Question and Answer Book,* J. P. Tarcher, 1982, revised edition published as *What Love Asks of Us,* Bantam, 1987.
If You Could Hear What I Cannot Say: Learning to Communicate with the Ones We Love, Bantam, 1983.
Honoring the Self: Personal Integrity and the Heroic Potentials of Human Nature, J. P. Tarcher, 1984.
How to Raise Your Self-Esteem, Bantam, 1987.
Experience High Self-Esteem, Simon & Schuster, 1988.
Judgment Day: Remembering Ayn Rand, Houghton, 1989.

Co-editor, with Ayn Rand, and contributor, *The Objectivist Newsletter,* 1962-65, and its successor, *The Objectivist* (monthly journal), 1966-68. Contributor of articles to anthologies and professional journals, including *Journal of Humanistic Psychology.*

SIDELIGHTS: One of the most frequent associations made when discussing psychologist Nathaniel Branden and his work involves Ayn Rand. Branden and the philosopher-novelist were close friends and professional colleagues for nearly two decades. During their association Branden was a major instrument in the popularization of the Objectivist philosophy described in Rand's novels. With Rand, he co-edited and contributed to *The Objectivist Newsletter* (which later became *The Objectivist*), a monthly publication which explained the application of the principles of Objectivism. He also founded and directed the Nathaniel Branden Institute and under its patronage presented a series of lectures on Rand's philosophy covering such topics as "What Is Reason?," "The Nature of Emotions," and "Social Metaphysics." Branden's first book, *Who Is Ayn Rand?,* is a study of Rand's thought.

Although Branden and Rand parted ways in 1968, some of the basic principles of Rand's philosophy are still contained in Branden's psychological theories. In *The Passion of Ayn Rand,* a biography of the novelist written by Barbara Branden, the psychologist explains his debt to Rand: "Intellectually . . . I learned more from Ayn Rand than I can possibly summarize. She used to say 'check your premises and watch your implications.' I really learned that from her, both with regard to my own thinking and statements and those of other people. . . . I feel she sharpened enormously my ability to think philosophically."

Egoism, or the importance of the self, an integral part of Rand's philosophy, is also a focal point of Branden's work. In particular, his books focus on how we see ourselves, how self-concept affects our sense of well-being, and how to improve our self-esteem. As Branden writes in the introduction to *Honoring the Self: Personal Integrity and the Heroic Potentials of Human Nature:* "At three o'clock in the morning, when we are alone with ourselves, we are aware that the most intimate and powerful of all relationships and the one we can never escape is the relationship to ourselves. No significant aspect of our thinking, motivation, feelings, or behavior is unaffected by our self-evaluation. We are organisms who are not only conscious but self-conscious. This is our glory and, at times, our burden."

CA INTERVIEW

CA interviewed Nathaniel Branden by telephone on January 22, 1988, at his home in Los Angeles, California.

CA: "Positive self-esteem," you say in the preface to your 1987 book How to Raise Your Self-Esteem, *"is a cardinal requirement of a fulfilling life." Is a lack of self-esteem at the root of most of the problems you see in your practice?*

BRANDEN: Wherever there are psychological problems, almost always there is a poor self-concept, generally developing through the years of childhood. The result is various behaviors that express low expectations, lack of confidence that one is able to get what one wants out of life or out of relationships. And the consequence of that is a string of disappointments or failures which have a feed-back effect worsening the self-concept. So the individual tends to be caught in a kind of vicious cycle.

CA: For people who have come through childhood relatively unharmed and are in general good health mentally, are there any common, everyday threats to self-esteem?

BRANDEN: I don't think so. I think there are challenges intrinsic to life which all of us come up against at one point or another. We all have to deal with the challenge of living consciously rather than living unconscious. High self-esteem is generated and sustained best by living consciously, and it is betrayed by living unconsciously—which, tragically, is the way too many people learn to live. Another challenge that has a lot to do with self-esteem is the challenge to stay open to life, the challenge to stay vulnerable. In the ordinary process of living, sooner or later all of us are going to be knocked on our butts, so to speak, in one way or another—we're going to be hurt, we might be betrayed by someone—and the challenge is not to shut down, not to close off emotionally, not to say *never again* and achieve that resolution by going dead inside. So one of the great challenges of mental health, of psychological well-being, is the ability to be resilient, to bounce back; the ability not to shut down, to stay open to the possibilities of life, open to the potential joy of life, even if we've been badly hurt in the past.

CA: Many people now are choosing to have children later in life than we were doing previously. Do you think this trend makes for stronger parents and happier children?

BRANDEN: I don't think the evidence is yet in, but I hope so, because it makes sense to me. In the past, too often what we've seen is children bringing up children. I hope what we may be seeing now is parents who, through waiting longer, are going to bring more maturity to the process.

CA: Your book The Psychology of Romantic Love *was published in 1980 and followed in 1982 by* The Romantic Love Question and Answer Book, *co-written with your wife E. Devers Branden and later reissued, with new material, as* What Love Asks of Us. *How do you think the sexual freedom that started in the 1960s has affected the concept of romantic love?*

BRANDEN: I don't think it has affected it in any important way. Most of the people that I have talked to ended up feeling that the sexual craziness of the sixties became a dead end, and that by the time people were in their late thirties, if not younger, and had the freedom to do things which would have been quite foreign to most members of an earlier generation, they came up against the question "And *now* what?" And they discovered that, still, the most extraordinary game in town, and perhaps the most challenging adventure, is to make love work with one individual. I'm thinking, for example, of Nena O'Neill, who, with her husband George O'Neill, wrote *Open Marriage* nearly two decades ago. Later, after her husband died, she wrote another book called *The Marriage Premise,* in which she made just the point I'm making now: it was her observation that many people—including herself—who "tried everything" ended up with the judgment that still, if you're interested in interacting with the opposite sex, the great adventure of life is one relationship. The good news about the sexual revolution, if one wants to call it that, was a greater freedom to discuss and explore these subjects; they were no longer forbidden. There was an attitude of far greater openness, which I think is very good and which I hope and expect will remain with us. But most people, at some time in their lives, come to the point where what they really want is to be in love with another human being who is in love with them. That remains a kind of perennial longing, and I don't think sociological fashions change that in any fundamental way.

CA: I think people whose ideas were fairly fixed before the sixties, however much they may have later experimented, given the new license to do so, may be luckier than the young people who grew up in the freer environment and didn't have the contrast.

BRANDEN: That's an important point, and I'm inclined to agree. What seems to be missing so often from young people today is passion. With all the talk about feelings, there's something incredibly shallow about most of the talk and, God knows, most of the behavior.

CA: How healthy do you feel the institution of marriage is now?

BRANDEN: It's not easy to say. We're seeing a decrease in divorce compared to a few years ago. Some of that probably has to do with fear of the various diseases that single people are more prone to. Some of it, perhaps, has to do with the realization that what's out there may not be that much better—or may not be better at all. We go back to my point about

many people coming to the realization that a lot of the sexual experimentation turned into a dead end, so there's a greater desire to see if there's a way to make a relationship work. There's no data to tell me one way or the other, but I hope that at least some of the drop in the divorce rate reflects an increase of knowledge or wisdom about what's needed to make a relationship successful.

CA: Guilt was one of the old bugaboos that the sixties were supposed to have freed us from, but we seem now as guilt-ridden as ever before. Do you think guilt has a rightful place in our emotional makeup?

BRANDEN: I don't think guilt is a good reason to remain in an unhappy marriage. I don't think guilt is an especially good reason to do anything. I think that, when people feel they have failed, what's important to know is what they mean by failure. Some regard any divorce as a failure. I don't. The failure might be choosing *not* to divorce. Two people who are thoroughly miserable with each other are not proving anything by electing to remain legally married and living under the same roof—except how little they may value their own lives. For such a couple, the marriage is the failure and divorce is the first step toward success.

On the other hand, there's a sense in which failure can be legitimately used and is conceivable relevant to guilt: that is the knowledge that you really have not done your best or given your best. Many people are scared to give their best. What if it doesn't work? they want to know. Their way of protecting themselves against a future pain or a future disappointment is never to go to the limit, never to give everything to a relationship they've got to give, so that if it doesn't work out, they won't have the pain of feeling, Well, I gave it everything I had, and that was not enough. So, often there is a guilt which is appropriate, but it's not what people will generally tell you about. It's something that, as a psychologist or a marriage counselor or a psychotherapist, one gets to see that one is not giving one's best, even while one is crying and suffering and complaining. And guilt can be valuable as an alarm system when it points to something that needs to be thought about, to be explored.

CA: Your eighteen-year association with Ayn Rand began when you were nearly twenty and was a tremendous influence on your thinking. What was the primary intellectual appeal in her work? What struck the first spark?

BRANDEN: The celebration of individualism, the central importance of productive work to human life, and the enormous emphasis placed on personal integrity.

CA: How much of your thinking on self-esteem did you bring to your association with Rand, and how much grew out of your work together—if it's possible to make that kind of separation between the two periods?

BRANDEN: That's not easy to do; it was a kind of parallel track. I met Miss Rand a month before I turned twenty, in March of 1950. At that time I was in school studying psychology. Later I began to work with people, while I was still in school, and I was looking for a common denominator that would help me to understand different problems. I was only twenty-four at this time, and I began to think about the fact that, regardless of what problem people spoke about, there was always the common denominator of low self-esteem. I remember one day running over to Ayn Rand's apartment to share with her some of my findings and ideas on this subject, and she was very excited, because just at that time she was writing John Galt's speech, which is the climax of *Atlas Shrugged*. She told me that in the novel she planned to say something about self-esteem that she thought was very important to her work. From that time on we did a lot of exploring and talking together. I'm writing a memoir of the years of our relationship, and I tell this story in the book.

CA: In her 1987 biography The Passion of Ayn Rand, *Barbara Branden described your painful break with Rand, after which you went to California and started the Biocentric Institute. Was it clear to you at the time of the break what direction your work should take?*

BRANDEN: At that time my whole mind was on breaking free of an environment that had become absolutely deadly for me emotionally, psychologically, and intellectually, and creating a new life with Patrecia in California. I knew that the first step was to get away and to handle and process the trauma of everything that had gone on in New York; and after that to discover what I wanted to do. So the direction was not clear except in a very general way. I went through a very productive period after settling in California; I published three books in as many years. It turned out to be a very creative period for me, and a wonderful period personally and emotionally. But I was still in the process of completing psychological projects that had been germinating in my mind year earlier, and then I went through a long hiatus of just thinking and studying, and didn't write for a number of years. After that I came back to writing with *The Psychology of Romantic Love*.

I often don't know exactly what I'm going to do next, which I rather enjoy. I've written seven books in the last seven or eight years, and it's been a very thrilling and a very creative period. Now, as I've mentioned, I'm working on the memoir. After that I'm contemplating a book on philosophy, I'm thinking about writing novels—I have so many projects in my brain, I really do not know what book I'll write next. I just know that I will be writing as long as I'm physically able, because I love the activity of writing more than any other activity in the world.

CA: What do you feel was Ayn Rand's greatest legacy to you?

BRANDEN: That's a tough question. A certain attitude of enormous respect for one's own life, the sense that one's own life is of the highest possible level of importance, and that what you will elect to do with it is, in the end, the supreme question. That was already part of my childhood orientation. Certain trends that were pronounced in me got magnified enormously in the relationship with Ayn Rand. And I always come back to the perception of productive work as a heroic activity. That feels very, very important.

CA: How would you assess the strength and importance of her influence today?

BRANDEN: There's a lot of evidence that it's quite powerful, first of all the sheer gigantic continuing sales of her books, both in hardback and paperback. Sales of her titles have passed twenty million; they sell several hundred thousand copies every year. The *New York Times* published a big article in the fall of 1987 devoted to key figures in government, all of whom acknowledged having been profoundly influenced by Ayn Rand.

More and more study groups are springing up all over the country. More and more books about her and her ideas are coming off the presses. There's been a great increase in the last several years. The success of Barbara Branden's biography itself was very interesting. The fact that it became a bestseller and continues to sell very strongly suggests that. In the concluding chapter of her book Barbara talks about Ayn Rand's influence world-wide, and my own information would suggest to me that, if anything, she understates it.

I think the influence is very powerful. I said when I was younger that Ayn would have to die for her philosophy really to take off. She had certain personality traits that made it very, very difficult for people—even people who loved and admired her—to work around her. Among other things, she required a degree of absolute and total agreement which is totally unrealistic. When you create something new, you must, in effect, send it out into the world, and different people will use it in different ways. That's the nature of life, and nothing you can do is going to change that. I felt that, when she was no longer active in the picture herself, the younger generations would read her and pick up what they liked and what they found valuable, and they would carry it further in their own ways. And I think that's what's happening.

CA: Her demand for complete agreement with her beliefs seems quite antithetical to her concept of individuality.

BRANDEN: It was. But she would have said, hearing you: "If I am convinced that I am right in what I'm saying, what do you expect me to think or feel if people are adapting me in ways which I judge mistaken, and false to the facts of reality?" But still—I think the most interesting years may lie ahead rather than behind us.

CA: Tell me about the work of the Biocentric Institute.

BRANDEN: Basically we're a psychological-psychotherapeutic clinic. We offer workshops and seminars additionally around the country. We offer training to mental health professionals who want to learn more about our particular way of doing therapy. We produce and distribute psychologically oriented educational audiocassettes.

CA: One of your seminars is called "Honoring the Present: Time, Mortality and Self-Esteem." Would you talk about your concept of honoring the present and its importance to mental health?

BRANDEN: One of the basic facts of life—much denied and evaded—is that we are all going to die. We are a culture that tends to deny the reality of death. In doing so, we unwittingly commit treason to life. We do not give each moment of our existence the respect that it deserves. We tell ourselves that we have all the time in the world—to accomplish the things we want to accomplish; to let those we love know that we love them; to make amends for errors; to experience what we want to experience; and so forth.

Some people choose never fully to participate in life, never commit to anything—either to work or to a person—on the unstated premise that if they do not enter the game, the clock does not begin to tick. But the clock is always ticking. To live fully and properly, we have to be aware of our own mortality as well as the mortality of others.

CA: In some of your psychology books you give very specific self-help directions. Do you hear directly from people whose lives have been greatly improved by your writing?

BRANDEN: People write frequently to report on what they're experiencing with the various things I recommend, and generally what we hear is quite favorable. And many people who write to us say that they wish we would write additionally on various problems.

CA: For people who would like psychotherapy but can't afford it or simply don't have access to it, are books and seminars the next best thing?

BRANDEN: I think so. I think they can be very helpful. But there, you know, everything depends on motivation. I am amazed at how well some people do. Some people have fabulous motivation. They pick up, let's say, one of by workbooks, such as *If You Could Hear What I Cannot Say,* and do magnificent things with it that even stun me. They really run with it. Other people need personal supervision. For those people, books are not the basic answer. They need a coach. They need to do what ever is necessary to get personal help.

CA: Will your memoir in progress be affected in any way by the 1987 publication of Barbara Branden's Rand biography?

BRANDEN: Not really. The concept of the memoir existed before the biography was written. I was under a contract to write several other psychology books and couldn't get to it earlier. It is a different kind of book in the sense that I'm not writing a history or a biography; I don't have the responsibility that Barbara had to give the history of a lot of different aspects of Ayn Rand's life. I am writing a memoir, which is a far more free and selective kind of project. But I probably do feel the benefit of knowing that the biography is out there. If you want to know about Rand's early career, before I met her, I don't have to tell all of that in my book. It's there in the biography for anybody who is interested, which is sort of relaxing for me.

CA: So the two books might complement each other?

BRANDEN: Yes. The stories will be different. Obviously my perspective on a lot of the events is different from Barbara's. There are factual mistakes in Barbara's book which I have to address. Her perception of certain events, or her psychological explanation of why certain things happened, is different from mine.

BIOGRAPHICAL/CRITICAL SOURCES:

BOOKS

Branden, Barbara, *The Passion of Ayn Rand,* Doubleday, 1986.
Branden, Nathaniel, *Honoring the Self: Personal Integrity and the Heroic Potentials of Human Nature,* J. P. Tarcher, 1984.
Branden, Nathaniel, *How to Raise Your Self-Esteem,* Bantam, 1987.
O'Neill, Nena and George O'Neill, *Open Marriage: A New Life Style for Couples,* M. Evans, 1972.

PERIODICALS

Chicago Tribune Book World, June 29, 1986.
Commentary, July, 1986.
Los Angeles Times, January 18, 1982.

Los Angeles Times Book Review, August 10, 1980, April 29, 1984.
New York Times, September 13, 1987.
Publishers Weekly, January 10, 1986.
San Francisco Chronicle, July 22, 1962.

—*Interview by Jean W. Ross*

*   *   *

BRASCH, Rudolph 1912-

PERSONAL: Born November 6, 1912, in Berlin, Germany; son of British citizens, Gustav and Hedwig (Mathias) Brasch; married Liselott Buchbinder, February 16, 1952. *Education:* Attended University of Berlin, 1931-35; University of Wurzburg, Ph.D. (summa cum laude), 1936; Jewish Theological Seminary, Berlin, Rabbi (with highest honors), 1938.

ADDRESSES: Home—14 Derby St., Vaucluse, Sydney, New South Wales, Australia.

CAREER: Rabbi of Progressive synagogues in London, England, 1938-48, and Dublin, Ireland, 1946-47; Johannesburg Reform Congregations, Johannesburg, South Africa, rabbi and director of public relations, 1948-49; Temple Emanuel, Woollahra, New South Wales, Australia, chief minister, 1949-79. Guest professor, University of Sydney, 1952-53; visiting rabbi in Montgomery, Ala., 1980; visiting professor at University of Hawaii, 1981. Lecturer on cruise ships. Life vice-president and chairman of ecclesiastical board, Australian and New Zealand Union for Progressive Judaism; member of governing body, World Union for Progressive Judaism; director of education, Liberal Education Board of New South Wales; justice of the peace and Civil Marriage celebrant, for Australia. *Military service:* Padre to Civil Defence during London blitz; received Coronation Medal (Queen Elizabeth II) for his work.

MEMBER: Royal Australian Historical Society, Society of Religious History (founding member), Rotary Club (Sydney).

AWARDS, HONORS: D.D., Hebrew Union College-Jewish Institute of Religion, Los Angeles, 1959; named Officer of the British Empire, 1967; Order of Australia, 1979; Peace Media Medal, Australian Association of the United Nations, 1979; made lieutenant-colonel in the Alabama militia.

WRITINGS:

(With Lily M. Montagu) *A Little Book of Comfort for Jewish People in Times of Sorrow,* [London], 1948.
The Star of David, Angus & Robertson, 1955.
The Eternal Flame, Angus & Robertson, 1958.
General Sir John Monash (biography), Royal Australian Historical Society, 1959.
How Did It Begin?, Longmans, Green, 1965, McKay, 1966, reprinted, Fontana, 1985.
Mexico: A Country of Contrasts, McKay, 1966.
Judaic Heritage, McKay, 1969.
The Unknown Sanctuary: The Story of Judaism, Its Teachings, Philosophy, and Symbols, Angus & Robertson, 1969.
How Did Sports Begin?: A Look at the Origins of Man at Play, McKay, 1970, reprinted, Fontana, 1986.
How Did Sex Begin?: The Sense and Nonsense of the Customs and Traditions that Have Separated Men and Women since Adam and Eve, McKay, 1973.
The Supernatural and You!, Cassell, 1976.
Strange Customs and How They All Began, McKay, 1976.
Australian Jews of Today and the Part They Have Played, Cassell, 1977.

There's a Reason for Everything, Fontana, 1982.
Mistakes, Misnomers and Misconceptions, Fontana, 1983.
Thank God I'm an Atheist, Fontana, 1987.

Also author of *The Midrash Shir Ha-shirim Zuta,* 1936, *The Jewish Question Mark,* 1945, and *The Symbolism of King Solomon's Temple,* 1954. Contributor to *This Is Australia,* Hamlyn, 1975, 1977, 1982, and to *The Australian Beef Eater's Diary,* 1977. Scriptwriter for Australian Broadcasting Commission. Regular columnist, "Religion and Life" in Australia's *Sun-Herald.* Contributor to *Mankind* and *Commentary* (both United States), and to other magazines and newspapers in Australia, Europe, and Africa. Editor, *Progressive Jew,* Johannesburg, 1948-49.

SIDELIGHTS: Rudolph Brasch is a master of twelve languages, among them Babylonic-Assyrian (Cuneiform), Syriac, Arabic, and Persian. From his early days, he has been active in inter-faith relations; in Ireland he stayed at a Franciscan monastery; in London he conducted a Hindu-Jewish service; in South Africa he addressed Bantus and held a Dutch Reformed-Jewish service; in Australia he has spoken in the Unitarian and Catholic churches of Sydney and at the Inland Mission Church at Alice Springs in the heart of the interior.

Several of Brasch's books have been translated into Japanese and German. He is a regular broadcaster and telecaster as a world authority on origins of customs, superstitions and phrases.

*   *   *

BREATHED, (Guy) Berke(ley)   1957-

PERSONAL: Surname rhymes with "method"; born June 21, 1957, in Encino, Calif.; son of John W. (an oil equipment executive) and Martha Jane (Martin) Breathed; married Jody Boyman (a photographer), May, 1986. *Education:* University of Texas at Austin, B.A., 1979. *Politics:* "Middle-winger."

ADDRESSES: Home—32062 Horseshoe Dr., Evergreen, Colo. 80439. *Agent*—Esther Newberg, International Creative Management, 40 West 57th St., New York, N.Y. 10019.

CAREER: University of Texas at Austin, photographer and columnist for *Daily Texan* (university newspaper), 1976-78; cartoonist and writer, 1978—.

AWARDS, HONORS: Harry A. Schweikert, Jr., Disability Awareness Award, Paralyzed Vets of America, 1982, for comic strip "Bloom County"; Pulitzer Prize for editorial cartooning, 1987, for "Bloom County."

WRITINGS:

COMICS

Bloom County: Loose Tails, Little, Brown, 1983.
'Toons for Our Times: A Bloom County Book of Heavy Metal Rump 'n' Roll, Little, Brown, 1984.
Penguin Dreams, and Stranger Things, Little, Brown, 1985.
Bloom County Babylon: Five Years of Basic Naughtiness, Little, Brown, 1986.
Billy and the Boingers Bootleg, Little, Brown, 1987.
Tales Too Ticklish to Tell, Little, Brown, 1988.

Author and artist of "Bloom County," a comic strip syndicated by Washington Post Writer's Group, 1980—.

SIDELIGHTS: "Since his comic strip, 'Bloom County,' debuted in 1980, Berke Breathed has consistently infuriated Christian fundamentalists, political conservatives and even his

fellow artists," writes Charles Solomon of the *Los Angeles Times.* "In the process, ironically, he's become one of the nation's most popular and successful newspaper cartoonists," winning the 1987 Pulitzer Prize for editorial cartooning. After initially appearing in less than two hundred papers, "Bloom County" first gained a larger following in 1983, when another two hundred dailies picked up the strip as a replacement for the vacationing "Doonesbury." Breathed's work now reaches an estimated 40 million readers in over twelve hundred newspapers; book collections of the strip have sold over four million copies. More recently, products such as T-shirts and stuffed dolls of the character "Opus" have further increased the "Bloom County" empire.

Although the strip first expanded as a replacement for Garry Trudeau's "Doonesbury," and has some similarities in format, Breathed told Gail Buchalter of *People* that the critics "who just see *Doonesbury* in my stuff aren't looking deep enough." The cartoonist once commented to *CA* that "the imagery of children's books (i.e. Dr. Seuss books, *The Phantom Tollbooth* by Norman Juster, and others) has had a long and overlooked influence on my approach to comic strips." This influence can be seen in the cast of "Bloom County," which includes the cynical Milo Bloom; the unassertive Michael Binkley, who is frequently visited by a closetful of anxieties; the sleazy lawyer Steve Dallas; Bill the Cat, a hairball-spitting feline whose favorite expression is "ACK!"; and Opus the penguin, who Solomon describes as "the perpetually befuddled observer of the world's descent into madness." The tone of the strip is frequently silly, demonstrating a keen sense of the absurd in everyday life. "Its freewheeling shenanigans contrast with Trudeau's sharply focused political satire," observes Solomon. "Breathed pokes fun at the gossip column elite more often than politicians."

Because "Bloom County" is more observant of social than political trends, Breathed's Pulitzer has sparked controversy among the cartooning community. Most outspoken of the critics has been Pat Oliphant, a Pulitzer-winner himself, who comments that the awarding was "a total aberration," reports Henry Allen in the *Washington Post.* "It's the final insult to what should be true cartooning." Oliphant also believes that Breathed's work is "negatively affecting what I would like to have taken as a serious form of commentary," he said to Solomon. But Breathed responds that in the work of artists like Oliphant, "day-to-day political events are talked about so much that we fool ourselves into thinking they're significant," as he told Solomon. "I'm more interested in longer, more subtle trends in society. . . . I won the Pulitzer for editorializing, which is a whole different matter," Breathed continued. "God knows, society needs its hard-bitten political commentators, but I've never seen that as my role."

Breathed's assertions notwithstanding, "Bloom County" manages to comment on a broad variety of current topics. But "instead of haranguing the reader from a soap box," notes Solomon in the *Los Angeles Times Book Review,* "Breathed makes the seemingly natural interactions of [his] characters into a vehicle for outrageous social and political satire." An example is the episode in which Oliver Wendell Jones, the young scientific wizard (who also happens to be black), develops an "electro photo pigment-izer" which will darken the skin color of its subject; an expedition is then dispatched to "test" the item on the South African ambassador. Other story lines have followed Bill the Cat's "affair" with conservative Jeane Kirkpatrick and the developments in the "Meadow" Party's presidential campaigns. And in addition to the unstereotypical Oliver Wendell Jones, ''Bloom County'' boasts Vietnam veteran Cutter John, the only handicapped character in a major strip today. But while the strip is not overtly political, it remains controversial and often generates strong and angry responses. For example, when an unflattering portrait of a religious fundamentalist appeared in the strip, the chairman of the National Federation for Decency wrote to ask Breathed's syndicate to fire him for ''religious hatred and bias,'' reports Solomon. In addition, when two episodes in one week used a slang word that some editors found objectionable, the strip was pulled; one newspaper chain has cancelled the strip entirely. But if Breathed alienates individual segments of society with his work, it hasn't affected his overall success. With its direct style and strong characters, ''Bloom County'' is ''one of the funniest and most relevant strips on the comics,'' according to Solomon. Drawing a comic strip, Breathed remarked to the critic, ''is not just a matter of getting a political point across or squeezing out a giggle from somebody: It's about creating your own universe, which is a real challenge. Few cartoonists succeed in doing it,'' concluded Breathed, ''but it's become my goal.''

BIOGRAPHICAL/CRITICAL SOURCES:

PERIODICALS

Detroit News, April 13, 1986.
Los Angeles Times, November 26, 1987.
Los Angeles Times Book Review, May 15, 1983, May 13, 1984, October 5, 1986.
People, August 6, 1984.
Washington Journalism Review, May, 1983.
Washington Post, May 9, 1987, November 12, 1987.
Washington Post Book World, April 24, 1983, August 24, 1986, August 23, 1987.

—*Sketch by Diane Telgen*

*   *   *

BRIN, Herb(ert Henry)   1915-

PERSONAL: Born February 17, 1915, in Chicago, Ill.; son of Sol (in sales) and Fannie (Goroway) Brin; married Selma Stone, December 25, 1940 (divorced, 1957); married Minna Burman, September 10, 1965 (divorced March 10, 1980); children: (first marriage) Stanley Richard, Glen David, Daniel Jeremy. *Education:* Attended Crane Junior College, 1932, Central YMCA College (now Roosevelt University), 1933, DePaul University, 1934-36, and University of Chicago, 1939-40. *Politics:* Liberal. *Religion:* Jewish.

CAREER: City News Bureau, Chicago, Ill., reporter, 1942-47; *Los Angeles Times*, Los Angeles, Calif., feature writer and reporter, 1947-54; Heritage Publishing Co., Los Angeles, owner and publisher, 1954-79, editor, 1954-79, editor emeritus, beginning 1979. Lecturer in journalism at several Californian universities. Attended and reported on the Paris Summit Conference, 1960, for KTTV, Los Angeles, and Eichmann Trial in Jerusalem, Israel, 1961, for the *Los Angeles Times;* reported on Suez and Syria war scenes for numerous leading newspapers. Founder of Pacific Southwest branches of Union of Orthodox Jewish Congregations of America, 1957. Former member of board of Hillel Academy and Beth Jacob Congregation. *Military service:* U.S. Army, Infantry, 1943-46; became sergeant.

MEMBER: World Federation of Jewish Journalists, American Jewish Press Association, American Jewish Committee, American Jewish Congress, Jewish War Veterans.

AWARDS, HONORS: Midwest Writers Conference Award, 1944, for best nonfiction article by a serviceman; award of merit from Jewish War Veterans, 1955; Three-Bell Award from California Association for Mental Health, 1958; Torch of Hope from City of Hope, 1959; Sigma Delta Chi, San Diego, awards for best feature story (3rd place) and for best news story (2nd place), both 1968; Communications Award from Anti-Defamation League of B'nai B'rith, 1971; Smolar Award for Overseas and Israel News from Council of Jewish Federations, 1977.

WRITINGS:

POETRY

Wild Flowers, Jonathan David, 1966.
Justice-Justice, Jonathan David, 1968.
Conflicts, Jonathan David, 1971.
Ich Bin Ein Jude, Jonathan David, 1982.
My Spanish Years and Other Poems, Jonathan David, 1985.

OTHER

The Eichmann Trial, Institute of Judaism, Department of Religious Studies, California State University, 1973.

Author of humorous articles. Contributor to *Army Times* and *Yankee* magazine.

*   *   *

BROOKS, Gwendolyn   1917-

PERSONAL: Born June 7, 1917, in Topeka, Kan.; daughter of David Anderson and Keziah Corinne (Wims) Brooks; married Henry Lowington Blakely, September 17, 1939; children: Henry Lowington, III, Nora. *Education:* Graduate of Wilson Junior College, 1936.

ADDRESSES: Home—7428 South Evans Ave., Chicago, Ill. 60619.

CAREER: Poet and novelist. Publicity director, NAACP Youth Council, Chicago, Ill., 1937-38. Taught poetry at numerous colleges and universities, including Columbia College, Elmhurst College, Northeastern Illinois State College (now Northwestern Illinois University), and University of Wisconsin—Madison, 1969; Distinguished Professor of the Arts, City College of the City University of New York, 1971. Member, Illinois Arts Council.

MEMBER: American Academy of Arts and Letters, National Institute of Arts and Letters, Society of Midland Authors (Chicago).

AWARDS, HONORS: Named one of ten women of the year, *Mademoiselle* magazine, 1945; National Institute of Arts and Letters grant in literature, 1946; American Academy of Arts and Letters award for creative writing, 1946; Guggenheim fellowships, 1946, 1947; Eunice Tietjens Memorial Prize, *Poetry* magazine, 1949; Pulitzer Prize in poetry, 1950, for *Annie Allen;* Robert F. Ferguson Memorial Award, Friends of Literature, 1964, for *Selected Poems;* Thormod Monsen Literature Award, 1964; Anisfield-Wolf Award, 1968, for *In the Mecca;* named Poet Laureate of Illinois, 1968—; Black Academy of Arts and Letters Award, 1971, for outstanding achievement in letters; Shelley Memorial Award, 1976; Poetry Consultant to the Library of Congress, 1985-86; forty-nine honorary degrees from universities and colleges, including Columbia College, 1964, Lake Forest College, 1965, and Brown University, 1974.

WRITINGS:

POETRY

A Street in Bronzeville (also see below), Harper, 1945.
Annie Allen (also see below), Harper, 1949, reprinted, Greenwood Press, 1972.
The Bean Eaters (also see below), Harper, 1960.
In the Time of Detachment, In the Time of Cold, Civil War Centennial Commission of Illinois, 1965.
In the Mecca (also see below), Harper, 1968.
For Illinois 1968: A Sesquicentennial Poem, Harper, 1968.
Riot (also see below), Broadside Press, 1969.
Family Pictures (also see below), Broadside Press, 1970.
Aloneness, Broadside Press, 1971.
Aurora, Broadside Press, 1972.
Beckonings, Broadside Press, 1975.
Primer for Blacks, Black Position Press, 1980.
To Disembark, Third World Press, 1981.
Black Love, Brooks Press, 182.
Mayor Harold Washington [and] *Chicago, The I Will City*, Brooks Press, 1983.
The Near Johannesburg Boy, and Other Poems, The David Co., 1987.

Also author of *A Catch of Shy Fish*, 1963.

JUVENILE

Bronzeville Boys and Girls (poems), Harper, 1956.
The Tiger Who Wore White Gloves, Third World Press, 1974, reissued, 1987.

FICTION

Maud Martha (novel; also see below), Harper, 1953, reprinted, The David Co., 1987.
(Contributor) Herbert Hill, editor, *Soon One Morning: New Writing by American Negroes, 1940-1962* (contains the short story "The Life of Lincoln West"), Knopf, 1963, published in England as *Black Voices*, Elek, 1964.
(Contributor) Langston Hughes, editor, *The Best Short Stories by Negro Writers: An Anthology from 1899 to the Present*, Little, Brown, 1967.

COLLECTED WORKS

Selected Poems, Harper, 1963.
The World of Gwendolyn Brooks (contains *A Street in Bronzeville, Annie Allen, Maud Martha, The Bean Eaters, In the Mecca*), Harper, 1971.
Blacks (includes *A Street in Bronzeville, Annie Allen, The Bean Eaters, Maud Martha, A Catch of Shy Fish, Riot, In the Mecca*, and most of *Family Pictures*), The David Co., 1987.

OTHER

(Author of foreword) Langston Hughes, editor, *New Negro Poets USA*, Indiana University Press, 1964.
(With others) *A Portion of that Field: The Centennial of the Burial of Lincoln*, University of Illinois Press, 1967.
(Editor) *A Broadside Treasury*, (poems), Broadside Press, 1971.
(Editor) *Jump Bad: A New Chicago Anthology*, Broadside Press, 1971.
Report from Part One: An Autobiography, Broadside Press, 1972.
(Author of introduction) Arnold Adoff, editor, *The Poetry of Black America: Anthology of the Twentieth Century*, Harper, 1973.

(With Keorapetse Kgositsile, Haki R. Madhubuti, and Dudley Randall) *A Capsule Course in Black Poetry Writing*, Broadside Press, 1975.
Young Poet's Primer (writing manual), Brooks Press, 1981.
Very Young Poets (writing manual), Brooks Press, 1983.

Also author of broadsides *The Wall* and *We Real Cool*, for Broadside Press, and *I See Chicago*, 1964. Contributor of poems and articles to *Ebony, McCall's, Nation, Poetry*, and other periodicals. Contributor of reviews to *Chicago Sun-Times, Chicago Daily News*, and *New York Herald Tribune*.

WORK IN PROGRESS: A sequel to *Maud Martha; Winnie*, poems interpreting Winnie Mandela of South Africa.

SIDELIGHTS: In 1950, Gwendolyn Brooks, a highly regarded poet, became the first black author to win the Pulitzer Prize. Her poems from this period, specifically *A Street in Bronzeville* and *Annie Allen*, were "devoted to small, carefully cerebrated, terse portraits of the Black urban poor," Richard K. Barksdale comments in *Modern Black Poets: A Collection of Critical Essays*. Jeanne-Marie A. Miller calls this "city-folk poetry" and describes Brooks's characters as "unheroic black people who fled the land for the city—only to discover that there is little difference between the world of the North and the world of the South. One learns from them," Miller continues in the *Journal of Negro Education*, "their dismal joys and their human griefs and pain." Audiences in Chicago, inmates in prisons around the country, and students of all ages have found her poems accessible and relevant. Haki Madhubuti, cited in Jacqueline Trescott's *Washington Post* article on Brooks, points out that Brooks "has, more than any other nationally acclaimed writer, remained in touch with the community she writes about. She lives in the core of Chicago's black community . . . . She is her work." In addition, notes Toni Cade Bambara in the *New York Times Book Review*, Brooks "is known for her technical artistry, having worked her word sorcery in forms as disparate as Italian terza rima and the blues. She has been applauded for revelations of the African experience in America, particularly her sensitive portraits of black women."

Though best known for her poetry, in the 1950s, Brooks published her first novel. *Maud Martha* presents vignettes from a ghetto woman's life in short chapters, says Harry B. Shaw in *Gwendolyn Brooks*. It is "a story of a woman with doubts about herself and where and how she fits into the world. Maud's concern is not so much that she is inferior but that she is perceived as being ugly." Eventually, she takes a stand for her own dignity by turning her back on a patronising, racist store clerk. "The book is . . . about the triumph of the lowly," comments Shaw. "[Brooks] shows what they go through and exposes the shallowness of the popular, beautiful white people with 'good' hair. One way of looking at the book, then, is as a war with . . . people's concepts of beauty." Its other themes include "the importance of spiritual and physical death," disillusionment with a marriage that amounts to "a step down" in living conditions, and the discovery "that even through disillusionment and spiritual death life will prevail," Shaw maintains. Other reviewers feel that Brooks is more effective when treating the same themes in her poetry, but David Littlejohn, writing in *Black on White: A Critical Survey of Writing by American Negroes*, feels the novel 'is a striking human experiment, as exquisitely written . . . as any of Gwendolyn Brook's poetry in verse. . . . It is a powerful, beautiful dagger of a book, as generous as it can possibly be. It teaches more, more quickly, more lastingly, than a thousand pages of protest.'' In a *Black World* review, Annette Oliver Shands appreciates the way in which *Maud Martha* differs from the works of other early black writers: ''Miss Brooks does not specify traits, niceties or assets for members of the Black community to acquire in order to attain their just rights. . . . So, this is not a novel to inspire social advancement on the part of fellow Blacks. Nor does it say *be poor, Black and happy.* The message is to accept the challenge of being human and to assert humanness with urgency.''

Although, as Martha Liebrum notes in the *Houston Post*, Brooks ''wrote about being black before being black was beautiful,'' in retrospect her poems have been described as sophisticated, intellectual, and European, or ''conditioned'' by the established literary tradition. Like her early favorites Emily Dickinson, John Keats, and Percy Bysshe Shelley, Brooks expresses in poetry her love of ''the wonders language can achieve,'' as she told Claudia Tate in an interview for *Black Women Writers at Work.* Barksdale states that by not directly emphasizing any ''rhetorical involvement with causes, racial or otherwise,'' Brooks was merely reflecting the ''the literary mood of the late 1940's.'' He suggests that there was little reason for Brooks to confront the problems of racism on a large scale since, in her work, ''each character, so neatly and precisely presented, is a racial protest in itself and a symbol of some sharply etched human dilemma.''

However, Brooks' later poems show a marked change in tone and content. Just as her first poems reflected the mood of their era, her later works mirror their age by displaying what *National Observer* contributor Bruce Cook calls ''an intense awareness of the problems of color and justice.'' Bambara comments that, at the age of fifty ''something happened [to Brooks], a something most certainly in evidence in 'In the Mecca' (1968) and subsequent works—a new movement and energy, intensity, richness, power of statement and a new stripped lean, compressed style. A change of style prompted by a change of mind.''

''Though some of her work in the early 1960s had a terse abbreviated style, her conversion to direct political expression happened rapidly after a gathering of black writers at Fisk University in 1967,'' Trescott reports. Brooks told Tate, ''They seemed proud and so committed to their own people. . . . The poets among them felt that black poets should write as blacks, about blacks, and address themselves *to* blacks.'' If many of her earlier poems had fulfilled this aim, it was not due to conscious intent, she said; but from this time forward, Brooks has thought of herself as an African who has determined not to compromise social comment for the sake of technical proficiency.

Although *In the Mecca* and later works are characterized as tougher and possess what a reviewer for the *Virginia Quarterly Review* describes as ''raw power and roughness,'' critics are quick to indicate that these poems are neither bitter nor vengeful. Instead, according to Cook, they are more ''about bitterness'' than bitter in themselves. *Dictionary of Literary Biography* essayist Charles Israel suggests that *In the Mecca*'s title poem, for example, shows ''a deepening of Brooks's concern with social problems.'' A mother has lost a small daughter in the block-long ghetto tenement, the Mecca; the long poem traces her steps through the building, revealing her neighbors to be indifferent, or insulated by their own personal obsessions. The mother finds her little girl, who ''never learned that black is not beloved,'' who ''Was royalty when poised, / sly, at the A and P's fly-open door,'' under a Jamaican resident's

cot, murdered. The *Virginia Quarterly Review* contributor compares the poem's impact to that of Richard Wright's fiction. R. Baxter Miller, writing in *Black American Poets Between Worlds, 1940-1960,* comments, ''*In the Mecca* is a most complex and intriguing book; it seeks to balance the sordid realities of urban life with an imaginative process of reconciliation and redemption.'' Other poems in the book, occasioned by the death of Malcolm X, or the dedication of a mural of black heroes painted on a Chicago slum building, express the poet's commitment to her people's awareness of themselves as a political as well as a cultural entity.

Her interest in encouraging young blacks to assist and appreciate fledgling black publishing companies led her to leave Harper & Row. In the seventies, she chose Dudley Randall's Broadside Press to publish her poetry (*Riot, Family Pictures, Aloneness, Aurura,* and *Beckonings*) and *Report from Part One,* the first volume of her autobiography. She edited two collections of poetry—*A Broadside Treasury* and *Jump Bad: A New Chicago Anthology*—for the Detroit-based press. The Chicago-based Third World Press, run by Haki R. Madhubuti (formerly Don L. Lee, one of the young poets she had met during the sixties), has also brought two Brooks titles into print. She does not regret having given her support to small publishers who dedicated themselves to the needs of the black community. Brooks was the first writer to read in Broadside's Poet's Theatre Series when it began, and was also the first poet to read in the second opening of the series when the press revived under new ownership in 1988.

Riot, Family Pictures, Beckonings, and other books brought out by black publishers were given brief notice by critics of the literary establishment who ''did not wish to encourage Black publishers,'' said Brooks. Some were disturbed by the political content of these poems. *Riot,* in particular, in which Brooks is the spokesman for the ''HEALTHY REBELLION'' going on then, as she calls it, was accused of ''celebrating violence'' by L. L. Shapiro in a *School Library Journal* review. Key poems from these books, later collected in *To Disembark,* call blacks to ''work together toward their own REAL emancipation,'' Brooks indicated. Even so, ''the strength here is not in declamation but in [the poet's] genius for psychological insight,'' claims J. A. Lipari in the *Library Journal.* Addison Gayle points out that the softer poems of this period—the ones asking for stronger interpersonal bonds among black Americans—are no less political: ''To espouse and exult in a Black identity, outside the psychic boundaries of white Americans, was to threaten . . . . To advocate and demand love between one Black and another was to begin a new chapter in American history. Taken together, the acknowledgment of a common racial identity among Blacks throughout the world and the suggestion of a love based upon the brotherhood and sisterhood of the oppressed were meant to transform Blacks in America from a minority to a majority, from world victims to, to use Madhubuti's phrase, 'world makers.'''

In the same essay, printed in *Black Women Writers (1950-1980): A Critical Evaluation,* Gayle defends *Riot* and the later books, naming them an important source of inspiration to a rising generation: ''It may well be . . . that the function of poetry is not so much to save us from oppression nor from Auschwitz, but to give us the strength to face them, to help us stare down the lynch mob, walk boldly in front of the firing squad. It is just such awareness that the poetry of Gwendolyn Brooks has given us, this that she and those whom she taught/ learned from have accomplished for us all. They have told us that for Black Americans there are no havens, that in the eyes of other Americans we are, each and every one of us, rioters. . . . These are dangerous times for Black people. The sensitive Black poet realizes that fact, but far from despairing, picks up his pen, . . . and echoes Gwendolyn Brooks: 'My aim . . . is to write poems that will somehow successfully "call" . . . all black people . . . in gutters, in schools, offices, factories, prisons, the consulate; I wish to teach black people in pulpits, black people in mines, on farms, on thrones." Brooks pointed out "a serious error" in this quote; she wants to "reach" people, not "teach" them. She added, "The times for Black people—when*ever* in the clutches of white *manipulation*, have ALWAYS been dangerous." She also advised young poets, "Walking in front of a firing squad is *crazy*. Your effort should be in preventing the *formation* of a firing squad."

The poet's search "for an *expression* relevant to all manner of blacks," as she described her change in focus to Tate, did not alter her mastery of her craft. "While quoting approvingly Ron Karenga's observation that 'the fact that we are black is our ultimate reality,' blackness did not, to her, require simplification of language, symbol, or mural perception," notes C. W. E. Bigsby in *The Second Black Renaissance: Essays in Black Literature*. It did include "the possibility of communicating directly to those in the black community." In the bars and on the street corners were an audience not likely to "go into a bookstore" to buy poetry by anyone, she told George Stavros in a *Contemporary Literature* interview reprinted in *Report from Part One: An Autobiography*. And in the late sixties, Brooks reported, "some of those folks DID" enter bookstores to buy poetry and read it "standing up." To better reach the street audience, Brooks's later poems use more open, less traditional poetic forms and techniques. Penelope Moffet of the *Los Angeles Times* records the poet's statement that since 1967, she has been "successfully escaping from close rhyme, because it just isn't natural. . . . I've written hundreds . . . of sonnets, and I'll probably never write another one, because I don't feel that this is a sonnet time. It seems to me it's a wild, raw, ragged free verse time." She told Stavros, "I want to write poems that will be non-compromising. I don't want to stop a concern with words doing good jobs, which has always been a concern of mine, but I want to write poems that will be meaningful to those people I described a while ago, things that will touch them." Speaking of later works aimed for that audience, Robert F. Kiernan offers in *American Writing since 1945: A Critical Survey*, "She remains, however, a virtuoso of the lyric and an extraordinary portraitist—probably the finest black poet of the post-Harlem generation."

When *Report from Part One* came out in 1972, some reviewers complained that it did not provide the level of personal detail nor the insight into black literature that they had expected. "They wanted a list of domestic spats," remarked Brooks. Bambara notes that it "is not a sustained dramatic narrative for the nosey, being neither the confessions of a private woman/poet or the usual sort of mahogany-desk memoir public personages inflict upon the populace at the first sign of a cardiac. . . . It documents the growth of Gwen Brooks." Other reviewers value it for explaining the poet's new orientation toward her racial heritage and her role as a poet. In a passage she has presented again in later books as a definitive statement, she writes: "I—who have 'gone the gamut' from an almost angry rejection of my dark skin by some of my brainwashed brothers and sisters to a surprised queenhood in the new Black sun—am qualified to enter at least the kindergarten of new consciousness now. New consciousness and trudge-toward-progress. I have hopes for myself. . . . I know now that I am

essentially an essential African, in occupancy here because of an indeed 'peculiar' institution. . . . I know that Black fellow-feeling must be the Black man's encyclopedic Primer. I know that the Black-and-white integration concept, which in the mind of some beaming early saint was a dainty spinning dream, has wound down to farce. . . . I know that the Black emphasis must be not *against white* but *FOR Black*. . . . In the Conference-That-Counts, whose date may be 1980 or 2080 (woe betide the Fabric of Man if it is 2080), there will be no looking up nor looking down." In the future, she envisions "the profound and frequent shaking of hands, which in Africa is so important. The shaking of hands in warmth and strength and union."

Brooks put some of the finishing touches on the second volume of her autobiography while serving as Poetry Consultant to the Library of Congress. Brooks was sixty-eight when she became the first black woman to be appointed to the post. Of her many duties there, the most important, in her view, were visits to local schools. "Poetry is life distilled," she told students in a Washington school, Schmich reports. "She urged them to keep journals. She read them a poem about teen suicide. She told them poetry exists where they might not recognize it," such as in John Lennon's song "Eleanor Rigby." Similar visits to colleges, universities, prisons, hospitals, and drug rehabilitation centers characterize her tenure as Poet Laureate of Illinois. In that role, she has sponsored and hosted annual literary awards ceremonies at which she presents prizes paid for "out of [her] own pocket, which, despite her modest means, is of legendary depth," Reginald Gibbons relates in *Tribune Books*. She has honored and encouraged many poets in her state through the Illinois Poets Laureate Awards and Significant Illinois Poets Awards programs. At one ceremony, says Gibbons, "poetry was, for a time, the vital center of people's lives."

Though her writing is "*to* Blacks," it is "*for* anyone who wants to open the book," she emphasized to Schmich. Brook's objectivity is perhaps the most widely acclaimed feature of her poetry. Janet Overmeyer notes in the *Christian Science Monitor* that Brooks' "particular, outstanding, genius is her unsentimental regard and respect for all human beings. . . . She neither foolishly pities nor condemns—she creates." Overmeyer continues, "From her poet's craft bursts a whole gallery of wholly alive persons, preening, squabbling, loving, weeping; many a novelist cannot do so well in ten times the space." Brooks achieves this effect through a high "degree of artistic control," claims Littlejohn. "The words, lines, and arrangements," he states, "have been worked and worked and worked again into poised exactness: the unexpected apt metaphor, the mock-colloquial asides amid jewelled phrases, the half-ironic repetitions—she knows it all." More importantly, Brooks' objective treatment of issues such as poverty and racism "produces genuine emotional tension," he writes.

This quality also provides her poems with universal appeal. Blyden Jackson states in *Black Poetry in America: Two Essays in Historical Interpretation* that Brooks "is one of those artists of whom it can truthfully be said that things like sex and race, important as they are, . . . appear in her work to be sublimated into insights and revelations of universal application." Although Brooks' characters are primarily black and poor, and live in Northern urban cities, she provides, according to Jackson, through "the close inspection of a limited domain, . . . a view of life in which one may see a microscopic portion of the universe intensely and yet, through that microscopic portion see all truth for the human condition wherever it is." And although the goals and adjustments of black nationalism have been her frequent topics, Houston A Baker, Jr., says of Brooks in the *CLA Journal*, "The critic (whether black or white) who comes to her work seeking only support for his ideology will be disappointed for, as Etheridge Knight pointed out, she has ever spoken the truth. And truth, one likes to feel, always lies beyond the boundaries of any one ideology. Perhaps Miss Brooks' most significant achievement is her endorsement of this point of view. From her hand and fertile imagination have come volumes that transcend the dogma on either side of the American veil." Baker feels that Brooks "represents a singular achievement. Beset by a double consciousness, she has kept herself from being torn asunder by crafting poems that equal the best in the black and white American literary traditions."

Proving the breadth of Brooks's appeal, poets representing a wide variety of "races and . . . poetic camps" gathered at the University of Chicago to celebrate the poet's 70th birthday in 1987, reports Gibbons. Brooks brought them together, he says, "in . . . a moment of good will and cheer." In recognition of her service and achievements, a junior high school in Harvey, Illinois has been named for her. She is also honored at Western Illinois University's Gwendolyn Brooks Center for African-American Literature.

Summing up the poet's accomplishments, Gibbons writes that, beginning with *A Street in Bronzeville*, Brooks has brought national attention to "a part of life that had been grossly neglected by the literary establishment. . . . "And because Brooks has been a deeply serious artist . . . , she has created works of special encouragement to black writers and of enduring importance to all readers."

BIOGRAPHICAL/CRITICAL SOURCES:

BOOKS

Authors in the News, Volume 1, Gale, 1976.
Baker, Houston A., Jr., *Singers of Daybreak: Studies in Black American Literature*, Howard University Press, 1974.
Bigsby, C. W. E., editor, *The Black American Writer, Volume II: Poetry and Drama*, Deland, 1969.
Bigsby, C. W. E., *The Second Black Renaissance: Essays in Black Literature*, Greenwood Press, 1980.
Brooks, Gwendolyn, *In the Mecca*, Harper, 1968.
Brooks, Gwendolyn, *Report from Part One: An Anthology*, Broadside Press, 1972.
Brown, Patricia L., Don L. Lee, and Francis Ward, editors, *To Gwen with Love: An Anthology Dedicated to Gwendolyn Brooks*, Johnson Publishing, 1971.
Concise Dictionary of Literary Biography, 1941-1968, Gale, 1985.
Contemporary Literary Criticism, Gale, Volume 1, 1973, Volume 2, 1974, Volume 4, 1975, Volume 5, 1976, Volume 15, 1980.
Dictionary of Literary Biography, Volume 5: *American Poets since World War II*, Gale, 1980.
Dembo, L. S. and Pondrom, C. N., editors, *The Contemporary Writer: Interviews with Sixteen Novelists and Poets*, University of Wisconsin Press, 1972.
Drotning, Philip T. and Wesley W. Smith, editors, *Up from the Ghetto*, Cowles, 1970.
Emanuel and Gross, editors, *Dark Symphony: Negro Literature in America*, Free Press, 1968.
Evans, Mari, editor, *Black Women Writers (1950-1980): A Critical Evaluation*, Anchor/Doubleday, 1984.
Gates, Henry Louis, Jr., editor, *Black Literature and Literary Theory*, Methuen, 1984.

Gayle, Addison, editor, *Black Expression*, Weybright & Talley, 1969.
Gibson, Donald B., editor, *Modern Black Poets: A Collection of Critical Essays*, Prentice-Hall, 1973.
Gould, Jean, *Modern American Women Poets*, Dodd, Mead, 1985.
Jackson, Blyden and Louis D. Rubin, Jr., *Black Poetry in America: Two Essays in Historical Interpretation*, Louisiana State University Press, 1974.
Kent, George, *Gwendolyn Brooks: A Life*, University Press of Kentucky, 1988.
Kufrin, Joan, *Uncommon Women*, New Century Publications, 1981.
Littlejohn, David, *Black on White: A Critical Survey of Writing by American Negroes*, Viking, 1966.
Madhubuti, Haki R., *Say that the River Turns: The Impact of Gwendolyn Brooks*, Third World Press, 1987.
Melhem, D. H., *Gwendolyn Brooks: Poetry and the Heroic Voice*, University Press of Kentucky, 1987.
Miller, R. Baxter, *Langston Hughes and Gwendolyn Brooks: A Reference Guide*, Hall, 1978.
Miller, R. Baxter, *Black American Poets between Worlds, 1940-1960*, University of Tennessee Press, 1986.
Mootry, Maria K. and Gary Smith, editors, *A Life Distilled: Gwendolyn Brooks, Her Poetry and Fiction*, University of Illinois Press, 1987.
Newquist, Roy, *Conversations*, Rand McNally, 1967.
Redmond, Eugene B., *Drumvoices: The Mission of Afro-American Poetry*, Doubleday, 1976.
Shaw, Harry F., *Gwendolyn Brooks*, Twayne, 1980.
Tate, Claudia, *Black Women Writers at Work*, Continuum, 1983.

PERIODICALS

Atlantic Monthly, September, 1960.
Best Sellers, April 1, 1973.
Black American Literature Forum, spring, 1977, winter, 1984.
Black Enterprise, June, 1985.
Black Scholar, March, 1981, November, 1984.
Black World, August, 1970, January, 1971, July, 1971, September, 1971, October, 1971, January, 1972, March, 1973, June, 1973, December, 1975.
Book Week, October 27, 1963.
Chicago Tribune, January 14, 1986, June 7, 1987.
Christian Science Monitor, September 19, 1968.
CLA Journal, December, 1962, December, 1963, December, 1969, September, 1972, September, 1973, September, 1977, December, 1982.
Contemporary Literature, March 28, 1969, winter, 1970.
Critique, summer, 1984.
Discourse, spring, 1967.
Ebony, July, 1968.
Essence, April, 1971, September, 1984.
Explicator, Volume 58, April, 1976, Volume 36, number 4, summer, 1978.
Houston Post, February 11, 1974.
Journal of Negro Education, winter, 1970.
Library Journal, September 15, 1970.
Los Angeles Times, November 6, 1987.
Los Angeles Times Book Review, September 2, 1984.
Modern Fiction Studies, winter, 1985.
Nation, September, 1962, July 7, 1969.
National Observer, November 9, 1968.
Negro American Literature Forum, fall, 1967, summer, 1974.

Negro Digest, December, 1961, January, 1962, August, 1962, July, 1963, June, 1964, January, 1968.

New Statesman, May 3, 1985.

New Yorker, September 22, 1945, December 17, 1949, October 10, 1953, December 3, 1979.

New York Times, November 4, 1945, October 5, 1953, December 9, 1956, October 6, 1963, March 2, 1969.

New York Times Book Review, October 23, 1960, October 6, 1963, March 2, 1969, January 2, 1972, June 4, 1972, December 3, 1972, January 7, 1973, June 10, 1973, December 2, 1973, September 23, 1984, July 5, 1987.

Phylon, Volume XXII, summer, 1961, Volume XXXVII, number 1, March, 1976.

Poetry, Volume 67, December, 1945, Volume 126, 1950, Volume 103, March, 1964.

Publishers Weekly, June 6, 1970.

Ramparts, December, 1968.

Saturday Review, January 19, 1946, September 17, 1949, February 1, 1964.

Saturday Review of Literature, May 20, 1950.

Southern Review, spring, 1965.

Studies in Black Literature, autumn, 1973, spring, 1974, summer, 1974, spring, 1977.

Tribune Books, July 12, 1987.

Virginia Quarterly Review, winter, 1969, winter, 1971.

Washington Post, May 19, 1971, April 19, 1973, March 31, 1987.

Washington Post Book World, November 3, 1968, November 11, 1973.

Women's Review of Books, December, 1984.

World Literature Today, winter, 1985.

*   *   *

BROWN, Cecil M(orris)   1943-

PERSONAL: Born July 3, 1943, in Bolton, N.C.; son of Cecil (a tobacco sharecropper) and Dorothy Brown. *Education:* Attended Agricultural and Technical State University, Greensboro, N.C., 1961; Columbia University, B.A., 1966, University of Chicago, M.A., 1967.

ADDRESSES: Office—1856 Dwight Way, Berkeley, Calif. 94703.

CAREER: Writer. University of Illinois at Chicago Circle, lecturer in English, 1968-69; University of California, Berkeley, lecturer in English, 1969-70; lecturer in English and producer of plays, Merrit College, Oakland, Calif. Screenwriter, Warner Brothers, 1977-79, and Universal Studios.

AWARDS, HONORS: Before Columbus Foundation American Book Award, 1984, for *Days Without Weather.*

WRITINGS:

The Life and Loves of Mr. Jiveass Nigger (novel), Farrar, Straus, 1970.

(With Carl Gottlieb) "Which Way is Up?" (screenplay; adapted from *The Seduction of Mimi* by Lina Wertmuller), Universal, 1977.

Days Without Weather, Farrar, Straus, 1982.

Author of plays, including "The African Shades: A Comedy in One Act," "The Gila Monster," and "Our Sisters Are Pregnant." Contributor of articles to *Partisan Review, Black World, Kenyon Review, Yardbird Reader, Evergreen Review, Negro Digest,* and other periodicals.

SIDELIGHTS: The major themes of Cecil Brown's work include stories of "black survival in a corrupt society" and how "a culture victimizes all its minorities if it denies a voice to any one of them," describes Jean M. Bright in a *Dictionary of Literary Biography* essay. *The Life and Loves of Mr. Jiveass Nigger,* Brown's first and probably best-known work, relates the story of George Washington, a young black who leaves the United States "to find out if everyone in the world lies as much as he lies in his dedicated search for invisibility," summarizes Richard Rhodes in the *New York Times Book Review.* Living in Copenhagen and drifting through various relationships with whites and blacks, Washington finally admits, as Bright relates it, "that he is a fool and a prodigal destroying himself by wallowing in a moral pigsty among swinish people."

Reception of Brown's novel was mixed, inviting comparisons to James Joyce on one hand and blunt criticism on the other. A *Times Literary Supplement* critic finds that woven into the story of Washington's "jiving" are subtleties which are "carefully placed. . . . Slowly but surely we pick up the idea that perhaps Jiveass is really on the losing side." Christopher Lehmann-Haupt writes in the *New York Times* that "at the beginning of 'The Life and Loves of Mr. Jiveass Nigger' we know that we are into good stuff. Mr. Brown has a hard, driving style that toys with the stereotypes of black verbal rhythms and punches when one isn't looking." Although Lehmann-Haupt admires the author's style, he faults the novel's plotting: "Gradually, as certain scenes (or the points of certain scenes) repeat themselves, the fictional illusion begins to wear thin . . . and one's attention wanders." An *Antioch Review* writer calls the work "crude," remarking that "neither is this soul novel very good reading, as a remembrance of *Invisible Man* could tell you." Rhodes draws a more favorable comparison, however, observing that the novel "recalls, in its form and language, other novels . . . [including] Joyce's 'Portrait of the Artist as a Young Man' and [Ralph] Ellison's 'Invisible Man.'" The critic continues: "The awareness of black invisibility and its uses (and its self-destructiveness) . . . creates a form reminiscent of Ellison's."

At the end of *Life and Loves,* Washington considers writing a novel upon his return to America; he says that "If you say something about sex and being a nigger then you got a best seller." Rhodes remarks that Washington's new vocation will still require him to work with lies and "jive"; in deciding to become an artist, Washington "knows that he must explain himself, must take on that ultimate jiving which is art." The *Times Literary Supplement* critic, however, finds a darker meaning in the novel's ending, one that reflects upon Brown's own career: "Mr. Brown's complaint, like that of Jiveass, is that his blackness forces him to attitudinize. He cannot be a writer, he has got to be a *black* writer, and this book, more than anything, is a bitter joke at its own expense."

It was thirteen years before Brown followed up *Life and Loves* with a second novel, *Days Without Weather.* In between these publications, Brown held a variety of positions, one of which was as a screenwriter for Warner Brothers and Universal. *Days Without Weather* draws upon Brown's own Hollywood experiences, relating the story of Jonah, a young black comedian whose attempts at bringing a friend's script about a historic slave revolt to the screen are corrupted by everyone involved. In the process of making the film, Jonah is betrayed by the producer, who breaks her promise to film the script intact, and his uncle Gadge, whose revisions transform the script into a work of exploitation. The worst corruption takes place when the playwright "visits the set, discovers the deception and protests, starting a riot between white actors and black actors," as David Bradley describes in the *New York Times Book Review*. The studio films the riot and releases the film, which is highly praised.

Days Without Weather is typical of the "Hollywood" novel, demonstrating the "classic quandary of the performing artist, whether to compromise his integrity to win applause," describes James Idema in the *Chicago Tribune Book World*. Art Seidenbaum, writing in the *Los Angeles Times Book Review*, sees the treatment of this subject as a flaw in the novel: "The trouble with Hollywood novels may be the way novelists moralize, setting up one pure soul sinking in a universal cesspool, alluding to fine art when frivolous amusement is more often the business at hand." David Bradley agrees with this assessment, noting in the *New York Times Book Review* that the hypocrisy of Jonah's own lies and betrayals are never fully explored. Both critics also believe that Jonah's comedic routines do not translate very well to written form. For Idema, however, Jonah's work on stage provides some of the best scenes in the book; "white or black," the critic comments, "you'll laugh at Jonah's raunchy routines." Bright believes that *Days Without Weather*, combined with Brown's *Life and Loves*, demonstrates that "he can use his outrageous sense of humor as an effective form of social protest, earning the praise of comedian Richard Pryor while pleasing social critic James Baldwin as well."

The Life and Loves of Mr. Jiveass Nigger has been translated into German.

BIOGRAPHICAL/CRITICAL SOURCES:

BOOKS

Dictionary of Literary Biography, Volume 33: *Afro-American Fiction Writers After 1955*, Gale, 1984.

PERIODICALS

Antioch Review, winter, 1970.
Atlantic Monthly, February, 1970.
Chicago Tribune Book World, January 23, 1983.
Los Angeles Times Book Review, January 16, 1983.
New Statesman, June 19, 1970.
New York Times, January 14, 1970.
New York Times Book Review, February 1, 1970, June 7, 1970, April 17, 1983.
Time, February 2, 1970.
Times Literary Supplement, July 31, 1970.*

*   *   *

BROWN, James   1934-

PERSONAL: Born May 1, 1934, in Boston, Mass.; son of Constantine (a businessman) and Sophia (Lucas) Brown; married Bonnie Jo Russell (a piano teacher), November 26, 1964; children: Shannon Sophia. *Education:* Texas Christian University, B.A., 1960, M.A., 1962; State University of New York at Buffalo, M.A., 1969, Ph.D., 1971.

ADDRESSES: Home—2733 Rosedale, Dallas, Tex. 75205. *Office*—Department of Political Science, Southern Methodist University, Dallas, Tex. 75222.

CAREER: Southern Methodist University, Dallas, Tex., instructor, 1969-70, assistant professor, 1970-74, associate professor, 1974-81, professor of political science, 1981—, director of graduate program, 1970-80, director of undergraduate

studies, 1983-86. Professor of national security affairs, Air Command and Staff College, Air University, 1979-80. Visiting lecturer at University of Erlangen-Nurnberg, University of Istanbul, University of Koln, Naval War College, and Panteos School of Political Science. Diplomat program scholar, U.S. State Department, 1971 and 1975; senior Fulbright scholar, University of Ankara, spring, 1985. Southwest area manager for News Election Service, 1972-82. Member of national selection committee of Institute of International Education. Organizer and chairman of conferences for Air University and Southern Methodist University. U.S. delegate to the International Wehrkunde-Encounters, Munich, West Germany, 1982, 1986, and 1987. Consultant to U.S. Senate Armed Services Committee, 1982; special assistant to the Deputy Undersecretary of Defense for Planning and Resources, Department of Defense, 1987-88. *Military service:* U.S. Army, Chemical Corps, 1954-57; became sergeant.

MEMBER: American Political Science Association, American Association of University Professors, Modern Greek Studies Association, Southern Political Science Association, Southwestern Political Science Association, Inter-University Seminar on Armed Forces and Society, Pi Sigma Alp.

AWARDS, HONORS: National Science Foundation travel grant and Arnold Foundation research grant, 1973 and 1981, for study in Greece.

WRITINGS:

(Contributor) Gerald A. Dorfman and Steffan W. Schmidt, editors, *The Military in Politics*, Geron-X, 1974.
(With Lee Vickers) *Small Cities Management Training Program*, International City Management Association, 1975.
(With Philip Seib) *The Art of Politics: Electoral Strategies and Campaign Management*, Aflred Publishing, 1976.
Military Ethics and Professionalism, National Defense University Press, 1981.
(Contributor) Nancy Goldman, editor, *Female Soldiers: Combatant or Noncombatant?*, Greenwood Press, 1982.
(With Michael J. Collins and Franklin Margiotta) *Changing Military Manpower Realities*, Westwood, 1982.
(Co-editor with William Snyder) *The Regionalization of Warfare: The Falkland Islands, Lebanese, and Iran-Iraq Conflicts*, Transaction Books, 1985.
(Contributor) Jerrold Elkins, editor, *The Military as a Vehicle for Social Integration*, Princeton University Press, 1987.
(Contributor) Constantine Danopoulos, editor, *Military Dictatorships in Retreat*, Westview, 1987.
(Co-editor with Snyder) *The Reagan Administration's Defense Policies: An Assessment*, Pergamon, 1987.

Also author of professional papers presented at various conferences. Contributor of numerous articles and book reviews to journals, including *Current History, Armed Forces and Society, International Journal of Public Administration, Journal of Middle East Studies, Journal of Communications*, and *Social Science Research Journal*.

WORK IN PROGRESS: NATO's Southern Flank: An American Dilemma; a sociological study of military academies.

*   *   *

BRUIN, John
See BRUTUS, Dennis

BRUTUS, Dennis 1924-
(John Bruin)

PERSONAL: Born November 28, 1924, in Salisbury, Southern Rhodesia (now Harare, Zimbabwe Rhodesia), Africa; came to the United States, 1971, granted political asylum, 1983; son of Francis Henry (a teacher) and Margaret Winifred (teacher, maiden name Bloemetjie) Brutus; married May Jaggers, May 14, 1950; children: Jacinta, Marc, Julian, Antony, Justina, Cornelia, Gregory, Paula. *Education:* Fort Hare University, B.A. (with distinction), 1947; University of the Witwatersrand, study of law, 1963-64.

ADDRESSES: Office—Department of Black Community Education Research and Development, University of Pittsburgh, Pittsburgh, Pa. 15260.

CAREER: Poet and political activist. High school teacher of English and Afrikaans in Port Elizabeth, South Africa, 1948-61; journalist in South Africa, 1960-61; imprisoned for anti-apartheid activities, Robben Island Prison, 1964-65; teacher and journalist in London, England, 1966-70; Northwestern University, Evanston, Ill., professor of English, 1971-85; Swarthmore College, Swarthmore, Pa., Cornell Professor of English Literature, 1985-86; University of Pittsburgh, Pittsburgh, Pa., professor of black studies and English, chairman of department of black community education research and development, 1986—. Visiting professor, University of Denver, 1970, University of Texas at Austin, 1974-75, Dartmouth College, 1983.

Secretary, South African Sports Association, 1959; president of South African Non-Racial Olympic Committee, 1963—; director, World Campaign for Release of South African Political Prisoners (London); United Nations representative, International Defense and Aid Fund (London), 1966-71; chairman of International Campaign Against Racism in Sport, 1972—; member of advisory board, ARENA: Institute for the Study of Sport and Social Analysis, 1975—; chairman, International Advisory Commission to End Apartheid in Sport, 1975—; member of board of directors, Black Arts Celebration (Chicago), 1975—; member, Emergency Committee for World government, 1978—; member of Working Committee for Action Against Apartheid (Evanston), 1978—; president of Third World Energy Resources Institute.

MEMBER: International Poetry Society (fellow), International Platform Association, Union of Writers of the African People (Ghana; vice-president, 1974—), Modern Language Association, African Literature Association (founding chairman, 1975—, member of executive committee, 1979—), United Nations Association of Illinois and Greater Chicago (member of board of directors, 1978).

AWARDS, HONORS: Chancellor's prize, University of South Africa, 1947; Mbari Award, CCF, 1962, for *Sirens, Knuckles, Boots;* Freedom Writers Award, Society of Writers and Editors, 1975; Kenneth Kaunda Humanism Award, 1979; awarded key to city of Sumter, S.C., 1979; L.H.D., Worcester State College and University of Massachusetts, 1984; Langston Hughes Award, City University of New York, 1987.

WRITINGS:

POETRY

Sirens, Knuckles, Boots, Mbari Publications, 1963.
Letters to Martha and Other Poems from a South African Prison, Heinemann, 1968.
Poems from Algiers, African and Afro-American Research Institute, University of Texas at Austin, 1970.
(Under pseudonym John Bruin) *Thoughts Abroad,* Troubadour Press, 1970.
A Simple Lust: Selected Poems Including "Sirens, Knuckles, Boots," "Letters to Martha," "Poems from Algiers," "Thoughts Abroad," Hill & Wang, 1973.
Strains, edited by Wayne Kamin and Chip Dameron, Troubadour Press, 1975, revised edition, 1982.
China Poems, translations by Ko Ching Po, African and Afro-American Studies and Research Center, University of Texas at Austin, 1975.
Stubborn Hope: New Poems and Selections from "China Poems" and "Strains," Three Continents Press, 1978.
Salutes and Censures, Fourth Dimension Publishers (Nigeria), 1984, Africa World Press, 1985.

WORK REPRESENTED IN ANTHOLOGIES

New Sum of Poetry from the Negro World, Presence Africaine (Paris), 1966.
Cosmo Pieterse, editor, *Seven South African Poets,* Heinemann, 1966, Humanities, 1973.
Gerald Moore and Ulli Beier, editors, *Modern Poetry from Africa,* Penguin, 1966.

OTHER

The American-South African Connection (sound recording), Iowa State University of Science and Technology, 1975.
Informal Discussion in Third World Culture Class (sound recording), Media Resources Center, Iowa State University of Science and Technology, 1975.

Contributor to journals. Member of editoral board, *Africa Today,* 1976—, and *South and West.* Guest editor, *The Gar,* 1978.

SIDELIGHTS: Describing Dennis Brutus as a "soft-spoken man of acerbic views," Kevin Klose suggests in the *Washington Post* that "he is one of English-speaking Africa's best-known poets, and also happens to be one of the most successful foes of the apartheid regime in South Africa." Born in Southern Rhodesia of racially mixed parentage, Brutus spent most of his early life in South Africa. Dismissed from his teaching post and forbidden to write by the South African government as a result of anti-apartheid activities, he was arrested in 1963 for attending a meeting in defiance of a ban on associating with any group. Seeking refuge in Swaziland following his release on bail, Brutus was apprehended in Mozambique by Portuguese secret police, who surrendered him to South African secret police. Fearing that he would be killed in Johannesburg, where he was subsequently taken, he again tried to escape. Pursued by police, Brutus was shot in the back, tortured, and finally sentenced to eighteen months of hard labor at Robben Island Prison—"the escape-proof concentration camp for political prisoners off the South African coast," remarks Klose in another *Washington Post* article. The time Brutus spent there, says Klose, "included five months in solitary confinement, which brought him to attempt suicide, slashing at his wrists with sharp stones."

After Brutus's release from prison, he was placed under house arrest and was prohibited from either leaving his home or receiving visitors. He was permitted to leave South Africa, however, "on the condition that he not return, according to court records, and he took his family to England," states William C. Rempel in the *Los Angeles Times.* Granted a conditional British passport because of Rhodesia's former colonial status,

Brutus journeyed to the United States, where temporary visas allowed him to remain. Rempel notes, however, that Brutus's "passport became snarled in technical difficulties when Rhodesia's white supremacist government was overthrown and Zimbabwe was created." In the process of applying for a new passport, Brutus missed his application deadline for another visa; and the United States government began deportation proceedings immediately. Brutus was ultimately granted political asylum because a return to Zimbabwe, given its proximity to South Africa, would place his life in imminent danger. Klose indicates that Brutus's efforts to remain in the United States have been at the expense of his art, though: "He has written almost no poetry, which once sustained him through the years of repression and exile."

Suggesting that Brutus's "poetry draws its haunting strength from his own suffering and from the unequal struggle of 25 million blacks, 'coloreds,' Indians and Orientals to throw off the repressive rule by the 4.5 million South African whites," Klose remarks that "there is no doubt in Brutus' mind of the power and relevance of his poetry to the struggle." Brutus's works are officially banned in South Africa. When, for example, his *Thoughts Abroad,* a collection of poems concerned with exile and alienation, was published under the pseudonym of John Bruin, it was immediately successful and was even taught in South African colleges; but when the government discovered that Brutus was the author, all copies were confiscated. The effectiveness of the South African government's censorship policies is evidenced by the degree to which Brutus's writing is known there. Colin Gardner, who thinks that "it seems likely that many well-read South Africans, even some of those with a distinct interest in South African poetry, are wholly or largely unacquainted with his writing," declares in *Research in African Literatures* that "Brutus as a writer exists, as far as the Pretoria government is concerned, as a vacuum, an absence; in the firmament of South African literature, such as it is, Brutus could be described as a black hole. But it is necessary to find him and read him, to talk and write about him, to pick up the light which in fact he does emit, because he is at his best as important as any other South African who has written poetry in English."

Deeming Brutus's poetry "the reaction of one who is in mental agony whether he is at home or abroad," R. N. Egudu suggests in Christopher Heywood's *Aspects of South African Literature* that "this agony is partly caused by harrassments, arrests, and imprisonment, and mainly by Brutus's concern for other suffering people." Brutus's first volume of poetry, *Sirens, Knuckles and Boots,* which earned him the Mbari Award, was published while he was incarcerated and includes a variety of verse, including love poems as well as poems of protest against South Africa's racial policies. Much of his subsequent poetry concerns imprisonment and exile. For example, *Letters to Martha and Other Poems from a South African Prison* was written under the guise of letters—the writing of which, unlike poetry, was not prohibited—and is composed of poems about his experiences as a political prisoner. His *A Simple Lust: Selected Poems Including "Sirens, Knuckles, Boots," "Letters to Martha," "Poems from Algiers," "Thoughts Abroad,"* represents "a collection of all Brutus' poetry relating to his experience of jail and exile," notes Paul Kameen in *Best Sellers.* Similarly, *Stubborn Hope: New Poems and Selections from "China Poems" and "Strains"* "contains several poems which deal directly with the traumatic period of his life when he was imprisoned on the island," states Jane Grant in *Index on Censorship.* Discussing the "interaction between the per-

sonal and political" in Brutus's poetry, Gardner points out that "the poet is aware that he has comrades in his political campaigns and struggles, but under intense government pressure, there is no real sense of mass movement. The fight for liberation will be a long one, and a sensitive participant cannot but feel rather isolated. This isolation is an important aspect of the poet's mode and mood."

Chikwenye Okonjo Ogunyemi thinks that although Brutus's writing is inspired by his imprisonment, it is "artistic rather than overtly propangandistic"; the critic observes in *Ariel* that "he writes to connect his inner life with the outside world and those who love him. . . . That need to connect with posterity, a reason for the enduring, is a genuine artistic feeling." Perceiving an early "inner conflict between Brutus, the activist against *apartheid,* and Brutus, the highly literate writer of difficult, complex and lyrical poetry," Grant suggests that "the months in solitary confinement on Robben Island seem to have led him to a radical reassessment of his role as poet." Moving toward a less complex poetry, "the trend culminates in the extreme brevity and economy of the *China Poems* (the title refers both to where they were written and to the delicate nature of the poems). . .," says Grant. "They are seldom more than a few lines long, and are influenced by the Japanese *haiku* and its Chinese ancestor, the *chueh chu.*" These poems, according to Hans Zell's *A New Reader's Guide to South African Literature,* evolved from Brutus's trip to the Republic of China, and were composed "in celebration of the people and the values he met there." Calling him "learned, passionate, skeptical," Gessler Moses Nkondo says in *World Literature Today* that "Brutus is a remarkable poet, one of the most distinguished South Africa has produced." Nkondo explains that "the lucidity and precision which he is at pains to develop in his work are qualities he admires from artistic conviction, as a humanist opposed both to romantic haze and conventional trends. But they also testify to a profound cultivation of spirit, a certain wholeness and harmony of nature, as they do too to a fine independence of literary fashion."

Influenced by the seventeenth-century metaphysical poets, Brutus employs traditional poetic forms and rich language in his work; Nkondo proposes that what "Brutus fastens on is a composite sensibility made up of the passionate subtleties and the intellectual sensuousness of the metaphysical poets and the masculine, ironic force of [John] Donne." Noting that Brutus assumes the persona of a troubadour throughout his poetry, Tanure Ojaide writes in *Ariel* that while it serves to unify his work, the choice of "the persona of the troubadour to express himself is particularly significant as the moving and fighting roles of the medieval errant, though romantic, tally with his struggle for justice in South Africa, a land he loves dearly as the knight his mistress. The movement contrasts with the stasis of despair and enacts the stubborn hope that despite the suffering, there shall be freedom and justice for those *now* unfree." And Gardner believes that "Brutus's best poetry has a resonance which both articulates and generalizes his specific themes; he has found forms and formulations which dramatize an important part of the agony of South Africa and of contemporary humanity."

Brutus "has traveled widely and written and testified extensively against the Afrikaner-run government's policies," remarks Klose. "In the world of activism, where talk can easily outweigh results, his is a record of achievement." For instance, Klose states that Brutus's voice against apartheid is largely responsible for South Africa's segregated sports teams having been "barred from most international competitions, including the Olympics since 1964.'' Egudu observes that in Brutus's ''intellectual protest without malice, in his mental agony over the apartheid situation in South Africa, in his concern for the sufferings of the others, and in his hope which has defied all despair—all of which he has portrayed through images and diction that are imbued with freshness and vision— Brutus proves himself a capable poet fully committed to his social responsibility.'' And according to Klose, Brutus maintains: ''You have to make it a two-front fight. You have to struggle inside South Africa to unprop the regime, and struggle in the United States—to challenge the U.S. role, and if possible, inhibit it. Cut off the money, the flow of arms, the flow of political and military support. You have to educate the American people. And that is what I think I'm doing.''

BIOGRAPHICAL/CRITICAL SOURCES:

BOOKS

Beier, Ulli, editor, *Introduction to African Literature,* Northwestern University Press, 1967.
Contemporary Literary Criticism, Volume 43, Gale, 1987.
Heywood, Christopher, editor, *Aspects of South African Literature,* Africana Publishing, 1976.
A History of Africa, Horizon Press, 1971.
Legum, Colin, editor, *The Bitter Choice,* World Publishing, 1968.
Pieterse, Cosmo, and Dennis Duerden, editors, *African Writers Talking,* Africana Publishing, 1972.
Zell, Hans M., and others, *A New Reader's Guide to African Literature,* 2nd revised and expanded edition, Holmes & Meier, 1983.

PERIODICALS

Ariel, October, 1982, January, 1986.
Best Sellers, October 1, 1973.
Index on Censorship, July/August, 1979.
Los Angeles Times, September 7, 1983.
New York Times, January 29, 1986.
Research in African Literatures, fall, 1984.
Washington Post, August 13, 1983, September 7, 1983.
World Literature Today, spring, 1979, autumn, 1979, winter, 1981.

—*Sketch by Sharon Malinowski*

*   *   *

BURTCHAELL, James Tunstead   1934-

PERSONAL: Born March 31, 1934, in Portland, Ore.; son of James Tunstead, Jr. (an executive) and Marion Margaret (Murphy) Burtchaell. *Education:* University of Notre Dame, A.B. (magna cum laude), 1956; Pontifical Gregorian University, Rome, Italy, S.T.B., 1958; Catholic University of America, S.T.L., 1960; Ecole Biblique et Archeologique Francaise de Jerusalem, graduate study, 1961-63; Pontifical Biblical Commission, Rome, S.S.B., 1961, S.S.L., 1964; Gonville and Caius College, Cambridge, Ph.D., 1966.

ADDRESSES: Home—141 Holy Cross Hall, University of Notre Dame, Notre Dame, Ind. 46556. *Office*—358 Decio Hall, University of Notre Dame, Notre Dame, Ind., 46556.

CAREER: Ordained Roman Catholic priest of Congregation of Holy Cross (C.S.C.), 1960; University of Notre Dame, Notre Dame, Ind., assistant professor, 1966-69, associate professor, 1969-75, professor of theology, 1975—, chairman of department, 1968-70, provost, fellow, and trustee, 1970-77. Cam-

bridge University, Gonville and Caius College, S.A. Cook Bye Fellow, 1965-66, St. Edmund's House, visiting fellow, 1965-66, senior Fulbright scholar, 1985-86; visiting fellow, Princeton University, 1980-81. Member of board of governors, Ave Maria Press, 1968-70; Danforth Foundation, associate, 1968-86, member of advisory council, 1970-74; chairman of constituting committee, Council on the Study of Religion, 1969-70; member of advisory screening committee in religion, Committee on International Exchange of Persons, 1970-73; member of commission of higher education, North Central Accrediting Association, 1972-75; National Endowment for the Humanities, panelist, 1975, member of national board of consultants, 1975-82; chairman of advisory board, Center for Constitutional Studies, 1977-79; member of advisory board, Our Sunday Visitor Institute, 1978-80; delegate, U.S. Roman Catholic-Presbyterian/Reformed Consultation, 1982-85; Council for the Retarded, member of protective services board, 1982-90, vice chairman, 1987—; center associate, Center on Religion and Society of the Rockford Institute, 1986—; member of JustLife education fund advisory board, 1988—. Member of board of directors, East Asia History of Science, Inc., 1980—.

MEMBER: American Academy of Religion (member of executive committee, 1969-74; vice president, 1969; president, 1970), Society for Values in Higher Education, Society for the Study of Egyptian Antiquities (honorary trustee), Associates for Religion and Intellectual Life, Catholic Commission on Intellectual and Cultural Affairs, Phi Beta Kappa, Phi Beta Delta.

AWARDS, HONORS: D.H.L. from St. Mary's College of California, 1974, Rose-Hulman Institute of Technology, 1976, and College of Mount St. Joseph, 1987; Christopher Book Award, 1984, for *Rachel Weeping, and Other Essays on Abortion.*

WRITINGS:

Catholic Theories of Biblical Inspiration since 1810, Cambridge University Press, 1969.
Philemon's Problem: The Daily Dilemma of the Christian, Life in Christ, 1973.
(Editor) *Marriage among Christians: A Curious Tradition,* Ave Maria Press, 1977.
(Editor) *Abortion Parley,* Andrews & McMeel, 1980.
Rachel Weeping, and Other Essays on Abortion, Andrews & McMeel, 1982.
For Better, for Worse: Sober Thoughts on Passionate Promises, Paulist Press, 1985.
Major Decisions: How to Pick Your Major in College, privately printed, 1986.
(Editor) *A Just War No Longer Exists: The Teaching and Trial of Don Lorenzo Milani,* University of Notre Dame Press, 1988.

CONTRIBUTOR

Cambridge Sermons in Christian Unity, Oldbourne, 1966.
Andrew Bauer, editor, *The Debate on Birth Control,* Hawthorne, 1969.
Peter Foote, John Hill, Laurence Kelly, John McCudden, and Theodore Stone, editors, *Church: Vatican II's Dogmatic Constitution on the Church,* Holt, 1969.
Willis W. Bartlett, editor, *Evolving Religious Careers,* Center for Applied Research in the Apostolate, 1970.
Paul T. Jersild and Dale A. Johnson, editors, *Moral Issues and Christian Response,* Holt, 1971.

Claude Welch, editor, *Religion in the Undergraduate Curriculum: An Analysis and Interpretation,* Association of American Colleges, 1972.

Ninian Smart, John Clayton, Steven Katz, and Patrick Sherry, editors, *Religious Thought in the Nineteenth Century,* Cambridge University Press, 1981.

The 1988 Catholic College and University Handbook, SMS Publications, 1987.

OTHER

Also author of tape cassettes, including "Bread and Salt: A Cassette Catechism," 1978. Contributor to *Ann Landers Encyclopedia A to Z,* 1978. Also contributor of book reviews and articles to *Commonweal, America, Christian Century,* and numerous other journals.

WORK IN PROGRESS: "Studies on the history of office in the earliest Christian Church."

SIDELIGHTS: Discussing his beliefs about the difference between sound and bad theology, James Tunstead Burtchaell says this in a *Commonweal* article: "We Christians . . . hold ourselves answerable to the more durable insights our ancestors in faith left us from their graced experience. But we think that we too have the Spirit, and that we never learn what the tradition has to teach us until we can see and say it sensibly shown in our own experience. Bad theology comes when we say in ancient words what ancients told, but cannot say it as something we relearned ourselves (at their cue)." Burtchaell concludes later in the article: "Sound theology must close the synapse between what ancients said to us and what we have seen for ourselves."

BIOGRAPHICAL/CRITICAL SOURCES:

PERIODICALS

Commonweal, January 30, 1981.
Los Angeles Times Book Review, September 19, 1982.

*   *   *

BUTTERICK, George F.   1942-

PERSONAL: Born October 7, 1942, in Yonkers, N.Y.; son of George W. (an electronic technician) and Kathleen (an account clerk; maiden name, Byrnes) Butterick; married Colette Marie Hetzel (an artist), June 19, 1965; children: George Adam, Aaron. *Education:* Manhattan College, B.A. (with honors), 1964; State University of New York at Buffalo, Ph.D., 1970.

ADDRESSES: Home—194 North St., Willimantic, Conn. 06226. *Office*—Literary Archives, University of Connecticut Library, Storrs, Conn. 06268.

CAREER: Wilson College, Chambersburg, Pa., instructor, 1968-69, assistant professor of English, 1969-70; University of Connecticut, Storrs, assistant professor, 1970-72, lecturer in English, 1972—, curator of Literary Archives, 1972—.

AWARDS, HONORS: Swedish Information Service Bicentennial Fund Grant for research in Sweden, 1985.

WRITINGS:

A Guide to the Maximus Poems of Charles Olson, University of California Press, 1978, revised edition, 1980.

Editing the Maximus Poems, University of Connecticut Library, 1983.
Editing the Postmodern Texts, Meckler, in press.

POETRY

The Norse, Institute of Further Studies, 1973.
Reading Genesis by the Light of a Comet, Ziesing Brothers, 1976.
Rune Power, Tin Man, 1983.
The Three-Percent Stranger, Zelot Press, 1986.
Repartee with the Mummy, Zelot Press, 1987.
Mummy Strands and Others, Am Here Books, 1987.
Collected Earlier Poems, Zelot Press, in press.

EDITOR

(With Albert Glover) *A Bibliography of Works by Charles Olson,* Phoenix Book Shop, 1967.
Charles Olson, *Poetry and Truth: The Beloit Lectures and Poems,* Four Seasons Foundation, 1970.
Olson, *Additional Prose,* Four Seasons Foundation, 1974.
(With Charles Boer) Olson, *The Maximus Poems, Volume Three,* Grossman, 1975.
Olson, *The Post Office,* Grey Fox Press, 1975.
Vincent Ferrini, *Selected Poems,* University of Connecticut Library, 1976.
Olson, *The Fiery Hunt and Other Plays,* Four Seasons Foundation, 1977.
Olson, *Muthologos: Collected Lectures and Interviews,* Four Seasons Foundation, 1978-79.
Charles Olson and Robert Creeley: The Complete Correspondence, five volumes, Black Sparrow Press, 1980.
(With Donald Allen) *The Postmoderns,* Grove Press, 1982.
Olson, *The Maximus Poems,* University of California Press, 1983.
The Collected Poems of Charles Olson, University of California Press, 1987.
A Nation of Nothing but Poetry, Black Sparrow Press, in press.

OTHER

Contributor of essays and reviews to numerous periodicals, including *American Literature, Chicago Review, Credences, Iowa Review, New England Quarterly,* and *Sagetrieb.* Co-editor of *Audit,* 1966-68; editor of *Olson: The Journal of the Charles Olson Archives,* 1974-78; contributing editor of *Magazine of Further Studies,* 1968-70, and *Athanor,* 1970-75.

WORK IN PROGRESS: Poems ("always the poem"); an edition of Olson's collected prose of his "witheld" or "auxiliary" *Maximus* poems; an Olson bibliography and a full biography of the poet.

AVOCATIONAL INTERESTS: Distance running.

BIOGRAPHICAL/CRITICAL SOURCES:

PERIODICALS

Los Angeles Times Book Review, May 10, 1981, September 4, 1983, July 7, 1985.
Times Literary Supplement, December 14, 1979.
Washington Post Book World, November 13, 1983.

C

CALIN, William (Compaine)   1936-

PERSONAL: Surname is pronounced *Kale*-in; born April 4, 1936, in Newington, Conn.; son of Jack and Nettie (Compaine) Calin; married Francoise Geffroy, January 5, 1971. *Education:* Studied in France, 1955-56; Yale University, B.A., 1957, Ph.D., 1960.

ADDRESSES: Office—Department of Romance Languages, University of Florida, Gainesville, Fla. 32611.

CAREER: Dartmouth College, Hanover, N.H., instructor, 1960-62, assistant professor of French, 1962-63; Stanford University, Stanford, Calif., assistant professor, 1964-65, associate professor, 1965-70, professor of French, 1970-73; University of Oregon, Eugene, professor of French, 1973-88, chairman of department of Romance languages, 1976-78; University of Florida, Gainesville, graduate research professor, 1988—. Visiting fellow, Clare Hall, Cambridge University, 1984-85; Arnold visiting professor, Whitman College, 1987—.

MEMBER: International Machaut Society (president), Modern Language Association of America, Societe Rencesvals.

AWARDS, HONORS: Guggenheim fellowship and American Council of Learned Societies grants, both 1963-64; Gilbert Chinard First Literary Prize, 1981; Fulbright award, 1982; Canada Federation in the Humanities grant, 1982; National Endowment for the Humanities grant, 1984-85; Fulbright senior research grant, 1988-89.

WRITINGS:

The Old French Epic of Revolt, Droz (Geneva), 1962.
(Editor with Michel Benamou) *Aux Portes du Poeme,* Macmillan, 1964.
The Epic Quest: Studies in Four Old French Chansons de Geste, Johns Hopkins Press, 1966.
(Editor) *La Chanson de Roland,* Appleton, 1968.
A Poet at the Fountain: Essays on the Narrative Verse of Guillaume de Machaut, University Press of Kentucky, 1974.
Crown, Cross and "Fleur-de-lis": An Essay on Pierre Le Moyne's Baroque Epic "Saint Louis," Stanford University Press, 1977.
A Muse for Heroes: Nine Centuries of the Epic in France, University of Toronto Press, 1983.

In Defense of French Poetry: An Essay in Reevaluation, Pennsylvania State University Press, 1987.

Contributor to journals.

WORK IN PROGRESS: A book on the French literary tradition and medieval English literature.

*   *   *

CARD, Orson Scott   1951-
(Brian Green)

PERSONAL: Born August 24, 1951, in Richland, Wash.; son of Willard Richards (a teacher) and Peggy Jane (a secretary and administrator; maiden name, Park) Card; married Kristine Allen, May 17, 1977; children: Michael Geoffrey, Emily Janice, Charles Benjamin. *Education:* Brigham Young University, B.A. (with distinction), 1975; University of Utah, M.A., 1981. *Politics:* Moderate Democrat. *Religion:* Church of Jesus Christ of Latter-day Saints (Mormon).

ADDRESSES: Home—546 Lindley Rd., Greensboro, N.C. 27410. *Agent*—Barbara Bova, 207 Sedgwick Rd., West Hartford, Conn. 06107.

CAREER: Volunteer Mormon missionary in Brazil, 1971-73; operated repertory theatre in Provo, Utah, 1974-75; Brigham Young University Press, Provo, editor, 1974-76; *Ensign,* Salt Lake City, Utah, assistant editor, 1976-78; free-lance writer and editor, 1978—. Senior editor, Compute! Books, Greensboro, N.C., 1983. Teacher at various universities and writers workshops. Local Democratic precinct election judge and Utah State Democratic Convention delegate.

AWARDS, HONORS: John W. Campbell Award for best new writer of 1977, World Science Fiction Convention, 1978; Hugo Award nominations, World Science Fiction Convention, 1978, 1979, 1980, for short stories, and 1986, for novelette, "Hatrack River"; Nebula Award nominations, Science Fiction Writers of America, 1979, 1980, for short stories; Utah State Institute of Fine Arts prize, 1980, for epic poem "Prentice Alvin and the No-Good Plow"; Nebula Award, 1985, and Hugo Award, 1986, both for novel *Ender's Game;* Nebula Award, 1986, and Hugo Award, 1987, both for novel *Speaker for the Dead;* World Fantasy Award, 1987, for novelette, "Hatrack River"; Hugo Award, and Locus Award nomination, both 1988, both for novella ''Eye for Eye''; Locus Award for best fantasy, Hugo Award nomination, and World Fantasy Award nomination, all 1988, all for novel *Seventh Son*.

WRITINGS:

SCIENCE FICTION/FANTASY

Capitol (collection), Ace Books, 1978.
Hot Sleep, Baronet, 1978.
A Planet Called Treason, St. Martin's, 1979, revised edition, Dell, 1980, published as *Treason*, St. Martin's, 1988.
Songmaster, Dial, 1980.
Unaccompanied Sonata and Other Stories, Dial, 1981.
(Editor) *Dragons of Darkness*, Ace Books, 1981.
Hart's Hope, Berkley Publishing, 1982.
The Worthing Chronicle, Ace Books, 1983.
(Editor) *Dragons of Light*, Ace Books, 1983.
Ender's Game (also see below), Tor Books, 1985.
Speaker for the Dead (also see below), Tor Books, 1986.
Ender's Game [and] *Speaker for the Dead*, Tor Books, 1987.
Wyrms, Arbor House, 1987.
(With others) *Free Lancers*, Baen Books, 1987.
Seventh Son (first novel in ''The Tales of Alvin Maker'' series), St. Martin's, 1987.
Red Prophet (second novel in ''The Tales of Alvin Maker'' series), Tor Books, 1988.
Prentice Alvin (third novel in ''The Tales of Alvin Maker'' series), Tor Books, 1989.
Folk of the Fringe (collection), Phantasia Press, 1989.

Contributor to numerous anthologies.

PLAYS

''The Apostate,'' produced in Provo, Utah, 1970.
''In Flight,'' produced in Provo, 1970.
''Across Five Summers,'' produced in Provo, 1971.
''Of Gideon,'' produced in Provo, 1971.
''Stone Tables,'' produced in Provo at Brigham Young University, 1973.
''A Christmas Carol'' (adapted from the story by Charles Dickens), produced in Provo, 1974.
''Father, Mother, Mother, and Mom,'' produced in Provo, 1974, published in *Sunstone*, 1978.
''Liberty Jail,'' produced in Provo, 1975.
(Under pseudonym Brian Green) ''Rag Mission,'' published in *Ensign*, July, 1977.

Also author of ''Fresh Courage Take,'' produced in 1978, ''Elders and Sisters'' (adapted from a work by Gladys Farmer), produced in 1979, and ''Wings'' (fragment), produced in 1982.

OTHER

Listen, Mom and Dad, Bookcraft, 1978.
Saintspeak: The Mormon Dictionary, Signature Books, 1981.
Ainge, Signature Books, 1982.
A Woman of Destiny (historical novel), Berkley Publishing, 1983, published as *Saints*, Tor Books, 1988.
Characters and Viewpoint, Writers Digest, 1988.

Also author of several hundred audio plays for Living Scriptures; co-author of animated videotapes. Author of regular review columns, ''You Got No Friends in This World,'' *Science Fiction Review*, 1979-86, ''Books to Look For,'' *Fantasy and Science Fiction*, 1987—, and ''Gameplay,'' *Compute!*, 1988—. Contributor of articles and reviews to periodicals, including *Washington Post Book World*, *Science Fiction Review*, and *Destinies*.

WORK IN PROGRESS: *Alvin Journeyman* and *Master Alvin*, Volumes IV and V of ''The Tales of Alvin Maker''; *Ender's Children*.

SIDELIGHTS: Since publishing the story that evolved into his award-winning novel *Ender's Game*, Orson Scott Card has become a prominent force in the science fiction and fantasy fields. In 1987, for example, Card became the first writer to win the genre's top awards, the Nebula and the Hugo, for consecutive novels in a continuing series. The first of these two, *Ender's Game*, concerns the training of Ender Wiggin, a six-year-old genius who is the Earth's only hope for victory over invading ''bugger'' aliens. While this plot appears to be standard science fiction fare, *New York Times Book Review* critic Gerald Jonas observes that ''Card has shaped this unpromising material into an affecting novel full of surprises that seem inevitable once they are explained.'' The difference, assert Jonas and other critics, is in the character of Ender Wiggin, who remains sympathetic despite his acts of violence. A *Kirkus Review* contributor, for example, while noting the plot's inherent weakness, admits that ''the long passages focusing on Ender are nearly always enthralling,'' concluding that *Ender's Game* ''is altogether a much more solid, mature, and persuasive effort'' than the author's previous work.

Other critics, however, believe that the character of Ender does not overcome the ''uninspired notions of Ender's training,'' as Michael Lassell describes in the *Los Angeles Times Book Review*. While Ender's character is ''likable,'' the critic remarks that he is ''utterly unbelievable as a child his age, genius or no.'' But *Analog Science Fiction/Science Fact* writer Tom Easton suggests that the reader ''reserve . . . skepticism of Ender's talent,'' for the novel ''succeeds because of its stress on the value of empathy. . . . The governmental agents who rule young Ender are as guilty of despicable acts, but they are saved by their ability to bleed for the souls they mangle.'' And Dan K. Moran, who calls *Ender's Game* ''the best novel I've read in a long time,'' adds in the *West Coast Review of Books* that ''Ender Wiggin is a unique creation. Orson Scott Card has created a character who deserves to be remembered with the likes of Huckleberry Finn. *Ender's Game* is *that* good.''

While *Ender's Game* garnered awards and popularity for Card, its sequel, *Speaker for the Dead*, ''is the most powerful work Card has produced,'' claims Michael R. Collings in *Fantasy Review*. ''*Speaker* not only completes *Ender's Game* but transcends it. . . . Read in conjunction with *Ender's Game*, *Speaker* demonstrates Card's mastery of character, plot, style, theme, and development.'' Ender Wiggin, now working as a ''Speaker for the Dead,'' travels the galaxy to interpret the lives of the deceased for their families and neighbors; as he travels, he also searches for a home for the eggs of the lone surviving ''hive queen'' of the race he destroyed as a child. When Ender is called to the colony planet of Lusitania, his visit coincides with the discovery of another intelligent race, re-opening the question of co-existence versus survival. ''[Card] has woven a constantly escalating storyline which deals with religion, alien/human viewpoints and perspectives on instinctual and cultural levels, the fate of three alien species . . . , and quite possibly the fate of mankind itself,'' describes *Science Fiction Review* editor Richard E. Geis. ''Like *Game*, *Speaker* deals with issues of evil and empathy, though not in so polarized a way,'' observes Easton in his review, concluding that ''less brash than *Ender's Game*, *Speaker for the Dead* may be a much better book.'' In addition, critics find an extra element of complexity in the ''Ender'' books; *Washington Post Book World* contributor Janrae Frank sees ''quasi-religious images and themes'' in the conclusions of both novels. Because Card combines these themes with traditional science fiction principles, Collings maintains that the novels ''succeed equally as straightforward SF adventure and as allegorical, analogical disquisitions on humanity, morality, salvation, and redemption.''

It is this symbolic, metaphorical aspect of Card's work that some critics feel distinguishes and intensifies his writing. ''It seemed that whenever Card drifted away from pure sf into the hazier realm of mythmaking, of allegory, he was far more successful,'' remarks Somtow Sucharitkul in the *Washington Post Book World,* ''for his gift lay not in the creation of vividly viable futures but in his ability to feel and transmit a timeless anguish.'' The critic explains that as Card has de-emphasized elaborate settings in his fiction, he has shown ''yet an ever-growing mastery of symbol, form and human emotional processes.'' In *Wyrms,* for example, a ''traditional'' quest adventure involving a deposed princess, ''there is nothing trite about this book, nothing swollen and contrived,'' asserts *Los Angeles Times Book Review* contributor Ingrid Rimland. ''[*Wyrms*] is many things at once: a parable, a heroic adventure, a philosophical treatise, a finely crafted masterpiece of stylistically honed paragraphs, [and] a careful and smart understatement on the rebellious theme that God might be evil and needs to be slain.''

Card continues using symbol and allegory in the ''Tales of Alvin Maker'' series; the first novel, *Seventh Son,* ''begins what may be a significant recasting in fantasy terms of the tall tale in America,'' describes *Washington Post Book World* reviewer John Clute. Set in a pioneer America where the British Restoration never happened, where the ''Crown Colonies'' exist alongside the states of Appalachia and New Sweden, and where folk magics such as hexes, dowsers, and torches exist, *Seventh Son* follows the childhood of Alvin Miller, who has enormous magical potential because of his birth as the seventh son of a seventh son. ''While this could easily have been another dull tale of the chosen child groomed to be the defender from evil,'' *Fantasy Review* contributor Martha Soukup believes that Card's use of folk magic and vernacular language, along with strongly realized characters, creates in *Seventh Son* ''more to care about here than an abstract magical battle.'' Collings similarly notes in the same issue that the novel continues Card's allegorical work, containing a re-working of the life of Joseph Smith, founder of the Mormon Church; nevertheless, comments the critic, Card depicts ''this community's people in such a masterly way that their allegorical functioning does not impede our involvement with and deep caring for them. *Seventh Son* is a moving novel.'' ''There is something deeply heart-wrenching about an America come true, even if it is only a dream, a fantasy novel,'' writes Clute; the critic concludes that ''the first volume of *The Tales of Alvin Maker* is sharp and clean and bracing.''

''Because we know it is a dream of an America we do not deserve to remember, Orson Scott Card's luminous alternate history of the early 19th century continues to chill as it soothes,'' Clute explains in a review of *Red Prophet,* the second volume of Alvin's story. The novel traces Alvin's kidnapping by renegade Reds employed by ''White Murderer'' William Henry Harrison, who wishes to precipitate a massacre of the Shaw-Nee tribe. Alvin is rescued by the Red warrior Ta-Kumsaw, however, and learns of Indian ways even as he attempts to prevent the conflict caused by his supposed capture and murder. While ''*Red Prophet* seems initially less ambitious'' than its predecessor, covering only one year of time, a *West Coast*

Review of Books contributor comments that ''in that year, Card creates episodes and images that stun with the power of their emotions.'' Sue Martin, however, believes that the setting is not enough to overcome the plot, which she describes in the *Los Angeles Times Book Review* as ''yet *another* tale of Dark versus Light.'' The critic states, however, that while Alvin ''seems almost Christlike'' in his ability to heal and bring people together, the allegory is drawn ''without the proselytizing.'' ''*Red Prophet* is the logical and emotional continuation of *Seventh Son,*'' maintains the *West Coast Review of Books* writer, ''surpassing the earlier volume in power and compassion, in cruelty and love.'' *Booklist* writer Sally Estes concurs: ''Harsher, bleaker, and more mystical than *Seventh Son,*'' Card's second volume displays his strong historical background, ''keen understanding of religious experience, and, most of all, his mastery of the art of storytelling.''

CA INTERVIEW

CA interviewed Orson Scott Card by telephone on June 17, 1988, while he was visiting his family in Utah.

CA: Early in your career you were writing plays and also working as an editor at Ensign *magazine in Salt Lake City. Did one job support the other?*

CARD: I began writing plays several years before I took the editing job. How to judge who is a professional playwright is a tricky question, because you don't make any money at it for years and years. But that was my primary occupation for quite a while. I was busy losing money hand over fist as an entrepreneur of plays while I was making a pathetic amount of money as an editor—the normal pattern.

CA: Did your experience as a playwright give you a well-honed sense of dramatic structure when you started writing fiction?

CARD: The overall structure of a story was still invisible to me at that time. I had a knack for dialogue, so that came easily. But the playwriting did teach me to keep it under control. Otherwise I would have my characters babble on—with great wit, of course, but the story didn't move. I had learned from the playwriting how to construct a scene, and in that sense I learned dramatic structure. I knew how to set it up so that a tension was created, and then how to heighten the tension and finally resolve it.

When I started writing fiction, I found that I was writing plays, only the stage directions were written out in past tense instead of present. It was hard to get over that and start discovering what fiction really was. And I very quickly learned what has since become probably the heart of my fiction style, which is a deep penetration into the point of view of the main character, so that it's almost indistinguishable from first-person narrative. I can drop into that character's thoughts and out again simply by changing person from third to first without ''he thought,'' ''she thought'' tags. I did that almost from the beginning, so that was probably the first breakthrough that I had in changing over from dramatic writing to prose writing. That's made it hard for me to go back to playwriting: all of the tricks I learned in playwriting for getting around the fact that you can't get inside a character's head are now very frustrating, because in fiction I've had the experience of being able to do that.

I really haven't stopped doing dramatic writing, even though I've stopped writing stage plays. Since 1978 I've been writing audio plays for Living Scriptures in Ogden, Utah, half-hour taped adaptations of stories from the Old Testament and the New Testament and Mormon scriptures, and from Mormon history and American history. I've done several hundred of those, so I'm still very much alert to and aware of what dramatic writing is and what it involves. That's a different medium entirely from stage plays because you can't show anything; it all has to be implied by sound. Recently I switched over to doing animated videotapes for the same outfit with Rick Rich, the animator who was in charge of "Black Cauldron" and a couple of other Disney films. That's the opposite art, in which the less said and the more shown by action, the better. I've had a lot of experience with different dramatic genres, but I still feel less adequate there than in fiction.

CA: You're best known as a writer of science fiction and fantasy. What was it about the genre that attracted you especially?

CARD: First of all, I knew the genre. While it was never even half my reading, I had read enough to be aware of the possibilities within it. It allowed the possibility of the kind of high drama that I'd been doing with religious plays for the Mormon market. If you're writing realistic contemporary fiction, you can't write about people doing big things unless you're writing about people in high office or something like that. Political thrillers didn't attract me, partly because I didn't know enough about how government worked at that time to deal with the kind of thing that a Robert Ludlum or a Tom Clancy writes now. In order to write the kind of intense romantic drama that I wanted to write, I needed the possibilities that science fiction and fantasy offered.

And then I had no idea whether I'd be successful or not at prose, so I wanted to try out with short stories, where I thought there was a smaller investment of time. I've since learned that writing a good short story takes about as much energy as writing a good novel; but starting out, everybody has the misconception that a short story is easy, that you whip one off, whereas a novel takes time. And I knew that science fiction had a living short-story market, not like the little literary magazines where you don't really get paid—and my impression is that most of them are read by people who are reading them only to find out how they can go about getting their own fiction published. I knew that I could break my heart trying to break into the *Atlantic* or *Harper's*. Science fiction had, and still has, a great opening in short stories for new writers, partly because the established writers move on to novels very quickly and then don't write that much short fiction anymore, and partly because short fiction is where science fiction happens; it's the cutting edge of science fiction. More than any other genre, science fiction thrives on new blood: we have to have fresh ideas and challenges to any kind of established view of the future. If we start with a consensus future, we're dead. New writers are the life blood of science fiction, and the result is that science fiction readers are not skeptical of them; they're eager to discover them. I found that that worked to my benefit. The first true science fiction story I wrote sold and received a lot of attention.

CA: Ender's Game, which got you the 1985 Nebula Award of the Science Fiction Writers of America and the 1986 Hugo, had in its earlier novelette version won you a John W. Campbell Award for Best New Writer of the Year (1977). How did the character and story of Ender Wiggin develop?

CARD: That was the very first science fiction story I did. Back when I was about sixteen years old, my brother's fiancee gave me Isaac Asimov's *Foundation* to read. That was my first exposure to Asimov; I had gone through a phase of not reading science fiction, and when she gave me that book I was really excited by it. I began to wonder if I could write science fiction. My impression then was that you had to have a neat scientific or futuristic idea. So I remember very clearly where I was at the time that I was daydreaming through a sort of futuristic idea, which was the battle room in *Ender's Game*. How would you train people for three-dimensional warfare, I wondered? What kind of war games would you train with? At that time I came up with just the battle room, the human beings playing those three-dimensional games.

That sat in the back of my mind as I worked through other story ideas over the next few years. All the time that I was a playwright, in fact, these science fictional ideas that never showed up in my plays were dancing around in the back of my mind. And while I was in Brazil on my Mormon missionary service I was writing stories that never made their way into *The Worthing Chronicle*, but were set in the same universe. Finally I sent one of those *Worthing Chronicle* stories off to Ben Bova, who was the editor of *Analog* at the time. It was a story that *I* knew was science fiction, but if you didn't know the setting, the overall picture surrounding it, it felt like fantasy. So Ben Bova sent it back to me saying, "I like the way you write; please send me more. But of course *Analog* only publishes science fiction, and your story 'The Tinker' is fantasy."

So I thought, Do I have any ideas that are *definitely* science fiction? And I thought back to this battle room idea. At that point I started developing it into a story that in some ways depended on some cliches, though I was naive enough in the field not to know that they were cliches. I wrote a seventy-five-page version and sent it to Ben Bova, and he asked me to cut it in half. I cut out five pages and made everything else more clearly pertinent and sent it back to him, and he published it. That story worked. It's still the most popular and the most reprinted of my stories, and I still have people tell me that they like it better than the novel—though I think maybe that's because they read the story first, so they came upon it with a great sense of surprise, and the novel can never do the same thing for them.

But I figured that was it for "Ender's Game." Years later, when I started working on the novel that became *Speaker for the Dead*, a breakthrough for me in that story was realizing that the main character should be Ender Wiggin. That made it a kind of sequel, although its plot had nothing to do with the original plot; it was just using a character. I signed a contract for that book and started trying to write it, and I realized that the first hundred pages were simply an effort to get people from the end of "Ender's Game" through a major moral transformation to start the actual story of *Speaker for the Dead*. It wasn't working, so I told the publisher, Tom Doherty, that I needed to do a novel version of "Ender's Game" just to set up *Speaker for the Dead*. That's the only reason "Ender's Game" ever became a novel. Once I got into transforming it, I did what I always do when I go from a short story version to a novel version of the same plot: I went back beyond the original story to start at its roots. It always happens that, by the time I do that, I've added so many characters and transformed so much of what was going on that not a word of the original story is usable. I give it a whole new set of meanings. And that's what I did with *Ender's Game*.

I was also, however, working out some theories that I had been developing. The novels that I had written in between, most recently *Hart's Hope* and *The Worthing Chronicle,* were extremely complex structurally, and challenging on a language level as well—especially *Hart's Hope.* They required more participation on the part of the reader in order to get what was going on and to hold it all in his head. I had been talking as a critic about how important it was to have absolute clarity and simplicity wherever possible, not putting any unnecessary barriers between the story and the reader. With *Ender's Game* I deliberately got rid of unnecessary barriers. For one thing, I cleaned up the language of the children, because I know that at least some readers find vulgar, crude language unpleasant. While there's still language that some people would consider vulgar and crude, you should have seen the first draft! I also presented the plot almost entirely in chronological order and used only a limited number of points of view. I kept it as clean and simple as possible without sacrificing any of what I thought of as the depth of the story and the moral transformations that I wanted to have clearly seen.

So I thought, and I still think, that what I did was to create a story that was at least as complex on a moral and subliminal level as anything I had done before, but on the surface was far cleaner and clearer and easier to receive. The fact that it's selling much better than any of my other work before it suggests that readers are finding it more accessible. It's now getting passed hand to hand.

The kinds of things happening in it are very similar on an emotional level to the things I had happening in *Worthing Chronicle* or *Hart's Hope,* but those didn't have that same kind of emotional impact. I think it's because I was interfering with the ability of readers to receive it, to respond to the story as I meant them to. I have since gone back occasionally to some structural complexity when I feel it's necessary; I'll never change what happens in a story to fit some literary theory. At the same time, I still strive for the kind of clarity I got in *Ender's Game,* because I think storytellers who expect to change the world have to talk to the people who live in the world.

CA: The story of Alvin Maker, which began in Seventh Son *and is now carried into the new book* Red Prophet, *is tied to this country's history and myth. It's more earth-bound than some of your earlier books.*

CARD: Yes. Each of the volumes in the "Tales of Alvin Maker" series is keyed to a major issue in American history. *Seventh Son* is tied to the issue of religion in America. *Red Prophet* has to do with our treatment of the Indians. *Prentice Alvin,* which I just finished, deals with the treatment of blacks under slavery. The following one, *Alvin Journeyman,* will probably deal mostly with the treatment of women, but it's also Alvin's *Wanderjahr.* Each one has a theme on that level that gets wrapped up by the end of the book, while other issues remain.

But there are a lot of different things going on in the "Tales of Alvin Maker." One of the most important is that it's a retelling of the spiritual life of Joseph Smith, the founder of Mormonism. Mormons who read these books almost instantly recognize elements from Joseph Smith's life. At the same time, I wanted to write them so that people who hadn't the faintest idea of what was going on in that respect would still be getting ninety percent of what's there. That's only one of the things I'm doing. It was the reason I started writing the books, but it's by no means the main purpose of writing them now.

This series began as an epic poem I was writing during graduate study at the University of Utah, when I was heavily influenced by Spenser and playing games with allegory. That epic poem won a prize from the Utah State Institute of Fine Arts, but I realized that there is very little future for an epic poem in terms of reaching an audience and telling a story to real people, so I converted it and expanded it and, I think, deepened and enriched it into something much longer and larger.

The main thing I'm working out now, more important even than the retelling of Joseph Smith's life, is trying to create a truly American fantasy. Most fantasy published in America today is dependent either on Tolkien or on the matter of the King Arthur legends. The variations seem to be in finding some other exotic locale that has its own mythology and using that mythology. It seemed to me that all of our fantasy writers were primarily devoting their attention to other people's myths and legends, and that that was rather a silly thing to do when no one was exploring our own. That's really *not* true in a sense: our contemporary myths and legends are being explored brilliantly by Stephen King, and the post-King generation of contemporary fantasists are creating a uniquely North American picture of the fantasy world. But I wanted to go into the American past; I wanted to write in the American vernacular. I'm trying to go back into the folk beliefs and practices, the gritty reality of frontier life.

I was deeply moved as a child by reading Conrad Richter's trilogy, *The Trees, The Fields,* and *The Town.* I think of it as one of the masterworks of American literature, and I think it's tragic that so much critical attention is spent on a showboater like Hemingway and so little on Conrad Richter. In a sense I'm revisiting the land that Richter gave me in his fiction, and discovering new things in it. There was always a hint of magic for me in Richter—not that he ever had anything magical happen, but it always seemed that more was going on under the surface than we could see; there was something else in control. That's what I try to hone and bring into greater focus in "The Tales of Alvin Maker." That's what fantasy is for, after all: to take the suggestion and make it concrete in the story so that you can clarify it, move the focus onto it. I'm doing the reality of the American past, trying to bring to life what the American people on the frontier *thought* the reality was; I'm including all the magic—the hexes, dowsing, and so forth—but really making it work, making it genuine within the story.

And I'm playing games with an alternate past, which is another way for me to focus what I think the truth of the American past is. For example, there was no Restoration in this past. The King is living in exile in Charleston, now called Camelot. In a way that was the truth of what was going on in the American South. People thought of themselves as the heirs of the Cavaliers; they had a manorial kind of life on their plantations, imitating a kind of noblesse oblige in their practice toward their slaves (called *servants*) and their neighbors and the cruelly-called "white trash" that lived around them. This wasn't true everywhere, but it was the attitude in the Tidewater country. So I'm telling something true about the American past even more clearly than it is told in the *real* American past.

Likewise, I'm having New England stay in the bondage of Puritanism much longer than it did in real life, and having the central colonies be a literal melting pot: New Sweden is ruled by Sweden right up to the end, and the Dutch colonies are still Dutch right up to the time that they join the American Compact sponsored by Benjamin Franklin. The country is an amalgam of many nations, including a state for the Iroquois. That's plain fantasy to incorporate the Indians peacefully into the United States, but it's what I think should have happened; here and there I write what I think we *should* have done. But by and large I'm trying to point out the different roles of those three primary regions of the original American colonies, and their different attitudes, in a way that is not as clear in American history.

CA: You also did the historical novel A Woman of Destiny, *which is concerned with Mormonism and centers on a woman who comes to America in the nineteenth century. Has that book fared well in the marketplace despite its bad treatment by the publisher?*

CARD: It fared quite well, but it was treated as a throwaway book. It's just been reprinted, by the way, under its true title, *Saints.* The story deals with a family in Industrial Revolution England who had joined the Mormon religion and crossed the Atlantic Ocean and come West. But I did not want to write a book where you had to decide whether you believed Mormonism was true or not. I wanted to write the story of people who *did* believe it, and once you accepted that they believed it, you would still care about what happened to them. So in the first three hundred pages of my original draft, I very carefully did not have one mention of Mormonism. There was no hint of any religion in particular; instead you saw the lives of these people. When Mormonism came in, it was something that fit what the characters were obviously already looking for. I didn't want the novel to be religious fiction: I wanted it to be fiction about religious people, which I think is a different thing entirely.

But an editor at Berkley recognized that along toward the last five hundred pages of the book I had this terrific love story between Joseph Smith and Dinah Kirkham, my main character. It's a disease among editors to try to make something look like something they've seen before. Mine said, "In a romance, you've got to have the two romantic figures introduced early. Joseph Smith seems to come out of nowhere. We need chapters about Joseph Smith from the beginning." Well, that was really a hideous idea because it would undo everything I was trying to do. I knew it, and I told her that. She said, "You can do it or you can give back the amount of the advance you've had so far." I know now that I could have said, "Sue me," and won—partly because she left the company four or five months later to get married; editors never take responsibility for their books the way authors do. But instead I bowed to what I thought was irresistible pressure and wrote what I thought of as the best possible dumb chapters I could.

I sent them in, hating it all the while, and then Berkley sent the book off to the book clubs. The book clubs took one look at it and said exactly what I had said to my editor: "This is a religious book. Religious books don't sell; that's not our market." And they sent it back. Berkley had been counting on the book club sales to make part of their money back, and the minute the books clubs rejected it, they thought, Oh, no. He's written a terrible book.

Well, at least I had permission now to get rid of all that religious stuff, so the text as it finally appeared was exactly what I wanted it to be. But now they were trying to find ways to "save the book." The only thing they could think of to do was to turn it into, not quite a bodice ripper, but definitely a women's historical novel. They put a really hideous cover on it; they changed the title to *Woman of Destiny,* which is a generic women's romance title. It was packaged so that any-

body who wanted what the cover promised would be disappointed, and anybody who wanted what the book *was* would never pick it up with that cover. Nevertheless, it sold decently.

In Utah, a few people who had been my friends for a long time saw the cover and were appalled, but picked it up anyway and read it; and a couple of key reviewers there said, "Hey, don't judge this book by its cover." So among the Mormon community the word began to spread, and that made the book sell very well in used copies—used paperbacks were going for fifteen or twenty dollars a copy, which is really unusual for a paperback. It became a cult favorite among Mormons. The new release, which came out about a month and a half ago, is one of the two or three top sellers in Utah, so it's having a decent life. It was picked up by critics in the Mormon community and some called it one of the foremost Mormon novels ever. That's what I meant it to be, so I was glad. But at the same time I wanted it to have a life outside of the Mormon community, and that's what I think Berkley cheated me out of.

CA: How well do you think fantasy is treated by reviewers?

CARD: It's treated very well by fantasy reviewers. Outside reviewers usually begin with an attitude of unhealthy contempt. They don't know the genre and they don't know what's going on in it, so they start with the assumption that it's escapist trash. No book can survive a hostile reading, no matter how great it is. I've seen Stephen King reviewed by people who are not fit to tie his literary shoelaces, sneering as if they were somehow better than him. These people are incapable of understanding that King is probably the foremost writer in America in the late twentieth century. If someone in the future wants to see what American life was like, what Americans cared about, what our stories were in the seventies and eighties, they'll read Stephen King; they'll never read John Updike. I expect Updike to be a forgotten footnote fifty or sixty years from now and King to be the person who is regarded as the dominant literary figure of the time. A lot of us feel that way.

There are a lot of other fantasy writers who are doing things that I think are far more interesting than just one more story about surrogate writer figures living in contemporary Manhattan or San Francisco or on some college campus somewhere. We treat the writers of that kind of fiction as badly as they treat us—as you can tell by my remarks!—and by and large we remain ignorant of each other, with the exception of a few of us who have tried to pass in both worlds. I have worked toward a doctorate in English literature, and I do know the language, at least; I just don't agree with the critical conclusions.

In another way, though, I'm glad that science fiction and fantasy have not been acceptable to literary reviewers, because I don't like what litterateurs are doing to their own fiction with their criticism. I think they're encouraging pre-killed fiction, fiction that fits a set of literary paradigms that, as far as I'm concerned, are inimical to good storytelling. The very fact that we fantasists have been despised and ignored has enabled us to create a far finer literature and a more useful literature than what's acceptable to the academic literary community. The academic literary establishment has taken American fiction by brute force, if nothing else, in the same direction as modern art and modern music: they've removed it from anything that volunteer audience members care about. The result is that they leave the volunteer audience to find its art and its stories from those who *will* give them something that untrained people can care about and understand; the academic literary establishment have consigned themselves, as far as I'm concerned, to the trash heap of history. The living art is the art that real people love. Any art that forsakes the volunteer audience, the untrained audience, is deciding to die. And any art that still attempts to reach real people and to have a real effect on the world will live. We're a living art; they're not.

CA: You've talked about the Alvin Maker books to come. In those books and on the broader scale, what do you consider the primary concerns of your fiction?

CARD: First of all, the issue that is probably most important in my fiction right now is what makes a community: what creates bonds among people, both at the micro level of the family and at the macro level of a city or a nation; what makes people surrender a part of themselves to become a greater whole. I also think that's closely tied with issues of good and evil. I don't like mindless struggles between good and evil, because I've never found pure good or pure evil in my life. But I do think there's a real struggle going on between good and evil in each person, and what I'm trying to do is bring a clear understanding of what that goodness is, that it consists in large measure of the willingness to sacrifice oneself for the good of others within a community.

I'm trying to show in the Alvin Maker series what it means to make something that wasn't there before, and to make it out of human beings rather than something else. In a way I'm playing games with anthropomorphizing the substances that Alvin Maker makes things out of, and I'm also having him makes things out of people, but not against their will—only by persuasion and what I think of as the legitimate *good* tools for creating communities.

BIOGRAPHICAL/CRITICAL SOURCES:

BOOKS

Contemporary Literary Criticism, Gale, Volume 44, 1987, Volume 47, 1988, Volume 50, 1988.

PERIODICALS

Analog Science Fiction/Science Fact, July, 1983, July, 1985, June, 1986, Mid-December, 1987.
Booklist, December 15, 1985, December 15, 1987.
Fantasy Review, April, 1986, June, 1987, July/August, 1987.
Kirkus Reviews, November 1, 1984.
Los Angeles Times Book Review, September 28, 1980, March 6, 1983, July 22, 1984, February 3, 1985, August 9, 1987, February 14, 1988.
New York Times Book Review, June 16, 1985, October 18, 1987.
Science Fiction and Fantasy Book Review, June, 1983.
Science Fiction Review, August, 1979, February, 1986.
Washington Post Book World, August 24, 1980, January 25, 1981, March 27, 1983, February 23, 1986, August 30, 1987, February 28, 1988.
West Coast Review of Books, March, 1984, July, 1986, Number 2, 1987, Number 4, 1988.

—*Sketch by Diane Telgen*
—*Interview by Jean W. Ross*

*   *   *

CARLSON, Ron(ald F.)   1947-

PERSONAL: Born September 15, 1947, in Logan, Utah; son of Edwin and Verna (Mertz) Carlson; married Georgia Elaine Craig (a teacher and editor), June 14, 1969; children: Nicholas, Colin. *Education:* University of Utah, B.A., 1970, M.A., 1972.

ADDRESSES: Home—2132 East Yale Dr., Tempe, Ariz. 85283. *Office*—Department of English, Arizona State University, Tempe, Ariz. 85287.

CAREER: Hotchkiss School, Lakeville, Conn., English teacher, 1971-81; full-time writer, 1981-86; Arizona State University, Tempe, writer in residence, 1986-87, assistant professor of creative writing, 1987—. Member of board, Writers at Work, Park City Writers Conference, 1985—; visiting artist and participant, Artist in the Schools programs for Utah, Idaho, and Alaska arts councils.

AWARDS, HONORS: Connecticut Commission on the Arts grant, 1978; Bread Loaf fellow, 1983; National Endowment for the Arts fellow, 1985.

WRITINGS:

Betrayed by F. Scott Fitzgerald (novel), Norton, 1977.
Truants (novel), Norton, 1981.
(Contributor) Shannon Ravenel, editor, *Best of the South 1986,* Algonquin, 1986.
(Contributor) George Murphy, editor, *Editor's Choice III,* Windstone, 1986.
(Contributor) Robert Shapard, editor, *Sudden Fiction,* Peregrine Smith, 1986.
(Contributor) Ann Beattie, editor, *Best American Short Stories 1987,* Houghton, 1987.
''The Tablecloth of Turin'' (one-act play), produced Off-Off Broadway at Manhattan Punch Line, January, 1987.
''Bigfoot Stole My Wife'' (one-act play), produced Off-Off Broadway at Manhattan Punch Line, May 30, 1987.
The News of the World (short stories), Norton, 1987.

WORK IN PROGRESS: A novel, *A Thousand People Later.*

SIDELIGHTS: Although Ron Carlson's fiction has ranged from a coming-of-age novel to stories dealing with families, all of his work is marked by witty observations that range from reflective to humorous. For example, *Betrayed by F. Scott Fitzgerald,* the story of a young graduate student's self-discovery, ''is written in a serio-comic vein, flecked with apt observations, often very funny, though more successful on the comic than it is on the serio side,'' observes Richard R. Lingeman in the *New York Times.* In *Truants,* his second novel, Carlson develops the theme of how ''most families, and their surrogates, wretchedly handle the business of nurturing and succoring,'' comments *New York Times Book Review* contributor Barry Yourgrau. Yet Carlson ''presents all of this in an affecting manner, with a very decent heart and a tart tongue,'' adds the critic. ''He practices a kind of wit that is at once tender, canny and vivid, capable of burnishing a passing moment with a quick touch.''

Like *Truants,* Carlson's story collection *The News of the World* also deals with family relations; ''the subject is domestic life, whose secrets [Carlson] tracks like a hunter, flushing them out with paranoid intensity,'' describes Nancy Forbes in the *New York Times Book Review. Washington Post Book World* contributor Alida Becker similarly remarks that the collection is ''an exuberant, wise and wonderfully inventive evocation of the kinds of love and longing that never really go out of style, no matter how much they're threatened by sentimentality on the one hand and cynicism on the other.'' Despite this opportunity for over-emotional treatment of "family" subjects, Carlson is "a writer who has acquired the technique to depict such values and situations with absolute integrity," asserts Alan Cheuse in Chicago *Tribune Books*. Richard Eder of the *Los Angeles Times Book Review* also sees a tendency toward "an outpouring instead of an evaporation of spirit," in Carlson's work, even though the outcomes of some stories are discouraging. The critic elaborates: "Carlson wants to find a design in things, even though this goes against the spirit if not the evidence of the times. Yet in his best stories, he does find it. And he finds it by a kind of magic, by a *credo quia absurdum* in which the will to believe is suddenly snatched up and transfigured." When this occurs, concludes Eder, "we experience a vision touched by wildness sometimes, by audacity sometimes, and sometimes by the sheer pleasure of inventiveness." It is this "blend of tragicomedy, sheer optimism, sharp perception, and almost manic energy that makes Carlson's work so distinctive—and so appealing," remarks Becker. Carlson is "a meat-and-potatoes writer," adds Becker, "a man who'll entertain you even as he's tricking you into swallowing that extra spoonful of understanding. And he'll never ever let you go away hungry."

Carlson told *CA*: "Just this, I write from my personal experience, whether I have had them or not. My writing, tenor and approach, changed after the arrival of my two sons. Many of my characters grew up, which was a relief, and I found myself suddenly doing a lot more work. Also, I took a job at Arizona State University, which was good in the way regular employment is good and bad exactly the same way. Right now I have several projects lined up and am quite optimistic about the future. My boys are [young]. Optimism seems the natural choice."

BIOGRAPHICAL/CRITICAL SOURCES:

PERIODICALS

Los Angeles Times Book Review, February 1, 1987.
New York Times, July 14, 1977, June 10, 1987.
New York Times Book Review, February 15, 1981, January 4, 1987.
Times Literary Supplement, March 26, 1982.
Tribune Books (Chicago), February 15, 1987.
Washington Post Book World, April 5, 1987.

*   *   *

CARPELAN, Bo (Gustaf Bertelsson) 1926-

PERSONAL: Surname is pronounced *Car*-pel-an; born October 25, 1926, in Helsinki, Finland; son of Bertel Gustaf (an engineer) and Ebba (Lindahl) Carpelan; married Barbro Eriksson (a reservations clerk for Finnair), April 13, 1954; children: Anders, Johanna. *Education:* University of Helsinki, Ph.D., 1960.

ADDRESSES: Home—Nyckelpigvaagen 2B, Tapiola, Finland.

CAREER: Writer. City Library, Helsinki, Finland, assistant chief librarian, 1963-80, professor of arts, 1980—.

MEMBER: PEN, Finnish-Swedish Authors Society.

AWARDS, HONORS: Finnish State Prize and Nils Holgersson Prize, 1969, for *Baagen;* Nordic Councils Prize, 1977, for *I de moerka rummen, i de ljusa;* Pro Finlandia Medal, 1980.

WRITINGS:

POETRY

Som en dunkel vaerme, Holger Schildt (Helsinki, Finland), 1946.
Du moerka oeverlevande, Bonnier (Stockholm, Sweden), 1948.
Variationer, Holger Schildt, 1950.
Minus sju, Bonnier, 1952.
Objekt foer ord, Bonnier, 1954.
Landskapets foervandlingar, Holger Schildt, 1957.
(Translator into Swedish with others) Eino S. Repo and Nils B. Stormbom, compilers, *Ny finsk lyrik* (anthology), Holger Schildt, 1960.
Den svala dagen, Holger Schildt, 1961.
Sjuttiotre dikter, Bonnier, 1966.
(Compiler) *Findlandssvenska lyrikboken* (anthology), Forum (Stockholm), 1967.
Gaarden, Holger Schildt, 1969.
Kaellan, Holger Schildt, 1973.
I de moerka rummen, i de ljusa, Holger Schildt, 1976.
Dihter fraen trettio aer (selected poems), Holger Schildt, 1980.
Dagen vaender, Holger Schildt, 1983.
(Compiler) *Modern finsk lyrik* (anthology), Holger Schildt, 1984.
Marginalia, Holger Schildt, 1984.
Room without Walls (selected poems), translated by Anne Born, Forest Books, 1987.

OTHER

Anders paa oen (juvenile), Bonnier, 1959.
(Contributor) *Jag lever i republiken Finland* (essays), Soederstroem (Helsinki), 1961.
Anders i stan (juvenile), Bonnier, 1962.
(With others) *Aaret i norden* (nonfiction), Bonnier, 1962.
Baagen: Beraettelsen om en sommar som var annorlunda (young adult), Bonnier, 1968, translation by Sheila La Farge published as *Bow Island: The Story of a Summer That Was Different*, Delacorte, 1972 (published in England as *The Wide Wings of Summer*, Heinemann, 1972).
Roesterna i den sena timmen (novel), Holger Schildt, 1971, translation published as *Voices at a Late Hour* (also see below), University of Georgia Press, 1988.
"Paluu nuoruuteen" (play), first produced in Helsinki at Kansallisteatteri, 1971.
Paradiset: Beraettelsen om Marvins och Johans vaenskap (young adult), Bonnier, 1973, translation by La Farge published as *Dolphins in the City*, Delacorte, 1976.
Din gestalt bakom doerren: En beraettelse (novel), Holger Schildt, 1975.
Vandrande skugga: En smaestadsberaettelse (novel), Holger Schildt, 1977.
Jag minns att jag droemde (short stories), Holger Schildt, 1979.
Julius Blom (juvenile), Bonnier, 1982.
Axel (also see below; novel), Holger Schildt, 1986.

A translation of *Axel* was published by Carcanet Press in 1989. Also author of works for television, theatre, and radio, including radio play, "Voices at a Late Hour," produced by Canadian Broadcasting Corp. (CBC-Radio).

BIOGRAPHICAL/CRITICAL SOURCES:

PERIODICALS

Swedish Book Review, May, 1984.

CARRIS, Joan Davenport 1938-

PERSONAL: Born August 18, 1938, in Toledo, Ohio; daughter of Roy (a sales manager) and Elfrid (an artist; maiden name, Nichols) Davenport; married Barr Tupper Carris (in data processing), December 28, 1960; children: Mindy, Leigh Ann, Bradley. *Education:* Iowa State University, B.S., 1960; graduate study at Duke University, 1970-71. *Politics:* "Greek 'Golden Mean' group." *Religion:* Protestant.

ADDRESSES: Home and office—Box 231, 48 Princeton Ave., Rocky Hill, N.J. 08553. *Agent*—Dorothy Markinko, McIntosh & Otis, Inc., 310 Madison Ave., New York, N.Y. 10017.

CAREER: High school English teacher in Nevada, Iowa, 1960-61; high school teacher of French, speech, and English in Des Moines, Iowa, 1963-65; private English tutor in Princeton, N.J., 1974—; author, 1977—. Member, New Jersey Council for Children's Literature.

MEMBER: National League of American Pen Women (president of Princeton, N.J., branch, 1980-84), Society of Children's Book Writers, Rocky Hill Community Group (member of executive board, 1974-78).

AWARDS, HONORS: Outstanding Science Book of 1984, *Science and Children* magazine, for *Pets, Vets and Marty Howard; When the Boys Ran the House* won an Iowa Children's Choice Award, Iowa Educational Media Association, 1984, a Tennessee Readers Award, 1985, and a Young Hoosier Book Award, Indiana Media Educators, 1986; New York Readers Award, Ethical Culture School, 1985, for *Witch-Cat.*

WRITINGS:

JUVENILES

The Revolt of 10-X (Junior Literary Guild selection), Harcourt, 1980.
When the Boys Ran the House, Harper, 1982.
Pets, Vets, and Marty Howard (sequel to *When the Boys Ran the House;* Junior Literary Guild selection), illustrations by Carol Newsom, Harper, 1984.
Witch-Cat (fantasy), illustrations by Beth Peck, Harper, 1984.
Rusty Timmons' First Million, illustrations by Kim Mulkey, Harper, 1985.
Hedgehogs in the Closet (sequel to *Pets, Vets, and Marty Howard*), Harper, 1988.

OTHER

(With Michael R. Crystal) *SAT Success: Peterson's Guide to English and Math Skills for College Entrance Examinations* (study guide), Peterson's Guides, 1982, revised edition with William R. McQuade, 1987.
Peterson's Success with Words, Peterson's Guides, 1987.

Author of "Tremendous Trifles," a humor column in the *Princeton Spectrum* and the *Trenton Times,* 1977-81. Contributor to magazines, including *Better Homes and Gardens, Think Magazine,* and to newspapers.

WORK IN PROGRESS: Moose Johnson and the Good Bad Cat; Personal Record, a young adult novel; two books for younger readers.

SIDELIGHTS: Joan Carris told *CA:* "I discovered the vast number of things I couldn't do pretty early in life. I couldn't do a handstand, jump rope past 'pepper,' skate without bloodying my entire body, or dance. I thought I might have to take my mother to college with me so that she could continue doing my hair—a feat I'd never managed alone.

"Just as I was about to declare myself a washout, I discovered that I could understand literature, really understand it. I could diagram sentences and spell—of all things. Moreover, I could write an analytical essay in English class, and some God-sent professor would read it aloud, or even publish it in a literary magazine. What a relief. Even my French was passable, and in a feeble way I can still communicate and read that sonorous language descended from Latin, my all-time favorite.

"Now that I am older, I am still involved with language, and my love for it grows, even though it *is* tricky to work those old spelling medals into a cocktail-party conversation.

"My impetus for writing was the glut of English teachers in the field at the time I wanted to return to teaching. There was no place for me—I'd been gone ten long years (whomping up three children) and it was too long. In a snit, I plunked my typewriter on the dining room table and said I'd try my hand at the only other possibility: education through writing for young people. But I didn't want to lure people to reading in the traditional way. I wanted to do it through humor, with as much warmth as I could transfer to paper, with that always-difficult goal of making readers laugh and say 'ah, yes' at the same time.

"Trying to teach young people to love and emulate good English is behind everything I do. For that reason I began teaching Scholastic Aptitude Test (SAT) preparation classes. In class we discuss old myths, the fascinating stories behind words, the power words have to take us anywhere we want to go. Out of this class has grown a book. I have a hunch it will be much like a house I would build—full of faults that get discovered only after I take possession.

"Writing children's books is my delight. If I can create even one character who truly comes to life, I'll feel immense satisfaction. And there will never be enough time for all the stories I want to tell about the kids who are like my kids, like the ones next door, like me when I was a kid. It is the hardest work I have ever done, the loneliest, the least rewarding financially, and the most frustrating.

"I wouldn't change it for anything."

MEDIA ADAPTATIONS: Witch-Cat was made into a Columbia Broadcasting System (CBS-TV) Story Hour Special in 1985.

AVOCATIONAL INTERESTS: Walking, playing tennis and bridge.

*   *   *

CARROLL, Christina
See HENDERSON, M(arilyn) R(uth)

*   *   *

CARTER, Nick
See HENDERSON, M(arilyn) R(uth) and STRATEMEYER, Edward L.

*   *   *

CARVAJAL, Ricardo
See MENESES, Enrique

*   *   *

CASE, Patricia J(une) 1952-

PERSONAL: Born July 24, 1952, in Hartford, Conn.; daughter of Howard C. (an automobile mechanic) and Virginia J. Case. *Education:* University of Connecticut, B.A., 1975; Southern Connecticut State College, M.L.S., 1981. *Politics:* None. *Religion:* None.

ADDRESSES: Home—Santa Barbara, Calif. *Office*—SourceNet, P.O. Box 6767, Santa Barbara, Calif. 93111.

CAREER: Long Island University, Brookville, N.Y., library assistant at B. Davis Schwartz Library, 1975-76; University of Connecticut, Storrs, special collections assistant, 1976-81, editor of *Harvest*, 1979-82; Temple University, Philadelphia, Pa., curator of Contemporary Culture Collection, 1982-84; free-lance indexer and editor, 1985—. Coordinator of Social Responsibilities Round Table's task force on alternatives in print, 1981-83.

MEMBER: American Library Association, Association of College and Research Libraries, American Society of Indexers.

WRITINGS:

(Editor with Elliott Shore and Laura Daly) *Alternative Papers: Selections from the Alternative Press, 1979-1980,* Temple University Press, 1982.
(Contributor) Shore and James P. Danky, editors, *Alternative Materials in Libraries,* Scarecrow, 1982.
(Editor) *Alternative Press Annual 1983-86,* Temple University Press, 1984-87.
(Editor with Tim Ryan) *Whole Again Resource Guide 1986/ 87,* SourceNet, 1986.

Compiler of "The Not in the New York Times Bibliography Series," Library, University of Connecticut, 1979-81, and "Newsworthy," Library, Temple University, 1983-84. Contributing editor of *New Pages: News and Reviews of the Progressive Book Trade,* 1979-84.

WORK IN PROGRESS: An index to the talks and writings of Jiddhu Krishnamurti.

BIOGRAPHICAL/CRITICAL SOURCES:

PERIODICALS

Voice Literary Supplement, February, 1983.

*   *   *

CAVANNA, Betty
   See HARRISON, Elizabeth Cavanna

*   *   *

CAVANNA, Elizabeth Allen
   See HARRISON, Elizabeth Cavanna

*   *   *

CAVERHILL, Nicholas
   See KIRK-GREENE, Anthony (Hamilton Millard)

*   *   *

CHADWICK, Lester
   [Collective pseudonym]

WRITINGS:

"BASEBALL JOE" SERIES

Baseball Joe of the Silver Stars; or, The Rivals of Riverside, Cupples & Leon, 1912.

. . . *on the School Nine; or, Pitching for the Blue Banner,* Cupples & Leon, 1912.
. . . *at Yale; or, Pitching for the College Championship,* Cupples & Leon, 1913.
. . . *in the Central League; or, Making Good as a Professional Pitcher,* Cupples & Leon, 1914.
. . . *in the Big League; or, A Young Pitcher's Hardest Struggles,* Cupples & Leon, 1915.
. . . *on the Giants; or, Making Good as a Twirler in the Metropolis,* Cupples & Leon, 1916.
. . . *in the World Series; or, Pitching for the Championship,* Cupples & Leon, 1917.
. . . *around the World; or, Pitching on a Grand Tour,* Cupples & Leon, 1918.
. . ., *Home Run King; or, The Greatest Pitcher and Batter on Record,* Cupples & Leon, 1922.
. . . *Saving the League; or, Breaking up a Great Conspiracy,* Cupples & Leon, 1923.
. . ., *Captain of the Team; or, Bitter Struggles on the Diamond,* Cupples & Leon, 1924.
. . ., *Champion of the League; or, The Record That Was Worth While,* Cupples & Leon, 1925.
. . ., *Club Owner; or, Putting the Home Town on the Map,* Cupples & Leon, 1926.
. . ., *Pitching Wizard; or, Triumphs on and off the Diamond,* Cupples & Leon, 1928.

"COLLEGE SPORTS" SERIES

The Rival Pitchers: A Story of College Baseball, Cupples & Leon, 1910.
A Quarterback's Pluck: A Story of College Football, Cupples & Leon, 1910.
Batting to Win: A Story of College Baseball, Cupples & Leon, 1911.
The Winning Touchdown: A Story of College Football, Cupples & Leon, 1911.
For the Honor of Randall: A Story of College Athletics, Cupples & Leon, 1912.
The Eight-Oared Victors: A Story of College Water Sports, Cupples & Leon, 1913.

SIDELIGHTS: Joe Matson, best known as "Baseball Joe," was the most popular sports figure featured in the books written under this pseudonym. The fourteen volumes in this series, according to Arthur Prager in *Rascals at Large; or, The Clue in the Old Nostalgia,* chronicled Joe's rise "up the Stratemeyer ladder from sand-lot ball to the New York Giants and on to immortality breaking every extant record on the way." Joe ended his career as captain of the Giants, leading the National League in both pitching and hitting, and retired to his hometown of Riverside to manage a semi-professional ball club of his own. Publisher's advertisements sometimes carried the notice that "Mr. Chadwick has played on the diamond and on the gridiron himself."

Howard Garis and Edward Stratemeyer both used this pseudonym to produce sports stories. For more information see the entries in this volume for Harriet S. Adams, Howard R. Garis, Edward L. Stratemeyer, and Andrew E. Svenson.

BIOGRAPHICAL/CRITICAL SOURCES:

BOOKS

Garis, Roger, *My Father Was Uncle Wiggily,* McGraw-Hill, 1966.
Johnson, Deidre, editor and compiler, *Stratemeyer Pseudonyms and Series Books: An Annotated Checklist of Stra-*

temeyer and Stratemeyer Syndicate Publications*, Greenwood Press, 1982.

Prager, Arthur, *Rascals at Large; or, The Clue in the Old Nostalgia*, Doubleday, 1971.

PERIODICALS

Sports Illustrated, April 23, 1962.

* * *

CHAMPLIN, John Michael 1937-
(Tim Champlin)

PERSONAL: Born October 11, 1937, in Fargo, N.D.; son of John B. (a veterinarian) and Elizabeth I. (a teacher; maiden name, Hushaw) Champlin; married Ellen Hosey (an artist), October 26, 1967; children: Christopher, Kenneth, Liz. *Education:* Middle Tennessee State College (now University), B.S., 1960; George Peabody College for Teachers, M.A., 1964. *Politics:* "Independent, but mostly Democrat." *Religion:* Roman Catholic.

ADDRESSES: Home—2926 Leatherwood, Nashville, Tenn. 37214. *Office*—Regional Office, Veterans Administration, 110 Ninth Ave. S., Nashville, Tenn. 37203.

CAREER: U.S. Department of the Interior, Washington, D.C., recreation resource specialist in Ann Arbor, Mich., 1967-68; Stewart Air Force Base, Smyrna, Tenn., civilian youth director, 1968-70; Veterans Administration, Nashville, Tenn., veterans' benefits counselor, 1970—. *Military service:* U.S. Naval Reserve, radar operator, 1955-63.

MEMBER: Western Writers of America (associate member).

AWARDS, HONORS: Citation from Catholic Press Association, 1978, for article "The Irish Travelers: Always on the Go, But Seldom Changing."

WRITINGS: Under name Tim Champlin

WESTERN NOVELS

Summer of the Sioux, Ballantine, 1982.
Dakota Gold, Ballantine, 1982.
Staghorn, Ballantine, 1984.
Shadow Catcher, Ballantine, 1985.
Great Timber Race, Ballantine, 1986.
Iron Horse, Ballantine, 1987.
Cult Lightning, Ballantine, 1989.

OTHER

Contributor of stories and articles to magazines, including *Bay and Delta Yachtsman, All Outdoors, Encounter, Seek, Great West*, and *Gracious Living*.

WORK IN PROGRESS: King of the Highbinders; three western novels.

SIDELIGHTS: John Michael Champlin, better known as Tim Champlin, told *CA:* "I have wanted to write ever since I was a little boy. At the age of twelve, I attempted to write a mystery similar to the 'Hardy Boys' books. I quit about two hundred handwritten pages into it, when I got my heroes into such a jam that I couldn't get them out.

"I started writing for publication in 1970, and had some success. I grew up in North Dakota, Nebraska, Missouri, and Arizona, and loved western history. In 1977 I decided to attempt a western historical novel. *Summer of the Sioux* was the result.

"The eight western novels I have written and the three I have in the planning stages are all set in the period between 1876 and 1890. From Indian campaigns to gold mining to riverboat trade to lumbering, I am attempting to portray aspects of frontier America as they really existed. In researching these things, I try to make my books more adventurous than violent. Certainly there was violence on the frontier, but it wasn't always the six-gun violence we have come to expect in western novels. There was the violence of the blizzard, of the plagues of grasshoppers, of prairie fires, and of epidemics of cholera. There were stampedes and mine cave-ins, accidental drownings, and broken bones from breaking horses.

"I see the American frontier west primarily as a huge, ever-changing block of space and time in which an individual had more freedom than the average person has today. True, it was a freedom to fail as well as to succeed, but the opportunities were there. A person then was not crushed by the burdens of personal income tax, a thirty-year mortgage, and the worry of trespassing on someone else's property if he stepped off his own. For the most part, the population was widely-spaced and transient. It was an era of building, of boom and bust and boom again. The resources and the future seemed unlimited. For those brave, and sometimes desperate, souls who ventured west looking for a better life, it must have been an exciting time to be alive. If I can capture even a little of this on paper for current readers I will be satisfied."

AVOCATIONAL INTERESTS: Travel, sailing, tennis, coin collecting.

* * *

CHAMPLIN, Tim
See CHAMPLIN, John Michael

* * *

CHANCE, Stephen
See TURNER, Philip (William)

* * *

CHAPMAN, Allen
[Collective pseudonym]

WRITINGS:

Bound to Rise; or, The Young Florists of Spring Hill [and] *Walter Loring's Career* (*Bound to Rise* originally serialized in *Bright Days*, 1896, under title "The Young Florists of Spring Hill; or, The New Heliotrope" by Albert Lee Ford; *Walter Loring's Career* originally serialized in *Bright Days*, 1896, under title "For Name and Fame; or, Walter Loring's Strange Quest"), Mershon, 1899.

"BOYS OF BUSINESS" SERIES

The Young Express Agent; or, Bart Stirling's Road to Success (also see below), Cupples & Leon, 1906, later published as part of the "Allen Chapman" series under title *Bart Stirling's Road to Success; or, The Young Express Agent* (also see below) by Goldsmith, and as part of the "Success" series under title *The Young Express Agent* by Donohue.

Two Boy Publishers; or, From Typecase to Editor's Chair (also see below), Cupples & Leon, 1906, later published as part of the "Allen Chapman" series under title *Work-*

ing Hard to Win; or, Adventures of Two Boy Publishers (also see below) by Goldsmith, and as part of the "Success" series under title *Two Boy Publishers* by Donohue.

Mail Order Frank; or, A Smart Boy and His Chances (also see below), Cupples & Leon, 1907, later published as part of the "Allen Chapman" series under title *Bound to Succeed; or, Mail-Order Frank's Chances* (also see below) by Goldsmith.

A Business Boy; or, Winning Success (also see below), Cupples & Leon, 1908, later published as part of the "Allen Chapman" series under title *The Young Storekeeper; or, A Business Boy's Pluck* (also see below) by Goldsmith, and as part of the "Success" series under title *A Business Boy's Pluck* by Donohue.

"BOYS OF PLUCK" SERIES

The Young Express Agent; or, Bart Stirling's Road to Success, Cupples & Leon, 1906.

Two Boy Publishers; or, From Typecase to Editor's Chair, Cupples & Leon, 1906.

Mail Order Frank; or, A Smart Boy and His Chances, Cupples & Leon, 1907.

A Business Boy's Pluck; or, Winning Success, Cupples & Leon, 1908.

The Young Land Agent; or, The Secret of the Borden Estate, Cupples & Leon, 1911, later published as part of the "Allen Chapman" series under title *Nat Borden's Find; or, The Young Land Agent* (also see below) by Goldsmith.

"BOY'S POCKET LIBRARY" SERIES

The Heroes of the School; or, The Darewell Chums through Thick and Thin (originally published as *The Darewell Chums; or, The Heroes of the School;* also see below), Cupples & Leon, 1917.

Ned Wilding's Disappearance; or, The Darewell Chums in the City (originally published as *The Darewell Chums in the City; or, The Disappearance of Nat Wilding;* also see below), Cupples & Leon, 1917.

Frank Roscoe's Secret; or, The Darewell Chums in the Woods (originally published as *The Darewell Chums in the Woods; or, Frank Roscoe's Secret;* also see below), Cupples & Leon, 1917.

Fenn Masterson's Discovery; or, The Darewell Chums on a Cruise (originally published as *The Darewell Chums on a Cruise; or, Fenn Masterson's Odd Discovery;* also see below), Cupples & Leon, 1917.

Bart Keene's Hunting Days; or, The Darewell Chums in a Winter Camp (originally published as *The Darewell Chums in a Winter Camp; or, Bart Keene's Best Shot;* also see below), Cupples & Leon, 1917.

Bart Stirling's Road to Success; or, The Young Express Agent, Cupples & Leon, 1917.

Working Hard to Win; or, Adventures of Two Boy Publishers, Cupples & Leon, 1917.

Bound to Succeed; or, Mail-Order Frank's Chances, Cupples & Leon, 1917.

The Young Storekeeper; or, A Business Boy's Pluck, Cupples & Leon, 1917.

Nat Borden's Find; or, The Young Land Agent, Cupples & Leon, 1917.

"DAREWELL CHUMS" SERIES

The Darewell Chums; or, The Heroes of the School, Cupples & Leon, 1908.

. . . in the City; or, The Disappearance of Nat Wilding, Cupples & Leon, 1908, later published as part of the "Success" series under title *The Darewell Chums in the City* by Donohue.

. . . in the Woods; or, Frank Roscoe's Secret, Cupples & Leon, 1908.

. . . on a Cruise; or, Fenn Masterson's Odd Discovery, Cupples & Leon, 1909.

. . . in a Winter Camp; or, Bart Keene's Best Shot, Cupples & Leon, 1911.

"FRED FENTON ATHLETIC SERIES"

Fred Fenton, the Pitcher; or, The Rivals of Riverport School, Cupples & Leon, 1913.

. . . in the Line; or, The Football Boys of Riverport School, Cupples & Leon, 1913.

. . . on the Crew; or, The Young Oarsmen of Riverport School, Cupples & Leon, 1913.

. . . on the Track; or, The Athletes of Riverport School, Cupples & Leon, 1913.

. . ., Marathon Runner; or, The Great Race at Riverport School, Cupples & Leon, 1915.

"RADIO BOYS" SERIES

The Radio Boys' First Wireless; or, Winning the Ferberton Prize, Grosset & Dunlap, 1922.

. . . at Ocean Point; or, The Message That Saved the Ship, Grosset & Dunlap, 1922.

. . . at the Sending Station; or, Making Good in the Wireless Room, Grosset & Dunlap, 1922.

. . . at Mountain Pass; or, The Midnight Call for Assistance, Grosset & Dunlap, 1922.

. . . Trailing a Voice; or, Solving a Wireless Mystery, Grosset & Dunlap, 1922.

. . . with the Forest Rangers; or, The Great Fire on Spruce Mountain, Grosset & Dunlap, 1923.

. . . with the Iceberg Patrol; or, Making Safe the Ocean Lanes, Grosset & Dunlap, 1924.

. . . with the Flood Fighters; or, Saving the City in the Valley, Grosset & Dunlap, 1925.

. . . on Signal Island; or, Watching for the Ships of Mystery, Grosset & Dunlap, 1926.

. . . in Gold Valley; or, The Mystery of the Deserted Mining Camp, Grosset & Dunlap, 1927.

. . . Aiding the Snowbound; or, Starvation Days at Lumber Run, Grosset & Dunlap, 1928.

. . . on the Pacific; or, Shipwrecked on an Unknown Island, Grosset & Dunlap, 1929.

. . . to the Rescue; or, The Search for the Barmore Twins, Grosset & Dunlap, 1930.

"RALPH OF THE RAILROAD" SERIES

Ralph of the Roundhouse; or, Bound to Become a Railroad Man (also see below), Mershon, 1906.

. . . in the Switch Tower; or, Clearing the Track (also see below), Mershon, 1907.

. . . on the Engine; or, The Young Fireman of the Limited Mail (also see below), Grosset & Dunlap, 1909.

. . . on the Overland Express; or, The Trials and Triumphs of a Young Engineer (also see below), Grosset & Dunlap, 1910.

. . ., the Train Dispatcher; or, The Mystery of the Pay Car, Grosset & Dunlap, 1911.

. . . on the Army Train; or, The Young Railroader's Most Daring Exploit, Grosset & Dunlap, 1918.

... *on the Midnight Flyer; or, The Wreck at Shadow Valley,*
     Grosset & Dunlap, 1923.
... *and the Missing Mail Pouch; or, The Stolen Government*
     Bonds, Grosset & Dunlap, 1924.
... *on the Mountain Division; or, Fighting both Flames and*
     Flood, Grosset & Dunlap, 1927.
... *and the Train Wreckers; or, The Secret of the Blue Freight*
     Cars, Grosset & Dunlap, 1928.
Ralph on the Railroad: Four Complete Adventure Books for
     Boys in One Big Volume (contains *Ralph of the Round-*
     house, Ralph in the Switch Tower, Ralph on the Engine,
     and *Ralph on the Overland Express*), Grosset & Dunlap,
     1933.

"TOM FAIRFIELD" SERIES

Tom Fairfield's School Days; or, The Chums of Elmwood Hall,
     Cupples & Leon, 1913.
Tom Fairfield at Sea; or, The Wreck of the Silver Star, Cup-
     ples & Leon, 1913.
Tom Fairfield in Camp; or, The Secret of the Old Mill, Cup-
     ples & Leon, 1913.
Tom Fairfield's Pluck and Luck; or, Working to Clear His
     Name, Cupples & Leon, 1913.
Tom Fairfield's Hunting Trip; or, Lost in the Wilderness, Cup-
     ples & Leon, 1915.

OTHER

Also pseudonym for *The Young Builders of Swiftdale,* for
Chatterton Peck. Contributor to periodical *Bright Days.*

SIDELIGHTS: Two of the series produced under this pseud-
onym, the "Ralph of the Railroad" stories and the "Radio
Boys" books, were based on mechanical and electronic inventions. Ralph Fairbanks was the hero of the "Ralph of the
Railroad" series, which "centered around the Great Northern
Railroad, a beleaguered line sorely beset with spies, 'sorehead
strikers' and unscrupulous competitors who used every kind
of skullduggery to wreck its schedules," according to Arthur
Prager in *Rascals at Large; or, The Clue in the Old Nostalgia.*
The Radio Boys were four young men, Bob Layton, Joe Atwood, Jimmy Plummer, and Herbert Fennington, all of whom
evinced an interest in radio, encouraged by their local pastor
Dr. Dale. "It wasn't easy to build thrills around stationary
apparatus instead of zippy vehicles, but the boys did very
well," says Prager. He continues, "Of course, there were
chases and daring rescues, and attempts by infamous bullies
to destroy the boys' apparatus, but the wonders of wireless,
as explained by genial Dr. Dale, launched the boys on thirteen
volumes of fun and adventure."

Some sources state that this pseudonym was used by Stratemeyer writer W. Bert Foster. For more information see the
entries in this volume for Harriet S. Adams, Edward L. Stratemeyer, and Andrew E. Svenson.

BIOGRAPHICAL/CRITICAL SOURCES:

BOOKS

Dizer, John T., *Tom Swift & Company: "Boy's Books" by*
     Stratemeyer and Others, McFarland & Co., 1982.
Johnson, Deidre, editor and compiler, *Stratemeyer Pseud-*
     onyms and Series Books: An Annotated Checklist of Stra-
     temeyer and Stratemeyer Syndicate Publications, Green-
     wood Press, 1982.
McFarlane, Leslie, *Ghost of the Hardy Boys,* Two Continents,
     1976.

Prager, Arthur, *Rascals at Large; or, The Clue in the Old*
     Nostalgia, Doubleday, 1971.

*   *   *

CHARLES, Louis
See STRATEMEYER, Edward L.

*   *   *

CHEEVER, John   1912-1982

PERSONAL: Born May 27, 1912, in Quincy, Mass.; died June
18, 1982, of cancer; son of Frederick and Mary (Liley) Cheever;
married Mary M. Winternitz (a poet and teacher), March 22,
1941; children: Susan, Benjamin Hale, Frederico. *Education:*
Attended Thayer Academy. *Religion:* Episcopal.

ADDRESSES: Home—Cedar Lane, Ossining, N.Y. 10562.

CAREER: Novelist and short story writer. Instructor, Barnard
College, 1956-57, Ossining (N.Y.) Correctional Facility, 1971-
72, and University of Iowa Writers Workshop, 1973; visiting
professor of creative writing, Boston University, 1974-75.
Member of cultural exchange program to the U.S.S.R., 1964.
Military service: U.S. Army Signal Corps, 1943-45; became
sergeant.

MEMBER: National Institute of Arts and Letters, Century Club
(New York).

AWARDS, HONORS: Guggenheim fellowship, 1951; Benja-
min Franklin Award, 1955, for "The Five-Forty-Eight";
American Academy of Arts and Letters award in literature,
1956; O. Henry Award, 1956, for "The Country Husband,"
and 1964, for "The Embarkment for Cythera"; National Book
Award in fiction, 1958, for *The Wapshot Chronicle;* Howells
Medal, American Academy of Arts and Letters, 1965, for *The*
Wapshot Scandal; Editorial Award, *Playboy,* 1969, for "The
Yellow Room"; honorary doctorate, Harvard University, 1978;
Edward MacDowell Medal, MacDowell Colony, 1979, for
outstanding contributions to the arts; Pulitzer Prize in fiction,
1979, National Book Critics Circle Award in fiction, 1979,
and American Book Award in fiction, 1981, all for *The Stories*
of John Cheever; National Medal for Literature, 1982.

WRITINGS:

NOVELS

The Wapshot Chronicle (also see below), Harper, 1957, re-
     printed, Franklin Library, 1978.
The Wapshot Scandal (also see below), Harper, 1964.
Bullet Park (Book-of-the-Month Club selection), Knopf, 1969.
Falconer, Knopf, 1977.
The Wapshot Chronicle [and] *The Wapshot Scandal,* Harper,
     1979.
Oh, What a Paradise It Seems, Knopf, 1982.

SHORT STORIES

The Way Some People Live: A Book of Stories, Random House,
     1943.
The Enormous Radio and Other Stories, Funk, 1953.
(With others) *Stories,* Farrar, Straus, 1956 (published in En-
     gland as *A Book of Stories,* Gollancz, 1957).
The Housebreaker of Shady Hill and Other Stories, Harper,
     1958.
Some People, Places and Things That Will Not Appear in My
     Next Novel, Harper, 1961.

The Brigadier and the Golf Widow, Harper, 1964.

Homage to Shakespeare, Country Squire Books, 1965.

The World of Apples, Knopf, 1973.

The Day the Pig Fell into the Well (originally published in the *New Yorker,* October 23, 1954), Lord John Press, 1978.

The Stories of John Cheever, Knopf, 1978.

The Leaves, the Lion-Fish and the Bear, Sylvester and Orphanos, 1980.

The Uncollected Stories of John Cheever: 1930-1981, Academy Chicago, in press.

OTHER

Also author of television scripts, including "Life with Father." Contributor to numerous anthologies, including *O. Henry Prize Stories,* 1941, 1951, 1956, 1964. Contributor to the *New Yorker, Collier's, Story, Yale Review, New Republic, Atlantic,* and other publications.

SIDELIGHTS: John Cheever has come to be considered among the finest American writers of the twentieth century, a master of the short story and a competent novelist. Cheever's long career as a short story writer began at the age of seventeen when he sold his first story to the *New Republic.* He became a regular contributor to the *New Yorker* five years later, a relationship that would last for decades and account for the publication of a majority of his stories. Cheever's short work, at times discounted because it was categorized as *New Yorker* style, earned a wider audience and greater recognition when his collection, *The Stories of John Cheever,* was awarded the Pulitzer Prize in fiction in 1979. The publication of this volume of sixty-one stories, including such titles as "The Enormous Radio," "The Country Husband," "The Chimera," and "The Swimmer," "revived singlehanded publishers' and readers' interest in the American short story," according to *Time*'s Paul Gray. Commenting on the author's place in American literature, John Leonard wrote in a 1973 *Atlantic* article, "I happen to believe that John Cheever is our best living writer of short stories: a[n Anton] Chekhov of the exurbs."

Cheever the novelist was not as widely praised, but even in this role he has had his champions. In 1977, fellow author John Gardner maintained that "Cheever is one of the few living American novelists who might qualify as true artists. His work ranges from competent to awesome on all the grounds I would count: formal and technical mastery; educated intelligence; what I would call 'artistic sincerity' . . . ; and last, validity." His novels—most notably *The Wapshot Chronicles, Bullet Park,* and *Falconer*—display "a remarkable sensitivity and a grimly humorous assessment of human behavior that capture[s] the anguish of modern man," commented Robert D. Spector in *World Literature Today,* "as much imprisoned by his mind as by the conventions of society."

Cheever was able to draw on the same confined milieu—geographical and social—in creating his five novels and numerous stories. "There is by now a recognizable landscape that can be called Cheever country," Walter Clemons observed in an article in *Newsweek.* It comprises "the rich suburban communities of Westchester and Connecticut," explained Richard Locke in the *New York Times Book Review,* "the towns [the author] calls Shady Hill, St. Botolphs and Bullet Park." In this country, Cheever found the source for his fiction, the lives of upwardly mobile Americans, both urban and suburban, lives lacking purpose and direction. His fictional representation of these lives captures what a *Time* reviewer termed the "social perceptions that seem superficial but somehow manage to reveal (and devastate or exalt) the subjects of his suburban scrutiny." Fashioned from the author's observations and presented in this manner, Cheever's stories have become, in the opinion of Jesse Kornbluth, "a precise dissection of the ascending middle class and the declining American aristocracy."

For the most part, the characters represented in Cheever's short stories and novels are white and Protestant; they are bored with their jobs, trapped in their lifestyles, and out of touch with their families. "Mr. Cheever's account of life in suburbia makes one's soul ache," Guy Davenport remarked in the *National Review.* Added the reviewer: "Here is human energy that once pushed plows and stormed the walls of Jerusalem . . . spent daily in getting up hung over, staggering drugged with tranquilizers to wait for a train to . . . Manhattan. There eight hours are given to the writing of advertisements about halitosis and mouthwash. Then the train back, a cocktail party, and drunk to bed." According to Richard Boeth of *Newsweek,* "what is missing in these people is not the virtue of their forebears . . . but the passion, zest, originality and underlying stoicism that fueled the Wasps' domination of the world for two . . . centuries. Now they're fat and bored and scared and whiny."

Critics have concluded that Cheever is not merely satirizing the upper middle class. According to John W. Aldridge in *Time to Murder and Create: The Contemporary Novel in Crisis,* Cheever "understands just what happens when a man making too much money awakens to the fact that there is nothing left to spend it on except some form of anesthesia against the knowledge that there is nothing left to spend it on." The author's ability to evoke this despair and treat it with compassion and humor is the reason he has been compared to Chekhov. Larry Woiwode explained in the *New York Times Book Review:* "Cheever is as much a master of the short form as Chekhov and should be recognized as such. He shares Chekhov's gentility, ingenuous warmth, humor, universality and all-seeing eye for the absurdities of the world and the foibles and weaknesses of humankind. Writing in *Twentieth Century Literature,* Clinton S. Burhans, Jr., called Cheever "a major chronicler of contemporary absurdity . . . who sees all too clearly into the gap between men's dreams and what they make of them." The critic added that "he sees . . . that men are born more than ever into a world of chance, complexity and ultimate loneliness. . . . Cheever reflects this world in whimsy and fantasy, in irony and extravagance, but never at the cost of his deep compassion for those who must live in it with him."

A recurring theme in Cheever's work is nostalgia, "the particular melancholia induced by long absence from one's country or home," Joan Didion explained in the *New York Times Book Review.* In her estimation, Cheever's characters have "yearned always after some abstraction symbolized by the word 'home,' after 'tenderness,' after 'gentleness,' after remembered houses where the fires were laid and the silver was polished and everything could be 'decent' and 'radiant' and 'clear.'" Even so, as Didion added: "Such houses were hard to find in prime condition. To approach one was to hear the quarreling inside. . . . There was some gap between what these Cheever people searching for home had been led to expect and what they got." What they got, the critic elaborated, was the world of the suburbs, where "jobs and children got lost." As Locke put it, Cheever's characters' nostalgia grows out of "their excruciating experience of present incivility, loneliness and moral disarray."

Throughout his tales of despair and nostalgia, Cheever offers an optimistic vision of hope and salvation. His main characters struggle to establish an identity and a set of values "in relation to an essentially meaningless—even absurd—world," Stephen C. Moore commented in the *Western Humanities Review*. Kornbluth found that "Cheever's stories and early novels are not really about people scrapping for social position and money, but about people rising toward grace." In his *Dictionary of Literary Biography* essay, Robert A. Morace came to a similar conclusion. Morace maintained that "while he clearly recognizes those aspects of modern life which might lead to pessimism, his comic vision remains basically optimistic. . . . Many of his characters go down to defeat, usually by their own hand. Those who survive . . . discover the personal and social virtues of compromise. Having learned of their own and their world's limitations, they can, paradoxically, learn to celebrate the wonder and possibility of life."

Cheever's straightforward language and vivid imagery have been widely praised. Robert Towers of the *New York Times Book Review* called the author "a precisionist of the senses" and explained: "Though his imagery of light has the strongest retinal impact, Cheever's evocation of color and texture and smell is also vivid and persistent. He shares with two very different writers, Lawrence and Faulkner, an extraordinary ability to fix the sensory quality of a particular moment, a particular place, and to make it function not as embellishment but as an essential element in the lives and moods of his characters." Locke commented, "Cheever's largest gift [is] the power to present a sensuous (especially a visual) detail that effortlessly carries intense emotional and symbolic force."

Critics have also been impressed by Cheever's episodic style. In a discussion of the author's first published work, "Expelled," Morace commented: "The opening paragraph lures the reader into a story which, like many of the later works, is a series of sketches rather than a linear narrative. The narrator, who remains detached even while recognizing his own expulsion, focuses on apparently disparate events which, taken together, create a single impression of what life at prep school is like." And in a review of *Bullet Park*, a *Time* critic notes that most of the novel "is composed of Cheever's customary skillful vignettes in which apparent slickness masks real feeling."

Some reviewers did find, however, that although this episodic structure works well in Cheever's short fiction, his novels "flounder under the weight of too many capricious, inspired, zany images," as Joyce Carol Oates remarked in the *Ontario Review*. John Updike once offered a similar appraisal: "In the coining of images and incidents, John Cheever has no peer among contemporary American fiction writers. His short stories dance, skid, twirl, and soar on the strength of his abundant invention; his novels fly apart under its impact." Moreover, Oates contended that though "there are certainly a number of powerful passages in *Falconer*, as in *Bullet Park* and the Wapshot novels, . . . in general the whimsical impulse undercuts and to some extent damages the more serious intentions of the works."

Clemons, among others, drew a different conclusion. He noted that "the accusation that Cheever 'is not a novelist' persists," despite the prestigious awards, such as the Howells Medal and the National Book Award, his novels have received. Clemons suggested that this lack of reviewer appreciation was due to Cheever's long affiliation with the *New Yorker*. "The recognition of Cheever's [work] has . . . been hindered by its steady appearance in a debonair magazine that is believed to publish something familiarly called 'the *New Yorker* story,'" he wrote, "and we think we know what *that* is." Clemons added: "Randall Jarrell once usefully [defined the novel] as prose fiction of some length that has something wrong with it. What is clearly 'wrong' with Cheever's . . . novels is that they contain separable stretches of exhilarating narrative that might easily have been published as stories. They are loosely knit. But so what?"

Over the years, the critical and popular response to Cheever's work has been decidedly favorable. Although some have argued that his characters are unimportant and peripheral and that the problems and crises experienced by the upper middle class are trivial, others, such as *Time*'s Gray, contended that the "fortunate few [who inhabit Cheever's fiction] are much more significant than critics seeking raw social realism will admit." Gray explained: "Well outside the mainstream, the Cheever people nonetheless reflect it admirably. What they do with themselves is what millions upon millions would do, given enough money and time. And their creator is less interested in his characters as rounded individuals than in the awful, comic and occasionally joyous ways they bungle their opportunities." John Leonard of the *New York Times* found the same merits, concluding that "by writing about any of us, Mr. Cheever writes about all of us, our ethical concerns and our failures of nerve, our experience of the discrepancies and our shred of honor."

Cheever's name is often raised by critics alongside the names of such highly regarded contemporaries as John O'Hara, Saul Bellow, Thomas Pynchon, and Philip Roth. Yet, as Peter S. Prescott noted in a *Newsweek* tribute on the occasion of Cheever's death, "His prose, unmatched in complexity and precision by that of any of his contemporaries . . . is simply beautiful to read, to hear in the inner ear—and it got better all the time." "More precisely than his fellow writers," added Prescott, "he observed and gave voice to the inarticulate agonies that lie just beneath the surface of ordinary lives." In the words of Gray, recorded in a *Time* tribute, Cheever "won fame as a chronicler of mid-century manners, but his deeper subject was always the matter of life and death."

For a *CA* Interview with this author, see earlier entry in *CA New Revision Series* Volume 5.

MEDIA ADAPTATIONS: Several of Cheever's short stories have been adapted for motion pictures and television. "The Swimmer" was produced by Columbia in 1968 and PBS-TV broadcast "The Sorrows of Gin," "The Five Forty-Eight," and "O Youth and Beauty!," all in 1979. The film rights to Cheever's novels *The Wapshot Chronicle*, *The Wapshot Scandal*, *Bullet Park*, and *Falconer* have been sold.

AVOCATIONAL INTERESTS: Sailing and skiing.

BIOGRAPHICAL/CRITICAL SOURCES:

BOOKS

Aldridge, John W., *Time to Murder and Create: The Contemporary Novel in Crisis*, McKay, 1966.
Bosha, Francis J., *John Cheever: A Reference Guide*, G. K. Hall, 1981.
Cheever, Susan, *Home before Dark*, Houghton, 1984.
Concise Dictionary of American Literary Biography, 1941-1968, Gale, 1987.
Contemporary Authors Bibliographical Series, Volume 1, Gale, 1986.

Contemporary Literary Criticism, Gale, Volume 3, 1975, Volume 7, 1977, Volume 8, 1978, Volume 11, 1979, Volume 15, 1980, Volume 25, 1983.
Dictionary of Literary Biography, Volume 2: *American Novelists since World War II*, Gale, 1978.
Dictionary of Literary Biography Yearbook, Gale, *1980*, 1981, *1982*, 1983.
Donaldson, Scott, editor, *Conversations with John Cheever*, University Press of Mississippi, 1987.
Donaldson, Scott, *John Cheever: A Biography*, Random House, 1988.
Hassan, Ihab, *Radical Innocence*, Princeton University Press, 1961.
Kazin, Alfred, *Bright Book of Life*, Atlantic-Little, Brown, 1973.
Short Story Criticism, Volume 1, Gale, 1988.
Updike, John, *Picked-Up Pieces*, Knopf, 1976.
Waldeland, L., *John Cheever*, G. K. Hall, 1979.

PERIODICALS

Atlantic, May, 1969, June, 1973.
Book Week, January 5, 1964.
Chicago Tribune Magazine, April 22, 1979.
Christian Century, May 21, 1969.
Christian Science Monitor, October 22, 1964.
Commonweal, May 9, 1969.
Critique, spring, 1963.
Detroit News, November 28, 1978.
Life, April 18, 1969.
Manchester Guardian, January 30, 1959.
Ms., April, 1977.
National Review, June 3, 1969.
New Leader, May 26, 1969.
New Republic, May 25, 1953, June 3, 1957, May 15, 1961, January 25, 1964, April 26, 1969.
Newsweek, March 14, 1977, October 30, 1978, June 28, 1982.
New York, April 28, 1969.
New York Herald Tribune Lively Arts, April 30, 1961.
New York Times, March 24, 1965, August 2, 1965, December 18, 1966, April 29, 1969, March 3, 1977, November 7, 1978.
New York Times Magazine, October 21, 1979.
New York Times Book Review, May 10, 1953, September 7, 1958, January 5, 1964, April 27, 1969, May 20, 1973, March 6, 1977, December 3, 1978, January 28, 1979.
Ontario Review, fall/winter, 1977-78.
Ramparts, September, 1969.
San Francisco Chronicle, May 24, 1953, March 25, 1957, April 28, 1961.
Saturday Review, May 27, 1961, April 26, 1969, April 2, 1977.
Time, March 27, 1964, April 25, 1969, February 28, 1977, October 16, 1978, June 28, 1982.
Times Literary Supplement, October 9, 1953, October 18, 1957, August 4, 1961.
Twentieth Century Literature, January, 1969.
Washington Post, April 29, 1969, October 8, 1979.
Washington Post Book World, March 30, 1980.
World Literature Today, autumn, 1977.

OBITUARIES:

PERIODICALS

New York Times, June 19, 1982.
Times (London), June 21, 1982.*

CHEEVER, Susan 1943-

PERSONAL: Born July 31, 1943, in New York, N.Y.; daughter of John (an author) and Mary (a poet and teacher; maiden name, Winternitz) Cheever; married Robert Cowley (an editor), 1967 (divorced); married Calvin Tomkins II (a *New Yorker* writer), 1981 (divorced); children: (second marriage) Sarah Liley. *Education:* Brown University, B.A., 1965.

ADDRESSES: Home—140 East 81st St., New York, N.Y. 10028. *Agent*—Andrew Wylie, Wylie, Aitken & Stone, 250 West 57th St., New York, N.Y.

CAREER: Taught English at the Colorado Rocky Mountain School and the Scarborough School, 1967-69; affiliated with *Queen* magazine, London, England, 1969-70; *Tarrytown Daily News*, Tarrytown, N.Y., reporter, 1971-72; *Newsweek*, New York, N.Y., 1974-78, began as religion editor, became lifestyle editor; writer. Instructor in creative writing, Hoffstra University, beginning 1980.

MEMBER: Authors Guild, Authors League of America, PEN American Center.

AWARDS, HONORS: Guggenheim fellowship, 1983; nomination for National Book Critics Circle Award in biography/autobiography, 1984, for *Home before Dark*; Lawrence L. Winship Book Award, *Boston Globe*, 1986, for *Home before Dark*.

WRITINGS:

Looking for Work (novel), Simon & Schuster, 1980.
A Handsome Man (novel), Simon & Schuster, 1981.
The Cage (novel), Houghton, 1982.
Home before Dark (biographical memoir of father, John Cheever), Houghton, 1984.
Doctors and Women (novel), C. N. Potter, 1987.
Elizabeth Cole (novel), Farrar, Straus, 1989.

SIDELIGHTS: Susan Cheever has had a long association with the craft of fiction writing. As the daughter of the late Pulitzer Prize-winning author John Cheever, she once explained to *CA*, "I grew up in a house where fiction was being written. . . . I saw how you did it. I saw that it was doable by a human being." Even with this background, however, she avoided becoming a fiction writer until, in her thirties, she found she "wanted to write something more personal" than what she was doing at the time for *Newsweek*. To this end, Cheever has written four novels which explore the lives of contemporary women dissatisfied with their marriages and their careers, women in search of something better. She has also written a biographical memoir of her father, the man who first modeled fiction writing for her.

In her first novel, *Looking for Work*, Cheever "paints the cheery saga of a spoiled, upper-middle-class brat who marries the wrong guy . . . has an affair, and finally gets ready for a steady job," writes Elizabeth Fox-Genovese in the *Antioch Review*. The story of Salley Gardens "is the one that so many writers regard as the story of our time," comments a reviewer for the *Atlantic*, "the demise of a marriage, told by a young wife who mistakenly assumed that she should and could find meaning in her life by helping her husband live his." In following her heroine's life from marriage to divorce to her eventual landing of a job on the staff of *Newsweek*, Cheever creates a novel that "belongs to a tradition of realism which sets itself the task of illuminating the way we all live now," observes Cheryl Rivers in a *Commonweal* article.

The view of contemporary America offered in *Looking for Work* is, in the words of *New York Times Book Review* contributor Robert Kiely, "very much like a certain kind of Hollywood film; brisk, bouncy, sharply focused, filled with primary colors and abrupt transitions. . . . [The] novel is easy to read. Nothing drags, nothing lingers, no one mopes." This ease, according to Jean Strouse of *Newsweek,* detracts from the overall impact of the book. "By merely *telling* us how Salley feels instead of giving those feelings dramatic life," writes Strouse, "Cheever has created something less than a novel." *New York Times* book reviewer Christopher Lehmann-Haupt offers a similar assessment: *Looking for Work* "is not really much of a story. . . . Nor has Miss Cheever found a metaphor to tie her narrative together." All the same, Lehmann-Haupt does admit that "Cheever shows considerable promise. She strikes a note of amusing rue that manages to avoid self-pity."

Though faulted for its story, *Looking for Work* did earn its author praise for its technical features. According to Susan Kennedy in a *Times Literary Supplement* review, "Cheever enlivens [the] well-trodden literary topography [of New York, Europe, and San Francisco] with some good descriptive writing; indeed, it is her unobtrusive technical assurance, her respect for the just use of words, that keeps the novel together." Rivers, too, finds that Cheever's inventive writing raises this novel above the level of cliche: "She plays with style, abruptly changing pace, mood, and vision. She is capable of intimate, wry commentary and of showy descriptions of events." Beyond this, continues the reviewer, "Cheever's very real accomplishment in *Looking for Work,* is the vividness with which she has observed the familiar plight of her heroine and the gentle affection with which she draws her cast of characters. She has avoided turning her characters into parodies; her belief in her characters allows us to believe in them and to care about their predicaments." Cheever succeeds in the end in showing the reader that "love, marriage, and even sex no longer have the redemptive qualities so widely advertised in popular culture, common sense, and our own psyches," concludes Rivers.

Cheever's second novel, *A Handsome Man,* focuses on a vacation in Ireland, shared by Hannah Bart, a divorcee in her thirties, her older lover, Sam, his teenage son, Travis, and Hannah's younger brother, Jake. "The work depends almost entirely upon the shifting dynamics between Hannah, Sam, and Travis," comments Susan Currier in the *Dictionary of Literary Biography Yearbook.* "Cheever moves the reader smoothly from one character's mind and feelings to another's, though Hannah's remains the dominant perspective." When revealing this young woman's character, in the opinion of *Washington Post* contributor Michele Slung, Cheever captures the interest of her readers: "Hannah is a real woman come alive on these pages. Both her doubts and her wisecracks ring true. But," adds the reviewer, "Sam and Travis added to Hannah make for a human equation that has less verisimilitude."

The novel "is meant as a study in the forms of selfishness afflicting lovers, father and son, the young and the not-so-young," observes Judith Chernaik in the *Times Literary Supplement.* Yet, in the end, concludes the reviewer, it "is marred by a pervading slickness, a tendency to slip into woman's-magazine banality." As Joyce Shaffer puts it in a *New Re-public* review, "It is like a faded color photograph: a brief moment of reality is accurately reproduced, but there is no movement or excitement." Slung attributes the novel's shortcomings to its having to compete with its own setting. Cheever's "prose, when it is good . . . is seductive and tightly phrased," she writes, "but it is not always strong enough to fight off the scene-stealing proclivities of things Irish."

"No youthful protagonist in search of either lover or work animates [*The Cage*, Cheever's third novel]," observes Currier. "It is a more tightly structured book than the first two, with a darker vision of a middle-aged couple trapped in mutual disappointment and destruction." The cage referred to in the book's title was once used to house the menagerie kept by Judith Bristol's late father on the grounds of his New Hampshire estate. Restoring this long-neglected pen has become a sort of therapy for Julia's husband, Billy, during the couple's summer vacation at the estate. The cage also plays a central part in the couple's final confrontation. This story of conflict simmering beneath the calm exterior of suburban America is reminiscent of the world of the author's father, John Cheever, a point on which Richard Eder comments in his *Los Angeles Times Book Review* article: "Susan Cheever has chosen deliberately, with some courage and less prudence, to start in her father's territory and walk her own wilder track out of it."

Cheever's detailed account of the uneventful surface features of suburban life is at the center of much of the criticism devoted to this book. "One of the problems with 'The Cage'—which seems not so much a novel as an extended story or even a television script . . . —is that it is mostly surface," comments Sheila Ballantyne in the *New York Times Book Review,* "embroidered with glittery and often repetitive detail." *New Statesman* contributor Bill Greenwell finds in the same features one of the novel's primary virtues. "What Cheever achieves with startling clarity is a surface naturalism, with a powerful eye for telling, insignificant detail and a feeling for the petty emotions of jealousy and depression." These mundane events are the pieces that build slowly toward the book's climax, he believes. "The novel's conclusion is masterly. As the final pages turn, the reader recalls a succession of brilliant images, sewn into the subtext, by which we have been prepared for the ending. Cheever is exceptionally talented," concludes Greenwell, "this novel superbly compulsive."

Although Cheever's first three novels all draw upon her experiences, none is as personal as her fourth novel, *Doctors and Women*. Its central character, Kate, like its author, has lost a father to cancer. But, Kate's fictional life is affected by a number of other complications: her mother is, at the time of the story, hospitalized with cancer; she is unhappy in her marriage; and, she is "fascinated by the charismatic power doctors seem to exercise over the lives of their patients," explains Susan Kenney in the *New York Times Book Review*. Her story offers, in the words of *Los Angeles Times Book Review* contributor Linsey Abrams, "a coming-of-age novel, all the more interesting because it documents that *second* coming of age, in one's 30s, when one chooses the life one is actually living over the fantasy lives that, like fiction, run parallel to it."

The novel had its genesis, as Cheever explains in her *CA Interview*, in the events of her father's illness. She was struggling to make sense of his battle with cancer when she became intrigued with the doctors attending to his and other cancer patients' day-to-day crises. She decided to learn more about these men, researching their professional duties and their personal lives. The information she gathered, intended originally for a nonfiction work, became instead the basis for this novel. "It is clear that Ms. Cheever has not only done her research, but also been there; her accounts of medical procedure and hospital ambience are authentic right down to the contents of IV bags and bulletin boards," writes Kenney. "Written in graceful prose, these scenes have the power and authority we associate with the best nonfiction."

In fact, it is in the arena of nonfiction that Cheever has enjoyed her greatest success, both in examining her personal concerns and in making a name for herself. After John Cheever's death from cancer, the younger Cheever decided to edit the log she was keeping of her thoughts. Her original intent was to distill this written mourning into a short memoir of the man she knew—father and author.

When she turned for supplementary material to her father's private journals—thirty volumes written over several decades—as she explained to Curt Suplee in a *Washington Post* interview, "I learned a lot of things I hadn't known before— how different life was for my father than we had imagined, how the humor he used was just transmuted pain." Her first reaction was to give up the memoir entirely, but as she explained to Suplee, "I knew that articles and a biography were going to be written. And I decided it'd be better if I presented these things myself, in context." The resultant book, *Home before Dark,* notes Suplee, "is a frank but frankly loving biographical memoir."

Yet, as Brigitte Weeks writes in the *Washington Post Book World,* "*Home before Dark* is much more than Susan Cheever's memoir of her famous author father: it is a portrait of the artist as a young man, a middle-aged man, an old man, a sick man. It is, in fact, one of the most moving and intimate books I have read in years." In looking back, Cheever follows her family's history from her grandfather's downfall during the Depression through her father's rise from struggling writer in the close quarters of the big city to respected author surrounded by the comforts of a suburban estate. This family history provides the backdrop for her close examination of John Cheever, the man, the author, and the father.

"The book seems to omit few unpleasant, even sordid details in its depiction of John Cheever as a tortured father, writer and man," suggests John Blades in a *Chicago Tribune* article, "telling of his turbulent marriage, his long and frustrating struggle to make a living as a writer, his alcoholism, his paternal inadequacies, his aristocratic pretensions and his confused sexual life." Though faulted by a number of reviewers for these revelations—what was considered by some a daughter's betrayal of her father—Cheever also received commendations for her sensitive handling of a subject so close to home. Weeks, for one, remarks that "the wonder of this book is the astonishing combination of dispassion and compassion with which Susan Cheever portrays her father." Eliot Fremont-Smith, writing in the *Village Voice,* describes Cheever's memoir in the following words: "She is not intrusive, only truthful; so this intimate, disturbing book is an act of mourning and forgiveness, of ultimate respect." And, he takes exception to some of the criticism of the book. "This is a deeply responsible and touching book," he concludes. "Those who find it shameful or lacking in respect know only the price of courage, not its necessity."

Home before Dark also provides insights into John Cheever, the author. "As important as tending to the actual facts," comments Ann Hulbert in the *New Republic,* "Susan Cheever emphasizes her father's zeal for imaginatively building upon past events." *New York Times* book reviewer Lehmann-Haupt notes that John Cheever "was a man tortured by his sense of inadequacy. His fiction was as much an attempt to reinvent himself as it was to give vent to marvelous imagination." In presenting her recollection of the lives—factual and fictional— of her father, Susan Cheever achieves a balance, finds Justin Kaplan in a *New York Times Book Review* article. "One of the many strengths of 'Home Before Dark' . . . is that in dealing with Cheever's versions of himself," writes Kaplan, "she holds them accountable mainly to internal consistency, to 'an inherent truth, outside of the facts.'" He continues, "She illuminates the conditions of his work and the price he paid to achieve it." In *Esquire* contributor Brett Singer's view, "If John Cheever deserves nothing else, he deserves a literary biography, and his daughter, a novelist in her own right, has given him nothing less."

Beyond the insights it offers into the father's work, *Home before Dark* provides evidence of the daughter's personal and professional development. In this book, writes Lehmann-Haupt, "we get to know a man we scarcely dreamed existed behind the elegant facade. It is a painful discovery, but it is to Miss Cheever's credit that she persevered. Not only has she finally identified her father, but in doing so she has faced up to the challenge of identifying herself." In his review, Kaplan touches upon the special effort required of the younger Cheever in writing this book: "'Home Before Dark' clearly demanded from its author more courage and force of heart than will be required of any biographer of John Cheever." Concludes Charles Champlin in the *Los Angeles Times Book Review,* "If the reader is touched, it is not by the mannered style but by the candor and insight that have gone before. There will be full-dress biographies of Cheever and his work in due course. All will be the more knowing for his daughter's paining portrait."

The world of Susan Cheever's writing is a personal world, one which focuses on the people, places, and concerns that reside close to home. Up to this point, she has best succeeded in capturing the profound contours of this world in her personal memoir of her father. If there is disappointment that her novels have not had the same success as has her own nonfiction, reviewers such as Chicago *Tribune Books* contributor Madeleine Blaise believe that it is "softened, somewhat, by the pleasure in hoping that her next novel will provide that breakthrough."

CA INTERVIEW

CA interviewed Susan Cheever by telephone on March 13, 1987, at her home in New York, New York.

CA: Until you were thirty-five, you told CA just after the publication of your first novel, Looking for Work, *you were "determined not to be a writer." With your fourth novel about to come out and the biographical memoir* Home before Dark *among your credits, do you feel established now in your identity as a writer?*

CHEEVER: Yes, I think I've given in to it.

CA: Do you think coming to your profession rather reluctantly might have worked as an advantage in some way?

CHEEVER: Absolutely. I think that was an incalculable benefit. For me, at least, it was important to have lived that much, to have experienced that much, in order to be seasoned enough to write a novel. I needed the confidence that I developed in the first thirty-five years of my life, or fifteen years of my professional life, to have the guts to write a novel. And in my situation, I think it took all those years to develop a voice of my own and a way of thinking of my own, considering that I was very close to someone who was very influential and had a tremendously strong style and vision of his own. In order to be an independent writer, as well as a writer at all, I needed every minute of that time. And I think, if there is a god in heaven, that he or she granted me that time of being absolutely sure that I would *never* be a writer to gather the strength that it takes to *be* a writer.

CA: Your latest novel, Doctors and Women, *is very much about cancer and the medical profession's ways of handling cancer patients. One of its points is how little incentive there is for doctors to show personal concern for cancer patients. Was this one of the main issues that prompted the book?*

CHEEVER: There were a lot of issues that prompted the book. Philip Roth said a wonderful thing: he said that a novel is the transformation of a personal emergency into a public act. For me, the personal emergency was having had a father with cancer and getting very involved. I had always been terrified of cancer. And I had always felt that if I didn't know anything about it, that would protect me; ignorance equalled immunity. I really made sure not to find anything out. Then when my father got cancer, the energy that had fueled that terror turned to obsession. All of a sudden I couldn't find out enough. I read everything I could find and talked to everyone I could talk to. At parties I would be off in a corner with someone else whose mother or father had died of cancer. I also started to talk with doctors—not about my father, but about them, about what they do and how it affects them. I got deeper and deeper into it.

I had been at this for four or five months before I said to myself, Maybe I should write something about it. There were a lot of things that I wanted to write about. One was what a hard time the doctors have. All those doctors are heroes—flawed heroes. Their incentive, really, is to help people. They don't make a lot of money. They work harder than anyone else. And yet, in a lot of ways, they're very, very imperfect. I had been in cancer hospitals not as a patient but as the child of a patient. Then I found out how complicated it was for the doctor. It was like stepping behind a curtain and seeing that the actors have costumes on. I suddenly saw the inner workings of something that had been very important in my life. So I wanted to write a book which would present both the doctor and the patient.

I do believe that if you write a book because you have messages, you can't write the book. I wrote the book because I *had* to write the book. Now, after the fact, I'm intellectualizing the reasons I might have written the book. Besides wanting to present both the patient's point of view and the doctor's point of view, another of those reasons was that I wanted to write a book that would force people to go through what I had gone through, defusing their fear and turning it into knowledge. I believe that fear is cancer's great friend, and I wanted to do something to dissipate that fear. So I wanted to write a book which was a compelling, obsessive love story that people would read in spite of themselves that would bring them into some kind of intimate relationship with knowledge about cancer that they need to have. People need to know about cancer. They need to know about doctors; they need to know how hospitals

work. I wanted to write a book that would tell them those things even if they didn't think they wanted to know. As I say in the book, about seventy percent of cancer is preventable. There are a lot of reasons why people don't do the things that they know perfectly well could prevent cancer, but one of them is fear. One of them is addiction.

What happened to me was that I got very close to some of the doctors. When I decided I was going to write about this, I talked with the Public Relations Director of the hospital and she gave me permission to start interviewing. I interviewed about eight doctors at length, and then I wasn't sure where this was going, what I was doing. At one point I went to interview one doctor and he said, "I can't tell you what I do; I can only show you." He gave me a white coat and his schedule, and he said, "Come when you can." Well, I put on the white coat and took off after him. I was riveted. I thought, I'll write a short nonfiction profile of this doctor. That's what we worked on for four months. Then I decided it couldn't just be a profile of him in the hospital; I had to see him at home. He had four kids. His wife was a surgeon; they had been at Harvard together. She had given up work to take care of the kids. I got very involved in this whole family situation, and then he said, "You can't write about me." So I found another doctor, followed him around, got very involved in his family situation. The same thing happened again.

But in the process of doing this I saw everything: I saw them operating; I saw them tell people they were going to die; I saw them tell people they were going to live; I saw them deal with the families; I saw them try to get permission for Do Not Resuscitate orders. It was fascinating, particularly given my obsessive interest. That's the information on which the novel is based. I spent basically a year talking to doctors and following them around, finding out everything I could. At that point—after I'd been working on this book for a year—I started writing a novel. The doctors in the novel aren't the doctors I followed around at all. Once it became a novel, it veered off, as fiction does, into my imagination—which by that time was pretty well stocked.

CA: Home before Dark *raised the question of whether you, as John Cheever's daughter, should have revealed much about him that you did in the book, including his bisexuality. At this remove, and with a biography due out soon, do you have any doubts that you did the right thing?*

CHEEVER: Here's how it all happened. I was pregnant, I had just gotten married, and we found out that my father was terminally ill. I was working on a novel, and I stopped work; I had a lot to take care of. I got involved in the hospital and started writing about my father to make myself feel better. I thought I'd just sit down and write whatever I was feeling, and I did, and it did make me feel better. It was really a kind of therapy while he was still sick, really a journal. It was a kind of mourning process. I started out writing about the experience of having him be so sick, and about the way he looked each day. I wanted to have a log of it; I knew I wouldn't remember it because it was too painful. More and more I found that I was writing about the past. By the time he died, which was six months after we found out how sick he was, I was writing quite a lot, both about what was happening from day to day and about my past with him. After he died, I kept on doing that. I had three other projects: the novel I had stopped, a screenplay I was writing, and something else—I forget what it was. And every day I would say to myself, Today I'm going to stop writing about my father and go on to these other projects; the time has come. Then every day I'd sit down at the typewriter and think, OK, one more day.

So these pages started to build up. By this time I had more than two hundred. Then came a big struggle. It was shapeless; it was all therapy. I believe that therapy and writing are very, very different, and if you mix them up, you're in trouble. I knew that what I had was no good in terms of writing. This was in August. My father had died in June, and after thirty days of still not being able to stop writing about him, I thought, I'll write a little memoir. I'll string together all the stories he ever told me, which is sort of what I was doing, and I'll write a little memoir, a hundred pages. Maybe we'll print it privately; maybe we won't. It was still for me. So I sat down with what I had already written and began to shape a little memoir. I wrote maybe a hundred and ten pages, and I know that I had decided I wanted to publish it, because at that point I had sold it to a publisher. I liked it. By this time it was fall.

One of the things my father had done that was interesting was keep journals. So I thought, I'll describe the journals. I did that, and then I thought that it would be great to throw in a couple of quotes from the journals to show what they were, to give my readers the texture of them, because these journals were so important to my father. They were in a vault in a moving company, where a friend of my father's had put them. I called him up and said, "I want to have a look at the journals," and he said, "Fine." We went to lunch and then went to the vault, and I grabbed about four of the journals. I took different years; I thought I'd just get a couple of paragraphs and quote them in my book. When I started reading them, I immediately realized that these journals shouldn't be in anybody else's vault. So the first thing I did was get my own vault and move them all. Then I read the four I had, and I was astonished, amazed . . . there's not a word for how I felt. I realized that I had never known my father, that I had never understood him.

I thought I'd read all the journals and then decide. It took me about a month, and it changed the whole way I looked at the world. I thought, I am not going to be the person to tell the world what my father was really like. But I thought too that neither could I publish some slim little memoir about him as a funny man, knowing what I knew now. So I abandoned the book. I also thought, Thanks, Dad. Now I'm going to have to tell the family. What I'd read wasn't just about his homosexuality; it was about everything—the depression, what alcoholism was really like, the whole thing. But by this time a lot of people were writing about him, including a biographer. I thought, what if they get it wrong? If somebody's going to break this, I don't want it to be one of my father's angry ex-lovers, and I don't want it to be the head of some English department who never knew him. I want it to be me. I want it to be someone who has read these journals, and has read his feelings about them. So I went back to the book with the idea that by presenting these things in context, in a sympathetic way, I was doing the most loving thing I could do. That was my intention. And the homosexuality is not even mentioned until three-quarters through the book. It's not as if his whole life was that at all.

CA: It's a very loving book, I think.

CHEEVER: I think so. I meant it as a eulogy. I really had serious doubts about it, but then I thought, Better someone who really loved him than a stranger.

CA: Your father had asked you to read some of his journals long before he died. When you finally read them after his death, did you have the feeling he had wanted you to know these things and perhaps had wanted your sanction?

CHEEVER: No question. He went to a psychiatrist when he had his first heart attack. His family doctor called me up afterward and said, "Do you know what he told the psychiatrist? He told the psychiatrist he was a homosexual." We both laughed, because we thought this was an expression of my father's disdain for psychiatry. I called my father up and said, "Daddy, why did you tell the doctor that you were gay?" My father just laughed. In the *Newsweek* interview, which was in 1977, I asked him if he'd ever had a homosexual experience, and he said he'd had many—all between the ages of nine and twelve. And he laughed. So he was sailing very close to the wind all of the time. There's also this thing in *Home before Dark* about my reading a letter he'd left in the pantry; it was from a man who was turning him down. I just didn't want to know. And it turned out that everyone else knew.

CA: Are there specific plans for the publication of your father's journals and letters at this point?

CHEEVER: It appears that the journals will be published. They are about a million and a half words, so it looks like a volume which will probably be from the journals but it will read like a novel, because the journals do. It will be published in 1991 or somewhere around there. This is all extremely tentative. My brother is working on the letters, and I think they will be published in a year or two.

CA: Talking with Helen Dudar for the Chicago Tribune Book World, *you called* Looking for Work *"a beginners book . . . a book in which I learned how to do a lot of things." Was* A Handsome Man *easier to write in any way, or was it the proverbial scary second novel?*

CHEEVER: I think it was the proverbial scary second novel. It was harder, much harder, and I actually think it was even more of a beginner's book. It doesn't just take one book, you know. I think in a way my first three novels were warm-ups for *Home before Dark*. By the time I got to writing *Home before Dark*, I knew how to do it. I never could have done it if I hadn't written those other three books. Although, I think *Looking for Work* is a very good first novel. But in a way *A Handsome Man* was more of a learning novel. It's hard to say. I don't want to disown my own work, but on the other hand, I feel as if I'm getting better.

CA: The Cage, the tragic story of the failed marriage of Billy and Julia Bristol, is a much more sombre book than the first two novels.

CHEEVER: Yes, and it's much more intellectual. *Looking for Work* is straight autobiographical. *A Handsome Man* is narrative biographical. And *The Cage* is metaphor. They're three very different kinds of novels.

CA: The actual cage that becomes the book's central metaphor is described in incredibly sharp detail—the design, the grillwork, the underground system through which Billy Bristol leaves it. Is it based on a real cage?

CHEEVER: No. I think it's so sharp because it doesn't exist. It might have something to do with the old lion house at the

Central Park Zoo, but that doesn't have any fancy grillwork or any underground system that I know about. There is a woodburning furnace in the cellar of the very small house that my grandparents left us in New Hampshire. But that house is not at all like Northwood. It's a little cabin. You couldn't possibly get into the underground furnace. I remember walking around New York looking at a lot of wrought iron work about the time I was writing the book, so I was trying to figure out what you could have in a grillwork. But there's not a cage like that.

CA: You've said in the past that you write on old metal-case portable Olivettis, and you do ten to twelve drafts. Have you changed in either regard? Do you use a word processor now?

CHEEVER: I bought a word processor and couldn't stand it and gave it away. But I've switched to an IBM electronic typewriter. I still write a lot of drafts, maybe eight to ten, though it's probably more like six to eight. Still a lot. When I'm finished with a book, there's a huge pile of paper.

CA: In 1980 you said that you didn't see much of other writers. But just in today's news you're twice in the company of other writers: once as a chairman of the upcoming Yaddo Second Annual Spring Gala and again as one of more than a hundred prominent people who signed a statement in support of surrogate mother Mary Beth Whitehead against William and Elizabeth Stern over the custody of Baby M. You obviously see more of other writers than you used to.

CHEEVER: Yes. That's changed. I think if you have any success as a writer at all you need other writers, and you also feel a tremendous obligation to help other writers in any way you can. Working for Yaddo is one of the ways I do that. I also love Yaddo; there's a selfish side. But I do think there's an obligation. I feel so lucky to be able to make a living as a writer today.

For another *CA* Interview with this author, see earlier entry in Volume 103.

BIOGRAPHICAL/CRITICAL SOURCES:

BOOKS

Cheever, Susan, *Home before Dark,* Houghton, 1984.
Contemporary Literary Criticism, Gale, Volume 18, 1981, Volume 48, 1988.
Dictionary of Literary Biography Yearbook: 1982, Gale, 1983.

PERIODICALS

American Spectator, January, 1982, February, 1985.
Antioch Review, spring, 1980.
Atlantic, January, 1980.
Chicago Tribune, October 21, 1984.
Chicago Tribune Book World, January 13, 1980, February 10, 1980, April 12, 1981.
Commonweal, July 4, 1980.
Esquire, February, 1985.
Globe and Mail (Toronto), June 20, 1987.
Los Angeles Times Book Review, October 3, 1982, October 24, 1984, May 17, 1987.
New Republic, May 16, 1981, November 12, 1984.
New Statesman, February 4, 1983.
Newsweek, January 14, 1980, October 22, 1984.
New York Review of Books, December 20, 1984.
New York Times, December 17, 1979, October 11, 1984, October 15, 1984.

New York Times Book Review, January 6, 1980, October 3, 1982, October 21, 1984.
People, November 5, 1984.
Publishers Weekly, November 2, 1984.
Spectator, February 2, 1985.
Time, December 24, 1979.
Times Literary Supplement, February 22, 1980, September 4, 1981, February 22, 1985, June 3, 1988.
Tribune Books (Chicago), May 3, 1987.
Village Voice, October 30, 1984.
Washington Post, July 19, 1981, October 15, 1984.
Washington Post Book World, October 7, 1984.

—*Sketch by Bryan Ryan*

—*Interview by Jean W. Ross*

*   *   *

CHERRY, Sheldon H(arold)   1934-

PERSONAL: Born March 31, 1934, in New York, N.Y.; son of Nathan and Fannie (Kasofsky) Cherry; married Gloria Barry, December 18, 1955 (divorced March, 1984); married Carolyn Runowicz (a physician), May, 1987; children: Sabrina, Dana, Pamela, Cara. *Education:* Columbia University, A.B., 1954, M.D., 1958. *Religion:* Jewish.

ADDRESSES: Office—1160 Park Ave., New York, N.Y. 10028.

CAREER: Private practice in obstetrics and gynecology, New York City, 1964—. Member of medical school faculty, Columbia University, 1964-69; Mount Sinai School of Medicine, New York City, associate professor, 1969—. *Military service:* U.S. Air Force, 1962-64; became captain.

MEMBER: American College of Obstetrics and Gynecology, American Board of Obstetrics and Gynecology, American College of Surgeons (fellow), New York Obstetrical Society, Alpha Omega Alpha.

AWARDS, HONORS: National Institutes of Health research grants, 1965-70.

WRITINGS:

Obstetrics and Gynecology, Volume IV, Medical Examination Publishing Co., 1967.
Understanding Pregnancy and Childbirth, Bobbs-Merrill, 1973, 2nd edition, 1984.
The Menopause Myth, Ballantine, 1975.
For Women of All Ages: A Gynecologist's Guide to Modern Female Health Care, Macmillan, 1979.
(Editor) *Rovinsky and Guttmacher's Medical, Surgical, and Gynecological Complications of Pregnancy,* 3rd edition (Cherry was not associated with previous editions), Williams & Wilkins, 1985.
Planning Ahead for Pregnancy, Viking, 1987.

Contributor of thirty-six research papers to medical journals.

*   *   *

CHEUSE, Alan   1940-

PERSONAL: Born January 23, 1940, in Perth Amboy, N.J.; son of Philip and Henrietta (Diamond) Cheuse; married Mary Agan, October 7, 1964 (divorced, 1974); married Marjorie Lee Pryse, June 22, 1975 (divorced, 1984); children: (first marriage) Joshua Todd; (second marriage) Emma Cordelia, Sonya Ruth. *Education:* Attended Lafayette College, 1957-58; Rutgers University, B.A., 1961, Ph.D., 1974.

ADDRESSES: Home—3307 Highland Place N.W., Washington, D.C. 20008. *Office*—Department of English, George Mason University, Fairfax, Va. 22030.

CAREER: Toll taker, New Jersey Turnpike Authority, 1961; reporter, Fairchild Publications, 1962-63; member of staff, Kirkus Review Service, 1963-64; Butler Institute, Guadalajara, Jalisco, Mexico, teacher of history and English, 1965-66; New York City Department of Welfare, New York, N.Y., case worker, 1966-67; Bennington College, Bennington, Vt., member of Division of Literature and Languages, 1970-78; University of the South, Sewanee, Tenn., writer in residence, 1984; University of Michigan, Ann Arbor, writer in residence, 1984-86; Bennington College, acting director of writing workshops, 1986-87; George Mason University, Fairfax, Va., member of writing faculty, 1987—. Visiting writer, University of Virginia, spring, 1987. Producer of radio magazine "Stories on the Air" for National Public Radio (NPR), 1989—.

MEMBER: National Book Critics Circle.

AWARDS, HONORS: National Endowment for the Arts writing fellowship, 1979-80.

WRITINGS:

(Editor with Richard M. Koffler) *The Rarer Action: Essays in Honor of Francis Fergusson*, Rutgers University Press, 1971.
Candace and Other Stories, Applewood Press, 1980.
The Bohemians: John Reed and His Friends Who Shook the World (novel), Applewood Books, 1982.
The Grandmothers' Club (novel), Peregrine Smith, 1986.
Fall Out of Heaven: An Autobiographical Journey, Peregrine Smith, 1987.

Contributor of short stories to *New Yorker, Black Warrior Review,* and other periodicals; contributor of articles and reviews to *Nation, New York Times Book Review, Los Angeles Times Book Review, Saturday Review, Chicago Tribune, Ms., Boston Globe,* and numerous other periodicals. Member of editorial board, *Studies on the Left,* 1964-65. Book commentator for NPR program "All Things Considered," 1982—.

WORK IN PROGRESS: Novels and stories; book-length essay on the work of Joan Didion.

SIDELIGHTS: In a broad sense, Alan Cheuse's novel *The Grandmothers' Club* relates the experience of the Jewish immigrant in America. More specifically, it discloses the life of misfortune of Rabbi Emmanuel (Manny) Bloch by his mother, Minnie. As Jerome Charyn explains in the *New York Times Book Review,* "this is an unlikely novel concerning a group of grandmothers who meet to trade stories about sons, daughters-in-law and whatever else is on this side of the moon. Minnie Bloch does most of the talking. She's the 'leading lady in the grandmothers' club.'" In her garrulous fashion, Minnie pieces together a record of her son's life; at age eight, we learn, Manny saw his father crushed to death beneath a milk wagon and that is why he has failed to move in rhythm with the rest of the world since. We also learn of Manny's more recent abandonment of his religious commitments for success on Wall Street, as well as his acceptance of a mistress when his wife experiences mental instability. Charyn believes *The Grandmothers' Club* "would be an ordinary Jewish family saga if Minnie were an ordinary woman.... It is this ... grandmother's ability to thrust herself into her son's surroundings, to soak up his past and dream her way into his future, to hallucinate a life for him, that is both the virtue and the

extraordinary sting of the book." Although in Charyn's opinion the novel is too long and at times overly melodramatic, he insists "we are all Jewish sons (and daughters) in Alan Cheuse's grip. His novel is a bitter, brilliant series of songs, heartless and tender, with a magical displacement of time and a language that rattles us and reminds us how close art and chaos really are."

Other critics value *The Grandmothers' Club* as well. In the *New York Times,* Christopher Lehmann-Haupt calls it a "haunting story.... A reader comes away from 'The Grandmothers' Club' with the sense that he has read an epic of Jewish life in America and of the sometimes tragic conflict between blessedness and wealth." If the reader is able to overcome some of Minnie's longwindedness and forced humor, "'The Grandmothers' Club' is bound to work its powerful incantatory effects on you," maintains Lehmann-Haupt. As for *Chicago Tribune* reviewer Judy Bass, Minnie Bloch is "a character of stunning authenticity, one whose nuances render her both lifelike and endearing.... Above all, it is Minnie's humaneness that emerges with aching clarity, and her abundant sympathy for all those who stumble into crucibles from which there is no escape."

BIOGRAPHICAL/CRITICAL SOURCES:

BOOKS

Cheuse, Alan, *The Grandmothers' Club*, Peregrine Smith, 1986.

PERIODICALS

Chicago Tribune, October 3, 1986.
Los Angeles Times, October 1, 1987.
Los Angeles Times Book Review, December 7, 1986.
New York Times, November 20, 1986.
New York Times Book Review, November 9, 1980, March 28, 1982, October 26, 1986.
Tribune Books (Chicago), September 20, 1987.
Washington Post Book World, March 14, 1982.

*   *   *

CHILDRESS, Alice 1920-

PERSONAL: Surname is pronounced *Chil*-dress; born October 12, 1920, in Charleston, S.C.; married second husband, Nathan Woodard (a musician), July 17, 1957; children: (first marriage) Jean (Mrs. Richard Lee). *Education:* Attended public schools in New York, N.Y.

ADDRESSES: Home—New York, N.Y. *Agent*—Flora Roberts, Inc., 157 West 57th St., Penthouse A, New York, N.Y. 10019.

CAREER: Playwright, novelist, actress, and director. Began career in theatre as an actress, with her first appearance in "On Strivers Row," 1940; actress and director with American Negro Theatre, New York, N.Y., for eleven years; played in "Natural Man," 1941, "Anna Lucasta," 1944, and her own play "Florence" (which she also directed), 1949; has also performed on Broadway and television. Lecturer at universities and schools; member of panel discussions and conferences on Black American theatre at numerous institutions, including New School for Social Research, 1965, and Fisk University, 1966; visiting scholar at Radcliffe Institute for Independent Study (now Mary Ingraham Bunting Institute), Cambridge, Mass., 1966-68. Member of governing board of Frances Delafield Hospital.

MEMBER: PEN, Dramatists Guild (member of council), American Federation of Television and Radio Artists, Writers Guild of America East (member of council), Harlem Writers Guild.

AWARDS, HONORS: Obie Award for best original Off-Broadway play, *Village Voice,* 1956, for "Trouble in Mind"; John Golden Fund for Playwrights grant, 1957; Rockefeller grant, 1967; *A Hero Ain't Nothin' but a Sandwich* was named one of the Outstanding Books of the Year by *New York Times Book Review,* 1973, and a Best Young Adult Book of 1975 by American Library Association; Woodward School Book Award, 1974, Jane Addams Children's Book Honor Award for young adult novel, 1974, National Book Award nomination, 1974, and Lewis Carroll Shelf Award, University of Wisconsin, 1975, all for *A Hero Ain't Nothin' but a Sandwich;* named honorary citizen of Atlanta, Ga., 1975, for opening of "Wedding Band"; Sojourner Truth Award, National Association of Negro Business and Professional Women's Clubs, 1975; Virgin Islands film festival award for best screenplay, 1977, for "A Hero Ain't Nothin' but a Sandwich"; first Paul Robeson Award for Outstanding Contributions to the Performing Arts, Black Filmmakers Hall of Fame, 1977, for "A Hero Ain't Nothin' but a Sandwich"; "Alice Childress Week" officially observed in Charleston and Columbia, S.C., 1977, to celebrate opening of "Sea Island Song"; *Rainbow Jordan* was named one of the "Best Books" by *School Library Journal,* 1981, one of the Outstanding Books of the Year by *New York Times,* 1982, and a notable children's trade book in social studies by National Council for the Social Studies and Children's Book Council, 1982; honorable mention, Coretta Scott King Award, 1982, for *Rainbow Jordan.*

WRITINGS:

Like One of the Family: Conversations from a Domestic's Life, Independence Publishers, 1956, reprinted with an introduction by Trudier Harris, Beacon Press, 1986.
(Editor) *Black Scenes* (collection of scenes from plays written by Afro-Americans about the Black experience), Doubleday, 1971.
A Hero Ain't Nothin' but a Sandwich (novel; also see below), Coward, 1973.
A Short Walk (novel), Coward, 1979.
Rainbow Jordan (novel), Coward, 1981.
Many Closets, Coward, 1987.

PLAYS

"Florence" (one-act), first produced in New York City at American Negro Theatre, directed by and starring Childress, 1949.
"Just a Little Simple " (based on Langston Hughes's short story collection *Simple Speaks His Mind*), first produced in New York City at Club Baron Theatre, September, 1950.
"Gold through the Trees," first produced at Club Baron Theatre, 1952.
"Trouble in Mind," first produced Off-Broadway at Greenwich Mews Theatre, directed by Childress, November 3, 1955, revised version published in *Black Theatre: A Twentieth-Century Collection of the Work of Its Best Playwrights,* edited by Lindsay Patterson, Dodd, 1971.
Wedding Band: A Love/Hate Story in Black and White (first produced in Ann Arbor, Mich., at University of Michigan, December 7, 1966; produced Off-Broadway at New York Shakespeare Festival Theatre, directed by Childress

and Joseph Papp, September 26, 1972; also see below), Samuel French, 1973.
"String" (one-act; based on Guy de Maupassant's story "A Piece of String"; also see below), first produced Off-Broadway at St. Mark's Playhouse, March 25, 1969.
"Mojo: A Black Love Story" (one-act; also see below), produced in New York City at New Heritage Theatre, November, 1970.
Mojo [and] *String,* Dramatists Play Service, 1971.
When the Rattlesnake Sounds: A Play (juvenile), illustrated by Charles Lilly, Coward, 1975.
Let's Hear It for the Queen: A Play (juvenile), Coward, 1976.
"Sea Island Song," produced in Charleston, S.C., 1977, produced as "Gullah" in Amherst, Mass., at University of Massachusetts—Amherst, 1984.
"Moms: A Praise Play for a Black Comedienne" (based on the life of Jackie "Moms" Mabley), music and lyrics by Childress and her husband, Nathan Woodard, first produced by Green Plays at Art Awareness, 1986, produced Off-Broadway at Hudson Guild Theatre, February 4, 1987.

Also author of "Martin Luther King at Montgomery, Alabama," music by Woodard, 1969, "A Man Bearing a Pitcher," 1969, "The African Garden," music by Woodard, 1971, and "Vashti's Magic Mirror"; author of "The Freedom Drum," music by Woodard, produced as "Young Martin Luther King" by Performing Arts Repertory Theatre (on tour), 1969-71.

SCREENPLAYS

Wine in the Wilderness: A Comedy-Drama (first produced in Boston by WGBH-TV, March 4, 1969), Dramatists Play Service, 1969.
"Wedding Band" (based on her play of the same title), American Broadcasting Companies (ABC-TV), 1973.
"A Hero Ain't Nothin' but a Sandwich" (based on her novel of the same title), New World Pictures, 1978.
"String" (based on her play of the same title), Public Broadcasting Service (PBS-TV), 1979.

CONTRIBUTOR

Langston Hughes, editor, *The Best Short Stories by Negro Writers: An Anthology from 1899 to the Present,* Little, Brown, 1967.
Plays to Remember (includes "The World on a Hill"), Macmillan, 1968.
Stanley Richards, editor, *The Best Short Plays of 1972,* Chilton, 1972.
The Young American Basic Reading Program, Lyons & Carnahan, 1972.
Success in Reading, Silver Burdette, 1972.
Richards, editor, *Best Short Plays of the World Theatre, 1968-1973,* Crown, 1973.
Patterson, editor, *Anthology of the Afro-American in the Theatre: A Critical Approach,* Publishers Agency, 1978.
R. Baxter Miller, editor, *Black American Literature and Humanism,* University of Kentucky Press, 1981.
Mari Evans, editor, *Black Women Writers (1950-1980): A Critical Evaluation,* Doubleday-Anchor, 1984.

Also contributor to *Keeping the Faith,* edited by Pat Exum.

OTHER

Author of "Here's Mildred" column in *Baltimore Afro-American,* 1956-58. Contributor of plays, articles, and reviews to *Masses and Mainstream, Black World, Freedomways, Essence, Negro Digest, New York Times,* and other publications.

SIDELIGHTS: Alice Childress's work is noted for its frank treatment of racial issues, its compassionate yet discerning characterizations, and its universal appeal. Because her books and plays often deal with such controversial subjects as miscegenation and teenage drug addiction, her work has been banned in certain locations. She recalls that some affiliate stations refused to carry the nationally televised broadcasts of ''Wedding Band'' and ''Wine in the Wilderness,'' and in the case of the latter play, the entire state of Alabama banned the telecast. Childress notes in addition that as late as 1973 the novel *A Hero Ain't Nothin' but a Sandwich* ''was the first book banned in a Savannah, Georgia school library since *Catcher in the Rye,* which the same school banned in the fifties.'' Despite such regional resistance, Childress has won praise and respect for writings that a *Variety* reviewer terms ''powerful and poetic.''

A talented writer and performer in several media, Childress began her career in the theater, initially as an actress and later as a director and playwright. Although ''theater histories make only passing mention of her,. . . she was in the forefront of important developments in that medium,'' writes *Dictionary of Literary Biography* contributor Trudier Harris. Rosemary Curb points out in another *Dictionary of Literary Biography* article that Childress's 1952 drama ''Gold Through the Trees'' was ''the first play by a black woman professionally produced on the American stage.'' Moreover, Curb adds, ''As a result of successful performances of [her 1950 play 'Just a Little Simple' and 'Gold Through the Trees'], Childress initiated Harlem's first all-union Off-Broadway contracts recognizing the Actors Equity Association and the Harlem Stage Hand Local.''

Partly because of her pioneering efforts, Childress is considered a crusader by many. But she is also known as ''a writer who resists compromise,'' says Doris E. Abramson in *Negro Playwrights in the American Theatre: 1925-1959.* ''She tries to write about [black] problems as honestly as she can.'' The problems Childress addresses most often are racism and its effects. Her ''Trouble in Mind,'' for example, is a play within a play that focuses on the anger and frustration experienced by a troupe of black actors as they try to perform stereotyped roles in a play that has been written, produced, and directed by whites. As Sally R. Sommer explains in the *Village Voice,* ''The plot is about an emerging rebellion begun as the heroine, Wiletta, refuses to enact a namby-Mammy, either in the play or for her director.'' In the *New York Times,* Arthur Gelb states that Childress ''has some witty and penetrating things to say about the dearth of roles for [black] actors in the contemporary theatre, the cutthroat competition for these parts and the fact that [black] actors often find themselves playing stereotyped roles in which they cannot bring themselves to believe.'' And of ''Wedding Band,'' a play about an interracial relationship that takes place in South Carolina during World War I, Clive Barnes writes in the *New York Times,* ''Childress very carefully suggests the stirrings of black consciousness, as well as the strength of white bigotry.''

Critics Sommer and the *New York Times*'s Richard Eder find that Childress's treatment of the themes and issues in ''Trouble in Mind'' and ''Wedding Band'' gives these plays a timeless quality. ''Writing in 1955,. . . Alice Childress used the concentric circles of the play-within-the-play to examine the multiple roles blacks enact in order to survive,'' Sommer remarks. She finds that viewing ''Trouble in Mind'' years later enables one to see ''its double cutting edge: It predicts not only the course of social history but the course of black playwriting.''

Eder states: ''The question [in ''Wedding Band''] is whether race is a category of humanity or a division of it. The question is old by now, and was in 1965, [when the play was written,] but it takes the freshness of new life in the marvelous characters that Miss Childress has created to ask it.''

The strength and insight of Childress's characterizations have been widely commented upon; critics contend that the characters who populate her plays and novels are believable and memorable. Eder praises the ''rich and lively characterization'' of ''Wedding Band.'' Similarly impressed, Harold Clurman writes in the *Nation* that ''there is an honest pathos in the telling of this simple story, and some humorous and touching thumbnail sketches reveal knowledge and understanding of the people dealt with.'' In the novel *A Short Walk,* Childress chronicles the life of a fictitious black woman, Cora James, from her birth in 1900 to her death in the middle of the century, illustrating, as *Washington Post* critic Joseph McLellan describes it, ''a transitional generation in black American society.'' McLellan notes that the story ''wanders considerably'' and that ''the reader is left with no firm conclusion that can be put into a neat sentence or two.'' What is more important, he asserts, is that ''the wandering has been through some interesting scenery, and instead of a conclusion the reader has come to know a human being—complex, struggling valiantly and totally believable.'' And of Childress's novel about teenage heroin addiction, *A Hero Ain't Nothin' but a Sandwich,* the *Lion and the Unicorn*'s Miguel Oritz states, ''The portrait of whites is more realistic in this book, more compassionate, and at the same time, because it is believable, more scathing.''

Some criticism has been leveled at what such reviewers as Abramson and Edith Oliver believe to be Childress's tendency to speechify, especially in her plays. ''A reader of the script is very much aware of the author pulling strings, putting her own words into a number of mouths,'' Abramson says of ''Trouble in Mind.'' According to Oliver in the *New Yorker,* ''The first act [of 'Wedding Band'] is splendid, but after that we hit a few jarring notes, when the characters seem to be speaking as much for the benefit of us eavesdroppers out front . . . as for the benefit of one another.''

For the most part, however, Childress's work has been acclaimed for its honesty, insight, and compassion. In his review of *A Hero Ain't Nothin' but a Sandwich,* Oritz writes: ''The book conveys very strongly the message that we are all human, even when we are acting in ways that we are somewhat ashamed of. The structure of the book grows out of the personalities of the characters, and the author makes us aware of how much the economic and social circumstances dictate a character's actions.'' Loften Mitchell concludes in *Crisis:* ''Childress writes with a sharp, satiric touch. Character seems to interest her more than plot. Her characterizations are piercing, her observations devastating.''

Alice Childress commented: ''Books, plays, tele-plays, motion picture scenarios, etc., I seem caught up in a fragmentation of writing skills. But an idea comes to me in a certain form and, if it stays with me, must be written out or put in outline form before I can move on to the next event. I sometimes wonder about writing in different forms; could it be that women are used to dealing with the bits and pieces of life and do not feel as [compelled to specialize]? The play form is the one most familiar to me and so influences all of my writing— I think in scenes.

''My young years were very old in feeling, I was shut out of so much for so long. [I] soon began to embrace the low-profile as a way of life, which helped me to develop as a writer. Quiet living is restful when one's writing is labeled 'controversial.'

"Happily, I managed to save a bit of my youth for spending in these later years. Oh yes, there are other things to be saved [besides] money. If we hang on to that part within that was once childhood, I believe we enter into a new time dimension and every day becomes another lifetime in itself. This gift of understanding is often given to those who constantly battle against the negatives of life with determination."

BIOGRAPHICAL/CRITICAL SOURCES:

BOOKS

Abramson, Doris E., *Negro Playwrights in the American Theatre, 1925-1959,* Columbia University Press, 1969.
Betsko, Kathleen and Rachel Koenig, *Interviews with Contemporary Women Playwrights,* Beech Tree Books, 1987.
Children's Literature Review, Volume 14, Gale, 1988.
Contemporary Literary Criticism, Gale, Volume 12, 1980, Volume 15, 1980.
Dictionary of Literary Biography, Gale, Volume 7: *Twentieth-Century American Dramatists,* 1981, Volume 38: *Afro-American Writers after 1955: Dramatists and Prose Writers,* 1985.
Donelson, Kenneth L. and Alleen Pace Nilson, *Literature for Today's Young Adults,* Scott, Foresman, 1980, 2nd edition, 1985.
Evans, Mari, editor, *Black Women Writers (1950-1980): A Critical Evaluation,* Doubleday-Anchor, 1984.
Hatch, James V. *Black Theater, U.S.A.: Forty-five Plays by Black Americans,* Free Press, 1974.
Mitchell, Loften, editor, *Voices of the Black Theatre,* James White, 1975.
Street, Douglas, editor, *Children's Novels and the Movies,* Ungar, 1983.

PERIODICALS

Crisis, April, 1965.
Freedomways, Volume 14, number 1, 1974.
Interracial Books for Children Bulletin, Volume 12, numbers 7-8, 1981.
Lion and the Unicorn, fall, 1978.
Los Angeles Times, November 13, 1978, February 25, 1983.
Los Angeles Times Book Review, July 25, 1982.
Ms., December, 1979.
Nation, November 13, 1972.
Negro Digest, April, 1967, January, 1968.
Newsweek, August 31, 1987.
New Yorker, November 4, 1972, Noyember 19, 1979.
New York Times, November 5, 1955, February 2, 1969, April 2, 1969, October 27, 1972, November 5, 1972, February 3, 1978, January 11, 1979, January 23, 1987, February 10, 1987, March 6, 1987, August 18, 1987, October 22, 1987.
New York Times Book Review, November 4, 1973, November 11, 1979, April 25, 1981.
Show Business, April 12, 1969.
Variety, December 20, 1972.
Village Voice, January 15, 1979.
Washington Post, May 18, 1971, December 28, 1979.*

*   *   *

CHISHOLM, Shirley (Anita St. Hill)   1924-

PERSONAL: Born November 30, 1924, in Brooklyn, N.Y.;
brought to Barbados, 1927; brought to U.S., 1934; daughter of Charles Christopher and Ruby (Seale) St. Hill; married Conrad Q. Chisholm (a social service investigator), October 8, 1949 (divorced February, 1977); married Arthur Hardwick (a businessman), November 26, 1977. *Education:* Brooklyn College (now Brooklyn College of the City University of New York), B.A. (cum laude), 1946; Columbia University, M.A., 1952. *Politics:* Democrat. *Religion:* Methodist.

ADDRESSES: Home—48 Crestwood Lane, Williamsville, N.Y. 14221. *Office*—Department of Sociology and Anthropology, Mount Holyoke College, South Hadley, Mass. 01075.

CAREER: Mt. Calvary Child Care Center, Harlem, N.Y., 1946-53, began as teacher's aide, became teacher; Friend in Need Nursery, Brooklyn, N.Y., director, 1953; Hamilton-Madison Child Care Center, New York City, director, 1954-59; New York City Bureau of Child Welfare, Division of Day Care, New York City, education consultant, 1959-64; New York State Assembly, Albany, member, 1964-68; U. S. Congress, representative from 12th District, New York City, 1968-83; Mt. Holyoke College, Department of Sociology and Anthropology, South Hadley, Mass., Purington Professor, 1983—. Fellow of School of Social Work, Adelphi University of Social Work. Unsuccessful Democratic presidential primary candidate, 1972. Founding member, National Women's Political Caucus. Former member of board of directors, Brooklyn Home for Aged. Consultant to Central Brooklyn Coordinating Council.

MEMBER: National Association of College Women, League of Women Voters, Americans for Democratic Action, Democratic Women Workshop, National Association for the Advancement of Colored People, United Negro College Fund, Advertising Council, Key Women, Inc. (president, Brooklyn chapter), Bedford-Stuyvesant Political League, Brooklyn College Alumnae, Delta Sigma Theta.

AWARDS, HONORS: Award for Outstanding Work in Field of Child Welfare, Women's Council of Brooklyn, 1957; Key Woman of the Year Award, 1963; Woman of Achievement Award, Key Women, Inc., 1965; Committee to Friends plaque, 1965; Human Relations Award, Central Nassau Club of Business and Professional Women, 1965; citation for outstanding service in the field of early childhood education and welfare, Sisterhood of Concord Baptist Church (Brooklyn), 1965; "Outstanding Service in Good Government" plaque, Christian Women's Retreat, 1965; Louise Waterman Wise Award, National Women's Division of the American Jewish Congress, 1969, for distinguished service in the cause of human rights; Award of Honor, Brooklyn College, 1969; Distinguished Service medal, Teachers College, 1969; Youth in Action Humanitarian Award of family counselling, 1969; Albert Einstein College of Medicine achievement award, 1969; Deborah Gannett Award, National Media Women, 1969; Meritorious Achievement award, Essex County college, 1971; Clairol's "Woman of the Year" Award, 1973, for outstanding achievement in public affairs; Civic and Community Leadership award, Council of Churches of New York City (Brooklyn Division), 1977; Certificate of Appreciation, College of Buffalo, State University of New York, 1981.

Honorary degrees from numerous colleges and universities in United States, including: L.H.D., North Carolina Central University, 1969, and Hampton Institute, 1970; LL. D., from Talladega College, 1969, Wilmington College, 1970, LaSalle College, William Patterson College of New Jersey, University of Maine, Capitol University, and Coppin State College, all

1971, Pratt Institute, 1972, Kenyon College, 1973, Aquinas College and Reed College, both 1974, University of Cincinnati, and Smith College, both 1975, Simmons College, 1977, Metropolitan State College, 1980, Mount Holyoke College and Villa Maria College, both 1981, Western Michigan University, Spelman College, and Saint Francis College, all 1982.

WRITINGS:

AUTOBIOGRAPHY

Unbought and Unbossed, Houghton, 1970.
The Good Fight, Haper, 1973.

CONTRIBUTOR

Lester Thomsen, editor, *Representative American Speeches, 1968-69*, Wilson, 1969.
Waldo H. Braden, editor, *Representative American Speeches, 1971-72*, Wilson, 1972.
Waldo H. Braden, editor, *Representative American Speeches, 1972-73*, Wilson, 1973.

OTHER

Contributor of articles to newspapers and periodicals.

SIDELIGHTS: "Shirley Chisholm is true grit," Susan Brownmiller writes in *Shirley Chisholm*. "Her cometlike rise from clubhouse worker to Representative in the United States Congress was no accident of the political heavens. It was accomplished by the wiles of a steely politician with a belief in her own abilities which at times approaches an almost Messianic fervor."

The title of Chisholm's first book, *Unbought and Unbossed* (also the campaign slogal of her first Congressional campaign), exemplifies the intense individualism of Chisholm's private and public life. Reviewers of the book express admiration for what it reveals about its author. Like Brownmiller, they applaud Chisholm's unflagging spirit which carried her from poverty to the Congress of the United States where she was the first black female member.

In *Catholic World*, for example, Sr. Elizabeth Kolmer comments: "Chisholm's story is a lively one. She herself is a petite woman, intelligent and dedicated with a fire twice her size. There is a singleness of purpose in her book just as there is in her life." Similarly, Jeffrey M. Elliot writes in the *Negro History Bulletin:* "Chisholm's *Unbought and Unbossed* is an absorbing, literate, revealing and inspiring account of those circumstances which made it possible for an idealist, an independent, a fighter; a woman of deep conviction, rare courage, and unquestionable honesty to do battle with party bosses, influence peddlers, and political hacks, and win."

Although while in college Chisholm had decided to dedicate herself to becoming a teacher of young children, the decision wasn't entirely her own. In *Unbought and Unbossed* she explains, "There was no other road open to a young black woman. Law, medicine, even nursing were too expensive, and few schools would admit black men, much less a woman."

While pursuing her childcare career, Chisholm became active in local politics, holding positions of leadership in several community groups. After ten years of doing everything from decorating cigar boxes to helping voters get to the polls, Chisholm decided to do the one thing she hadn't done, run for office. Although she encountered much opposition to her candidacy—mainly because of her sex—she won her first campaign by a wide margin and became a member of the New York State Assembly.

During her four years in Albany she learned more about the intricacies of politics and her constituents learned more about her political priorities. In *Unbought and Unbossed*, Chisholm points with pride to the eight bills she saw passed of the fifty she introduced. "Two I was especially satisfied with," she writes. "One created a program called SEEK, to make it possible for young men and women from disadvantaged backgrounds to go to college, by seeking them out and assisting them while they go to school.... The other was a bill to set up the state's first unemployment insurance coverage for personal and domestic employees."

As these two bills reveal, among Chisholm's causes are better educational opportunities for minority groups, programs for the poor and disadvantaged, and a constant push for equality for ethnic minorities and for women. After her election to Congress in 1968, she introduced, co-sponsored, and ardently supported many important measures linked to these causes including proposals to create a study commission on Afro-American history and culture, to enlarge the powers of the Department of Housing and Urban Development, to establish a Department of Consumer Affairs at a full Cabinet level, and several anti-poverty and welfare programs.

While election to Congress was the realization of a dream for Chisholm, she soon focused on another goal, running for President of the United States. Her second book, *The Good Fight*, details her campaign for the Democratic presidential nomination in 1972.

Although Chisholm failed in her presidential bid, *Best Sellers* contributor Norman Lederer maintains that her candidacy was an important political event. "Chisholm's campaign was unusual," he observes, "in that it stressed real issues omitted from the platforms of the major candidates and obscured by dogma among minority candidates.... Chisholm's failure to obtain the nomination was a foregone conclusion but through her intrepid effort a new life and vitality was infused into the American political scene."

Chisholm also sees her candidacy in a positive light. In *The Good Fight* she notes, "The mere fact that a black woman dared to run for President, *seriously,* not expecting to win but sincerely trying to, is what it was all about. 'It can be done'; that was what I was trying to say, by doing it."

"We Americans," she adds, "have a chance to become someday a nation in which all racial stocks and classes can exist in their own selfhoods, but meet on a basis of respect and equality and live together, socially, economically, and politically.... I hope I did a little to make it happen. I am going to keep trying to make it happen as long as I am able. I will not run for President again, but in a broad sense my campaign will continue. In fact, it is just beginning."

BIOGRAPHICAL/CRITICAL SOURCES:

BOOKS

Brownmiller, Susan, *Shirley Chisholm*, Doubleday, 1970.
Chisholm, Shirley, *Unbought and Unbossed*, Houghton, 1970.
Chisholm, Shirley, *The Good Fight*, Harper, 1973.
Contemporary Issues Criticism, Volume 2, Gale, 1984.

PERIODICALS

Atlantic, November, 1970.
Best Sellers, October 15, 1970, July 15, 1973.

Catholic World, February, 1971.
Congressional Digest, January, 1971.
Ebony, February, 1969.
Freedomways, first quarter, 1974.
Los Angeles Times, December 18, 1983.
McCall's, August, 1970.
Nation, January 26, 1970.
Negro History Bulletin, May, 1972.
New York Times Book Review, November 1, 1970, October 21, 1973.
New York Times Magazine, April 13, 1969.
Time, November 2, 1970.
Washington Post, October 10, 1970.*

—*Sketch by Marian Gonsior*

*   *   *

CHISHOLM, William S(herman), Jr.   1931-

PERSONAL: Born February 2, 1931, in Detroit, Mich.; married Marian Moutoux, 1953; children: Susan, James, Thomas. *Education:* Baldwin-Wallace College, A.B., 1953; Western Reserve University (now Case Western Reserve University), M.A., 1955; University of Michigan, Ph.D., 1964. *Politics:* Radical left. *Religion:* Atheist.

ADDRESSES: Office—Department of English, Cleveland State University, Cleveland, Ohio 44114.

CAREER: University of Toledo, Toledo, Ohio, instructor, 1956-59, assistant professor of English, 1959-61; Wayne State University, Detroit, Mich., instructor in English, 1961-63; pronunciation editor, *Webster's New World Dictionary* (2nd edition), 1963-65; Western Illinois University, Macomb, associate professor of English, 1965-69; Cleveland State University, Cleveland, Ohio, associate professor, 1969-72, professor of English, 1972—. High school lecturer, 1972-74.

MEMBER: Linguistic Society of America.

WRITINGS:

The New English, Funk, 1969.
(Editor with David Guralnik and others) *Webster's New World Dictionary*, 2nd edition (Chisholm not associated with earlier edition), World Publishing, 1970.
Syllabus and Video Instruction: English 101, Department of English, Cleveland State University, 1970.
(Contributor) Lance Buhl, editor, *Innovative Teaching: Issues, Strategies, and Evaluation*, Cleveland State University, 1973.
(With Louis T. Milic) *The English Language: Form and Use*, McKay, 1974.
Essentials of English Linguistics, Longman, 1981.
(Editor) *Interrogativity: A Colloquium on the Grammar, Typology, and Pragmatics of Questions in Seven Diverse Languages, Cleveland, Ohio, October 5th, 1981-May 3rd, 1982*, J. Benjamins, 1984.
Webster's New World Guide to Pronunciation, Simon & Schuster, 1984.

Also author of sound recording, "Webster's New World Phonoguide," 1970, and audio-visual presentation, "Language Yes," 1973. Contributor to professional journals.

SIDELIGHTS: William S. Chisholm, Jr., describes himself as a "transformationalist-integrationist linguist with emphasis on pedagogy." He once wrote: "The mind and how it controls language should be pursued in school. But this is impossible in a society that promotes only conformism, racism, mediocrity."

*   *   *

CIRCUS, Anthony
See HOCH, Edward D(entinger)

*   *   *

CLARK, William Bedford   1947-

PERSONAL: Born January 23, 1947, in Oklahoma City, Okla.; son of William B. (a pipeliner) and Florine (Griggs) Clark; married Charlene Kerne (a library development professional), December 22, 1972; children: Mary Frances, Eleanor Kerne. *Education:* University of Oklahoma, B.A., 1969, Louisiana State University, M.A., 1971, Ph.D., 1973.

ADDRESSES: Home—2304 Burton, Bryan, Tex. 77802. *Office*—Department of English, Texas A&M University, College Station, Tex. 77843.

CAREER: North Carolina Agricultural and Technical State University, Greensboro, assistant professor of English, 1974-77; Texas A&M University, College Station, 1977—, began as assistant professor, became professor of English.

MEMBER: Modern Language Association of America, Society for the Study of Southern Literature, Conference on Christianity and Literature, South Central Modern Language Association.

AWARDS, HONORS: Grants from National Endowment for the Humanities, 1973-74, 1977, 1980.

WRITINGS:

(Contributor) George Carter and Bruce Mouser, editors, *Identity and Awareness: Selected Proceedings of the First and Second Minorities Studies Conferences*, [La Crosse], 1975.
(Editor and author of introduction) *Critical Essays on Robert Penn Warren*, G. K. Hall, 1981.
(Co-editor with W. Craig Turner) *Critical Essays on American Humor*, G. K. Hall, 1984.
(Contributor) Ann Abadie and Doreen Fowler, editors, *Faulkner and Humor*, University of Mississippi, 1985.

Contributor of about forty articles and reviews to literature journals and literary magazines, including *Southern Review, Antioch Review, American Literature, Renascence, South Atlantic Quarterly, Kenyon Review, Sewanee Review*, and *Studies in American Humor*. Editor of *South Central Review*, 1984-87.

WORK IN PROGRESS: Continuing research on the career and writings of Robert Penn Warren and the literature of the American West.

SIDELIGHTS: William Bedford Clark told *CA:* "For me, literary criticism is not only the exploration of a text but a mode of self-exploration. I am often surprised by the degree to which my own writings represent an implicit autobiography."

*   *   *

CLAYPOOL, Jane
See MINER, Jane Claypool

CLEAGE, Pearl (Michelle) 1948-

PERSONAL: Indexed in some sources under married name, Pearl Lomax; surname is pronounced Clegg; born December 7, 1948, in Springfield, Mass.; daughter of Albert Buford (a minister) and Doris (a teacher; maiden name, Graham) Cleage; married Michael Lucius Lomax (an elected official of Fulton County, Ga.), October 31, 1969; children: Deignan Njeri. *Education:* Attended Howard University, 1966-69, Yale University, 1969, and University of the West Indies, 1971; Spelman College, B.A., 1971; graduate study at Atlanta University.

ADDRESSES: Home—1665 Havilon Dr. S.W., Atlanta, Ga. 30311.

CAREER: Playwright, poet. Martin Luther King, Jr., Archival Library, Atlanta, Ga., member of field collection staff, 1969-70; Southern Education Program, Inc., Atlanta, assistant director, 1970-71; WQXI, Atlanta, writer and associate producer, 1972-73; City of Atlanta, director of communications, 1974-76; Brown/Gray, Ltd., Atlanta, writer, beginning 1976; Just Us Theater Co., Atlanta, began as playwright-in-residence, currently artistic director. Hostess and interviewer, "Black Viewpoints," produced by Clark College, WETV, Atlanta, 1970-71; staff writer and interviewer, *Ebony Beat Journal,* WQXI, Atlanta, 1972; executive producer, WXIA, Atlanta, 1972-73. Instructor, Emory University, 1978. Member of board of directors, Atlanta Center for Black Art, 1970-71.

MEMBER: Writers Guild of America (East), Southern Collective of African American Writers.

AWARDS, HONORS: Five Audelco Recognition Awards for a member of the black theater, 1983, for "Hospice"; Seed grant from Coordinating Council of Literary Magazines, 1987, for *Catalyst.*

WRITINGS:

We Don't Need No Music (poetry), Broadside Press, 1971.
One for the Brothers (chapbook), privately printed, 1983.

PLAYS

"Hymn for the Rebels" (one-act), first produced in Washington, D.C., at Howard University, 1968.
"Duet for Three Voices" (one-act), first produced in Washington, D.C., at Howard University, 1969.
"The Sale" (one-act), first produced in Atlanta, Ga., at Spelman College, 1972.
"puppetplay," first produced in Atlanta by Just Us Theater Co., 1983.
"Good News," first produced in Atlanta by Just Us Theater Co., 1984.
"Essentials," first produced in Atlanta by Just Us Theater Co., 1985.

Also author of the play "Hospice," first produced in 1983.

CONTRIBUTOR

John Mahoney and John Schmittroh, editors, *The Insistent Present,* Houghton, 1970.
Orde Coombs, editor, *We Speak as Liberators: Young Black Poets,* Dodd, 1970.
Lindsay Patterson, editor, *A Rock against Black America,* Dodd, 1973.

Also contributor to *The Poetry of Black America,* edited by Adoff, and *Dues,* edited by Welburn.

OTHER

Also author, with Zaron Burnett, of *Live at Club Zebra: The Book,* Volume I, Just Us Theater Press. Author-performer of several performance pieces, including "My Father Has a Son," 1986, "Love and Trouble," with Burnett, 1987, "A Little Practice," 1987, "Live at Club Zebra!" with Burnett, 1987-88, and "The Final Negro Rhythm and Blues Revue," with Burnett, 1988. Columnist for *Atlanta Gazette,* 1976—, *Atlanta Constitution,* 1977, and *Atlanta Tribune.* Contributor to various periodicals and journals, including *Readers and Writers, Promethean, Afro-American Review, Journal of Black Poetry, Dues, Essence, Pride, Black World, Ms., Atlanta Magazine, New York Times Book Review, Southern Voices,* and *Black Collegian.* Editor, *Catalyst,* 1987—.

WORK IN PROGRESS: Short story collection for Third World Press.

SIDELIGHTS: Pearl Cleage once told *CA:* "As a black female writer living and working in the United States, my writing of necessity reflects my blackness and my femaleness. I am convinced that this condition of double-oppression based on race and sex gives me a unique perspective that, hopefully, adds energy and a certain creative tension to my work. Here's hoping. . . ."

Cleage later added: "Amiri Baraka said the tradition of the black writer is to write something so ba-a-a-a-d that they have to ban it. It is within the wondrous energy of that tradition that I work."

*   *   *

CLEGG, Stewart (Roger) 1947-

PERSONAL: Born September 4, 1947, in Bradford, England; son of Willie (a sales representative) and Joyce Sylvia (Rogers) Clegg; married Caroline Lynne Bowker (a teacher), August 7, 1971; children: Jonathan James. *Education:* University of Aston, B.Sc. (with honors), 1971; University of Bradford, Ph.D., 1974. *Politics:* Social democratic. *Religion:* None.

ADDRESSES: Office—Department of Sociology, University of New England, Armidale, NSW 2351, Australia. *Agent*—A. D. Peters & Co., 10 Buckingham St., London WC2N 6BU, England.

CAREER: Lecturer for Faculty of Business and Professional Studies, Trent Polytechnic, 1974-75; University of Bradford, Bradford, England, research fellow of European Group for Organization Studies at Management Centre, 1975-77; Griffith University, Brisbane, Australia, reader in sociology, beginning 1977; currently professor of sociology, University of New England, Armidale, Australia.

MEMBER: Australian and Pacific Researchers in Organization Studies, European Group for Organization Studies, British Sociological Association, Sociological Association of Australia and New Zealand, American Sociological Association.

WRITINGS:

Power, Rule and Domination: A Critical and Empirical Understanding of Power in Sociological Theory and Organizational Life, Routledge & Kegan Paul, 1975.
(Editor with David Dunkerley) *Critical Issues in Organizations,* Routledge & Kegan Paul, 1977.
The Theory of Power and Organization, Routledge & Kegan Paul, 1979.

(With Dunkerley) *Organization, Class and Control,* Routledge & Kegan Paul, 1980.

(Editor with Geoff Dow and Paul Boreham) *Politics, the State and Recession,* St. Martin's, 1983.

(With Dow and Boreham) *Class, Politics and the Economy,* Routledge & Kegan Paul, 1986.

(Editor with Dunkerley and S. G. Redding) *The Enterprise and Management in East Asia,* Centre of Asian Studies, University of Hong Kong, 1986.

Contributor to professional journals. Editor of *Australian and New Zealand Journal of Sociology* and of *Organization Studies.*

WORK IN PROGRESS: Research on the class structure of Australia in comparative perspective, power in modernity and post-modernity, and organization theory; cross-cultural research.

*   *   *

COALE, Samuel Chase   1943-

PERSONAL: Born July 26, 1943, in Hartford, Conn.; son of Samuel Chase (a photographer) and Harriet (Kimberly) Coale; married Gray Emory, June 24, 1972; children: Samuel Chase. *Education:* Trinity College, Hartford, Conn., B.A., 1965; Brown University, M.A. and Ph.D., both 1970.

ADDRESSES: Office—Department of English, Wheaton College, Norton, Mass. 02766.

CAREER: Wheaton College, Norton, Mass., instructor, 1968-71, assistant professor, 1971-76, associate professor, 1976-81, professor of American literature, 1981—. Instructor, Poznan Summer Seminar, Poznan, Poland, 1977, 1978, 1979, 1984, and 1985; instructor, English Literature and Language Seminar in Czechoslavakia, 1983, 1984, 1985, 1986, and 1988; lecturer in Sweden, Pakistan, India, Egypt, and Israel, 1981—. Trinity Square Repertory Theatre, coordinating humanist and moderator, 1977—, member of board of directors; member of board of directors, Looking Glass Theatre and Rhode Island Dance Repertory Theatre.

MEMBER: Modern Language Association of America, English-Speaking Union (president, 1975-78; program chair, 1978-83; scholarship chair, 1986—), Hawthorne Society, Frost Society, Poe Society, National Book Critics Circle, Phi Beta Kappa.

AWARDS, HONORS: Grants for study in England, 1969, 1970, 1972; Ford Foundation summer grants, 1970, 1971; Fulbright fellowship in Greece, 1976-77; elected Knight of Mark Twain for book *John Cheever;* named outstanding young man, U.S. Jaycees, 1978; National Endowment for the Humanities fellowship, 1981-82.

WRITINGS:

John Cheever, Ungar, 1977.

Anthony Burgess, Ungar, 1981.

In Hawthorne's Shadow: American Romance from Melville to Mailer, University Press of Kentucky, 1985.

Paul Theroux, Twayne, 1987.

"Providence's Muse; or, It's Muse to Me" (play), produced by Trinity Repertory Company, 1987.

CONTRIBUTOR TO ANTHOLOGIES

Jack Tharpe, editor, *Frost: Centennial Essays,* University Press of Mississippi, 1974.

Robert Morris and Kathryn Van Spanckeren, editors, *John Gardner: Critical Perspectives,* Southern Illinois University Press, 1982.

Robert Collins, editor, *Critical Essays on John Cheever,* G. K. Hall, 1982.

Frank Magill, editor, *Critical Study of Long Fiction,* Salem Press, 1983.

Jeff Henderson, editor, *Thor's Hammer: Essays on John Gardner,* University of Central Arkansas Press, 1985.

OTHER

Contributor of articles and reviews to literature journals such as *American Literature, Modern Fiction Studies,* and *Essays in Literature.* Book reviewer, *Providence Journal;* theater and film reviewer, *East Side* (Providence, R.I.) and *Newport: This Week.* Contributing editor, *Critique: Studies in Modern Fiction,* 1982—.

WORK IN PROGRESS: Shadow Lives, a novel; a critical book on William Styron, for Twayne; a work on a 1987 visit to the Mideast; a work on the American Romance as a reenactment of Western myths.

SIDELIGHTS: Speaking of his writing, Samuel Chase Coale told *CA:* "I like alternating between fiction and nonfiction, between novels and articles on contemporary writers. Travelling recently to Egypt and Israel has opened other possibilities. I'm now writing reviews, interviews, and articles for newspapers and magazines about my experiences there; and I hope to travel for a year or two in 1990-91. Writing remains compulsive and incessant. I couldn't get through a day without it. I work every day at any odd moment. It requires self-discipline and daily 'slog.' Just don't stop!''

BIOGRAPHICAL/CRITICAL SOURCES:

PERIODICALS

Los Angeles Times Book Review, January 10, 1982.
Times Literary Supplement, May 22, 1987.

*   *   *

COHEN, William S(ebastian)   1940-

PERSONAL: Born August 28, 1940, in Bangor, Me.; son of Reuben and Clara (Hartley) Cohen; children: Kevin, Christopher. *Education:* Bowdoin College, B.A. (cum laude), 1962; Boston University, LL.B., 1965. *Politics:* Republican. *Religion:* Unitarian-Universalist.

ADDRESSES: Home—Bangor, Me. 04401. *Office*—U.S. Senate, 322 Hart Senate Office Building, Washington, D.C. 20510.

CAREER: Admitted to Maine Bar, 1965; Paine, Cohen, Lynch, Weatherbee & Kobritz (law firm), Bangor, Me., partner, 1966-72; U.S. House of Representatives, Washington, D.C., Republican representative from Maine, 1973-79; U.S. Senate, Washington, D.C., Republican senator from Maine, 1979—. Instructor at Husson College, 1966, and University of Maine, 1968-72. Member of board of trustees of Unity College and board of overseers of Bowdoin College, 1973-85. Member of Bangor zoning board of appeals, 1967-69, member of city council, 1969-72, chairman of finance committe, 1970-71, member of school board, 1970-71, mayor, 1972. Assistant county attorney of Penobscot County, 1968-70. Member of Governor's State Credit Research Committee, 1968.

MEMBER: American Trial Lawyers Association, Maine Trial Lawyers Association (vice-president, 1970-72).

AWARDS, HONORS: Fellow of John F. Kennedy Institute of Politics, 1972; LL.D., St. Joseph's College, 1974, University of Maine, 1975, Western New England College, 1975, Bowdoin College, 1975, and Nasson College, 1975; named Outstanding Young Man of the Year, National Jaycees, 1975; Alumni Award, Boston University, 1976, for distinguished public service; Silver Anniversary Medal, National Collegiate Athletic Association, 1987; Balfour Silver Anniversary All-American Team selection, National Association of Basketball Coaches of the United States, 1987.

WRITINGS:

Of Sons and Seasons (poetry), Simon & Schuster, 1978.
Roll Call: One Year in the United States Senate, Simon & Schuster, 1981.
Getting the Most out of Washington, Facts on File, 1982.
(With Gary Hart) *The Double Man* (novel), Morrow, 1985.
A Baker's Nickel (poetry), Morrow, 1986.

Contributor to magazines. Assistant editor in chief, journal of American Trial Lawyers Association, 1965-66, co-editor of volumes 32 and 33; editor, journal of Maine Trial Lawyers Association.

SIDELIGHTS: Republican Senator William S. Cohen first found himself in the national limelight when in 1974, as a freshman representative from Maine, he crossed party lines to cast the deciding vote on the House Judiciary Committee motion to subpoena President Richard Nixon's Watergate tapes. More recently Cohen has gained attention for *The Double Man,* a mystery novel written with former presidential candidate and senator Gary Hart. The idea for the novel sprung from a late-night meeting between the two senators, when each confessed they would rather be writing a novel than waiting for the end of a filibuster. "Within about 25 minutes we wrote an outline that never changed," Cohen told *Washington Post Book World* reporter Bill Peterson. "It was a spontaneous kind of thing. A lark really. If I hadn't run into Gary that night it never would have happened." The resultant thriller, which took the two over four years to finish, follows the investigations of Senator Tom Chandler into possible connections between assassinations of the Secretary of State's family, murders of both suspects and agents, and the KGB and CIA.

Reaction to this novel by two novices has been mixed; Nicholas von Hoffman writes in the *New Republic* that *The Double Man* "is one thriller dull enough to be sent out under the franking privilege," adding that "every page, every paragraph, every sentence has been scoured and scrubbed clean of life and interest by two men dedicated to making sure that nothing appears between the covers that their opponents can use against them in the next campaign." But other critics find the novel interesting for its insights into the workings of the Senate: "What is lacking in style and flow," remarks *Los Angeles Times* writer Dick Roraback, "is made up in insight into the works, quirks and perks of the U.S. Congress and, in particular, the Senate Intelligence Committee, on which both authors have served." *Detroit News* contributor Jay Carr similarly notes that "the senators expertly and matter-of-factly limn the complicated and pressure-ridden workings of a senator's staff." The critic also observes, however, that "oddly enough, the talk between senators—even senators who are supposed to be longtime friends—is stilted and calculated." In contrast to criticisms of the book's plot, *Washington Post Book World* contributor Jack Beatty finds that "*The Double Man* is as crammed with surprises as a rigged box of Cracker Jacks. . . . [Cohen and Hart] advance a frighteningly informed hypothesis about the reason for killing intelligence agents." And Carr admits that "in the end, it isn't the senators' inside information that makes their book stand up and march; it's their enthusiasm and their giddy escalation of Cold War heroics that William Buckley Jr. hasn't thought of yet." Concludes the critic: "One can't help feeling it took Cohen and Hart a while before they began having fun writing this book. When they finally do, we do, too."

Cohen's collaboration with Hart is not his first venture into publishing, however, for he has also written two volumes of poetry, the first of which, *Of Sons and Seasons,* was a best seller in his home state of Maine. "I write about common themes and try to arrange words in a way to create a maximum emotional effect with a minimum of words—I get a great pleasure out of writing—period," Cohen told Barbara Gamarekian in the *New York Times.* "The fact is, I spend most of my time writing legislation, and I used to even like writing briefs—using language to create a visual image." Cohen never intended on publishing his poetry, as he told Gamarekian: "It's really just a hobby. It's not great poetry—but for me it is important to try to freeze time, to hold in my mind the memory of an event." Cohen concluded by comparing his poetry to "photographs—I can go back and read them and experience the whole sensation I felt when I wrote it."

BIOGRAPHICAL/CRITICAL SOURCES:

PERIODICALS

Detroit News, May 5, 1985.
Los Angeles Times, June 27, 1985.
Los Angeles Times Book Review, February 1, 1981.
New Republic, June 3, 1978, May 27, 1985.
New York Times, April 12, 1978.
New York Times Book Review, March 1, 1981, May 5, 1985.
Time, November 20, 1978, May 6, 1985.
Washington Post, December 22, 1987.
Washington Post Book World, April 7, 1985.

*   *   *

COLEMAN, J(ohn) Winston, Jr.   1898-1983

PERSONAL: Born November 5, 1898, in Lexington, Ky.; died May 4, 1983, in Lexington, Ky.; son of John Winston and Mary (Payne) Coleman; married Burnetta Z. Mullen, October 15, 1930. *Education:* University of Kentucky, B.S., 1920, M.E., 1929. *Politics:* Democrat. *Religion:* Presbyterian.

ADDRESSES: Home—2048 Blairmore Rd., Lexington, Ky. 40502.

CAREER: Engaged in engineering in New York and other states, 1920-23; Coleman & Davis, Inc. (general contractors and builders), Lexington, Ky., organizer and president, 1924-36; Winburn Farm, Lexington, owner and operator, 1936-66. President of board of directors, Lexington Cemetery Co., beginning 1948; member of board of directors, Henry Clay Memorial Foundation, 1948-73, Kentucky Civil War Round Table, beginning 1953, Kentucky Heritage Commission, 1961-63, Kentucky Civil War Centennial Commission, 1961-65.

MEMBER: Society of American Historians (fellow), American Antiquarian Society, Bibliographical Society of America, American Geographical Society, Southern Historical Association, Mississippi Valley Historical Association, Kentucky Historical Society, Cincinnati Historical Society, Kentucky Society—Sons of the Revolution (president, 1944-46), Sigma

Nu, Omicron Delta Kappa, Phi Alpha Theta, Masons, Shriners, Filson Club, Rotary Club.

AWARDS, HONORS: Litt.D., Lincoln Memorial University, 1945, University of Kentucky, 1947; University of Kentucky Distinguished Alumni Award, 1967; LL.D., Transylvania University, 1969, D.Litt., Eastern Kentucky University, 1976.

WRITINGS:

Masonry in the Bluegrass, Transylvania Press, 1933.
Stage-Coach Days in the Bluegrass, Standard Press, 1935.
Lexington during the Civil War, Commercial Printing Co., 1938, revised edition, Henry Clay Press, 1968.
Slavery Times in Kentucky, University of North Carolina Press, 1940, reprinted, Johnson Reprint, 1970.
A Bibliography of Kentucky History, University of Kentucky Press, 1949.
The Beauchamp-Sharp Tragedy: An Episode of Kentucky History during the Middle 1820's, Roberts Printing Co., 1950.
Old Homes of the Blue Grass, Kentucky Society, 1950.
Famous Kentucky Duels: The Story of the Code of Honor in the Bluegrass State, Roberts Printing Co., 1953, reprinted, Henry Clay Press, 1969.
A Centennial History of Sayre School, 1854-1954, Winburn Press, 1954.
An Autobiographical Sketch, with a List of Writings, Winburn Press, 1954.
The Springs of Kentucky, Winburn Press, 1955.
Historic Kentucky, Henry Clay Press, 1967, 2nd edition, 1968.
The Collected Writings of J. Winston Coleman, Jr., Winburn Press, 1969.
(Editor) *Kentucky: A Pictorial History* (based on Coleman's photographs), University of Kentucky Press, 1971, 2nd edition, 1972.
The Squire's Sketches of Lexington, Henry Clay Press, 1972.
(Editor) *Life in the Bluegrass,* Historic Records Association, 1974.
Three Kentucky Artists: Hart, Price and Troye, University of Kentucky Press, 1974.
The Squire's Memoirs, Winburn Press, 1976.
Sketches of Kentucky's Past: A Series of Essays Concerning the State's History, introduction by Thomas D. Clark, Winburn Press, 1979.
Lexington, Winburn Press, 1981.
Nathan B. Stubblefield, Winburn Press, 1982.
Here I Have Lived, Winburn Press, 1982.
The Historical Writings of J. Winston Coleman, Jr., Winburn Press, 1982.
An Outdoor Hall of Fame, Winburn Press, 1982.
The Book Thieves Club, Winburn Press, 1983.

A Bibliography of Kentucky History has been reprinted by UMI Press. Also author of numerous pamphlets on Kentucky history.

SIDELIGHTS: J. Winston Coleman, Jr. owned the largest private collection of literature by and about Kentucky.*

*   *   *

COLEMAN, Terry   1931-

PERSONAL: Born February 13, 1931, in Bournemouth, England; married first wife, Lesley Fox-Strangways-Vane, 1954; married second wife, Vivien Rosemary Lumsdaine-Wallace, 1981; children: (first marriage) Tigre and Eleanor (daughters); (second marriage) Eliza and Jack. *Education:* Attended University of Exeter; University of London, LL.B., 1958.

ADDRESSES: Agent—A. D. Peters, 10 Buckingham St., London WC2N 6BU, England.

CAREER: University College, Cork, Ireland, Lyon Lecturer in Medieval Law, 1959; former journalist of five English newspapers and onetime editor of *Savoir Faire* (women's magazine, now defunct); *Guardian* (formerly *Manchester Guardian*), London, England, reporter, arts correspondent, and chief feature writer, 1961-74; *Daily Mail,* London, special writer, 1974-76; *Guardian,* political interviewer, 1976-79, special correspondent in New York, N.Y., 1981-82, special correspondent in London, 1982—.

AWARDS, HONORS: Yorkshire Post prize for best first book, 1965, for *The Railway Navvies;* British Press Award for feature writer of the year, 1982; Granada Award for journalist of the year, 1987.

WRITINGS:

The Railway Navvies (nonfiction), Hutchinson, 1965, revised edition, Penguin, 1968, reprinted, 1987.
A Girl for the Afternoons (novel), Elek, 1965.
(With Lois Deacon) *Providence and Mr. Hardy* (biographical study of Thomas Hardy), Hutchinson, 1966.
The Only True History (collected journalism), Hutchinson, 1969.
Going to America (social history), Pantheon, 1972, new edition, Genealogical Publishing, 1987 (published in England as *Passage to America,* Hutchinson, 1972).
The Pantheretti (poems), [London], 1972.
The Liners (social history), Putnam, 1976.
(Editor) Thomas Hardy, *An Indiscretion in the Life of an Heiress* (Hardy's previously unpublished first novel), Hutchinson, 1976.
Southern Cross (novel; Book-of-the-Month Club selection), Viking, 1979.
Thanksgiving (novel), Simon & Schuster, 1981.
Movers and Shakers: Conversations with Uncommon Men (collected interviews), Deutsch, 1987.
Thatcher's Britain: A Jouney through the Promised Lands (nonfiction), Bantam (London), 1987.

SIDELIGHTS: As a journalist, historian, and novelist, Terry Coleman focuses on the human side of current and historical events. His first book, *The Railway Navvies,* tells the history of England's nineteenth-century railroads and the people who made them possible. In another nonfiction work, *Going to America,* the author describes the hazardous travelling conditions endured by English immigrants who came to America in the mid-nineteenth century. Noting that *Going to America* could have been set into a "more solid historical matrix," an *Economist* reviewer feels that this novel is, nevertheless, "a worthy, readable book." Stanley Kauffmann, in a *New Republic* article, praises *Going to America* and calls the author "a journalist, but also a thoughtful social historian and a first-rate writer." This idea is echoed by a *Times Literary Supplement* reviewer, who writes: "This is a book which is essential reading for British social historians."

In keeping with Coleman's preference for social history books, *The Liners* is a study of the great ships that have sailed the North Atlantic, from Isambard Brunel's Great Eastern line in 1858 to the modern *Queen Elizabeth 2,* one of the last liners afloat. Coleman concentrates on the ships themselves, the men who captained them, and the variety of passengers who sailed on them. E. S. Turner, writing in the *Times Literary Supplement,* says that Coleman "brings it all vividly back . . . [and] he quotes amusingly from promotional and sailing literature."

Turner also adds praise for the author's "delightful stories, as of the French Caribbean island which regularly asked the unmistakable Mauretania 'What ship are you?' and was answered with 'What island are you?'"

In the role of reporter and interviewer, Coleman has covered both British and American election campaigns and has interviewed seven British prime ministers. From these experiences he has garnered information for his two journalistic books: *Movers and Shakers: Conversations with Uncommon Men* and *Thatcher's Britain: A Journey through the Promised Lands.* The former is a collection of newspaper interviews, while the latter, as *Times Literary Supplement* contributor Gillian Peele summarizes, "uses observations of the 1987 campaign trail to illuminate the very different perceptions of the Thatcher 'revolution' to be found in the contrasting subcultures of contemporary Britain." In this way, the author offers a commentary on the state of British life and politics. Adds Peele: "The final impression which Coleman leaves of the quality of life and democracy in Britain is a depressing one." Edward Pierce of the London *Times* says about *Thatcher's Britain:* "The dismal nature of that election comes over brilliantly—the arrogance of the Tories, the hired felicity of Labour." The reviewer concludes that Coleman "is an excellent guide along the melancholy contours" of the political process.

Coleman's predilection for writing about events of historical significance is also carried over into his novels. However, he does not approach his fiction with the same gravity of his nonfiction, permitting himself to embellish historical fact. David Malouf of the *Washington Post,* in a review on *Southern Cross,* criticizes this "tampering with the truth," but *Publishers Weekly* contributor Barbara Bannon feels that Coleman's work is "richly romantic." In her opinion, *Southern Cross* "could almost be called an Australian *Gone with the Wind.*"

AVOCATIONAL INTERESTS: Cricket, opera, travel (Coleman has been to sixty countries).

BIOGRAPHICAL/CRITICAL SOURCES:

PERIODICALS

Economist, April 15, 1972.
New Republic, March 25, 1972.
Publishers Weekly, April 23, 1979.
Times (London), November 15, 1987.
Times Literary Supplement, September 22, 1972, November 26, 1976, May 28, 1982, February 19, 1988.
Washington Post, July 5, 1979.

*   *   *

COLLINS, Max
  See COLLINS, Max Allan (Jr.)

*   *   *

COLLINS, Max Allan (Jr.)   1948-
  (Max Collins)

PERSONAL: Born March 3, 1948, in Muscatine, Iowa; son of Max Allan, Sr. (an executive) and Patricia Ann Collins; married Barbara Jane Mull (a secretary), June 1, 1968; children: Nathan Allan. *Education:* Muscatine Community College, A.A., 1968; University of Iowa, B.A., 1970, M.F.A., 1972. *Politics:* Independent.

ADDRESSES: Home and office—M.A.C. Productions, 117 Lord Ave., Muscatine, Iowa 52761. *Agent*—Dominick Abel Literary Agency, Inc., 498 West End Ave., New York, N.Y. 10024.

CAREER: Professional musician, 1966-72; Muscatine Community College, Muscatine, Iowa, instructor in English, journalism, and creative writing, 1971-77; professional musician, 1977-79; writer, 1972—. Instructor at Mississippi Valley Writers Conference.

MEMBER: Mystery Writers of America, Private Eye Writers of America.

AWARDS, HONORS: Inkpot Award for outstanding achievement in comic arts, San Diego Comic Convention, 1982; Shamus Award for best hardcover novel, Private Eye Writers of America, 1983, for *True Detective;* Edgar Allan Poe Special Award for critical/biographical work, Mystery Writers of America, 1984, for *One Lonely Knight: Mickey Spillane's Mike Hammer;* distinguished alumnus award, Muscatine Community College, 1985.

WRITINGS:

(Co-editor) Mickey Spillane, *Mike Hammer: The Comic Strip,* Ken Pierce, Volume 1, 1982, Volume 2, 1985.
Midnight Haul, Foul Play, 1986.

"NOLAN" SUSPENSE NOVEL SERIES

(Under name Max Collins) *Bait Money,* Curtis Books, 1973, revised edition, Pinnacle Books, 1981.
(Under name Max Collins) *Blood Money,* Curtis Books, 1973, revised edition, Pinnacle Books, 1981.
(Under name Max Collins) *Fly Paper,* Pinnacle Books, 1981.
(Under name Max Collins) *Hush Money,* Pinnacle Books, 1981.
(Under name Max Collins) *Hard Cash,* Pinnacle Books, 1982.
(Under name Max Collins) *Scratch Fever,* Pinnacle Books, 1982.
Spree, Tor Books, 1987.

"QUARRY" SERIES

(Originally published under name Max Collins) *The Broker,* Berkley Publishing, 1976, reprinted as *Quarry,* Foul Play, 1985.
(Originally published under name Max Collins) *The Broker's Wife,* Berkley Publishing, 1976, reprinted as *Quarry's List,* Foul Play, 1985.
(Originally published under name Max Collins) *The Dealer,* Berkley Publishing, 1976, reprinted as *Quarry's Deal,* Foul Play, 1986.
(Originally published under name Max Collins) *The Slasher,* Berkley Publishing, 1977, reprinted as *Quarry's Cut,* Foul Play, 1986.
Primary Target, Foul Play, 1987.

"MALLORY" SERIES

(Under name Max Collins) *The Baby Blue Rip-Off,* Walker & Co., 1983.
No Cure for Death, Walker & Co., 1983.
Kill Your Darlings, Walker & Co., 1984.
A Shroud for Aquarius, Walker & Co., 1985.
Nice Weekend for a Murder, Walker & Co., 1986.

"MEMOIRS OF NATHAN HELLER" HISTORICAL PRIVATE EYE SERIES

True Detective, St. Martin's, 1983.
True Crime, St. Martin's, 1984.
The Million-Dollar Wound, St. Martin's, 1986.

Neon Mirage, St. Martin's, 1988.

"ELIOT NESS" HISTORICAL NOVEL SERIES

The Dark City, Bantam, 1987.
Butcher's Dozen, Bantam, 1988.
Bullet Proof, Bantam, 1989.

NONFICTION

(With Ed Gorman) *Jim Thompson: The Killers Inside Him*, Fedora Press, 1983.
(With James L. Traylor) *One Lonely Knight: Mickey Spillane's Mike Hammer*, Bowling Green University, 1984.
(With John Javna) *The Best of Crime and Detective TV*, Harmony, 1988.

COMIC STRIP COLLECTIONS

(Under name Max Collins) *Dick Tracy Meets Angeltop*, Ace Books, 1980.
(Under name Max Collins) *Dick Tracy Meets the Punks*, Ace Books, 1980.
(Under name Max Collins) *The Mike Mist Minute Mist-eries*, Eclipse Enterprises, 1981.
(With Terry Beatty) *The Files of Ms. Tree*, Volume 1, Aardvark-Vanaheim, 1984, Volume 2: *The Cold Dish*, Renegade Press, 1985.
(With Dick Locher) *Dick Tracy: Tracy's Wartime Memories*, Ken Pierce, 1986.
(With Beatty) *Ms. Tree*, Paper Jacks, 1988.

OTHER

Writer, under name Max Collins, of comic strip "Dick Tracy," distributed by Chicago Tribune/New York News Syndicate, 1977—; writer of "The Comics Page," 1979-80, and of monthly *Ms. Tree* comic book. Contributor of scripts to *Batman* and *DC* comic books; co-creator, with Beatty, of "Wild Dog" comic-book feature. Movie columnist for *Mystery Scene*. Contributor of articles to magazines, including *Armchair Detective*, *Comics Feature*, and *Mystery Scene*.

SIDELIGHTS: Max Allan Collins wrote to *CA:* "While I am still active scripting comics, I have been placing more and more emphasis on novels, particularly of the historical detective variety. With *True Detective* I have moved into a subgenre of (I think) my own creation: the 'period' private eye novel dealing with historical events. I am hardly the first to set a private eye tale in the 1930s or 1940s, but I believe my Nathan Heller novels, each of which to date has in excess of 100,000 words, are the first such novels whose stories are essentially true. *True Detective* deals with the assassination of Mayor Cermak, while the immediate sequel, *True Crime*, explores the shooting of John Dillinger. [*The Million-Dollar Wound* from the "Memoirs of Nathan Heller" series] examines the infiltration of the Chicago mob into Hollywood movie unions, as well as Heller's own combat experiences on Guadalcanal. Research for these novels is extensive and begins at least a year in advance of writing.

"The Heller novels have led to another series of books about real-life gangbuster Eliot Ness, but I also continue to write about my other contemporary series characters, Nolan, Quarry, and Mallory, and the occasional 'non-series' novel, such as *Midnight Haul*, which concerns the illegal dumping of hazardous chemicals, or my forthcoming novel about Bobby Kennedy and Jimmy Hoffa.

"My interest in comics had previously been reflected by the character Jon, a young aspiring cartoonist who is a sidekick

of sorts to the fifty-ish, semi-retired thief Nolan. Cartooning had been my childhood ambition, and 'Dick Tracy' was my favorite comic strip. As I grew older my fondness for Tracy led me quite naturally into the works of Dashiell Hammett, Mickey Spillane, and other 'tough guy' crime writers, and I put drawing aside and concentrated on writing.

"I am a former rock musician (I recorded with the Daybreakers in Nashville, Tennessee, and in 1968 signed a songwriting contract with Tree Publishing of Nashville), and I am still interested in music in general rock 'n' roll in particular (probably always will be). I collect original comic art and have assembled one of the major collections in the United States (or anywhere), with an excess of one hundred originals hanging in my home. I am an avid movie buff and have a growing library of old movies on video tape.

"My literary heroes within the suspense field include Dashiell Hammett, James M. Cain, Mickey Spillane, and Jim Thompson; mainstream influences include William March, Calder Willingham, and Mark Harris."

*　　　*　　　*

COOPER, John R.
[Collective pseudonym]

WRITINGS:

"MEL MARTIN BASEBALL STORIES"

The Mystery at the Ball Park, Cupples & Leon, 1947.
The Southpaw's Secret, Cupples & Leon, 1947.
The Phantom Homer, Garden City, 1952.
First Base Jinx, Garden City, 1952.
The College League Mystery, Garden City, 1953.
The Fighting Shortstop, Garden City, 1953.

SIDELIGHTS: Mel Martin was described in Books, Inc. advertisements as a "young right-hander with a quick-breaking curve, plenty of hop on his fast ball, and good control when the going gets tough." When not involved in sports, Mel was solving mysteries. Andrew E. Svenson worked on this series before joining the Stratemeyer Syndicate as a full-time writer and editor. For more information see the entries in this volume for Harriet S. Adams, Edward L. Stratemeyer, and Andrew E. Svenson.

BIOGRAPHICAL/CRITICAL SOURCES:

BOOKS

Johnson, Deidre, editor and compiler, *Stratemeyer Pseudonyms and Series Books: An Annotated Checklist of Stratemeyer and Stratemeyer Syndicate Publications*, Greenwood Press, 1982.

*　　　*　　　*

COPPARD, Audrey　1931-

PERSONAL: Born July 5, 1931; daughter of Alexander Sherwood and Doris (Beamont) Begbie; married Christopher Dirk Coppard (an editor); children: Harriet, Tim, Abbie. *Politics:* "Conservative revolutionary."

ADDRESSES: Agent—Sheila Watson, Suite 8, 26 Charing Cross Rd., London WC2H 0DG, England.

CAREER: Research assistant, London University; writer.

WRITINGS:

Who Has Poisoned the Sea? (young adult science fiction), S. G. Phillips, 1970.
This Could Be the Start of Something, Heinemann, 1970.
Sending Secrets: An Introduction to Codes, illustrations by Jane Hickson, Heinemann, 1972.
Nancy of Nottingham, Heinemann, 1973.
Don't Panic!, illustrations by Alison Prince and Samantha Perry, Heinemann, 1975.
Get Well Soon, illustrations by Prince, Heinemann, 1978.
(With Bernard Crick) *Orwell Remembered,* Facts on File, 1984.

Also collaborated on recording of English folksongs produced by Folkways. Contributor of poems to periodicals.

BIOGRAPHICAL/CRITICAL SOURCES:

PERIODICALS

Los Angeles Times Book Review, January 13, 1985.

*   *   *

COSBY, Bill
See COSBY, William Henry, Jr.

*   *   *

COSBY, William Henry, Jr. 1937-
(Bill Cosby)

PERSONAL: Born July 12, 1937, in Philadelphia, Pa.; son of William Henry (a U.S. Navy mess steward) and Anna Cosby (a domestic worker); married Camille Hanks, January 25, 1964; children: Erika Ranee, Erinn Chalene, Ennis William, Ensa Camille, Evin Harrah. *Education:* Attended Temple University, 1961-62; University of Massachusetts, M.A., 1972, Ed. D., 1977.

ADDRESSES: Agent—The Brokaw Co., 9255 Sunset Blvd., Los Angeles, Calif. 90069.

CAREER: Comedian, actor, and recording artist. Performer in nightclubs, including The Cellar, Philadelphia, Pa., Gaslight Cafe, New York City, Bitter End, New York City, and Hungry i, San Francisco, 1962—; performer in television series for National Broadcasting Co. (NBC-TV), including "I Spy," 1965-68, "The Bill Cosby Show," 1969-71, and "The Cosby Show," 1984—, for Columbia Broadcasting System (CBS-TV), "The New Bill Cosby Show," 1972-73, and American Broadcasting Co. (ABC-TV), "Cos," 1976; actor in motion pictures, including "Hickey and Boggs," 1972, "Man and Boy," 1972, "Uptown Saturday Night," 1974, "Let's Do It Again," 1975, "Mother, Jugs, and Speed," 1976, "A Piece of the Action," 1977, "California Suite," 1978, "The Devil and Max Devlin," 1981, "Bill Cosby Himself," 1985, and "Leonard Part VI," 1987; creator of animated children's programs "The Fat Albert Show" and "Fat Albert and the Cosby Kids," CBS-TV, 1972-84. Performer on "The Bill Cosby Radio Program," television specials "The First Bill Cosby Special" and "The Second Bill Cosby Special," in animated feature "Aesop's Fables," in "An Evening with Bill Cosby" at Radio City Music Hall, 1986, and in videocassette "Bill Cosby: 49," sponsored by Kodak, 1987. Guest on Public Broadcasting Co. (PBS-TV) children's programs "Sesame Street" and "The Electric Company," and NBC-TV's "Children's Theatre"; host of Picture Pages segment of CBS-TV's "Captain Kangaroo's Wake Up." Commercial spokesman for

Jell-O Pudding (General Foods Inc.), Coca-Cola Co., Ford Motor Co., Texas Instruments, E.F. Hutton, and Kodak Film. President of Rhythm and Blues Hall of Fame, 1968. Member of Carnegie Commission for the Future of Public Broadcasting, board of directors of National Council on Crime and Delinquency, Mary Holmes College, and Ebony Showcase Theatre, board of trustees of Temple University, advisory board of Direction Sports, communications council at Howard University, and steering committee of American Sickle Cell foundation. *Military service:* U.S. Navy Medical Corps, 1956-60.

AWARDS, HONORS: Eight Grammy Awards for best comedy album from National Society of Recording Arts and Sciences, including 1964, for "Bill Cosby Is a Very Funny Fellow . . . Right!," 1965, for "I Started Out as a Child," 1966, for "Why Is There Air?," 1967, for "Revenge," and 1969, for "To Russell, My Brother, Whom I Slept With"; Emmy Award for best actor in a dramatic series from Academy of Television Arts and Sciences, 1965-66, 1966-67, and 1967-68, for "I Spy"; named "most promising new male star" by *Fame* magazine, 1966; Emmy Award, 1969, for "The First Bill Cosby Special"; Seal of Excellence, Children's Theatre Association, 1973; Ohio State University award, 1975, for "Fat Albert and the Cosby Kids"; NAACP Image Award, 1976; named "Star Presenter of 1978" by *Advertising Age*; Gold Award for Outstanding Children's Program, International Film and Television Festival, 1981, for "Fat Albert and the Cosby Kids"; Emmy Award for best comedy series, 1985, for "The Cosby Show"; honorary degree, Brown University; Golden Globe Award, Hollywood Foreign Press Association; four People's Choice Awards; voted "most believable celebrity endorser" three times in surveys by Video Storyboard Tests Inc.

WRITINGS—Under name Bill Cosby:

The Wit and Wisdom of Fat Albert, Windmill Books, 1973.
Bill Cosby's Personal Guide to Tennis Power; or, Don't Lower the Lob, Raise the Net, Random House, 1975.
(Contributor) Charlie Shedd, editor, *You Are Somebody Special,* McGraw, 1978, 2nd edition, 1982.
Fatherhood, Doubleday, 1986.
Time Flies, Doubleday, 1987.

Also author of *Fat Albert's Survival Kit.* Author of recordings, including "Bill Cosby Is a Very Funny Fellow . . . Right!," 1964, "I Started Out as a Child," 1965, "Why Is There Air?," 1966, "Wonderfulness," 1967, "Revenge," 1967, "To Russell, My Brother, Whom I Slept With," 1969, "Bill Cosby Is Not Himself These Days, Rat Own, Rat Own, Rat Own," 1976, "My Father Confused Me . . . What Must I Do? What Must I Do?," 1977, "Disco Bill," 1977, "Bill's Best Friend," 1978, and also "It's True, It's True," "Bill Cosby Himself," "200 MPH," "Silverthroat," "Hooray for the Salvation Army Band," "8:15, 12:15," "For Adults Only," "Bill Cosby Talks to Kids About Drugs," and "Inside the Mind of Bill Cosby."

WORK IN PROGRESS: A book on love and marriage.

SIDELIGHTS: "When I was a kid I always used to pay attention to things that other people didn't even think about," claims William H. Cosby, Jr. "I'd remember funny happenings, just little trivial things, and then tell stories about them later. I found I could make people laugh, and I enjoyed doing it because it gave me a sense of security. I thought that if people laughed at what you said, that meant they like you." As an adult, Bill Cosby has developed his childhood behavior into a comedic talent that earns him millions of dollars annually for his work in films, television, and commercials.

What Cosby calls his "storytelling knack" may have had its roots in his mother's nightly readings of Mark Twain and the Bible to her three sons. Their father, a Navy cook, was gone for long stretches of time, but Anna Cosby did her best to provide a strong moral foundation for the family she raised in Philadelphia's housing projects. Bill Cosby helped with the family's expenses by delivering groceries and shining shoes. His sixth-grade teacher described him as "an alert boy who would rather clown than study"; nevertheless, he was placed in a class for gifted students when he reached high school. His activities as captain of the track and football teams and member of the baseball and basketball teams continued to distract him from academics, however, and when his tenth-grade year ended, Cosby was told he'd have to repeat the grade. Instead of doing so, he quit school to join the Navy. It was a decision he soon came to regret, and during his four-year hitch in the Navy, Cosby earned his high school diploma through a correspondence course. He then won an athletic scholarship to Temple University in Philadelphia, where he entered as a physical education major in 1961.

Cosby had continued to amuse his schoolmates and shipmates with his tales. He first showcased his humor professionally while a student at Temple, in a five-dollar-a-night job telling jokes and tending bar at "The Cellar," a Philadelphia coffeehouse. More lucrative engagements soon followed; before long Cosby's budding career as an entertainer was conflicting with his school schedule. Forced to choose between the two, Cosby dropped out of Temple, although the university eventually awarded him a bachelor's degree on the basis of "life experience." His reputation as a comic grew quickly as he worked in coffeehouses from San Francisco to New York City. Soon he was playing the biggest nightclubs in Las Vegas, and shortly after signing a recording contract in 1964, he became the best-selling comedian on records, with several of his recordings earning over one million dollars in sales.

His early performances consisted of about 35 percent racial jokes, but Cosby came to see this kind of humor as something that perpetuated racism rather than relieving tensions, and he dropped all such jokes from his act. "Rather than trying to bring the races together by talking about the differences, let's try to bring them together by talking about the similarities," he urges. Accordingly, he developed a universal brand of humor that revolved around everyday occurrences. A long-time jazz devotee, the comedian credits the musical improvisations of Miles Davis, Charles Mingus and Charlie Parker with inspiring him to come up with continually fresh ways of restating a few basic themes. "The situations I talk about people can find themselves in . . . it makes them glad to know they're not the only ones who have fallen victims of life's little ironies," states Cosby.

The comedian first displayed his skill as an actor when he landed the co-starring lead in "I Spy," a popular NBC-TV program of the late 1960s that featured suspense, action, and sometimes humor. Cosby portrayed Alexander Scott, a multilingual Rhodes scholar working as part of a spy team for the United States. Scott and his partner (played by Robert Culp) travelled undercover in the guises of a tennis pro and his trainer. The Alexander Scott role had not been created especially for a black actor, and Cosby's casting in the part was hailed as an important breakthrough for blacks in television.

"The Bill Cosby Show" followed "I Spy." In this half-hour comedy, Cosby portrayed Chet Kincaid, a high-school gym teacher—a role closer to his real-life persona than that of Alexander Scott. In fact, at this time Cosby announced that he was considering quitting show business to become a teacher. Although he never followed through on that statement, Cosby did return to college and earned a doctorate in education in 1977. His doctoral thesis, "An Integration of the Visual Media via Fat Albert and the Cosby Kids into the Elementary School Curriculum as a Teaching Aid and Vehicle to Achieve Increased Learning," analyzed an animated Saturday-morning show that Cosby himself had created. "Fat Albert and the Cosby Kids" had its roots in the comedy routines about growing up in Philadelphia. It attempted to entertain children while encouraging them to confront moral and ethical issues, and it has been used as a teaching tool in schools.

During the 1970s, Cosby teamed with Sidney Poitier and several other black actors to make a highly successful series of comedies, including "Uptown Saturday Night," "Let's Do It Again," and "A Piece of the Action." These comedies stood out in a time when most of the films for black audiences were oriented to violence. Critics are generous in their praise of Cosby's acting; Tom Allen notes his "free-wheeling, jiving, put-down artistry," and Alvin H. Marritt writes that, in "Let's Do It Again," Cosby "breezes through the outrageous antics."

Concern over his family's television viewing habits led Cosby to return to prime-time in 1984. "I got tired of seeing TV shows that consist of a car crash, a gunman and a hooker talking to a black pimp," Jane Hall quotes him in *People*. "It was cheaper to do a series than to throw out my family's six TV sets." But Cosby found that network executives were resistant to his idea for a family-oriented comedy. He was turned down by both CBS and ABC on the grounds that a family comedy—particularly one featuring a black family—could never succeed on modern television. NBC accepted his proposal and "The Cosby Show" very quickly became the top-rated show on television, drawing an estimated 60 million weekly viewers.

Like most of Bill Cosby's material, "The Cosby Show" revolves around everyday occurrences and interactions between siblings and parents. Cosby plays obstetrician Cliff Huxtable, who with his lawyer wife Claire has four daughters and one son—just as Cosby and wife Camille do in real life. Besides entertaining audiences, Cosby aims to project a positive image of a family whose members love and respect one another. The program is hailed by some as a giant step forward in the portrayal of blacks on television. Writes Lynn Norment in *Ebony*, "This show pointedly avoids the stereotypical Blacks often seen on TV. There are no ghetto maids or butlers wisecracking about Black life. Also, there are no fast cars and helicopter chase scenes, no jokes about sex and boobs and butts. And, most unusual, both parents are present in the home, employed and are Black."

"The Cosby Show" has not been unanimously acclaimed, however. As Norment explains, "Despite its success, the show is criticized by a few for not being 'Black enough,' for not dealing with more controversial issues, such as poverty and racism and interracial dating, for focusing on a Black middle-class family when the vast majority of Black people survive on incomes far below that of the Huxtables." Cosby finds this type of criticism racist in itself. "Does it mean only white people have a lock on living together in a home where the father is a doctor and the mother is a lawyer and the children are constantly being told to study by their parents?" Hall quotes

Cosby in *People*. "This is a black American family. If anybody has difficulty with that, it's their problem, not ours."

The paternal image of Cliff Huxtable led a publisher to ask Cosby for a humorous book to be called *Fatherhood*. Cosby obliged, making notes for the project with shorthand and tape recorder between his entertainment commitments. The finished book sold a record 2.6 million hardcover copies and was quite well-received by critics. *Newsweek* book reviewer Cathleen McGuigan states that it "is like a prose version of a Cosby comedy performance—informal, commiserative anecdotes delivered in a sardonic style that's as likely to prompt a smile of recognition as a belly laugh. . . . [But] it's not all played for laughs. There's a tough passage in which he describes the only time he hit his son, and a reference to a drinking-and-driving incident involving a daughter and her friends that calls upon him to both punish and forgive. Cosby's big strength, though, is his eye and ear for the everyday event—sibling squabbles, children's excuses." Jonathan Yardley concurs in the *Washington Post Book World:* "Cosby has an extraordinarily keen ear for everyday speech and everyday event, and knows how to put just enough of a comic spin on it so that even as we laugh we know we are getting a glimpse of the truth."

Following the huge success of *Fatherhood*, Doubleday published *Time Flies*, in which Cosby treats the subject of aging in the same style as his earlier book. Toronto *Globe & Mail* reviewer Leo Simpson comments, "Decay and the drift into entropy wouldn't get everyone's vote as a light-hearted theme, yet Time Flies is just as illuminating, witty and elegantly hilarious as . . . Fatherhood." Although Cosby complains in *Time Flies* that he is slowing down with age, his performing, directing, writing and devotion to charitable projects provide him with a very busy schedule. As he told the *Los Angeles Times*, "I think one of the most important things to understand is that my mother, as a domestic, worked 12 hours a day, and then she would do the laundry, and cook the meals and serve them and clean them up, and for this she got $7 a day. So 12 hours a day of whatever I do is as easy as eating a Jell-O Pudding Pop."

AVOCATIONAL INTERESTS: Tennis.

BIOGRAPHICAL/CRITICAL SOURCES:

BOOKS

Adams, Barbara Johnston, *The Picture Life of Bill Cosby*, F. Watts, 1986.
Johnson, Robert E., *Bill Cosby: In Words and Pictures*, Johnson Publishing (Chicago), 1987.
Smith, R. L., *Cosby*, St. Martin's, 1986.
Woods, H., *Billy Cosby, Making America Laugh and Learn*, Dillon, 1983.

PERIODICALS

Chicago Tribune, September 14, 1987.
Chicago Tribune Books, May 3, 1987.
Ebony, May, 1964, June, 1977, April, 1985, February, 1986, February, 1987.
Films in Review, November, 1975.
Globe & Mail (Toronto), July 5, 1986, October 24, 1987.
Jet, January 12, 1987, January 19, 1987, February 9, 1987, February 23, 1987, March 9, 1987.
Ladies Home Journal, June, 1985.
Los Angeles Times, September 25, 1987, December 20, 1987, January 24, 1988.

Los Angeles Times Book Review, June 15, 1986.
National Observer, January 6, 1964.
Newsweek, November 5, 1984, September 2, 1985, May 19, 1986, September 14, 1987.
New York Post, February 23, 1964.
New York Times Book Review, September 20, 1987.
New York Times Magazine, March 14, 1965.
People, December 10, 1984, September 14, 1987.
Playboy, December, 1985.
Saturday Evening Post, April, 1985, April, 1986.
Time, September 28, 1987.
Village Voice, November 3, 1975.
Washington Post, September 7, 1987.
Washington Post Book World, April 27, 1986.*

—Sketch by Joan Goldsworthy

*   *   *

COTTON, John 1925-

PERSONAL: Born March 7, 1925, in London, England; son of Arthur Edmund (a structural engineer) and Florence (Mandy) Cotton; married Peggy Midson (a secretary), December, 1948; children: Toby, Bevis. *Education:* University of London, B.A. (with honors), 1956.

ADDRESSES: Home—37 Lombardy Dr., Berkhamsted, Hertfordshire HP4 2LQ, England.

CAREER: Middlesex Education Authority, England, teacher of English, 1947-57; Southall Grammar Technical School, England, head of English department, 1957-63; Highfield Comprehensive School, Hemel Hempstead, England, headmaster, 1963-85. Tutor for the Arvon Foundation, Tarleigh Barton, Devon; member of literature panel, Eastern Arts. *Military service:* Royal Naval Commandos, 1942-46; served in the Far East.

MEMBER: National Poetry Society (member of council; chairman of council, 1973-75, and 1977; treasurer, 1986—).

AWARDS, HONORS: Publication award from Arts Council of Great Britain, 1971, for *Old Movies and Other Poems;* Page scholarship from English Speaking Union, 1975.

WRITINGS:

POETRY

Fourteen Poems, Priapus, 1967.
Outside the Gates of Eden and Other Poems, Taurus Press, 1969.
Ampurias, Priapus, 1969.
Old Movies and Other Poems, Chatto & Windus, 1971.
The Wilderness Priapus, 1971.
Columbus on St. Dominica, Sceptre Press, 1972.
Photographs, Sycamore Press, 1973.
A Sycamore Press Broadsheet, Sycamore Press, 1973.
British Poetry since 1965: A Selected List, National Book League, 1973.
Kilroy Was Here (Poetry Book Society selection), Chatto & Windus, 1974.
Places, Priapus, 1981.
Day Books, Priapus, 1981.
Catullus at Sirmione, Priapus, 1982.
The Storyville Portraits, Headland Press, 1984.
The Crystal Zoo, Oxford University Press, 1985.
Dust, Starwheel Press, 1986.
Oh Those Happy Feet!, Poet and Printer, 1986.

The Poetry File, Macmillan, 1988.

CONTRIBUTOR TO ANTHOLOGIES

Poetry Introduction 1, Faber & Faber, 1969.
Edward Lucie-Smith, editor, *Holding Your Eight Hands*, Doubleday, 1969.
Michael Horovitz, editor, *Children of Albion*, Penguin, 1969.
Harry Harrison and Brian Aldiss, editors, *Best Science Fiction, 1972*, Putnam, 1972.
New Poetry, Hutchinson, Number 1, 1975, Number 2, 1976, Number 3, 1977, Number 7, 1981, Number 8, 1982, Number 9, 1983.
John Loveday, editor, *Over the Bridge*, Kestrel Books, 1981.

Also contributor to PEN poetry annuals, 1965, 1967, 1974, and 1975; and *Poems for Shakespeare 1987*, Bishopsgate Press.

OTHER

Editor of *Priapus*, 1962-72, and *Private Library*, 1970-80. Advisory editor for *Contemporary Poets of the English Language*.

WORK IN PROGRESS: *Here's Looking At You, Kid*, a collection of poems.

BIOGRAPHICAL/CRITICAL SOURCES:

PERIODICALS

Hertfordshire Countryside, July, 1973.
Poetry Book Society Bulletin, Number 69, summer, 1971, Number 84, spring, 1975.
Stand, Volume 14, number 1, 1972.
Teacher, May, 1973.
Times Literary Supplement, September 6, 1985.

*   *   *

CRAIN, Jeff
See MENESES, Enrique

*   *   *

CRANNY, Titus (Francis)   1921-1981
(Daniel Francis)

PERSONAL: Born April 15, 1921, in Sioux City, Iowa; died April 28, 1981; son of Daniel Joseph (a farmer) and Theresa P. (Clarke) Cranny. *Education:* Catholic University of America, B.A., 1944, M.A., 1948, S.T.L., 1948, S.T.D., 1952. *Politics:* Democrat.

ADDRESSES: Home and office—League of Prayer for Unity, Graymoor, Garrison, N.Y. 10524.

CAREER: Roman Catholic clergyman, member of Franciscan Friars of the Atonement (S.A.). Howard University, Washington, D.C., chaplain for Roman Catholic students, 1948-49; Atonement Seminary, Washington, D.C., rector, 1951-54; affiliated with Unity Apostolate, Graymoor, Garrison, N.Y., 1954-58; League of Prayer for Unity, Graymoor, director, beginning 1956. Member of staff, Rhode Island Council of Churches, 1968-70. Lecturer at Marist College, St. Francis College, Brooklyn, N.Y., St. John's University, Jamaica, N.Y., and Manhattan College.

MEMBER: International Marian Academy, International Scotists Society, Catholic Theological Society.

AWARDS, HONORS: Marian Library award, 1963, for *Our Lady and Reunion*.

WRITINGS:

The Moral Obligation of Voting, Catholic University of America Press, 1953.
Father Paul, Apostle of Unity, Graymoor Press (Peekskill, N.Y.), 1956, revised edition, 1965.
Our Lady and Reunion, Chair of Unity Apostolate (Graymoor, Garrison, N.Y.), 1962.
Franciscan Contributions to Christian Unity, Chair of Unity Apostolate, 1962.
John 17: As We Are One, Graymoor Press, 1966.
Mary, Mother of the Church, Kenedy, 1968.
Is Mary Relevant?: A Commentary on Chapter 8 of Lumen Gentium, Exposition, 1970.

EDITOR

Meditations for Use of the Society of the Atonement, Compiled According to the Spirit of Father Paul and from His Words, G. K. Hall, 1960.
A Franciscan View of the Spiritual and Religious Life, Franciscan Friars of the Atonement (Garrison), 1962.
(And compiler) Pope Joannes XXIII, *Pope John and Christian Unity* (pamphlet), Chair of Unity Apostolate, 1962.
(And compiler) Father Paul James Francis, *Father Paul and Christian Unity* (anthology), Chair of Unity Apostolate, 1963.
Episcopate and Christian Unity, Graymoor Press, 1964.
St. Bonaventure on Religious and Spiritual Life, Graymoor Press, 1965.
(And compiler) *The Episcopate and Christian Unity*, Chair of Unity Apostolate, 1965.

Also editor of *Words of Father Paul*, sixteen volumes of the writings of Father Paul of Graymoor, 1951-56, and co-editor of *One Fold*, 1959.

OTHER

Also author of *Meditations from Father Paul*, 1960. Associate editor, *Lamp*, 1954-59.

*   *   *

CROSS, Theodore L(amont)   1924-

PERSONAL: Born February 12, 1924, in Newton, Mass; son of Gorham Lamont and Margaret Moore (Warren) Cross; married Sheilah Burr Ross, September 16, 1950 (divorced, 1972); married Mary Warner, 1974; children: (first marriage) Amanda Burr, Lisa Warren. *Education:* Amherst College, A.B., 1947; Harvard University, J.D., 1950.

ADDRESSES: Home—233 Carter Rd., Princeton, N.J. 08540. *Office*—870 7th Ave., New York, N.Y. 10019.

CAREER: Admitted to the Bar of Massachusetts, 1950, and to the Bar of New York State, 1953; Hale & Dorr (law firm), Boston, Mass., associate, 1950-52; treasurer, secretary, vice-president of legal affairs, and member of finance committee board of directors, Sheraton Corporation of America, 1953-69; Warren, Gorham & Lamont, Inc. (publisher of periodicals for bankers and accountants), New York City, 1957-80, co-founder, editor, treasurer, secretary, became chairman of the board and chief executive officer; *Investment Dealer's Digest*, New York City, owner, 1982-86. Director, Bank Tax Institute, 1964, Management Reports, Inc., Record Publishing Co., International Thomson Organization, Inc., and International

Thomson Holdings, Inc. Public governor, American Stock Exchange, New York City, 1972-77. Founder of Banking Law Institute, 1965, chairman, 1965—. Lecturer, Harvard University, Cornell University, and University of Virginia. Trustee, Amherst College, 1973. Consultant, Health, Education, and Welfare (HEW) Federal Office of Economic Opportunity, 1964-69. *Military service:* U.S. Navy, 1942-46; became ensign.

AWARDS, HONORS: McKinsey Foundation Book Award, 1969, for *Black Capitalism: Strategy for Business in the Ghetto.*

WRITINGS:

Black Capitalism: Strategy for Business in the Ghetto, Atheneum, 1969.
(With wife, Mary Cross) *Behind the Great Wall: A Photographic Essay on China,* Atheneum, 1979.

The Black Power Imperative: Racial Inequality and the Politics of Nonviolence, Faulkner Books, 1984, revised edition, 1986.

Editor of *Atomic Energy Law Journal,* beginning 1959, *Bankers Magazine,* beginning 1962, and *Business and Society Review,* beginning 1971.

AVOCATIONAL INTERESTS: Bird photography.

BIOGRAPHICAL/CRITICAL SOURCES:

PERIODICALS

Business Week, January 8, 1972.
Fortune, January 5, 1987.
Newsday, October 26, 1971.
New York Times, February 25, 1973.*

D

DALY, Jim
   See STRATEMEYER, Edward L.

* * *

DANIELS, Arlene Kaplan   1930-

PERSONAL: Born December 10, 1930, in New York, N.Y.;
daughter of Jacob (a storekeeper) and Elizabeth (Rathstone)
Kaplan; married Richard Rene Daniels (a hospital administrator), June 9, 1956. *Education:* University of California, Berkeley, B.A. (with honors), 1952, M.A., 1954, Ph.D., 1960.
Politics: Democrat. *Religion:* Agnostic.

ADDRESSES: Office—Department of Sociology, Northwestern University, Evanston, Ill. 60208.

CAREER: University of California, Berkeley, principal investigator for School of Public Health, 1957-58, instructor in
speech, 1959-61; Mental Research Institute, Palo Alto, Calif.,
research associate, 1968-75; Northwestern University, Evanston, Ill., professor of sociology, 1974—, director of program
on women, 1974-79.

MEMBER: American Sociological Association, Society for the
Study of Social Problems, Sociologists for Women in Society.

WRITINGS:

(Contributor) Gideon Sjober, editor, *Politics, Ethics and So-
   cial Research,* Schenkman, 1967.
(Editor with Rachel Kahn-Hut) *Academics on the Line,* Jossey-
   Bass, 1970.
(Contributor) Tamotsu Shibutani, editor, *Human Nature and
   Collective Behavior,* Prentice-Hall, 1970.
(Contributor) Hans P. Dreitzel, editor, *Recent Trends in So-
   ciology,* Macmillan, 1970.
(Contributor) Eliot Freidson and Judith Lorber, editors, *Med-
   ical Men and Their Work,* Atherton, 1971.
A Survey of Research Concerns on Women's Issues, Associ-
   ation of American Colleges, 1975.
(Contributor) Marcia Millman and Rosabeth Kanter, editors,
   Another Voice, Doubleday, 1975.
(Editor with Gaye Tuchman and James Benet) *Hearth and
   Home,* Oxford University Press, 1978.
(Editor with Benet) *Education: Straitjacket or Opportunity?,*
   Transaction Books, 1980.

(Editor with Kahn-Hut and Richard Colvard) *Women and Work,*
   Oxford University Press, 1980.
(Editor with Alice Cook and Val Lorwin) *Women and Trade
   Unions in Eleven Industrialized Countries,* Temple, 1984.
(Co-author with Odendahl and Boris) *Working in Foundations,*
   Foundation Press, 1986.
Invisible Careers: Women Leaders in the Volunteer World,
   University of Chicago Press, 1988.

Contributor to psychiatry, sociology, and feminist journals.

SIDELIGHTS: Arlene Kaplan Daniels wrote *CA:* "For me
writing is a byproduct of research. The writing is hard to do—
sometimes painful, because it is a problem to write for both a
sociological audience and for the people one has studied. I
hope I solved the problem in my latest book *Invisible Careers:
Women Leaders in the Volunteer World.* So far both social
scientists and the volunteer women I studied seem to think
well of the work. That makes all the labor of trying to create
a document without compromising either set of interests
worthwhile.''

* * *

DAS, Kamala   1934-

PERSONAL: Born March 31, 1934, in the district of Malabar,
India (now part of the state of Kerala); daughter of V. M. (an
editor) and Balamani Amma (a poet; maiden name, Nalapat)
Nair; married K. Madhava Das (a banker), February 4, 1949;
children: Monu Nalapar, Chinnen, Jaisurya (all sons). *Education:* Educated privately. *Politics:* "Once upon a time believed in the Indian National Congress." *Religion:* Hindu.

ADDRESSES: Home—Nalapat House, Nalapat Rd., Punna-
yurkulam, Kerala, India. *Office*—Book Point, Ballard Estate,
Bombay, India.

CAREER: Writer. Director of Book Point, Bombay, India.
Member of governing council, Indian National Trust for Cultural Heritage, New Delhi, India. Founding president, Bahu-
tantrika Group. Vice-president, State Council for Child Welfare, Trivandrum, India. Forestry Board, Kerala, India, chairman
of the board and chairman of Committee for Environmental
Education council. Conducts seminars on environmental protection for rural groups. Former president, Jyotsha Art and
Education Academy; former president, Kerala Children's Film

Society; former member, State Planning Board Committee on Art, Literature, and Mass Communications. Independent candidate for Parliament, 1984.

MEMBER: International PEN, World Poetry Society (Orient editor).

AWARDS, HONORS: Prize from International PEN, 1964; fiction award from Kerala Sahitya Academy, 1969, for *Thanuppu;* Chaiman Lau Award for Journalism, 1971; honorary doctorate in literature, World Academy of Arts and Culture (Taiwan), 1984; Asan World Prize for Literature, 1985.

WRITINGS:

IN ENGLISH

Summer in Calcutta: Fifty Poems, Everest Press (Delhi, India), 1965, InterCulture, 1975.
The Descendants (poems), Writers Workshop (Calcutta, India), 1967, Ind-US, 1975.
The Old Playhouse and Other Poems, Orient Longman (Madras, India), 1973.
Alphabet of Lust (novel), Orient Paperbacks (New Delhi), 1976.
My Story (autobiography), Sterling Publishers (Jullundur, India), 1976, Ind-US, 1977.
A Doll for the Child Prostitute (stories), India Paperbacks (New Delhi), 1977.
Tonight This Savage Rite: The Love Poetry of Kamala Das and Pritish Nandy, Arnold-Heinemann (New Delhi), 1979.
The Heart of Britain (nonfiction), Firma KLM (Calcutta), 1983.
Kamala Das: A Collage (collection of one-act plays), compiled by Arun Kuckreja, Vidja Prakashan Mandir (New Delhi), 1984.
Collected Poems, privately printed, 1984.

Also author of *Towards the Twenty-first Century, Collected Stories,* and *The Smell of the Bird.*

OTHER

Draksakshi Panna (juvenile; title means ''Eyewitness''), Longman, 1973.
Madhavikkuttiyute munnu novalukal (three novels), Navadhara (Trivandum, India), 1977.
Anoraniyan (novel), Paribesaka Natha Bradarsa (Calcutta), 1985.
Ente cerukathakal: Madhavikkutti (stories), Matrbhumi (Calcutta), 1985.

Also author of several books published by Current Books (Trichur, India), 1953-72, including *Pathu kathakal* (title means ''Ten Stories''), *Tharisunilam* (stories; title means ''Fallow Fields''), *Narachirukal parakkumbol* (stories; title means ''When the Bats Fly), *Ente snehita aruna* (stories; title means ''My Friend Aruna''), *Chuvanna pavada* (stories; title means ''The Red Skirt''), *Thanuppu* (stories; title means ''Cold''), *Rajavinte premabajanam* (stories; title means ''The King's Beloved''), *Premathinte vilapa kavyam* (stories; title means ''Requiem for a Love''), *Mathilukal* (stories; title means ''Walls''). Contributor of stories, plays, and political commentaries to journals. Poetry editor, *Illustrated Weekly of India,* 1971-72 and 1978-79.

WORK IN PROGRESS: A book on herbs and medicinal plants used as cures in ancient India; research on witchcraft for a book on sorcery in Malabar; poems.

SIDELIGHTS: Kamala Das told *CA:* ''I believe in the ancient religion of Love which is the root of the tree of religions. If a branch is severed and removed it must soon wither and die.

This is the reason why I oppose religious revivals. Like drugs, religions and political systems too have an expiry date. If they outlive that date they become poisonous. The prevalent religions and political systems have outlived their expiry dates.''

Das ran as an independent candidate for the Indian Parliament in 1984. Regarding her interest in politics, she comments: ''I believe that the strength accumulated over the years by a writer should be utilized in public service, ultimately. Merely writing cannot change the social system.'' Das writes that she also is ''interested in producing children's films in order to draw the young ones' attention from terrorist-attitudes now so prevalent in our country.'' Das has served as president of the Kerala Children's Film Society, a group which screens films at schools free of cost.

AVOCATIONAL INTERESTS: Tree-planting.

BIOGRAPHICAL/CRITICAL SOURCES:

BOOKS

Dwivedi, A. N., *Kamala Das and Her Poetry,* Doaba (New Delhi), 1983.
Jussawalla, Feroza F., *Family Quarrels: Towards a Criticism of Indian Writing in English,* Peter Lang, 1985.
Kohli, Devindra, *Kamala Das,* Arnold-Heinemann, 1975.
Rahman, Anisur, *Expressive Form in the Poetry of Kamala Das,* Abhinav (New Delhi), 1981.

PERIODICALS

Times Literary Supplement, February 3, 1978.

*   *   *

DAVIDSON, Marion
  See GARIS, Howard R(oger)

*   *   *

DAWE, (Donald) Bruce   1930-

PERSONAL: Born February 15, 1930, in Geelong, Australia; son of Alfred (a laborer) and Mary Ann (Hamilton) Dawe; married Gloria Desley, January 1, 1964; children: Brian, Jamie, Katrina, Melissa. *Education:* University of Queensland, B.A., 1969, M.A., 1975, Ph.D., 1980; University of New England, Litt.B., 1973. *Religion:* Roman Catholic.

ADDRESSES: Home—30 Cumming St., Toowoomba, Queensland, Australia 4350. *Office*—School of Arts, Institute of Advanced Education, Darling Heights, Toowoomba, Queensland, Australia 4350.

CAREER: Has worked as a laborer, postman, and gardener; Institute of Advanced Education, Toowoomba, Australia, lecturer in literature, 1971—. *Military service:* Royal Australian Air Force, 1959-68; became sergeant.

AWARDS, HONORS: Myer Award for poetry, 1966, for *A Need of Similar Name,* and 1969, for *An Eye for a Tooth;* Ampol Arts Award for Creative Literature, 1967; Dame Mary Gilmore Medal, 1971, for *Condolences of the Season;* Grace Leven Poetry Prize, 1978, and Braille Book of the Year award, 1979, both for *Sometimes Gladness: Collected Poems, 1954-1978;* Patrick White Literary Award for contributions to Australian poetry, 1980.

WRITINGS:

No Fixed Address, Cheshire (Melbourne), 1962.

A Need of Similar Name, Cheshire, 1965.
An Eye for a Tooth, Cheshire, 1968.
Beyond the Subdivision, Cheshire, 1969.
Heat-Wave, Sweeny Reed (Melbourne), 1970.
Condolences of the Season, Cheshire, 1971.
Bruce Dawe Reads from His Own Work, University of Queensland Press, 1971.
(Editor) *Dimensions*, McGraw, 1974.
Just a Dugong at Twilight, Cheshire, 1975.
Sometimes Gladness: Collected Poems, 1954-1978, Longman Cheshire (Melbourne), 1979, revised edition published as *Sometimes Gladness: Collected Poems, 1954-1982*, 1983, 2nd revised edition published as *Sometimes Gladness: Collected Poems, 1954-1987*, 1988.
Over Here, Harv! and Other Stories, Penguin, 1983.
Towards Sunrise: Poems, 1979-1986, Longman Cheshire, 1986.
Speaking in Parables: A Reader, Longman Cheshire, 1987.

SIDELIGHTS: Australian Bruce Dawe's "poetry sounds easy . . . but it represents a feat of strength," Clive James asserts in the *Times Literary Supplement*. James praises Dawe's ability to show his country's relationship to, and assimilation of, American culture. "Dawe was the first Australian poet to take measure of the junk media and find poetry in their pathos," James continues. "He wrote better about the Vietnam War than any other poet, including American poets; and he could do so because he wrote better about television."

Dawe writes: "One of the reasons why the use of various verse forms may help me to capture something of the evanescence of the contemporary Australian idiom is that the use of various traditional rhyme-forms and some metrical regularity together with elements of the contemporary scene and idiom provide a 'mix' of past and present in an acceptable form overall."

In response to *CA*'s question as to how he chose the dramatic monologue as one of his major poetic forms, Dawe said: "I never *consciously* chose the dramatic monologue form—it just occurred as a form frequently enough to confirm its possibilities. I am sure this is the general way things happen—forms choose us."

"Regional poetry," Dawe continued, "is not (as in the United States) a very obvious and characteristic kind of poetry here, Australian society being culturally and linguistically far more homogeneous than American—urban and rural are the significant 'regions' rather than the Southwest, West, Midwest, East, etc. This is one of our greatest losses, I feel, artistically."

BIOGRAPHICAL/CRITICAL SOURCES:

BOOKS

Goodwin, K. L., *Adjacent Worlds: A Literary Life of Bruce Dawe*, Longman Cheshire, 1988.
Goodwin, K. L., *Selected Poems of Bruce Dawe*, Longman York Press, 1983.
Hansen, Ian Victor, editor, *Bruce Dawe: The Man down the Street*, Victorian Association for the Teaching of English, 1972.
Shaw, Basil, editor, *Times and Seasons: An Introduction to Bruce Dawe*, Cheshire, 1973.

PERIODICALS

Times Literary Supplement, November 27-December 3, 1987.

DAWSON, Elmer A.
[Collective pseudonym]

WRITINGS:

"BUCK AND LARRY" BASEBALL STORIES

The Pick-up Nine; or, The Chester Boys on the Diamond, Grosset & Dunlap, 1930.
Buck's Winning Hit; or, The Chester Boys Making a Record, Grosset & Dunlap, 1930.
Larry's Fadeaway; or, The Chester Boys Saving the Nine, Grosset & Dunlap, 1930.
Buck's Home Run Drive; or, The Chester Boys Winning against Odds, Grosset & Dunlap, 1931.
Larry's Speedball; or, The Chester Boys and the Diamond Secret, Grosset & Dunlap, 1932.

"GARRY GRAYSON" FOOTBALL STORIES

Garry Grayson's High Street Eleven; or, The Football Boys of Lenox, Grosset & Dunlap, 1926.
Garry Grayson at Lenox High; or, The Champions of the Football League, Grosset & Dunlap, 1926.
Garry Grayson's Football Rivals; or, The Secret of the Stolen Signals, Grosset & Dunlap, 1926.
Garry Grayson Showing His Speed; or, A Daring Run on the Gridiron, Grosset & Dunlap, 1927.
Garry Grayson at Stanley Prep; or, The Football Rivals of Riverview, Grosset & Dunlap, 1927.
Garry Grayson's Winning Kick; or, Battling for Honor, Grosset & Dunlap, 1928.
Garry Grayson Hitting the Line; or, Stanley Prep on a New Gridiron, Grosset & Dunlap, 1929.
Garry Grayson's Winning Touchdown; or, Putting Passmore Tech on the Map, Grosset & Dunlap, 1930.
Garry Grayson's Double Signals; or, Vanquishing the Football Plotters, Grosset & Dunlap, 1931.
Garry Grayson's Forward Pass; or, Winning in the Final Quarter, Grosset & Dunlap, 1932.

SIDELIGHTS: The sports stories produced under the pseudonym Elmer A. Dawson included the "Garry Grayson" series. Garry, described by Arthur Prager in *Rascals at Large; or, The Clue in the Old Nostalgia* as "an athletic male Nancy Drew, perfect and infallible," was about fourteen years old when the series began. The books themselves, continues Prager, were "long detailed chronicles like the games in [Lester Chadwick's] Baseball Joe series. Plot was unimportant, shoved in to give us a breather between halves. Most of the plots were lifted from other Stratemeyer series. There were frame-ups, missing money, fathers faced with ruin, abduction of stars before the game, and all the tried and true situations [found in other Stratemeyer Syndicate work]."

For more information see the entries in this volume for Harriet S. Adams, Edward L. Stratemeyer, and Andrew E. Svenson.

BIOGRAPHICAL/CRITICAL SOURCES:

BOOKS

Johnson, Deidre, editor and compiler, *Stratemeyer Pseudonyms and Series Books: An Annotated Checklist of Stratemeyer and Stratemeyer Syndicate Publications*, Greenwood Press, 1982.
Prager, Arthur, *Rascals at Large; or, The Clue in the Old Nostalgia*, Doubleday, 1971.

DAY, Richard B(ruce) 1942-

PERSONAL: Born July 22, 1942, in Toronto, Ontario, Canada; son of Raymond V. (a businessman) and Dorothy M. (Witney) Day; married Judith Sheffield, August 5, 1969; children: Tara Nicole, Geoffrey Bruce, Christine Michelle. *Education:* University of Toronto, B.A., 1965, M.A., 1967, Dip. REES, 1967; University of London, Ph.D., 1970.

ADDRESSES: Home—2601 Truscott Dr., Mississauga, Ontario, Canada. *Office*—Department of Political Economy, University of Toronto, Toronto, Ontario, Canada M5S 1A1.

CAREER: University of Toronto, Toronto, Ontario, assistant professor, 1970-73, associate professor, 1974-78, professor of political economy, 1979—.

WRITINGS:

Leon Trotsky and the Politics of Economic Isolation, Cambridge University Press, 1973.
The Crisis and the Crash: Soviet Studies of the West (1917-1939), NLB, 1981.
(Editor, translator, and author of introduction) Nicholas I. Bukharin, *Selected Writings on the State and the Transition to Socialism,* M. E. Sharpe, 1982.
(Editor, translator, and author of introduction) E. A. Preobrazhenskii, *The Decline of Capitalism,* M. E. Sharpe, 1985.
(Editor with Ronald Beiner and Joseph Masculli) *Democratic Theory and Technological Society,* M. E. Sharpe, 1988.

WORK IN PROGRESS: Volume II (1945-73) of "Soviet Studies of the West," entitled *The Capitalist State and Keynesian Planning: Soviet Studies of Western Economics.*

*   *   *

DELANY, Samuel R(ay, Jr.) 1942-

PERSONAL: Born April 1, 1942, in New York, N.Y.; son of Samuel R. (a funeral director) and Margaret Carey (a library clerk; maiden name, Boyd) Delany; married Marilyn Hacker (a poet), August 24, 1961 (divorced, 1980); children: Iva Alyxander. *Education:* Attended City College (now of the City University of New York), 1960 and 1962-63.

ADDRESSES: Agent—Henry Morrison, Inc., Box 235, Bedford Hills, N.Y. 10507.

CAREER: Writer. Butler Professor of English, State University of New York at Buffalo, 1975; senior fellow at the Center for Twentieth Century Studies, University of Wisconsin—Milwaukee, 1977; senior fellow at the Society for the Humanities, Cornell University, 1987; professor of comparative literature, University of Massachusetts—Amherst, 1988.

AWARDS, HONORS: Nebula Award, Science Fiction Writers of America, 1967, for best novel, *Babel-17,* 1968, for best short story, "Aye and Gomorrah," and for best novel, *The Einstein Intersection,* and 1970, for best novelette, "Time Considered as a Helix of Semi-Precious Stones"; Hugo Award, Science Fiction Convention, for "Time Considered as a Helix of Semi-Precious Stones"; American Book Award nomination, 1980, for *Tales of Neveryon;* Pilgrim Award, Science Fiction Research Association, 1985.

WRITINGS:

SCIENCE FICTION

The Jewels of Aptor (abridged edition bound with *Second Ending* by James White), Ace Books, 1962, hardcover edi-

tion, Gollancz, 1968, complete edition published with an introduction by Don Hausdorff, Gregg Press, 1976.
Captives of the Flame (first novel in trilogy; bound with *The Psionic Menace* by Keith Woodcott), Ace Books, 1963, revised edition published under author's original title *Out of the Dead City* (also see below), Sphere Books, 1968.
The Towers of Toron (second novel in trilogy; also see below; bound with *The Lunar Eye* by Robert Moore Williams), Ace Books, 1964.
City of a Thousand Suns (third novel in trilogy; also see below), Ace Books, 1965.
The Ballad of Beta-2 (also see below; bound with *Alpha Yes, Terra No!* by Emil Petaja), Ace Books, 1965, hardcover edition published with an introduction by David G. Hartwell, Gregg Press, 1977.
Empire Star (also see below; bound with *The Three Lord of Imeten* by Tom Purdom), Ace Books, 1966, hardcover edition published with an introduction by Hartwell, Gregg Press, 1977.
Babel-17, Ace Books, 1966, hardcover edition, Gollancz, 1967, published with an introduction by Robert Scholes, 1976.
The Einstein Intersection, slightly abridged edition, Ace Books, 1967, hardcover edition, Gollancz, 1968, complete edition, Ace Books, 1972.
Nova, Doubleday, 1968.
The Fall of the Towers (trilogy; contains *Out of the Dead City, The Towers of Toron,* and *City of a Thousand Suns*), Ace Books, 1970, hardcover edition published with introduction by Joseph Milicia, Gregg Press, 1977.
Driftglass: Ten Tales of Speculative Fiction, Doubleday, 1971.
The Tides of Lust, Lancer Books, 1973.
Dhalgren, Bantam, 1975, hardcover edition published with introduction by Jean Mark Gawron, Gregg Press, 1978.
The Ballad of Beta-2 [and] *Empire Star,* Ace Books, 1975.
Triton, Bantam, 1976.
Empire: A Visual Novel, illustrations by Howard V. Chaykin, Berkley Books, 1978.
Distant Stars, Bantam, 1981.
Stars In My Pocket Like Grains of Sand, Bantam, 1984.
The Complete Nebula Award-Winning Fiction, Bantam, 1986.

"RETURN TO NEVERYON" SERIES; SWORD AND SORCERY NOVELS

Tales of Neveryon, Bantam, 1979.
Neveryona; or, The Tale of Signs and Cities, Bantam, 1983.
Flight from Neveryon, Bantam, 1985.
The Bridge of Lost Desire, Arbor House, 1987.

OTHER

The Jewel-Hinged Jaw: Notes on the Language of Science Fiction, Dragon Press, 1977, revised edition, Berkley Publishing, 1978.
The American Shore: Meditations on a Tale of Science Fiction by Thomas M. Disch—"Angouleme" (criticism), Dragon Press, 1978.
Heavenly Breakfast: An Essay on the Winter of Love (memoir), Bantam, 1979.
Starboard Wine: More Notes on the Language of Science Fiction, Dragon Press, 1984.
The Motion of Light in Water: Sex and Science Fiction Writing in the East Village, 1957-1965, Arbor House, 1988.
Wagner/Artaud: A Play of Nineteenth and Twentieth Century Critical Fictions, Ansatz Press, 1988.
Straits of Messina (essays), Serconia Press, 1988.

Also author of scripts, director, and editor for two short films, "Tiresias," 1970, and "The Orchid," 1971; author of two scripts for the ''Wonder Woman Comic Series,'' 1972, and of the radio play ''The Star Pit,'' based on his short story of the same title.

Editor, *Quark,* 1970-71.

SIDELIGHTS: ''Samuel R. Delany is one of today's most innovative and imaginative writers of science-fiction,'' comments Jane Branham Weedman in her study of the author, *Samuel R. Delany.* In his science fiction, which includes over fifteen novels and two collections of short stories, the author ''has explored what happens when alien world views intersect, collide, or mesh,'' writes Greg Tate in the *Voice Literary Supplement.* Delany first appeared on the science-fiction horizon in the early 1960s and in the decade that followed he established himself as one of the stars of the genre. Like many of his contemporaries who entered science fiction in the 1960s, he is less concerned with the conventions of the genre, more interested in science fiction as literature, literature which offers a wide range of artistic opportunities. As a result, maintains Weedman, ''Delany's works are excellent examples of modern science-fiction as it has developed from the earlier and more limited science-fiction tradition, especially because of his manipulation of cultural theories, his detailed futuristic or alternate settings, and his stylistic innovations.''

''One is drawn into Delany's stories because they have a complexity,'' observes Sandra Y. Govan in the *Black American Literature Forum,* ''an acute consciousness of language, structure, and form; a dextrous ability to weave together mythology and anthropology, linguistic theory and cultural history, gestalt psychology and sociology as well as philosophy, structuralism, and the adventure story.'' At the center of the complex web of personal, cultural, artistic, and intellectual concerns that provides the framework for all of his work is Delany's examination of how language and myth influence reality. ''According to [the author],'' writes Govan in the *Dictionary of Literary Biography,* ''language identifies or negates the self. It is self-reflective; it shapes perceptions.'' By shaping perceptions, language in turn has the capacity to shape reality. Myths can exercise much the same power. In his science fiction, Delany ''creates new myths, or inversions of old ones, by which his protagonists measure themselves and their societies against the traditional myths that Delany includes,'' Weedman observes. In this way, as Peter S. Alterman comments in the *Dictionary of Literary Biography,* the author confronts ''the question of the extent to which myths and archetypes create reality.''

In societies in which language and myth are recognized as determinants of reality, the artist—one who works in language and myth—plays a crucial part. For this reason, the protagonist of a Delany novel is often an artist of some sort. ''The role which Delany defines for the artist is to observe, record, transmit, and question paradigms in society,'' explains Weedman. But Delany's artists do more than chronicle and critique the societies of which they are a part. His artists are always among those at the margin of society; they are outcasts and often criminals. ''The criminal and the artist both operate outside the normal standards of society,'' observes Alterman, ''according to their own self-centered value systems.'' The artist/criminal goes beyond observation and commentary. His actions at the margin push society's values to their limits and beyond, providing the experimentation necessary to prepare for eventual change.

Delany entered the world of science fiction in 1962 with the publication of his novel, *The Jewels of Aptor.* Over the next

six years, he published eight more, including *Babel-17, The Einstein Intersection,* and *Nova,* his first printed originally in hardcover. Douglas Barbour, writing in *Science Fiction Writers,* describes these early novels as ''colorful, exciting, entertaining, and intellectually provocative to a degree not found in most genre science fiction.'' Barbour adds that although they do adhere to science-fiction conventions, they ''begin the exploration of those literary obsessions that define [Delany's] oeuvre: problems of communication and community; new kinds of sexual/love/family relationships; the artist as social outsider . . . ; cultural interactions and the exploration of human social possibilities these allow; archetypal and mythic structures in the imagination.''

With the publication of *Babel-17* in 1966, Delany began to gain recognition in the science fiction world. The novel, which earned its author his first Nebula Award, is a story of galactic warfare between the forces of the Alliance, which includes the Earth, and the forces of the Invaders. The poet Rydra Wong is enlisted by Alliance intelligence to decipher communications intercepted from its enemy. When she discovers that these dispatches contain not a code but rather an unknown language, her quest becomes one of learning this mysterious tongue labeled Babel-17. While leading an interstellar mission in search of clues, Rydra gains insights into the nature of language and, in the process, discovers the unique character of the enigmatic new language of the Invaders.

Babel-17 itself becomes an exploration of language and its ability to structure experience. A central image in the novel, as George Edgar Slusser points out in his study, *The Delany Intersection: Samuel R. Delany Considered as a Writer of Semi-Precious Words,* is that of ''the web and its weaver or breaker.'' The web, continues Slusser, ''stands, simultaneously, for unity and isolation, interconnectedness and entanglement.'' And, as Peter Alterman points out in *Science-Fiction Studies,* ''the web is an image of the effect of language on the mind and of the mind as shaper of reality.'' Weedman elaborates in her essay on the novel: ''The language one learns necessarily constrains and structures what it is that one says.'' In its ability to connect and constrain is the power of the language/web. ''Language . . . has a direct effect on how one thinks,'' explains Weedman, ''since the structure of the language influences the processes by which one formulates ideas.'' At the center of the language as web ''is one who joins and cuts—the artist-hero,'' comments Slusser. And, in *Babel-17,* the poet Rydra Wong demonstrates that only she is able to master this new language weapon and turn it against its creators.

Delany followed *Babel-17* with another Nebula winner, *The Einstein Intersection.* This novel represents a ''move from a consideration of the relationship among language, thought, action and time to an analytic and imaginative investigation of the patterns of myths and archetypes and their interaction with the conscious mind,'' writes Alterman. Slusser sees this development in themes as part of a logical progression: ''[Myths] too are seen essentially as language constructs: verbal scenarios for human action sanctioned by tradition or authority.'' Comparing this novel to *Babel-17,* he adds that ''Delany's sense of the language act, in this novel, has a broader social valence.''

The Einstein Intersection relates the story of a strange race of beings that occupies a post-apocalyptic Earth. This race assumes the traditions—economic, political, and religious—of the extinct humans in an attempt to make sense of the remnant world in which they find themselves. ''While they try to live by the myths of man,'' writes Barbour in *Foundation,* ''they cannot create a viable culture of their own. . . . Their more profound hope is to recognize that they do not have to live out the old myths at all, that the 'difference' they seek to hide or dissemble is the key to their cultural and racial salvation.''

''Difference is a key word in this novel,'' Weedman explains, ''for it designates the importance of the individual and his ability to make choices, on the basis of being different from others, which affect his life, thus enabling him to question the paradigms of his society.'' The artist is the embodiment of this difference and in *The Einstein Intersection* the artist is Lobey, a musician. The power of Lobey's music is its ability to create order, to destroy the old myths and usher in the new. At its core, then, ''*The Einstein Intersection* is . . . a novel about experiments in culture,'' Weedman comments.

Delany's next novel, *Nova,* ''stands as the summation of [his] career up to that time,'' writes Barbour in *Science Fiction Writers: Critical Studies of the Major Authors from the Early Nineteenth Century to the Present Day.* ''Packing his story full of color and incident, violent aciton and tender introspective moments, he has created one of the grandest space operas ever written.'' In this novel, Delany presents a galaxy divided into three camps, all embroiled in a bitter conflict caused by a shortage of the fuel illyrion on which they all depend. In chronicling one group's quest for a new source of the fuel, the author examines, according to Weedman, ''how technology changes the world and philosophies for world survival. Delany also explores conflicts between and within societies, as well as the problems created by people's different perceptions and different reality models.''

''In developing this tale,'' notes Slusser, ''Delany has inverted the traditional epic relationship, in which the human subject (the quest) dominates the 'form.' Here instead is a 'subjunctive epic.' Men do not struggle against an inhuman system so much as *inside* an unhuman one.'' The system inside which these societies struggle is economic; the goal of the quester, who is driven by selfishness, is a commodity. Whether the commodity is abundant or scarce, as Jeanne Murray Walker points out in *Extrapolation,* this ''is a world where groups are out of alignment, off balance, where some suffer while others prosper, where the object of exchange is used to divide rather than to unite.'' Walker concludes in her essay that ''by ordering the action of *Nova* in the quest pattern, but assuming a value system quite different from that assumed by medieval romance writers, Delany shows that neither pattern nor action operate as they once did. Both fail.'' Even so, as she continues, ''individuals must continue to quest. Through their quests they find meaning for themselves.''

After the publication of *Nova,* Delany turned his creative urges to forms other than the novel, writing a number of short stories, editing four quarterlies of speculative fiction, and dabbling in such diverse media as film and comic books. Also at this time, he engaged himself in conceiving, writing, and polishing what would become his longest, most complex, and most controversial novel, *Dhalgren*—a work that would earn him national recognition. On its shifting surface, this novel represents the experience of a nameless amnesiac, an artist/criminal, during the period of time he spends in a temporally and spatially isolated city scarred by destruction and decay. As Alterman relates in the *Dictionary of Literary Biography,* ''it begins with the genesis of a protagonist, one so unformed that he has no name, no identity, the quest for which is the

novel's central theme.'' The critic goes on to explain that ''at the end Kid has a name and a life, both of which are the novel itself; he is a persona whose experience in *Dhalgren* defines him.''

Dhalgren's length and complexity provide a significant challenge to readers, but as Gerald Jones observes in the *New York Times Book Review,* ''the most important fact about Delany's novel . . . is that nothing in it is clear. Nothing is *meant* to be clear.'' He adds: ''An event may be described two or three times, and each recounting is slightly disconcertingly different from the one before.'' What is more, continues the reviewer, ''the nameless narrator experiences time discontinuously; whole days seem to be excised from his memory.'' According to Weedman, ''Delany creates disorientation in *Dhalgren* to explore the problems which occur when reality models differ from reality.'' And in Jonas's estimation, ''If the book can be said to be *about* anything, it is about nothing less than the nature of reality.''

''*Dhalgren* has drawn more widely divergent critical response than any other Delany novel,'' comments Govan in her *Dictionary of Literary Biography* essay. ''Some reviewers deny that it is science fiction, while others praise it for its daring and experimental form.'' For instance, the *Magazine of Fantasy and Science Fiction* book reviewer Algis Budrys contends that ''this book is not science fiction, or science fantasy, but allegorical quasi-fantasy on the [James Gould] Cozzens model. Thus, although it demonstrates the breadth of Delany's education, and many of its passages are excellent prose, it presents no new literary inventions.'' In his *Science Fiction Writers* essay, Barbour describes the same novel as ''the very stuff of science fiction but lacking the usual structural emblems of the genre.'' ''One thing is certain,'' offers Jonas, '''Dhalgren' is not a conventional novel, whether considered in terms of S.F. or the mainsream.''

Following the exhaustive involvement with Kid necessary to complete *Dhalgren,* Delany chose to do a novel in which he distanced himself from his protagonist, giving him a chance to look at the relationship between an individual and his society in a new light. ''I wanted to do a psychological analysis of someone with whom you're just not in sympathy, someone whom you watch making all the wrong choices, even though his plight itself is sympathetic,'' Delany explained in an interview with Larry McCaffery and Sinda Gregory published in their book *Alive and Writing: Interviews with American Authors of the 1980s.* The novel is *Triton;* its main character is Bron.

''*Triton* is set in a sort of sexual utopia, where every form of sexual behavior is accepted, and sex-change operations (not to mention 'refixations,' to alter sexual preference) are common,'' observes Michael Goodwin in *Mother Jones.* In this world of freedom lives Bron, who Govan describes in *Black American Literature Forum* as ''a narrow-minded, isolated man, so self-serving that he is incapable of reaching outside himself to love another or even understand another despite his best intentions.'' In an attempt to solve his problems, he undergoes a sex-change operation, but finds no happiness. ''Bron is finally trapped in total social and psychological stasis, lost in isolation beyond any help her society can offer its citizens,'' comments Barbour in *Science Fiction Writers.*

In this novel, once again Delany creates an exotic new world, having values and conventions that differ from ours. In exploring this fictional world, he can set up a critique of our present-day society. In *Triton,* he casts a critical eye, as Weedman points out, on "sexual persecution against women, ambisexuals, and homosexuals." She concludes that the work is "on the necessity of knowing one's self despite sexual identification, knowing one's sexual identity is not one's total identity."

In the 1980s, Delany has continued to experiment in his fiction writing. In his "Neveryon" series, which includes *Tales of Neveryon, Neveryona; or, The Tale of Signs and Cities, Flight from Neveryon,* and *The Bridge of Lost Desire,* he chooses a different setting. "Instead of being set in some imagined future, [they] are set in some magical, distant past, just as civilization is being created," observes McCaffery in a *Science-Fiction Studies* interview of Delany. Their focus, suggests Gregory in the same interview, is "power—all kinds of power: sexual, economic, even racial power via the issue of slavery."

Throughout these tales of a world of dragons, treasures, and fabulous cities, Delany weaves the story of Gorgik, a slave who rises to power and abolishes slavery. In one story, the novel-length "Tale of Plagues and Carnivals," he shifts in time from his primitive world to present day New York and back to examine the devastating effects of a disease such as AIDS. And, in the appendices that accompany each of these books, he reflects on the creative process itself. Of the four, it is *Neveryona,* the story of Pryn—a girl who flees her mountain home on a journey of discovery—that has received the most attention from reviewers. *Science Fiction and Fantasy Book Review* contributor Michael R. Collings calls it "a stirring fable of adventure and education, of heroic action and even more heroic normality in a world where survival itself is constantly threatened." Faren C. Miller finds the book groundbreaking; she writes in *Locus:* "Combining differing perspectives with extraordinary talent for the *details* of a world—its smells, its shadows, workaday furnishings, and playful frills—Delany has produced a sourcebook for a new generation of fantasy writers." The book also "presents a new manifestation of Delany's continuing concern for language and the magic of fiction, whereby words become symbols for other, larger things," Collings observes.

In *Stars in My Pocket Like Grains of Sand,* Delany returns to distant worlds of the future. The book is "a densely textured, intricately worked out novelistic structure which delights and astonishes even as it forces a confrontation with a wide range of thought-provoking issues," writes McCaffery in *Fantasy Review.* Included are "an examination of interstellar politics among thousands of far flung worlds, a love story, a meandering essay on the variety of human relationships and the inexplicability of sexual attractiveness, and a hypnotic crash-course on a fascinating body of literature which does not yet exist," notes H. J. Kirchhoff in the Toronto *Globe and Mail.*

Beneath the surface features, as Jonas suggests in the *New York Times Book Review,* the reader can discover the fullness of this Delany novel. The reviewer writes: "To unpack the layers of meaning in seemingly offhand remarks or exchanges of social pleasantries, the reader must be alert to small shifts in emphasis, repeated phrases or gestures that assume new significance in new contexts, patterns of behavior that only become apparent when the author supplies a crucial piece of information at just the proper moment." Here in the words and gestures of the characters and the subtle way in which the author fashions his work is the fundamental concern of the novel. "I take the most basic subject here to be the nature of information itself," McCaffery explains, "the way it is processed, stored and decoded symbolically, the way it is dis-

torted by the present and the past, the way it has become a commodity . . . the way that the play of textualities defines our perception of the universe."

"This is an astonishing new Delany," according to Somtow Sucharitkul in the *Washington Post Book World,* "more richly textured, smoother, more colorful than ever before." Jonas commends the novel because of the interaction it encourages with the reader. "Sentence by sentence, phrase by phrase, it invites the reader to collaborate in the process of creation, in a way that few novels do," writes the reviewer. "The reader who accepts this invitation has an extraordinarily satisfying experience in store for him/her." "*Stars in My Pocket Like Grains of Sand . . .* confirms that [Delany] is American SF's most consistently brilliant and inventive writer," McCaffery claims.

Critics often comment on Delany's use of fiction as a forum to call for greater acceptance of women's rights and gay rights; yet, as Govan maintains in her *Dictionary of Literary Biography* contribution, "a recurring motif frequently overlooked in Delany's fiction is his subtle emphasis on race. Black and mixed-blood characters cross the spectrum of his speculative futures, both as a testimony to a future Delany believes will change to reflect human diversity honestly and as a commentary on the racial politics of the present."

In novels such as *Babel-17,* Delany demonstrates how language can be used to rob the black man of his identity. "White culture exerts a great influence because it can force stereotypic definitions on the black person," writes Weedman. She adds that "if the black person capitulates to the definition imposed on him by a force outside of his culture, then he is in danger of losing his identity." In his other novels, Govan points out, "Delany utilizes existing negative racial mythologies about blacks, but, in all his works, he twists the commonplace images and stereotypes to his own ends." In using his fiction to promote awareness of the race issue, he and other black writers like him "have mastered the dominant culture's language and turned it against its formulators in protest," writes Weedman.

"Delany is not only a gifted writer," claims Barbour in his *Foundation* article, "he is one of the most articulate theorists of sf to have emerged from the ranks of its writers." In such critical works as *The Jewel-Hinged Jaw, The American Shore,* and *Starboard Wine,* "he has done much to open up critical discussion of sf as a genre, forcefully arguing its great potential as art," adds the reviewer. In his nonfiction, Delany offers a functional description of science fiction and contrasts it with other genres such as naturalistic fiction and fantasy. He also attempts to expand "the domain of his chosen genre by claiming it the modern mode of fiction *par excellence,*" comments Slusser, "the one most suited to deal with the complexities of paradox and probability, chaos, irrationality, and the need for logic and order."

Samuel R. Delany is not a simple man: a black man in a white society, a writer who suffers from dyslexia, an artist who is also a critic. His race, lifestyle, chosen profession, and chosen genre keep him far from the mainstream. "His own term 'multiplex' probably best describes his work (attitudes, ideas, themes, craftsmanship, all their inter-relations, as well as his relation, as artist, to them all)," Barbour suggests. And, adds the reviewer, "His great perseverance in continually developing his craft and never resting on his past achievements is revealed in the steady growth in [his] artistry." In Weedman's estimation,

"Few writers approach the lyricism, the command of language, the powerful combination of style and content that distinguishes Delany's works. More importantly," she concludes, "few writers, whether in science fiction or mundane fiction, so successfully create works which make us question ourselves, our actions, our beliefs, and our society as Delany has helped us do."

BIOGRAPHICAL/CRITICAL SOURCES:

BOOKS

Bleiler, E. F., editor, *Science Fiction Writers: Critical Studies of the Major Authors from the Early Nineteenth Century to the Present Day*, Scribner, 1982.
Contemporary Literary Criticism, Gale, Volume 8, 1978, Volume 14, 1980, Volume 38, 1986.
Delany, Samuel R., *The Jewel-Hinged Jaw: Notes on the Language of Science Fiction*, Dragon Press, 1977, revised edition, Berkley Publishing, 1978.
Delany, Samuel R., *Heavenly Breakfast: An Essay on the Winter of Love*, Bantam, 1979.
Delany, Samuel R., *The Motion of Light in Water: Sex and Science Fiction Writing in the East Village, 1957-1965*, Arbor House, 1988.
Dictionary of Literary Biography, Gale, Volume 8: *Twentieth-Century American Science Fiction Writers*, 1981, Volume 33: *Afro-American Fiction Writers after 1955*, 1984.
McCaffery, Larry, and Sinda Gregory, editors, *Alive and Writing: Interviews with American Authors of the 1980s*, University of Illinois Press, 1987.
Peplow, Michael W., and Robert S. Bravard, *Samuel R. Delany: A Primary and Secondary Bibliography, 1962-1979*, G. K. Hall, 1980.
Platt, Charles, editor, *Dream Makers: The Uncommon People Who Write Science Fiction*, Berkley Books, 1980.
Slusser, George Edgar, *The Delany Intersection: Samuel R. Delany Considered as a Writer of Semi-Precious Words*, Borgo, 1977.
Weedman, Jane Branham, *Samuel R. Delany*, Starmont House, 1982.

PERIODICALS

Analog Science Fiction/Science Fact, April, 1985.
Black American Literature Forum, summer, 1984.
Commonweal, December 5, 1975.
Extrapolation, fall, 1982.
Fantasy Review, December, 1984.
Foundation, March, 1975.
Globe and Mail (Toronto), February 9, 1985.
Locus, summer, 1983.
Los Angeles Times Book Review, March 13, 1988.
Magazine of Fantasy and Science Fiction, November, 1975, June, 1980.
Mother Jones, August, 1976.
New York Times Book Review, February 16, 1975, March 28, 1976, October 28, 1979, February 10, 1985.
Publishers Weekly, January 29, 1988.
Science Fiction and Fantasy Book Review, July/August, 1983.
Science Fiction Chronicle, November, 1987.
Science-Fiction Studies, Volume 4, number 11, Volume 14, number 2, 1987.
Voice Literary Supplement, February, 1985.
Washington Post Book World, January 27, 1985.

—*Sketch by Bryan Ryan*

DENTINGER, Stephen
See HOCH, Edward D(entinger)

*   *   *

DERWENT, Lavinia

PERSONAL: Born in Jedburgh, Scotland. *Religion:* Protestant.

ADDRESSES: Home—1 Great Western Ter., Glasgow G12 OUP, Scotland. *Agent*—Campbell Thomson & McLaughlin, 31 Newington Green, London N16 9PU, England.

CAREER: Writer, 1950—. Has appeared on television; storyteller in schools.

MEMBER: International PEN, Society of Authors, Writers Guild, Soroptimists.

AWARDS, HONORS: Member of Order of the British Empire.

WRITINGS:

(Compiler with John Redgwick Crossland) *Ten Modern Mystery Stories*, Collins, 1935.
(Compiler) *My Own Book of Animals*, Collins, 1937.
Brer Rabbit (adapted from *Uncle Remus* by Joel Chandler Harris), Collins, 1938.
More Brer Rabbit (adapted from *Uncle Remus* by Harris), Collins, 1940.
The Woodland Readers, Collins, 1940.
The Witch (verse play), Thomas Nelson, 1941.
Brer Rabbit Again (adapted from *Uncle Remus* by Harris), Collins, 1942.
The Book of Fables (adapted from *Fables* be Aesop), Collins, 1945.
Clashmaclavers: A Mixty-Maxty of Prose and Verse in the Couthy Tradition, Oliver & Boyd, 1947.
Kirk Moose, Maclellan, 1951.
Children's Picture Dictionary, Collins, 1957.
Macpherson, Bobbs-Merrill, 1961.
The Coat of Many Colours, Burke Publishing, 1965.
The Story of Hiawatha (adapted from *Hiawatha* by Henry Wadsworth Longfellow), Collins, 1965.
The Boy and the Giant, Burke Publishing, 1967.
The Boy in the Basket, Burke Publishing, 1968.
Macpherson's Skyscraper, Burke Publishing, 1969.
Sula (juvenile), Gollancz, 1969.
Fisher Boy, Burke Publishing, 1969.
Picture Dictionary, Burke Publishing, 1969.
Macpherson's Island, Burke Publishing, 1970.
Return to Sula (juvenile), Gollancz, 1971.
Boy Named Samuel, Burke Publishing, 1972.
Macpherson's Winter Sports, Burke Publishing, 1972.
The Boy from Sula (juvenile), Gollancz, 1973.
The Adventures of Tammy Troot, Holmes-McDougall, 1975.
Further Adventures of Tammy Troot, Holmes-McDougall, 1975.
A Breath of Border Air, Hutchinson, 1975.
Song of Sula (juvenile), Gollancz, 1976.
Another Breath of Border Air, Hutchinson, 1977.
Macpherson's Lighthouse Adventure, Blackie (Glasgow), 1977.
Joseph and the Coat of Many Colors, Scholastic Book Services, 1979.
Macpherson's Caravan, Blackie, 1979.
A Border Bairn, Hutchinson, 1979.
Macpherson's Highland Fling, Blackie, 1980.
God Bless the Borders!, Hutchinson, 1981.
The Boy in the Bible, Piccolo, 1981.
Macpherson's Mystery Adventure, Blackie, 1981.

Lady of the Manse, Hutchinson, 1983.
The Tale of Greyfriars Bobby, Puffin, 1986.

Also author of *Macpherson in America*, 1965, *Macpherson Sails the Seas*, 1966, and *Macpherson on the Farm*, 1967.

SIDELIGHTS: Lavinia Derwent spent her childhood on a Scottish farm; her books deal with her experiences of farm life.

AVOCATIONAL INTERESTS: Travel.*

* * *

DEWDNEY, Selwyn (Hanington)   1909-1979

PERSONAL: Born October 22, 1909, in Prince Albert, Saskatchewan, Canada; died November 18, 1979; son of Alfred Daniel Alexander (an Anglican bishop) and Alice Ashwood (Hanington) Dewdney; married Irene Maude Donner (a psychiatric art therapist), October 3, 1936; children: Donner, Alexander Keewatin, Peter North, Christopher. *Education:* University of Toronto, B.A., 1931, education certificate, 1932; Ontario College of Art, associateship (with honors), 1936. *Politics:* "A skeptical socialist." *Religion:* "Humanist."

ADDRESSES: *Office*—Royal Ontario Museum, Toronto, Ontario, Canada M5S 2C6.

CAREER: Aboriginal art researcher. Collegiate-Vocational Institute, Owen Sound, Ontario, art specialist and teacher of English and geography, 1932-34; Sir Adam Beck Collegiate Institute, London, Ontario, head of art and geography departments, 1936-45; Westminster Hospital, London, part-time psychiatric art therapist, 1953-72; Ontario College of Art, Toronto, Ontario, lecturer on aboriginal art, 1975-79. President of Western Art League, 1957-60; executive director of Artists Workshop of London, 1960-62; member of board of directors of N'Amerind (Indian Friendship Centre), 1966-69, Indian Crafts of Ontario, 1970-72, and Western Ontario Therapeutic Community Hostel (founding member), 1970-72. Royal Ontario Museum, research associate in pictography, 1966-79, research assistant in archaeology, 1970-71; co-founder and senior associate of Canadian Rock Art Research Associates, 1969-79; coordinator of Trent University Rock Art Research Project, 1972-74. Book illustrator, 1947-59. Conducted field research all over Canada since 1957. Reproductions of rock paintings and petroglyphs represented in collections at Royal Ontario Museum, Glenbow-Alberta Institute, and National Museum of Man.

MEMBER: Indian-Eskimo Association (member of Ontario board of directors, 1968-69).

WRITINGS:

Wind without Rain (novel), Copp Clark (Toronto), 1946, reprinted with an introduction by John Stevens, McClelland & Stewart, 1974.
(Editor and author of introduction) Audrey Saunders, *Algonquin Story*, Ontario Department of Lands and Forests, 1946.
The Map that Grew (juvenile; self-illustrated), Oxford University Press, 1960.
(Illustrator) Mabel Dunham, *Kristli's Trees*, McClelland & Stewart, 1960.
The St. Lawrence (juvenile), Oxford University Press, 1961.
(With Kenneth E. Kidd) *Indian Rock Paintings of the Great Lakes*, University of Toronto Press, 1962, revised and enlarged edition, 1967.

(Editor and author of introduction) Norval Morriseau, *Legends of My People: The Great Ojibway*, Ryerson (Toronto), 1965.
They Shared to Survive: The Native Peoples of Canada, Macmillan, 1975.
The Sacred Scrolls of the Southern Ojibway, University of Toronto Press, 1975.
(With Gilles Tasse) *Releves et travaux recents sur l'art rupestre amerindien*, Laboratoire d'archeologie de l'Universite du Quebec (Montreal), 1977.
Christopher Breton: A Novel, McClelland & Stewart, 1978.
The Hungry Time, illustrated by Olena Kassian, Lorimer, 1980.

Illustrator of numerous textbooks. Contributor of articles on pictography, ethnology and ethnohistory, education, geography, art therapy, and native artists to journals and popular periodicals.

A collection of over seven thousand of Dewdney's works, including manuscripts, diaries, correspondence, slides, artwork, pictograph reproductions, and historical photographs is housed at the Royal Ontario Museum in Toronto.

SIDELIGHTS: In 1928, Selwyn Dewdney accompanied his father, the bishop of Keewatin on a thirty-eight-hundred-mile journey to northern Indian and Eskimo missions, traveling eight hundred miles by canoe. In 1929 and 1930 he worked as an Anglican student missionary at Lac Seul Post. In 1933 he was traverse man on a Geological Survey of Canada crew in Kapuskasing district. In 1937 he helped lead a Schools Exploration Society expedition to survey an unmapped area in the Cassiar Mountains of British Columbia. In 1940 he was a member of a timber-cruising party for a timber company northeast of Lake Superior.

Dewdney conducted field work in aboriginal pictography for Royal Ontario Museum, Quetico Foundation, Glenbow Foundation, Canada Council, Saskatchewan Museum of Natural History, Quetico-Superior Wilderness Research Center, Manitoba Department of Mines and Natural Resources, and Ontario Ministry of Natural Resources. He examined hide and bark pictography in British, French, and Soviet museums and in private collections in Canada and the United States.

BIOGRAPHICAL/CRITICAL SOURCES:

BOOKS

Dictionary of Literary Biography, Volume 68: *Canadian Writers, 1920-59*, First Series, Gale, 1988.*

* * *

DEWHURST, Eileen (Mary)   1929-

PERSONAL: Born May 27, 1929, in Liverpool, England. *Education:* Attended Huyton College, 1938-47; St. Anne's College, Oxford, B.A., 1951, M.A., 1958.

ADDRESSES: *Agent*—Sheila Watson, Watson & Little, 26 Charing Cross Rd., London WC2H 0DG, England.

CAREER: Writer.

MEMBER: Society of Authors, Crime Writers Association, Oxford Society.

WRITINGS:

CRIME NOVELS

Death Came Smiling, R. Hale, 1975.

After the Ball, Macmillan (London), 1976.

Curtain Fall (U.S. Detective Book Club Inner Circle selection), Macmillan (London), 1977, Doubleday, 1982.

Drink This (U.S. Detective Book Club Inner Circle selection), Collins Crime Club (London), 1980, Doubleday, 1981.

Trio in Three Flats, Doubleday, 1981.

Whoever I Am, Collins Crime Club, 1982, Doubleday, 1983.

The House That Jack Built, Collins Crime Club, 1983.

There Was a Little Girl, Collins Crime Club, 1984, Doubleday, 1986.

Playing Safe, Collins Crime Club, 1985, Doubleday, 1987.

A Private Prosecution, Collins Crime Club, 1986, Doubleday, 1987.

A Nice Little Business, Doubleday, 1987.

The Sleeper, Doubleday, 1988.

WORK IN PROGRESS: A murder mystery set on the fringe of the Edinburgh festival.

SIDELIGHTS: Eileen Dewhurst told *CA:* "As a crime writer I have of course portrayed a variety of violent deaths, but always contain them within an overall structure which tends toward the triumph of good. Perhaps in fact, I feel at home in the crime genre because its basic theme is the disclosing and routing of the bad!

"Despite writing crime novels exclusively (apart from journalistic articles and a few plays which have been produced by amateur companies in England), my chief concern is human relationships and everyday life—out of which the frightening, the suspenseful, the mysterious can arise with peculiar shock.

"My main interests apart from writing are the fine arts (particularly pictures and furniture), painting, and animals."

BIOGRAPHICAL/CRITICAL SOURCES:

PERIODICALS

Booklist, December 1, 1984.

Chicago Tribune Book World, February 23, 1986.

Times (London), August 7, 1986.

Washington Post Book World, June 21, 1981.

Wilson Library Bulletin, January, 1985.

*   *   *

DICKSON, Paul (Andrew) 1939-

PERSONAL: Born July 30, 1939, in Yonkers, N.Y.; son of William A. and Isabelle (Cornell) Dickson, Jr.; married Nancy Hartman, April 13, 1968; children: Andrew Cary, Alexander Hartman. *Education:* Wesleyan University, B.A., 1961.

ADDRESSES: Home—Box 80, Garrett Park, Md. 20896. *Agent*—Helen Brann Agency, 157 West 57th St., New York, N.Y. 10019.

CAREER: McGraw-Hill Book Co., New York, N.Y., regional editor, 1966-69. *Military service:* U.S. Navy, 1962-65.

MEMBER: Washington Independent Writers (board member and treasurer).

AWARDS, HONORS: American Political Science Association fellowship for reporters, 1969-70.

WRITINGS:

Think Tanks, Atheneum, 1971.

The Great American Ice Cream Book, Atheneum, 1973.

The Future of the Workplace, Weybright, 1975.

The Electronic Battlefield, Indiana University Press, 1976.

The Mature Person's Guide to Kites, Frisbees, Yo-Yos and Other Childlike Diversions, New American Library, 1977.

Out of This World: American Space Photography, foreword by R. Buckminster Fuller, Delacorte, 1977.

Future File: A Handbook for People with One Foot in the Twenty-first Century, Rawson, 1977.

Chow: A Cook's Tour of Military Food, New American Library, 1978.

The Official Rules, illustrated by Kenneth Tiews, Delacorte, 1978.

The Official Explanations, Delacorte, 1980.

Toasts: The Complete Book of the Best Toasts, Sentiments, Blessings, Curses, and Graces, Delacorte, 1981.

Words: A Connoisseur's Collection of Old and New, Weird and Wonderful, Useful and Outlandish Words, Delacorte, 1982.

(With Joseph C. Goulden) *There Are Alligators in Our Sewers, and Other American Credos*, Delacorte, 1983.

Jokes: Outrageous Bits, Atrocious Puns, and Ridiculous Routines for Those Who Love Jests, illustrated by Don Addis, Delacorte, 1984.

On Our Own: A Declaration of Independence for the Self-Employed, Facts on File, 1985.

Names: A Collector's Compendium of Rare and Unusual, Bold and Beautiful, Odd and Whimsical Names, Delacorte, 1986.

The Library in America: A Celebration in Words and Pictures, Facts on File, 1986.

Too Much Saxon Violence, Dell, 1986.

Waiter, There's a Fly in My Soup, Dell, 1986.

Family Words, Addison-Wesley, 1988.

Contributor to national magazines, including *Progressive*, *Town and Country*, *American Heritage*, *Esquire*, and *Washington Monthly*.

SIDELIGHTS: Paul Dickson has written several unusual, lighthearted works, including *The Great American Ice Cream Book*, *The Mature Person's Guide to Kites, Frisbees, Yo-Yos and Other Childlike Diversions*, and *Names: A Collector's Compendium of Rare and Unusual, Bold and Beautiful, Odd and Whimsical Names*. Dickson's book of words entitled *Words: A Connoisseur's Collection of Old and New, Weird and Wonderful, Useful and Outlandish Words* contains such rarities as borborygmite, wamble, vomer, and psithurism. Writes Charles Champlin for the *Los Angeles Times Book Review*, "it is unquestionably a word man's word book, a treasury for anyone whose love of words approaches (and indeed overtakes) the obsessive. . . . You realize afresh what an astonishing arsenal of invective English is." Additionally, *Time* reviewer Otto Friedrich believes the "novelty" of Dickson's word book lies in its organization. Dickson arranges his book into categories, like Outdoors Words, Alimentary (food-related) Words, Sexy Words, and so forth. As for "new" words, Dickson presents words that have been deliberately developed to fill a void. A "nork," for instance, is, as Dickson defines it, "a product that looks especially appealing in its original context—an ad, a catalogue, a hotel gift shop—but then loses its appeal very shortly after you get it." In the end, Champlin concludes: "Once you've dipped . . . [into *Words*], only the steel-willed can stop."

BIOGRAPHICAL/CRITICAL SOURCES:

BOOKS

Dickson, Paul, *Words: A Connoisseur's Collection of Old and New, Weird and Wonderful, Useful and Outlandish Words*, Delacorte, 1982.

PERIODICALS

Book World, October 31, 1971.
Chicago Tribune Book World, July 31, 1986.
Los Angeles Times, March 10, 1983.
Los Angeles Times Book Review, August 29, 1982.
New York Times, February 12, 1979, August 9, 1982, February 17, 1983, August 15, 1986.
New York Times Book Review, October 15, 1972.
Saturday Review, March 18, 1972.
Time, August 23, 1982.
Washington Post Book World, October 15, 1972.

*　　*　　*

DIMOND, Stuart J. 1938-1981

PERSONAL: Born April 30, 1938, in Bristol, England; died May 16, 1981, in Wales; son of William Henry (a businessman) and Dorothea Madge Dimond; married Bridgit Carolyn Price, March 30, 1968; children: Clare, Rebecca. *Education:* University of Bristol, B.Sc., 1960, Ph.D., 1963. *Politics:* Socialist.

ADDRESSES: Home—16 Highfields, Llandaff, Cardiff, Wales. *Office*—Department of Psychology, University College, University of Wales, Cardiff, Wales.

CAREER: University of Wales, University College, Cardiff, beginning 1966, began as lecturer, became reader in psychology.

MEMBER: European Brain and Behaviour Society, British Psychological Society, Association for the Study of Animal Behavior, Experimental Psychological Society.

AWARDS, HONORS: M.A., Trinity College, 1966; senior scientist award, North Atlantic Treaty Organization (NATO); Xavier Bichat Medal, for "Cerebral Crossroads."

WRITINGS:

The Social Behavior of Animals, Harper, 1970.
The Double Brain, Churchill Livingstone, 1972.
(With J. E. Beaumont) *Hemisphere Function of the Human Brain*, Elek, 1974.
(Editor with David A. Blizard) *Evolution and Lateralization of the Brain*, New York Academy of Sciences, 1977.
Introducing Neuropsychology: The Study of Brain and Mind, C. C Thomas, 1978.
Neuropsychology: A Textbook of Systems and Psychological Functions of the Human Brain, Butterworth, 1980.

Also author of a film, "Cerebral Crossroads."

AVOCATIONAL INTERESTS: Music, travel, reading, walking, gardening.

*　　*　　*

DIXON, Franklin W.
[Collective pseudonym]

WRITINGS:

"HARDY BOYS MYSTERY STORIES" SERIES

The Tower Treasure (also see below), Grosset & Dunlap, 1927, revised edition, 1959.
The House on the Cliff (also see below), Grosset & Dunlap, 1927, revised edition, 1959.

The Secret of the Old Mill (also see below), Grosset & Dunlap, 1927, revised edition, 1962.
The Missing Chums, Grosset & Dunlap, 1928, revised edition, 1962.
Hunting for Hidden Gold, Grosset & Dunlap, 1928, revised edition, 1963.
The Shore Road Mystery, Grosset & Dunlap, 1928, revised edition, 1964.
The Secret of the Caves, Grosset & Dunlap, 1929, revised edition, 1965.
The Mystery of Cabin Island, Grosset & Dunlap, 1929, revised edition, 1966.
The Great Airport Mystery, Grosset & Dunlap, 1930, revised edition, 1965.
What Happened at Midnight, Grosset & Dunlap, 1931, revised edition, 1967.
While the Clock Ticked, Grosset & Dunlap, 1932, revised edition, 1962.
Footprints under the Window, Grosset & Dunlap, 1933, revised edition, 1965.
The Mark on the Door, Grosset & Dunlap, 1934, revised edition, 1967.
The Hidden Harbor Mystery, Grosset & Dunlap, 1935, revised edition, 1961.
The Sinister Signpost, Grosset & Dunlap, 1936, revised edition, 1968.
A Figure in Hiding, Grosset & Dunlap, 1937, revised edition, 1965.
The Secret Warning, Grosset & Dunlap, 1938, revised edition, 1966.
The Twisted Claw, Grosset & Dunlap, 1939, revised edition, 1969.
The Disappearing Floor, Grosset & Dunlap, 1940, revised edition, 1964.
The Mystery of the Flying Express, Grosset & Dunlap, 1941, revised edition, 1970.
The Clue of the Broken Blade, Grosset & Dunlap, 1942, revised edition, 1970.
The Flickering Torch Mystery, Grosset & Dunlap, 1943, revised edition, 1971.
The Melted Coins, Grosset & Dunlap, 1944, revised edition, 1970.
The Short-Wave Mystery, Grosset & Dunlap, 1945, revised edition, 1966.
The Secret Panel, Grosset & Dunlap, 1946, revised edition, 1969.
The Phantom Freighter, Grosset & Dunlap, 1947, revised edition, 1970.
The Secret of Skull Mountain, Grosset & Dunlap, 1948, revised edition, 1966.
The Sign of the Crooked Arrow, Grosset & Dunlap, 1949, revised edition, 1970.
The Secret of the Lost Tunnel, Grosset & Dunlap, 1950, revised edition, 1968.
The Wailing Siren Mystery, Grosset & Dunlap, 1951, revised edition, 1968.
The Secret of Wildcat Swamp, Grosset & Dunlap, 1952, revised edition, 1969.
The Crisscross Shadow, Grosset & Dunlap, 1953, revised edition, 1969.
The Yellow Feather Mystery, Grosset & Dunlap, 1953, revised edition, 1971.
The Hooded Hawk Mystery, Grosset & Dunlap, 1954, revised edition, 1971.

The Clue in the Embers, Grosset & Dunlap, 1955, revised edition, 1972.
The Secret of Pirates' Hill, Grosset & Dunlap, 1957, revised edition, 1972.
The Ghost at Skeleton Rock, Grosset & Dunlap, 1958, revised edition, 1966.
The Mystery at Devil's Paw, Grosset & Dunlap, 1959, revised edition, 1973.
The Mystery of the Chinese Junk, Grosset & Dunlap, 1960.
The Mystery of the Desert Giant, Grosset & Dunlap, 1961.
The Clue of the Screeching Owl, Grosset & Dunlap, 1962.
The Viking Symbol Mystery, Grosset & Dunlap, 1963.
The Mystery of the Aztec Warrior, Grosset & Dunlap, 1964.
The Haunted Fort, Grosset & Dunlap, 1965.
The Mystery of the Spiral Bridge, Grosset & Dunlap, 1966.
The Secret Agent on Flight 101, Grosset & Dunlap, 1967.
The Mystery of the Whale Tattoo, Grosset & Dunlap, 1968.
The Arctic Patrol Mystery, Grosset & Dunlap, 1969.
The Bombay Boomerang, Grosset & Dunlap, 1970.
Danger on Vampire Trail, Grosset & Dunlap, 1971.
The Masked Monkey, Grosset & Dunlap, 1972.
The Shattered Helmet, Grosset & Dunlap, 1973.
The Clue of the Hissing Serpent, Grosset & Dunlap, 1974.
The Mysterious Caravan, Grosset & Dunlap, 1975.
The Witchmaster's Key, Grosset & Dunlap, 1976.
The Jungle Pyramid, Grosset & Dunlap, 1977.
The Firebird Rocket, Grosset & Dunlap, 1978.
The Sting of the Scorpion, Grosset & Dunlap, 1979.
Night of the Werewolf, Wanderer, 1979.
Mystery of the Samurai Sword, Wanderer, 1979.
The Pentagon Spy, Wanderer, 1979.
The Apeman's Secret, Wanderer, 1980.
The Mummy Case, Wanderer, 1980.
Mystery of Smuggler's Cove, Wanderer, 1980.
The Stone Idol, Wanderer, 1981.
The Vanishing Thieves, Wanderer, 1981.
The Outlaw's Silver, Wanderer, 1981.
Deadly Chase, Wanderer, 1981.
The Four-Headed Dragon, Wanderer, 1981.
The Infinity Clue, Wanderer, 1981.
Track of the Zombie, Wanderer, 1982.
The Voodoo Plot, Wanderer, 1982.
The Billion Dollar Ransom, Wanderer, 1982.
Tic-Tac-Terror, Wanderer, 1982.
Trapped at Sea, Wanderer, 1982.
Game Plan for Disaster, Wanderer, 1982.
The Crimson Flame, Wanderer, 1983.
Cave-In!, Wanderer, 1983.
Sky Sabotage, Wanderer, 1983.
The Roaring River Mystery, Wanderer, 1984.
The Demon's Den, Wanderer, 1984.
The Blackwing Puzzle, Wanderer, 1984.
The Swamp Monster, Wanderer, 1985.
Revenge of the Desert Phantom, Wanderer, 1985.
The Skyfire Puzzle, Wanderer, 1985.
The Mystery of the Silver Star, Minstrel, 1987.
Program for Destruction, Minstrel, 1987.
Tricky Business, Minstrel, 1988.
The Sky Blue Frame, Minstrel, 1988.
Danger on the Diamond, Minstrel, 1988.
Shield of Fear, Minstrel, 1988.
The Shadow Killers, Minstrel, 1988.
The Serpent's Tooth Mystery, Minstrel, 1988.
Breakdown in Axeblade, Minstrel, 1989.
Danger on the Air, Minstrel, 1989.

"HARDY BOYS CASE FILES" SERIES

Dead on Target, Archway, 1986.
Evil, Inc., Archway, 1986.
Cult of Crime, Archway, 1986.
The Lazarus Plot, Archway, 1987.
Edge of Destruction, Archway, 1987.
The Crowning Terror, Archway, 1987.
Deathgame, Archway, 1987.
See No Evil, Archway, 1987.
The Genius Thieves, Archway, 1987.
Hostages of Hate, Archway, 1987.
Brother against Brother, Archway, 1988.
Perfect Getaway, Archway, 1988.
The Borgia Dagger, Archway, 1988.
Too Many Traitors, Archway, 1988.
Blood Relations, Archway, 1988.
Line of Fire, Archway, 1988.
The Number File, Archway, 1988.
A Killing in the Market, Archway, 1988.
Nightmare in Angel City, Archway, 1988.
Witness to Murder, Archway, 1988.
Street Spies, Archway, 1988.
Double Exposure, Archway, 1988.
Disaster for Hire, Archway, 1989.
Scene of the Crime, Archway, 1989.
The Borderline Case, Archway, 1989.
Trouble in the Pipeline, Archway, 1989.
Nowhere to Run, Archway, 1989.
Countdown to Terror, Archway, 1989.
Thick as Thieves, Archway, 1989.
The Deadliest Dare, Archway, 1989.
Without a Trace, Archway, 1989.

"TED SCOTT FLYING STORIES" SERIES

Over the Ocean to Paris; or, Ted Scott's Daring Long Distance Flight, Grosset & Dunlap, 1927.
Rescued in the Clouds; or, Ted Scott, Hero of the Air, Grosset & Dunlap, 1927.
Over the Rockies with the Air Mail; or, Ted Scott Lost in the Wilderness, Grosset & Dunlap, 1927.
First Stop Honolulu; or, Ted Scott over the Pacific, Grosset & Dunlap, 1927.
The Search for the Lost Flyers; or, Ted Scott over the West Indies, Grosset & Dunlap, 1928.
South of the Rio Grande; or, Ted Scott on a Secret Mission, Grosset & Dunlap, 1928.
Across the Pacific; or, Ted Scott's Hop to Australia, Grosset & Dunlap, 1928.
The Lone Eagle of the Border; or, Ted Scott and the Diamond Smugglers, Grosset & Dunlap, 1929.
Flying against Time; or, Ted Scott Breaking the Ocean to Ocean Record, Grosset & Dunlap, 1929.
Over the Jungle Trails; or, Ted Scott and the Missing Explorers, Grosset & Dunlap, 1929.
Lost at the South Pole; or, Ted Scott in Blizzard Land, Grosset & Dunlap, 1930.
Through the Air to Alaska; or, Ted Scott's Search in Nugget Valley, Grosset & Dunlap, 1930.
Flying to the Rescue; or, Ted Scott and the Big Dirigible, Grosset & Dunlap, 1930.
Danger Trails of the Sky; or, Ted Scott's Great Mountain Climb, Grosset & Dunlap, 1931.
Following the Sun Shadow; or, Ted Scott and the Great Eclipse, Grosset & Dunlap, 1932.

Battling the Wind; or, Ted Scott Flying around Cape Horn, Grosset & Dunlap, 1933.

Brushing the Mountain Top; or, Aiding the Lost Traveler, Grosset & Dunlap, 1934.

Castaways of the Stratosphere; or, Hunting the Vanquished Balloonists, Grosset & Dunlap, 1935.

Hunting the Sky Spies; or, Testing the Invisible Plane, Grosset & Dunlap, 1941.

The Pursuit Patrol; or, Chasing the Platinum Pirates, Grosset & Dunlap, 1943.

WITH CAROLYN KEENE

Nancy Drew and the Hardy Boys: Super Sleuths! (short stories), Wanderer, Volume 1, 1981, Volume 2, 1984.

Nancy Drew and the Hardy Boys Camp Fire Stories, Wanderer, 1984.

Nancy Drew & the Hardy Boys Be a Detective Mystery Stories: The Secret of the Knight's Sword, edited by Betty Schwartz, Wanderer, 1984.

Nancy Drew & the Hardy Boys Be a Detective Mystery Stories: Danger on Ice, edited by Schwartz, Wanderer, 1984.

Nancy Drew & the Hardy Boys Be a Detective Mystery Stories: The Feathered Serpent, edited by Schwartz, Wanderer, 1984.

Nancy Drew & the Hardy Boys Be a Detective Mystery Stories: Secret Cargo, edited by Schwartz, Wanderer, 1984.

Nancy Drew & the Hardy Boys Be a Detective Mystery Stories: The Alaskan Mystery, edited by Diane Arico, Wanderer, 1985.

Nancy Drew & the Hardy Boys Be a Detective Mystery Stories: The Missing Money Mystery, edited by Arico, Wanderer, 1985.

Nancy Drew & the Hardy Boys Be a Detective Mystery Stories: Jungle of Evil, edited by Arico, Wanderer, 1985.

Nancy Drew & the Hardy Boys Be a Detective Mystery Stories: Ticket to Intrigue, edited by Arico, Wanderer, 1985.

OTHER

(With D. A. Spina) *The Hardy Boys' Detective Handbook* (short stories and police procedures), Grosset & Dunlap, 1959, revised edition, 1972.

The Tower Treasure, The House on the Cliff, [and] *The Secret of the Old Mill* (three-in-one reprint), Grosset & Dunlap, 1959.

(Contributor) Stephen Dunning and Henry B. Maloney, editors, *A Superboy, Supergirl Anthology: Selected Chapters from the Earlier Works of Victor Appleton, Franklin W. Dixon, and Carolyn Keene,* Scholastic Book Services, 1971.

The Hardy Boys and Nancy Drew Meet Dracula (based on episodes of "The Hardy Boys/Nancy Drew Mysteries"), Grosset & Dunlap, 1978.

The Haunted House and Flight to Nowhere (based on episodes of "The Hardy Boys/Nancy Drew Mysteries"; *Flight to Nowhere* adapted from *The Flickering Torch Mystery*), Grosset & Dunlap, 1978.

(With Sheila Link) *The Hardy Boys' Handbook: Seven Stories of Survival* (short stories), Wanderer, 1980.

The Hardy Boys' Who-Dunnit Mystery Book, Wanderer, 1980.

The Hardy Boys: Ghost Stories, edited by Schwartz, Wanderer, 1984.

SIDELIGHTS: In 1927 Edward Stratemeyer, head of the productive literary syndicate that bore his name, proposed a new series to Leslie McFarlane, a Canadian journalist and freelance writer who had worked for him on other titles. "He had

observed . . . that detective stories had become very popular in the world of adult fiction. He instanced the works of S. S. Van Dine, which were selling in prodigious numbers as I was well aware,'' McFarlane reminisces in *Ghost of the Hardy Boys.* "It had recently occurred to him . . . that the growing boys of America might welcome similar fare.'' Stratemeyer enclosed an outline of the first volume in the new series, which he wanted McFarlane to write. "What Stratemeyer had in mind was a series of detective stories on the juvenile level, involving two brothers of high-school age who would solve such mysteries as came their way,'' McFarlane continues. "To lend credibility to their talents, they would be the sons of a professional private investigator, so big in his field that he had become a sleuth of international fame. His name—Fenton Hardy. His sons, Frank and Joe, would therefore be known as. . . The Hardy Boys!''

Thus began what is certainly one of the most popular series in the history of children's fiction. The Hardy Boys, their parents Fenton and Laura Hardy, as well as the inimitable Aunt Gertrude, their friends Chet Morton, Tony Prito, Biff Hooper, Phil Cohen, Callie Shaw and Iola Morton, are still going strong over sixty years after their creation, and show no sign of stopping. "Reprinted, revised, and rewritten for more than half a century,'' states Jonathan Cott in *Esquire,* "works like *The Mystery at Devil's Paw, The Haunted Fort,* and *Hunting for Hidden Gold* still sell remarkably well; they are, in fact, the most popular boys' books of all time.'' Carol Billman, in her 1986 book *The Secret of the Stratemeyer Syndicate: Nancy Drew, the Hardy Boys, and the Million Dollar Fiction Factory,* reports that "over seventy million Hardy Boys novels have been purchased,'' and, she adds, "in the last three years over two and a half million paperback copies of their mysteries were sold.''

Although earlier series had introduced the young-detective motif, the Hardys novels were innovative in introducing detection as their primary focus. "The essential ingredients of a Hardys title,'' says Billman, "are fast-paced investigative action and a large dollop of the conventional gimmickry of pulp magazine detection that began with Nick Carter: disguises, ciphers to be puzzled out, rude thugs to be put in their places, crime kits, secret messages, and passwords.'' Yet adventure—long a mainstay of children's fiction—also plays a significant role in the Hardys books. Billman sees them as "everyboy's fantasy adventure, the fantasy that explains in large part the thrill the fast-paced adventure genre has held for boys since the days of *Robinson Crusoe, The Coral Island,* and *Treasure Island.*'' "The secret the Stratemeyer Syndicate hit upon in the Hardy Boys books,'' she continues, "was the *packing* of timeless adventure-story action into a distinctive, and repeatable, detective fiction pattern. Thus, the novel lure of the detective mystery had at last been thoroughly fused with the earlier adventure tale tradition.''

Neither the Hardy Boys themselves nor the places they frequent are fully depicted in the books, and they do not develop as the series progresses. Billman recognizes that Bayport, the Hardys' home town, is "not a place that fires readers' imaginations, as settings so often do in literature for the young.'' "So different from the messy, unfragrant world depicted relentlessly in hard-boiled detective fiction,'' she concludes, "Bayport superficially looks like a real place but is actually a fantasy island.'' "In Dixon's oeuvre, the characters do exactly the same things year after year,'' Billman declares. "They find another cave to explore, another international smuggling ring to smash open.'' Although crammed with a criminal element that is the Hardys' sworn enemies, Bayport remains to the reader a secure small town.

Yet this lack of depth seems to add, rather than subtract, from readers's enjoyment of the series. Cott recalls, "Still, what I *remembered* having liked about the Hardy Boys books was that paradoxical sense that the series had given me of living in a familiar, secure, protected world, in which one could imagine oneself being as curious, fearless, ingenious, risk-taking, courageous, and righteous as the Hardy Boys themselves—those two action-driven, brotherly ciphers, whose lack of interiority was in fact their most rewarding and positive attribute." A reader can identify with the boys; they are "paradoxically, average guys," says Billman, "'fellows like yourself' as the publicity went, even as they perform wondrous feats of detection. They can be likened to Wally and The Beaver or David and Ricky Nelson . . . average fellows from a town that is depicted as a quaint Everytown, U.S.A., right down to the smiling policemen and helpful shopkeepers. But *these* ordinary boys get mixed up in high-level detection and dangerous adventure."

Harriet Adams, Stratemeyer's daughter, continued the Hardy Boys series after her father's death in 1930. Many of the volumes—up to and including 1947's *The Phantom Freighter*—were written by Leslie McFarlane, the same man who originally created the characters for Stratemeyer. By the late 1950s, however, these earlier stories seemed dated to new readers. Volumes originally written in the 1920s did not reflect the faster paced postwar juvenile lifestyle. To eliminate this contrast, Adams and her co-workers modernized the Hardy Boys. Although they remained all-American and squeaky-clean, by the mid-1960s Frank and Joe were chasing around the world after international spies, rescuing American astronauts, and exhibiting a taste for rock music. In 1959, in order to reflect the changing times, the Stratemeyer Syndicate began to rewrite the earlier volumes of the series, bringing them up-to-date, and removing disparaging references to minority groups and other objectionable material.

Many readers of the original versions protested the changes Adams and her co-workers had made. "The leisurely pace, the sense of having world enough and time," says Cott, "—all of this had been excised or eviscerated in the flatter or more high-tech versions of recent times." "If anyone still doubts that the world is a profoundly different place than it was when we were children, consider this: Frank Hardy has encountered a groupie," declares Ed Zuckerman in *Rolling Stone*. "If word came that Abe Lincoln turned up on *Let's Make a Deal* dressed as a carrot, it could not be more unsettling." "The extent of this literary sacrilege is overwhelming," he asserts. "Every Hardy Boys book up to and including *The Mystery at Devil's Paw* (number 38) is not the same as it used to be. . . . The Hardy Boys have entered the new age."

Frank and Joe were modernized once again when Simon & Schuster launched the "Hardy Boys Casefiles" in 1986. The new pocket-sized paperbacks offered grittier, more contemporary action; Frank and Joe now fought terrorists and drug-dealers rather than smugglers and counterfeiters. Again, the changes upset some series followers. One irate reader complained to *Columbus Dispatch* columnist Mike Harden, "If I wanted Ian Fleming, I would buy Ian Fleming and read it." A more drastic alteration was the murder of Iola Morton, killed by a terrorist's bomb planted in the Hardy's car. The brutal realism of Iola's death shocked long-time Hardys fans. "In the old novels, girls were never killed, never even bruised," said John Corr in the *Chicago Tribune*. "They were just nice, slow people the Boys could be patient with and explain things to." Trying to understand the negative reaction, Harden explained, "There was something comfortable, even predictable, about the Hardy Boys. Evil never went unpunished. The good guys always prevailed. The innocent never died young. Though Frank and Joe kept the same girlfriends for 50 years . . . they remained—for all of their curiosity and sense of adventure—innocently celibate."

"But life has changed," Harden admits. "Hardy Boys' creator Edward Stratemeyer fashioned Frank and Joe's world the year Lindberg flew the Atlantic. Bayport was a million miles from mass death at the hands of terrorists, the threat of nuclear annihilation. The world had yet to hear of crack addiction. Teen pregnancy was an exception, not an epidemic. It took something more than a Rambo or a Mad Max to earn a spot on youth's pedestal of idolatry." But for some the Hardy's attraction remains. In his book *Rascals at Large; or, The Clue in the Old Nostalgia* Arthur Prager remembers, "Rascals were at large, and the Hardys would fight on until the very last criminal was behind bars. The old readers are grown up and scattered now, and Stratemeyer has gone to whatever special Heaven exists for people who make children happy, but the boy detectives go on thrilling new generations, rewritten, brought 'up to date,' but still fearlessly making their dad proud of them."

Stratemeyer also used the pseudonym Franklin W. Dixon for another series launched in 1927: the "Ted Scott Flying Stories." "Ted Scott, intrepid airman, was a lanky, soft-spoken Middle-Westerner of twenty-one who had achieved world celebrity (and the nickname the 'Lone Eagle') by making the first flight across the Atlantic solo from New York to Paris," explains Prager. Based on Charles Lindberg's exploits, the series progressed "with the aviation industry until it met the fate of most long-run series," Prager concludes. "Its little readers grew up and got involved in the apocalyptic events of the 1930s and 1940s and Ted Scott ceased to be an 'active property.'" Edward L. Stratemeyer, Andrew E. Svenson, Harriet S. Adams, and James Duncan Lawrence were among the authors who contributed to the "Hardy Boys" and "Ted Scott" series. For more information, see the entries in this volume for Harriet S. Adams, James Duncan Lawrence, Edward L. Stratemeyer, and Andrew E. Svenson.

MEDIA ADAPTATIONS: Walt Disney Productions filmed two Hardy Boys serials for the "Mickey Mouse Club Show." Both starred Tommy Kirk and Tim Considine as Frank and Joe Hardy: "The Hardy Boys," also known as "The Applegate Treasure," was loosely based on *The Tower Treasure,* and its first episode aired on October 1, 1956, on ABC-TV. An original story, not based on any of the series volumes, began September 30, 1957, on ABC; it was called "The Mystery of Ghost Farm." A pilot film, called "The Mystery of the Chinese Junk," and based on the series book of that title, was made for a series that never materialized. It was first broadcast on September 8, 1967, and starred Rick Gates as Frank and Tim Mathieson as Joe. Filmation Associates made an animated version of the Hardy Boys for the Saturday morning television market that starred the voices of Dallas McKennon, Jane Webb, and Byron Kane; the title of the show was "The Hardy Boys," and it ran on ABC from 1969-71. More recently, Parker Stevenson and Shaun Cassidy have portrayed the sleuths in "The Hardy Boys/Nancy Drew Mysteries," which ran on ABC from 1977 to 1979, and then went into syndication.

Three different Hardy Boys games have been published: *Walt Disney's Hardy Boys Treasure Game*, published by Walt Disney Productions and Parker Brothers in 1957; Milton Bradley's *The Hardy Boys Game*, linked to the Filmation series, 1969; and *The Secret of Thunder Mountain: The Hardy Boys Mystery Game*, published by Parker Brothers in 1978, and linked to the Parker Stevenson/Shaun Cassidy series. Recordings: Two original stories, "The Disco Conspiracy" and "The Mystery of the Missing Iceman," were recorded for Wonderland Records in 1978. The Cassette Book Company presently offers recordings of Frank and Joe's adventures, read by Eve Plumb.

Several comic books were released in conjunction with the Walt Disney serials. They were published by Dell from 1956 to 1959. Other comic books were published by Gold Key in 1970-71 in relation to the Filmation animated series. The Whitman Publishing Company brought out the first Hardy Boys coloring book in 1957; related to the Disney serial, it featured Tommy Kirk and Tim Considine on the cover. In 1977, at the time "The Hardy Boys/Nancy Drew Mysteries" were first broadcast, Grosset & Dunlap's imprint Treasure Books began publishing a variety of coloring and activity (puzzles, mazes, and word games) books featuring the Hardy Boys.

BIOGRAPHICAL/CRITICAL SOURCES:

BOOKS

Billman, Carol, *The Secret of the Stratemeyer Syndicate: Nancy Drew, the Hardy Boys, and the Million Dollar Fiction Factory*, Ungar, 1986.
Johnson, Deidre, editor and compiler, *Stratemeyer Pseudonyms and Series Books: An Annotated Checklist of Stratemeyer and Stratemeyer Syndicate Publications*, Greenwood Press, 1982.
McFarlane, Leslie, *Ghost of the Hardy Boys*, Two Continents, 1976.
Nye, Russel B., *The Unembarrassed Muse: The Popular Arts in America*, Dial, 1970.
Prager, Arthur, *Rascals at Large; or, The Clue in the Old Nostalgia*, Doubleday, 1971.

PERIODICALS

Chicago Tribune, July 5, 1987.
Columbus Dispatch, April 15, 1987.
Esquire, June, 1986.
New Yorker, August 18, 1986.
Publishers Weekly, March 5, 1979.
Rolling Stone, September 9, 1976.
TV Guide, June 25, 1977.
Washington Post Book World, February 8, 1981.
Yellowback Library, May/June, 1983, July/August, 1987, February, 1988.

—*Sketch by Kenneth R. Shepherd*

*   *   *

DOBSON, James (Clayton, Jr.)   1936-

PERSONAL: Born April 21, 1936, in Shreveport, La.; son of James C. and Myrtle (G.) Dobson; married Shirley Deere, August 27, 1960; children: Danae, Ryan. *Education:* Pasadena College, B.A., 1958; University of Southern California, M.S., 1962, Ph.D., 1967; graduate study, University of California, Berkeley, 1963, University of California, Los Angeles, 1964.

ADDRESSES: Home—348 Harvard Dr., Arcadia, Calif. 91006. *Office*—Focus on the Family, Pomona, Calif. 91799.

CAREER: Teacher and counselor in public schools in Hacienda, Calif. and Covina, Calif., 1960-64; Charter Oak Unified School District, Covina, Calif., psychologist and coordinator of Pupil Personnel Services, 1964-66; University of Southern California, School of Medicine, Los Angeles, 1966-83, began as assistant professor, became associate clinical professor of pediatrics; Focus on the Family, Pomona, Calif., founder, 1977, president, 1977—. Co-director of Research, Division of Medical Genetics, Children's Hospital of Los Angeles. Appointed by President Carter to task force for White House conferences on the family, and by President Reagan to National Advisory Council, Office of Juvenile Justice and Delinquency Prevention, 1983.

WRITINGS:

Dare to Discipline, Tyndale, 1970.
(Editor and contributor with Richard Koch) *The Mentally Retarded Child and His Family: A Multidisciplinary Handbook*, Brunner, 1971.
Symposium on Phenylketonuria: Present Status and Future Developments, Verlag Thieme Publications (Heidelberg), 1971.
Discipline with Love, Tyndale, 1972.
Hide or Seek, Revell, 1974, 3rd edition, 1979.
What Wives Wish Their Husbands Knew about Women, Tyndale, 1975.
Prescription for a Tired Homemaker, Tyndale, 1978.
The Strong-Willed Child: Birth through Adolescence, Tyndale, 1978.
Preparing for Adolescence, Vision House, 1978.
(With daughter, Danae Dobson) *Woof!: A Bedtime Story about a Dog*, illustrations by Dennis Bellile, Word, 1979.
Emotions: Can You Trust Them?, Regal, 1980.
Straight Talk to Men and Their Wives, illustrations by Bellile, Word, 1980.
Dr. Dobson Answers Your Questions, Tyndale, 1982.
Love Must Be Tough: New Hope for Families in Crisis, Word, 1983.
Dr. Dobson Answers Your Questions about Confident, Healthy Families, Tyndale, 1986.
Dr. Dobson Answers Your Questions about Marriage and Sexuality, Tyndale, 1986.
Dr. Dobson Answers Your Questions about Raising Children, Tyndale, 1986.
Temper Your Child's Tantrums, Tyndale, 1986.
Love for a Lifetime: Building a Marriage That Will Go the Distance, Multnomah, 1987.
Parenting Isn't for Cowards, Word, 1987.

Contributor to *Educational and Psychological Measurement*, *Journal of Developmental Reading*, *New England Journal of Medicine*, *Hospital Topics*, *Lancet*, and *Journal of Pediatrics*. Consulting editor, *Journal of International Neurosciences Abstracts*.

SIDELIGHTS: Child psychologist and author James Dobson is also founder and president of Focus on the Family, an organization that produces nationally broadcast radio programs on domestic issues. Dobson's books cover such topics as helping adolescents understand their sexuality and building stronger marital relationships. Dobson once told *CA:* "My mission in writing is to help preserve the health and vitality of the American family, which is undergoing a serious threat to its survival. It is my view that our society can be no more stable than the foundation of individual family units upon which it rests. Our government, our institutions, our schools . . . indeed, our way of life is dependent on healthy marriages and loyalty to the vulnerable little children around our feet. Thus, my professional life is devoted to the integrity of the family and the God who designed it.''

*   *   *

DODGE, H(arry) Robert 1929-

PERSONAL: Born September 17, 1929, in St. Louis, Mo.; son of Harry Varnum (a sales manager) and Jeanne (Groeinger) Dodge; married Donna Broughman, August 6, 1960; children: Melody Jean, Kevin Robert. *Education:* Ohio State University, B.Sc., 1951, M.B.A., 1954, Ph.D., 1962. *Politics:* Republican. *Religion:* Presbyterian.

ADDRESSES: Office—Department of Marketing, Youngstown State University, 410 Wick Ave., Youngstown, Ohio 44555.

CAREER: University of Nebraska, Lincoln, instructor in business organization, 1954-55; Ohio State University, Columbus, instructor in business organization, 1955-57; Florida State University, Tallahassee, assistant professor of marketing, 1957-58; Knox Associates, Inc. (consultants), Toledo, Ohio, research associate, 1958-59; California State College, Los Angeles (now California State University, Los Angeles), assistant professor of marketing, 1959-64; Arlington State College (now University of Texas at Arlington), associate professor of marketing, 1964-65; Memphis State University, Memphis, Tenn., professor of marketing, 1965-76; Northern Illinois University, De Kalb, professor of marketing and chairman of department, beginning 1976; currently affiliated with Youngstown State University, Youngstown, Ohio. Officer and managing director, Market Consultants, Inc., 1967-69; vice-president, Curriculum Aids, 1975-76. Consultant to various businesses, banks, and civic organizations. *Military service:* U.S. Army, 1951-53. U.S. Army Reserve, 1953-59; became captain.

MEMBER: American Marketing Association (vice-president of industrial marketing, 1974-75), American Institute of Decision Sciences, Southern Marketing Association, Phi Kappa Tau, Beta Gamma Sigma.

WRITINGS:

Industrial Marketing, McGraw, 1970.
Field Sales Management, Business Publications, 1973.
(Co-author) *Professional Selling*, Business Publication, 1976, 4th edition, 1985.
(With Louis E. Boone) *Contemporary Business*, 2nd edition, Dryden Press, 1979.
(Editor with William G. Zikmund) *A Collection of Cases in Marketing Management*, West Publishing, 1979, 2nd edition, 1987.
(With Sam Fullerton and David Rink) *Marketing Research*, Merrill, 1982.

Contributor to *Journal of Retailing, A.I.D.S. Journal, Journal of the Bank Public Relations and Marketing Association.*

WORK IN PROGRESS: New Production Management, for Grid Publishing; *Positioning Selling Strategies to the Product-Life Cycle; The Corporate Life Cycle and Attendant Management Decisions; Faculty Ratings of Marketing and Management Publications.*

SIDELIGHTS: H. Robert Dodge once told *CA:* ''Books are an expression of self and the ultimate in professionalism. Authors are those who are better disciplined, not necessarily more intelligent.''*

DONALDSON, Scott 1928-

PERSONAL: Born November 11, 1928, in Minneapolis, Minn.; son of Frank A. (a manufacturer) and Ruth E. (Chase) Donaldson; married Winifred M. Davis, December 27, 1953 (died July 28, 1954); married Janet K. Mikelson, April 12, 1958 (divorced February, 1982); married Vivian Breckenridge, March 5, 1982; children: (second marriage) Matthew Chase, Stephen Scott, Andrew Wilson; stepchildren: (third marriage) Janet Breckenridge, Britt Breckenridge. *Education:* Yale University, B.A., 1951; University of Minnesota, M.A., 1952, Ph.D., 1966.

ADDRESSES: Home—240 West Tazewell's Way, Williamsburg, Va. 23185. *Office*—College of William and Mary, Williamsburg, Va. 23185.

CAREER: Minneapolis Star, Minneapolis, Minn., reporter, 1956-58; *Bloomington Sun-Surburbanite,* Bloomington, Minn., editor-publisher, 1959-63; University of Minnesota, Minneapolis, instructor in humanities and American literature, 1963-66; College of William and Mary, Williamsburg, Va., assistant professor, 1966-69, associate professor, 1969-74, professor, 1974—, Louise G. T. Cooley Professor of English, 1984—. Fulbright lecturer in Turku, Finland, 1970-71; visiting professor, University of Leeds, Leeds, England, 1972-73; visiting fellow, Princeton University, 1978; Fulbright senior lecturer, Milan, Italy, 1979; fellow, MacDowell Colony, 1980-81; research fellow, Villa Serbelloni, Italy, 1982. *Military service:* U.S. Army, 1953-56.

MEMBER: American Studies Association, Modern Language Association of America, Organization of American Historians, Fulbright Alumni Association, Sigma Delta Chi.

WRITINGS:

The Making of a Suburb, Bloomington (Minn.) Historial Society, 1964.
The Suburban Myth, Columbia University Press, 1969.
Poet in America: Winfield Townley Scott, University of Texas Press, 1972.
By Force of Will: The Life and Art of Ernest Hemingway, Viking, 1977.
(With Ann Massa) *American Literature: Nineteenth and Early Twentieth Centuries*, Barnes & Noble, 1978.
(Editor) Jack Kerouac, *On the Road*, Viking, 1979.
(Contributor) *American Writers*, Supplement I, Part I, Scribner, 1979.
(Contributor) *American Literary Scholarship*, Duke University Press, 1980-83.
Fool for Love: F. Scott Fitzgerald, Congdon & Weed, 1983.
(Editor) *Critical Essays on ''The Great Gatsby,''* G.K. Hall, 1983-84.
(Editor) Harold Frederic, *The Damnation of Theron Ware*, Viking, 1984.
(Editor) *Conversations with John Cheever*, University Press of Mississippi, 1987.
John Cheever: A Biography, Random House, 1988.

Contributor to *Sewanee Review, American Literature, Modern Fiction Studies*, and other journals.

WORK IN PROGRESS: A biography of Archibald MacLeish.

SIDELIGHTS: Scott Donaldson told *CA:* ''American literary biography is what I have been doing for the past two decades and what I seem likely to continue doing. It is at once the most fascinating and frustrating of crafts, the fascination deriving from the frustrating knowledge that it is quite impossible to encompass, to come fully to understand, the life and work of our gifted writers. But I can't seem to stop trying.''

BIOGRAPHICAL/CRITICAL SOURCES:

PERIODICALS

Chicago Tribune Book World, June 5, 1988.
Los Angeles Times, November 25, 1983.
New York Times, April 19, 1977.
New York Times Book Review, April 24, 1977, January 15, 1984, July 10, 1988.
Washington Post Book World, June 19, 1988.

*   *   *

DOODY, Margaret (Anne) 1939-

PERSONAL: Born September 21, 1939, in St. John, New Brunswick, Canada; daughter of Hubert (an Anglican clergyman) and Anne (a social worker; maiden name, Cornwall) Doody. *Education:* Dalhousie University, B.A. (with honors), 1960; Lady Margaret Hall, Oxford, B.A. (with first class honors), 1962, D.Phil, 1968. *Politics:* "Much the same as Dr. Johnson's." *Religion:* Anglican.

ADDRESSES: Residence—Princeton, N.J. *Office*—Department of English, McCosh 22, Princeton University, Princeton, N.J. 08544.

CAREER: University of Victoria, Victoria, British Columbia, Canada, instructor, 1962-64, assistant professor of English, 1968-69; University of Wales, University College, Swansea, lecturer in English, 1969-76; University of California, Berkeley, visiting associate professor, 1976-77, associate professor of English, 1977-80; Princeton University, Princeton, N.J., professor of English, 1980—.

MEMBER: Modern Language Association (member of eighteenth-century panel).

AWARDS, HONORS: Guggenheim fellowship, 1978; American Philosophical Society research grant, 1982; Rose Mary Crawshay Prize, British Academy, 1986, for *The Daring Muse: Augustan Poetry Reconsidered.*

WRITINGS:

NONFICTION

A Natural Passion: A Study of the Novels of Samuel Richardson, Clarendon Press, 1974.
(Contributor) Ricks and Michaels, editors, *The State of the Language,* University of California Press, 1980.
(Author of introduction) Samuel Richardson, *Pamela,* edited by Peter Sabor, Penguin, 1981.
(Contributor) Martin and Mullen, editors, *No Alternative: The Prayer Book Controversy,* Basel Blackwell, 1981.
The Daring Muse: Augustan Poetry Reconsidered, Cambridge University Press, 1985.
Frances Burney: The Life in the Works, Rutgers University Press, 1988.
(Editor with Peter Sabor) Frances Burney, *Cecilia,* Oxford University Press, 1988.

DETECTIVE NOVELS

Aristotle Detective, Bodley Head, 1978, Harper, 1980.
The Alchemists, Bodley Head, 1980.

OTHER

(With Florian Stuber and John Sgueglia) "Clarissa: The Encounter" (one-act; based on Richardson's *Clarissa*), first produced in New York City at Circle Repertory Lab, May 26, 1983.
(With Stuber) "Clarissa: A Theatre Work, Part One," first produced as three-act in New York City at Douglas Fairbanks Theatre, March 12, 1984, produced as two-act in New York City at West End Theatre, October 26, 1984.

Aristotle Detective has been translated into Italian, French, and German. Contributor to *Times Literary Supplement.* Advisor to *Studies in English Literature.*

WORK IN PROGRESS: *The Customs of Fiction* (on the history of the novel) for Rutgers University Press; editing, with Sabor, a book of essays on Richardson for Cambridge University Press, and an edition of Burney's *The Wanderer,* for Oxford University Press; *Aristotle and Poetic Justice* (detective novel); a detective novel set in the eighteenth century; *Bath Cats* (for children); a drama based on eighteenth-century court cases; with Stuber, parts two and three of "Clarissa: A Theatre Work"; a film script of *The Alchemists.*

SIDELIGHTS: Margaret Doody once told *CA:* "I find that the academic life and the writing of detective stories mesh quite nicely. I look forward to escaping from the eighteenth century from time to time (it seems so very modern to me) and going back to ancient Greece with Aristotle, my Sherlock Holmes. A recent venture into drama has convinced me that I want to stay there. I have several plans for plays, but first Florian Stuber and I must complete our dramatization of Richardson's *Clarissa*—a monumental undertaking, and totally rewarding. I am very grateful for the chance of working with professional actors under the aegis of Circle Rep Directors' Lab in May, 1983.''

AVOCATIONAL INTERESTS: Detective stories, children's books, theatre, travel.

BIOGRAPHICAL/CRITICAL SOURCES:

PERIODICALS

Christian Science Monitor, October 21, 1986.
Times Literary Supplement, November 10, 1978, April 25, 1980, March 14, 1986.

*   *   *

DOVE, Rita (Frances) 1952-

PERSONAL: Born August 28, 1952, in Akron, Ohio; daughter of Ray (a chemist) and Elvira (Hord) Dove; married Fred Viebahn (a writer); children: Aviva Chantal Tamu Dove-Viebahn. *Education:* Miami University, Oxford, Ohio, B.A. (summa cum laude), 1973; attended Universitaet Tuebingen, West Germany, 1974-75; University of Iowa, M.F.A., 1977.

ADDRESSES: Office—Department of English, Arizona State University, Tempe, Ariz. 85287.

CAREER: Arizona State University, Tempe, assistant professor, 1981-84, associate professor, 1984-87, professor of English, 1987—. Writer-in-residence at Tuskegee Institute, 1982. National Endowment for the Arts, member of literature panel, 1984-86, chair of poetry grants panel, 1985. Commissioner, Schomburg Center for the Preservation of Black Culture, New York Public Library, 1987—.

MEMBER: PEN, Associated Writing Programs (member of board of directors, 1985-88, president, 1986-87), Academy of American Poets, Poetry Society of America, Poets and Writers, Phi Beta Kappa, Phi Kappa Phi.

AWARDS, HONORS: Fulbright fellowship, 1974-75; grants from National Endowment for the Arts, 1978, and Ohio Arts Council, 1979; International Working Period for Authors fellowship for West Germany, 1980; Portia Pittman fellowship at Tuskegee Institute from National Endowment for the Humanities, 1982; John Simon Guggenheim fellowship, 1983; Peter I. B. Lavan Younger Poets Award, Academy of American Poets, 1986; Pulitzer Prize in poetry, 1987, for *Thomas and Beulah;* General Electric Foundation Award for Younger Writers, 1987; Honorary Doctor of Letters, Miami University, 1988; Bellagio (Italy) residency, Rockefeller Foundation, 1988; Mellon fellowship, National Humanities Center, North Carolina, 1988-89.

WRITINGS:

Ten Poems (chapbook), Penumbra Press, 1977.
The Only Dark Spot in the Sky (poetry chapbook), Porch Publications, 1980.
The Yellow House on the Corner (poems), Carnegie-Mellon University Press, 1980.
Mandolin (poetry chapbook), Ohio Review, 1982.
Museum (poems), Carnegie-Mellon University Press, 1983.
Fifth Sunday (short stories), Callaloo Fiction Series, 1985.
Thomas and Beulah (poems), Carnegie-Mellon University Press, 1986.
The Other Side of the House (poems), photographs by Tamarra Kaida, Pyracantha Press, 1988.

Work represented in anthologies. Contributor of poems, stories, and essays to magazines, including *Agni Review, Antaeus, Georgia Review, Nation,* and *Poetry.* Member of editorial board, *National Forum,* 1984—; poetry editor, *Callaloo,* 1986—; advisory editor, *Gettysburg Review,* 1987—, and *TriQuarterly,* 1988—.

SIDELIGHTS: Black American writer Rita Dove is best known for her book of poems *Thomas and Beulah,* which garnered her the 1987 Pulitzer Prize in poetry. Dove has been described as a quiet leader, a poet who does not avoid race issues, but does not make them her central focus. As Dove herself explains in the *Washington Post:* "Obviously, as a black woman, I am concerned with race. . . . But certainly not every poem of mine mentions the fact of being black. They are poems about humanity, and sometimes humanity happens to be black. I cannot run from, I *won't* run from any kind of truth."

The poems in *Thomas and Beulah* are loosely based on the lives of Dove's maternal grandparents, and are arranged in two sequences: one devoted to Thomas, born in 1900 in Wartrace, Tennessee, and the other to Beulah, born in 1904 in Rockmart, Georgia. *Thomas and Beulah* is viewed as a departure from Dove's earlier works in both its accessibility and its chronological sequence that has, to use Dove's words, "the kind of sweep of a novel." On the book's cover is a snapshot of the author's grandparents, and *New York Review of Books* contributor Helen Vendler observes that "though the photograph, and the chronology of the lives of Thomas and Beulah appended to the sequence, might lead one to suspect that Dove is a poet of simple realism, this is far from the case. Dove has learned . . . how to make a biographical fact the buried base of an imagined edifice."

In the *Washington Post,* Dove describes the poems this way: "The poems are about industrialization, discrimination sometimes—and sometimes not—love and babies—everything. It's not a dramatic story—nothing absolutely tragic happened in my grandparents' life. . . . But I think these are the people who often are ignored and lost." Peter Stitt expresses a similar view in the *Georgia Review:* "The very absence of high drama may be what makes the poems so touching—these are ordinary people with ordinary struggles, successes, and failures." He concludes: "There is a powerful sense of community, residing both in a family and in a place, lying at the heart of this book, and it is this that provides a locus to the poems. Rita Dove has taken a significant step forward in each of her three books of poems; she must be recognized as among the best young poets in the country today."

AVOCATIONAL INTERESTS: Travel (Israel, southern Europe, West Germany).

BIOGRAPHICAL/CRITICAL SOURCES:

PERIODICALS

American Book Review, July, 1985.
American Poetry Review, January, 1982.
Callaloo, winter, 1986.
Georgia Review, summer, 1984, winter, 1986.
New York Review of Books, October 23, 1986.
North American Review, March, 1986.
Poetry, October, 1984.
Washington Post, April 17, 1987.

*　　　*　　　*

DOZOIS, Gardner R(aymond)   1947-

PERSONAL: Born July 23, 1947, in Salem, Mass.; son of Raymond (a factory worker) and Dorothy (McSwiggin) Dozois. *Education:* Educated in the United States.

ADDRESSES: Home and office—526 Spruce St., Philadelphia, Pa. 19106. *Agent*—Virginia Kidd, Box 278, Milford, Pa. 18337.

CAREER: Writer and editor, 1966—. *Isaac Asimov's Science Fiction Magazine,* associate editor, 1976-77, editor, 1985—. Editor of *Isaac Asimov Presents* novel line. *Military service:* U.S. Army, 1966-69; served as military journalist.

MEMBER: Science Fiction Writers of America.

AWARDS, HONORS: Nebula Award for best short story, Science Fiction Writers of America, 1983, for "The Peacemaker," and 1984, for "Morning Child."

WRITINGS:

(With George Alec Effinger) *Nightmare Blue,* Berkley Publishing, 1975.
The Fiction of James Tiptree, Jr., Algol Press, 1977.
Visible Man, Berkley Publishing, 1977.
Strangers, Berkley Publishing, 1978.

EDITOR; SCIENCE FICTION SHORT STORY ANTHOLOGIES

A Day in the Life, Harper, 1972
(With Jack M. Dann) *Future Power,* Random House, 1976.
Another World, Follett, 1977.
Best Science Fiction Stories of the Year: Sixth Annual Collection, Dutton, 1977.
Best Science Fiction Stories of the Year, 1978: Seventh Annual Collection, Dutton, 1978.

Best Science Fiction Stories of the Year, 1979: Eighth Annual Collection, Dutton, 1979.

(With Dann) *Aliens!*, Pocket Books, 1980.

Best Science Fiction Stories of the Year, 1980: Ninth Annual Collection, Dutton, 1980.

Best Science Fiction Stories of the Year, 1981: Tenth Annual Collection, Dutton, 1981.

(With Dann) *Unicorns!*, Ace Books, 1982.

(With Dann) *Magicats!*, Ace Books, 1984.

The Year's Best Science Fiction: First Annual Collection, Bluejay, 1984.

(With Dann) *Beastiary!*, Ace Books, 1985.

The Year's Best Science Fiction: Second Annual Collection, Bluejay, 1985.

(With Dann) *Mermaids*, Ace Books, 1986.

(With Dann) *Sorcerers!*, Ace Books, 1986.

The Year's Best Science Fiction: Third Annual Collection, Bluejay, 1986.

(With Dann) *Demons!*, Ace Books, 1987.

The Year's Best Science Fiction: Fourth Annual Collection, St. Martin's, 1987.

The Best from Isaac Asimov's Science Fiction Magazine, Ace Books, 1988.

(With Dann) *Dogtails!*, Ace Books, 1988.

The Year's Best Science Fiction: Fifth Annual Collection, St. Martin's, 1988.

OTHER

Contributor of science fiction short stories to periodicals, including *Playboy, Omni, Penthouse, Oui, Analog,* and *Isaac Asimov's Science Fiction Magazine.*

WORK IN PROGRESS: Flash Point, a novel; co-authorship of another novel; *Seaserpents!*, with Jack M. Dann, and *Time-Travellers and Temponauts*, short story anthologies for Ace Books; a collection of original short stories, tentatively entitled *Virgin Territory*, for Ace Books.

*   *   *

DRURY, Michael

PERSONAL: Born in Sacramento, Calif.; daughter of Davis (in advertising) and Lucile (Rood) Drury; married John S. Calderwood, 1942 (divorced, 1961). *Education:* Stanford University, A.B., 1940. *Politics:* Independent. *Religion:* Protestant.

ADDRESSES: Home—Newport, R.I.

CAREER: Life, New York City, editorial assistant, 1941-43; *Harper's Monthly,* New York City, editorial assistant, 1943-44; *McCall's,* New York City, assistant fiction editor, 1946-47; free-lance writer, 1947—. Visiting instructor at University of Missouri, 1958; volunteer teacher at Women's Correctional Institution, New York City, 1959-60.

MEMBER: Authors Guild (council member, 1956-74), Authors League of America, Theta Sigma Phi.

AWARDS, HONORS: Headliner award from Theta Sigma Phi, 1958; Freedoms Foundation award, 1973.

WRITINGS:

(Editor with Helen Hull) *The Writers' Roundtable*, Harper, 1959.

How to Get Along with People, Doubleday, 1965.

Advice to a Young Wife from an Old Mistress, Doubleday, 1968.

The Inward Sea, Doubleday, 1972.

The Everyday Miracles, Hallmark Editions, 1972.

This Much and More, Pocket Books, 1973.

Every Whit Whole: The Adventure of Spiritual Healing, Dodd, 1978.

Counterclockwise: Reflections of a Maverick, Walker, 1987.

Also author of a novelette, *The Cheese Stands Alone.* Contributor of more than four hundred articles, short stories, and poems to magazines, journals, and anthologies, including *Good Housekeeping, McCall's, Woman's Day, Reader's Digest, Atlantic,* and *Redbook.*

SIDELIGHTS: Michael Drury told *CA:* "I don't often give myself reasons for writing—the doing of a thing and the analysis of it are two quite different skills. But I rather think I do it out of a fathomless respect for the human spirit, which staggers me. From a ladybug to Prometheus, from an Indian paintbrush to the Rocky Mountains, from a kitten to man—that spirit exalts and humbles me. That's why I write both fiction and nonfiction, and poetry. The human being lives in a staggering, beautiful, orderly universe, and the two of them taken together make something that is called God.

"I've been writing since childhood and have the tremendous blessing—pure luck—of being in love with what I do. It chose me long before I chose it consciously. That impulse is not, I think, just writing—it's a deep urge to give back to the world something you feel it is pouring out upon you, and the form of that giving has as many shapes as there are people. If I were to advise young writers, I would say, Get the ablest teachers you can—not writing teachers as such, but general education teachers. When I look back at the women and men who educated me from grade school through college, I am stunned at their quality. And they weren't sentimental about it; it was tough, powerful teaching with a good deal of love thrown in.

"My main aim as far as readers are concerned is to touch others minds and hearts with a single spark of their own capacities and then let them take it from there. I admire some other writers but am much more influenced by composers and painters than by particular writers. To be successful as a writer, I think one has to have a taste for loneliness and discipline; they're both exciting if you happen to like them."

AVOCATIONAL INTERESTS: Theater, the outdoors, cooking, comparative religion, modern philosophers, music.

*   *   *

DUCAS, Dorothy   1905-1987

PERSONAL: Born June 9, 1905, in New York, N.Y.; died September 23, 1987 in Valhalla, N.Y.; daughter of Charles and Doris L. (Pottlitzer) Ducas; married James B. Herzog (a foreign trade executive), June 7, 1926 (died January, 1964); children: John Ducas, Thomas Ducas. *Education:* Attended Connecticut College for Women (now Connecticut College), 1922-23; Columbia University, B.Litt., 1926; also attended London School of Economics and Political Science and Kings College for Women.

ADDRESSES: Home—Box 21A, Spring St., South Salem, N.Y. 10590.

CAREER: Reporter for *New York Herald Tribune, New York Evening Post,* and *London Express*, 1925-29; *McCall's* (magazine), New York, N.Y., associate editor, 1929-30; correspondent for International News Service, 1930-35; U.S. Office of War Information, Washington, D.C., founder and chief of magazine bureau, 1942-44; National Foundation for Infantile Paralysis, consultant, 1944-45, director of public relations, 1949-60; self-employed public relations consultant, beginning 1960. Public service director, Lobsenz Public Relations, 1962-68; National Cystic Fibrosis Research Foundation, public relations director, 1968-71, consultant, 1971-87. Instructor in public relations, New York University, 1961-63; lecturer in public relations, New School for Social Research. Special consultant to American Museum of Natural History and National Health Council, 1968-69; consultant to Rockefeller Public Service Awards program of Princeton University, National Jewish Hospital at Denver, Goodwill Industries of America, and the U.S. Public Health Service.

MEMBER: Public Relations Society of America (member of board of directors), Authors League of America, Overseas Club, New York Newspaper Women's Club, Washington Press Club, Theta Sigma Phi.

AWARDS, HONORS: Pulitzer traveling scholarship, 1926; Headliners' Award from Theta Sigma Phi, 1943.

WRITINGS:

(With Elizabeth Gordon) *More House for Your Money*, Morrow, 1936.
Modern Nursing, Walck, 1962.
(Editor) *National Voluntary Health Agencies*, National Health Council, 1969.

Contributor of articles to *Collier's, American, Good Housekeeping, Woman's Day, Mademoiselle, Parent's*, and other magazines.

WORK IN PROGRESS: Works on medical and nursing subjects.*

*　　*　　*

DUNCAN, Julia K.
[Collective pseudonym]

WRITINGS:

"DORIS FORCE" SERIES

Doris Force at Locked Gates; or, Saving a Mysterious Fortune, H. Altemus, 1931.
. . . at Cloudy Cove; or, The Old Miser's Signature, H. Altemus, 1931.
. . . at Raven Rock; or, Uncovering the Secret Oil Well, H. Altemus, 1932.
. . . at Barry Manor; or, Mysterious Adventures between Classes, H. Altemus, 1932.

SIDELIGHTS: Occasionally publishers have created fictional biographies for Stratemeyer pseudonyms. According to a publicist for the Harry Atlemus company, says Carol Billman in *The Secret of the Stratemeyer Syndicate*, the author "based her stories on events from her own life." Mildred Augustine Wirt Benson wrote the first two volumes in the "Doris Force" series for the Stratemeyer Syndicate. Walter Karig also contributed to the series. For more information see the entries in this volume for Harriet S. Adams, Edward L. Stratemeyer, and Andrew E. Svenson.

BIOGRAPHICAL/CRITICAL SOURCES:

BOOKS

Billman, Carol, *The Secret of the Stratemeyer Syndicate: Nancy Drew, the Hardy Boys, and the Million Dollar Fiction Factory*, Ungar, 1987.
Johnson, Deidre, editor and compiler, *Stratemeyer Pseudonyms and Series Books: An Annotated Checklist of Stratemeyer and Stratemeyer Syndicate Publications*, Greenwood Press, 1982.
Paluka, Frank, *Iowa Authors: A Bio-Bibliography of Sixty Native Authors*, Friends of the University of Iowa Libraries, 1967.

*　　*　　*

DUVERGER, Maurice　1917-

PERSONAL: Born June 5, 1917, in Angouleme, France; son of Georges (a businessman) and Anna (Gobert) Duverger; married Odile Batt, June 7, 1949. *Education:* University of Bordeaux, Agrege des Facultes de Droit, 1942.

ADDRESSES: Home—24 rue des Fosses Saint Jacques, 75005 Paris, France. *Office*—La Sorbonne, 17 rue de la Sorbonne, 75005 Paris, France.

CAREER: University of Poitiers, Poitiers, France, professor of law, 1942; University of Bordeaux, Bordeaux, France, professor of law, 1943-55; University of Paris I, Paris, France, professor of political sociology and economics, 1955-85, professor emeritus, 1985—. Director of Institute for Political Studies, Bordeaux, 1946-55; director of studies of National Foundation of Political Science, Paris.

MEMBER: American Academy of Arts and Sciences.

AWARDS, HONORS: Chevalier de la Legion d'honneur.

WRITINGS:

IN ENGLISH OR ENGLISH TRANSLATION

Les Partis politiques, Librairie Armand Colin, 1951, translation by Barbara North and Robert North published as *Political Parties: Their Organization and Activity in the Modern State*, Wiley, 1954, revised edition, Methuen, 1964, 10th French edition, 1981.
The Political Role of Women, UNESCO (Paris), 1955.
The French Political System, translation by B. North and R. North, University of Chicago Press, 1958.
Methodes de la science politique, Presses universitaires de France, 1959, 2nd edition, 1961, translation by Malcolm Anderson published as *An Introduction to the Social Sciences, with Special Reference to Their Methods*, Praeger, 1964.
Introduction a la politique, Gallimard, 1964, translation by R. North and Ruth Murphy published as *The Idea of Politics: The Uses of Power in Society*, Regnery, 1966.
Sociologie politique, Presses universitaires de France, 1966, 3rd edition, 1968, translation by Robert Wagoner published as *The Study of Politics*, Crowell, 1972.
Party Politics and Pressure Groups: A Comparative Introduction, Crowell, 1972.
Modern Democracies: Economic Power vs. Political Power, translation by Charles L. Markmann, Holt, 1974.

OTHER

L'Affectation des immeubles domaniaux aux services publics: Traite theorique et practique, Librairie generale de droit et de jurisprudence, 1941.

La Situation des fonctionnaires depuis la revolution de 1940, Librairie generale de droit et de jurisprudence, 1941.

Les Constitutions de la France, Presses universitaires de France, 1944, 10th edition, 1983.

Cours de droit constitutionnel, Recueil Sirey, c. 1946, 5th edition published as *Manuel de droit constitutionnel et de science politique*, Presses universitaires de France, 1948.

Les Regimes politiques, Presses universitaires de France, 1948, 7th edition, 1965.

Les Finances publiques, Presses universitaires de France, 1950, 9th edition, 1978.

(With Francois Goguel and others) *L'Influence des systemes electoraux sur la vie politique*, Librairie Armand Colin, 1950.

Amme maliyesi, [Ankara], 1955.

Droit constitutionnel et institutions politiques, two volumes, Presses universitaires de France, 1955, 5th edition published as *Institutions politiques et droit constitutionnel*, 1960, 18th revised edition published as *Le systeme politique francais*, 1985.

Institutions financieres, Presses universitaires de France, 1956, 8th edition published as *Finances publiques*, 1975.

Constitutions et documents politiques, Presses universitaires de France, 1957, 9th edition, 1981.

Cours de vie politique en France et a l'entranger, Cours de droit, 1957.

(With Goguel and Jean Touchard) *Les Elections du 2 janvier 1956*, Librairie Armand Colin, 1957.

Demain, la Republique, Editions Rene Julliard, 1958.

La Cinquieme Republique, Presses universitaires de France, 1959, 5th edition, 1974.

Cours de science politique, Cours de droit, 1959.

(With Pierre Lalumiere) *Droit public*, Presses universitaires de France, 1959, 6th edition published as *Elements de droit public*, 1970, 10th edition, 1983.

Cours de sociologie politique, Cours de droit, 1960, 3rd semi-annual edition published as *Sociologie politique: Licence 1re annee, 1964-1965*, 1965.

De la dictature, Editions Rene Julliard, 1961.

La Sixieme Republique et la regime presidentiel, Librairie Artheme Fayard, 1961.

Les Institutions francaises, Presses universitaires de France, 1962.

(With Manuel Bridier) *Evolution des structures de l'etat*, Centre d'etudes socialistes (Paris), 1963.

Introduction a la sociologie politique, Cours de droit, 1963, 2nd edition, 1964.

La Democratie sans le peuple, Editions du Seuil, 1967, new edition, 1971.

Janus: Les deux faces de l'Occident, Librairie Artheme Fayard, 1972.

Sociologie de la politique: Elements de science politique, Presses universitaires de France, 1973.

La Monarchie republicaine: Comment les democraties se donnent des rois, Laffont, 1974.

Elements de fiscalite, Presses universitaires de France, 1976.

La Constitution de la Republique portugaise: 2 avril, 1976, Documentation francaise, 1977.

Echec au roi, A. Michel, 1977.

Les Orangers du lac Balaton, Seuil, 1980.

Le Concept d'empire, Presses universitaires de France, 1980.

La Republique des citoyens, Editions Ramsay (Paris), 1982.

(Editor) Pierre Avril and others, *Les Regimes semi-presidentiels*, Presses universitaires de France, 1986.

Breviaire de la cohabitation, Presses universitaires de France, 1986.

Also author of *Lettre ouverte aux socialistes*, 1976, and *L'autre cote des choses*, 1977. Daily writer for *Le Monde*, 1946—, *Express*, 1954-65, and *Nouvel Observateur*, 1966—.

SIDELIGHTS: Some of Maurice Duverger's books are available in Chinese and Spanish.

AVOCATIONAL INTERESTS: Theatre.

E

EARNSHAW, Brian 1929-

PERSONAL: Born December 26, 1929, in Wrexham, Wales; son of Eric and Annie (Barker) Earnshaw. *Education:* Cambridge University, B.A., 1952, M.A., 1955; University of Bristol, Certificate in Education, 1957; University of London, Diploma of Education, 1970; University of Warwick, Ph.D., 1983. *Politics:* "Smugly patriotic since Mrs. Thatcher arrived." *Religion:* Church of England.

ADDRESSES: Home and office—21 Cotham Vale, Bristol BSG GHS, England. *Agent*—Jonathan Clowes Ltd., 22 Prince Albert Rd., London, NW1 7ST, England.

CAREER: Taught English at a public school, a grammar school, and a comprehensive school, 1952-65; St. Paul's College, Cheltenham, England, creative writing teacher, 1965-85; architectural historian and free-lance writer, 1985—.

WRITINGS:

And Mistress Pursuing, Hodder & Stoughton, 1966.
At St. David's a Year (poems), Hodder & Stoughton, 1968.
Planet in the Eye of Time (science fiction), Hodder & Stoughton, 1968.
Starclipper and the Songwars, illustrations by Roger W. Walker, Methuen Children's Books, 1985.
(With Tim Mowl) *Trumpet at a Distant Gate: The Lodge as Prelude to the Country House,* Waterston (London), 1985.
Starclipper and the Snowstone, illustrated by Walker, Methuen Children's Books, 1986.
Starclipper and the Galactic Final, Methuen Children's Books, 1987.
The Rock Dog Gang, illustrated by Joanna Carey, Methuen Children's Books, 1987.
John Wood: Architect of Obsession, Millstream Books, 1988.

"DRAGONFALL FIVE" SERIES

Dragonfall Five and the Space Cowboys, Methuen Children's Books, 1972, Lothrop, 1975.
. . . and the Royal Beast, Lothrop, 1972.
. . . and the Empty Planet, Lothrop, 1973.
. . . and the Hijackers, Methuen Children's Books, 1974.
. . . and the Master Mind, Methuen Children's Books, 1975.
. . . and the Superhorse, Methuen Children's Books, 1977.
. . . and the Haunted Planet, Methuen Children's Books, 1979.

WORK IN PROGRESS: An architectural history of the Neo-Norman Revival, eighteenth and nineteenth centuries.

SIDELIGHTS: Brian Earnshaw told *CA:* "It is not easy to understand what matters in what I write. I spent years, off and on, writing a 'masterwork' novel with strong autobiographical undertone. Now I think it a blessing that publishers turned it down. On the other hand, a science fiction series which I began in three books written in three weeks still rolls the money in and still seems fresh, witty, and unpretentious when I reread it."

The author recently added: "I became bored with lecturing full-time and now write architectural history. This I find an exhilarating change after relying on imagination for so many years. I am, frankly, disenchanted with the English literary criticism industry since it began to indulge itself in pretentious terminology. Stones are more satisfying than theories."

BIOGRAPHICAL/CRITICAL SOURCES:

PERIODICALS

New York Times Book Review, December 8, 1985.
Punch, March 27, 1968.
Times Literary Supplement, August 23, 1985.

*   *   *

EAST, Ben 1898-

PERSONAL: Born July 18, 1898, in Oakland County, Mich.; son of Darwin (a farmer) and Cora (Dorn) East; married Eleanor Lee, July 29, 1919 (divorced, 1946); married Helen Gorski, August 16, 1946; children: (first marriage) Barbara Lee (Mrs. Roger Pope, deceased), David Carnes. *Education:* Attended high school in Holly, Mich.

CAREER: Booth Newspapers, Inc. (a chain of eight Michigan daily newspapers), Grand Rapids, Mich., outdoor editor, 1926-46; *Outdoor Life* (magazine), Holly, Mich., Midwest field editor, 1946-66, senior field editor, 1966-70, contributing field editor, 1970—. Travel lecturer for many organizations, including the National Geographic Society and the American Museum of Natural History.

MEMBER: Explorer's Club (New York), Adventurer's Club (Chicago).

AWARDS, HONORS: Most popular lecturer of the year, World Adventure Series, 1946; first place in big-game photography competition, Boone and Crockett Club, 1948; honored in a concurrent resolution for distinguished contribution to the conservation of natural resources, Michigan Senate and House of Representatives, 1973; Award of Merit and Passenger Pigeon Award, Michigan United Conservation Clubs; Sparky Hale Award, Michigan Bear Hunters Association; Golden Mallard Awards, Arkansas Wildlife Federation; annual award of the Michigan Environmental Association.

WRITINGS:

Narrow Escapes and Wilderness Adventures, Popular Science-Outdoor Life Books, 1960.
Survival: 23 True Sportsmen's Adventures, Popular Science-Outdoor Life Books, 1968.
Danger: Explosive True Adventures of the Great Outdoors, Popular Science-Outdoor Life Books, 1970.
(With Olive Fredrickson) *The Silence of the North,* Crown, 1972.
The Last Eagle, Crown, 1974.
The Ben East Hunting Book, Popular Science-Outdoor Life Books, 1974.
(With Anton Money) *This Was the North,* Crown, 1975.
The Bears of North America, Popular Science-Outdoor Life Books, 1977.

"SURVIVAL" SERIES

Danger in the Air, illustrated and designed by Jack Dahl, edited by Howard Schroeder and Jerolyn Nentl, Crestwood, 1979.
Desperate Search, illustrated by Dahl, edited by Schroeder and Nentl, Crestwood, 1979.
Forty Days Lost, illustrated by Dahl, edited by Schroeder and Nentl, Crestwood, 1979.
Found Alive, illustrated by Dahl, edited by Schroeder and Nentl, Crestwood, 1979.
Frozen Terror, illustrated by Dahl, edited by Schroeder and Nentl, Crestwood, 1979.
Grizzly!, illustrated by Dahl, edited by Schroeder and Nentl, Crestwood, 1979.
Mistaken Journey, illustrated by Dahl, edited by Schroeder and Nentl, Crestwood, 1979.
Trapped in Devil's Hole, illustrated by Dahl, edited by Schroeder and Nentl, Crestwood, 1979.

SIDELIGHTS: Ben East is well known as a writer, photographer, and filmer of the North American wilderness. "I have covered much of the back country of North America," he once told *CA,* "from the eastern seaboard to the Aleutian Islands of Alaska, and from the Canadian arctic to the southern United States." Initially, East gained recognition as the first person to film an Alaskan sea otter in color (he did so in 1941), and has continued to record his adventures in writing and on film since then.

About his later years as a writer, he added: "Much of my writing has dealt with major conservation problems confronting the nation. I have produced . . . articles for *Outdoor Life* on such environmentally destructive practices as strip mining, channelization, unethical use of aircraft to take trophy game, political interference in wildlife affairs, the indiscriminate use of pesticides, and the damming of wild and scenic rivers and streams. One of my most widely discussed articles was a three-parter on the growth of the anti-hunting movement that ran in *Outdoor Life* in 1970 under the title 'The Big Lie.'" Though

no longer directly employed with this magazine, East has contributed to *Outdoor Life* as a non-staff field editor since 1970.*

* * *

EASTON, Robert (Olney) 1915-

PERSONAL: Born July 4, 1915; son of Robert Eastman (a business executive) and Ethel (Olney) Easton; married Jane Faust, September 24, 1940; children: Joan (Mrs. Gilbert W. Lentz), Katherine (Mrs. Armand Renga), Ellen (Mrs. Gregory W. Brumfiel), Jane. *Education:* Attended Stanford University, 1933-34, graduate study, 1938-39; Harvard University, B.S., 1938; University of California, Santa Barbara, M.A., 1960.

ADDRESSES: Home—2222 Las Canoas Rd., Santa Barbara, Calif. 93105. *Agent*—Sandra Dijkstra Literary Agency, 1237 Camino del Mar, Suite 515C, Del Mar, Calif. 92104.

CAREER: Writer. Formerly employed as ranch hand, day laborer, civil engineer, magazine and newspaper editor; *Lampasas Dispatch,* Lampasas, Tex., co-publisher and editor, 1946-50; radio station KHIT, Lampasas, co-owner and manager, 1948-50; Santa Barbara City College, Santa Barbara, Calif., instructor in English, 1959-65; U.S. Naval Civil Engineering Laboratory, Port Hueneme, Calif.; writing and publishing consultant, 1961-69. Co-chairman, Committee for Santa Barbara; trustee, Santa Barbara Museum of Natural History. *Military service:* U.S. Army, Field Artillery, Tank Destroyer Command, Infantry, 1942-46; became first lieutenant; received Combat Infantryman's Badge.

AWARDS, HONORS: This Promised Land was chosen as a Books-across-the-Sea selection by English Speaking Union, 1983.

WRITINGS:

The Happy Man (novel), Viking, 1943, reprinted, University of New Mexico Press, 1977.
(Contributor) Harry E. Maule, editor, *Great Tales of the American West,* Modern Library, 1944.
(Contributor) Joseph Henry Jackson, editor, *Continent's End,* McGraw, 1944.
(Contributor) Jack Schaefer, editor, *Out West,* Houghton, 1955.
(Contributor) Charles N. Barnard, editor, *A Treasury of True,* A. S. Barnes, 1956.
(With Mackenzie Brown) *Lord of Beasts,* University of Arizona Press, 1961.
(With Jay Monaghan and others) *The Book of the American West,* Messner, 1963.
The Hearing (novel), McNally & Loftin, 1964.
(With Dick Smith) *California Condor: Vanishing American,* McNally & Loftin, 1964.
(Editor) *Max Brand's Best Stories,* Dodd, 1967.
(Editor and author of introduction with Brown) Charles F. Lummis, *Bullying the Moqui,* Prescott College Press, 1968.
Max Brand: "The Big Westerner," University of Oklahoma Press, 1970.
Black Tide: The Santa Barbara Oil Spill and Its Consequences, introduction by Ross MacDonald, Delacorte, 1972.
Guns, Gold, and Caravans, Capra, 1978.
China Caravans: An American Adventurer in Old China, Capra, 1982.
This Promised Land (historical novel), Capra, 1982.
(Contributor) Ralph Sipper, editor, *Inward Journey: Ross Macdonald,* Cordelia Editions, 1984.
Power and Glory (historical novel), Capra, 1988.

Contributor of stories and articles to magazines, including *Atlantic, Reader's Digest,* and *New York Times Magazine.* Associate editor, *Coast Magazine,* 1939-40.

WORK IN PROGRESS: "The Saga of California," a series of historical novels.

SIDELIGHTS: Robert Easton's work as a novelist, biographer, and ecologist displays a concern for the American West. Easton "writes about the land he loves with the gentleness of a romancer, the dedication of a researcher and the confidence of a trail-blazer. . . . He's a creative writer with a researcher's pen handy beside him," states Helene Rivers in the *San Francisco Chronicle Review.* Easton's novel *The Happy Man* chronicles the deeds of Dynamite, a ranch hand who, according to an *Atlantic* reviewer, "stepped right out of Remington's drawings into the present. . . . [*The Happy Man*] is a colorful, authentic narrative." A *Commonweal* critic commends Easton for "weaving a happy spell about the rough and thankless round [of the cowhand]. It is his marvelous tales of the ranch house and saloon that do the trick." G. R. Stewart of the *New York Times* finds the novel has "what is necessary—quick narrative, infallible regional feeling, and a not often approached rendition of the vernacular," while H. M. Jones of *Saturday Review* is impressed with Easton's "capacity to observe and put down sharply rich, significant detail. Almost any one of the sketches [of Dynamite] is a pleasurable experience." And in his introduction to the reprinted edition of the book, Jack Schaefer writes of *The Happy Man:* "It has a timeless, enduring quality. . . . It is a one-of-a-kind book, not derivative in any way, completely itself, the work of a young writer who had the stubbornness and great good sense to ignore the literary fashions of the period and to write his book in his way—and thus create one of the authentic classics of the American west."

Easton's biography of his father-in-law Frederick Faust (better known by his pseudonym Max Brand) is acclaimed as "the standard work on 'Max Brand,'" by a *Choice* reviewer. Faust, the creator of *Destry Rides Again* and "Doctor Kildare" and one of the most prolific writers of our time, was famous for his western tales which, according to Easton, were laced with mythological metaphors and allusions. Easton is as "solemn as an owl, but he manages to be extremely readable. He takes Faust dead seriously and thinks that he introduced, from his wide reading, a tone of mythology that elevated the Western," a *Times Literary Supplement* reviewer comments. *Max Brand: "The Big Westerner,"* David Dempsey writes in the *New York Times Book Review,* "supplies the 'everyday reality' with sympathy but without idolatry. Although other books have been written on Faust, none that I know of portrays so thoroughly the man behind the legend. The style is altogether that of a company history, but his can be a virtue when you are writing about productivity: 22 million Faustian words that break down into 196 novels, 226 novelettes, 162 stories, 44 poems, 56 motion pictures associated with Faust's name." This literary outpouring and the popularity of Max Brand did little to satisfy Faust, who wanted desperately to be a serious poet and scholar of ancient mythology. "Easton draws a fascinating picture of Faust as a man torn between the necessity of writing the popular fiction he detested and his desire to write serious poetry," a *Choice* reviewer states, and William Decker reaches a similar conclusion in *Saturday Review:* "This is a fascinating book about a fascinating man who lived a tormented life. Whatever his final place in American literature may be, there can be no doubt that he left his mark on it, and merits this worthwhile study." In the *St. Louis Post-Dispatch,* Deirdre

LaRouche observes that "delineating the myriad facets of the life of Frederick Faust must have been a challenging and difficult task. . . . Easton has handled [it] more than competently. His biography of Faust manages to convey the unbelievable energy of the man. . . . [*Max Brand*] is an exhilarating and exhausting book to read."

This Promised Land is the first volume of a Western trilogy that begins with the Spaniards extending their empire into the area that is now California, as their hold on past conquests loosens. While Easton features historical figures, including the Spanish commander Gaspar de Portola, his main characters are a Spanish soldier and a Chumash Indian princess, who eventually meet and fall in love. "It's a good plot," notes Rivers. "The action is slow to begin, but then it reaches a pace strong enough to sustain continued interest throughout. . . . The book ends with impact." But *Los Angeles Times* contributor James D. Houston believes that Easton sometimes loses his story in a mass of historical detail: "Too often character and story run second to the author's love of historical lore for its own sake. For the reader who prefers to be captured by the story-teller's art, this book probably will not serve. But for the reader who delights in details from this region's rich and volatile past, the book may work . . . as another kind of history, with nuggets of insight and reclaimed information gathered around the lives of his imagined characters. His re-creation of Portola's first march is in itself worth the book."

Easton wrote *CA* that he intends to call his trilogy "The Saga of California," and plans to extend it from the state's "conquest and settlement by Europeans in 1769 down to the present. It in a way complements and incorporates my first book and novel, *The Happy Man,* published in 1943, which deals with the California of about that time—and is in effect an unintended beginning to the series I began in 1982 with the publication of *This Promised Land,*" he explained. "I believe that all of us may have a place, a piece of land, where we write best and which we write best of, and this for me is true of California where I was born and where my people have been since the 1849 Gold Rush days."

Easton has also investigated various ecological issues. His environmental studies, specifically his books *The California Condor* and *Black Tide: The Santa Barbara Oil Spill and Its Consequences,* have established him, a *Library Journal* reviewer notes, as "a national leader among ecologists." A *Kirkus Reviews* writer calls *Black Tide* "an unusually adept blend of personalities, statistics, politics, idealism, issues, and crisp understanding. . . . [Easton's dismay] is balanced with an appreciation of the complexities and exigencies involved. . . . Easton avoids the knee-jerk reductionism so characteristic of pollution case histories—a noteworthy accomplishment."

The author changed settings from North America to Asia in *China Caravans,* the story of American explorer, trader, and adventurer Fred Schroder, who lived in and around Mongolia and Tibet at the beginning of the twentieth century. Arthur Zich in the *Los Angeles Herald Examiner* describes the tale as "a fresh glimpse of a face of China that will never be seen again—and an account so brimming with derring-do one can only lament it isn't longer than its slim, trimly written 155 pages." The book includes "an insightful eyewitness account of a tumultuous period of Chinese history that ushered in Sun Yat Sen's revolution, the crumbling of the Manchu Empire, and the abortive coup to restore the Manchu Boy Emperor," reports *San Francisco Chronicle* contributor Robert Lee, who also states, "rarely does one read a book as captivating, as filled with drama, excitement and adventure as 'China Caravans.'''

BIOGRAPHICAL/CRITICAL SOURCES:

BOOKS

Easton, Robert, *The Happy Man,* reprinted edition, University of New Mexico Press, 1977.

PERIODICALS

Atlantic, April, 1943.
Choice, October, 1970.
Commonweal, February 26, 1943.
Kirkus Reviews, April 1, 1972.
Library Journal, March 1, 1973.
Los Angeles Herald Examiner, August 15, 1982.
Los Angeles Times, November 7, 1982.
New York Times, February 21, 1943.
New York Times Book Review, May 3, 1970.
San Francisco Chronicle, August 2, 1982.
San Francisco Chronicle Review, July 3, 1983.
Saturday Review, March 28, 1970.
Saturday Review of Literature, February 27, 1943.
St. Louis Post-Dispatch, March 8, 1970.
Times Literary Supplement, December 4, 1970.
Westways, October, 1978.

*   *   *

EDGAR, Ken(neth Frank)   1925-

PERSONAL: Born May 23, 1925, in Bedford, Ind.; son of Frank O. (a businessman) and Eileen (Davis) Edgar; married Mary A. Edgar; children: Mike, Mark. *Education:* Pennsylvania State University, B.A., 1947; University of Pittsburgh, M.A. and Ph.D., 1961; post-doctoral study, University of Chicago, California State University, Long Beach, and Institute for Rational Living, New York City; also studied at University of Arkansas, 1944.

ADDRESSES: Office—Department of Psychology, Indiana University of Pennsylvania, Clark Hall, Indiana, Pa. 15705-1068. *Agent*—Alex Jackinson Agency, 156 Fifth Ave., New York, N.Y. 10036.

CAREER: Allegheny County, Pittsburgh, Pa., school psychologist, 1956-61; Slippery Rock State College, Slippery Rock, Pa., director of counseling center, 1961-66; Indiana University of Pennsylvania, Indiana, Pa., 1966—, now professor of psychology. Private practice in psychotherapy; clinical psychologist at Indiana County Guidance Center, part-time, 1971—. Play director, Cain Park Creative Theatre, Cleveland Heights, Ohio, summers, 1956-57. *Military service:* U.S. Army, infantry, 1943-45.

MEMBER: American Psychological Association.

WRITINGS:

The Starfire (juvenile novel), Boxwood Press, 1961.
End and Beginning, Prentice-Hall, 1972.
As If (novel), Prentice-Hall, 1973.
(Contributor) J. J. Leedy, editor, *Poetry Therapy,* Lippincott, 1969.
Frogs at the Bottom of a Well: A Novel, Playboy Press, 1976.
Mirrors: A Novel, Methuen, 1978.
''A Coat upon a Stick'' (play), first produced at Landers Theatre in Springfield, Mo., 1986.

WORK IN PROGRESS: Dead Letters, a novel about ''a serial killer''; *Demon Guest,* a novel about ''demonic possession''; ''House on Sweet Hill,'' a play.

SIDELIGHTS: Ken Edgar writes: ''I believe we are in a critical time in our history, similar to that of ancient Greece and Rome when they began to collapse because of greed, the deterioration of the family, and the weakening of authority.''

AVOCATIONAL INTERESTS: Dogs.

*   *   *

EDGAR, Neal Lowndes   1927-1983

PERSONAL: Born June 21, 1927, in New York, N.Y.; died April 2, 1983; son of William J. B. (a professor) and Margaret B. (an editor; maiden name, Thomas) Edgar; married Susanna Jane Capper (a librarian), May 7, 1966. *Education:* Trinity College, Hartford, Conn., A.B., 1950; State University of New York at Albany, M.A. and M.S.L.S., both 1958; University of Michigan, A.M.L.S., 1964, Ph.D., 1965.

ADDRESSES: Home—1378 Athena Dr., Kent, Ohio 44240. *Office*—Library, Kent State University, Kent, Ohio 44242.

CAREER: State University of New York at Albany, acquisitions librarian, 1958-61; University of Michigan, Ann Arbor, coordinating librarian for Residence Hall Libraries, 1961-65; Library of Congress, Washington, D.C., serials cataloger in Descriptive Cataloging Division, 1965-66; Kent State University, Kent, Ohio, acquisitions librarian, 1967-68, serials librarian, 1968-77, research librarian, 1977-79, associate curator of special collections, beginning 1979, associate professor of library administration, 1969-74, professor of library science, beginning 1972, professor of library administration, beginning 1974. Has served as institutional representative to professional organizations, including Ohio College Library Center, Northeast Ohio Major Academic Libraries, and Ohio Inter-University Library Council's Technical Services Group.

MEMBER: American Library Association, American Association of University Professors, Tri-State Association of College and Research Librarians, Academic Librarians Association of Ohio, Northern Ohio Technical Services Librarians, Akron Area Librarians Association.

AWARDS, HONORS: Received yearly grants from Kent State University, beginning 1975.

WRITINGS:

A History and Bibliography of American Magazines, 1810-1820, Scarecrow, 1975.
(Contributor) Sidney L. Jackson, editor, *A Century of Service: Librarianship in the United States and Canada,* American Library Association, 1976.
(Compiler) *AACR2 and Its Impact on Libraries,* Ohio State University Libraries, 1980.
(With Wendy Yu Ma) *Travel in Asia: A Guide to Information Sources,* Gale, 1983.
AACR2 and Serials: The American View, Haworth Press, 1983.

Also contributor to *Anglo-American Cataloguing Rules,* 2nd edition, 1978. Contributor of about twenty-five articles to professional magazines. Member of editorial board, *Serials Librarian.*

SIDELIGHTS: Neal Lowndes Edgar once told *CA* that his ''career in librarianship has focused on technical services, especially in serials and cataloging. The highlight has been selection as a member of the American Library Association's RTSD Catalog Code Revision Committee.''

OBITUARIES:

PERIODICALS

Library Journal, July, 1983.

*   *   *

EDISON, Theodore
    See STRATEMEYER, Edward L.

*   *   *

EDSALL, Marian (Stickney)   1920-

PERSONAL: Born April 24, 1920, in Chicago, Ill.; daughter of Harry Foster and Hazel (Dickover) Stickney; married James VanAllen Edsall (director emeritus, university planning and construction), November 20, 1943; children: Sandra Lee (Mrs. Dennis Allen). *Education:* Wellesley College, B.A., 1941; graduate study, Art Institute of Chicago and University of Wyoming.

ADDRESSES: Home—7996 Deer Run Heights, Cross Plains, Wis. 53528.

CAREER: Meyer Both Advertising Agency, Chicago, Ill., copywriter, 1941-43; Community Plan Office, Champaign, Ill., publications director, 1953-54; University of Illinois, Champaign, publicity director for WILL-TV, 1961-63; Visual Educational Consultants, Middleton, Wis., editor, 1967-68; Division for Library Services, Madison, Wis., director of Coordinated Library Information Program, 1970-78; free-lance writer, 1980—. Lecturer, University of Wisconsin Library School. Former trustee of library boards in Champaign, Ill., and Middleton and Dane Counties, Wis.

MEMBER: American Library Association, National Audubon Society, Nature Conservancy, Society of American Unitarians, Wisconsin Library Association, Friends of Wisconsin Libraries.

AWARDS, HONORS: Wisconsin Library Trustee of the Year, 1971; certificate of distinction, 1977, from *Art Directions Magazine.*

WRITINGS:

JUVENILES

Our Auto Trip, Rand McNally, 1953.
Battle on the Rosebush: Insect Life in Your Backyard, Follett, 1972.

OTHER

The Harried Librarian's Guide to Public Relations Resources, Being a Compendium of Useful References and a Miscellany of Aids and Materials, Coordinated Library Information Program, 1976.
Library Displays, Coordinated Library Information Program, 1977.
Library Promotion Handbook, Oryx Press, 1980.
(Editor) *Library Public Relations Audio Tapes,* Oryx Press, 1981.
Practical PR for School Library Media Centers, Neal-Schuman, 1984.
Roadside Plants and Flowers: A Traveler's Guide to the Midwest and Great Lakes Area, University of Wisconsin Press, 1985.

Contributor to journals and magazines. Editor, *Camping Horizons,* 1960-62, *Channel 12 Newsletter* (University of Illinois radio station), 1962-63, *Tips from CLIP,* 1970-76, *Library PR News,* 1978-80.

WORK IN PROGRESS: Wildflower Guide/Diary.

SIDELIGHTS: Marian Edsall told *CA:* ''It has been particularly rewarding to share my life-long interest in photography and wildflowers through my books and articles, and with the audiences of my slide programs. I hope that this has contributed, in a small measure, to an increased awareness of our environmental and conservation problems, and to a willingness to work toward solutions.''

AVOCATIONAL INTERESTS: Outdoor life and nature, extensive U.S. and foreign travel.

*   *   *

EDWARDS, Julia
    See STRATEMEYER, Edward L.

*   *   *

EDWARDS, Page (Lawrence, Jr.)   1941-

PERSONAL: Born January 15, 1941, in Gooding, Idaho; son of Page Lawrence (a mining engineer) and Mary Elizabeth (a botanist; maiden name, Smith) Edwards; married Frances deForest Smith, June 10, 1967 (divorced, 1981); married Diana Selson, August 29, 1987; children: (first marriage) Amy deForest, Benjamin Carter. *Education:* Stanford University, B.A., 1963; University of Iowa, M.F.A., 1973; Simmons College, M.L.S., 1982.

ADDRESSES: Home—P.O. Box 1117, St. Augustine, Fla. 32085. *Office*—St. Augustine Historical Society, 271 Charlotte, St. Augustine, Fla. 32084. *Agent*—Elaine Markson, 44 Greenwich Ave., New York, N.Y. 10011.

CAREER: Viking Press, New York City, editor, 1968; Grossman Publishers, New York City, editor, 1969-71; University Press of New England, Hanover, N.H., assistant director, 1972-73; David R. Godine, Publishers, Boston, Mass., editor, 1974-75; Haverhill Public Library, Haverhill, Mass., reference librarian, 1975-81; Massachusetts Institute of Technology, Cambridge, archivist, 1981-82; St. Augustine Historical Society, St. Augustine, Fla., director, 1984—. Staff associate, Bread Loaf Writers' Conference, 1982-83. *Military service:* U.S. Navy, 1964-67; became lieutenant junior grade.

MEMBER: Society of American Archivists, Society of Florida Archivists, Florida Historical Society.

WRITINGS:

The Mules That Angels Ride, J. P. O'Hara, 1972.
Touring, Marion Boyars, 1976.
Staking Claims: Stories, Marion Boyars, 1980.
Peggy Salte, Marion Boyars, 1983.
Scarface Joe (juvenile), Four Winds, 1984.
The Lake: Father and Son, Marion Boyars, 1986.

Contributor to *Library Journal* and the *St. Petersburg Times.*

WORK IN PROGRESS: Benjamin Cooke, a novel set in northeast Florida on the St. Johns and St. Mary rivers.

SIDELIGHTS: Although he has written four novels, Page Edwards first gained critical attention for his short stories. In a

Spectator review of *Staking Claims: Stories,* Mary Hope observes that "if you look for genuinely good writing, instinctive truth rather than word-spinning, again and again, you are more likely to find it in the short story. . . . Edwards is a distinguished practitioner and this collection is a model." *Times Literary Supplement* contributor Kate Flint, however, feels that "although there is a deliberate sparseness to the prose, giving greater weight to the suggestive power of material detail than to subjective speculation, the experimentation of Edward's earlier novels . . . is notably lacking [in this collection]." The critic also notes that the protagonists of the stories often "seem paralysed by a want of daring," and subsequently "retreat into chilly and silent resignation." But Peter Tinniswood remarks in the London *Times* that *Staking Claims* is "an impressive and enjoyable collection." Dealing with the lives of "ordinary" people, the stories are made interesting by the author's "sure style. His stories remind me of [Sherwood Anderson's] *Winesburg, Ohio.*"

Similarly, Edwards's novel *Peggy Salte* is presented as "cameos of specific incidents in Peggy's life, with little linking explanation," describes Brian Morton in the *Times Literary Supplement.* "The book can even be read as a cycle of independent but linked short stories." But Diane Cole, while she remarks in the *New York Times Book Review* that "some chapters can be enjoyed as independent, gemlike short stories," maintains that this format detracts from the continuity of the work. "When tensions introduced in one chapter are forgotten or resolved superficially in the next, the novel loses its compelling quality," remarks the critic. Morton, however, believes that this construction reflects the idea that "life is a series of 'camps,' more or less temporary holds on place." As demonstrated through her diary entries, "Peggy Salte still manages to traverse great areas of dramatic time before finally 'breaking camp,'" comments Morton. "The novel is, among other things, an extended speculation on time, space, and mutual dependence and is an impressive step forward in Edwards's work."

AVOCATIONAL INTERESTS: Paintings of Edward Hopper and C. F. Childs, landscapes, long-distance running, cross-country skiing.

BIOGRAPHICAL/CRITICAL SOURCES:

PERIODICALS

New Statesman, January 28, 1977, July 18, 1980.
New York Times Book Review, December 11, 1983.
Spectator, January 29, 1977, August 23, 1980.
Times (London), June 26, 1980.
Times Literary Supplement, February 4, 1977, July 18, 1980, November 25, 1983, April 18, 1986.

*   *   *

EICHORN, Dorothy H(ansen)   1924-

PERSONAL: Born November 8, 1924, in Montpelier, Vt.; daughter of George Marinus (an accountant) and Lula (Ryan) Hansen; married Herman Eichorn (a chaplain), June 28, 1947; children: Eric Hansen. *Education:* University of Vermont, B.A., 1947; Boston University, M.A., 1949; Northwestern University, Ph.D., 1951.

ADDRESSES: Home—Box 7125, Napa, Calif. 94558. *Office*—Society for Research in Child Development, Inc., University of California, Berkeley, Calif. 94720.

CAREER: University of California, Institute for Human Development, Berkeley, junior research psychologist, 1952-54, assistant research psychologist, 1954-60, associate research psychologist, 1960-67, research psychologist, 1967—, administrator, Child Study Center, 1962-75, associate director, 1975-89; Society for Research in Child Development, Inc., University of California, Berkeley, lecturer in physiology, 1952—, executive officer, 1971-1990.

MEMBER: Inter-American Society of Psychology, American Psychological Association (fellow; member of board of directors, 1969-72), American Association for the Advancement of Science (fellow), Psychonomic Society, Society for Psychophysiological Research, Western Psychological Association (president, 1987).

WRITINGS:

(Co-editor) *Youth: Transition to Adulthood,* University of Chicago Press, 1973.
Longitudinal Research: Alternative Methods and Major Findings (cassette), American Psychologial Association, 1976.
(Editor, with others) *Present and Past in Middle Life,* Academic Press, 1982.

Also editor, with D. Stern, of *Adolescence and Work: Influences of Social Structure, Labor Markets and Culture,* 1989. Contributor of chapters to thirty-five books, and of articles to journals.

WORK IN PROGRESS: Research on two-generation similarities in developmental patterns.

*   *   *

EIDELBERG, Paul   1928-

PERSONAL: Born June 21, 1928, in Brooklyn, N.Y.; son of Harry and Sarah (Leimseider) Eidelberg; married Phyllis Leif, December 27, 1947; children: Steven, Sharen, Sarah Elizabeth. *Education:* University of Chicago, M.A., 1957, Ph.D., 1966. *Religion:* Hebrew.

ADDRESSES: Home—Shabtai Negbi, Gilo 63/32, Jerusalem, Israel.

CAREER: Sweet Briar College, Sweet Briar, Va., visiting professor of political science, 1966-67; North Carolina State University at Raleigh, assistant professor of politics, 1967-68; Kenyon College, Gambier, Ohio, associate professor of political science, 1968-70; University of Dallas, Irving, Tex., associate professor of political science, 1970-74; Claremont Men's College, Claremont, Calif., research professor of political science, 1974-76; Bar-Ilan University, Ramat-Gan, Israel, professor of political science, 1976—. Visiting professor of political science, Yeshiva University, New York, N.Y., 1987-88. Visiting lecturer at colleges and universities, including Kenyon College, 1973, Claremont Men's College, 1975 and 1976, and St. Thomas Aquinas College, 1976. Co-founder, Institute of Statesmanship and Torah-Philosophy, Jerusalem, Israel. *Military service:* U.S. Air Force, 1946-53; became first lieutenant.

MEMBER: American Political Science Association.

AWARDS, HONORS: Earhart Foundation grant, 1974 and 1977; Salvatori Center grant, 1976.

WRITINGS:

The Philosophy of the American Constitution: A Reinterpretation of the Intentions of the Founding Fathers, Free

Press, 1968, (paperback edition) University Press of America, 1986.

A Discourse of Statesmanship: The Design and Transformation of the American Polity, University of Illinois Press, 1974.

On the Silence of the Declaration of Independence, University of Massachusetts Press, 1976.

Beyond Detente: Toward an American Foreign Policy, Sherwood Sugden, 1977.

Hamazema shel Sadat, Reshafim (Tel Aviv), 1978.

Sadat's Strategy, Dawn Publishing (Montreal), 1979.

Jerusalem vs. Athens: In Quest of a General Theory of Existence, University Press of America, 1983.

Israel's Return and Restoration, [Jerusalem], 1987.

Beyond the Secular Mind, Greenwood Press, 1989.

Contributor to periodicals, including *Midstream, International Behavioral Scientist, Congressional Record, Review of Politics,* and *Journal of Nuclear Medicine.* Contributor of articles to newspapers in various countries, including the United States, Israel, and several European and South American nations.

WORK IN PROGRESS: A book, contracted for publication by Greenwood Press.

*   *   *

EIDUSON, Bernice T(abackman)   1921-1985

PERSONAL: Born August 21, 1921, in Buffalo, N.Y.; died July, 1985; daughter of Max and Tillie (Cohen) Tabackman; married Samuel Eiduson (a professor of chemistry and psychiatry), 1942. *Education:* University of Buffalo (now State University of New York at Buffalo), B.A., 1943, M.A., 1944; University of California, Los Angeles, Ph.D., 1957.

ADDRESSES: Home—941 Stonehill Ln., Los Angeles, Calif. *Office*—Department of Psychiatry, Neuropsychiatric Institute, University of California, Los Angeles, Calif. 90024.

CAREER: Guidance Center of Buffalo, Buffalo, N.Y., clinical internship, 1944, psychologist, 1944-46; Hacker Foundation for Psychiatric Research and Education, Beverly Hills, Calif., research psychologist, 1957-59; Reiss-Davis Clinic for Child Guidance, Los Angeles, Calif., chief clinical psychologist, 1959-61, director of research, 1961-70; University of California, Los Angeles, associate professor, 1970-72, professor of psychiatry, 1972-85.

MEMBER: American Psychological Association, American Orthopsychiatric Association, Society for Projective Techniques, American Association for the Advancement of Science, Western Psychological Association, California State Psychological Association, Southern California Psychological Association, Phi Beta Kappa, Sigma Xi.

WRITINGS:

Scientists: Their Psychological World, Basic Books, 1962.

(Contributor) *Biochemistry and Behavior,* D. Van Nostrand, 1964.

(Editor with Linda Beckman) *Science as a Career Choice: Theoretical and Emperical Studies,* Russell Sage, 1974.

Bringing up the Only Child, Hawthorne, 1976.

Author of more than ninety professional papers in psychology.*

EINSTEIN, Elizabeth (Ann)   1939-

PERSONAL: Born October 7, 1939, in Loyal, Wis.; daughter of Andrew (a farmer) and Betty Mae (a bookkeeper; maiden name, Lee) Weyer; married Billy Ralston Matteson (divorced); married Walter O. Einstein, February 14, 1969 (divorced); children: Christopher Alan, Jeffrey Scott; stepchildren: Beverly V. Einstein Grulke, Brenda Einstein Wilcox, Kurt W. *Education:* Onondaga Community College, A.A. (with highest honors), 1974; Syracuse University, B.A., 1977, M.A., 1980. *Religion:* Christian.

ADDRESSES: Home and Office—P.O. Box 6760, Ithaca, N.Y. 14851. *Agent*—Jean Nagger, 336 East 73rd St., New York, N.Y. 10021.

CAREER: Robert Fulton Printing Co., Sacramento, Calif., office manager, 1967-70; State University of New York College of Environmental Science and Forestry, Syracuse, intern feature writer, 1976, staff writer, 1977, editorial assistant, 1977-78; free-lance writer, 1978—; lecturer, workshop leader, and community educator on stepfamilies, 1982—.

MEMBER: Stepfamily Association of America (member of national board of directors), Society of Professional Journalists, Parents without Partners, Alpha Sigma Lambda, Phi Kappa Phi.

AWARDS, HONORS: National media awards from American Psychological Association, 1978, for newspaper series on behavior modification techniques, and 1980, for *The Stepfamily: Living, Loving, and Learning;* Breadloaf Writers Conference fellow, 1983.

WRITINGS:

The Stepfamily: Living, Loving, and Learning, Macmillan, 1982.

(Co-author) *Stepfamily Living* (series of four booklets), privately printed, 1983.

(Co-author) *Strengthening Stepfamilies,* American Guidance Service, 1986.

Author of "Cook of the Week," a column in *Chittenango-Bridgeport Times,* 1976-78. Correspondent for *Human Behavior,* 1978-79. Author of text for "Stepfamily Living" (three audiocassettes), 1987. Contributing editor of *Outlook,* 1975, associate editor, 1976; founding editor of *Stepfamily Buletin,* 1980-82. Contributor to magazines and newspapers, including *Empire, Air Progress, Parents, Marriage and Family,* and *National Observer.*

WORK IN PROGRESS: "Families in Transition," a nationally syndicated column; two books, *New Connections: Preparing for Remarriage and Other Relationships* and *Changing: Essays of More Gentle Journeys of Growth.*

SIDELIGHTS: Elizabeth Einstein told *CA:* "Both my first book and works in progress are an integration of personal experience with journalistic research with others in similar situations, and with the professionals working with them. Empathy can provide both pitfalls and possibilities for the writer. It provides insights and personal anecdotes, but it also makes hooking into selective perception easier.

"The same is true for stepfamilies. When they have the information most of us lack about how living in a stepfamily is different, they can accept those differences and make them work for them. The inherent pitfalls in stepfamily living become possibilities after this acceptance occurs. But like writing, becoming a stepfamily is a process, and it takes time—a lot of time—to get it right.

"Many times I think I write for growth reasons. Writing about universal experiences that have personally touched my life forces me to work things through, and sometimes that means in deep ways that I never dreamed of. Completing *The Stepfamily,* for instance, meant going back to the drawing board after a very perceptive author rejected the manuscript 'because my subjectiveness caused my writing to be unclear.' Rewriting the manuscript until I got it right meant yielding my biases and dumping my selective perception from the interviews until I got it right.

"Likewise with *New Connections.* The book changed as rapidly as I did because, at first, I thought the goal was merely remarriage. Now I understand it to be becoming a whole, healthy, and independent being. Changes have touched my life in a profound way, and researching and writing them through is changing me still. First comes confusion—in the research, the organization, and the writing. But that leads to curiosity, and that cannot help but create growth—in my writing and in me as a person."

BIOGRAPHICAL/CRITICAL SOURCES:

PERIODICALS

Baltimore Sun, September 9, 1982.
Buffalo Evening News, January 6, 1983.
Los Angeles Times, June 10, 1982.
New York Times, January 10, 1983.
Philadelphia Inquirer, September 26, 1982.
U.S. News and World Report, January 17, 1983.
Washington Post, August 3, 1982.

*   *   *

EISENBUD, Jule   1908-

PERSONAL: Born November 20, 1908, in New York, N.Y.; son of Abraham and Sarah (Abramson) Eisenbud; married Molly Lewis, January 1, 1937; children: Joanna (Mrs. Raymond Moldow), John, Eric. *Education:* Columbia University, B.A., 1929, M.D., 1934, Med. Sci. Dr., 1939. *Religion:* Hebrew.

ADDRESSES: Home and office—4634 East Sixth Ave., Denver, Colo. 80220.

CAREER: Private practice of psychiatry in New York City, 1938-50, and Denver, Colo., 1950—. Columbia University, Columbia College of Physicians and Surgeons, New York City, associate in psychiatry, 1938-50; University of Colorado Medical School, Denver, associate clinical professor of psychiatry, 1950—. Lecturer at New York School of Social Work, 1938-41, and New York Psychoanalytic Institute, 1940-41.

MEMBER: American Psychiatric Association (fellow), American Psychoanalytic Association, Parapsychological Association, American Society for Psychical Research (founding member of medical section).

WRITINGS:

The World of Ted Serios: Thoughtographic Studies of an Extraordinary Mind, Morrow, 1967.
Psi and Psychoanalysis, Grune, 1970.
(Contributor) Edgar D. Mitchell and John White, editors, *Psychic Exploration: A Challenge for Science,* Putnam, 1974.
(Contributor) B. B. Wolman, editor, *Handbook of Parapsychology,* Van Nostrand, 1981.
Paranormal Foreknowledge: Problems and Perplexities, Human Sciences Press, 1982.

Parapsychology and the Unconscious, North Atlantic, 1984.

Contributor to psychiatric, psychoanalytic, and parapsychological journals.

*   *   *

EMECHETA, (Florence Onye) Buchi   1944-

PERSONAL: Born July 21, 1944, in Yaba, Lagos, Nigeria; daughter of Jeremy Nwabudike (a railway worker and molder) and Alice Ogbanje (Okwuekwu) Emecheta; married Sylvester Onwordi, 1960 (separated, 1966); children: Florence, Sylvester, Jake, Christy, Alice. *Education:* University of London, B.Sc. (with honors), 1972. *Religion:* Anglican.

ADDRESSES: Home—144 Craney Gardens, Muswell Hill, London N10 3AH, England.

CAREER: British Museum, London, England, library officer, 1965-69; Inner London Education Authority, London, youth worker and sociologist, 1969-76; community worker, Camden, N.J., 1976-78. Writer and lecturer, 1972—. Visiting professor at several universities throughout the United States, including Pennsylvania State University, University of California, Los Angeles, and University of Illinois at Urbana-Champaign, 1979; senior resident fellow and visiting professor of English, University of Calabar, Nigeria, 1980-81; lecturer, Yale University, 1982, London University, 1982—. Fellow, London University, 1986. Proprietor, Ogwugwu Afor Publishing Company, 1982-83. Member of Home Secretary's Advisory Council on Race, 1979—, and of Arts Council of Great Britain, 1982-83.

AWARDS, HONORS: Jock Campbell Award for literature by new or unregarded talent from Africa or the Caribbean, *New Statesman,* 1978; selected as the Best Black British Writer, 1978, and one of the Best British Young Writers, 1983.

WRITINGS:

In the Ditch, Barrie and Jenkins, 1972.
Second-Class Citizen (novel), Allison & Busby, 1974, Braziller, 1975.
The Bride Price: A Novel (paperback published as *The Bride Price: Young Ibo Girl's Love; Conflict of Family and Tradition*), Braziller, 1976.
The Slave Girl: A Novel, Braziller, 1977.
The Joys of Motherhood: A Novel, Braziller, 1979.
Destination Biafra: A Novel, Schocken, 1982.
Naira Power (novelette directed principally to Nigerian readers), Macmillan (London), 1982.
Double Yoke (novel), Schocken, 1982.
The Rape of Shavi (novel), Ogwugwu Afor, 1983, Braziller, 1985.
Adah's Story: A Novel, Allison & Busby, 1983.
Head above Water (autobiography), Ogwugwu Afor, 1984, Collins, 1986.
A Kind of Marriage (novelette), Macmillan, 1987.

JUVENILE

Titch the Cat (based on story by daughter Alice Emecheta), illustrated by Thomas Joseph, Allison & Busby, 1979.
Nowhere to Play (based on story by daughter Christy Emecheta), illustrations by Peter Archer, Schocken, 1980.
The Moonlight Bride, Oxford Univesity Press in association with University Press, 1981.
The Wrestling Match, Oxford University Press in association with University Press, 1981, Braziller, 1983.

Family Bargain (publication for schools), British Broadcasting Corp., 1987.

OTHER

(Author of introduction and commentary) Maggie Murray, *Our Own Freedom* (book of photographs), Sheba Feminist (London), 1981.
A Kind of Marriage (teleplay; produced by BBC-TV), Macmillan (London), 1987.

Also author of teleplays ''Tanya, a Black Woman,'' produced by BBC-TV, and ''The Juju Landlord.'' Contributor to journals, including *New Statesman, Times Literary Supplement,* and the *Guardian.*

SIDELIGHTS: Although Buchi Emecheta has resided in London since 1962, she is ''Nigeria's best-known female writer,'' comments John Updike in the *New Yorker.* ''Indeed, few writers of her sex . . . have arisen in any part of tropical Africa.'' Emecheta enjoys much popularity in Great Britain, and she has gathered an appreciative audience on this side of the Atlantic as well. Although Emecheta has written children's books and teleplays, she is best known for her historical novels set in Nigeria, both before and after independence. Concerned with the clash of cultures and the impact of Western values upon agrarian traditions and customs, Emecheta's work is strongly autobiographical; and, as Updike observes, much of it is especially concerned with ''the situation of women in a society where their role, though crucial, was firmly subordinate and where the forces of potential liberation have arrived with bewildering speed.''

Born to Ibo parents in Yaba, a small village near Lagos, Nigeria, Emecheta indicates that the Ibos ''don't want you to lose contact with your culture,'' writes Rosemary Bray in the *Voice Literary Supplement.* Bray explains that the oldest woman in the house plays an important role in that she is the ''big mother'' to the entire family. In Emecheta's family, her father's sister assumed this role, says Bray: '' 'She was very old and almost blind,' Buchi recalls, 'And she would gather the young children around her after dinner and tell stories to us.' '' The stories the children heard were about their origins and ancestors; and, according to Bray, Emecheta recalls: ''I thought to myself 'No life could be more important than this.' So when people asked me what I wanted to do when I grew up I told them I wanted to be a storyteller—which is what I'm doing now.''

Orphaned as a young child, Emecheta lived with foster parents who mistreated her. She attended a missionary high school for girls on a scholarship until she was sixteen, and then wed a man to whom she had been betrothed since the age of eleven. A mother at seventeen, she had two sons and three daughters by the time she was twenty-two. After the birth of her second child, Emecheta followed her husband to London, where she endured poor living conditions, including one-room apartments without heat or hot water, to help finance his education. ''The culture shock of London was great,'' notes Bray, ''but even more distressing was her husband's physical abuse and his constant resistance to her attempts at independence.'' The marriage ended when he read and then burned the manuscript of her first book. Supporting herself and five children on public assistance and by scrubbing floors, Emecheta continued to write in the mornings before her children arose, and also managed to earn an honors degree in sociology. *In the Ditch,* her first book, originally appeared as a series of columns in the *New Statesman.* Written in the form of a diary, it ''is based

on her own failed marriage and her experiences on the dole in London trying to rear alone her many children,'' state Charlotte and David Bruner in *World Literature Today.* Called a ''sad, sonorous, occasionally hilarious . . . extraordinary first novel,'' by Adrianne Blue in the *Washington Post Book World,* it details her impoverished existence in a foreign land, as well as her experience with racism, and ''illuminates the similarities and differences between cultures and attitudes,'' remarks a *Times Literary Supplement* contributor, who thinks it merits ''special attention.''

Similarly autobiographical, Emecheta's second novel, *Second-Class Citizen,* ''recounts her early marriage years, when she was trying to support her student-husband—a man indifferent to his own studies and later indifferent to her job searches, her childbearing, and her resistance to poverty,'' observe the Bruners. The novel is about a young, resolute and resourceful Nigerian girl who, despite traditional tribal domination of females, manages to continue her own education; she marries a student and follows him to London, where he becomes abusive toward her. ''Emecheta said people find it hard to believe that she has not exaggerated the truth in this autobiographical novel,'' reports Nancy Topping Bazin in *Black Scholar.* ''The grimness of what is described does indeed make it painful to read.'' Called a ''brave and angry book'' by Marigold Johnson in the *Times Literary Supplement,* Emecheta's story, however, ''is not accompanied by a misanthropic whine,'' notes Martin Levin in the *New York Times Book Review.* Alice Walker, who thinks it is ''one of the most informative books about contemporary African life'' that she has read, observes in *Ms.* that ''it raises fundamental questions about how creative and prosaic life is to be lived and to what purpose.''

''Emecheta's women do not simply lie down and die,'' observes Bray. ''Always there is resistance, a challenge to fate, a need to renegotiate the terms of the uneasy peace that exists between them and accepted traditions.'' Bray adds that ''Emecheta's women know, too, that between the rock of African traditions and the hard place of encroaching Western values, it is the women who will be caught.'' Concerned with the clash of cultures, in *The Bride Price: A Novel,* Emecheta tells the story of a young Nigerian girl ''whose life is complicated by traditional attitudes toward women,'' writes Richard Cima in the *Library Journal.* The young girl's father dies when she is thirteen; and, with her brother and mother, she becomes the property of her father's ambitious brother. She is permitted to remain in school only because it will increase her value as a potential wife. However, she falls in love with her teacher, a descendant of slaves; and because of familial objections, they elope, thereby depriving her uncle of the ''bride price.'' When she dies in childbirth, she fulfills the superstition that a woman would not survive the birth of her first child if her bride price had not been paid; and Susannah Clapp maintains in the *Times Literary Supplement,* that the quality of the novel ''depends less on plot or characterization than on the information conveyed about a set of customs and the ideas which underlay them.'' Calling it ''a captivating Nigerian novel lovingly but unsentimentally written, about the survival of ancient marriage customs in modern Nigeria,'' Valerie Cunningham adds in *New Statesman* that this book ''proves Buchi Emecheta to be a considerable writer.''

Emecheta's *Slave Girl: A Novel* is about ''a poor, gently raised Ibo girl who is sold into slavery to a rich African marketwoman by a feckless brother at the turn of the century,'' writes a *New Yorker* contributor. Educated by missionaries, she joins the new church where she meets the man she eventually marries. In the *Library Journal*, Cima thinks that it provides an "interesting picture of Christianity's impact on traditional Ibo society." Perceiving parallels between marriage and slavery, Emecheta explores the issue of "freedom within marriage in a society where slavery is supposed to have been abolished," writes Cunningham in the *New Statesman,* adding that the book indicts both "pagan and Christian inhumanity to women." And although a contributor to *World Literature Today* suggests that the "historical and anthropological background" in the novel tends to destroy its "emotional complex," another contributor to the same journal believes that the sociological detail has been "unobtrusively woven into" it and that *The Slave Girl* represents Emecheta's "most accomplished work so far. It is coherent, compact and convincing."

"Emecheta's voice has been welcomed by many as helping to redress the somewhat one-sided picture of African women that has been delineated by male writers," according to *A New Reader's Guide to African Literature*. Writing in *African Literature Today*, Eustace Palmer indicates that "the African novel has until recently been remarkable for the absense of what might be called the feminine point of view." Because of the relatively few female African novelists, "the presentation of women in the African novel has been left almost entirely to male voices . . . and their interest in African womanhood . . . has had to take second place to numerous other concerns," continues Palmer. "These male novelists, who have presented the African woman largely within the traditional milieu, have generally communicated a picture of a male-dominated and male-oriented society, and the satisfaction of the women with this state of things has been . . . completely taken for granted." Palmer adds that the emergence of Emecheta and other "accomplished female African novelists . . . seriously challenges all these cosy assumptions. The picture of the cheerful contented female complacently accepting her lot is replaced by that of a woman who is powerfully aware of the unfairness of the system and who longs to be fulfilled in her self, to be a full human being, not merely somebody else's appendage." For instance, Palmer notes that *The Joys of Motherhood: A Novel* "presents essentially the same picture of traditional society . . . but the difference lies in the prominence in Emecheta's novel of the female point of view registering its disgust at male chauvinism and its dissatisfaction with what it considers an unfair and oppressive system."

The Joys of Motherhood is about a woman "who marries but is sent home in disgrace because she fails to bear a child quickly enough," writes Bazin. "She then is sent to the city by her father to marry a man she has never seen. She is horrified when she meets this second husband because she finds him ugly, but she sees no alternative to staying with him. Poverty and repeated pregnancies wear her down; the pressure to bear male children forces her to bear child after child since the girls she has do not count." Palmer observes that "clearly, the man is the standard and the point of reference in this society. It is significant that the chorus of countrymen say, not that a woman without a child is a failed woman, but that a woman without a child *for her husband* is a failed woman." Bazin observes that in Emecheta's novels, "a woman must accept the double standard of sexual freedom: it permits polygamy and infidelity for both Christian and non-Christian men but only monogamy for women. These books reveal the extent to which the African woman's oppression is engrained in the African mores."

Acknowledging that "the issue of polygamy in Africa remains a controversial one," Palmer states that what Emecheta stresses in *The Joys of Motherhood* is "the resulting dominance, especially sexual, of the male, and the relegation of the female into subservience, domesticity and motherhood." Nonetheless, despite Emecheta's "angry glare," says Palmer, one can "glean from the novel the economic and social reasons that must have given rise to polygamy. . . . But the author concentrates on the misery and deprivation polygamy can bring." Palmer praises Emecheta's insightful psychological probing of her characters's thoughts: "Scarcely any other African novelist has succeeded in probing the female mind and displaying the female personality with such precision." In the *Washington Post Book World*, Adrianne Blue suggests that Emecheta "tells this story in a plain style, denuding it of exoticism, displaying an impressive, embracing compassion." Calling it a "graceful, touching, ironically titled tale that bears a plain feminist message," Updike adds in the *New Yorker* that "in this compassionate but slightly distanced and stylized story of a life that comes to seem wasted, she sings a dirge for more than African pieties. The lives within 'The Joys of Motherhood' might be, transposed into a different cultural key, those of our own rural ancestors."

Emecheta's "works reveal a great deal about the lives of African women and about the development of feminist perspectives," observes Bazin, explaining that one moves beyond an initial perspective of "personal experience," to perceive "social or communal" oppression. This second perspective "demands an analysis of the causes of oppression within the social mores and the patriarchal power structure," adds Bazin. Finding both perspectives in Emecheta's work, Bazin thinks that through her descriptions of "what it is like to be female in patriarchal African cultures," she provides a voice for "millions of black African women." Although her feminist perspective is anchored in her own personal life, says Bazin, she "grew to understand how son preference, bride price, polygamy, menstrual taboos, . . . wife beating, early marriages, early and unlimited pregnancies, arranged marriages, and male dominance in the home functioned to keep women powerless." The Bruners write that "obviously Emecheta is concerned about the plight of women, today and yesterday, in both technological and traditional societies, though she rejects a feminist label." Emecheta told the Bruners: "The main themes of my novels are African society and family; the historical social, and political life in Africa as seen by a woman through events. I always try to show that the African male is oppressed and he too oppresses the African women . . . I have not committed myself to the cause of African women only. I write about Africa as a whole."

Emecheta's *Destination Biafra: A Novel* is a story of the "history of Nigeria from the eve of independence to the collapse of the Biafran secessionist movement," writes Robert L. Berner in *World Literature Today*. The novel has generated a mixed critical response, though. In the *Times Literary Supplement*, Chinweizu feels that it "does not convey the feel of the experience that was Biafra. All it does is leave one wondering why it falls so devastatingly below the quality of Buchi Emecheta's previous works." Noting, however, that Emecheta's publisher reduced the manuscript by half, Berner suggests that "this may account for what often seems a rather elliptical narrative and for the frequently clumsy prose which too often blunts the novel's satiric edge." Finding the novel "different from any of her others . . . larger and more substantive," the Bruners state: "Here she presents neither the life story of a single character nor the delineation of one facet of a culture, but the whole perplexing canvas of people from diverse ethnic groups, belief systems, levels of society—all caught in a disastrous civil war.'' Moreover, the Bruners feel that the ''very objectivity of her reporting and her impartiality in recounting atrocities committed by all sides, military and civilian, have even greater impact because her motivation is not sadistic.''

The Rape of Shavi represents somewhat of a departure in that ''Emecheta attempts one of the most difficult of tasks: that of integrating the requirements of contemporary, realistic fiction with the narrative traditions of myth and folklore,'' writes Somtow Sucharitkul in the *Washington Post Book World.* Roy Kerridge describes the novel's plot in the *Times Literary Supplement:* ''A plane crashes among strange tribespeople, white aviators are made welcome by the local king, they find precious stones, repair their plane and escape just as they are going to be forcibly married to native girls. The king's son and heir stows away and has adventures of his own in England.'' Called a ''wise and haunting tale'' by a *New Yorker* contributor, *The Rape of Shavi* ''recounts the ruination of this small African society by voracious white interlopers,'' says Richard Eder in the *Los Angeles Times.* A few critics suggest that in *The Rape of Shavi,* Emecheta's masterful portrayal of her Shavian community is not matched by her depiction of the foreigners. Eder, for instance, calls it a ''lopsided fable,'' and declares: ''It is not that the Shavians are noble and the whites monstrous; that is what fables are for. It is that the Shavians are finely drawn and the Westerners very clumsily. It is a duet between a flute and a kitchen drain.'' However, Sucharitkul thinks that portraying the Shavians as ''complex individuals'' and the Westerners as ''two dimensional, mythic types'' presents a refreshing, seldom expressed, and ''particularly welcome'' point of view.

Although in the *New York Times* Michiko Kakutani calls *The Rape of Shavi* ''an allegorical tale, filled with ponderous morals about the evils of imperialism and tired aphorisms about nature and civilization,'' Sucharitkul believes that ''the central thesis of [the novel] is brilliantly, relentlessly argued, and Emecheta's characters and societies are depicted with a bittersweet, sometimes painful honesty.'' Sucharitkul also praises Emecheta's ''persuasive'' prose: ''It is prose that appears unusually simple at first, for it is full of the kind of rhythms and sentence structures more often found in folk tales than in contemporary novels. Indeed, in electing to tell her multilayered and often very contemporary story within a highly mythic narrative framework, the author walks a fine line between the pitfalls of preciosity and pretentiousness. By and large, the tightrope act is a success.''

''Emecheta has reaffirmed her dedication to be a full-time writer,'' say the Bruners. ''Her culture and her education at first were obstacles to her literary inclination. She had to struggle against precedent, against reluctant publishers, and later against male-dominated audiences and readership.'' Her fiction is intensely autobiographical, drawing on the difficulties she has both witnessed and experienced as a woman, and most especially as a Nigerian woman. Indicating that in Nigeria, however, ''Emecheta is a prophet without honor,'' Bray adds that ''she is frustrated at not being able to reach women—the audience she desires most. She feels a sense of isolation as she attempts to stake out the middle ground between the old and the new.'' Remarking that ''in her art as well as in her life, Buchi Emecheta offers another alternative,'' Bray continues: ''What I am trying to do is get our profession back,'' Emecheta told Bray. ''Women are born storytellers. We keep the history. We are the true conservatives—we conserve things and we never forget. What I do is not clever or unusual. It is

what my aunt and my grandmother did, and their mothers before them.''

AVOCATIONAL INTERESTS: Gardening, attending the theatre, listening to music, reading.

BIOGRAPHICAL/CRITICAL SOURCES:

BOOKS

Contemporary Literary Criticism, Volume 14, Gale, 1980.
Zell, Hans M., and others, *A New Reader's Guide to African Literature,* 2nd revised and expanded edition, Holmes & Meier, 1983.

PERIODICALS

African Literature Today, Number 3, 1983.
Atlantic, May, 1976.
Black Scholar, November/December, 1985, March/April, 1986.
Library Journal, September 1, 1975, April 1, 1976, January 15, 1978, May 1, 1979.
Listener, July 19, 1979.
Los Angeles Times, October 16, 1983, March 6, 1985.
Ms., January, 1976, July, 1984, March, 1985.
New Statesman, June 25, 1976, October 14, 1977, June 2, 1978, April 27, 1979.
New Yorker, May 17, 1976, January 9, 1978, July 2, 1979, April 23, 1984, April 22, 1985.
New York Times, February 23, 1985.
New York Times Book Review, September 14, 1975, November 11, 1979, January 27, 1980, February 27, 1983, May 5, 1985.
Times Literary Supplement, August 11, 1972, January 31, 1975, June 11, 1976, February 26, 1982, February 3, 1984, February 27, 1987.
Voice Literary Supplement, June, 1982.
Washington Post Book World, May 13, 1979, April 12, 1981, September 5, 1982, September 25, 1983, March 30, 1985.
World Literature Today, spring, 1977, summer, 1977, spring, 1978, winter, 1979, spring, 1980, winter, 1983, autumn, 1984, winter, 1985.

—*Sketch by Sharon Malinowski*

*   *   *

EMERSON, Alice B.
[Collective pseudonym]

WRITINGS:

(Contributor) *Mystery and Adventure Stories for Girls* (includes *Betty Gordon at Bramble Farm;* also see below), Cupples & Leon, 1934.
(Contributor) *Popular Stories for Girls* (includes *Ruth Fielding of the Red Mill;* also see below), Cupples & Leon, 1934.

''BETTY GORDON'' SERIES

Betty Gordon at Bramble Farm; or, The Mystery of a Nobody, Cupples & Leon, 1920.
. . . in Washington; or, Strange Adventures in a Great City, Cupples & Leon, 1920.
. . . in the Land of Oil; or, The Farm That Was Worth a Fortune, Cupples & Leon, 1920.
. . . at Boarding School; or, The Treasure of Indian Chasm, Cupples & Leon, 1921.
. . . at Mountain Camp; or, The Mystery of Ida Bellethorne, Cupples & Leon, 1922.

. . . *at Ocean Park; or, School Chums on the Boardwalk*, Cupples & Leon, 1923.

. . . *and Her School Chums; or, Bringing the Rebels to Terms*, Cupples & Leon, 1924.

. . . *at Rainbow Ranch; or, Cowboy Joe's Secret*, Cupples & Leon, 1925.

. . . *in Mexican Wilds; or, The Secret of the Mountains*, Cupples & Leon, 1926.

. . . *and the Lost Pearls; or, A Mystery of the Seaside*, Cupples & Leon, 1927.

. . . *on the Campus; or, The Secret of the Trunk Room*, Cupples & Leon, 1928.

. . . *and the Hale Twins; or, An Exciting Vacation*, Cupples & Leon, 1929.

. . . *at Mystery Farm; or, Strange Doings at Rocky Ridge*, Cupples & Leon, 1930.

. . . *on No-Trail Island; or, Uncovering a Queer Secret*, Cupples & Leon, 1931.

. . . *and the Mystery Girl; or, The Secret at Sundown Hall*, Cupples & Leon, 1932.

"RUTH FIELDING" SERIES

Ruth Fielding of the Red Mill; or, Jasper Parloe's Secret, Cupples & Leon, 1913.

. . . *at Briarwood Hall; or, Solving the Campus Mystery*, Cupples & Leon, 1913.

. . . *at Snow Camp; or, Lost in the Backwoods*, Cupples & Leon, 1913.

. . . *at Lighthouse Point; or, Nita, the Girl Castaway*, Cupples & Leon, 1913.

. . . *at Silver Ranch; or, Schoolgirls among the Cowboys*, Cupples & Leon, 1913.

. . . *on Cliff Island; or, The Old Hunter's Treasure Box*, Cupples & Leon, 1915.

. . . *at Sunrise Farm; or, What Became of the Ruby Orphans*, Cupples & Leon, 1915.

. . . *and the Gypsies; or, The Missing Pearl Necklace*, Cupples & Leon, 1915.

. . . *in Moving Pictures; or, Helping the Dormitory Fund*, Cupples & Leon, 1916.

. . . *Down in Dixie; or, Great Days in the Land of Cotton*, Cupples & Leon, 1916.

. . . *at College; or, The Missing Examination Papers*, Cupples & Leon, 1917.

. . . *in the Saddle; or, College Girls in the Land of Gold*, Cupples & Leon, 1917.

. . . *in the Red Cross; or, Doing Her Best for Uncle Sam*, Cupples & Leon, 1918.

. . . *at the War Front; or, The Hunt for the Lost Soldier*, Cupples & Leon, 1918.

. . . *Homeward Bound; or, A Red Cross Worker's Ocean Perils*, Cupples & Leon, 1919.

. . . *Down East; or, The Hermit of Beach Plum Point*, Cupples & Leon, 1920.

. . . *in the Great Northwest; or, The Indian Girl Star of the Movies*, Cupples & Leon, 1921.

. . . *on the St. Lawrence; or, The Queer Old Man of the Thousand Islands*, Cupples & Leon, 1922.

. . . *Treasure Hunting; or, A Moving Picture That Became Real*, Cupples & Leon, 1923.

. . . *in the Far North; or, The Lost Motion Picture Company*, Cupples & Leon, 1924.

. . . *at Golden Pass; or, The Perils of an Artificial Avalanche*, Cupples & Leon, 1925.

. . . *in Alaska; or, The Miners of Snow Mountain*, Cupples & Leon, 1926.

. . . *and Her Great Scenario; or, Striving for the Motion Picture Prize*, Cupples & Leon, 1927.

. . . *at Cameron Hall; or, A Mysterious Disappearance*, Cupples & Leon, 1928.

. . . *Clearing Her Name; or, The Rivals of Hollywood*, Cupples & Leon, 1929.

. . . *in Talking Pictures; or, The Prisoners of the Tower*, Cupples & Leon, 1930.

. . . *and Baby June*, Cupples & Leon, 1931.

. . . *and Her Double*, Cupples & Leon, 1932.

. . . *and Her Greatest Triumph; or, Saving Her Company from Disaster*, Cupples & Leon, 1933.

. . . *and Her Crowning Victory; or, Winning Honors Abroad*, Cupples & Leon, 1934.

SIDELIGHTS: ''Edward Stratemeyer's Ruth Fielding,'' states Carol Billman in *The Secret of the Stratemeyer Syndicate: Nancy Drew, the Hardy Boys, and the Million Dollor Fiction Factory*, ''was the preeminent 'charity child' on the go.'' She is one of the best representative heroines of early twentieth-century girls' series fiction, Billman suggests, ''because of her series' popularity and because of her own position as a pivotal figure in fiction for American girls. Ruth is the orphan, a carry-over from the nineteenth-century sentimental tradition, turned movie star and sleuth, two new roles for fictional heroines of the 1900s.'' In her sleuthing capacity, Billings suggests, Ruth Fielding serves as a prototype for other female detectives, especially Nancy Drew.

Yet Nancy Drew is still published today, while the last Ruth Fielding volume appeared in 1934. Part of the reason the series' success diminished, Billman declares, is because Ruth was unable to balance her career and her domestic life successfully after her marriage to her long-time suitor, Tom Cameron. Ruth's marriage, says Billman, altered the nature of the series; it lost the adventure orientation it had once had. ''Ruth Fielding settles down to a quiet family life imbued with the strength of her conquests and discoveries in the wide world, and the desire for more such excitement,'' Billman asserts. ''And the result is unsettling, for both her and her readers, who had come to expect in a Fielding title the tale of an independent and glamorous supergirl.''

Ruth's dilemma lies in the fact that she is trying to be a working executive, a wife, and a mother all at once. ''In her youth Ruth had no . . . qualms [about her future life],'' states Billman, ''for she knew she would grow up to do exactly what she chose. But her later conflict as an adult woman demonstrated that even when enormous talent, strong character, and indomitable will are available, there was reason for girls to be unsure. 'Having it all'—interesting work, marriage, and children—didn't come easily.''

Mildred Augustine Wirt Benson wrote the last seven volumes of the ''Ruth Fielding'' series at Edward Stratemeyer's request. Stratemeyer writer W. Bert Foster also worked under the pseudonym on both Ruth Fielding and the Betty Gordon books, a series that capitalized on Ruth's popularity. For more information see the entries in this volume for Harriet S. Adams, Edward L. Stratemeyer, and Andrew E. Svenson.

BIOGRAPHICAL/CRITICAL SOURCES:

BOOKS

Billman, Carol, *The Secret of the Stratemeyer Syndicate: Nancy Drew, the Hardy Boys, and the Million Dollar Fiction Factory*, Ungar, 1986.

Dizer, John T., *Tom Swift & Company: "Boy's Books" by Stratemeyer and Others,* McFarland & Co., 1982.

Johnson, Deidre, editor and compiler, *Stratemeyer Pseudonyms and Series Books: An Annotated Checklist of Stratemeyer and Stratemeyer Syndicate Publications,* Greenwood Press, 1982.

Paluka, Frank, *Iowa Authors: A Bio-Bibliography of Sixty Native Writers,* Friends of the University of Iowa Libraries, 1967.

PERIODICALS

Books at Iowa, November, 1973.
New York Times Book Review, September 28, 1986.
Yellowback Library, July, 1983, September, 1986.

*　　　*　　　*

ENTHOVEN, Alain C(harles)　1930-

PERSONAL: Born September 10, 1930, in Seattle, Wash.; son of Richard Frederick and Jacqueline (Camerlynck) Enthoven; married Rosemary Fenech, July 28, 1956; children: Eleanor, Richard, Andrew, Martha, Nicholas, Daniel. *Education:* Stanford University, B.A., 1952; Oxford University, M.Phil., 1954; Massachusetts Institute of Technology, Ph.D., 1956.

ADDRESSES: Home—One McCormick Lane, Atherton, Calif. 94025. *Office*—Graduate School of Business, Stanford University, Stanford, Calif. 94305.

CAREER: Massachusetts Institute of Technology, Cambridge, instructor in economics, 1955-56; Rand Corporation, Santa Monica, Calif., economist, 1956-60; U.S. Department of Defense, Washington, D.C., operations research analyst in Office of the Director of Defense Research and Engineering, 1960, deputy comptroller and deputy assistant secretary of defense, 1961-65, assistant secretary of defense for systems analysis, 1965-69; Litton Industries, Beverly Hills, Calif., vice president for economic planning, 1969-71; Litton Medical Products, Beverly Hills, president, 1971-73; Stanford University, Stanford, Calif., Marriner S. Eccles Professor of Public and Private Management, and professor of health care economics, 1973—, member of computer science advisory committee, 1968-73. Director, Hotel Investors Trust, 1986-87, and PCS Inc., 1987. Member of board of directors, Georgetown University, 1968-73; member of board of regents, St. John's Hospital, Santa Monica, 1971-73; member of visiting committee in economics at Massachusetts Institute of Technology, 1971-78, visiting committee on environmental quality laboratory at California Institute of Technology, 1972-75, and of Harvard University School of Public Health, 1974-80. Visiting associate professor of economics at University of Washington, 1958; visiting professor, University of Paris, 1985; visiting fellow, St. Catherine's College, Oxford University, 1985. Consultant to Brookings Institution, 1956-60, Rand Corp., 1969—, and Kaiser Foundation Health Plan, Inc., 1973—.

MEMBER: American Economic Association, Institute of Medicine of the National Academy of Sciences, Council on Foreign Relations, American Association of Rhodes Scholars, Sierra Club, Phi Beta Kappa.

AWARDS, HONORS: President's Award for Distinguished Federal Civilian Service, 1963; Department of Defense Medal for Distinguished Public Service, 1969; L.H.D., Sierra Nevada College, 1987.

WRITINGS:

(Contributor) John G. Gurley and Edward S. Shaw, *Money in a Theory of Finance,* Brookings Institution, 1960.

(Contributor) C. J. Hitch and R. N. McKean, *The Economics Defense in the Nuclear Age,* Harvard University Press, 1960.

(With Robert S. McNamara and C. J. Hitch) *A Modern Design for Defense Decision: A McNamara-Hitch-Enthoven Anthology,* National War College, 1966.

(With K. Wayne Smith) *How Much Is Enough?: Shaping the Defense Program 1961-1969,* Harper, 1971.

Health Plan: The Only Practical Solution to the Soaring Cost of Medical Care, Addison-Wesley, 1980.

(Contributor) Cotton M. Lindsay, editor, *New Directions in Public Health Care: A Prescription for the 1980s,* 3rd edition, Transaction Books, 1980.

Financing Health Care in America, Touche Ross, 1984.

Theory and Practice of Managed Competition in Health Care Finance, North Holland, 1988.

Also author, with Myrick Freeman III, of *Pollution, Resources and the Environment,* 1973. Contributor to journals in his field.

*　　　*　　　*

ESSLIN, Martin (Julius)　1918-

PERSONAL: Born June 8, 1918, in Budapest, Hungary; came to Great Britain, 1939; naturalized British citizen, 1947; son of Paul (a journalist) and Charlotte (Schiffer) Pereszlenyi; married Renate Gerstenberg, 1947; children: one daughter. *Education:* Attended University of Vienna, 1936-38; received degree from Reinhardt Seminar of Dramatic Art, Vienna, 1938.

ADDRESSES: Home—66 Loudoun Rd., London NW 8, England; and Ballader's Plat, Winchelsea, Sussex, England. *Office*—Department of Drama, Stanford University, Stanford, Calif. 94305. *Agent*—Curtis Brown Ltd., 162-168 Regent St., London W1R 5TB, England.

CAREER: Director and writer on theatre, British Broadcasting Corp. (BBC), London, England, 1940-77, producer and scriptwriter for European services, 1941-55, became assistant head of European productions, 1955, became assistant head of drama (sound), 1961, head of drama (radio), 1963-77; Stanford University, Stanford, California, professor of drama, 1977—. Visiting professor of theatre at Florida State University, 1969-76.

MEMBER: Arts Council of Great Britain (member of drama panel), Garrick Club.

AWARDS, HONORS: Title of Professor by president of Austria, 1967; member of the Order of the British Empire, 1972; D.Litt., Kenyon College, 1978.

WRITINGS:

Brecht: A Choice of Evils; A Critical Study of the Man, His Work, and His Opinions, Eyre & Spottiswoode, 1959, published as *Brecht: The Man and His Work,* Doubleday, 1960, 4th revised edition, Methuen, 1984.

The Theatre of the Absurd, Doubleday, 1961, third revised edition, Penguin, 1983.

(Editor with others) *Sinn oder Unsinn? Das Groteske im Modernen Drama,* Basilius, 1962.

(Editor) *Samuel Beckett: A Collection of Critical Essays,* Prentice-Hall, 1965.

(Editor) *Absurd Drama,* Penguin (London), 1965.

Harold Pinter, Friedrich Verlag, 1967.

(Editor and author of introduction) *The Genius of the German Theater,* New American Library, 1968.

Bertolt Brecht, Columbia University Press, 1969.

Reflections: Essays on Modern Theatre, Doubleday, 1969 (published in England as *Brief Chronicles: Essays on Modern Theatre,* Maurice Temple Smith, 1970).

(Editor) *The New Theatre of Europe,* Volume IV, Dell, 1970.

The Peopled Wound: The Work of Harold Pinter, Doubleday, 1970, revised edition published as *Pinter: A Study of His Plays,* Methuen, 1973, 4th revised edition, 1982.

An Anatomy of Drama, T. Smith, 1976, Hill & Wang, 1977.

Artaud, J. Calder, 1976, Penguin, 1977.

(Editor and author of introduction) *The Encyclopedia of World Theater,* Scribner, 1977 (published in England as *The Illustrated Encyclopaedia of World Theatre,* Thames & Hudson, 1977).

Mediations: Essays on Brecht, Beckett, and the Media, Louisiana University Press, 1980.

The Age of Television, Stanford, 1981.

(Author of introduction) Jan Kott, *The Theater of Essence and Other Essays,* Northwestern University Press, 1984.

The Field of Drama, Methuen, 1987.

Contributor of reviews and essays on theatre to numerous periodicals. Advisory editor of *Drama Review;* drama editor of *Kenyon Review.*

SIDELIGHTS: Martin Esslin has been a prominent, and sometimes controversial, critic of contemporary theatre. Besides volumes on individual playwrights such as Bertolt Brecht, Antonin Artaud, and Harold Pinter, he has written and edited numerous other books on theatre, most notably, *The Theatre of the Absurd.*

Esslin's *The Theatre of the Absurd* is considered a major study of the school of avant-garde dramatists who emerged in the late 1950's and early 1960's. Such playwrights as Samuel Beckett, Jean Genet, and Eugene Ionesco had bewildered many critics and audiences who found no recognizable plot, theme, characterization, or any other "typical" elements of drama in their work. Instead, in Esslin's words, viewers saw an expression "of the senselessness of the human condition and the inadequacy of the rational approach by the open abandonment of rational devices and discursive thought." To better comprehend these works, then, a new set of judgments had to be used, those which Esslin sought to define and clarify in his book.

One of Esslin's major theses expressed in *The Theatre of the Absurd* held that these plays, often dismissed as "nonsense or mystification, *have* something to say and *can* be understood." Essentially, he said, the theatre of the absurd reflected the absurdity of human life not by argument or theory, but by actually presenting the experience; it strove for "an integration between the subject matter and the form." Esslin cited changing critical response to *Waiting for Godot* as evidence that audiences have come to look past their preconceived notions of what a play should be: While the 1955 premier of Beckett's play met with "a wide measure of incomprehension," its 1964 London revival was criticized for having "one great fault: its meaning and symbolism were a little too obvious."

Another playwright whose avant-garde style warrants Esslin's attention is Pinter. With such plays as *The Caretaker* and *The Birthday Party,* Pinter creates a stage where domination and self-doubt boil together into a hazy neo-reality. In Esslin's study *The Peopled Wound: The Work of Harold Pinter,* the author "has moved in on Pinter as remorselessly as one Pinter character moves in on another Pinter character," according to *New York Review of Books* critic Nigel Dennis. And while Dennis doesn't claim to agree with Esslin's assessments of Pinter's work, the reviewer notes that among Pinter scholars, Esslin is "the kindest and gentlest." *New York Times Book Review* writer Richard Gilman expresses similar mixed feelings, remarking that Esslin is a critic "whose usefulness lies less in original thinking or insightfulness than in lucid exposition, the kind of critic who possesses thoroughness in place of brilliance, breadth instead of depth." While citing Esslin's tendency to "encircle the [Pinter] plays with [descriptive] terminology and his narrow experience of them as sensuous, independent, unprogrammatic works," Gilman also finds that "at his best . . . Esslin is able to offer some helpful illustrations of how Pinter's dialogue achieves its effects and some minor illumination of the way he departs from traditional dramaturgy." And in a *Times Literary Supplement* critic's opinion, *The Peopled Wound* (published in a revised edition as *Pinter: A Study of His Plays*) "holds its place as the most straightforwardly useful account of Pinter's work to date."

With such works as *Brief Chronicles, Mediations: Essays on Brecht, Beckett, and the Media,* and *The Field of Drama,* Esslin draws the usual mixed critical reaction. All three books contain the author's thoughts on the direction of modern drama in its many manifestations. "In *Brief Chronicles* the best pieces are those in which [Esslin] focuses on a play, a playwright or a performance," says another *Times Literary Supplement* critic. "He provides, for example, a fine structural analysis of Ibsen's *Hedda Gabler.* Another excellent piece deals with three plays by Edward Bond: The remarks on *Early Morning* are a first-rate exposition of that mordant piece." And while London *Times* writer Peter Ackroyd acknowledges that some of Esslin's views are controversial, he says of *The Field of Drama:* "It is not necessary to agree with this book in order to be impressed by it. It is engagingly written, elegantly argued, and filled with those genuine perceptions which spring from what might be described as cross-cultural magnanimity."

AVOCATIONAL INTERESTS: Reading, book-collecting.

BIOGRAPHICAL/CRITICAL SOURCES:

BOOKS

Esslin, Martin, *The Theatre of the Absurd,* Doubleday, 1961, 3rd revised edition, Penguin, 1983.

PERIODICALS

Books and Bookmen, January, 1977, March, 1978.
Drama Review, winter, 1970, spring, 1974.
Economist, October 23, 1976.
New York Review of Books, December 17, 1970, June 3, 1971.
New York Times, December 14, 1984.
New York Times Book Review, January 23, 1966, September 13, 1970, July 17, 1977.
Times (London), July 2, 1987.
Times Literary Supplement, July 23, 1970, July 6, 1973, December 17, 1976, April 10, 1981.
World Literature Today, summer, 1978, winter, 1982.

*   *   *

ESTLEMAN, Loren D.   1952-

PERSONAL: Born September 15, 1952, in Ann Arbor, Mich.; son of Leauvett Charles (a truck driver) and Louise (a postal clerk; maiden name, Milankovich) Estleman; married Carole

Ann Ashley (a marketing and public relations specialist), September 5, 1987. *Education:* Eastern Michigan University, B.A., 1974.

ADDRESSES: Home—Whitmore Lake, Mich. *Agent*—Barbara Puechner, Ray Peekner Literary Agency, 3418 Shelton Ave., Bethlehem, Pa. 18017.

CAREER: Writer. *Michigan Fed*, Ann Arbor, Mich., cartoonist, 1967-70; *Ypsilanti Press*, Ypsilanti, Mich., reporter, 1973; *Community Foto-News*, Pinckney, Mich., editor in chief, 1975-76; *Ann Arbor News*, Ann Arbor, special writer, 1976-77; *Dexter Leader*, Dexter, Mich., staff writer, 1977-80. Has been an instructor for Friends of the Dexter Library, and a guest lecturer at colleges.

MEMBER: Western Writers of America, Private Eye Writers of America.

AWARDS, HONORS: American Book Award nomination, 1980, for *The High Rocks; Motor City Blue* named most notable book of 1980 by *New York Times Book Review;* Golden Spur Award for best western historical novel, Western Writers of America, 1982, for *Aces & Eights; The Midnight Man* was named most notable book of 1982 by *New York Times Book Review;* Shamus Award nomination for best private eye novel, Private Eye Writers of America, 1984, for *The Glass Highway;* Pulitzer Prize in Letters nomination, 1984, for *This Old Bill;* Shamus Awards, Private Eye Writers of America, for *Sugartown,* and for short story "Eight Mile and Dequindre," both 1985; Golden Spur Award for best western short story, Western Writers of America, 1986, for "The Bandit"; Michigan Arts Foundation Award for Literature, 1986.

WRITINGS:

The Oklahoma Punk (crime novel), Major Books (Canoga Park, Calif.), 1976.
Sherlock Holmes vs. Dracula; or, The Adventure of the Sanguinary Count (mystery-horror novel), Doubleday, 1978.
Dr. Jekyll and Mr. Holmes (mystery-horror novel), Doubleday, 1979.
The Wister Trace: Classic Novels of the American Frontier (criticism), Jameson Books, 1987.
Red Highway (novel), PaperJacks, 1988.
Peeper (mystery novel), Bantam, 1989.

"AMOS WALKER" MYSTERY SERIES

Motor City Blue, Houghton, 1980.
Angel Eyes, Houghton, 1981.
The Midnight Man, Houghton, 1982.
The Glass Highway, Houghton, 1983.
Sugartown, Houghton, 1984.
Every Brilliant Eye, Houghton, 1986.
Lady Yesterday, Houghton, 1987.
Downriver, Houghton, 1988.
General Murders (short story collection), Houghton, 1988.
Silent Thunder, Houghton, 1989.

"PETER MACKLIN" MYSTERY SERIES

Kill Zone, Mysterious Press, 1984.
Roses Are Dead, Mysterious Press, 1985.
Any Man's Death, Mysterious Press, 1986.

WESTERN NOVELS

The Hider, Doubleday, 1978.
Aces & Eights (first book in historical western trilogy), Doubleday, 1981.

The Wolfer, Pocket Books, 1981.
Mister St. John, Doubleday, 1983.
This Old Bill (second book in historical western trilogy), Doubleday, 1984.
Gun Man, Doubleday, 1985.
Bloody Season, Bantam, 1988.
Western Story, Doubleday, 1989.

"PAGE MURDOCK" WESTERN SERIES

The High Rocks, Doubleday, 1979.
Stamping Ground, Doubleday, 1980.
Murdock's Law, Doubleday, 1982.
The Stranglers, Doubleday, 1984.

OTHER

(Contributor) Robert J. Randisi, editor, *The Eyes Have It: The First Private Eye Writers of America Anthology*, Mysterious Press, 1984.
(Contributor) Edward D. Hoch, editor, *The Year's Best Mystery and Suspense Stories, 1986*, Walker & Co., 1986.

Contributor to periodicals, including *Alfred Hitchcock's Mystery Magazine, Baker Street Journal, Fiction Writers Magazine, A Matter of Crime, Mystery, New Black Mask, Pulpsmith, Roundup, Saint Magazine, TV Guide, Writer,* and *Writer's Digest.*

WORK IN PROGRESS: A novel about George Armstrong Custer to complete the historical western trilogy; historical trilogy of city of Detroit from Prohibition to the present.

SIDELIGHTS: Loren D. Estleman, the prolific author of what James Kindall describes in *Detroit* as "hard-bitten mysteries, a herd of reality-edged westerns and an occasional fantasy or two," is perhaps best known for his series of hard-boiled mysteries that unravel in an authentically evoked Detroit. "A country boy who has always lived outside of Detroit, he writes with convincing realism about inner city environments," states Kindall, adding that "probably no other area pensmith can lay as convincing a claim to the title of Detroit's private eye writer as Estleman." Had it not been for the success of fellow Detroiter and mystery writer Elmore Leonard, pronounces William A. Henry in *Time,* "Estleman would doubtless be known as the poet of Motor City."

Trained as a journalist, Estleman researches his work thoroughly and draws deeply from his experience as a reporter who covered the police beat of a small-town newspaper: He "killed a lot of time . . . just listening to cops," notes Beauford Cranford in a *Detroit News* interview with the author; and according to Kindall, he "sometimes rode with police and held shotgun during arrests." Kindall proposes that Estleman's "affection for the street life which permeates his detective books" can be attributed partially to the stories he heard as a child from his family: "His mother nearly married a member of Detroit's Purple Gang and his father told tales of his rowdy but harmless past. Only after talking to his Austrian-born grandmother, a professional cook who took hotel jobs across the country, in later years did he find out her roving was because of an insatiable thirst for gambling, he says. And one of her casino acquaintances was Al Capone."

For Estleman, writing is an avowed compulsion: "Can't not write," he admits to Kindall. Devoting six hours a day, seven days a week to his craft, he tries to produce five pages of manuscript daily. "Clarity distinguishes Estleman's writing," declares Bob McKelvey in the *Detroit Free Press.* "Just what you'd expect from a guy who sneers at murky, avant-garde authors who go in for what Estleman calls 'ropy subjunctives and diarrhetic stream-of-consciousness.'" Estleman concurs with *CA* interviewer Jean W. Ross that his style, which he characterizes in *Twentieth-Century Western Writers* as "highly visual," has been influenced by television and motion pictures. Critics commend the clarity, good dialogue, and cinematic framing that hallmark Estleman's writing and frequently compare him to his predecessors in the genre, Dashiell Hammett and Raymond Chandler. However, Estleman is "a genre writer with ambitious intent," discerns Cranford, to whom Estleman explains: "I'm trying to delve into crime as a metaphor for society. One of the reasons crime novels are so popular now is that crime isn't something that always happens to the other guy any more. Everybody has been touched by crime, and you can't turn on the television without hearing about it. So more and more, crime and law and cops and robbers tend to become a metaphor for the way we live. Crime is probably our basic conflict."

Estleman has crafted an increasingly popular series of mysteries around the character of Amos Walker, a witty and rugged Detroit private investigator who recalls Chandler's Philip Marlowe and Hammett's Sam Spade. Considered "one of the best the hard-boiled field has to offer" by Kathleen Maio in *Wilson Library Bulletin*, "Walker is the very model of a Hammett-Chandler descendant," observes the *New York Times Book Review*'s Newgate Callendar. "He is a big man, very macho, who talks tough and is tough. He hates hypocrisy, phonies and crooks. He pretends to cynicism but is a teddy bear underneath it all. He is lonely, though women swarm all over him." Conceding to Ross that the character represents his "alter ego," Estleman once refused a six-figure offer from a major film company for exclusive rights to Walker, explaining to Kindall: "Twenty years from now, the money would be spent and I'd be watching the umpteenth movie with Chevy Chase or Kurt Russell playing Amos with the setting in Vegas or L.A. and blow my brains out."

Amos Walker "deals with sleaze from top to bottom—Motor City dregs, cop killers and drug dealers," remarks Andrew Postman in *Publishers Weekly,* and reviewers admire the storytelling skills of his creator. Walker made his debut searching the pornographic underworld of Detroit for the female ward of an aging ex-gangster in *Motor City Blue,* a novel that Kristiana Gregory appraises in the *Los Angeles Times Book Review* as "a dark gem of a mystery." About *Angel Eyes,* in which a dancer who anticipates her own disappearance hires Walker to search for her, the *New Republic*'s Robin W. Winks believes that "Estleman handles the English language with real imagination . . . so that one keeps reading for the sheer joy of seeing the phrases fall into place." In *Midnight Man,* which Callendar describes as "tough, side-of-the-mouth stuff, well written, positively guaranteed to keep you awake," Walker encounters a contemporary bounty hunter in his pursuit of three cop killers; and writing about *The Glass Highway,* in which Walker is hired to locate the missing son of a television anchor and must contend with a rampaging professional killer, Callendar believes that Estleman "remains among the top echelon of American private-eye specialists."

Although critics generally enjoy Estleman's narrative skill, plots, dialogue, and well-drawn characters, they are especially fond of his realistic portraits of the Motor City. Estleman and his private-eye character "share a unique view" of the city of Detroit, observes Kindall: "The things I like about Detroit are everything the mayor hates," states Estleman. "I love the warehouse district, for instance; that's Detroit to me . . . I like

the character of a city that grew up without anybody's help." According to Jean M. White in a *Washington Post Book World* review of *Angel Eyes:* "Estleman knows the seamy underworld of Detroit's mean streets. He has a nice touch for its characters and language. His knife-sharp prose matches the hurtling pace of the action." Bill Ott suggests in *Booklist* that "Detroit becomes more than merely a setting" in Estleman's Shamus Award-winning *Sugartown,* in which an elderly Polish immigrant hires Walker to find her grandson who has been missing for nineteen years: "As the city's neighborhoods fall prey to the wrecker's ball, the dreams and even the very histories of its residents become part of the rubble." Maio believes that "Estleman writes so well of the threadworn respectability of working people stranded on the edge of an urban wasteland. His vivid and merciless descriptions of the revitalized Detroit root his complex story in reality."

As "one of the major current practitioners of the tough-guy private-eye novel," proclaims Callendar, Estleman is "at his best" in *Downriver,* a novel in which Walker investigates the claim of an intimidating black ex-convict that he was framed for the murder that sent him to prison for twenty years. "The dialogue is crackling, the writing is unpadded," Callendar continues, "and one can smell and even taste the city of Detroit." In a Chicago *Tribune Books* review of the novel, Kevin Moore considers Estleman a "polished craftsman," commending especially his "sharp, cleanly defined writing." Reviewing *Every Brilliant Eye,* in which Walker searches for a vanished friend, Callendar thinks that there exists "a kind of poetry in his snapshots of the underside of a city with which he so clearly has a love-hate relationship." Despite praise for the novel itself, Marcel Berlins adds in the London *Times* that he nonetheless wishes "Walker would move elsewhere." Resolved, according to Kindall, to continue the series until "it begins to be [like] pulling boxcars to write another one," Estleman intends to keep Walker in Detroit, remarking to Cranford: "If L.A. was where the American dream went wrong, then Detroit is where it bellied up dead. But there's still a nobility to Detroit, a certain kind of grittiness among people who can live here from day to day that may not be so true for L.A."

Although some reviewers fault Estleman's tough-guy fiction for occasional cliched conventionality, most find his Walker novels especially well-written and riveting. Henry, for instance, faults Estleman for generally resolving his plots "unsatisfyingly" through withheld information, but nevertheless believes that Estleman's "ear for diverse patois seems impeccable, and so does the inner mechanism that tells him when an unlikely escape can be plausible." Estleman's vibrant renderings of Detroit's jazz world also elicit a favorable critical response. For example, in a *Washington Post Book World* review of *Lady Yesterday,* in which Walker helps an ex-prostitute hunt for her missing father, Alan Ryan praises the novel's "great narrative and dialogue," adding: "All of this is good. I'm caught up in the story, but best of all is the way Estleman writes about jazz, the sound of it, the smoky clubs it lives in and the musicians who play it. . . . Well done. I like Estleman." And although Kindall regards Estleman as "one of those rare people who can write about deadly things in poetic terms," he perceives that a few critics have difficulty determining "who's zoomin' who," especially since Walker himself seems to border on parody rather than a realistic portrayal. "There are some critics out there who don't know what I'm doing," Estleman responds. "Some don't know if I'm parodying the form, if I'm being serious or what. The only answer to that is I'm doing both.''

In another series of mysteries, Estleman slants the perspective to that of a criminal, Peter Macklin, who also free-lances out of Detroit. ''Macklin is the result of my wanting to do an in-depth study of a professional killer,'' Estleman tells Mc-Kelvey. ''It presents a challenge to keep a character sympathetic who never has anything we would call morals.'' Kindall suggests that ''although a killer, he always seems to end up facing opponents even lower on the evolutionary scale, which shades him into the quasi-hero side.'' However, in a review of *Kill Zone*, the first novel in the Macklin series, Callendar feels that ''not even Mr. Estleman's considerable skill can hide the falsity of his thesis'' that even hired killers can be admirable characters. The plot of the novel concerns the seizure of a Detroit riverboat by terrorists who hold hundreds of passengers hostage, attracting other professional killers from organized crime and a governmental agency as well—a plot that a *Publishers Weekly* contributor finds ''confusing and glutted with a plethora of minor characters who detract from the story's credibility.'' And although Peter L. Robertson detects an implausibility of plot in the second of the series' novels, *Roses Are Dead*, in which Macklin tries to determine who and why someone has contracted to kill him, he says in *Booklist* that the novel is ''a guaranteed page-turner that features an intoxicating rush of brutal events and a fascinating anti-hero in Macklin.'' Describing the action of *Any Man's Death*, in which Macklin is hired to guard the life of a television evangelist and is caught in the struggle between rival mob families for control of a proposed casino gambling industry in Detroit, Wes Lukowsky suggests in *Booklist* that Estleman ''has created a surprisingly credible and evolving protagonist.'' And as a *Time* contributor remarks: ''For urban edge and macho color . . . nobody tops Loren D. Estleman.''

Estleman explains to Kindall that the hard-boiled mystery genre is particularly popular in this country because ''America has always tended to revere the revolutionary types . . . who are not allied with any official organization . . . someone who lives pretty much according to his own rules.'' Estleman's work enjoys popularity in several other countries as well, though, including West Germany, Holland, Great Britain, Spain, and Japan, where his Detroit-based mysteries are enthusiastically received, notes Kindall. ''Genre fiction is just American literature,'' Estleman tells Cranford, adding that ''mysteries and westerns are our contribution to world literature.'' He further suggests to Ross that ''private-eye fiction is the modern counterpart of the western story'' because its solitary hero, when confronted with dreadful odds, must depend solely on his own ''wits and personal sense of integrity.'' Estleman alternates between writing mysteries and westerns to keep the ideas fresh, he tells Ross, dubbing it ''literary crop rotation.''

The Hider, a novel about the last buffalo hunt in America, was Estleman's first western novel and was purchased immediately—a rarity in the genre. He has since written several other successful western novels plus a critical analysis of western fiction itself, *The Wister Trace: Classic Novels of the American Frontier*; and several of his books about the American West have earned critical distinction. *The High Rocks*, for instance, which is set in the mountains of Montana and relates the story of a man's battle with the Indians who murdered his parents, was nominated for an American Book Award. And the first two books of his proposed historical western trilogy have also earned honors: *Aces & Eights*, about the murder of Wild Bill Hickok, was awarded the Golden Spur;

and *This Old Bill*, a fable based on the life of William Frederick ''Buffalo Bill'' Cody, was nominated for a Pulitzer Prize.

In the *Los Angeles Times Book Review*, David Dary discusses Estleman's *Bloody Season*, an extensively researched historical novel about the gunfight at the O.K. Corral: ''The author's search for objectivity and truth, combined with his skill as a fine writer, have created a new vision of what happened in Tombstone. . . , and he avoids the hackneyed style that clutters the pages of too many Westerns.'' Dary concludes that although it is a fictional account, the novel ''probably comes closer to the truth'' than anything else published on the subject. In *Twentieth-Century Western Writers*, Bill Crider observes: ''All of Estleman's books appear solidly researched, and each ends in a way which ties all the story threads together in an effective pseudo-historical manner, giving each an air of reality and credibility.''

Estleman once wrote *CA*: ''The three writers whose works have had the most profound influence on my writing are all dead, which should prove some indication of my opinion of most writers who have since arisen. Edgar Allan Poe, Jack London, and Raymond Chandler have impressed me since childhood with their lyrical, poetical approach to action and adventure. The literature of violence is purely an American development and only the English language, that most elusive, infinitely fascinating of tongues, fulfills all the requirements for its proper expression. The icy deliberation of the murderer in Poe's 'A Cask of Amontillado,' the tortured psyche of the brutal Wolf Larsen in London's *The Sea Wolf*, and the parade of grotesques that march through all of Chandler's best works are products of the American experience beside which the elements of the great fiction of Europe seem tame as a houseplant. That there is a prejudice in literary circles against these three masters is evidence of how far we still have to go to cast off the shackles forged by those potentially great writers who accepted the restrictions of Victorian society during literature's so-called Golden Age. Shakespeare was aware of the importance of violence in human nature, as were Homer and Dostoevski, but today's civilization prefers to forget that it even exists.

''All of this may sound strange coming from the author of *Sherlock Holmes vs. Dracula*. Indeed, one or two reviewers commented upon a rather bloody scene in that book and said that Conan Doyle would have been repelled by it. If they'd taken the trouble to read one or two of the original Holmes adventures, they'd have recognized his debt to Poe and his own 'morbid' fascination with brutality and the grotesque.

''I've never killed anyone off the written page. I am, however, a hunter, and I doubt that I'm being original in saying that people and animals die similarly. I'm a good boxer, a fair wrestler, and with a name like Loren I saw my share of schoolyard fights. Although I hardly appreciated it then, those tussles have come in handy every time I've sat down to write a fight scene. Since we have no memory of pain, though, I've occasionally had to remind myself of certain sensations, which has entailed slugging myself in the jaw while seated at the typewriter. Writing was never more painful than this.''

MEDIA ADAPTATIONS: The Amos Walker mysteries *Motor City Blue*, *Angel Eyes*, *The Midnight Man*, *Sugartown*, *The Glass Highway*, and *Every Brilliant Eye* were recorded on audio cassettes in unabridged readings by David Regal for Brilliance Corp. (Grand Haven, Mich.) in 1988. *Sherlock Holmes vs. Dracula* was broadcast by the British Broadcasting

Corporation. One of Estleman's western novels has been optioned by a California film company.

CA INTERVIEW

CA interviewed Loren D. Estleman by telephone on December 18, 1987, at his home in Whitmore Lake, Michigan.

CA: You've built up a considerable reputation with your Amos Walker private eye books, the Peter Macklin series, and a number of westerns that include the Golden Spur Award-winning Aces & Eights. *Let's talk about Amos Walker first. How did he incubate in your mind, and how long, before you actually began to write about him?*

ESTLEMAN: I'd say he'd been incubating all my life. He began to take concrete form and a name a couple of years before I sat down to write *Motor City Blue.* I had come up with the name Walker, which seemed perfect for me: it's common, it's ordinary, it has that Everymannish quality. Also it has a good lonely, single, pedestrian sound to it. But I didn't have a Christian name for him. Then I was writing a western, *The High Rocks,* and thought I would try out the name Walker on a character there. It took place in the Old West, so I thought I'd give him an Old Testament first name, which was common back then. I came up with the name Amos Walker, and I realized that was the name I wanted. It was too good to waste on a minor character in a western, so I named him something else and saved Amos Walker for my detective. He really had been incubating all my life. I think he's still incubating. I still don't know everything about him.

CA: That must be what keeps him fresh.

ESTLEMAN: For me it does.

CA: Is Walker in some ways your alter ego?

ESTLEMAN: Definitely. In many ways he's what I would like to be, and I often say that what we are and what we would like to be say the same things about us, though they're not the same thing, obviously. I always like to paraphrase what Ross Macdonald said about Lew Archer: Amos Walker is me, but I am not Amos Walker.

CA: Walker's home territory is Detroit, which you described to Twentieth-Century Crime and Mystery Writers *as "the place where the American Dream stalled and sat rusting in the rain," and which you can, in a few words, evoke for the reader with almost photographic realism. Do Walker's feelings about Detroit pretty much reflect your own?*

ESTLEMAN: Yeah. I decided early on that, if I had Walker have different opinions from mine, I would constantly be having to go back and check the earlier books to find out if he likes this or doesn't like that. So we feel the same. He's my conduit, the way I have of expressing my emotions about life in general, the world, people, and especially Detroit.

CA: In the Detroit Free Press's Detroit *magazine for an article James Kindall wrote about you, photographer George Waldman pictured you in a Detroit alley. Do you roam about the city a lot, either on foot or in a car, for the settings of your stories?*

ESTLEMAN: I do a lot of that—however, always in broad daylight. I'm no hero. I leave the midnight meetings in Mt. Elliott to Walker.

CA: Before you left newspaper work to write full-time, you were, among other things, a police-beat writer. How much of a help has that work been to you in writing your fiction?

ESTLEMAN: It's been a lot of help. Working that closely with the different police officers, I got to be pretty close to a lot of them. And they told wonderful stories, some of which have worked their way into my fiction, things that I knew I couldn't use in the news stories I was writing at the time if I wanted to maintain the good working relationship we had. Also the special language they speak, the cadence of their speech, and the world view that every police officer I've ever known shares—these have all gone into the books.

CA: In Kill Zone *you introduced as a protagonist the professional hit man Peter Macklin, and within pages managed to establish him as a truly sympathetic figure. Did you take him on as a deliberate challenge?*

ESTLEMAN: Yes, definitely as a challenge. I could never believe the old schoolboy saw that a lot of the critics still cling to, that your main character must be sympathetic to be interesting. I always believed he need merely be interesting, and Macklin is certainly that. I think in the beginning I had some idea of setting out to make him as nonsympathetic as possible, but it didn't work out that way because he kept getting human on me as I got along. I think it's something I knew going into the series that professional killers are human and many of them face a lot of the same problems we all face; the main difference is that they kill for a living. That probably means that they lack something that the rest of us have—I don't know if it's conscience or what, maybe just that last little bit of mercy that the rest of us have and they don't. Aside from that, he's just like you and me. I wondered starting out if I could sustain that interest for the length of a book, and eventually for the length of a series. I think I have.

CA: Does a plot for the next mystery often occur while you're doing the current one?

ESTLEMAN: Very often I'll get ideas. I'll jot them down or stick them away someplace in my head and let them germinate for a while. At any given time I have far more ideas and plots in my mind than I could ever do anything with.

CA: Do you plot the books out carefully in advance, or do you just know what's going to happen?

ESTLEMAN: Actually, *no* to both of those things. I do not plot them out in detail before I begin writing, and I seldom know how a book's going to end. Very often I don't even know what direction it's going to take. A novel is an organic thing that can just grow. I will get hold of one little scene or something that catches my fancy, something that I want to do something with, and I begin writing. I may have some other little things sketched about here and there, some ideas of the general direction or things I want to incorporate. The writing itself is a matter of getting from one of those things to the other, sometimes by a pretty circuitous route, and seldom a predictable one.

CA: That must make it fun.

ESTLEMAN: It really is fun, and I figure that if I don't know what's going to happen from one page to the next, neither will my readers. And I have surprised myself. I have had characters die on me whom I liked and hadn't expected to die. I've had someone I didn't think would be the murderer turn out to be the murderer. I've had people who I thought were going to be sympathetic characters turn out to be villains, and vice versa. It's always a learning process.

CA: There's a lot of history and biography in your westerns— Aces & Eights, *for example, being about Wild Bill Hickok and* This Old Bill, *which was nominated for a Pulitzer, telling the life of Buffalo Bill Cody. Has the research for the westerns taken you far from Detroit?*

ESTLEMAN: Yes, it has. The westerns take place just about everywhere, the Northwest, the Southwest, some of them in the Midwest, which we don't consider the West now but it was at that time. I had published five westerns and won my first Golden Spur before I ever went west of Kalamazoo. That meant I had to do a lot more research than the average person who got out there more often. Since then I have made many trips out there and learned things I wouldn't have known otherwise. There's a great deal of reading, of course. But going to a place you're going to be writing about, talking to people who have lived there for a length of time, and getting some feeling of living there yourself is very important.

CA: Do you find—if it's possible to know—that you have two separate readerships for the mysteries and the westerns, or is there a large crossover?

ESTLEMAN: It's pretty much separate. There is some crossover; I think there's more now than there used to be. I will have people come up to me at mystery conventions and other mystery events to tell me how much they like my westerns. They say they've never read westerns before, but because they like my mysteries, they wanted to try them out. I'm getting some crossover in that way. But I've always had a pretty strong cult following in the two separate areas.

CA: Does alternating between the two genres serve to keep each one fresh for you as a writer?

ESTLEMAN: Yes, it always has. I've always called it literary crop rotation. It does keep me from getting burned out. The two genres are just different enough that each one is a vacation from the other.

CA: Do you just need a rest from Amos Walker sometimes?

ESTLEMAN: It's not so much that I need a rest as that I make myself take a rest from him because I don't want to get tired of him. Beginning a new Walker is always an exciting experience for me, and I would hate to see that feeling go away. I would never want to write a Walker just to write a Walker. I want it always to be just the way it is now, so that every time I start a new one, it's like seeing an old friend.

CA: You draw a connection between your genres rather than making a sharp distinction between them as publishers, reviewers, and librarians do.

ESTLEMAN: Yes. Certainly private eye fiction is the modern counterpart of the western story. You can draw a straight line from the dime novels of Ned Buntline and Prentiss Ingraham

right on through the more modern detective novels of Raymond Chandler, Dashiell Hammett, Ross Macdonald, John D. MacDonald, and Robert Parker. They have very concrete links. For one thing, Street & Smith Publications, who put out the Buffalo Bill novels in the last century, which were very popular, in turn brought out the *Black Mask* and many other popular magazines in this century. Also, we're dealing in both genres with a purely American type of hero, the revolutionary type. We're a country that was born in revolution and we've always tended to revere the loner, the man with no organization to fall back on, who is up against tremendous odds and has no weapons but his wits and his personal sense of integrity. This is almost purely an American concept, and it's found in both the gunfighter hero and the private detective. There's very little difference between Shane and Philip Marlowe.

CA: Crime stories and mysteries are enjoying tremendous popularity now in this country, both in book form and as television series. Judging from the reception of your foreign editions, does that seem to be true abroad also?

ESTLEMAN: It does seem to be. There are some places where it's more true than others. The French, although they don't have all that much regard for Americans, do tend to like things American particularly well; they like our rock 'n' roll, they like our jazz, they like our western stories, they like our detective stories. The whole *noir* movement—*film noir, serie noir,* detective stories, even the name *noir* was bestowed upon them by the French. They tend to recognize things in our literature and culture before we do ourselves. And that's been true of the Germans too. They're very big on our detective stories and espionage. Probably because they're living at the back door of Russia and they live with that kind of thing every day, they like to read about it as entertainment in which the good guy can win.

It seems to be true too with the Japanese. The books are pretty popular in Japan. It's always hard to predict or to understand or to analyze a culture that is as alien to the Occidental culture as the Oriental is. It's hard to say what their reasons are, but they do tend to like this kind of thing that's American. The books are starting to get into Spain now, and that kind of surprises me because the Spanish were never particularly interested in this sort of thing. England seems to be very big on the American hard-boiled form; they seem to be getting away from the old Agatha Christie mode. Some of the English writers who are working in what I call the American school are now extremely good. Dick Francis could teach a lot of Americans things about their own medium. And there are a lot of other good English writers coming up.

CA: You've named Raymond Chandler, Edgar Allan Poe, and Jack London as your major literary influences. Do you thing movies and television have played a shaping part in your style of writing?

ESTLEMAN: Oh yes. "The Untouchables" changed my life when I was a kid. That show fascinated me. It showed me how violence could be a medium not only of entertainment, but a powerful message. I've always thought that my life directed itself from that point. Definitely I'm a big fan of the *film noir* movement, which, again, made use of American detective stories. Those things have influenced the way I will very often frame a scene in almost cinematographic terms— more so, I think, in something like the Macklins, which are told from a semi-omniscient point of view. The movement can be very camera-like, and I use that device without any thought of it. I've seem other writers do it too; I'm sure they don't even know they're doing it, but it comes from movies.

CA: I think most all of us were so influenced by movies that we think in movie terms a lot of the time and sometimes maybe even live as if we were in a movie.

ESTLEMAN: I think one of the big reasons the Gothic movement was so big a few years ago was that so many people of my generation used to come home in the afternoons to watch "Dark Shadows." I think the whole Star Wars movement came out of "Star Trek." That generation—the baby-boomers or whatever—has started to see a lot of these things we saw before in different forms, with a new twist added to them.

CA: You told James Kindall for the Detroit *piece that you try to do five pages a day. Does that include the short stories as well as the novels?*

ESTLEMAN: The short stories are different. They're a very intensive form. I'm happy if I can do two pages of a story a day, and that can take all day long. A lot more happens, of course, within two pages of a short story than happens in the same space in a novel. You have to nail down characters in a few lines; you have to know where your story is going from the beginning. Every line has a significance. That isn't always so true with a novel. In a novel, you can have a little more fun, wander around a bit and flesh it out with some other things. With a short story, it has to be pretty intensive or it doesn't work.

CA: Do you usually do stories between novels?

ESTLEMAN: Yes, very often. Sometimes, on rare occasions, I will chip away at a story while I'm doing a novel. I might work on the novel during the day and do a page or two of a short story at night. But that's pretty rare. Usually I put all my energy into the project of the moment.

CA: Your dialogue is one of the things I especially like in your writing. It reads as if you toss it off quite easily. Is that a deception?

ESTLEMAN: It is and it isn't. Certainly when the flow gets going, it's one of the easiest kinds of writing there is. When you have two characters talking to each other, one line will trigger the next line and so on. You can really pile up the pages that way, more than, say, with description. But it can also be very difficult because what I'm actually writing is an illusion of the way people really talk, with a little tiny bit of repetition and a certain use of slang—timeless slang, I hope, so it will read as well ten years down the road as it does today. And I try to use what will sound like my characters' kind of jargon. If I don't know the jargon, I make it up. I think most of the time I come pretty close.

But it can be hard. Every now and then I get stalled. Walker sometimes drives me crazy because he's telling the story, and I want to keep it sort of conversational so that it doesn't sound too formal. At the same time, I don't want anybody to think that I don't know the rules of grammar. I'm always getting in fights over things like the word *whom*. To Walker, that's a dead word. The only time I get violently angry with copyeditors is when they screw around with my dialogue. I know when I've broken the rules, but it's because they got in my

way. I sometimes have to prove to the copyeditors that I really do know grammar, and in some cases I know it a lot better than they do.

CA: In an interview for the New Black Mask *you said, "I've had a series of very good editors along the way who have well understood what it is I'm trying to do and have known how much to take part and when to back off and defer to me." Would you talk more about who has been especially helpful to you in your writing, and how?*

ESTLEMAN: I think the editor I may have learned the most from, at least about the whole publishing process, is the lady who edited my first novel, *The Oklahoma Punk*, over at Major Books, which no longer exists. Her name is Yvonne Mac-Manus. She's a wonderful lady, and a very aggressive lady who generally taught me a lot by editing my book the way she thought it would work best. Ruth Hapgood, my editor at Houghton Mifflin, has been an angel from the start. She has gone to bat for me many times. At a point early on when it looked like the sales department weren't happy with the sales and might drop the series, she got them to pick it up again. And we've just been very artistically compatible right down the line. And she's pointed out some things from time to time that I wouldn't have noticed myself, being as close to the book as I was.

I've had a lot of very good copyeditors along the way, and that's the hardest job in the world. A lady especially whom I've had a lot of fights with, but because of whom I think each book was at least ten percent better, had to be Georgia Remer over at Doubleday. A very tough, very thorough lady. When a manuscript came back from her, it would be packed full of these little yellow tabs on which she wrote her comments. She double-checked or triple-checked everything. Once, for *Sherlock Holmes vs. Dracula,* she had me go back and change their whole train schedule from London to Whitby because she bothered to find out when the trains ran between those two places in 1890. Not many copyeditors would go to that length.

Pat Lo Brutto, over at Doubleday with my westerns, has been a very close friend and an artistic angel straight through. I always liked working with Pat. It's nice to work with an editor who's enthusiastic about your work and wants to contribute something. Louisa Rudeen over at Fawcett, who does the Amos Walker paperbacks, is terrific, probably the oldest twenty-eight-year-old editor I'll ever know. And there's Greg Tobin too, over at Bantam. I've had a lot of good editors. A few clinkers, but not as many as some other writers I know. I've been pretty lucky.

CA: You're said to have quite a book collection. What are your main interests as a collector?

ESTLEMAN: Everything, absolutely everything. I set out very early on—a foolish, foolish notion, but I'm still pursuing it— to gather all of human knowledge in one room so I'll never have to step out to get anything. Judging by the volume of stuff up there, I must be pretty close to that. Every now and then I come across something that I don't have handy information on, so I have to go out and get it, but that happens less and less as I go along. As far as the things that I love to read and collect, naturally, of course, they include great mysteries, or even bad mysteries, which I also have fun with. I have a lot of mysteries from both the English and the American schools and other strange schools that nobody knows anything about. A lot of Sherlock Holmes, because I'm a Sherlockian from way back. I'm big on the occult, especially vampires and vampirism and Dracula and all the pretenders. I have a military library I've been working on for a long time; I have the wars of history going back to the beginning. A lot of fine general fiction, good literature from all countries. My three favorites are American and English and Russian literature. I'm still learning about Tolstoy and Dostoevski. Just about anything you can think of you'll find up there, but these are a few of my pets.

CA: What's ahead that you'd like to talk about?

ESTLEMAN: I am at this point putting together a proposal for a trilogy about Detroit that I would really like to do, all centered around a crime theme and dealing with the city in three different portions of its history: Prohibition, the mid-1960s, and today. I haven't even approached a publisher with it yet, but it's something I'm excited about, that I would like to do and I would spend some time with. Continuing with Amos Walker, I have many more ideas for him and some new directions I want to go in. He'll always stay in Detroit, of course, but personally speaking, I want him to spread his wings a little bit more. I want to go deeper into his background and what he is as a person, never forgetting the mysteries along the way. I want to continue with the westerns. Now that Bantam is doing *Bloody Season* in hardcover, I'd like to pursue that and get my westerns into the mainstream. It would be nice to have people reading my westerns who weren't previously western fans. And I also want to tackle some larger things, some things that don't necessarily have to do with crime but would touch on things that I've learned and want to learn along the way.

BIOGRAPHICAL/CRITICAL SOURCES:

BOOKS

Contemporary Literary Criticism, Volume 48, Gale, 1988.
Twentieth-Century Crime and Mystery Writers, 2nd edition, St. Martin's, 1985.
Twentieth-Century Western Writers, Gale, 1982.

PERIODICALS

Ann Arbor News, September 24, 1978.
Ann Arbor Observer, July, 1978.
Booklist, November 15, 1984, September 1, 1985, October 15, 1986.
Chicago Tribune Book World, January 18, 1981, August 10, 1986.
Detroit, March 8, 1987.
Detroit Free Press, September 26, 1984.
Detroit News, May 18, 1979, August 21, 1983.
Eastern Echo, September 8, 1978.
Los Angeles Times Book Review, August 21, 1983, January 19, 1986, January 24, 1988.
New Black Mask, Number 4, 1986.
New Republic, November 25, 1981.
New York Times Book Review, November 11, 1979, October 26, 1980, November 1, 1981, August 22, 1982, August 14, 1983, October 23, 1983, December 2, 1984, December 23, 1984, March 24, 1985, November 24, 1985, April 20, 1986, October 26, 1986, March 6, 1988.
Publishers Weekly, August 23, 1985, January 22, 1988.
Time, July 31, 1978, December 22, 1986, August 17, 1987, February 1, 1988.
Times (London), November 20, 1986, November 29, 1986, December 31, 1987.

Times Literary Supplement, March 14, 1986, April 10, 1987.
Tribune Books (Chicago), January 31, 1988.
Village Voice, February 24, 1987.
Washington Post Book World, October 18, 1981, May 17, 1987.
Wilson Library Bulletin, March, 1985.

—Sketch by Sharon Malinowski
—Interview by Jean W. Ross

*   *   *

ETEROVICH, Adam S(lav) 1930-

PERSONAL: Born November 27, 1930, in San Francisco, Calif.; son of Ivan and Ana (Cvitanich) Eterovich; married Danica Kralj, April 15, 1957; children: Karen. *Education:* San Francisco State College (now University), B.A., 1955; graduate study at University of Zagreb, 1956-57. *Politics:* Democrat. *Religion:* Roman Catholic.

ADDRESSES: Home—1372 Rosewood Ave., San Carlos, Calif. 94070. *Office*—936 Industrial Ave., Palo Alto, Calif. 94303.

CAREER: Home Insurance Co., San Francisco, Calif., insurance underwriting manager, 1958-69; publisher-owner, Century Twenty-one Publishing, 1968—; Ragusan Press, Palo Alto, Calif., publisher-owner, 1976—. Member of International Hospitality House of San Francisco. *Military service:* U.S. Army, 1949-52; became sergeant first class.

MEMBER: Croatian Genealogical Society (president), California Historical Society, Slavonic Mutual and Benevolent Society of San Francisco of 1857, Croatian Fraternal Union.

WRITINGS:

(Compiler) *Irish Slavonians in California, 1849-1880*, Slavonic American Historical and Genealogical Society, 1964.
Orthodox Church Directory of the United States, Ragusan Press, 1968.
Dalmatians from Croatia and Montenegrin Serbs in the West and South, 1800-1900, Ragusan, 1971.
Yugoslav Survey of California, Nevada, Arizona, and the South, 1830-1900, Ragusan, 1971.
Yugoslavs in Nevada, 1859-1900, Ragusan, 1973.
Croatian and Dalmatian Coats of Arms, Ragusan, 1978.
A Guide and Bibliography to Research on Yugoslavs in the United States and Canada, Ragusan, 1978.
Croatian Pioneers in America, 1685-1900, Ragusan, 1980.
The Slavonic Mutual and Benevolent Society: One Hundred Twenty-five Years in San Francisco, 1857-1985, Ragusan, 1984.

Author of the weekly column "Croatian Roots" in *Croatian Fraternal Weekly* and *Catholic Twin Circle Magazine*. Contributor of more than one hundred articles to journals.*

*   *   *

EVANS, Howard Ensign 1919-

PERSONAL: Born February 23, 1919, in East Hartford, Conn.; son of Archie J. and Adella (Ensign) Evans; married Mary Alice Dietrich, June 6, 1954; children: Barbara, Dorothy, Timothy. *Education:* University of Connecticut, B.A., 1940; Cornell University, M.S., 1941, Ph.D., 1949.

ADDRESSES: Home—79 McKenna Ct., Livermore, Colo. 80536. *Office*—Department of Zoology and Entomology, Colorado State University, Fort Collins, Colo. 80523.

CAREER: Kansas State University (now Kansas State University of Agriculture and Applied Science), Manhattan, assistant professor, 1949-52; Cornell University, Ithaca, N.Y., assistant professor of entomology, 1954-59; Harvard University, Cambridge, Mass., associate curator, Museum of Comparative Zoology, 1959-64, curator, 1964-70, Alexander Agassiz Professor of Zoology, 1970-73; Colorado State University, Fort Collins, professor of entomology, 1973-85, professor emeritus, 1986—. *Military service:* U.S. Army, 1942-45; became second lieutenant.

MEMBER: National Academy of Sciences, Animal Behavior Society.

AWARDS, HONORS: National Book Award nomination, 1964, for *Wasp Farm*.

WRITINGS:

The Song I Sing: Verses, Humphries, 1951.
(With Cheng Shan Lin) *Studies on the Larvae of Digger Wasps (Hymenoptera, Sphecidae)*, [Philadelphia], 1956.
Studies on the Comparative Ethology of Digger Wasps of the Genus Bembix, Cornell University Press, 1957.
A Revision of the Genus Pseudisobrachium in North and Central America, Museum of Comparative Zoology, Harvard University, 1961.
A Revision of the Genus Apenesia in the Americas (Hymenoptera, Bethylidae), Museum of Comparative Zoology, Harvard University, 1963.
Wasp Farm, Natural History Press, 1963, reprinted, Cornell University Press, 1985.
A Revision of the Genus Pristocera in the Americas (Hymenoptera, Bethylidae), Museum of Comparative Zoology, Harvard University, 1963.
A Synopsis of the American Bethylidae (Hymenoptera, Aculeata), Museum of Comparative Zoology, Harvard University, 1964.
A Revision of the Genus Rhabdepyris in the Americas (Hymenoptera, Bethylidae), Museum of Comparative Zoology, Harvard University, 1965.
The Comparative Ethology and Evolution of the Sand Wasps, Harvard University Press, 1966.
A Revision of the Mexican and Central American Spider Wasps of the Subfamily Pompilinae (Hymenoptera: Pompilidae), American Entomological Society, 1966.
Life on a Little-Known Planet, Dutton, 1968, reprinted, University of Chicago Press, 1984.
Ecological-Behavioral Studies of the Wasps of Jackson Hole, Wyoming, Museum of Comparative Zoology, Harvard University, 1970.
(With Mary Jane West Eberhard) *The Wasps*, University of Michigan Press, 1970.
(With wife, Mary Alice Evans) *William Morton Wheeler, Biologist*, Harvard University Press, 1970.
(With Robert W. Matthews) *Systematics and Nesting Behavior of Australian Bembix Sand Wasps (Hymenoptera, Sphecidae)*, American Entomological Institute, 1973.
A Revision of Spider Wasps of the Genus Ctenostegus (Hymenoptera Pompilidae), Commonwealth Scientific and Industrial Research Organization, 1976.
The Bethylidae of America North of Mexico, American Entomological Institute, 1978.
(Editor with Michael D. Breed and Charles D. Michener) *The Biology of Social Insects: Proceedings of the Ninth Congress of the International Union for the Study of Social Insects*, Westview Press, 1982.

(With Mary Alice Evans) *Australia: A Natural History*, Smithsonian Institution Press, 1983.
A Revision of Spider Wasps of the Genus Turneromyia (Hymenoptera: Pompilidae), Australian Journal of Zoology, 1984.
Insect Biology, Addison-Wesley, 1984.
The Pleasures of Entomology, Smithsonian Institution Press, 1985.

Contributor to scientific journals.

SIDELIGHTS: Howard Ensign Evans' *Life on a Little-Known Planet* describes the life histories and mating habits of several common insects. *New York Times Book Review* writer Robert W. Stock comments: ''Evans, a skilled writer in the unlikely guise of a Harvard University entomologist, has the wit and charm to make us care about the life-styles of locusts and bedbugs.'' ''The 'little-known planet' of the title is earth,'' he continues, ''and Evans is pleading for a greater understanding of earth life—even unto the smallest bug. Seldom, if ever, has the case for the natural sciences—and for conservation—been presented with such reasoned, convincing eloquence.''

AVOCATIONAL INTERESTS: Photography, backpacking, fishing.

BIOGRAPHICAL/CRITICAL SOURCES:

PERIODICALS

Christian Century, March 3, 1971.
Natural History, October, 1979, December, 1981.
Nature, March 7, 1985.
New York Times Book Review, November 17, 1968.
Times Literary Supplement, April 8, 1965, May 28, 1970.

*   *   *

EVANS, Mari   1923-
(E. Reed)

PERSONAL: Born July 16, 1923, in Toledo, Ohio; divorced; children: two sons. *Education:* Attended University of Toledo.

ADDRESSES: *Home*—P.O. Box 483, Indianapolis, Ind. 46206. *Office*—Department of English, State University of New York—Albany, Albany, N.Y. 12203.

CAREER: Worked as an editor for a chain manufacturing company. Indiana University—Purdue University at Indianapolis, instructor in black literature and writer-in-residence, 1969-70; Indiana University at Bloomington, assistant professor of black literature and writer-in-residence, 1970-78; State University of New York—Albany, associate professor, 1985—. Visiting assistant professor, Northwestern University, 1972-73, Purdue University, West Lafayette, Ind., 1978-80, Washington University, St. Louis, 1980, Cornell University, 1981-84. Producer, director, writer for television program, ''The Black Experience,'' WTTV, Indianapolis, 1968-73; has lectured and read at numerous colleges and universities. Consultant to Discovery Grant Program, National Endowment for the Arts, 1969-70; consultant in ethnic studies, Bobbs-Merrill Co., 1970-73. Member of literary advisory panel, Indiana State Arts Commission, chairperson, 1976-77; chairman, Statewide Committee for Penal Reform; member of board of management, Fall Creek Parkway YMCA, 1975-80; member, Indiana Corrections Code Commission, 1978-79; member of board of directors, 1st World Foundation.

MEMBER: Authors Guild, Authors League of America, African Heritage Studies Association.

AWARDS, HONORS: John Hay Whitney fellow, 1965-66; Woodrow Wilson Foundation grant, 1968; Indiana University Writers' Conference award, and Black Academy of Arts and Letters first annual poetry award, both 1970, for *I Am a Black Woman;* L.H.D., Marian College, 1975; MacDowell fellow, 1975; Builders Award, Third World Press, Chicago, 1977; Indiana Committee for the Humanities grant, 1977; Black Liberation Award, Kuumba Theatre Workshop, Chicago, 1978; Copeland Fellow, Amherst College, 1980; Black Arts Celebration Poetry Award, Chicago, 1981; National Endowment for the Arts Creative Writing Award, 1981; Yaddo Writers Colony fellow, 1984.

WRITINGS:

Where Is All the Music? (poems), P. Breman, 1968.
I Am a Black Woman (poems), Morrow, 1970.
J. D. (juvenile), Doubleday, 1973, Avon, 1982.
I Look at Me (juvenile), Third World Press, 1974.
Rap Stories (juvenile), Third World Press, 1974.
Singing Black (juvenile), Reed Visuals, 1976.
"River of My Song" (play), first produced in Indianapolis, Ind., at Lilly Theatre, May, 1977, produced in Chicago, Ill., at Northeastern Illinois University, Center for Inner City Studies, 1977.
Jim Flying High (juvenile), Doubleday, 1979.
Night Star: 1973-1978 (poems), Center for African American Studies, University of California, Berkeley, 1980.
"Eyes" (a musical; adapted from Zora Neale Hurston's *Their Eyes Were Watching God*), first produced in New York at the Richard Allen Cultural Center, 1979, produced in Cleveland at Karamu Theatre of the Performing Arts, March, 1982.
(Editor and contributor) *Black Women Writers (1950-1980): A Critical Evaluation,* Doubleday-Anchor, 1984, published in England as *Black Women Writers, 1950-1980: Arguments and Interviews,* Pluto, 1985.

Also author of *Portrait of a Man,* 1979, "Boochie" (a play), 1979, "The Way They Made Beriani," and "Glide and Sons" (a musical).

CONTRIBUTOR TO ANTHOLOGIES

James A. Emanuel and Theodore L. Gross, editors, *Dark Symphony: Negro Literature in America,* Free Press,1968.
Abraham Chapman, editor, *Black Voices: An Anthology of Afro-American Literature,* American Library, 1968.
Anita Dore, editor, *The Premier Book of Major Poets: An Anthology,* Fawcett, 1970.
Edna Johnson, editor, *Anthology of Children's Literature,* 4th edition, Houghton, 1970.
Alan Lomax and Raoul Abdul, editors, *3000 Years of Black Poetry: An Anthology,* Dodd, Mead, 1970.
Richard A. Long and Eugenia Collier, editors, *Afro-American Writing: An Anthology of Prose and Poetry,* New York University Press, 1972.
Chapman, editor, *New Black Voices: An Anthology of Contemporary Afro-American Literature,* New American Library, 1972.
Raoul Abdul, editor, *The Magic of Black Poetry,* Dodd, Mead, 1972.
Stephen Henderson, *Understanding the New Black Poetry: Black Speech and Black Music as Poetic References,* Morrow, 1973.
Arnold Adoff, editor, *Black Out Loud: An Anthology of Modern Poems by Black Americans,* Dell, 1975.

Poetry is represented in more than two hundred anthologies and textbooks.

OTHER

Writer for television program, "The Black Experience." Contributor to *Phylon, Black World* (formerly *Negro Digest*), *Dialog, Black Enterprise* (under the pseudonym E. Reed), *First World,* and other periodicals.

SIDELIGHTS: When a story Mari Evans wrote in the fourth grade was accepted for publication in her school paper, her father expressed his pride by marking the occasion as an important event in their family history. Just a few years later, the young Evans read *Weary Blues* by Langston Hughes and identified with the black literature that was to become her vocation. These two influences, she says in *Black Women Writers (1950-1980): A Critical Evaluation,* gave her the confidence she needed to become a professional writer despite the racism that plagued her apprenticeship as an editor for a chain manufacturing plant. Inspired by their early faith in her abilities, Evans has also endured frequent rejection from publishers who take issue with the strong social comment that characterizes her works. These obstacles, she relates, have taught her the importance of discipline in the writer's life. And they have not prevented her from becoming an award-winning writer who is a well-known advocate of the growth of black pride and the construction of the black community in America. As Wallace R. Peppers notes about Evans in the *Dictionary of Literary Biography,* "Her volumes of poetry, her books for adolescents, her work for television and other media, and her . . . volume on black women writers between 1950 and 1980 ensure her a lasting place among those who have made significant contributions to Afro-American life and culture."

The author's first book of poems, *Where Is All the Music?,* came out in 1968, the same year that Evans began to write, direct, and produce "The Black Experience," a program for WTTV in Indianapolis. While the program met with critical acclaim, the book received little notice from critics. Pepper feels it is significant, nonetheless, because of its "well-crafted first-person personae, effective linguistic devices, apt diction, and strong characterizations." The poet's ambition, he observes, is "to record the emotional vicissitudes of the individual soul; and to document the difficult, but necessary struggle to form meaningful human relationships." The book "barely suggests Evans's eventual concern for social relevancy," he comments, noting that only three of its poems treat "activist" themes.

Evans's focus on social issues becoms sharper in later volumes. *I Am a Black Woman,* her second book, "heralded the arrival of a poet who took her subject matter from the black community, and who celebrated its triumphs, . . . and who would mourn its losses, especially the deaths of Martin Luther King, Jr. and Malcolm X," Peppers relates. David Dorsey's essay on Evans's work in *Black Women Writers* comments on the obvious political intent of poems that declare "i / will not sit / in Grateful meetings," and others that address the need for social change in "more strident terms." But the last poem, notes Dorsey, emphasizes the positive foundation of her political stance when it asks, "Who can be born black and not exult!" *I Am a Black Woman* won Indiana University's Writers' Conference award and the Black Academy of Arts and Letters first annual poetry award in 1970.

The poet's commitment to the concerns of Black Americans grows stronger in *Nightstar,* say the critics, in poems that also show an improvement in poetic technique. Dorsey comments that his analysis of *Nightstar* "cannot suggest the humane grace that pervades this book." Yet he means for the reader to see "that mechanical means, poetic design, and didactic import are so interconnected [in it] that to separate them is to dismember an organism." A *Virginia Quarterly Review* writer has similar praise for Evans: "Mari Evans is a powerful poet. Her craftsmanship does not interfere with the subject she treats with a fullness born of deep caring. She subtly interweaves private and public Black frustration and dignity with an infectious perception. Sparseness of speech belies a command of the language and knowledge of the Black experience.... We need to hear this authentic voice again and again, for there is strength in exquisitely revealing expressions of ghetto dynamics."

Evans's command of Black idioms is one reason why her works should be valued, suggests Dorsey: "There are several reasons why the corpus of Evans's published works to date [1984] are extremely illuminating for anyone interested in considering the nature of art in the Black American tradition. The first is that her creative works are of unquestionable artistic excellence.... Similarly, her adaptation of Black idiom in children's stories, in poetry, and in drama shows how the writer must manipulate idiom to achieve reader identification with the speaker, rather than aesthetic (and ideological) alienation." In her statement for *Black Women Writers,* Evans explains the role of idiom in her works: "Idiom is larger than geography; it is the hot breath of a people—singing, slashing, explorative. Imagery becomes the magic denominator, the language of a passage, saying the ancient unchanging particulars, the connective currents that nod Black heads from Maine to Mississippi to Montana. No there ain't nothin universal about it. So when I write, I write reaching for all that. Reaching for what will nod Black heads over common denominators.... If there are those outside the Black experience who hear the music and can catch the beat, that is serendipity; I have no objections. But when I write, I write according to the title of poet Margaret Walker's classic: 'for my people.'"

Evans "celebrates the known and the unsung among us," says *Black Women Writers* contributor Solomon Edwards. "She writes of Wes Montgomery and Yusef Lateef, jazz titans. She asserts that Black education should begin in a loving Black home where concern for learning can mature in a friendly atmosphere of belonging rather than in a threatening often alien environ. Hence, the highly personalized preprimer, *I Look at Me,* was created." Using only forty-six vocabulary words, *I Look at Me* presents the black citizens of America in a variety of professions as "a Beautiful nation." Evans has written other children's books helpful in the education of young readers to Black cultural values, he notes. "*Singing Black* provides alternative nursery rhymes for the Black child's first encounter with the music of Black values. In . . . *Jim Flying High,* [a West Indian dialect] underscores a humorous tale of problem identification, and interdependence that requires unselfish participation in order to strengthen the Black community."

In essays and in plays as well, "Evans maintains her unequivocal stride for Black autonomy," observes Edwards. "She has tenderly sorted out the sweet, sour, salt, and bitter experiences of Black people and dramatized the suffering and shouts of Black strength." Earlier, he comments that Evans "has a passion for the dramatic," seen in the fact that her poems generally focus specifically on well-drawn characters, and more so in the plays and musicals she has written. "There is an intimate relation between Evans's poetry and her theater works,"

namely, their didactic intent, states Dorsey. "River of My Song," produced in Indianapolis, and later in Chicago in 1977, is written for four musicians, three dancers, and four actresses. "The use of poetry and music, the choice of instruments, the coordination of . . . 'movement, text, music' . . . all reflect adherence to traditional and genuine Black theatrical ritual," the essayist adds. "Portrait of a Man" and "Boochie" are more conventional but not less ritualistic. "Portrait" allows the audience to develop "determination, pride, courage, and comprehension" in the face of white indifference to human suffering, says Dorsey; and through the monologue of the one character in "Boochie," the audience is "led to a very specific and incisive recognition of the effects of social forces (unemployment, alcohol, welfare) on the Black woman, the Black man, the Black child."

Observing that information on black women writers was scarce though their ranks held many accomplished poets, novelists, and two Pulitzer prize winners since the 1940s, Evans compiled new critical articles and personal statements from fifteen authors to make *Black Women Writers (1950-1980)*. The book, according to *World Literature Today* contributor Bettina L. Knapp, "not only fills a vacuum, but it also makes for exciting and provocative reading." Zhana especially values each "author's own writings, which were done in response to a questionnaire.... It is useful and informative to me, as a Black woman writer, to read of the joys, pains, blood, ecstasy of writers plying their craft," she says in the *New Statesman.* Writing in the *New York Times Book Review,* Rosellen Brown appreciates the opening essay by Stephen E. Henderson, which "puts this exposition of talent into historical perspective." Brown also applauds "a biography and bibliography so detailed that it . . . names the nine cities that have given their keys to Nikki Giovanni." For the first time, notes Brown, Margaret Walker, Alice Childress, and the other women in *Black Women Writers* are given the scholarly attention that is their due. Furthermore, the collection makes an important amendment to the literary canon, which she hopes will no longer exclude the black woman writer: "[Evans's] book is a cause for delight to anyone who wants to share or, from a distance, to discover the world of black women writers, with the knowledge that there are many more waiting their turns. Partly by their efforts, the map of significance has been irrevocably changed."

Translated versions of Evans's poetry have been published in Swedish, French, Russian, German, Italian, and Dutch textbooks and anthologies.

MEDIA ADAPTATIONS: Evans's poetry has been choreographed and used on record albums, filmstrips, television specials, and in two Off-Broadway productions, "A Hand Is on the Gate" and "Walk Together Children."

BIOGRAPHICAL/CRITICAL SOURCES:

BOOKS

Dictionary of Literary Biography, Volume 41: *Afro-American Poets since 1955*, Gale, 1985.
Evans, Mari, *I Am a Black Woman*, Morrow, 1970.
Evans, Mari, *I Look at Me*, Third World Press, 1974.
Evans, Mari, editor and contributor, *Black Women Writers (1950-1980): A Critical Evaluation*, Doubleday/Anchor, 1984.

PERIODICALS

Black American Literature Forum, winter, 1984.

Black Scholar, March, 1981.
Black World, January, 1971, July, 1971.
Book World, November 11, 1973, September 14, 1975.
Ebony, March, 1974.
Essence, September, 1984.
Freedomways, Volume XXIV, number 4, 1984.
Los Angeles Times Book Review, September 2, 1984.
Modern Fiction Studies, winter, 1985.
New Statesman, May 3, 1985.
New Yorker, September 3, 1979.
New York Times Book Review, September 23, 1984.
Publishers Weekly, July 6, 1970.
Virginia Quarterly Review, winter, 1971.
World Literature Today, winter, 1985.*

—*Sketch by Marilyn K. Basel*

*   *   *

EWALD, William Bragg, Jr.   1925-

PERSONAL: Born December 8, 1925, in Chicago, Ill.; son of
William Bragg (a lawyer) and Ann (a concert pianist; maiden
name, Niccolls) Ewald; married Mary Cecilia Thedieck (a
writer), December 6, 1947; children: William Bragg III, Charles
Ross, Thomas Hart Benton. *Education:* Washington University, St. Louis, Mo., A.B., 1946; Harvard University, M.A.,
1947, Ph.D., 1951. *Politics:* Republican. *Religion:* Episcopalian.

ADDRESSES: Home—Dewart Rd., Greenwich, Conn. 06830.
Office—International Business Machines Corp., Armonk, N.Y.
10504. *Agent*—Knox Burger Associates Ltd., 39 1/2 Washington Sq. S., New York, N.Y. 10012.

CAREER: Harvard University, Cambridge, Mass., instructor
in English and humanities, 1951-54; The White House, Washington, D.C., special assistant, 1954-56, assistant to Secretary
of the Interior, 1957-61; assistant to Dwight D. Eisenhower,
1961-64; International Business Machines Corp., Armonk,
N.Y., director of studies, 1964—. President of Bruce Museum
Associates; vice-chairman of board of directors of Bruce Museum.

MEMBER: Cosmos Club, 1925 F Street Club, Round Hill
Club, Phi Beta Kappa.

AWARDS, HONORS: Grants from American Philosophical
Society and Harvard Foundation for Advanced Study and Research, both 1952-53; Eisenhower exchange fellowship, 1959-
60.

WRITINGS:

The Masks of Jonathan Swift, Harvard University Press, 1954.

Rogues, Royalty and Reporters, Houghton, 1957.
Eisenhower the President: Crucial Days, 1951-60, Prentice-
Hall, 1981.
Who Killed Joe McCarthy?, Simon & Schuster, 1984.
McCarthyism and Consensus, University Press of America,
1987.

Contributor to newspapers.

SIDELIGHTS: William Bragg Ewald, Jr., told *CA:* "My book
The Masks of Jonathan Swift came out of my doctoral dissertation at Harvard. *Rogues, Royalty and Reporters* resulted from
my research, principally in the British Museum, on early eighteenth-century newspapers. My books on Eisenhower and
McCarthy reflect my own experience on the Eisenhower White
House staff, my association with the former president in the
preparation of his memoirs after he left the White House—a
five-year association that gave me unique access to his private
papers and his recollections—and independent research which
I began with his enthusiastic encouragement after we finished
the memoirs."

Although *Washington Post* critic James E. Clayton writes that
he has "no trouble commending" Ewald's book *Who Killed
Joe McCarthy?* because "it re-creates that spring of 30 years
ago better than anything else I have read," he nevertheless
feels that Ewald answers the book's title question "almost as
an afterthought. And it is an afterthought many people will
disagree with." According to Ewald, it was President Eisenhower who brought McCarthy down, albeit with what Ewald
deems a slow, careful strategy. In the opinion of *New York
Times Book Review* writer Jack Rosenthal, "The trouble with
this admiring contention is not that it's admiring but that Mr.
Ewald's book, though it draws on a file cabinet full of hitherto
undisclosed documentation, does not support it. . . . The memos,
phone transcripts and White House and Defense Department
papers hint at some interesting Administration intrigue against
McCarthy. They do not, however, give much evidence of the
Eisenhower strategy perceived by the author." Similarly,
Clayton maintains that the "real value of Ewald's work rests
in the new material he injects to expand our understanding of
the Army-McCarthy fight, not the conclusion he draws."

AVOCATIONAL INTERESTS: Playing piano recitals.

BIOGRAPHICAL/CRITICAL SOURCES:

PERIODICALS

Los Angeles Times, May 15, 1984.
New York Times Book Review, June 28, 1981, October 7,
1984.
Wall Street Journal, June 18, 1981.
Washington Post, June 12, 1984.

F

FAST, Julius 1919-
(Adam Barnett)

PERSONAL: Born April 17, 1919, in New York, N.Y.; son of Barnett A. (a pattern maker) and Ida (Miller) Fast; married Barbara Hewitt Sher (a novelist), June 8, 1946; children: Jennifer, Melissa, Timothy H. *Education:* New York University, B.A., 1942.

ADDRESSES: Home—P.O. Box 81, Southbury, Conn. 06488. *Agent*—Bob Markel, 424 Madison Ave., New York, N.Y. 10017.

CAREER: Smith, Kline & French (drugs), Philadelphia, Pa., writer, 1952-54; Purdue Frederick (drugs), New York City, research associate, 1954-61; *Medical News*, New York City, feature editor, 1961-62; *Medical World News*, New York City, editor and writer, 1962-63; *Ob-Gyn Observer*, New York City, editor, 1963-75. *Military service:* U.S. Army, 1943-46; became staff sergeant.

AWARDS, HONORS: Edgar Allan Poe Award for best first mystery novel, from Mystery Writers of America, 1946, for *Watchful at Night.*

WRITINGS:

(Editor) *Out of This World*, Penguin, 1944.
Watchful at Night, Farrar & Rinehart, 1945.
Bright Face of Danger, Rinehart, 1946.
Walk in Shadow, Rinehart, 1947, published as *Down through the Night*, Fawcett, 1956.
A Model for Murder, Rinehart, 1956.
Street of Fear, Rinehart, 1958.
(Self-illustrated) *Blueprint for Life: The Story of Modern Genetics*, St. Martin's, 1964.
What You Should Know about Human Sexual Responses, Putnam, 1966.
The Beatles: The Real Story, Putnam, 1968.
How to Stop Smoking and Lose Weight, National Education Association, 1969.
League of Grey-Eyed Women, Lippincott, 1969.
Body Language, M. Evans, 1970.
You and Your Feet, St. Martin's, 1970.
The Incompatibility of Men and Women, M. Evans, 1971.
The New Sexual Fulfillment, Berkley Publishing, 1972.
Bisexual Living, M. Evans, 1975.

The Pleasure Book, Stein & Day, 1975.
Creative Coping, Morrow, 1976.
The Body Language of Sex, Power, and Aggression, M. Evans, 1976.
Psyching Up, Stein & Day, 1978.
Weather Language, Wyden Books, 1979.
Body Politics, Tower, 1980.
The Body Book, Tower, 1981.
(With Paul Henreid) *Ladies Man*, St. Martin's, 1983.
Sexual Chemistry, M. Evans, 1983.
Trial Communication Skills, McGraw, 1986.
The Omega 3 Breakthrough, Body Press, 1987.
What Should We Do about Davey?, St. Martin's, 1988.

UNDER PSEUDONYM ADAM BARNETT

(With Larry Alexander) *Iron Cradle*, Crowell, 1954.
Doctor Harry: The Story of Dr. Harry Lorber, Crowell, 1958.

SIDELIGHTS: H. S. Resnik of *Saturday Review* writes of Julius Fast's *Body Language:* "Although he pays far too much homage to other people's studies and published papers, Fast does make some interesting points about the ways in which people's bodies communicate their feelings and needs. . . . His book is actually a crash course in sensitivity, and some people can probably benefit from reading it."

Reviewing *The Incompatibility of Men and Women* for *Best Sellers*, Joseph Szuhay states that Fast "has presented an authoritative how-to-do-it course on incompatibility. . . . Basically the research cited may be a beginning of a scientific basis for the theoretical relationship between aggression, fear, and sexuality in man. . . . The book offers us a good, hard look at the sexual equality which according to all research cited is greatly misapprehended. The final section on marriage presents a plea to all readers to focus on what in our concept a male-female relationship should be, and how this concept should be answered. . . . The book should be recommended reading for all adults, married or not, for it provides an interesting understanding of human relationships at the most important levels. It no doubt could provide building blocks for better relationships for couples on the brink of separation or divorce."

BIOGRAPHICAL/CRITICAL SOURCES:

PERIODICALS

American Journal of Public Health, April, 1972.

Best Sellers, June 1, 1970, December 1, 1971.
Newsweek, June 22, 1970.
New York Times Book Review, October 25, 1970.
Saturday Review, July 25, 1970.

*   *   *

FELDMAN, Gerald D(onald) 1937-

PERSONAL: Born April 24, 1937, in New York, N.Y.; son of Isadore and Lillian (Cohen) Feldman; married Philippa Blume, June 22, 1958 (divorced, 1982); married Norma von Ragenfeld, November 30, 1983; children: (first marriage) Deborah Eve, Aaron. *Education:* Columbia University, B.A. (magna cum laude), 1958; Harvard University, M.A., 1959, Ph.D., 1964. *Politics:* Democrat. *Religion:* Jewish.

ADDRESSES: Home—Berkeley, Calif. *Office*—Department of History, University of California, Berkeley, Calif. 94720.

CAREER: University of California, Berkeley, assistant professor, 1963-68, associate professor, 1968-70, professor of history, 1970—, Institute of International Studies, member of advisory and program committees, 1969-70, member of executive committee, 1975-76 and 1979-81, acting chairman of committee on Advanced Industrial Societies and West European Studies, 1971-72. Delegate to Council for European Studies, 1971-72; member of Curatorium for State and the Economy in the Weimer Republic conference, 1973; co-chairman of conference on twentieth-century capitalism, 1974; participant in consultation program, Historische Kommission zu Berlin, summer, 1976; Stephen Allen Kaplan Memorial Lecturer, University of Pennsylvania, 1984.

MEMBER: American Historical Association, Historische Kommission zu Berlin (corresponding member), Phi Beta Kappa.

AWARDS, HONORS: Woodrow Wilson fellow, 1958-59; Harvard fellow, 1961-63; Social Science Research Council fellow, 1961-63; honorary Sheldon traveling fellow, 1961-62; American Council of Learned Societies fellow, 1966-67, 1970-71; Social Science Research Council grant, 1966-67; honorary mention for best article, Conference Group on Central European History, 1970; University of California Humanities research fellow, 1970-71; Guggenheim fellow, 1973-74; Newcomen Prize (with Ulrich Nocken) for best essay in *Business History Review*, 1975; National Endowment for the Humanities fellow, 1977-78; Volkswagen Foundation grant, 1979-82; Lehrman Institute fellow, 1981-82; German Marshall Fund fellow, 1981-82; stipendiat and prize of the Historisches Kolleg, Munich, 1982-83; ACLS grants, 1986; appointment to the Wissenschaftskolleg, Berlin, 1987-88.

WRITINGS:

Army, Industry and Labor in Germany, 1914-1918, Princeton University Press, 1966, revised version published in German translation as *Armee, Industrie und Arbeiterschaft in Deutschland 1914 bis 1918*, J. H. Dietz (Berlin/Bonn), 1985.
Iron and Steel in the German Inflation, 1916-1923, Princeton University Press, 1977.
(With Heidrun Homburg) *Industrie und Inflation: Studien und Dokumente zur Politik der deutschen Unternehmer 1916 bis 1923*, Hoffman und Campe (Hamburg), 1977.
Vom Weltkrieg zur Weltwirtschaftskrise: Studien zur deutschen Wirtschafts- und Sozialgeschichte 1914-32, Vandehoeck & Ruprecht (Goettingen), 1984.

(With Irmgard Steinisch) *Industrie und Gewerkschaften 1918-1924: Die ueberforderte Zentralarbeitgemeinschaft*, Oldebourg (Stuttgart), 1985.

EDITOR

German Imperialism, 1914-1917: The Development of a Historical Debate, Wiley, 1972.
(With Thomas G. Barnes) *A Documentary History of Europe*, Volume III: *Nationalism, Industrialization, and Democracy, 1814-1914*, Volume IV: *Breakdown and Rebirth, 1914 to the Present*, Little, Brown, 1972.
(With Otto Beusch, and contributor) *Historische Prozesse der deutschen Inflation 1914-1924: Ein Tangungsbericht*, Colloquium-Verlag (Berlin), 1978.
(With Carl-Ludwig Holtfrerich, Gerhard A. Ritter, and Peter-Christian Witt, and contributor) *The German Inflation: A Preliminary Balance*, De Gruyter, 1982, published as *The German Inflation Reconsidered: A Preliminary Balance*, 1984.
(With Holtfrerich, Ritter, and Witt) *The Experience of Inflation: International and Comparative Studies*, De Gruyter, 1984.
(With Elizabeth Mueller-Luckner, and contributor) *Die Nachwirkungen der Inflation auf die deutsche Geschichte 1924-1933*, Oldenbourg, 1985.
(With Holtfrerich, Ritter, and Witt, and contributor) *The Adaption to Inflation/Die Anpassung an die Inflation*, De Gruyter, 1986.

CONTRIBUTOR

Ritter, editor, *Entsehung und Wandel der modernen Gesellschaft: Festschrift fuer Hans Rosenberg zum 65. Geburtstag*, De Gruyter, 1970.
I. Geiss and B. Wendt, editors, *Deutschland in der Weltpolitik des 19. und 20. Jahrhunderts: Fritz Fischer zum 65. Geburtstag*, Bertelsmann Universitaetsverlag, 1973.
Hans-Ulrich Wehler, editor, *Sozialgeschichte heute: Festschrift fuer Hans Rosenberg zum 70. Geburtstag*, Vandenhoeck & Ruprecht, 1974.
Henrich Winkler, editor, *Organisierter Kapitalismus: Voraussetzungen und Anfange*, Vandenhoeck & Ruprecht, 1974.
Heinz Oskar Vetter, editor, *Vom Sozialistengesetz zur Mitbestimmung: Zum 100. Geburtstag von Hans Boeckler*, Bund-Verlag (Cologne), 1975.
Dirk Stegmann and others, editors, *Industrielle Gesellschaft und politisches System. Beitraege zur politischen Sozialgeschichte: Festschrift fuer Fritz Fisher*, Verlag Neue Gesellschaft (Bonn), 1978.
Karl Holl, editor, *Wirtschaftskrise und liberale Demokratie*, Vandenhoeck & Ruprecht, 1978.
Gene Brucker, editor, *People and Communities in the Western World*, Volume II, Dorsey, 1979.
Hans Mommsen and Ulrich Borsdorf, editors, *Gluck auf, Kameraden! Die Bergarbeiter und ihre Organisationen in Deutschland*, Bund-Verlag, 1979.
Suzanne Berger, editor, *Organizing Interests in Western Europe*, Cambridge University Press, 1981.
Klaus Tenfelde and Heinrich Volkmann, editors, *Streik: Zur Geschichte des Arbeitskampfes in Deutschland waehrend der Industrialisierung*, C. H. Beck (Munich), 1981.
Nathan Schmukler and Edward Marcus, editors, *Inflation through the Ages: Economic, Social, Psychological and Historical Aspects*, Brooklyn College Press, 1983.
Dieter Langewiesche, editor, *Ploetz: Das deutsche Kaiserreich 1867/71 bis 1918. Bilanz einer Epoche*, A. G. Ploetz (Freiburg), 1984.

Giovanni Battimelli and others, editors, *La Ristrutturazione delle scienze tra le due guerre mondiali,* La Goliardica (Rome), 1984.

Juergen Kocka, editor, *Arbeiter und Buerger im 19. Jahrhundert,* Oldenbourg, 1986.

Charles Meier, editor, *The Changing Boundaries of the Political,* Cambridge University Press, 1987.

OTHER

Contributor to proceedings and historical journals in the United States and Germany. Member of editorial boards, *Journal of Social History,* 1970—, *Central European History,* 1973-75, *Journal of Modern History,* 1973-75, *Geschichte und Gesellschaft,* 1974—, and *German Yearbook on Business History,* 1982—.

WORK IN PROGRESS: The Great Disorder: A Political and Social History of the German Inflation and an accompanying volume of documents for the German edition.

*   *   *

FERRIS, James Cody
[Collective pseudonym]

WRITINGS:

"X BAR X BOYS" SERIES

The X Bar X Boys on the Ranch, Grosset & Dunlap, 1926.
. . . in Thunder Canyon, Grosset & Dunlap, 1926.
. . . on Whirlpool River, Grosset & Dunlap, 1926.
. . . on Big Bison Trail, Grosset & Dunlap, 1927.
. . . at the Round-up, Grosset & Dunlap, 1927.
. . . at Nugget Camp, Grosset & Dunlap, 1928.
. . . at Rustlers' Gap, Grosset & Dunlap, 1929.
. . . at Grizzly Pass, Grosset & Dunlap, 1929.
. . . Lost in the Rockies, Grosset & Dunlap, 1930.
. . . Riding for Life, Grosset & Dunlap, 1931.
. . . in Smoky Valley, Grosset & Dunlap, 1932.
. . . at Copperhead Gulch, Grosset & Dunlap, 1933.
. . . Branding the Wild Herd, Grosset & Dunlap, 1934.
. . . at the Strange Rodeo, Grosset & Dunlap, 1935.
. . . with the Secret Rangers, Grosset & Dunlap, 1936.
. . . Hunting the Prize Mustangs, Grosset & Dunlap, 1937.
. . . at Triangle Mine, Grosset & Dunlap, 1938.
. . . and the Sagebrush Mystery, Grosset & Dunlap, 1939.
. . . in the Haunted Gully, Grosset & Dunlap, 1940.
. . . Seeking the Lost Troopers, Grosset & Dunlap, 1941.
. . . Following the Stampede, Grosset & Dunlap, 1942.

SIDELIGHTS: The X Bar X Boys, Roy and Teddy Manley, were "a reasonably accurate facsimile of the Hardy Boys, but moved out West and riveted firmly into the saddle," comments Arthur Prager in *Rascals at Large; or, The Clue in the Old Nostalgia.* Sons of Bradwell Manley, a ranch owner and cattle breeder, the Manleys were, like the Hardys, a year apart in age. Roy, the older, had dark hair and eyes, while Teddy, like Joe Hardy, was fair and had blue eyes.

However, unlike the Hardys, who had a variety of criminal life to deal with, the Manleys had to be content with pursuing cattle rustlers. The boys met danger mostly in the form of natural disasters; Prager remarks that "each book held a number of danger's disasters for the lads, much more to be feared than the human kind. [These included] forest fires, rapids, snowstorms, quicksand, timber wolves, rattlesnakes, cougars and many more, evenly distributed to keep us reading while

the boys pursued cardboard badmen of the stamp of 'Three Lip' Denger.''

Leslie McFarlane, Walter Karig, and Roger Garis, son of Howard R. Garis, the creator of Uncle Wiggily, are known to have used this pseudonym and contributed volumes to this series. For more information see the entries in this volume for Harriet S. Adams, Howard R. Garis, Edward L. Stratemeyer, and Andrew E. Svenson.

BIOGRAPHICAL/CRITICAL SOURCES:

BOOKS

Garis, Roger, *My Father Was Uncle Wiggily,* McGraw-Hill, 1966.

Johnson, Deidre, editor and compiler, *Stratemeyer Pseudonyms and Series Books: An Annotated Checklist of Stratemeyer and Stratemeyer Syndicate Publications,* Greenwood Press, 1982.

McFarlane, Leslie, *Ghost of the Hardy Boys,* Two Continents, 1976.

Prager, Arthur, *Rascals at Large; or, The Clue in the Old Nostalgia,* Doubleday, 1971.

*   *   *

FIELDS, Rick   1942-

PERSONAL: Born May 16, 1942, in Manhattan, N.Y.; son of Allen D. (a publicist) and Reva (Fried) Fields. *Education:* Attended Harvard University, 1960-63, and University of New Mexico, 1964. *Politics:* "Interdependence of all sentient beings." *Religion:* Buddhist.

ADDRESSES: Office—1526 5th St., Boulder, Colo. 80302.

CAREER: Has worked as an English teacher for Berlitz in Guadalajara, Mexico, as an apple picker, a street theatre writer and actor, a warehouse worker, a reporter, an editor, a plumber's helper, a furniture mover, and a teacher at University of Colorado, Naropa Institute, and at Loretto College. Special projects editor, *New Age Magazine;* currently editor in chief, *Vajradhatu Sun* (international Buddhist newspaper).

MEMBER: American Society of Journalists and Authors.

AWARDS, HONORS: Fellow in nonfiction, Bread Loaf Writers Conference, 1984.

WRITINGS:

(Editor) *Loka: A Journal from Naropa Institute,* Doubleday, 1974.

(Editor) *Loka II,* Doubleday, 1975.

How the Swans Came to the Lake: A Narrative History of Buddhism in America, Shambhala Publications, 1981, revised edition, 1986.

(With Peggy Taylor, Rex Weyler, and Rick Ingrasci) *Chop Wood, Carry Water: A Guide to Spiritual Fulfillment in Everyday Life,* J. P. Tarcher, 1984.

(With Lucy Beale) *The Win-Win Way,* Harcourt, 1987.

Taking Refuge in L.A.: Life in a Vietnamese Buddhist Temple, photographs by Don Farber, Aperture Books, 1987.

SIDELIGHTS: In *How the Swans Came to the Lake: A Narrative History of Buddhism in America,* Rick Fields documents the rise of Buddhism in the modern West. According to *Washington Post Book World* reviewer Nancy Wilson Ross, the book is "literally crammed with the sort of lively and accurate information in its special field which I had for years been longing to find assembled in an orderly manner. . . . Not only has [Fields] thoroughly researched the rich lode of material at his disposal. . ., but he also possesses first-hand knowledge of how Buddhist practice 'works,' and further, he is blessed with a flair for characterization and the perceptive turn of phrase which give his unusual material all the elements of a 'good read.'''

BIOGRAPHICAL/CRITICAL SOURCES:

PERIODICALS

Washington Post Book World, April 25, 1982.

*   *   *

FILBY, P(ercy) William   1911-

PERSONAL: Born December 10, 1911, in Cambridge, England; came to United States in 1957, naturalized in 1961; son of William Lusher (a builder) and Florence Ada (Stanton) Filby; married Nancie Elizabeth Giddens, August 20, 1936 (divorced, 1957); married Vera Ruth Weakliem (a U.S. Government research analyst), May 23, 1957; children: (first marriage) Ann Veronica (Mrs. Ward Chesworth), Jane Vanessa (Mrs. Anthony Maisley), Roderick, Guy. *Education:* Attended Cambridge University, 1928-29. *Politics:* Democrat. *Religion:* Church of England.

ADDRESSES: Home—8944 Madison St., Savage, Md. 20763. *Office*—201 West Monument, Baltimore, Md. 21201.

CAREER: Cambridge University, Cambridge, England, member of library staff, 1930-37, Cambridge Philosophical Library (natural science), director, 1937-40; British Foreign Office, London, England, senior archivist, 1946-57; Peabody Institute Library, Baltimore, Md., assistant director, 1957-65; Maryland Historical Society, Baltimore, librarian and assistant director, 1965-72, director, 1972-78; Gale Research Inc., Detroit, Mich., consultant, 1978—. Secretary to Sir James G. Frazer, 1935-40. Lecturer at universities on calligraphy, fine printing, genealogy, heraldry, and Sir James G. Frazer. Fellow, Society of Genealogists, London, and National Genealogical Society, Manuscript Society, Evergreen House, La Casa del Libro. *Military service:* British Army, Intelligence Corps, 1940-46; became captain.

MEMBER: American Library Association, Special Libraries Association (president, Baltimore chapter), Bibliographical Society of America, Manuscript Society (director, 1972-75; president, 1976-78), Baltimore Bibliophiles (president, 1963-65), New York Typophiles, Grolier Club (member of library committee, 1965-84), Wynkyn de Worde Society.

WRITINGS:

EDITOR

Cambridge Papers, Cambridge University Library, 1935.
Calligraphy and Handwriting in America, 1710-1962, Italimuse, 1963, reprinted, 1985.
(With others) *Two Thousand Years of Calligraphy*, Walten Art Gallery, 1965.
American and British Genealogy and Heraldry: A Selected List of Books, American Library Association, 1970, 3rd edition, New England Historic Genealogical Society, 1983, *1982-1985 Supplement*, 1987.
(With Edward G. Howard) *Star-Spangled Books: Books, Sheet Music, Newspapers, Manuscripts, and Persons Associated with The Star-Spangled Banner*, Maryland Historical Society, 1972.

(With Mary Keysor Meyer) *Passenger and Immigration Lists Index: A Guide to Published Arrival Records of About 500,000 Passengers Who Came to the United States and Canada in the Seventeen, Eighteenth, and Nineteenth Centuries*, Gale, three volumes, 1980, *1983 Supplement*, 1984, *1984 Supplement*, 1985, *1985 Supplement*, 1985, *1986 Supplement* with Dorothy M. Lower, 1986, *1987 Supplement*, 1987, *1988 Supplement*, 1988.
Passenger and Immigration Lists Bibliography, 1538-1900: Being a Guide to Published Lists of Arrivals in the United States and Canada, Gale, 1980, *First Supplement*, 1984, 2nd edition, 1988.
Philadelphia Naturalization Records: An Index to Records of Aliens' Declarations of Intention and/or Oaths of Allegiance, 1789-1880, in United States Circuit Court, United States District Court, Supreme Court of Pennsylvania, Quarter Sessions Court of Common Please, Philadephia, Gale, 1982.
(With Meyer) *Who's Who in Genealogy and Heraldry*, Gale, Volume 1, 1985.
A Bibliography of American County Histories, Genealogical Publishing, 1985.
Directory of American Libraries with Genealogy of Local History Collections, Scholarly Research Inc., 1988.
Germans to America: Lists of Passengers Arriving at U.S. Ports, 1850-1855, ten volumes, Volumes 1-3, Scholarly Research Inc., 1988.

OTHER

(Contributor) John James Doyle, *Genealogical Use of Catholic Records*, Indiana Historical Society, 1978.
(Author of introduction) Arlene H. Eakle and Johni Cerny, *The Source: A Guidebook of American Genealogy*, Ancestry, 1984.
(Author of introduction) Cerny and Wendy Elliott, editors, *The Library: A Guide to the LDS Family History Library*, Ancestry, 1988.

Contributor to *American Reference Books Annual*, and of articles on genealogy for *Funk & Wagnall's Encyclopedia*, 1982. Also author of hundreds of book reviews and at least one hundred articles on genealogy and military intelligence.

WORK IN PROGRESS: Passenger and Immigration Lists supplements; *American and British Genealogy and Heraldry*, 1985-1988 supplement.

SIDELIGHTS: P. William Filby tells *CA:* "Having been a cryptographer during World War II and later, my opportunities for authorship were nil because of the Official Secrets Act. But once I came to America and returned to my original profession, that of librarianship, I found the opportunities limitless. Because of the ignorance in genealogy exhibited by librarians, usually nongenealogists, I determined to compile a reference work especially for them, and this has been updated regularly.

"Tiring of fund-raising as director of the Maryland Historical Society, in 1978 I accepted an offer to join Gale Research Company and to head the genealogical effort of the company. Such was the enthusiasm of Gale's former president, Frederick G. Ruffner, no fewer than sixteen major works have been published in the intervening years. This happy chance meeting with the former president of Gale has altered the face of genealogy; and the passenger and immigration lists are rated as perhaps the greatest genealogical work of the 1970s and 1980s." In the *Gale Gazette*, Filby states that five hundred thousand names comprise the initial three volumes of passenger and immigration lists, and the annual supplements augment that total by one hundred and twenty-five thousand each. Indicating that more than twenty-five hundred sources have been culled for this project, Filby adds, "I currently have over one million names awaiting [the index] and I am adding to the list daily."

Filby comments to *CA*: "I am fortunate in never having to 'sell' my writings; all are commissioned and I am generally two or three books behind requests. Working hours are generally 7-10, 1-4, 8-11, but I allow anything to cause changes in this schedule. But when there is nothing in the way, I generally try to put in six to eight hours during the weekdays."

AVOCATIONAL INTERESTS: Researching genealogy and heraldry, particularly British sources; collector of fine printing, and of cricketana.

BIOGRAPHICAL/CRITICAL SOURCES:

PERIODICALS

Gale Gazette, fall, 1987.

*   *   *

FINOCCHIARO, Mary (Bonomo)   1913-

PERSONAL: Born April 21, 1913, in New York, N.Y.; daughter of Anthony and Josephine (Billone) Bonomo; married Santo Finocchiaro (a surgeon), September 21, 1940 (died April 25, 1975); children: Salvatore, Rosemary (Mrs. Andreas Bartsch). *Education:* Hunter College (now Hunter College of the City University of New York), B.A., 1932, M.A., 1934; additional study at Sorbonne, University of Paris, 1934; Columbia University, Ph.D., 1948.

ADDRESSES: Office—United States Information Service, Army Post Office, New York, N.Y. 09994.

CAREER: New York City Public Schools, teacher of foreign language, 1932-47, guidance counselor, 1947-49, curriculum assistant for Division of Curriculum Research, 1949-50, supervisory instructor for PR education, 1950-54, chairman of foreign language in the secondary schools, 1954-57, elementary school principal, 1957; Hunter College of the City College of New York (now of the City University of New York), New York City, 1957—, began as associate professor, emeritus professor of education, 1972—, director of foreign language institute, 1957-72. Fulbright professor in Italy, 1954, in Spain, 1961; Fulbright lecturer in Italy, 1968-70. Director, associate director, or speaker at language-teaching seminars in Morocco, Turkey, Poland, Spain, and Germany. Co-director, U.S. Government's Bilingual Readiness Project; educational consultant to Migration Division, Commonwealth of Puerto Rico. English language consultant to Georgetown University, 1961-62, to American Embassy in Rome, 1975—.

MEMBER: American Association of University Professors, National Council of Administrative Women Educators, Teachers of English to Speakers of Other Languages (president, 1970-71), American Association of Teachers of French, American Association of Teachers of Italian, Foreign Language Chairman's Association, New York State Association for Curriculum Development, State Federation of Foreign Language Teachers (member of board of executives), Experimental Society (New York).

AWARDS, HONORS: Educator service award, 1956.

WRITINGS:

(With Theodore Huebener) *English for Spanish Americans*, Henry Holt, 1950.
Teaching English as a Second Language in Elementary and Secondary Schools, Harper, 1958, revised edition, 1974.
Children's Living Spanish Picture Dictionary, Crown, 1960.
Children's Living Spanish Illustrated Lesson Book, Crown, 1960.
Teaching Children Foreign Languages, McGraw, 1964.
English as a Second Language: From Theory to Practice (synthesis of Finocchiaro's lectures and demonstrations for U.S. Department of State, 1960-64), Regents Publishing, 1964, 3rd edition published as *English as a Second/Foreign Language: From Theory to Practice*, 1986.
(With Harold J. McNally) *Educator's Vocabulary Handbook for Administrators, Supervisors, Teachers, Students, and Others Learning and Using English as a Foreign Language*, American Book Co., 1965.
Teachers Manual for Learning to Use English, two volumes, Regents Publishing, 1966.
Learning to Use English, two volumes, Regents Publishing, 1967.
Let's Talk, Regents Publishing, 1968.
(With M. Bonomo) *The Foreign Language Learner: A Guide for Teachers*, Regents Publishing, 1974.
Hablemos Espanol, Regents Publishing, 1976.
Viewpoints on English as a Second Language in Honor of James E. Alatis, Regents Publishing, 1977.
(With Violet H. Lavanda) *Growing in English Language Skills*, Regents Publishing, 1977.
The Second Language Classroom, Oxford University Press, 1981.
(With Christopher Brumfit) *The Functional-Notional Approach: From Theory to Practice*, Oxford University Press, 1983.
(With Sydney Sako) *Foreign Language Testing: A Practical Approach*, Regents Publishing, 1983.
Living Language Advanced Conversational French, Crown, 1986.
(Editor) *Children's Living Spanish*, Crown, 1986.

Contributor to education journals.

WORK IN PROGRESS: College Subjects Self-Taught and *Tales from Everywhere*.

*   *   *

FORBES, Graham B.
[Collective pseudonym]

WRITINGS:

"BOYS OF COLUMBIA HIGH" SERIES

The Boys of Columbia High; or, The All Around Rivals of the School (also see below), Grosset & Dunlap, 1912.
. . . *on the Diamond; or, Winning Out by Pluck* (also see below), Grosset & Dunlap, 1912.
. . . *on the River; or, The Boat Race Plot That Failed* (also see below), Grosset & Dunlap, 1912.
. . . *on the Gridiron; or, The Struggle for the Silver Cup* (also see below), Grosset & Dunlap, 1912.
. . . *on the Ice; or, Out for the Hockey Championship* (also see below), Grosset & Dunlap, 1912.
. . . *in Track Athletics; or, A Long Run That Won* (also see below), Grosset & Dunlap, 1913.

. . . *in Winter Sports; or, Stirring Doings on Skates and Ice-boats* (also see below), Grosset & Dunlap, 1915.
. . . *in Camp; or, The Rivalry of the Old School League* (also see below), Grosset & Dunlap, 1920.

"FRANK ALLEN" SERIES

Frank Allen's Schooldays; or, The All Around Rivals of Columbia High (originally published as *The Boys of Columbia High; or, The All Around Rivals of the School*), Garden City, 1926.
Frank Allen Playing to Win; or, The Boys of Columbia High on the Ice (originally published as *The Boys of Columbia High on the Ice; or, Out for the Hockey Championship*), Garden City, 1926.
. . . *in Winter Sports; or, Columbia High on Skates and Ice-boats* (originally published as *The Boys of Columbia High in Winter Sports; or, Stirring Doings on Skates and Ice-boats*), Garden City, 1926.
. . . *and His Rivals; or, The Boys of Columbia High in Track Athletics* (originally published as *The Boys of Columbia High in Track Athletics; or, A Long Run That Won*), Garden City, 1926.
. . . —*Pitcher; or, The Boys of Columbia High on the Diamond* (originally published as *The Boys of Columbia High on the Diamond; or, Winning out by Pluck*), Garden City, 1926.
. . . —*Head of the Crew; or, The Boys of Columbia High on the River* (originally published as *The Boys of Columbia High on the River; or, The Boat Race Plot That Failed*), Garden City, 1926.
. . . *in Camp; or, Columbia High and the School League Rivals* (originally published as *The Boys of Columbia High in Camp; or, The Rivalry of the Old School League*), Garden City, 1926.
. . . *at Rockspur Ranch; or, The Old Cowboy's Secret*, Garden City, 1926.
. . . *at Gold Fork; or, Locating the Lost Claim*, Garden City, 1926.
. . . *and His Motor Boat; or, Racing to Save a Life*, Garden City, 1926.
. . . —*Captain of the Team; or, The Boys of Columbia High on the Gridiron* (originally published as *The Boys of Columbia High on the Gridiron; or, The Struggle for the Silver Cup*), Garden City, 1926.
. . . *at Old Moose Lake; or, The Trail in the Snow*, Garden City, 1926.
. . . *at Zero Camp; or, The Queer Old Man of the Hills*, Garden City, 1926.
. . . *Snowbound; or, Fighting for Life in the Big Blizzard*, Garden City, 1927.
. . . *after Big Game; or, With Guns and Snowshoes in the Rockies*, Garden City, 1927.

OTHER

Also author of *Frank Allen with the Circus; or, The Old Ring-master's Secret*, Garden City, and *Frank Allen Pitching His Best; or, The Baseball Rivals of Columbia High*, Garden City.

SIDELIGHTS: Author St. George Rathborne helped Edward Stratemeyer with some of the books produced under this pseudonym. For more information see the entries in this volume for Harriet S. Adams, Edward L. Stratemeyer, and Andrew E. Svenson.

BIOGRAPHICAL/CRITICAL SOURCES:

BOOKS

Johnson, Deidre, editor and compiler, *Stratemeyer Pseud-onyms and Series Books: An Annotated Checklist of Stra-temeyer and Stratemeyer Syndicate Publications*, Green-wood Press, 1982.

*   *   *

FORD, Albert Lee
    See STRATEMEYER, Edward L.

*   *   *

FORREST, A(lfred) C(linton)   1916-1978

PERSONAL: Born May 24, 1916, in Mariposa Township, Ontario, Canada; died December 27, 1978; son of Alexander James (a farmer) and Jennie May (Greenaway) Forrest; married Esther Harriet Clipsham, January 31, 1941; children: Ann, Susan, Wendy, Diane. *Education:* Attended University of Toronto; Victoria University, B.A., 1937; Emmanuel College, Toronto, B.D., 1941; Huntington University, D.D., 1960.

ADDRESSES: Home—21 Dale Ave., Toronto, Ontario M4G 1K3. *Office*—United Church Observer, 85 St. Clair Ave., Toronto, Ontario M4T 1M8.

CAREER: Ordained minister of United Church of Canada, 1940; minister of Mt. Hamilton Church, Mt. Hamilton, Ontario, 1941-48; minister of First United Church, Port Credit, Ontario, 1948-55; editor, *United Church Observer*, Toronto, Ontario, 1954-78. Lecturer and broadcaster on the Middle East. *Military service:* Royal Canadian Air Force, chaplain, 1944-46; became flight lieutenant.

AWARDS, HONORS: Canadian centennial medal, 1967.

WRITINGS:

Not Tomorrow—Now, Ryerson, 1960.
(With William Kilbourne and Patrick Watson) *Religion in Canada*, McClelland & Stewart, 1968.
The Unholy Land, McClelland & Stewart, 1971, Devin-Adair, 1972, 2nd edition, 1974.
The Parables of Jesus, Christian Journals, 1979.

Author of weekly syndicated newspaper column "A Cleric Comments," appearing in Canadian newspapers. Regular columnist, *Ottawa Journal*, 1949-78. Contributor to religious periodicals in Canada and the United States. Editor-in-chief, *Varsity* magazine (University of Toronto), 1938-39.

WORK IN PROGRESS: Castro's Hot Little Island.

SIDELIGHTS: A. C. Forrest traveled in Europe, Asia, and Africa, and at one time lived in Lebanon.

*   *   *

FOX, Richard Wightman   1945-

PERSONAL: Born November 27, 1945, in Boston, Mass.; son of Matthew Bernard (a television producer and writer) and Lucy (Pope) Fox; married Frances Diane Nieblack, September 16, 1967; children: Rachel, Christopher. *Education:* Stanford University, B.A., 1966, M.A., 1974, Ph.D., 1975; attended Yale University, 1966-67.

ADDRESSES: Home—3946 Northeast Davis St., Portland, Ore. 97232. *Office*—Department of History, Reed College, Portland, Ore. 97202.

CAREER: Chinese University of Hong Kong, Chung Chi College, Hong Kong, instructor in western civilization, 1967-68; Lycee Ibn Rouchd, Blida, Algeria, teacher of English, 1968-70; Yale University, New Haven, Conn., assistant professor of history and American studies, 1975-81; Reed College, Portland, Ore., associate professor of history and humanities, 1981-88, Cornelia Marvin Pierce Professor of American Institutions and Humanities, 1988—.

MEMBER: Organization of American Historians, American Studies Association.

AWARDS, HONORS: Fellowship from Stanford University, 1977; Morse fellowship from Yale University, 1979-80; research fellowship for college teachers from National Endowment for the Humanities, 1984-85; Graves Award in the humanities from Pomona College, 1986; Burlington Northern Award from Reed College, 1986; fellowship from Oregon Committee for the Humanities, summer, 1986; fellowship from American Council of Learned Societies, 1987-88; Guggenheim fellowship, 1988-89.

WRITINGS:

So Far Disordered in Mind: Insanity in California, 1870-1930, University of California Press, 1978.
(Editor with T. J. Jackson Lears) *The Culture of Consumption: Critical Essays in American History, 1880-1980*, Pantheon, 1983.
Reinhold Niebuhr: A Biography, Pantheon, 1986.

CONTRIBUTOR

Carolyn Buan, editor, *How Human a Yardstick*, Oregon Committee for the Humanities, 1983.
John Witte, editor, *2084: Looking beyond Orwell*, Oregon Committee for the Humanities, 1984.
Michael Lacey, editor, *Religion and American Intellectual Life*, Woodrow Wilson Center, 1988.
Charles Reynolds, editor, *Community in America: The Challenge of Habits of the Heart*, University of California Press, 1988.

OTHER

Contributor of about fifty articles and reviews to scholarly and popular journals, including *American Quarterly, Wilson Quarterly*, and *New York Times Book Review*.

WORK IN PROGRESS: Gospel of Modernity: Liberal Protestantism in American Culture, for Pantheon; co-editor and contributor, *The Production of Culture: Essays in American Cultural History*, for Pantheon.

SIDELIGHTS: Reinhold Niebuhr: A Biography is Richard Wightman Fox's critical look at one of America's most influential religious liberalists. Niebuhr was a Protestant theologian and author who preferred viewing himself as a teacher of ethics rather than a theologian. His approach to Christianity has become known as "Christian Realism." As Julian N. Hartt proclaims in the *Washington Post Book World*, Niebuhr was "for at least two generations, until his death in 1971,. . . religious liberalism's main American public figure." Also according to Hartt, "never has [Niebuhr's] life been so richly delineated as . . . Fox has drawn it here. Fox has written not only an excellent biography but a notable chapter in the history of American religious thought. It is also a notable feat of the imagi-

nation. Fox never saw or heard Niebuhr. Yet his portrayal of the man will surely strike many readers as executed from life. The moral passion, the formidable intellectual energy, the drive for domination, even the idiosyncratic pulpit and rostrum gestures, are all there." Additionally, a number of reviewers identify significant ambiguities in Niebuhr's thinking through the decades and the fact that Fox has skillfully brought them into focus. In the *New York Times Book Review*, for instance, Harvey Cox remarks: "Fox has given us a colorful account of Niebuhr's life that is at once scrupulous and warmhearted. He gently undercuts some of the myths that Niebuhr himself did so little to challenge. . . . He also wisely refuses to smooth over Niebuhr's contradictions or unravel his inconsistencies." Overall, Fox's biography is highly esteemed as a work that "comes as close to being comprehensive as we are likely to see in an imperfect, Niebuhrian world. Based on meticulous research. . ., the book is written with a verve, grace, and depth of understanding worthy of its subject," writes David Brion Davis for the *New York Review of Books*.

Fox wrote to *CA*: "The most pressing concern for the scholarly writer in an age of over-specialized disciplines is to cultivate a style accessible to nonspecialists. Like Reinhold Niebuhr, I am trying to bridge the gap between journalism and scholarship, between a wide audience of ordinary readers and a narrow one of academic professionals. There are few models in America of the serious 'writer' in the British sense. We tend to equate 'writer' with 'writer of fiction' rather than 'essayist.' What we need are more essayists who are equally comfortable with scholarly methods and literate, nonesoteric expression."

BIOGRAPHICAL/CRITICAL SOURCES:

PERIODICALS

Globe and Mail (Toronto), May 10, 1986.
Los Angeles Times, December 2, 1983.
Los Angeles Times Book Review, March 30, 1986.
Nation, January 14, 1984.
New Republic, March 31, 1986.
New York Review of Books, February 13, 1986.
New York Times, January 2, 1986.
New York Times Book Review, January 5, 1986.
Time, January 20, 1986.
Washington Post Book World, March 23, 1986.

*   *   *

FRANCIS, Daniel
    See CRANNY, Titus (Francis)

*   *   *

FRANKLIN, Jon (Daniel)   1942-

PERSONAL: Born January 13, 1942, in Enid, Okla.; son of Benjamin Max and Wilma (a copyreader; maiden name, Winburn) Franklin; married Nancy Creevan, December 12, 1959 (divorced, 1975); children: Teresa June, Catherine Cay. *Education:* University of Maryland, B.S. (with high honors), 1970.

ADDRESSES: Agent—Dominick Abel Literary Agency, 498 West End Ave., No. 12C, New York, N.Y. 10024.

CAREER: U.S. Navy, journalist in the Far East, 1959-67; *Prince Georges Post*, Hyattsville, Md., editor and reporter, 1967-70; *Baltimore Evening Sun*, Baltimore, Md., rewrite man, 1970-72, science writer, 1972-86; University of Maryland,

School of Journalism, College Park, associate professor, 1986—. Visiting associate professor, Towson State University. Member of unit council of Newspaper Guild at Baltimore Sunpapers.

MEMBER: National Association of Science Writers, National Press Club, Newspaper Guild, Maryland Press Club.

AWARDS, HONORS: James T. Grady Medal, American Chemical Society, 1975, for popularizing science; Pulitzer Prize for feature writing, 1979, and for explanatory journalism, 1985, for series ''The Mind Fixers.''

WRITINGS:

NONFICTION

(With Alan Doelp) *Shocktrauma* (Book-of-the-Month Club alternate selection), St. Martin's, 1980.
(With Doelp) *Not Quite a Miracle: Brain Surgeons and Their Patients on the Frontier of Medicine,* Doubleday, 1983.
(With John Sutherland) *Guinea Pig Doctors: The Drama of Medical Research through Self-Experimentation,* Morrow, 1984.
Writing for Story: Craft Secrets of Dramatic Nonfiction, Atheneum, 1986.
Molecules of the Mind: The Brave New Science of Molecular Psychology, Atheneum, 1987.

SIDELIGHTS: Pulitzer Prize-winning Jon Franklin, formerly a science writer with the *Baltimore Evening Sun,* brings his journalistic skills to his several nonfiction books about medical advances and the medical profession. *Shocktrauma,* written with Alan Doelp, details the creation of an Emergency Medical Services unit to deal with severely traumatized accident victims. ''The product of five years of research, this painstakingly documented nonfiction'' nevertheless contains ''a powerful and realistic drama, as informative as it is intriguing,'' writes John Charnay in the *Los Angeles Times Book Review.* ''The dialogue is enthralling and the narrative compelling.'' *Guinea Pig Doctors: The Drama of Medical Research through Self-Experimentation,* co-written with physician John Sutherland, follows eight doctors who experimented on themselves to advance their theories. Like *Shocktrauma,* it combines a ''mass of scientific information'' with ''background material on the times and places of the various episodes,'' notes Ronald Sutherland in the Toronto *Globe and Mail.* The result, concludes the critic, is ''a highly readable and captivating book.''

Similarly, Franklin's second collaboration with Doelp, *Not Quite a Miracle: Brain Surgeons and Their Patients on the Frontier of Medicine,* recreates the ordeals of four patients and their surgeons. Summarizes *Washington Post Book World* contributor Robin Marantz Henig: ''[The co-authors] recount in painstaking detail the brain operations, and the lives and hopes, of four brave patients.... The awesome stakes of neurosurgery are what keep us reading this impressive book.'' In this ''reconstructive reporting,'' however, ''scenes not observed by a writer [are] pieced together or guessed at later and written as though witnessed,'' relates Charles Leroux in the *Chicago Tribune.* Even though this process fleshes out the story, Leroux feels that the authors ''don't need to be hussying up this story. It's a natural beauty.'' Henig expresses similar reservations, but admits that ''the personal background supplied for our heroes might have been awkwardly handled, but it did indeed turn them into more than cardboard actors.'' Adds the critic: ''By the end of the book, I really cared about the patients.''

More recently, Franklin has turned his talents to investigating the field of molecular psychology. *Molecules of the Mind: The Brave New Science of Molecular Psychology* details the development of these theories, which postulate the existence of brain chemicals that encourage various types of behavior. Thus psychological disorders such as depression, schizophrenia, or psychosis can be a matter of confused chemical signals. Franklin again creates a compelling portrait of his subject; *New York Times Book Review* contributor Barry L. Jacobs remarks that the author ''spends the first two-thirds of the book describing, in lucid and riveting fashion, the scientific advances in molecular psychology.... He captures the excitement and explosive nature of research in this field.'' Similarly, Richard M. Restak writes in the *Washington Post Book World* that ''molecular psychology provides an exciting story that Franklin sets out in riveting detail. The prose is often sparkling, and he tells us things we're not likely to have read in a magazine article.'' But Restak also faults the author for not keeping ''to himself his sometimes wildly speculative predictions and oftentimes dingbat opinions about the implications of molecular psychology.'' Skip Kaltenhauser, however, defends these ideas as stimulating: ''Franklin has been criticized for speculative predictions,'' the critic writes in the *Washington Post,* ''but such musings are labeled as such and provoke examination of the decisions society will confront as a result of the new science.'' Such examinations serve the author's purpose, for as Jacobs describes, Franklin's ''goal is to make us aware of this revolution so that we can monitor it and especially so that we can take part in it and make decisions.''

BIOGRAPHICAL/CRITICAL SOURCES:

PERIODICALS

Chicago Tribune, March 23, 1983.
Christian Science Monitor, September 10, 1986.
Globe and Mail (Toronto), April 8, 1984.
Los Angeles Times Book Review, June 1, 1980.
New York Times Book Review, April 22, 1984, February 8, 1987.
Washington Post, February 29, 1988.
Washington Post Book World, April 17, 1983, February 22, 1987.

*   *   *

FRASER, J(ulius) T(homas)   1923-

PERSONAL: Born May 7, 1923, in Budapest, Hungary; came to United States in 1946, naturalized in 1953; son of Francis (an attorney) and Olga (Szigethy) Fraser; married Margaret Cameron (a musician), 1948 (divorced, 1970); married Jane Hunsicker (a teacher), 1973; children: Thomas C. Fraser, Anne-Marie C. Fraser, Carol Hunsicker, Margaret C. Fraser, Ann Hunsicker. *Education:* Cooper Union School of Engineering, B.E.E., 1951; Technische Universitaet Hannover, Ph.D., 1970. *Politics:* ''A Jeffersonian independent.'' *Religion:* ''Christian by private creed.''

ADDRESSES: Office—International Society for the Study of Time, P.O. Box 815, Westport, Conn. 06881.

CAREER: Worked as a machinist, technician, and draftsman in Budapest, Hungary, 1941-44; Allied Control Commission, Rome, Italy, English correspondent, 1945-46; cataloger at Columbia University Libraries, contract inspector for Electrolux Vacuum Cleaners, and laboratory foreman at North American Philips, Inc., 1947-50; Rangertone, Inc., Newark, N.J., design draftsman, 1950-51; Westinghouse Electric Corp., Baltimore, Md., junior engineer, 1951-53; General Precision Laboratory (now Singer-Kearfott, Inc.), Pleasantville, N.Y., staff member, 1955-57, senior staff member, 1957-62, senior scientist in physics department of Research Division, 1962-71; independent scholar in the study of time, 1971—. Visiting lecturer, Massachusetts Institute of Technology, 1966-67, and Mt. Holyoke College, 1967-69; visiting professor, University of Maryland, 1969-70; adjunct professor, Fordham University, 1971-84. Has lectured extensively on various aspects of the study of time.

MEMBER: International Society for the Study of Time (founder and secretary).

WRITINGS:

Of Time, Passion, and Knowledge: Reflections on the Strategy of Existence, Braziller, 1975.
Time as Conflict: A Scientific and Humanistic Study, Birkhauser, 1978.
The Genesis and Evolution of Time: A Critique of Interpretation in Physics, University of Massachusetts Press, 1982.
Time, the Familiar Stranger, University of Massachusetts Press, 1987.

EDITOR AND CONTRIBUTOR

The Voices of Time: A Cooperative Survey of Man's Views of Time as Expressed by the Sciences and the Humanities, Braziller, 1966, 2nd enlarged edition, University of Massachusetts Press, 1981.
(With F. C. Haber and G. H. Mueller) *The Study of Time I,* Springer-Verlag, 1972.
(With N. Lawrence) *The Study of Time II,* Springer-Verlag, 1975.
(With Lawrence and D. Park) *The Study of Time III,* Springer-Verlag, 1978.
(With Lawrence and Park) *The Study of Time IV,* Springer-Verlag, 1981.
(With Lawrence) *Time, Science, and Society in China and the West: The Study of Time V,* University of Massachusetts Press, 1986.
Time and Mind: The Study of Time VI, University of Massachusetts Press, 1988.

OTHER

Contributor to *Britannica Yearbook of Science and the Future,* 1970, and to numerous scientific and scholarly books and journals.

WORK IN PROGRESS: Revolt of the Caged Mind, a novel; editing *Time and Process: Essays on Change and Permanence.*

SIDELIGHTS: In his pioneering 1966 work *The Voices of Time: A Cooperative Survey of Man's Views of Time as Expressed by the Sciences and the Humanities,* J. T. Fraser "has managed to bring together a most impressive collection of materials bearing on his subject, such as notions of time in the history of philosophy and religions, the rhythms of language and music, time-perception in children," and many other areas, notes J. Ben Lieberman in the *Saturday Review.* In gathering together various studies of time, "what Fraser is really after is an interdisciplinary understanding of time itself, and he has broken new ground in bringing out its role in almost every conceivable field of study," adds Lieberman. Despite the work's scholarly nature, *Observer Review* contributor Philip Toynbee finds *The Voices of Time* accessible to the general reader: "For a non-scientist reader a principal source of pleasure comes from having his mind stretched to the uttermost limits of its

capacity." Lieberman concurs, asserting that the lay reader "can still profit from the book"; in addition, the critic finds that "the ramifications of time are both so profound and so superficial, so pervasive and so personal, that the sensitive reader or conversationalist may well find himself pursuing the subject more and more deeply, until he is confronted with all those questions about the meaning of his own life." Toynbee concludes that *The Voices of Time* is "one of the most fascinating books I have read for a long time."

Since the appearance of *The Voices of Time,* Fraser has founded the International Society for the Study of Time (of which he is secretary); he has also published several books on the nature of time. *Of Time, Passion, and Knowledge,* his first, covers much of the same ground as *The Voices of Time,* but attempts to integrate the various themes into a single theory. "J. T. Fraser would have earned our gratitude if his new book provided a lucid and encompassing guide to this complex topic— period! But that is only one of his achievements," claims Robert Kastenbaum in *Social Science.* "More than a scholarly treatise, this volume delights with its play of mind upon the most varied and challenging of materials. Fraser's style and wit, his gift for integrating unexpected elements, and the enthusiasm he obviously feels for this topic come across on every page. And yet," continues the critic, "the book has still another, and possibly even more significant, contribution to make. Fraser concludes with the outlines of a systematic theory of time. It is a bold and welcome attempt."

Fraser's most recent work, *Time, the Familiar Stranger,* "is the best available discussion of time for a general audience," remarks H. C. Byerly in a *Choice* review, adding that the work "provides an excellent introduction to more specialized studies." Discussing the use of time in different cultures, *Time, the Familiar Stranger*'s "unifying theme is the difference between psychological time and time in modern physics," describes David Gordon in *Library Journal.* "It is not a new idea that time is multiple, that there is more than one structure to which the word refers," notes *Nature* contributor C. J. S. Clarke; "this explains why the discussion of time is so fraught with paradox. But Fraser is the first to have developed the idea into a universal vision, condensed into the modest space of this book." Concludes the critic: "As well as setting the context for future work on time, this book will add to our understanding of the choice before us for the future direction of humanity."

"As a young child growing up in the Hungarian countryside, I liked to tell people that I would be a blacksmith, explorer, and everyone's friend," J. T. Fraser told *CA.* "The 'blacksmith' progressed through technician, draftsman, engineer, inventor, physicist and philosopher to the writer of both fiction and nonfiction. The 'explorer' still travels around the world, in search of ideas and feelings. The 'friend' is manifest in a profound empathy for people, and in an unremitting concern with the responsibility of being human.

"All three parts are joined in my dedication to the study of time which spans over thirty-five years. In my early writings I formulated a new system of natural philosophy—the theory of time as conflict. In my subsequent writings I have been working out the practical significance of the new philosophical system for our understanding of matter, life, and society.

"The moving power of this single passion—the analysis of time—to which I have given my life, is, not surprisingly, experiential. As an adolescent in World War II, I watched the clash of cultures and the attendant release of primordial emotions. As a young man I observed America, this land of promise, through extensive travels—but always returning in body and spirit to my home along the Hudson.

"Integrating these two families of impressions, I could not help but note how thoroughly the spectacular achievements of science and industry have undermined all traditional assessments of the position of man in the scheme of things. The consequent absence of ideals, inspiring as well as intelligible to the majority of people, makes our epoch an uninformed one.

"An analysis of the social forces at work, carried out through the theory of time as conflict suggests that this regression is, metaphorically, a withdrawal before the leap. We are witnessing around the earth a 'revolt of the caged mind,' a radical alteration in the texture of human life itself. The march is not to the tune of Dies Irae, not even to that of the Communist Internationale, but to a more elemental call. We have reached an evolutionary dead-end, comparable in its dynamics to the one that was reached by inorganic evolution just before the birth of life, and by organic evolution just before the emergence of the human mind.

"As a writer, philosopher and scientist I see my task as one of chronicling and interpreting these profound changes, becoming a part of the motive forces behind them, and pursuing them toward their unknown end."

BIOGRAPHICAL/CRITICAL SOURCES:

PERIODICALS

Choice, March, 1983, May, 1988.
Library Journal, November 15, 1987.
Nature, December 24, 1987.
Observer Review, February 18, 1968.
Saturday Review, January 29, 1966.
Social Science, autumn, 1975.
Washington Post Book World, August 17, 1975.

* . * *

FRASER, Jane
See PILCHER, Rosamunde

* * *

FREED, Lynn (R.) 1945-

PERSONAL: Born July 18, 1945, in Durban, South Africa; came to the United States in 1967, naturalized in 1977; daughter of Harold Derrick (an actor) and Anne (a theatre director; maiden name, Moshal) Freed; married Gordon Gamsu (a physician), July 9, 1967 (divorced, 1986); children: Jessica Peta. *Education:* University of the Witwatersrand, B. A., 1966; Columbia University, M. A., 1968, Ph. D., 1972.

ADDRESSES: Home—57 Ashbury Ter., San Francisco, Calif. 94117. *Agent*—Lois Wallace, Wallace & Sheil Agency Inc., 177 East 70th St., New York, N.Y. 10021.

CAREER: Writer, 1975—.

AWARDS, HONORS: Bay Area Book Reviewers Association award for fiction, 1986, for *Home Ground;* National Endowment for the Arts fellowship, 1987; Yaddo and MacDowell fellowship.

WRITINGS:

Heart Change (novel), New American Library, 1982.

Home Ground (novel), Summit Books, 1986.

Contributor of stories to magazines for adults and children, including *Harper's, New York Times,* and *Zyzzyva.*

WORK IN PROGRESS: A novel.

SIDELIGHTS: Home Ground, Lynn Freed's novel about Ruth Frank, a young white girl coming of age in South Africa in the 1950s and 1960s, is proclaimed a "rarity" by *Washington Post Book World* critic Jonathan Yardley. In Yardley's opinion, this is "a novel about childhood and adolescence that never lapses into self-pity, that rings true in every emotion and incident, that regards adults sympathetically if unsparingly, that deals with serious thematic material, and that is quite deliciously funny. *Home Ground* is all this and more: it is also the flip side of rites-of-passage literary tradition, for its narrator is not a boy but a girl." Although Yardley and other critics, like *New York Times Book Review* contributor Janette Turner Hospital, stress that *Home Ground* is not a political novel, they are of the opinion that Ruth and her theatrical family are essentially a metaphor for South Africa. Writes Hospital: "The Franks are South Africa in miniature. They are a theater family: second-rate, self-obsessed, histrionic, always requiring an audience. . . . More than 20 years later the reader feels a shiver of recognition: South African politics as soap opera; P. W. Botha's Government as second-rate stage director, casting itself in the grand melodramas, convinced of its own tragic and misunderstood role."

When *Home Ground* first appeared in South Africa, newspaper headlines hinted that it might be banned. This did not occur, but in an interview with Harriet Stix in the *Los Angeles Times,* Freed told of how disconcerted some people were with the work: "Very little has been written about middle-class South Africans," and people were "just horrified. . . . I was considered a traitor, and this by people who are highly critical of the government." Even so, *Home Ground* has been a financial and critical success. As Hospital maintains, "Freed's guileless child-narrator takes us *inside* the neurosis of South Africa. We experience it in a way that is qualitatively different from watching the most graphic of news clips. . . . Freed may not have quite the literary reach of Nadine Gordimer, but her vantage point of privileged outcaste gives, I think, a more disturbing inner view of that awful, intricate symbiosis between black and white."

Freed wrote to *CA:* "All fiction is betrayal. All fiction is revenge. The problem, for the writer, is to find the proper voice, the proper object for both. When I began [*Home Ground*], I received some good advice from an editor. 'Don't show it to anyone involved,' she said. 'And if you hold back, it'll show.'"

BIOGRAPHICAL/CRITICAL SOURCES:

PERIODICALS

Los Angeles Times, December 14, 1986.
New York Times Book Review, August 17, 1986.
Times Literary Supplement, May 9, 1986.
Village Voice, October 28, 1986.
Washington Post Book World, August 24, 1986.

* * *

FREUDENTHAL, Hans 1905-

PERSONAL: Born September 17, 1905, in Luckenwalde, Germany; son of Joseph and Elsbeth (Ehmann) Freudenthal; married Susanna Johanna Catharina Lutter, July 20, 1932; children: Jedidja, Matthijs, Thomas, Mirjam. *Education:* University of Berlin, Ph.D., 1930.

ADDRESSES: Home—Franz Schubertstraat 44, Utrecht, Netherlands.

CAREER: Jahrbuch Forstschritte der Mathematik, Berlin, Germany, assistant, 1930; University of Amsterdam, Mathematical Institute, Amsterdam, Netherlands, assistant, 1931-37, conservator, 1937-46; State University of Utrecht, Mathematical Institute, Utrecht, Netherlands, professor, 1946-76, director of institute curriculum development in mathematics, 1971-76. Lecturer at American universities. President, International Committee on Mathematical Instruction.

MEMBER: Royal Netherlands Academy of Sciences, American Mathematical Society.

AWARDS, HONORS: De Gauden Ganzeveer (the Golden Goosequill), 1985; D.Sc., Humboldt University in Berlin; Ph.D. from Erlangen University, Free University, Brussels, York University, and University of Amsterdam.

WRITINGS:

Oktaven, Ausnahmegruppen, Oktavengeometric, [Utrecht], 1951, 2nd edition, 1960.
Inleiding tot het denken van Albert Einstein, Assen, 1952.
Waarschijnlijkheid en statistiek, Bohn, 1957, translation published as *Probability and Statistics,* Elsevier, 1965.
Logique mathematique appliquee, Gauthier-Villars (Paris), 1958.
(Editor) *Report on Methods of Initiation into Geometry,* J. B. Wolters, 1958.
Lie Groups and Foundations of Geometry, University of New Brunswick, 1959.
(Editor) *Colloquium on Algebraic and Topological Foundations of Geometry,* Utrecht, 1959, Pergamon, 1962.
(Compiler) *Lincos, Design of a Language for Cosmic Intercourse,* North-Holland Publishing, 1960.
Lie Groups: Mathematics S-283, Associated Students' Store, University of California, 1960.
Exacte Logica, Bohn, 1961, translation published as *The Language of Logic,* Elsevier, 1966.
Lie Groups, Department of Mathematics, Yale University, 1961.
(Editor) *The Concept and the Role of the Model in Mathematics and Natural and Social Sciences,* Gordon & Breach, 1961.
(Editor) *Report on the Relations between Arithmetic and Algebra in Mathematical Education up to the Age of 15 Years,* J. B. Wolters, 1962.
De Eerste Ontmoeting tussen de Wiskunde en de Sociale Wetenschappen, [Brussels], 1966.

Mathematics Observed, translation by Stephen Rudolpher and I. N. Baker, McGraw, 1967, original German version published as *Mathematik in Wissenschaft und Alltag,* Kinder Verlag, 1968.
(With H. de Vries) *Linear Lie Groups,* Academic Press, 1969.
Vijjentwintig jaar Wiskundige ideen en methoden, Math. Centrum., 1972.
Mathematics as an Educational Task, Reidel, 1973.
(Editor) L. E. J. Brouwer, *Collected Works II,* North-Holland Publishing, 1976.
Weeding and Sowing: Preface to a Science of Mathematics Education, Reidel, 1978, 2nd edition, 1980.
(Editor) *Raumtheorie,* Wissenschaftliche Buchgesellschaft, 1978.
Fiabilite, validite, pertinence: Criteres sur la recherche de l'enseignement mathematique, Journees didactiques, 1980.
Didactical Phenomenology of Mathematical Structures, Reidel, 1983.
Appels en Peren: Wiskunde en Psychologie, Van Walraven, 1984.
(Author of introduction) Phillip J. Davis and Reuben Hersch, *Erfahrung Mathematik,* Birkhaeuser, 1986.
Berlin 1923-30: Studienerinnerungen, Walter de Gruyter, 1986.
Schrijf dat op Hans, Meulenhoff, 1986.

Also author of fiction printed in Dutch. Editor-in-chief of *Educational Studies in Mathematics,* nine volumes, Reidel, 1968-79, and *Geometricae Dedicata,* 1972.

SIDELIGHTS: Hans Freudenthal told *CA:* "Although my writings extend from poetry to mathematics, from formal publications to informal letters, from fiction to fact-finding reports, I have pursued both rigor and art in all of them even when I knew it was unfeasible. Neither as a speaker nor as a writer do I master any language as well as I would like or even as others would expect me to. The worst is the one I invented myself, and the worst but that one is English, which is the easiest language to be written at a low level and the most difficult for high aspirations to be satisfied. I started publishing at the age of thirteen; now seventy years later my pace is still accelerating. I doubt whether anybody ever took such a pleasure in reading my work as I did in writing it. Fortunately nobody is obliged to read all I am writing, and nobody remembers any substantial part of my writings—myself included. If I will ever be remembered, I will be so as the one who is not worth being remembered."

*   *   *

FREY, Marlys
See MAYFIELD, Marlys

G

GALENSON, Walter 1914-

PERSONAL: Born December 5, 1914, in New York, N.Y.; son of Louis P. (a certified public accountant) and Libby (Mishell) Galenson; married Marjorie Spector (a professor), June 27, 1940; children: Emily, Alice, David. *Education:* Columbia University, A.B., 1934, Ph.D., 1940.

ADDRESSES: Home—1150 Park Ave., New York, N.Y. 10128. *Office*—School of Industrial and Labor Relations, Cornell University, Ithaca, N.Y. 14850.

CAREER: Hunter College (now Hunter College of the City University of New York), New York, N.Y., assistant professor of economics, 1938-41; economist with U.S. Office of Strategic Services, 1942-44, and U.S. Foreign Service, 1944-46; Harvard University, Cambridge, Mass., assistant professor of economics, 1946-51; University of California, Berkeley, professor of economics, 1951-66; Cornell University, Ithaca, N.Y., 1966—, began as professor of economics, currently professor emeritus.

MEMBER: Association for Comparative Economic Studies.

AWARDS, HONORS: Fulbright fellow, 1950; Guggenheim fellow, 1954-55.

WRITINGS:

Rival Unionism in the United States, American Council on Public Affairs, 1940, reprinted, Russell & Russell, 1966.
Labor in Norway, Harvard University Press, 1949, reprinted, Russell & Russell, 1970.
Unemployment Compensation in Massachusetts, State of Massachusetts, 1950.
The Danish System of Labor Relations, Harvard University Press, 1952.
(Editor) *Comparative Labor Movements,* Prentice-Hall, 1952.
Labor Productivity in Soviet and American Industry, Columbia University Press, 1955.
(Editor) *Labor and Economic Development,* Wiley, 1959.
The CIO Challenge to the AFL, Harvard University Press, 1960.
(With S. M. Lipset) *Labor and Trade Unionism: An Interdisciplinary Reader,* Wiley, 1960.
Trade Union Democracy in Western Europe, University of California Press, 1961.

(Editor) *Labor in Developing Economies,* University of California Press, 1962.
(WIth F. G. Pyatt) *The Quality of Labor and Its Impact on Economic Development,* International Labour Office, 1964.
A Primer on Employment and Wages, Random House, 1966.
(Editor with Alexander Eckstein and T. C. Liu) *Economic Trends in Communist China,* Aldine, 1968.
(With Nai-Ruenn Chen) *The Chinese Economy under Communism,* Aldine, 1969.
The Labor Force and Labor Problems, Fontana, 1975.
Labor in the Twentieth Century, Academic Press, 1978.
Economic Growth and Structural Change in Taiwan, Cornell University Press, 1979.
The International Labor Organization, University of Wisconsin Press, 1981.
The United Brotherhood of Carpenters, Harvard University Press, 1983.
(Editor) *Foreign Trade and Investment: The Newly Industrializing Asian Countries,* University of Wisconsin Press, 1985.
A Welfare State Strikes Oil: The Norwegian Experience, University Press of America, 1986.

Contributor to economics journals.

*   *   *

GALLAGHER, Patricia

PERSONAL: Born in Lockhart, Tex.; daughter of Frank (in construction business) and Martha (Rhody) Bienek; married James D. Gallagher (a television engineer; died, 1966); children: James C. *Education:* Attended Trinity University, San Antonio, Tex., 1951.

ADDRESSES: Home—3111 Clearfield Dr., San Antonio, Tex. 78230. *Agent*—Scott Meredith Literary Agency, Inc., 845 Third Ave., New York, N.Y. 10022.

CAREER: Writer, 1949—. Limited operator for KTSA-Radio, 1950-51; has appeared on television and radio programs in Texas, Charleston, S.C., and other cities.

MEMBER: Authors Guild, Authors League of America, Romance Writers of America, Golden Triangle Writers Guild.

WRITINGS:

NOVELS

The Sons and the Daughters, Messner, 1961.
Answer to Heaven, Avon, 1964.
The Fires of Brimstone, Avon, 1966.
Shannon, Avon, 1967.
Shadows of Passion, Avon, 1971.
Summer of Sighs, Avon, 1971.
The Thicket, Avon, 1974.
Castles in the Air, Avon, 1976.
Mystic Rose, Avon, 1977.
No Greater Love, Avon, 1979.
All for Love, Avon, 1981.
Echoes and Embers, Avon, 1983.
On Wings of Dreams, Berkley Publishing, 1985.
A Perfect Love, Berkley Publishing, 1987.

OTHER

Member of advisory council for *San Antonio* magazine.

WORK IN PROGRESS: More novels.

SIDELIGHTS: Patricia Gallagher wrote *CA:* "I've been interested in writing since childhood, wrote short stories in high school, and walked three miles each way to the Public Library. 'Making it' was a long hard struggle, writing on a small portable on my kitchen table between the chores of housewife and mother, and often late at night when my family was asleep, and the kitchen was the quietest place in the house."

Gallagher's works have been published in French, German, Spanish, Portuguese, Italian, Dutch, Danish, Swedish, and Norwegian. Her book *Castles in the Air* was used as a text at Penn State University and was rated by students as second only to *Gone with the Wind*.

AVOCATIONAL INTERESTS: Traveling, reading, and gardening.

BIOGRAPHICAL/CRITICAL SOURCES:

PERIODICALS

Affaire de Coeur, September, 1987.
Bride's Magazine, February-March, 1983.
Dallas News, April 16, 1961, May 27, 1976.
Houston Post, April 1, 1962, June 1, 1976.
Romantic Times, September, 1987.
San Antonio Light, May 23, 1976.
San Antonio Magazine, October, 1976.

*　　　*　　　*

GALLUP, Donald (Clifford)　1913-

PERSONAL: Born May 12, 1913, in Sterling, Conn.; son of Carl Daniel (a lumberman) and Lottie (Stanton) Gallup. *Education:* Yale University, B.A., 1934, Ph.D., 1939.

ADDRESSES: Home—216 Bishop St., New Haven, Conn. 06511.

CAREER: Southern Methodist University, Dallas, Tex., instructor in English, 1937-41; Yale University, New Haven, Conn., assistant professor of bibliography, curator of Yale Collection of American Literature, and fellow of Jonathan Edwards College, 1947-80. *Military service:* U.S. Army, 1941-46; became lieutenant colonel; received Croix de Guerre.

MEMBER: Bibliographical Society of America, Elizabethan Club (Yale), Grolier Club and Yale Club (both New York).

AWARDS, HONORS: Guggenheim fellowships, 1961, 1968-69; Litt.D., Colby College, 1971.

WRITINGS:

(Compiled with Robert Bartlett Haas) *A Catalogue of the Published and Unpublished Writings of Gertrude Stein,* Yale University Library, 1941, reprinted, Folcroft Library Editions, 1974.
T. S. Eliot: A Bibliography, Faber, 1952, Harcourt, 1953, revised edition, 1969.
(Editor) *The Flowers of Friendship: Letters Written to Gertrude Stein,* Knopf, 1953.
(Editor) Eugene O'Neill, *Inscriptions,* Yale University Library, 1960.
Ezra Pound: A Bibliography, Hart-Davis, 1963, revised edition, University Press of Virginia, 1983.
(Editor) O'Neill, *More Stately Mansions,* Yale University Press, 1964.
On Contemporary Bibliography, with Particular Reference to Ezra Pound (booklet), University of Texas Press, 1970.
T. S. Eliot and Ezra Pound: Collaborators in Letters, C. A. Stonehill, 1970.
(Editor) Gertrude Stein, *Fernhurst, Q.E.D., and Other Early Writings,* Liveright, 1971.
(Editor) Thornton Niven Wilder, *The Alcestiad: or, a Life in the Sun* (three-act play), Harper, 1977.
(Editor) Wilder, *American Characteristics and Other Essays,* Harper, 1979.
(Editor) O'Neill, *Poems, 1912-1944,* Ticknor & Fields, 1980.
Work Diary, Yale Library, 1981.
The Calms of Capricorn, Ticknor & Fields, 1982.
(Editor) Kathryn Hulme, *Of Chickens and Plums,* Yale Library, 1982.
At the Circulo de Recreo with Ezra Pound, Beinecke Library, 1985.
(Editor) *The Journals of Thornton Wilder: 1939-1961,* Yale University Press, 1985.
Pigeons on the Granite: Memories, Beinecke Library, 1988.

Contributor to *Times Literary Supplement* and *Atlantic.* Contributor and editor, *Yale University Library Gazette,* 1947-80.

WORK IN PROGRESS: A study of the cycle plays of Eugene O'Neill; an edition of the letters of Gertrude Stein.

SIDELIGHTS: As curator of the Beinecke Library Collection of American Literature at Yale, Donald Gallup's interests went "beyond the conservation of books to the conservation of literature," the *New York Times* reports. "He . . . prepared definitive bibliographies—an ordering and tidying of the clutter that creeps into the printed record of any major author—for T. S. Eliot, [Ezra] Pound, and Gertrude Stein."

According to the *Times Literary Supplement,* Gallup's *Ezra Pound: A Bibliography* "has been frequently cited as the model bibliography of a modern author," while the 1952 edition of *T. S. Eliot: A Bibliography* is "at once acclaimed for its thoroughness and clarity." When the latter was revised to reflect the effect of a Nobel Prize on the author's literary standing and to meet the increasingly sophisticated demands of Eliot scholars, the *Times Literary Supplement* proclaimed the resulting edition "one of the classics of its type."

AVOCATIONAL INTERESTS: Book-collecting (T. S. Eliot, Ezra Pound, Gertrude Stein, Edward Lear, Lawrence Durrell, Graham Greene).

BIOGRAPHICAL/CRITICAL SOURCES:

PERIODICALS

American Theatre, July/August, 1986.
New York Times, April 24, 1980.
New York Times Book Review, April 24, 1980, October 13, 1985.
Times Literary Supplement, March 7, 1969, May 3, 1970, March 20, 1981, March 14, 1986.
Washington Post Book World, October 20, 1985, September 13, 1987.

*   *   *

GARDNER, Richard Kent 1928-

PERSONAL: Born December 7, 1928, in New Bedford, Mass.; son of Francis and Millicent Annetta (Kent) Gardner. *Education:* Middlebury College, Middlebury, Vermont, A.B. (cum laude), 1950; University of Paris, diploma in literature, 1954; Western Reserve University (now Case Western Reserve University), M.S.L.S., 1955, Ph.D., 1968. *Religion:* Episcopalian.

ADDRESSES: Home—3328 Ave. Troie, Apt. 405, Montreal, Quebec, Canada H3V 1B1. *Office*—Ecole de bibliotheconomie et des sciences de l'information, University of Montreal, C.P. 6128, Succursale A, Montreal, Quebec, Canada H3C 3J7.

CAREER: Case Institute of Technology (now Case Western Reserve University), Cleveland, Ohio, assistant librarian, 1955-57; Michigan State University, East Lansing, library adviser for Vietnam project, 1957-58; Marietta College, Marietta, Ohio, librarian and associate professor, 1959-63; *Choice* Magazine, Middletown, Conn., founding editor, 1963-66; Case Western Reserve University, School of Library Science, associate professor, 1966-69; University of Montreal, Montreal, Quebec, associate professor, 1969-70, professor of library science and director of Graduate School of Library Science, 1970-72; *Choice* Magazine, editor, 1972-77; University of California, Graduate School of Library and Information Science, Los Angeles, professor of library and information science, 1977-82; University of Montreal, Ecole de bibliotheconomie et des sciences de l'information, professor, 1983—, director, 1983-87. Consultant to college and university libraries, 1966—. Trustee, Lake Placid Club Educational Foundation, 1972-87, and Russell Library, 1975-77. *Military service:* U.S. Army, 1951-53.

MEMBER: American Library Association, Canadian Library Association, Association of College and Research Libraries, Music Library Association, Association pour l'Avancement des Sciences et des Techniques de la Documentation, Corporation des Bibliothecaires Professionels du Quebec (member of administrative council, 1970-72), Ohio Library Association (member of executive board, 1962-63), Ohio College Association (library section; vice-president, 1962-63; president, 1963), Tudor Singers (Montreal; vice-president, 1970-72), Beta Phi Mu, Phi Beta Kappa.

WRITINGS:

(With Nguyen Xuan Dao) *Bibliography of Periodicals Published in Viet Nam*, Michigan State University, 1958.
(Editor) Nguyen thi Cut, translator, *The Cataloging and Classification of Books*, Asia Foundation (Saigon), 1959, revised edition, 1966.
(Editor with others) *Opening Day Collection*, Choice Magazine, 1965, 3rd edition, 1974.

(With Dorothy Sinclair, Mary Ann Hanna, and John Rowell) *Cooperative Services for "Big Country" Libraries: Report of a Survey with Recommendations for Cooperation among Libraries of All Types in Thirty-Six Counties of West Central Texas*, [Cleveland], 1969.
(Editor with Phyllis Grumm) *Choice: A Classified Cumulation*, Volumes 1-10, March, 1964-February, 1974, Rowman & Littlefield, 1976-77.
Library Collections: Their Origin, Selection, and Development, McGraw, 1981.
(Editor) *Education of Library and Information Professionals: Present and Future Prospects*, Libraries Unlimited, 1987.

Also author of *Education for Librarianship in France: An Historical Survey*, 1968.

*   *   *

GARIS, Howard R(oger) 1873-1962
(Marion Davidson, Raymond Sperry)

PERSONAL: Born April 25, 1873, in Binghamton, N.Y.; died of heart failure, November 6, 1962, in Northampton, Mass.; son of Simeon Harris (a railroad dispatcher) and Ellen A. (Kimball) Garis; married Lilian C. (a writer and newspaperwoman; maiden name, McNamara), April 26, 1900 (died, 1954); children: Roger C., Cleo F. Garis Clancy. *Education:* Attended Stevens Institute of Technology, and a printing school in New York, N.Y. *Religion:* Roman Catholic.

ADDRESSES: Home—Amherst, Mass.

CAREER: Worked briefly as a seal-examiner for the Lackawanna Railroad in Hoboken, N.J., 1894; *Newark Evening News*, Newark, N.J., reporter and special writer, 1896-1947; author of books for children, including work under various pseudonyms for the Stratemeyer Syndicate, 1902-1962. Creator of "Uncle Wiggily Longears" character, and of games for children, including the Uncle Wiggily game, the Mr. Doodle's Dog game, the Witch Magic game, the Get Well game, and, with son, Roger C. Garis, the 100 Red Convertibles game.

MEMBER: Authors League of America, National Press Club, Reptile Study Society.

WRITINGS:

With Force and Arms: A Tale of Love and Salem Witchcraft, J. S. Ogilvie, 1902.
The King of Unadilla: Stories of Court Secrets Concerning His Majesty, J. S. Ogilvie, 1903.
Isle of Black Fire: A Tale of Adventure for Boys, Lippincott, 1904.
The White Crystals: Being an Account of the Adventures of Two Boys, illustrated by Bertha Corson Day, Little, Brown, 1904.
Dick Hamilton's Fortune; or, The Stirring Doings of a Millionaire's Son, Grosset & Dunlap, 1909.
Dick Hamilton's Cadet Days; or, The Handicap of a Millionaire's Son, Grosset & Dunlap, 1910.
Those Smith Boys; or, The Mystery of the Thumbless Man, R. F. Fenno, 1910.
Dick Hamilton's Steam Yacht, Goldsmith, 1911.
Dick Hamilton's Football Team, Goldsmith, 1912.
The Island Boys; or, Fun and Adventures on Lake Modok, R. F. Fenno, 1912.
Those Smith Boys on the Diamond; or, Nip and Tuck for Victory, R. F. Fenno, 1912.

Three Little Trippertrots, How They Ran Away, and How They Got Back Again, Graham & Matlack, 1912.

Three Little Trippertrots on Their Travels, the Wonderful Things They Saw, and the Wonderful Things They Did, Graham & Matlack, 1912.

(Under pseudonym Marion Davidson) *The Camp Fire Girls; or, The Secret of an Old Mill*, R. F. Fenno, 1913.

(Under pseudonym Marion Davidson) *The Camp Fire Girls on the Ice; or, The Mystery of a Winter Cabin*, R. F. Fenno, 1913.

Snarlie the Tiger, R. F. Fenno, 1916.

The Venture Boys Afloat; or, The Wreck of the Fausta, illustrated by Perc E. Cowan, Harper, 1917.

Umboo the Elephant, R. F. Fenno, 1918.

Woo-Uff the Lion, R. F. Fenno, 1918.

The Venture Boys in Camp; or, The Mystery of Kettle Hill, Harper, 1918.

Tom Cardiff's Circus, illustrated by King, Milton Bradley Co., 1926.

Tom Cardiff in the Big Top, illustrated by King, Milton Bradley Co., 1927.

Tam of the Fire Cave, Appleton, 1927.

Tuftoo the Clown, Appleton, 1928.

Chad of Knob Hill: The Tale of a Lone Scout, illustrated by Paul Martin, Little, Brown, 1929.

The Mystery Boys in Ghost Canyon, illustrated by H. G. Nichols, M. Bradley, 1930.

The Mystery Boys at Round Lake, illustrated by Nichols, M. Bradley, 1931.

"GREAT NEWSPAPER" SERIES

From Office Boy to Reporter; or, The First Step in Journalism (also see below), Chatterton-Peck, 1907, published in the "Young Reporter" series as *The Young Reporter at the Big Flood; or, The Perils of News Gathering*, G. Sully.

Larry Dexter, the Young Reporter; or, Strange Adventures in a Great City (also see below), Chatterton-Peck, 1907, published in the "Young Reporter" series as *The Young Reporter and the Land Swindlers; or, Queer Adventures in a Great City*, G. Sully.

Larry Dexter's Great Search; or, The Hunt for a Missing Millionaire (also see below), Grosset & Dunlap, 1907, published in the "Young Reporter" series as *The Young Reporter and the Missing Millionaire; or, A Strange Disappearance*, G. Sully.

Larry Dexter and the Bank Mystery; or, A Young Reporter in Wall Street (also see below), Grosset & Dunlap, 1912, published in the "Young Reporter" series as *The Young Reporter and the Bank Mystery; or, Stirring Doings in Wall Street*, G. Sully.

Larry Dexter and the Stolen Boy; or, A Young Reporter on the Lakes (also see below), Grosset & Dunlap, 1912, published in the "Young Reporter" series as *The Young Reporter and the Stolen Boy; or, A Chase on the Great Lakes*, G. Sully.

Larry Dexter in Belgium; or, A Young War Correspondent's Double Mission (also see below), Grosset & Dunlap, 1915, published in the "Young Reporter" series as *The Young Reporter at the Battle Front; or, A War Correspondent's Double Mission*, G. Sully.

"BEDTIME STORIES" SERIES

Sammie and Susie Littletail, R. F. Fenno, 1910.

Johnnie and Billie Bushytail, illustrated by Louis Wisa, R. F. Fenno, 1910.

Jackie and Peetie Bow Wow, illustrated by Wisa, R. F. Fenno, 1912.

Lulu, Alice, and Jimmie Wibblewobble, illustrated by Wisa, R. F. Fenno, 1912.

Buddy and Brighteyes Pigg, illustrated by Wisa, A. L. Burt, 1913.

Charlie and Arabella Chick, R. F. Fenno, 1914.

Joie, Tommy, and Kittie Kat, R. F. Fenno, 1914.

Bully and Bawly No-Tail, the Jumping Frogs, illustrated by Wisa, R. F. Fenno, 1915.

Jacko and Jocko Kinkytail, illustrated by Wisa, A. L. Burt, 1917.

Toodle and Noodle Flat-Tail, the Jolly Beaver Boys, illustrated by Wisa, A. L. Burt, 1919.

"UNCLE WIGGILY LONGEARS" BOOKS

Uncle Wiggily's Adventures, illustrated by Wisa, R. F. Fenno, 1912, reprinted with illustrations by Elmer Rache, Platt & Munk, 1940.

Uncle Wiggily Longears, illustrated by Edward Bloomfield, R. F. Fenno, 1915.

Uncle Wiggily and Mother Goose, illustrated by Bloomfield, R. F. Fenno, 1916.

Uncle Wiggily's Arabian Nights, R. F. Fenno, 1916.

Uncle Wiggily in the Woods, illustrated by Wisa, A. L. Burt, 1917.

Uncle Wiggily and Alice in Wonderland, illustrated by Bloomfield, R. F. Fenno, 1918.

Uncle Wiggily and Baby Bunty, illustrated by Wisa, A. L. Burt, 1920.

Uncle Wiggily's Rheumatism, illustrated by Wisa, A. L. Burt, 1920.

Uncle Wiggily: Indian Hunter, illustrated by Lang Campbell, Graham & Matlack, 1922.

Uncle Wiggily on the Farm, illustrated by Campbell, Graham, 1922, reprinted with illustrations by Elmer Rache, Platt & Munk, 1939.

Uncle Wiggily's Ice Cream Party, illustrated by Campbell, Graham & Matlack, 1922.

Uncle Wiggily's June Bug Friends, illustrated by Campbell, Graham & Matlack, 1922.

Uncle Wiggily's Silk Hat, illustrated by Campbell, Graham & Matlack, 1922.

Uncle Wiggily's Woodland Games; or Uncle Wiggily Thought He Could Skip the Grape Vine Rope and A Party in the Woodlands, also Uncle Wiggily Makes a Kite, illustrated by Campbell, Graham & Matlack, 1922.

The Adventures of Uncle Wiggily, the Bunny Rabbit Gentleman with the Twinkling Pink Nose, illustrated by Campbell, Graham, 1924.

Uncle Wiggily and the Pirates, illustrated by Campbell, Graham, 1924.

Uncle Wiggily at the Beach, illustrated by Campbell, Graham, 1924.

Uncle Wiggily Goes Swimming, illustrated by Campbell, Graham, 1924.

Uncle Wiggily on Roller Skates, illustrated by Campbell, Graham, 1924.

Uncle Wiggily on the Flying Rug, illustrated by Campbell, Graham, 1924.

Uncle Wiggily's Funny Auto, illustrated by Campbell, Graham, 1924.

Uncle Wiggily's Painting Fun, illustrated by Campbell, Graham, 1924.

Uncle Wiggily's Painting Play, illustrated by Campbell, Graham, 1924.

The Second Adventures of Uncle Wiggily, the Bunny Rabbit Gentleman and His Muskrat Lady Housekeeper, illustrated by Campbell, Graham, 1925.

The Uncle Wiggily Book, illustrated by Campbell, Appleton, 1927.

Uncle Wiggily's Water-Spout, illustrated by Campbell, Graham, 1927.

Uncle Wiggily's Puzzle Book, illustrated by Campbell, puzzles by Cleo Garis, A. L. Burt, 1928.

Uncle Wiggily and the Alligator, illustrated by William Weaver, Graham, 1929.

Uncle Wiggily's Ice Boat, illustrated by Campbell, Graham, 1929.

Uncle Wiggily's Make Believe Tarts, illustrated by Campbell, Graham, 1929.

Uncle Wiggily's Rolling Hoop, illustrated by Campbell, Graham, 1929.

Uncle Wiggily's Squirt Gun, illustrated by Campbell, Graham, 1929.

Uncle Wiggily's Wash Tub Ship, illustrated by Campbell, Graham, 1929.

Uncle Wiggily Plays Storekeeper, illustrated by Campbell, Graham, 1929.

Uncle Wiggily's Bungalow, A. L. Burt, 1930.

Uncle Wiggily's Airship, illustrated by Wisa, A. L. Burt, 1931.

Uncle Wiggily's Icicle Spear; or, The Battle with the Two Bad Chaps and Uncle Wiggily Captures the Skee, also Uncle Wiggily's Trick Skating, illustrated by Campbell, Graham, 1931.

Uncle Wiggily's Jumping Boots; or, The Wild Trip to the Starry Sky and Uncle Wiggily Builds a Snow House, also Uncle Wiggily Catches the Alligator, illustrated by Campbell, Graham, 1931.

Uncle Wiggily's Travels, illustrated by Wisa, A. L. Burt, 1931.

Uncle Wiggily's Picnic Party, A. L. Burt, 1933.

Uncle Wiggily's Auto Sled, illustrated by Campbell, Whitman, 1936.

Uncle Wiggily's Holidays, illustrated by Campbell, Whitman, 1936.

Uncle Wiggily's Visit to the Farm, illustrated by Campbell, Whitman, 1936.

Uncle Wiggily's Surprises, Blue Ribbon Books, 1937.

Uncle Wiggily's Automobile, illustrated by Rache, Platt & Munk, 1939.

Uncle Wiggily in the Country, illustrated by Rache, Platt & Munk, 1940.

Uncle Wiggily's Picture Book, illustrated by Campbell, Platt & Munk, 1940, reprinted, 1960.

Uncle Wiggily and the Littletails, illustrated by Rache, Platt & Munk, 1942.

Uncle Wiggily's Fortune, illustrated by Rache, Platt & Munk, 1942.

Uncle Wiggily's Happy Days, illustrated by George Carlson, Platt & Munk, 1947, new edition, 1976.

Uncle Wiggily & Jackie and Peetie Bow Wow, Platt & Munk, 1952.

The Little Golden Book of Uncle Wiggily, illustrated by Mel Crawford, Simon & Schuster, 1953.

The Uncle Wiggily Book, illustrated by Carl and Mary Hauge, Grosset & Dunlap, 1955.

Uncle Wiggily and His Friends, Platt & Munk, 1955, reprinted, Putnam, 1978.

Uncle Wiggily Stories, illustrated by Art Seiden, Grosset & Dunlap, 1965.

Uncle Wiggily and the Runaway Cheese, illustrated by Aldren Watson, Platt & Munk, 1977.

Uncle Wiggily and the Sugar Cookie, illustrated by Watson, Platt & Munk, 1977.

Uncle Wiggily and His Woodland Friends, illustrated by Jaroslav Bradac, edited by M. R. Garis, Wildwood House, 1977.

Uncle Wiggily's Story Book, Platt & Munk, 1987.

''DADDY'' SERIES

Daddy Takes Us Camping, R. F. Fenno, 1916.
. . . Fishing, R. F. Fenno, 1916.
. . . to the Circus, R. F. Fenno, 1916.
. . . Skating, R. F. Fenno, 1916.
. . . Coasting, R. F. Fenno, 1916.
. . . Hunting Flowers, R. F. Fenno, 1916.
. . . Hunting Birds, R. F. Fenno, 1916.
. . . to the Woods, R. F. Fenno, 1916.
. . . to the Farm, R. F. Fenno, 1916.
. . . to the Garden, R. F. Fenno, 1916.

''CURLYTOPS'' SERIES

The Curlytops at Uncle Frank's Ranch, illustrated by Julia Greene, Cupples & Leon, 1918.
. . . on Star Island, illustrated by Greene, Cupples & Leon, 1918.
. . . Snowed In; or, Grand Fun with Skates and Sleds, illustrated by Greene, Cupples & Leon, 1918.
. . . and Their Pets, Cupples & Leon, 1921.
. . . and Their Playmates, illustrated by Greene, Cupples & Leon, 1922.
. . . in the Woods; or, Fun at the Lumber Camp, illustrated by Greene, Cupples & Leon, 1923.
. . . at Sunset Beach; or, What Was Found in the Sand, illustrated by Greene, Cupples & Leon, 1924.
. . . Touring Around, Cupples & Leon, 1925.
. . . Growing Up; or, Winter Sports and Summer Pleasures, illustrated by Greene, Cupples & Leon, 1928.
. . . at Happy House; or, The Mystery of the Chinese Vase, Cupples & Leon, 1931.
. . . at the Circus; or, The Runaway Elephant, Cupples & Leon, 1932.

''RICK AND RUDDY'' SERIES

Rick and Ruddy: The Story of a Boy and His Dog, illustrated by John Goss, Milton Bradley Co., 1920.
. . . in Camp: The Adventures of a Boy and His Dog, illustrated by Milo Warner, Milton Bradley Co., 1921.
. . . Afloat: The Cruise of a Boy and His Dog, illustrated by W. B. King, Milton Bradley Co., 1922.
. . . out West, Milton Bradley Co., 1923.
. . . on the Trail, illustrated by King, Milton Bradley Co., 1924.
The Face in the Dismal Cavern, McLoughlin, 1930.
The Mystery of the Brass Bound Trunk, McLoughlin, 1930.
On the Showman's Trail, McLoughlin, 1930.
The Secret of Lost River, McLoughlin, 1930.
Swept from the Storm, McLoughlin, 1930.

''TWO WILD CHERRIES'' SERIES

Two Wild Cherries; or, How Dick and Janet Lost Something, illustrated by John M. Foster, Milton Bradley Co., 1924.

. . . in the Country; or, How Dick and Janet Saved the Mill, illustrated by Foster, Milton Bradley Co., 1924.

. . . in the Woods; or, How Dick and Janet Caught the Bear, illustrated by Foster, Milton Bradley Co., 1924.

. . . at the Seashore, Milton Bradley Co., 1925.

"LARRY DEXTER" SERIES; UNDER PSEUDONYM RAYMOND SPERRY

Larry Dexter at the Big Flood; or, The Perils of a Reporter (originally published as *From Office Boy to Reporter; or, The First Step in Journalism* by Howard R. Garis), Garden City, 1926.

. . . and the Land Swindlers; or, Queer Adventures in a Great City (originally published as *Larry Dexter, the Young Reporter; or, Strange Adventures in a Great City* by Howard R. Garis), Garden City, 1926.

. . . and the Missing Millionaire; or, The Great Search (originally published as *Larry Dexter's Great Search; or, The Hunt for a Missing Millionaire* by Howard R. Garis), Garden City, 1926.

. . . and the Bank Mystery; or, Exciting Days in Wall Street (originally published as *Larry Dexter and the Bank Mystery; or, A Young Reporter in Wall Street* by Howard R. Garis), Garden City, 1926.

. . . and the Stolen Boy; or, A Chase on the Great Lakes (originally published as *Larry Dexter and the Stolen Boy; or, A Young Reporter on the Lakes* by Howard R. Garis), Garden City, 1926.

. . . the Battle Front; or, A War Correspondent's Double Mission (originally published as *Larry Dexter in Belgium; or, A Young War Correspondent's Double Mission* by Howard R. Garis), Garden City, 1926.

. . . and the Ward Diamonds; or, The Young Reporter at Sea Cliff, Garden City, 1927.

Larry Dexter's Great Chase; or, The Young Reporter across the Continent, Garden City, 1927.

"HAPPY HOME" SERIES

The Adventures of the Galloping Gas Stove, Grosset & Dunlap, 1926.

. . . of the Runaway Rocker, Grosset & Dunlap, 1926.

. . . of the Sailing Sofa, Grosset & Dunlap, 1926.

. . . of the Sliding Foot Stool, Grosset & Dunlap, 1926.

. . . of the Traveling Table, Grosset & Dunlap, 1926.

. . . of the Prancing Piano, Grosset & Dunlap, 1927.

"BUDDY" SERIES

Buddy in School; or, A Boy and His Dog, Cupples & Leon, 1929.

. . . on the Farm; or, A Boy and His Prize Pumpkin, Cupples & Leon, 1929.

. . . and His Winter Fun; or, A Boy in a Snow Camp, Cupples & Leon, 1929.

. . . at Rainbow Lake; or, A Boy and His Boat, Cupples & Leon, 1930.

. . . and His Chum; or, A Boy's Queer Search, Cupples & Leon, 1930.

. . . and His Flying Balloon; or, A Boy's Mysterious Airship, Cupples & Leon, 1931.

. . . at Pine Beach; or, A Boy on the Ocean, Cupples & Leon, 1931.

. . . on Mystery Mountain; or, A Boy's Strange Discovery, Cupples & Leon, 1932.

. . . on Floating Island; or, A Boy's Wonderful Secret, Cupples & Leon, 1933.

. . . and the Secret Cave; or, A Boy and the Crystal Hermit, Cupples & Leon, 1934.

. . . and His Cowboy Pal; or, A Boy on a Ranch, Cupples & Leon, 1935.

. . . and the Indian Chief; or, A Boy among the Navajos, Cupples & Leon, 1936.

. . . and the Arrow Club; or, A Boy and the Long Bow, Cupples & Leon, 1937.

. . . at Lost River; or, A Boy and a Gold Mine, Cupples & Leon, 1938.

. . . on the Trail; or, A Boy among the Gypsies, Cupples & Leon, 1939.

. . . in Deep Valley; or, A Boy on a Bee Farm, Cupples & Leon, 1940.

. . . at Red Gate; or, A Boy on a Chicken Farm, Cupples & Leon, 1941.

. . . in Dragon Swamp; or, A Boy on a Strange Hunt, Cupples & Leon, 1942.

Buddy's Victory Club; or, A Boy and a Salvage Campaign, Cupples & Leon, 1943.

. . . and the G-Man Mystery; or, A Boy and a Strange Cipher, Cupples & Leon, 1944.

. . . and His Fresh-Air Camp; or, A Boy and the Unlucky Ones, Cupples & Leon, 1947.

"DICK AND JANET CHERRY" SERIES

The Gypsy Camp, McLoughlin, 1930.

Saving the Old Mill, McLoughlin, 1930.

The Bear Hunt, McLoughlin, 1930.

Shipwrecked on Christmas Island, McLoughlin, 1930.

"ROCKET RIDERS" SERIES

Rocket Riders across the Ice; or, Racing against Time, A. L. Burt, 1933.

. . . in Stormy Seas; or, Trailing the Treasure Divers, A. L. Burt, 1933.

. . . over the Desert; or, Seeking the Lost City, A. L. Burt, 1933.

. . . in the Air; or, A Chase in the Clouds, A. L. Burt, 1934.

"TEDDY" SERIES

Teddy and the Mystery Dog, Cupples & Leon, 1936.

. . . and the Mystery Monkey, Cupples & Leon, 1936.

. . . and the Mystery Cat, Cupples & Leon, 1937.

. . . and the Mystery Parrot, Cupples & Leon, 1938.

. . . and the Mystery Pony, Cupples & Leon, 1939.

. . . and the Mystery Deer, Cupples & Leon, 1940.

. . . and the Mystery Goat, Cupples & Leon, 1941.

OTHER

Also author of *The Curlytops at the Cherry Farm, The Curlytops at Silver Lake,* and *The Curlytops in Summer Camp,* for Cupples & Leon. Author of books under various pseudonyms for the Stratemeyer Syndicate, including the "Tom Swift" series (as Victor Appleton), the "Baseball Joe" series (as Lester Chadwick), the "Bunny Brown and His Sister Sue" series and the "Six Little Bunkers" series (as Laura Lee Hope), the "Great Marvel" series (as Roy Rockwood), and the "Motor Boys" series (as Clarence Young). Contributor of stories to periodicals, including *St. Nicholas, Argosy,* and *Collier's.*

SIDELIGHTS: "To say that the writer Howard Roger Garis was prolific is an understatement," declares *Dictionary of Literary Biography* contributor Douglas Street. "To say, as some have, that he was a literary hack or a 'fiction machine,'" he continues, "is to demean the man who created countless hours of literary enjoyment for generations of American children who eagerly devoured his popular boys' adventure series, his animal stories, and, most of all, his Uncle Wiggily stories.'' In a writing career stretching well over half a century, Garis produced books and stories featuring some of the best-loved fictional characters of all time. ''He considered it no great feat,'' confides his son Roger Garis in his biography *My Father Was Uncle Wiggily*, ''to become one of the most famous authors of children's stories, completing—besides more than 15,000 Uncle Wiggily adventures which sold over 18 million books, and are still selling widely—at least 700 other books, including (many of them under pen names) some volumes of the Tom Swift series; The Motor Boys; Baseball Joe; the Dick Hamilton series; the Teddy series; and many whose titles I have forgotten—or possibly never knew.''

Howard R. Garis was never encouraged to become a writer. His father, a railroad dispatcher, felt that writing was not profitable, and sent his son to the Stevens Institute in Hoboken, New Jersey, to study engineering. There Garis failed every subject except elocution and English, and, as Roger Garis puts it, ''Stevens Institute gave him his unconditional release.'' Garis's father then sent him to a printer's school in New York City, but his printing career was cut short by his father's death. In 1896, however, Garis landed a job with the *Newark Evening News*, where he met Lilian McNamara, a pioneering woman reporter. Garis married her in 1900.

Lilian and Howard Garis were drawn together not only by their newspaper experiences, but also by their common interest in writing for children. Lilian Garis was nearly as prolific a writer as her husband, reports their son Roger; she ''wrote the early Bobbsey Twins, The Motor Girls, The Outdoor Girls—these under pen names . . . and some 250 more books, many of them under her own name.'' Later their children Roger and Cleo also began to write fiction, and the entire Garis family worked at one time for Edward Stratemeyer and the Stratemeyer Syndicate, generating manuscript from plot outlines provided by Stratemeyer. ''I'd say that among us four we turned out more than a thousand books,'' decides Roger Garis. In the years between 1905 and 1935 alone, he continues, the Garis family contributed to the ''Dorothy Dale,'' ''Judy Jordan,'' ''Connie Loring,'' ''Gloria,'' ''Melody Lane,'' ''Nancy Brandon,'' ''X Bar X Boys,'' ''Outboard Boys,'' and ''Barbara Hale'' series, among many others.

Although the Garises' work for Stratemeyer represented a large part of their output, most of these books were written under Syndicate pseudonyms. The writers received neither credit nor royalties, but instead a flat rate per book; for instance, Howard Garis collected $100 per book for his work on the very popular ''Tom Swift'' series, later increased to $125. ''Stratemeyer provided the nom de plume and titles, plus a general sketch of what he wanted a given book to be,'' reports Street. ''Stratemeyer also stipulated that each book in the series was to be thirty chapters of roughly seven pages each.'' Yet despite these restrictions Garis and Stratemeyer maintained a cordial relationship. Harriet Adams, Stratemeyer's daughter, recalled to the *New Yorker*, ''Mr. Garis would hide behind the sofa, pretending he was the skillery-scallery alligator dry-gulching Uncle Wiggily, or Father would get behind a chair, pretending he was Dan Baxter dry-gulching Dick Rover.''

Garis conceived his own claim to fame in 1910. Edward M. Scudder, editor of the *Newark Evening News*, ''wanted to publish some type of children's story daily, as an extra to the regular children's features,'' explains Street, and he asked Garis to write some short stories. While pondering the problem on a walk in the nearby woods, the author met a rabbit who sat behind a nearby log and wiggled its ears at him. That, Garis claimed, was the inspiration for Uncle Wiggily Longears, the rheumatic bunny rabbit gentleman with the twinkling pink nose and the barber-pole-striped crutch.

''Great Britain has Beatrix Potter's immortal Peter Rabbit,'' asserts Street, but, he adds, ''America possesses the no less immortal Uncle Wiggily.'' The rabbit gentleman has had thousands of adventures with his friends: Nurse Jane Fuzzy Wuzzy, the muskrat lady who kept his Hollow Stump Bungalow for him, Doctor Possum, who treated Uncle Wiggily when his Epizootis acted up, Mr. Whitewash, the polar bear gentleman, and especially the animal children, the Littletails, Notails, Bushytails, Bow Wows, and Baby Bunty. Often Uncle Wiggily was threatened by one or more of the Bad Chaps, who wanted to nibble his ears: the Skeezicks, Pipsisewah, Skillery Scallery Alligator, Fuzzy Fox, Woozie Wolf, Bad Old Blue-Nosed Baboon, Skuddlemagoon, Bushy Bear, Bob Cat, the Bad Old Bazumpus and the Worse Old Crozocus.

Beginning January 30, 1910, and continuing to the day of his death, Garis wrote Uncle Wiggily stories averaging seven hundred words in length, six days a week. The rabbit gentleman's adventures sold over eighteen million copies in the next fifty years. Around 1914 the author started a practice of reading the stories over the radio, which brought Uncle Wiggily to the attention of thousands who had not read the books. In addition, Garis created the Uncle Wiggily Game in 1917, which soon became the largest selling children's game in the world, and is still marketed today. Other Uncle Wiggily products also appeared—dolls, dishes, dress patterns, toys, wallpaper, and phonograph records—making Uncle Wiggily one of the most famous and best loved rabbits of all time. Since Garis's death, more Uncle Wiggily stories have been written by members of his family.

Although Garis the writer, states Street, ''may well be forgotten as tastes change and more and better authors continue to flood the popular children's book market,'' his place among children's authors is assured thanks to Uncle Wiggily. Howard Garis was almost as popular with children as his creation. ''He was like the Pied Piper of Hamelin—wherever he went, he drew children,'' Roger Garis recalls. ''Garis wrote for the children, not for the critics,'' Street concludes, ''and whereas critics tossed his writing aside as 'literary hack work,' the children responded with praise, laughter, and written orders for more. Garis seemed to know what they wanted and how best to give it to them.''

For more information about the Stratemeyer Syndicate and the pseudonyms used by Garis and his family, see the entries in this volume for Harriet S. Adams, Edward L. Stratemeyer, and Andrew E. Svenson, and for the following pseudonyms: Victor Appleton, Lester Chadwick, Laura Lee Hope, Roy Rockwood, and Clarence Young.

BIOGRAPHICAL/CRITICAL SOURCES:

BOOKS

Dictionary of Literary Biography, Volume 22: *American Writers for Children, 1900-1960*, Gale, 1983.

Garis, Roger, *My Father Was Uncle Wiggily*, McGraw-Hill, 1966.

Johnson, Deidre, editor and compiler, *Stratemeyer Pseudonyms and Series Books: An Annotated Checklist of Stra-*

temeyer and Stratemeyer Syndicate Publications, Greenwood Press, 1982.

PERIODICALS

Better Homes & Gardens, April, 1947.
Fortune, April, 1934.
Look, July 3, 1962.
Newsweek, October 14, 1946, November 7, 1966.
New Yorker, March 20, 1954.
Saturday Evening Post, December 19, 1964.

OBITUARIES:

PERIODICALS

Newsweek, November 19, 1962.
New York Times, November 6, 1962.
Publishers Weekly, November 19, 1962.
Time, November 16, 1962.*

—*Sketch by Kenneth R. Shepherd*

*   *   *

GATCH, Milton McC(ormick, Jr.)   1932-

PERSONAL: Born November 22, 1932, in Cincinnati, Ohio; son of Milton M. (a banker) and Mary (Curry) Gatch; married Ione G. White (a college dean of students), August 25, 1956; children: Ione W., Lucinda McC., George C. W. *Education:* Haverford College, A.B., 1953; University of Cincinnati, law student, 1953-55; Episcopal Theological School, B.D., 1960; Yale University, M.A., 1961, Ph.D., 1963. *Politics:* Democrat. *Religion:* Episcopalian.

ADDRESSES: Home—606 West 122nd St., New York, N.Y. 10027. *Office*—Union Theological Seminary, 3041 Broadway, New York, N.Y. 10027.

CAREER: Educator. Ordained Episcopalian clergyman; Wooster School, Danbury, Conn., master in Latin and acting chaplain, 1963-64; Shimer College, Mount Carroll, Ill., member of humanities faculty and chaplain, 1964-66, chairman of humanities faculty, 1966-67; Northern Illinois University, DeKalb, associate professor of English, 1967-68; University of Missouri, Columbia, associate professor, 1968-72, professor of English, 1972-78, chairman of department, 1971-74; Union Theological Seminary, New York City, academic dean and professor of church history, 1978—, provost, 1986—. Senior fellow, National Endowment for the Humanities, and associate, Clare Hall, Cambridge University, 1974-75. *Military service:* U.S. Army, 1965-67.

MEMBER: Modern Language Association of America (executive committee for Old English, member, 1975—, chairman, 1977), Mediaeval Academy of America, Early English Text Society, American Society of Church History, American Academy of Religion, Century Association, Yale Club (New York City).

WRITINGS:

Death: Meaning and Mortality in Christian Thought and Contemporary Culture, Seabury, 1969.
(Contributor) Liston O. Mills, editor, *Perspectives on Death*, Abingdon, 1969.
Loyalties and Traditions: Man and His World in Old English Literature, Pegasus, 1971.
Preaching and Theology in Anglo-Saxon England: Aelfric and Wulfstan, University of Toronto Press, 1977.

(Editor with C. T. Berkhout) *Anglo-Saxon Scholarship: The First Three Centuries*, G. K. Hall, 1982.

Contributor to literary and religious journals.

WORK IN PROGRESS: Studies of the relationship of literature to the liturgy in the Anglo-Saxon period; studies in English antiquarianism; an edition of the Old English Blickling Homilies; a bibliography of W. B. and Jack B. Yeats.

*   *   *

GAY, Carlo T(eofilo) E(berhard)   1913-

PERSONAL: Born July 12, 1913, in Villar Pellice, Torino, Italy; son of Lino Renato (a physician) and Letizia (Malan) Gay; married Claudia Boyd, July 4, 1948; children: Oliver Robin. *Education:* Institute of Oriental Languages of Naples, diploma in Amaric, 1938; University of Naples, Ph.D. (economics), 1940.

ADDRESSES: Home—80-71 Grenfell St., Kew Gardens, New York, N.Y. 11415.

CAREER: Dalmine (steel pipe manufacturers), Milan, Italy, executive, 1940-55, vice-president of subsidiary Dalminter, Inc., and president of Canadian subsidiary Dalminter Ltd., New York, N.Y., 1955-61; researcher and writer on art and history of ancient Mexico, 1962-88. *Military service:* Italian Army, Alpine Corps, 1934-35; became lieutenant.

MEMBER: Royal Anthropological Institute of Great Britain and Ireland, Institutum Canarium (Austria), New York Academy of Sciences.

WRITINGS:

Guerrero: Stone Sculpture from the State of Guerrero, Mexico (exhibition catalogue), edited by Elayne H. Varian, Finch College Museum of Art, 1965.
Mezcala Stone Sculpture: The Human Figure, Museum of Primitive Art, 1967.
Chalcacingo, Akademische Druck, 1971.
Xochipala: The Beginnings of Olmec Art, Art Museum, Princeton University, 1972.
Ceramic Figures of Ancient Mexico: Guerrero, Mexico, Guanajuato, Michoacan, 1600 B.C.-300 A.D. (illustrations by Frances Pratt), Akademische Druck, 1979.
Mezcala Architecture in Miniature, Academie Royale de Belgique, 1987.

Contributor to *Natural History, Archaeology, Antike Welt, Raggi,* and *Almogaren*.

WORK IN PROGRESS: Further research on Olmec culture and related lithic traditions indigenous to the Middle Balsas River region in Guerrero, Mexico; research on the stone-tool industries of the Lower and Middle Paleolithic of Europe and Africa; research on "cupules" dating from the Middle Paleolithic to the present. Books in preparation include comprehensive studies of the Mezcala and Chontal lithic traditions of Guerrero.

AVOCATIONAL INTERESTS: Mountain climbing; travel in Europe and North America, including the Yukon and Alaska; exploring Mexico; photography of ancient architecture and monuments.

BIOGRAPHICAL/CRITICAL SOURCES:

PERIODICALS

Christian Science Monitor, February 9, 1973.

Corriere della Sera, April 15, 1967.
L'Europeo, December, 1967.
Life, May 12, 1967.
Life en Espanol, May 22, 1967.
New York Times, April 14, 1967.

*   *   *

GEISLER, Norman L(eo) 1932-

PERSONAL: Born July 21, 1932, in Warren, Mich.; son of Alphonso H. (a factory worker) and Bertha (Rottmann) Geisler; married Barbara Jean Cate (a pianist), June 24, 1955; children: Ruth, David, Daniel, Rhoda, Paul, Rachel. *Education:* Wheaton College, Wheaton, Ill., B.A., 1958, M.A., 1960; Detroit Bible College (now William Tyndale College), Th.B., 1964; Loyola University, Chicago, Ill., Ph.D., 1970. *Politics:* Republican.

ADDRESSES: Office—Dallas Theological Seminary, Dallas, Tex. 75204.

CAREER: Ordained minister, 1956. Pastor of Dayton Center Church, Silverwood, Mich., 1955-57, River Grove Bible Church, River Grove, Ill., 1958-59, and Memorial Baptist Church, Warren, Mich., 1960-63; Detroit Bible College, Detroit, Mich., instructor, 1959-62, assistant professor, 1963-66, chairman of Bible-Theology department, 1965; Trinity College, Deerfield, Ill., assistant professor of Bible, 1967-69, associate professor of philosophy, 1970-71; Trinity Evangelical Divinity School, Mundelein, Ill., visiting professor of philosophy of religion, 1969-70, chairman of department, 1970-79; Dallas Theological Seminary, professor of systematic theology, 1979—. Interim pastor in Michigan, Illinois, and Texas, 1965—. International lecturer at universities, churches, retreats, and pastors' conferences. Member of Mundelein High School Board of Education, beginning 1971.

MEMBER: American Philosophical Association, Evangelical Theological Society (president, 1976), Evangelical Philosophical Society (president, 1976), American Academy of Religion, American Scientific Affiliation, Alumni of Detroit Bible College (president, 1961-62).

AWARDS, HONORS: Outstanding Educator of America, 1975; Choice Evangelical Book of the Year, *Christianity Today,* 1975, for *Philosophy of Religion;* elected member of Wheaton Scholastic Honor Society, 1977; Alumnus of the Year, William Tyndale College, 1982.

WRITINGS:

(Co-author) *General Introduction to the Bible,* Moody, 1968, revised edition, 1986.
Christ: The Theme of the Bible, Moody, 1968.
Ethics: Alternatives and Issues, Zondervan, 1971.
The Christian Ethic of Love, Zondervan, 1973.
(With Winfried Cordvan) *Philosophy of Religion,* Zondervan, 1974, revised edition, Baker Book, 1988.
(With William E. Nix) *From God to Us,* Moody, 1974.
Christian Apologetics, Baker Book, 1976.
A Popular Survey of the Old Testament, Baker Book, 1977.
The Roots of Evil, Zondervan, 1978.
To Understand the Bible, Look for Jesus, Baker Book, 1979.
Introduction to Philosophy: A Christian Perspective, Baker Book, 1980.
(Editor) *Inerrancy,* Zondervan, 1980.
(Editor) *Decide for Yourself: How History Views the Bible,* Zondervan, 1981.

(Editor) *Biblical Errancy: Its Philosophical Roots,* Zondervan, 1981.
Options in Contemporary Christian Ethics, Baker Book, 1981.
The Creator in the Courtroom: "Scopes II," foreword by Duane T. Gish, Mott Media, 1982.
(Contributor) Saint Augustine, *What Augustine Says,* Baker Book, 1982.
Miracles and Modern Thought, Zondervan, 1982.
Is Man the Measure: An Evaluation of Humanism, Baker Book, 1982.
Cosmos: Carl Sagan's Religion for the Scientific Mind, Quest Publishing, 1983.
The Religion of the Force, Quest Publishing, 1983.
(With William D. Watkins) *Perspectives: Understanding and Evaluating Today's World Views,* Here's Life, 1984, revised edition published as *A Handbook on World Views,* Baker Book, 1988.
False Gods of Our Time, Harvest House, 1985.
Christianity under Attack, Quest Publishing, 1985.
(With J. Yutaka Amano) *The Reincarnation Sensation,* Tyndale, 1986.
(With J. Kerby Anderson) *Origin Science: A Proposal for the Creation-Evolution Controversy,* Baker Book, 1987.
To Drink or Not to Drink: A Sober Look at the Question, revised edition, Quest Publishing, 1987.

Contributor to philosophical and religious periodicals.

AVOCATIONAL INTERESTS: Collecting rocks and fossils, skiing, sailing, wood working.

*   *   *

GEORGE, Jonathan
See THEINER, George (Fredric)

*   *   *

GILBERT, Russell Wieder 1905-1985

PERSONAL: Born September 3, 1905, in Emmaus, Pa.; died, 1985; son of John Mathias (a business executive) and Meda (Wieder) Gilbert; married Viola Kemmerer, June 25, 1931; children: Joyce K. (died April 11, 1979), Arlan K. *Education:* Muhlenberg College, A.B., 1927; University of Pennsylvania, M.A., 1929, Ph.D., 1943. *Politics:* Republican. *Religion:* Lutheran.

ADDRESSES: Home—100 Susquehanna Ave., Selinsgrove, Pa. 17870.

CAREER: Lehigh University, Bethlehem, Pa., assistant in German, 1927-29; Muhlenberg College, Allentown, Pa., instructor in German, 1929-30; Susquehanna University, Selinsgrove, Pa., 1930-70, began as instructor, became professor of German and professor of speech, 1940-70, chairman of department of modern languages, 1959-70, professor emeritus, 1970—.

MEMBER: Pennsylvania German Society (member of board of directors, 1966-75; vice-president), Pennsylvania Historical Association, Theta Chi.

AWARDS, HONORS: Fellow of Carl Schurz Memorial Foundation; citations from Pennsylvania German Society, 1963, 1975.

WRITINGS:

(Editor with Arthur Herman Wilson) Frederic Brush, *Walk the Long Years,* Susquehanna University Press, 1946.

A Picture of the Pennsylvania Germans, Pennsylvania Historical Association, 1947, 3rd edition, 1962, reprinted, 1972.

Pennsylvania German Wills, Pennsylvania German Folklore Society, 1951.

(Editor) M. Walter Dunmore, *The Saga of the Pennsylvania Germans in Wisconsin,* Pennsylvania German Folklore Society, 1954.

(Editor with William Adam Russ, Jr. and Wilson) William S. Clark and Wilson, *The Story of Susquehanna University,* Susquehanna University Press, 1958.

Bilder un Gedanke: Poems, Pennsylvania German Society, 1975.

Glotz un Schliwwere, Pennsylvania German Society, 1987.

Contributor to speech and history journals, and to *Susquehanna University Studies.* Member of editorial board of *Susquehanna University Studies,* 1944-46. Consultant, *Britannica World Language Dictionary,* 1954-55.

WORK IN PROGRESS: A fourth edition of *A Picture of the Pennsylvania Germans;* another volume of original dialect poems; *The Humor of the Pennsylvania Germans.*

AVOCATIONAL INTERESTS: Sports.*

*   *   *

GINZBERG, Eli 1911-

PERSONAL: Born April 30, 1911, in New York, N.Y.; son of Louis (a Talmudist) and Adele (Katzenstein) Ginzberg; married Ruth Szold, July 14, 1946; children: Abigail, Jeremy, Rachel. *Education:* Attended University of Heidelberg and University of Grenoble, 1928-29; Columbia University, A.B., 1931, A.M., 1932, Ph.D., 1934.

ADDRESSES: Home—845 West End Ave., New York, N.Y. *Office*—Graduate School of Business, Columbia University, New York, N.Y. 10027.

CAREER: Columbia University, Graduate School of Business, New York, N.Y., member of faculty, 1935—, A. Barton Hepburn Professor of Economics, 1967-79, professor emeritus, 1979—, director of Research Economists on Group Behavior, 1939-42 and 1948-49, Staff Studies of National Manpower Council, 1941-61, Conservation of Human Resources Project, 1950—, and Revson Fellows Program on the Future of New York City, 1979—. Honorary member of faculty, Industrial College of the Armed Forces, 1971—. Adjunct professor of health and society, Barnard College.

Chairman of board (emeritus), Manpower Demonstration Research Corp. Research director, United Jewish Appeal, 1941; member of Committee on Wartime Requirements for Scientific and Specialized Personnel, 1942; special assistant to chief statistician, U.S. Department of War, 1942-47; director of Resources Analysis Division, Surgeon General's Office, 1944-46; U.S. Representative, Five Power Conference on Reparations for Non-Repatriable Refugees, 1946; member of medical advisory board, Secretary of War, 1946-48; director, New York State Hospital Study, 1948-49; member of board of governors, Hebrew University of Jerusalem, 1953-59; member, National Advisory Mental Health Council, 1959-63, and National Advisory Allied Health Professions Council, 1969-72; chairman of studies committee, White House Conference on Children and Youth, 1960; National Commission for Manpower Policy, chairman of advisory committee, 1962-74, chairman of commission, 1974-79; chairman of task force on manpower research, Defense Science Board, 1970-71; member of scientific advisory board, U.S. Air Force, 1970-74; chairman, National Commission for Employment Policy, 1979-81; member of personnel advisory committee, National Academy of Sciences Office of Science and Engineering; National Commission for Full Employment, member of advisory council and co-chairman of advisory committee; advisor, International Institute Management Science Center, Berlin.

Consultant to U.S. Department of the Army, 1946-70, Department of State, 1953, 1956, 1965-69, Department of Labor, 1954—, Department of Defense, 1964-71, Department of Commerce, 1965-66, General Accounting Office, 1973—, and Department of Health, Education, and Welfare; consultant to General Electric, Western Electric, Du Pont, and International Business Machines; consultant to Federation of Jewish Philanthropies of New York, Rockefeller Foundation, Robert Wood Johnson Foundation, Ford Foundation, and McKinsey Foundation for Management Research; medical consultant, Hoover Commission, 1952.

MEMBER: American Association for the Advancement of Science (fellow), American Economic Association, Academy of Political Science, American Academy of Arts and Sciences (fellow), American Association of University Professors, Society of Medical Consultants to the Armed Forces (associate member), Industrial Relations Research Association, Institute of Medicine, Allen O. Whipple Surgical Society (honorary member), National Academy of the Sciences, Phi Beta Kappa, Beta Gamma Sigma.

AWARDS, HONORS: U.S. Department of War Medal, 1946, for exceptional civilian service; International University of Social Studies Medal (Rome), 1957, for research contributions to the study of human resources; McKinsey Management Journal Award, University of California, 1964; D.Litt., Jewish Theological Seminary of America, 1966; LL.D., Loyola University (Chicago), 1969; certificate of merit, U.S. Department of Labor, 1972; Litt.D., Columbia University, 1982; Special Service Award, Department of Labor, 1982; Distinguished Service Award, Teachers College, Columbia University, 1984; L.H.D., Rush University, 1985.

WRITINGS:

Studies in the Economics of the Bible, Jewish Publication Society, 1932.

The House of Adam Smith, Columbia University Press, 1934, reprinted, Octagon, 1964, new edition published as *The House of Adam Smith Revisited,* Temple University Press, 1977.

The Illusion of Economic Stability, Harper, 1939.

Grass on the Slag Heaps: The Story of the Welsh Miners, Harper, 1942.

Report to American Jews on Overseas Relief, Palestine, and Refugees in the United States, Harper, 1942.

(With Ethel L. Ginsberg, Dorothy L. Lynn, and others) *The Unemployed,* Harper, 1943.

(With Joseph Carwell) *The Labor Leader,* Macmillan, 1948.

Program for the Nursing Profession, Macmillan, 1949.

A Pattern for Hospital Care, Columbia University Press, 1949.

Agenda for the American Jews, King's Crown Press, 1950.

(With others) *Occupational Choice,* Columbia University Press, 1951.

(With John L. Herma and Sol W. Ginsberg) *Psychiatry and Military Manpower Policy: A Reappraisal of the Experience in World War II,* King's Crown Press, 1953.

(With Douglas W. Bray) *The Uneducated,* Columbia University Press, 1953.

(With others) *What Makes an Executive?* (symposium), Columbia University Press, 1955.

(With Bray, James K. Anderson, and Robert W. Smuts) *The Negro Potential*, Columbia University Press, 1956.

(With Ewing W. Reilley, Bray, and Herma) *Effecting Change in Large Organizations*, Columbia University Press, 1957.

Human Resources: The Wealth of a Nation, Simon & Schuster, 1958, reprinted, Greenwood Press, 1973.

(With Anderson) *Manpower for Government: A Decade's Forecast*, Public Personnel Association (Chicago), 1958.

(With Anderson and others) *The Ineffective Soldier: Lessons for Management and the Nation*, Volume 1: *The Lost Divisions*, Volume 2: *Breakdown and Recovery*, Volume 3: *Patterns of Performance*, Columbia University Press, 1959, reprinted, Greenwood Press, 1975.

(With Peter Rogatz) *Planning for Better Hospital Care*, King's Crown Press, 1961.

(With Anderson and Herma) *The Optimistic Tradition and American Youth*, Columbia University Press, 1962.

(With Ivar E. Berg) *Democratic Values and the Rights of Management*, Columbia University Press, 1963.

(With Hyman Berman) *The American Worker in the Twentieth Century: A History through Autobiographies*, Free Press of Glencoe, 1964.

(With Alfred S. Eichner) *The Troublesome Presence: American Democracy and the Negro*, Free Press of Glencoe, 1964.

(With Herma) *Talent and Performance*, Columbia University Press, 1964.

(With Dale L. Hiestand and Beatrice G. Reubens) *The Pluralistic Economy*, McGraw, 1965.

Louis Ginzberg: Keeper of the Law, Jewish Publication Society, 1966.

(With others) *Life Styles of Educated Women: Self-Portraits* (also see below), Columbia University Press, 1966.

(With Alice M. Yohalem) *Educated American Women: Self-Portraits* (also see below), Columbia University Press, 1966.

(With Herbert A. Smith) *Manpower Strategy for Ethiopia*, Central Press (Addis Ababa), 1966, enlarged edition published as *Manpower Strategy for Developing Countries: Lessons from Ethiopia*, Columbia University Press, 1967.

The Development of Human Resources, McGraw, 1966.

(With others) *The Middle-Class Negro in a White Man's World*, Columbia University Press, 1967.

(With Carol A. Brown) *Manpower for Library Services*, Columbia University Press, 1967.

(With Hiestand) *Mobility in the Negro Community: Guidelines for Research on Social and Economic Progress*, U.S. Commission on Civil Rights, 1968.

Manpower Agenda for America, McGraw, 1968.

(With others) *Manpower Strategy for the Metropolis*, Columbia University Press, 1968.

People and Progress in East Asia, Columbia University Press, 1968.

One Fifth of the World: Manpower Reports on Iran and South Asia, Conservation of Human Resources Project, Columbia University, 1969.

(With Miriam Ostow) *Men, Money, and Medicine*, Columbia University Press, 1969.

Manpower for Development: Perspectives on Five Continents, Praeger, 1971.

Educated American Women: Life Styles and Self-Portraits (contains *Life Styles of Educated Women* and *Educated American Women: Self-Portraits*), Columbia University Press, 1971.

Career Guidance: Who Needs It, Who Provides It, Who Can Improve It, McGraw, 1971.

Perspectives on Indian Manpower, Employment, and Income, [New Delhi], 1971.

(With others) *Urban Health Services: The Case of New York*, Columbia University Press, 1971.

Manpower Advice for Government, U.S. Department of Labor, 1972.

The Outlook for Educated Manpower, Engineering Manpower Commission (New York), 1972.

Federal Manpower Policy in Transition, U.S. Department of Labor, 1974.

The Manpower Connection: Education and Work, Harvard University Press, 1975.

The Human Economy, McGraw, 1976.

The Limits of Health Reform: The Search for Realism, Basic Books, 1977.

Health Manpower and Health Policy, Allanheld, Osmun, 1978.

Good Jobs, Bad Jobs, No Jobs, Harvard University Press, 1979.

The School/Work Nexus, Phi Delta Kappa, 1980.

(In Hebrew) *American Jews: The Building of Voluntary Community*, Schocken, 1980.

Home Health Care: Its Role in the Changing Health Services Market, Rowman & Allanheld, 1984.

The Coming Physician Surplus: In Search of a Policy, Rowman & Allanheld, 1985.

American Medicine: The Power Shift, Rowman & Allanheld, 1985.

Local Health Policy in Action: The Municipal Health Services Program, Rowman & Allanheld, 1985.

(With George Vojta) *Beyond Human Scale: The Large Corporation at Risk*, Basic Books, 1985.

Understanding Human Resources: Perspectives, People and Policy, Abt Books, 1985.

From Health Dollars to Health Services: New York City 1965-85, Rowan & Allanheld, 1986.

Technology and Employment: Concepts and Clarifications, Westview Press, 1986.

Medicine and Society, Westview Press, 1987.

The Skeptical Economist, Westview Press, 1987.

Tomorrow's Executives, Wiley, 1988.

EDITOR

The Nation's Children, Volume 1: *The Family and Social Change*, Volume 2: *Development and Education*, Volume 3: *Problems and Perspectives*, Columbia University Press, 1960.

Values and Ideals of American Youth, with foreword by John W. Gardner, Columbia University Press, 1961, new edition, Books for Libraries, 1972.

The Negro Challenge to the Business Community, McGraw, 1964.

Technology and Social Change, Columbia University Press, 1964.

Business Leadership and the Negro Crisis, McGraw, 1968.

(With Yohalem) *Corporate Lib: Women's Challenge to Management*, Johns Hopkins Press, 1973.

New York Is Very Much Alive: A Manpower View, McGraw, 1973.

(With Robert M. Solow) *The Great Society: Lessons for the Future*, Basic Books, 1974.

(With Yohalem) *The University Medical Center and the Metropolis*, Josiah Macy, Jr. Foundation, 1974.

The Future of the Metropolis: People, Jobs, Income, Olympus, 1975.

Economic Impact of Large Public Programs: The NASA Story, Olympus, 1976.

Jobs for Americans, Prentice-Hall, 1976.

Regionalization and Health Policy, U.S. Department of Labor, 1977.

Employing the Unemployed, Basic Books, 1980.

The U.S. Health Care System: A Look to the 1990s, Rowan & Allanheld, 1985.

From Physician Shortage to Patient Shortage: The Uncertain Future of Medical Practice, Westview Press, 1986.

OTHER

Also author of *The Skilled Work Force of the United States*, 1955, *The Negro and His Work*, 1961, and *Kavim le-heker haye ka-kalkalah shel Yehude ha-tefutsot*, 1972. Author of manpower studies for Israeli Ministry of Labor, 1961, 1964, and 1968, for Industrial College of the Armed Forces, 1964, and for National Commission on Productivity, 1971. Contributor to *Public Interests*.

SIDELIGHTS: Eli Ginzberg and co-author George Vojta discuss the problems of multinational corporations in *Beyond Human Scale: The Large Corporation at Risk*. Their thesis, an *Economist* reviewer relates, "is that huge firms are losing their competitive edge because they can no longer motivate workers enough." The problem is "bigness," writes Robert Krulwich. In the *New York Times Book Review* he summarizes, "As companies grow, they create internal monitoring systems to keep the boss aware of what is going on below—but after a while these systems take on a life of their own, and division chiefs and would-be division chiefs spend their days filling out reports and holding endless meetings instead of focusing on what counts in the business: the product, the customer, and the competition." According to Ginzberg and Vojta, today's managerial talent may prefer attachment to smaller companies where they don't spend as much time stalled in middle-management positions attending, for the most part, to corporate politics. Smaller companies offer higher productivity incentives and advancement opportunity; therefore, say the authors, large corporations are at risk unless they learn to reward talented managers with a greater voice in decision making to compensate for other missing motivators. To redirect energy from infighting back to the outside competitors, they prescribe a renewed emphasis on company-wide growth, and a decentralization of power. The multinational company may not be as endangered as Ginzberg and Vojta depict, states Krulwich, but he agrees that its survival will depend on its ability to attract and keep "the best recruits" in the manner that *Beyond Human Scale* suggests.

BIOGRAPHICAL/CRITICAL SOURCES:

PERIODICALS

American Journal of Sociology, March, 1981.
Business Week, April 22, 1985.
Current History, July, 1985.
Economic Books: Current Selections, September, 1985, June, 1986, September, 1986.
Economist, May 10, 1986.
Industrial and Labor Relations Review, January, 1965, July, 1965, October, 1969, July, 1973, July, 1977.

International Labour Review, July, 1966, May, 1967, October, 1968, August, 1972.
Journal of Economic Literature, March, 1977, March, 1981, September, 1986.
Nation, January 23, 1967.
New Leader, December 9, 1974.
New Republic, December 8, 1979.
New York, May 7, 1973.
New York Review of Books, December 17, 1970, December 16, 1971.
New York Times, January 11, 1965, August 4, 1965.
New York Times Book Review, February 21, 1965, January 15, 1967, July 14, 1985.
Personnel and Guidance Journal, June, 1965, April, 1972, December, 1982.
Personnel Psychology, winter, 1985.
Publishers Weekly, March 8, 1985.
Saturday Review, April 17, 1965, April 23, 1966, January 25, 1969, January 22, 1972.
SciTech Book News, February, 1986.
Times Literary Supplement, February, 25, 1965, October 21, 1965.
Washington Post Book World, January 26, 1969.
West Coast Review of Books, March 1978.
Wilson Quarterly, winter, 1980, spring, 1981, spring, 1982.

*   *   *

GLUECK, William F(rank)   1934-1980

PERSONAL: Surname is pronounced "Glick"; born December 24, 1934, in Cincinnati, Ohio; died May, 1980; son of Frank Charles (a businessman) and Alice (Buxsel) Glueck; children: William, Jr., Lisa, David, Melissa. *Education:* Xavier University, B.S. (magna cum laude), 1956, M.B.A., 1963; Michigan State University, Ph.D., 1966.

CAREER: Employed in sales, sales management, and management positions in the food industry, 1958-63; Michigan State University, East Lansing, assistant instructor in management, 1963-64, assistant to associate dean for graduate programs in business administration, 1964-66; University of Texas at Austin, assistant professor of management, 1966-68; University of Missouri—Columbia, associate professor of management, faculty research associate at Business and Public Administration Research Center, and faculty research associate at Space Sciences Research Center, all 1968-70, professor of management and faculty research professor, 1972-76; University of Georgia, Athens, distinguished professor of management, 1976-80. Visiting research fellow, University of Aston, Birmingham, England, 1970-71; Fulbright visiting professor, University of Belgrade, 1971. Consultant to Aluminum Company of America, American Management Association, American College of Hospital Administrators, and Missouri Regional Medical Programs. *Military service:* U.S. Army, 1956-58; became first lieutenant.

MEMBER: American Association of University Professors, Academy of Management (past president), Institute of Management Sciences, Industrial Relations Research Association, Beta Gamma Sigma, Phi Kappa Phi, Alpha Sigma Nu, Tau Kappa Alpha, Sigma Pi.

AWARDS, HONORS: University of Texas Excellence Fund award, 1968.

WRITINGS:

Hemisphere West: El Futuro, Bureau of Business Research, University of Texas, 1968.

(With Cary D. Thorp) *Organization Planning and Development,* American Management Association, 1971.

The Management of Scientific Research: An Annotated Bibliography and Synopsis, Research Center, School of Business and Public Administration, University of Missouri, 1971.

Business Policy: Strategy Formation and Management Action, McGraw, 1971, 3rd edition published as *Business Policy and Strategic Management,* 1980, 4th edition (with Lawrence R. Jauch), 1984, 5th revised edition, 1987.

The Teaching of Business Policy, McGraw, 1971, 2nd edition, 1976.

Personnel: A Diagnostic Approach, Business Publications, 1974, 3rd edition (with George T. Milkovich), 1982, 4th edition published as *Personnel-Human Resources Management: A Diagnostic Approach,* 1985.

Cases and Exercises in Personnel, Business Publications, 1974, 3rd edition (with George E. Stevens), published as *Cases and Exercises in Personnel-Human Resources Management,* 1983, 4th edition, 1986.

Management (study guide also available), Dryden, 1977, 3rd edition (with Arthur G. Bedeian), 1983.

(With Jauch and Sally Coltrin) *The Managerial Experience: Cases, Exercises, and Readings,* Dryden, 1977, 3rd edition, 1983.

(Editor) *Readings in Personnel,* Business Publications, 1977.

(Editor) *Readings in Business Policy from "Business Week,"* McGraw, 1978, 2nd revised edition (with Neil H. Snyder), published as *Readings in Business Policy and Strategy from "Business Week,"* 1982.

Foundations of Personnel, Business Publications, 1979, 2nd revised edition (with John M. Ivancevich) published as *Foundations of Personnel: Human Resource Management,* 1983, 3rd edition, 1986.

Management Essentials, Dryden, 1979.

Strategic Management and Business Policy, McGraw, 1980, 2nd edition (with Jauch), 1984, 3rd edition, 1987.

CONTRIBUTOR

William G. Scott, editor, *Organization Concepts and Analysis,* Dickenson, 1969.

Dale S. Beach, editor, *Readings in Personnel,* Macmillan, 1970.

Elmer Burack and James Walker, editors, *Manpower Planning,* Allyn & Bacon, 1971.

Robert W. Siroka and others, editors, *Sensitivity Training Reader,* Grosset, 1971.

OTHER

Contributor to *Academy of Management Journal, Management Science, Personnel Psychology,* and over thirty other publications.*

*   *   *

GODDEN, Jon 1906-1984

PERSONAL: Born August 3, 1906, in Bengal, India; died April 10, 1984; daughter of Arthur Leigh (a steamship agent) and Katherine Norah (Hingley) Godden; married Nigel Baughan, September 14, 1930 (died, 1931); married Roland Oakley, October 26, 1936 (divorced). *Education:* Attended art school in England, 1922-25.

ADDRESSES: Agent—Curtis Brown Ltd., 162-168 Regent St., London W1R 5TA, England.

CAREER: Writer.

MEMBER: PEN.

WRITINGS:

NOVELS

The Bird Escaped, Rinehart, 1947.
The House by the Sea, Rinehart, 1948.
The Peacock, Rinehart, 1950.
The City and the Wave, Rinehart, 1950.
The Seven Islands, Knopf, 1956.
Mrs. Panopoulis, Knopf, 1959.
A Winter's Tale, Knopf, 1961 (published in England as *Told in Winter,* Chatto & Windus, 1961).
In the Sun, Knopf, 1965.
Kitten with Blue Eyes, Chatto & Windus, 1971.
Mrs. Starr Lives Alone, Knopf, 1972.
Ahmed's Lady, Chatto & Windus, 1975, published in the United States as *Ahmed and the Old Lady,* Knopf, 1976.
In Her Garden, Knopf, 1981.

WITH SISTER, RUMER GODDEN

Two under the Indian Sun (autobiography), Knopf, 1966, reprinted, Morrow, 1987.
Shiva's Pigeons: An Experience of India (nonfiction), Knopf, 1972.

SIDELIGHTS: Jon Godden was well known for her finely crafted novels of British and Indian life. She and her sister, novelist Rumer Godden, spent several childhood years in India when it was still ruled by the British Raj. The experience colored many of the sisters' later writings, including their two collaborations, *Two under the Indian Sun* and *Shiva's Pigeons: An Experience of India.* In their first collaboration, the Goddens evoke five years of their Indian sojourn. Reviewer G. Parthasarathi calls *Two under the Indian Sun* "remarkably sensitive" in the *Saturday Review.* "It is based on reminiscence, but it is far more than an autobiography; for it tells not only what happened to these two young girls but pictures life around them, carrying the reader back over the decades, in delicately fluent prose, to a child's world of wonder."

New York Times Book Review contributor Virgilia Peterson points out that while the Goddens describe India in the early twentieth century, their book does not seem dated: "Between religions and classes, between men and women, between rich and poor, sharp lines still divide the Indian people. These things that the Godden sisters describe so vividly have no more vanished than the great canopy of the Indian sky which has given them, they say, their sense of space." Peterson further comments: "Within the framework of this childhood memoir, 'Two under the Indian Sun' is actually a many-storied edifice in which the authors move lightly but purposefully. Built upon the foundation of an English household in colonial India, it reaches down into the deep rivalry and tension between the two sisters and the well-springs of creative instincts which bubbled out in both of them.... Here, too, is a panoramic view of the India they knew and loved. Implicitly, and most important, it is also a book about an education for life."

Jon and Rumer Godden also collaborated on a narrative portrait of India entitled *Shiva's Pigeons: An Experience of India.* By following the life of their fictional protagonist, Amar, from birth to death, the Goddens explore many aspects of Indian life. A *Times Literary Supplement* writer comments, ''Although both [women] are better known as novelists, their narrative displays a perception and a sense of history which many Indologists might envy; the result gives a clearer idea of what life is like for many of the inhabitants of India than can be gathered from the writings of most professional sociologists.'' Thomas Lask of the *New York Times* writes that *Shiva's Pigeons* is ''a book of observation, not political comment, of understanding and empathy, not of judgement. When they describe the prevalence of beggars, they try to show how these people appear to the Indians; when they tell about those who, having no place of their own, sleep on mats in the streets, they try to make sense of this phenomenon to westerners who might be inclined to be censorious and superior. They do not defend either practice as being quaint or picturesque. But they do not lecture the Indians on their shortcomings or tell them how to do things better. They do not, to sum up, tell them how to live their lives, only to understand them.''

The novel *Ahmed's Lady* (published in the United States as *Ahmed and the Old Lady*) concerns an eighty-year-old Englishwoman's expedition into the mountains between Kashmir and Pakistan. She is accompanied only by Ahmed, her native guide. The formidable social barriers between the two mountain climbers dissolve as their expedition progresses. ''Jon Godden, always a superb storyteller, gets unusual shadings out of her characters,'' asserts a *New York Times Book Review* writer. ''The old adventurer is admittedly 'foolish, headstrong and rash.' And gallant. Ahmed is an ambivalent charmer out of Kipling. The two know the best and worst of one another—and their symbiosis makes an irresistable fable.'' In the *Times Literary Supplement*, Victoria Glendinning allows that while ''[*Ahmed's Lady*] is an old-fashioned novel,'' it is ''none the worse for that.'' She deems the novel ''as gallant and Kiplingesque as its heroine.''

AVOCATIONAL INTERESTS: Travel in India, Africa, and Japan.

BIOGRAPHICAL/CRITICAL SOURCES:

BOOKS

Godden, Jon and Rumer Godden, *Two under the Indian Sun*, Knopf, 1966, reprinted, Morrow, 1987.

PERIODICALS

Atlantic Monthly, July, 1966.
Los Angeles Times, April 14, 1981.
New York Times, June 22, 1966, August 26, 1972.
New York Times Book Review, June 12, 1966, April 4, 1976.
Saturday Review, August 28, 1965, July 23, 1966.
Time, April 19, 1976.
Times Literary Supplement, August 4, 1966, December 8, 1972, September 19, 1975.
Washington Post Book World, December 27, 1987.

OBITUARIES:

PERIODICALS

Times (London), April 17, 1984.*

* * *

GODDEN, (Margaret) Rumer 1907-

PERSONAL: Born December 10, 1907, in Sussex, England; daughter of Arthur Leigh (a steamship agent) and Katherine Norah (Hingley) Godden; married Laurence S. Foster, 1934 (deceased); married James Haynes Dixon, November 11, 1949 (died, 1973); children: (first marriage) Jane, Paula. *Education:* Attended Moira House, Eastbourne; studied dancing privately. *Religion:* Roman Catholic.

ADDRESSES: Home—Ardnacloich, Dumfriesshire, Moniaive, Scotland. *Agent*—Curtis Brown Ltd., 10 Astor Pl., New York, N.Y. 10003.

CAREER: Novelist, poet, and author of books for children. Founded and operated a children's dancing school in Calcutta, India.

AWARDS, HONORS: Commended for Carnegie Medal, 1962, for *Miss Happiness and Miss Flower;* Children's Book of the Year Awards from the Child Study Association, 1969, for *Operation Sippacik*, 1972, for *The Diddakoi* and *The Old Woman Who Lived in a Vinegar Bottle*, and 1975, for *Mr. McFadden's Hallowe'en;* Whitbread Award, 1973, for *The Diddakoi; Horn Book* Honor List citations, for *Miss Happiness and Miss Flower, Little Plum, Home Is the Sailor, The Kitchen Madonna*, and *The Old Woman Who Lived in a Vinegar Bottle;* American Library Association Notable Books citations, for *The Doll's House, The Mousewife, Impunity Jane: The Story of a Pocket Doll, The Fairy Doll, Miss Happiness and Miss Flower, The Kitchen Madonna, The Old Woman Who Lived in a Vinegar Bottle, A Kindle of Kittens*, and *The Dragon of Og*.

WRITINGS:

NOVELS

Chinese Puzzle, P. Davies, 1936.
The Lady and the Unicorn, P. Davies, 1938, reprinted, 1969.
Black Narcissus (also see below), Little, Brown, 1939, reprinted, New American Library, 1968.
Gypsy, Gypsy, Little, Brown, 1940, reprinted, Macmillan (London), 1965.
Breakfast with the Nikolides, Little, Brown, 1942.
Rungli-Rungliot (Thus Far and No Further), P. Davies, 1944, published as *Rungli-Rungliot Means in Parharia "Thus Far and No Further,"* Little, Brown, 1946, 2nd edition, Macmillan, 1961.
Take Three Tenses: A Fugue in Time, Little, Brown, 1945 (published in England as *A Fugue in Time*, M. Joseph, 1945, reprinted, Macmillan, 1976).
The River (also see below), Little, Brown, 1946, reprinted, Macmillan, 1967.
A Candle for St. Jude, Viking, 1948, reprinted, Avon, 1975.
A Breath of Air, M. Joseph, 1950, Viking, 1951.
Kingfishers Catch Fire, Viking, 1953.
An Episode of Sparrows (also see below), Viking, 1955, large type edition, 1968, reprinted, Perennial Library, 1981.
The Greengage Summer (also see below), Viking, 1958.
China Court: The Hours of a Country House, St. Martin's, 1961.
The Battle of Villa Fiorita, Viking, 1963, published with *An Episode of Sparrows* and *The Greengage Summer*, 1969.
In This House of Brede, Viking, 1969.
The Peacock Spring: A Western Progress, Macmillan, 1975, Viking, 1976.
Five for Sorrow, Ten for Joy, Viking, 1979.
The Dark Horse, Viking, 1981.
Thursday's Children, Viking, 1984.

JUVENILE

The Doll's House (illustrated by Dana Saintsbury), M. Joseph, 1947, Viking, 1948, new edition illustrated by Tasha Tudor, Viking, 1962.

The Mousewife (illustrated by Saintsbury), Viking, 1951, new edition illustrated by Heidi Holder, Viking, 1982.

Impunity Jane: The Story of a Pocket Doll (illustrated by Adrienne Adams; also see below), Viking, 1954.

The Fairy Doll (illustrated by Adams; also see below), Viking, 1956.

Mouse House (illustrated by Adams), Viking, 1957.

The Story of Holly and Ivy (illustrated by Adams; also see below), Viking, 1958.

Candy Floss (illustrated by Adams; also see below), Viking, 1960.

St. Jerome and the Lion (poems; illustrated by Jean Primrose), Viking, 1961.

Miss Happiness and Miss Flower (illustrated by Primrose), Viking, 1961.

Little Plum (illustrated by Primrose), Viking, 1963.

Home Is the Sailor (illustrated by Primrose), Viking, 1964.

The Kitchen Madonna (illustrated by Carol Barker), Viking, 1967.

Operation Sippacik (illustrated by James Bryan; Junior Literary Guild selection), Viking, 1969.

The Diddakoi (illustrated by Creina Glegg), Viking, 1972.

(Adaptor) *The Old Woman Who Lived in a Vinegar Bottle* (illustrated by Mairi Hedderwick), Viking, 1972.

Mr. McFadden's Hallowe'en (illustrated by Ann Strugnell), Viking, 1975.

The Rocking Horse Secret (illustrated by Juliet S. Smith), Macmillan, 1977, Viking, 1978.

A Kindle of Kittens (illustrated by Lynne Byrnes), Macmillan, 1978, Viking, 1979.

The Dragon of Og (illustrated by Pauline Baynes), Viking, 1981.

The Valiant Chatti-Maker (illustrated by Jeroo Roy), Viking, 1983.

Four Dolls (includes *Impunity Jane: The Story of a Pocket Doll, The Fairy Doll, The Story of Holly and Ivy* and *Candy Floss*), Greenwillow, 1983.

EDITOR

(with Margaret Bell) *Round the Day: Poetry Programmes for the Classroom or Library*, Macmillan, 1966.

(With Bell) *Round the Year: Poetry Programmes for the Classroom or Library*, Macmillan, 1966.

(With Bell) *The World Around: Poetry Programmes for the Classroom or Library*, Macmillan, 1966.

Emily Dickinson, *A Letter to the World: Poems for Young People* (illustrated by Prudence Seward), Bodley Head, 1968.

Olga Manders, *Mrs. Manders' Cook Book*, Macmillan, 1968.

Raphael, *The Raphael Bible*, Viking, 1970.

OTHER

Bengal Journey: A Story of the Part Played by Women in the Province, 1939-1945, Longmans, Green, 1945.

In Noah's Ark (narrative poem), Viking, 1949.

(Adaptor with Jean Renoir) "The River" (screenplay; based on her novel of same title), United Artists, 1951.

Hans Christian Andersen: A Great Life in Brief (biography), Knopf, 1954.

Mooltiki: Stories and Poems from India, Viking, 1957 (published in England as *Mooltiki, and Other Stories and Poems from India*, Macmillan, 1957).

(Translator) Carmen de Gasztold, *Prayers from the Ark* (poems), Viking, 1962.

(Translator) de Gasztold, *The Creatures' Choir* (poems), Macmillan, 1962, Viking, 1965, published as *The Beasts' Choir*, Macmillan, 1967.

(Adaptor) Hans Christian Andersen, *The Feather Duster: A Fairy-Tale Musical*, music by Kai Normann Andersen, Dramatic Publishing, 1964.

(With sister, Jon Godden) *Two under the Indian Sun* (autobiography), Knopf, 1966, reprinted, Morrow, 1987.

Gone: A Thread of Stories, Viking, 1968 (published in England as *Swans and Turtles: Stories*, Macmillan, 1968).

The Tale of the Tales: The Beatrix Potter Ballet, Warne, 1971.

(With J. Godden) *Shiva's Pigeons: An Experience of India*, Viking, 1972.

The Butterfly Lions: The Story of the Pekingese in History, Legend and Art, Macmillan, 1978.

Gulbadan, Portrait of a Rose Princess at the Mughal Court (biography), Viking, 1981.

A Time to Dance, No Time to Weep (autobiography), Beech Tree Books, 1988.

Also author of dramatization of *Black Narcissus*. Contributor to publications in England and the United States.

SIDELIGHTS: Rumer Godden is well known for both her novels and her award-winning children's books. Critics have praised her complex, poetic style in such novels as *Thursday's Children, The Peacock Spring,* and *The Dark Horse*. Themes of childhood upheavals and clashing cultures are common for Godden, reflecting the circumstances of her own life as an Englishwoman in India at the time of the Raj. Born in England, she was taken to India by her parents with her three sisters when she was nine months old. Her father's position as a steamship agent took the family all over the subcontinent and brought them into contact with the natives of India far more frequently than most of their fellow Englishmen. Writing was a family preoccupation for the Goddens. Rumer created her first books when she was seven, but turned to dancing as a means of overcoming serious injuries she suffered in an accident. In 1921 all four of the Godden sisters were sent to boarding school in England. "It was a multiple shock," writes Ann Chisholm in the *Times Literary Supplement*. "Not only were the warmth, light and space of India replaced by dark, cold, cramped England, but conscientious and often chilly relatives or teachers took over from loving parents." Unable to conform to the restrictive atmosphere, Godden went to five schools in two years before settling at Moira House, a progressive institution. Emma Fisher quotes her in *The Pied Pipers*: "The vice-principal [at Moira House] was a remarkable woman . . . who was very interested in the stage, and theatre and writing; and after my first week there, she took me out of school, and I only learnt French, and literature, and music. She let me work with her. And did she make me work, in no uncertain terms! . . . What I owe to her is beyond words. She gave me a really thorough training in English, and technique."

Godden returned to India in the 1930s. She opened a dancing school there, married a stockbroker, and began to work on novels. Her first, *Chinese Puzzle*, was published in 1936. "In those days I was very precious, and I wrote [*Chinese Puzzle*] in longhand—and I used capitals for the nouns," Fisher quotes the author. "I suppose I thought it would give a sort of Chinoiserie context to it, and of course when it was printed it looked too terrible for words. It absolutely killed the book, though it got very good reviews." Godden achieved her first commercial success with a story about nuns, *Black Narcissus*. It was a runaway best seller in the United States, but the prosperity it brought Godden was short-lived, for her husband soon gambled away the profits from the book, then abandoned her. Godden and her two daughters lived for a time in a hotel for army wives, but found the cramped conditions there intolerable. The author then defied convention by taking her children to a remote village in Kashmir. There they lived in peasant style, and ran a herb farm. The experience deepened Godden's love and understanding of India.

After World War II ended, Godden left Kashmir and sailed for England. She was penniless and took with her only her children, a precious Oriental rug, and the manuscript of a new book. She soon reestablished her career as a novelist; in 1947 she published a children's story, *The Doll's House*. She wrote the book to see if she could successfully set an entire novel within the confines of a toy house. *The Doll's House* was the first of many acclaimed children's books by Godden. She followed it up in 1951 with *The Mousewife*. This tale of a mouse looking for a new home was based on a story Godden found in the journal of Dorothy Wordsworth, sister of the poet William Wordsworth. "It takes courage to tell a story, to endure the discipline of writing it, and doing that for children is a far more difficult art than writing a novel," remarked Godden in *The Writer*.

Many critics note that even in her novels for adults, Godden displays a profound understanding of children and their view of the world. Her book *Thursday's Children* shows how a mother's ambition forces her two children to compete in the world of classical dance. Crystal is determined to become a member of Her Majesty's Ballet, but has only average talent; her younger brother, Doone, is naturally gifted but ignored. Alexandra Marshall applauds *Thursday's Children* in the *New York Times Book Review*: "This novel, being about both art and life, is both exotic and mundane. [It] is rich in symbolic gesture, formal and intricately stylized, graceful in presentation, intensely emotional and even, at times, like a good ballet—transporting." Parents' hypocritical attitudes toward their children are illustrated in Godden's novel *The Peacock Spring*. In this story, a British envoy in Delhi summons his two daughters to join him from England. Once in India, the girls realize that their father has uprooted them only to chaperone his fiancee, Alix, a half-caste who hides her background. One of the daughters eventually falls in love with an Indian boy, but in spite of their similar circumstances, the older couple rejects the union to protect their own social standing. A *Newsweek* writer reviewing *The Peacock Spring* states: "Rumer Godden remains among the last British novelists to be influenced by the colonial experience in India. . . . [Her books] have reflected the enlightenment and catholic vision acquired from those early years along the banks of the great accepting rivers of the subcontinent. At the sametime, her writing, sometimes lightly nostalgic, sometimes darkly romantic, takes its moral and melodramatic conventions from the tradition of Henry James and E. M. Forster, if on a smaller scale. Drawing on the best of East and West, she produces a deeply satisfying fable of innocence lost and romance strangled."

Nuns are another of Godden's favorite subjects; they figure prominently in her first best seller, *Black Narcissus*, and in many of her other novels, including *The Dark Horse*, *Five for Sorrow, Ten for Joy*, and *In This House of Brede*. The latter is perhaps her most serious book, according to numerous commentators. Through the story of Phillipa Talbot, a successful businesswoman and widow who joins the Benedictine order of nuns, Godden examines the contemplative life in detail. Hassell A. Simpson assesses *In This House of Brede* as Godden's "longest and most varied" book in the *Saturday Review*,

and he believes that it may also be "her richest and most moving." The many intertwining threads in her plot "are woven so closely that the fabric appears seamless, and there are no loose ends left dangling. The religious life has scarcely ever received so careful a presentation in fiction, and the main impression we take away is of very real women attempting without ever completely achieving the perfect life."

Godden's own colorful life has provided the material for two volumes of autobiography: *Two under the Indian Sun*, written with her sister, novelist Jon Godden, and *A Time to Dance, No Time to Weep*, in which she traces her life from her adolescent exile to England to her departure from her Kashmir village at the end of World War II. Sharon Dirlam of the *Los Angeles Times* praises *A Time to Dance, No Time to Weep*: "This wonderful autobiography is full of Godden's spirit, her courage and passion, her acceptance of fate and her love of life. It will be embraced by all who have read her works; for others, it will be a compelling introduction to a remarkable writer."

MEDIA ADAPTATIONS: Six of Godden's novels have been adapted for motion pictures and television: "Black Narcissus," produced by Universal, 1947; "Enchantment" (adapted from *Take Three Tenses*), produced by RKO, 1948; "Innocent Sinners" (adapted from *An Episode of Sparrows*), produced by Rank Organisation Film Products, 1957; "Loss of Innocence" (adapted from *Greengage Summer*), produced by Columbia, 1961; "The Battle of Villa Fiorita," produced by Warner Brothers, 1965; and "In This House of Brede," produced by Learning Corp. of America, televised on CBS, 1975.

BIOGRAPHICAL/CRITICAL SOURCES:

BOOKS

Arbuthnot, May Hill, *Children and Books*, 3rd edition, Scott, Foresman, 1964.
Books for Children, 1960-1965, American Library Association, 1966.
Cameron, Eleanor, *The Green and Burning Tree*, Atlantic-Little, Brown, 1969.
Doyle, Brian, *The Who's Who of Children's Literature*, Schocken, 1968.
Fisher, Margery, *Who's Who in Children's Books*, Holt, 1975.
Godden, Jon and Rumer Godden, *Two under the Indian Sun*, Knopf, 1966, reprinted, Morrow, 1987.
Godden, Rumer, *A Time to Dance, No Time to Weep*, Beech Tree Books, 1988.
Haviland, Virginia, *Children and Literature: Views and Reviews*, Lothrop, 1974.
Larrick, Nancy, *A Parent's Guide to Children's Reading*, 3rd edition, Doubleday, 1969.
Wintle, Justin and Emma Fisher, *The Pied Pipers*, Paddington Press, 1975.

PERIODICALS

Atlantic Monthly, October, 1969.
Best Sellers, October 1, 1969.
Book Week, September 29, 1963.
The Calendar, September/December, 1972.
Christian Science Monitor, December 15, 1955, December 11, 1969.
Horn Book, December, 1969, August, 1976.
Library Journal, June 15, 1969.
Life, August 5, 1966.
Los Angeles Times, June 8, 1981, September 5, 1984, February 21, 1988.

New Republic, November 24, 1979, June 23, 1982.
New Statesman, November, 1968.
Newsweek, September 30, 1963, April 12, 1976.
New Yorker, March 23, 1981.
New York Times Book Review, July 9, 1939, June 12, 1966, January 7, 1968, June 30, 1968, September 21, 1969, May 7, 1972, April 25, 1976, December 16, 1979, June 24, 1984, January 3, 1988.
Observer Review, July, 1968.
Publishers Weekly, February 3, 1975.
Saturday Review, October 4, 1969.
Spectator, October 17, 1981.
Times Literary Supplement, January 30, 1976, February 26, 1988.
Washington Post, November 29, 1969, December 3, 1979, January 30, 1982.
The Writer, July, 1977.

—*Sketch by Joan Goldsworthy*

*   *   *

GOEDICKE, Patricia (McKenna) 1931-
(Patricia McKenna, Patricia Robinson)

PERSONAL: Born June 21, 1931, in Boston, Mass.; daughter of John Bernard (a psychiatrist) and Helen (Mulvey) McKenna; married Victor Goedicke (a professor), September 12, 1956 (divorced, 1968); married Leonard Wallace Robinson (a writer), June 3, 1971. *Education:* Middlebury College, B.A. (cum laude), 1953; studied under W. H. Auden at Young Men's Hebrew Association, New York, N.Y., 1955; Ohio University, M.A. in creative writing and poetry, 1965.

ADDRESSES: Home—310 McLeod Ave., Missoula, Mont. 59801. *Office*—Department of English, University of Montana, Missoula, Mont. 59812.

CAREER: Harcourt, Brace & World, New York City, editorial assistant, 1953-54; T. Y. Crowell (publishers), New York City, editorial assistant, 1955-56; co-editor, *Page* (poetry broadsheet), 1961-66; Ohio University, Athens, instructor in English, 1963-68; reader-writer, Book-of-the-Month Club, 1968-69; Hunter College of the City University of New York, New York City, lecturer in English, 1969-71; Instituto Allende, Guanajuato, Mexico, associate professor of creative writing, 1972-79; Sarah Lawrence College, Bronxville, N.Y., guest faculty member in writing program, 1980-81; University of Montana, Missoula, visiting poet in residence, 1981-83, associate professor of English, 1983—. Has given poetry readings at the Library of Congress, the Young Men's Hebrew Association Poetry Center in New York, the New England Poetry Club, and the San Francisco State Poetry Center, as well as at colleges and universities, including State University of New York College at Brockport, Columbia University, New York University, Dartmouth College, Kalamazoo College, Washington University, Lake Forest College, San Francisco State University, Queens College of the City University of New York, Bucknell University, Wells College, and the Universities of Kansas, Arkansas, Alaska, Oregon, Minnesota, and Nevada. Panel member, Ohio Poetry Association annual meeting, 1974.

MEMBER: PEN, Academy of American Poets, Associated Writing Programs, Poetry Society of America, MacDowell Colony (fellow), Phi Beta Kappa.

AWARDS, HONORS: Emily Clark Balch Poetry Contest second prize and National Endowment for the Arts award, both 1968, both for poem ''You Could Pick It Up''; National Endowment for the Arts creative writing fellowship, 1976-77; Coordinating Council of Literary Magazines prize, 1976, for poem ''Lost''; Duncan Frazier Prize, *Loon,* fall, 1976; William Carlos Williams Prize for poetry, *New Letters,* spring, 1977; *Quarterly West* Prize for poetry, 1977; Pushcart Prize, 1977; Carolyn Kizer Prize, Monmouth Institute, 1987; Strousse Award, *Prairie Schooner,* 1987; Hohenberg Award, *Memphis State Review,* 1987.

WRITINGS:

POEMS

Between Oceans, Harcourt, 1968.
For the Four Corners, Ithaca House, 1976.
The Trail That Turns on Itself, Ithaca House, 1978.
The Dog That Was Barking Yesterday, Lynx, 1980.
Crossing the Same River, University of Massachusetts Press, 1980.
The Wind of Our Going, Copper Canyon Press, 1985.
Listen, Love, Barnwood Press, 1986.

CONTRIBUTOR

The American Literary Anthology, Volume 3, Viking, 1970.
William Cole, editor, *And Be Merry,* Grossman, 1972.
Psyche: The Feminine Poetic Consciousness, Dell, 1975.
William Cole, editor, *The Ardis Anthology of New American Poetry,* Ardis, 1976.
Bill Henderson, editor, *The Pushcart Prize, II: Best of the Small Presses,* Pushcart, 1978.
Tangled Vines, Beacon Press, 1978.
The Treasury of American Poetry, Doubleday, 1978.
A Geography of Poets, Bantam, 1979.
Editor's Choice, Spirit That Moves Us, 1980.
Walt Whitman: The Measure of His Song, Holy Cow Press, 1981.
Of Silence and Solitude, Beacon Press, 1982.
Writing in a Nuclear Age, New England Review, 1984.
Women Brave in the Face of Danger: Photographs of and Writings by Latin and North American Women, The Crossing Press, 1985.
Strong Measures, Harper, 1986.
Sutured Words, Aviva Press, 1987.
This Sporting Life, Milkweed Editions, 1987.

Also contributor to *New Letters Reader 1,* 1983, and *Crossing the River: Poets of the Western U.S.,* 1987.

OTHER

(Contributor of translations) *IXOK AMARGO* (poems), Granite Press, 1987.

Contributor to periodicals, including *Open Places, New Yorker, American Poetry Review, Antioch Review, Saturday Review, Nation,* and *Harper's.*

SIDELIGHTS: Patricia Goedicke's poetry is described in the *Times Literary Supplement* by David Kirby as ''intensely emotional, intensely physical.'' ''More than any contemporary woman poet, perhaps, she exhibits a Whitmanesque exuberance,'' claims *Small Press Review* contributor Hans Ostrom. According to Peter Schjeldahl in the *New York Times Book Review,* Goedicke ''bears down hard on the language, frequently producing exact ambiguities of phrasing that are startling and funny.'' And *Harper's* reviewer Hayden Carruth believes that Goedicke's poems ''have a hard truthful ring, like parables of survival.'' Goedicke's collection, *The Wind of Our*

Going, "is distinguished by its use of lavish images and multiple comparisons," describes Lex Runciman in *Western American Literature.* "Her poems delight in their connections, in the sheer physical length and amplitude of their sentences." Ostrom also likes the book, and writes, "*The Wind of Our Going* shows [Goedicke] to be a confident poet and a poet who has reason to be confident. Although she could benefit from a lighter touch and more varied forms, this is an engaging, vital book."

BIOGRAPHICAL/CRITICAL SOURCES:

PERIODICALS

Chicago Sun-Times, July 9, 1978.
Harper's, December, 1980.
Los Angeles Times Book Review, April 27, 1980.
Modern Poetry Studies, winter, 1976.
New York Times Book Review, December 17, 1978, February 9, 1986.
Small Press Review, November, 1985.
Southern Humanities Review, fall, 1971.
Times Literary Supplement, June 13, 1980.
Western American Literature, fall, 1986.

*   *   *

GOODRUM, Charles A(lvin)   1923-

PERSONAL: Born July 21, 1923, in Pittsburg, Kan.; son of Bernie Loy (a city director) and Mae (Beaver) Goodrum; married Donna Belle Mueller, September 2, 1950; children: Christopher Kent, Julia Belle, Geoffrey Paul. *Education:* University of Wichita (now Wichita State University), student, 1941-43, 1945-46, B.A., 1964; attended Princeton University, 1943-44; Columbia University, M.A., 1949.

ADDRESSES: Home—2808 Pierpont St., Alexandria, Va. 22302.

CAREER: University of Wichita (now Wichita State University), Wichita, Kan., librarian in charge of circulation, 1947-48; Library of Congress, Washington, D.C., Legislative Reference Service, reference librarian, 1949-50, political science bibliographer, 1950-53, librarian, 1953-62, coordinator of research, 1963-70, Congressional Research Service, assistant director, 1970-76, Office of the Librarian of Congress, director of Office of Planning and Development, 1976-78. Writer and consultant, 1978—. *Military service:* U.S. Army, 1943-46.

WRITINGS:

I'll Trade You an Elk, Funk, 1967.
The Library of Congress, Praeger, 1974, 2nd revised edition, with Helen W. Darymple, Westview, 1982.
Dewey Decimated (mystery novel), Crown, 1977.
(Contributor) Dilys Winn, *Murderess Ink,* Workman Publishing, 1979.
Carnage of the Realm (mystery novel), Crown, 1979 (published in England as *Dead for a Penny,* Gollancz, 1979).
Treasures of the Library of Congress, Abrams, 1980.
(With Darymple) *Guide to the Library of Congress,* Library of Congress, 1983.
(Contributor) Daniel J. Boorstin, *Books in Our Future: A Report from the Librarian of Congress to the Congress,* Library of Congress, 1984.
The Best Cellar (mystery novel), St. Martin's, 1987.
(Contributor) *Respectfully Quoted: A Dictionary of Quotations Requested from the Congressional Research Service,* Library of Congress, 1989.

American Advertising: The First 200 Years, Abrams, 1989.

Contributor to *Atlantic, New Yorker,* and library journals.

WORK IN PROGRESS: A revised edition of *Treasures of the Library of Congress;* a historical biography; two murder mysteries.

SIDELIGHTS: Charles A. Goodrum told *CA:* "I try to keep a little variety going by doing a non-fiction, reasonably serious research book, immediately followed by a light, hopefully humorous mystery novel—and then starting the cycle over again. Regrettably, the money is in the non-fiction, while the fun is in the detective stories." Goodrum's mystery novels have all been detective stories set in a famous library of rare books. One of Goodrum's nonfiction books, *Treasures of the Library of Congress,* is described by *New York Times Book Review* critic Frances Taliaferro as "a large handsome volume whose text suggests the remarkable range of the Library's 76 million items; abundant photographs document the richness of books and objects that are the best of their kind." *Washington Post Book World* reviewer Herman W. Liebert reports that, here, Goodrum "writes with humor, a sure feel for the little-known and the unexpected, and a sense of the ticking of history's clock. No one who cares about our present as the child of its past and the parent of its future can read his book without being freshly instructed and deeply moved."

MEDIA ADAPTATIONS: I'll Trade You an Elk was produced by Walt Disney Studios as a made-for-television movie.

BIOGRAPHICAL/CRITICAL SOURCES:

PERIODICALS

New York Times Book Review, February 8, 1981.
Washington Post Book World, November 16, 1980.

*   *   *

GORDON, John (William)   1925-

PERSONAL: Born November 19, 1925, in Jarrow, England; son of Norman (a teacher) and Margaret (Revely) Gordon; married Sylvia Ellen Young, January 9, 1954; children: Sally, Robert. *Education:* Educated in Jarrow and Wisbech, England.

ADDRESSES: Home—99 George Borrow Rd., Norwich, Norfolk NR4 7HU, England.

CAREER: Isle of Ely and Wisbech Advertiser, Wisbech, England, reporter, 1947-49, sub-editor, 1949-51; *Bury Free Press,* Bury St. Edmunds, Suffolk, England, 1951-58, began as chief reporter, became sub-editor; *Western Evening Herald,* Plymouth, England, sub-editor, 1958-62; *Eastern Evening News,* Norwich, England, columnist and sub-editor, 1973-85. *Military service:* Royal Navy, 1943-47.

WRITINGS:

FOR CHILDREN

The Giant under the Snow, Hutchinson, 1968, Harper, 1970.
The House on the Brink, Hutchinson, 1970, Harper, 1971, revised edition, Patrick Hardy Books, 1983.
The Ghost on the Hill, Kestrel, 1976.
The Waterfall Box, Kestrel, 1978.
The Spitfire Grave and Other Stories, Kestrel, 1979.
The Edge of the World, Patrick Hardy Books, 1983, Atheneum, 1983.
Catch Your Death and Other Ghost Stories, Patrick Hardy Books, 1984, Methuen, 1985.

The Quelling Eye, Bodley Head, 1986, Fontana, 1988.
The Grasshopper, Bodley Head, 1987.

CONTRIBUTOR

M. R. Hodgkin, editor, *Young Winter's Tales,* Macmillan, Number 2, 1971, Number 4, 1974, Number 6, 1975.
Edward Blishen, editor, *The Thorny Paradise,* Kestrel, 1975.
Jean Russell, editor, *The Methuen Book of Strange Tales,* Methuen, 1980.
Deborah Shine, editor, *Ghost Stories,* Octopus, 1980.
Shine, editor, *Detective Stories,* Octopus, 1980.
A. Smith and F. Mann, editors, *Englishcraft,* University Tutorial Press, 1981.
Aidan Chambers, editor, *Ghost after Ghost,* Kestrel, 1982.
Karl Edward Wagner, editor, *The Year's Best Horror Stories,* DAW, 1985.
Chambers, editor, *Shades of Dark,* Patrick Hardy Books, 1984, Puffin Books, 1985.
Bryan Newton, editor, *Spook: Stories of the Unusual,* Collins, 1985.
Chambers, editor, *A Sporting Chance,* Bodley Head, 1985.
Dennis Pepper, editor, *Oxford Book of Christmas Stories,* Oxford University Press, 1986.
Mick Gower, editor, *Twisted Circuits,* Hutchinson, 1987.
Chambers, editor, *A Quiver of Ghosts,* Bodley Head, 1987.
Jean Richardson, editor, *Beware! Beware!,* Hamish Hamilton, 1987.
Gower, editor, *Electric Heroes,* Bodley Head, 1988.
Chambers, editor, *Love All,* Bodley Head, 1988.

Work represented in numerous anthologies.

OTHER

Contributor of articles to periodicals.

WORK IN PROGRESS: Ride the Wind, a children's novel.

SIDELIGHTS: John Gordon, whose work has been translated into Japanese, Danish, Swedish, German, and Norwegian, wrote *CA:* "Stories are dreams in disguise. There are dreams hidden in all my stories. They are necessary, but they must remain hidden because they are mine and mean nothing to anybody else. The stories that surround them are meant to make you have similar dreams, your *own* dreams, which will again be secret. Stories are a way of sharing secrets too deep to mention.

"It is because I have to share this kind of feeling with other people that I write stories. And a story, no matter how strange the events in it, must be largely a matter of fact. So the places are real. I was brought up in the Fen Country of England, the eastern part that was once all marshes (or fens), but is now fields of rich black earth that stretch away as flat as the sea from horizon to horizon. It is a place full of stories already. There was a giant killer called Hickathrift; nearer the coast a ghost dog called Old Shuck pads the roads at night; King John is said to have lost his Crown Jewels in the marsh and people still dig for them. I use the places I know. The people become real to me as I write.

"I said I use dreams. Dreams reach into strange areas. *The House on the Brink* is a kind of ghost story and it led me into one of the strangest experiences I have had. The house of the title is an actual old house on the brink of an actual river. The 'ghost', a stump of wood that may be a body, is found in the mud of a river and it exerts a powerful influence over the woman who lives in the house.

"I invented everything except the house and the river, and I had not been in the house for fifteen years when I wrote the book and did not revisit it until after the book was published. When I did so, I discovered a part of the garden I had not known existed. It was to one side, behind a wall, and stretched away a considerable distance from the house. In the farthest part of it, on the far side of a lawn and almost in the trees, stood a stump. It was very much the shape of the stump I had described in the book but when I went closer I discovered it was stone and not wood. However, at the blunt, rounded top, which in the story contains a skull, there was carved, very faintly and almost worn away by time, the face of a man.

"Everything fitted so close to my story I went back to the house, which is a showplace open to visitors, and asked about the stump. The custodian told me that it was the shaft of an ancient stone cross that had once stood in the road behind the house, and that seemed to be the end of the matter. She did not know me nor the story I had written, but then she said, 'About a century ago they dredged that old stump from the mud of the river outside.'

"The fens, as I said, are full of stories."

BIOGRAPHICAL/CRITICAL SOURCES:

PERIODICALS

Times Literary Supplement, March 30, 1984.

*   *   *

GOULD, Peter R(obin) 1932-

PERSONAL: Born November 18, 1932, in Coulesdon, England; son of Ralph Graham and Helene (Hanson) Gould; married Johanna Stuyck, July 10, 1956; children: Katherine, Richard, Andrew. *Education:* Colgate University, B.A. (summa cum laude), 1956; Northwestern University, M.A., 1957, Ph.D., 1960.

ADDRESSES: Home—921 Oak Ridge Ave., State College, Pa. 16801. *Office*—306 Walker Building, Pennsylvania State University, University Park, Pa. 16802.

CAREER: Syracuse University, Syracuse, N.Y., assistant professor, 1960-63; Pennsylvania State University, University Park, Pa., assistant professor, 1963-64, associate professor, 1964-68, professor, 1968-86, Evan Pugh Professor, 1986—. Visiting lecturer at numerous universities in the United States, Canada, the Caribbean, and Europe. Chairman of numerous professional conferences. Consultant to various governmental agencies, universities, and private firms. Member of numerous committees at Pennsylvania State University. *Military service:* British Army, Infantry (Gordon Highlanders), 1951-53, became lieutenant.

MEMBER: Social Science Research Council, Phi Beta Kappa.

AWARDS, HONORS: Ford Foundation fellowship, 1959-63; National Science Foundation grants, 1965-84; award for meritorious contribution, American Association of Geographers, 1975; faculty research medal, Pennsylvania State University, 1981; D.Sc. (honoris causa), Universite Louis Pasteur, Strasbourg, 1982.

WRITINGS:

The Development of the Transportation Pattern in Ghana (monograph), Department of Geography, Northwestern University, 1960.

(Editor) *Africa: Continent of Change*, Wadsworth, 1961.

On Mental Maps, Michigan Inter-University Community of Mathematical Geographers, 1966.

Space Searching Procedures in Geography and the Social Sciences, Social Science Research Institute, University of Hawaii, 1966.

Spatial Diffusion, Association of American Geographers, 1969, published as *Spacial Diffusion: The Spread of Ideas and Innovations in Geographic Space*, Learning Resources in International Studies, 1975.

(With E. J. Taaffe, N. Ginsburg Burton, F. Lukermann, and P. L. Wagner) *Geography*, Prentice-Hall, 1970.

(With Ronald Abler and John S. Adams) *Spatial Organization: The Geographer's View of the World*, Prentice-Hall, 1971.

(With G. Tornqvist, S. Nordbeck, and B. Rystedt) *Multiple Location Analysis*, Gleerup (Lund, Sweden), 1972.

(With Rodney White) *Mental Maps*, Penguin, 1974, 2nd edition, Allen & Unwin, 1986.

People in Information Space: The Mental Maps and Information Surfaces of Sweden, Gleerup, 1975.

(With G. Olsson) *A Search for Common Ground*, Pion, 1982.

(With A. Pires, I. Boura, J. Gaspar, and R. Jacinto) *Estrutura agraria e inovacao na cova da beira*, Comissao de Coordenacao da Regiao Centro (Coimbra, Portugal), 1983.

(With J. Johnson and G. Chapman) *The Structure of Television*, Volume I: *Television, the World of Structure*, Volume II: *Structure, the World of Television*, Pion, 1984.

The Geographer at Work, Routledge & Kegan Paul, 1985.

(With R. Golledge and H. Couclelis) *A Ground for Common Search*, Santa Barbara Geographical Press, 1988.

Also author of *Fire in the Rain: The Democratic Consequences of Chernobyl*, 1988.

OTHER

(With K. Bassett) "The Spatial Dynamics of a Regional Taxonomy" (animated film), [produced in University Park, Pa.], 1968.

Also contributor of articles to over fifty books; also contributor to organization annals. Has delivered over fifty papers to conferences and meetings. Contributor of over ninety articles to periodicals, including *Harper's*. Consulting editor to journals, including *Environment and Planning, Geographical Analysis, L'Espace Geographique, Geografia, Journal of Geography in Higher Education, Journal of Geography*, and *Mappemonde*.

WORK IN PROGRESS: Global epidemiology of AIDS.

SIDELIGHTS: Peter R. Gould's book *Mental Maps*, co-written with Rodney White, analyzes perception of place, i.e. how people perceive geographic locales other than their own. A reviewer for the *Times Literary Supplement* writes that "the authors' approach, full of zest and zeal, is not of theoretical interest alone. It has implications for planners and policy-makers, administrators and educationists."

Gould enjoys travel and has visited Europe, Africa, Asia, and Latin America.

AVOCATIONAL INTERESTS: Reading, wine.

BIOGRAPHICAL/CRITICAL SOURCES:

PERIODICALS

Choice, October, 1974.
Times Literary Supplement, June 14, 1974.

GOULD, Stephen Jay   1941-

PERSONAL: Born September 10, 1941, in New York, N.Y.; son of Leonard (a court reporter) and Eleanor (an artist; maiden name, Rosenberg) Gould; married Deborah Lee (an artist and writer), October 3, 1965; children: Jesse, Ethan. *Education:* Antioch College, A.B., 1963; Columbia University, Ph.D., 1967.

ADDRESSES: Office—Museum of Comparative Zoology, Harvard University, Cambridge, Mass. 02138.

CAREER: Antioch College, Yellow Springs, Ohio, instructor in geology, 1966; Harvard University, Cambridge, Mass., assistant professor, 1967-71, associate professor, 1971-73, professor of geology and curator of invertebrate paleontology at Museum of Comparative Zoology, 1973—, Alexander Agassiz Professor of Zoology, 1982—. Harvard University, assistant curator, 1967-71, associate curator of invertebrate paleontology, 1971-73.

MEMBER: American Association for the Advancement of Science, American Academy of Arts and Sciences, American Society of Naturalists (president, 1979-80), Paleontological Society (president, 1985-86), Society for the Study of Evolution (vice president, 1975, president, 1990), Society of Systematic Zoology, Society of Vertebrate Paleontology, History of Science Society, Linnaean Society of London (foreign member), European Union of Geosciences (honorary foreign fellow), Sigma Xi.

AWARDS, HONORS: National Science Foundation, Woodrow Wilson, and Columbia University fellows, 1963-67; principal investigator for various grants, National Science Foundation, 1969—; Schuchert Award, Paleontological Society, 1975; National Magazine Award in essays and criticism, 1980, for "This View of Life"; "Notable Book" citation, American Library Association, 1980, and American Book Award in science, 1981, both for *The Panda's Thumb;* "Scientist of the Year" citation, *Discover,* 1981; National Book Critics Circle Award in general nonfiction, 1981, American Book Award nomination in science, 1982, and outstanding book award, American Educational Research Association, all for *The Mismeasure of Man;* MacArthur Foundation Prize fellowship, 1981-86; medal of excellence, Columbia University, 1982; F. V. Haydn Medal, Philadelphia Academy of Natural Sciences, 1982; Joseph Priestley Award and Medal, Dickinson College, 1983; Neil Miner Award, National Association of Geology Teachers, 1983.

Silver medal, Zoological Society of London, 1984; Bradford Washburn Award and gold medal, Museum of Science (Boston), 1984; distinguished service award, American Humanists Association, 1984; Tanner Lectures, Cambridge University, 1984, and Stanford University, 1989; meritorious service award, American Association of Systematics Collections, 1984; Founders Council Award of Merit, Field Museum of Natural History, 1984; John and Samuel Bard Award, Bard College, 1984; Phi Beta Kappa Book Award in science, 1984, for *Hen's Teeth and Horse's Toes;* Sarah Josepha Hale Medal, 1986; creative arts award (citation in nonfiction), Brandeis University, 1986; Terry Lectures, Yale University, 1986; distinguished service award, American Geological Institute, 1986; Glenn T. Seaborg Award, International Platform Association, 1986; In Praise of Reason Award, Committee for the Scientific Investigation of Claims of the Paranormal, 1986; H. D. Vursell Award, American Academy and Institute of Arts and Letters, 1987; National Book Critics Circle Award nomination in general nonfiction, 1987, for *Time's Arrow, Time's Cycle;*

Anthropology in Media Award, American Anthropological Association, 1987; History of Geology Award, Geological Society of America, 1988; T. N. George Medal, University of Glasgow, 1989. Recipient of over twenty honorary degrees from colleges and universities.

WRITINGS:

An Evolutionary Microcosm: Pleistocene and Recent History of the Land Snail P. (Poecilozonites) in Bermuda, [Cambridge, Mass.], 1969.
Ontogeny and Phylogeny, Belknap Press, 1977.
Ever since Darwin: Reflections in Natural History (essays), Norton, 1977.
The Panda's Thumb: More Reflections in Natural History (essays), Norton, 1980.
(With Salvador Edward Juria and Sam Singer) *A View of Life,* Benjamin-Cummings, 1981.
The Mismeasure of Man, Norton, 1981.
Hen's Teeth and Horse's Toes: Further Reflections in Natural History (essays), Norton, 1983.
The Flamingo's Smile: Reflections in Natural History (essays), Norton, 1985.
(With Rosamund Wolff Purcell) *Illuminations: A Bestiary,* Norton, 1986.
Time's Arrow, Time's Cycle: Myth and Metaphor in the Discovery of Geological Time, Harvard University Press, 1987.
An Urchin in the Storm: Essays about Books and Ideas, Norton, 1987.

Author of monthly column, ''This View of Life,'' in *Natural History.*

OTHER

(Contributor with Niles Eldredge) T. J. M. Schopf, editor, *Models in Paleobiology,* Freeman, Cooper, 1972.
(Contributor) Ernst Mayr, editor, *The Evolutionary Synthesis: Perspectives on the Unification of Biology,* Harvard University Press, 1980.
(General editor) *The History of Paleontology* (contains thirty-four different works), twenty volumes, Ayer, 1980.
(Editor with Eldredge) Mayr, *Systematics and the Origin of Species,* Columbia University Press, 1982.
(Editor with Eldredge) Theodosius Dobzhansky, *Genetics and the Origin of Species,* Columbia University Press, 1982.
(Contributor) Charles L. Hamrum, editor, *Darwin's Legacy: Nobel Conference XVIII, Gustavus Adolphus College, St. Peter, Minnesota,* Harper, 1983.
(Author of foreword) Gary Larson, *The Far Side Gallery 3,* Andrews & McMeel, 1988.

Contributor to proceedings of International Congress of Systematic and Evolutionary Biology Symposium, 1973; contributor to *Bulletin of the Museum of Comparative Zoology,* Harvard University. Contributor of more than one hundred articles to scientific journals. Associate editor, *Evolution,* 1970-72; member of editorial board, *Systematic Zoology,* 1970-72, *Paleobiology,* 1974-76, and *American Naturalist,* 1977-80; member of board of editors, *Science,* 1986—. Member of advisory board, Children's Television Workshop, 1978-81, and ''Nova,'' 1980—.

WORK IN PROGRESS: ''A large-scale technical book on the structure of evolutionary theory''; *The Burgess Shale* (tentative title), a book on ''the nature of history and its vicissitudes and contingencies . . . focus[ing] on the early evolution of animals groups, particularly the fauna of the Burgess Shale.''

SIDELIGHTS: Harvard University professor and evolutionary biologist Stephen Jay Gould is renowned for his ability to translate difficult scientific theories into understandable terms. In his books and essays on natural history, Gould, a paleontologist and geologist by training, popularizes his subjects without trivializing them, ''simultaneously entertaining and teaching,'' writes James Gorman in the *New York Times Book Review.* With his essay collections *Ever since Darwin, The Panda's Thumb, Hen's Teeth and Horse's Toes,* and *The Flamingo's Smile,* in addition to book-length studies on specific topics, such as *The Mismeasure of Man* and *Time's Arrow, Time's Cycle,* Gould has won critical acclaim for bridging a gap between the front lines of science and the literary world. ''As witty as he is learned, Gould has a born essayist's ability to evoke the general out of fascinating particulars and to discuss important scientific questions for an audience of educated laymen without confusion or condescension,'' Gene Lyons comments in *Newsweek.* ''He is a thinker and writer as central to our times as any whose name comes to mind.'' Lee Dembart offers similar praise in the *Los Angeles Times:* ''Stephen Jay Gould is one of our foremost expositors of science, a man of extraordinary intellect and knowledge and an uncanny ability to blend the two. He sees familiar things in fresh ways, and his original thoughts are textured with meaning and powerfully honed. . . . The publication of a new book by Gould is a cause for celebration.''

Gould's essay collections feature pieces written for his popular monthly column, ''This View of Life,'' which appears in the magazine *Natural History.* His column ''communicates the excitement of Gould's field of evolutionary biology in superbly witty and literate fashion to anyone willing to grapple with slippery and subtle ideas,'' David Graber comments in the *Los Angeles Times Book Review.* As both his column and books demonstrate, a frequent technique of Gould's is to illuminate scientific principles by way of interesting, often peculiar, examples within nature. ''When he writes about such biological oddities as the inverted jellyfish Cassiopea, the praying mantis's mating habits, the giant panda's extra 'thumb' or the flamingo's inverted jaw, he does so with a double purpose—to entertain us with fascinating details while teaching us a few general concepts,'' remarks David Quammen in the *New York Times Book Review.* ''Every oddity he describes stands on its own as a discrete fact of nature, an individual mystery, as well as yielding an example of some broader principle.''

Gould's focus on the unexpected within nature reflects a view that permeates his work: that natural history is significantly altered by events out-of-the-ordinary and is largely revealed by examining its ''imperfections.'' ''Catastrophes contain continuities,'' explains Michael Neve in the *Times Literary Supplement.* ''In fact Gould has made it his business to see the oddities and small-scale disasters of the natural record as the actual historical evidence for taking evolution seriously, as a real event.'' Through imperfections, ''we can . . . see how things have altered by looking at the way organic life is, as it were, cobbled together out of bits and pieces some of which work, but often only just.'' The panda's ''thumb,'' highlighted in Gould's 1981 American Book Award-winning essay collection *The Panda's Thumb: More Reflections in Natural History,* particularly demonstrates this. Not really a thumb at all, the contraption on the panda's paw is actually an enlarged wristbone that enables the panda to strip leaves from bamboo shoots. ''If one were to design a panda from scratch, one would not adapt a wrist bone to do the job of a thumb,'' observes *Times Literary Supplement* reviewer D. M. Knight.

An imperfection, the appendage "may have been fashioned by a simple genetic change, perhaps a single mutation affecting the timing and rate of growth."

That nature does not always display the expected is also behind "punctuated equilibrium," the noted evolutionary theory formulated by Gould with paleontologist Niles Eldredge. Punctuated equilibrium, familiarly known as "punk eke," holds that evolution does not occur in the steady incremental stages assumed by adherents of "gradualism"—but in rapidly sweeping leaps of change initiated in small segments of a population. Gould and Eldredge's theory proposes that "new species usually arise, not by the slow and steady transformation of entire ancestral populations, but by the splitting off of small isolates from an unaltered parental stock," continues Knight. Adds Richard Rhodes in the *Chicago Tribune Book World:* "They don't run from one to the next like melting cheese. They're more revolutionary than that: changing at the edges and the changed forms lying in wait to overwhelm the main body when it fails." Punctuated equilibrium also highlights a discrepancy that for years has daunted the traditionalists of Darwinian studies. According to Knight, "Gradualism should lead to the finding of transitional forms in the fossil record, but there are extremely few. . . . [Punctuated equilibrium] raises the problem of what is the use of a half-developed organ; and it seems as though some more jerky mechanism must be invoked, the evolution of a species being a matter of rapid changes in small populations followed by long periods of stability."

The sway that gradualism has held over the field of evolution is something Gould attributes to human expectations of harmony and progress. "Our standard view of the history of life is more based on our hopes and expectations than the realities of nature," he told Michelle Green in *People.* "We try so hard to see nature as a progressive process leading in a predictable and determined way towards us—the pinnacle of creation . . . but a closer examination . . . shows nothing of the sort. History is quirky, full of random events." In a *New York Times Magazine* profile of Gould, James Gleick reports: "For *Homo sapiens,* Gould and some of his colleagues believe, biological evolution is already over." He quotes Gould: "We're not just evolving slowly,. . . for all practical purposes we're not evolving. There's no reason to think we're going to get bigger brains or smaller toes or whatever—we are what we are."

Gould's writings emphasize science as a discipline "culturally embedded." "Science is not a heartless pursuit of objective information," he is quoted in the *New York Times Book Review,* "it is a creative human activity." Raymond A. Sokolov, in the same publication, remarks that Gould's "method is at bottom, a kind of textual criticism of the language of earlier biologists, a historical analysis of their 'metaphors,' their concepts of the world." Gould frequently examines science as the output of individuals working within the confines of specific time periods and cultures. In a *New Yorker* review of *The Flamingo's Smile: Reflections in Natural History,* John Updike writes of "Gould's evangelical sense of science as an advancing light [which] gives him a vivid sympathy with thinkers in the dark." Updike continues: "Gould chastens us ungrateful beneficiaries of science with his affectionate and tactile sense of its strenuous progress, its worming forward through fragmentary revelations and obsolete debates, from relative darkness into relative light. Even those who were wrong win his gratitude." Sue M. Halpern notes in *Nation:* "Gould is both a scientist and a humanist, not merely a scientist whose literary abilities enable him to build a narrow-bridge between the two

cultures in order to export the intellectual commodities of science to the other side. [His writing] portrays universal strivings, it expresses creativity and it reveals Gould to be a student of human nature as well as one of human affairs."

Gould also demonstrates instances where science, by factually "verifying" certain cultural prejudices, has been misused. *The Flamingo's Smile* contains several accounts of individuals victimized as a result of cultural prejudices used as scientific knowledge, such as the "Hottentot Venus," a black southern African woman whose anatomy was put on public display in nineteenth-century Europe, and Carrie Buck, an American woman who was legally sterilized in the 1920s because of a family history of mentally "unfit" individuals. And in *The Mismeasure of Man,* his 1981 National Book Critics Circle Award-winning study, Gould focuses on the development of IQ testing and debunks the work of scientists purporting to measure human intelligence objectively. "This book," writes Gould, "is about the abstraction of intelligence as a single entity, its location within the brain, its quantification as one number for each individual, and the use of these numbers to rank people in a single series of worthiness, invariably to find that oppressed or disadvantaged groups—races, classes or sexes—are innately inferior and deserve their status." Halpern points out a theme that runs throughout Gould's work: "Implicit in Gould's writing is a binding premise: while the findings of science are themselves value-free, the uses to which they are put are not."

In a *London Review of Books* essay on *Hen's Teeth and Horse's Toes: Further Reflections in Natural History,* John Hedley Brooke summarizes some of the major themes, all pointing "towards a critique of neo-Darwinian gradualism," that appear in Gould's writings. He cites: "The 'fact' of evolution is 'proved' from those imperfections in living organisms which betray a history of descent. The self-styled 'scientific creationists' have no leg to stand on and are simply playing politics. Natural selection must not be construed as a perfecting principle in any strong sense of perfection. Neo-Darwinists who look to adaptive utility as the key to every explanation are as myopic as the natural theologians of the early 19th century who saw in the utility of every organ the stamp of its divine origin. . . . Another recurrent theme is the extent to which the course of evolution has been constrained by the simple fact that organisms inherit a body structure and style of embryonic development which impose limits on the scope of transformation." This last principle is enhanced by Gould's field work with the Bahamian land snail genus *Cerion,* a group that displays a wide variety of shapes, in addition to a permanent growth record in its shell. "More orthodox evolutionists would assume that the many changes of form represent adaptations," notes Gleick. "Gould denies it and finds explanations in the laws of growth. Snails grow the way they do because there are only so many ways a snail *can* grow."

Some reviewers have commented that Gould's writings display a repetition of key principles and themes—in reviewing *Hen's Teeth and Horse's Toes,* Hedley remarks that "the big implications may begin to sound familiar"—however, Gould earns consistent praise for the diversity of his interests and subject matter through which he illustrates evolutionary principles. "Gould entices us to follow him on a multifaceted Darwinian hunt for answers to age-old questions about ourselves and the rest of the living world," writes John C. McLoughlin in the *Washington Post Book World.* "Like evolution itself, Gould explores possibilities—any that come to hand—and his range of interest is stupendous. . . . Throughout, he displays with force and elegance the power of evolutionary theory to link the phenomena of the living world as no other theory seems able.'' Steven Rose writes in the *New York Times Book Review:* ''Exploring the richness of living forms, Mr. Gould, and we, are constantly struck by the absurd ingenuity by which fundamentally inappropriate parts are pressed into new roles like toes that become hooves, or smell receptors that become the outer layer of the brain. Natural selection is not some grandiose planned event but a continual tinkering. . . . Mr. Gould's great strength is to recognize that, by demystifying nature in this way, he increases our wonder and our respect for the richness of life.''

CA INTERVIEW

CA interviewed Stephen Jay Gould by telephone on March 17, 1988, at his office at Harvard University in Cambridge, Massachusetts.

CA: One of the joys of your writing is that it makes the excitement of science accessible to educated general readers. Isn't it sometimes a hefty challenge to put scientific concepts into understandable prose for the lay reader?

GOULD: I think that's a myth. I don't see why it should be that difficult—or at least not more difficult than doing it for any other field. Every field has its jargon. I think scientists hide behind theirs perhaps more than people in other professions do—it's part of our mythology—but I don't think the concepts of science are intrinsically more difficult than the professional notions in any other field. The main reason why the impression may persist that it's more difficult in science is just that good writers are self-selected out of science. They tend to be channeled into other areas, so most scientists end up without skill in writing, without thinking about it very much.

CA: Your writing is full of metaphor and literary allusions. Are there other writers, scientific or not, who have been in some way models or inspirations for your writing?

GOULD: I've always written very intuitively. I was never trained in writing. And I'm not nearly so well-read as some people might think from the kinds of quotations I use; I just have the ability not to forget what I've read. What I've developed is a style that more or less grew with my practice of it. There are people whose writings I admire, mostly T. H. Huxley and Peter Medawar, but I came to them after I started writing myself.

CA: It's a well-known story how you decided at the age of five, when you first saw Tyrannosaurus rex *at the American Museum of Natural History, to become a paleontologist, though you didn't know the word yet. . . .*

GOULD: It's a very stale story. It's stale because it's true. There's nothing unique about it. A lot of paleontologists began life as dinosaur nuts.

CA: But how and when did you pick a Bahamian land snail as the focus of your continuing study of evolution?

GOULD: I decided that I wanted to study evolutionary pattern in a statistical way, and you can't do that with dinosaurs. There are only two *Tyrannosaurus* skeletons in the entire world, so you could not do a rigorous study of rates of evolution in tyrannosaurs. If you want to study rates and patterns, you need material that comes in thousands rather than handful as specimens. That meant invertebrates rather than vertebrates. Snails suit my own interest because I'm concerned with the relationship between growth and evolution, and snails preserve in their shell the record of their entire growth from babyhood to adult. Most organisms don't.

CA: Were there other organisms that you considered using?

GOULD: You don't really approach these kinds of things as a logical exercise in an armchair. You get into organisms by odd sets of personal circumstances. When I was at Antioch College, I worked for the Woods Hole Oceanographic Institution. I went to Bermuda when I was stationed on one of the ships there, and while I was in Bermuda I learned about these land snails—not the ones I study now, but another group that became the subject of my Ph.D. thesis. I just drifted into it, and it was appropriate so I stayed with it.

CA: Much of your writing is related to the theory of punctuated equilibrium, change by fits and starts rather than a gradual and logical evolution, that you and Niles Eldredge presented in a 1972 paper. Has that theory gained any ground among your colleagues?

GOULD: It certainly has. It was new in 1972, and now it's a part of any paleontological discussion of the nature of pattern in life's history. I don't think anyone would deny that it happens often. The remaining issue is its relative frequency. Naturally I think that its relative frequency is predominant, or at least very high. Not everybody agrees with me. But I don't think you will find many paleontologists who doubt the reality of the process.

CA: Do you feel the academic scientist has an obligation to the community? I'm thinking specifically of the example of your going to court to support the teaching of evolution in public schools, opposing those who demand equal time for what they call ''creation science.''

GOULD: The stock phrase is ''duty to the community.'' Wonder why it's always asked that way? But that's not why I went to court in Little Rock. I'm an evolutionary biologist, and we were threatened. It was very personal. Of course I believe in the First Amendment and of course I don't want to see nonsense taught as science in schools. But the reaction of evolutionists to creation is very personal. We are a small profession. Some three thousand people in this country spend their professional lifetimes studying evolution, and creationism is a direct threat to one of the most exciting things scientists have ever learned. Of course we had to fight it. It wasn't public service—though aspects of it turned out to be public service.

CA: How would you rate us as a nation on scientific literacy?

GOULD: I don't really know. If you go out on the street and choose a Mr. or Mrs. John Q. American Public, obviously the amount of scientific knowledge is dismally low, and disconcertingly and disappointingly so, and scientists tend to bemoan it. On the other hand, I'm not nearly so pessimistic as the standard statement. First of all, you've got to realize that although it is true that among educated people a hundred years ago general sophistication in science was high, you've got to remember that education was available to only a tiny fraction of people back then. An elite was educated, and they knew something about science. If you looked at that elite today, they'd probably still be reasonably well informed. But now education is available to so many people, I'm happy for whatever knowledge they have.

Also, I think there's a very bad mistake made when people think that scientific knowledge is abysmal. It may be true that formal, academic knowledge of science isn't high, but there's a lot in popular culture that really is a form of science that many people understand very well. Seventy million people every year go to the horse races. You've got a hundred million poker players. There's a lot of very sophisticated knowledge on the nature of probability. Sure, a lot of people bet on a horse because it has the same name as their granddaughter, but a lot of people who bet are really quite sophisticated. There's a large knowledge of probability out there that we generally don't call science. That's one of the most important of all subjects. Take the amateur telescope makers, the collecting of tropical fish in blue-collar communities, dog fancying—that's all part of science. There's so much. I'm not happy with the general knowledge of science, but I don't think it's nearly so abysmal as the doomsayers would have it.

CA: Would you like to see more science taught on the elementary and high-school levels, or to see science courses taught differently?

GOULD: I don't know a lot about high schools. The one time I ever made an effort to find out, when I read through all the high-school textbook chapters on evolution, it was a very disappointing experience because they're very poor. I wrote about this in ''The Case of the Creeping Fox Terrier Clone'' in the January, 1988, issue of *Natural History*. It's not so much that they've kowtowed to creationist pressure, because that's not the major problem; most of them haven't. It's just that the material's old and it's repetitious. It's presented in practically the same way in every textbook—in the same sequence, often using the same style of argument and even the same anecdotes, as I said in that *Natural History* article. And that doesn't excite students.

CA: Another thing you teach is the history of science. Is that flourishing as a profitable and useful field of study?

GOULD: It's very popular here. It's one of the largest undergraduate concentrations, and it's a very good way for students to mix, as many of them have, an interest in science with a concern for society and the humanities.

CA: How well does the combination of teaching and writing work for you?

GOULD: It would be nice if days had fifty hours, but otherwise it's fine.

CA: In The Mismeasure of Man *you analyze some of the fallacies and injustices of various means of measuring intelligence. Can you envision a workable educational system that would allow all children the chance to develop to their individual capacities without labelling or pigeonholing them?*

GOULD: You have to have some form of assessment, and nobody's really opposed to that. One of the points I tried to make in the book is that Alfred Binet himself, who invented what was later called the IQ test, had no intention of its being used as a labeling device, but merely as an aid to the identi-

fication of children who needed special help so that the help could be given in the hope that they would do the best they possibly could. If tests were used to identify merely in order to aid, that would be fine. When they're used to categorize, then they become objectionable. But it would be the height of hubris for me to claim to know how seven-year-old children or high-schoolers should be dealt with. I'm not an expert in education.

CA: Genetic engineering is more and more in the news, and it raises a lot of ethical questions. How do you feel about it, generally speaking? Are there legitimate uses?

GOULD: Of course. You don't throw out the printing press because it once printed *Mein Kampf*. It's too broad a topic, really, to comment on in a general way. You don't turn off academic professions. There are enormously beneficial medical and agricultural uses that are potential and even actual, and there are other things like cloning that you would not want to do. All technology has power, and power can be used in good and bad ways. It has to be scrutinized, but you don't turn off the power because of its potential misuse.

CA: In forming my question so generally, I was thinking of Jeremy Rifkin, who is opposed to any form of genetic engineering and about whom you've written.

GOULD: What Jeremy Rifkin is against in principle is the transference of the genetic material of one creature into another. I don't see where that becomes a high ethical principle. If in fact, for example, you could take a bacterial gene that conferred frost-resistance upon plants—and I don't make that up; it's an actual case that's a possibility—then why shouldn't you do it in a world that's suffering from malnutrition if there are no other harmful consequences? I don't see any inherent ethical principle about cross-species transfer, especially since it probably happens in nature. Probably viruses are carrying genes across borders all the time.

CA: You've said one of your greatest pleasures is to discover something new to learn about and tell others about in your writing. Considering all the topics you've come up with over the years, isn't that getting harder and harder?

GOULD: Oh no. Knowledge in science is so close to the starting line relative to what there is to know, there's no prospect that in the limited course of a human life you could ever get anywhere close to satisfactory knowledge about any large issue.

CA: You continue to teach, write the column for Natural History *and articles for other magazines, and publish essay collections and books with incredible regularity. What's ahead in your work that you'd like to talk about?*

GOULD: There's a large-scale technical book on the structure of evolutionary theory which I'll write during 1989. Then there's a book that's really about the nature of history and its vicissitudes and contingencies, but it will focus on the early evolution of animal groups, particularly the fauna of the Burgess Shale, which is the oldest evidence we have of soft-bodied invertebrate animals and therefore is really the most important of all fossil localities. I'll finish that this summer. It will probably be called *The Burgess Shale*, but it's a very general book about the nature of history, how different life undoubtedly be if you could play the tape again, and how improbable therefore our evolution was.

BIOGRAPHICAL/CRITICAL SOURCES:

BOOKS

Gould, Stephen Jay, *The Mismeasure of Man*, Norton, 1981.

PERIODICALS

America, May 24, 1986.
Antioch Review, spring, 1978.
Chicago Tribune, December 2, 1981, January 20, 1988.
Chicago Tribune Book World, November 30, 1980, June 26, 1983.
Christian Science Monitor, July 15, 1987.
Detroit News, May 22, 1983.
Economist, May 16, 1987.
Listener, June 11, 1987.
London Review of Books, December 1, 1983.
Los Angeles Times, June 2, 1987.
Los Angeles Times Book Review, July 17, 1983, November 29, 1987.
Nation, June 18, 1983, November 16, 1985.
Natural History, January, 1988.
Nature, November 19, 1987.
New Republic, December 3, 1977, November 11, 1981.
Newsweek, November 9, 1981, August 1, 1983.
New Yorker, December 30, 1985.
New York Review of Books, June 1, 1978, February 19, 1981, October 22, 1981, May 28, 1987.
New York Times, October 17, 1987.
New York Times Book Review, November 20, 1977, September 14, 1980, November 1, 1981, May 8, 1983, September 22, 1985, December 7, 1986, September 11, 1987, November 15, 1987.
New York Times Magazine, November 20, 1983.
People, June 2, 1986.
Rolling Stone, January 15, 1987.
Science, May, 1983.
Time, May 30, 1983, September 30, 1985.
Times Literary Supplement, May 22, 1981, February 10, 1984, October 25, 1985, June 6, 1986, September 11-17, 1987.
Voice Literary Supplement, June, 1987.
Washington Post Book World, November 8, 1981, May 8, 1983, September 29, 1985, April 26, 1987.

OTHER

"Stephen Jay Gould: This View of Life" (segment of television series, "Nova"), first aired on Public Broadcasting System (PBS-TV), December 18, 1984.

—*Sketch by Michael E. Mueller*

—*Interview by Jean W. Ross*

* * *

GRANBECK, Marilyn
See HENDERSON, M(arilyn) R(uth)

* * *

GRANT, Ben
See HENDERSON, M(arilyn) R(uth)

GREEN, Brian
See CARD, Orson Scott

* * *

GREEN, Paul E(dgar) 1927-

PERSONAL: Born April 4, 1927, in Glenolden, Pa.; son of Joseph (a law book dealer) and Lucy Mae (Gordy) Green; married Elizabeth Ann Weamer; children: three. *Education:* University of Pennsylvania, A.B., 1950, A.M., 1953, Ph.D., 1961.

ADDRESSES: Office—Department of Marketing, Wharton School, Suite 1400, Steinberg Hall-Dietrich Hall, University of Pennsylvania, Philadelphia, Pa. 19104-6371.

CAREER: Sun Oil Co., Philadelphia, Pa., statistician, 1950-53; Lukens Steel Co., Coatesville, Pa., commercial research analyst, 1953-54; University of Pennsylvania, Wharton School, Philadelphia, instructor in statistics, 1954-55; Lukens Steel Co., supervisor of operations research group and senior market analyst, 1955-58; E. I. duPont DeNemours & Co., Wilmington, Del., market planning consultant, 1958-62; University of Pennsylvania, Wharton School, deputy director of Management Science Center and associate professor, 1962-65, professor, 1965-71, S. S. Kresge Professor of Marketing, 1971—. Guest lecturer at more than seventy colleges and universities in the United States and abroad, including University of Delaware, University of Pittsburgh, Washington University, Massachusetts Institute of Technology, Stanford University, University of Tel Aviv, University of London, University of Leiden, University of Grenoble, and University of Paris. Chairman of Institute of Management Sciences' College on Marketing, 1970-71. Member of advisory council, Association for Consumer Behavior, 1970-74; member of Census Advisory Committee, 1980-83.

MEMBER: European Marketing Research Society, American Association for the Advancement of Science, American Marketing Association (member of local executive council, 1965-67, 1968-69, and local board of directors, 1976-77), Operations Research Society of America, Institute of Management Sciences, American Institute of Decision Sciences (fellow), Society of Multivariate Experimental Psychology, American Statistical Association (fellow), Psychometric Society, Academy of Marketing Sciences (member of policy board, 1982-85), Association of Consumer Research (member of advisory council, 1970-74).

AWARDS, HONORS: Award from Alpha Kappa Psi, 1963, for "Bayesian Decision Theory in Pricing Strategy," and 1981, for "A General Approach to Optimal Product Design via Conjoint Analysis"; silver medal from J. Walter Thompson Agency, 1970, for "Advertisement Perception and Evaluation: An Application of Multidimensional Scaling"; honorable mention in research design contest from American Marketing Association, 1971, for "On the Measurement of Judgmental Responses to Multi-Attribute Stimuli"; first prize in research design competition from American Psychological Association, 1972; Parlin Award for the advancement of science in marketing from American Marketing Association, 1977; Paul D. Converse Award in marketing theory, 1978; distinguished lecturer award from Beta Gamma Sigma, 1978; elected to Attitude Research Hall of Fame, 1981; special award from Marketing Science Institute, 1986, for "Contributions to Multidimensional Scaling"; finalist for O'Dell Award from

Journal of Marketing Research, 1987; finalist for Franz Edelman Award, 1988.

WRITINGS:

(With Wroe Alderson) *Planning and Problem Solving in Marketing,* Irwin, 1964.

(With D. S. Tull) *Research for Marketing Decisions,* Prentice-Hall, 1966, 5th edition, 1988.

(With P. T. FitzRoy and P. J. Robinson) *Experiments on the Value of Information in Simulated Marketing Environments* (monograph), Allyn & Bacon, 1967.

(With R. E. Frank) *A Manager's Guide to Marketing Research: Survey of Recent Developments,* Wiley, 1967.

(With Frank) *Quantitative Methods in Marketing Analysis,* Prentice-Hall, 1967.

(With F. J. Carmone) *Multidimensional Scaling and Related Techniques in Marketing Analysis,* Allyn & Bacon, 1970.

(With V. R. Rao) *Applied Multidimensional Scaling,* Holt, 1972.

(With Yoram Wind) *Multi-Attribute Decisions in Marketing,* Holt, 1973.

(Editor with Martin Christopher) *Brand Positioning,* EJM Publishers (London), 1973.

Mathematical Tools for Applied Multivariate Analysis, Academic Press, 1976.

Analyzing Multivariate Data, Dryden, 1978.

(With P. K. Kedia and R. S. Nikhil) *Electronic Questionnaire Design and Analysis with CAPPA,* Scientific Press, 1985.

CONTRIBUTOR

Alderson and Stanley Shapiro, editors, *Marketing and the Computer,* Prentice-Hall, 1963.

Alderson, Shapiro, and Cox, editors, *Theory in Marketing,* Irwin, 1964.

Peter Langhoff, editor, *Models, Measurement, and Marketing,* Prentice-Hall, 1964.

Michael Halbert, editor, *The Nature and Sources of Marketing Theory,* McGraw, 1965.

Patrick Robinson, editor, *Promotional Decision Making: Practice and Theory,* McGraw, 1965.

J. W. Newman, editor, *On Knowing the Consumer,* Wiley, 1966.

George Fisk, editor, *The Psychology of Management Decision,* C.W.K. Gleerup (Sweden), 1967.

Frank Bass, Charles King, and Edgar Pessemier, editors, *Applications of the Sciences in Marketing,* Wiley, 1967.

P. J. Robinson and C. L. Hinkle, editors, *Sales Promotion Analysis: Some Applications of Quantitative Techniques,* Allyn & Bacon, 1967.

Almarin Phillips, editor, *Pricing Theories, Practices, and Policies,* University of Pennsylvania Press, 1968.

Montrose Sommers and Jerome Kernan, editors, *Explorations in Consumer Behavior,* University of Texas Press, 1968.

Irving Crespi, editor, *Attitude Research on the Rocks,* American Marketing Association, 1968.

R. L. King, editor, *Proceedings of the Denver Conference of the American Marketing Association,* American Marketing Association, 1968.

Fisk, editor, *Essays in Marketing Theory,* Allyn & Bacon, 1971.

C. King, editor, *Attitude Research Reaches New Heights,* American Marketing Association, 1971.

R. N. Shepard, K. Romney, and Sara Nerlove, editors, *Multidimensional Scaling,* Academic Press, 1972.

W. D. Wells, editor, *Life Style and Psychographies,* American Marketing Association, 1973.

Studies in Multiple Criterion Decision Making, University of South Carolina Press, 1973.

J. N. Sheth, editor, *Multivariate Procedures in Marketing,* American Marketing Association, 1975.

Sheth, editor, *Research for Marketing,* Jai Press, 1977.

Wind and Marshall Greenberg, editors, *Moving Ahead with Attitude Research,* American Marketing Association, 1977.

Wind, editor, *Product Policy: Concepts, Methods, and Strategies,* Addison-Wesley, 1981.

Wind, V. Mahajan, and R. Cardozo, editors, *New Product Forecasting: Models and Applications,* Lexington Books, 1981.

Encyclopedia of the Statistical Sciences, McGraw, 1983.

OTHER

Co-editor of a marketing series, Holt, 1967-78. Contributor to *Handbook of Marketing Management, Handbook of Marketing Research,* and *Marketing Handbook.* Contributor of more than a hundred articles to technical journals, including *Business Horizons, Journal of Marketing, Applied Statistics, Management Science, Wharton Quarterly,* and *Journal of Consumer Research.* Member of editorial board of *Journal of Marketing Research,* 1965—, *Journal of Consumer Research,* 1973-87, *Journal of Business Research,* 1973-75, *Journal of Marketing,* 1978—, *Journal of the Market Research Society,* 1981—, *International Journal of Research in Marketing,* 1985-86, and *Marketing Science,* 1985—; referee for *Psychometrika, Journal of the Operations Research Society, Management Science, Academy of Marketing Science, International Journal of Research in Marketing,* and *Decision Sciences.*

WORK IN PROGRESS: Research on multi-attribute choice theory in marketing.

*   *   *

GREENE, Bert   1923-1988

PERSONAL: Born October 16, 1923, in Flushing, N.Y.; died June 10, 1988 of a heart attack in Manhattan, New York, N.Y.; son of Samuel Michael (an electrical contractor) and Paula (a pianist; maiden name, Cohn) Greene. *Education:* Attended College of William and Mary, Richmond Professional Institute, Pratt Institute, and Yale University. *Politics:* "Independent, with Democrat bias." *Religion:* None.

ADDRESSES: Home—240 West 12th St., New York, N.Y. 10014; and Main St., Amagansett, Long Island, N.Y. 11930. *Agent*— Nat Sobel Associates, 128 East 56th St., New York, N.Y. 10022.

CAREER: Helena Rubenstein, Inc. (beauty preparations), New York City, art director, 1950-53; I. Miller & Sons (shoe firm), New York City, art director, 1954-60; *Esquire* magazine, New York City, art director in promotion, beginning 1970; food editor, *Gentleman's Quarterly* magazine, 1977-84. Founder and co-owner of The Store in Amagansett, 1966-76.

AWARDS, HONORS: R. T. French Tastemaster Awards, American Recipes Collection category, 1982, for *Honest American Fare,* and Specialty category, 1985, for *Greene on Greens.*

WRITINGS:

(With Denis Vaughan) *The Store Cookbook,* Regnery, 1974.

(With Philip Stephen Schulz) *Pity the Poor Rich*, Contemporary Books, 1978.

Bert Greene's Kitchen Bouquets, Contemporary Books, 1979, revised edition, Simon & Schuster, 1986.

Honest American Fare, Contemporary Books, 1981.

Greene on Greens, Workman Publishing, 1982.

(With Phyllis Stephen Schulz) *Cooking for Giving*, Irena Chalmers, 1984.

PLAYS

(Adaptor with Aaron Fine) Franz Kafka, ''The Trial'' (two-act), first produced Off-Broadway at Provincetown Playhouse, June 19, 1955.

(Adaptor) Frank Wedekind, ''Spring's Awakening'' (three-act), first produced Off-Broadway at Provincetown Playhouse, November 1, 1956.

''The Summer of Daisy Miller'' (two-act), first produced Off-Broadway at Phoenix Theatre, May 17, 1964.

TELEVISION PLAYS

(Adaptor) Colette, ''My Mother's House'' (three-act), produced on WNET-TV, New York, 1969.

''Colette,'' produced on National Educational Television's ''Playhouse,'' February, 1971.

OTHER

Author of weekly column, ''Bert Greene's Kitchen,'' syndicated in numerous newspapers, including *New York Daily News*, *Los Angeles Times*, and *Dallas Times Herald*. Contributor to periodicals, including *Vogue*, *Chocolatier*, *Good Food*, and *Family Circle*.

WORK IN PROGRESS: Greene on Grains.

SIDELIGHTS: Bert Greene told *CA:* ''I began to write early on, but the conflict of a double talent waylaid me into graphics where I strayed too long. My formal career as a wage-earning writer began in 1976. My single greatest influence has always been women writers. I love Elizabeth Bowen, Rosamund Lehmann and Colette dearly and have an ongoing friendship with M. F. K. Fisher—who inducted me into the mysteries of taste and smell. I am a gourmand who loves to cook and eat well and takes enormous pleasure in writing about food.''

AVOCATIONAL INTERESTS: Travel, especially to England, France, and Haiti.

*   *   *

GREENE, Bob
    See GREENE, Robert Bernard, Jr.

*   *   *

GREENE, Robert Bernard, Jr.   1947-
    (Bob Greene)

PERSONAL: Born March 10, 1947, in Columbus, Ohio; son of Robert Bernard (a business executive) and Phyllis Ann (Harmon) Greene; married Susan Bonnet Koebel (a paralegal), February 13, 1971; children: Amanda Sue. *Education:* Northwestern University, B.J., 1969.

ADDRESSES: Home—Chicago, Ill. *Office*—*Chicago Tribune*, 435 North Michigan Ave., Chicago, Ill. 60611.

CAREER: Chicago Sun-Times, Chicago, Ill., reporter, 1969-71, columnist, 1971-78; *Chicago Tribune*, Chicago, columnist, 1978—. Syndicated columnist, Field Newspaper Syndicate, Irvine, Calif., 1976-81, and Tribune Media Services, Orlando, Fla., 1981—. Contributing correspondent to ABC-TV's ''Nightline,'' 1981—. Fine arts lecturer, University of Chicago.

AWARDS, HONORS: Best newspaper column in Illinois, Associated Press, 1975; best sustaining feature in Chicago, Chicago Newspaper Guild, 1976; National Headliner Award, 1977, for best newspaper column in the United States; Peter Lisagor Award, 1981, for exemplary journalism.

WRITINGS: Under name Bob Greene

We Didn't Have None of Them Fat Funky Angels on the Wall of Heartbreak Hotel and Other Reports from America, Regnery Gateway, 1971.

Running: A Nixon-McGovern Campaign Journal, Regnery Gateway, 1973.

Billion Dollar Baby, Atheneum, 1974.

Johnny Deadline, Reporter: The Best of Bob Greene (columns), Nelson-Hall, 1976.

(With Paul Galloway) *Bagtime*, Popular Library, 1977.

American Beat (columns), Atheneum, 1983.

Good Morning, Merry Sunshine: A Father's Journal of His Child's First Year (Literary Guild alternate selection; excerpted in *Reader's Digest*, *Redbook*, and *Esquire*), Atheneum, 1984.

Cheeseburgers (columns), Atheneum, 1985.

Be True to Your School: A Diary of 1964 (excerpted in *Family Circle* and *Esquire*), Atheneum, 1987.

Homecoming: When the Soldiers Returned from Vietnam (excerpted in *Esquire*), Putnam, 1989.

Author of column in *Esquire*, 1980—. Contributor of news stories, articles, and columns to newspapers and magazines, including *New York Times*, *Harper's*, *Rolling Stone*, and *Newsweek*. Contributing editor for *Esquire*, 1980—.

SIDELIGHTS: Syndicated columnist Bob Greene ''is a talented storyteller with an acute eye and ear,'' states Taffy Cannon in the *Los Angeles Times*, who also writes, ''Greene has a gift for finding the fresh angle, the offbeat circumstance, the fascinating story begging to be written.'' Rather than following major news items, Greene's *Chicago Tribune* and *Esquire* pieces cover unusual events or people who never appear in the typical news story. ''Greene has an excellent eye for the Everyman Anecdote in his columns,'' states Bob Levey in the *Washington Post*. But Greene generally keeps his feelings and judgments out of the picture: ''Greene rarely editorializes,'' comments Ron Grossman in the *Chicago Tribune*. ''For their bite, his columns usually depend upon a reporter's eye rather than a critic's tongue. Even when he does deal in imperatives, either philosophical or psychological, he's usually measuring himself as much as his subject.''

Many of Greene's books are compilations of favorite columns. In 1971, he published a collection of magazine-length pieces under the title *We Didn't Have None of Them Fat Funky Angels on the Wall of Heartbreak Hotel*. A *Variety* reviewer describes the book as ''an unusually perceptive look at cafe society and its discontents'' and lauds Greene a ''rare newspaperman.'' Greene's second book, *Running: A Nixon-McGovern Campaign Journal*, contains his observations on the 1972 presidential campaign, which he came to view as a kind of road show. *New York Times Book Review* critic Leonard C. Lewin thinks that *Running* captures the mood of a typical political campaign: ''The detail is rich and the observations sharp, albeit without more than casual political insights.... And it is impossible not to share Greene's wonderment, to which he returns time and again, at the apparently total lack of connection between what was happening in the campaign organizations and what was going on outside.''

Greene joined a different type of road show in 1973 when he toured with the rock group Alice Cooper, which at the time labeled itself "the sickest, most degenerate band in America." Greene wanted to experience the life of a rock star; he sat in on one of the band's recording sessions, then joined their tour. Greene had "always been attracted by the fantasy, of being a wealthy superstar, of performing on a stage before 20,000 adoring fans," reports a *Publishers Weekly* contributor, who also quotes Greene's experiences with the band: "I became another band member, performing with them every night and sharing their luxurious yet boring life on the road." But Greene's fantasy probably hadn't included playing Santa Claus in Alice Cooper's show, beaten to death every night by the band members as part of their holiday theme.

Greene's account of his experiences with the band, *Billion Dollar Baby,* is a study in the achievement of the modern American Dream through media image manipulation. The reporter took pains to portray not only the public image of the band, but also the private reality. Greene depicts Vince Furnier, the band's front man and the personification of Alice Cooper, as a normal, intelligent young man who consciously set out to create a controversial, unsavory public image in order to attract attention. The band's strategy proved successful, but, according to Greene, the members paid a price: the nights of glory and adulation they enjoyed were offset by days of boredom spent in hotel rooms watching television and drinking beer.

Most critics commend Greene for seeing through the glitter and presenting a balanced view of the inside reality of the superstars' lives. *New York Times* reviewer Christopher Lehmann-Haupt describes Greene as "a cultural explorer in search of the gap between the image and the reality, and a mapmaker trying to prove that the gap is nonexistent. Mr. Greene may look like a good-natured lightweight. But when he swings, he hits; when he hits, he hurts; and 'Billion Dollar Baby' knocks you out." The book satisfies other critics as well: "Greene's provocative inside account," writes *Newsweek* reviewer Maureen Orton, "is neither the sycophantic gush of much rock writing nor the supercilious put-down of the Establishment journalist.... 'Billion Dollar Baby' is to rock idols what 'The Selling of the President' was to politics." *New York Times Book Review* critic John Rockwell calls the book "the most exhaustive rock-tour book yet, full of doggedly detailed information on everything from taping an album to the thoughts of the star to the tensions in the band to the camaraderie of the roadies." And a *New Yorker* contributor praises *Billion Dollar Baby* as an "intelligent, unpretentious, and compelling account of a rock supergroup and its world."

Greene returned to the streets of Chicago with his next book, *Johnny Deadline, Reporter.* The book is a collection of his newspaper columns on a variety of topics best described by the broad heading, "human interest." *Rolling Stone* reviewer Greil Marcus was impressed by Greene's ability to create insightful portraits: "When Greene deals with people on and off the street they come alive, and they are memorable.... What is best about Greene is that he writes as if he thinks there are still things for him to learn about. His columns will not live as literature.... But as a journalist who seems most interested

in connecting with individuals, with uncovering his city and his country person by person, he seems to be doing better work than anyone else these days.''

American Beat compiles more of Greene's favorite columns. According to Grossman the assortment "give us instant-replay access to the crazy-quilt times through which we have been passing." The book also reflects Greene's nostalgia for the fifties and sixties. Carolyn See observes in the *Los Angeles Times* that Greene's "writing is vibrant and strong. But he's also a person beginning to consider himself as an old man. Several of his columns deal with traditional 'where are the snows of yesteryear?' themes.... It is as a young/old man newly bowed down by the exigencies of daily life that Greene writes." *Christian Science Monitor* contributor Jim Bencivenga praises Greene's ability as a reporter: "I make a deep bow to Bob Greene as a man who can write the simple declarative sentence, the sine qua non of readable journalism. He's mastered the craft of clarity." And Grossman finds in Greene "that capacity—to recognize the common ground between 'we' and 'you,' and to own up to reactions from which others shrink—[which] has always been the benchmark of good journalism. It's doubly so in this age when, as 'American Beat' shows, Bob Green is one of the very few syndicated columnists who still faithfully practices his craft according to that demanding measure.''

At the age of thirty-five, Greene became a father for the first time. The birth of his daughter, Amanda, became the springboard for his next project: a record of his child's first year. The daily journal of both Amanda's and her parents' growth, *Good Morning, Merry Sunshine,* became Greene's most popular book to date. *Publishers Weekly* contributor Janis Graham calls the book "an intensely personal, day-by-day diary of the emotions Greene experienced as a first-time father." By publishing the journal, which included both Greene's and his wife Susan's readjustments to one another as well as to Amanda, Greene dropped some of his prior reserve and opened his life to his audience. Jim Spencer observes in the *Chicago Tribune* that "Greene has never revealed much about his family or private life in his columns.... He frequently refers to himself in his work, but what he reveals about himself is purposely limited.... One part of Greene revels in having created and sustained this mysterious persona. That is why [*Good Morning, Merry Sunshine*] seems ironic. This man, who spent years carefully avoiding saying very much about his private life, has written a book providing the intimate details of that most personal bond between father and daughter and throwing in several related family tidbits to boot.''

Greene first hit upon the idea of writing the diary when he combed bookstores for "anything that dealt on a human level with what happens when a man and a woman bring a new baby home—when a house that held two people suddenly holds three," he explains in *Good Morning, Merry Sunshine.* As Greene later told reporters, he did not intend to set himself up as a perfect father, but wanted to share with readers the common incidents in becoming a parent. Greene found his introduction to fatherhood a struggle since, as he later told Graham, "I've always been ambitious and, to use a negative term, selfish. The number one obligation in my life was always to get the story.... When you are expecting a child, everyone tells you how your life is going to change. My problem was that I liked my life the way it was." His attitude however, changed after Amanda's birth. Greene added to Graham that "my job is still a huge part of my life, but now there is a part that is even bigger.''

Still, despite the apparent openness, some critics felt Greene was holding back emotionally when describing his relationship with his family. "He hides behind the reporter's habit of just-the-facts ma'am, where exploring or hypothesizing would have added to the book immeasurably," claims Levey, who continues, "Greene doesn't deliver when it comes to researching the core of his own feelings." And other critics object that Greene's observations of Amanda were not always first-hand. David Owen claims in the *New Republic* that "many of his journal entries are simple recountings of things Susan has pointed out to him about their baby. Even when Bob is physically present, he isn't altogether there." But *New York Times Book Review* contributor James Carroll finds the book conveys immediacy and warmth: "I relished Bob Greene's 'Good Morning, Merry Sunshine,' for the company and the comfort," he writes. "At times I had the feeling it was one of those rare late-night conversations with an old friend and, at other times, a startling exchange with a stranger on an airplane." And Levey recalls, "To read the book in public is to have others wonder why you're nodding and grinning so much."

Overall, the book was highly successful. *Chicago Tribune Book World* contributor Larry L. King also praises Greene's effort, concluding that *Good Morning, Merry Sunshine* is "an honest and valuable book, one dealing with new career conflicts, the changing relationships with his own parents, the complex and painful evolutions between married lovers when a strong new force intervenes—all based on [Amanda's] becoming a part of the world. He has also written a basic guide to the uninitiated—other new parents and those yet to face the thrilling terrors of parenthood—that could prove as useful as anything written by Dr. Spock."

Greene later published another diary. He had written *Be True to Your School,* however, when he was a seventeen-year-old intent on honing his writing and reporting skills. After working on the journal for a year during high school, Greene had packed it away. Years later, he writes in the book, "I realized that what I had here was something money could not buy: time preserved." As the entries were often scribbled, he rewrote many of them and connected the episodes with narrative, but still tried to retain the work's original teenage voice. Daniel B. Wood explains in the *Christian Science Monitor* that "doing his best as a 'glorified rewrite man,' . . . he has taken the cryptic sentence fragments, disjointed conversations and hurriedly written descriptions of emotions to reconstruct a publishable manuscript—a full, readable narrative on what might be called the purgatory of teendom. . . . On one level, the book is a document of pure nostalgia. . . . On another, it is a daily dissection of the hopes, loves, and fears of a fragile 17-year-old, riding the emotional roller coaster of dating, while trying to discover himself, 'achieve,' and develop independence all at the same time. The book represents a tableau of memories for past generations. . . . And it represents a chronicle of the teenage Everyman for the present."

Despite his upper-middle-class suburban background, Greene feels that almost anyone can relate to his high school experiences. He told Paul Galloway for the *Chicago Tribune,* "I don't think it matters where anyone went to high school or when. Everyone was 17 once, and the emotions you feel at that age are universal. Although this is the life of one boy in one town in the middle of the country in the middle of the century, everyone has the same experiences and the same feelings. This is how most of the country grew up. Everyone falls in love and has his first beer and a best friend and cruises his town in a car and maybe gets into a fight."

Some critics object to the inclusion of minor happenings. A *Booklist* contributor finds that "along with the 'big' moments there is plenty of 'I went to the icebox and drank a Coke out of the bottle.'" But most agree that Greene has captured the flavor of the early sixties and the emotions of his younger self, although *Globe and Mail* contributor Jeffrey Zaslow thinks that "because the book is now very readable, it is also suspect. Many observations are so astute that you have to wonder who is responsible for them, the 17-year-old Bobby or the 39-year-old Bob." He continues, "the finished work is sensitively written, often amusing, even gripping. There is a voyeuristic charge to eavesdropping on this boy's life in 1964. It's as if you've stolen his diary." And Zaslow concludes that Greene "has a gift for writing vivid, heartfelt prose, for revelling in the memories that tug at us all."

CA INTERVIEW

CA interviewed Bob Greene by telephone on January 24, 1988, while he was in Lincolnwood, Illinois, making a videotape for television.

CA: You're in "an enviable line of work," as you said in the introduction to your collection American Beat—*writing stories about things that interest you for the* Chicago Tribune *and* Esquire, *and working as a correspondent for ABC News "Nightline." What's the best part of it? What makes it absolutely worth the time at the typewriter and the nights away from home?*

GREENE: Obviously the combination of the newspaper column and the *Esquire* column plus "Nightline" plus the books (I do about one a year) plus speeches is a lot of work. But I'm not a pundit and I'm not a political philosopher. I really see myself as a storyteller, and the best thing a storyteller can have is an audience on the other end. I think what makes it worth it is that, through all these different avenues of communication, I reach the audiences in different ways. Some people don't read the newspaper, but maybe they'll see me in *Esquire.* If they don't see me in *Esquire,* maybe they'll come to a speech. The combination gives me the opportunity to reach more and more people.

CA: There's an immediate response in some of those areas of communication.

GREENE: Yes, although it's sort of an incremental thing. Over the years, if somebody saw you speak somewhere or read one of your books or saw you on "Late Night with David Letterman," they all seem to feed into each other. If the goal is to get people to pay attention to your work, I think all those things work in conjunction with one another.

CA: In Be True to Your School *you described your work on the high school newspaper and your summer job with the Citizen-Journal in Columbus, Ohio. How early did you know that you wanted to be a journalist?*

GREENE: In seventh grade we had this little punch-out test, the Kuder Preference Test, that tells you what career you're supposed to go into. Mine said I was supposed to be either a forest ranger or a journalist. Sometimes I feel I made the wrong decision! I did indeed start working on the junior high school paper in the seventh grade, so I guess I knew it when I was twelve years old.

CA: What was the first real break, the job or the story that gave you the feeling you were going to make it?

GREENE: Back when I was in seventh grade there was a star Ohio State basketball player named Jerry Lucas. He was supposed to be impossible to reach; the local papers hadn't gotten interviews, even though he seemed to be the hottest basketball star in the country. But Jack Roth and I (he was the *J* in ABCDJ, our group, which I wrote about in *Be True to Your School*) heard that he was a member of the Beta Theta Pi fraternity at Ohio State, so we called the Beta house one night and asked for him. He just came up from dinner, and we said we were from the Bexley Junior High School *Beacon,* and he talked to us. Here two twelve-year-old kids had a national exclusive.

As far as having people really pay attention to my work for the first time is concerned, it was when I wrote about my feelings a year after President Kennedy died. I referred to it in *Be True to Your School.* It was published in a local magazine for teenagers, *Junior Prom,* and then the *Citizen-Journal* printed it. All of a sudden, for the first time, people all over the city were reading my work.

CA: The stories you tell cover an almost incredible range of people and topics. Do you see common denominators among them besides the fact that they simply attracted your attention?

GREENE: No, that's really it. If they interest me not as a "journalist" but viscerally, as a person, then I'll write about them. That's why I don't take assignments from editors. Either you're enthusiastic about something or you're not, and I think about ninety percent of the success of what I do is due to the story selection. If a story is the first thing I would tell my best friend on the phone at the end of the day, then I know it's good to write a column about. I think so many columnists write about what's on page one of the *Washington Post* or the *New York Times* and assume people are interested. I never make that assumption. My assumption is that if it interests me as a person, I should write about it.

CA: For Esquire's *"American Beat" and your syndicated* Chicago Tribune *column, are there any restrictions on what you can write, either stated or implied?*

GREENE: At the *Tribune,* more so than *Esquire,* there's obviously a restriction on space. At *Esquire* I can sometimes get an extra couple of columns of space. But as far as topics go, no. I can't use obscenities in the paper—that applies to any writer for a general-circulation newspaper. And while I wouldn't do that gratuitously at *Esquire,* if it's important to the story I can. But I've never had them tell me what to write about or what not to write about.

CA: Some of your stories are very offbeat. I think one of the best examples is "Jesus on a Tortilla."

GREENE: That's the sort of thing you hear about; I saw a one-paragraph item somewhere and I thought, Hey, this is interesting, so I followed up on it. Every other columnist in the country that day would have probably been looking at page one of the *New York Times* and writing about the MX missile debate. The fact is that people at the dinner table don't talk about politics; they don't talk about international relations. They talk about things that interest them. That story is a good example. That day, had I gone out and talked with friends, I wouldn't have said to them, Did you see what the Senate did

today in caucus? I would have said, There's this woman out in New Mexico who has this tortilla and she thinks the face of Jesus is on it. If it's the kind of story I would tell anyway, I just write it down.

CA: Do many ideas for stories come from being in the newsroom and seeing reports come in?

GREENE: They used to, but I'm not really in the newsroom anymore. I'm in my little office or I'm on the road. And for syndication that's been good. When I first started on the paper and my work was strictly in Chicago, it made sense for me to watch the city news wire. But now my job is to appeal not just to readers in Chicago, but to readers in Denver and Dallas and Tampa and Columbus and wherever. So it's almost good that I'm not watching that local news wire. Even when I do write a Chicago column, it had better have a universal theme.

CA: Do you still find Chicago a great place to be working from?

GREENE: Chicago's fine, but I consider myself much more midwestern than from Chicago. After all these years of having my home in Chicago, still, when people say "Where are you from?" I say, "Columbus" or "Ohio." When we came up with the name for the *Esquire* column, it was no coincidence that we called it "American Beat." I write about the whole country. I think being based in the Midwest is important, but I don't think it's essential that I be based in Chicago. Obviously O'Hare Airport is handy; you can get anywhere in the nation from there. But I don't like it when I go on a talk show and somebody says I write a Chicago column. That's not what I do. I think the fact that people can enjoy my work all over the country is indicative of the fact that I've been able to universalize.

CA: Do you feel a responsibility to your readers beyond entertaining them?

GREENE: Beyond entertaining or informing them, the only responsibility I feel is to myself, and that is to make sure that they get to the last period of the last sentence of the last paragraph of the story. I'd say that people don't read ninety-five percent of newspaper stories to the end. I feel I have a responsibility to make the story interesting enough for them to read all the way through it.

CA: In "Paper Boy" (collected in American Beat*) you wrote a bit about the changing nature of newspapers as television became a provider of instant news. What are your primary concerns for newspapers now and in the near future?*

GREENE: I think the dominant newspaper in each city will probably remain in an even stronger position than it's ever been in. But I think the others are in trouble. Back in Columbus, where I grew up, the *Citizen-Journal* is no more. It used to be that there were at least two competing newspapers in large towns, and even more. When I came to Chicago, there were four competing dailies. When I was growing up in Columbus there were three. In New York there were many more than that at one time. But I think the function of the newspaper is changing because of TV. People usually have seen the news the night before, so when they pick the newspaper up in the morning, they either purposely or subliminally turn to the columnists to see what they have to say, because that's the one thing they're not getting on TV.

CA: For Billion Dollar Baby *you joined Alice Cooper as a performing member. In the diary that became* Be True to Your School *you wrote a lot about the Kingston Trio and the Beatles; you've also written about Elvis Presley, Bob Seger, and other musicians. Do you find time to relax and enjoy music now?*

GREENE: Yes, I always have. Most people, when they go to their hotel rooms on the road, flip their televisions on first of all. But I'll usually look for the best rock'n'roll radio station. If I hadn't ended up doing what I'm doing, my fantasy probably would have been to be a singer with a band. I've always thought that would have been a lot of fun. I think you have to be a little more extroverted to be able to do that, but, writing a column, I sort of understand what it must be like to go out there on stage and perform for all those people. Often when I'd be on the road with one of those bands and I'd see ten or fifteen or twenty thousand people out there in the audience, it would occur to me that I reach a lot more people than that. Of course they're not there in front of you; you can't see them.

CA: Your work must be an amazing juggling act. Is there ever a feeling of panic, a feeling that you can't keep going from one thing to the next, or that you'll run out of ideas?

GREENE: No, but it really is hectic. I'm up here in Lincolnwood on a Sunday morning because I had to tape something for television last night. Before I did that I had to go into office at the *Tribune* and work on a new book project. Saturday's supposed to be your day off, but the first thing I did was go in and work on the book and then I came up here and did the TV thing. I've never missed a deadline, so I know I can turn the stuff out. The question is, how long do you keep doing it? And that's the decision I have to make somewhere along the line.

CA: In Good Morning, Merry Sunshine *you chronicled the everyday joys and shocks of daughter Amanda Sue's first year. The book got raves from such people as Erma Bombeck and Phil Donahue. Was there an overwhelming response from gerneral readers?*

GREENE: Yes, to that book and to *Be True to Your School* also. Everyone was aware that *Good Morning, Merry Sunshine* might get that kind of response, but what's surprising to me is how strong the reaction has been to *Be True to Your School.* What it teaches me is that, if you're very specific about what you write about, the universality will come through. In both of those cases the argument could have been made, who wants to read your diary? If you wrote a general book about the growing-up experience in high school in the sixties, I think it would be sort of boring. But by being very specific about one boy's life growing up in the middle of the country in the middle of the century, it was possible to capture the emotions. Other people's experiences may not have been the same as mine, but the emotions were the same. And I think the only way you can capture the emotions is to be very specific. I thought the "big" stories in *Be True to Your School* would get a response—the older woman at Cedar Point, the girl I was in love with, my friend losing his virginity while the rest of us were in the adjacent bathroom listening. But I've been amazed at the response some of the little things got, instances that I thought were almost throwaway things, like when my dad yelled at me because I was eating a cheeseburger for breakfast at the Pancake House. Maybe other people didn't

eat cheeseburgers for breakfast, but that was such a good example of the authoritarian father.

CA: When you contemplated turning your 1964 high school diary into a book for publication, what problems did you see?

GREENE: I had been carrying the diary around for twenty years, and finally it occurred to me that I really did have time preserved here. But I thought there would be two problems. One was maintaining the voice of the seventeen-year-old kid. I didn't want to sound like a forty-year-old man writing the book. But clearly the book had to be a writing job, because the diary was just bits and pieces and notes. So it was, to use the phrase I used in the introduction, very much like restoring a cracked and faded old photograph. But the writing had to be so seamless, almost invisible, that you really would get the impression that it was the voice of the seventeen-year-old boy. I think it worked in that sense. The other problem was the worry about whether there was a story. And finally I figured, "Yes, it's the story of growing up in the middle of the country, and it's not necessary to look for a grand plot. Let's just tell what happened that year."

CA: I think it was brave of you to do Be True to Your School *in that it would likely reveal to your parents things you'd done in high school that they didn't know about. How did they like the book?*

GREENE: I was more concerned about, for example, how my dad would react to the portrait of him than what he would think of what I did when I was seventeen. Other people have said they thought it was brave too. I don't think it was that brave twenty-three years later. Obviously I lay my emotions bare in that book. But they were the emotions of a seventeen-year-old kid. As soon as I got my first bound books, I Federal Expressed my parents two copies. And they liked it. My dad said, "I was probably even tougher than you portrayed me."

CA: In her Publishers Weekly *interview, Janis Graham noted that* Good Morning, Merry Sunshine *was a sharp change from "Greene's journalistic trademark: a flair for keeping himself out of the story." So indeed was* Be True to Your School.

GREENE: It's funny. Those books were very personal, and they were the ones that turned into national bestsellers. I don't know what the lesson there is.

CA: Do you feel, since those books, somehow closer to your readers?

GREENE: No, not really. As I've said, I really like the work I do for *Esquire* and the newspaper column, but usually I'm telling other people's stories. Or when I use myself in them, it's a device to tell a story about something else. All of a sudden these two very personal books that became bestsellers. It was surprising; it wouldn't have figured. Maybe in book form that's how it works. It's interesting. Nobody could have predicted that *Good Morning, Merry Sunshine* would have become a bestseller, and then *Be True to Your School* did too. So obviously there are people out there who read my stuff.

CA: It's hard to imagine, but is there something you've wanted very much to do in your work that has so far eluded you—a story you haven't gotten to write, an interview you haven't been able to pin down?

GREENE: Not a story so much. I had three people that I really wanted to interview: Patty Hearst when she was in prison, Richard Nixon, and mass murderer Richard Speck. I got all three of them. The only person I ever wanted to interview that I never did and obviously never will was Elvis Presley. He never really sat down and talked to anybody. I think I could have done a great job of drawing him out, and I would have loved that opportunity.

I do wish that I had the right television forum. "Nightline" is fun—especially going on live is fun—and David Letterman's show is fun. But I would like to find a television forum that would have the same sort of impact on people that the writing does. It seems that there must be some way to translate the column into a television format without doing it literally; to go out in front of the camera and rephrase a piece I'd write is not the same thing. If you're a writer and you want people to see your stuff, TV is a good way to reach a lot of people. And there's no question that TV is very good for getting people interested in reading your books and magazine stories, because if they see you on TV they get to recognize your name.

Whenever TV producers hire print journalists, they say, "We're hiring you because you're such a good writer." But "good writers" often don't work on TV because sometimes the most elegant writing is stilted on TV. I try to explain to them whenever they hire me to do something that they're really hiring me not because I'm a good writer but for my powers of observation. I'll often tell them I don't want to write a script; I just want to sit here and talk the way I'm talking now. And they'll say, "But everybody uses a script—especially you, because you're a writer." Well, that doesn't get it. So I do wish I could find the perfect television forum. There must be a way, and I'm still trying to figure it out.

BIOGRAPHICAL/CRITICAL SOURCES:

BOOKS

Greene, Bob, *Good Morning, Merry Sunshine: A Fathers Journal of His Child's First Year*, Atheneum, 1984.
Greene, Bob, *Be True to Your School: A Diary of 1964*, Atheneum, 1987.

PERIODICALS

Booklist, February 15, 1987.
Chicago Tribune, June 14, 1984, April 3, 1987, April 5, 1987.
Chicago Tribune Book World, October 16, 1983, May 6, 1984.
Christian Science Monitor, November 4, 1983, April 28, 1987.
Globe and Mail (Toronto), April 4, 1987.
Los Angeles Times, November 24, 1983, December 6, 1985.
Newsweek, January 13, 1975.
New Yorker, December 9, 1974.
New York Times, November 14, 1974.
New York Times Book Review, May 20, 1973, December 22, 1974, June 10, 1984, January 22, 1989.
Publishers Weekly, August 5, 1974, May 4, 1984.
Rolling Stone, July 1, 1976.
Saturday Review/World, December 14, 1974.
Tribune Books (Chicago), January 22, 1989.
Variety, July 10, 1978.
Washington Post, May 26, 1984, May 14, 1987.

—*Sketch by Jani Prescott*

—*Interview by Jean W. Ross*

GRIFFIN, Susan   1943-

PERSONAL: Born January 26, 1943, in Los Angeles, Calif.; daughter of Walden and Sarah (Colvin) Griffin; married John Levy, June 11, 1966 (divorced, 1970); children: Rebecca Siobhain. *Education:* Attended University of California, Berkeley, 1960-63; San Francisco State College (now University), B.A. (cum laude), 1965; California State University, San Francisco (now San Francisco State University), M.A., 1973. *Politics:* "Feminist." *Religion:* None.

ADDRESSES: Home—1400 Hawthorne Terrace, Berkeley, Calif. 94708. *Agent*—Frances Goldin, 305 East 11th St., New York, N.Y. 10003.

CAREER: Poet. *Ramparts* (magazine), San Francisco, Calif., assistant editor, 1966-68; San Francisco State College (now University), San Francisco, instructor in English, 1970-71; Poetry in the Schools program, teacher of poetry in Oakland, Calif. high schools, 1972-73; University of California, Berkeley, extension school, instructor in English and women's studies, 1973-75; San Francisco State University, instructor, 1974-75. Visiting writer, Delta College of San Joaquin and Cazenovia College.

AWARDS, HONORS: Ina Coolbrith Prize in Poetry, 1963; Emmy Award, 1975, for *Voices;* National Endowment for the Arts grant, 1976; Malvina Reynolds Award for cultural achievement, 1982; Kentucky Foundation for Women grant, 1987; Commonwealth Club Silver Medal, 1988; Schumacher fellow; Ph.D., Starr King School for the Ministry.

WRITINGS:

Dear Sky (poetry), Shameless Hussy Press, 1971.
(Contributor) *Women Feminist Stories by New Fiction Authors*, Eakins, 1971.
Le Viol, L'Etincelle (Canada), 1972.
Let Them Be Said, Mama Press, 1973.
Letters, Twowindows Press, 1973.
The Sink, Shameless Hussy Press, 1973.
(Contributor) Florence Howe and Ellen Bass, editors, *No More Masks: An Anthology of Poems by Women*, Doubleday, 1973.
Voices (a play in poetry; first produced in San Francisco, 1974), Feminist Press, 1975.
(Author of foreword) Karen Brodine and others, *Making the Park*, Kelsey St. Press, 1976.
Like the Iris of an Eye (poetry), Harper, 1976.
Woman and Nature: The Roaring inside Her, Harper, 1978.
Rape: The Power of Consciousness, Harper, 1979.
Pornography and Silence: Culture's Revolt against Nature, Harper, 1981.
(Author of introduction) Valerie Miner, *Movement*, Crossing Press, 1982.
Made from This Earth: Selections from Her Writing, 1967-82, Women's Press, 1982, published as *Made from This Earth: An Anthology of Writings*, Harper, 1983.
Unremembered Country, Copper Canyon Press, 1987.

Contributor to many periodicals, including *Ramparts, Sundance, Shocks, Ms.,* and *Aphra.*

WORK IN PROGRESS: The First and the Last: A Woman Thinks about War, a book on warfare in this century.

SIDELIGHTS: In a *Library Journal* review of Susan Griffin's collection of poetry *Like the Iris of an Eye*, A. B. Eaglen states: "If there is a stronger, better, more forceful feminist poem than Griffin's 'An Answer to a Man's Question, "What Can I Do about Women's Liberation"'" I'd like to see it—and that is only one excellent poem in a uniformly excellent collection by one of the most-quoted feminist poets writing today." Eaglen adds that the book is a "fine anthology of work that has been available before this only in anthologies and small press offerings, for collections serving women and/or lovers of good contemporary poetry."

More recently, Griffin has turned to theorizing and writing about issues important to women. In her *Ms.* review of *Woman and Nature: The Roaring inside Her,* Valerie Miner characterizes the book as "feminist philosophy written in poetic prose. Susan Griffin explores woman's traditional identification with the earth—both as sustenance for humanity and victim of male ravage. The book is cultural anthropology, visionary prediction, literary indictment, and personal claim. Griffin's testimony about the lives of women throughout Western civilization reveals extensive research from Plato to Galileo to Freud to Emily Carr to Jane Goodall to Adrienne Rich." Concludes the critic: "Griffin moves us from pain to anger to communion with and celebration of the survival of woman and nature."

In *Pornography and Silence: Culture's Revolt against Nature,* Griffin explores the nature and function of pornography, claiming that it is the manifestation of the male's desire to separate emotion, desire, and feeling from himself. In a dialogue related in *Women Writers of the West Coast,* Griffin elaborates on this theory: "All the qualities that women are accused of—passivity, wantonness or prudery, both the fear of sex and nymphomania—all of these qualities are human qualities, human possibilities, and they are projected onto a woman." In portraying women in this manner, pornography allows men to "disassociate these parts" from themselves and conquer them physically. For the purposes of her analysis, Griffin does not limit her definition of pornography to works that are violent or sadistic, but also includes "the idea that woman is submissive; that she is pretty but dumb; that she likes to be dominated; that she's an object for somebody's pleasure; that she likes to serve." In the process of developing her thesis, Griffin refutes the concept of pornography as a sexual liberator; instead, she sees it as an attempt to deny sexuality.

Pornography and Silence has drawn a variety of responses from critics. While many critics agree that her hypothesis is interesting, they also fault the author for her method. In his *New Republic* review, Irving Kristol notes that while Griffin's "polemic against pornography and its apologists . . . is shrewd, vigorous, and leaves little unsaid," he also comments that "she seems sadly unaware" of the precedents for her argument. In addition, Kristol criticizes the author's vehement attitude, remarking that "much of her book is an autodidact's brash exploration of cultural history that is occasionally very perceptive, more often painfully sophomoric." *Village Voice* contributor Robert Christgau also questions Griffin's methods, finding the details of her hypothesis lacking. "As one theory of pornography," writes Christgau, "this is fairly insightful, but it's only one theory, partial at best. First of all, it doesn't apply to all pornography, although since Griffin never defines the term . . . it's hard to pin her down." In her *Ms.* review, however, Marcia Yudkin praises the author's analysis as "surprising, deep, and unsettling. Her soundings not only connect

seemingly disparate aspects of our culture; they transform one's questions and answers about sex, history, the self, and nature."

Other critics, while admiring Griffin's analysis, remark that her political, angry delivery detracts from the message of the book. In the *Washington Post Book World,* Lewis H. Lapham observes that while "*Pornography and Silence* convincingly dissects the dehumanizing character of pornography, . . . it would have been a kindness to the reader if Griffin had resisted the temptation to make of her observations a political theory." In taking an unmovable stance, Lapham writes, "she makes so many doubtful statements . . . that her more useful remarks about the nature of pornography lose their force and urgency." Critic Ellen Willis expresses a similar opinion, noting in the *New York Times Book Review* that "the passages she devotes to condemning pornography, rather than analyzing it, are reductive and heavy-handed in a way the rest of the book is not."

Whatever faults it may contain, reviewers still find that *Pornography and Silence* contains an important message. By refuting the myth that women enjoy being dominated and helpless, as they are often portrayed in pornographic works, *New Statesman* contributor Marion Glastonbury writes that "those of us to whom this is dangerous nonsense can take heart from Susan Griffin's subtle, lucid, and compelling book. Pornography is exposed as a system of censorship which serves not to enhance but to vilify pleasure, perpetuating error by suppressing half the evidence." Yudkin similarly concludes that the book "is profound, stimulating, sophisticated, far-reaching in its implications. Although feminists are still left wondering about the First Amendment and a conscionable strategy for making pornography disappear, we are much enriched by Susan Griffin's graceful, clear, unrhetorical book."

Summing up her philosophy of writing, Griffin once told *CA:* "As a woman, I struggle to write from my life, to reflect all the difficulties, angers, joys of my existence in a culture that attempts to silence women, or that does not take our work, or words or our lives seriously. In this, I am a fortunate woman, to be published, to be read, to be supported, and I live within a cultural and social movement aiming toward the liberation of us all. And within and also beyond all this I experience the transformations of my soul through the holy, the ecstatic, the painfully born or joyously made *word.* I know now that never when I begin to write will I truly know what or how my vision will become."

MEDIA ADAPTATIONS: "Voices" was adapted for television and aired in 1974.

BIOGRAPHICAL/CRITICAL SOURCES:

BOOKS

Yalom, Marilyn, editor, *Women Writers of the West Coast,* Capra Press, 1983.

PERIODICALS

Library Journal, December 1, 1976.
Ms., April, 1979, January, 1982.
New Republic, July 25, 1981.
New Statesman, November 6, 1981.
New York Times Book Review, July 12, 1981.
Quill & Quire, September, 1981.

Times Literary Supplement, January 1, 1982.
Village Voice, July 15, 1981.
Washington Post Book World, June 21, 1981.

*   *   *

GROSS, S(amuel Harry) 1933-

PERSONAL: Born August 7, 1933, in Bronx, N.Y.; son of Max (an accountant) and Sophie (Heller) Gross; married Isabelle Jaffe (a social work supervisor), June 7, 1959; children: Michelle. *Education:* College of the City of New York (now City College of the City University of New York), B.B.A., 1954.

ADDRESSES: Home—115 East 89th St., New York, N.Y. 10128.

CAREER: Accountant, 1956-62; free-lance cartoonist, 1962—. Designer of greeting cards and lithograph prints; has written for Public Broadcasting System's ''Sesame Street''; former senior contributing artist, *National Lampoon*. Works exhibited at Foundry Gallery, Washington, D.C., 1983, and Master Eagle Gallery, New York City, 1984 and 1985. Former vice-president and president, Cartoonists Guild. *Military service:* U.S. Army, 1954-56.

MEMBER: Cartoonists Association.

AWARDS, HONORS: Inkpot Award, San Diego Comicon, 1980.

WRITINGS:

CARTOONS

How Gross, Dell, 1973.
I Am Blind and My Dog Is Dead, Dodd, 1977.
An Elephant Is Soft and Mushy, Dodd, 1980.
More Gross, Congdon & Weed, 1982.
Love Me, Love My Teddy Bear, Perigee, 1986.

No More Mr. Nice Guy: A New Collection of Outrageous Cartoons, Perigee, 1987.

EDITOR

(And author of foreword) *Why Are Your Papers in Order?: Cartoons for 1984*, Avon, 1983.
Dogs, Dogs, Dogs: A Collection of Great Dog Cartoons, Harper, 1985.
Cats, Cats, Cats: A Collection of Great Cat Cartoons, Harper, 1986.
All You Can Eat: A Collection of Great Food Cartoons, Harper, 1987.
(With Jim Charlton) *Books, Books, Books: A Hilarious Collection of Literary Cartoons*, Harper, 1988.
Golf, Golf, Golf: A Collection of Great Golf Cartoons, Harper, 1989.

CONTRIBUTOR

Bob Abel, editor, *Best Cartoons of the World*, Dell, 1969.
Gerald T. Counihan, editor, *Post Mortems*, Bantam, 1969.
New Cartoon Laughs from ''True,'' Fawcett, 1970.
Lawrence Larier, editor, *Best Cartoons of the Year*, Dodd, 1970.
Bill Lee, editor, *Absolutely No U.S. Personnel Permitted beyond This Point*, Delta, 1972.
Best Cartoons from the New Yorker, 1925-1975, Viking, 1975.
George Booth and Gahan Wilson, editors, *Animals, Animals, Animals*, Harper, 1979.
Sean Kelly and John Weidman, editors, *National Lampoon's Cartoons Even We Wouldn't Dare Print*, Simon & Schuster, 1979.
Jumping Up and Down on the Roof, Throwing Bags of Water on People, Doubleday, 1980.

Also contributor to numerous periodicals, including *New Yorker, Esquire, National Lampoon, Cosmopolitan,* and *Saturday Review*.

H

H. M. S.
See KIRK-GREENE, Anthony (Hamilton Millard)

* * *

HAHN, Emily 1905-

PERSONAL: Born January 14, 1905, in St. Louis, Mo.; daughter of Isaac Newton and Hannah (Schoen) Hahn; married Charles Ralph Boxer, November 28, 1945; children: Carola Vecchio, Amanda. *Education:* University of Wisconsin, B.S., 1926; graduate study, Columbia University, 1928, and Oxford University, 1934-35.

ADDRESSES: Home and office—16 West 16th St., Apt. 12 N South, New York, N.Y. 10011. *Agent*—Andrew Wylie Agency, 250 West 57th St., Suite 2331, New York, N.Y. 10019.

CAREER: Free-lance writer, 1938—. Deko Oil Co., St. Louis, Mo., mining engineer, 1926; courier in Santa Fe, N.M., 1927-28; Hunter College (now Hunter College of the City University of New York), New York City, instructor in geology, 1929-30; worked with Red Cross in Belgian Congo (now Zaire), 1930-31; writer of stories and scenarios in New York City and Hollywood, Calif., and correspondent in England, Europe, and Central Africa for various newspapers, 1931-32; Customs College, Shanghai, China, instructor in English and writing, 1935-38, and Chungking, China, instructor in English and writing, 1940; Customs University, Hong Kong, instructor, 1941. Former correspondent for the *New Yorker.*

MEMBER: American Academy and Institute of Arts and Letters, Authors League of America.

WRITINGS:

Seductio ad Absurdum: The Principles and Practices of Seduction—A Beginner's Handbook, Brewer & Warren, 1930.
Beginner's Luck, Brewer & Warren, 1931.
Mr. Pan (short stories), Doubleday, 1942.
Love Conquers Nothing: A Glandular History of Civilization, Doubleday, 1952 (published in England as *Love Conquers Nothing: A New Look at Old Romances,* Dobson, 1959), reprinted, Books for Libraries, 1971.
(With Charles Roetter and Harford Thomas) *Meet the British,* N. Neame, 1953.
Spousery, F. Watts, 1956.

Diamond: The Spectacular Story of Earth's Rarest Treasure and Man's Greatest Greed, Doubleday, 1956.
The Tiger House Party: The Last Days of the Maharajas, Doubleday, 1959.
China Only Yesterday, 1850-1950: A Century of Change, Doubleday, 1963.
Indo, Doubleday, 1963.
Romantic Rebels: An Informal History of Bohemianism in America, Houghton, 1967.
Animal Gardens, Doubleday, 1967 (published in England as *Zoos,* Secker & Warburg, 1968).
The Cooking of China, Time-Life, 1968.
Recipes: Chinese Cooking, Time-Life, 1968.
Breath of God: A Book about Angels, Demons, Familiars, Elementals and Spirits, illustrated by Barton L. Benes, Doubleday, 1971.
Fractured Emerald: Ireland, Doubleday, 1971.
On the Side of the Apes: A New Look at the Primates, the Men Who Study Them and What They Have Learned, Crowell, 1971.
Once Upon a Pedestal: An Informal History of Women's Lib, Crowell, 1974.
Look Who's Talking! New Discoveries in Animal Communication, Crowell, 1978.
Love of Gold, Lippincott and Crowell, 1980.
The Islands: America's Imperial Adventures in the Philippines, Coward, McCann, 1981.
Eve and the Apes, Weidenfeld & Nicolson, 1988.
The Emily Hahn Reader, Knopf, 1989.

AUTOBIOGRAPHIES

Congo Solo: Misadventures Two Degrees North, Bobbs-Merrill, 1933.
China to Me: A Partial Autobiography, Doubleday, 1944, reprinted, Beacon Press, 1988.
Hong Kong Holiday, Doubleday, 1946.
England to Me, Doubleday, 1949.
Kissing Cousins, Doubleday, 1958.
Africa to Me: Person to Person, Doubleday, 1964.
Times and Places, Crowell, 1970.

BIOGRAPHIES

The Soong Sisters, Doubleday, 1941, reprinted, Greenwood Press, 1970.

Raffles of Singapore, Doubleday, 1946, reprinted, University of Malaya Press, 1968.

A Degree of Prudery: A Biography of Fanny Burney, Doubleday, 1950.

James Brooke of Sarawak: A Biography of Sir James Brooke, Arthur Barker, 1953.

Chiang Kai-shek: An Unauthorized Biography, Doubleday, 1955.

Lorenzo: D. H. Lawrence and the Women Who Loved Him, Lippincott, 1975.

Mabel: A Biography of Mabel Dodge Luhan, Houghton, 1977.

NOVELS

With Naked Foot, Bobbs-Merrill, 1934.

Affair, Bobbs-Merrill, 1935.

Steps of the Sun, Dial, 1940.

Miss Jill, Doubleday, 1947, published as *House in Shanghai,* Fawcett, 1958.

Purple Passage: A Novel About a Lady Both Famous and Fantastic, Doubleday, 1950.

JUVENILE

China A to Z, F. Watts, 1946.

The Picture Story of China, Reynal & Hitchcock, 1946.

Francie, F. Watts, 1951.

Francie Again, F. Watts, 1953.

Mary, Queen of Scots, illustrated by Walter Buehr, Random House, 1953.

The First Book of India, F. Watts, 1955.

Francie Comes Home, F. Watts, 1956.

Leonardo da Vinci, illustrated by Mimi Korach, Random House, 1956.

Aboab: First Rabbi of the Americas, Farrar, Straus, 1959.

Around the World with Nellie Bly, Houghton, 1959.

June Finds a Way, F. Watts, 1960.

OTHER

Contributor to *New Yorker* and other periodicals.

SIDELIGHTS: "I have deliberately chosen the uncertain path whenever I had the chance," Emily Hahn once stated. This firm resolve to avoid the commonplace has rewarded her with what a *New York Times* interviewer characterizes as "a ground-breaking, breathtaking life in which she has thumbed her nose at convention all the way." Hahn, who is known as "Mickey" to her friends, first confronted convention in the early 1920s at the University of Wisconsin. She became the first woman there to graduate as a mining engineer, despite opposition from the all-male student body and the dean of the College of Engineering. Her actual career in engineering, however, was somewhat short-lived because of her frustration with superiors who would not allow her to venture out into the field. Still intending to be an engineer, Hahn worked briefly in New Mexico and then taught at Hunter College in New York City. But an article she wrote for the *New York World* as a favor for a friend one day marked the beginning of a change in the young engineer's plans: it would eventually lead to a successful writing career.

Despite selling the article and the three that followed, Hahn remembers: "I [still] thought of myself as an engineer, and continued to work at it with one hand, while writing with the other, until I suppose the balance simply shifted." Having managed to bank the $500 advance she received for her first book, *Seductio ad Absurdum,* Hahn decided in 1930 that it was time to pursue a dream she had had for a long time—a

trip to Africa. Arriving in the Belgian Congo, she worked in a hospital outpost for two years "to earn her keep" and lived with a tribe of Pygmies for a year. In 1935, Hahn was hired as the *New Yorker*'s China Coast correspondent at a time when that country was suffering through the double effects of revolution and war with the Japanese. During her turbulent nine-year stay, she became a confidante of the Soong sisters (one married Sun Yat-sen, another Chiang Kai-shek) and got to know such future notables as Mao Tse-tung and Chou En-lai. In addition, she found time for several much-talked about love affairs, including one with Sinmay Zau, an aristocratic Chinese intellectual who served as her first "cultural and political guide to China."

A subsequent liaison with Major Charles Boxer, a married English officer who was in charge of British intelligence in the Far East, produced a daughter, Carola. But when Hong Kong was captured by the Japanese, Boxer was imprisoned, and Hahn, having avoided repatriation by claiming to be Eurasian, smuggled food to him during the next few years. Hahn and Carola eventually were repatriated to the United States in 1943. Boxer, on the other hand, was not released from prison until late 1945. Several months before his release, rumors of his execution had circulated through the American press, but Hahn refused to believe they were true. It was not long after his return that the couple was married in New Haven, Connecticut.

Hahn's autobiographies discuss these experiences in her life with a characteristically calm tone that nevertheless does not camouflage her excitement about life. One *Publishers Weekly* reviewer considers her autobiographies "to be an extended confessional or self-portrait by a courageous and unusual woman." In an interview with the author in another *Publishers Weekly* article, Katherine Weber notes that Hahn has an ability to stay calm in the worst circumstances, as well as a tendency for offering "droll" reflections on personal matters like her year-long opium addiction in Shanghai. Her book *China to Me* relates the story of her affairs with Sinmay and Boxer, but mostly tells about "her struggle to survive after the Japanese invasion," says Weber. The interviewer remarks that the author's "sense of humor and ability to remain fascinated in the face of danger make *China to Me* a frontline report on life in China during World War II as well as a revealing account of the unusual outlook of its author." Besides this book, Hahn has written several other books concerning China and its people, including *China Only Yesterday, 1850-1950: A Century of Change, Chiang Kai-shek: An Unauthorized Autobiography,* and *The Soong Sisters.*

In addition to her personal accounts about her days in China and a book about her travels in Africa entitled *Africa to Me: Person to Person,* Hahn has written a historical work about the Philippines. This publication required more research, since the events described in *The Islands: America's Imperial Adventure in the Philippines* occurred while the author was still in China, her knowledge of the country coming largely from observing Filipinos in China and a trip to the islands after World War II. This book is concerned with the "calmer history" of these islands, as Carolyn See phrases it in the *Los Angeles Times.* Unlike other publications on the subject, Hahn does not focus on the injustices and cruelties that occurred in the Philippines at the time, but rather "concentrates on decent American men like Dean Conant Worcester, a young zoologist from the University of Michigan, who simply came out to the islands and fell in love with them," says See.

After the United States took possession of the Philippines from the Spanish as a consequence of the Spanish-American War, the Americans concentrated mainly upon improving the sanitation and education for the islanders. It is this part of the occupation on which the author concentrates, rather than the more brutal side, as in Russell Roth's *Muddy Glory,* which describes the battles fought on the islands, or Stephen Rosskamm Shalom's *The United States and the Philippines: A Study in Neocolonialism,* which discusses America's collaboration with the Filipino elite. Because of Hahn's altered focus on Philippine history, she fails to mention some of the less philanthropic aspects of America's involvement. For example, John Leonard points out in the *New York Times* that "there is no mention whatsoever of 'Howling Jake' Smith, the American general who conducted the notorious Samar campaign ordering his men to kill 'everything over 10' years old.''

Leonard also notes the author's lack of attention to American support of the elite Filipinos, who later collaborated with the Japanese, and to "the role of American corporations." Furthermore, Leonard feels that Hahn exaggerates the success of American efforts to increase the literacy level among the natives ("as high as 87 percent" Hahn claims), and fails to comment on the importance of drama in Filipino culture. See argues, however, that Hahn is taking the "tea table" approach to describing the islands under American domination; that is, by discussing the school teachers, missionaries, doctors, and others who worked there and the results of that work, we may perceive the "true horror" of the situation as a "delayed reaction." "Emily Hahn has applied this precept with such deftness," declares See, "that this reader, at least, is still waiting for the horror of 'America's Imperial Adventure in the Philippines' to set in." A *New Yorker* reviewer also believes that the author's perspective on America's involvement is "exactly right, and her style, as ever, is easy and entertaining."

Another source of material from Hahn's own past, her former ownership of a number of apes and monkeys, has become the foundation for several books about animals. "I'm very fond of apes. I've always liked apes," she told Weber in *Publishers Weekly.* Hahn's book *Eve and the Apes,* published in 1988, tells about the noted women who have owned or worked with apes in the past. She does not, however, pay much attention to such luminaries as Jane Goodall and Diane Fossey, because, "she explains, they have written their own stories," says *Los Angeles Times Book Review* contributor Bettyann Kevles. Instead, the author discusses such people as former San Diego Zoo director Belle Benchley, Penny Patterson, who taught gorillas sign language, and Augusta Hoyt, a wealthy woman who came into the possession of a gorilla by accident while looking for gorilla specimens for the American Museum of Natural History.

In comparison to the author's book, *On the Side of the Apes: A New Look at the Primates, the Men Who Study Them and What They Have Learned,* which looks at primatologists and their work in laboratories, Greene feels that "*Eve and the Apes* is in some respects the lighter counterpart." However, Greene thinks that Hahn quotes from the autobiographies of her subjects too often, adding that "the chapters that contain fresh research and first-hand observation tend to be stronger. Still, because Hahn's focus is so novel, and the material she uncovers so truly eccentric, the book must be counted a modest success." On a more enthusiatic note, Ray calls *Eve and the Apes* "fascinating," while Kevles remarks that Hahn "moves deftly in more or less chronological order, dropping some of the best tidbits in captivating digressions."

Eve and the Apes and *On the Side of the Apes,* along with Hahn's book about zoos, *Animal Gardens,* and her volume on animal communications, *Look Who's Talking!,* "abundantly testify to her profound empathy for all manner of animate beings,'' observes Thomas Sebeok in a *Times Literary Supplement* review of *Look Who's Talking!* In this book on communication between man and animal, the author does not go so far as to claim that animals such as chimpanzees are capable of language, but she is quoted by Sebeok as saying: "Many people are satisfied that the apes' productions are certainly relative to the language behavior of man."

Sebeok believes, however, that Hahn favors those who are optimistic about the language capabilities of animals, while "the opposing view is hardly represented at all." He concludes, "The impression of idyllic concord" between humans and animals "is quite misleading." In a *Time* magazine article, R. Z. Sheppard also senses Hahn's predilection for presenting only one side of the argument, but maintains that she still keeps "her professional distance and differentiates between communication that is characterized by animal instinct and communication that is conceptual and learned from humans." By citing examples about chimps and other apes (the animals with which she has had the most experience) which can communicate by using symbols (Yerkish) or sign language (Ameslan), Hahn supports the belief that the apes' ability to form concepts using these methods is evidence for a human-like capacity for language. "The linguistic exchanges now happening will serve to underscore the close biological relationship between the two," she says in *Look Who's Talking!*

Although many of her books relate to her own personal experiences, Hahn does not restrain herself from branching out into other areas which she has not previously explored. "That's no accident," she tells Weber in her *Publishers Weekly* interview. "As an actress might, early on, I made a decision to avoid being type cast." Towards this end she has also written novels, such as *With Naked Foot* (1934) and *Miss Jill* (1947), and children's books like *The Picture Story of China* (1946) and the "Francie" books (1951-56), as well as other nonfiction works. Besides her autobiographical publications, she has also written a number of biographies. The subjects for these books have been as diverse as the events portrayed in her autobiographies. Besides the Soong sisters and Chiang Kai-shek, she has written about James Brooke, the nineteenth-century, Indian-born British soldier who was a raja of Sarawak (now a state of Malaysia), a book for children on Leonardo de Vinci, and works about D. H. Lawrence, and Mabel Dodge Luhan, a former amorist of Lawrence's.

Hahn's biography of Lawrence, *Lorenzo: D. H. Lawrence and the Women Who Loved Him,* is "a lively, entertaining, and, above all, humane account of the tragicomic romantic career of modern literature's evangelist of sexuality," says a *New Yorker* critic. Laurie Stone describes the book in *Village Voice* as "literary gossip," though not "first-rate . . . literary gossip like Quentin Bell's 'Virginia Woolf,' James Mellow's 'Charmed Circle' and Lillian Hellman's brilliant 'Pentimento.'" Stone feels that the documents the author cites, specifically the letters and books that Lawrence's lovers wrote about him, are "fascinating material," but that Hahn's weakness lies in her attempts to compare Lawrence's life to his works. However, the author does not spend much time on such analyses, instead detailing Lawrence's relationships with Lady Ottoline Morrell, Katherine Mansfield, Mabel Dodge, and others. "Although Hahn does not assess them," remarks Stone, "Lawrence's obsessive, repetitive patterns of behavior and his ambivalent identification with and outrage at women emerge clearly.''

Among Lawrence's adorers, ''Mabel Dodge Luhan's story is among the most intriguing,'' says Stone. Hahn, too, found Mabel intriguing enough to write a biography on this woman. During her life, Mabel Dodge married a Buffalo society man, an architect, a Jewish painter, and finally an American Indian, in search of ''a source of genuine spiritual power,'' according to *New York Times Book Review* contributor Julian Moynahan. Mabel Dodge wrote four autobiographies which Hahn uses as sources, ''plus,'' Moynahan continues, ''much unpublished material deposited at Yale.'' The reviewer describes the author's work as ''an expert, swiftly paced biography that is only occasionally marred by a facetious tone perhaps masking dislike of some sides of her subject.''

The biographer treats her subject with what Andrew Field labels in the *Times Literary Supplement* as ''offensive intimacy,'' because she calls Mrs. Luhan and others in the book by their first names. This ''first sin of biography'' has some justification in Field's view, since ''Mabel Dodge Luhan was a metaphysically vulgar person.'' Her third husband, Maurice Sterne, rephrases this description with less objectivity in a quote from the article by Moynahan: ''Mabel had no vitality or creative power of her own. She was a dead battery who needed constantly to recharge with the juice of some man, though she might leave him 'dead' in the process.'' In spite of such invectives against Mrs. Luhan by others, a *New Yorker* reviewer believes that the author manages to treat her subject ''calmly'' and without a patronizing attitude. Furthermore, the critic maintains that Hahn represents both sides of Mrs. Luhan's character fairly, though she is sympathetic to her subject's ambition ''in an age when being a woman of her class was looked upon as merely one of the decorative arts.'' She was a manipulative woman, testifies Moynahan, but one with ''legitimate aspirations to be someone in her own right and to understand what was going on in the political, artistic and literary worlds.''

During her lifetime, the author has herself run across barriers similar to those Mabel Luhan came across. Hahn's degree in engineering was, at the time, a novel achievement which ran against the grain of society. Her travels around the world, bigamous relationship with Sinmay, deliverance of Boxer's illegitimate daughter, and use of opium in Shanghai, are described by her with characteristic matter-of-factness. ''Clearly,'' concludes Weber, ''Emily Hahn has never minded being a maverick.'' She does not, however, consider herself a feminist; neither does the eclectic and adventurous lifestyle she has led seem ''extreme'' to her, Hahn tells Weber. She explains simply that all the things she has done during her life ''always seemed natural at the time.''

CA INTERVIEW

CA interviewed Emily Hahn by telephone on June 15, 1988, at her office at the *New Yorker* in New York, New York.

CA: Eve and the Apes has been published this year, and the 1944 autobiography China to Me *has recently been made available in two new editions. Do these expressions of such major interests in your life make 1988 seem like a celebratory year?*

HAHN: Yes, I suppose so. It's good to have two books in one year, although one is a reprint.

CA: In Eve and the Apes *you write about women who have worked successfully and lovingly with great apes. In the prologue to the book you point out that the trend for women to work with apes started in the 1920s. Do you see more and more women going into this field?*

HAHN: Yes. I haven't gone around an awful lot in the last few months, because the book was finished. But before that I'm sure more and more women were going into that kind of work. They're good at it, of course. And since things are opening up, even in the zoo field, you do see more women.

They haven't quite reached the state here that they have in Russia, by the way. When I visited Russia to see their zoos, practically everybody doing any work with the animals was female. The woman who was taking me around was awfully good at stirring up the chimps, making them laugh and making them run—she ran up and down the length of their cage, and they raced with her. I'll never forget one woman I watched who had nothing to do with apes. She had on some sort of uniform, and she was giving the tiger a drink of water. She was holding a pail just close to the bars so the tiger could lap through them. They both seemed quite used to that. I can't speak very well for Russian zoos. I've seen only two of them, and they seem to me very backward, rather Victorian. That's probably from lack of money.

CA: You've described again in the new book how you met Chimpo, your first ''nonzoo chimpanzee,'' and since that time you've had several primates for companions. Do you think your petless early years, when you weren't allowed to have even dogs or cats, had something to do with your later strong feelings for animals?

HAHN: A lot, yes. Mother was afraid for us—well, she said she was afraid for the dogs and cats! We were not supposed to own any pets until we were twelve. But when I was eleven, a suitor of my older sister did break down mother's defenses and I got a puppy. That was the first one I ever had.

CA: What sort of advice or warnings would you give people about having primates for pets?

HAHN: Never try to keep one in a town; you need a lot of space, both for you and for the primate. And it ought to be a good climate for the primate. I wouldn't dream of trying to keep anything except a Japanese snow monkey in very cold weather. I think it's safe to say that mostly primates like hot weather. And you have to be patient.

CA: I've read that many people get primates for pets without realizing how much time and affection they need.

HAHN: Yes. I can see why Norway passed a law that nobody can keep an exotic pet, anything apart from dogs and cats. And there are no zoos in Norway.

CA: Eve and the Apes *is a very nice companion to the 1971 book* On the Side of the Apes. *Both books deal with the study of primates, and in part with the question of using them in medical and other scientific experiments. There's a growing public concern about experimentation on animals. Where do you stand? Where do you think the lines should be drawn?*

HAHN: I never liked it. I hated the way the researchers kept some of their animals in very small cages, and I believe they are being forced now to spend more money and give more space to them. I realize that we cannot do without the help of the animals generally—unwilling help.

CA: As part of the concern for animals now there's a push for something called animals' rights. Do you have any thoughts about how we should change our treatment of animals?

HAHN: We certainly should change our treatment of animals, and we can if we try. The animals' rights thing goes too far. But perhaps you have to go too far to get anywhere.

CA: Reading China to Me *and the later autobiography* Times and Places, *I was struck by the ingenuous and matter-of-fact tone in which you wrote about the most exciting, and sometimes frightening, events, such as your World War II experiences in China when the Japanese arrived, and choosing to have a child without being married to her father. Is that tone of writing something you worked artfully toward, or rather a reflection of some incredible calm you managed to feel about things as they happened?*

HAHN: I try to be calm. I never planned most of this. I did plan having a baby, and in those days it was very shocking. Now, of course, I would be one among many. I don't think I work for that calm tone; I just think I *am* that way.

CA: While you were living in China, you wrote a biography of the Soong sisters, one of whom married Chiang Kai-shek and another married Sun Yat-sen. What is the status of that book now?

HAHN: I think it's still in print, but I'm not sure. Of course, two of the ladies are dead, and Madame Chiang is not well. She's ninety years old, I think, and she's decided to go back; she's living in Taiwan. She didn't get on with one of Chiang Kai-shek's sons by an earlier marriage. I think it's noticeable that, after he died, she went back.

CA: Is China to Me, *in its new editions, attracting a whole new generation of readers?*

HAHN: Yes, I think so. I'm glad that it came out in England too, in the Virago edition; the one here is Beacon. They look alike except the Beacon one is a little bit bigger. I've been getting more letters again from the new edition, some of them from readers who are sort of appalled and questioning. It's news. All you have to do is live long enough, and what you had to say is news again.

CA: How recently have you been back to China, or to Africa?

HAHN: Four years ago I went back to China with my husband. We had a month there. I've been back to Africa rather a lot, though not exactly the place where I lived. When Tanzania and Nigeria were given their independence, I covered both of them for the *New Yorker.* That was fun. Coming back by Sabena Airlines we made a forced landing in the middle of the Congo—Zaire now—and it looked very much the same. We weren't there for long, only a few hours.

In China I was able to check up on some of my old friends. I'm afraid to say that a couple of them were all ready bedridden with age. And Sinmay died two years before we went—I knew that—so it's six years he's been dead. I had kept up with him, kind of, because his sister married a banker who ran away to Taiwan; and I saw her, so I knew more or less what had happened.

CA: Your autobiographical writings tell of a great love not only of travel, but of certain cities where you've lived, such as Shanghai. What made Shanghai so special and exciting for you?

HAHN: The same thing that makes New York exciting, I think: it was so cosmopolitan. People from every country in the world were there. And of course it was full of Chinese, and I discovered that I am very, very fond of them. I saw a marvelous play lately, *M. Butterfly.* It's a very exciting play written by a young San Franciscan playwright, David Henry Hwang.

CA: Did it bring back a lot of memories?

HAHN: Yes, it did.

CA: Your book The Islands: America's Imperial Adventure in the Philippines *was published in 1981. How did you become so interested in Philippine history? Was that also connected with your being in Asia during World War II?*

HAHN: Of course. There were many Filipinos in Hong Kong then, and I got well acquainted with them as we all roamed the streets. Later I visited the islands, so I was glad to go again when I wrote the book.

CA: Katharine Weber noted in her Publishers Weekly *article about you that your "enormous capacity for adventure and . . . unusual gift for both enjoying and writing about the oddities that life brings are undiminished." What makes life exciting for you on a daily basis?*

HAHN: I don't know. I go over in my mind before I get up what's going to happen. It's just that I am normally full of zest.

CA: Will you tell the story of how you proceeded from writing a newspaper article for a busy friend to getting published by the New Yorker, *becoming a writer by mistake, as you've described it?*

HAHN: In my family we all wrote a little bit; we all scribbled and nobody took it as anything extraordinary. But I was determined to be an engineer, and I did become a mining engineer. I was in New York teaching geology at Hunter College, when a friend of mine had to go away and asked me to do an article that he was supposed to do for the old *New York World* about Helen Morgan. So I did that and was paid $25, which to me was a very large sum. And of course it was more then than it is now. I was paid $25 for a week's teaching, and I thought, What am I doing here? Teaching, when it comes to giving grades, is no fun.

Then I was writing letters home, full of myself. My brother-in-law had always thought I should be writing instead of teaching, and he sent a couple of these letters to the *New Yorker,* which had not been running more than three years. He just took off "Dear Mitchell" and "Love, Mickey." And the *New Yorker* bought them. At the end of the term, I got to work and started writing instead.

CA: It's ironic how that happened, because so many writers try forever to get published by the New Yorker.

HAHN: Yes. And I hadn't even been reading the magazine! Mind you, they didn't take everything. After they take three they'll pay attention to you, but they did turn down the next three. However, little by little, I was doing more for them.

CA: Would you like to comment on your long and surely happy relationship with the magazine?

HAHN: Well, it certainly has been long, and it's been happy!

CA: I think one of the good things about the magazine is that they'll let writers work on whatever they want to work on, within reason.

HAHN: Yes, that's the secret of it; you're supposed to make suggestions about what you want to do, and either they say yes or they say no. They don't harry you—you can take as long as you like doing it. That's something important. It's not like working on a paper.

CA: Also they'll give you whatever space you need.

HAHN: That's right. Katharine Weber once asked me, ''What can we do not to have such long pieces?'' Because she thought they were too long; so did I. I said, ''As long as you pay by the word, you're going to get long pieces.''

CA: In China to Me *there are some poems you've written. Is writing poetry a leisure activity for you?*

HAHN: It used to be; I don't do it now. I think it's a young thing. Real poets go on, of course.

CA: Your own ''liberation,'' long before the feminist movement that began in the 1960s, could very well give you a unique view on the whole range of problems women have been struggling with publicly for the last twenty-five years or so.

HAHN: That's true. Every time they come out with something new, I think, Oh, yes! Yes!

CA: Any special observations on where we stand and where we need to go from here?

HAHN: I think we've got very far. I don't really know why we keep on yelling for—what is that thing with initials that everybody wants?—ERA. I believe it's all included in what we have, if we knew how to use it. I can't go into the technicalities of it, but I can't think of anything that we haven't got, really, except the right attitude on the part of some people. I've been interested, for instance, in the subject of prostitution: how it got started, why. Somebody said, in a rather careless manner, the law of supply and demand. Yes, that's the easy way out, if you want to make a living. But that's one of the things about the whole attitude toward women, which I do think is changing, but maybe it never will completely.

CA: What thoughts do you have about prostitution?

HAHN: I used to think we could stamp it out, because I didn't like it. It offended me, my idea of independence and so forth. But I saw it happen once in Zaire. One of the wives of the head man didn't like him and left. He wouldn't take her back, which was natural—they usually won't. People said that ''she walked and walked by the river,'' meaning that she walked out and gathered clients. I don't think she knew anything of the history of prostitution; she just did that and made what money she could, and she managed. I thought, This is probably the way it all began. It was a primitive village; I'm sure she'd never read anything about it—she couldn't read.

CA: What's in the future for you that you'd like to mention?

HAHN: I'm doing a very long study for the *New Yorker* on students abroad. And there's a book coming out in 1989, *The Emily Hahn Reader.* A couple of people at Knopf have gone over everything I've written, which is pretty awful—think how long it would take!—and they've picked out what they think would make a good picture of me. I didn't always agree, but I've just made a few emendations. There are things I never would have thought of. But of course it should make a fair picture; it shouldn't be just what I'd pick out.

BIOGRAPHICAL/CRITICAL SOURCES:

BOOKS

Hahn, Emily, *China to Me: A Partial Autobiography,* Doubleday, 1944, reprinted, Beacon Press, 1988.
Hahn, *Hong Kong Holiday,* Doubleday, 1946.
Hahn, *England to Me,* Doubleday, 1949.
Hahn, *Kissing Cousins,* Doubleday, 1958.
Hahn, *Africa to Me: Person to Person,* Doubleday, 1964.
Hahn, *Times and Places,* Crowell, 1970.

PERIODICALS

Best Sellers, July 1, 1971.
Book World, November 5, 1967.
Los Angeles Times, November 2, 1981.
Los Angeles Times Book Review, June 12, 1988.
New York Times, April 5, 1968, June 23, 1978, October 2, 1981.
New York Times Book Review, November 19, 1967, September 21, 1975, June 26, 1977, July 16, 1978, May 22, 1988.
New Yorker, September 29, 1975, May 16, 1977, October 19, 1981.
Publishers Weekly, October 5, 1970, March 18, 1988.
Saturday Review, November 15, 1975.
Time, June 26, 1978.
Times Literary Supplement, June 17, 1965, December 30, 1977, September 22, 1978.
Village Voice, October 27, 1975.
Virginia Quarterly Review, winter, 1976.
Washington Post Book World, July 3, 1988.

—*Sketch by Kevin S. Hile*

—*Interview by Jean W. Ross*

*   *   *

HALL, (Frederick) Leonard   1899-

PERSONAL: Born October 30, 1899, in Seneca, Mo.; son of Frederick Bagby and Corinne (Steele) Hall; married Frances Mabley, April, 1923 (died, 1937); married Virginia Watson, May 28, 1941; children: Frederick Leonard. *Education:* Attended Washington University, St. Louis, Mo., 1920, and University of Wisconsin—Madison, 1921-22. *Religion:* Protestant.

ADDRESSES: Home—Possum Trot Farm, Caledonia, Mo. 63631.

CAREER: Affiliated with R. R. Donnelley and Sons Co., Chicago, Ill., 1930-45; *St. Louis Post Dispatch,* St. Louis, Mo., columnist, 1943-59; *St. Louis Globe Democrat,* St. Louis, columnist, 1959-80; owner and operator of livestock farm, Possum Trot Farm, 1964-85; free-lance writer, 1980—. Conservation lecturer for National Audubon Society, 1944-64; chairman of advisory commission of Ozark National Scenic Riverways, 1965-69. *Military service:* U.S. Naval Reserve, active duty, 1917-19.

MEMBER: Wilderness Society, Sierra Club, National Audubon Society, National Parks Association (member of board of trustees), American Forestry Association, Defenders of Wildlife (past member of board of directors), Humane Society of the United States (past member of board of directors), Missouri Nature Conservancy (past member of board of directors), Missouri Conservation Federation (member of board of directors), Missouri Parks Association (member of board of directors), Sigma Delta Chi.

AWARDS, HONORS: Named Master Conservationist in Missouri, 1948; LL.D. from Westminster College, Fulton, Mo., 1950, and Washington University, St. Louis, Mo., 1970; Thomas Stokes Award from Nieman Fellows of Harvard University, 1959; named Missouri State Conservationist, 1966; member of Governor's Academy of Missouri Squires, 1967; award for outstanding environmental leadership from Missouri Botanical Garden, 1982.

WRITINGS:

Stars Upstream: Life Along an Ozark Stream, University of Chicago Press, 1962, 4th edition, 1987.
A Journal of the Seasons on an Ozark Farm (originally published as *Country Year,* 1957), illustrations by George Conrey, University of Missouri Press, 1980.
Earth's Song: "What Makes the Crops Rejoice, Beneath What Star to Plow, Of These I Sing," foreword by Howard F. Baer, University of Missouri Press, 1981.

Also author of *Possum Trot Farm,* 1948, *Stars Upstream,* 1962, 1963, 1967, 1987, and *Ozark Wildflowers,* 1969; author of film scripts "An Ozark Anthology," 1960, "Audubon's Wilderness," 1962, "Forever Yours," 1966, "Birds Over Florida," 1967, and "Country Year," 1971. Contributor to magazines.

*   *   *

HAMILTON, Adam
    See HENDERSON, M(arilyn) R(uth)

*   *   *

HAMILTON, Ralph
    See STRATEMEYER, Edward L.

*   *   *

HARKABI, Yehoshafat   1921-

PERSONAL: Born September 21, 1921, in Haifa, Israel; son of Zidkiahv (a judge) and Haya (Stamper) Harkabi; married Miryam Manzon (a medical secretary), March 23, 1953; children: Irit, Dan. *Education:* Hebrew University of Jerusalem, M.A., 1949, Ph.D., 1968; Harvard University, M.P.A., 1960. *Religion:* Jewish.

ADDRESSES: Home—6 Bar Kokhva St., French Hill, Jerusalem, Israel. *Office*—Department of International Relations, Hebrew University of Jerusalem, Jerusalem, Israel.

CAREER: Israel Defence Forces, secretary to foreign minister, 1949-50, director of military intelligence, 1950-59, leaving service as major general; Ministry of Defence, Tel-Aviv, Israel, in strategic research, 1963-68; Hebrew University of Jerusalem, Jerusalem, Israel, 1968—, professor of international relations and Middle Eastern studies, 1973—. Assistant to minister of defence strategic policy, 1974-75; advisor to prime minister for intelligence, 1977.

WRITINGS:

Nuclear War and Nuclear Peace, Israel Program for Scientific Translations, 1964.
Arab Attitudes to Israel, translated by Misha Louvish, Israel University Press, 1971.
Palestinians and Israel, Keter Publishing House, 1974.
Arab Strategies and Israel's Response, Free Press, 1977.
The Palestinian Covenant and Its Meaning, Biblio Distribution, 1979.
The Bar Kokhba Syndrome: Risk and Realism in International Relations, translated by Max Ticktin, Rossel, 1983.
The Arab-Israeli Conflict: Future Perspective, International Center for Peace in the Middle East (Tel Aviv), 1985.
Israel's Fateful Hour, Harper, 1988, originally published in England as *Israel's Fateful Decisions.*

WORK IN PROGRESS: A textbook on war and strategy; a textbook on the philosophy of international relations.

BIOGRAPHICAL/CRITICAL SOURCES:

PERIODICALS

Christian Science Monitor, April 18, 1988.
Financial Times (London), June 23, 1988.
Jewish Chronicle (London), July 1, 1988.
Los Angeles Times Book Review, May 22, 1983.
New Republic, September 5, 1983.
New York Review of Books, June 12, 1980.

*   *   *

HARKAWAY, Hal
    See STRATEMEYER, Edward L.

*   *   *

HARRIS, (Theodore) Wilson   1921-
    (Kona Waruk)

PERSONAL: Born March 24, 1921, in New Amsterdam, British Guiana (now Guyana); immigrated to England, 1959; son of Theodore Wilson (an insurer and underwriter) and Millicent Josephine (Glasford) Harris; married Cecily Carew, 1945; married second wife, Margaret Nimmo Burns (a writer), April 2, 1959. *Education:* Queen's College, Georgetown, British Guiana, 1934-39; studied land surveying and geomorphology under government auspices, 1939-42.

ADDRESSES: Home—London, England. *Office*—c/o Faber and Faber, 3 Queen Square, London WC1N 3AU, England.

CAREER: British Guiana Government, government surveyor, 1942-54, senior surveyor, 1955-58; full-time writer in London, England, 1959—. Visiting lecturer, State University of New York at Buffalo, 1970, Yale University, 1979; guest lecturer, Mysore University (India), 1978; regents' lecturer, University of California, 1983; writer-in-residence, University of West Indies, 1970, University of Toronto, 1970, Newcastle University, Australia, 1979, University of Queensland, Australia, 1986; visiting professor, University of Texas at Austin, 1972, 1981-82, 1983, University of Aarhus, Denmark, 1973, and in Cuba. Delegate, UNESCO Symposium on Caribbean Literature in Cuba, 1968, National Identity Conference in Brisbane, Australia, 1968.

AWARDS, HONORS: English Arts Council grants, 1968 and 1970; Commonwealth fellow at University of Leeds, 1971; Guggenheim fellow, 1972-73; Henfield writing fellow at University of East Anglia, 1974; Southern Arts fellow, Salisbury, 1976; D.Lit., University of West Indies, 1984.

WRITINGS:

NOVELS

Palace of the Peacock (Book I of the ''Guiana Quartet''; also see below), Faber, 1960.
The Far Journey of Oudin (Book II of the ''Guiana Quartet''; also see below), Faber, 1961.
The Whole Armour (Book III of the ''Guiana Quartet''; also see below), Faber, 1962.
The Secret Ladder (Book IV of the ''Guiana Quartet''; also see below), Faber, 1963.
The Whole Armour [and] *The Secret Ladder,* Faber, 1963.
Heartland, Faber, 1964.
The Eye of the Scarecrow, Faber, 1965.
The Waiting Room, Faber, 1967.
Tamatumari, Faber, 1968.
Ascent to Omai, Faber, 1970.
Black Marsden: A Tabula Rasa Comedy, Faber, 1972.
Companions of the Day and Night, Faber, 1975.
Da Silva da Silva's Cultivated Wilderness [and] *Genesis of the Clowns* (also see below), Faber, 1977.
Genesis of the Clowns, Faber, 1978.
The Tree of the Sun, Faber, 1978.
The Angel at the Gate, Faber, 1982.
Carnival, Faber, 1985.
The Guyana Quartet (contains *Palace of the Peacock, The Far Journey of Oudin, The Whole Armour,* and *The Secret Ladder;* issued as a boxed set), Faber, 1985.

SHORT STORIES

The Sleepers of Roraima, Faber, 1970.
The Age of the Rainmakers, Faber, 1971.

POETRY

(Under pseudonym Kona Waruk) *Fetish,* privately printed (Georgetown, Guyana), 1951.
The Well and the Land, British Guiana, 1952.
Eternity to Season, privately printed (Georgetown), 1954, 2nd edition, New Beacon Books, 1978.

NONFICTION

Tradition and the West Indian Novel (lecture), introduction by C.L.R. James, New Beacon, 1965.
Tradition, the Writer and Society: Critical Essays, New Beacon, 1967.
History, Fable and Myth in the Caribbean and Guianas (booklet), National History and Arts Council, (Georgetown), 1970.
Fossil and Psyche (criticism), African and American Studies and Research Center, University of Texas, 1974.

(Contributor) J. T. Livingston, editor, *Caribbean Rhythms: The Emerging English Literature of the West Indies,* Washington Square Press, 1974.
(Contributor) Anna Rutherford and Kirsten Holst Petersen, editors, *Enigma of Values: An Introduction,* Dangaroo Press, 1975.
(Contributor) Edward Baugh, editor, *Critics on Caribbean Literature: Readings in Literary Criticism,* St. Martin's, 1978.
Explorations: A Series of Talks and Articles, 1966-1981, Hena Maes-Jelinek, editor and author of introduction, Dangaroo Press, 1981.
The Womb of Space: The Cross-Cultural Imagination, Greenwood Press, 1983.
The Infinite Rehearsal, Faber, 1987.

Also contributor to *Literary Half-Yearly, Kyk-over-al,* and *New Letters.*

SIDELIGHTS: Novelist Wilson Harris blends philosophy, poetic imagery, symbolism and myth to create new visions of reality. His fiction shows the reader a world where the borders between physical and spiritual reality, life and death have become indistinguishable. In *World Literature Today,* Richard Sander states that Harris has ''realized a new, original form of the novel that in almost all respects constitutes a radical departure from the conventional novel.'' Reed Way Dasenbrock, also writing in *World Literature Today,* claims that Harris ''has always operated at a very high level of abstraction, higher than any of his fellow West Indian novelists, higher perhaps than any other contemporary novelist in English. . . . And whether one regards Harris's evolution as a rich and exciting development or a one-way trip down an abstractionist cul-de-sac, there is no denying his unique vision or dedication to that vision.'' The constant use of abstraction has brought Harris both praise and criticism; while some find his work rewarding and challenging, others think his unorthodox methods alienate the reader.

Harris is perhaps best known to the general public for *The Guyana Quartet.* Important to all four works of the quartet is the landscape of the Guyanese interior, which Harris came to know well during his years as a government surveyor. ''Two major elements seem to have shaped Harris's approach to art and his philosophy of existence: the impressive contrasts of the Guyanese landscapes, . . . and the successive waves of conquest which gave Guyana its heterogeneous population polarised for centuries into oppressors and their victims. The two, landscape and history, merge in his work into single metaphors symbolising man's inner space saturated with the effects of historical—that is, temporal—experiences,'' writes Hena Maes-Jelinek in *West Indian Literature.*

Harris's works are frequently difficult for critics to summarize because they move so far from the accepted definition of a novel. Harris uses dream, hallucination, psychic experiences, and various historical times without clearcut divisions, and critics often find it necessary to invent a genre for Harris's works in order to discuss them. Michael Thorpe in *World Literature Today* calls the author's more recent books ''psychical 'expeditions.''' A *Times Literary Supplement* contributor terms *Palace of the Peacock,* the first volume of the ''Guyana Quartet,'' ''a 150-page definition of mystical experience given in the guise of a novel.'' And an *Encounter* contributor describes Harris's work as ''a metaphysical shorthand on the surface of a narrative whose point cannot readily be grasped by any but those thoroughly versed in his previous work and able at once to recognise the recurrent complex metaphors.''

Reviewers frequently mention that to fully grasp Harris's work it is necessary to be familiar with his metaphors, since the elaborately written passages and complex symbolism can make the writing nearly impenetrable for readers used to more traditional fiction. A *Times Literary Supplement* contributor warns, "no reader should attempt Mr. Harris's novels unless he is willing to work at them." Reviewing *Palace of the Peacock*, another *Times Literary Supplement* contributor says it is "a difficult book to read, yet it is the very concreteness of Mr. Harris's imagery that makes its denseness so hard to penetrate." Thorpe agrees, writing, "The uninitiated reader may become discouraged, wrestling with opaque ideas attached to tantalizing shadows of what he seeks in fiction: engagement with deeply apprehended lives and moving action." But according to J. P. Durix, also a *Times Literary Supplement* contributor, the reader who stays with Harris is rewarded by his "dense style and meticulous construction, his attention to visual and rhythmic effects, [which] are matched by an inventiveness which few contemporary novelists can equal."

Harris also writes literary criticism; in *The Womb of Space*, he expands upon many of the ideas contained in his novels. But in his general theory as well as in his fictional works, Harris's points can be hard to understand. Steven G. Kellman writes in *Modern Fiction Studies*, "I take it that Wilson Harris' theme is the ability of consciousness to transcend a particular culture. But his articulation of that theme is so turgid, so beset by mixed and obscure metaphors and by syntactical convolutions that much of the book simply remains unintelligible even to a sympathetic reader." Harris's goal in the work is to establish parallels between writers of various cultural backgrounds. He observes in *The Womb of Space* that "literature is still constrained by regional and other conventional but suffocating categories." His vision is of a new world community, based on cultural heterogeneity, not homogeneity, which, "as a cultural model, exercised by a ruling ethnic group, tends to become an organ of conquest and division because of *imposed* unity that actually subsists on the suppression of others." Sander believes that *The Womb of Space* is "an attack on the traditional critical establishment." A *Choice* contributor agrees, claiming, "*The Womb of Space* issues a direct challenge to the intellectual provincialism that often characterises literary study in the US."

But critics who applaud Harris's work believe he has contributed greatly to the understanding of art and consciousness. John Hearne writes in *The Islands in Between*, "No other British Caribbean novelist has made quite such an explicit and conscious effort as Harris to reduce the material reckonings of everyday life to the significance of myth." And speaking of the breadth of Harris' work, Louis James states in the *Times Literary Supplement*, "The novels of Wilson Harris . . . form one ongoing whole. Each work is individual; yet the whole sequence can be seen as a continuous, ever-widening exploration of civilization and creative art."

BIOGRAPHICAL/CRITICAL SOURCES:

BOOKS

Baugh, Edward, editor, *Critics on Caribbean Literature: Readings in Literary Criticism*, St. Martin's, 1978.
Contemporary Literary Criticism, Volume 25, Gale, 1983.
Dance, Daryl Cumber, editor, *Fifty Caribbean Writers: A Bio-Bibliographical Critical Sourcebook*, Greenwood Press, 1986.
Drake, Sandra E., *Wilson Harris and the Modern Tradition: A New Architecture of the World*, Greenwood Press, 1986.
Fletcher, John, *Commonwealth Literature and the Modern World*, Didier (Brussels), 1975.
Gilkes, Michael, *The West Indian Novel*, Twayne Publishers, 1981.
Gilkes, Michael, *Wilson Harris and the Caribbean Novel*, Longman, 1975.
Harris, Wilson, *The Tree of the Sun*, Faber, 1978.
Harris, Wilson, *The Womb of Space: The Cross-Cultural Imagination*, Greenwood Press, 1983.
James, Louis, editor, *The Islands In Between*, Oxford University Press, 1968.
King, Bruce, editor, *West Indian Literature*, Archon Books, 1979.
Maes-Jelinek, Hena, *The Naked Design*, Dangaroo Press, 1976.
Maes-Jelinek, Hena, *Wilson Harris*, Twayne, 1982.
Moore, Gerald, *Chosen Tongue*, Longman, 1969.
Munro, Ian and Reinhard Sander, editors, *Kas-Kas: Interviews with Three Caribbean Writers in Texas*, African and Afro-American Research Institute, The University of Texas at Austin, 1972.
Ramchand, Kenneth, *An Introduction to the Study of West Indian Literature*, Nelson Caribbean, 1976.
Van Sertima, Ivan, *Enigma of Values*, Dangaroo Press, 1975.

PERIODICALS

Choice, March, 1984.
Encounter, May, 1987.
Journal of Commonwealth Literature, July, 1969, June, 1971, April, 1975.
Language and Literature, autumn, 1971.
Literary Half-Yearly, January, 1972.
Modern Fiction Studies, summer, 1984.
Observer, July 7, 1985.
Quill and Quire, October, 1985.
Spectator, March 25, 1978.
Times Educational Supplement, July 19, 1985.
Times Literary Supplement, December 9, 1965, July 4, 1968, May 21, 1970, October 10, 1975, May 25, 1977, May 19, 1978, October 15, 1982, July 12, 1985, September 25-October 1, 1987.
World Literature Today, winter, 1984, summer, 1985, spring, 1986.*

—*Sketch by Jani Prescott*

*   *   *

HARRISON, Elizabeth Cavanna   1909-
(Betty Cavanna, Elizabeth Allen Cavanna, Elizabeth Headley; pseudonym: Betsy Allen)

PERSONAL: Born June 24, 1909, in Camden, N.J.; daughter of Walter and Emily (Allen) Cavanna; married Edward Headley, August 5, 1940 (died, 1952); married George Russell Harrison (a university dean of science), March 9, 1957 (died July 27, 1979); children: (first marriage) Stephen. *Education:* Douglass College (now part of Rutgers, The State University—New Brunswick Campus), A.B., 1929. *Religion:* Protestant.

ADDRESSES: Home—45 Pasture Lane, Bryn Mawr, Pa. 19010 (winter); R.D. Box 459, Edgartown, Mass. 02539 (summer).

CAREER: Bayonne Times, Bayonne, N.J., reporter, 1929-31; Westminster Press, Philadelphia, Pa., began as advertising manager, became art director, 1931-41; full-time writer, 1941—.

MEMBER: Writers Guild, Boston Museum of Fine Arts, Philadelphia Art Alliance, Technology Matrons (program chairman, 1961-62), Phi Beta Kappa, Women's Travel Club of Boston (2nd vice-president, 1972-73), Cosmopolitan Club (New York).

WRITINGS:

UNDER NAME BETTY CAVANNA

Puppy Stakes, Westminster, 1943.

The Black Spaniel Mystery, Westminster, 1945.

Secret Passage, John C. Winston, 1946.

Going on Sixteen, Westminster, 1946, revised edition, Morrow, 1985.

Spurs for Suzanna, Westminster, 1947.

A Girl Can Dream, Westminster, 1948.

Paintbox Summer, Westminster, 1949, reprinted, Harmony Raine, 1981.

Spring Comes Riding, Westminster, 1950.

Two's Company, Westminster, 1951.

(Compiler) *Pick of the Litter: Favorite Dog Stories*, Westminster, 1952.

Lasso Your Heart, Westminster, 1952.

Love, Laurie, Westminster, 1953.

Six on Easy Street, Westminster, 1954.

The First Book of Seashells, F. Watts, 1955.

Passport to Romance, Morrow, 1955.

The Boy Next Door, Morrow, 1956.

Angel on Skis, Morrow, 1957.

Stars in Her Eyes, Morrow, 1958.

The Scarlet Sail, Morrow, 1959.

Accent on April, Morrow, 1960.

A Touch of Magic, Westminster, 1961.

Fancy Free, Morrow, 1961.

The First Book of Wildflowers, F. Watts, 1961.

A Time for Tenderness, Morrow, 1962.

Almost Like Sisters, Morrow, 1963.

Jenny Kimura, Morrow, 1964.

Mystery at Love's Creek, Morrow, 1965.

A Breath of Fresh Air, Morrow, 1966.

The First Book of Wool (photographs by husband, George Russell Harrison), F. Watts, 1966 (published in England as *Wool*, F. Watts, 1972).

The Country Cousin, Morrow, 1967.

Mystery in Marrakech, Morrow, 1968.

Spice Island Mystery, Morrow, 1969.

The First Book of Fiji (photographs by G. R. Harrison), F. Watts, 1969 (published in England as *Fiji*, F. Watts, 1972).

The First Book of Morocco (photographs by G. R. Harrison), F. Watts, 1970.

Mystery on Safari, Morrow, 1971.

The Ghost of Ballyhooly, Morrow, 1971.

Mystery in the Museum, Morrow, 1972.

Petey, Westminster, 1973.

Joyride, Morrow, 1974.

Ruffles and Drums, Morrow, 1975.

Mystery of the Emerald Buddha, Morrow, 1976.

Stamp Twice for Murder, Morrow, 1981.

The Surfer and the City Girl, Westminster, 1981.

Storm in Her Heart, Westminster, 1983.

Romance on Trial, Westminster, 1984.

Wanted: A Girl for the Horses, Morrow, 1984.

Banner Year, Morrow, 1987.

UNDER NAME ELIZABETH HEADLEY

A Date for Diane (also see below), Macrae Smith, 1946.

Take a Call, Topsy!, Macrae Smith, 1947, reprinted under name Betty Cavanna as *Ballet Fever*, Westminster, 1978.

She's My Girl!, Macrae Smith, 1949, reprinted under name Betty Cavanna as *You Can't Take Twenty Dogs on a Date*, Westminster, 1979.

Catchpenny Street, Macrae Smith, 1951, reprinted under name Betty Cavanna, Westminster, 1975.

Diane's New Love (also see below), Macrae Smith, 1955.

Toujours Diane (also see below), Macrae Smith, 1957.

The Diane Stories: All about America's Favorite Girl Next Door (contains *A Date for Diane*, *Diane's New Love*, and *Toujours Diane*), Macrae Smith, 1964.

"AROUND THE WORLD TODAY" SERIES; UNDER NAME BETTY CAVANNA

Arne of Norway, photographs by G. R. Harrison, F. Watts, 1960.

Lucho of Peru, photographs by G. R. Harrison, F. Watts, 1961.

Paulo of Brazil, photographs G. R. Harrison, F. Watts, 1962.

Pepe of Argentina, photographs by G. R. Harrison, F. Watts, 1962.

Lo Chau of Hong Kong, photographs by G. R. Harrison, F. Watts, 1963.

Chico of Guatemala, photographs by G. R. Harrison, F. Watts, 1963.

Noko of Japan, photographs by G. R. Harrison, F. Watts, 1964.

Carlos of Mexico, photographs by G. R. Harrison, F. Watts, 1964.

Tavi of the South Seas, photographs by G. R. Harrison, F. Watts, 1965.

Doug of Australia, photographs by G. R. Harrison, F. Watts, 1965.

Ali of Egypt, photographs by G. R. Harrison, F. Watts, 1966.

Demetrios of Greece, photographs by G. R. Harrison, F. Watts, 1966.

"CONNIE BLAIR MYSTERY" SERIES; UNDER PSEUDONYM BETSY ALLEN

Puzzle in Purple, Grosset, 1948.

The Secret of Black Cat Gulch, Grosset, 1948.

The Riddle in Red, Grosset, 1948.

The Clue in Blue, Grosset, 1948.

The Green Island Mystery, Grosset, 1949.

The Ghost Wore White, Grosset, 1950.

The Yellow Warning, Grosset, 1951.

The Gray Menace, Grosset, 1953.

The Brown Satchel Mystery, Grosset, 1954.

Peril in Pink, Grosset, 1955.

The Silver Secret, Grosset, 1956.

OTHER

Contributor of serials to *American Girl* and other magazines.

SIDELIGHTS: Books by Elizabeth Cavanna Harrison (best known as Betty Cavanna) often concern junior high school girls. Cavanna explains this as the result of "an almost total emotional recall for this particular period of my own life, which made it possible for me to identify with a teenage heroine. Fashions in clothes and speech change, but the hopes, dreams, and fears of the young remain fairly constant, and over the years I have explored all sorts of youthful problems—among them loneliness, shyness, jealousy, social maladjustment, and the destructiveness of alcoholism, divorce, race prejudice, and mother-daughter rivalry within family situations.''

Dwight L. Burton of *English Journal* writes: ''Books by Betty Cavanna have been among the most popular with young high school readers.'' He cites *Going on Sixteen* as particularly ''noteworthy.'' The novel, Burton explains, ''rests upon its genuineness and sincerity rather than upon melodrama. Julie, the heroine, is a somewhat shy, nondescript girl who lives on a farm with her father.'' Burton notes that as the story follows Julie's progress through three years of high school, Cavanna ''avoids the easy assumptions present in many books with a similar theme.... There is realistic evolution of character brought about by Julie's own efforts and recognition of her faults and by the sympathetic guidance of a teacher.'' In 1985, Morrow published a revised edition of *Going on Sixteen* as a ''Morrow Junior Classic.''

Cavanna has travelled to the Caribbean, Mexico, Europe, South America, Australia, Japan, the South Seas, Iran, Nepal, Afghanistan, Sri Lanka, Indonesia, China, and eastern Africa.

AVOCATIONAL INTERESTS: Art, antiques.

BIOGRAPHICAL/CRITICAL SOURCES:

BOOKS

Contemporary Literary Criticism, Volume 12, Gale, 1980.
Something about the Author Autobiography Series, Volume 4, Gale, 1987.
Thomison, Dennis, editor, *Readings about Adolescent Literature,* Scarecrow, 1970.

PERIODICALS

Atlantic, December, 1946.
Book Week, November 29, 1964.
Christian Science Monitor, November 4, 1965.
English Journal, September, 1951.
New York Herald Tribune Book Review, June 10, 1945, May 5, 1946, April 11, 1948, June 17, 1951.
New York Times Book Review, January 5, 1947, July 20, 1947, May 15, 1949, November 15, 1953, December 15, 1957.
Saturday Review, August 13, 1949.

*   *   *

HARRISON, George Russell   1898-1979

PERSONAL: Born July 14, 1898, San Diego, Calif.; died July 27, 1979, in Concord, Mass.; son of Ernest (a dry goods merchant) and Magda (Lincke-Tiesel) Harrison; married Florence Kent, 1922 (died, 1955); married Elizabeth Cavanna Headley (a writer; professionally known as Betty Cavanna), March 9, 1957; children: (first marriage) Mary Lou, Nancy, David Kent. *Education:* Stanford University, B.S., 1919, M.A., 1920, Ph.D., 1922.

CAREER: Stanford University, Stanford, Calif., instructor in physics, 1919-1923; Harvard University, Cambridge, Mass., research fellow, 1923-25; Stanford University, assistant professor, 1925-27, associate professor of physics, 1927-30, research associate, 1930-31; Massachusetts Institute of Technology, Cambridge, professor of physics, 1930-64, dean of science, 1942-64, dean emeritus, 1964-79. National Defense Research Committee, chief of optics division, 1942-46, chief of physics division, 1945-46; chief of research section, General MacArthur's headquarters, 1944. Director, Bausch & Lomb, Inc., and Colt Industries. Trustee, Boston Museum of Science, Corning Glass Museum, and Babson Institute.

MEMBER: Optical Society of American (president, 1946-48), American Philosophical Society, American Academy of Arts and Sciences (vice-president, 1944-46), American Association for the Advancement of Science (vice-president, 1953).

AWARDS, HONORS: Rumford Medal of American Academy of Arts and Sciences, 1939; Medal of Freedom, 1946; Presidential Medal of Merit, 1948; Ives Medal, 1949; Cresson Medal of Franklin Institute, 1953; Pittsburgh Spectrographic Award, 1957; C. E. K. Mees Medal of Optical Society of America. D.Sc., Northwestern University, 1943, and St. Lawrence University, 1952; LL.D., Middlebury College, 1955; D.Eng., Drexel Institute of Technology, 1956.

WRITINGS:

Atoms in Action, Morrow, 1938, 3rd edition, 1955.
M.I.T. Wavelength Tables, Wiley, 1938, 2nd edition published as *Wavelength Tables,* MIT Press, 1970.
How Things Work, Morrow, 1941.
(With Lord and Loofbourow) *Practical Spectroscopy,* Prentice-Hall, 1948.
What Man May Be, Morrow, 1956.
First Book of Light, F. Watts, 1962.
First Book of Energy, F. Watts, 1965.
The Conquest of Energy, Morrow, 1968.
Lasers, F. Watts, 1971.
Research Directed toward the Development of an Improved Process for Optical Grating Ruling: Final Report, three volumes, [Cambridge, Mass.], 1972-73.

Illustrator (photographs) of ''Around the World Today'' series, twelve books written by wife, Elizabeth Cavanna Harrison (under name Betty Cavanna), published by F. Watts, 1960-70.

SIDELIGHTS: The George Russell Harrison Spectroscopy Laboratory was dedicated in 1980 by the Massachusetts Institute of Technology.

OBITUARIES:

PERIODICALS

New York Times, July 29, 1979.*

[Sketch reviewed by wife, Elizabeth Cavanna Harrison]

*   *   *

HART-DAVIS, Duff   1936-

PERSONAL: Born June 3, 1936, in London, England; son of Rupert (a publisher and author) and Comfort (Turner) Hart-Davis; married Phyllida Barstow (an author), April 22, 1961; children: Alice, Guy. *Education:* Attended Eton College, 1949-54; Oxford University, B.A. (second class honors), 1960.

ADDRESSES: Home—Owlpen Farm, Uley, Dursley, Gloucestershire, England. *Agent*—Curtis Brown Ltd., 575 Madison Ave., New York, N.Y. 10022.

CAREER: Worked as a deckhand on a cargo boat on the West African coast and pioneered a motor route to Moscow and Crimea, 1957; *Sunday Telegraph,* London, England, feature writer, 1969-75, literary editor, 1975-76, assistant editor, 1977-78; writer. *Military service:* British Army, 1955-57; became second lieutenant.

WRITINGS:

Behind the Scenes on a Newspaper, Dent, 1964.

The Megacull, Constable, 1968.

The Gold Trackers, Doubleday, 1970 (published in England as *The Gold of St. Matthew,* Constable, 1970).

Spider in the Morning, Doubleday, 1972.

Ascension: The Story of a South Atlantic Island, Constable, 1972, Doubleday, 1973.

Peter Fleming: A Biography, J. Cape, 1974.

Monarchs of the Glen: A History of Deerstalking in the Scottish Highlands, J. Cape, 1978.

The Heights of Rimring, J. Cape, 1980, Atheneum, 1981.

(With Colin Strong) *Fighter Pilot,* Queen Anne Press, 1981.

Level Five, Atheneum, 1982.

Fire Falcon, J. Cape, 1983.

The Man-Eater of Jassapur, J. Cape, 1985.

Hitler's Games: The 1936 Olympics, Harper, 1986.

(Editor) *End of an Era: Letter and Journals of Sir Alan Lascelles, 1887-1920,* David & Charles, 1987.

Country Matters, illustrated by George Tute, Weidenfeld & Nicolson, 1988.

(Editor) *The Prince of Wales,* Hamish Hamilton, 1988.

SIDELIGHTS: As a reporter for the *Sunday Telegraph,* writer Duff Hart-Davis has visited many parts of the world, including Nepal, India, Afghanistan, Iran, the Persian Gulf, Turkey, Europe, and the Caribbean. These experiences provide Hart-Davis with strong backdrop for much of his fiction and nonfiction. In the espionage novel *The Heights of Rimring,* for example, Hart-Davis's hero is propelled into a Himalayan setting; his portrait of the Tibetans who live there is "sensitive and convincing," comments Jack Sullivan in the *Washington Post Book World.* Although the critic finds the author's heroes somewhat stereotyped, "his description of the magisterial Himalayas and the people who somehow survive in them is consistently stirring and evocative," admits Sullivan. Similarly, "a sense of atmosphere and place are the strengths" of *The Man-Eater of Jassapur,* writes Gillian Greenwood in the London *Times.* "Set on the border of Nepal, [the book] is also strong on character," adds the critic. But while the setting of the Indian jungle "with its impressive dawns and sunsets, sounds and silence, is drawn with skill," Greenwood notes that it "is always subservient to the exciting narrative." The reviewer concludes by calling *The Man-Eater of Jassapur* a "thrilling, exotic, even humorous tale."

A strong sense of location also marks *Hitler's Games: The 1936 Olympics,* for "Hart-Davis has revealed in detail how the Nazis exploited this opportunity for their political ends," observes Vane Ivanovic in the *Spectator.* "The young should thank the author for recalling the mood of the Thirties in western Europe and America." The 1936 Olympic Games were to take place in Berlin, Germany, during the height of Hitler's power; the Nazi leader saw the Games as an opportunity to promote his regime and theories of Aryan supremacy. Because of the regime's controversial domestic crimes and breaches of international law, many Western governments questioned the wisdom of participating in the Berlin games. "The story of the bitter and protracted debate that took place before the athletes departed for Germany constitutes the most interesting part" of the book, comments *New York Times Book Review* contributor Gordon A. Craig. "This is not to say that the Games themselves are inadequately treated," continues the critic, for Hart-Davis "has lively accounts of [both] the winter Games . . . and of the exploits of such outstanding athletes as the American Jesse Owens, [and] the New Zealand metric miler Jack Lovelock," among others. And while Ivanovic believes the author places too much emphasis on the idea of a deliberate and substantial German deception, "nothing can take away from Mr. Hart-Davis's masterly exposure of the appalling story of complacency and fear of war that prevailed in the Thirties that were highlighted by Hitler's Games."

AVOCATIONAL INTERESTS: Deer (study, conservation, and hunting).

BIOGRAPHICAL/CRITICAL SOURCES:

PERIODICALS

New York Times Book Review, May 10, 1981, June 15, 1986.

Spectator, July 5, 1986.

Times (London), September 8, 1983, July 18, 1985.

Times Literary Supplement, February 12, 1982.

Washington Post, July 7, 1986.

Washington Post Book World, May 3, 1981, July 4, 1982.*

*   *   *

HART-DAVIS, Phyllida
   See BARSTOW, Phyllida

*   *   *

HASLAM, Gerald W.   1937-

PERSONAL: Born March 18, 1937, in Bakersfield, Calif.; son of Fred M. (an oil worker) and Lorraine (Johnson) Haslam; married Janice E. Pettichord, July 1, 1961; children: Frederick, Alexandra, Garth, Simone, Carlos. *Education:* San Francisco State College (now University), A.B., 1963, M.A., 1965; Washington State University, additional study, 1965-66; Union Graduate School, Ph.D., 1980.

ADDRESSES: Home—Box 969, Penngrove, Calif. 94951. *Office*—Sonoma State University, 1801 East Cotati Ave., Rohnert Park, Calif. 94928.

CAREER: Before and during his college years, Haslam worked as a roustabout in oilfields, picked, plowed, irrigated, and packed crops in the San Joaquin Valley, and was employed in stores, banks, and shops; San Francisco State College (now University), San Francisco, Calif., instructor in English, 1966-67; Sonoma State University, Rohnert Park, Calif., professor of English, 1967—. *Military service:* U.S. Army, 1958-60.

MEMBER: Western Writers of America, College Language Association, National Council of Teachers of English, Western Literature Association (vice-president, 1982; president-elect, 1983-84), California Teachers Association, California Association of Teachers of English, Nature Conservancy, Sierra Club, Trout Unlimited, Valley of the Moon Track Club, Napa Valley Runners' Club, Little Hills Striders.

AWARDS, HONORS: Arizona Quarterly nonfiction award, 1969, for "The Subtle Thread"; General Semantics Foundation grant; Joseph Henry Jackson Award, 1970, for *Okies;* Pushcart Prize, 1982; Bernard Ashton Raborg Award, 1985; Spur Award finalist, 1988.

WRITINGS:

(Editor) *Forgotten Pages of American Literature,* Houghton, 1970.

William Eastlake, Steck, 1970.

The Language of the Oilfields, Old Adobe Press, 1972.

Okies: Selected Stories, New West Publications, 1973, revised and enlarged edition, Peregrine Smith, 1975.

(Editor) *Western Writings,* University of New Mexico Press, 1974.

Jack Schaefer, Boise State College Western Writers, 1976.
Masks: A Novel, Old Adobe Press, 1976.
(Editor with James D. Houston) *California Heartland*, Capra, 1978.
The Wages of Sin, Duck Down Press, 1980.
Hawk Flights: Visions of the West, Seven Buffaloes Press, 1983.
Snapshots: Glimpses of the Other California, Devil Mountain Books, 1985.
The Man Who Cultivated Fire, Capra Press, 1987.
Voices of a Place, Devil Mountain Books, 1987.
(Co-editor) *A Literary History of the American West*, Texas Christian University Press, 1987.

OTHER

(Contributor) Gary Elder, editor, *The Far Side of the Storm*, Holmgangers, 1975.
(Contributor) Jonathan Eisen and David Fine, editors, *Unknown California*, Macmillan, 1985.
(Contributor) Gary Soto, editor, *California Childhood*, Creative Arts Books, 1988.

Also contributor to *Father Me Home Wind* and *American Ethnic Stories*. General editor, ''Western American Writers'' series, Everett/Edwards. Contributor to *Arizona Quarterly, College English, Western American Literature, Negro American Literature Forum, Nation, American History Illustrated, New Society, Southwest Review, Los Angeles Times Magazine, Pacific Discovery, This World, Sierra*, and other periodicals; has had many short stories and poems published. Former production editor, *ETC: A Review of General Semantics*. Editor, *Ecolit*.

WORK IN PROGRESS: The Great Central Valley: California's Heartland for University of California Press; *In the War Zone*, a novel; ''most attention being given to short stories, with continued forays into interpretive journalism.''

SIDELIGHTS: Gerald W. Haslam told *CA:* ''Most of my time and energy goes to the crafting of short stories, the large majority of which are set in the American West. I hope to achieve universality through original presentation of the particular, and to expand regional vistas and perceptions in the process.

''I was raised in a richly varied area—California's San Joaquin Valley—where oral tale-telling was a fine art. I was a good listener and I still am. Since no one ever told me a novel, I have always considered the story, not its longer counterpart, to be fiction's most natural expression. It is a continuing source of both wonder and satisfaction to me that I have evolved into a storyteller.

''Perhaps because I came to writing directly from the oral tradition, I've never yearned to be an *Author*, although I'm certainly pleased to see my work published. No, for me the act of writing is the most important thing, experiencing the emergence of a new reality. Like love, it remains an enduring thrill. I can't wait to face the typewriter each morning. I'm always amazed at what's in there. It's a great privilege to be able to write.''

AVOCATIONAL INTERESTS: Backpacking, flyfishing, competitive running, cycling.

                              *   *   *

HAULE, James M(ark)   1945-

PERSONAL: Born November 26, 1945, in Detroit, Mich.; son of Robert P. and Eileen M. Haule; married Margaret Ann

Cyzeska (an elementary school teacher), November 29, 1968; children: Patricia, Katherine. *Education:* University of Michigan, B.A., 1968; Wayne State University, M.A., 1970, Ph.D., 1974.

ADDRESSES: Home—1505 Hawk Ave., McAllen, Tex. 78504. *Office*—Department of English, Pan American University, Edinburg, Tex. 78539.

CAREER: Wayne State University, Detroit, Mich., instructor, 1974-75, assistant professor of English, 1975; Detroit College of Business, Dearborn, Mich., faculty coordinator, 1975-76; Detroit College of Business, Flint, Mich., associate professor of English and associate academic dean, 1976-78; Pan American University, Edinburg, Tex., associate professor, 1978-85, professor of English, 1985—, assistant dean, 1978-80, director of Humanities Community Services, 1980-84. Member of James Joyce Foundation.

MEMBER: Modern Language Association of America, Conference of College Teachers of English, Virginia Woolf Society (founding member), James Joyce Foundation, South Central Modern Language Association, Rio Grande Valley Conference of Teachers of English.

AWARDS, HONORS: Distinguished Faculty award, Pan American University, 1985.

WRITINGS:

(Contributor) Patricia De La Fuente, Jan Seale, and Donald Fritz, editors, *James Dickey: Splintered Sunlight*, Pan American University, 1979.
(With P. H. Smith, Jr.) *A Concordance to ''The Waves'' by Virginia Woolf*, Oxford Microform Publication, 1981.
(With Smith) *A Concordance to ''Between the Acts'' by Virginia Woolf*, Oxford Microform Publications, 1983.
(With Smith) *A Concordance to ''To the Lighthouse'' by Virginia Woolf*, Oxford Microform Publications, 1983.
(With Smith) *A Condordance to ''The Years'' by Virginia Woolf*, Oxford Microform Publications, 1984.
(With Smith) *A Concordance to ''Mrs. Dalloway'' by Virginia Woolf*, Oxford Microform Publications, 1985.
(With Smith) *A Concordance to ''Orlando'' by Virginia Woolf*, Oxford Microform Publications, 1985.
(With Smith) *A Concordance to ''Night and Day'' by Virginia Woolf*, Oxford Microform Publications, 1986.
(With Smith) *A Concordance to ''Jacob's Room'' by Virginia Woolf*, University of Michigan Press, 1988.
(With Smith) *A Concordance to ''The Voyage Out'' by Virginia Woolf*, University of Michigan Press, 1988.

General editor of ''Living Author Series,'' Pan American University, 1980—. Contributor of articles and reviews to literature journals, including *James Joyce Quarterly, Contemporary Literature, Literature and Pschology, Colby Library Quarterly*, and *Critique: Studies in Modern Fiction*.

WORK IN PROGRESS: A union concordance to all of the novels of Virginia Woolf for Garland Publishing; production of a data base of Woolf's fiction on CD/ROM.

SIDELIGHTS: James M. Haule commented in *Contemporary Literature* on the practice of studying an author's letters, diaries, and discarded drafts: ''The value of searching through the clutter of creative effort lies not in the secrets revealed about the life of the author, but rather in what we learn about the process of creation, the nature of style and, ultimately, what the search tells us about ourselves.''

Haule discovered a Virginia Woolf typescript of an early version of the "Time Passes" section of *To the Lighthouse,* which many had thought lost. Edited and with commentary, this section was published in *Twentieth Century Literature* in the fall of 1983.

BIOGRAPHICAL/CRITICAL SOURCES:

PERIODICALS

Contemporary Literature, winter, 1982.

*   *   *

HEADLEY, Elizabeth
    See HARRISON, Elizabeth Cavanna

*   *   *

HEBBLETHWAITE, Brian Leslie   1939-

PERSONAL: Born January 3, 1939, in Bristol, England; son of Cyril H. and Sarah Anne (Nash) Hebblethwaite. *Education:* Magdalen College, Oxford, B.A., 1961, M.A., 1967; Magdalene College, Cambridge, B.A., 1964, M.A., 1968. *Politics:* Social Democrat. *Religion:* Church of England.

ADDRESSES: Home and office—Queens' College, Cambridge University, Cambridge, England.

CAREER: Ordained priest of Church of England, 1966; Church of England, Bury, England, curate, 1965-68; Cambridge University, Cambridge, England, fellow and dean of chapel at Queens' College, 1969—, assistant lecturer in divinity, 1972-77, lecturer in divinity, 1977—.

MEMBER: Aristotelian Society, Societas Ethica, Society for the Study of Theology, Royal Institute of Philosophy.

WRITINGS:

Evil, Suffering, and Religion, Sheldon Press, 1976.
The Problems of Theology, Cambridge University Press, 1980.
(Editor with John Hick) *Christianity and Other Religions,* Collins, 1980.
Christian Ethics in the Modern Age, Westminster, 1982.
(Editor with Stewart Sutherland) *The Philosophical Frontiers of Christian Theology,* Cambridge University Press, 1982.
The Christian Hope: An Introduction to Eschatology, Marshall, Morgan & Scott, 1984.
Preaching through the Christian Year 10: Sermons from Queens' College, Cambridge, Mowbrays, 1985.
The Incarnation: Collected Essays in Christology, Cambridge University Press, 1987.
The Ocean of Truth: A Defence of Objective Theism, Cambridge University Press, 1988.

Ethics editor for *Theologische Realenzyklopaedie,* 1980—.

SIDELIGHTS: Brian Leslie Hebblethwaite wrote: "I am interested in the critical study of Christian theology, in the context of the comparative study of religion, and in its relation to modern philosophy and science. The ethical implications of Christian theology are also my concern."

Sarah Coakley, in a *Time Literary Supplement* review, described Hebblethwaite's *The Problems of Theology* as "an introductory methodological work [which] provides an admirably lucid discussion of the place of theology in the university, and at the same time (though this is not a stated intention) reads something like a defense of the present Cambridge tripos in theology and religious studies." The book opens with Hebblethwaite's definition of his discipline as "*rational* thought about God" and goes on to indicate how such fields as comparative religion, philosophy, sociology, and anthropology relate to modern theological study. The remaining text is devoted to a discussion of varying points of view on general theological topics, such as revelation and ethics, and concludes with Hebblethwaite's arguments for specific Christian doctrines (Trinity, incarnation) which he believes can be proved; as Coakley observed, the author "recommends the 'cumulative case' method whereby a range of arguments, none of them individually conclusive, can none the less convince cumulatively."

AVOCATIONAL INTERESTS: Music (especially opera), literature, fell-walking, travel.

BIOGRAPHICAL/CRITICAL SOURCES:

PERIODICALS

Interpretation, January, 1982.
New Blackfriars, February, 1982.
Theologia Evangelica, September, 1981.
Times Literary Supplement, October 31, 1980.

*   *   *

HEBERT, Jacques   1923-

PERSONAL: Surname pronounced Hay-bear; born June 21, 1923, in Montreal, Quebec, Canada; son of Louis-Philippe (a doctor) and Denise (Saint-Onge) Hebert; married Therese DesJardins, October 20, 1951; children: Michel, Pascale, Isabelle, Bruno, Sophie. *Education:* Attended College Sainte-Marie, Montreal, and University St. Dunstan, Charlottetown; Ecole Des Hautes Etudes Commercials de Montreal, license en sciences commerciales.

ADDRESSES: Home—3480 Prud-homme, Montreal, Quebec, Canada H4A 3H4. *Office*—Senate Parliament Bldg., Ottawa, Ontario, Canada K1A 0A4.

CAREER: Editions de l'Homme, Montreal, Quebec, founder, 1958; Editions du Jour, Montreal, founder, president, and director general, 1961-74; Canada World Youth, Montreal, founder and president, beginning 1971; member of senate, Canadian Parliament, Ottawa, Ontario, 1983. Founder and president, Katimavik, 1976—. Commissioner, Canadian Radio Television Commission, 1971-81. Co-chairman, Federal Cultural Review Committee, 1981-82. Order of Canada, officer, 1979.

WRITINGS:

Autour des trois Ameriques, Beauchemin, 1948.
Autour de l'Afrique, Fides, 1950.
Aicha l'Africaine (stories), Fides, 1950.
Aventure autour du Monde, Fides, 1952.
Nouvelle aventure en Afrique, Fides, 1953.
Coffin etait innocent, Editions de l'Homme, 1958.
Scandale a Bordeaux, Editions de l'Homme, 1959.
(With Pierre Elliott Trudeau) *Deux innocents en Chine rouge,* Editions de l'Homme, 1960, translation published as *Two Innocents in Red China,* Oxford University Press (Toronto), 1968.
J'accuse les assassins de Coffin, Editions du Jour, 1963, translation published as *I Accuse the Assassins of Coffin,* 1964.
Trois jours en prison, Club du Livre du Quebec, 1965.

Les Ecoeurants (novel), Editions du Jour, 1966, translation published as *The Temple on the River*, Harvest House, 1967.

Ah! mes Aieux!, Editions du Jour, 1968.

Obscenite et Liberte, Editions du Jour, 1970.

Blablabla du bout de monde, Editions du Jour, 1971.

The World Is Round, McClelland & Stewart, 1976.

Have Them Build a Tower Together, McClelland & Stewart, 1979.

(With Maurice F. Strong) *The Great Building-Bee*, General Publishing, 1980.

L'Affaire Coffin, Domino, 1980, translation published as *The Coffin Affair*, General Publishing, 1982.

La jeunesse des annees 80: Etat d'urgencer, Editions Heritage, 1982.

Voyager en pays tropical, Boreal Express, 1984, translation published as *Travelling in Tropical Countries*, Hurtig Publishers, 1986.

Trois semaines dans le hall du Senat, Editions de l'Homme, 1986, translation published as *Twenty-one Days: One Man's Fight for Canada's Youth*, Optimum Publishing, 1986.

*   *   *

HEILMAN, Robert Bechtold   1906-

PERSONAL: Born July 18, 1906, in Philadelphia, Pa.; son of Edgar James (a clergyman) and Mary Alice (Bechtold) Heilman; married Elizabeth Wiltbank, 1927 (divorced, 1934); married Ruth Delavan Champlin, July 31, 1935; children: (second marriage) Champlin. *Education:* Lafayette College, A.B., 1927; Tufts University, graduate study, 1927-28; Ohio State University, M.A., 1930; Harvard University, M.A., 1931, Ph.D., 1935. *Politics:* "Swing voter." *Religion:* Lutheran.

ADDRESSES: Home—4554 45th Ave. N.E., Seattle, Wash. 98105. *Office*—Department of English, GN-30, University of Washington, Seattle, Wash. 98195.

CAREER: University of Maine, Orono, instructor in English, 1930-33, 1934-35; Louisiana State University, Baton Rouge, instructor, 1935-36, assistant professor, 1936-42, associate professor, 1942-46, professor of English, 1946-48; University of Washington, Seattle, professor of English, 1948-76, professor emeritus, 1976—, chairman of department, 1948-71. Arnold Professor of English, Whitman College, 1977.

MEMBER: International Association of University Professors of English, International Shakespeare Association, Modern Language Association of America (member of national executive council, 1966-69), National Council of Teachers of English (distinguished lecturer, 1968), American Association of University Professors (member of national executive council, 1962-65), Shakespeare Association of America (trustee, 1977-80), Philological Association of Pacific Coast (president, 1958), Phi Beta Kappa (senator, 1967-85; member of executive committee, 1973-82; visiting scholar, 1983-84).

AWARDS, HONORS: Arizona Quarterly Essay Prize, 1956, for an essay on *Othello; Explicator* Award (for criticism), 1957, for *Magic in the Web: Action and Language in Othello;* Huntington Library grant, 1959; Longview Award, 1960, for essay in *Texas Quarterly;* Guggenheim fellowship, 1964-65, and 1975-76; D.Litt., Lafayette College, 1967; National Endowment for the Humanities senior fellow, 1971-72; LL.D., Grinnell College, 1971; L.H.D., Kenyon College, 1973; HH.D., Whitman College, 1977; Litt.D., University of the South, 1978;

Christian Gauss Prize of Phi Beta Kappa, 1979, for *The Ways of the World: Comedy and Society*.

WRITINGS:

America in English Fiction, 1760-1800, Louisiana State University Press, 1937, reprinted, Hippocrene Books, 1968.

This Great Stage: Image and Structure in King Lear, Louisiana State University Press, 1948, reprinted, Greenwood, 1976.

Magic in the Web: Action and Language in Othello, University Press of Kentucky, 1956, reprinted, Greenwood Press, 1977.

Tragedy and Melodrama: Versions of Experience, University of Washington Press, 1968.

The Iceman, the Arsonist, and the Troubled Agent: Tragedy and Melodrama on the Modern Stage, University of Washington Press, 1973.

The Ghost on the Ramparts and Other Essays in the Humanities, University of Georgia Press, 1973.

The Ways of the World: Comedy and Society, University of Washington Press, 1978.

EDITOR AND AUTHOR OF CRITICAL INTRODUCTION

Jonathan Swift, *Gulliver's Travels*, Modern Library, 1950, revised edition, 1969.

Swift, *A Tale of a Tub* [and] *The Battle of the Books*, Modern Library, 1950.

An Anthology of English Drama before Shakespeare, Rinehart, 1952.

Joseph Conrad, *Lord Jim*, Rinehart, 1957.

Thomas Hardy, *The Mayor of Casterbridge*, Riverside, 1962.

George Eliot, *Silas Marner*, Riverside, 1962.

William Shakespeare, *Cymbeline*, Pelican, 1964.

Euripides, *Alcestis*, Chandler, 1965.

Hardy, *Jude the Obscure*, Harper, 1966.

Shakespeare, *The Taming of the Shrew*, Signet, 1966.

Hardy, *Tess of the D'Ubervilles*, Bantam, 1971.

Shakespeare; the Tragedies: Twentieth Century Views, New Perspectives, Prentice-Hall, 1984.

EDITOR

Aspects of Democracy, Louisiana State University Press, 1941, reprinted, Ayer, 1968.

Aspects of a World at War, Louisiana State University Press, 1943.

(With Cleanth Brooks) *Understanding Drama* (textbook), Henry Holt, 1945, enlarged edition, 1948.

Modern Short Stories: A Critical Anthology (textbook), Harcourt, 1950, reprinted, Greenwood Press, 1971.

CONTRIBUTOR

T. A. Kirby and N. M. Caffee, editors, *Studies for W. A. Read*, Louisiana State University Press, 1941.

Allen Tate, editor, *A Southern Vanguard*, Prentice-Hall, 1947.

Louis Rubin and Robert Jacobs, editors, *Southern Renascence*, Johns Hopkins Press, 1953.

Robert Rathburn and Martin Steinman, editors, *From Jane Austen to Joseph Conrad*, University of Minnesota Press, 1958.

James G. McManaway, editor, *Shakespeare 400*, Holt, 1964.

Edward A. Bloom, editor, *Shakespeare 1564-1964*, Brown University Press, 1965.

Gerald W. Chapman, editor, *Essays on Shakespeare*, Princeton University Press, 1966.

Kenneth Muir, editor, *Shakespeare Survey 19*, Cambridge University Press, 1966.

Kirby and W. Olive, editors, *Essays in Honor of E. L. Marilla*, Louisiana State University Press, 1970.

David Madden, editor, *American Dreams, American Nightmares*, Southern Illinois University Press, 1970.

Brom Weber, *Sense and Sensibility in Twentieth-Century Writings*, Southern Illinois University Press, 1970.

John Halperin, editor, *The Theory of the Novel: New Essays*, Oxford University Press, 1974.

Halperin, editor, *Jane Austen: Bicentenary Essays*, Cambridge University Press, 1975.

Lewis P. Simpson, editor, *The Possibilities of Order: Cleanth Brooks and His Work*, Louisiana State University Press, 1976.

Walter Edens and others, editors, *Teaching Shakespeare*, Princeton University Press, 1976.

William H. New, editor, *A Political Art: Essays and Images in Honour of George Woodcock*, University of British Columbia Press, 1978.

Anne Smith, editor, *The Novels of Thomas Hardy*, Vision Press (London), 1979.

Peggy W. Prenshaw, editor, *Eudora Welty: Critical Essays*, University Press of Mississippi, 1979.

John Alvis and Thomas G. West, editors, *Shakespeare as Political Thinker*, Carolina Academic Press, 1981.

Philip Highfill, editor, *Shakespeare's Craft: Eight Lectures*, Southern Illinois Press, 1982.

William C. Harvard and Walter Sullivan, editors, *A Band of Prophets: The Vanderbilt Agrarians after Fifty Years*, Louisiana State University Press, 1982.

Gordon S. Haight and Rosemary T. VanArdsel, editors, *George Eliot: A Centenary Tribute*, Macmillan, 1982.

Charlton Laird, editor, *Walter Van Tilberg Clark: Critiques*, University of Nevada Press, 1983.

Donald K. Anderson, Jr., editor, *Concord in Discord: Essays on John Ford*, AMS Press, 1986.

OTHER

Also author of the *Charliad* (verse), 1973. Contributor to *English Institute Annual*, Columbia University Press, 1949, and *The Range of English: NCTE Distinguished Lectures*, National Council of Teachers of English, 1968, and *Dictionary of American Biography*, 1981. Contributor of essays and reviews to journals. Member of editorial board, *Poetry Northwest*, 1962, *Studies in the Novel*, 1966—, *Shakespeare Studies*, 1966—, *Modern Language Quarterly*, 1973-77, *Sewanee Review*, 1974—, *Mississippi Studies in English*, 1981—, and *Interim*, 1987—. Regular reviewer for Phi Beta Kappa *Key Reporter*, 1959—.

WORK IN PROGRESS: A book-length study of farce and its relation to other dramatic forms.

AVOCATIONAL INTERESTS: Watching football games; doing chores at a hideaway shack on a high bank overlooking Puget Sound.

*   *   *

HEMMINGS, F(rederic) W(illiam) J(ohn)   1920-

PERSONAL: Born December 13, 1920, in Southampton, England; son of Frederick James (a schoolmaster) and Ethel (Jones) Hemmings; married Rona Thomas, April 18, 1942 (divorced, 1970); married Margaret Neilson (an advertising executive),

July 10, 1972; children: Iona Hemmings Seymour, Julian. *Education:* Exeter College, Oxford, B.A., 1941, D.Phil., 1949.

ADDRESSES: Home—46 Southernhay Rd., Leicester LE2 3TJ, England. *Agent*—A. D. Peters & Co. Ltd., 10 Buckingham St., London WC2N 6BU, England.

CAREER: University of Leicester, Leicester, England, assistant lecturer, 1948-50, lecturer, 1950-54, reader, 1954-63, professor of French, 1963-85. Visiting professor, Yale University, 1966-67. *Military Service:* British Army, Intelligence Corps, 1941-46; became captain.

MEMBER: Society for French Studies, Society of Authors.

WRITINGS:

The Russian Novel in France, 1884-1914, Oxford University Press, 1950.

Emile Zola, Oxford University Press, 1953, 2nd edition, 1970.

Stendhal: A Study of His Novels, Oxford University Press, 1964.

Balzac: An Interpretation of "La Comedie Humaine," Random House, 1967.

Culture and Society in France, 1848-1898: Dissidents and Philistines, Scribner, 1971.

(Editor) *The Age of Realism*, Penguin, 1974.

The Life and Times of Emile Zola, Scribner, 1977.

(Translator) Charles Baudelaire, *City Blues*, St. Bernard Press, 1977.

Alexandre Dumas: The King of Romance, Scribner, 1979 (published in England as *The King of Romance: A Portrait of Alexandre Dumas*, H. Hamilton, 1979).

Baudelaire the Damned: A Biography, Scribner, 1982.

Culture and Society in France, 1789-1848, Leicester University Press, 1987.

Reviewer for magazines and newspapers, including *New Statesman* and *Listener*.

WORK IN PROGRESS: The Theatre Industry in France, 1760-1910.

SIDELIGHTS: A former professor of French at the University of Leicester, F. W. J. Hemmings has written several biographies on famous French literary figures. In his *The Life and Times of Emile Zola*, for example, Hemmings "has collated the new material now available to scholars," writes V. S. Pritchett in the *New York Review of Books*. The critic calls the book "thoughtful, inquiring, and well-written, . . . command[ing] a very necessary perspective. It puts the light and shade on a complex character whom we had seen only in black and white." *Times Literary Supplement* contributor Colin Smethurst similarly believes that "this biography is decidedly not an academic's compendium of all the known facts about Zola, but rather a synthesis of them," making it "a thoroughly readable book." Hemmings's treatment in *Alexandre Dumas: The King of Romance* likewise "makes the story fresh, handling his larger-than-life subject with humor and warmth," comments Jean Strouse in *Newsweek*. "As an experienced biographer," comments Robert Atwan in the *Los Angeles Times Book Review*, in *Baudelaire the Damned* "Hemmings knows how to serve up a highly satisfying mixture of life story and literary career." Victor Brombert also sees an appropriate symmetry to the author's portrait of Baudelaire: "Mr. Hemmings keeps his balance in this crisp biography," the critic remarks in the *New York Times Book Review*. "He does not overstate any theme or any one problem in Baudelaire's life. His judgments are always objective and sound and he has firm command of the work of his predecessors, yet his writing is not lacking in incisiveness or fervor.'' Brombert concludes by calling *Baudelaire the Damned* ''a gracefully written and very useful book.''

Hemmings told *CA:* ''I regard myself as an uninventive or noncreative writer. The business of planning, researching, and composing is what interests me, much more than what I am writing about; and the subjects of my books have all arisen out of my professional work as an academic specialist in French literature, simply because, as it happened, they were the easiest things for me to write about. Probably I am not, by nature, very imaginative, which is why I cannot see myself ever writing a novel, not even a campus-novel. But writing biographies, which is what I have been tending to do over the past few years, is a good halfway house between pure creative writing, for which I lack the gift, and writing 'lit-crit,' which is how I started, but which I feel has too circumscribed a market and too ingrown a public to provide much satisfaction for an author these days.''

BIOGRAPHICAL/CRITICAL SOURCES:

PERIODICALS

Los Angeles Times Book Review, December 5, 1982.
Newsweek, March 10, 1980.
New Yorker, January 30, 1978, October 18, 1982.
New York Review of Books, November 10, 1977, December 2, 1982.
New York Times Book Review, November 21, 1982.
Times Literary Supplement, February 24, 1978, November 23, 1979, January 21, 1983.
Washington Post, March 20, 1980.
Washington Post Book World, October 30, 1977.

*   *   *

HENDERSON, G. D. S.
See HENDERSON, George (David Smith)

*   *   *

HENDERSON, George (David Smith)   1931-
(G. D. S. Henderson)

PERSONAL: Born May 7, 1931, in Aberdeen, Scotland; son of George David (a professor of ecclesiastical history) and Janet (Smith) Henderson; married Isabel Bisset Murray (a librarian at National Library of Scotland), September 6, 1957; children: Matthew Magnus Murray, Katherine Isabella Murray. *Education:* University of Aberdeen, M.A., 1953; University of London, B.A., 1956; Cambridge University, M.A. and Ph.D., 1961. *Politics:* Conservative. *Religion:* Christian.

ADDRESSES: Home—15 Hills Ave., Cambridge, England. *Office*—Department of the History of Art, 1-5 Scroope Terrace, Cambridge CB2 1PX, England.

CAREER: Research fellow at Barber Institute of Fine Art, University of Birmingham, Birmingham, England, 1960-61, and Downing College, Cambridge University, Cambridge, England, 1961-64; University of Manchester, Manchester, England, lecturer in history of art, 1963-66; University of Edinburgh, Edinburgh, Scotland, lecturer in history of art, 1966-73; Cambridge University, lecturer in the history of art and fellow of Downing College, 1974—.

AWARDS, HONORS: Reginald Taylor Prize of British Archaeological Association, 1962, for paper ''The Sources of the Genesis Cycle at St.-Savin-sur-Gartempe.''

WRITINGS:

Gothic, Penguin, 1967.
Chartres, Penguin, 1968.
Early Medieval, Penguin, 1972, revised edition, 1977.
(Editor with Giles Robertson) *Studies in Memory of David Talbot Rice,* Edinburgh University Press, 1975.
Bede and the Visual Arts, Parish of Jarrow, 1980.
(Under name G. D. S. Henderson) *Losses and Lacunae in Early Insular Art: The Third G. N. Garmonsway Memorial Lecture Delivered on 9 May, 1975 in the University of York,* appendix by T. J. Brown, Ebor, 1982.
Studies in English Bible Illustration, two volumes, Pindar, 1985.
From Durrow to Kells, Thames & Hudson, 1988.

Contributor of articles on the style and iconography of English medieval manuscripts to professional journals.*

*   *   *

HENDERSON, M(arilyn) R(uth)   1927-
(Marilyn Granbeck; pseudonyms: Christina Carroll, Nick Carter, Ben Grant, Adam Hamilton, Clayton Moore, Van Saxon)

PERSONAL: Born September 7, 1927, in Brooklyn, N.Y.; daughter of Rudolph (a machinist) and Irene (Jacobsen) Podesta; married Robert Granbeck, December 31, 1949 (divorced, 1972); married Morrice R. Henderson, December 28, 1979 (died, 1986); children: (first marriage) Christine Ellen, Leslie Carolyn, Robert Alan, Laurie Ann. *Education:* Brooklyn College (now Brooklyn College of the City University of New York), B.A., 1947.

ADDRESSES: Home—Reno, Nev.

CAREER: Institute of Paper Chemistry, Appleton, Wis., research chemist, 1947-48; Krimko Corp., Chicago, Ill., research chemist, 1948-50; University of Minnesota, Minneapolis, research chemist, 1952-58; writer, 1962—.

MEMBER: Mystery Writers of America (regional vice-president of Southern California chapter, 1976-79), Authors Guild, Minneapolis Writers Workshop (president, 1967-68).

WRITINGS:

If I Should Die, Doubleday, 1985.
By Reason Of. . . , Doubleday, 1986.

UNDER NAME MARILYN GRANBECK

Finding Your Job Workbook, Finney (Minneapolis), 1969, reprinted as *Finding Your Job Skillbook,* 1980.
Metals and Plastics, Dillon, 1974.
The Hidden Box Mystery, Scholastic Book Services, 1975.
Social Work Careers, photographs by Chuck Freedman, F. Watts, 1977.
Summer at Ravenswood, Scholastic Book Services, 1977.
The Magician's Daughter, Manor, 1977.
Celia, Jove, 1977.
Elena, Jove, 1977.
Winds of Desire, Jove, 1978.
The Mystery of the Jade Princess, Scholastic Book Services, 1979.

Also author of *Maura, Lorielle,* and *The Fifth Jade of Heaven.*

UNDER PSEUDONYM ADAM HAMILTON; WITH ARTHUR MOORE

Zaharan Pursuit, Berkley Publishing, 1974.
Xander Pursuit, Berkley Publishing, 1974.
Yashar Pursuit, Berkley Publishing, 1975.

UNDER PSEUDONYM CLAYTON MOORE

End of Reckoning, Berkley Publishing, 1974.
The Corrupters, Berkley Publishing, 1974.

UNDER PSEUDONYM VAN SAXON; WITH ARTHUR MOORE

Wyss Pursuit, Berkley Publishing, 1975.
Hollywood Hit Man, Zebra Publications, 1975.

OTHER

(Under pseudonym Ben Grant) *Alice Dies Twice,* Major, 1975.
(Under pseudonym Nick Carter) *Assignment Intercept,* Award, 1976.
(Under pseudonym Christina Carroll) *Paris,* Ace Books, 1986.

WORK IN PROGRESS: A historical romance set in New York, Pittsburgh, and Cairo, Ill. in 1849.

SIDELIGHTS: M. R. Henderson once told *CA:* "A recurrent back injury that made it impossible for me to stand in a laboratory was the incentive to turn to writing. I believe in keeping fit by jogging, swimming, regular exercise. I love to travel and find that the most interesting (and easy) part of getting into a book. I have no competency in foreign languages, though I have been struggling with Spanish since my high school days. I was not a good history student and am now learning all the history I didn't in school."

*   *   *

HENDERSON, Michael (Douglas)   1932-

PERSONAL: Born March 15, 1932, in London, England; came to the United States, 1978; son of Arthur Douglas (a businessman) and Erina (Tilly) Henderson; married Erica Mildred Hallowes, March 16, 1966; children: Juliet Rachel Erina. *Education:* Attended schools in England and the United States. *Religion:* Christian.

ADDRESSES: Home—10605 Southwest Terwilliger Place, Portland, Ore. 97219.

CAREER: KOAP-TV, Portland, Ore., moderator of "World Press in Review" program, 1979-81; KBOO-Radio, Portland, commentator, 1981—; Oregon Public Broadcasting Radio (KOAC/KOAP-FM), Portland, 1987—. Columnist, *Lake Oswego Review,* Lake Oswego, Ore. Voluntary religious worker with Moral Re-Armament, 1950—. Cable television host and free-lance journalist.

MEMBER: World Affairs Council of Oregon (president, 1983—), English-speaking Union (president, 1982-83), Willamette Writers (president, 1983), Institute of Journalists, Society of Professional Journalists, Sigma Delta Chi.

AWARDS, HONORS: George Washington Honor Medal, Freedoms Foundation at Valley Forge, 1986, for *A Different Accent;* Academy of Religions Broadcasting Award of Excellence for radio commentary, 1987.

WRITINGS:

From India With Hope, Grosvenor, 1972.

Experiment With Untruth: India Under Emergency, Macmillan (India), 1977, South Asia Books, 1979.
A Different Accent (a collection of transcripted radio talks), Grosvenor, 1985.
On History's Coat-tails, Grosvenor, 1988.

SIDELIGHTS: Michael Henderson once told *CA:* "I was interviewed by a journalist ... who asked me, 'What is your philosophy of writing?' I was a bit taken aback. I suppose I shouldn't have been. I had just never been asked it like that before, never really taken time to think out why I write what I write. I had taken my writing philosophy for granted; seen it simply as an extension of how I lived and what I lived for.

"That journalist's question to me," continued Henderson, "has caused me to consider the why of my commentaries. Basically I write and speak to change the way people live and think. I write to share insights, lessons, attitudes, and hopes I have gleaned as the fruit of contact with very fine men and women all over the world, many of them associated with the program of Moral Re-Armament.

"One motive I have [for writing] is to enlarge horizons. In this dangerous age in which we live it is vital to be knowledgeable about other countries and what motivates their peoples. We are, whether we like it or not, interdependent. What is in the world interest is in our national interest, though we don't always realize it.

Henderson concludes: "There are so many ways in which society gets polarized, and I would like to work for a greater tolerance and understanding of those who differ from us. I would like in my writing to reduce the us and them syndrome. In the peace movement people who should be working together are at odds.... As Peter Howard, the English journalist to whom I owe most of what I know about writing, said about his own work: 'I write to encourage men to accept the growth in character that is essential if civilization is to survive.'

BIOGRAPHICAL/CRITICAL SOURCES:

PERIODICALS

Christian Science Monitor, September 20, 1985.
The Oregonian, February 6, 1983.

*   *   *

HICKS, Harvey
See STRATEMEYER, Edward L.

*   *   *

HILL, Clifford S.   1927-

PERSONAL: Born June 23, 1927, in London, England; son of Horace William (a London telephone manager) and Miriam (Cooper) Hill; married Monica Ford, August 10, 1957; children: Jennifer, Alison, Stephen. *Education:* Attended Paton Theological College, Nottingham, England, 1949-52; University of London, B.D., 1960; London School of Economics and Political Science, M.A., 1964; University of Nottingham, Ph.D., 1972.

ADDRESSES: Home—35 Dorchester Ct., London SE24 9OX, England. *Office*—*Prophecy Today,* 175 Tower Bridge Rd., London SE1 2AB, England.

CAREER: Ordained Congregational minister. Electronics research scientist on radar and guided missiles, British government, 1943-49; Harlesden Congregational Church, London, England, minister, 1952-57; High Cross Congregational Church, Tottenham, London, minister, 1957-68; University of London, London, senior lecturer in sociology, 1968-75; Newham County Renewal Programme, Newham, England, director, 1970-78; national director of evangelism, Decade of Evangelism, Evangelical Alliance, 1978-80; New Way London, London, director, 1981-83; director of British Parliamentary Group Video Enquiry, 1983-85; *Prophecy Today* (international magazine), editor in chief, 1985—. Broadcaster on race relations. Adviser on race relations for British Television. *Military service:* British Army, research with Royal Electrical and Mechanical Engineers, 1947-49.

MEMBER: Institute of Race Relations, Convocation of the University of London.

WRITINGS:

Black and White in Harmony, Hodder & Stoughton, 1958.
West Indian Migrants and the London Churches, Oxford University Press, 1963.
How Colour Prejudiced Is Britain?, Gollancz, 1965.
(Editor) *Race: A Christian Symposium,* Gollancz, 1968.
Immigration and Integration: A Study of the Settlement of Coloured Minorities in Britain, Pergamon, 1969.
Black Churches: West Indian & African Sects in Britain, British Council of Churches, 1971.
Renewal in the Inner City, Methodist Home Mission Department, 1976.
Towards the Dawn, Collins & World, 1980.
The Day Comes, Collins & World, 1982.
Tell My People I Love Them, Collins & World, 1984.
A Prophetic People, Collins & World, 1986.

Also author of *Family and Marriage,* a symposium on West Indians in England. Author of weekly religion column for *Willesden Chronicle,* 1953-57. Contributor of articles on religion and sociology to newspapers and periodicals.

SIDELIGHTS: Clifford S. Hill has traveled extensively in the West Indies. He took a leading role in organizing West Indian immigrants after the Notting Hill riots in London. Hill commented on his work for *CA:* "My writings are basically in the field of the sociology of religion, bringing together sociological insights of modern society and a biblical perspective aimed at discovering what God is saying today with the immense racial, social, economic and political issues facing mankind."

*   *   *

HIRSCH, E(ric) D(onald), Jr.   1928-

PERSONAL: Born March 22, 1928, in Memphis, Tenn.; son of Eric Donald (a businessman) and Leah (Aschaffenburg) Hirsch; married Mary Pope, 1958; children: John, Frederick, Elizabeth. *Education:* Cornell University, B.A., 1950; Yale University, M.A., 1953, Ph.D., 1957.

ADDRESSES: Home—2006 Pine Top Rd., Charlottesville, Va. 22903. *Office*—Department of English, University of Virginia, Charlottesville, Va. 22901.

CAREER: Yale University, New Haven, Conn., instructor, 1956-60, assistant professor, 1960-63, associate professor of English, 1963-66; University of Virginia, Charlottesville, professor, 1966-72, William R. Kenan Professor of English, 1973—, chairman of department, 1968-71, 1981-82, director of composition, 1971—. Member of faculty, School of Crit-

icism and Theory, Northwestern University, summer, 1981; Bateson Lecturer, Oxford University, 1983. Trustee and founder, Cultural Literacy Foundation. *Military service:* U.S. Naval Reserve, 1950-54; active duty, 1950-52.

MEMBER: American Academy of Arts and Sciences (fellow), Modern Language Association of America, Keats-Shelley Association, Byron Society, American Rhododendron Society.

AWARDS, HONORS: Fulbright fellow, 1955; Morse fellow, 1960-61; Guggenheim fellow, 1964-65; *Explicator* (magazine) Prize, 1964, for *Innocence and Experience: An Introduction to Blake;* National Endowment for the Humanities senior fellow, 1971-72, 1980-81; Wesleyan University Center for the Humanities fellow, 1973, 1974; Princeton University Council of the Humanities fellow, 1976; Stanford University Center for Advanced Study in the Behavioral Sciences fellow, 1980-81; Australian National University Humanities Research Centre fellow, 1982.

WRITINGS:

Wordsworth and Schelling: A Typological Study of Romanticism, Yale University Press, 1960.
Innocence and Experience: An Introduction to Blake, Yale University Press, 1964.
(Contributor) Harold Bloom and Frederick W. Hilles, editors, *From Sensibility to Romanticism: Essays Presented to Frederick A. Pottle,* Oxford University Press, 1965.
Validity in Interpretation, Yale University Press, 1967.
The Aims of Interpretation, University of Chicago Press, 1976.
The Philosophy of Composition, University of Chicago Press, 1977.
(Contributor) Thomas F. Rugh and Erin R. Silva, editors, *History as a Tool in Critical Interpretation: A Symposium,* Brigham Young University Press, 1978.
(Contributor) Paul Hernadi, editor, *What Is Literature?,* Indiana University Press, 1978.
Cultural Literacy: What Every American Needs to Know, Houghton, 1987.
(With Joseph Kett and James Trefil) *The Dictionary of Cultural Literacy: What Every American Needs to Know* (Literary Guild selection), Houghton, 1988.

OTHER

Contributor of essays and articles to *American Educator, Times Literary Supplement, Critical Inquiry, College English,* and *American Scholar.*

SIDELIGHTS: After spending a quarter of a century publishing works that have had a "significant impact on recent American literary criticism and theory," according to Brian G. Caraher of the *Dictionary of Literary Biography,* E. D. Hirsch, Jr., published *Cultural Literacy: What Every American Needs to Know,* a book that hit the bestseller lists and raised a storm of controversy. Hirsch argues in the book that many Americans are ignorant of the shared terms and concepts of their society, and that this renders them incapable of participating fully in that society. *Cultural Literacy* brought Hirsch to the attention of a wide reading audience and pushed him into founding the Cultural Literacy Foundation, an organization promoting the teaching of a shared core of knowledge in the nation's schools.

Cultural Literacy begins with a recitation of just how ill-informed contemporary students are. Hirsch quotes studies showing that the majority of high school students do not know when the American Civil War took place; half cannot identify Winston Churchill or Joseph Stalin; three-fourths do not recognize Walt Whitman or Henry David Thoreau; and many are unaware of when Christopher Columbus discovered America. Their knowledge of science, geography, the arts, and other subjects is also weak. Such a lack of basic information renders much of what these students read meaningless. They are not illiterate, but they are unable to identify people and places discussed in what they read, and are baffled by historic, scientific, and literary terms or allusions. "That so many people should be stumbling around in this kind of fog," writes John Gross in the *New York Times,* "is an obvious cause for concern. It implies a coarsening in the quality of life, and a drying-up of invaluable common traditions. It makes it harder for us to communicate with one another. For the children of the poor and disadvantaged, it represents a formidable barrier to progress." "Most Americans can make out the words," James W. Tuttleton explains in *Commentary*. "The literacy we need, according to Hirsch, is *cultural* literacy."

As a means of identifying some of the information that cultural illiterates lack, Hirsch includes a 63-page list of 5,000 names, terms, and phrases he considers to be essential to cultural literacy. Compiled with the assistance of two academic colleagues, historian Joseph Kett and physicist James Trefil, the list includes such varied items as "absolute zero," "flapper," "Sherlock Holmes," "critical mass," and "empiricism." A complete and thorough knowledge of each item is not needed, Hirsch explains. To understand a text a reader needs schemata, thumbnail explanations of these terms. David Gates in *Newsweek* defines schemata as "simple, superficial ideas suggested by words." Studies show that these are enough to allow a literate person to comprehend newspapers, books, and other media, and more importantly, to participate in his society. According to Tuttleton, Hirsch "points out that the culturally illiterate—and the same goes for those not having a command of standard English—can exercise no effect on discourse concerning social policy." As Hirsch writes in the book, "We will be able to achieve a just and prosperous society only when our schools ensure that everyone commands enough shared background knowledge to be able to communicate effectively with everyone else."

To reach this goal, Hirsch calls for a drastic change in America's educational system. He argues that the idea of reading as an abstract skill divorced from any specific content is a major cause of the present dilemma. According to Hirsch, content is essential to reading and is especially vital for comprehending what is read. Citing recent studies of how we read, Hirsch explains that "every text, even the most elementary, implies information that it takes for granted and doesn't explain. Knowing such information is *the* decisive skill of reading." He calls for schools to supply that necessary background information as it teaches students reading skills. To assist in this effort, Hirsch founded the Cultural Literacy Foundation.

Not all critics have appreciated *Cultural Literacy;* some claim that the book calls for a return to "teaching names, dates and places by rote and providing a context later," as Stefan Kanfer of *Time* puts it. And the list of needed cultural information has prompted "accusations of elitism," Charles Trueheart reports in the *Washington Post*. Robert Pattison of *Nation* argues that "a culture index poses a fundamental political question: How far are the wishes of the people to be consulted in determining the nature of culture itself?" But even harsh critics admit that the book raises some serious questions about the failure of American education.

In *The Dictionary of Cultural Literacy: What Every American Needs to Know,* written with Kett and Trefil, Hirsch provides definitions of the items listed in his earlier book, along with the definitions of many other terms. "The dictionary is more ambitious and really more important," Hirsch tells Trueheart, "because it will suggest to people who are outsiders in the literate culture, 'What do these characters really know that I'm being excluded from?'" The book is arranged into twenty-three sections which cover the major categories of knowledge, providing definitions of hundreds of terms, ideas, events, and names.

Many of Hirsch's ideas about cultural literacy are derived from his years as a literary critic, during which time he has shown "an enduring concern for *types* and for the *typicality* of expressive and interpretive behavior," according to Caraher. As a critic, Hirsch does not isolate a text from its author. Rather, he focuses his attention on the author's worldview, knowledge, and cultural situation. In order to understand an author's work, a critic "must familiarize himself with the typical meanings of the author's mental and experiential world," as Hirsch states in *Validity in Interpretation*. That is, a critic must enter into the author's perceptual framework. Caraher finds that Hirsch's "most singular contribution to modern American criticism and theory . . . might very well be his persistent iteration of the philosophical inevitability and the heuristic power of *typology*."

CA INTERVIEW

CA interviewed E. D. Hirsch, Jr., by telephone on November 17, 1987, at the Cultural Literacy Foundation in Charlottesville, Virginia.

CA: You've been much in the news lately for your book Cultural Literacy, *a term you define as "that middle ground of cultural knowledge possessed by the 'common reader.'" You're going far beyond why Johnny can't read to say that we're not teaching basic information about our culture that constitutes a vocabulary in itself. Are you greatly encouraged by the book's having made the bestseller lists and provoked a lively public response?*

HIRSCH: I am, but I have to say that I'm more encouraged by the response of teachers and superintendents and education professors. The public response is hard to gauge; you can't be sure of why they are buying the book. But it's very clear from the letters I've gotten from teachers, and from talking to school people, that they are by and large strongly for universal cultural literacy and generally agree with the thesis of the book.

CA: Are there any real stumbling blocks among the ideas you presented in the book for revamping our teaching?

HIRSCH: The chief stumbling block has been an ideological one: people are worried that this concept would impose a white Anglo-Saxon Protestant culture on minorities. That worry has not been expressed by everybody, but by some people. Whenever I have had three hours with such people, though, I've never failed to persuade them that their fears are groundless. First of all, I tell them we are revising our list of what literate Americans know, so the things they were worried about our not having on the list are now there. So that issue has been removed. The second thing I make clear to the objectors is that this approach is a lot more socially progressive than the fragmented, multicultural approach has been. And, given enough time, we can make this clear to anyone.

CA: In Cultural Literacy *you invited readers to send comments and suggestions on your list. What sort of responses have you received?*

HIRSCH: I've had at least two hundred responses with suggestions, and they've been very useful. They've come from all kinds of people.

CA: According to your list, which was drawn up in collaboration with history professor Joseph Kett and physics professor James Trefil, many of us older people are revealed to be woefully deficient in scientific knowledge. Do our children outshine us in that area?

HIRSCH: Yes, they do. They do remarkably well in some of those terms that we do less well on, so obviously our scientific literacy is improving. But I think it's important to remember that the scientific part of that list is international; it's not just American cultural literacy but what literate people have to know, I would say, in any modern culture, no matter where they are.

CA: Do you perceive among many professional people in the humanities a kind of prejudice against the sciences?

HIRSCH: Yes. Some of them fear natural science, fear its success and prestige. In some complaints about the soullessness of science there is a tinge of envy. But, in fact, science is one of the humanities, one of our noblest enterprises as a species. And, unlike much in the humanities, science is universally human—international.

CA: You and your collaborators are now preparing a dictionary of the terms on the list, which will include not only definitions but the associations that the terms call up in our minds. Are the associations a problem in any way? Is there some subjectivity about them?

HIRSCH: Not that we've discovered. It has gone through a process of being read and proofread by great numbers of people, and there doesn't seem to be much disagreement. The reason for that isn't hard to see: what we're trying to provide is shared associations, and if the associations genuinely are shared by literate people, then there will be agreement. That's built into the whole concept of shared knowledge.

CA: You don't blame television for our illiteracy; in fact, you give it credit for some benefits, if it is not watched excessively. Do you think that eventually some television-related terms will become a part of the literate cultural vocabulary?

HIRSCH: Of course. Television-related terms are probably already in our vocabulary. But there's a difference between television-related terms and the regular content that comes out over the television. Since there are so many channels, the idea that there is a television culture is not really accurate; different people have different cultures from television, and also television culture is rather ephemeral. What I hope to see happen is some help from television in conveying literate culture, and I think as soon as television feels the need or the obligation to do that, it probably will. It can be a genuine help in that way.

CA: You believe that much of the basic stuff of cultural literacy can be taught to students by fifth grade, and that full cultural literacy should be acquired by the time students graduate from high school. *If this were achieved, what would the implications be for university studies?*

HIRSCH: I think university studies would be much more productive. There's a general principle that the more you know, the more easily you can learn and the *more* you can learn. If students come to the university with a general background, good general knowledge, first of all they'll understand their textbooks and their lectures better. They will be able to get much more out of college. It won't be so disastrous for them to pursue specialized studies, because they will have a good background; you won't have the phenomenon of the person who is one-sided just because he has majored in engineering. Of course, one of the problems now, and one of the reasons there's so much interest in liberal arts in the universities, is that there's so much remedial work that the universities have to do.

CA: In addition to your teaching at the University of Virginia, you are now also a trustee of the Cultural Literacy Foundation. Could you tell us something about the Foundation, how it began and how it works?

HIRSCH: I created the Foundation to be the owner of the Cultural Literacy Tests, because I wanted to put them in the public sector. So one of the things we're going to do is issue lists and tests for twelfth grade. Those are already made and field-tested. But we'll ultimately publish tests for third, sixth, and ninth grades as well. The idea is to influence the school curriculum. The Foundation's fundamental aim is to enhance literacy, and to do it by affecting the school curriculum, particularly in the very early grades.

CA: Your work on cultural literacy seems to be a logical flowering of much of your philosophy on literary criticism. Do you see a direct progression of thought from your earlier views on criticism to the present time?

HIRSCH: One theme is consistent: language is saying more than appears on the page, or in the sounds we make. The actual words are able to convey meaning only because of all sorts of implications that are *not* said. The reader must bring those meanings to the words by virtue of background knowledge. That principle, which is one that dates way back to the 1950s and early '60s in my work, forms a principle of continuity with my work on literacy. But I didn't really see that myself until after the fact.

CA: In the afterword to The Aims of Interpretation *you wrote, "The job of criticism is both to illuminate meaning (when necessary) and to indicate some valuable application of meaning, some special charm or use or wisdom for the present time." By this standard, how well do you think literary criticism is being done today?*

HIRSCH: I think that, unfortunately, as far as being effective in the society at large, it has made itself marginal. Literary criticism, as published, is not read by very many people. It's a highly specialized domain, and therefore, in a social sense, it's marginal. Some of it may indeed have influence on what's done in other disciplines. One hears that that's so. I'm not hostile toward literary criticism, even though I think it's marginal, because I think you do need to have some kind of theory, some sort of arrangement that keeps giving the people who preserve the tradition—that is, English teachers—something to do in the way of publication at the university level.

Because universities require publication. And I think that has been, in fact, the underlying reason for changes in literary criticism and literary theory. You need new theories to keep the presses rolling. I'm afraid that's not something I object to. There's no way, as far as I can see, that universities can work except by having professors and graduate students publish things. My own feeling is that it's OK if the primary function of current literary criticism is to keep the presses rolling, as long as we don't make literature itself marginal. How many people read astrophysics journals? You can say about criticism and theory what Dr. Johnson said about writing books in general: it's a harmless activity like gardening.

CA: But it would be a pleasure to see more literary criticism that's accessible to the general educated reader.

HIRSCH: There are book reviews that are well done; the kind you read in the *New York Times* fulfill that purpose. I don't know that we need a lot of other kinds of literary criticism in the general sphere. We might need criticism that says, ''Dear Reader: This is why you should read Wordsworth.'' But in general, book reviewing is the principal job of criticism for the society at large.

CA: Are new trends developing in literary criticism?

HIRSCH: They happen every six months. The current trend (besides women's studies, which is very interesting—and it's been around for quite a little while now) is something that goes on at Berkeley called the New Historicism. That's a good change to the extent that it brings history back into literary criticism.

CA: What do you enjoy reading either for use in your teaching or for your own pleasure?

HIRSCH: I only read for pleasure. I get pleasure from any writing that teaches me something. I do take a guilty pleasure in reading adventure novels. I read philosophy and poetry, and I devour *Scientific American* every month. It's my connection with reality and progress, it's an antidote to literary theory.

CA: Beyond the upcoming publication of your dictionary, are there projects on your desk or in your mind that you'd like to talk about?

HIRSCH: These tests I've mentioned earlier are occupying my mind a lot. They're very demanding. I'm also considering making some temporary materials that the schools can use right away. It takes five or six years to develop a textbook, and we need to have better materials, more classical and rational materials, in the schools in the meantime. It seems to me that for the early grades the job can be done with supplementary materials, so I'm working on those. I'm not doing all those things myself, but I'm overseeing the various efforts. And just getting this Foundation operating is very time-consuming too.

BIOGRAPHICAL/CRITICAL SOURCES:

BOOKS

Dictionary of Literary Biography, Volume 67: *Modern American Critics since 1955*, Gale, 1988.
Hirsch, E. D., Jr., *Validity in Interpretation*, Yale University Press, 1967.
Hirsch, E. D., Jr., *Cultural Literacy: What Every American Needs to Know*, Houghton, 1987.

Lentricchia, Frank, *After the New Criticism*, University of Chicago Press, 1980.
Ray, William, *Literary Meaning: From Phenomenology to Deconstruction*, Blackwell, 1984.

PERIODICALS

College English, November, 1977.
Commentary, July, 1987.
Journal of Aesthetics and Art Criticism, fall, 1984.
Journal of Reading, May, 1988.
Nation, May 30, 1987.
Newsweek, April 20, 1987.
New York Times, April 17, 1987, June 14, 1987.
New York Times Book Review, March 15, 1987.
Partisan Review, fall, 1967.
Pre/Text, Number 1, spring/fall, 1980.
Time, July 20, 1987.
Virginia Quarterly Review, summer, 1967, winter, 1988.
Washington Post, April 20, 1987.

—*Sketch by Thomas Wiloch*
—*Interview by Jean W. Ross*

*   *   *

HOCH, Edward D(entinger)   1930-
(Irwin Booth, Anthony Circus, Stephen Dentinger, Pat McMahon, Mister X, R. L. Stevens)

PERSONAL: Surname rhymes with ''coke''; born February 22, 1930, in Rochester, N.Y.; son of Earl G. (a banker) and Alice (Dentinger) Hoch; married Patricia McMahon, June 5, 1957. *Education:* Attended University of Rochester, 1947-49. *Politics:* Liberal Republican. *Religion:* Roman Catholic.

ADDRESSES: Home—2941 Lake Ave., Rochester, N.Y. 14612.

CAREER: Rochester Public Library, Rochester, N.Y., researcher, 1949-50, member of board of trustees, 1982—; Pocket Books, Inc., New York, N.Y., staff member in adjustments department, 1952-54; Hutchins Advertising Co., Rochester, copy writer, 1954-68; full-time author, 1968—. *Military service:* U.S. Army, Military Police, 1950-52.

MEMBER: Mystery Writers of America (president, 1982-83), Authors Guild, Authors League of America, Science Fiction Writers of America.

AWARDS, HONORS: Edgar Allan Poe (''Edgar'') Award of Mystery Writers of America for best mystery short story of 1967, for ''The Oblong Room.''

WRITINGS:

The Shattered Raven, Lancer, 1969.
The Transvection Machine, Walker & Co., 1971.
The Judges of Hades, Leisure Books, 1971.
The Spy and the Thief, Davis Publications, 1971.
City of Brass, Leisure Books, 1971.
The Fellowship of the Hand, Walker & Co., 1973.
The Frankenstein Factory, Warner Books, 1975.
The Thefts of Nick Velvet, Mysterious Press, 1978.
The Monkey's Clue [and] *The Stolen Sapphire* (juvenile), Grosset, 1978.
The Quests of Simon Ark, Mysterious Press, 1984.
Leopold's Way, Southern Illinois University Press, 1985.

EDITOR

Dear Dead Days, Walker & Co., 1973.

Best Detective Stories of the Year, annual, Dutton, 1976-81.
All But Impossible!, Ticknor & Fields, 1981.
The Year's Best Mystery and Suspense Stories, annual, Walker & Co., 1982-88.

OTHER

Contributor, sometimes under a pseudonym, of more than seven hundred short stories to periodicals, including *Antaeus, Argosy, Ellery Queen's Mystery Magazine,* and *Alfred Hitchcock's Mystery Magazine.*

MEDIA ADAPTATIONS: Fourteen of Edward D. Hoch's stories have been adapted for television, including three for the NBC-TV series ''McMillan and Wife.''

AVOCATIONAL INTERESTS: The contemporary motion picture as an art form.

BIOGRAPHICAL/CRITICAL SOURCES:

PERIODICALS

Ellery Queen's Mystery Magazine, August, 1976.
New York Times Book Review, June 29, 1968, March 11, 1973.
Rochester Democrat and Chronicle, September 7, 1969.
Writer, April, 1974.

*   *   *

HOCH, Paul L(awrence) 1942-

PERSONAL: Born October 16, 1942, in London, England; came to the United States in 1950; naturalized citizen.

ADDRESSES: Home—2599 Le Conte Ave., Berkeley, Calif. 94709.

CAREER: Writer.

WRITINGS:

Academic Freedom in Action, Sheed, 1970.
Rip Off the Big Game: The Exploitation of Sports by the Power Elite, Anchor Books, 1972.
The Newspaper Game: The Political Sociology of the Press, Calder & Boyars, 1974.
(Editor with Peter Dale Scott and Russell Stetler) *The Assassinations: Dallas and Beyond,* Random House, 1976.*

*   *   *

HOEXTER, Corinne K. 1927-

PERSONAL: ''O'' in surname is silent; born November 3, 1927, in Scranton, Pa.; daughter of Edward D. (a manufacturer) and Aimee Helen (Rosenfelder) Katz; married Rolf Hoexter (an engineering and management consultant), December 25, 1955; children: Vivien, Michael Frederic. *Education:* Wellesley College, B.A. (with high honors in English), 1949; University of Chicago, M.A., 1950.

ADDRESSES: Office—67 Spring Lane Englewood, N.J. 07631.

CAREER: Experiment in International Living, Putney, Vt., promotion assistant, 1950-51; *Parent's Magazine,* New York City, editorial assistant, 1951-53; Magazine Management, New York City, associate editor, 1953-54; Pines Publications, New York City, 1954-57, began as associate editor, became managing editor; J. J. Little & Ives, New York City, picture editor, 1957-59; *Portfolio and Art News Annual,* New York City, managing editor, 1959-60; *Asia,* New York City, 1978-84,

began as managing editor, became executive editor; *New York Times,* travel section editor, 1984-85; free-lance writer/editor, 1985—. Trustee, Flat Rock Brook Nature Association, 1973-78.

MEMBER: Authors League of America, League of Women Voters, National Organization for Women, Common Cause, Legal Defense Fund of the NAACP, Chinese Historical Society of America, Asian American Legal Defense Fund, New York Zoological Society, Friends of the New York Public Library, Museum of Modern Art, Metropolitan Museum of Art, Friends of Carnegie Hall, Whitney Museum of American Art, South Street Seaport Museum, Englewood Social Service Federation, Chatham Yacht Club (Chatham, Mass.), Wellesley Club of Englewood, Wellesley Club of New York City, Phi Beta Kappa.

AWARDS, HONORS: Fulbright fellowship at University of Bologna, 1953.

WRITINGS:

(With Ira Peck) *A Nation Conceived and Dedicated,* Scholastic Book Services, 1970.
Black Crusader: Frederick Douglass (Child Study Association book list), Rand McNally, 1970.
From Canton to California: The Epic of Chinese Immigration, Four Winds, 1976.

Contributor of articles on travel, culture, and personality profiles to newspapers, including the *New York Times,* and to periodicals, including *Connoisseur* and *Modern Bride.*

WORK IN PROGRESS: A book based on the author's articles for the *New York Times* about nature and the survival of unspoiled tracts of land in the American Northeast and West Coast and in Florida; a long-term project concerning the performing arts, especially the Asian performing arts.

SIDELIGHTS: Corinne K. Hoexter says: ''As a child . . . many of my favorite books were histories or historical novels. . . . Since history was always so real to me and threw so much light on our own world and problems, I felt it could be equally real to other people today. I have tried to show the historical people in my books as people, after all, struggling with many of the same problems we face today, involved in the old and continuing human battle against injustice. At the same time I have tried to show individuals in relation to the great events and movements of history.

''In our small city of Englewood and the nearby metropolis, New York, my family and I have been interested in a variety of urban problems. With the aid of many citizen groups, we succeeded in saving a beautiful piece of wild land on the west slope of the Palisades, one of the last in Englewood, and turned it into a nature center for the benefit of the whole city. A solar-heated interpretive center has been opened and is working to educate both children and adults in preserving our threatened natural environment.''

AVOCATIONAL INTERESTS: Reading, bicycling, skiing, sailing, playing the piano, family singing and chamber music, walking in the city and hiking in the country, visiting places of historical and artistic interest, concerts, dance performances, the theater, art museums.

*   *   *

HOFFER, William 1943-

PERSONAL: Born June 11, 1943, in Cleveland, Ohio; son of

Frank and Lucile (Koeblitz) Hoffer; married Edie Bauer, June 12, 1966; children: Jennifer, Amanda. *Education:* Columbia Union College, B.A., 1969.

ADDRESSES: Agent—Julian Bach Literary Agency, 747 3rd Ave., New York, N.Y. 10017.

CAREER: PHC Business Magazine, Washington, D.C., associate editor, 1968-69; *Life Association News,* Washington, D.C., associate editor, 1969-70; free-lance writer, 1970—.

MEMBER: American Society of Journalists and Authors (director-at-large, 1976-78), Authors Guild.

WRITINGS:

NONFICTION

(With William W. Pearce) *Caught in the Act,* Stein & Day, 1976.
(With Billy Hayes) *Midnight Express,* Dutton, 1977.
Saved!: The Story of the Andrea Doria, the Greatest Sea Rescue in History, Summit Books, 1979.
Volcano: The Search for Vesuvius, Summit Books, 1982.
(With Betty Mahmoody) *Not without My Daughter,* St. Martin's, 1987.

OTHER

Contributor to *True, Popular Science, House Beautiful, Mechanix Illustrated, Today's Health, Saga, Family Health, Modern Medicine,* and other magazines.

SIDELIGHTS: William Hoffer is the author and co-author of several popular nonfiction works. He is noted for co-authoring books that recreate the terror and confusion of Americans held against their will in foreign countries. In 1977, for example, he wrote *Midnight Express* with Billy Hayes, who was held in a Turkish prison on drug charges, and in 1987, he worked on *Not without My Daughter* with Betty Mahmoody, who went on a vacation to Iran with her daughter and Iranian-born husband, then discovered her husband had no intention of returning to America.

Hoffer also wrote *Saved!: The Story of the Andrea Doria, the Greatest Sea Rescue in History. Washington Post* contributor Robert J. Serling comments: "'Saved!' is so superbly written, with such tautness, dramatic timing and calculated suspense, that it comes close to matching that classic of sea disaster stories—Walter Lord's 'A Night to Remember,' about the Titanic. Hoffer manages to put the reader aboard the doomed liner and into the minds and hearts of its passengers and crew.''

BIOGRAPHICAL/CRITICAL SOURCES:

PERIODICALS

Los Angeles Times Book Review, November 1, 1987.
Newsweek, March 7, 1977.
New York Times, February 25, 1977.
Saturday Review, March 5, 1977.
Washington Post, August 16, 1979, September 21, 1987.*

*   *   *

HOGARTH, (Arthur) Paul 1917-

PERSONAL: Born October 4, 1917, in Kendal, Westmorland, England; son of Arthur and Janet (Bownass) Hogarth; married Phyllis Daphne Pamplin; married Patricia Douthwaite, February 14, 1959; children: (first marriage) Virginia; (second marriage) Toby. *Education:* Attended Manchester College of Art, 1936-38, St. Martin's School of Art, 1938-40.

ADDRESSES: Home and office—The Studio, 61 Auden Place, Manley St., London NW1 8ND, England. *Agent*—(Literary) Tessa Sayle Agency, 11 Jubilee Place, London SW3 3TE, England; (artistic) Edward T. Riley, 215 East 31st St., New York, N.Y. 10016.

CAREER: Free-lance artist and illustrator. London Dounty Council Central School of Arts and Crafts, London, England, visiting lecturer, 1951-54; Cambridge School of Art, Cambridge, England, senior tutor of drawing, 1959-61; Royal College of Art, London, tutor, 1964-70, visiting lecturer in Department of Illustration, Faculty of Graphic Design, 1971—. Visiting associate professor, Philadelphia College of Art, 1968-69. Hogarth has exhibited his work at several London locations, including Leicester Gallery, the American Embassy, and Kyle Gallery. *Military service:* Royal Engineers.

MEMBER: Royal Designers for Industry, Royal Academy of Fine Arts, Chartered Society of Designers (fellow), Association of Illustrators (honorary president, 1982), Reform Club (London).

AWARDS, HONORS: Francis Williams Illustration Award, 1982, for *Poems; Yorkshire Post* award for best art book, 1986, for the revised edition of *The Artist as Reporter.*

WRITINGS:

Defiant People: Drawings of Greece Today, Lawrence & Wishart, 1953.
Drawings of Poland, Wydawnictwo Artystczno-Graficzne (Warsaw), 1953.
Looking at China, Lawrence & Wishart, 1956.
People Like Us: Drawings of South Africa and Rhodesia, Dobson, 1958, published as *The Sons of Adam,* Thomas Nelson, 1960.
Irish Sketchbook, Verlagder Kunst, 1962.
Creative Pencil Drawing, Watson, 1964, 6th edition, 1979.
The Artist as Reporter, Reinhold, 1967, revised and enlarged edition, Gordon Fraser, 1986.
Creative Ink Drawing, Watson, 1968.
Drawing People, Watson, 1971.
Artists on Horseback: The Old West in Illustrated Journalism, 1857-1900, Watson, 1972.
Drawing Architecture, Watson, 1973.
Paul Hogarth's American Album, Lion and Unicorn Press, 1974.
Paul Hogarth's Walking Tours of Old Philadelphia, Barre Publications, 1976.
Paul Hogarth's Walking Tours of Old Boston: Through North End, Downtown, Beacon Hill, Charleston, Cambridge, and Back Bay, Dutton, 1978.
Arthur Boyd Houghton, Gordon Fraser, 1982.
Paul Hogarth's Walking Tours of Old Washington and Alexandria, EPM Publications, 1985.
(With Graham Greene) *Graham Greene Country,* Pavillion Books, 1986.
(With Lawrence Durrell) *The Mediterranean Shore: Travels in Lawrence Durrell Country,* Pavillion Books, 1988.

ILLUSTRATOR

Charlotte Bronte, *Jane Eyrova* (title means "Jane Eyre"), Mlada Fronta (Prague), 1953.
Charles Dickens, *Pan Pickwick,* Statni Nakladatelstvi Detske Knihy (Prague), 1956.
Doris Lessing, *Going Home,* M. Joseph, 1957.
Arthur Catherall, *Jungle Trap,* Roy, 1958.

Arthur Conan Doyle, *The Adventures of Sherlock Holmes*, Folio Society, 1958.

R. Haggard, *King Solomon's Mines*, Penguin, 1958.

P. Knight, *The Gold of the Snow Geese*, Thomas Nelson, 1958.

O. Henry, *Selected Short Stories*, Folio Society, 1960.

Elizabeth Gaskell, *Marie Bartonova* (title means "Mary Barton"), Mlada Fronta, 1960.

Olive Schreiner, *The Story of an African Farm*, Limited Editions Club, 1961.

Jean Jacques Salomon, *Prehistory: Civilizations Before Writing*, Dell, 1962.

Brendan Behan, *Brendan Behan's Island*, Geis, 1962.

Behan, *Brendan Behan's New York*, Geis, 1964.

Robert Graves, *Majorca Observed*, Doubleday, 1965.

(And author of captions) Malcolm Muggeridge, *London a la Mode*, Hill & Wang, 1967.

Alaric Jacob, *A Russian Journey: From Suzdal to Samarkand*, Hill & Wang, 1969.

James D. Atwater and R. E. Ruiz, *Out from Under*, Doubleday, 1969.

Doris Whitman, *The Hand of Apollo*, Follet, 1969.

Elizabeth Sheppard-Jones, *Stories of Wales: Told for Children*, Academy Chicago, 1978.

Siegfried Sassoon, *Memoirs of a Fox-Hunting Man*, Limited Editions Club, 1978.

James Joyce, *Ulysses*, Franklin Library, 1978.

Nigel Buxton, *America*, Cassell, 1979.

Stephen Spender, *America Observed*, Potter, 1979.

Robert Graves, *Poems*, Limited Editions Club, 1980.

Siegfried Sassoon, *Memoirs of an Infantry Officer*, Limited Editions Club, 1981.

Hugh Johnson, *Hugh Johnson's Wine Companion*, Simon & Schuster, 1984.

Joseph Conrad, *Nostromo*, Folio Society, 1984.

William Trevor, *Night at the Alexandria*, Century Hutchinson, 1987.

OTHER

Contributor to *Penrose Annual* of Hastings House, and to *Daily Telegraph Magazine*, *Sports Illustrated*, *House and Garden*, and other periodicals. Art editor, *Contact*, 1950-51.

AVOCATIONAL INTERESTS: Travel (Hogarth has been to Poland, Czechoslovakia, the U.S.S.R., Rhodesia, Central and South America, China, South Africa, Ireland, Canada, and the United States), sailing.

*   *   *

HOGE, Dean R(ichard)   1937-

PERSONAL: Surname rhymes with "stogie"; born May 27, 1937, in Ohio; son of Arthur F. (a lumber dealer) and Meta (Meckstroth) Hoge; married Josephine Jacobson, June 27, 1965; children: Christopher, Elizabeth. *Education:* Ohio State University, B.S. (summa cum laude), 1960; graduate study at University of Bonn, 1960-61; Harvard University, B.D. (cum laude), 1964, M.A., 1966, Ph.D., 1970. *Religion:* Presbyterian.

ADDRESSES: Home—7314 Holly Ave., Takoma Park, Md. 20012. *Office*—Department of Sociology, Catholic University of America, Washington, D.C. 20064.

CAREER: Princeton Theological Seminary, Princeton, N.J., assistant professor of sociology, 1969-74; Catholic University of America, Washington, D.C., associate professor of sociology, 1974—.

MEMBER: American Sociological Association, Society for the Scientific Study of Religion, Religious Research Association (president, 1979-80), Religious Education Association, Association for the Sociology of Religion, Common Cause.

AWARDS, HONORS: Catholic Book Award for best professional book, Catholic Press Association, 1987, for *The Future of Catholic Leadership: Responses to the Priest Shortage*.

WRITINGS:

Commitment on Campus: Changes in Religion and Values over Five Decades, Westminster, 1974.

Division in the Protestant House: The Basic Reasons behind Intra-Church Conflicts, Westminster, 1976.

(Editor with David A. Roozen, and contributor) *Understanding Church Growth and Decline*, Pilgrim Press, 1979.

(With others) *Converts, Dropouts, Returnees: A Study of Religious Change among Catholics*, with technical supplement, Pilgrim Press, 1981.

(With others) *Research on Men's Vocations to the Priesthood and the Religious Life*, U.S. Catholic Conference, 1984.

(With Eugene Hembrick) *Seminarians in Theology: A National Profile*, U.S. Catholic Conference, 1986.

The Future of Catholic Leadership: Responses to the Priest Shortage, Sheed & Ward, 1987.

Contributor to religion and sociology journals.

WORK IN PROGRESS: Research on religious education and self-esteem of youth.

*   *   *

HOLLOWAY, (Percival) Geoffrey   1918-

PERSONAL: Born May 23, 1918, in Birmingham, England; married Joyce Mildred Broom, 1951 (died, 1974); married Patricia Pogson, 1977; children: (first marriage) Catherine Rowan, Susan Bryony. *Education:* University of Southampton, certificate in social science, 1948. *Politics:* Liberal.

ADDRESSES: Home—4 Gowan Cres., Staveley near Kendal, Cumbria LA8 9NF, England. *Office*—County Hall, Kendal, Cumbria, England.

CAREER: Salop County Council, Shrewsbury, England, library assistant, 1935-39, 1946; Hatton Psychiatric Hospital, Warwick, England, social worker, 1946-48; Prisoner's Aid Society, Lincoln, England, officer, 1950-51; hospital porter at Lincoln Sanitorium, 1951-53; Westmorland County Council, Kendal, England, mental health worker, 1953-74; Cumbria County Council, Kendal, England, social worker, 1974-83.

WRITINGS:

POEMS

To Have Eyes, Anvil Press, 1973.

Rhine Jump (Poetry Book Society selection), London Magazine Editions, 1974.

All I Can Say, Anvil Press, 1978.

Salt, Roses, Vinegar, Grapheme Press, 1985.

The Crones of Aphrodite, Free Man's Press Editions, 1985.

Percepts without Deference, Aquila Publishing, 1987.

My Ghost in Your Eye, Littlewood Press, 1988.

The Last Snowflake, Iolaire Arts Association, 1988.

OTHER

(Editor) *Trio 2*, Cumbria Poetry Society, 1977.

AVOCATIONAL INTERESTS: Walking, gurning (the sport of making faces).

* * *

HOLMES, Kenneth L(loyd) 1915-

PERSONAL: Born January 14, 1915, in Montreal, Quebec, Canada; naturalized U.S. citizen; son of James Sails (a clergyman) and Ruby Alice (Renshaw) Holmes; married Inez L'Adelle Rawlings, August 23, 1941; children: Donald Clifford, Stephen Lloyd. *Education:* University of Redlands, B.A., 1938; Berkeley Baptist Divinity School, B.D., 1945, M.A., 1948; University of Oregon, Ph.D., 1962. *Politics:* Democrat. *Religion:* Society of Friends (Quaker).

ADDRESSES: Home—410 Orchard St., Monmouth, Ore. 97361. *Office*—Department of History, Western Oregon State College, Monmouth, Ore. 97361.

CAREER: American Baptist Convention, pastor in Moscow, Idaho, 1948-53; Linfield College, McMinnville, Ore., assistant professor, 1954-61, associate professor, 1961-64, professor of history, 1964-67, dean of men, 1955-59; Western Oregon State College, Monmouth, professor of history, 1967-79, professor emeritus, 1979—.

MEMBER: English-Speaking Union, American Historical Association, American Association for the Advancement of Science, Royal Geographical Society (fellow), Fellowship of Reconciliation, Northwest Scientific Association (president, 1976-77), Oregon Historical Society (honorary life member of the board), Hudson's Bay Record Society.

WRITINGS:

(Editor and contributor) *Linfield's Hundred Years* (centennial history), Binfords, 1956.
(Contributor) LeRoy R. Hafen, editor, *Mountain Men and the Fur Trade*, Arthur Clark, Volumes II, III, VI, VII, VIII, IX, 1964-72.
Ewing Young, Master Trapper, Binfords, 1967.
(With Judith Farmer) *Historical Atlas of Early Oregon*, text edition, Geographic & Area Study Publications, 1973.
Mount St. Helens: Lady with a Past, Salem Press, 1980.
(Editor and compiler) *Covered Wagon Women: Diaries and Letters from the Western Trails, 1840-1890*, Arthur H. Clark, Volume I: *1840-1849*, 1983, Volume II: *1850*, 1983, Volume III: *1851*, 1984, Volume IV: *1852*, 1985, Volume V: *1852—The Oregon Trail*, 1986, Volume VI: *1853-1854*, 1987, Volume VII: *1854-1860*, in press.

Contributor to *Encyclopedia Americana* and *Dictionary of Canadian Biography*. Author of column, "Pages from the Past," appearing in twenty Pacific Northwest newspapers, 1962-66. Also contributor to *Geographical Bulletin* and to other magazines, Quaker journals, and newspapers. Special writer, *Portland Oregonian*, 1967—.

WORK IN PROGRESS: Covered Wagon Women, Volume VIII: *1862-1864*.

SIDELIGHTS: "There is a demand on professors to 'produce' research and writing," Kenneth L. Holmes told *CA*. "I have been writing for years because it is my highest joy to do so. Research is my detective work, comparable to the pursuits of my most famous 'relative,' Sherlock Holmes."

BIOGRAPHICAL/CRITICAL SOURCES:

PERIODICALS

American Historical Review, February, 1968.

* * *

HOOBLER, Dorothy

PERSONAL: Born in Philadelphia, Pa.; daughter of Frederick and Eleanor (Bystrom) Law; married Thomas Hoobler (a writer and editor), December 18, 1971; children: Ellen Marie. *Education:* Wells College, A.B., 1963; New York University, M.A., 1971.

ADDRESSES: Home—320 West 83rd St., Apt. 6-C, New York, N.Y. 10024.

CAREER: Has worked as an editor and genealogist; free-lance writer, 1973—.

WRITINGS:

WITH HUSBAND, THOMAS HOOBLER

Frontier Diary, Macmillan, 1974.
Margaret Mead: A Life in Science, Macmillan, 1974.
House Plants, Grosset, 1975.
Vegetable Gardening and Cooking, Grosset, 1975.
Pruning, Grosset, 1975.
An Album of World War I, F. Watts, 1976.
The Year in Bloom, Bantam, 1977.
Photographing History: The Career of Mathew Brady, Putnam, 1977.
An Album of World War II, F. Watts, 1977.
The Trenches: Fighting on the Western Front in World War I, Putnam, 1978.
Photographing the Frontier, Putnam, 1980.
U.S.-China Relations since World War II, F. Watts, 1981.
An Album of the Seventies, F. Watts, 1981.
The Social Security System, F. Watts, 1982.
The Voyages of Captain Cook, Putnam, 1983.
Stalin, Chelsea House, 1985.
Your Right to Privacy, F. Watts, 1986.
Zhou Enlai, Chelsea House, 1986.
Cleopatra, Chelsea House, 1986.
Nelson and Winnie Mandela, F. Watts, 1987.
Drugs and Crime, Chelsea House, 1988.

WORK IN PROGRESS: The Vietnam War, a book for young adults, with T. Hoobler.

AVOCATIONAL INTERESTS: Oriental, American, and European medieval history, music, photography, gardening, and travel.

* * *

HOOBLER, Thomas

PERSONAL: Born in Cincinnati, Ohio; son of John T. (a printer) and Jane Frances (Pachoud) Hoobler; married Dorothy Law (a writer), December 18, 1971; children: Ellen Marie. *Education:* University of Notre Dame, A.B., 1964; attended University of Iowa, Writer's Workshop, 1965.

ADDRESSES: Home—320 West 83rd St., Apt. 6-C, New York, N.Y. 10024.

CAREER: Worked in various positions at private schools in Cincinnati, Ohio, including teacher of English and photography, audio-visual coordinator, and basketball coach, 1965-70; trade magazine editor, 1971-76; free-lance writer and editor, 1976—.

WRITINGS:

(With Burt Wetanson) *The Hunters*, Doubleday, 1978.
(With Wetanson) *The Treasure Hunters*, Playboy Press, 1983.
Dr. Chill's Project, Putnam, 1987.
The Revenge of Ho-tai, Walker, in press.

WITH WIFE, DOROTHY HOOBLER

Frontier Diary, Macmillan, 1974.
Margaret Mead: A Life in Science, Macmillan, 1974.
House Plants, Grosset, 1975.
Vegetable Gardening and Cooking, Grosset, 1975.
Pruning, Grosset, 1975.
An Album of World War I, F. Watts, 1976.
The Year in Bloom, Bantam, 1977.
Photographing History: The Career of Mathew Brady, Putnam, 1977.
An Album of World War II, F. Watts, 1977.
The Trenches: Fighting on the Western Front in World War I, Putnam, 1978.
Photographing the Frontier, Putnam, 1980.
U.S.-China Relations since World War II, F. Watts, 1981.
An Album of the Seventies, F. Watts, 1981.
The Social Security System, F. Watts, 1982.
The Voyages of Captain Cook, Putnam, 1983.
Stalin, Chelsea House, 1985.
Your Right to Privacy, F. Watts, 1986.
Zhou Enlai, Chelsea House, 1986.
Cleopatra, Chelsea House, 1986.
Nelson and Winnie Mandela, F. Watts, 1987.
Drugs and Crime, Chelsea House, 1988.

WORK IN PROGRESS: The Vietnam War, a book for young adults, with D. Hoobler.

AVOCATIONAL INTERESTS: Oriental, American, and European medieval history, music, photography, gardening, and travel.

*   *   *

HOPE, Laura Lee
[Collective pseudonym]

WRITINGS:

"BLYTHE GIRLS" SERIES

The Blythe Girls: Helen, Margy, and Rose; or, Facing the Great World, Grosset & Dunlap, 1925.
. . . *Margy's Queer Inheritance; or, The Worth of a Name*, Grosset & Dunlap, 1925.
. . . *Rose's Great Problem; or, Face to Face with a Crisis*, Grosset & Dunlap, 1925.
. . . *Helen's Strange Boarder; or, The Girl from Bronx Park*, Grosset & Dunlap, 1925.
. . . *Three on a Vacation; or, The Mystery at Peach Farm*, Grosset & Dunlap, 1925.
. . . *Margy's Secret Mission; or, Exciting Days at Shadymore*, Grosset & Dunlap, 1926.
. . . *Rose's Odd Discovery; or, The Search for Irene Conroy*, Grosset & Dunlap, 1927.
. . . *The Disappearance of Helen; or, The Art Shop Mystery*, Grosset & Dunlap, 1928.

. . . *Snowbound in Camp; or, The Mystery at Elk Lodge*, Grosset & Dunlap, 1929.
. . . *Margy's Mysterious Visitor; or, Guarding the Pepper Fortune*, Grosset & Dunlap, 1930.
. . . *Rose's Hidden Talent*, Grosset & Dunlap, 1931.
. . . *Helen's Wonderful Mistake; or, The Mysterious Necklace*, Grosset & Dunlap, 1932.

"BOBBSEY TWINS" SERIES

The Bobbsey Twins; or, Merry Days Indoors and Out, Mershon, 1904, new and enlarged edition, Grosset & Dunlap, 1928, published as *Laura Lee Hope's "The Bobbsey Twins,"* retold by Bennett Kline, Whitman, 1940, revised edition published as *The Bobbsey Twins* (also see below), Grosset & Dunlap, 1950, published as *Meet the Bobbsey Twins*, Wonder Books, 1954, published as *The Bobbsey Twins of Lakeport* (also see below), Grosset & Dunlap, 1961, reprinted, Wanderer, 1979.
. . . *in the Country* (also see below), Mershon, 1904, revised edition, Grosset & Dunlap, 1950, published as *The Bobbsey Twins' Adventures in the Country* (also see below), reprinted, Wanderer, 1979.
. . . *at the Seashore* (also see below), Chatterton-Peck, 1907, revised edition, Grosset & Dunlap, 1950, published as *The Bobbsey Twins' Secret at the Seashore* (also see below), Grosset & Dunlap, 1962, reprinted, Wanderer, 1979.
. . . *at School*, Grosset & Dunlap, 1913, reprinted, 1941, revised edition published as *The Bobbsey Twins' Mystery at School*, 1962.
. . . *at Snow Lodge*, Grosset & Dunlap, 1913, revised edition published as *The Bobbsey Twins and the Mystery at Snow Lodge*, 1960.
. . . *on a Houseboat*, Grosset & Dunlap, 1915, revised edition, 1955.
. . . *at Meadow Brook*, Grosset & Dunlap, 1915, revised edition published as *The Bobbsey Twins' Mystery at Meadowbrook*, 1963.
. . . *at Home*, Grosset & Dunlap, 1916, reprinted, 1944, revised edition published as *The Bobbsey Twins' Big Adventure at Home*, 1960.
. . . *in a Great City*, Grosset & Dunlap, 1917, reprinted, 1945, revised edition published as *The Bobbsey Twins' Search in the Great City*, Grosset & Dunlap, 1960.
. . . *on Blueberry Island*, Grosset & Dunlap, 1917, reprinted, 1945, revised edition, 1959.
. . . *on the Deep Blue Sea*, Grosset & Dunlap, 1918, reprinted, 1946, revised edition published as *The Bobbsey Twins' Mystery on the Deep Blue Sea*, 1965.
. . . *in Washington*, Grosset & Dunlap, 1919, reprinted, 1945, revised edition published as *The Bobbsey Twins' Adventure in Washington*, 1963.
. . . *in the Great West*, Grosset & Dunlap, 1920, revised edition published as *The Bobbsey Twins' Visit to the Great West*, 1966.
. . . *at Cedar Camp*, Grosset & Dunlap, 1921, revised edition published as *The Bobbsey Twins and the Cedar Camp Mystery*, 1967.
. . . *at the County Fair*, Grosset & Dunlap, 1922, revised edition published as *The Bobbsey Twins and the County Fair Mystery*, 1960.
. . . *Camping Out*, Grosset & Dunlap, 1923, revised edition, 1955.
. . . *and Baby May*, Grosset & Dunlap, 1924, revised edition published as *The Bobbsey Twins' Adventures with Baby May*, 1968.

. . . *Keeping House*, Grosset & Dunlap, 1925, revised edition published as *The Bobbsey Twins and the Play House Secret*, 1968.

. . . *at Cloverbank*, Grosset & Dunlap, 1926, revised edition published as *The Bobbsey Twins and the Four-Leaf Clover Mystery*, 1968.

. . . *at Cherry Corners*, Grosset & Dunlap, 1927, revised edition published as *The Bobbsey Twins' Mystery at Cherry Corners*, 1971.

. . . *and Their Schoolmates*, Grosset & Dunlap, 1928.

. . . *Treasure Hunting*, Grosset & Dunlap, 1929.

. . . *at Spruce Lake*, Grosset & Dunlap, 1930.

The Bobbsey Twins' Wonderful Secret, Grosset & Dunlap, 1931, revised edition published as *The Bobbsey Twins' Wonderful Winter Secret*, 1962.

. . . *at the Circus*, Grosset & Dunlap, 1932, revised edition published as *The Bobbsey Twins and the Circus Surprise*, 1960.

. . . *on an Airplane Trip*, Grosset & Dunlap, 1933.

. . . *Solve a Mystery*, Grosset & Dunlap, 1934.

. . . *on a Ranch*, Grosset & Dunlap, 1935.

. . . *in Eskimo Land*, Grosset & Dunlap, 1936.

. . . *in a Radio Play*, Grosset & Dunlap, 1937.

. . . *at Windmill Cottage*, Grosset & Dunlap, 1938.

. . . *at Lighthouse Point*, Grosset & Dunlap, 1939.

. . . *at Indian Hollow*, Grosset & Dunlap, 1940.

. . . *at the Ice Carnival*, Grosset & Dunlap, 1941.

. . . *in the Land of Cotton*, Grosset & Dunlap, 1942.

. . . *in Echo Valley*, Grosset & Dunlap, 1943.

. . . *on the Pony Trail*, Grosset & Dunlap, 1944.

. . . *at Mystery Mansion*, Grosset & Dunlap, 1945.

. . . *at Sugar Maple Hill*, Grosset & Dunlap, 1946.

. . . *in Mexico*, Grosset & Dunlap, 1947.

The Bobbsey Twins' Toy Shop, Grosset & Dunlap, 1948.

. . . *in Tulip Land*, Grosset & Dunlap, 1949.

. . . *in Rainbow Valley*, Grosset & Dunlap, 1950.

The Bobbsey Twins' Own Little Railroad, Grosset & Dunlap, 1951.

. . . *at Whitesail Harbor*, Grosset & Dunlap, 1952.

. . . *and the Horseshoe Riddle*, Grosset & Dunlap, 1953.

. . . *at Big Bear Pond*, Grosset & Dunlap, 1954.

. . . *on a Bicycle Trip*, Grosset & Dunlap, 1955.

The Bobbsey Twins' Own Little Ferryboat, Grosset & Dunlap, 1956.

. . . *at Pilgrim Rock*, Grosset & Dunlap, 1957.

The Bobbsey Twins' Forest Adventure, Grosset & Dunlap, 1958.

. . . *at London Tower*, Grosset & Dunlap, 1959.

. . . *in the Mystery Cave*, Grosset & Dunlap, 1960.

. . . *in Volcano Land*, Grosset & Dunlap, 1961.

. . . *and the Goldfish Mystery*, Grosset & Dunlap, 1962.

. . . *and the Big River Mystery*, Grosset & Dunlap, 1963.

. . . *and the Greek Hat Mystery*, Grosset & Dunlap, 1964.

The Bobbsey Twins' Search for the Green Rooster, Grosset & Dunlap, 1965.

. . . *and Their Camel Adventure*, Grosset & Dunlap, 1966.

The Bobbsey Twins' Mystery of the King's Puppet, Grosset & Dunlap, 1967.

. . . *and the Secret of Candy Castle*, Grosset & Dunlap, 1968.

. . . *and the Doodlebug Mystery*, Grosset & Dunlap, 1969.

. . . *and the Talking Fox Mystery*, Grosset & Dunlap, 1970.

. . . *The Red, White, and Blue Mystery*, Grosset & Dunlap, 1971.

. . . *Dr. Funnybone's Secret*, Grosset & Dunlap, 1972.

. . . *and the Tagalong Giraffe*, Grosset & Dunlap, 1973.

. . . *and the Flying Clown*, Grosset & Dunlap, 1974.

. . . *on the Sun-Moon Cruise*, Grosset & Dunlap, 1975.

. . . *The Freedom Bell Mystery*, Grosset & Dunlap, 1976.

. . . *and the Smoky Mountain Mystery*, Grosset & Dunlap, 1977.

. . . *in a TV Mystery Show*, Grosset & Dunlap, 1978.

. . . *The Coral Turtle Mystery*, Grosset & Dunlap, 1979.

. . . *The Blue Poodle Mystery*, Wanderer, 1980.

. . . *The Secret in the Pirate's Cave*, Wanderer, 1980.

. . . *The Dune Buggy Mystery*, Wanderer, 1980.

. . . *The Missing Pony Mystery*, Wanderer, 1981.

. . . *The Rose Parade Mystery*, Wanderer, 1981.

. . . *The Camp Fire Mystery*, Wanderer, 1982.

. . . *Double Trouble*, Wanderer, 1982.

. . . *Mystery of the Laughing Dinosaur*, Wanderer, 1983.

. . . *The Music Box Mystery*, Wanderer, 1983.

. . . *The Ghost in the Computer*, Wanderer, 1984.

. . . *The Scarecrow Mystery*, Wanderer, 1984.

. . . *The Haunted House Mystery*, Wanderer, 1985.

. . . *Mystery of the Hindu Temple*, Wanderer, 1985.

. . . *The Grinning Gargoyle Mystery*, Wanderer, 1986.

''NEW BOBBSEY TWINS'' SERIES

The Secret of Jungle Park, Minstrel, 1987.

The Case of the Runaway Money, Minstrel, 1987.

The Clue That Flew Away, Minstrel, 1987.

The Secret in the Sand Castle, Minstrel, 1988.

The Case of the Close Encounter, Minstrel, 1988.

Mystery on the Mississippi, Minstrel, 1988.

Trouble in Toyland, Minstrel, 1988.

The Secret of the Stolen Puppies, Minstrel, 1988.

The Clue in the Classroom, Minstrel, 1988.

The Chocolate-Covered Clue, Minstrel, 1989.

The Case of the Crooked Contest, Minstrel, 1989.

The Secret of the Sunken Treasure, Minstrel, 1989.

The Case of the Crying Clown, Minstrel, 1989.

''BUNNY BROWN AND HIS SISTER SUE'' SERIES

Bunny Brown and His Sister Sue, Grosset & Dunlap, 1916.

. . . *on Grandpa's Farm*, Grosset & Dunlap, 1916.

. . . *Playing Circus*, Grosset & Dunlap, 1916.

. . . *at Camp Rest-A-While*, Grosset & Dunlap, 1916.

. . . *at Aunt Lou's City Home*, Grosset & Dunlap, 1916.

. . . *in the Big Woods*, Grosset & Dunlap, 1917.

. . . *on an Auto Tour*, Grosset & Dunlap, 1917.

. . . *and Their Shetland Pony*, Grosset & Dunlap, 1918.

. . . *Giving a Show*, Grosset & Dunlap, 1919.

. . . *at Christmas Tree Cove*, Grosset & Dunlap, 1920.

. . . *in the Sunny South*, Grosset & Dunlap, 1921.

. . . *Keeping Store*, Grosset & Dunlap, 1922.

. . . *and Their Trick Dog*, Grosset & Dunlap, 1923.

. . . *at a Sugar Camp*, Grosset & Dunlap, 1924.

. . . *on the Rolling Ocean*, Grosset & Dunlap, 1925.

. . . *on Jack Frost Island*, Grosset & Dunlap, 1927.

. . . *at Shore Acres*, Grosset & Dunlap, 1928.

. . . *at Berry Hill*, Grosset & Dunlap, 1929.

. . . *at Sky Top*, Grosset & Dunlap, 1930.

. . . *at the Summer Carnival*, Grosset & Dunlap, 1931.

''MAKE-BELIEVE STORIES'' SERIES

The Story of a Sawdust Doll, Grosset & Dunlap, 1920.

. . . *White Rocking Horse*, Grosset & Dunlap, 1920.

. . . *Lamb on Wheels*, Grosset & Dunlap, 1920.

. . . *Bold Tin Soldier*, Grosset & Dunlap, 1920.

. . . *Candy Rabbit*, Grosset & Dunlap, 1920.

. . . *Monkey on a Stick*, Grosset & Dunlap, 1920.
. . . *Calico Clown*, Grosset & Dunlap, 1920.
. . . *Nodding Donkey*, Grosset & Dunlap, 1921.
. . . *China Cat*, Grosset & Dunlap, 1921.
. . . *Plush Bear*, Grosset & Dunlap, 1921.
. . . *Stuffed Elephant*, Grosset & Dunlap, 1922.
. . . *Woolly Dog*, Grosset & Dunlap, 1923.

"MOVING PICTURE GIRLS" SERIES

The Moving Picture Girls; or, First Appearances in Photo Dramas, Grosset & Dunlap, 1914.
. . . *at Oak Farm; or, Queer Happenings While Taking Rural Plays*, Grosset & Dunlap, 1914.
. . . *Snowbound; or, The Proof on the Film*, Grosset & Dunlap, 1914.
. . . *under the Palms; or, Lost in the Wilds of Florida*, Grosset & Dunlap, 1914.
. . . *at Rocky Ranch; or, Great Days among the Cowboys*, Grosset & Dunlap, 1914.
. . . *at Sea; or, A Pictured Shipwreck That Became Real*, Grosset & Dunlap, 1915.
. . . *in War Plays; or, The Sham Battles at Oak Farm*, Grosset & Dunlap, 1916.

"OUTDOOR GIRLS" SERIES

The Outdoor Girls of Deepdale; or, Camping and Tramping for Fun and Health, Grosset & Dunlap, 1913.
. . . *at Rainbow Lake; or, The Stirring Cruise of the Motor Boat Gem*, Grosset & Dunlap, 1913.
. . . *in a Motor Car; or, The Haunted Mansion of Shadow Valley*, Grosset & Dunlap, 1913.
. . . *in a Winter Camp; or, Glorious Days on Skates and Iceboats*, Grosset & Dunlap, 1913.
. . . *in Florida; or, Wintering in the Sunny South*, Grosset & Dunlap, 1913.
. . . *at Ocean View; or, The Box That Was Found in the Sand*, Grosset & Dunlap, 1915.
. . . *on Pine Island; or, A Cave and What It Contained*, Grosset & Dunlap, 1916.
. . . *in Army Service; or, Doing Their Bit for the Soldier Boys*, Grosset & Dunlap, 1918.
. . . *at the Hostess House; or, Doing Their Best for the Soldiers*, Grosset & Dunlap, 1919.
. . . *at Bluff Point; or, A Wreck and a Rescue*, Grosset & Dunlap, 1920.
. . . *at Wild Rose Lodge; or, The Hermit of Moonlight Falls*, Grosset & Dunlap, 1921.
. . . *in the Saddle; or, The Girl Miner of Gold Run*, Grosset & Dunlap, 1922.
. . . *around the Campfire; or, The Old Maid of the Mountains*, Grosset & Dunlap, 1923.
. . . *at Cape Cod; or, Sally Ann of Lighthouse Rock*, Grosset & Dunlap, 1924.
. . . *at Foaming Falls; or, Robina of Red Kennels*, Grosset & Dunlap, 1925.
. . . *along the Coast; or, The Cruise of the Motor Boat Liberty*, Grosset & Dunlap, 1926.
. . . *at Spring Hill Farm; or, The Ghost of the Old Milk House*, Grosset & Dunlap, 1927.
. . . *at New Moon Ranch; or, Riding with the Cowboys*, Grosset & Dunlap, 1928.
. . . *on a Hike; or, The Mystery of the Deserted Airplane*, Grosset & Dunlap, 1929.
. . . *on a Canoe Trip; or, The Secret of the Brown Mill*, Grosset & Dunlap, 1930.

. . . *at Cedar Ridge; or, The Mystery of the Old Windmill*, Grosset & Dunlap, 1931.
. . . *in the Air; or, Saving the Stolen Invention*, Grosset & Dunlap, 1932.
. . . *in Desert Valley; or, Strange Happenings in a Cowboy Camp*, Grosset & Dunlap, 1933.

"SIX LITTLE BUNKERS" SERIES

Six Little Bunkers at Grandma Bell's, Grosset & Dunlap, 1918.
. . . *at Aunt Jo's*, Grosset & Dunlap, 1918.
. . . *at Cousin Tom's*, Grosset & Dunlap, 1918.
. . . *at Grandpa Ford's*, Grosset & Dunlap, 1918.
. . . *at Uncle Fred's*, Grosset & Dunlap, 1918.
. . . *at Captain Ben's*, Grosset & Dunlap, 1920.
. . . *at Cowboy Jack's*, Grosset & Dunlap, 1921.
. . . *at Mammy June's*, Grosset & Dunlap, 1922.
. . . *at Farmer Joel's*, Grosset & Dunlap, 1923.
. . . *at Miller Ned's*, Grosset & Dunlap, 1924.
. . . *at Indian John's*, Grosset & Dunlap, 1925.
. . . *at Happy Jim's*, Grosset & Dunlap, 1928.
. . . *at Skipper Bob's*, Grosset & Dunlap, 1929.
. . . *at Lighthouse Nell's*, Grosset & Dunlap, 1930.

OTHER

Six Little Bunkers (four-in-one reprint), Grosset & Dunlap, 1933.
The Bobbsey Twins, The Bobbsey Twins in the Country, [and] *The Bobbsey Twins at the Seashore*, Donohue, ca. 1940.
The Bobbsey Twins Mystery Stories (contains *The Bobbsey Twins of Lakeport, The Bobbsey Twins' Adventures in the Country*, and *The Bobbsey Twins' Secret at the Seashore*), Grosset & Dunlap, ca. 1960.

SIDELIGHTS: In 1904 Edward Stratemeyer's new literary syndicate began to produce the "Bobbsey Twins." This first series produced by the new coalition was published under the house pseudonym Laura Lee Hope, "in the final analysis one of the most productive of all Stratemeyer Syndicate noms de plume," according to Carol Billman in *The Secret of the Stratemeyer Syndicate: Nancy Drew, the Hardy Boys, and the Million Dollar Fiction Factory*. The Bobbseys proved very popular, outselling all previous Stratemeyer series, and their popularity continues today with new adventures produced and old adventures rewritten for a modern juvenile audience. Glenn Collins, writing in the *New York Times* in 1987, described the series of more than 70 books for children seven to nine years old as having "sold more than 50 million copies worldwide." Each copy, adds Arthur Prager in *Saturday Review*, is "enjoyed by an average of two readers."

"The 'Bobbseys' were aimed at a younger market [than previous Stratemeyer series] and covered both male and female readers," explains Prager. "There were two sets of twins, Flossie and Freddie, who were four years old, and Nan and Bert, who were eight (they were later raised to six and twelve). They had a beloved dog, Snap, and a mischievous cat, Snoop." Their parents, Richard and Mary Bobbsey, the Bobbsey's cook and gardener, Dinah and Sam Johnson, and the bully Danny Rugg also figured in the books. But why twins? Bobbie Ann Mason, author of *The Girl Sleuth: A Feminist Guide*, suggests that "the Bobbsey Twins . . . are archetypal: they stroke the deepest longings of a child for a soulmate. The double theme is recurrent in children's literature, and the Bobbseys, more than others, have capitalized on this desire children have for a mirror-image that talks, sure proof that one has an identity."

Many of the earlier volumes chronicled the Bobbseys' adventures on vacation at various sites in and around the country. "Most of the excitement in the [earlier volumes of the] series was at the under-ten level," Prager continues. "Flossie saw a snake at a Sunday School picnic, but it turned out to be only an old dead stick. Mr. Bobbsey's wallet was stolen by a tramp. The littlest Bobbseys, however, were often caught in real danger: lost, caught in thunderstorms, trapped in a runaway balloon, or facing some similar peril." However, "at about the time the Hardy Boys and Nancy Drew first began their investigations," Billman observes, the Bobbsey Twins books "took on some of the traits of the mystery genre."

Some critics perceive unfortunate consequences in this trend. "The Bobbseys are now known as amateur detectives and there is a purpose to childhood after all," says Mason. She sees that purpose as a defense of the upper-middle-class values that she calls "Bobbsey Bourgeois." "There used to be a lot of simple fun in the childlike defense of innocence, but nowadays the twins are super-serious," she concludes. "They must defend that station-wagon scene like crazy." "Why don't the Bobbseys investigate some truly destructive social force, such as the David Letterman show?" complains Margot Dougherty of *People* magazine. In some of the most recent volumes the twins foil arsonists, shoplifters, kidnapping and blackmail, states Michael Kernan of the *Washington Post*. "It's one thing for Nancy Drew and the Hardy Boys and all the children on public TV to be detectives," he protests, "but somehow I didn't expect it from the Bobbseys."

Although the series has been undeniably popular, some readers consider the Bobbseys overly moralistic and sentimental. Russel Nye, for instance, writing in *The Unembarrassed Muse: The Popular Arts in America*, calls the books "surely the most syrupy" of their genre. Mason disagrees; she declares that the volumes "supplant sentiment with action. The characters are morally upright and the books end happily, but sloppy emotions and meaningful moralities are shunned in favor of zestful pursuits. The characterizations are so slim and the language so sparse it is hard to say that they are ever drippy." Mason detects other, more ominous defects in the books: "Models of authority are insisted upon in the Bobbsey Twins series, not only through obvious sexism but through red-white-and-blue patriotism and through extensive racism." Gypsies and other racial minorities are frequently characterized as malign or threatening, but this, she feels, is a result of the milieu from which the stories came. "The racist assumptions are basic to most of the series books I read as a child," she concludes, "but the series stories were merely a barometer of society, rather than deliberate propaganda."

In the 1950s, the Stratemeyer Syndicate began to rewrite the "Bobbsey Twins" in order to eliminate some of these outdated racial and ethnic prejudices. In this, declares Mason, they were partly successful; but, she adds, they "could not remove the fundamental assumptions without abandoning the Bobbseys and starting over again." The stories were showing their age in other ways as well. Characters, plots, and settings, says Billman, "evoked an *earlier* era, and that was bad." In 1987, Simon & Schuster again updated the Bobbseys in a new paperback series that, according to Collins, "fast-forwarded" the family into the 1980s. Mrs. Bobbsey has a part-time job as a reporter for the *Lakeport News*, and Sam Johnson has become foreman at Mr. Bobbsey's lumber mill. Nan wears silver eyeshadow, a miniskirt, and purple lipstick, and she and Bert belong to a punk rock band. "But one character has hardly been touched: Danny Rugg," states an article in *Pub-*

lishers Weekly. "It seems that once a bully, always a bully, whether in 1904 or 1987."

Besides the "Bobbsey Twins," the pseudonym Laura Lee Hope was used on books intended for young children ("Make-Believe Stories," "Bunny Brown and His Sister Sue," "Six Little Bunkers") and teen-aged girls ("Blythe Girls," "Moving Picture Girls," "Outdoor Girls"). Harriet S. Adams, former Stratemeyer Syndicate partner Nancy Axelrad, Lilian and Howard R. Garis, James Duncan Lawrence, Edward L. Stratemeyer, and Andrew E. Svenson were among the authors who used this pseudonym to write "Bobbsey Twins" books and others. For more information, see the sketches in this volume for Harriet S. Adams, Howard R. Garis, James Duncan Lawrence, Edward L. Stratemeyer, and Andrew Svenson.

BIOGRAPHICAL/CRITICAL SOURCES:

BOOKS

Billman, Carol, *The Secret of the Stratemeyer Syndicate: Nancy Drew, the Hardy Boys, and the Million Dollar Fiction Factory*, Ungar, 1986.
Garis, Roger, *My Father Was Uncle Wiggily*, McGraw-Hill, 1966.
Johnson, Deidre, editor and compiler, *Stratemeyer Pseudonyms and Series Books: An Annotated Checklist of Stratemeyer and Stratemeyer Syndicate Publications*, Greenwood Press, 1982.
Mason, Bobbie Ann, *The Girl Sleuth: A Feminist Guide*, Feminist Press, 1975.
Nye, Russel B., *The Unembarrassed Muse: The Popular Arts in America*, Dial, 1970.

PERIODICALS

New York Times, August 17, 1987.
New York Times Book Review, April 26, 1981.
People, September 14, 1987.
Publishers Weekly, August 28, 1987.
Saturday Review, July 10, 1971.
Washington Post, September 5, 1987.
Washington Post Book World, August 17, 1980.

—Sketch by Kenneth R. Shepherd

*   *   *

HOPKIN, Alannah 1949-

PERSONAL: Born September 6, 1949, in Singapore; daughter of Denis Arthur Buxton (an anesthesiologist) and Angela Mary (Foley) Hopkin. *Education:* Queen Mary College, London, B.A. (with honors), 1974; University of Essex, M.A., 1976. *Religion:* Roman Catholic.

ADDRESSES: Home—2 Higher O'Connell St., Kinsdale, County Cork, Ireland. *Agent*—Aeg Davis-Poynter, 118 St. Pancras, Chichester, West Sussex PO19 4LH, England.

CAREER: Free-lance journalist in London, England, 1976-82; writer, 1982—.

MEMBER: International PEN, National Union of Journalists.

WRITINGS:

A Joke Goes a Long Way in the Country (novel), Hamish Hamilton, 1982, Atheneum, 1983.
The Out-Haul (novel), Hamish Hamilton, 1985.
In the Footsteps of St. Patrick (historical study), Grafton Books, 1988.

Contributor of articles and reviews to magazines and newspapers, includng the *Irish Times*. Area editor of Fodor's *Ireland* (travel guide), 1986—.

SIDELIGHTS: Alannah Hopkin told *CA:* "I earned my living by writing for six years before I started work on my first novel. I worked on it for a year on weekends and wrote features and book reviews during the week."

AVOCATIONAL INTERESTS: "I live beside the sea. When I am not reading or writing, I go sailing or horseback riding or take long walks. I also like sitting in bars and talking to people and playing poker, and I enjoy cooking and gardening."

BIOGRAPHICAL/CRITICAL SOURCES:

PERIODICALS

Irish Times, February 9, 1985.
Los Angeles Times, April 13, 1983.
New Statesman, July 16, 1982.
New Yorker, May 2, 1983.
New York Times Book Review, December 22, 1985.
Spectator, March 9, 1985.

* * *

HOROWITZ, Joseph   1948-

PERSONAL: Born February 12, 1948, in New York, N.Y.; son of Jacob (a doctor) and Leah (a psychiatric social worker; maiden name, Lurie) Horowitz. *Education:* Swarthmore College, B.A., 1970; University of California, Berkeley, M.J., 1975.

ADDRESSES: Home—49 West 96th St., No. 6G, New York, N.Y. 10025. *Agent*—Robert Cornfield Literary Agency, 145 West 79th St., New York, N.Y. 10024.

CAREER: New York Times, New York City, music critic, 1976-80; Kaufmann Concert Hall of 92nd St., New York City, program editor and chief annotator, 1981—.

AWARDS, HONORS: ASCAP-Deems Taylor Award, 1983, for *Conversations with Arrau;* National Book Critics Circle nomination for best criticism, 1987, for *Understanding Toscanini: How He Became an American Culture-God and Helped Create a New Audience for Old Music.*

WRITINGS:

Conversations with Arrau, Knopf, 1982.
Understanding Toscanini: How He Became an American Culture-God and Helped Create a New Audience for Old Music, Knopf, 1987.

Contributor to periodicals, including *High Fidelity, Musical America, New York Times Magazine,* and *Opus.*

WORK IN PROGRESS: A book on piano competitions.

SIDELIGHTS: Former *New York Times* music critic Joseph Horowitz brings his talent for analysis to his surveys of two notable musicians. *Conversations with Arrau* is a retrospective look at the life and career of Chilean pianist Claudio Arrau. It includes interviews with Arrau and his associates, among them Daniel Barenboin, Garrick Ohlsson, and Sir Colin Davis. In his *Washington Post* review, music critic Joseph McLellan notes that the book "is informative and readable on [Arrau's] performing preferences, techniques and quirks, his attitudes toward various composers and colleagues, his drives and superstitions, even the often harrowing details of his biography and his psyche." Although the musician's life is presented through a series of interviews, Horowitz's "skillful questions and sensitive editing produce a smooth narrative of the pianist's life and capture his passion for music," observes *New York Times Book Review* contributor GraceAnne Andreassi DeCandido. Linda Sanders believes these refinements are due to the author's critical background: "Horowitz's knowledge-able grasp of Arrau's playing and history allows him to bypass the more pedestrian forms of information-gathering and go directly to the heart of each subject," the critic comments in the *Nation.* "*Conversations with Arrau,*" summarizes Sanders, "is quite simply the best book I've ever read about a performing musician."

Understanding Toscanini: How He Became an American Culture-God and Helped Create a New Audience for Old Music "does not aim to explore Toscanini's psyche as much as to chart the development of his public image—a myth, even a fetish—that was brilliantly exploited by the organizations employing him," describes Rupert Christiansen in the *Listener.* Although conductor Arturo Toscanini began his career in Europe, his almost three decades with the New York Philharmonic and the NBC Symphony (created especially for him) had a great influence on both the American public and his musical peers. Horowitz's main thesis is that "the Toscanini legend . . . had much less to do with the appreciation of art than with a response to the peculiarly American sort of hucksterism practiced by P. T. Barnum," recounts Herbert Glass in the *Los Angeles Times Book Review.* The result, asserts Horowitz, was a standardization of orchestral repertoire that ironically limited the scope of music being brought to the American public at the same time it was supposedly "democratizing" classical music.

The book contains analyses of various elements of the American culture and music scenes, including the periods before and after 1926-54, the years of Toscanini's most powerful influence. "In digesting countless reviews," writes Michael Walsh in *Time,* "Horowitz has provided a valuable look at the state of American music criticism during the first half of the century." In addition, some of the analyses "reproduce in discursive language the highly charged effect of Toscanini's performances," observes Edward W. Said in the *New York Times Book Review.* Nevertheless, Said finds that the author "is simply too linear and repetitive, too single-minded and too homogenizing in his analyses." *Washington Post Book World* contributor Samuel Lipman also sees a single-mindedness in Horowitz's assessment of Toscanini himself: "[The] tendentious formulation of a real problem unfortunately confuses the victim with the perpetrator," ultimately blaming Toscanini for all the attention the public lavished on him. Similarly, Christiansen wonders about "[Toscanini's] own views on the gigantic shadow he cast over the American musical scene, and why has Horowitz, otherwise an impeccable researcher, not interviewed anyone who knew or even played for him?" But whatever its shortcomings, *Understanding Toscanini* "provides at once a comprehensive portrait of Toscanini's adopted musical milieu and an outspoken caveat on the dangers of commercializing high culture," concludes John von Rhein of Chicago *Tribune Books.* "It represents an important, substantial addition to the literature," adds the critic, "one that will be read and argued over long after the superficial, fatuous or fawning volumes that have been written on Toscanini have disappeared."

BIOGRAPHICAL/CRITICAL SOURCES:

PERIODICALS

Christian Science Monitor, December 7, 1984.
Listener, July 23, 1987.
Los Angeles Times Book Review, April 26, 1987.
Nation, June 11, 1987.
New Republic, June 1, 1987.
New Statesman, July 31, 1987.
Newsweek, March 2, 1987.
New York Review of Books, April 9, 1987.
New York Times Book Review, March 20, 1983, March 8, 1987.
Time, March 9, 1987.
Times Literary Supplement, September 4, 1987.
Tribune Books (Chicago), February 15, 1987.
Washington Post, October 23, 1982.
Washington Post Book World, March 1, 1987.

*   *   *

HOTCHNER, A(aron) E(dward)   1920-

PERSONAL: Born June 28, 1920, in St. Louis, Mo.; son of Samuel (a jeweler) and Sally (a Sunday school administrator; maiden name, Rossman) Hotchner; married Geraldine Mavor, May 15, 1949 (died January, 1969); married Ursula Robbins (a magazine researcher), April 18, 1970; children: Tracy, Holly, Timothy Aaron. *Education:* Washington University, St. Louis, Mo., A.B., LL.B., 1941. *Politics:* Democrat.

ADDRESSES: Home and office—14 Hillandale Rd., Westport, Conn. 06880. *Agent*—Owen Laster, Wiiliam Morris Agency, 1350 Sixth Ave., New York, N.Y. 10019.

CAREER: Admitted to Missouri State Bar, 1941; practiced law in St. Louis, Mo., 1941-42; *Cosmopolitan* (magazine), New York City, articles editor, 1948-50; free-lance writer, 1950—. Vice-president and treasurer, Newman's Own, Inc. *Military service:* U.S. Army Air Forces, 1942-46; Anti-submarine command, North African Theater of Operations; became major.

MEMBER: Authors League of America, Dramatists Guild, Writer's Guild of America, PEN, Missouri Bar Association.

WRITINGS:

The Dangerous America (novel), Random House, 1958.
Papa Hemingway: A Personal Memoir, Random House, 1966, reprinted as *Papa Hemingway: The Ecstasy and Sorrow*, Morrow, 1983.
Treasure (novel), Random House, 1970.
King of the Hill (memoir), Harper, 1973.
Looking for Miracles, Harper, 1975.
Doris Day: Her Own Story, Morrow, 1976.
Sophia, Living and Loving: Her Own Story, Morrow, 1979.
The Man Who Lived at the Ritz (novel), Putnam, 1982.
Choice People: The Greats, Near-Greats, and Ingrates I Have Known, Morrow, 1984.

PLAYS

"The Capital of the World" (ballet), first produced in New York at Metropolitan Opera House, October, 1954.
"A Short Happy Life" (two-act), first produced in Los Angeles at Huntington Hartford Theatre, November, 1961.
The White House (two-act; first produced in New York at Henry Miller's Theatre, May 19, 1964), Samuel French, 1965.
"The Hemingway Hero" (two-act), first produced in New Haven, Conn., at Shubert Theatre, September, 1967.
"Do You Take This Man?" (two-act), first produced in New York at Experimental Theatre, April, 1970.
"Sweet Prince" (two-act), first produced in St. Louis at the Loretto-Hilton, 1980, produced in New York at the Theater Off Park, 1982.
(With Cy Coleman) "Let 'Em Rot!" (musical), first produced in Miami at the Coconut Grove Playhouse, February, 1988.

OTHER

Author of screenplay, "Adventures of a Young Man," released by 20th Century Fox; also author of teleplays for "Playhouse 90," 1958-60, including "Last Clear Chance," and "The Killers of Mussolini," and teleplays adapted from major works of Ernest Hemingway, including "For Whom the Bell Tolls," 1958, and "The Killers," 1959.

Contributor of more than 300 articles and short stories to magazines, including *Reader's Digest, Esquire,* and *Saturday Evening Post.*

SIDELIGHTS: Although A. E. Hotchner has written best-selling biographies of Doris Day and Sophia Loren and has associated with and written about such luminaries as Clark Gable, Frank Sinatra, Candace Bergen, and Burt Reynolds, he is best known for his 1966 biography of "Papa" Ernest Hemingway, based on his thirteen-year friendship with the Nobel Prize-winning author. Their association began in 1948, when Hotchner was assigned by a *Cosmopolitan* editor to travel to Cuba and persuade Hemingway to contribute to the magazine. While his editor was insistent on getting a Hemingway story, Hotchner remarks in his memoir *Choice People: The Greats, Near-Greats, and Ingrates I Have Known* that "I was just as intent on avoiding this assignment, for I had a worshipful awe of Hemingway that bordered on the fearful—this gargantuan literary god, omnivorous, immortal, impervious to the ravages of war, pestilence, rampant bulls, and debauchery." After receiving Hotchner's apologetic note explaining his assignment, Hemingway invited the young editor for drinks and later extended the invitation to fishing on his boat. These meetings developed into a relationship that continued until Hemingway's death, and during this time Hotchner took notes and tape recordings of their conversations. These notes and tapes led to *Papa Hemingway: A Personal Memoir*, which sparked controversy as some critics questioned its validity and Hemingway's widow Mary sued to prevent the sale of the book. Nevertheless, the book was a best-seller and many critics find it an enlightening account of Hemingway's life, especially of the years leading to the author's suicide in 1961.

Papa Hemingway is presented mainly in the form of a dialogue, based on Hotchner's recollections of their many conversations. Hotchner's method of presentation has been criticized, for many reviewers are uncomfortable with the accuracy of a straight "repetition" of conversation. For example, a *Times Literary Supplement* critic comments that "Mr. Hotchner is to be congratulated on his assiduity, but he is to be sharply blamed for not discriminating by even the simplest of footnotes between those dialogues that were written down afterwards and those that were directly captured on tape." The critic also adds that "the conversations are often so extended that the reader would be more willing to accept them if he knew the method that had been employed."

Other reviewers think that the material Hotchner presents does not contribute much that is new to histories about Hemingway;

New York Review of Books contributor John Thompson writes that "much of the material has been published before in other forms, in interviews, in [brother] Leicester Hemingway's book . . . and notably in *A Moveable Feast*." Thompson also complains that what the book does add is "only the black side of the fame, the legends of bragging, drinking, picking fights, and then finally, the bad last years." Hemingway scholar Philip Young goes further in his criticism, accusing Hotchner of actually taking his material from these other sources, and citing instances where he believes the author has misrepresented himself. Writing in the *Atlantic,* Young comments that "it is awfully difficult to believe that Mr. Hotchner has accurately described the matter out of which his book was made, and just as hard to resist the notion that this *Personal Memoir* is less by than compiled by him." The *Times Literary Supplement* critic is less harsh, however, remarking only that "Hotchner does not even remind the reader that [one excerpt] is a quotation, though he is far too familiar with Hemingway's writings not to have recognized it."

Other critics, however, find Hotchner's work to be a believable source of information about Hemingway's life, due to his special association with the author. Writing in the *Saturday Review,* Granville Hicks comments that "Hotchner's style is journalistic, and some of his stories—he tells many good ones—may be touched up a little. And of course no one can be expected to repeat conversations verbatim. But I think that in essentials Hotchner is to be depended on, and I think so because his devotion to Hemingway is so obviously genuine." Because Hotchner acted as a type of agent for Hemingway, and was the one writer permitted to adapt his works for television, some critics believe that Hotchner is uniquely qualified to write about the great author. "Hemingway soon took Hotchner into his confidence and made him a literary executor of sorts, commissioning him to tell the world everything he would not have the time to put into writing," writes George Wickes in the *New Republic.* Wickes also observes that the dialogue "sounds like Hemingway alright, with some bad patches that make it sound all the more genuine." Vance Bourjaily, commenting on some of the "stories" related in the memoir, adds in the *New York Times Book Review* that "generally these things come from Hemingway, talking to Hotchner, who in turn passes along to us what was said. Thus, once we agree, and there seems no reason not to, that Hotchner must be repeating what he heard, the question of veracity returns to the subject."

Even though Hotchner's relationship with his subject may make the memoir credible, many observers find that this same relationship prevents him from objectively assessing Hemingway's recollections. Even after the biographer concludes that one of Hemingway's tales was mathematically impossible, *Atlantic* contributor Edward Weeks is still unsure "whether Hotchner believed the stories or mistrusted them as much as I do." Bourjaily expresses a similar opinion: "Hotchner may seem a little credulous, though it doesn't seem to me to happen often." The reviewer offsets this criticism by remarking that "after all, it is probably more important to believe that that's what the man said, than to have to believe that every word he said, in high spirited conversation, was true. And indeed, at one such point Hotchner makes his own disclaimer." Bourjaily also notes that "if there is a touch of hero-worship required for total belief of [some] observations . . . , it's a state of mind many readers will bring to the book, and there is not so much of that kind of thing as to be constantly irritating to the more skeptical."

For all the criticism of *Papa Hemingway,* many reviewers still find it a definitive portrait of the Nobel laureate. *New York Times* writer Conrad Knickerbocker expresses the opinion that Hotchner "has moved as close as anyone with a tape recorder can toward defining the intricate character of a man who, for better or worse, was a giant." Similarly, Wickes remarks that "it is unlikely that we shall ever get a better portrait of Hemimgway as he was in his latter years." The reviewer adds, "Hotchner is not only a good reporter, he is an intelligent admirer with an honest concern for presenting the man he observed." In contrast to the criticism that the book details only the dark side of Hemingway, Bourjaily writes that "it is one of the pleasures of Hotchner's book that we find Hemingway for once allowed to display his gentleness, his gift for casual phrase-making, his gift for delighting in things and thereby making them delightful to others." Weeks speculates that "Hemingway, who sought legal protection against such biographers as Charles Fenton, must have suspected that this book was coming and wished it to be of the best vintage. One is captivated by his enormous zest, his wonderful talk, his quick friendships, and his hatred of cant." And Hicks, remarking on the lawsuit of Hemingway's widow, comments that "Hotchner helps us to feel what the things were that Hemingway couldn't stand. I am grateful for the book, and I think that in the long run Mary Hemingway may be. For one thing," continues the critic, "I feel a little better about some of the bad work Hemingway did in his later years; it's still bad, but I don't, so to speak, hold it up against him."

Hotchner told *CA* that "my long association with Hemingway was the overriding influence on me as a writer and as a person. His sense of values was extraordinary and infectious." This influence is evident in some of Hotchner's later works, which include a play titled "The Hemingway Hero" and the 1982 novel *The Man Who Lived at the Ritz*, which includes an appearance by Hemingway in the story. Like his Hemingway biography, Hotchner's novel inspires a variety of critical responses. Larry Jonas of the *West Coast Review of Books* calls it a "first-rate book [that] elevates its author to the first rank of contemporary novelists," while James Campbell writes in the *New Statesman* that the novel "goes from the ridiculous to the even more ridiculous." Set in Paris during the Nazi occupation, *The Man Who Lived at the Ritz* follows expatriate American Philip Weber as he goes from apathetic collaboration with the Nazis to active resistance against them. The novel eventually develops into an all-out thriller, with Philip attempting to escape from the Nazis he has betrayed.

In placing the novel in World War II France, Hotchner attempts to recreate the atmosphere of an era. As part of his method, the author makes several period references and "interposes a body of actual personages in his story to enhance its sense of timeliness and lend validity and interest to *roman a clef* situations," describes Jonas. Reviewers differ as to the effectiveness of this technique; for example, while *Washington Post* contributor Charles Naylor finds Hotchner "competent" in his general knowledge, he complains of "a tendency to display conspicuous period consumerism . . . all to no positive effect. Ditto the people." In contrast, Monty Haltrecht writes that "the background detail is carefully researched, and convincing. . . . It is easy to believe in the Paris of the period," continues the writer in the *Times Literary Supplement*, "and in Philip as a long-time resident. The complexities of the spy system and Philip's gradual enmeshment are excitingly detailed [and] characters from real life abound."

In the course of Philip Weber's gradual change, many reviewers see the influence of Hemingway in Hotchner's story, although they again disagree upon its value. In the *Los Angeles Times Book Review*, David Shaw writes that Hotchner "still seems preoccupied with the man." He elaborates: "Hemingway never actually appears in the novel, but he is often referred to—as in . . . 'Hemingway was the man Philip would have liked to be, but he didn't have the courage or imagination or talent.'" Haltrecht observes that "one senses a submerged serious theme. . . . Hemingway is the prototype of the artist confronting the reality of his century by involving himself in it as a man of action and embracing violence." The critic speculates that "Hotchner has remained obsessed by this figure, no less so because he chooses to present a hero who is the obverse of Hemingway." Perhaps taking this observation further, Alan Cheuse writes in the *New York Times Book Review* that during the course of the novel, Philip is inspired "to become the kind of hero Papa Hemingway would be proud of." Overall, Cheuse finds *The Man Who Lived at the Ritz* to be an "entertaining homage to a literary hero and to the genre of spy fiction. . . . [It] is more than a merely classy little 'head fake.'" And Jonas concludes by calling the novel "a story of incompromising tension and high-level interest. It's Hotchner's best work—by far."

Although he has received much attention for his work on Hemingway, Hotchner has not limited himself by focusing on this one influence. Throughout his career, as he writes in a *New York Times* article, "I have roamed the writing landscape, going from novels to biographies to short stories to television dramas to ballets to Broadway plays." He also writes of a new ambition: "Despite all that variety, for as long as I can remember I have coveted what I secretly considered the ultimate but elusive spice—writing a musical comedy." In 1988 Hotchner realized that goal as well, with the premiere of "Let 'Em Rot," which he wrote with composer Cy Coleman. As he recalls in the *New York Times*, the experience was something completely different for him: "For a guy who has spent his life sitting alone in a small room confronted with a blank piece of paper in an inanimate typewriter, collaborating with all these lively singers and dancers has been a welcome tonic."

MEDIA ADAPTATIONS: A reading by Robert Stack of an abridged form of *Papa Hemingway: A Personal Memoir* was recorded on cassette for Listen for Pleasure in 1986; "The Man Who Lived at the Ritz," a two-part television series based on Hotchner's novel, aired on WWOR on November 28, 1988.

BIOGRAPHICAL/CRITICAL SOURCES:

BOOKS

Hotchner, A. E., *Papa Hemingway: A Personal Memoir*, Random House, 1966.
Hotchner, A. E., *King of the Hill*, Harper, 1973.
Hotchner, A. E., *Choice People: The Greats, Near-Greats, and Ingrates I Have Known*, Morrow, 1984.

PERIODICALS

Atlantic, May, 1966, August, 1966.
Chicago Tribune, April 22, 1984, April 23, 1984.
Chicago Tribune Book World, May 20, 1979.
Esquire, June, 1966.
Harper's, June, 1966.
Los Angeles Times Book Review, May 9, 1982, April 8, 1984.
National Review, June 28, 1966.
New Republic, April 23, 1966.
New Statesman, September 23, 1966, March 26, 1982.

Newsweek, April 11, 1966, December 19, 1966.
New Yorker, June 20, 1970, September 9, 1972.
New York Review of Books, April 28, 1966.
New York Times, April 2, 1966, January 23, 1982, September 25, 1982, March 27, 1988.
New York Times Book Review, April 3, 1966, July 26, 1970, August 13, 1972, February 28, 1982, January 22, 1984, April 8, 1984.
Publishers Weekly, February 2, 1976, May 10, 1976, August 16, 1976.
Quill & Quire, August, 1986.
Saturday Review, April 9, 1966, April 19, 1967, June 27, 1970, November 28, 1970.
Spectator, July 8, 1966.
Time, April 15, 1966.
Times Literary Supplement, September 29, 1966, April 9, 1982.
Washington Post, January 22, 1982.
Washington Post Book World, September 3, 1972, April 6, 1975, February 18, 1979.
West Coast Review of Books, April, 1982.

—*Sketch by Diane Telgen*

*   *   *

HOUTON, Kathleen
See KILGORE, Kathleen

*   *   *

HOWE, Russell Warren   1925-

PERSONAL: Born August 1, 1925, in London, England. *Education:* Attended Cambridge University; Sorbonne, University of Paris, D-es-E.C.F., 1948.

ADDRESSES: Home—P.O. Box 32221, Washington, D.C. 20007. *Agent*—Jacques de Spoelberch, Shagbark Rd., Wilson Point, South Norwalk, Conn. 06854.

CAREER: Reuters Ltd., London, England, foreign correspondent, 1948-52; *Sunday Times*, London, foreign correspondent, 1955-58; *Washington Post*, Washington, D.C., bureau chief in Africa, 1958-65; Columbia University, New York City, Ford Foundation fellow in advanced reporting, 1965-66; *Christian Science Monitor*, Boston, Mass., foreign correspondent, 1968-69; *The Sun*, Baltimore, Md., bureau chief in Africa, 1969-72; Delegation of the European Community, Washington, D.C., media director, 1972-75; *Events*, Beirut, Lebanon, Washington correspondent, 1978-79; Washington correspondent for Middle East publication *Eight Days*, 1979-82; *Washington Times*, defense correspondent, 1982-83, diplomatic correspondent, 1983-85; *Al Qabas*, Kuwait City, Kuwait, Washington correspondent, 1985-87; American Broadcasting Co. (ABC-TV/Radio), New York City, roving correspondent, 1987—. Free-lance investigative reporter and magazine, radio, and television correspondent, 1952-55, 1966-68, and 1975-78; internationally syndicated columnist, 1987—. Special counsel to Premier Sylvanus Olympio of Togo, 1960-61; visiting professor at Dakar University, 1967-71; guest scholar at Woodrow Wilson International Center of the Smithsonian Institution, 1972.

MEMBER: International Press Institute, PEN, Authors League of America, Institute of Journalists, Foreign Correspondents Association of Washington (president), Washington Independent Writers, Foreign Correspondent Clubs of Tokyo, Seoul, Hong Kong, and Bangkok, Aircraft Owners and Pilots Association, Sigma Delta Chi.

AWARDS, HONORS: Venus Award for documentary production, Houston International Film Festival, 1981.

WRITINGS:

The Light and the Shadows (stories), Secker & Warburg, 1952.
Behold, the City (novel), Secker & Warburg, 1953.
Theirs the Darkness (African travel book), Jenkins, 1955.
Black Star Rising (African travel and politics), Jenkins, 1958.
Black Africa: A History in Two Volumes, Walker & Co., Volume I, 1966, Volume II, 1967.
The African Revolution, Barnes & Noble, 1968.
Along the Afric Shore: An Historical Review of Two Centuries of U.S.-African Relations, Barnes & Noble, 1968.
(With Sarah Hays Trott) *The Power Peddlers: How Lobbyists Mold U.S. Foreign Policy,* Doubleday, 1977.
Weapons: The International Game of Arms, Money, and Diplomacy, Doubleday, 1980.
Mata Hari: The True Story, Dodd, 1986.
The Koreans: Passion and Grace, Harcourt, 1988.

Contributor to periodicals, including *Foreign Affairs, Look, New Republic, Economist,* and *Saturday Review.*

WORK IN PROGRESS: Flight of the Cormorants, a novel; *Witch Hunt: The Crucifixion of "Tokyo Rose"; The Swallow's Story: Sleeping with the F.B.I.*

AVOCATIONAL INTERESTS: Light plane flying, sport fishing.

*   *   *

HUGHES, Catharine R(achel)   1935-1987

PERSONAL: Born September 4, 1935, in Newark, N.J.; daughter of John (a glassblower) and Eleanor (a nurse; maiden name Woodworth) Hughes. *Education:* Attended schools in Lancaster, Pa. *Religion:* Roman Catholic.

ADDRESSES: Home—79 West 12th St., Apt. 6B, New York, N.Y. 10011.

CAREER: L. B. Herr & Son (distributors of school supplies and equipment), Lancaster, Pa., assistant to president, 1952-57; Sheed & Ward, New York City, director of advertising and publicity, 1957-63; Frederick A. Praeger, New York City, merchandising coordinator, 1963-67; *Publishers Weekly,* New York City, fiction reviewer and specialist in Soviet and Eastern European affairs, 1966-83; *America,* New York City, drama critic, 1967-87; *Plays and Players,* London, England, American theatre critic, 1969-75, 1981-84. Off- and Off-Off-Broadway reviewer for *Show Business,* 1968-70; arts columnist for *Holiday,* 1976-77; contributing editor for *Stages,* 1984-87; New York columnist for *Plays,* 1984-87; free-lance editor in New York City. Hughes was assistant director for Off-Broadway plays, theatre consultant for New York State Council on the Arts, editorial consultant to book publishers, and film columnist for *Critic.*

MEMBER: New Drama Forum Association (chairman of awards committee), Drama Desk, American Theatre Critics Association.

WRITINGS:

Plays, Politics, and Polemics, DBS Publications, 1973.
American Playwrights: 1945-75, Pitman Publishing (London), 1976.

PLAYS

"Madame Lafayette" (historical drama), first produced at the Blackfriar's Theatre, New York, N.Y., March 3, 1960.

EDITOR; "MYSTICISM AND MODERN MAN" SERIES

Darkness and Light: Selections from St. John of the Cross, Sheed, 1972.
The Prison of Love: Selections from St. Teresa of Avila, Sheed, 1972.
The Clouded Hills: Selections from William Blake, Sheed, 1973.
Dreams and Regrets: Selections from the Russian Mystics, Sheed, 1973.
The Weeping Sky (Jewish mystics), Sheed, 1973.
Leaves in the Dust (American Indian mystics), Sheed, 1973.

EDITOR AND PHOTOGRAPHER

The Secret Shrine: Islamic Mystical Reflections, Seabury, 1974.
The Smokeless Fire: Hindu Mystical Reflections, Seabury, 1974.
The Solitary Journey: Buddhist Mystical Reflections, Seabury, 1974.
Shadow and Substance: Taoist Mystical Reflections, Seabury, 1974.

PHOTOGRAPHER

Sister Mary Roger Thibodeaux, *A Black Nun Looks at Black Power,* Sheed, 1972.
F. J. Sheed, *The Lord's Prayer,* Seabury, 1975.
Sheed, *Our Hearts Are Restless,* Seabury, 1976.
Sheed, *Death into Life,* Arena Lettres, 1978.
Helen Thomas, *Personal Prayers,* Arena Lettres, 1978.
Richard Liddy, *In God's Gentle Arms,* Arena Lettres, 1979.

OTHER

(Adapter) Francis Peter LeBuffe, *My Changeless Friend,* Arena Lettres, 1974.
(Adapter) LeBuffe, *Friends Aren't Kept Waiting,* Sheed, 1975, revised edition, 1978.
(Adapter) LeBuffe, *More of My Changeless Friend,* Arena Lettres, 1977.
(Editor and author) *American Theater Annual,* four volumes, Gale, 1978-81.

Contributor to *Nation, Playbill, Ebony, Progressive, After Dark, Commonweal, Christian Century, Congress Bi-Weekly, Critic, Saturday Review, Antioch Review, Arts in Society, New York Times,* and other periodicals.

AVOCATIONAL INTERESTS: Travel to Russia, eastern and western Europe, Britain and Ireland, Canada, and the Caribbean.

OBITUARIES:

PERIODICALS

Publishers Weekly, August 7, 1987.*

*   *   *

HUSEN, Torsten   1916-

PERSONAL: Born March 1, 1916, in Lund, Sweden; son of Johan S. (an executive director) and Betty Maria (Prawitz) Husen; married Ingrid Joensson (a language teacher), April 10, 1940; children: Sven-Torsten, Mats O., Goerel. *Education:* University of Lund, B.A., 1937, M.A., 1938, Fil.lic., 1941, Ph.D., 1944.

ADDRESSES: Home—Armfeltsgatan 10, S-11534 Stockholm, Sweden. *Office*—University of Stockholm, S-10691 Stockholm, Sweden.

CAREER: University of Lund, Lund, Sweden, instructor and research assistant, 1938-44; University of Stockholm, Stockholm, Sweden, associate professor, 1947-52, professor of educational psychology, 1953-56, professor of education and director of Institute of Educational Research, 1959-71, professor of international education, 1971-81, professor emeritus, 1982—. Visiting professor, University of Chicago, 1959, University of Hawaii, 1968, Ontario Institute for Studies in Education, 1971, Stanford University, 1981, and University of California, Berkeley, 1984. Chairman of governing boards of universities and of international education associations. Participant in international seminars. Expert and consultant on various Swedish government commissions. Consultant to many world organizations. *Military service:* Swedish Armed Forces, psychologist, 1942-44, senior psychologist, 1944-51.

MEMBER: International Association for the Evaluation of Educational Achievement (chairman), International Council for Educational Development, International Academy of Education (chairman), American Academy of Arts and Sciences, National Academy of Education (United States; foreign associate), Swedish Royal Academy of Sciences, Finnish Academy, Polish Academy.

AWARDS, HONORS: Prize for educational authorship, Swedish Literary Foundation, 1961; fellow, Center for Advanced Study of the Behavioral Sciences, 1965-66, and 1973-74; honorary degrees from University of Chicago, 1967, Brunel University, 1974, University of Glasgow, 1974, University of Rhode Island, 1975, University of Joensuu, 1979, University of Amsterdam, 1982, and Ohio State University, 1985; medal for distinguished service, Teachers College, Columbia University, 1969; fellow, National Center for the Humanities, 1978-79; Swedish cultural prize, Natur & Kultur Publishing House, 1979; Gold Medal, National Institute of Educational Research (Tokyo), 1983; honorary professor, University of Shanghai, 1984.

WRITINGS:

Psykologisk krigfoering, C.W.K. Gleerup, 1942.
Adolescensen: Undersoekningar roerande manlig svensk ungdom i aaldern 17-20 aar, Almqvist & Wiksell, 1944.
Studier roerande de eidetiska fenomenen, C.W.K. Gleerup, Volume I, 1946, Volume II, 1952.
Begavning och miljo: Studier i begavningsutvecklingens och begavningsurvalets psykologiskpedagogiska och sociala problem, H. Gerber, 1948.
Om innerborden av psykologiska matningar: Nagra bidrag till psykometrikens metdlara, C.W.K. Gleerup, 1949.
Anders Berg under folkskolans pionjaeraar, Erlanders Bookstore, 1949.
Raettstavningsfoermagans psykologi: Nagra experimentella bidrag, Svensk Lararetidnings Forlag, 1950.
Testresultatens prognosvarde: En Undersokning av den teoretiska skolningens inverkan pa testresultaten, intelligenstedens prognosvarde och de sociala faktorernas inverkan pa urvalet till hogre laroanstalter, H. Gerber, 1950.
(With Sven-Eric Henricson) *Some Principles of Construction of Group Intelligence Tests for Adults: A Report on Construction and Standardization of the Swedish Induction Test (the I-test),* Almqvist & Wiksell, 1951.
Tvillingstudier: Undersoekningar roerande begavningsforhallanden, skolprestationer, intraparrelationer, antropometriska matt, handstilslikhet samt diagnosproblem m.m. inom

e reprensentativ population likkonade tvillingar, Almqvist & Wiksell, 1953.
Psykologi, Svenska Bokforlaget, 1954, 5th edition with Lars Larsson, 1966.
(With others) *Betyg och standardprov: En orientering for foraldrar och larare,* Almqvist & Wiksell, 1956.
(With others) *Standardproven: En redogoerelse foer konstruktion och standardisering,* Almqvist & Wiksell, 1956.
Militart och civilt, Norstedt, 1956.
Ur psykologisk synvinkel, Almqvist & Wiksell, 1957.
Pedagogisk psykologi, Svenska Bokforlaget, 1957, 4th edition, 1968.
(With Artur Olsson) *Akademiska studier: Studieteknik for studenter,* Svenska Bokforlaget, 1958.
Psychological Twin Research: A Methodological Study, Almqvist & Wiksell, 1959.
Att undervisa studenter, Almqvist & Wiksell, 1959.
(Editor with Sten Henrysson) *Differentiation and Guidance in the Comprehensive School: Report on the Sigtuna Course Organized by the Swedish Government under the Auspices of the Council of Europe, August, 1958,* Almqvist & Wiksell, 1959.
(With Urban Dahllof) *Matematik och modersmaalet i skola och yrkesliv: Studier av kunskapskrav, kunskapbehallning och undervisningens upplaggning,* Studieforbundet Naringsliv och Samhalle, 1960, translation published as *Mathematics and Communication Skills in School and Society: An Empirical Approach to the Problem of Curriculum Contest,* Industrial Council for Social and Economic Studies, 1960.
Psykologi, introduktion til psykologien af i dag, A. Busck, 1960.
Skolan i ett foranderligt samhalle, Almqvist & Wiksell, 1961, 2nd edition, 1963.
De Farliga psykologerna, Raben & Sjogren, 1961.
Studieteknik foer gymnasiet, Svenska Bokforlaget, 1961.
(With Elvy Johanson) *Fysik och kemi i skola och yrkesliv,* Studienfoerbundet Naaringsliv och Samhalle, 1961.
School Reform in Sweden, U.S. Department of Health, Education, and Welfare, 1961.
Tonaaringarna i utbildningssamhaelle—Nagra maenniska ocho miljoe: Studier i Amerikansk pedagogik, Almqvist & Wiksell, 1962.
(With Gosta Ekman) *Att studera psykologi och pedagogik,* Svenska Bokforlaget, 1962.
Problems of Differentiation in Swedish Compulsory Schooling, Svenska Bokforlaget, 1962.
(With Malcolm Shepherd Knowles) *Erwachsene lernen,* E. Klett, 1963.
Skola foer 60-talet, Almqvist & Wiksell, 1963.
(With Gunnar Boalt) *Skolans sociologi,* Almqvist & Wiksell, 1964, 3rd edition, 1967.
Det nya gymnasiet: Information och debatt, Almqvist & Wiksell, 1964.
(With Karl-Erik Warneryd) *Psykologi for fackskolan,* Svenska Bokforlaget, 1966.
Skola i foervandling, Almqvist & Wiksell, 1966.
(Editor with Ingvar Carlson) *Tonaringarna och skolan,* Almqvist & Wiksell, 1966.
(Editor) *International Study of Achievement in Mathematics: A Comparison of Twelve Countries,* Wiley, 1967.
(With Boalt) *Educational Research and Educational Change: The Case of Sweden,* Wiley, 1968.
Skola foer 80-talet, Almqvist & Wiksell, 1968.

(Compiler) *Livsaaskaadning och religion,* Svenska Bokforlaget, 1968.

*Talent, Opportunity and Career: A Twenty-Six Year Follow-
up of 1500 Individuals,* Almqvist & Wiksell, 1969.

(Compiler with Sune Askaner) *Literatur: Konst och musik,*
Laromedelsforlaget, 1969.

(Contributor) D. F. Swift, editor, *Basic Readings in the Sociology of Education,* Routledge & Kegan Paul, 1970.

(Compiler with Ulf Hard af Segerstad) *Samhaallsfraagor: Pla-
nering ocho miljoe,* Laromedelsforlaget, 1971.

*Present Trends and Future Developments in Education: A Eu-
ropean Perspective,* Ontario Institute for Studies in Education, 1971.

Utbildning ar 2000, Bonniers, 1971.

*Social Background and Educational Career: Research Per-
spectives on Equality of Educational Opportunity,* Organization for Economic Co-operation and Development,
1972.

Skolans kris ocha andra uppsatser om utbildning, Almqvist &
Wiksell, 1972.

*Svensk skola i internationell belysning: Naturorienterande am-
nen,* Almqvist & Wiksell, 1973.

Talent, Equality and Meritocracy, Nijhoff, 1974.

The Learning Society, Methuen, 1974.

Social Influences on Educational Attainment, Organization for
Economic Co-operation and Development, 1975.

Universiteten och forskningen, Natur och Kultur, 1975.

(Contributor) Jerome Karable and A. H. Halsey, *Power and
Ideology in Education,* Oxford University Press, 1977.

The School in Question, Oxford University Press, 1979.

The Future of Formal Education, Almqvist & Wiksell, 1980.

En obotlig akademiker: En professors memoarer, Natur och
Kultur, 1981, translation published as *An Incurable Academic: Memoirs of a Professor,* Pergamon Press, 1983.

(Contributor) Manfred Niessen and Jules Peschar, *International Comparative Research: Problems of Theory, Methodology, and Organization in Eastern and Western Europe,* Pergamon Press, 1982.

(Editor with S. Opper) *Multicultural and Multilingual Education in Immigrant Countries,* Pergamon Press, 1983.

(Editor with M. Kogan) *Educational Research and Policy:
How Do They Relate?,* Pergamon Press, 1984.

Devenir Adulte dans une societe en mutation, OECD, 1985,
translation published as *Becoming Adult in a Changing
Society,* OECD, 1985.

(Contributor) Bjoern Engholm, editor, *Demokratie faengt in
der Schule an,* Eichborn Verlag, 1985.

Also contributor of chapters, introductions, and forewords to
many studies in psychology and education. Co-editor-in-chief,
*International Encyclopedia of Education: Research and Stud-
ies;* editor, *Scandinavian Encyclopedia of Psychology and Education;* member, international board of consultants, *World
Book Encyclopedia.*

*WORK IN PROGRESS: The Relationships between Research-
ers and Policymakers in Education in Sweden, 1944-1962.*

SIDELIGHTS: In an article entitled "Marriage to Higher Education" in the *Journal of Higher Education,* Torsten Husen
writes, "I can hardly think of any other group in society to
which the principle of lifelong learning applies more ade-
quately than to academics involved in advanced teaching and
research. In essence, to be involved in research means that
one constantly has to revise ideas and restructure models of
reality and incessantly move into new intellectual territory. A
university professor is never 'fully prepared' or 'competent.'

One has to prove oneself continuously. The most salient feature of the professorial role is that of a permanent student who
is involved in continuous learning, not least from one's own
students of whom the more able often are the initiators of new
paradigms of thinking in the discipline."

Utbildning ar 2000 has been translated into Polish, Russian,
Arabic, and Hindi. *The Learning Society* has been translated
into Dutch, Italian, and Spanish, and *The School in Question*
has been translated into Swedish, Danish, Portugese, Chinese,
French, German, Spanish, and Japanese.

AVOCATIONAL INTERESTS: Collecting old books.

BIOGRAPHICAL/CRITICAL SOURCES:

BOOKS

Husen, Torsten, *An Incurable Academic: Memoirs of a Professor,* Pergamon Press, 1983.

PERIODICALS

Journal of Higher Education, volume 51, number 6, 1980.

*   *   *

HUTTON, James   1902-1980

PERSONAL: Born November 30, 1902, in Airth, Stirlingshire,
Scotland; died October 29, 1980; son of John and Elizabeth
(Arthur) Hutton. *Education:* Cornell University, B.A., 1924,
M.A., 1925, Ph.D., 1927.

ADDRESSES: Office—Department of Classics, Cornell University, Goldwin Smith Hall, Ithaca, N.Y. 14853.

CAREER: Columbia University, New York, N.Y., instructor
in Greek and Latin, 1926-27; Cornell University, Ithaca, N.Y.,
instructor, 1927-29, assistant professor, 1929-38, professor,
1938-61, Kappa Alpha Professor of Classics, 1961-68, professor emeritus, 1968-80, chairman of department, 1946-52,
member of department of comparative literature, 1927-43.

MEMBER: Modern Language Association of America, American Philological Association, Society for the Humanities (fellow), American Council of Learned Societies (member of
committee on Renaissance studies), Phi Beta Kappa, Phi Kappa
Phi.

AWARDS, HONORS: Guggenheim fellow, 1958-59.

WRITINGS:

The Greek Anthology in Italy, Cornell University Press, 1935.

*The Greek Anthology in France and in Latin Writers of the
Netherlands,* Cornell University Press, 1946, revised edition, Johnson Reprint, 1967.

Essays on Renaissance Poetry, edited by Rita Guerlac, Cornell
University Press, 1980.

(Editor) *Aristotle's Poetics,* Norton, 1982.

(Editor with Rita Guerlac) *Themes of Peace in Renaissance
Poetry,* Cornell University Press, 1984.

Co-editor of "Cornell Studies in Classical Philology." Contributor of articles and reviews to scholarly periodicals.*

*   *   *

HYDE, Mary (Morley Crapo)   1912-

PERSONAL: Born July 8, 1912, in Detroit, Mich.; daughter
of Stanford Tappan (an executive) and Emma Caroline (Morley) Crapo; married Donald Frizell Hyde, September 16, 1939

(died February 6, 1966); married David McAdam Eccles, September 26, 1984. *Education:* Vassar College, A.B., 1934, Columbia University, M.A., 1936, Ph.D., 1947.

ADDRESSES: Home—Four Oaks Farm, 350 Burnt Mills Rd., Somerville, N.J. 08876. *Office*—Room 424, One Palmer Sq., Princeton, N.J. 08540.

CAREER: Writer. Council member, Friends of Columbia University Libraries, 1954—; member, humanities visiting committee of University of Chicago, 1956—; member, board of governors of Johnson House (London), 1963—; member, English department and library advisory councils of Princeton University, 1965—; member, English department and libraries visiting committees of Harvard University, 1966—. Trustee, Pierpont Morgan Library, 1966—; trustee, Yale Library Associates, 1970—; American trustee, British Library, 1980.

MEMBER: Association Internationale de Bibliophile (vice-president, 1983), Bibliographical Society of America, Johnsonians, Keats-Shelley Association of America (director, 1967—), Johnson Society of Lichfield, England (president, 1957), Royal Society of Arts (London; Benjamin Franklin fellow), Zamorano (Roxburgh, England), Boswell Society (Auchinleck, Scotland; vice-president, 1982), Lambeth Palace Library, Grolier Club (council member, 1979; vice-president, 1982), Hroswitha Club, Phi Beta Kappa.

AWARDS, HONORS: D.Litt., Douglas College, 1965; Litt.D., Brown University, 1968, University of Birmingham, 1969; D.H.L., Union College, 1979; Officier de l'Ordre de la Couronne, Belgium, 1979; honorary fellow, Pembroke College, Oxford University, 1986.

WRITINGS:

Playwriting for Elizabethans, Columbia University Press, 1949, new edition, 1973.
(Editor with E. L. McAdam and Donald Hyde) *Johnson's Diaries, Prayers, and Annals,* Yale University Press, 1958.
Four Oaks Farm and Its Library, Clarke & Way, 1967.
The Impossible Friendship: Boswell and Mrs. Thrale, Harvard University Press, 1973.
(Editor) Hester Lynch Salusbury Thrale Piozzi, *The Thrales of Streatham Park,* Harvard University Press, 1977.
(Editor) *Bernard Shaw and Alfred Douglas: A Correspondence,* Ticknor & Fields, 1982.

Member of editorial committee of "Yale Works of Johnson," 1957, and "Private Papers of James Boswell," 1966—.

HYNDMAN, Donald W(illiam)   1936-

PERSONAL: Born April 15, 1936, in Vancouver, British Columbia, Canada; son of Andrew William (a high school principal) and Joan (MacDonald) Hyndman; married Shirley Boyes, August 25, 1960; children: Karen, David. *Education:* University of British Columbia, B.A.Sc., 1959; University of California, Berkeley, Ph.D., 1964.

ADDRESSES: Home—615 Hastings, Missoula, Mont. 59801. *Office*—Department of Geology, University of Montana, Missoula, Mont. 59801.

CAREER: University of Montana, Missoula, assistant professor, 1964-68, associate professor, 1968-72, professor of geology, 1972—. Technical officer of Geological Survey of Canada in British Columbia, summers, 1959-62.

MEMBER: Mineralogical Association of Canada, Geological Association of Canada (fellow), Association of Professional Geologists, Geological Society of America (fellow), Mineralogical Society of America (fellow), Sigma Xi.

WRITINGS:

Petrology and Structure of Nakusp Map-Area, British Columbia, Geological Survey of Canada, 1969.
Petrology of Igneous and Metamorphic Rocks, McGraw, 1972, 2nd edition, 1985.
(With David D. Alt) *Roadside Geology of the Northern Rockies,* Mountain Press, 1972.
(With Alt) *Rocks, Ice, and Water: Geology of Watertow Glacier Park,* Mountain Press, 1973.
(With Alt) *Roadside Geology of Northern California,* Mountain Press, 1974.
(With Alt) *Roadside Geology of Oregon,* Mountain Press, 1978.
(With Alt) *Roadside Geology of Washington,* Mountain Press, 1984.
(With Alt) *Roadside Geology of Montana,* Mountain Press, 1986.
(Editor with Alt) Keith Frye, *Roadside Geology of Virginia,* Mountain Press, 1986.
(Editor with Alt) Bradford B. Van Diver, *Roadside Geology of New Hampshire-Vermont,* Mountain Press, 1987.
(Editor with Alt) Halka Chronic, *Roadside Geology of New Mexico,* Mountain Press, 1987.
(With Alt) *Roadside Geology of Idaho,* Mountain Press, 1988.
(Editor with Alt, Cathy Connor, and Daniel O'Haire) *Roadside Geology of Alaska,* Mountain Press, 1988.

Contributor to journals.

I-J

INGALLS, Jeremy 1911-

PERSONAL: Born April 2, 1911, in Gloucester, Mass.; daughter of Charles Augustine and May-Estelle (Dodge) Ingalls. *Education:* Tufts University, A.B., 1932, A.M., 1933; University of Chicago, Oriental Institute, advanced Chinese studies, 1945-47. *Religion:* Episcopalian.

ADDRESSES: Home—6269 East Rosewood, Tucson, Ariz. 85711.

CAREER: Western College, Oxford, Ohio, assistant professor, 1941-43; Rockford College, Rockford, Ill., resident poet, 1947, assistant professor of English literature, 1948-50, associate professor, 1953-55, professor of English and Asian studies, 1955-60, chairman of literature department, 1953-60; full-time writer, 1960—. Visiting lecturer at more than fifty colleges and universities, 1941—; Fulbright professor in American literature, Kobe College, Japan, 1957-58; Rockefeller Foundation lecturer, Kyoto, Japan, 1958; Steinman Foundation lecturer on poetry, 1960; University of Arizona Poetry Center lecturer, 1964; senior guest poet, Tucson Poetry Festival, 1985.

MEMBER: Poetry Society of America, Modern Language Association of America (chairman of Asian literature conference, 1959-60), Association for Asian Studies, Authors Guild, Authors League of America, Dante Society, New England Poetry Society, Phi Beta Kappa, Chi Omega.

AWARDS, HONORS: Yale Series of Younger Poets Prize, 1941, for *The Metaphysical Sword;* Guggenheim fellow, 1943-44; American Academy of Arts and Letters grant, 1944-45; classical Chinese research fellowship from Republic of China, 1945-47; Shelley Memorial Award for Poetry, 1950; Lola Ridge Memorial Award for Poetry, 1951, 1952; Ford Foundation faculty fellow, 1952-53; L.H.D., Rockford College, 1960; Litt.D., Tufts University, 1965; named honorary epic poet laureate, United Poets Laureate International, 1965; named Distinguished American Woman of Letters by Republic of Philippines, 1967.

WRITINGS:

A Book of Legends (short stories), Harcourt, 1941.
The Metaphysical Sword (poetry), Yale University Press, 1941, reprinted, AMS Press, 1970.
Tahl (narrative poem), Knopf, 1945.
The Galilean Way (prose), Longmans, Green, 1953.

(Editor and translator with S. Y. Teng) Li Chien-nung, *A Political History of China,* Van Nostrand, 1956.
The Woman from the Island (poetry), Regnery, 1958.
These Islands Also (poetry), Tuttle, 1959.
(Translator) Yao Hsin-nung, *The Malice of Empire,* University of California Press, 1970.
(Translator and author of commentary) Yoichi Nakagawa, *Nakagawa's Tenno Yugao,* Twayne, 1975.
This Stubborn Quantum: Sixty Poems, Capstone Editions, 1983.
A Summer Liturgy: A Verse Play, Capstone Editions, 1985.
The Epic Tradition and Related Essays, Capstone Editions, 1988.

Contributor of poems to anthologies and more than one hundred magazines and literary reviews. Contributor to professional journals.

WORK IN PROGRESS: Seacross and *Patmos,* long poems, Volumes 2 and 3 of the trilogy of which *Tahl* is the first; *Mao's Poems: The Political Legacy,* an analysis of the Chinese texts, new English translations, and an explication of the poems' literary and political contexts.

SIDELIGHTS: Jeremy Ingalls's poem, ''Ballad of the Times of Men,'' from *The Metaphysical Sword,* was set to music for symphony orchestra and women's chorus by composer Everett Helm, and performed by the Cincinnati Symphony Orchestra. Other poems have been published in Italian, French, Japanese, and Korean.

*   *   *

JABBER, Fuad (Amin)
See JABBER, Paul

*   *   *

JABBER, Paul 1943-
(Fuad [Amin] Jabber)

PERSONAL: Surname is accented on first syllable; original name, Fuad Amin Jabber; name legally changed, February, 1976; born November 22, 1943, in Buenos Aires, Argentina; came to the United States in 1970, naturalized citizen, 1976; son of Amin (a businessman) and Najla (a businesswoman; maiden name, Sefa) Jabber; married Tania Leovin, July 2,

1966 (divorced, 1981); married Diana W. Woods (a marketing executive), January 1, 1984; children: Eva. *Education:* American University of Beirut, B.A., 1967, M.A., 1969; University of California, Los Angeles, Ph.D., 1974.

ADDRESSES: Home—515 East 79th St., New York, N.Y. 10021. *Office*—Bankers Trust, P.O. Box 318, Church Street Station, New York, N.Y. 10015.

CAREER: Adlai Stevenson Institute of International Affairs, Chicago, Ill., research fellow in international affairs, 1973-75; University of California, Los Angeles, assistant professor, 1974-80, associate professor of political science, 1980-82; Bankers Trust, New York, N.Y., vice president of political assessment group and senior political analyst, 1982—. Consultant to RAND Corp., U.S. Department of State, and U.S. Arms Control and Disarmament Agency.

MEMBER: International Institute of Strategic Studies, International Studies Association.

AWARDS, HONORS: First Prize from Arab Cultural Circle, Beirut, Lebanon, 1971, for Arabic edition of *Israel and Nuclear Weapons*.

WRITINGS:

(Editor under name Fuad Jabber) *International Documents on Palestine, 1967*, Institute for Palestine Studies, 1970.
(Under name Fuad Jabber) *Israel and Nuclear Weapons*, Chatto & Windus, 1971.
(Under name Fuad Jabber, with William B. Quandt and Ann M. Lesch) *The Politics of Palestinian Nationalism*, University of California Press, 1973.
Not by War Alone: Security and Arms Control in the Middle East, University of California Press, 1981.

CONTRIBUTOR

J. C. Hurewitz, editor, *Oil, the Arab-Israel Dispute, and the Industrial World: Horizons of Crisis*, Westview, 1976.
Milton Leitenberg and Gabriel Sheffer, editors, *Great Power Intervention in the Middle East*, Pergamon, 1979.
Stephen S. Kaplan, editor, *Diplomacy of Power: Soviet Armed Forces as a Political Instrument*, Brookings Institution, 1981.
Malcolm H. Kerr and El-Sayyed Yassin, editors, *Rich and Poor States in the Middle East: Egypt and the New Arab Order*, Westview, 1982.

OTHER

Contributor to *Palestine Yearbook*. Contributor to scholarly journals.

SIDELIGHTS: Paul Jabber told *CA:* "In my new banking career, I am currently responsible for determining political and economic risk in some thirty countries spanning southern Europe and the Middle East, from Portugal and Morocco to Pakistan. My writing output is copious, but also extremely sensitive and restricted in circulation to those with a need-to-know within the bank. I have no major work-in-progress for publication due to heavy corporate responsibilities and frequent travel to the countries I monitor. My job does provide me with rich opportunities for comparative observation of how disparate societies cope with similar economic and political problems, and I plan to publish on the subject as time and circumstances permit."*

JACKSON, Jesse   1908-1983

PERSONAL: Born January 1, 1908, in Columbus, Ohio; died April 14, 1983, in Boone, N.C.; son of Jesse (a trucker) and Mable (Rogers) Jackson; married Ann Newman (a social worker), September 19, 1938; children: Judith Ann. *Education:* Attended Ohio State University, 1927-29. *Politics:* Independent. *Religion:* Baptist.

ADDRESSES: Home—80 La Salle St., New York, N.Y. 10027. *Office*—Duncan Hall, Appalachian State University, Boone, N.C. 28608. *Agent*—Anita Diamant, Writers' Workshop, Inc., 51 East 42nd St., New York, N.Y. 10017.

CAREER: Writer. Worked as juvenile probation officer, in Columbus, Ohio, beginning 1936; worked for the U.S. Postal Service in Columbus; worked for H. Wolfe Book Manufacturing Company; worked as a reader for National Bureau of Economic Research, 1951-68; Appalachian State University, Boone, N.C., 1974-83, instructor, lecturer, and writer in residence.

MEMBER: Authors Guild, Authors League of America, Kiwanis Club.

AWARDS, HONORS: Award from Child Study Association for *Call Me Charley;* commendation from Council of Christians and Jews for *Anchor Man;* MacDowell Colony fellowship; Carter G. Woodson Book Award, National Council for the Social Studies, 1975, for *Make a Joyful Noise unto the Lord!: The Life of Mahalia Jackson, Queen of Gospel Singers;* LL.D., Appalachian State University, 1982.

WRITINGS:

YOUNG ADULT NOVELS

Call Me Charley, illustrated by Doris Spiegel, Harper, 1945, Dell, 1968.
Anchor Man, illustrated by Spiegel, Harper, 1947, Dell, 1968.
Room for Randy, Friendship Press, 1957.
Charley Starts from Scratch, illustrated by Frank C. Nicholas, Harper, 1958.
Tessie, illustrated by Harold James, Harper, 1968.
Tessie Keeps Her Cool, Harper, 1970.
The Sickest Don't Always Die the Quickest, Doubleday, 1971.
The Fourteenth Cadillac, Doubleday, 1972.

YOUNG ADULT NONFICTION

I Sing Because I'm Happy (biography of Mahalia Jackson), Rutledge Books, 1972.
(With Elaine Landau) *Black in America: A Fight for Freedom*, Messner, 1973.
Make a Joyful Noise unto the Lord!: The Life of Mahalia Jackson, Queen of Gospel Singers, Crowell, 1974.

OTHER

Contributor of articles and reviews to periodicals, including *Crisis.*

SIDELIGHTS: For more than three decades, Jesse Jackson wrote books directed towards black adolescents growing up in America. His landmark novel *Call Me Charley*, first published in 1945, stands as one of the first books for young adults that openly dealt with racial prejudice. The story of Charles Moss, a young black boy who lives in an all-white neighborhood and attends an all-white school, *Call Me Charley* "was the first book to present anything resembling a genuine black-white confrontation," notes Dorothy M. Broderick in *Image of the*

Black in Children's Fiction. In a memorable scene from the book, Charles responds to a white boy's calling him "Sambo" by answering, "My name is Charles. Charles Moss." The novel charts the young boy's experiences and struggles as he sets out to gain respect and acceptance from the whites he lives among.

Call Me Charley was praised as a sincere account of a young black boy's experiences in a racially discriminatory world. "The hurt and bewilderment of a boy who is treated differently because of the color of his skin gets across to the reader with an impact he is not likely to forget," wrote a reviewer for *Book Week.* May Hill Arbuthnot and Zena Sutherland commented in *Children and Books* that "Jesse Jackson has given a full and moving account of the kind of discriminations a black child may encounter.... It is a touching story made more poignant by Charley's quiet, patient acceptance of his lot.... The author has too realistic an approach to suggest a complete solution, but he tells a good story of a brave, likeable boy in a difficult world." Calling the novel "a contribution to understanding," May Lamberton Becker in the *New York Herald Tribune Book World* added that "the young author, whose ear is uncommonly sensitive, reproduces the staccato touch and distinctive turn of Negro speech without attributing dialect to educated Northern negroes."

In a 1977 profile by Ruby J. Lanier for *Language Arts,* Jackson commented on how he decided to write books for young people. While working as a juvenile probation officer in the 1930s, Jackson encountered the case of three Ohio boys who had been convicted of the robbery and murder of a restaurant owner. "Investigation of their case brought out that all three boys had dropped out of school because they were ashamed to tell their teachers they could not read. Their ages ran from fourteen to sixteen when this occurred. How to write something non-readers would want to read became an obsession of mine and still is." In the same profile, Jackson discussed the origins of *Call Me Charley* and the objectives he set for his first novel: "Prior to this time most blacks were lost like peas in a pod under such titles as George, Sam, Sambo, Coon, Nigger.... So with this *Call Me Charley* it was my aim to single out one black boy, to have him fight for at least the respect of being called Charles Moss. Charley had a game plan and the game plan began with recognize me as an individual and then we will go on from there and I'll try to get into the boys' club and try to win admission to the swimming pool and try to get a part in the school play."

Call Me Charley remains a popular book among adolescents, yet some recent criticism has pointed out that the story now appears dated. In *Written for Children: An Outline of English-Language Children's Literature,* John Rowe Townsend remarks that "the black characters bear injustice with a patience which now appears Uncle Tommish.... There is some resemblance to the treatment of the poor in books by well-meaning Victorians. Just as the poor were expected to rely on and be grateful for the beneficence of the rich, so the black must rely on and be grateful for the beneficence of the white." Townsend concedes, however, that in its time, *Call Me Charley* was a step in the right direction; he states, "We have no right to sneer from our vantage-point in the 1970s at advice which was sensible when it was given." In his later novel *Tessie,* Jackson again presents a character trying to live between two worlds. *Tessie* is the story of a young girl from Harlem who wins a scholarship to an all-white private school. In her new situation, Tessie "encounters an entirely different city and an entirely different world," notes Jane H. Clarke in *Book World,* adding

that Jackson "writes compassionately of a girl's struggle to face a strange world and be true to herself."

Jackson's young adult writings hold special relevance for black adolescents, yet both his fiction and nonfiction display a simplicity, honesty, and readability that can appeal to a wide range of readers. Regarding Jackson's novel *The Fourteenth Cadillac,* John W. Conner writes in *English Journal:* "Jesse Jackson has a talent for combining description and fast-paced narrative.... *The Fourteenth Cadillac* is great fun to read. It will touch many adolescents where their weaknesses in familial relationships occur." Jackson's 1974 biography of Mahalia Jackson, *Make a Joyful Noise unto the Lord!,* prompted the following comments from Lorain Alterman in the *New York Times Book Review:* "Jesse Jackson tells the story well—explaining vividly why Miss Jackson stuck with gospel rather than singing the blues.... On the whole [the book] will induce young readers to listen to some of Mahalia Jackson's recordings and to discover for themselves what made her gift so special."

BIOGRAPHICAL/CRITICAL SOURCES:

BOOKS

Arbuthnot, May Hill, and Zena Sutherland, *Children and Books,* Scott, Foresman, 1947, 4th edition, 1972.
Broderick, Dorothy M., *Image of the Black in Children's Fiction,* Bowker, 1973.
Contemporary Literary Criticism, Volume 12, Gale, 1980.
Jackson, Jesse, *Call Me Charley,* Harper, 1945, Dell, 1968.
Townsend, John Rowe, *Written for Children: An Outline of English-Language Children's Literature,* Lippincott, 1965, revised edition, 1974.

PERIODICALS

Book Week, November 11, 1945.
Book World, May 5, 1968.
Bulletin of the Center for Children's Books, April, 1974.
English Journal, May, 1971, Febraury, 1973.
Language Arts, March, 1977.
Library Journal, October 15, 1968.
New York Herald Tribune Book Review, November 11, 1945.
New York Times, December 23, 1945.
New York Times Book Review, May 26, 1968, February 14, 1971, June 16, 1974.
Saturday Review, June 15, 1968.
School Library Journal, October, 1968, January, 1975.
Washington Post Book World, May 19, 1974.

OBITUARIES:

PERIODICALS

Publishers Weekly, June 3, 1983.
School Library Journal, September, 1983.*

*   *   *

JAMES, Captain Lew
   See STRATEMEYER, Edward L.

*   *   *

JASEN, David A(lan) 1937-

PERSONAL: Born December 16, 1937, in New York, N. Y.; son of Barnet (a dentist) and Gertrude (Cohen) Jasen; married Susan Pomerantz (a registered nurse), December 30, 1963;

children: Raymond Douglas. *Education:* American University, B. A., 1959; Long Island University, M. S., 1972.

ADDRESSES: Home—225 East Penn St., Long Beach, N. Y. 11561. *Office*—C. W. Post Center, Long Island University, Greenvale, N. Y. 11548.

CAREER: Columbia Broadcasting System, New York City, supervisor of news videotape, 1959-66; American Educational Theatre Association, Washington, D.C., administrative assistant, 1967; Florists' Transworld Delivery Association, Detroit, Mich., field service representative, 1968-69; Reading Development Center, Inc., New York City, assistant to president, 1969-70; Long Island University, C. W. Post Center, Greenvale, N. Y., assistant professor, 1971-77, associate professor in School of Art, 1977—, professor of cmmunication arts, 1982—, director of communication arts, 1975—, chairman of communication arts department, 1979—. Ragtime composer and pianist; record producer; public speaker.

MEMBER: American Library Association, Ragtime Society, Maple Leaf Club, Pi Delta Epsilon, Alpha Psi Omega.

WRITINGS:

Bibliography and Reader's Guide to the First Editions of P. G. Wodehouse, Archon, 1970.
Recorded Ragtime, 1897-1958 (discography), Archon, 1973.
P. G. Wodehouse: A Portrait of a Master, Mason & Lipscomb, 1974, revised edition, Continuum, 1981.
(Editor) *The Uncollected Wodehouse,* Seabury, 1976.
(With Trebor Jay Tichenor) *Rags and Ragtime: A Musical History,* Seabury, 1978.
(Editor) *Ragtime: 100 Authentic Rags* (music), Big 3 Music, 1979.
(Editor) P. G. Wodehouse, *The Swoop! and Other Stories,* Seabury, 1979.
The Theatre of P. G. Wodehouse, Batsford, 1979.
(Editor) Wodehouse, *The Eighteen-Carat Kid, and Other Stories,* Continuum, 1980.
(Editor) Wodehouse, *Not George Washington: An Autobiographical Novel,* Continuum, 1980.
(Editor) George Barr McCutcheon, *Brewster's Millions,* Continuum, 1980.
(Editor) Jerome K. Jerome, *Three Men in a Boat,* Continuum, 1980.
(Editor) *P. G. Wodehouse: Four Plays,* Methuen, 1983.
Alexander's Ragtime Band and Other Favorite Song Hits, 1901-1911, Dover, 1987.
Tin Pan Alley, Fine, 1988.

Also author of several ragtime pieces, included in his sound recordings "Creative Ragtime," Euphonic Sound (1206), "Fingerbustin' Ragtime," Blue Goose Records (3001), "Rompin' Stompin' Ragtime," Blue Goose Records (3002), and "Rip-Roarin' Ragtime," Folkways (FG3561). Contributor to *Ragtimer.*

SIDELIGHTS: In editing the collection *The Swoop! and Other Stories,* "David A. Jasen has performed a valuable service in combing through turn-of-the-century popular British periodicals . . . in search of pieces from the earliest years of [P. G.] Wodehouse's long career," remarks *New York Times Book Review* contributor Robert Kiely. "The result is a collection of fresh and delightful entertainments, many of which had been thought lost and none of which has been published in book form in this country," continues the critic. Jasen has edited several volumes of Wodehouse's work, and was the first to publish a biography of the great British humorist. How-

ever, Jasen is also a composer, performer, and producer of ragtime music. Jasen has written and recorded several albums of ragtime, and has helped propogate the popularity of rags through concerts, radio shows, university classes, and books. His discography, *Recorded Ragtime, 1897-1958,* "is a landmark of ragtime scholarship," notes *Washington Post* writer Joseph McLellan. And his historical work, *Rags and Ragtime,* written with fellow composer-performer Trebor Jay Tichenor, is "commendably lucid, accurate, detailed, and well-arranged, with interesting illustrations," comments McLellan. The critic adds that the work helps "fill widespread needs which have begun to be felt only in the last generation and have reached their peak in the present decade."

BIOGRAPHICAL/CRITICAL SOURCES:

PERIODICALS

Los Angeles Times, June 1, 1980.
New York Times, November 14, 1971, February 10, 1985.
New York Times Book Review, July 1, 1979.
Time, May 4, 1981.
Washington Post, July 24, 1978.

*   *   *

JELLISON, Charles Albert, Jr.   1924-

PERSONAL: Born March 1, 1924, in Bangor, Me.; son of Charles A. (a postmaster) and Glennie (Noddin) Jellison; married Phyllis Gift, January 19, 1952; children: Jody Lee, Thomas Martin, Sally. *Education:* Attended University of Maine, 1941-43; Stanford University, A.B., 1947, M.A., 1948; attended University of Wisconsin, 1949-50; University of Virginia, Ph.D., 1956. *Politics:* Republican. *Religion:* Congregationalist.

ADDRESSES: Home—Mill Pond Rd., Durham, N.H. 03824. *Office*—History Department, University of New Hampshire, Durham, N.H. 03824.

CAREER: University of New Hampshire, Durham, from instructor to associate professor, 1956-69, professor of United States history, 1969—. Ernest J. King professor of maritime history, Naval War College, 1961-62; Fulbright professor of history, University of Witwatersrand, South Africa, 1970, and University of Malta, 1977-78.

MEMBER: American Historical Association, New England Association of Social Studies Teachers, Phi Beta Kappa.

AWARDS, HONORS: DuPont Senior Research fellowship, University of Virginia, 1955; Best Book Award, University Press of New England, and co-winner of Best Book Award, New England Historical Association, both 1985, for *Besieged: The World War II Ordeal of Malta, 1940-1942.*

WRITINGS:

Fessenden of Maine, Civil War Senator, Syracuse University Press, 1962.
Ethan Allen: Frontier Rebel, Syracuse University Press, 1969.
Tomatoes Were Cheaper: Tales of the 1930s, Syracuse University Press, 1977.
Besieged: The World War II Ordeal of Malta, 1940-1942, University Press of New England, 1985.

BIOGRAPHICAL/CRITICAL SOURCES:

PERIODICALS

American Historical Review, June, 1970, December, 1977, June, 1986.

Journal of American History, June, 1970.
New England Quarterly, March, 1970.
Pacific Historical Review, November, 1970.
Saturday Review, February 7, 1970.
Times Literary Supplement, May 17, 1985.
William & Mary Quarterly, July, 1970.

* * *

JEZER, Marty 1940-

PERSONAL: Surname is pronounced *Jay*-zer; born November 21, 1940, in Bronx, N.Y.; son of Meyer (a lawyer) and Blanche (Litzky) Jezer; children: Kathryn Ruth. *Education:* Lafayette College, A.B., 1961; graduate study at Boston University, 1961-62. *Politics:* Democratic socialist. *Religion:* Jewish.

ADDRESSES: Home and office—R.D. 3, Box 328, Brattleboro, Vt. 05301.

CAREER: Gimbel's Department Store, New York City, advertising copywriter, 1963-65; Crowell-Collier Educational Corp., New York City, staff writer and editor of *Merit Student Encyclopedia*, 1963-67; farmer, 1968—. Solar technician with Solar Applications Co., 1979-82. Draft resistance organizer, 1967-69; organizer of symposium on the future of the peace movement, 1986.

WRITINGS:

(Editor of revision) *The Food Garden*, Signet, 1971.
Power for the People: Active Nonviolence in the United States, Peace Press, 1977, revised edition published as *Power for the People: A Pictorial History of the Nonviolent Movement in America*, MNS Press, 1987.
The Dark Ages: Life in the United States, 1945-1960, South End Press, 1982.
Rachel Carson (biography for teens), Chelsea House, 1988.

CONTRIBUTOR

David Manning White and Robert Abel, editors, *The Funnies: An American Idiom*, Free Press, 1963.
Alice Lynd, editor, *We Won't Go*, Beacon Press, 1968.
Herbert H. Blumberg and A. Paul Hare, editors, *Nonviolent Direct Action*, Corpus, 1968.
Jane Gormley, editor, *The Prophetic Generation*, Catholic Art Association, 1970.
Mitchell Goodman, editor, *Movement for a New America*, Knopf, 1970.
Richard Wizansky, editor, *Home Comfort: Life on the Total Loss Farm*, Saturday Review Press, 1973.
Sally Freeman, editor, *The Green World*, Putnam, 1975.
Jon Snodgrass, editor, *Men against Sexism*, Times Change Press, 1977.
Frank Lindenfeld, editor, *Radical Perspectives on Social Problems*, 3rd edition, General Hall, 1986.

OTHER

Contributor to magazines and newspapers, including *Nation*, *Village Voice*, *Vermont Vanguard Press*, *Seven Days*, *The Natural Farmer*, *In These Times*, *Music Journal*, and *Radical America*. Founder and editor of *Win*, 1966-84, member of editorial board, 1966—; contributing editor of *Liberation*, 1967-68.

WORK IN PROGRESS: Bohos, Beats, Hipsters and Freaks: A History of the Bohemian Left in the United States; and, with Randy Kehler, *The Time is Now! A Handbook for Electoral Reform.*

SIDELIGHTS: Marty Jezer wrote: "I am a political activist; most of my writing is inspired by a commitment to peace, economic justice, human rights and social change. To augment my income from writing, I work in the trades: solar installations, home renovations, carpentry, [and] the like."

* * *

JONES, Faustine Childress
See JONES-WILSON, Faustine C(hildress)

* * *

JONES, Gayl 1949-

PERSONAL: Born November 23, 1949, in Lexington, Ky.; daughter of Franklin (a cook) and Lucille (Wilson) Jones. *Education:* Connecticut College, B.A., 1971; Brown University, M.A., 1973, D.A., 1975.

ADDRESSES: Office—c/o Beacon Press, 25 Beacon St., Boston, Mass. 02108.

CAREER: University of Michigan, Ann Arbor, 1975-83, began as assistant professor, became professor of English.

MEMBER: Authors Guild, Authors League of America.

AWARDS, HONORS: Award for best original production in the New England region, American College Theatre Festival, 1973, for "Chile Woman"; playwriting grant from Shubert Foundation, 1973-74; grant from Southern Fellowship Foundation, 1973-75; fellowship from Yaddo, 1974; grant from Rhode Island Council on the Arts, 1974-75; award from Howard Foundation, 1975; fiction award from *Mademoiselle*, 1975; fellowship from National Endowment of the Arts, 1976; fellowship from Michigan Society of Fellows, 1977-79; Henry Russell Award from University of Michigan, 1981.

WRITINGS:

FICTION

Corregidora (novel), Random House, 1975.
Eva's Man (novel), Random House, 1976.
White Rat (short stories), Random House, 1977.

POETRY

Song for Anninho, Lotus Press, 1981.
The Hermit-Woman, Lotus Press, 1983.
Xarque and Other Poems, Lotus Press, 1985.

OTHER

Chile Woman (play), Shubert Foundation, 1974.
(Contributor) Amiri Baraka and Amina Baraka, editors, *Confirmation*, Morrow, 1983.

Also contributor to *Chants of Saints; Keeping the Faith; Midnight Birds; Norton Anthology;* and *Soulscript*. Contributor to *Massachusetts Review*.

WORK IN PROGRESS: Research on sixteenth- and seventeenth-century Brazil and on settlements of escaped slaves, such as Palmares.

SIDELIGHTS: "Though not one of the best-known of contemporary black writers, Gayl Jones can claim distinction as the teller of the most intense tales," Keith E. Byerman writes in *Dictionary of Literary Biography*. Jones's novels *Corregidora* and *Eva's Man*, in addition to many of the stories in her collection *White Rat*, offer stark, often brutal accounts of black women whose psyches reflect the ravages of accumulated sexual and racial exploitation. In *Corregidora*, Jones reveals the tormented life of a woman whose female forebears—at the hands of one man—endured a cycle of slavery, prostitution, and incest over three generations. *Eva's Man* explores the deranged mind of a woman institutionalized for poisoning and sexually mutilating (by dental castration) a male acquaintance. And in "Asylum," a story from *White Rat*, a young woman is confined to a mental hospital for a series of bizarre behaviors that protest a society she sees bent on personal violation. "The abuse of women and its psychological results fascinate Gayl Jones, who uses these recurring themes to magnify the absurdity and the obscenity of racism and sexism in everyday life," comments Jerry W. Ward, Jr., in *Black Women Writers (1950-1980): A Critical Evaluation*. "Her novels and short fictions invite readers to explore the interior of caged personalities, men and women driven to extremes." Byerman elaborates: "Jones creates worlds radically different from those of 'normal' experience and of storytelling convention. Her tales are gothic in the sense of dealing with madness, sexuality, and violence, but they do not follow in the Edgar Allan Poe tradition of focusing of private obsession and irrationality. Though her narrators are close to if not over the boundaries of sanity, the experiences they record reveal clearly that society acts out its own obsessions often violently."

Corregidora, Jones's first novel, explores the psychological effects of slavery and sexual abuse on a modern black woman. Ursa Corregidora, a blues singer from Kentucky, descends from a line of women who are the progeny, by incest, of a Portuguese slaveholder named Corregidora—the father of both Ursa's mother and grandmother. "All of the women, including the great-granddaughter Ursa, keep the name Corregidora as a reminder of the depredations of the slave system and of the rapacious natures of men," explains Byerman. "The story is passed from generation to generation of women, along with the admonition to 'produce generations' to keep alive the tale of evil." Partly as a result of this history, Ursa becomes involved in abusive relationships with men. The novel itself spawns from an incident of violence; after being thrown down a flight of stairs by her first husband and physically injured so that she cannot bear children, Ursa "discharges her obligation to the memory of Corregidora by speaking [the] book," notes John Updike in the *New Yorker*. The novel emerges as Ursa's struggle to reconcile her heritage with her present life. *Corregidora* "persuasively fuses black history, or the mythic consciousness that must do for black history, with the emotional nuances of contemporary black life," Updike continues. "The book's innermost action . . . is Ursa's attempt to transcend a nightmare black consciousness and waken to her own female, maimed humanity."

Corregidora was acclaimed as a novel of unusual power and impact. "No black American novel since Richard Wright's *Native Son* (1940)," writes Ivan Webster in *Time*, "has so skillfully traced psychic wounds to a sexual source." Darryl Pinckney in *New Republic* calls *Corregidora* "a small, fiercely concentrated story, harsh and perfectly told. . . . Original, superbly imagined, nothing about the book was simple or easily digested. Out of the worn themes of miscegenation and diminishment, Gayl Jones *excavated* the disturbingly buried damage of racism." Critics particularly praised Jones's treatment of sexual detail and its illumination of the central character. "One of the book's merits," according to Updike, "is the ease with which it assumes the writer's right to sexual specifics, and its willingness to explore exactly how our sexual

and emotional behavior is warped within the matrix of family and race." In the book's final scene, Ursa comes to a reconciliation with her first husband Mutt by envisioning an ambivalent sexual relationship between her great-grandmother and the slavemaster Corregidora. *Corregidora* is a novel "filled with sexual and spiritual pain," writes Margo Jefferson in *Newsweek:* "hatred, love and desire wear the same face, and humor is blues-bitter. . . . Jones's language is subtle and sinewy, and her imagination sure."

Jones's second novel, *Eva's Man,* continues her exploration into the psychological effects of brutality, yet presents a character who suffers greater devastation. Eva Medina Canada, incarcerated for the murder and dental castration of a male acquaintance, narrates a personal history which depicts the damaging influences of a society that is sexually aggressive and hostile. Updike describes the exploitative world that has shaped the mentally deranged Eva: "Evil permeates the erotic education of Eva Canada, as it progresses from Popsicle-stick violations to the witnessing of her mother's adultery and a growing awareness of the whores and 'queen bees' in the slum world around her, and on to her own reluctant initiation through encounters in buses and in bars,where a man with no thumb monotonously propositions her. The evil that emanates from men becomes hers." In a narrative that is fragmented and disjointed, Eva gives no concrete motive for the crime committed; furthermore, she neither shows remorse nor any signs of rehabilitation. More experimental than *Corregidora, Eva's Man* displays "a sharpened starkness, a power of ellipsis that leaves ever darker gaps between its flashes of rhythmic, sensuously exact dialogue and visible symbol," according to Updike. John Leonard adds in the *New York Times* that "not a word is wasted" in Eva's narrative. "It seems, in fact, as if Eva doesn't have enough words, as if she were trying to use the words she has to make a poem, a semblance of order, and fails of insufficiency." Leonard concludes: "'Eva's Man' may be one of the most unpleasant novels of the season. It is also one of the most accomplished."

Eva's Man was praised for its emotional impact, yet some reviewers found the character of Eva extreme or inaccessible. June Jordan in the *New York Times Book Review* calls *Eva's Man* "the blues that lost control. This is the rhythmic, monotone lamentation of one woman, Eva Medina, who is nobody I have ever known." Jordan explains: "Miss Jones delivers her story in a strictly controlled, circular form that is wrapped, around and around, with ambivalence. Unerringly, her writing creates the tension of a problem unresolved." In the end, however, Jordan finds that the fragmented details of Eva's story, "do not mesh into illumination." On the other hand, some reviewers regard the gaps in *Eva's Man* as appropriate and integral to its meaning. Pinckney calls the novel "a tale of madness; one exacerbated if not caused by frustration, accumulated grievances" and comments on aspects that contribute to this effect: "Structurally unsettled, more scattered than *Corregidora, Eva's Man* is extremely remote, more troubling in its hallucinations. . . . The personal exploitation that causes Eva's desperation is hard to appreciate. Her rage seems never to find its proper object, except, possibly, in her last extreme act." Updike likewise holds that the novel accurately portrays Eva's deranged state, yet points out that Jones's characterization skills are not at their peak: "Miss Jones apparently wishes to show us a female heart frozen into rage by deprivation, but the worry arises, as it did not in 'Corregidora,' that the characters are dehumanized as much by her artistic vision as by their circumstances."

Jordan raises a concern that the inconclusiveness of *Eva's Man* harbors a potentially damaging feature. "There is the very real, upsetting accomplishment of Gayl Jones in this, her second novel: sinister misinformation about women—about women, in general, about black women in particular." Jones comments in *Black Women Writers (1950-1980)* on the predicament faced in portraying negative characters: "To deal with such a character as Eva becomes problematic in the way that 'Trueblood' becomes problematic in [Ralph Ellison's] *Invisible Man*. It raises the questions of possibility. Should a Black writer ignore such characters, refuse to enter 'such territory' because of the 'negative image' and because such characters can be misused politically by others, or should one try to reclaim such complex, contradictory characters as well as try to reclaim the idea of the 'heroic image'?" In an interview with Claudia Tate for *Black Women Writers at Work*, Jones elaborates: "'Positive race images' are fine as long as they're very complex and interesting personalities. Right now I'm not sure how to reconcile the various things that interest me with 'positive race images.' It's important to be able to work with a range of personalities, as well as with a range within one personality. For instance, how would one reconcile an interest in neurosis or insanity with positive race image?"

Although Jones's subject matter is often charged and intense, a number of critics have praised a particular restraint she manages in her narratives. Regarding *Corregidora*, Updike remarks: "Our retrospective impression of 'Corregidora' is of a big territory—the Afro-American psyche—rather thinly and stabbingly populated by ideas, personae, hints. Yet that such a small book could seem so big speaks well for the generous spirit of the author, unpolemical where there has been much polemic, exploratory where rhetoric and outrage tend to block the path." Similarly, Jones maintains an authorial distance in her fiction which, in turn, makes for believable and gripping characters. Byerman comments: "The authority of [Jones's] depictions of the world is enhanced by [her] refusal to intrude upon or judge her narrators. She remains outside the story, leaving the reader with none of the usual markers of a narrator's reliability. She gives these characters the speech of their religion, which, by locating them in time and space, makes it even more difficult to easily dismiss them; the way they speak has authenticity, which carries over to what they tell. The results are profoundly disturbing tales of repression, manipulation, and suffering."

Reviewers have also noted Jones's ability to innovatively incorporate Afro-American speech patterns into her work. In *Black Women Writers (1950-1980)*, Melvin Dixon contends that "Gayl Jones has figured among the best of contemporary Afro-American writers who have used Black speech as a major aesthetic device in their works. Like Alice Walker, Toni Morrison, Sherley Williams, Toni Cade Bambara, and such male writers as Ernest Gaines and Ishmael Reed, Jones uses the rhythm and structure of spoken language to develop authentic characters and to establish new possibilities for dramatic conflict within the text and between readers and the text itself." In her interview with Tate, Jones remarks on the importance of storytelling traditions to her work: "At the time I was writing *Corregidora* and *Eva's Man* I was particularly interested—and continue to be interested—in oral traditions of storytelling—Afro-American and others, in which there is always the consciousness and importance of the hearer, even in the interior monologues where the storyteller becomes her own hearer. That consciousness or self-consciousness actually determines my selection of significant events."

Jones's 1977 collection of short stories, *White Rat*, received mixed reviews. A number of critics noted the presence of Jones's typical thematic concerns, yet also felt that her shorter fiction did not allow enough room for character development. Diane Johnson comments in the *New York Review of Books* that the stories in *White Rat* "were written in some cases earlier than her novels, so they confirm one's sense of her direction and preoccupations: sex is violation, and violence is the principal dynamic of human relationships." Mel Watkins remarks in the *New York Times*, however, on a drawback to Jones's short fictions: "The focus throughout is on desolate, forsaken characters struggling to exact some snippet of gratification from their lives. . . . Although her prose here is as starkly arresting and indelible as in her novels, except for the longer stories such as 'Jeveta' and 'The Women,' these tales are simply doleful vignettes—slices of life so beveled that they seem distorted."

While Jones's writing often emphasizes a tormented side of life—especially with regards to male-female relationships—it also raises the possibility for more positive interactions. Jones points out in the Tate interview that "there seems to be a growing understanding—working itself out especially in *Corregidora*—of what is required in order to be genuinely tender. Perhaps brutality enables one to recognize what tenderness is." Some critics have found ambivalence to be at the core of Jones's fiction. Dixon remarks: "Redemption . . . is most likely to occur when the resolution of conflict is forged in the same vocabulary as the tensions which precipitated it. This dual nature of language makes it appear brutally indifferent, for it contains the source and the resolution of conflicts. . . . What Jones is after is the words and deeds that finally break the sexual bondage men and women impose upon each other."

BIOGRAPHICAL/CRITICAL SOURCES:

BOOKS

Contemporary Literary Criticism, Gale, Volume 6, 1976, Volume 9, 1978.

Dictionary of Literary Biography, Volume 33: *Afro-American Fiction Writers after 1955*, Gale, 1984.

Evans, Mari, editor, *Black Women Writers (1950-1980): A Critical Evaluation*, Anchor Books, 1984.

Tate, Claudia, editor, *Black Women Writers at Work*, Continuum, 1986.

PERIODICALS

Black World, February, 1976.
Esquire, December, 1976.
Kliatt, spring, 1986.
Literary Quarterly, May 15, 1975.
Massachusetts Review, winter, 1977.
National Review, April 14, 1978.
New Republic, June 28, 1975, June 19, 1976.
Newsweek, May 19, 1975, April 12, 1976.
New Yorker, August 18, 1975, August 9, 1976.
New York Review of Books, November 10, 1977.
New York Times, April 30, 1976, December 28, 1977.
New York Times Book Review, May 25, 1975, May 16, 1976.
Time, June 16, 1975.
Washington Post, October 21, 1977.
Yale Review, autumn, 1976.*

—*Sketch by Michael E. Mueller*

JONES, Jack
See JONES, James Larkin

*   *   *

JONES, James Larkin   1913-
  (Jack Jones)

PERSONAL: Born March 29, 1913, in Liverpool, England; son of George and Anne Jones; married Evelyn Mary Taylor (a factory worker and voluntary social worker); children: Jack, Michael. *Education:* Attended technical school and labor college.

ADDRESSES: Home—74 Ruskin Park House, Champion Hill, London SE5 8TH, England.

CAREER: Apprentice engineer and dock worker, 1927-39; Transport and General Workers Union, London, England, secretary of Coventry district, 1939-55, and Midlands region, 1955-63, assistant executive secretary, 1963-69, general secretary, 1969-78; vice-president of Age Concern, 1978—. Member of Liverpool City Council, 1936-39; city magistrate in Coventry, 1950-63. Trades Union Congress, member of general council, 1968-78, former chairman of international and industrial committees, chairman of Midlands advisory committee, 1948-63. Member of Midland Regional Board for Industry, 1942-46, 1954-63; chairman of Birmingham Productivity Committee, 1957-63; member of national executive committee of Labour Party, 1964-67, chairman of special committee on industrial democracy, 1967; member of National Committee on Commonwealth Immigrants, 1965-69; deputy chairman of National Ports Council, 1967-79; member of Lord Bullock Committee on Industrial Democracy, 1978; fellow of Chartered Institute of Transport. *Military service:* International Brigade, British Batallion, political commissar, 1937-38.

AWARDS, HONORS: Named to Order of the British Empire, 1950; Companion of Honor, 1978; D. Litt. from University of Warwick, 1979; fellow of London School of Economics and Political Science, London.

*WRITINGS—*Under name Jack Jones:

(With Charles Levinson) *Industry's Democratic Revolution,* Allen & Unwin, 1974.
The Human Face of Labour, BBC Publications, 1977.
Bevin: Revolutionary by Consent, Department of Employment Gazette, 1981.
(With Max Morris) *A-Z Trade Unionism and Industrial Relations,* Heinemann, 1982.
Union Man: The Autobiography of Jack Jones, Collins, 1986.
"Twentieth Century Remembered" (television series), British Broadcasting Corporation (BBC-TV), 1986.

Contributor to magazines and newspapers.

SIDELIGHTS: "My main interest has been strengthening trade unionism and improving industrial relations," Jack Jones told *CA.* About his book, *Union Man: The Autobiography of Jack Jones,* Jones explained: "I tried to deal with my outlook on life, as well as my many and varied abilities in the cause of trade unionism, hopefully as an encouragement to others." Jones described his earlier work in the following manner: "The work is each case has reflected some of my own experiences. For example, my writing on Ernest Bevin (former British Minister of Labour and Foreign Secretary) arose from my own knowledge of him. *The Human Face of Labour* is intended to provide shop stewards and trade union officials with a comprehensive guide in trade union practice and policy and on industrial legislation."

BIOGRAPHICAL/CRITICAL SOURCES:

PERIODICALS

Economist, September 6, 1986.
Listener, September 18, 1986.

*   *   *

JONES, LeRoi
See BARAKA, Amiri

*   *   *

JONES-WILSON, Faustine C(hildress)   1927-
  (Faustine Childress Jones)

PERSONAL: Born December 3, 1927, in Little Rock, Ark.; daughter of James Edward Thomas and Perrine Marie (Childress) Thomas Patterson; married James Theoplius Jones, June 20, 1948 (divorced, June, 1977); married Edwin L. Wilson, Sr., July 10, 1981; children: (first marriage) Yvonne Dianne, Brian Vincent. *Education:* Dunbar Junior College, diploma, 1946; Arkansas Agricultural, Mechanical and Normal College (now University of Arkansas at Pine Bluff), A.B. (summa cum laude), 1948; University of Illinois, A.M., 1951, Ed.D., 1967; also attended University of Chicago and Indiana University, Gary. *Politics:* Democrat. *Religion:* Methodist.

ADDRESSES: Home—908 Dryden Ct., Silver Spring, Md. 20901. *Office*—School of Education, Howard University, 2400 Sixth St. N.W., Washington, D.C. 20059.

CAREER: Junior and senior high school teacher in public schools in Gary, Ind., 1955-62, 1964-67; Indiana University, Gary, part-time member of associate faculty, 1965-66; University of Illinois at Chicago Circle, Chicago, assistant professor of education, 1967-69; Howard University, Washington, D.C., assistant professor of education, 1969-70; Federal City College, Washington, D.C., associate professor of adult education, 1970-71; Howard University, associate professor, 1971-73, professor of education, 1973—, chairman of School of Education foundations department, 1972-73, 1976-78, area coordinator social foundations, 1973-77, senior fellow at Institute for the Study of Educational Policy, 1974-77, director of Bureau of Educational Research, 1978—. Workshop leader and participant. Regular speaker at Washington International Center. Has appeared on national and local television and radio programs, including the "Today" show. East Coast Steering Committee Chairman, National Conference on Educating Black Children, 1986-88. Member of advisory council, Charlotte Hawkins Brown Historical Foundation, Inc., 1984—.

MEMBER: American Educational Studies Association (president, 1984-85), John Dewey Society (member of executive board, 1976-78, 1988-91), Society of Professors of Education (member of executive council, 1981-87), National Association for the Advancement of Colored People (NAACP), South Atlantic Philosophy of Education Society, Phi Delta Kappa (president of Howard University chapter, 1986-87), Alpha Kappa Mu, Kappa Delta Pi, Delta Tau Kappa.

AWARDS, HONORS: Outstanding Alumnus Award, Dunbar High School National Alumni Association, 1973, from Detroit chapter, 1979, from Little Rock chapter, 1983, from Seattle chapter, and 1985, from Washington, D.C., chapter; selected as outstanding teacher of the year, Howard University School of Education, 1975, 1978; Frederick Douglass Award, National Black Press Association, 1979; outstanding alumnus of Arkansas A. M. & N. College, National Association for Equal Opportunity in Higher Education, Washington, D.C., chapter, 1984; Distinguished Teacher-Scholar Award, Howard University, 1985; Exemplary Leadership Award, American Association for Higher Education Black Caucus, Washington, D.C., chapter, 1988.

WRITINGS:

UNDER NAME FAUSTINE CHILDRESS JONES

(Contributor) Lawrence E. Gary and Aaron Favors, editors, *Restructuring the Educational Process: A Black Perspective,* Institute for Urban Affairs and Research, Howard University, 1975.

(Contributor) Maurice M. Martinez, Jr., and Josepha M. Weston, editors, *School and Community: Issues and Alternatives,* Kendall/Hunt, 1976.

(Contributor) Warren Marr II and Maybelle Ward, editors, *Minorities and the American Dream: A Bicentennial Perspective,* Arno Press, 1976.

The Changing Mood in America: Eroding Commitment?, Howard University Press, 1977.

(Contributor) Cynthia J. Smith, editor, *Advancing Equality of Opportunity: A Matter of Justice,* Institute for the Study of Educational Policy, 1978.

(Contributor) Helen R. Houston and others, editors, *Through a Glass Darkly,* Contemporary Publishing, 1979.

(Contributor) Daniel S. Parkingson and Charles E. Skipper, editors, *Readings in the Cultural Foundations of Education,* Ginn Custom, 1979.

A Traditional Model of Excellence: Dunbar High School of Little Rock, Arkansas, Howard University Press, 1981.

OTHER

(Contributor) *The State of Black America 1984,* National Urban League, Inc., 1984.

(Contributor) Alan H. Jones, editor, *Civic Learning for Teachers: Capstone for Educational Reform,* Prakken, 1985.

(Contributor with Nancy L. Arnez) Diana Slaughter and Deborah Johnson, editors, *Visible Now: Blacks in Private Schools,* Greenwood Press, 1989.

Also contributor to *Negro Almanac,* 1983. Contributor of more than eighty articles to education and black studies journals, including *Urban Review, Howard Law Journal, Educational Studies,* and *Journal of Teacher Education.* Editor, *Journal of Negro Education,* 1978—. Member of editorial board, *New Directions,* 1978—, *Urban Review,* 1978—, *Review of Research in Education,* 1981-84, *Sage, Educational Studies,* and *Education Digest.*

SIDELIGHTS: Faustine C. Jones-Wilson told *CA:* "Growing up in Arkansas with a concerned, strong family and with dedicated teachers, I was shaped to enjoy learning and to appreciate its value. It was deemed an obligation to know, and to use knowledge in behalf of one's people. That love of knowledge and sense of obligation has carried over to my adult life and shaped my rearing of my own children and my relationship with students over time.

"In contemporary society our American democracy faces the challenge of attaining authenticity in education. True quality in education must be provided to all the children of all the people if our democracy is to attain its promises of equality and justice for all. Currently the literature stresses the need to educate the children of minorities and/or immigrants for economic reasons. As we approach the year 2000 these youth are the pool of potential employees; further, their earnings and contributions to federal/state tax revenues as well as to the Social Security system are very much needed to maintain these systems. Therefore, a human capital mind-set is critical to the development of our citizens, and education is the chief instrument for the human development that is needed to make ours a more democratic, more productive, competent, internationally competitive society."

*　　*　　*

JUDD, Frances K.
[Collective pseudonym]

WRITINGS:

"KAY TRACEY MYSTERY STORIES"

The Secret of the Red Scarf, Cupples & Leon, 1934, reprinted as Volume 15 of series, Garden City, 1953.

The Strange Echo, Cupples & Leon, 1934, reprinted as Volume 7 of series, Berkley, 1964.

The Mystery of the Swaying Curtains, Cupples & Leon, 1935.

The Shadow on the Door, Cupples & Leon, 1935.

The Six-Fingered Glove Mystery, Cupples & Leon, 1936, reprinted as Volume 3 of series, Bantam, 1980.

The Green Cameo Mystery, Cupples & Leon, 1936, reprinted as Volume 5 of series, Bantam, 1980.

The Secret at the Windmill, Cupples & Leon, 1937, reprinted as Volume 8 of series, Garden City, 1952.

Beneath the Crimson Briar Bush, Cupples & Leon, 1937, reprinted under title *The Crimson Briar Bush* as Volume 12 of series, Garden City, 1952, reprinted under title *The Crimson Brier Bush* as Volume 7 of series, Books, Inc.

The Message in the Sand Dunes, Cupples & Leon, 1938, reprinted as Volume 6 of series, Bantam, 1980.

The Murmuring Portrait, Cupples & Leon, 1938, reprinted as Volume 9 of series, Garden City, 1951.

When the Key Turned, Cupples & Leon, 1939, reprinted as Volume 6 of series, Garden City, 1951.

In the Sunken Garden, Cupples & Leon, 1939, reprinted as Volume 2 of series, Bantam, 1980.

The Forbidden Tower, Cupples & Leon, 1940.

The Sacred Feather, Cupples & Leon, 1940, reprinted as Volume 4 of series, Berkley, 1961.

The Lone Footprint, Cupples & Leon, 1941, reprinted as Volume 10 of series, Garden City, 1952.

The Double Disguise, Cupples & Leon, 1941, reprinted as Volume 1 of series, Bantam, 1980.

The Mansion of Secrets, Cupples & Leon, 1942, reprinted as Volume 4 of series, Bantam, 1980.

The Mysterious Neighbors, Cupples & Leon, 1942, reprinted as Volume 2 of series, Berkley, 1961.

SIDELIGHTS: Sixteen-year-old Kay Tracey starred in a series launched after the phenomenal success of Nancy Drew. "Some of the titles still in print," remarks Carol Billman in *The Secret of the Stratemeyer Syndicate,* "intimate this series' link with the Gothic mysteries [Carolyn] Keene wrote around Nancy Drew: *In the Sunken Garden, The Mansion of Secrets, The Green Cameo Mystery.*" She adds that the series has had five reprint publishers, thus exhibiting "noteworthy lasting power."

Mildred Augustine Wirt Benson is credited with having written eleven of the "Kay Tracey" detective stories. For more information see the entries in this volume for Harriet S. Adams, Edward L. Stratemeyer, and Andrew E. Svenson.

BIOGRAPHICAL/CRITICAL SOURCES:

BOOKS

Billman, Carol, *The Secret of the Stratemeyer Syndicate: Nancy Drew, the Hardy Boys, and the Million Dollar Fiction Factory,* Ungar, 1986.

Johnson, Deidre, editor and compiler, *Stratemeyer Pseudonyms and Series Books: An Annotated Checklist of Stratemeyer and Stratemeyer Syndicate Publications,* Greenwood Press, 1982.

Paluka, Frank, *Iowa Authors: A Bio-Bibliography of Sixty Native Writers,* Friends of the University of Iowa Libraries, 1967.

Prager, Arthur, *Rascals at Large; or, The Clue in the Old Nostalgia,* Doubleday, 1971.

PERIODICALS

Ohio Magazine, December, 1987.
Washington Post Book World, October 19, 1980.

K

KAHN, James 1947-

PERSONAL: Born December 30, 1947, in Chicago, Ill.; son of Alfred J. (a physician) and Judith (an artist; maiden name, Pesmen) Kahn; married Jill Alden Littlewood (an illustrator), August 30, 1975. *Education:* University of Chicago, B.A., 1970, M.D., 1974.

ADDRESSES: Agent—Jane Jordan Browne, Multimedia Product Development, Inc., 410 South Michigan Ave., Suite 724, Chicago, Ill. 60605.

CAREER: University of Wisconsin—Madison, intern, 1974-75; Los Angeles County Hospital, Los Angeles, Calif., emergency medicine resident, 1976-77; University of California, Los Angeles, emergency medicine resident, 1978-79; Rancho Encino Hospital, Los Angeles, emergency room physician, 1978—; writer. Worked as consultant to Steven Spielberg for film "E.T."

MEMBER: American College of Emergency Physicians.

WRITINGS:

(With Jerome McGann) *Nerves in Patterns* (poems), X Press, 1978.
Diagnosis: Murder (mystery), Carlyle, 1978.
World Enough and Time (first novel in "New World" science fiction trilogy), Ballantine, 1980.
Time's Dark Laughter (second novel in "New World" trilogy), Ballantine, 1982.
"A Pig Too Far" (teleplay for "St. Elsewhere" series), National Broadcasting Co., 1983.
Timefall (third novel in "New World" trilogy), St. Martin's, 1987.
The Echo Vector (suspense novel), St. Martin's, 1988.

SCREENPLAY NOVELIZATIONS

Poltergeist, Warner Books, 1982.
Revenge of the Jedi, Ballantine, 1983.
Indiana Jones and the Temple of Doom, Ballantine, 1984.
The Goonies, Warner Books, 1985.
Poltergeist II, Warner Books, 1986.

OTHER

Also author of teleplays for "E/R" series, CBS-TV, 1984-85. Contributor of stories to magazines, including *Playboy.*

SIDELIGHTS: Trauma specialist Dr. James Kahn spent six days on the set of the film "E.T.: The Extra-Terrestrial" helping director Steven Spielberg with the scenes in which E.T. is dying and then resuscitated. While on the set, Kahn noticed that the famed director had a copy of his first novel, *World Enough and Time;* after introducing himself as its author, Spielberg offered Kahn a chance to work on the novelization of another film, "Poltergeist." Since then Kahn has added the book versions of many other Spielberg projects to his credits, as well as two other fiction titles. Despite his success, Kahn remains dedicated to medicine: "It's very exciting," he said of his specialty, trauma medicine, to the *Chicago Tribune*'s Arthur Shay. "Saving someone from certain death or preserving an arm or leg someone else might have amputated, saving a child or just alleviating pain—all these are why I trained as a doctor."

About his writing, Kahn once told *CA:* "I'm basically a storyteller. I stretch for metaphors at times, but only if they make good stories themselves. The way the story is told is the art, the craft, the game of it—what makes the writing (and reading) fun." He added that he "would like to be a man of letters, involved in all literary forms—the novel, short story, essay, screenplay, and poetry." Kahn has achieved almost all of these, for he has written several scripts for the television medical shows "St. Elsewhere" and "E/R." As he commented to Marian Smith Holmes in a *People* interview, "I'm following in the tradition of doctor writers. I see myself as a cross between Chekhov, Conan Doyle, and Michael Crichton."

BIOGRAPHICAL/CRITICAL SOURCES:

PERIODICALS

Chicago Tribune, August 22, 1983.
Los Angeles Times Book Review, December 6, 1987.
New York Times Book Review, April 26, 1987.
People, October 4, 1982.

*   *   *

KAHN, Michael D. 1936-

PERSONAL: Born March 11, 1936, in Israel; son of Lester (an executive) and Helen (Baum) Kahn; married Ruth Jacobson (a special educator), March 29, 1958; children: Kim Lee, Tamara Regina, Benjamin Alexander. *Education:* City College (now City College of the City University of New York), B.A., 1960; New School for Social Research, M.A., 1965; University of North Carolina, Ph.D., 1970. *Politics:* Democrat. *Religion:* Jewish.

ADDRESSES: Home—54 Mountain Brook Rd., West Hartford, Conn. 06117. *Office*—Department of Psychology, University of Hartford, 200 Bloomfield Ave., West Hartford, Conn. 06032.

CAREER: University of Hartford, West Hartford, Conn., assistant professor, 1970-78, associate professor, 1979-84, professor of psychology, 1984—. Associate clinical professor at University of Connecticut, Farmington, 1974—. Private practice of psychology in Hartford, 1971—. Family Study Center of Connecticut, member of board of directors, 1975—, president, 1982—; consultant to Hartley Salmon Child Guidance Clinic and Veterans Administration Hospital, Newington, Conn.

MEMBER: American Psychological Association, American Orthopsychiatric Association (fellow), American Family Therapy Association (charter member), Connecticut Psychological Association.

WRITINGS:

(With Stephen P. Bank) *The Sibling Bond,* Basic Books, 1982.
(Editor with Karen G. Lewis) *Siblings in Therapy: Life Span and Clinical Issues,* Norton, 1988.
Towards the Integration of Individual and Family Therapy: A Dialectical Theory of Change, Guilford, 1989.

Advisory editor of *Family Process;* member of editorial board of *International Journal of Family Therapy* and *Journal of Marital and Family Therapy.*

WORK IN PROGRESS: A book on "the interface of the psychodynamic theory of individual therapy with the systems process theory of family therapy"; research on the effects of immigration to a new culture on one's own identity.

SIDELIGHTS: Michael D. Kahn once wrote *CA:* "I am an only child. The subject of siblings has always fascinated me, and the interaction of my own children gave me living evidence that brothers and sisters could be caring and loving to one another.

"Thus, my choice of topics to initially write about began with a satisfying conviction that I wanted to undo prevailing myths regarding sibling rivalry and fratricide. In addition, as a psychotherapist, I have had the privilege of being witness to the interior of people's lives. But that experience is sometimes overwhelming in its collective implications to me of the cultural, historical, social, and psychological changes that we all face in the latter part of the twentieth century.

"Therefore putting some of those thoughts to paper through my writing has afforded me the opportunity to gain a much needed larger perspective, transcending the personal and comprehending the contextual nature of things. Writing is a way of bringing order out of randomness in further investigations. These attempts at creative transformation, in spite of the grueling pain inherent in any creative process are often joyous. When I can reach a level of aesthetic symmetry, when I can connect to other contributor of knowledge, and when I believe I am able to state some principle which affords others an appreciation of the complexity of things, allows me a great measure of satisfaction. I thank life for it."

AVOCATIONAL INTERESTS: Sailing, travel, playing alto and tenor saxophone in jazz groups.

KAPTCHUK, Ted J(ack)   1947-

PERSONAL: Born August 17, 1947, in Brooklyn, N.Y.; son of Harry and Nina Kaptchuk. *Education:* Columbia University, B.A., 1968; Macau Institute of Chinese Medicine, O.M.D., 1975.

ADDRESSES: Home—27 Bay St., Cambridge, Mass. 02139. *Office*—Lemuel Shattuck Hospital, 170 Morton St., Jamaica Plain, Boston, Mass. 02139. *Agent*—Nancy Trichter, 137 Riverside Dr., New York, N.Y. 10024.

CAREER: Overseas Chinese Medical Clinic, Macau, China, doctor of Oriental medicine, 1975-76; Sanskrit University, Ayura Vedic Hospital, Varanasi, India, doctor of Oriental medicine, 1976; private practice of Oriental medicine, Cambridge, Mass., 1976—; Lemuel Shattuck Hospital, Cambridge, acupuncturist, 1980-81, director of Pain and Stress Clinic, 1981—. Acupuncturist at Solomon Carter Fuller Mental Health Center, Boston University, 1978-79, and Long Island Hospital, 1979-80. Lecturer at Sanskrit University, 1976; member of faculty at Pacific College of Naturopathic Medicine, 1979—, and Santa Fe College of Natural Medicine, 1981—; supervisor of preceptorship program at National College of Naturopathic Medicine, 1979—; advisor to colleges of acupuncture. Consultant to British Broadcasting Corp. Speaker at workshops and seminars.

MEMBER: Societe Internationale d'Acupuncture, North American Acupuncture Association, American Association of Acupuncture and Oriental Medicine, American Acupuncture Association, British Acupuncture Association, Acupuncture Association of India, Traditional Acupuncture Society (England), Massachusetts Acupuncture Association.

WRITINGS:

The Web That Has No Weaver: Understanding Chinese Medicine, Congdon & Weed, 1983.
(With Michael Croucher) "The Healing Arts" (nine-hour television series), first broadcast by British Broadcasting Corp. (BBC-TV), summer, 1986, accompanying book (with Croucher) published as *The Healing Arts: Exploring the Medical Ways of the World,* Summit Books, 1987.
(Contributor) Richard Carlson and Benjamin Shield, editors, *Healers on Healing,* J. P. Tarcher, 1989.

Contributor to *Science Digest* and *East-West Journal.*

WORK IN PROGRESS: A History of the Experience of Pain; also working "on cross-cultural and historical pieces concerned with the shifting boundary between theological suffering and physical pain . . . [and] on a piece concerned with 'healing.'"

SIDELIGHTS: In *The Healing Arts: Exploring the Medical Ways of the World,* Ted J. Kaptchuk and Michael Croucher "analyze the great healing systems through history and extract meaning from each of them," explains Carol Eron in the *Washington Post Book World.* Kaptchuk, specifically, "while cautioning that ultimately every healing art falls in love with itself, . . . envisions a system that is greater than any individual system, one that takes into account the fact that the human body is more than the sum of its parts; thus, the art of healing must also involve the unknown." Eron goes on to call the book "both provocative and filled with delightful detail."

BIOGRAPHICAL/CRITICAL SOURCES:

PERIODICALS

Washington Post Book World, October 25, 1987.

KASHNER, Rita 1942-

PERSONAL: Born March 10, 1942, in Mount Vernon, N. Y.; daughter of Ludwig (in business) and Mildred (a teacher; maiden name, Saretsky) Danziger; married Howard Kashner (an attorney), August 19, 1962; children: Elizabeth Anne, Megan Rachel. *Education:* Smith College, B.A., 1963; Brandeis University, M.A., 1965. *Religion:* Jewish.

ADDRESSES: Home—Scarsdale, N.Y. *Agent*—Jonathan Dolger, 49 East 96th St., New York, N.Y. 10128.

CAREER: Mamaroneck High School, Mamaroneck, N.Y., English teacher, 1976-77; Sunburst Communications, Pleasantville, N.Y., filmstrip writer, 1977-78; writer, 1979—. Teacher at Women's Institute, 1974-75, and Scarsdale Alternative School, 1975-76; member of executive boards of parent teacher associations in Scarsdale, N.Y.; member of school board nominating committee of Scarsdale, 1977-79; Temple Israel Center, member of board of trustees, 1979-82, and chairman of school board, 1980-82.

MEMBER: Authors Guild.

WRITINGS:

Bed Rest (novel), Macmillan, 1981.
To the Tenth Generation (novel), Putnam, 1984.

Author of filmstrip series on grammar, "How to Write a Really Good Paragraph," Sunburst Communications. Contributor of short stories to *Hadassah.*

WORK IN PROGRESS: Another novel, a black comedy.

SIDELIGHTS: In remarks published by the *Library Journal,* Rita Kashner described how her first book evolved: "*Bed Rest* started with the image I had of someone who made her bed so comfortable that she became increasingly reluctant to leave it." As Beth, a wife and mother in her early thirties, retreats deeper and deeper under the covers, cutting herself off from family and friends, fear and guilt begin to exert a debilitating effect on her life. "Trying to re-create the feeling of safety she remembers from her childhood, she begins putting herself to bed—eventually for whole days," Kashner explained. "And with gathering desperation she seeks her mother (whom she has never laid to rest) in her friends, her husband, her children, a potential lover and, finally, in herself."

Brigitte Weeks, editor of the *Washington Post Book World,* comments: "We spend only a few weeks with Beth, luxuriating in the fresh talcum powder and the line-dried sheets. We meet her array of friends, her children—portrayed with fiendish accuracy, her almost-but-not-quite lover, her teachers. Her humor, guts and willingness to love won me over."

Kashner's second novel, *To the Tenth Generation,* differs significantly from *Bed Rest. To the Tenth Generation* is set in modern day Israel and Palestine, and "encompasses such complex themes as the legacy of the Holocaust in the lives of middle-aged survivors, the growing self-sufficiency and changing needs of women in society, the bonds that develop between men at war, the rootlessness of the new generation of Israelis, and evolving sexual mores," writes Michael J. Bandler in *Newsday.* The novel's protagonist, Racheli Kovner, is obsessed with having someone who belongs to her alone, and who is completely devoted to her. As a child, Racheli had to share her parents' affections with the other children in the

kibbutz where she was raised; later as a wife and mother, Racheli had to share her children's devotion with her husband, Dov. Racheli satisfies her obsession by taking a lover and bearing a son, Daniel, whom she forbids her lover to see. According to Orthodox Jewish law, Daniel's illegitimacy prevents him from marrying a legitimate Jew, and marks his children as illegitimate unto the tenth generation.

While Racheli is in the hospital recuperating from giving birth, Daniel and another newborn are temporarily confused. This chance occurence forges a lasting bond between the two mothers and their offspring. Unlike Racheli, the other mother, Chava, is a concentration camp survivor who is still plagued by guilt and painful recollections of the war. *New York Times Book Review* contributor Cheri Fein finds Chava's story more compelling than that of Racheli. Writes Fein: "Kashner recreates the horror and complexity of surviving such a trauma with impressive freshness." *Washington Post Book World* contributor Elizabeth Ward similarly notes that Chava's story draws in the other characters, "and though each reacts individually, with impatience or sympathy or indifference, the general lesson is that in postwar Israel the Holocaust is above all what determines meaning, or absurdity, in the life of every Jew, survivor or otherwise."

Ward adds that while the novel's impact is lessened by "a lot of what might politely be described as graphic passion, . . . this is really a minor quibble in view of Kashner's larger achievement. *To the Tenth Generation* is not only a responsible and thought-provoking novel, but a compellingly readable one." Bandler concludes: "By all tests, this volume confirms Rita Kashner as an exemplary American Jewish novelist."

BIOGRAPHICAL/CRITICAL SOURCES:

PERIODICALS

Library Journal, June 15, 1981.
Los Angeles Times Book Review, January 6, 1985.
Newsday, October 14, 1984.
New York Times Book Review, December 16, 1984.
Washington Post Book World, September 27, 1981, December 23, 1984.

*   *   *

Ka-TZETNIK 135633

PERSONAL: Ka-Tzetnik 135633, a pseudonym, is the author's concentration camp number; born in Poland; married Nina De-Nur (an author).

ADDRESSES: Home—7 Pineles St., Tel Aviv 62265, Israel. *Agent*—Curtis Brown Ltd., 10 Astor Place, New York, N.Y. 10003.

CAREER: Writer; was imprisoned in concentration camp by Nazis during World War II.

WRITINGS:

NOVELS

Salamandra, Dvir Publishing, 1946, reprinted, 1977, translation from the Hebrew by wife, Nina De-Nur, published as *Sunrise over Hell,* W. H. Allen, 1977.
Beit Ha-Bubot, Dvir Publishing, 1953, translation from the Hebrew by Moshe M. Kohn and De-Nur published as *House of Dolls,* Simon & Schuster, 1955.

Ha-Shaon, Bialik Institute for Classics (Jerusalem), 1960, translation published as *Kohav Ha-efer* (title means ''Star of Ashes''; trilingual edition in Hebrew, Yiddish, and English), Gershon Kispel Lithographs (Tel Aviv), 1967, published as *Star Eternal*, Arbor House, 1971.

Kar'oo Lo Piepel, Am Ha'Sefer (Tel Aviv), 1961, translation from the Hebrew by Kohn published as *They Called Him Piepel*, Anthony Blond, 1961, published as *Atrocity*, edited by Lyle Stuart, Lyle Stuart, 1963, published as *Moni*, Citadel, 1987.

Ka-hol Me-effer (sequel to *House of Dolls*), Am Oved, 1966, translation from the Hebrew by De-Nur published as *Phoenix over the Galilee*, Harper, 1969, published as *House of Love*, W. H. Allen, 1971.

Shivitti, Ha-Kibbutz Ha-Meoohad, 1988.

SIDELIGHTS: A survivor of Auschwitz, Ka-Tzetnik 135633 (''ka-tzetnik'' was the slang name used for Nazi concentration camp prisoners) has focused on the horror of the Holocaust in a quintet of compelling novels. These works were actually part of the official documentation used to convict Nazi leader Karl Eichmann in 1961. In English translation this quintet includes *Sunrise over Hell, House of Dolls, Star Eternal, They Called Him Piepel*, and *Phoenix over the Galilee*, of which *House of Dolls* is by far Ka-Tzetnik's most celebrated work. With its depiction of Nazi sexual exploitation of Jewish girls, *House of Dolls* has sold over five million copies and has been translated into more than twenty languages. According to Ka-Tzetnik's wife and translator, Nina De-Nur, ''*House of Dolls* is the life-and-death story of Daniella Prelshnik, interlocked with her brother, Harry's. Daniella, a blond, blue-eyed beauty, is one of the countless Jewish belles captured by the Gestapo for field-whores, prostitutes put at the use of German soldiers on furlough from the battlefronts. In order to cauterize the subject matter of any trace of pornography and get at the quintessence of this unprecedented grief, Ka-Tzetnik rewrote the book five times. *House of Dolls* is the fifth and final version, hailed by Israel's senior writer, Gershon Shoffman, as 'a holy book.'''
In addition, a *Nation* reviewer responds to *House of Dolls* as follows: ''Here is prose at once memorable and merciless, controlled and explosive. This novel, in a fine translation from the Hebrew. . ., records a degeneration of humanity the world has too soon forgotten.''

De-Nur further wrote to *CA:* ''Ka-Tzetnik 135633 regards his work as 'an act of faith in humanity, faith in the Fourth Dimension.' This is born of the belief that survival was granted him by God-at-Auschwitz in exchange for The Vow: 'To continue telling of this Other Planet even unto the last of my breath.'''

Since the early 1960s, Ka-Tzetnik and his wife, who is also Jewish, have opened their home in Tel Aviv, Israel, for weekly meetings between Jews and Arabs. With other such homes in Israel, Ka-Tzetnik and his wife formed the Israeli Movement for Arab-Jewish Cooperation in 1965. This is a nonpolitical, grass roots organization whose ideological basis stemmed from the contents of Ka-Tzetnik's writing.

BIOGRAPHICAL/CRITICAL SOURCES:

PERIODICALS

Books Abroad, autumn, 1970.
Nation, August 6, 1955.
Saturday Review, March 13, 1971.

KEENE, Carolyn
[Collective pseudonym]

WRITINGS:

''DANA GIRLS'' MYSTERY SERIES

By the Light of the Study Lamp, Grosset & Dunlap, 1934.
The Secret at Lone Tree Cottage, Grosset & Dunlap, 1934.
In the Shadow of the Tower, Grosset & Dunlap, 1934.
A Three-Cornered Mystery, Grosset & Dunlap, 1935.
The Secret at the Hermitage, Grosset & Dunlap, 1936.
The Circle of Footprints, Grosset & Dunlap, 1937.
The Mystery of the Locked Room, Grosset & Dunlap, 1938.
The Clue in the Cobweb, Grosset & Dunlap, 1939.
The Secret at the Gatehouse, Grosset & Dunlap, 1940.
The Mysterious Fireplace, Grosset & Dunlap, 1941.
The Clue of the Rusty Key, Grosset & Dunlap, 1942.
The Portrait in the Sand, Grosset & Dunlap, 1943.
The Secret in the Old Well, Grosset & Dunlap, 1944.
The Clue in the Ivy, Grosset & Dunlap, 1952.
The Secret of the Jade Ring, Grosset & Dunlap, 1953.
The Mystery at the Crossroads, Grosset & Dunlap, 1954.
The Ghost in the Gallery, Grosset & Dunlap, 1955, reprinted as Volume 13 of series, 1975.
The Clue of the Black Flower, Grosset & Dunlap, 1956.
The Winking Ruby Mystery, Grosset & Dunlap, 1957, reprinted as Volume 12 of series, 1974.
The Secret of the Swiss Chalet, Grosset & Dunlap, 1958, reprinted as Volume 7 of series, 1973.
The Haunted Lagoon, Grosset & Dunlap, 1959, reprinted as Volume 8 of series, 1973.
Mystery of the Bamboo Bird, Grosset & Dunlap, 1960, reprinted as Volume 9 of series, 1973.
The Sierra Gold Mystery, Grosset & Dunlap, 1961, reprinted as Volume 10 of series, 1973.
The Secret of Lost Lake, Grosset & Dunlap, 1963, reprinted as Volume 11 of series, 1974.
Mystery of the Stone Tiger, Grosset & Dunlap, 1963, reprinted as Volume 1 of series, 1972.
The Riddle of the Frozen Fountain, Grosset & Dunlap, 1964, reprinted as Volume 2 of series, 1972.
The Secret of the Silver Dolphin, Grosset & Dunlap, 1965, reprinted as Volume 3 of series, 1972.
Mystery of the Wax Queen, Grosset & Dunlap, 1966, reprinted as Volume 4 of series, 1972.
The Secret of the Minstrel's Guitar, Grosset & Dunlap, 1967, reprinted as Volume 5 of series, 1972.
The Phantom Surfer, Grosset & Dunlap, 1968, reprinted as Volume 6 of series, 1972.
The Curious Coronation, Grosset & Dunlap, 1976.
The Hundred-Year Mystery, Grosset & Dunlap, 1977.
The Mountain-Peak Mystery, Grosset & Dunlap, 1978.
The Witch's Omen, Grosset & Dunlap, 1979.

''NANCY DREW MYSTERY STORIES''

The Secret of the Old Clock (also see below), Grosset & Dunlap, 1930, revised edition, 1959.
The Hidden Staircase (also see below), Grosset & Dunlap, 1930, revised edition, 1959.
The Bungalow Mystery, Grosset & Dunlap, 1930, revised edition, 1960.
The Mystery at Lilac Inn, Grosset & Dunlap, 1930, revised edition, 1961.
The Secret at Shadow Ranch, Grosset & Dunlap, 1930, revised edition, 1965.

The Secret of Red Gate Farm, Grosset & Dunlap, 1931, revised edition, 1961.

The Clue in the Diary, Grosset & Dunlap, 1932, revised edition, 1962.

Nancy's Mysterious Letter, Grosset & Dunlap, 1932, revised edition, 1968.

The Sign of the Twisted Candles, Grosset & Dunlap, 1933, revised edition, 1968.

The Password to Larkspur Lane, Grosset & Dunlap, 1933, revised edition, 1966.

The Clue of the Broken Locket, Grosset & Dunlap, 1934, revised edition, 1965.

The Message in the Hollow Oak, Grosset & Dunlap, 1935, revised edition, 1972.

The Mystery of the Ivory Charm, Grosset & Dunlap, 1936, revised edition, 1974.

The Whispering Statue, Grosset & Dunlap, 1937, revised edition, 1970.

The Haunted Bridge, Grosset & Dunlap, 1937, revised edition, 1972.

The Clue of the Tapping Heels, Grosset & Dunlap, 1939, revised edition, 1969.

The Mystery of the Brass Bound Trunk, Grosset & Dunlap, 1940, revised edition, 1976.

The Mystery at the Moss-Covered Mansion, Grosset & Dunlap, 1941, revised edition, 1971.

The Quest of the Missing Map, Grosset & Dunlap, 1942, revised edition, 1969.

The Clue in the Jewel Box, Grosset & Dunlap, 1943, revised edition, 1972.

The Secret in the Old Attic, Grosset & Dunlap, 1944, revised edition, 1970.

The Clue in the Crumbling Wall, Grosset & Dunlap, 1945, revised edition, 1973.

The Mystery of the Tolling Bell, Grosset & Dunlap, 1946, revised edition, 1973.

The Clue in the Old Album, Grosset & Dunlap, 1947, revised edition, 1977.

The Ghost of Blackwood Hall, Grosset & Dunlap, 1948, revised edition, 1967.

The Clue of the Leaning Chimney, Grosset & Dunlap, 1949, revised edition, 1967.

The Secret of the Wooden Lady, Grosset & Dunlap, 1950, revised edition, 1967.

The Clue of the Black Keys, Grosset & Dunlap, 1951, revised edition, 1968.

The Mystery at the Ski Jump, Grosset & Dunlap, 1952, revised edition, 1968.

The Clue of the Velvet Mask, Grosset & Dunlap, 1953, revised edition, 1969.

The Ringmaster's Secret, Grosset & Dunlap, 1953, revised edition, 1974.

The Scarlet Slipper Mystery, Grosset & Dunlap, 1954, revised edition, 1974.

The Witch Tree Symbol, Grosset & Dunlap, 1955, revised edition, 1975.

The Hidden Window Mystery, Grosset & Dunlap, 1957, revised edition, 1975.

The Haunted Showboat, Grosset & Dunlap, 1958.

The Secret of the Golden Pavilion, Grosset & Dunlap, 1959.

The Clue in the Old Stagecoach, Grosset & Dunlap, 1960.

The Mystery of the Fire Dragon, Grosset & Dunlap, 1961.

The Clue of the Dancing Puppet, Grosset & Dunlap, 1962.

The Moonstone Castle Mystery, Grosset & Dunlap, 1963.

The Clue of the Whistling Bagpipes, Grosset & Dunlap, 1964.

The Phantom of Pine Hill, Grosset & Dunlap, 1965.

The Mystery of the 99 Steps, Grosset & Dunlap, 1966.

The Clue in the Crossword Cipher, Grosset & Dunlap, 1967.

The Spider Sapphire Mystery, Grosset & Dunlap, 1968.

The Invisible Intruder, Grosset & Dunlap, 1969.

The Mysterious Mannequin, Grosset & Dunlap, 1970.

The Crooked Bannister, Grosset & Dunlap, 1971.

The Secret of Mirror Bay, Grosset & Dunlap, 1972.

The Double Jinx Mystery, Grosset & Dunlap, 1973.

The Mystery of the Glowing Eye, Grosset & Dunlap, 1974.

The Secret of the Forgotten City, Grosset & Dunlap, 1975.

The Sky Phantom, Grosset & Dunlap, 1976.

The Strange Message in the Parchment, Grosset & Dunlap, 1977.

The Mystery of Crocodile Island, Grosset & Dunlap, 1978.

The Thirteenth Pearl, Grosset & Dunlap, 1979.

The Triple Hoax, Wanderer, 1979.

The Flying Saucer Mystery, Wanderer, 1980.

The Secret in the Old Lace, Wanderer, 1980.

The Greek Symbol Mystery, Wanderer, 1981.

The Swami's Ring, Wanderer, 1981.

The Kachina Doll Mystery, Wanderer, 1981.

The Twin Dilemma, Wanderer, 1981.

Captive Witness, Wanderer, 1981.

Mystery of the Winged Lion, Wanderer, 1982.

Race against Time, Wanderer, 1982.

The Sinister Omen, Wanderer, 1982.

The Elusive Heiress, Wanderer, 1982.

Clue in the Ancient Disguise, Wanderer, 1982.

The Broken Anchor, Wanderer, 1983.

The Silver Cobweb, Wanderer, 1983.

The Haunted Carousel, Wanderer, 1983.

Enemy Match, Wanderer, 1983.

The Mysterious Image, Wanderer, 1984.

The Emerald-Eyed Cat Mystery, Wanderer, 1984.

The Eskimo's Secret, Wanderer, 1985.

The Bluebeard Room, Wanderer, 1985.

Phantom of Venice, Wanderer, 1985.

The Double Horror of Fenley Place, Minstrel, 1987.

The Case of the Disappearing Diamonds, Minstrel, 1987.

The Mardi Gras Mystery, Minstrel, 1988.

The Clue in the Camera, Minstrel, 1988.

The Case of the Vanishing Veil, Minstrel, 1988.

The Joker's Revenge, Minstrel, 1988.

The Secret of Shady Glen, Minstrel, 1988.

The Mystery of Misty Canyon, Minstrel, 1988.

The Case of the Rising Stars, Minstrel, 1989.

The Search for Cindy Austin, Minstrel, 1989.

"NANCY DREW FILES" MYSTERY SERIES

Secrets Can Kill, Archway, 1986.

Deadly Intent, Archway, 1986.

Murder on Ice, Archway, 1986.

Smile and Say Murder, Archway, 1986.

Hit and Run Holiday, Archway, 1986.

White Water Terror, Archway, 1987.

Deadly Doubles, Archway, 1987.

Two Points for Murder, Archway, 1987.

False Moves, Archway, 1987.

Buried Secrets, Archway, 1987.

Heart of Danger, Archway, 1987.

Fatal Ransom, Archway, 1987.

Wings of Fear, Archway, 1987.

This Side of Evil, Archway, 1987.

Trial by Fire, Archway, 1987.

Never Say Die, Archway, 1987.
Stay Tuned for Danger, Archway, 1987.
Circle of Evil, Archway, 1987.
Sisters in Crime, Archway, 1988.
Very Deadly Yours, Archway, 1988.
Recipe for Murder, Archway, 1988.
Fatal Attraction, Archway, 1988.
Sinister Paradise, Archway, 1988.
Til Death Do Us Part, Archway, 1988.
Rich and Dangerous, Archway, 1988.
Playing with Fire, Archway, 1988.
Most Likely to Die, Archway, 1988.
The Black Widow, Archway, 1988.
Pure Poison, Archway, 1988.
Death by Design, Archway, 1988.
Trouble in Tahiti, Archway, 1989.
High Marks for Malice, Archway, 1989.
Danger in Disguise, Archway, 1989.
Vanishing Act, Archway, 1989.
Bad Medicine, Archway, 1989.
Over the Edge, Archway, 1989.
Last Dance, Archway, 1989.
The Final Scene, Archway, 1989.
The Suspect Next Door, Archway, 1989.

WITH FRANKLIN W. DIXON

Nancy Drew and the Hardy Boys: Super Sleuths! (short stories), Wanderer, Volume 1, 1981, Volume 2, 1984.
Nancy Drew and the Hardy Boys Camp Fire Stories, Wanderer, 1984.
Nancy Drew & the Hardy Boys Be a Detective Mystery Stories: The Secret of the Knight's Sword, edited by Betty Schwartz, Wanderer, 1984.
Nancy Drew & the Hardy Boys Be a Detective Mystery Stories: Danger on Ice, edited by Schwartz, Wanderer, 1984.
Nancy Drew & the Hardy Boys Be a Detective Mystery Stories: The Feathered Serpent, edited by Schwartz, Wanderer, 1984.
Nancy Drew & the Hardy Boys Be a Detective Mystery Stories: Secret Cargo, edited by Schwartz, Wanderer, 1984.
Nancy Drew & the Hardy Boys Be a Detective Mystery Stories: The Alaskan Mystery, edited by Diane Arico, Wanderer, 1985.
Nancy Drew & the Hardy Boys Be a Detective Mystery Stories: The Missing Money Mystery, edited by Arico, Wanderer, 1985.
Nancy Drew & the Hardy Boys Be a Detective Mystery Stories: Jungle of Evil, edited by Arico, Wanderer, 1985.
Nancy Drew & the Hardy Boys Be a Detective Mystery Stories: Ticket to Intrigue, edited by Arico, Wanderer, 1985.

OTHER

(Contributor) Stephen Dunning and Henry B. Maloney, editors, *A Superboy, Supergirl Anthology: Selected Chapters from the Earlier Works of Victor Appleton, Franklin W. Dixon, and Carolyn Keene,* Scholastic Book Services, 1971.
The Nancy Drew Cookbook: Clues to Good Cooking, Grosset & Dunlap, 1973.
Mystery of the Lost Dogs (Nancy Drew picture book), Grosset & Dunlap, 1977.
The Secret of the Twin Puppets (Nancy Drew picture book), Grosset & Dunlap, 1977.
The Hardy Boys and Nancy Drew Meet Dracula (based on episodes of "The Hardy Boys/Nancy Drew Mysteries"), Grosset & Dunlap, 1978.

The Haunted House and Flight to Nowhere (based on episodes of "The Hardy Boys/Nancy Drew Mysteries"), Grosset & Dunlap, 1978.
The Nancy Drew Sleuth Book: Clues to Good Sleuthing (short stories and police procedures), Grosset & Dunlap, 1979.
Nancy Drew Book of Hidden Clues, Wanderer, 1980.
Nancy Drew Ghost Stories (short stories), edited by Meg Schneider, Wanderer, Volume 1, 1983, Volume 2, 1985.
Nancy Drew Mystery Stories: Back-to-Back Edition, Putnam, 1987.
Double Crossing: A Nancy Drew & Hardy Boys Supermystery, Archway, 1988.
A Crime for Christmas: A Nancy Drew & Hardy Boys Supermystery, Archway, 1988.
Shock Waves: A Nancy Drew & Hardy Boys Supermystery, Archway, 1989.

Also author of *The Secret of the Old Clock* [and] *The Hidden Staircase,* revised editions, published in the early 1970s.

SIDELIGHTS: Of all the Stratemeyer Syndicate series stars, perhaps none has shone as brightly as Nancy Drew. "Since the '30s," declares Deborah Kaplan in the *Detroit Free Press,* "she has steered the Silent Generation, Woodstock Generation and Me Generation of women through their tender years as the model of a Junior Leaguer." Supported by her lawyer father, Carson Drew, aided by chums George Fayne and Bess Marvin as well as boyfriend Ned Nickerson, driving her blue roadster around River Heights, Nancy has sleuthed her way into the hearts of millions of young readers for more than fifty years. Nancy is "the most popular girl detective in the world," says Bobbie Ann Mason in her book *The Girl Sleuth: A Feminist Guide.* "There had been nothing in children's books like the success of Nancy Drew." She began her detecting career in 1929, Mason declares, "serenely ignoring the world crashing all around." By 1933, she adds, Nancy was outselling the most popular boys' series by nearly two to one. Today, more than fifty years after her debut, Nancy's adventures continue to attract readers; more than eighty million copies of her books have been sold.

Part of Nancy's success, critics believe, derives from the way her adventures mix elements of three different genres: detective, series, and Gothic fiction. Russel B. Nye reports in *The Unembarrassed Muse: The Popular Arts in America* that all of Nancy's exploits "are based on the mystery-adventure-Gothic pattern developed by Mary Roberts Rinehart, geared to the level of the early teen." Nancy is locked in Heath Castle's dusty tower in *The Clue in the Crumbling Wall. The Witch Tree Symbol* interweaves Pennsylvania Dutch hex signs and a thief who pursues Nancy with deadly intent, while in *The Invisible Intruder,* the young detective and her friends search for a ghost. "This seesaw pattern of pursuit, confinement, and release, in turn," Carol Billman asserts in *The Secret of the Stratemeyer Syndicate: Nancy Drew, the Hardy Boys, and the Million Dollar Fiction Factory,* "wrings out readers' emotions by exciting alternating feelings of tension and exhilaration."

Often these elements are used repeatedly in different volumes of the series, sometimes—in the opinion of certain critics—to the detriment of the reader's imagination. "A common complaint" of reviewers, notes *New York Times Book Review* contributor Karla Kuskin, "is that 'Nancy Drew books are the same books written over and over again.'" Proponents of series fiction recognize this; Mason observes, "The plots of Nancy Drew mysteries are like sonnets—endless variations on an inflexible form." But some of Nancy's supporters see this repetitiousness as a positive factor in the series' success. "Perhaps," Kuskin continues, "that is also part of the charm they hold for their readers. A series combines the excitement of the unknown cushioned by the known." "In a world of gaudy exhibitionism," declares Arthur Prager in *Rascals at Large; or, The Clue in the Old Nostalgia,* "sub-teens find refuge in Nancy's enviable, secure, conservative world."

Another part of the series' attraction lies in the figure of the girl sleuth herself. Anita Susan Grossman, writing in *Ohio Magazine,* states, "Nancy represents an ideal: Well-to-do, attractive, intelligent, she is eternally poised on the edge of adulthood, without ever having to take on grown-up worries and responsibilities." "At the same time," she adds, "Nancy is endowed with any number of skills . . . and is mature beyond her years." Nancy has her own car and is largely free of parental supervision; she can do anything, and does it superbly well. The young investigator, says Mason, "is as immaculate and self-possessed as a Miss America on tour. She is as cool as Mata Hari and as sweet as Betty Crocker." In *The Password to Larkspur Lane* she makes a championship dive while at a swank resort, then rescues a small child who has fallen in the lake. She shoots a lynx with a revolver in *The Secret at Shadow Ranch,* and even repairs her car in *The Sign of the Twisted Candles.* "As a symbolic figure," declares Billman, "the young female private eye is everything girl readers could ask for."

Yet Nancy also has a certain accessibility and appeal that other, more exotic, heroines lack. Prager reports, "When I asked my daughter why she had loved Nancy, she thought for a moment, and then said simply, 'You can *identify* with her.' She meant that a little girl can plausibly pretend to be Nancy. She is an example of the fantasy world in which pre-pubescent girls live in day-dreams." Carol King, a regional director of the National Organization for Women, told Kaplan, "You could relate to a young woman who wasn't just timidly sitting back playing dolls, watching life go by, waiting for her knight in armor to come and sweep her off her feet." "She gave girls the idea you could be something other than Pollyanna or the Bobbsey Twins. Nancy Drew *did* stuff," women's studies librarian Pat Padala informed Kaplan. She is a paragon of young women's aspirations. Young readers, says Nye, "find in her what they hope soon to be—a poised, capable, self-sufficient girl in control of her life; one who can take care of herself and who needs neither guidance nor exhortation."

Although Nancy has her proponents as a symbol of female liberation, some critics note that she fails as a role model. Nora Faires, a woman's historian, told Kaplan that Nancy "never seemed to have a future." "Totally protected from want, gainful employment, boredom and despair," says Kuskin, "Nancy would seem to be more of a suburban princess than a symbol of liberation from anything except real life." "Living in the nearly fantastic land of River Heights, she is hermetically sealed off from change, growth, failure," asserts Billman. "Yet," she continues, "it is precisely because [Nancy] is so far removed from the little qualms and the big frustrations and decisions facing real girls and women that she cannot be considered a helpful fictional model of successful womanhood." "Cool Nancy Drew figures it is better to be locked in the timeless role of girl sleuth—forever young, forever tops, above sex, above marriage—an inspiring symbol of freedom," states Mason. "But was she?. . . She always has it both ways—protected and free. She is an eternal girl, a stage which is a false ideal for women in our time." "Maybe in the end that's why I didn't like her," Faires concludes. "Her world never

gets more complicated. Like Peter Pan, she never had to grow up."

If Nancy has never had to grow up, still she has evolved over the years. Juvenile lifestyles changed after the Second World War, and volumes written in the 1930s seemed dated to later readers. In 1959 Harriet Adams, head of the Stratemeyer Syndicate, began rewriting the earlier series books in order to bring Nancy up-to-date and to eliminate racial stereotypes. Villains lost their ethnic qualities and dialect-speaking characters switched to standard English, but the young sleuth herself stayed basically the same. In 1986, however, Simon & Schuster launched the "Nancy Drew Files" series, which featured an entirely revamped Nancy. "In keeping with Eighties feminism," says Grossman, "Nancy has become more a professional detective who is hired for 'cases' and has a 'career.'" Nancy Wartik writes in *Ms.,* "The blue roadster is now a Mustang GT convertible, Ned Nickerson's demure pecks on the cheek have turned into lingering kisses and romantic liaisons in a Jacuzzi." "To some readers," relates Grossman, "it has all been too much." One reviewer, she continues, "blasted the new Nancy Drew as a '*Dynasty* bimbo,' finding her 'a hot little number looking for "hunks" who acts like something out of a Jackie Collins novel.'"

Revised, revamped, and renewed, Nancy seems destined to continue forever. Although many critics agree that her adventures lack literary quality, they continue to enthrall readers—and, Kuskin emphasizes, "they have helped lead many children past River Heights or Bayport further into the bewitched byways of reading for pleasure. It's a destination well worth the trip." Librarians, executives, and authors such as Frances Fitzgerald, Ellen Goodman, and Eileen Goudge Zuckerman all have acknowledged Nancy's influence in their early years. "Whatever literary or life experiences readers graduate to," Billman declares, "Nancy does seem to be in American girls' bloodstream; and as part of their larger reading and developmental pattern, she not only has won—but *has*—her place."

The Stratemeyer Syndicate also used the Carolyn Keene pseudonym for the "Dana Girls" series, combining elements of Nancy Drew and the Hardy Boys in the adventures of two sister sleuths, Louise and Jean Dana. Mildred Augustine Wirt Benson originated the "Nancy Drew" series for Edward Stratemeyer, and also contributed volumes to the "Dana Girls." Walter Karig, Leslie McFarlane, Harriet S. Adams, James Duncan Lawrence, and Nancy Axelrad were among the other writers who contributed to these series. For more information, see the entries in this volume for Harriet S. Adams, James Duncan Lawrence, and Edward L. Stratemeyer.

MEDIA ADAPTATIONS: Four black and white films featuring Nancy Drew were made in 1938-39. They all starred Bonita Granville as Nancy, John Litel as Carson Drew, and Frankie Thomas as "Ted" Nickerson: "Nancy Drew—Detective" (loosely based on *The Password to Larkspur Lane*), Warner Bros., 1938; "Nancy Drew—Reporter," Warner Bros., 1939; "Nancy Drew, Trouble Shooter," Warner Bros., 1939; and "Nancy Drew and the Hidden Staircase," Warner Bros., 1939. More recently, Pamela Sue Martin and Janet Louise Jackson have portrayed the girl sleuth in "The Nancy Drew Mysteries," which later became "The Hardy Boys/Nancy Drew Mysteries," and ran on ABC-TV from 1977 to 1979, and then went into syndication. Four Nancy Drew filmstrips, each an adaptation of a Nancy Drew book, appeared in 1979 from the Society for Visual Education: "The Secret of the Old Clock," "Nancy's Mysterious Letter," "The Mysterious Mannequin,'' and ''The Sky Phantom.'' The girl sleuth has also appeared in other media. Parker Brothers released a *Nancy Drew Mystery Game* in 1958. ''The Clue in the Old Stagecoach,'' a recording of the novel of the same title, was issued in 1972, and recently actress Eve Plumb has narrated Nancy's adventures for the Cassette Book Company. In 1979, Grosset & Dunlap published two coloring books and Wanderer issued a Nancy Drew diary and date book.

BIOGRAPHICAL/CRITICAL SOURCES:

BOOKS

Authors in the News, Volume 2, Gale, 1976.
Bargainnier, Earl F., editor, *Ten Women of Mystery,* Bowling Green State University Popular Press, 1981.
Billman, Carol, *The Secret of the Stratemeyer Syndicate: Nancy Drew, the Hardy Boys, and the Million Dollar Fiction Factory,* Ungar, 1986.
Johnson, Deidre, editor and compiler, *Stratemeyer Pseudonyms and Series Books: An Annotated Checklist of Stratemeyer and Stratemeyer Syndicate Publications,* Greenwood Press, 1982.
Mason, Bobbie Ann, *The Girl Sleuth: A Feminist Guide,* Feminist Press, 1975.
Nye, Russel B., *The Unembarrassed Muse: The Popular Arts in America,* Dial, 1970.
Penzler, Otto, editor, *The Great Detectives,* Little, Brown, 1978.
Prager, Arthur, *Rascals at Large; or, The Clue in the Old Nostalgia,* Doubleday, 1971.

PERIODICALS

Americana, September-October, 1986.
Ann Arbor News, February 19, 1980.
Chicago Tribune, July 10, 1986.
Children's Literature, Volume 7, 1978.
Detroit Free Press, October 10, 1975, June 17, 1986, September 7, 1986.
Detroit News, February 17, 1980, August 13, 1986.
Family Weekly, August 10, 1980.
Hobbies, March, 1981.
Journal of Popular Culture, spring, 1973.
Language Arts, November-December, 1975.
Ms., January, 1974, September, 1986.
New Yorker, August 18, 1986.
New York Times, April 4, 1968, March 27, 1977.
New York Times Book Review, May 4, 1975.
Ohio Magazine, December, 1987.
People, April 28, 1980.
Publishers Weekly, March 5, 1979, May 30, 1986.
Redbook, April, 1980.
San Francisco Chronicle, August 21, 1988.
Saturday Review, January 25, 1969.
Seventeen, December, 1979.
TV Guide, June 25, 1977.
Vogue, May, 1980.

—*Sketch by Kenneth R. Shepherd*

*   *   *

KEESING, Nancy (Florence) 1923-

PERSONAL: Born September 7, 1923, in Sydney, New South Wales, Australia; daughter of Gordon Samuel (an architect) and Margery Louise (Hart) Keesing; married A. M. Hertzberg, February 2, 1955; children: Margery, John. *Education:* Uni-

versity of Sydney, Diploma of Social Studies. *Religion:* Jewish.

ADDRESSES: Home—3 Garrick Ave., Hunter's Hill, New South Wales NSW 2110, Australia.

CAREER: Writer. Department of Navy, Sydney, Australia, clerk, 1942-45; Royal Alexandra Hospital for Children, Sydney, social worker, 1947-51. Member of literature board of Australia Council, 1973-74; member of board of governors of Winifred West Schools Ltd., 1973—. Member of council, Kuring-gai College of Advanced Education.

MEMBER: English Association (vice-president of Sydney branch, 1979—), Australian Society of Authors (executive member; member of management committee, 1969-73).

AWARDS, HONORS: Order of Australia.

WRITINGS:

Garden Island People (memoir), Wentworth, 1975.
John Lang and ''The Forger's Wife'' (biography), John Ferguson, 1979.
Lily on the Dustbin: Slang of Australian Women and Families, illustrated by Victoria Roberts, Penguin, 1982.
Just Look out the Window: Superstitions, Odd Beliefs, and Possibly the Truth about the Weather and Your Future, illustrated by Roberts, Penguin, 1985.
Riding the Elephant: A Memoir, Allen & Unwin, 1988.

POETRY

Imminent Summer, Lyrebird Writers, 1951.
Three Men and Sydney, Angus & Robertson, 1955.
Showground Sketchbook and Other Poems, Angus & Robertson, 1968.
Hails and Farewells, Edwards & Shaw, 1977.

LITERARY CRITICISM

(Author of commentary) *Elsie Carew: Australian Primitive Poet,* Wentworth, 1965.
Douglas Stewart, Lansdowne Press, 1965, revised edition, Oxford University Press, 1969.
(Editor) *Australian Post-War Novelists,* Jacaranda, 1975.

NOVELS FOR CHILDREN

By Gravel and Gum: The Story of a Pioneer Family, Macmillan, 1963.
The Golden Dream, Collins, 1974.

EDITOR OR COMPILER

(With Douglas Stewart) *Australian Bush Ballads,* Angus & Robertson, 1955.
(With Stewart) *Old Bush Songs and Rhymes of Colonial Times,* Angus & Robertson, 1957.
Australian Poetry: 1959, Angus & Robertson, 1959.
(With Stewart) *The Pacific Book of Bush Ballads,* Angus & Robertson, 1967, published as *Bush Songs, Ballads, and Other Verses,* Discovery Press, 1968, revised edition published as *Favourite Bush Ballads,* Angus & Robertson, 1977.
(And author of introduction and notes) *Gold Fever: The Australian Goldfields, 1851 to 1890s* (anthology), Angus & Robertson, 1967, published as *A History of the Australian Gold Rushes,* 1976.
(And author of introduction) *Transition* (anthology), Angus & Robertson, 1970.
The Kelly Gang, Ure Smith, 1975.

The White Chrysanthemum, Angus & Robertson, 1977, published in paperback as *Dear Mum,* 1985.
Henry Lawson: Favourite Verse, Thomas Nelson, 1978.
Shalom: Australian Jewish Short Stories, Collins, 1978.

CONTRIBUTOR

Australia Writes, F. W. Cheshire, 1953.
Australian Signpost, F. W. Cheshire, 1956.
A Book of Australian Verse, Oxford University Press, 1956.
Australian Poets Speak, Rigby (Adelaide), 1961.
Poetry in Australia: 2, Angus & Robertson, 1964.
Songs for All Seasons, Angus & Robertson, 1967.
James McAuley, editor, *A Map of Australian Verse,* Oxford University Press, 1975.
Australian Verse from 1805, Rigby, 1976.
The Collins Book of Australian Poetry, Collins, 1981.
The New Oxford Book of Australian Verse, Oxford University Press, 1986.
The Penguin Book of Australian Women Poets, Penguin, 1986.

OTHER

Contributor to *Bulletin, Southerly, Bridge, Overland,* and other periodicals, and to Australian Broadcasting Commission programs. Editor, *Australian Author,* 1971-73.

SIDELIGHTS: Nancy Keesing told *CA:* "My main interest is poetry. More or less by accident I seem to find myself writing mostly criticism and 'popular' history."

AVOCATIONAL INTERESTS: Reading, gardening, walking.

*   *   *

KELLEY, Kitty   1942-

PERSONAL: Born April 4, 1942, in Spokane, Wash.; daughter of William V. (an attorney) and Adele (Martin) Kelley; separated. *Education:* University of Washington, Seattle, B.A. (cum laude), 1964.

ADDRESSES: *Home and office*—3037 Dumbarton Ave. N.W., Washington, D.C. 20007.

CAREER: World's Fair, New York, N.Y., VIP hostess for General Electric exhibit, 1964-65; press assistant to U.S. Senator Eugene McCarthy in Washington, D.C., 1966-69; *Washington Post,* Washington, D.C., researcher for editorial page staff, 1969-71; *Washingtonian,* Washington, D.C., contributing editor, 1971-73; free-lance writer, 1973—. Has also worked as a schoolteacher in Seattle, Wash. Member of board of directors of Richmund Fellowship.

MEMBER: Women's Forum, American Newspaperwomen's Club, Washington Independent Writers (member of advisory board), Washington Press Club, Lotos Club.

WRITINGS:

The Glamour Spas, Simon & Schuster, 1975.
Jackie Oh!, Lyle Stuart, 1978.
Elizabeth Taylor: The Last Star, Simon & Schuster, 1981.
His Way: The Unauthorized Biography of Frank Sinatra, Bantam, 1986.

Editor of "Today is Sunday," appearing weekly in *Chicago Sun Times* and *Philadelphia Bulletin,* 1978. Contributor to magazines, including *Newsweek, McCall's, Ladies' Home Journal, Cosmopolitan,* and *Family Circle,* and to newspapers. Assistant editor of *The Berkshires,* 1976.

WORK IN PROGRESS: The unauthorized biography of Nancy Reagan, for Simon & Schuster.

SIDELIGHTS: As a biographer of a trio of celebrated Americans, Kitty Kelley has become almost as famous in her own right. While a Kelley biography often receives a lukewarm critical reception, the book inevitably heads for the bestseller lists. One work, *His Way: The Unauthorized Biography of Frank Sinatra,* made headlines even before a word of it was published. That's because Sinatra, in an effort to stop his life's story reaching the public via Kelley, filed an order of prior restraint. In response, a coalition of writers' groups leapt to Kelley's defense, citing the author's First Amendment rights. "Sinatra's suit is a chilling example of how a powerful public figure using money and influence can orchestrate what the public shall know about him," said the coalition in a prepared statement. "Sinatra, who has thrived in the public limelight for decades, has now concluded that it is within his exclusive power to let the public know what he wants it to know about his life."

Eventually, the singer dropped his $2 million suit after some of his allegations about Kelley's work habits proved unfounded. And after years of research, including interviewing more than 800 subjects connected to Sinatra, Kelley published *His Way* to a flurry of publicity and controversy. Much of the talk centered on a brace of new information about Sinatra's past, including Kelley's revelation that the entertainer's mother was an abortionist who worked many New Jersey cities, and that Sinatra's tempestuous romance with actress Ava Gardner culminated in the pregnant Gardner's seeking an abortion herself, because "she hated Frankie so much," as the book puts it, that she couldn't bear his child. Sinatra's psychological tics also enter into the biography. In a show of affection toward a friend, Kelley reports, the singer once said, "Bill, sometimes I wish someone would really hurt you so I could kill them."

His Way's incendiary tone sparked many critical flames. "There is so much cruel, actionable, semi-rational behavior recounted here that a reader can't help wondering if there isn't another side. Won't someone close to the man make a case for him?" writes *Los Angeles Times* reviewer David Freeman, adding, "No one expects an artist to be a Boy Scout or a member of the Chamber of Commerce, but it is astounding to consider that a man capable of evoking such ache and longing through his music could be so cruel and insensitive." "Kelley details [Sinatra's] often-rumored and undeniably extensive mob connections, his shocking tirades against the press . . . his callous disregard for others and his casual and regular brutality toward anyone who gets in the way of his massive ego and legendary temper," according to Joy Fielding in a Toronto *Globe and Mail* article.

"Assuming that this biography of one of President Reagan's Medal of Freedom winners is accurate, is it also fair?" asks *Time*'s John Skow. "Kelley takes pains to point out that Sinatra's callousness has often been balanced by a swaggering generosity. . . . What *His Way* acknowledges but cannot really convey is the gift that made Sinatra famous and kept him that way; the meticulous phrasing that changed the intonation of popular music."

Of Kelley's three biographies, *His Way* is probably the best known, stemming from its extensive lawsuit-generated publicity and its two excerpts published as cover stories in *People* magazine. The author honed her biographical research skills on two previous books, *Jackie Oh!,* a version of Jacqueline Kennedy Onassis's life, and *Elizabeth Taylor: The Last Star.*

Both unauthorized, the books feature the same sweeping background work that characterizes *His Way*. For the Taylor story, for instance, Kelley interviewed more than 400 people. She was accused of mudslinging in her descriptions of the actress's private life, and responded to the charges in a *Chicago Tribune* interview with Clarence Peterson: "It would be dishonest of me to write a book that makes Elizabeth Taylor sound like Mother Teresa of Calcutta because she is *not* Mother Teresa of Calcutta, and I don't think a biographer has a right to edit anyone's life." She goes on to say that for all the controversial material she includes, "I don't think I'm venomous. I still think Elizabeth Taylor is sensational, and I'm still fascinated by her because she is one woman who has really made it in a man's world, and she's a star by every definition and has been for 40 years. There's no malice in the book. I went in loving her and came out, ah, liking her."

Kelley's biographical technique, as Fielding sees it, "is relatively simple: she does mountains of research, . . . and then presents this information in a straightforward manner, uncomplicated by style or literary grace, as though it were indisputable fact. Kelley writes with the authority and assurance of someone who has been at her subject's side since the moment he was born, . . . and maybe even before that." To remarks that her biographies are no more than long gossip pieces, Kelley has responded humorously that "if it hadn't been for gossip, we wouldn't have three books of the Bible because Mark, Luke and John never knew Jesus. They wrote 100 years after the guy died. At least I got to people who are still kicking," as Betty Cuniberti quotes the author in a *Los Angeles Times* article. And *Washington Post Book World* critic Peter Collier states that "while it is true that her work bears approximately the same relation to the art of biography that the rap sheet has to the completed prosecution," it would be "shortsighted to dismiss Kitty Kelley as a simple gossipmonger or hatchet lady." Collier concludes: "Her work is marked by a vigor, thoroughness and an odd integrity. These virtues were on display in her biography of Jacqueline Kennedy and can be seen again in [*His Way*]. From the opening pages of this book, one can see why Sinatra went to such extremes . . . to keep Kelley from writing about him. He must have dreaded the symbiosis—he, more than most stars, had something to hide, and she, more than most writers, would be sure to ferret it out."

CA INTERVIEW

CA interviewed Kitty Kelley by telephone on October 10, 1987, at her home in Washington, D.C.

CA: You've been in the news recently because of your biography of Frank Sinatra, His Way, *and before that there were the celebrity biographies* Jackie Oh! *and* Elizabeth Taylor: The Last Star. *One of the difficulties common to all three books was that they were unauthorized, which meant that you had to depend entirely on secondary sources for your information. What attracted you to these difficult subjects?*

KELLEY: I suppose it was the impact they've had on the world in which they live. Jacqueline Kennedy Onassis, Elizabeth Taylor, and Frank Sinatra are all very powerful people who have influenced millions, and I was fascinated by how they came to that power and how they used it.

CA: You had taught school in Seattle, worked for Senator Eugene McCarthy, and been with the Washington Post *before you became a free-lance writer. Was writing your goal all along, or did you happen into it and find that you liked it?*

KELLEY: I'm embarrassed to say that I didn't have any specific life-goals or directions other than doing interesting things. Looking at the three positions you just mentioned, though—education, politics, and writing—you can see a relationship, but I didn't realize it at the time.

CA: Before His Way *was even written, Sinatra brought a two-million-dollar lawsuit against you to stop the book. That suit was later dropped. Was the agony the suit must have caused you in any way compensated for in the publicity it gave the book?*

KELLEY: The publicity of the lawsuit came three years before the book was published. The lawsuit was quite frightening in many respects, but I was very gratified that so many writers' groups around the country stepped forward to say that what Frank Sinatra was doing was a matter of prior restraint and should be dismissed on its face by the courts. I certainly came to a greater appreciation of the First Amendment. The lawsuit was a controversial issue because there were a lot of people who would side with Frank Sinatra; they would say, "Whose life is it anyway—his or hers?" The very easy answer to that question, I learned, is *Neither*. It's yours. The life of a public figure belongs to everybody.

The *Baltimore Sun* wrote a very eloquent editorial about this at the time. They said that "a public person affects everyone else's life, whether that person is an entertainer, journalist, officeholder or consort of an officeholder. If all the public can learn of the person is what the person himself wants it to learn, then ours will become a very closed and ignorant society, unable to correct its ills, quite unlike what the drafters and subsequent generations of defenders of the free speech First Amendment had in mind." That is really an endorsement of the unauthorized biography, too. The *Sun* also said, "No biographer has the right to damage subjects with malicious falsehoods. There are ways for damaged subjects to get their due after publication of such reporting. But prior restraint of the sort Mr. Sinatra is seeking is censorship, no matter how you dress it up. In the interest of the public, that is constitutionally impermissible, as the courts surely will make clear, promptly and unequivocally."

William Safire in the *New York Times* called for the same thing. So did an editorial-page piece in the *Washington Post*. As a free-lance writer, I didn't have the resources of a huge newspaper behind me, so I was very fortunate that so many writers' groups—the American Society of Journalists and Authors, Washington Independent Writers, the National Writers' Union, the Reporters' Committee for Freedom of the Press, PEN, and the Newspaper Guild—stepped forward to back me in this suit. That was very, very helpful and I'll be forever grateful.

It was a serious issue, and also very expensive. I don't think the publicity helped the book at the time, because there was no book to help in 1983. However, when the book was published three years later, it probably helped in that people could say, "This is the book that Frank Sinatra wanted to stop, and now we'll see why." Possibly it had that effect. In any event, people certainly remembered me. Up to that point—I laugh and I say this kiddingly—I could go to a party, be introduced as Kitty Kelley, and put people to sleep. Now, when I'm introduced as the woman who wrote the Frank Sinatra book, I can clear the room!

CA: Were you ever afraid physically while you were researching and writing His Way?

KELLEY: I was never afraid physically, but there was a different, more insidious kind of fear. The most frightening thing that happened to me in doing this book—and it really made me take more care than I've ever taken in my life—was this: Frank Sinatra had said in his court papers that he and he alone could write his book; nobody else could, unless they were authorized by him, and I certainly wasn't authorized. Midway into the lawsuit he claimed that he had a tape recording of me calling somebody in New York and leaving a message on their answering machine saying that Frank had told me to call, that I was his authorized biographer and he wanted this person to give me an interview.

That was terrifying. I knew I hadn't done it, but I began to wonder, and I stayed up all night worrying. Why would he say he had a tape if I hadn't left such a message? The lawyers soon descended upon my house to listen to the tape—I'd had to hire lawyers in California because that was where the suit was filed; I have a lawyer here in Washington; and the publisher's lawyers are in New York. All of them arrived so we could listen to this tape recording together. It was a phony. It sounded like Boy George imitating Joan Rivers. You have never seen such a roomful of relieved lawyers in your life. But I was terrorized. I thought, If somebody would go to those lengths, what are they going to do next to try to discredit me? That someone would do something so illegal to frame me was very frightening.

I interviewed over eight hundred people and worked four years on the book. I always take notes and tape record where possible, but this taught me something else. From that point forward, I was very careful. When I went to interview Frank Sinatra, Jr., I had tapes, I had notes, but I also had a photographer with me, who took a picture of me with Frank Sinatra, Jr., which I thought was silly at the time, but he said to me, "Listen: when this book comes out, they're going to deny everything. A picture is proof." I thought the photographer was paranoid, but when the book came out and Frank Sinatra, Jr., tried to deny giving me that interview, I was very grateful when my friend released his photograph to the press.

There was a time in Los Angeles—June 15, 1983—when I went to interview Frank Sinatra's former valet. I had never met him, so when he suggested that we meet at a bar, I asked my photographer friend to go there ahead of me. My friend was at the bar when I walked in to interview the valet. This way I had a witness to the interview, plus my notes and the American Express receipt for the drinks. I later wrote the valet a letter thanking him for giving me that short interview—all of which was very helpful three years later when the valet tried to deny he had ever met me.

CA: You've said previously that some people even cancelled or refused interviews because of fear of Frank Sinatra. Who were the hardest people to get to?

KELLEY: Everybody was hard—every single person. There wasn't one easy interview for this book. Nobody stepped forward to say, May I help you? Nobody offered information. People refused. They thought their careers would be ruined, their children would be harmed; some feared losing their lives. Even a benign questions like "What was your experience with Frank Sinatra?" frightened them. So it meant going back to people repeatedly.

When you do an unauthorized biography, you're not working with your subject, so you have an obligation to get to as many people as possible who are or have been close to the subject—his relatives, neighbors, classmates, employers, co-stars, girl friends, wives and ex-wives, producers, directors, songwriters, musicians, and other singers. In the case of Frank Sinatra, who has been associated with organized crime, I also had to interview past and present law enforcement officials. There are pivotal people in everybody's life: their mother, their first love, their best friend growing up, a high school teacher, a grade school teacher; but when you're writing about someone who is already seventy years old, some of the most important people in his life may have died.

In planning the interviews, I took an overview of Frank Sinatra's life. I divided it up into decades: people who knew him in the '40s, people who were close to him in the '50s, and so on. In each year there are pivotal people. For example, in 1964 there was a man by the name of Brad Dexter. He was an actor in Hollywood and the man who saved Frank Sinatra's life. I had been told that Sinatra later turned on him, but I didn't know why. So Mr. Dexter was someone I had to get to, and at first he didn't want to participate: he had never really talked before, never given an interview on the subject of his friendship with Sinatra. He was wealthy and influential in his own right so he wasn't afraid of Sinatra, but he just didn't want to get involved. I had to keep going back to him several times and begging him to talk to me. He finally agreed and he was a very important source. I felt I needed his story to do the book. But I felt that way about Peter Lawford, Nelson Riddle, and everyone else I interviewed!

CA: It's hard to imagine handling the sheer mass of material you must gather for your books. How do you organize and store it?

KELLEY: I create a filing system that's very detailed. In doing a biography, for the most part you're doing it chronologically. And doing an unauthorized book, you have no right to say, *He felt . . .* or *he thought . . .* or *he believed . . .* unless the subject has gone on the public record about his feelings, his thoughts and his beliefs. (If you cite such, I feel you should have the source as part of the chapter notes in the back of the book saying where you got your information.) Because I couldn't say, Frank Sinatra felt . . . , I had to do in-depth reporting so the reader could understand what Frank Sinatra was going through at the time.

To give you an example: Frank Sinatra's mother ran an abortion mill in Hoboken, New Jersey. That's not the only thing she did in life, but it was one of her occupations. Many people in Hoboken say that she performed a humane service; others were more judgemental. Mrs. Sinatra was arrested several times for performing illegal abortions, so she had a police record, which was public information. But it was still a difficult thing to write, because you're writing about someone's mother who is no longer alive, and about something that has been hidden for many years. Knowing that the information would bring a great deal of hurt and humiliation to the Sinatra family, I tried to handle it as sensitively as I could.

Mrs. Sinatra's abortion business was a real source of shame to her son but I couldn't say that Frank Sinatra *felt* ashamed, because Frank Sinatra didn't tell me he felt ashamed. That information came from interviewing other people—classmates who remembered how scandalized their parents were by Mrs. Sinatra's activities; how the Catholic church refused to let

Frank bring his record player for the high school dance because of his mother; how upset he would get if anyone referred to his mother's "business." Girl friends remembered the crippling headaches Frank developed and the moodiness that could suddenly overtake him, especially when his mother was around. Friends recalled how embarrassed he was, how he refused to acknowledge his mother's activities. You begin to see how his mother's activities affected Frank Sinatra, while at the same time bringing the family a great deal of money during the Depression. As you go through the book, you understand why Frank Sinatra at the age of seventy-one still needs to bathe himself in respectability.

CA: Suppose you get completely conflicting information from different interview subjects? How do you deal with that problem?

KELLEY: You *do* get conflicting information. For instance, Frank Sinatra had a home in Palm Springs when he was breaking up with Ava Gardner. He had loaned that home to Lana Turner and her manager. Ava showed up there and Frank showed up later. Each has a different story about what happened here; they were conflicting in parts and they agreed in parts. And I put them all in. You have to say in the book that this is the way Ava remembered it, and this is the way Lana remembered it. They *all* remembered there was a violent fight between Ava and Frank; they simply had different versions. Another dilemma concerned Nick Sevano, who grew up with Frank Sinatra in Hoboken and went on to work with him in the Dorsey days. I quoted him saying that Sinatra fired him. Since you can't take just one person's view and report it as fact, you have to put it in their words.

CA: Do you wait until you feel you have everything before you start the actual writing?

KELLEY: Yes, and even then I keep interviewing.

CA: Did your feelings about Jacqueline Onassis and Liz Taylor change over the course of your writing the books about them? Were you tired of them by the time you got to the end?

KELLEY: My feelings about them did change, but I wasn't tired of them. I saw after I finished *Jackie Oh!* that what I was dealing with was a very, very shrewd woman, who purposely created a mystery with which to surround herself, perhaps making her more interesting, and certainly more complex than Elizabeth Taylor. Your feelings change as you do more research and reporting because you come to know your subjects so much better. I do think you have to start out from a basis of respect or affection, because you're going to spend so much time with these people. In the case of Frank Sinatra, I felt that I was dealing with a story of real power, with the best and the worst of the American Dream. I finally realized a little bit about the American Dream when I walked the streets of Hoboken, New Jersey. I had been to the library and looked up pictures of what Hoboken was like when Frank Sinatra was growing up, and although I was there forty years later the streets in Little Italy are still the same and there are many people who grew up with Sinatra who have *never* been able to get out. Once I walked the same streets, I understood better the driving ambition and talent that catapulted Frank Sinatra out of Hoboken, New Jersey, to the top of the world.

CA: Do you feel there are gaps in any of the books, issues that you couldn't get enough information on or verify to your satisfaction?

KELLEY: Absolutely! But there's enough in each book to give you the *essence* of the subject. As President Kennedy once said, "What makes journalism so fascinating and biography so interesting is that single question: 'What's he like?'"

CA: Many people give you high marks for your work. As one example, Peter Range, a reporter for U.S. News and World Report *who was quoted in a* Los Angeles Times *article, called you "a deadly serious researcher. . . . first, last and always a reporter." On the other side of the coin, you are sometimes called a gossip writer. Does the negative criticism bother you a great deal?*

KELLEY: Yes, it does, but then I always try to remember the sage who said that gossip is merely history running down the street in a red satin dress!

CA: Would you ever be interested in doing a more traditional biography, perhaps about someone who is safely dead?

KELLEY: "Safely" meaning that the dead can't sue? It's true that writing about famous people who are alive makes the job much harder because you have to deal with battalions of lawyers before your book can be published. But it's a great challenge. Still, I'm not going to say I would *never* do the other kind of biography; I just haven't thought of doing it. Or rather, no one has asked me to do it. I'd probably enjoy it very much, though, because it's history.

CA: Has history always been one of your strong interests?

KELLEY: It is now. I'd never want to do another Hollywood biography because most movie stars seem so one-dimensional, but doing the Elizabeth Taylor biography gave me a chance to capture a bit of Hollywood history at the time when movies were so formative in all of our lives. It was interesting because it *was* history. And I suppose that's the only way I can justify spending as much time as I do writing books.

CA: What about a novel? You said some years ago that you'd love to try one someday.

KELLEY: I *would* love to, absolutely. But I haven't yet. I think it would be very difficult for someone like me who is wedded to the facts. One good thing would be the business of *he felt, he believed, he thought,* which you don't have to worry about with fiction. But you must tell quite a story, and I don't know if I'd be able to do that. Then again . . .

CA: Have you decided on your next book subject yet?

KELLEY: Right now I'm working on a magazine article that's rather important historically on Judith Exner. She's finally going to tell the truth about her involvement with President Kennedy and the mobster Sam Giancana. That's an article that I hope to have done by the end of the year. Then I'll start thinking of the next book.

BIOGRAPHICAL/CRITICAL SOURCES:

BOOKS

Kelley, Kitty, *His Way: The Unauthorized Biography of Frank Sinatra,* Bantam, 1986.

PERIODICALS

Baltimore Sun, December 4, 1983.
Chicago Tribune, January 3, 1982, September 26, 1986.
Globe and Mail (Toronto), November 8, 1986.
Los Angeles Times, March 24, 1985, September 26, 1986, October 22, 1986.
Nation, May 5, 1979.
New York Daily News, September 25, 1984.
New York Times, February 9, 1979, October 6, 1981, October 13, 1983, December 1, 1983, October 10, 1986.
New York Times Book Review, October 18, 1981, November 26, 1986.
People, September 15, 1986, September 22, 1986.
Time, November 30, 1981, November 3, 1986.
Times Literary Supplement, October 31, 1986.
Washington Post, October 14, 1981, October 8, 1983.
Washington Post Book World, October 8, 1978, November 9, 1986.

—*Interview by Jean W. Ross*

*   *   *

KELLEY, William Melvin   1937-

PERSONAL: Born November 1, 1937, in New York, N.Y.; son of William (an editor) and Narcissa Agatha (Garcia) Kelley; married Karen Isabelle Gibson (a designer), December, 1962; children: Jessica, Ciratikaiji. *Education:* Attended Harvard University, 1957-61.

ADDRESSES: Office—P.O. Box 2658, New York, N.Y. 10027.

CAREER: Free-lance writer and photographer. Writer in residence, State University of New York at Geneseo, spring, 1965; instructor, New School for Social Research, 1965-67; guest lecturer in American literature, University of Paris, Nanterre, 1968; guest instructor, University of West Indies, Mona, 1969-70.

AWARDS, HONORS: Dana Reed Prize from Harvard University, 1960; Bread Loaf Scholar, 1962; John Hay Whitney Foundation Award and Rosenthal Foundation Award, 1963, both for *A Different Drummer; Transatlantic Review* Award, 1964, for *Dancers on the Shore;* fiction award from Black Academy of Arts and Letters, 1970, for *Dunfords Travels Everywheres.*

WRITINGS:

FICTION

A Different Drummer (novel), Doubleday, 1962.
Dancers on the Shore (short stories), Doubleday, 1964, reprinted (introduction by Mel Watkins), Howard University Press, 1984.
A Drop of Patience (novel), Doubleday, 1965.
dem (novel), Doubleday, 1967, reprinted (introduction by Willie E. Abraham), Collier Books, 1969.
Dunfords Travels Everywheres (novel), Doubleday, 1970.

CONTRIBUTOR TO ANTHOLOGIES

Langston Hughes, editor, *The Best Short Stories by Negro Writers: An Anthology from 1899 to the Present*, Little, Brown, 1967.
Richard Kostelanetz, editor, *The Young American Writers*, Funk, 1967.
James A. Emanuel and Theodore Gross, editors, *Dark Symphony: Negro Literature in America*, Free Press, 1968.

Edward Margolies, editor, *Native Sons: A Critical Study of Twentieth-Century Negro American Authors*, Lippincott, 1968.
Arnold Adoff, editor, *Brothers and Sisters: Modern Stories by Black Americans*, Macmillan, 1970.
Lettie J. Austin, Lewis W. Fenderson, and Sophia P. Nelson, editors, *The Black Man and the Promise of America*, Scott, Foresman, 1970.
Bradford Chambers and Rebecca Moon, editors, *Right On!: Anthology of Black Literature*, New American Library, 1970.
John Henrik Clarke, editor, *Harlem: Voices from the Soul of Black America*, New American Library, 1970.
Charles L. James, editor, *From the Roots: Short Stories by Black Americans*, Dodd, 1970.
Francis E. Kearns, editor, *Black Experience: An Anthology of American Literature for the 1970's*, Viking, 1970.
Darwin T. Turner, editor, *Black American Literature: Essays, Poetry, Fiction, Drama*, Merrill, 1970.
Houston A. Baker, Jr., editor, *Black Literature in America*, McGraw-Hill, 1971.
Arthur P. Davis and J. Saunders Reddings, editors, *Cavalcade: Negro American Writing from 1760 to the Present*, Houghton, 1971.
Nick Aaron Ford, editor, *Black Insights: Significant Literature by Black Americans, 1760 to the Present*, Ginn, 1971.
Richard K. Barksdale and Kenneth Kinnamon, editors, *Black Writers of America: A Comprehensive Anthology*, Macmillan, 1972.
Abraham Chapman, editor, *New Black Voices*, New American Library, 1972.
Richard A. Long and Eugenia W. Collier, editors, *Afro-American Writing: An Anthology of Prose and Poetry*, New York University Press, 1972.
William Smart, editor, *Women and Men, Men and Women*, St. Martin's, 1975.

OTHER

"Excavating Harlem" (video), produced by Manhattan Cable/Channel D, 1988.

Contributor to periodicals, including *Accent, Canto, Jazz and Pop, Mademoiselle, Negro Digest, New York Times Magazine, Partisan Review, Playboy, Quilt, River Styx, Urbanite,* and *Works in Progress.*

WORK IN PROGRESS: Days of Our Lives.

SIDELIGHTS: The fiction of William Melvin Kelley published between 1962 and 1970—spanning the most tumultuous years of the civil rights movement—displays the author's evolving perceptions of black and white in American society. Kelley's fiction undergoes noticeable transformations from his first novel, *A Different Drummer*, supportive of nonviolence as a means to affect social change, to his later works which become increasingly experimental in structure and more vehemently critical of social injustice. Kelley begins with "a vision of racial coexistence," explains Valerie M. Babb in *Dictionary of Literary Biography*, yet as he "became more aware of the systematic degradation of blacks throughout American history, the themes and concerns of his writing took on a more radical stance. He shifted from characters making quiet protests to regain their lost dignity to characters angrily avenging past wrongs." This progression in Kelley's fiction offers a paradigm to changes within the 1960s civil rights movement itself. "In his personal development, we can see a chapter of our nation's history," contends Babb, "and in his literary development, we can note some of the clearest articulations of American culture at the time.''

Kelley's four novels, along with his short story collection *Dancers on the Shore,* are often collectively examined as a saga of contemporary Afro-American experience. Robert Bone notes in the *New York Times Book Review* that Kelley's ''books are unified in over-all design,'' comparing the effect to a ''reverse'' variation on William Faulkner's Yoknapatawpha County legend: ''an epic treatment of American history from a Negro point of view.'' Jill Weyant similarly comments in *CLA Journal:* ''The purpose of writing a serious saga . . . is to depict impressionistically a large, crowded portrait, each individual novel presenting enlarged details of the whole, each complete in itself, yet evoking a more universal picture than is possible in a single volume.'' Weyant elaborates that the ''Kelley saga is an attempt to redefine the Complete Man and to overturn inaccurate racial stereotypes that, in Kelley's opinion, have too long held sway.'' Kelley himself has commented on a goal of interrelatedness in his fiction, telling Roy Newquist in *Conversations:* ''Perhaps I'm trying to follow the Faulknerian pattern—although I guess it's really Balzacian when you connect everything. I'd like to be eighty years old and look up at the shelf and see that all of my books are really one big book.''

Throughout his fiction, Kelley emphasizes the worth and intrinsic rights of humans as individuals. Babb comments on the early stages of Kelley's outlook: ''In the beginning stages of his writing career, Kelley saw that to be black in America was an amalgam of many experiences, yet many white and even black leaders sought to view black consciousness as a single entity. The individual has an obligation, Kelley believed, to focus more on 'what we really are: human beings, not simply members of a race.''' This belief exists behind the title of Kelley's first novel, *A Different Drummer,* recalling the famous lines of Henry David Thoreau: ''If a man does not keep pace with his companions, perhaps it is because he hears a different drummer. Let him step to the music which he hears, however measured or far away.'' Hugh J. Ingrasci comments on the resilience of Kelley's concept of individuality: ''The world Kelley portrays . . . projects a life of possibilities, one wherein the struggle to eliminate racial inequities is viable, but only for the individual who hammers away at exploitation with one irrestible conviction: that each human person has too great a value to allow others to regard him as a mere social commodity.'' It matters little, Ingrasci continues, if one ''wins his battle with the society he finds. . . . It is his belief that he is humanly equal to anyone else that has set him free, and not the prospect of attaining social justice.''

In the preface to his short story collection *Dancers on the Shore,* Kelley likewise emphasizes an approach to writing that focuses on the individual. He criticizes those who would lump all black authors into a single category, the ''Negro literary ghetto,'' as he describes it. ''An American writer who happens to have brown skin faces this unique problem,'' Kelley explains: ''Solutions and answers to the Negro Problem are very often read into his work. At the instant they open his book, the readers begin to search fervently, and often with honest concern, for some key or answer to what is happening today between black and white people in America.'' Kelley likewise applies an emphasis on individuality to his own characters: ''At this time, let me say for the record that I am not a sociologist or a politician or a spokesman. Such people try to give answers. A writer, I think, should ask questions. He should depict people, not symbols or ideas disguised as people.''

Critical response to Kelley's individual books has been divided. He is often noted for maintaining a controlled and calculated distance from his subject matter, yet at times is criticized for writing too facilely, or—in seeming contradiction to his stated intentions—from too ideological a perspective. Regarding *Dancers on the Shore,* Louis Rubin, Jr., comments in the *New York Herald Tribune Book Week* that Kelley's stories ''bear all the earmarks of having been written while the author was still searching for his true subject'' and that they suffer in two main areas: ''Either they are underdeveloped, with the author having worked only at the surface of his material, or else (and sometimes at the same time) they are content with presenting aspects of what Mr. Kelley said he wasn't going to try to solve, The Negro Problem.'' Michele Murray in *Commonweal,* on the other hand, praises Kelley's perspective in *Dancers on the Shore,* writing that the stories benefit from ''a fineness that comes from the *tone* of the telling—very spare, very quiet, very honest.'' Kelley's third book, *A Drop of Patience,* similarly received mixed comments. The story of a black jazz musician who is blind, *A Drop of Patience* ''is a moving, painful and stinging experience,'' writes David Boroff in the *New York Times Book Review:* ''Kelley's prose is tight and spare, the novel's anger and bitterness straining against the stripped-down language.'' He concludes, however, that Kelley's main character is ''in the end . . . too simple a figure, a slice of folklore rather than a convincing human being.'' Likewise, Whitney Balliett in the *New Yorker,* although in praise of Kelley's going ''about his work calmly'' while working with subject matter that can ''turn well-meaning novelists into polemicists,'' comments on over-ideologized characters: ''Kelley's characters . . . tend to spring from his ideas, rather than the other way around. If he were to press deeper into the ordinary hearts he writes of, instead of forcing them to grow on intellectual trellises, he would help us to know our own hearts.''

Kelley's fourth book, the novel *dem,* takes a distinctly radical approach in communicating the destructive influences of racism in America. An ''overt satire of the ways of white people,'' according to Bone, Kelley's novel is the story of a white couple who, through a rare fertilization process, become the parents of twin boys, one white and one black. Calling the book ''a jarring surprise,'' Henry S. Resnik in the *Saturday Review* describes *dem*'s major characters: ''The protagonist, Mitchell Pierce, is upper-middle-class white, an advertising copy-writer, emotionally and sexually impotent, a travesty of a man. His wife, Tam, is a domineering bitch whose principal characteristics are her penchant for ridicule and her preoccupation with her hairdo.'' Resnik adds: ''The book is an angry, if not always original, portrait of American society. . . . Kelley is not only angry at savagery, racism, emasculation, and matriarchy; he takes a good hard crack at our slim hold on reality.''

As with Kelley's previous fiction, some reviewers objected to a level of superficiality in the novel. Dan Jaffe remarks in *Prairie Schooner:* ''The texture of the language, the settings, and the dialogue, give the reader a sense of life, of the alienation of a confused white man who suspects he is on the periphery of a life-rhythm more natural and substantial than his own. Unfortunately, the rest of the novel is slick and stagey by comparison.'' Frank C. Shapiro comments in *Book World* that the main character of *dem* is not quite believable: ''There are good scenes in this unsatisfying book, and good writing, too, but on the whole, reading *dem* is like watching a basketball player, in perfect form, fake out a guard, arch for a pivot shot, and miss.'' Bone, however, praises Kelley's use of satire to effectively communicate his message: "[Kelley's] present mood is bitter, disillusioned, alienated to the point of secession from American society. The expatriate impulse, however, has found in satire a controlling form. Kelley's images are able to encompass his negative emotions. The result is a sharp increase in perception for the victims of his satire." Babb commends Kelley's innovative approach in that it "represents a reordering of the social history of America. Rather than having blacks as the victims, in [*dem*] it is the whites who suffer as Kelley parodies their traditions and their values. . . . Kelley suggests that white America is sterile in the values it pursues and is consciously, deliberately cruel."

Kelley's next novel, *Dunfords Travels Everywheres,* is his most experimental. "Inspired by *Finnegans Wake* and the problem [James] Joyce faced as an Irish writer within a larger English context," notes Babb, "*Dunfords Travels Everywheres* is constructed from a language derived from Bantu, Pidgin English, and Harlem argot, among other forms of black speech." In the novel, Kelley combines this experimental, collective language ("Langleash") with that of standard English prose to relate the internal exploration of Chig Dunford, a contemporary Harvard-educated black. In his self-exploration, Dunford comes upon an aspect of himself embodied in a character named Carlyle Bedlow, a Harlem-raised black; these twin aspects of the same person converge along common bonds that are understood through their secret language. Michael Wood explains in the *New York Review of Books:* "In the half-gibberish of their dreams, represented in the novel by Joycean metalanguage, . . . they know the truth which escapes them in waking life—shown here by Kelley in more conventional prose, as a place of assassinations and deceit, where slaves are suddenly encountered on a lower deck of a modern liner, where vast competing conspiracies, secret societies of whites against blacks and vice versa, are glimpsed beneath the surfaces of an innocent-looking world." Dunford emerges as a far-reaching representative of the Afro-American, according to David Galloway in *The Black American Short Story in the Twentieth Century: A Collection of Critical Essays:* "Just as Joyce's hero, H. C. E., metamorphoses into 'Here comes Everybody,' so Dunford is a kind of 'everybody' traveling everywhere—Harlem spade, Ivy League Negro, crook and cowboy and lover and artist and pilgrim."

Regarding *Dunfords Travels Everywheres* critical opinion was again divided on Kelley. Wood comments that like Joyce, Kelley "as a black American and a writer, is caught in the language and culture of an enemy country, and his use of *Finnegans Wake* reflects a legitimate distress: it is a mockery both of 'good English' and of black manglings of it." Wood concludes, however, that "the effort looks in the wrong direction. The experimental idiom is ingenious, but it is, also, thin and obscure." On the other hand, Christopher Lehmann-Haupt notes in the *New York Times* that the "black form of the dream language of James Joyce's *Finnegans Wake* . . . has released in Kelley a creative exuberance that was being choked with bitterness in his last book." Although Lehmann-Haupt agrees that some aspects of the novel "seem curiously cryptic and incomplete," he commends Kelley for "the way the 'real' surface is undermined, so that finally it threatens to splinter into hallucination at every moment. Chief among the myriad themes . . . is that the way to the black man's roots is not over Harlem and out, but back to the streets of the ghetto and in through its language."

Regarding possible political statements in his fiction, Kelley remarked in his 1967 *Conversations* interview: "I simply want

to try to write good books. It isn't that I'm naive, that I'm trying to divorce myself from the racial struggle, but I don't think it should enter into my art in such a way that my writing becomes propagandistic. If my novels are so strongly tied to the times the book would have no reason to live once the present struggles are over—if indeed, they ever will be over. I want my books to have reason to exist." Galloway comments that, as enduring literature, Kelley's novels and short stories "manage to carve a reasonably secure niche for themselves within the American system; the trials to which they are submitted have as much to do with being human as they do, specifically, with being black." Galloway notes a particular relevance of Kelley's fiction: "The dilemma he frequently underscores is that the black's destiny is in many ways indistinguishable from the destiny of the entire post-modern American society, but that participation in such a destiny must not be allowed to submerge entirely the ethnic, cultural, and personal identity of the black."

BIOGRAPHICAL/CRITICAL SOURCES:

BOOKS

Bruck, Peter, editor, *The Black American Short Story in the Twentieth Century: A Collection of Critical Essays,* Gruener, 1977.
Contemporary Literary Criticism, Volume 22, Gale, 1982.
Dictionary of Literary Biography, Volume 33: *Afro-American Fiction Writers after 1955,* Gale, 1984.
Kelley, William Melvin, *Dancers on the Shore,* Doubleday, 1964.
Kelley, William Melvin, *dem,* Doubleday, 1967.
Kelley, William Melvin, *Dunfords Travels Everywheres,* Doubleday, 1970.
Littlejohn, David, *Black on White,* Grossman, 1966.
Newquist, Roy, editor, *Conversations,* Rand McNally, 1967.
Whitlow, Roger, *Black American Literature: A Critical History,* Nelson Hall, 1973.
Williams, Sherley Anne, *Give Birth to Brightness,* Dial, 1972.

PERIODICALS

America, April 17, 1965.
American Literature, January, 1973.
Best Sellers, April 15, 1964, April 15, 1965, October 1, 1970.
Booklist, July 1, 1962.
Book World, October 22, 1967.
CLA Journal, December, 1975.
Commonweal, July 3, 1964.
Critique: Studies in Modern Fiction, fall, 1984.
Esquire, August, 1963.
Harper's, December, 1969.
Negro Digest, October, 1962, January, 1967, March, 1967, May, 1968, November, 1969.
Newsweek, April 12, 1965.
New Yorker, May 22, 1965.
New York Herald Tribune Books, June 17, 1962.
New York Herald Tribune Book Week, March 22, 1964.
New York Review of Books, March 11, 1971.
New York Times, April 9, 1965, September 7, 1970.
New York Times Book Review, June 17, 1962, May 2, 1965, September 24, 1967, November 8, 1970.
Partisan Review, spring, 1968.
Prairie Schooner, spring, 1968.
Reporter, May 21, 1964.
Saturday Review, April 17, 1965, October 28, 1967.
Studies in Black Literature, summer, 1971, fall, 1972, winter, 1974, fall, 1975.

Times Literary Supplement, March 17, 1966.

—*Sketch by Michael E. Mueller*

*   *   *

KELLNER, Bruce 1930-

PERSONAL: Born March 17, 1930, in Indianapolis, Ind.; son of Gordon (an insurance executive) and Lillian (Zumbrunn) Kellner; married Margaret Wilcox, December 28, 1961; children: Hans Karl, Kate Hein. *Education:* Colorado College, B.A., 1955; University of Iowa, M.F.A., 1958. *Politics:* Democrat. *Religion:* None.

ADDRESSES: Home—514 North School Lane, Lancaster, Pa. 17603. *Office*—Department of English, Millersville University, Millersville, Pa. 17551.

CAREER: Coe College, Cedar Rapids, Iowa, assistant professor of English, 1955-60; Hartwick College, Oneonta, N.Y., assistant professor of English and drama director, 1960-69; Millersville University, Millersville, Pa., professor of English, 1969—. *Military service:* U.S. Navy, 1951-54.

MEMBER: Modern Language Association of America, American Association of University Professors, NAACP, Alpha Psi Omega, Pi Delta Kappa, Kappa Sigma.

WRITINGS:

Carl Van Vechten and the Irreverent Decades, University of Oklahoma Press, 1968.
(Editor) *''Keep A-Inchin' Along'': Selected Writings of Carl Van Vechten about Black Arts and Letters,* Greenwood Press, 1979.
A Bibliography of the Work of Carl Van Vechten, Greenwood Press, 1980.
The Harlem Renaissance: A Historical Dictionary for the Era, Greenwood Press, 1984, revised edition, Routledge & Kegan Paul, 1987.
Letters of Carl Van Vechten, Yale University Press, 1987.
(Author of introduction) Carl Van Vechten, *The Tattooed Countess,* University of Iowa Press, 1987.
Content With the Example: A Gertrude Stein Companion, Greenwood Press, 1988.

CONTRIBUTOR

James Vinson, editor, *Great Writers of the English Language,* Scribner, 1979.
A. Walton Litz, editor, *American Writers,* Scribner, 1981.
Steven Ford Brown, editor, *Heart's Invention: On the Poetry of Vassar Miller,* Ford-Brown Publishers, 1988.

OTHER

Contributor to reference books, including *Contemporary Photographers, Dictionary of Literary Biography,* and *Reference Guide to America.* Author of essays and articles on modern Irish poetry, obscure literary figures, and bibliography.

WORK IN PROGRESS: The Bookshelf Onstage, scripts based on literary texts for reader's theater; a biography of Ralph Barton.

SIDELIGHTS: "Like Joanne Trautmann, who may have coined the phrase to describe herself when she was editing Virginia Woolf's letters, I am a 'footnote fetishist,'" Bruce Kellner told *CA.* "My natural habitat is the library, but I care passionately about language and believe that scholarly writing can be as handsomely constructed as other literary forms. Craft

and art are not the especial possessions of poetry and fiction. Regardless of the form, however, I believe that craft must precede art. Our greatest critics, like our greatest poets, have always known that."

BIOGRAPHICAL/CRITICAL SOURCES:

PERIODICALS

Callalou, spring, 1987.
Journal of Negro Education, fall, 1985.
New York Times Book Review, February 16, 1969.
Variety, March 26, 1969.

*   *   *

KEVAN, Martin 1949-

PERSONAL: Born March 19, 1949, in Nairobi, Kenya; son of Douglas Keith (an entomologist) and Kathleen (Luckin) Kevan. *Education:* McGill University, B.Comm., 1969, teaching certificate, 1972; Concordia University, M.A., 1988.

ADDRESSES: Home—128 Clermont Ave., Montreal, Quebec, Canada H2T 2N1.

CAREER: Jim Buck's School of Dogs, New York, N.Y., dog walker, 1969; Sadler's Wells Theatre, London, England, assistant manager, 1970; Toras Moishe Rabbinical College, Montreal, Quebec, Canada, teacher, 1982-84; Concordia University, Montreal, instructor of creative writing and English composition, 1986—. Actor (film, stage, and radio) in French and English productions, Montreal, 1970—.

MEMBER: Association of Canadian Television and Radio Artists, Union des Artistes.

AWARDS, HONORS: Award for most imaginative radio broadcast, New York International Radio Awards, 1977, for "The Music of New France"; nomination for best original film script, ETROG Awards, 1978, for "Happiness Is Loving Your Teacher."

WRITINGS:

"The Rainbow Show" (children's theatrical production), produced in Montreal at Magic Mountain Theatre, 1974.
"Le spectacle des patates" (children's theatrical production), produced in Montreal at Magic Mountain Theatre, 1975.
"The Music of New France," produced by Canadian Broadcasting Corp. (CBC-Radio), 1977.
Racing Tides ("historical faction" novel), Stoddart, 1982, Beaufort Books, 1985.
"Escape from the Citadel" (play), produced in Montreal by St. Urbain Group, 1984.
(With Larry-Michel Demers) "Hommage a Rene-Daniel Dubois" (play), produced in Montreal at Theatre Quat' Sous, 1985.
(Contributor) John Metcalfe, editor, *The Council: The Bumper Book,* ECW Press (Toronto), 1986.
(Translator) Rene-Daniel Dubois, *Dialogue,* Canadian Artists against Apartheid (Toronto), 1986.
(Contributor) Robert Wallace, editor, *Three Quebec Playwrights* (contains Dubois's "Don't Blame the Bedouins," translated by Kevan), Coach House Press (Toronto), 1986.

Also author of *Psy Spy,* 1988, a satirical novel; also author and broadcaster of programs for Canadian Broadcasting Corp. (CBC-TV) and CINQ-Radio (Montreal). Contributor of poetry to anthologies. Contributor to periodicals, including *Zynergy,*

Poetry Montreal, Cahier de theatre JEU, X=Ero Magazine, and *Essays on Canadian Writing.*

WORK IN PROGRESS: Rough Terrain, a historical novel dealing with Romanticism, rebellion, and Utopianism in Scotland, the United States, Canada, and Australia during the years 1805-39; *And the Gods Came Down,* a novel dealing with neofascism, psychiatry, and theatre, set in Montreal during 1938.

SIDELIGHTS: Martin Kevan told *CA:* "I started writing at age 30 after a long period of illness. My career as an actor was faltering in part because I refused to move from my adopted city, Montreal, which was in the throes of an independence movement. The first book, *Racing Tides,* now classified by me as historical faction, was an attempt to inform anglophones of Canada's French and Amerindian histories. It is written in the first person in the form of a journal (I was tempted to foist in on the world as a genuine historical document). It almost wrote itself. I would go to the library to search for likely events to fill in the duller periods of the true history, and books magically opened onto usable ideas, observations and philosophies.

"After the publication of *Racing Tides* I became aware that I had broken the standard conventions of writing both histories and novels. I researched a second historical faction centered on the Quebec uprisings of 1837, but unable to get financial support, I decided to write a true novel about today's rivalry between capitalism and communism. I felt that I needed to understand this rivalry and to also address the American market. The result was *Psy Spy,* a satire. I wrote it in the third person in order to explore the techniques used by the omnipresent author. *Psy Spy* was not a gift; I had to work very hard."

*   *   *

KEVLES, Bettyann 1938-

PERSONAL: Surname is pronounced *Kev*-less; born August 20, 1938, in New York, N.Y.; daughter of David Marshal (a lawyer) and Sondra (a theatrical producer; maiden name, Alosoroff) Holtzmann; married Daniel Jerome Kevles (a historian), May 18, 1961; children: Beth, Jonathan. *Education:* Vassar College, B.A., 1959; Columbia University, M.A., 1961.

ADDRESSES: Home—575 La Loma Rd., Pasadena, Calif. 91105.

CAREER: Editor and writer. *Sunbeam,* Northridge, Calif., editor and writer, 1967-69; Westridge School, Pasadena, Calif., history instructor, 1970-76; *Los Angeles Times,* Los Angeles, Calif., columnist, 1982-88. Sponsoring editor, University of California Press, Los Angeles, 1984-87; consulting editor, Stanford University Press, 1988—.

AWARDS, HONORS: Award for best older juvenile book, New York Academy of Science, 1977, and for best nonfiction book, *Boston Globe/Horn Book,* 1978, both for *Watching the Wild Apes: The Primate Studies of Goodall, Fossey, and Galdikas.*

WRITINGS:

Watching the Wild Apes: The Primate Studies of Goodall, Fossey, and Galdikas, Dutton, 1976.
Thinking Gorillas: Testing and Teaching the Greatest Ape, Dutton, 1980.
Listening In, Scholastic Book Services, 1981.
Females of the Species: Sex and Survival in the Animal Kingdom, Harvard University Press, 1986.

OTHER

(Contributor) Alice Lawrance, editor, *Cassandra Rising: Science Fiction by Women,* Doubleday, 1978.

Contributor of other science fiction to anthologies; also contributor of spy stories to anthologies.

WORK IN PROGRESS: "A detective novel set in the rarified world of a major research library and the computer industry."

SIDELIGHTS: Bettyann Kevles's *Females of the Species: Sex and Survival in the Animal Kingdom* has been praised for its detailed account of the contributions female animals make to the evolutionary process—an area obscured for many years by science's focus on male animals. "*Females of the Species* is a survey of how female animals in nature play the Darwinian game of struggle for personal reproductive success," notes Stephen Jay Gould in the *New York Review of Books,* adding: "This work concentrates on demolishing a reverse fallacy— the long tradition, now thankfully fading (with a substantial push to oblivion from this book), for interpreting what female animals do in the light of supposed role models imposed by sexist societies upon human females." Sara Neustadtl comments in the *Women's Review of Books* that "[Kevles's] purpose, which she presents in a fluid and graceful style that will encourage reading by non-biologists, is to provide a compendium of the female behaviors biologists discovered once they opened their eyes, and the conclusions they have chosen to draw from their results." Gould goes on to praise *Females of the Species* as an "unrelenting bestiary of examples from beetles to baboons—hundreds and hundreds of tales about female behavior, orgainzed in sections on courtship, mating, motherhood, and sisterhood, and all aimed to reinforce the point that females participate in the Darwinian struggle for reproductive success as actively and as assiduously as males, only differently." He adds: "Anyone can wax eloquent about diversity as nature's theme; Kevles has sunk years of work into its documentation."

Although primarily a science writer, Kevles is currently working on a detective novel. In the past, she has also written science fiction and spy stories. Kevles comments to *CA* on the overlap among these venues: "Writing about science has led me into writing fiction again. There's just a thin line, and the real becomes preposterous."

BIOGRAPHICAL/CRITICAL SOURCES:

PERIODICALS

London Review of Books, May 22, 1986.
Los Angeles Times Book Review, April 20, 1986.
New Yorker, July 21, 1986.
New York Review of Books, September 25, 1986.
New York Times Book Review, October 5, 1986.
Times Literary Supplement, January 16, 1987.
Women's Review of Books, August, 1986.

*   *   *

KEVLES, Daniel J(erome) 1939-

PERSONAL: Surname is pronounced *Kev*-less; born March 2, 1939, in Philadelphia, Pa.; son of David (a teacher) and Anne (Rothstein) Kevles; married Bettyann Holtzmann (an editor and writer), May 18, 1961; children: Beth, Jonathan. *Education:* Princeton University, B.A., 1960, Ph.D., 1964; graduate study at Oxford University, 1960-61. *Politics:* Liberal.

ADDRESSES: Home—575 La Loma Rd., Pasadena, Calif. 91105. *Office*—Division of Humanities and Social Sciences, California Institute of Technology, 1201 East California Blvd., Pasadena, Calif. 91125.

CAREER: California Institute of Technology, Pasadena, assistant professor, 1964-68, associate professor, 1968-78, professor of history, 1978-86, J. O. and Juliette Koepfli Professor of the Humanities, 1986—. Visiting professor, University of Pennsylvania, 1979. Visiting research fellow, University of Sussex, 1976; Charles Warren Fellow, Harvard University, 1981-82; fellow, Center for Advanced Study in the Behavioral Sciences, 1986-87. Member of White House staff, Washington, D.C., 1964; member of committee on scientific autobiography, Alfred P. Sloan Foundation.

MEMBER: Organization of American Historians, History of Science Society (president of West Coast Branch, 1978-80), American Association for the Advancement of Science, PEN, Authors Guild, Authors League of America, Phi Beta Kappa.

AWARDS, HONORS: National Science Foundation fellowship, 1960-61; Woodrow Wilson fellowship, 1961-62; National Science Foundation grants, 1965, 1973-74, and 1978-80; American Council of Learned Societies grant, 1973; National Historical Society Book Prize, 1979, and American Book Award nomination in history, 1980, both for *The Physicists: The History of a Scientific Community in Modern America;* National Endowment for the Humanities senior fellowship, 1981-82; Sloan Foundation grants, 1982-84 and 1985-87; Guggenheim fellowship, 1983; Page One Award, Newspaper Guild of New York, 1985, for "Annals of Eugenics"; American Book Award nomination in nonfiction, 1985, for *In the Name of Eugenics: Genetics and the Uses of Human Heredity.*

WRITINGS:

The Physicists: The History of a Scientific Community in Modern America, Knopf, 1978.
In the Name of Eugenics: Genetics and the Uses of Human Heredity, Knopf, 1985.

OTHER

(Editor) *The George Ellery Hale Papers, 1882-1937, at the Mount Wilson and Palomar Observatories Laboratory, Pasadena, California* (microfilm), Carnegie Institute of Washington, 1967.

Contributor of articles and reviews to periodicals, including *Scientific American, Harper's,* and *New Yorker.*

SIDELIGHTS: A professor of history at the California Institute of Technology, Daniel J. Kevles is the author of two critically praised scientific histories, both nominated for American Book Awards. *The Physicists: The History of a Scientific Community in Modern America* traces American physics since the Civil War, profiling its most influential figures while also offering insights into the role of science within American society. A "carefully assembled work," according to Deborah Shapley in the *New York Times Book Review, The Physicists* "examines the intrinsic elitism of scientific research and traces the conflict of that elitism with America's democratic traditions." John Leonard similarly comments in the *New York Times* that Kevles's book, "ultimately and significantly, is about how a kind of intelligence and a species of need are forced to accommodate themselves to the broader intelligence and needfulness of pluralistic, democratic community." Leonard adds: "Calmly,

with a sharp eye for the telling anecdote, Mr. Kevles paints a picture of aristocrats who managed unconsciously to translate a laissez-faire attitude toward their science . . . into an attitude about society, government, [and] capitalism." A reviewer for the *New Yorker* calls *The Physicists* a "fascinating and meticulously documented study."

Kevles's 1985 book, *In the Name of Eugenics: Genetics and the Uses of Human Heredity,* examines the history of eugenics, the controversial branch of science founded in the late nineteenth century by Francis Galton with the belief of improving society through selective human breeding. According to Leon J. Kamin in the *New York Times Book Review,* Kevles "makes clear in his well-written narrative the symbiotic relations between the genuine science of genetics—the branch of biology that deals with heredity and variation in similar or related animals and plants—and the political programs and prejudices of the eugenicists." In addition to examining the relationship of eugenic principles to modern-day medical genetics, Kevles cites examples where eugenic theories have influenced U.S. and British governmental policy, as in the establishment of immigration quotas according to race. "A book that is at once impressive and deeply disturbing," according to James H. Jones in the *Washington Post Book World, In the Name of Eugenics* "is a skillful revelation of the ease with which a pseudo-science can elevate gross social prejudices to official public policies, and it stands as a powerful warning against anyone today who would use the fruits of legitimate science to bolster arguments and policies that echo the social and racial prejudices of the past."

Kevles once commented on his objectives as a scientific historian: "In my writing I generally aim to interpret scientists, who are as human as anyone else; science, which is one of man's greatest intellectual achievements; and their combined role in society, both contemporary and historical. I like to dramatize my subjects as much as possible, to include anecdote along with analysis. Books about science should be as readable and as accessible as books about, say, politics or culture, especially since science and technology affect our lives in so many ways. I'm an old Jeffersonian: the healthiest way to deal with even abstruse issues of public policy is not by courts of experts alone but through an informed public."

AVOCATIONAL INTERESTS: Swimming, playing guitar and piano, "cooking, eating, and drinking with good company," and "endlessly" restoring his 1956 Jaguar XK-140.

BIOGRAPHICAL/CRITICAL SOURCES:

PERIODICALS

American Historical Review, June, 1986.
Book World, March 12, 1978, July 14, 1985.
Commonweal, February 27, 1987.
London Review of Books, March 5, 1987.
Los Angeles Time Book Review, August 11, 1985, October 11, 1987.
New Republic, August 5, 1985.
Newsweek, January 23, 1978.
New Yorker, February 13, 1978.
New York Review of Books, June 28, 1979.
New York Times, January 6, 1978, May 23, 1985.
New York Times Book Review, February 12, 1978, June 9, 1985.
Psychology Today, June, 1985.
Scientific American, January, 1986.

KILGORE, Kathleen   1946-
(Kathleen Houton)

PERSONAL: Born July 11, 1946, in Washington, D.C.; daughter of Lowell Berry (a chemist) and Helen (a teacher; maiden name, Ford) Kilgore; married Daniel J. Houton (a contract administrator), September 7, 1969 (divorced, February, 1988); children: Hong phung Duong (adopted), Mariah Gifford. *Education:* Oberlin College, A. B., 1968; Fletcher School of Law and Diplomacy, M.A., 1969. *Politics:* Liberal Democrat. *Religion:* Unitarian-Universalist.

ADDRESSES: Home—9 Alban St., Dorchester, Mass. 02124. *Agent*—Llewellyn Howland III, 100 Rockwood St., Jamaica Plain, Mass. 02130.

CAREER: Harbridge House (business consultants), Boston, Mass., editor, 1969-70; *Metro: Boston* (magazine), Boston, contributing editor, 1970-71; *Boston,* Boston, contributing editor, 1972-75; free-lance writer, 1975-78; Word Guild, Cambridge, Mass., subcontractor, 1978-85; Childrens' Centers, Inc. (social service agency), Boston, clerk, 1986-87, president and executive director, 1987-88; *Metropolitan Real Estate Journal,* Boston, editor, 1987—. Trustee of First Parish Unitarian Church, 1978-82; member of board of directors of Benevolent Fraternity of Unitarian Churches, 1979—; secretary of advisory committee of Unitarian-Universalist Legal Ministry in Dorchester, 1982—.

MEMBER: Irish National Caucus, Massachusetts Bay District Unitarian-Universalist Association (secretary, 1981-83), Lower Mills Civil Association, Dorchester Residents for Racial Harmony, Friendly Sons of St. Patrick of Boston.

WRITINGS:

The Wolfman of Beacon Hill (young adult), Little, Brown, 1982.
The Sorcerer's Apprentice (young adult), Houghton, 1984.
John Volpe: The Immigrant's Son (biography), Yankee Press, 1987.

Contributor of more than one hundred articles and stories, some written under name Kathleen Houton, to magazines and newspapers, including *Yankee, Phoenix, New Englander,* and *Boston Herald-American.*

WORK IN PROGRESS: A novel about the Vietnamese in America with the tentative title *The Kingdom of the Flowery Flag;* a history of Boston University.

SIDELIGHTS: Kathleen Kilgore wrote to *CA:* "I grew up in Chevy Chase, Maryland, and spent some of my childhood in Geneva, Switzerland, where my father was a delegate to the General Agreements on Tariff and Trade, and where I served as his translator. I had intended to pursue a career in the U.S. Foreign Service but became involved in Boston politics instead when my husband ran for Congress in 1970. For the past eighteen years I have lived in Dorchester, a working-class neighborhood that seems much farther from Chevy Chase than any foreign service post. I have been involved in local politics, especially around issues of racial conflict. Much of my fiction has dealt with these themes. My daughter Mariah began school in Roxbury, Massachusetts, at the height of the busing crisis. Then, in 1981, we became the parents of a fourteen-year-old Vietnamese refugee who spoke no English.

"My life and work changed abruptly in 1986 when I took over the operation of Childrens' Centers, Inc., a large social service agency on whose board I served. The executive director had disappeared, leaving behind him a massive debt and 150 children (over 50% abuse-neglect cases) in need of care. I ran the corporation until all of the children were placed, closed it, and spent over a year putting together an agreement to sell the real estate to pay the debts. At the same time, I finished a biography of John Volpe [entitled *John Volpe: The Immigrant's Son*]. My husband and I separated, and I took a job as editor of a monthly real estate newspaper, *Metropolitan Real Estate Journal.* In January, 1988, I was selected to write a history of Boston University for its one hundred fiftieth anniversary.

"I am also working on a novel about Vietnamese people in America. There has been a great deal about the experience of Americans in Vietnam, yet almost nothing about the experience of nearly half a million Vietnamese in America. In novels and films, they appear only as figures in an exotic landscape, or as stereotypical villains and victims. Yet they are, of course, real people with a very old culture. I hope I can capture some of their reality and the personalities of Americans involved with the Vietnamese today in the book I am working on now."

*   *   *

KING, Coretta Scott   1927-

PERSONAL: Born April 27, 1927, in Marion, Ala.; daughter of Obidiah (a pulpwood dealer) and Bernice (McMurry) Scott; married Martin Luther King, Jr. (Baptist minister and civil rights activist), June 18, 1953 (died April 4, 1968); children: Yolanda Denise, Martin Luther III, Dexter Scott, Bernice Albertine. *Education:* Antioch College, B.A., New England Conservatory of Music, Mus.B., 1954, Mus.D., 1971. *Religion:* Baptist.

ADDRESSES: Office—Martin Luther King, Jr. Center for Nonviolent Social Change, Inc., 449 Auburn Ave., N.E., Atlanta, Ga. 30312; Press Relations, Cable News Network, 1050 Techwood Dr., N.W., Atlanta, Ga. 30318.

CAREER: Affiliated with Martin Luther King, Jr. Foundation and Martin Luther King, Jr. Memorial Center for Nonviolent Social Change, Atlanta, Ga., 1968—; Cable News Network, Atlanta, Ga., news commentator, 1980—. Singer, beginning 1948; Morris Brown College, Atlanta, voice instructor, 1962; presenter of "freedom concerts" in which she sings, recites poetry and lectures, beginning 1964; narrator of Aaron Copeland's "A Lincoln Portrait" with Washington National Symphony Orchestra in Washington, D.C., and New York City, 1968, and with San Francisco Symphony, in San Francisco, Calif., 1970. Lecturer, writer and delegate to White House Conference on Children and Youth, 1960. Sponsor, Sane Nuclear Policy, Committee on Responsibility, Inc., and Mobilization to End the War in Viet Nam, 1966-67, and Margaret Sanger Memorial Foundation. Member of board of directors, Southern Christian Leadership Conference, National Organization of Women, and Martin Luther King, Jr. Foundation—Great Britain; member of executive board, National Health Insurance Commission. Trustee, Robert F. Kennedy Memorial Center.

MEMBER: Women's International League for Peace and Freedom, National Council of Negro Women, Women's Strike for Peace, United Church Women (member of board of managers), Alpha Kappa Alpha.

AWARDS, HONORS: Annual Brotherhood Award, National Council of Negro Women, 1957; Outstanding Citizenship Award, Montgomery (Ala.) Improvement Association, 1959;

Merit Award, St. Louis *Argus,* 1960; Woman of the Year Award, Utility Club (New York City), 1962; Distinguished Achievement Award, National Organization of Colored Women's Clubs, 1962; citation for work in peace and freedom, Women's Strike for Peace, 1963; Louise Waterman Wise Award, American Jewish Congress Women's Auxiliary, 1963; Human Dignity and Human Rights Award, Norfolk Chapter of Links, Inc., 1964; Myrtle Wreath Award, Cleveland Hadassah, 1965; Wateler Peace Prize, 1968; named "Woman of the Year," National Association of Radio and TV Announcers, 1968; Women of Conscience Award, National Council of Women, 1968; selected in national college student poll as most admired woman, 1968, 1969; Pacem in Terris Award, International Overseas Service Foundation, 1969; Dag Hammarskjoeld Award and diploma as academicien, World Organization of the Diplomatic Press-Academie Diplomatique de la Paix, 1969; Candace Award, National Coalition of 100 Black Women, 1987; Human Relations Award, Academia Nazionale Del Lincei (Italy). Honorary doctorates from Boston University, Marymount Manhattan College, and Brandeis University, all 1969, Morehouse College, Wilberforce University, University of Bridgeport, Morgan State College, Bethune-Cookman College, Keuka College, and Princeton University, all 1970, Northeastern University and Bates College, both 1971.

WRITINGS:

AUTOBIOGRAPHY

My Life with Martin Luther King, Jr. (Book-of-the-Month Club selection), Holt, 1969.

AUTHOR OF INTRODUCTION OR FOREWORD

Martin Luther King, Jr., *Where Do We Go From Here: Chaos or Community?,* memorial edition, Bantam, 1968 (published in England as *Chaos or Community?,* Hodder & Stoughton, 1968).
Martin Luther King, Jr., *Trumpet of Conscience,* Harper, 1968.
Schulke, Flip, editor, *Martin Luther King, Jr.: A Documentary . . . : Montgomery to Memphis,* Norton, 1976.
(And editor) Martin Luther King, Jr., *The Words of Martin Luther King, Jr.,* Newmarket Press, 1983.
Dorothy S. Strickland, *Listen Children: An Anthology of Black Literature,* Bantam, 1986.

OTHER

Contributor of articles to magazines, including *Good Housekeeping, New Lady, McCall's, Theology Today,* and *Ebony.*

SIDELIGHTS: "My husband," writes Coretta Scott King in her introduction to *The Words of Martin Luther King, Jr.,* "was a man who hoped to be a Baptist preacher to a large, Southern, urban congregation. Instead, by the time he died in 1968, he had led millions of people into shattering forever the Southern system of segregation of the races."

Like her husband's life, Coretta Scott King's own life took a dramatically different turn than the one she had planned. As she relates in her autobiography, *My Life with Martin Luther King, Jr.,* when Coretta Scott first met the young preacher, she was studying music at the New England Conservatory in Boston and had already begun a career as a concert singer. Although she had thought that she would never consider being a preacher's wife, she found her future husband to be different than the stereotyped man of God she had imagined. As she observes in her introduction to *The Words of Martin Luther King, Jr.,* "Martin was an unusual person. . . . He was so alive and so much fun to be with. He had strength that he imparted to me and others that he met."

Coretta Scott married Martin Luther King, Jr., giving up her personal career plans to join him as a civil rights activist. Side by side with her husband she led marches and gave speeches, but as the spouse of a popular public figure, she also endured many hours alone. In *My Life with Martin Luther King, Jr.* she notes that "in spite of Martin's being away so much, he was wonderful with his children, and they adored him. When Daddy was home it was something special."

While the book is filled with many such personal glimpses of the civil rights leader, reviewers find it flawed by its portrayal of Dr. King as a man without human weaknesses. "Understandably enough," Patricia Canham writes in the *Christian Science Monitor,* "it is the public image, the 'noble servant of humanity' that Mrs. King wishes to perpetuate." A *Time* critic, however, notes that "dispassionate reportage is not her real purpose. Rather, she has undertaken to bear witness to his life, and she has done so with great warmth and skill." A *Publishers Weekly* contributor deems the autobiography "one of the noblest and most moving human documents of this or any season."

The success of *My Life with Martin Luther King, Jr.* added to Coretta King's prominence as a public figure in her own right but her fame had spread even before the book's publication as she led a silent memorial march of more than 50,000 people through the streets of Memphis on April 8, 1968, just four days after her husband's death. The following day, at Dr. King's funeral, she shared her grief with an estimated 120 million people who watched on television and crowds of mourners who filled the streets of Atlanta.

In *King Remembered,* Flip Shulke and Penelope O. McPhee praise Coretta King's ability to continue her husband's work so soon after his death. "As she would prove many times in the future," they write, "she was prepared to take up her late husband's cause. . . . But it came as no surprise to her friends or to her husband's associates. They knew she had always lent a quiet support and calming spirit to everything Martin had undertaken."

Her leadership capabilities were further tested soon thereafter as King strove to preserve her husband's memory with the foundation in 1968 of both the Martin Luther King, Jr. Memorial Center for Nonviolent Social Change and the Martin Luther King, Jr. Federal Holiday Commission. As chairperson of both organizations King made hundreds of speeches, logged thousands of miles traveling around the world, and met with countless national and local leaders proclaiming her husband's message of nonviolence. Her energies became focused on two goals: the opening of a scholarly center dedicated to her husband where nonviolence could be taught and studied and the celebration of his birthday as a national holiday.

The first of these two projects to be realized, the Martin Luther King, Jr. Center for Nonviolent Social Change, became a reality in 1981 when the $8.4 million center was dedicated in Atlanta, Georgia. The complex includes exhibit areas, a 250-seat auditorium, a 90-seat theater, administrative offices, a library, archives and the Martin Luther King, Jr. gravesite.

In an *Ebony* article, King explains some of the Center's activities. "Since it was founded," she writes, "the King Center has trained thousands of future leaders in the spirit and tradition of its namesake through a series of wide-ranging programs and workshops in the philosophy and strategy of nonviolence.

The Center has also emerged as a catalyst for massive social change coalitions, including the National Committee for Full Employment and the 1983 mobilization of the 20th Anniversary March on Washington, which brought more than a half-million demonstrators to the nation's capitol.''

King also observes that the Center's library and archives contain over one million documents related to the civil rights movement, including a vast collection of personal King items, which are examined by nearly 5,000 scholars annually.

The Center has been instrumental in the achievement of Coretta King's second goal, the establishment of a Martin Luther King, Jr. national holiday. The Center led a campaign that collected six million signatures to present to Congress in support of the proposed holiday and sponsored annual national programs celebrating the holiday during the years between Martin Luther King, Jr.'s death and the first official celebration of the day in January, 1986.

Talking about her work in an *Ebony* interview, Coretta King notes, ''I will always be out here doing the things I do, and I'm not going to stop talking about Martin and promoting what I think is important in terms of teaching other people, particularly young people, his meaning so they can live in such a way to make a contribution to our advancement and progress.''

BIOGRAPHICAL/CRITICAL SOURCES:

BOOKS

King, Coretta Scott, *My Life with Martin Luther King, Jr.*, Holt, 1969.
King, Martin Luther, Jr., *The Words of Martin Luther King, Jr.*, edited by and with an introduction by Coretta Scott King, Newmarket Press, 1983.
Schulke, Flip, and Penelope O. McPhee, *King Remembered*, Norton, 1986.

PERIODICALS

American Visions, January/February, 1986.
Book World, September 28, 1969.
Christian Science Monitor, September 25, 1969.
Ebony, September, 1968, January, 1986, January, 1987.
Good Housekeeping, June, 1964.
Jet, January 20, 1986.
Ladies Home Journal, January, 1987.
New Statesman, January 23, 1970.
Newsweek, April 22, 1968.
New York Times, September 29, 1969.
Publishers Weekly, August 18, 1969.
Saturday Review, October 11, 1969.
Time, October 3, 1969, September 22, 1986.
Times Literary Supplement, June 11, 1970.*

—*Sketch by Marian Gonsior*

*   *   *

KING, Martin Luther, Jr.   1929-1968

PERSONAL: Given name, Michael, changed to Martin; born January 15, 1929, in Atlanta, Ga.; assassinated April 4, 1968, in Memphis, Tenn.; originally buried in South View Cemetery, Atlanta; reinterred at Martin Luther King, Jr. Center for Nonviolent Social Change, Atlanta; son of Martin Luther (a minister) and Alberta Christine (a teacher; maiden name, Williams) King; married Coretta Scott (a concert singer), June 18, 1953; children: Yolanda Denise, Martin Luther III, Dexter Scott, Bernice Albertine. *Education:* Morehouse College, B.A.,

1948; Crozer Theological Seminary, B.D., 1951; Boston University, Ph.D., 1955, D.D., 1959; Chicago Theological Seminary, D.D., 1957; attended classes at University of Pennsylvania and Harvard University.

CAREER: Ordained Baptist minister, 1948; Dexter Avenue Baptist Church, Montgomery, Ala., pastor, 1954-60; Southern Christian Leadership Conference (S.C.L.C.), Atlanta, founder, 1957, and president, 1957-68; Ebenezer Baptist Church, Atlanta, co-pastor with his father, 1960-68. Vice-president, National Sunday School and Baptist Teaching Union Congress of National Baptist Convention; president, Montgomery Improvement Association.

MEMBER: National Association for the Advancement of Colored People (NAACP), Alpha Phi Alpha, Sigma Pi Phi, Elks.

AWARDS, HONORS: Selected one of ten outstanding personalities of 1956 by *Time*, 1957; Spingarn Medal, National Association for the Advancement of Colored People, 1957; L.H.D., Morehouse College, 1957, and Central State College, 1958; L.L.D., Howard University, 1957, and Morgan State College, 1958; Anisfield-Wolf Award, 1958, *Stride toward Freedom; Time* Man of the Year, 1963; Nobel Prize for Peace, 1964; Judaism and World Peace Award, Synagogue Council of America, 1965; Brotherhood Award, 1967, for *Where Do We Go from Here: Chaos or Community?;* Nehru Award for International Understanding, 1968; Presidential Medal of Freedom, 1977; received numerous awards for leadership of Montgomery Movement; two literary prizes were named in his honor by National Book Committee and Harper & Row.

WRITINGS:

Stride Toward Freedom: The Montgomery Story, Harper, 1958, reprinted, 1987.
The Measure of a Man, Christian Education Press (Philadelphia), 1959, memorial edition, Pilgrim Press, 1968, reprinted, Fortress, 1988.
Letter from Birmingham City Jail, American Friends Service Committee, 1963, published as *Letter from Birmingham Jail* (also see below), Overbrook Press, 1968.
Why We Can't Wait (includes ''Letter from Birmingham Jail''), Harper, 1964, reprinted, New American Library, 1987.
Where Do We Go from Here: Chaos or Community?, Harper, 1967, memorial edition with an introduction by wife, Coretta Scott King, Bantam, 1968 (published in England as *Chaos or Community?*, Hodder & Stoughton, 1968).
(Author of introduction) William Bradford Huie, *Three Lives for Mississippi*, New American Library, 1968.
(Contributor) John Henrik Clarke and others, editors, *Black Titan: W.E.B. Du Bois*, Beacon Press, 1970.

OMNIBUS VOLUMES

''Unwise and Untimely?'' (letters; originally appeared in *Liberation*, June, 1963), Fellowship of Reconciliation, 1963.
Strength to Love (sermons), Harper, 1963, reprinted, Walker, 1985.
A Martin Luther King Treasury, Educational Heritage (New York), 1964.
The Wisdom of Martin Luther King in His Own Words, edited by staff of Bill Alder Books, Lancer Books, 1968.
''*I Have a Dream*'': *The Quotations of Martin Luther King, Jr.*, edited and compiled by Lotte Hoskins, Grosset, 1968.
The Trumpet of Conscience (transcripts of radio broadcasts), introduction by C. S. King, Harper, 1968.
We Shall Live in Peace: The Teachings of Martin Luther King, Jr., edited by Deloris Harrison, Hawthorn, 1968.

Speeches about Vietnam, Clergy and Laymen Concerned about Vietnam (New York), 1969.

A Martin Luther King Reader, edited by Nissim Ezekiel, Popular Prakashan (Bombay), 1969.

Words and Wisdom of Martin Luther King, Taurus Press, 1970.

Speeches of Martin Luther King, Jr., commemorative edition, Martin Luther King, Jr. Memorial Center (Atlanta), 1972.

Loving Your Enemies, Letter from Birmingham Jail [and] *Declaration of Independence from the War in Vietnam* (also see below), A. J. Muste Memorial Institute, 1981.

The Words of Martin Luther King, Jr., edited and with an introduction by C. S. King, Newmarket Press, 1983.

A Testament of Hope: The Essential Writings of Martin Luther King, Jr., edited by James Melvin Washington, Harper, 1986.

SPEECHES

The Montgomery Story, [San Francisco, Calif.], 1956.

I Have a Dream, John Henry and Mary Louise Dunn Bryant Foundation (Los Angeles), 1963.

Nobel Lecture, Harper, 1965.

Address at Valedictory Service, University of the West Indies (Mona, Jamaica), 1965.

The Ware Lecture, Unitarian Universalist Association (Boston), 1966.

Conscience for Change, Canadian Broadcasting Co., 1967.

Beyond Vietnam, Altoan Press, 1967.

Declaration of Independence from the War in Vietnam, [New York], 1967.

A Drum Major for Justice, Taurus Press, 1969.

A Testament of Hope (originally appeared in *Playboy,* January, 1969), Fellowship of Reconciliation, 1969.

CONTRIBUTOR TO ANTHOLOGIES

H. John Heinz III, editor, *Crisis in Modern America,* Yale University, 1959.

Robert A. Goldwin, editor, *Civil Disobedience: Five Essays,* Public Affairs Conference Center, Kenyon College, 1968.

William B. Thomas, editor, *Shall Not Perish: Nine Speeches by Three Great Americans,* Gyldendalske Boghandel, 1969.

William M. Chace and Peter Collier, editors, *Justice Denied: The Black Man in White America,* Harcourt, 1970.

Leslie H. Fishel, Jr., and Benjamin Quarles, editors, *The Black American: A Documentary History,* Morrow, 1970.

Richard K. Barksdale and Kenneth Kinnamon, editors, *Black Writers of America: A Comprehensive Anthology,* Macmillan, 1972.

Also contributor to many other anthologies.

OTHER

Pilgrimage to Nonviolence (monograph; originally appeared in *Christian Century*), Fellowship of Reconciliation, 1960.

Contributor to periodicals, including *Harper's, Nation,* and *Christian Century.*

WORK IN PROGRESS: King's papers are being edited by Clayborn Carson to be published in a twelve-volume set over a fifteen-year period.

SIDELIGHTS: "We've got some difficult days ahead," civil rights activist Martin Luther King, Jr., told a crowd gathered at Memphis's Clayborn Temple on April 3, 1968, in a speech now collected in *The Words of Martin Luther King, Jr.* "But it really doesn't matter to me now," he continued, "because I've been to the mountaintop. . . . And I've seen the promised land. I may not get there with you. But I want you to know tonight that we as a people will get to the promised land." Uttered the day before his tragic assassination, King's words were prophetic of his death. They were also a challenge to those he left behind to see that his "promised land" of racial equality became a reality; a reality to which King devoted the last twelve years of his life.

Just as important as King's dream was the way he chose to achieve it: nonviolent resistance. He embraced nonviolence as a method for social reform after being introduced to the nonviolent philosophy of Mahatma Gandhi while doing graduate work at Pennsylvania's Crozer Seminary. Gandhi had led a bloodless revolution against British colonial rule in India. According to Stephen B. Oates in *Let the Trumpet Sound: The Life of Martin Luther King, Jr.,* King became "convinced that Gandhi's was the only moral and practical way for oppressed people to struggle against social injustice."

What King achieved during the little over a decade that he worked in civil rights was remarkable. "Rarely has one individual," noted Flip Shulke and Penelope O. McPhee in *King Remembered,* "espousing so difficult a philosophy, served as a catalyst for so much significant social change. . . . There are few men of whom it can be said their lives changed the world. But at his death the American South hardly resembled the land where King was born. In the twelve years between the Montgomery bus boycott and King's assassination, Jim Crow was legally eradicated in the South."

The first public test of King's adherence to the nonviolent philosophy came in December, 1955, when he was elected president of the Montgomery [Alabama] Improvement Association (M.I.A.), a group formed to protest the arrest of Rosa Parks, a black woman who refused to give up her bus seat to a white. Planning to end the humiliating treatment of blacks on city bus lines, King organized a bus boycott that was to last more than a year. Despite receiving numerous threatening phone calls, being arrested, and having his home bombed, King and his boycott prevailed. Eventually, the U.S. Supreme Court declared Montgomery's bus segregation laws illegal and, in December, 1956, King rode on Montgomery's first integrated bus.

"Montgomery was the soil," wrote King's widow in her autobiography, *My Life with Martin Luther King, Jr.,* "in which the seed of a new theory of social action took root. Black people found in nonviolent, direct action a militant method that avoided violence but achieved dramatic confrontation which electrified and educated the whole nation."

King was soon selected to be president of an organization of much wider scope than the M.I.A., the Southern Christian Leadership Conference (S.C.L.C.). The members of this group were black leaders from throughout the South, many of them ministers like King, himself. Their immediate goal was for increased black voter registration in the South with an eventual elimination of segregation.

1957 found King drawn more and more into the role of national and even international spokesman for civil rights. In February a *Time* cover story on King called him "a scholarly . . . Baptist minister . . . who in little more than a year has risen from nowhere to become one of the nation's remarkable leaders of men." In March, he was invited to speak at the ceremonies marking the independence from Great Britain of the new African republic of Ghana.

The following year, King's first book, *Stride Toward Freedom: The Montgomery Story,* which told the history of the boycott, was published. *New York Times* contributor Abel Plenn called the work "a document of far-reaching importance for present and future chroniclings of the struggle for civil rights in this country." A *Times Literary Supplement* writer quoted U.S. Episcopalian Bishop James Pike's reaction to the book: *Stride Toward Freedom* "may well become a Christian classic. It is a rare combination: sound theology and ethics, and the autobiography of one of the greatest men of our time."

In 1959, two important events happened. First, King and his wife were able to make their long-awaited trip to India where they visited the sites of Gandhi's struggle against the British and met face-to-face with people who had been acquainted with the Indian leader. Second, King resigned as pastor of Dexter Avenue Baptist Church in Montgomery so he could be closer to S.C.L.C.'s headquarters in Atlanta and devote more of his time to the civil rights effort.

King's trip to India seemed to help make up his mind to move to Atlanta. The trip greatly inspired King as Oates observed: "He came home with a deeper understanding of nonviolence and a deep commitment as well. For him, nonviolence was no longer just a philosophy and a technique of social change; it was now a whole way of life."

Despite his adherence to the nonviolent philosophy, King was unable to avoid the bloodshed that was to follow. Near the end of 1962, he decided to focus his energies on the desegregation of Birmingham, Alabama. Alabama's capital was at that time what King called in his book *Why We Can't Wait,* "the most segregated city in America," but that was precisely why he had chosen it as his target.

In *Why We Can't Wait* King detailed the advance planning that was the key to the success of the Birmingham campaign. Most important was the training in nonviolent techniques given by the S.C.L.C.'s Leadership Training Committee to those who volunteered to participate in the demonstrations. "The focus of these training sessions," King noted in his book, "was the socio-dramas designed to prepare the demonstrators for some of the challenges they could expect to face. The harsh language and physical abuse of the police and self-appointed guardians of the law were frankly presented, along with the non-violent creed in action: to resist without bitterness; to be cursed and not reply; to be beaten and not hit back."

One of the unusual aspects of the Birmingham campaign was King's decision to use children in the demonstrations. When the protests came to a head on May 3, 1963, it was after nearly one thousand young people had been arrested the previous day. As another wave of protestors, mostly children and teenagers, took to the streets, they were suddenly hit with jets of water from powerful fire hoses. Police dogs were then released on the youngsters.

The photographs circulated by the media of children being beaten down by jets of water and being bitten by dogs brought cries of outrage from throughout the country and the world. President Kennedy sent a Justice Department representative to Birmingham to work for a peaceful solution to the problem. Within a week negotiators produced an agreement that met King's major demands, including desegregation of lunch counters, restrooms, fitting rooms and drinking fountains in the city and hiring of blacks in positions previously closed to them.

Although the Birmingham campaign ended in triumph for King, at the outset he was criticized for his efforts. Imprisoned at the beginning of the protest for disobeying a court injunction forbidding him from leading any demonstrations in Birmingham, King spent some of his time in jail composing an open letter answering his critics. This document, called "Letter from Birmingham Jail," appeared later in his book *Why We Can't Wait.* Oates viewed the letter as "a classic in protest literature, the most elegant and learned expression of the goals and philosophy of the nonviolent movement ever written."

In the letter King addressed those who said that as an outsider he had no business in Birmingham. King reasoned: "I am in Birmingham because injustice is here. . . . I cannot sit idly by in Atlanta and not be concerned about what happens in Birmingham. Injustice anywhere is a threat to justice everywhere. We are caught in an inescapable network of mutuality, tied in a single garment of destiny."

Another important event of 1963 was a massive march on Washington, D.C., which King planned together with leaders of other civil rights organizations. When the day of the march came, an estimated two hundred and fifty thousand people were on hand to hear King and other dignitaries speak at the march's end point, the Lincoln Memorial.

While King's biographers noted that the young minister struggled all night writing words to inspire his people on this historic occasion, when his turn came to speak, he deviated from his prepared text and gave a speech that Schulke and McPhee called "the most eloquent of his career." In the speech, which contained the rhythmic repetition of the phrase "I have a dream," King painted a vision of the "promised land" of racial equality and justice for all that he would return to often in speeches and sermons in the years to come, including his final speech in Memphis. Schulke and McPhee explained the impact of the day: "The orderly conduct of the massive march was an active tribute to [King's] philosophy of non-violence. Equally significant, his speech made his voice familiar to the world and lives today as one of the most moving orations of our time."

On January 3, 1964, King was proclaimed "Man of the Year" by *Time,* the first black to be so honored. Later that same year, King's book, *Why We Can't Wait,* was published. In the book King gave his explanation of why 1963 was such a critical year for the civil rights movement. He believed that celebrations commemorating the one-hundredth anniversary of Lincoln's Emancipation Proclamation reminded American blacks of the irony that while Lincoln made the slaves free in the nineteenth century, their twentieth-century grandchildren still did not feel free.

Reviewers generally hailed the work as an important document in the history of the civil rights movement. In *Book Week,* J. B. Donovan called it "a basic handbook on non-violent direct action." *Critic* contributor C. S. Stone praised the book's "logic and eloquence" and observed that it aimed a death blow "at two American dogmas—racial discrimination, and the even more insidious doctrine that nourishes it, gradualism."

In December of 1964, King received the Nobel Peace Prize, becoming the twelfth American, the third black, and the youngest—he was thirty-five—person ever to receive the award. He donated the $54,600 prize to the S.C.L.C. and other civil rights groups. The Nobel Prize gave King even wider recognition as a world leader. "Overnight," commented Shulke and

McPhee, "King became . . . a symbol of world peace. He knew that if the Nobel Prize was to mean anything, he must commit himself more than ever to attaining the goals of the black movement through peace."

The next two years were marked by both triumph and despair. First came King's campaign for voting rights, concentrating on a voters registration drive in Selma, Alabama. Selma would be, according to Oates, "King's finest hour."

Voting rights had been a major concern of King's since as early as 1957 but, unfortunately, little progress had been made. In the country surrounding Selma, for example, only 335 of 32,700 blacks were registered voters. Various impediments to black registration, including poll taxes and complicated literacy tests, were common throughout the South.

Demonstrations continued through February and on into early March, 1965, in Selma. One day nearly five hundred school children were arrested and charged with juvenile delinquency after they cut classes to show their support for King. In another incident, over a hundred adults were arrested when they picketed the county courthouse. On March 7, state troopers beat nonviolent demonstrators who were trying to march from Selma to Montgomery to present their demands to Governor Wallace.

Angered by such confrontations, King sent telegrams to religious leaders throughout the nation calling for them to meet in Selma for a "ministers' march" to Montgomery. Although some 1500 marchers assembled, they were again turned back by a line of state troopers, but this time violence was avoided.

King was elated by the show of support he received from the religious leaders from around the country who joined him in the march, but his joy soon turned to sorrow when he learned later that same day that several of the white ministers who had marched with him had been beaten by club-wielding whites. One of them died two days later.

The brutal murder of a clergyman seemed to focus the attention of the nation on Selma. Within a few days, President Johnson made a televised appearance before a joint session of Congress in which he demanded passage of a voting rights bill. In the speech Johnson compared the sites of revolutionary war battles such as Concord and Lexington with their modern-day counterpart, Selma, Alabama.

Although Johnson had invited King to be his special guest in the Senate gallery during the address, King declined the honor, staying instead in Selma to complete plans to again march on Montgomery. A federal judge had given his approval to the proposed Selma-to-Montgomery march and had ordered Alabama officials not to interfere. The five-day march finally took place as hundreds of federal troops stood by overseeing the safety of the marchers.

Later that year, President Johnson signed the 1965 Voting Rights Act into law, this time with King looking on. The act made literacy tests as a requirement for voting illegal, gave the Attorney General the power to supervise federal elections in seven southern states, and urged the Attorney General to challenge the legality of poll taxes in state and local elections in four Southern states. "Political analysts," Oates observed, "almost unanimously attributed the voting act to King's Selma campaign. . . . Now, thanks to his own political sagacity, his understanding of how nonviolent, direct-action protest could stimulate corrective federal legislation, King's long crusade to gain southern Negroes the right to vote . . . was about to be realized."

By this time, King was ready to embark on his next project, moving his nonviolent campaign to the black ghettoes of the North. Chicago was chosen as his first target, but the campaign did not go the way King had planned. Rioting broke out in the city just two days after King initiated his program. He did sign an open-housing agreement with Chicago Mayor Daley but, according to Oates, many blacks felt it accomplished little.

Discord was beginning to be felt within the civil rights movement. King was afraid that advocates of "black power" would doom his dream of a nonviolent black revolution. In his next book, *Where Do We Go from Here: Chaos or Community?*, published in 1967, he explored his differences with those using the "black power" slogan.

According to *New York Times Book Review* contributor Gene Roberts, while King admitted in the volume that black power leaders "foster[ed] racial pride and self-help programs," he also expressed regret that the slogan itself produced "fear among whites and [made] it more difficult to fashion a meaningful interracial political coalition. But above all, he [deplored] . . . an acceptance of violence by many in the movement."

In *Saturday Review* Milton R. Knovitz noted other criticisms of the movement which King voiced in the book. King saw black power as "negative, even nihilistic in its direction," "rooted in hopelessness and pessimism" and "committed to racial—and ethical—separatism." In *America*, R. F. Drinan wrote, "Dr. King's analysis of the implications of the black power movement is possibly the most reasoned rejection of the concept by any major civil rights leader in the country."

Where Do We Go from Here touched on several issues that became King's major concerns during the last two years of his life. He expressed the desire to continue nonviolent demonstrations in the North, to stop the war in Vietnam, and to join underprivileged persons of all races in a coalition against poverty.

His first wish never materialized. Instead of nonviolent protest, riots broke out in Boston, Detroit, Milwaukee and more than thirty other U.S. cities between the time King finished the manuscript for the book and when it was published in the late summer.

By that time, King had already spoken out several times on Vietnam. His first speech to be entirely devoted to the topic was given on April 15, 1967, at a huge anti-war rally held at the United Nations Building in New York City. Even though some of King's followers begged him not to participate in anti-war activities, fearful that King's actions would antagonize the Johnson administration which had been so supportive in civil rights matters, King could not be dissuaded.

In *The Trumpet of Conscience,* a collection of radio addresses published posthumously, King explained why speaking out on Vietnam was so important to him. He wrote: "I cannot forget that the Nobel Prize for Peace was also a commission—a commission to work harder than I ever worked before for the 'brotherhood of man.' This is a calling which takes me beyond national allegiances."

Commenting on King's opposition to the war, Coretta King observed that her husband's "peace activity marked incontestably a major turning point in the thinking of the nation. . . . I think history will mark his boldness in speaking out so early and eloquently—despite singularly virulent opposition—as one of his major contributions."

When King was assassinated in Memphis on April 4, 1968, he was in the midst of planning his Poor People's Campaign. Plans called for recruitment and training in nonviolent techniques of 3,000 poor people from each of fifteen different parts of the country. The campaign would culminate when they were brought to Washington, D.C., to disrupt government operations until effective anti-poverty legislation was enacted.

On hearing of King's death, angry blacks in one hundred and twenty-five cities across the nation rioted. As a result, thirty people died, hundreds suffered injuries, and more than thirty million dollars worth of property damage was incurred. But, fortunately, rioting was not the only response to his death. Accolades came from around the world as one by one world leaders paid their respects to the martyred man of peace. Eventually, King's widow and other close associates saw to it that a permanent memorial—the establishment of Martin Luther King, Jr.'s birthday as a national holiday in the United States—would assure that his memory would live on forever.

In her introduction to *The Trumpet of Conscience,* Coretta King quoted from one of Martin Luther King, Jr.'s most famous speeches as she gave her thoughts on how she hoped future generations would remember her husband. "Remember him," she wrote, "as a man who tried to be 'a drum major for justice, a drum major for peace, a drum major for righteousness.' Remember him as a man who refused to lose faith in the ultimate redemption of mankind."

BIOGRAPHICAL/CRITICAL SOURCES:

BOOKS

Bennett, Lerone, Jr., *What Manner of Man,* Johnson Publishing (Chicago, Ill.), 1964.

Bishop, Jim, *The Days of Martin Luther King, Jr.,* Putnam, 1971.

Bleiweiss, Robert M., editor, *Marching to Freedom: The Life of Martin Luther King, Jr.,* New American Library, 1971.

Clayton, Edward T., *Martin Luther King, Jr.: The Peaceful Warrior,* Prentice-Hall, 1968.

Collins, David R., *Not Only Dreamers: The Story of Martin Luther King, Sr. and Martin Luther King, Jr.,* Brethren Press, 1986.

Davis, Lenwood G., *I Have a Dream: The Life and Times of Martin Luther King, Jr.,* Adams Book Co., 1969.

Frank, Gerold, *An American Death: The True Story of the Assassination of Dr. Martin Luther King, Jr. and the Greatest Manhunt of Our Time,* Doubleday, 1972.

Garrow, David J., *Bearing the Cross: Martin Luther King, Jr. and the Southern Christian Leadership Conference,* Morrow, 1986.

Harrison, Deloris, editor, *We Shall Live in Peace: The Teachings of Martin Luther King, Jr.,* Hawthorn, 1968.

King, Coretta Scott, *My Life with Martin Luther King, Jr.,* Holt, 1969.

King, Martin Luther, Jr., *The Trumpet of Conscience,* with an introduction by Coretta Scott King, Harper, 1968.

King, Martin Luther, Jr., *The Words of Martin Luther King, Jr.,* edited and with an introduction by Coretta Scott King, Newmarket Press, 1983.

Lewis, David, L., *King: A Critical Biography,* Praeger, 1970.

Lincoln, Eric C., editor, *Martin Luther King, Jr.: A Profile,* Hill & Wang, 1970, revised edition, 1984.

Lokos, Lionel, *House Divided: The Life and Legacy of Martin Luther King,* Arlington House, 1968.

Lomax, Louis E., *To Kill a Black Man,* Holloway, 1968.

Martin Luther King, Jr.: The Journey of a Martyr, Universal Publishing & Distributing, 1968.

Martin Luther King, Jr., 1929-1968, Johnson Publishing (Chicago, Ill.), 1968.

Martin Luther King, Jr., Norton, 1976.

Miller, William Robert, *Martin Luther King, Jr.: His Life, Martyrdom, and Meaning for the World,* Weybright, 1968.

Oates, Stephen B., *Let the Trumpet Sound: The Life of Martin Luther King, Jr.,* Harper, 1982.

Paulsen, Gary and Dan Theis, *The Man Who Climbed the Mountain: Martin Luther King,* Raintree, 1976.

Playboy Interviews, Playboy Press, 1967.

Schulke, Flip, editor, *Martin Luther King, Jr.: A Documentary . . . Montgomery to Memphis,* with an introduction by Coretta Scott King, Norton, 1976.

Schulke, Flip and Penelope O. McPhee, *King Remembered,* with a foreword by Jesse Jackson, Norton, 1986.

Small, Mary Luins, *Creative Encounters with "Dear Dr. King": A Handbook of Discussions, Activities, and Engagements on Racial Injustice, Poverty, and War,* edited by Saunders Redding, Buckingham Enterprises, 1969.

Smith, Kenneth L. and Ira G. Zepp, Jr., *Search for the Beloved Community: The Thinking of Martin Luther King, Jr.,* Judson, 1974.

Westin, Alan, and Barry Mahoney, *The Trial of Martin Luther King,* Crowell, 1975.

Witherspoon, William Roger, *Martin Luther King, Jr.: To the Mountaintop,* Doubleday, 1985.

PERIODICALS

A B Bookman's Weekly, April 22, 1968.

America, August 17, 1963, October 31, 1964, July 22, 1967, April 20, 1968.

American Vision, January/February, 1986.

Antioch Review, spring, 1968.

Books Abroad, autumn, 1970.

Book World, July 9, 1967, September 28, 1969.

Choice, February, 1968.

Christian Century, August 23, 1967, January 14, 1970, August 26,1970.

Christian Science Monitor, July 6, 1967.

Commonweal, November 17, 1967, May 3, 1968.

Critic, August, 1964.

Ebony, April, 1961, May, 1968, July, 1968, April, 1984, January, 1986, January, 1987, April, 1988.

Economist, April 6, 1968.

Esquire, August, 1968.

Harper's, February, 1961.

Life, April 19, 1968, January 10, 1969, September 12, 1969, September 19, 1969.

Listener, April 11, 1968, April 25, 1968.

Los Angeles Times Book Review, December 11, 1983.

National Review, February 13, 1987, February 27, 1987.

Negro Digest, August, 1968.

Negro History Bulletin, October, 1956, November, 1956, May, 1968.

New Republic, February 3, 1986, January 5, 1987.

New Statesman, March 22, 1968.

Newsweek, January 27, 1986.

New Yorker, June 22, 1967, July 22, 1967, April 13, 1968, February 24, 1986, April 6, 1987.

New York Herald Tribune, October 16, 1964.

New York Post, October 15, 1964.

New York Review of Books, August 24, 1967, January 15, 1987.

New York Times, October 12, 1958, October 15, 1964, July 12, 1967, April 12, 1968, April 13, 1968.
New York Times Book Review, September 3, 1967, February 16, 1969, February 16, 1986, November 30, 1986.
Punch, April 3, 1968.
Ramparts, May, 1968.
Saturday Review, July 8, 1967, April 20, 1968.
Time, February 18, 1957, January 3, 1964, February 5, 1965, February 12, 1965, April 19, 1968, October 3, 1969, January 27, 1986, January 19, 1987.
(London) *Times,* April 6, 1968.
Times Literary Supplement, April 18, 1968.
Virginia Quarterly Review, autumn, 1968.
Washington Post, January 14, 1970.
Washington Post Book World, January 19, 1986, January 18, 1987.

OBITUARIES:

PERIODICALS

New York Times, April 5, 1968.
Time, April 12, 1968.
(London) *Times,* April 5, 1968.*

—*Sketch by Marian Gonsior*

*   *   *

KIRK-GREENE, Anthony (Hamilton Millard)   1925-
(Anthony H. M. Kirk-Greene; pseudonyms:
Nicholas Caverhill, H. M. S., P. L. K., Yerima
Yola)

PERSONAL: Born May 16, 1925, in Tunbridge Wells, England; son of Leslie (a civil engineer) and Helen (Millard) Kirk-Greene; married Helen Margaret Sellar (a personal secretary), April 22, 1967. *Education:* Clare College, Cambridge, B.A. (with first class honors), 1949, M.A., 1954; Oxford University, M.A., 1964; graduate study at Cambridge University, 1955-56, Northwestern University and University of California, Los Angeles, 1958-59, and Edinburgh University, 1965-66.

ADDRESSES: Home—34 Davenant Rd., Oxford, England. *Office*—St. Antony's College, Oxford University, Oxford OX2 6JF, England.

CAREER: British Colonial Administrative Service, Northern Nigeria, district officer, 1950-57; Institute of Administration, Zaria, Nigeria, senior lecturer in government, 1957-60; Ahmadu Bello University, Zaria, associate professor of government and head of department, 1961-66; Oxford University, St. Antony's College, Oxford, England, senior research fellow in African studies, 1967-81, University Lecturer in the Modern History of Africa, 1982—, director of Oxford Colonial Records and Research Project, 1980-84, director of foreign service program, 1986-87. Visiting professor, Syracuse University, 1961, University of California, Los Angeles, 1962, 1963, 1967, and 1968, University of Paris, 1971, 1973, and 1975, Scandinavian Institute of African Studies, 1974, and University of Calgary, 1977, and 1985; Hans Wolff Memorial Lecturer, University of Indiana, 1973; visiting fellow, Hoover Institution on War, Revolution, and Peace, 1975—; scholar in residence, Trent University, 1975. Consultant to Kenya Government, 1961, East African Staff College, 1969 and 1970, East African Community, 1972, and African Association for Public Administration and Management, 1975. *Military service:* Royal Warwickshire Regiment, 1943-44. Indian Army, 8th Punjab Regiment, 1944-47; became captain.

MEMBER: International African Institute, African Studies Association (vice-president, 1986-88; president, 1988—), Royal African Society (vice-president, 1986—), Royal Commonwealth Society (member of council, 1984—), Royal Historical Society (fellow), Hawks Club, Oxford and Cambridge United University Club.

AWARDS, HONORS: Harkness fellowship, 1958-59; member, Order of the British Empire, 1963; Canada Council fellowship, 1975.

WRITINGS:

This Is Northern Nigeria: Background to an Invitation, Government Printer of Northern Nigeria (Kaduna), 1956.
Maiduguri and the Capitals of Bornu, bilingual edition, Northern Regional Literature Agency (Zaria, Nigeria), 1958.
Adamawa, Past and Present: An Historical Approach to the Development of a Northern Cameroons Province, Oxford University Press for the International African Institute, 1958, new edition, Humanities, 1969.
(With Caroline Sassoon) *The Cattle People of Nigeria,* Oxford University Press, 1959.
(With Sassoon) *The Niger,* Oxford University Press, 1961.
Barth's Travels in Nigeria, Oxford University Press, 1962.
The Principles of Native Administration in Nigeria: Selected Documents, 1900-1947, Oxford University Press, 1965.
(With Sidney Hogben) *The Emirates of Northern Nigeria,* Oxford University Press, 1966.
(Compiler and translator) *Hausa ba dabo ba ne: A Collection of 500 Proverbs,* Oxford University Press, 1966.
(With Yahaya Aliyu) *A Modern Hausa Reader,* McKay, 1967.
(Editor) *Lugard and the Amalgamation of Nigeria: A Documentary Record,* Cass, 1968.
(Translator with Paul Newman) *West African Travels and Adventures: Two Autobiographical Narratives from Northern Nigeria,* Yale University Press, 1971.
Crisis and Conflict in Nigeria: A Documentary Sourcebook, two volumes, Oxford University Press, 1971.
(Editor and author of introduction and preface) *Gazetteers of the Northern Provinces of Nigeria,* revised edition, Volume I: *The Hausa Emirates,* Volume II: *The Eastern Kingdoms,* Volume III: *The Central Kingdoms,* Volume IV: *The Highland Chieftaincies,* Cass, 1972.
(With Charles Kraft) *Teach Yourself Hausa,* University of London Press, 1973.
Mutumin Kirkii: The Concept of the Good Man in Hausa (monograph), University of Indiana, 1974.
The Genesis of the Nigerian Civil War (monograph), University of Uppsala, 1975.
(With Pauline Ryan) *Faces North: Some Peoples of Nigeria,* Pitkin Publications, 1975.
(Editor) *The Transfer of Power: The African Administrator in the Age of Decolonization,* Oxford University Press, 1978.
A Biographical Dictionary of the British Colonial Governor, Volume I: *Africa,* Hoover Institution, 1980.
"Stay by Your Radios": Documentation for a Study of Military Government in Tropical Africa, University of Leiden Press, 1981.
(With Douglas Rimmer) *Nigeria since 1970: A Political and Economic Outline,* Holmes & Meier, 1981.
The Sudan Political Service: A Profile in the Sociology of Empire, Oxford University Press, 1982.

(Editor and author of introduction) Margery Perham, *West African Passage: A Journey through Nigeria, Chad, and the Cameroons, 1931-1932*, P. Owen, 1983.
(Editor with Mahdi Adamu) *Pastoralists of the West African Savanna*, Manchester University Press, 1986.
(Editor and author of introduction) Perham, *Pacific Prelude*, P. Owen, 1988.

CONTRIBUTOR

Donald C. Stone, editor, *Education and Public Administration*, International Institute of Administrative Sciences, 1963.
James S. Coleman, editor, *Education and Political Development*, Princeton University Press, 1965.
L. Franklin Blitz, editor, *The Politics and Administration of Nigeria*, Praeger, 1966.
H. Schiffers, editor, *Heinrich Barth Festschrift*, Steiner (Hamburg), 1967.
Arnold Rivkin, editor, *Nations by Design*, Doubleday, 1968.
John Spencer, editor, *The English Language in West Africa*, Longmans, Green, 1968.
Robert Rotberg, editor, *African Explorers and Exploration*, Harvard University Press, 1971.
C. Fyfe and G. Shepperson, editors, *The Exploration of Africa in the Eighteenth and Nineteenth Centuries*, Edinburgh University, 1972.
K. Ingham, editor, *Foreign Relations of African States*, Butterworth & Co., 1974.
A. Adedeji and C. Baker, editors, *Education and Research in Public Administration in Africa*, Hutchinson, 1974.
Adedeji and G. Hyden, editors, *Developing Research on African Administration*, [Nairobi], 1975.
Fyfe, editor, *African Studies since 1945*, Longman, 1976.
L. H. Gann and Peter Duignan, editors, *African Proconsuls: European Governors in Africa*, Hoover Institution, 1978.
D. K. Fieldhouse and A. F. Madden, *Oxford and Empire*, Croom Helm, 1982.
Prosser Gifford and W. Roger Louis, editors, *The Transfer of Power in Africa: Decolonization 1940-1960*, Yale University Press, 1982.
Duignan and Robert Jackson, *Politics and Government in African States, 1960-1985*, Croom Helm, 1986.
William Baker and J. A. Mengan, *Sport in Africa*, Holmes & Meier, 1987.
Graham Furniss and Philip Jagger, *Studies in Hausa*, Routledge & Kegan Paul, 1988.
Gifford and Louis, editors, *The Transfer of Power in Africa: Causes and Consequences*, Yale University Press, 1988.
W. Mommsen and R. E. Robinson, *The Berlin West Africa Conference of 1885*, Oxford University Press, 1988.

AUTHOR OF INTRODUCTION

C. J. Orr, *The Making of Northern Nigeria*, 2nd edition, Cass, 1965.
Heinrich Barth, *Travels and Discoveries in North and Central Africa*, centenary edition, Barnes & Noble, 1965.
Sonia Graham, *Government and Mission Education in Northern Nigeria*, Ibadan University Press, 1966.
P. A. Benton, *The Languages and People of Bornu*, Cass, 1968.
Barth, *The Vocabularies of Central African Languages*, Cass, 1970.
Frederick Lugard, *Political Memoranda*, Cass, 1971.
J. A. Burdon, *History of the Emirates of Northern Nigeria*, Gregg, 1973.

OTHER

Also author of pamphlets and research papers on African history, governmental institutions, politics, and languages. Contributor of several hundred articles and reviews to African and historical journals. General editor, ''Studies in African History'' series, Methuen, 1971—; co-editor of ''Colonial History Series,'' Hoover Institution, 1975—. Editorial advisor, *Journal of African Administration*, 1957-67, *African Affairs*, 1975—, and *Culture et Developpement*, 1976—.

WORK IN PROGRESS: A history of the British Colonial Administrative Service; the political history of modern Nigeria; colonial rule and decolonization.

BIOGRAPHICAL/CRITICAL SOURCES:

PERIODICALS

Times (London), June 11, 1981.
Times Literary Supplement, September 25, 1981, January 20, 1984.

*   *   *

KIRK-GREENE, Anthony H. M.
See KIRK-GREENE, Anthony (Hamilton Millard)

*   *   *

KORNBLATT, Joyce Reiser   1944-

PERSONAL: Born May 29, 1944, in Boston, Mass.; daughter of Morris (in sales) and Shirley (in sales; maiden name, Nathansen) Reiser; children: Sara. *Education:* Carnegie-Mellon University, B.A., 1966; Western Reserve University (now Case Western Reserve University), M.A., 1969.

ADDRESSES: Home— 8101 Custer Rd., Bethesda, Md. 20814. *Office—*Department of English, University of Maryland, College Park, Md. 20742. *Agent—*Ellen Levine Literary Agency Inc., 432 Park Ave. S., Suite 1205, New York, N.Y. 10016.

CAREER: University of Maryland, College Park, 1975—, currently associate professor of English. Member of board of directors of Glen Echo Park Writer's Center.

AWARDS, HONORS: Maryland Arts Council fellowship, 1980; creative arts performance award from University of Maryland, 1981; National Endowment for the Arts fellowship, 1985.

WRITINGS:

Nothing to Do with Love (short stories and novella), Viking, 1981.
White Water (novel), Dutton, 1985.
Breaking Bread (novel), Dutton, 1987.

SIDELIGHTS: After publishing *Nothing to Do with Love*, a well-received collection of short stories which focus predominantly on the way individuals deal with painful life situations, Joyce Reiser Kornblatt published her first novel, *White Water*, the story of three generations of a family pulling together in a crisis. ''This 'white water' is the turbulence stirred up by family conflict, and the novel charts the hazardous course which the members of one particular family must negotiate,'' explains Susan Wood in the *Washington Post Book World*. Because of the upcoming marriage, and eventual kidnapping, of the Fry family's youngest member, this family is moved to reassess their past, having been split for years by what London *Times* writer Gillian Greenwood labels ''sibling distrust, divorce, and lonely children.'' Greenwood views *White Water* as a '''therapeutic' novel in the sense that its characters . . . mostly come to a greater degree of acceptance and understanding of themselves.''

In the opinion of *Saturday Review* critic Bruce Van-Wyngarden, *White Water* ''is one of the best conceived and movingly executed works of fiction of this or any other year.'' VanWyngarden is particularly fond of Reiser's narrative format in which five separate family members speak their minds: ''Like soloists in a jazz band, they testify, each giving a singular self-portrait and point of view of the others. We thus see each character from five perspectives. . . . We become omniscient by degrees. It's a marvelous plot device, and it's complemented by Kornblatt's marvelous prose.'' In contrast, Wood believes there is too much going on in the novel, thus preventing Kornblatt from fully developing her characters and plot: ''The ambition is admirable, but alas, though the novel has interesting moments, in the end it fails to convince us—in large part because its slender frame (210 pages) will not bear the weight of its structure, plot and theme.'' From a different angle, *Los Angeles Times Book Review* contributor James Kaufmann questions the book's ''neat'' resolution: ''Is family harmony restored so easily? Does it take something horrible like a kidnaping to pull a family back together?. . . Hard questions, the answers to which are not forthcoming, at least not in many words, in 'White Water.''' The critic adds that ''Kornblatt seems more interested in demonstrating that, in a family, point of view is everything.'' Finally, although Kathryn Morton detects certain flaws in this novel, she writes in the *New York Times Book Review* that *White Water*, like some first novels ''by the most promising authors, lift the reader over the rough structure on the strength of their wit and insight, the rich sound of voices and the energetic flow of invention. These things can't be learned and can't be faked. A writer who has them is a writer to enjoy and watch.''

Kornblatt followed *White Water* with *Breaking Bread*, a journal-like novel in which Kornblatt's narrator reconstructs the lives of five individuals, now deceased, who had a lasting impact on her life. The book's title and theme come from W. H. Auden's proclamation that ''through art, we are able to break bread with the dead, and without communion with the dead a fully human life is impossible.'' There is some question as to whether *Breaking Bread* is a semi-autobiographical endeavor. Barbara Thompson professes in the *New York Times Book Review* that ''the lives in 'Breaking Bread' are the narrator's sacred dead,'' but she is uncertain as to whether they are Kornblatt's own. Thompson maintains that ''of the many pleasures [of *Breaking Bread*] is the richness of detail, the layering of meanings—and the suggestive uncertainty whether this is augmented memoir or elegant fiction sculpted on the slight armature of memory.'' *Los Angeles Times* contributor Elaine Kendall is more convinced that the five portraits represent individuals who ''counted most to the author. . . . Remarkably objective, lyrical but unsentimental, 'Breaking Bread' is autobiography by refraction, so subtle that we're unaware until the last page that the book is in fact a classic journal of self-discovery, valid not just for this particular author but for many women of the same generation and background.''

Kornblatt told *CA*: ''During the 1960s and early 1970s I worked as a community organizer and technical writer for the city of Cleveland. I wrote speeches and campaign materials for Carl Stokes, Eugene McCarthy, and Harold Hughes. After this immersion in the 'real world' I returned to literary pursuits more conscious of how human beings live in this culture. I am concerned with the ways humans break out of the isolation imposed on them by culture and by historical circumstance. What moves me are the extremes to which people will go in order to experience love. Hate comes easily, indifference comes easily. I am no sentimentalist. Still, I watch my fellows risk intimacy over and over again, and I am trying in my fiction to record, as an anthropologist might, those courageous gestures of affection, those sorties into devotion.''

BIOGRAPHICAL/CRITICAL SOURCES:

PERIODICALS

Chicago Tribune Book World, August 23, 1981.
Los Angeles Times, May 14, 1981, January 23, 1987.
Los Angeles Times Book Review, August 18, 1985.
New Republic, April 25, 1981.
New York Times Book Review, April 12, 1981, July 7, 1985, January 18, 1987.
Saturday Review, July-August, 1985.
Times (London), January 16, 1986.
Washington Post Book World, July 14, 1985, February 8, 1987.

*   *   *

KRAMMER, Arnold Paul   1941-

PERSONAL: Born August 15, 1941, in Chicago, Ill.; son of David and Eva (Vas) Krammer; married Rhoda Miriam Nudelman, June 19, 1968 (divorced, 1980); children: Adam. *Education:* University of Wisconsin—Madison, B.S., 1963, M.S., 1965, Ph.D., 1970; University of Vienna, diploma, 1964. *Religion:* Jewish.

ADDRESSES: Home—725 Meadow Ln., Bryan, Tex. 77802. *Office*—Department of History, Texas A & M University, College Station, Tex. 77843.

CAREER: Rockford College, Rockford, Ill., assistant professor of history, 1970-74; Texas A & M University, College Station, associate professor, 1974-79, professor of history, 1979—, principal investigator on German Documents Retrieval Project, Center for Energy and Mineral Resources, 1975—. Visiting professor at Rice University, 1980, 1982. Has presented numerous radio and television lectures throughout the United States; testified before Congress, 1977. Consultant to Nebraska Educational Television Network, 1978, and Greenwich Film Co.

MEMBER: Society for Historians of American Foreign Relations, American Historical Association, American Committee of Historians of the Second World War, National Institute on the Holocaust, Southern Historical Association, Phi Alpha Theta.

AWARDS, HONORS: American Council of Learned Societies grant, 1972, 1975, 1980; American Philosophical Society grant, 1973, 1976, 1979; National Endowment for the Humanities research grant, 1975; *The Forgotten Friendship: Israel and the Soviet Bloc, 1947-53* was named ''book of the year'' by Jewish Book Council in 1975; Congressional Award, Missouri House of Representatives, 1980, for research on German synthetic fuel; National Science Foundation research grant, 1982; study abroad appointments in Italy, 1985, and Germany, 1989.

WRITINGS:

The Forgotten Friendship: Israel and the Soviet Bloc, 1947-1953, University of Illinois Press, 1974.
Nazi Prisoners of War in America, Stein & Day, 1979.

(Contributor) L. J. Perelman and others, editors, *Energy Transitions: Long-Term Perspectives*, American Association for the Advancement of Science, 1981.

(Contributor) Ronald H. Bailey, editor, *Prisoners of War*, Time-Life, 1981.

(Contributor) Samuel R. Williamson, Jr. and Peter Pastor, editors, *War and Society in East Central Europe*, Volume 5, Columbia University Press, 1981.

(With Georg Gaertner) *Hitler's Last Soldier in America*, Stein & Day, 1985.

Contributor to *Proceedings of the American Society for Engineering Education*, 1982; contributor of articles and reviews to more than forty history and technical journals. Editorial consultant to *Southwestern Historical Quarterly* and *German Studies Review*.

WORK IN PROGRESS: Prisoner of War Art in the U.S.; studies of the German P.O.W. generals at Camp Clinton, Miss., and the Mexican Nazi Party: Gold Shirts.

SIDELIGHTS: Arnold Paul Krammer told *CA:* "I was born and raised in a Hungarian household where European history and its languages and customs were as vivid as Chicago's North Side beyond the window. Surviving the rigors of Chicago's public school systems, I pursued the study of history first as a student, and now as a teacher, and [I] try to present history with a storyteller's verve and a scholar's care."

As the principal investigator on the German Documents Retrieval Project at the Center for Energy and Mineral Resources at Texas A & M University, Krammer is in the process of analyzing nearly 173 tons of captured World War II German industrial records on synthetic fuel for possible use by the American energy industry.

Krammer's book, *Nazi Prisoners of War in America*, attracted the attention of Georg Gaertner, a fugitive German soldier who escaped from a prisoner-of-war camp in New Mexico in 1945. An article by Ralph Blumenthal in the *New York Times* tells that Gaertner contracted Krammer after reading his book, "with a desire to tell his story. Mr. Krammer said he encouraged Mr. Gaertner to come forward as a way 'of easing his transition into legality' and helping him 'come in from the cold.'" Together, Gaertner and Krammer wrote Gaertner's story, *Hitler's Last Soldier in America*.

BIOGRAPHICAL/CRITICAL SOURCES:

PERIODICALS

Christian Science Monitor, July 26, 1977.
Newsweek, July 4, 1977.
New York Times, September 11, 1985.
Time, April 18, 1977.

*   *   *

KUNIHOLM, Bruce Robellet   1942-

PERSONAL: Born October 4, 1942, in Washington, D.C.; son of Bertel E. (a diplomat) and Berthe E. (a government employee; maiden name, Robellet) Kuniholm; married Elizabeth Fairbank (a lawyer), June 29, 1968; children: Jonathan Fairbank, Erin Fairbank. *Education:* Dartmouth College, B.A., 1964; Duke University, M.A., 1972, M.A.P.P.S. and Ph.D., both 1976.

ADDRESSES: Home—1719 Tinsdale St., Durham, N.C. 27705. *Office*—Institute of Policy Sciences and Public Affairs, Duke University, 4875 Duke Station, Durham, N.C. 27706.

CAREER: Robert College, Istanbul, Turkey, instructor in English at Robert Academy, 1964-67; Duke University, Durham, N.C., lecturer, 1975-77, assistant professor, 1977-84, associate professor of policy sciences and history, 1984—, director of undergraduate studies, 1977—. Instructor with Peace Corps in Istanbul, Turkey, 1966. U.S. Department of State, Bureau of Intelligence and Research, political analyst for Arabian Peninsula and Persian Gulf, 1979; member, policy planning staff, 1979-80. Guest scholar, Woodrow Wilson Center for International Scholars, 1982. *Military service:* U.S. Marine Corps, 1967-71; became captain; received Bronze Star with "V" and Navy Achievement medal.

MEMBER: American Historical Association, Organization of American Historians, Society for Historians of American Foreign Relations, Middle East Institute, Council on Foreign Relations, Phi Beta Kappa.

AWARDS, HONORS: International Affairs fellow of Council on Foreign Relations, National Endowment for the Humanities, 1978-79; Stuart L. Bernath prize, Society for Historians of American Foreign Relations, 1981, for *The Origins of the Cold War in the Near East: Great Power Conflict and Diplomacy in Iran, Turkey, and Greece*.

WRITINGS:

The Origins of the Cold War in the Near East: Great Power Conflict and Diplomacy in Iran, Turkey, and Greece, Princeton University Press, 1980.
The Persian Gulf and United States Policy: A Guide to Issues and References, Regina Books, 1984.
The Near East Connection: Greece and Turkey in the Reconstruction and Security of Europe, 1946-1952, Hellenic College Press, 1984.
(With Michael Rubner) *The Palestinian Problem and United States Policy: A Guide to Issues and References*, Regina Books, 1985.

CONTRIBUTOR

Richard Burns, editor, *Guide to American Foreign Relations since 1700*, American Bibliographical Center-Clio Press, 1983.
Walter Isaacson, editor, *Pros and Cons*, Putnam, 1983.
Lawrence Kaplan, editor, *NATO and the Mediterranean*, Scholarly Resources, 1984.
Sam Wells and Mark Bruzonsky, editors, *Security in the Middle East: Prospects and Problems in the 1980s*, Westview Press, 1985.

OTHER

Editor, *Golden Horn*, 1966-67. Referee and reader for various presses and publications.

WORK IN PROGRESS: An edited volume on Cyprus; a diplomatic history of U.S.-Turkish relations from World War II to the present.

BIOGRAPHICAL/CRITICAL SOURCES:

PERIODICALS

New York Review of Books, October 8, 1981.
Times Literary Supplement, May 23, 1980.

L

LADD, Veronica
See MINER, Jane Claypool

* * *

LAKOFF, George 1941-

PERSONAL: Born May 24, 1941; son of Herman and Ida (Rosenfeld) Lakoff; married Robin Tolmach (a professor), June 9, 1963; children: Andrew. *Education:* Massachusetts Institute of Technology, B.S., 1962; Indiana University, Ph. D., 1966. *Politics:* "Yes." *Religion:* "No."

ADDRESSES: Office—Department of Linguistics, University of California, 2120 Oxford St., Berkeley, Calif. 94720.

CAREER: Harvard University, Cambridge, Mass., research fellow and lecturer, 1965-69; University of Michigan, Ann Arbor, associate professor of linguistics, beginning 1969; currently faculty member in department of linguistics at University of California, Berkeley.

WRITINGS:

Pronouns and Reference, Indiana University Linguistics Club, 1968.
Repartee; or, A Reply to Negation, Conjunction, and Quantifiers, Center for Applied Linguistics, 1969.
On Generative Semantics, Indiana University Linguistics Club, 1969.
Irregularity in Syntax, Holt, 1970.
Linguistik und natuerliche Logik, translated from the original English by Udo Frie and Harald Mittermann, Athenaeum, 1971.
(With Mark Johnson) *Metaphors We Live By,* University of Chicago Press, 1980.
(Editor with John R. Ross) Ann Borkin, *Problems in Form and Function,* Ablex Publishing, 1984.
Women, Fire, and Dangerous Things: What Categories Reveal about the Mind, University of Chicago Press, 1987.

Contributor to professional journals.

SIDELIGHTS: "One approaches *Metaphors We Live By,* fruit of a collaboration between a linguist and a philosopher, with caution," observes *Times Literary Supplement* contributor Liam Hudson. It is "all the more pleasant the discovery, then, that what George Lakoff and Mark Johnson write makes sense.

Their text is plain, . . . [and] what [they] say is not only true, it needs to be said," adds the critic. By using examples from everyday language, the authors claim that the use of metaphor is an everyday event rather than an extraordinary occurence. Although Hudson thinks the later parts of the book tend to be obscure, he admits that "their own argument holds water, avoids going around in circles, and gets purposively from A to B." And a reviewer for *Choice* comments that for a premise "so bold and comprehensive the book is remarkably short . . . but the argument is clear, if somewhat schematic, and the writing is full of examples that make it eminently readable." The critic concludes by giving *Metaphors We Live By* his "highest recommendation."

BIOGRAPHICAL/CRITICAL SOURCES:

PERIODICALS

Choice, May, 1981.
Times Literary Supplement, March 13, 1981.*

* * *

LAKOFF, Robin Tolmach 1942-

PERSONAL: Born November 27, 1942, in Brooklyn, N.Y.; married George Lakoff (a professor), June 9, 1963; children: Andrew. *Education:* Radcliffe College, B.A., 1964; Indiana University, M.A., 1965; Harvard University, Ph.D., 1967.

ADDRESSES: Office—Department of Linguistics, University of California, 2120 Oxford St., Berkeley, Calif. 94720.

CAREER: Language Research Foundation, Cambridge, Mass., textbook editor, 1968-69; University of Michigan, Ann Arbor, assistant professor of linguistics, 1969-71; Stanford University, Stanford, Calif., fellow of Center for Advanced Study of Behavioral Sciences, 1971-72; University of California, Berkeley, associate professor of linguistics, 1972—. Lecturer in classics and linguistics, University of Illinois, 1968; visiting associate professor, University of Michigan Linguistics Institute, 1973.

MEMBER: Linguistics Society of America.

WRITINGS:

Abstract Syntax and Latin Complementation, M.I.T. Press, 1968.

Language and Woman's Place, Harper, 1975.
(With Raquel L. Scherr) *Face Value: The Politics of Beauty*, Methuen, 1984.
(With Mandy Aftel) *When Talk Is Not Cheap: Or, How to Find the Right Therapist When You Don't Know Where to Begin*, Warner Books, 1985.

SIDELIGHTS: Robin Tolmach Lakoff's book *Language and Woman's Place* discusses language's part in indicating and reinforcing society's attitudes toward women. Reviewer Ann Scott of the *English Journal* notes that *"Language and Woman's Place* goes a long way toward elucidating for the open-minded reader the reasons for the feminist attack upon language use, separating the sense from the nonsense. . . . Less controversial, but probably more socially revealing, are Lakoff's observations about the language spoken by women themselves." Lakoff identifies certain speech patterns and word choices found almost exclusively in the linguistic behavior of women; she observes, for example, that women more frequently than men add a tag question at the end of a declarative assertion, such as "He's with the Philharmonic, isn't he?" The tag question diminishes the force of the sentence and may be indicative of a sense of subordination, claims Lakoff. The author notes other areas in which women's language is both characteristic and socially revealing. Her analysis is based on personal observation and interpretation rather than scientifically collected data; thus Scott concludes that "in the absence of experimental proof [Lakoff] invites the reader to make his (?!) own observations and draw his own conclusions."

Lakoff and co-author Raquel L. Scherr use a similar method in *Face Value: The Politics of Beauty*, drawing from anthropology, philosophy, psychology, art, surveys, and personal experience to explain conventional ideas of beauty. While attractiveness has traditionally been perceived as a form of power, Lakoff told *Los Angeles Times* writer Harriet Stix that "beauty comes from what the observer observes. It has to be a passive trait." Because of this passivity, Lakoff explained to Stix that "beauty is a nice tool precisely because you don't have to take responsibility for it, whereas if you go out in the world and do something, you are responsible. That can be very troubling for a lot of women," she continued, "especially if they were brought up not to be particularly self-confident." Even though changing attitudes about beauty can be frightening because they are new, "the important thing is that we somehow transcend the issue of looks and have something else," Lakoff declared. "If we can feel good about what we accomplish, then we can have looks to play with as an additional attraction."

BIOGRAPHICAL/CRITICAL SOURCES:

PERIODICALS

English Journal, May, 1976.
Los Angeles Times, August 16, 1985.
Nation, December 8, 1984.
New Statesman, January 11, 1985.*

*   *   *

LANCER, Jack
[Collective pseudonym]

WRITINGS:

"CHRISTOPHER COOL/TEEN AGENT" SERIES

X Marks the Spy, Grosset & Dunlap, 1967.

Mission: Moonfire, Grosset & Dunlap, 1967.
Department of Danger, Grosst & Dunlap, 1967.
Ace of Shadows, Grosset & Dunlap, 1968.
Heads You Lose, Grosset & Dunlap, 1968.
Trial by Fury, Grosset & Dunlap, 1969.

SIDELIGHTS: Christopher Cool/TEEN Agent was a series which appeared in the wave of popularity following the "I Spy," "Get Smart," and "The Man from U.N.C.L.E." television programs. A sophomore at an Ivy League university, Christopher Cool, his Apache Indian roommate Geronimo Johnson and red haired co-ed espionage agent Spice Carter carried out undercover assignments for the U. S. Intelligence Agency—TEEN, an acronym for Top-Secret Educational Espionage Network.

Stratemeyer Syndicate writer James Duncan Lawrence developed this series, which was continued by Andrew Svenson. For more information, see the entries in this volume for Harriet S. Adams, James Duncan Lawrence, Edward L. Stratemeyer, and Andrew E. Svenson.

BIOGRAPHICAL/CRITICAL SOURCES:

BOOKS

Johnson, Deidre, editor and compiler, *Stratemeyer Pseudonyms and Series Books: An Annotated Checklist of Stratemeyer and Stratemeyer Syndicate Publications*, Greenwood Press, 1982.

PERIODICALS

Yellowback Library, January/February, 1986.

*   *   *

LANE, William L(ister)   1931-

PERSONAL: Born January 16, 1931, in New Britain, Conn.; son of William J. (a production supervisor) and Evelyn (Moore) Lane; married Brenda Whitaker, August 7, 1974; children: William John, Kristine Ruth, Mark Timothy, David Eric. *Education:* Wesleyan University, Middletown, Conn., B.A., 1952; Gordon Divinity School. B.D., 1955; Westminster Theological Seminary, Th.M., 1956; Harvard University, Th.D., 1962. *Politics:* Republican. *Religion:* American Baptist.

ADDRESSES: Home—1338 Park St., Bowling Green, Ky. 42101. *Office*—Department of Philosophy and Religion, Western Kentucky University, Bowling Green, Ky. 42101.

CAREER: Hebrew Union College-Jewish Institute of Religion, Cincinnati, Ohio, Christian research fellow, 1959-60; Gordon Divinity School (now Gordon-Conwell Theological Seminary), South Hamilton, Mass., assistant professor, 1960-63, associate professor, 1963-68, professor of New Testament and Judaic studies, 1968-73, chairman of New Testament department, 1972-73; Western Kentucky University, Bowling Green, Ky., professor of religious studies, 1974—.

MEMBER: Society of Biblical Literature, Evangelical Theological Society, Studiorum Novi Testamenti Societas, Near East Archeological Society, Phi Beta Kappa, Phi Alpha Chi.

WRITINGS:

(With Glenn W. Barker and J. Ramsey Michaels) *The New Testament Speaks*, Harper, 1969.
Ephesians, Philippians, Colossians, 1 Thessalonians, 2 Thessalonians (Bible study book), Scripture Union (London), 1969, A. J. Holman, 1978.

Righteousness in Christ, Scripture Union, 1973.
(Author of introduction, exposition, and notes) *Commentary on the Gospel of Mark,* Eerdmans, 1974.
(Contributor) R. N. Longenecker and M. C. Tenney, editors, *New Dimensions in New Testament Study,* Zondervan, 1974.
(Contributor) J. H. Skilton, editor, *The New Testament Student and Theology,* Presbyterian and Reformed, 1976.
Righteousness, Eerdmans, 1978.
Highlights of the Bible: The New Testament, Regal Books, 1980.
Call to Commitment: Responding to the Message of Hebrews, Thomas Nelson, 1985.

Also author of *World Biblical Commentary,* 1986. Bibliographical editor, *Encyclopedia of Christianity,* Christian Educational Foundation, 1964; associate editor, *Encyclopedia of Modern Christian Missions,* Thomas Nelson, 1967.

WORK IN PROGRESS: Paul in the Perspective of His Mission.

SIDELIGHTS: William Lane once told *CA:* "I have gradually come to understand that my primary task as a writer of technical biblical studies is to listen to the text, and to the discussion it has prompted over the course of the centuries, as a child who needs to be made wise. I view my writing as a response to the discipline of responsible listening."

AVOCATIONAL INTERESTS: Stamp collecting, with emphasis on Scandinavia.*

*   *   *

LARSEN, Carl 1934-
(Edna Poots-Booby)

PERSONAL: Born August 28, 1934, in Orange County, Calif.; son of Carl T. (a clerk) and Lucille (Porter) Larsen; married Celeste Rhodes (a college instructor), May 30, 1970; children: Catherine, Shoshana, David, Adam, Jason. *Education:* Attended El Camino College, 1954-56, and Actor's Studio, 1960-61. *Politics:* Liberal. *Religion:* None.

ADDRESSES: Home and office—147 North Coalter St., Staunton, Va., 24401.

CAREER: Western Freight Association, New York, N.Y., dispatcher, 1960-75; free-lance writer, 1975—.

MEMBER: Dramatists Guild, Authors Guild.

AWARDS, HONORS: National Endowment for the Arts grant, 1978-79.

WRITINGS:

Notes from a Machine Shop (poems), Hennypenny Press, 1956.
The Journal of an Existentialist Villain (poems), Hennypenny Press, 1957.
Arrows of Longing (poems), Hearse Chapbooks, 1958.
Onan's Seed (novel), Seven Poets Press, 1960.
(With Jim Singer) *The Beat Generation Cook Book,* Seven Poets Press, 1961.
The Plot to Assassinate the Chase Manhattan Bank (poems), Seven Poets Press, 1962.
The Naked and the Dead and the Catcher in the Rye and the Sick and the Sad and the Sorry Meet Frankenstein (poems), Hors Commerce Press, 1963.
The Book of Eric Hammerscoffer (novel), Tarot Press, 1964.
The Toad King (poems), Goosetree Press, 1964.

The Popular Mechanics Book of Poetry, Mimeo Press, 1966.
Ol' Peckerhead (fiction), Samasdat, 1975.
The Midvale Chronicle (fiction), New Earth Books, 1977.
The Amalgamated Lugwart Company Spare Parts Catalogue (fiction), Cornerstone Press, 1977.
(With Michael Milts) *Only a Gringo Would Die for an Anteater: The Adventures of a Veterinarian* (biography), illustrated by Pete Hironaka, Norton, 1979.
Even the Dog Won't Eat My Meatloaf: An Even Hundred of the Author's Syndicated Column, "Frying Pan Follies," Media Ventures, 1980.

PLAYS

"The Census Bureau" (one-act), first produced in New York City at Riverdale Church, 1962.
"The Plot to Assassinate the Chase Manhattan Bank" (one-act), first produced in New York City at Theatre East, 1963.
"Who's Afraid of Edward Albee?" (one-act), first produced in New York City at Theatre East, 1963.
"The Clocks" (one-act), first produced in New York City at Fulton Theatre, 1965.
"Funny Side Up" (one-act), first produced in San Francisco, Calif., at Revue Theater, 1965.
"You Guys Kill Me" (one-act), first produced in New York City at Fulton Theater, 1969.
"Sue Loves Frankenstein" (one-act), first produced in New York City at Fulton Theater, 1970.
"Several Objects Passing Charlies Greeley" (one-act), first produced in Milwaukee, Wis., at Milwaukee Repertory Theatre, 1972.

OTHER

Also author of two other plays, "Bury My Knee at Wounded Groin" and "Centipede." Writer and co-producer for radio series, "The Sowbelly Show," for WBPZ-AM-FM Radio, 1975-76. Author of syndicated weekly column, "Frying Pan Follies," 1977—. Contributor to literary magazines, sometimes under pseudonym Edna Poots-Booby.

WORK IN PROGRESS: "Museum Pieces," a play; *Warm Bodies,* a novel.

SIDELIGHTS: Carl Larsen writes: "An avowed humorist is either funny, or not. And I've found that social protest goes down a lot easier with a teaspoon of sugar. I've always felt like a sort of tourist on this funny planet; here to take pictures, to gather a few anecdotes (for the folks back on Betelgeuse), and—The Writer's Sacred Responsibility—to spread as much Chaos and Confusion as is possible, amongst the natives."*

*   *   *

LAWRENCE, J. D.
See LAWRENCE, James Duncan

*   *   *

LAWRENCE, James Duncan 1918-
(J. D. Lawrence, Jim Lawrence)

PERSONAL: Born October 22, 1918, in Detroit, Mich.; son of Charles Wilbert (a salesman) and Pearl Susan (Best) Lawrence; married Marie Catherine Blum, December 30, 1939; children: Sherry, Liane, James D., Jr., John William, Vivian, Gillian. *Education:* Attended U.S. Naval Academy; Wayne University (now Wayne State University), B.A. in Education,

1939; Detroit Institute of Technology, B.S. in Mechanical Engineering, 1939.

ADDRESSES: Home—63 Tall Oaks Dr., Summit, N.J. 07901.

CAREER: Free-lance writer for radio and for newspaper comic strips. Stratemeyer Syndicate (creators of juvenile books), East Orange, N.J., writer-editor, 1954-67.

WRITINGS:

Davy Crockett and the Indian Secret: Adventures of a Boy Pioneer (juvenile), Books, Inc., 1955.
(Under name J. D. Lawrence) *Barnaby's Bells* (juvenile), illustrated by Michael Lowenbein, Macmillan, 1965.
Binky Brothers: Detectives (juvenile), illustrated by Leonard Kessler, Harper, 1968.
Binky Brothers and the Fearless Four (juvenile), illustrated by Kessler, Harper, 1970.
(Under name Jim Lawrence) *Buck Rogers in the 25th Century,* foreword by Buster Crabbe, illustrated by Gray Morrow, Quick Fox, 1981.
(Under name Jim Lawrence) *ESP McGee and the Haunted Mansion* (juvenile), illustrated by Larry Ross, Avon, 1983.

OTHER

Also author of radio scripts for programs including "Sergeant Preston of the Yukon," "Sky King," "The Lone Ranger," "The Green Hornet," and "Jack Armstrong"; writer for newspaper comic strips, including "Buck Rogers," "James Bond," "Joe Palooka," "Friday Foster," "Captain Easy," "Barbara Cartland's Romances," and "Dallas"; author of interactive fiction computer software.

Contributor of books to "Tom Swift Jr." series under pseudonym Victor Appleton II, to "Hardy Boys" series under pseudonym Franklin W. Dixon, to "Bobbsey Twins" series under pseudonym Laura Lee Hope, and to "Nancy Drew" series under pseudonym Carolyn Keene. Originator of "Christopher Cool—TEEN Agent" series, under pseudonym Jack Lancer.

SIDELIGHTS: For many years James Duncan Lawrence worked on series books for the Stratemeyer Syndicate. He told Geoffrey S. Lapin in an interview for *Yellowback Library* magazine that after the radio shows he wrote for went off the air in the early 1950s, he noticed an article in the *New Yorker* announcing the start of a new "Tom Swift" series: "Of course I'd wanted to be a writer all my life, and radio died in 1954, so I was looking around for new areas. Since I actually had been educated as an engineer I had technical background, so I wrote to them and asked if they were interested in working with free-lance writers and they said they were. So, I began writing Tom Swift Jr. Series for them." Lawrence states that he wrote all the "Tom Swift Jr." series books, beginning with the fifth and excluding the eighth, until he left the Syndicate in 1967.

While working for the Syndicate, Lawrence created the "Christopher Cool—TEEN Agent" series in response to the spy craze of the 1960s. He also revised several of the early "Hardy Boys" titles. In recent years he has written volumes in the "Nancy Drew" and "Bobbsey Twins" series for Simon & Schuster. For more information see the sketches in this volume for Harriet S. Adams, Edward L. Stratemeyer, Andrew E. Svenson, and for the following pseudonyms: Victor Appleton II, Franklin W. Dixon, Laura Lee Hope, Carolyn Keene, and Jack Lancer.

MEDIA ADAPTATIONS: A movie based on Lawrence's comic strip "Friday Foster" was produced by American-International in 1975. It starred Pam Grier, Yaphet Kotto, and Godfrey Cambridge.

BIOGRAPHICAL/CRITICAL SOURCES:

PERIODICALS

Christian Science Monitor, May 2, 1968.
New Yorker, March 20, 1954, March 21, 1970.
New York Times Book Review, June 6, 1965, May 24, 1970.
Science Fiction and Fantasy Book Review, April, 1982.
Yellowback Library, January/February, 1986.*

*   *   *

LAWRENCE, Jim
See LAWRENCE, James Duncan

*   *   *

LAX, Robert   1915-

PERSONAL: Born November 30, 1915, in Olean, N.Y.; son of Sigmund and Betty (Hotchner) Lax. *Education:* Columbia University, B.A., 1938. *Politics:* Democrat. *Religion:* Roman Catholic.

ADDRESSES: Home—Patmos, Greece. *Office*—c/o Marcia Kelly, 70 Riverside Dr., New York, N.Y. 10024.

CAREER: New Yorker, New York City, member of editorial staff, 1941-42; University of North Carolina at Chapel Hill, instructor in English, 1943-44; *Time,* New York City, film critic, 1945-46; Samuel Goldwyn Studio, Hollywood, Calif., script writer, 1946-48; Connecticut College for Women (now Connecticut College), New London, instructor in English and comparative literature, 1948-49; *Jubilee,* New York City, 1953-67, began as roving editor, became executive editor; free-lance writer, 1967—. Exhibitions of poetry, films and drawings at Victoria and Albert Museum, London, England, 1967, Zano Gallery, Florence, Italy, 1972, Neue Staatsgalerie Stuttgart, Stuttgart, West Germany, 1985, Nigel Greenwood Books, London, England, 1987, and Bach Julius, Stuttgart, 1987.

AWARDS, HONORS: National Council of the Arts award, 1969.

WRITINGS:

POETRY

The Juggler, Hand Press, 1956.
Oedipus, lithographs by Emil Antonucci, Hand Press, 1958.
Ian Hamilton Finlay, editor, *Poor Old Tired Horse: "The Stone, the Sea,"* drawings by E. Antonucci, Wild Hawthorn Press (Lanark, Scotland), 1965.
Sea and Sky (offprint), Lugano Review, 1965.
(Contributor) Stephen Bann, editor, *Concrete Poetry: An International Anthology,* Secker & Warburg, 1967.
Sea Poems, Wild Hawthorn Press, 1967.
David Kilburn, editor, *Abstract Poem,* Green Island (London), 1968.
Lo, La, General Beadle State College, 1968.
Black and White #10, General Beadle State College, 1968.
(Contributor) Ron Schrieber, editor, *Thirty-One New American Poets,* Hill & Wang, 1969.
D. Kilburn, editor, *Shower Girl Song,* Green Island, 1969.
D. Kilburn, editor, *You Will Dissolve,* photographs by D. Kilburn, Green Island, 1970.
Ktaadn Volume 1, #3: "Hill Poems," drawings by E. Antonucci, Lional Basney (Houghton, New York), 1970.

(Contributor) George Plimpton and others, editors, *American Literary Anthology*, Viking, 1970.

Homage to Wiggenstein, [Kalymnos], 1970.

(Contributor) Richard Kostelanetz, editor, *Imaged Words and Worded Images*, Outerbridge & Dientsfrey, 1970.

(Contributor) Emmett Williams, editor, *Expanded Poetry*, Simon & Schuster, 1970.

(Contributor) Mary Ellen Solt, editor and author of introduction, *Concrete Poetry: A World View*, Indiana University Press, 1970.

(Contributor) *Sound*, Random House, 1971.

4 Boats, 3 People (postcard), Tarasque Press, 1971.

Able Charlie Baker Dance, drawings by E. Antonucci, Tarasque Press, 1971.

Wasser = Water = L'Eau (German, English, and French text), German translation by Alfred Kuoni, photographs by Bernard Moosbrugger, Pendo-Verlag (Zurich), 1973.

Spring Song, Kontexts Publications, 1974.

D. Kilburn, editor, *Rosebud Is*, Green Island, 1976.

101: The Point of It All, [Patmos, Greece], 1977.

(With Thomas Merton) *A Catch of Anti-Letters*, drawings by T. Merton, Sheed Andrews and McMeel, 1978.

A Poem (Round and Turning), Zona (Firenze, Italy), 1978.

Selections, X-Press (Hove, England), 1978.

A Suite for Jiri Valoch, Falkynor Books (Davie, Florida), 1978.

Color, Exempla Editione (Florence), . 1979.

(Contributor) Claudio Parmiggiani, editor, *TAU/MA 7*, [Bologna], 1981.

Circus = Zirkus = Cirque = Circo (German, English, French, and Spanish text), German translation by A. Kuoni, French translation by Catherine Mauger, Spanish translation by Ernesto Cardenal, photographs by B. Moosbrugger, Pendo Verlag, 1981.

Ten Poems, Patmos Press, 1981.

Robert Butman, editor, *Episodes Episoden* (English and German text), German translation by A. Kuoni, Pendo Verlag, 1983.

The Blue Boat #1: "Nine Poems," Moschatel Press, 1983.

Ennia Poihmata (Nine Poems), translation by M. Lagouvardos, Moschos Lagouvardos, 1983.

21 Pages = 21 Seiten (English and German text), German translation by A. Kuoni, Pendo Verlag, 1984.

Aggie Weston's #21: "Light," Stuart Mills (Belper, England), 1984.

Cloning for Yellow, Seedorn Verlag, 1984.

D. Kilburn, editor, *The Port Was Longing*, Green Island, 1984.

Journal A = Tagebuch A (English and German text), German translation by A. Kuoni, Pendo Verlag, 1986.

Heinz Gappmayr, editor, *New Poems (1962/1985)*, Coracle Press (London), 1986.

Journal B, illustrations by R. Lax, Pendo Verlag, 1988.

Thomas Kellein, editor, *33 Poems*, edition hansjoerg mayer (London), 1987, New Directions Publishing, 1988.

POETRY; PUBLISHED BY JOURNEYMAN BOOKS; ILLUSTRATIONS BY EMIL ANTONUCCI, EXCEPT AS NOTED

The Circus of the Sun, 1959, new edition with facing translations in German, French, and Spanish published as *Circus*, photographs by B. Moosbrugger, Pendo Verlag, 1981.

New Poems, 1962.

3 or 4 Poems about the Sea, 1966.

How Does the Sun's Ray Seek the Flower?, 1966.

Thought, 1966.

The Angel and the Little Old Lady, 1969.

A Poem for Thomas Merton, 1969.

Three Poems, 1969.

Fables, 1970.

Tree, 1970.

Red Circle-Blue Square, 1971.

Another Red Red Blue Poem, 1971.

Black and White, 1971.

An Evening at Webster Hall, 1971.

A Guide for the Perplexed, 1971.

A Moment, 1971.

Mostly Blue, 1971.

Circus Black-Circus White, 1974.

More Black and Whites, 1974.

Pictures of Reality, 1974.

Poem (Does the Grass Fear the Dark), 1974.

Poem (Try to See the Air), 1974.

Star Dialogue, 1974.

13 Poems, 1974.

Black Earth-Blue Sky, 1975.

"Journeyman Series": *#1: Bird Against the Cloud, #3: Oedipus, #5: Dr. Shakesprop, #7: Sandra's Dream, #9: Game on the Beach, #12: Red Blue*, all 1975.

G'bye Flo, I Tell Her (broadside), 1975.

I Like Get F'd (broadside), 1975.

My Dog Has Fleas (broadside), 1975.

Five Broadsides: Untitled, drawings by R. Lax, 1975.

Poemes des Collines, translation by Catherine Mauger, 1975.

Red Blue, 1976.

Color Poems, 1976.

Fables, 1970, published as *Fables (Mythoi = Myths)*, translated from original English manuscript into Greek by M. Lagouvardos, [Salonika, Greece], 1980.

POETRY; MICHAEL LASTNITE, EDITOR; PUBLISHED BY FURTHERMORE PRESS

At the Top of the Night, 1983.

Clouds, 1983.

In and Out of Purdah, drawings by R. Lax, 1983.

Shepherd's Calendar, 1983.

Tiger (booklet), 1983.

The Way (booklet), 1983.

Whole (booklet), 1983.

Said's, 1983.

Act in This Moment (broadside), 1984.

Arc, 1984.

As Long As, drawings by R. Lax, 1984.

Astrophysical Masterpieces, 1984.

Cloud over Hill, 1984.

Fat Ladies, drawings by R. Lax, 1984.

From the Top of the Ferris Wheel, 1984.

In His Dreams, 1984.

Just Midnight, 1984.

The Love that Comes, 1984.

Snowflake, 1984.

Water Sunlight Writes, 1984.

Spider, 1984.

Dark Earth, Bright Sky, 1985.

Ghost, 1985.

I Can't See You, 1985.

The Nights the Days, 1985.

Above the Rock, 1985.

Some Short Notes, 1985.

Other Notes, 1985.

OTHER

Postcard Drawings of Robert Lax, Furthermore Press, 1983.

Also author of *Question*, Hand Press, *New Poems 1962-85*, selected by Heinz Gappmayer, Coracle Press, and *Jerusalem (Above All Joy)*, 1969. Author of one-page magazines from 1956-62, and 1985—. Also contributor of poems to numerous periodicals, including *New Yorker, Commonweal, Lines, Beloit Poetry Journal, Artes Hispanicas, New York Quarterly, London Magazine, Merton Annual*, and *Proteus*. Author of poetry on audio cassettes, edited by Michael Lastnite, for On the Other Hand Productions.

MEDIA ADAPTATIONS: "New Film," 1969, "Red and Blue," 1971, and "Shorts," are 16mm films based on Lax's poetry and were produced by Emil Antonucci. "Robert Lax: Word and Image," featuring Lax reading and talking about his work, was produced by On the Other Hand Productions in 1988.

WORK IN PROGRESS: "A poem-journal or journal poem, and abstract poems."

SIDELIGHTS: "Most of my books to date," writes Robert Lax, "have been published by other poets, or by graphic artists who have discovered the work in small press editions in America, Europe, or Australia, and have undertaken to do small editions of their own, designing and illustrating them, each according to his ideas. The results have been most gratifying: a series of often slim, inexpensive but life-breathing books, warmly conceived and lovingly designed. They go out of print almost as fast as they come into it, but each is beautiful while it lasts.

"The first of these artists to produce my work, and the most prodigious, is Emil Antonucci, the publisher of Journeyman Books. He has designed and published at least twenty-five of my books, large and small, and has produced three or four short films in black and white and in color based on poems he had already published. [Among the films are 'New Film,' 'Shorts' and 'Red & Blue.'] Maurizio Nannucci—poet, artist, and demiurge in Florence—has designed and published other of my books and produced a cassette of my readings, [*Sea and Sky*]. Bernhard Moosbrugger, an outstanding Swiss photographer and publisher of Pendo Verlag, Zurich, has designed and illustrated several of my books (in English, with German translation) and has still others in the works." Other artists and poets who have been instrumental in getting Lax's work published, broadcast, or filmed include John Ashbery, Thomas Merton, Mark Van Doren, Theodore Weiss, Richard Kostelanetz, Thomas A. Clark, Stephen Bann, Mario Diacono, Jiri Valoch and Ernesto Cardenal.

Lax has recorded his poems for the Lamont Poetry Room at Harvard University. In 1968, a double issues of *Voyages* was devoted to his work.

BIOGRAPHICAL/CRITICAL SOURCES:

PERIODICALS

Art International, January 20, 1971.

FILMS

"Robert Lax: Neue Staatsgalerie, Exhibition and Reading," On the Other Hand Productions, 1985.
"Robert Lax: Word and Image," On the Other Hand Productions, 1988.

*   *   *

LEADER, Shelah Gilbert 1943-

PERSONAL: Born December 26, 1943, in New York, N.Y.; daughter of Sanford Forest (in sales) and Betty (a secretary; maiden name, Unterman) Gilbert; married Stefan Hugh Leader (a defense analyst), June 11, 1967; children: Lauren. *Education:* Attended University of Paris, 1963-64; Hofstra University, B.A., 1965; State University of New York at Buffalo, Ph.D., 1970; additional study at Cornell University, 1971.

ADDRESSES: Office—American Association of Retired Persons, 1909 K St. N.W., Washington, D.C. 20049. *Agent*—Gloria Stern Agency, 1230 Park Ave., New York, N.Y. 10028.

CAREER: Rutgers University, New Brunswick, N.J., research associate at Eagleton Institute, 1973-74; equal opportunity specialist with U.S. Justice Department, 1974-75; senior policy analyst with National Commission in the Observance of International Women's Year, 1975-78; senior analyst for U.S. Department of Health, Education, and Welfare, 1978-80; L & L Associates (consulting firm), Washington, D.C., partner, 1980-83; National Consumers League, Washington, D.C., director of education, 1983-84; American Association of Retired Persons, Washington, D.C., health policy analyst, 1986—. Former member of board of directors of Cornell University's women's studies program and advisory committee of George Washington University's women's studies program; member of advisory board of Women's Institute, American University.

MEMBER: National Organization for Women (president of Buffalo, N.Y., chapter, 1968; chairperson of Montgomery County insurance task force, 1983-85), Women's Caucus for Political Science (past treasurer), National Women's Political Caucus, National Association for Repeal of Abortion Laws, American Civil Liberties Union, American Public Health Association, Association for Health Services Research, Women in Government Relations, Sigma Kappa Alpha, Pi Gamma Mu.

WRITINGS:

(With Sheila Tobias, Peter Gouinoff, and husband, Stefan Leader) *What Kinds of Guns Are They Buying for Your Butter?: A Beginner's Guide to Defense, Weaponry, and Military Spending*, Morrow, 1982.
(With Marilyn Moon) *Changing America's Health Care System: Proposals for Legislative Action*, Scott, Foresman, 1988.

CONTRIBUTOR

The Role of Women in Politics, University of Delaware Press, 1974.
Louis Maisel and Joseph Cooper, editors, *The Impact of the Electoral Process*, Sage Publications, 1977.
Irene Diamond, editor, *Families, Politics, and Public Policy*, Longman, 1983.
Marion Eiwlewin and Sean Sullivan, *The Economics and Ethics of Long Term Care and Disability*, University Press, 1988.

OTHER

Author of "Public Opinions," a monthly column published in *Spring*. Contributor to magazines, including *Ms., Asian Survey*, and *World Politics*, and newspapers, including *Christian Science Monitor* and *Newsday*.

WORK IN PROGRESS: Research on health policy, women, and the aged.

SIDELIGHTS: Shelah Gilbert Leader told *CA:* "I am primarily an educator. My writings reflect my own curiosity and my need to understand what is happening in America. I wrote

What Kinds of Guns Are They Buying for Your Butter?: A Beginner's Guide to Defense, Weaponry, and Military Spending, after my co-author, Sheila Tobias, asked me if I was as ignorant as she about defense policy. She forced me to confront my aversion to the subject and to learn enough to be able to explain it to others. Learning about defense didn't change my basic values or attitudes, but it did make me more confident in debate and more aware of how complex are the problems we face. I feel that if I could learn this subject, so can other interested-but-intimidated people.

"My *Newsday* article, 'Social Security's Poor Portfolio,' evolved from a question posed by formed NOW president, Ellie Smeal: 'Where did all the money go?' I found it went into cheap loans to other federal programs and efforts (like the Vietnam War) and that the borrowing goes in only one direction. A lot of mumbo jumbo is used to hide the reality of these cash flows."

* * *

LEAVITT, Judith A(nn) 1947-

PERSONAL: Born November 21, 1947, in Washington, Iowa; daughter of David Elwood (a farmer) and Ada (a secretary; maiden name, Denison) Kleese; married David Leavitt (a personnel manager), August 30, 1969; children: Joseph David, John Richard. *Education:* University of Iowa, B.A. (with honors), 1970; Indiana University, M.L.S., 1977. *Politics:* Democrat. *Religion:* Unitarian-Universalist.

ADDRESSES: Home—1223 38th St. N.W., Cedar Rapids, Iowa 52405. *Office*—Collins Division, Rockwell International, 400 Collins Rd. N.E., Cedar Rapids, Iowa 52498.

CAREER: Purdue University Libraries, West Lafayette, Ind., acquisitions librarian, 1970-76; Ball State University, Muncie, Ind., secretary for Institute for Community Education Development, 1978-79, instructor in library service and catalog librarian, Bracken Library, 1979-81; Rockwell International, Cedar Rapids, Iowa, supervisor of Information Center at Collins Divisions, 1982—. Lecturer.

MEMBER: American Library Association, Special Libraries Association, American Management Association, Women Library Workers, League of Women Voters (member of board of directors of committee on international relations, 1979-81; member of board of directors, 1979-83), Iowa Library Association, Beta Phi Mu, Toastmasters International.

WRITINGS:

(Compiler) *Women in Management, 1970-1979: An Annotated Sourcelist,* Oryx, 1982.
Dual-Career Families, Council of Planning Libraries, 1982.
American Women Managers and Administrators: Twentieth-Century Leaders in Business, Education, and Government, Greenwood Press, 1985.
Women in Administration and Management: An Information Sourcebook, Oryx, 1988.

Also editor of bibliographies. Contributor of bibliographies to *Library Hi-Tech;* also contributor of articles and reviews to library journals, including *Women Library Workers* and *Behavioral and Social Sciences Librarian.*

WORK IN PROGRESS: Research on dual-career families, Iowa's women writers, and women's studies in general.

SIDELIGHTS: "It was natural that I should choose librarianship as a career," Judith Leavitt told *CA,* "because I have

always been an avid reader. Even as a child I was so eager to read everything that, at the age of ten, I read a geography book from cover to cover.

"My love for books and learning led me to work in an academic library after taking an undergraduate degree in French, and in my mid-twenties I became interested in women's studies. Earning a graduate degree in the late 1970's made it possible to combine my vocation, librarianship, with my avocation, women's studies.

"My roles of wife, mother, and professional librarian have been the impetus for publishing works on dual-career families and women in management. I plan to continue using my library skills to research and write about women's issues."

AVOCATIONAL INTERESTS: Travel (France, England, Austria, Germany, Italy, Switzerland).

* * *

LEITHAUSER, Brad 1953-

PERSONAL: Born February 27, 1953, in Detroit, Mich.; son of Harold Edward (an attorney) and Gladys (a professor and author; maiden name, Garner) Leithauser; married Mary Jo Salter (a writer), August 2, 1980. *Education:* Harvard University, B.A., 1975, J.D., 1980.

ADDRESSES: Home—122 Elm Park, Pleasant Ridge, Mich. 48069. *Office*—c/o Knopf, Inc., 201 East 50th St., New York, N.Y. 10022.

CAREER: Poet, novelist. Kyoto Comparative Law Center, Kyoto, Japan, research fellow, 1980-83. Visiting writer, Amherst College, 1984-85. Lecturer, Mount Holyoke College, 1987-88.

AWARDS, HONORS: Academy of American Poets prize from Harvard University for best poems by an undergraduate, 1973, 1975; Lloyd McKim Garrison Prize for best poems by a Harvard University undergraduate, 1974, 1975; Amy Lowell travel scholarship in poetry, 1981-82; Guggenheim fellowship, 1982-83; National Book Critics Circle poetry nominations for *Hundreds of Fireflies,* 1982, and *Cats of the Temple,* 1986; Peter I. B. Lavan Younger Poets Award from Academy of American Poets, 1983; MacArthur Foundation research fellow, 1983-87.

WRITINGS:

Hundreds of Fireflies (poems), Knopf, 1982.
Equal Distance (novel), Knopf, 1985.
Cats of the Temple (poems), Knopf, 1986.
Between Leaps: Poems 1972-85, Oxford University Press, 1987.
Hence (novel), Knopf, 1989.

Contributor to periodicals and newspapers, including *New Yorker, Atlantic, New Republic,* and *New York Review of Books.*

WORK IN PROGRESS: A fourth volume of poetry.

SIDELIGHTS: Although formerly a lawyer, Brad Leithauser has more recently gained recognition as a poet and novelist. In just over one decade, Leithauser has become a notable figure on the American poetry scene. Two of his poetry collections, *Hundreds of Fireflies* and *Cats of the Temple,* were nominated for National Book Critics Circle awards in 1982 and 1986 respectively, and Leithauser's writing has already garnered an array of prestigious commendations, including the Peter I. B. Lavan Younger Poets Award from the Academy of American Poets and a MacArthur Foundation research fellowship. In the opinion of *New York Times* critic John Gross, Leithauser's *Cats of the Temple* makes it "clear that [Leithauser] is one of the most gifted American poets to have come over the horizon in years."

Reviewer descriptions of Leithauser's first poetry collection, *Hundreds of Fireflies,* include such adjectives as "meticulous," "mature," "calculated," "exhilarating," "exuberant," "sensuous," and "life-affirming." According to Bruce Bennett in the *New York Times Book Review,* the hallmark of *Hundreds of Fireflies* is "meticulous examination of particulars," like those found in nature—its landscapes, its creatures, its rebirths. In fact, various reviewers compare Leithauser's poetry to that of Marianne Moore, Elizabeth Bishop, and others. Helen Vendler notes in the *New York Review of Books* that Leithauser has "learned from Marianne Moore a form of compressed emblem description, from Elizabeth Bishop an unassuming visual scanning, from Robert Frost a love of rural scenes, from A. R. Ammons a telling use of modesty of voice, and from James Merrill a worldly form of narrative verse. These lessons have been assimilated beyond pastiche, on the whole, and have been brought into a tone distinguished by its mildness. Mildness is in fact Leithauser's chief personal form of stylization. Mild poets are rare." In addition, *Washington Post Book World* contributor Joel Conarroe believes Leithauser's poem "Giant Tortoise" is a homage to Moore while "Birches" is one to Frost. But *Hundreds of Fireflies* "is no mere echo chamber," assures Conarroe; "Leithauser has a distinctive voice, an altogether appealing one."

One aspect that sets Leithauser's *Hundreds of Fireflies* apart from most contemporary verse is its formal structure. Leithauser counts every syllable and employs complex rhyming schemes. In the *New Boston Review,* Sven Birkerts comments that *Hundreds of Fireflies* "is an overtly formal book.... Leithauser's work is proof that the heritage of formal verse is more arsenal than obstacle, that the problem, where there is a problem, lies not in the rigidity of the forms but in the rigidity of their user. Here is a clear case of a supple and subtle intellect deriving maximum benefit from its interaction with formal strictures. The maturity of these poems is to some extent derived from the maturity of poetic form itself." In a similar respect, *Poetry* critic Robert B. Shaw declares: "There must be very few poets as young as Leithauser in such absolute command of their instrument. In particular his handling of rhyme, sometimes in extremely intricate patterns, is remarkable in avoiding distortion of diction or syntax." Criticism of Leithauser's *Hundreds of Fireflies* is sparse and minor; on the whole, writes *New Leader* reviewer Phoebe Pettingell, "this is an exciting debut from an ambitious and brilliant poet."

A few years after *Hundreds of Fireflies,* Leithauser published his first novel, *Equal Distance.* Although considered by some reviewers to be short on plot and characterization, the book is nevertheless rich in detail, perceptions, and poetic prose. In the novel, protagonist Danny Ott takes a year off from his Harvard law studies to live in Japan. He goes there to assist a Japanese professor with a study on international law, but also to learn more of life. Kunio Francis Tanabe writes in the *Washington Post Book World* that *Equal Distance* is, "in many ways, a sequel to [a poem in *Hundreds of Fireflies*]—a young man's search for the big S (something, someone, somewhere)—and, as in the poem, the writing is sprightly, sprinkled throughout with wit and humor, and a delight to read.... As this first novel shows clearly, Leithauser is on the right track toward something BIG." The novel also impressed *New*

York Times critic Christopher Lehmann-Haupt. He calls *Equal Distance* a "remarkable first novel. For rarely does one come across a work of fiction so singular for the variety of pungent flavors it succeeds in conveying—the flavors of food, of drink, of travel, of nature, of friendship, of family, of youth, of love and most particularly of contemporary Kyoto, Japan.... It is the flavors of 'Equal Distance' that make it such a pleasure to read."

Equal Distance is additionally valued for its look at American culture via its expatriate theme. Although the book's setting is Japan, all of the book's main characters are American. Shortly after arriving in Kyoto, Danny encounters the witty, intelligent, but disillusioned Harvard graduate Greg Blaising, whom Tanabe describes as a "veteran expatriate bum.... [Greg has] ended up teaching English in Kyoto after failing to find nirvana in Mexico, Europe, Africa, India or Nepal." Danny subsequently meets and falls in love with a wealthy Ivy Leaguer named Carrie. According to Anatole Broyard in the *New York Times Book Review,* Carrie "camps out in other cultures. She is even less *present* in Japan, less responsive to it, than Greg. She has come there to exist *outside* of things.... In a foreign country it's unnecessary to feel love or pity becuase she can't perceive the connections that would create those emotions." According to Lehmann-Haupt, *Equal Distance* "leaves you with the sense that you've been touched by a whole new generation of young Americans—the post-1960's generation—children disillusioned with the sins of the American past, yet bent on overcoming them with the force of their intelligence and ambition." However, Darryl Pinckney, a critic for the *New York Review of Books,* does not sense this same move toward redressing the past. Rather, in Pinckney's opinion, "the novel is about Danny's acceptance of his parents' values, not his rejection of them, not even his challenge to them. His biggest worry in wooing Carrie is that he has only a middle-class background to offer. Despite its *Bildungsroman* tone, the novel is mostly a portrait of the acceptability of conventional class aspirations among the young."

Unlike *Hundreds of Fireflies, Equal Distance* failed to receive full-scale acceptance. In terms of evocation of place, Anne Tyler proclaims in her *New Republic* contribution that "most believable of all is the country that surrounds [Danny]. It's proof of the book's persuasiveness that from now on, if anyone asks me whether I've been to Japan, I'll be tempted to say yes." However, Pinckney questions: "Why Japan for this story of love and anxiety among the Doonesbury generation? Maybe it's just for the hip of being on location, so to speak.... Danny's courtship does not gain much from the exotic setting. He and his friends might as well have met at a sushi bar in Manhattan." Other complaints arise concerning characterization. D. D. Guttenplan maintains in *Village Voice:* "Danny Ott is an a—. This shouldn't matter—literature is rich with people you wouldn't want to invite over for dinner—but it does. Perhaps because Leithauser is trying so hard to be ingratiating, Ott's character becomes an issue. He's meant to be not just smart and successful but *sensitive* as well.... Without our affection, he just isn't interesting enough to carry the novel." Guttenplan furthers his stance by calling Danny a "naive prig, pompous bore, [and] neoconservative," which coincides with the opinion of Frank Gannon in the *Saturday Review.* In Gannon's mind, *Equal Distance* is "without a single appealing character, including the hero: the priggish, pedantic and tiresome Danny Ott." In the end, Guttenplan surmises: "If Leithauser is to improve as a novelist, he will have to learn that prose fiction is more than just poetry with the net down....

He will have to learn the hard lessons of structure and character and imagination. He is already an exceptional observer, but that isn't enough.'' For other reviewers, it is enough. Like Lehmann-Haupt and Tanable, *Los Angeles Times Book Review* critic Brian Stonehill finds the book ''excellent in itself and, as a first novel, an event.''

As previously noted, upon reading Leithauser's second poetry collection, *Cats of the Temple,* critic Gross professed Leithauser ''one of the most gifted American poets to have come over the horizon in years.'' In Gross's viewpoint, *Cats of the Temple* shows an extended range when compared to *Hundreds of Fireflies* and, as previously, the poet displays ''a keen delight in language, in disclosing its hidden recesses and its as-yet unrealized powers.... Leithauser's observations are wonderfully meticulous and precise. Whether he is evoking flora or fauna, landscapes or incidents, he will settle for nothing less than the distinctive gesture, the exact nuance.'' *Cats of the Temple* is similar to *Hundreds of Fireflies* in its nature studies, its frequent use of internal and external rhyme, and its polished, elaborate imagery. The setting of *Cats of the Temple* is more global, however, with several poems set in Japan, for instance.

Although *Cats of the Temple* is celebrated by some critics, it has not received praise across the board. According to some reviewers, Leithauser's meticulousness is more vice than virtue. *Washington Post Book World* contributor Bruce Bawer writes: ''Some of Leithauser's descriptions of nature are quite accomplished. Too often, though, there appears to be little or no real emotion beneath the highly polished surfaces.'' The poem ''Sea Horses,'' Bawer maintains, is a ''sparkling but largely soulless exercise in versification.... One comes away from [Leithauser's] poems impressed with his technical facility, but one *feels* nothing.'' In his *New York Times Book Review* article, Richard Tillinghast detects ''slightness and impersonality of material'' and D. J. Enright for *New Republic* believes Leithauser can ''irritate by a self-defeating overmeticulousness or finicky attenuation, or when the cleverness of how-it-is-said exceeds the cleverness of what-is-said, and the truth of imagination sinks into the embroidery of fancy.'' However, once this is said, Enright commends Leithauser for verse which contains ''enough to elicit jealous carping from fellow practitioners. He satisfies what he terms, in lines from 'Seaside Greetings,' 'our appetite for play at the stone heart of things.''' Finally, Vendler expresses both disapproval and delight for *Cats of the Temple* in her second *New York Review of Books* article. According to Vendler, Leithauser's poetry is too imitative of Marianne Moore's: ''If Leithauser did not adopt Marianne Moore's manner so strenuously one would read him in a less distracted way. One is often made so conscious of the perfectly mimicked model that the poem begins to seem a form of ventriloquism.'' At the same time, Vendler welcomes Leithauser's movement away from the confessional poetry of the 1960s and 1970s, and explains: ''What I find most interesting in Leithauser's work is . . . his investigation into his own kind of maleness, into the sort of man he is and would like to be. He often uses one of his symbolic animals as a way to write on both maleness and the enterprise of being an artist.'' According to Vendler, ''it is not clear what [Leithauser] will become when he sheds his dependency on Moore; he will still, I assume, have a self-effacing poetic, and it will be interesting to see how he embodies it next.''

BIOGRAPHICAL/CRITICAL SOURCES:

BOOKS

Contemporary Literary Criticism, Volume 27, Gale, 1984.

PERIODICALS

Detroit News, January 27, 1985.
Los Angeles Times Book Review, February 17, 1985.
Nation, April 12, 1986.
New Boston Review, June, 1982.
New Leader, May 3, 1982.
New Republic, April 14, 1982, January 21, 1985, October 27, 1986.
New Yorker, March 11, 1985.
New York Review of Books, September 23, 1982, May 29, 1986, October 23, 1986.
New York Times, January 3, 1985, March 21, 1986.
New York Times Book Review, March 14, 1982, December 30, 1984, July 13, 1986.
Poetry, December, 1982.
Saturday Review, March-April, 1985.
Times Literary Supplement, January 9, 1987, November 20, 1987.
Village Voice, April 23, 1985.
Washington Post Book World, February 21, 1982, January 13, 1985, March 26, 1986.

—*Sketch by Cheryl Gottler*

* * *

LEITHAUSER, Gladys Garner 1925-

PERSONAL: Born February 11, 1925, in Detroit, Mich.; daughter of Herbert Neil and Carolyn (Speer) Garner; married Harold E. Leithauser (a lawyer; died, 1985); children: Lance, Mark, Brad, Neil. *Education:* Wayne (now Wayne State) University, B.S., 1946, M.A., 1969, Ph.D., 1977. *Politics:* Democrat. *Religion:* Presbyterian.

ADDRESSES: Home—122 Elm Park, Pleasant Ridge, Mich. 48069. *Office*—Humanities Department, University of Michigan—Dearborn, 4901 Evergreen Rd., Dearborn, Mich. 48128.

CAREER: Detroit Institute of Cancer Research, Detroit, Mich., biochemistry research assistant, 1961-66; Highland Park Community College (now Highland Park College), Highland Park, Mich., teacher of English, 1967-68; Wayne State University, Detroit, Mich., member of English department faculty, 1969-77; University of Michigan—Dearborn, member of humanities department faculty, 1978—. Instructor, University of Michigan, Ann Arbor, 1987-88. Technical writer, Cleveland Institute of Electronics.

MEMBER: Detroit Women Writers.

AWARDS, HONORS: Wayne State University graduate fellow, 1972-74.

WRITINGS:

(With Lois Breitmeyer) *The Dinosaur Dilemma* (juvenile), Golden Gate Junior Books, 1964.
(With Breitmeyer) *The Rabbit Is Next,* Western Publishing, 1978.
(With Marilyn Powe Bell) *The World of Science: An Anthology for Writers* (instructor's manual available), Holt, 1987.
(Contributor) *Voices on Writing Fiction,* DWW Press, 1987.

Contributor of juvenile poems and short stories to magazines and to the electronic publishing program of Scott, Foresman & Co.; contributor of scholarly articles to *English Language Notes, Modern Fiction Studies, Russell: The Journal of the Bertrand Russell Archives,* and *English Journal.*

L'ESPERANCE, Wilford L(ouis) III   1930-1982

PERSONAL: Born December 9, 1930, in New York, N.Y.; died in 1982; son of Wilford L., Jr. (a clerk) and Marguerite (Destephen) L'Esperance; married Barbara Manochio, May 4, 1957 (died, January, 1977); children: Annette, Suzanne, Claire, Wilford IV. *Education:* Columbia University, A.B., 1951, M.S., 1952; University of Michigan, Ph.D., 1963.

ADDRESSES: Home—Columbus, Ohio. *Office*—Department of Economics, Ohio State University, Columbus, Ohio 43214.

CAREER: General Electric Co., New York, N.Y., and Fort Wayne, Ind., marketing research analyst, 1952-53, 1955-60, consultant, 1965; U.S. Army, Guided Missile Development Division, Ordnance Corps, Huntsville, Ala., mathematics analyst, 1953-55; University of Michigan, Department of Economics, Ann Arbor, research assistant, 1961-63; U.S. Department of the Interior, Bureau of Commercial Fisheries, Ann Arbor, economist, 1962-63, Sandusky, Ohio, consultant, 1963-65; Ohio State University, Columbus, assistant professor, 1963-66, associate professor, 1966-70, professor of economics, 1970-82, instructor in the executive development program of the division of continuing education, 1970-75; Midwest Econometrics, Inc., Columbus, president, 1973-79. Lecturer, Indiana University, 1956-60. Member, Ohio Governor's Task Force on Lake Erie Fishery, 1973-74; member, Population Study Group, Environmental Health Commission, Office of Comprehensive Health Planning, Ohio Department of Health, 1973-76; member of technical advisor group, Columbus Mayor's Economic Development Council, 1975. Economic advisor to John Glenn, Ohio Democratic candidate for the U.S. Senate, 1974.

MEMBER: American Economic Association, American Statistical Association (president of Columbus chapter, 1968), Econometric Society, Regional Science Association, New York State Society, Cincinnati Historical Society, Worthington Historical Society (Ohio), Hoover Yacht Club (trustee), Columbus Metro Club (trustee).

AWARDS, HONORS: Department of the Interior, Bureau of Commercial Fisheries grant, 1963-64; College Research Commission, College Commerce and Administration grant, 1965-66, College Social and Behavioral Sciences grant, 1969, 1976; Ohio Department of Development grant, 1967-68.

WRITINGS:

Modern Statistics for Business and Economics, Macmillan, 1971.
The Structure and Control of the State Economy, Methuen, 1981.

Also author, with others, of *Columbus Area Economy-Structure and Growth, 1950-85,* 1966. Associate editor of the *Journal of Regional Science,* 1978-82. Contributor to professional journals.*

*   *   *

LEVENTHAL, Lance A.   1945-

PERSONAL: Born November 29, 1945, in Victoria, British Columbia, Canada; came to the United States in 1951, naturalized in 1959; son of Max (in business) and Ruby (a secretary; maiden name, Cramer) Leventhal; married Donna Rosen, August 19, 1971; children: Elizabeth, Stacy. *Education:* Washington University, St. Louis, Mo., B.A., 1966; University of California, San Diego, M.S., 1969, Ph.D., 1973.

ADDRESSES: Home—P.O. Box 1258, Rancho Sante Fe, Calif. 92067. *Office*—Emulative Systems Co., 11722-D Sorrento Valley Rd., San Diego, Calif. 92121.

CAREER: Naval Electronic Laboratory, San Diego, Calif., scientist, 1972-73; I.R.T. Corp., San Diego, scientist, 1973-74, Linkabit Corp., San Diego, senior scientist, 1974-75; Emulative Systems Co., San Diego, computer consultant, 1975—. Consultant to Rockwell International, Anderson-Jackson, Disney, and Cordura Corp.

MEMBER: Institute of Electrical and Electronics Engineers, Association for Computing Machinery, Society for Computer Simulation, American Society for Engineering Education.

WRITINGS:

Introduction to Microprocessors: Software, Hardware, Programming, Prentice-Hall, 1978.
8080A/8085 Assembly Language Programming, Osborne (Berkeley, Calif.), 1978.
6800 Assembly Language Programming, Osborne, 1978.
The 6800 Microprocessor: A Self-Study Course with Applications, Hayden, 1978.
Z80 Assembly Language Programming, Osborne, 1979.
6502 Assembly Language Programming, Osborne/McGraw, 1979, 2nd edition, 1982.
(With Colin Walsh) *Microcomputer Experimentation with the Intel SDK-85,* Prentice-Hall, 1980.
(With Adam Osborne and Chuck Collins) *Z8000 Assembly Language Programming,* Osborne/McGraw, 1980.
6809 Assembly Language Programming, Osborne/McGraw, 1981.
Microcomputer Experimentation with the Motorola MEK6800D2, Prentice-Hall, 1981.
(With Irvin Stafford) *Why Do You Need a Personal Computer?,* Wiley, 1981.
(With Gerry Kane and Doug Hawkins) *68000 Assembly Language Programming,* Osborne/McGraw, 1981.
(With Winthrop Saville) *6502 Assembly Language Subroutines,* Osborne/McGraw, 1982.
Microcomputer Experimentation with the MOS Technology KIM-1, Prentice-Hall, 1982.
Microcomputer Experimentation with the Synertek SYM-1, Prentice-Hall, 1982.
(Editor) *Modeling and Simulation on Microcomputers,* Society for Computer Simulation, 1982.
(With Saville) *Z80 Assembly Language Subroutines,* Osborne/McGraw, 1983.
(With Saville) *8080/8085 Assembly Language Subroutines,* Osborne/McGraw, 1983.
(With Sally Cordes) *6809 Assembly Language Subroutines,* McGraw, 1985.
8086 Assembly Language Subroutines, McGraw, 1986.
(With Fred Cordes) *68000 Assembly Language Subroutines,* McGraw, 1987.
Microcomputer Experimentation with the Intel SDK-86, Holt, 1987.
Microcomputer Experimentation with the Rockwell AIM-65, Prentice-Hall, 1987.
Microcomputer Experimentation with the IBM PC, Holt, 1988.
80386 Programming Guide, Bantam, 1988.
Quick C Programmer's Guide, Bantam, 1988.
Microcomputer Experimentation with the Motorola MC68000ECB, Holt, 1988.

Contributor of more than sixty articles to computer magazines. Technical editor for Society for Computer Simulation, 1976-83, and for Consortium for Space/Terrestrial Automation and Robotics newsletter, 1987—. Series editor for personal computing, Prentice-Hall, 1982-85, and for computer science, Slawson Communications, 1986—. Contributing editor, *Digital Design*.

SIDELIGHTS: Lance A. Leventhal told *CA:* "Through both editing and writing, I continue to emphasize the development of computer books that are clearly written, interesting, enjoyable, technically accurate, and useful."

*   *   *

LIFTON, Betty Jean

PERSONAL: Born in New York, N.Y.; adopted daughter of Oscar and Hilda Kirschner; married Robert Jay Lifton (a professor of psychiatry), March 1, 1952; children: Kenneth Jay, Karen, Natasha. *Education:* Barnard College, B.A., 1948.

ADDRESSES: Agent—Berenice Hoffman, Berenice Hoffman Literary Agency, 215 West 75th St., New York, N.Y. 10023.

CAREER: Children's author, playwright, journalist, and biographer.

AWARDS, HONORS: New York Herald Tribune award, 1960, for *Kap the Kappa,* and 1970, for *Return to Hiroshima;* National Book Award nomination, 1975, for *Children of Vietnam.*

WRITINGS:

JUVENILES

Joji and the Dragon, illustrated by Eiichi Mitsui, Morrow, 1957.
Mogo the Mynah, illustrated by Anne Scott, Morrow, 1958.
Joji and the Fog, illustrated by Mitsui, Morrow, 1959.
Kap the Kappa (also see below), illustrated by Mitsui, Morrow, 1960.
The Dwarf Pine Tree, illustrated by Fuku Akino, Atheneum, 1963.
Joji and the Amanojaku, illustrated by Mitsui, Norton, 1965.
The Cock and the Ghost Cat, illustrated by Akino, Atheneum, 1965.
The Rice-Cake Rabbit, illustrated by Mitsui, Norton, 1966.
The Many Lives of Chio and Goro, illustrated by Yasuo Segawa, Norton, 1966.
Taka-Chan and I: A Dog's Journey to Japan, by Runcible, illustrated with photographs Eikoh Hosoe, Norton, 1967.
Kap and the Wicked Monkey, illustrated by Mitsui, Norton, 1968.
The Secret Seller, illustrated by Etienne Delessert, Norton, 1968.
The One-Legged Ghost (Junior Literary Guild selection), illustrated by Akino, Atheneum, 1968.
A Dog's Guide to Tokyo, illustrated with photographs by Hosoe, Norton, 1969.
Return to Hiroshima (Junior Literary Guild selection), illustrated with photographs by Hosoe, Atheneum, 1970.
The Mud Snail Son, illustrated by Akino, Atheneum, 1971.
The Silver Crane, illustrated by Laszlo Kubinyi, Seabury Press, 1971.
(With Thomas C. Fox) *Children of Vietnam,* Atheneum, 1972.
Good Night, Orange Monster, illustrated by Cyndy Szekeres, Atheneum, 1972.

Jaguar, My Twin, illustrated by Ann Leggett, Atheneum, 1976.

OTHER

"Moon Walk" (children's play), first produced on Broadway at City Center, November 26, 1970.
(Editor and contributor) *Contemporary Children's Theater* (includes "Kap the Kappa," an adaptation of her story), Avon, 1974.
Twice Born: Memoirs of an Adopted Daughter, McGraw-Hill, 1975.
Lost and Found: The Adoption Experience, Dial, 1979.
I'm Still Me (young adult), Knopf, 1981.
A Place Called Hiroshima, Kodansha, 1985.
The King of Children: A Biography of Janusz Korczak, Farrar, Straus, 1988.

Contributor to newspapers and periodicals.

SIDELIGHTS: Betty Jean Lifton is an author of books for and about children. Many of her stories are drawn from traditional Japanese folktales, reflecting her travels in the Far East. *The One-Legged Ghost,* for instance, tells of a strange creature with a round body, a single bamboo leg, paper-like skin, and forty wooden ribs that suddenly appears in an isolated mountain village. The tale has "simplicity, pathos, humor, and a barely perceptible comment on human nature," declares Jerome Beatty, Jr., in the *New York Times Book Review.* Other books by Lifton also draw on her experiences in the Orient—especially those that explore the lives of survivors of the Hiroshima atomic bomb and the children of the war-torn country of Vietnam. Sada Fretz of *Library Journal* calls *Return to Hiroshima* "a moving, eloquent account in words and pictures of the lingering effects of the first atomic bomb on survivors and families of victims."

Another aspect of the author's concern with children lies in her experience with adoption. Lifton sees the institution of legal adoption as a system built on pretense and deception, calling it in *Lost and Found: The Adoption Experience,* "The Game of As If." Her own experience as an adopted child, chronicled in *Twice Born: Memoir of an Adopted Daughter,* convinced her that the typical "identity crisis" of adolescence is complicated and prolonged by being adopted. "What [Lifton] didn't know, all wisdom to the contrary, *did* hurt her," writes Julia Whedon in the *New York Times Book Review.* "She worried about herself. She felt ashamed, counterfeit. She hid her doubts and feelings until they festered. To save herself she had to find herself; she began her own rescue at thirty." Whedon believes that Lifton "makes a very strong case for open access to adoption records and common cause with those relatively new private agencies organized to help others as Mrs. Lifton, independently and courageously, helped herself."

More recently, Lifton explores the impact of the Holocaust on children's lives in a biography of Janusz Korczak. "In 'The King of Children,'" reports Elie Wiesel in *Tribune Books,* "Betty Jean Lifton has recreated, with passion and generosity, the life of an extraordinary man who, until the end of his life, dreamed and worked only for his unfortunate children, and who lost his life hand-in-hand with the Jewish children he had tried to protect." Korczak was a Polish-Jewish educator whose writings and work with the orphans of the Warsaw ghettos broke with traditional views of family life. In 1942, during the Nazi occupation of Poland, Korczak and his charges were arrested and shipped to the Treblinka concentration camp, where they were all gassed. "Though Korczak's story has a melancholy ending, he lived a memorable and edifying life—one well worth a biography,'' declares Robert Coles in the *Los Angeles Times Book Review*. ''He was an exemplary intellectual and spiritual figure, and Betty Jean Lifton does a fine job of evoking his lively mind, his generous heart.''

BIOGRAPHICAL/CRITICAL SOURCES:

BOOKS

Lifton, Betty Jean, *Twice Born: Memoir of an Adopted Daughter,* McGraw-Hill, 1975.
Lifton, Betty Jean, *Lost and Found: The Adoption Experience,* Dial, 1979.

PERIODICALS

Library Journal, May 15, 1970.
Los Angeles Times Book Review, May 22, 1988.
New York Times Book Review, November 3, 1968, December 1, 1972, November 2, 1975, July 15, 1979, April 26, 1981.
Tribune Books (Chicago), May 1, 1988.
Washington Post Book World, April 22, 1979, June 19, 1988.

*   *   *

LIFTON, Robert Jay 1926-

PERSONAL: Born May 16, 1926, in Brooklyn, N.Y.; son of Harold A. (a businessman) and Ciel (Roth) Lifton; married Betty Jean Kirschner (a writer), March 1, 1952; children: Kenneth Jay, Karen, Natasha. *Education:* Attended Cornell University, 1942-44; New York Medical College, M.D., 1948.

ADDRESSES: Office—John Jay College, City University of New York, 444 West 56th St., New York, N.Y. 10019.

CAREER: Washington School of Psychiatry, Washington, D.C., and Hong Kong, member of faculty, 1954-55; Harvard University, Cambridge, Mass., research associate in psychiatry, 1956-61; Yale University, New Haven, Conn., associate professor, 1961-67, professor of psychiatry, beginning 1967, Foundations' Fund for Research in Psychiatry, research professor, beginning 1967; affiliated with John Jay College, City University of New York. Gay Lecturer, Harvard Medical School, 1976; Messenger Lecturer, Cornell University, 1980. Research psychiatrist, Walker Reed Army Institute of Research, 1956; research associate in psychiatry, Massachusetts General Hospital, 1956-61, Tokyo University, 1960-61; candidate, Boston Psychoanalytic Institute, 1957-60; affiliated with Mt. Sinai Medical Center. Organizer of redress group opposing Vietnam War, International Atomic Energy Agency, Vienna, Austria, 1975. Member, Council on East Asian Studies, Yale University, 1964—. Consultant to behavioral studies study section, National Institute of Mental Health, 1962-64, to New York Bar Association Committee on the Invasion of Privacy, 1963-64, to Columbia seminars on modern Japan and Oriental thought and religion, 1965—, to Arnold and Porter concerning 1972 Buffalo Flood Creek disaster, 1973-74, and to Harmon and Weiss and David Berger, P.A., on psychological effects of 1979 Three Mile Island nuclear accident. *Military service:* U.S. Air Force, 1951-53; became captain.

MEMBER: American Psychiatric Association (fellow), Group for the Advancement of Psychiatry, Association for Asian Studies, American Anthropological Association, American Association for the Advancement of Science, American Academy of Arts and Sciences (fellow), Group for the Study of Psychohistorical Process (coordinator), American Academy of Psychoanalysis, Physicians for Social Responsibility, Medical Committee for Human Rights.

AWARDS, HONORS: National Book Award for sciences, and Van Wyck Brooks Award for nonfiction, both 1969, for *Death in Life: Survivors of Hiroshima;* public service award, New York Society of Clinical Psychologists, and Alumni Medal, New York Medical College, both 1970; D.Sc., Lawrence University, 1971, and Merrimack College, 1973; Karen Horney Lecture Award, Association for the Advancement of Psychoanalysis, 1972; distinguished service award, Society for Adolescent Psychology, 1972; Mount Airy Foundation Gold Medal for excellence in psychiatry, 1973; National Book Award nomination, 1974, for *Home from the War: Vietnam Veterans— Neither Victims nor Executioners;* Hiroshima Gold Medal, 1975; D.H.L., Wilmington College, 1975, New York Medical College, 1977, Marlboro College, 1983, Maryville College, 1983; Guggenheim fellowship, 1983; Gandhi Peace Award, 1984; Bertrand Russell Society award, 1985; *Los Angeles Times* Book Prize for history, 1987, for *The Nazi Doctors: Medical Killing and the Psychology of Genocide.*

WRITINGS:

Thought Reform and the Psychology of Totalism: A Study of ''Brainwashing'' in China, Norton, 1961.
Death in Life: Survivors of Hiroshima, Random House, 1968.
Revolutionary Immortality: Mao Tse-Tung and the Chinese Cultural Revolution, Random House, 1968.
Birds, Words and Birds (cartoons), Random House, 1969.
History and Human Survival: Essays on the Young and the Old, Survivors and the Dead, Peace and War, and on Contemporary Psychohistory, Random House, 1970.
Boundaries, Canadian Broadcasting Corp. (Toronto), 1969, published as *Boundaries: Psychological Man in Revolution,* Random House, 1970.
Home from the War: Vietnam Veterans—Neither Victims nor Executioners, Simon & Schuster, 1973, reprinted, Basic Books, 1985.
(With Eric Olson) *Living and Dying,* Praeger, 1974.
The Life of the Self: Toward a New Psychology, Simon & Schuster, 1976.
Psychobirds, Countryman Press, 1978.
(With Shuichi Kato and Michael Reich) *Six Lives/Six Deaths: Portraits from Modern Japan* (originally published in Japanese as *Nihonjin no shiseikan,* 1977), Yale University Press, 1979.
The Broken Connection: On Death and the Continuity of Life, Simon & Schuster, 1979.
(With Richard A. Falk) *Indefensible Weapons: The Political and Psychological Case against Nuclearism,* Basic Books, 1982.
The Nazi Doctors: Medical Killing and the Psychology of Genocide, Basic Books, 1986.
The Future of Immortality and Other Essays for a Nuclear Age, Basic Books, 1987.

EDITOR

The Woman in America, Houghton, 1965.
America and the Asian Revolutions, Trans-Action Books, 1970, 2nd edition, 1973.
(With Falk and Gabriel Kolko) *Crimes of War: A Legal, Political-Documentary, and Psychological Inquiry into the Responsibilities of Leaders, Citizens, and Soldiers for Criminal Acts of War,* Random House, 1971.
(With Olson) *Explorations in Psychohistory: The Wellfleet Papers,* Simon & Schuster, 1975.

(With Eric Chivian, Susanna Chivian, and John E. Mack) *Last Aid: The Medical Dimensions of Nuclear War*, W. H. Freeman, 1982.

(With Nicholas Humphrey) *In a Dark Time: Images for Survival*, Harvard University Press, 1984.

OTHER

Contributor of articles and reviews to *New York Times Book Review, New York Times Magazine, New York Review of Books, Atlantic Monthly, Daedalus, Transaction/Society, American Scholar, New Republic, Partisan Review,* and to *American Journal of Psychiatry, Psychiatry,* and other professional journals in the fields of psychiatry, psychology, history, and Asian studies.

SIDELIGHTS: Robert Jay Lifton "is an indefatigable author with a lively sense of history and a considerable capacity for assimilating and reordering huge amounts of information," declares Anthony Storr in the *Washington Post Book World.* "What chiefly interests him," the reviewer continues, "is the reaction of human beings to extreme situations." Outstanding among his interests is the question of how people come to terms with mortality—how they face death individually and collectively. "Whether grappling with the experience of mass destruction suffered by the survivors of Hiroshima, with nuclear weapons' potential for genocide, or with the adverse emotional sequelae in American veterans of the Vietnamese war," states Sidney Bloch in the *Times Literary Supplement,* "Lifton has steadfastly striven to comprehend the seemingly incomprehensible."

Lifton studies these questions using the techniques of psychohistory, a discipline that *New York Times* contributor Christopher Lehmann-Haupt defines as an "endeavor to define how individual human behavior interacts with the historical currents of a given age." This discipline found its modern form in the work of psychologist Erik Erikson, whose biographies *Young Man Luther: A Study in Psychoanalysis and History* and *Gandhi's Truth: On the Origins of Militant Nonviolence* broke new ground by integrating history and psychology in order to understand historical figures in the context of their times. Although Lifton's own work also attempts to understand history through the application of psychoanalysis, it differs from that of Erikson because it concentrates not on influential individuals who affect history, but rather on the historical processes that impact on the individual.

Psychohistory is not universally accepted by historians as a discipline in its own right. Lehmann-Haupt declares in a review of Lifton's psychohistorical *History and Human Survival* that "as Lifton points out, the two [areas of study] have been traditionally opposed to the degree 'that psychoanalysis seeks to eliminate history, and history seeks to eliminate psychological man.'" This is not reasonable, Lehmann-Haupt claims; after all, "no individual is free of history and no history is free of individuals." Instead, Lifton suggests that history and psychology complement each other. In a different review—of *Home from the War: Vietnam Veterans—Neither Victims nor Executioners*—Lehmann-Haupt states, "What is provocative about Dr. Lifton's long, complex study [are] . . . the conclusions he draws that even in contemporary situations, history and psychology cannot be separated, and that therefore psychiatrists must henceforth take history into account when treating their patients—not only history as it relates to the patient, but also as it relates to the therapist."

Death in Life: Survivors of Hiroshima, Lifton's award-winning study of the psychoses and behavior patterns of the more than ninety thousand survivors of the atom bomb dropped on the city at the close of the Second World War, uses psychohistorical methods to understand the impact the bomb had on the people who survived it—called *hibakusha,* or "explosion-affected persons," in Japanese. All survivors, Lifton found, share feelings of a close association with catastrophe and a feeling of guilt at having survived, coupled with a profound death-wish. In a *New York Times* article entitled "On the Nuclear Altar," Lifton explains the *hibakusha*'s reactions more fully: "But their basic feeling was that they had been made into historical guinea pigs—had been victimized by a weapon so new, powerful, and mysterious that its effects could not be known until it had been 'tried' on a particular population. One survivor put the matter bitterly: 'There exist no words in any human language that can comfort guinea pigs who do not know the cause of their death.'" "Perhaps [*Death in Life*'s] most significant message," suggests Jerome D. Frank in the *New York Times Book Review,* "is that the long-term psychological crippling of survivors, and the profound societal disruption caused by a nuclear attack, are at least as severe a threat to the continued existence of organized society as the extent of biological and physical destruction."

Lifton sees the possibility of nuclear holocaust as a significant factor in modern concepts of life and death. Emile Capouya in *Saturday Review* says of *Boundaries,* a series of essays focussing on this theme, "The possibility that civilization and life itself may be ended, deliberately or accidentally, through the exercise of our scientific and technical powers, has been present to us all through the modern period and has given rise at last to a real crisis of morale, of the animal faith that we must have if we are to carry on." Although people have always had to face their own mortality, Capouya states, "even those persons who had had no revelation about a universal resurrection . . . might hope to survive biologically, through their children, or spiritually, through their contribution to human culture and history." Now, they may no longer have that option. David Gates, writing in *Newsweek* about a later Lifton book, *The Future of Immortality,* has a parallel view; Lifton's theory, he says, is "that we all yearn for immortality, whether in an afterlife or in the idea that we live on through our children—or simply humankind. The threat of nuclear holocaust, therefore, has done unique psychic damage." One symptom of this damage, Gates states, is the behavior of many young adults who are preparing for marriage and children yet doubting that they will live that long. "Traditional apocalyptic visions, says Lifton, at least saw the end of the world as redemptive," declares Gates; "nuclear self-immolation doesn't even offer that cold comfort."

One way people deal with a profound psychic disturbance such as nuclear devastation, Lifton has found, is through the device he calls "psychic numbing" or "psychic closing-off." "Human beings, Lifton observes, 'are unable to remain open to emotional experience of this intensity for any length of time, and very quickly—sometimes within minutes—there began to occur what we may term psychic closing-off; that is, people simply ceased to feel,'" explains Henry S. Resnik in *Saturday Review.* Many of the Hiroshima *hibakusha* exhibit psychic numbing, and Lifton observed similar symptoms in Jewish survivors of Nazi Germany, in the veterans of the Vietnam War, and in student rebels in the West—all victims of an emotional overload.

Doctors in the Nazi concentration camps, Lifton has found, underwent a similar process. Lifton's study *The Nazi Doctors: Medical Killing and the Psychology of Genocide* asks the question, "How did doctors, devoted to relieving human suffering, justify the treatment of the Jews incarcerated in the camps?" The book shows that there were several factors responsible. In Germany at the time the Nazi party came to power, there was already a concept of "racial purity" that, combined with radical concepts of "euthanasia," helped lead to an organized extermination of the Jews. Doctors, says Neal Ascherson in the *New York Review of Books,* were envisioned as "biological soldiers," fighting to preserve the purity of the state. They "were invited to see their task as a supreme expression of medical responsibility, its value only emphasized by the fact that most doctors initially found it difficult to carry out—and some found it impossible." Another attitude, used to justify experimentation on living bodies, was that the prisoners were "in practice already dead by virtue of their presence in camp"; they could therefore be regarded simply as very fresh cadavers.

When actually faced with the horrors of giving injections and choosing people for experimentation, the doctors resorted to "psychic numbing," usually accomplished by means of heavy drinking, and a technique that Lifton calls "doubling"—the temporary formation of another self in order to adapt to the extreme conditions of the camp. Michael R. Marrus states in the Toronto *Globe and Mail* about *The Nazi Doctors,* "Lifton's analysis is unsettling because he concludes that the mechanisms used by the most grotesque experimenters and killers are much more common than we might like to admit. In particular, we may have invented an entire era of 'doubling' by living with and using the threat of nuclear weaponry. Reflecting on our common humanity, the example set throughout this remarkable work may be our only hope."

These means of adapting to the thought of ultimate destruction has resulted in the emergence of a psychological type that Lifton calls Protean Man. "In 'Protean Man' Lifton advances, with admirable conciseness, the idea that various conditions of contemporary life are contributing to the emergence of a new kind of man," explains Resnik. "The two principal historical developments Lifton cites are 'historical . . . dislocation, the break in the sense of connection which men have long felt with the vital and nourishing symbols of their cultural tradition,' and 'the flooding of imagery produced by the extraordinary flow of post-modern cultural influences over mass-communication networks.'" "It is simply impossible, in short," he concludes, "to hold on to an identity or a world these days—youngsters who grew up with television scarcely know how to try—and the only acceptable alternative, not necessarily an evil one, is to live life as 'an interminable series of experiments and explorations.'" "By means of the modern information media, Protean Man can be everywhere, experience everything," asserts Anthea Lahr in *Nation.* "The phenomena that created and nurtured him are still present and, healthy or pathological, to be Protean is still a survival tactic."

Lifton's strongly expressed opinions and analyses of these processes have aroused considerable controversy among critics. A reviewer for the *Chicago Tribune Book World* remarks of *Indefensible Weapons: The Political and Psychological Case against Nuclearism,* "For all [the authors'] interesting insights, they are so transparently polemical that they provoke the reader's defenses rather than penetrate them." Gates sees Lifton's work as "supercritical when he starts exhorting." And Richard Locke, writing in the *New York Times Book Review* about *Home from the War,* declares, "The book lacks the sensitive precision that gave tragic power to much of his first work, 'Totalism and the Psychology of Thought Reform,' where he was scrupulously attentive to individual experience and moved from

the particular to the general with great care." However, other critics disagree with these assessments. Resnik, writing about *History and Human Survival,* maintains, "Whatever his method or its inconsistencies, Lifton has superb talent as a journalist; there is virtually no psychohistorical content in his description of a week's visit to Vietnam, but the essay, which stands somewhat apart from the rest, is a bitingly understated indictment of the American presence in Southeast Asia, and is worthwhile reading in any context." Frank calls *Death in Life* "an impressive, trail-breaking contribution in describing and conceptualizing the experience of surviving a taste of man's nuclear war on his own species—an experience which may fall to the lot of everyone alive today."

While Lifton's arguments may prove controversial to some readers, others see justification in his stance. "His subjects are too morally and mythically fraught to afford him the luxury of scientific detachment," asserts *Village Voice* contributor Mark Caldwell. "They've led him to redefine psychological paradigms, pushing them ever further toward ethics." "Lifton is trying to persuade us that we are living in mortal sin. Some of us may not feel the guilt, but that is because we have been numbed," contends Locke. The author, states the reviewer, feels he must cure us out of our moral numbness. "Lifton argues that what we have to feel . . . is what he calls 'animating guilt,'" says Locke, "a sense that one has violated ultimate moral boundaries; that one must analyze the personal and social forces that led one into sin; that one must come to terms with these facts and then not merely go and sin no more but expose to all mankind the falsity of guiltlessness, the hypocrisy and deathliness of the current social order; and finally that one must exhort one's fellow man to confess his sins and convert to 'Protean' nonviolence."

CA INTERVIEW

CA interviewed Robert Jay Lifton by telephone on September 15, 1987, at his home on Cape Cod, Massachusetts.

CA: Would it be accurate to say that your study of Hiroshima survivors, which resulted in the 1968 book Death in Life, *was a turning point in your personal and professional life?*

LIFTON: Yes, it would. I had been interested in nuclear weapons issues prior to going to Hiroshima. I had, in fact, belonged to a small informal group at Harvard concerned with these matters. But going to Hiroshima, living there for six months, interviewing survivors, and then writing my book on Hiroshima all changed me in ways that were quite powerful.

CA: You were studying to be a psychoanalyist before that, weren't you?

LIFTON: I was already a psychiatrist and had residency work. Prior to *Death in Life,* I had written *Thought Reform and the Psychology of Totalism: A Study of "Brainwashing" in China,* so I was already doing research involving psychology in history. But the Hiroshima work was different from anything I had undertaken. What I subsequently wrote, and what I believe to be true, is that when you take something like Hiroshima seriously, when you let it in, so to speak, to your own imagination, you take on survivor-like emotions and a responsibility to that event. That's the way I felt. Once I had lived in Hiroshima for six months and done that work interviewing survivors, it simply remained with me as a fundamental set of images and a source of much that I've done afterwards.

CA: What made you decide to undertake the study of the Hiroshima tragedy?

LIFTON: I had gone to Japan earlier for other reasons, to study Japanese youth and the relationship of individual psychology and historical change as reflected by Japanese youth. But I was, as I said before, part of that small informal group around the sociologist David Riesman at Harvard, and we had begun to think about some of the nuclear weapons-related issues that were active at that time, in the late '50s, including extensive shelter building and certain ethical questions that arose in connection with shelters. Riesman was the main figure in putting out a small newsletter, and a few of us wrote pieces for that newsletter. So I had some interest in the subject in a very preliminary way, enough to lead me to go on what I though would be a visit of a few days to Hiroshima, just to look into what I could of the atomic bombing there. When I got there—this was in April, 1962—I realized quickly from talking to people there that nobody had studied the general human effects of the atomic bomb, the psychological and social effects. People had studied the physical after-effects, but that was quite different. I was very impressed by the absence of any such study. Since I had done some work before on Chinese thought reform and the whole subject of extreme situations, I felt I would be able to do such a study. The combination of my earlier interest and my surprising discovery that nobody had studied that question led me to make arrangements to stay. I was just then beginning my work at Yale; I had been given a chair there and was able to write to my colleagues and arrange for funds to do some research and arrange to stay in Japan for six months.

CA: Did you already have some knowledge of Japanese, so that you could interview the survivors?

LIFTON: Yes. I've never been a bona fide Japanologist; I've never been really fluent in Japanese. But, in connection with the work on Japanese youth, I had spent some months studying the Japanese language rather intensively, and I could understand quite a bit of it. Although I always used an interpreter in my interviews, the knowledge I did have of Japanese helped a great deal. For instance, I selected research subjects randomly from a list that was given to me at the University of Hiroshima. I would pay a visit to most of them in their homes, together with a Japanese social worker, and I could chat with them in a limited way in Japanese—explain to them why I wanted to interview them, and invite them to come see me in a little office I set up in the middle of Hiroshima. This way I was able at least to give them a feeling of my interest in their culture and their experience.

CA: It seems that there would be a lot of interest in following up on what's happened to those people since you talked with them.

LIFTON: I don't know that anyone has ever done that in any fully systematic way, but I have made a number of visits back to Hiroshima since the original study in 1962, and in 1975 I went back there with Robert Voss, who made a film for BBC that was an adaptation of *Death in Life*. I was able to find some of the people I had originally interviewed thirteen years before and to interview them again on camera. That was just a series of impressions, not a systematic study, but to that extent I was able to get a sense of what had happened to them in the intervening years.

CA: Since the after-effects of the bombing can go through more than one generation, I imagine we won't know all of them for some time.

LIFTON: That's the fear. It's known, first of all, that radiation effects can appear decades later in people who seemed perfectly all right earlier. That's been shown by studies that have been continued in Hiroshima. It's also known that radiation effects can be transmitted to subsequent generations. The systematic studies comparing populations don't show any definite increase in radiation effects in the next generation, but it's impossible to guarantee that there won't be such effects. When I went there five or six years ago, one man who was rather close to the problem put the matter in a very clear and poignant way when he said to me, "It looks as though the second generation is OK, but we don't know about the third generation." The fear is endless.

CA: You have been working in psychohistory for some time. How did it begin?

LIFTON: I became interested in the psychological approach to historical questions long before we used the term "psychohistory." I conducted my first study, the one I did in the mid-'50s on Chinese thought reform, in Hong Kong, interviewing people coming out of the mainland. I sensed very quickly in doing that study that, in order to understand their experience in being put through an emotionally and sometimes physically pressured process of so-called thought reform, so-called brainwashing, I had to understand a lot about Chinese history and the Chinese Communist Revolution and much about Chinese culture. As I began to try to put together psychological and historical matters, I was influenced by the work of Erik Erikson, who had done something like that in developing ideas about individual and collective identity. I've been concerned about psychology and history ever since. Over the years, the name psychohistory has emerged, but that really means simply a psychological approach to historical questions.

CA: How do you differ with Erikson in approach to psychohistory? His concentration, I believe, is mainly on the great man in history.

LIFTON: That's right. For instance, in his two great psychobiographies, of Luther and Gandhi, his approach is to look at the life of a man who brought about a significant change in our sense of what it is to be human, and how one could understand the interaction of the man and his times—how the inner struggles of the great individual coincide with the struggles of large numbers of people of that era, and how, in solving those questions for himself, he solves them for a large collectivity. That's the so-called "great person in history" approach. What I've done is to modify that somewhat and look at groups of people who have been through or helped create certain historical events of great importance. That approach I call "shared themes." That's what I did in Hiroshima, and I also did that in another way in my more recent work *The Nazi Doctors*. In one study I did, a short book called *Revolutionary Immortality*, I combined both approaches by looking at Mao Tse-Tung's life and also the Cultural Revolution, how Mao's personal struggles were interwoven with shared themes in Chinese Communist society. But by and large I've used the shared themes approach rather than the great man, or great person, approach.

CA: It must have been extremely difficult emotionally for you to work on The Nazi Doctors. *Were there specific findings you expected to make in your examination?*

LIFTON: Before I undertook the study, I did a lot of reading and I began to realize that the doctors were a much more important group in perpetrating the Holocaust than people realized. But I wasn't sure what I would find. I wanted to learn more about just what they did, how they did it, and how individual doctors reversed the healing commitment. In undertaking the study, I was concerned about the reversal of healing and killing. But I didn't know exactly how that had come about. It was demanding and often quite difficult, but it was also very rewarding to complete the study.

CA: Would you talk about ''doubling,'' the term you invented and used to explain one of the key ways doctors were able to do their work at Auschwitz and the other concentration camps?

LIFTON: Yes. I believe that concept helps us a great deal to understand how Nazi doctors could do what they did and how other people could participate in genocide. I probably invented the term, at least in the way that I've used it, but there are precedents for it. There's an important book written in the 1920s by Otto Rank, a gifted psychoanalyst, called *The Double,* based mainly on German Romantic literature. In that he talked about a kind of inner division which was reflected not only in German literature but literature throughout the world, though he concentrated on German literature. In addition to that, in interviewing Nazi doctors and in probing their behavior through other sources—studying trial records and talking to various people who knew them and so on—I realized that in the killings at Auschwitz or in so-called ''euthanasia,'' which always has to have quotes around it when it's used to mean killing mental patients or other people deemed incurable, there really was formed a second self; or a portion of the self would act as though it were an independent self involved with the killing and the rationale for killing, so that a Nazi doctor at Auschwitz would adjust to the Auschwitz environment and form an Auschwitz self while at the same time he would retain his prior self when he went back and visited his family outside and was again a father and a husband. I've tried to develop the concept as to how it might help explain what Nazi doctors did. I would add that it isn't only the doubling that explains it, however. You need the extreme ideology of the Nazis to promote the process and to create the killing institutions like Auschwitz. But doubling is a mechanism by which they could do it.

CA: Weren't the Nazi doctors somewhat reluctant to talk with you about what they had done? Weren't they ashamed?

LIFTON: I wish I had encountered more shame—or more *overt* shame—or guilt in them. I was somewhat surprised at their willingness to talk to me, but I would have to explain that. I had to approach them very carefully and indirectly. Something in them wanted to talk, wanted to explore things, but never fully, never with a complete moral confrontation. It was rather more characteristic for them to explore things with me in a way that would find justification or, in many cases, to convey to me a sense of themselves as people who were caught up in a very difficult situation and behaved as well as they could. That isn't the way I understood them to be at all, but that was partly their motivation in agreeing to see me. And some arrangements were made indirectly through German physicians and scholars who were very committed to helping me in my research, and who did so through introductions and through helping to sponsor my work. It was done very carefully and with considerable help.

CA: In your essay ''Dreaming Well: Frontiers of Form,'' collected in The Future of Immortality, *you report a conversation that you had with an Auschwitz survivor, in which you told him that you had many nightmares and he said they were a sign that your work was getting beyond the intellectual stage.*

LIFTON: What he said was more cryptic: ''Good. Now you can do the work.'' That seemed to me exactly right. What I was trying to illustrate in telling that story in the essay is that dreams reflect one's immersion in experiences. In this case, one *has* to have bad dreams if one is sufficiently immersed to convey in depth something of what happened. You need that immersion and, if you have that immersion, you're going to dream about it.

CA: You've said that throughout your studies you have tried constantly to employ Martin Buber's rule of ''imagining the real.'' That reminded me of St. Ignatius Loyola's urging that we should picture the horrors of hell to the extent of seeing flames and smelling burning flesh. So many of us understand Hiroshima or Auschwitz only in an intellectual way.

LIFTON: Buber meant ''imagining the real,'' as I understand it, very broadly, in terms of any kind of authenticity we have to imagine our way into experience, into events. I think the Loyola example you've mentioned is getting closer. What that seems to say is that, if you're to be a genuinely moral or spiritual person, you have to be able to imagine evil, because evil is real in our world. I feel this quite strongly in a secular sense, but it's very parallel to the religious equivalent and is, though I call it secular, a spiritual sense in every meaning of that word. There is a lot of evil in the twentieth century, and a great deal of it very recent. I think we can extricate ourselves from that evil only by first allowing our imaginations to take it in so that we can then transcend it by wise decisions, at least to some degree. But that can't be done without taking it in.

CA: You have *taken it in. For many of us, it would be overpowering and would perhaps lead to suicide or just giving up on life in some other way. Obviously there are lessons to be learned from dealing with it the way you have.*

LIFTON: Yes. I think what has happened is that, by having developed a combination of personal commitment to combating some of these destructive forces on the one hand and, on the other, a certain professional approach which I try to make as rigorous and systematic as possible, it has become right for me—putting it in the most simple but the most accurate language I know—to pursue this path. It has become part of my sense of myself, my identity. It's not just a matter of courage or even exclusively morality; it has to do with an inner sense of what's right for me to do. That's what took me to the study of the Nazi doctors, which obviously involved some great difficulties and a lot of pain. But if one can struggle to find what is right for one, I'm sure it's what, in religious terms, is meant by a calling. Then one can follow it, precisely because it does feel right, and one can move into very difficult areas.

CA: Throughout your studies the reader finds a compelling interest in symbols and myths. Have you drawn a lot from the writings of Jung?

LIFTON: I've been interested in Jung right along, and I've learned a lot from him. But he's not a central part of my intellectual formation. It's partly just a matter of what has happened to form one intellectually, which is in my case more a sequence of Freud and Erikson with a great influence from Otto Rank. But Jung has been very valuable to me too because of his early interest in symbolization as such and his interest in the self and in collective behavior.

CA: You have talked with many Vietnam veterans and have written about them in the 1973 book Home from the War. *Since that war, there's been a feeling among the veterans that they have been ignored. Have such recent initiatives as the building of the monument in Washington called* The Wall *made Vietnam veterans feel more appreciated?*

LIFTON: Vietnam is another one of those searing events that never fully leaves you once you become seriously involved in it—nor should it. In my new introduction to my book on Vietnam, which has been reissued, I said that The Wall is, to me, a perfect symbol of that war; and I think it's a beautiful and very poignant monument that has meant a great deal to veterans because it's so simple and makes no pretense of heroic dimensions but has appropriate quietude, one might say. I think there has been a series of commendable efforts to recognize the pain and losses, the sacrifices, that Vietnam veterans have made, and I've been very sympathetic to those. The difficulty is that some groups have sought to combine that very worthy enterprise with a revisionist view that seeks to justify the war as a noble American enterprise. That seems to me all wrong and a very misbegotten approach. And sometimes it's hard to sort out these two things—the honoring of the veterans, which is necessary and right, and the attempt to revise the American sense of the war and render it a noble enterprise, which I think is wrong and dangerous.

On the question of just how much these efforts have helped the veterans, it's hard to judge. The main monument in Washington and other monuments elsewhere have made a difference to them. It's been a long time now. A lot of veterans are in national office, and moving into the society at various levels. And I think there is a growing sense among them of being recognized and appreciated. That's the general trend, though there are many exceptions and there's still a lot of pain and psychological conflict in many Vietnam veterans. But I think the vast outreach program has been very commendable. I think it's had a very good response. And I think that, by and large, veterans have felt further recognition of a kind that they have needed.

CA: Although you spend much of your time in research and writing, you still apparently feel that it's very important to take an active, even militant stand on such issues as disarmament and civil rights.

LIFTON: That's true. I'm a very dedicated scholar. I spend a lot of hours in my study, I've written a lot of books and papers, and I try to be as scholarly and as accurate as I can be. But I don't think that precludes taking an active stand in one's own culture in favor of those things that one believes in and against those things that one thinks are dangerous and awful to human beings in general. So I have been an activist in various ways at various times. I've been very active in the doctors' antinuclear movement and hope to continue to be. I was very active in the anti-Vietnam War protest movement. It happens that in recent years I've focused very intensely on writing and,

though I've taken public stands, I haven't been quite as active as perhaps I had been before. I find that my life, as I suppose must be true of the lives of many people like me, has its own rhythms. This is a phase where I'm focusing a lot on writing, but on issues that are related to these moral and political questions on which I have been active.

CA: That's true of the book you're writing now, isn't it?

LIFTON: Yes. It's a book that tries to look at the Nazi Holocaust in terms of the lessons it might have for us in regard to nuclear threat.

CA: Do you think more and more people are taking an active interest in the nuclear threat?

LIFTON: There's no doubt about it. Even though our nuclear policies haven't changed as much as one would have hoped, it has been recorded by various surveys and polls that there's been a significant and gratifying increase in awareness of nuclear danger, and an increasing conviction on the part of Americans in general that something should be done. Americans disagree on *what* should be done, and they're still deeply concerned about the Russians, but nonetheless there's been a marked increase in the last decade or so in interest in nuclear weapons issues and of opposition to at least an unrestricted arms race. That was of course reflected in the freeze movement and in other elections. Now the near-signing of at least one form of nuclear weapons treaty is a reflection of that trend. There are many things involved in that, including the needs of both leaders involved. But it also reflects an increasing recognition that has to be, at a certain point, a political recognition that the American people want something like this.

MEDIA ADAPTATIONS: Death in Life: Survivors of Hiroshima was adapted for BBC-TV by Richard Voss in 1975.

AVOCATIONAL INTERESTS: Tennis, films, and cartooning.

BIOGRAPHICAL/CRITICAL SOURCES:

BOOKS

Erikson, Erik, *Young Man Luther: A Study in Psychoanalysis and History,* Norton, 1958.
Erikson, Erik, *Gandhi's Truth: On the Origins of Militant Nonviolence,* Norton, 1968.
Rank, Otto, *Der Doppelgaenger: Eine Psychoanalytische Studie,* Internationaler Psychoanalytischer Verlag, 1925, translation by Harry Tucker, Jr., published as *The Double: A Psychoanalytic Study,* University of North Carolina Press, 1971.

PERIODICALS

Chicago Tribune Book World, October 24, 1982, December 12, 1982.
Globe and Mail (Toronto), November 1, 1986.
Harper's Magazine, February, 1983.
Los Angeles Times Book Review, January 24, 1980, September 9, 1984, October 12, 1986, October 18, 1987, November 8, 1987, March 20, 1988.
Nation, May 6, 1968, November 9, 1970.
Newsweek, February 19, 1968, October 7, 1968, June 18, 1973, March 2, 1987.
New York Review of Books, March 25, 1968, January 16, 1969, June 28, 1973, October 31, 1974, May 28, 1987.
New York Times, September 30, 1968, February 6, 1970, August 6, 1973, July 26, 1979, November 4, 1979, March

1, 1981, March 28, 1981, April 13, 1981, March 15, 1982, September 25, 1986.

New York Times Book Review, March 31, 1968, August 2, 1970, December 6, 1970, June 24, 1973, December 2, 1973, March 10, 1974, July 21, 1974, November 4, 1979, November 25, 1979, July 27, 1980, March 1, 1981, October 10, 1982, December 26, 1982, January 16, 1983, December 18, 1983, February 17, 1985, October 5, 1986, April 5, 1987, March 20, 1988.

Partisan Review, winter, 1968.

Publishers Weekly, November 7, 1986.

Saturday Review, February 3, 1968, March 15, 1969, February 21, 1970, February 20, 1971, September 25, 1971.

Spectator, February 7, 1969.

Time, February 16, 1968, October 18, 1968, July 9, 1973, June 25, 1979.

Times Literary Supplement, April 10, 1969, July 18, 1975, December 7, 1979, June 12, 1987.

Village Voice, August 15, 1974, October 14, 1986.

Virginia Quarterly Review, winter, 1971.

Washington Post Book World, March 24, 1968, October 20, 1968, January 25, 1970, June 24, 1973, May 16, 1976, April 1, 1979, November 5, 1979, December 23, 1979, February 20, 1983, October 5, 1986.

—Sketch by Kenneth R. Shepherd

—Interview by Walter W. Ross

*   *   *

LINCOLN, C(harles) Eric   1924-

PERSONAL: Born June 23, 1924, in Athens, Ala.; son of Less and Mattie (Sowell) Lincoln; married second wife, Lucy Cook (a teacher), July 1, 1961; children: (first marriage) Cecil Eric, Joyce Elaine; (second marriage) Hilary Anne, Less Charles II. *Education:* LeMoyne College, A.B., 1947; Fisk University, M.A., 1954; University of Chicago Divinity School, B.D., 1956; Boston University, M.Ed., 1960, Ph.D., 1960.

ADDRESSES: Office—Department of Religion, Duke University, Durham, N.C. 27706.

CAREER: LeMoyne College, Memphis, Tenn., director of public relations, 1950-51; Fisk University, Nashville, Tenn., associate personnel dean, 1953-54; Clark College, Atlanta, Ga., assistant professor of religion and philosophy, 1954-57, associate professor of social philosophy, 1960-61, professor of social relations, 1961-64, administrative assistant to president, 1961-63, director of Institute for Social Relations, 1963-65, assistant personnel dean; Portland State College (now University), Portland, Ore., professor of sociology, 1965-73; Union Theological Seminary, New York, N.Y., professor of sociology of religion, 1973-76; Fisk University, professor of religion and sociology and chairman of department of religious and philosophical studies, 1973-76; Duke University, Durham, N.C., professor of religion and culture, 1976—. Boston University, Human Relations Center, director of Panel of Americans, 1958-60, adjunct professor, 1963-65; Dartmouth College, lecturer-in-residence, 1962, visiting professor, 1962-63; visiting professor, Spelman College, 1966; adjunct professor, Vassar College, 1969-70; visiting professor at State University of New York at Albany, 1970-72, and Queens College of the City University of New York, 1972; adjunct professor of ethics and society, Vanderbilt University, 1973-76. Lecturer; has made numerous appearances on local and national television and on radio. Member of boards of directors

or boards of trustees of several institutions, including Boston University, Jewish Theological Seminary, Institute for Religious and Social Studies, Clark Atlanta University, and Association of Theological Schools. Consultant in human relations. *Military service:* U.S. Navy, 1944-45.

MEMBER: American Academy of Arts and Sciences (fellow), American Sociological Association, Society for the Psychological Study of Social Issues, American Academy of Political and Social Science, Society for the Scientific Study of Religion, National Association of University Professors, National Education Association, Association for the Study of Negro Life and History, Black Academy of Arts and Letters (founding president; member of board of directors), American Association of Intergroup Relations Officials, Authors Guild, Authors League of America, National Geographic Society, Southern Sociological Society, New York Academy of Arts and Sciences, New York Academy of Sciences, Kappa Alpha Psi, Free and Accepted Masons, International Frontiers Club.

AWARDS, HONORS: John Hay Whitney fellow, 1957; Crusade fellow, Methodist Church, 1958; Lilly Endowment fellow, 1959; human relations fellow, Boston University, 1959-60; L.L.D. from Carleton College, 1968, Lane College, 1982, and Clark College, 1983; Creative Communications Award, Art Institute of Boston, 1970; L.H.D. from St. Michael's College, 1972; research grants from Society for the Psychological Study of Social Issues, Anti-Defamation League of B'nai B'rith, Fund for the Advancement of Education, Lilly Endowment, and Ford Foundation.

WRITINGS:

The Black Muslims in America, Beacon Press, 1961, 2nd revised edition, 1982.

My Face Is Black, Beacon Press, 1964.

Sounds of the Struggle, Morrow, 1967.

The Negro Pilgrimage in America: The Coming of Age of the Blackamericans, Bantam, 1967.

Is Anybody Listening?, Seabury, 1968.

(With Langston Hughes and Milton Meltzer) *A Pictorial History of the Negro in America,* Crown, 1968, 5th revised edition, 1983.

A Profile of Martin Luther King, Jr., Hill & Wang, 1969, revised edition, 1984.

The Blackamericans, Bantam, 1969.

The Black Church since Frazier, Schocken, 1974.

(Editor) *The Black Experience in Religion: A Book of Readings,* Doubleday, 1974.

Race, Religion, and the Continuing American Dilemma, Hill & Wang, 1984.

The Avenue: Clayton City, Morrow, 1988.

EDITOR; "C. ERIC LINCOLN SERIES IN BLACK RELIGION"

James H. Cone, *A Theology of Black Liberation,* Lippincott, 1970.

Henry Mitchell, *Black Preaching,* Lippincott, 1970.

Gayraud Wilmore, *Black Religion and Black Radicalism,* Doubleday, 1972.

Joseph R. Washington, Jr., *Black Sects and Cults,* Doubleday, 1972.

William R. Jones, *Is God a White Racist?,* Doubleday, 1973.

Leonard E. Barrett, *Soul-Force,* Doubleday, 1973.

CONTRIBUTOR

Alice Horowitz, editor, *The Outlook for Youth,* H. W.Wilson, 1962.

Earl Raab, editor, *New Frontiers in Race Relations*, Doubleday, 1962.

Mulford Sibley, editor, *The Quiet Battle*, Doubleday, 1963.

Louis Lomax, editor, *When the Word Is Given*, New American Library, 1963.

Arnold Rose, editor, *Assuring Freedom to the Free*, Wayne State University Press, 1963.

Rolf Italiaander, editor, *Die Herasforderung des Islam*, Muster-Schmidt-Verlag (Gottingen), 1965.

Arnold Rose and Caroline Rose, editors, *Minority Problems*, Harper, 1965.

Gerald H. Anderson, editor, *Sermons to Men of Other Faiths*, Abingdon, 1966.

John P. Davis, editor, *The American Negro Reference Book*, Prentice-Hall, 1966.

Nils Petter Gleditsch, editor, *Kamp Uten Vapen*, Eides Boktrykkeri (Bergen), 1966.

Edgar A. Shuler and others, editors, *Readings in Sociology*, Crowell, 1967.

William C. Kvaraceus and others, editors, *Poverty, Education and Race Relations*, Allen & Bacon, 1967.

Milgon L. Barron, editor, *Minorities in a Changing World*, Knopf, 1967.

Bradford Chambers, editor, *Chronicles of Negro Protest*, New American Library, 1968.

Peter T. Rose, editor, *Old Memories, New Moods*, Atherton Press, 1970.

David Reimers, editor, *The Black Man in America since Reconstruction*, Crowell, 1970.

Benjamin Brawley, editor, *A Social History of the American Negro*, Macmillan, 1970.

George Ducas, editor, *Great Documents in Black American History*, Praeger, 1970.

Robert Weisbard and Arthur Stein, editors, *The Bittersweet Encounter*, Negro Universities Press, 1970.

Scott G. McNall, editor, *The Sociological Perspective*, Little, Brown, 1971.

Michael V. Namorato, editor, *Have We Overcome?: Race Relations since Brown*, University Press of Mississippi, 1979.

OTHER

Contributor to *Encyclopaedia Britannica, Encyclopedia Americana, Encyclopedia of Southern Religion, World Book Encyclopedia,* and *Encyclopdia of World Biography.* Contributor of articles, poetry, and reviews to numerous journals and popular periodicals.

SIDELIGHTS: C. Eric Lincoln has long been considered an important and respected sociologist studying such topics as race relations in the United States, the historical development of black protest and black nationalism, the growth and importance of the Black church, the Black Muslim movement, and the backgrounds and influence of Black leaders on the civil rights cause. Many reviewers feel that through his lectures, his appearances on national television and radio programs, and his writings, Lincoln has examined the various elements of black life in America in an intelligent, insightful, and thorough manner. As Herbert Mitgang remarks in the *Saturday Review,* "[Lincoln] writes dispassionately and from the inside about where the Negro stands and what he hopes for today."

The publication of his first book, *The Black Muslims in America,* gained Lincoln and his work national attention. As one of the first sociological accounts of the Black Muslim movement in the United States, this book explores the movement's beginnings, doctrines, goals, strengths, leaders, and the powerful influence the group has had on the black American. P. J. Gleason writes in the *San Francisco Chronicle* that "Lincoln's study of the pseudo-Islamic sect of Black Muslims is timely, fascinating . . . to read." Gleason continues to note that "the story of the rise of this sect is logically and deftly told by Dr. Lincoln. . . . This is the first survey in depth on one of the most important, as well as one of the most significant, movements in contemporary America and it is well done."

"As an objective study of a social phenomenon [*The Black Muslims in America*] is outstanding," remarks K. B. Clark in the *Saturday Review.* "The author is at his best when he is describing the ideas, manner, ambiguities—intentional or unintentional—of the leaders and the appeals to and techniques of control of their followers. . . . [Lincoln] writes with clarity, with compassion, and with some evidence of deep personal conflict." And M. E. Burgess states in *Social Forces* that "whatever course the Movement takes in years ahead, it bears close watching. Dr. Lincoln's insightful analysis of the rationale, the appeal, and the implications of such a movement is a valuable contribution to the literature."

BIOGRAPHICAL/CRITICAL SOURCES:

PERIODICALS

Atlanta Journal/Constitution, March 13, 1988.
Best Sellers, February 15, 1970.
Commonweal, August 9, 1985.
Fayetteville Observer, April 3, 1988.
Greensboro News and Record, April 22, 1988.
Library Journal, January 15, 1970.
New York Review of Books, February 11, 1965.
New York Times Book Review, April 23, 1961.
San Francisco Chronicle, May 7, 1961.
Saturday Review, May 13, 1961, January 16, 1965, January 27, 1968, February 14, 1970.
Social Forces, December, 1961.*

*   *   *

LINDARS, Barnabas   1923-

PERSONAL: Name originally Frederick Chevallier Lindars; born June 11, 1923, in Leighton Buzzard, Bedfordshire, England; son of Walter St. John (a clergyman) and Rose (Chevallier) Lindars. *Education:* St. John's College, Cambridge, B.A. (with honors), 1944, M.A., 1947; additional study at Westcott House, Cambridge, 1946-48.

ADDRESSES: Home—Hulme Hall, Oxford Place, Manchester M14 5RR, England. *Office*—Faculty of Theology, Victoria University of Manchester, Manchester M13 9PL, England.

CAREER: Ordained Anglican deacon, 1948, priest, 1949; curate in Pallion, Sunderland, England, 1948-52; became member of Society of St. Francis, taking the name of Barnabas, 1952; Cambridge University, Cambridge, England, assistant lecturer, 1961-66, lecturer in Old Testament studies, 1966-78, fellow and dean of Jesus College, 1976-78; Victoria University of Manchester, Manchester, England, Rylands Professor of Biblical Criticism and Exegesis, 1978—. *Military service:* British Army, Intelligence Corps, 1944-45; became lieutenant.

MEMBER: Studiorum Novi Testamenti Societas (assistant secretary, 1962-76), Society for Old Testament Study (president, 1986).

AWARDS, HONORS: B.D. from Cambridge University, 1961, for *New Testament Apologetic;* D.D. from Cambridge University.

WRITINGS:

(Contributor) F. L. Cross, editor, *Studies in the Fourth Gospel,* Mowbray, 1957.
New Testament Apologetic, Westminster, 1961.
(Contributor) C. F. D. Moule, editor, *Miracles,* Mowbray, 1965.
(Editor with P. R. Ackroyd and contributor) *Words and Meanings,* Cambridge University Press, 1968.
(Editor) *Church without Walls,* Society for Promoting Christian Knowledge, 1968.
Behind the Fourth Gospel, Society for Promoting Christian Knowledge, 1971.
The Gospel of John, Oliphants, 1972.
(Editor with S. S. Smalley and contributor) *Christ and Spirit in the New Testament,* Cambridge University Press, 1974.
(Contributor) G. R. Dunstan, editor, *Duty and Discernment,* Society for Promoting Christian Knowledge, 1975.
(Contributor) J. A. Emerton, editor, *Studies in the Historical Books of the Old Testament,* E. J. Brill, 1979.
(Contributor) M. Santer, editor, *Their Lord and Ours,* Society for Promoting Christian Knowledge, 1982.
Jesus Son of Man, Society for Promoting Christian Knowledge, 1983.
(Contributor) C. E. Cox, editor, *VI Congress of International Organisation for Septuagint and Cognate Studies,* Scholars Press, 1987.
(Contributor) P. Avis, editor, *The Threshold of Theology,* Marshall-Pickering, 1988.
(Editor and contributor) *Law and Religion,* James Clarke, 1988.
(With J. W. Rogerson and C. J. Rowland) *The Study and Use of the Bible,* Marshall-Pickering, 1988.

Contributor to magazines and theological journals.

WORK IN PROGRESS: Commentary on Judges for *The International Critical Commentaries,* for T. & T. Clark; a study of the theology of Hebrews, for Cambridge University Press.

SIDELIGHTS: Barnabas Lindars told *CA:* "As a follower of St. Francis of Assisi teaching biblical criticism in a great university, I stand at a point of tension for faith today: how can the gospel of Jesus Christ be retained when the Bible is subjected to searching critical and historical analysis? I believe that the search for truth at the scholarly level is not opposed to the religious call, but an essential part of the pursuit of the vision of God and his will for humanity."

*   *   *

LINDBERG, Richard 1953-

PERSONAL: Born June 14, 1953, in Chicago, Ill.; son of Oscar Waldemar (a contractor) and Helen (a clerk; maiden name, Stone) Lindberg; married Denise Janda (a claims supervisor), July 1, 1978. *Education:* Northeastern Illinois University, B.A., 1974, M.A., 1987. *Politics:* "Moderate Republican." *Religion:* Methodist.

ADDRESSES: Home—465 Beech Dr., Wheeling, Ill. 60090. *Office*—Americall Corp., 3010A Wood Creek Dr., Downers Grove, Ill. 60515. *Agent*—Jane Jordan Browne Multimedia Product Development, Inc., 410 South Michigan Ave., Chicago, Ill. 60605.

CAREER: Sears, Roebuck & Co., Inc., Chicago, Ill., beginning 1971, department manager, 1982-84; The Signature Group, Schaumburg, Ill., senior scriptwriter, 1984-88; Chicago White Sox, Chicago, Ill., team historian, 1985—; Americall Corp., Downers Grove, Ill., account executive, 1988—. Reporter for Lerner Newspaper Chain, 1977-81.

MEMBER: Society for the Study of American Baseball Research, Phi Alpha Theta (Pi Gamma chapter president, 1988-89).

AWARDS, HONORS: Robert Zegger Memorial Award, Phi Alpha Theta, Pi Gamma chapter, 1987, for graduate thesis "The Impact of Politics, Gambling, and Vice on the Chicago Police Department, 1855-1920."

WRITINGS:

Stuck on the Sox, Sassafrass Press, 1978.
(With Cindy Cooney, Ron Pazola, Fritz Plous, and Linda Warner) *A Kid's Guide to Chicago,* G. T. Nelson Publishing, 1980.
Who's on Third?: The Chicago White Sox Story, Icarus, 1983.
The Macmillan White Sox Encyclopedia, Macmillan, 1984.
Chicago Ragtime: Another Look at Chicago, 1880-1920, Icarus, 1985.
(Contributor) *The Baseball Biographical Encyclopedia,* Morrow, in press.

Contributor to periodicals, including *Chicago History,* and *Inside Chicago;* contributor to newspapers, including the *Chicago Sun Times,* and the *Chicago Tribune.*

WORK IN PROGRESS: To Serve and Collect: A History of the Chicago Police Department; Sister Kathy, a novel.

SIDELIGHTS: Richard Lindberg told *CA:* "As a boy I was somewhat of a loner, insecure, nervous, and picked on by my school classmates. Coming from a broken home, I turned inward and expressed my private thoughts in a diary which I maintain to this day. This practical experience provided the foundation for my future writing endeavors.

"I am a Chicago writer—born years after the city 'Renaissance.' They say the creative flourish died when James T. Farrell caught the last train to New York, sometime around 1935. Chicago today is a literary wasteland, some New Yorkers will tell you. But the soul of the city pulsates in the works of Theodore Dreiser, Farrell, Upton Sinclair, Nelson Algren, and a score of 'post-Renaissance' writers working in Chicago today. It is up to this new generation to keep the earlier tradition alive. In my previous books I have chronicled the exploits of a broken down baseball team from the grimy, industrial south side. Now I look toward new directions.

"I hope to explore the theme of wealth and despair in my future writings. There exists Gold Coast parties, trendy Rush Street night spots, and posh gallery openings within the shadow of some of the city's most squalid housing projects. Dreiser's 'walled city' of privilege and the people who aspire to its glitter [are] the directions my future writing will take me."

*   *   *

LINDE, Gunnel 1924-

PERSONAL: Born October 14, 1924, in Stockholm, Sweden; daughter of Gunnar E. and Liv (Nordenstrom) Af Geijerstam; married Einar Linde (a television producer), January 6, 1949 (died May 2, 1983); children: Liv, Vysse Gunnel, Sunniva (all daughters). *Education:* Attended Anders Beckmans Reklamskola, Stockholm, 1943-44, and Stockholms Konstskola, 1953.

ADDRESSES: Home—Grindavagen 9, Waxholm, Sweden. *Office*—Sveriges Televisions AB, Oxenstiernsgatan 2, Stockholm, Sweden.

CAREER: Journalist with newspapers in Katrineholm, Linkoping, Halsingborg, Sweden, 1945-47, and with Roster i Radio, Stockholm, Sweden, 1948-49; Sveriges Radio, Stockholm, producer of radio programs for children, 1957-63, and television programs for children, 1964—.

MEMBER: Sveriges Foerfattarfoerbund, Svenska Journalistfoerbund, Publicistklubben, Sveriges Dramatikfoerbund, Samfundet Visans Vanner, Stim Foereningen TV-Producenterna, Foereningen Idun, Foereningen Barnens Raetti Samhaellet (BRIS), International Society for Prevention of Child Abuse and Neglect.

AWARDS, HONORS: Diploma of merit (as runner-up), International Hans Christian Anderson Award, 1964, for *Till aventyrs i Skorstengrand;* Nils Holgersson Award, 1965, for *Den vita stenen;* the translation of *Den vita stenen, The White Stone,* was chosen by the American Library Association as one of the notable children's books of 1966; Foerfatterfondens premium, 1970; Club 100 Prize, and *Expressen* (newspaper) prize, 1974, both for the best family television program of the year, "The White Stone"; Astrid Lindgren prize, 1978; Natur och Kultur prize, 1979.

WRITINGS:

Osynliga klubben och honshusbaten, Albert Bonniers, 1958.
Tacka vet jag Skorstensgrand, Albert Bonniers, 1959, translation by Lise Soemme McKinnon published as *Chimney Top Lane,* Harcourt, 1965.
Lurituri, Albert Bonniers, 1959.
Osynliga klubben och kungliga spoket, Albert Bonniers, 1960, translation by Anne Parker published as *The Invisible League and the Royal Ghost,* Harcourt, 1970.
Lurituri reser bort, Albert Bonniers, 1961.
Till aventyrs i Skorstensgrand, Albert Bonniers, 1962.
Froken Ensam Hemma aker gungstol, Albert Bonniers, 1963.
Den vita stenen, Albert Bonniers, 1964, translation by Richard Winston and Clara Winston published as *The White Stone,* Harcourt, 1966.
Med Lill-Klas i Kappsacken, Albert Bonniers, 1965, translation by Parker published as *Pony Surprise,* Harcourt, 1968.
Den olydiga ballongen, Albert Bonniers, 1966.
I Eviga skogen, International Book Production, 1966.
I Evasjams land, Albert Bonniers, 1967.
Evasjam och Nalle, Albert Bonniers, 1968.
Evasjam och Lua, Albert Bonniers, 1968.
Pellepennan och suddagumman, Sveriges Radios Foerlag, 1968.
Pellepennan och suddagumman och kluddabarnen, Sveriges Radios Foerlag, 1969.
Loejliga familjerna, Albert Bonniers, 1971.
Jag aer en varulvsunge, Albert Bonniers, 1972.
Om man misstaenker barnmisshandel-vad goer man?, Almaenna Barnhuset, 1975.
Mamm-och pappsagor, Albert Bonniers, 1976.
Om livet aer dig kaert, Albert Bonniers, 1977.
Lita pa det ovaentade, Albert Bonniers, 1979.
Dingo, rymmare utan fasttagare, Albert Bonniers, 1981.
Foersta laeseboken, Almquist & Wiksells Foerlag, 1982.
Audra laeseboken, Albert Bonniers, 1982.
Telefonen i underjorden, Albert Bonniers, 1983.

Hur natten ser uf pa mitten, Albert Bonniers, 1983.
Tredje laeseboken, Albert Bonniers, 1984.
Barndomens boecker, Albert Bonniers, 1984.
Raedda Joppe: Thoed eller levande, Albert Bonniers, 1985.
Skraecknatten i Fasenbo, Albert Bonniers, 1986.
TV-taemjarna, Albert Bonniers, 1987.
Ga pa vattnet, Raben & Sjogrens Foelag, 1987.
Solkatter, Albert Bonniers, 1987.

Author of radio scripts, including features for adults and children, dramatizations, and serials; also author of more than one hundred television plays, mainly for children and families. Has had eight recordings issued by Decca, Barben, Warner Bros., and others, 1958-65. Author of an opera, "Froeken Ensam Hemma," for the Royal Swedish Opera, 1969-70.

WORK IN PROGRESS: A book for Albert Bonniers; a television film and cinema film based on *Trust in the Unexpected.*

SIDELIGHTS: In addition to the English translations, some of Gunnel Linde's books have been published in Danish, Finnish, Norwegian, German, French, Czech, Spanish, Polish, Yugoslavian, Dutch, Chinese, and Japanese.

*   *   *

LORD, Shirley
   See ROSENTHAL, Shirley Lord

*   *   *

LOXTON, (Charles) Howard   1934-

PERSONAL: Surname originally Loxston; born July 10, 1934, in Birmingham, England; son of Percy (a clerk) and Florence (Howard) Loxston. *Education:* Attended Birmingham Theatre School, 1949-51; Polytechnic of North London, M.A., 1985.

ADDRESSES: Home—21 Alma St., London NW5 3DJ, England.

CAREER: Author and editor. Performer and stage director, working in theatre, films, and television in England, 1950-58; joint founder and editor, *Viewpoint, a Television Quarterly,* 1956-59. Has held editorial posts with several British publishing houses, including editorial director of Jackdaw Publications, Jonathan Cape Ltd., London, England, 1964-71. Chairman, Society of Young Publishers, 1967-68; served on Arts Council Working Party investigating the Obscene Publication Acts, 1968-69.

MEMBER: National Union of Journalists.

WRITINGS:

(Editor) *Dogs, Dogs, Dogs, Dogs, Dogs, Dogs,* Paul Hamlyn, 1962.
Railways, Paul Hamlyn, 1962, revised edition, 1970, reprinted, 1986.
Pompeii and Herculaneum, Spring Books, 1966.
(Compiler) *The Battle of Agincourt: A Collection of Contemporary Documents,* Cape, 1966.
(Compiler with Lawrence E. Tanner and Nicholas H. MacMichael) *Westminster Abbey: A Collection of Contemporary Documents,* Jackdaw Publications, 1967.
(Compiler and designer, with Michael Rand and Len Deighton) *The Assassination of President Kennedy,* Jackdaw Publications, 1970.
(Compiler) *Christmas: A Collection of Documents,* Jackdaw Publications, in association with Grossman, 1970.

The Murder of Thomas Beckett: A Collection of Contemporary Documents, Grossman, 1971.

The Beauty of Cats, Ward, Lock, 1972.

(Compiler) *Shakespeare's Theatre,* Jackdaw Publications, 1972.

The Beauty of Big Cats, Ward Lock, 1973.

All Colour Book of Kittens, Octopus Books, 1974.

Caring for Your Cat, illustrations by Lawrence Easden, Arco, 1975.

Guide to the Cats of the World, illustrations by Peter Warner, Elsevier Phaidon, 1975, Exeter Books, 1983.

World of Cats, Omega, 1976.

Pilgrimage to Canterbury, David and Charles, 1978.

Train Your Human: A Manual for Caring Dogs, David and Charles, 1979.

Cats: A Colour Guide to the Pedigree Cat Breeds of the World, illustrations by Denys Ovenden, Sundial, 1979.

Spotters Guide to Cats, Usborne, 1980.

Beautiful Cats, Crescent Books, 1980.

Cats, illustrations by David Nockels and others, Ward Lock, 1981.

(Editor) *How to Hold a Crocodile,* Ballantine, 1981.

Cats, illustrations by Gwen Green and John Green, Granada, 1983.

Cats, illustrations by Ryozo Kohira, Collins, 1985.

Cat Repair Handbook: The Practical Guide to Feline Health Care, Macdonald, 1985.

Theatre, Wayland, 1988.

Contributor to encyclopedias and theatre guides, and to story collections for children.

WORK IN PROGRESS: Book on promenade theatre; historical and topographic projects; a feline anthology.

* * *

LUDMERER, Kenneth M. 1947-

PERSONAL: Born January 13, 1947, in Long Beach, Calif.; son of Sol (a physician) and Norma (Helfer) Ludmerer. *Education:* Harvard University, A.B., 1968; Johns Hopkins University, M.A., 1971, M.D., 1973. *Politics:* Independent. *Religion:* Jewish.

ADDRESSES: Home—23 Portland Pl., St. Louis, Mo. 63108.

CAREER: Barnes Hospital, St. Louis, Mo., intern and resident, 1973-76, chief resident in internal medicine, 1978-79; Washington University, St. Louis, fellow in medicine, 1976-78, assistant director of General Medical Service, 1978-79, assistant professor of medicine, School of Medicine, 1979—, assistant professor of history, Faculty of Arts and Sciences, 1979—.

AWARDS, HONORS: American College of Physicians teaching and research scholar, 1980-83.

WRITINGS:

Genetics and American Society: A Historical Appraisal, Johns Hopkins Press, 1972.

Learning to Heal: The Development of American Medical Education, Basic Books, 1985.

Contributor to *Journal of the History of Biology, Bulletin of the History of Medicine,* and *Journal of the History of Medicine and Allied Sciences.*

SIDELIGHTS: From 1870 to 1920 American medical education was transformed from being among the worst in the Western world to the best. In *Learning to Heal: The Development of American Medical Education,* Kenneth M. Ludmerer describes the process of this transformation "with accuracy, clarity and the descriptive skill of a first-rate storyteller," writes Sherman Mellinkoff in the *Los Angeles Times Book Review.*

Learning to Heal reveals that, initially, American medical schools were run as proprietary schools and were not affiliated with any university. Students learned primarily from textbooks and lectures, rarely participating in any laboratory research or clinical training. During the second half of the nineteenth century, however, American universities became interested in establishing medical schools. They teamed up with American physicians who had been trained in German universities, and together they developed quality medical institutions.

New York Times Book Review contributor James H. Jones comments: "Far from serving as a cheerleader for the changes he chronicles, Dr. Ludmerer points out their unexpected and often damaging social consequences. For example, he notes with obvious regret how rising standards worked to the disadvantage of blacks, women, and the poor, who saw their chances for becoming doctors vastly diminished. Nor is he blind to the fact that training thinking physicians proved difficult in the 1920's and remains so." *Science* contributor Joseph F. Kett similarly observes: "Though recognizing the darker side of medical reform, Ludmerer resists the fashion of carping at medical education. His immersion in the past gives him a wise respect for the present, warts and all. *Learning to Heal* is richly informative, arrestingly insightful, and judiciously balanced." Jones concludes: "With admirable patience and great skill, Dr. Ludmerer weaves medical history into the larger fabric of American social and intellectual history. 'Learning to Heal' is the best study yet of the origins of modern medical education."

BIOGRAPHICAL/CRITICAL SOURCES:

PERIODICALS

Los Angeles Times Book Review, January 19, 1986.

New Leader, January 27, 1986.

New York Times Book Review, December 22, 1985.

Science, February 21, 1986.

* * *

LUTTRELL, Ida (Alleene) 1934-

PERSONAL: Surname is accented on first syllable; born April 18, 1934, in Laredo, Tex.; daughter of Pelton Bruce (a rancher) and Helen (a teacher and rancher; maiden name, Sewell) Harbison; married William S. Luttrell (in real estate and insurance), January 20, 1959; children: Robert, Anne, Billy, Richard. *Education:* University of Texas, B.A., 1955; also attended University of Houston, 1960, and Houston Baptist University, 1969, 1970, 1971. *Religion:* Protestant.

ADDRESSES: Home—12211 Beauregard, Houston, Tex. 77024.

CAREER: University of Texas, Main University (now University of Texas at Austin), laboratory technician at Biochemical Institute, 1954-55; Texas Children's Hospital, Houston, bacteriologist, 1955-63; Luttrell Insurance Agency, Houston, Tex., part-time secretary, 1963—. Writer.

MEMBER: Authors Unlimited of Houston.

WRITINGS:

(Contributor) A. Christian Revi, editor, *Collectible Glass,* Everybody's Press, 1980.

(Contributor) Phyllis Prokop, editor, *Three Ingredient Cookbook*, Broadman, 1981.
Not Like That, Armadillo (juvenile), Harcourt, 1982.
One Day at School (juvenile), Harcourt, 1984.
Lonesome Lester (juvenile), Harper, 1984.
Tillie and Mert (juvenile), Harper, 1985.
Mattie and the Chicken Thief (juvenile), Dodd, 1988.
Ottie Slockett (juvenile), Dial, 1989.
Milo's Toothache (juvenile), Dial, 1989.
The Neighbors (juvenile), Harper, 1989.

Contributor to *Antique Trader, Collectible Glass,* and *Spinning Wheel.*

SIDELIGHTS: Ida Luttrell commented to *CA:* "I grew up on a small ranch in south Texas, in a family where children were plentiful and money was scarce. We could not buy books, but I can still remember the thrill of checking out my first book from the county library—*Angus and the Ducks* by Marjorie Flack, the even greater thrill when I could finally read it, and the longing to have A. A. Milne's *Winnie the Pooh* for my very own. Because ranch life was so isolated, books were a great diversion for us, as well as taming baby rabbits, mice, quail, owls, or ground squirrels for pets, and the joy we found in the profusion of wild flowers that bloomed in the fields and pastures.

"Both parents stressed the importance of an education, and there was never any doubt that we would all go to college. So I went to the University of Texas and became a bacteriologist. During the time I worked at Texas Children's Hospital I met my husband, and we now have four children. Through my children I once again became interested in children's books. I have very happy memories of reading to my children when they were small, and the closeness that sharing pleasures brings.

"Because books and reading have been so important to me, it distresses me to hear of the cutbacks in funding for public libraries. Citizens whose only source of reading material is the public library are being robbed of the enrichment books provide. With test scores declining, we need more exposure to books, and I feel the cutbacks could be made in other areas."

AVOCATIONAL INTERESTS: "One of my favorite activities is helping in the school library and reading to the primary grades. I also enjoy gardening, plays, family get-togethers, and sharing my husband's interest in old and contemporary art glass. I also like to do needlework occasionally, including designing and stitching quilts."

BIOGRAPHICAL/CRITICAL SOURCES:

BOOKS

Goettsche, Jacque and Phyllis Prokop, *A Kind of Splendor,* Broadman, 1980.

*   *   *

LYNN, Kenneth S(chuyler) 1923-

PERSONAL: Born June 17, 1923, in Cleveland, Ohio; son of Ernest Lee (a newspaperman) and Edna (Marcey) Lynn; married Valerie Ann Roemer, September 23, 1948; children: Andrew Schuyler, Elisabeth, Sophia. *Education:* Harvard University, A.B., 1947, M.A., 1950, Ph.D., 1954.

ADDRESSES: Home—1709 Hoban Rd. N.W., Washington, D.C. 20007. *Office*—Department of History, Johns Hopkins University, Baltimore, Md. 21218.

CAREER: Harvard University, Cambridge, Mass., instructor, 1954-55, assistant professor, 1955-59, associate professor, 1959-63, professor of English, 1963-68, chairman of American civilization program, 1964-68; Federal City College, Washington, D.C., professor of American studies, 1968-69; Johns Hopkins University, Baltimore, Md., professor of history, 1969-86, Arthur O. Lovejoy Professor of History, 1986—. Fulbright lecturer in Denmark, 1958; visiting professor, University of Madrid, 1963-64; Phi Beta Kappa visiting scholar, 1976-77. *Military service:* U.S. Army Air Forces, 1943-46; became second lieutenant.

MEMBER: American Historical Association, American Studies Association, Modern Language Association of America, Massachusetts Historical Society.

AWARDS, HONORS: Los Angeles Times Book Prize in biography, 1987, for *Hemingway: The Life and the Work.*

WRITINGS:

The Dream of Success: A Study of the Modern American Imagination, Little, Brown, 1955, reprinted, Greenwood Press, 1972.
(Editor) Theodore Dreiser, *Sister Carrie,* Henry Holt, 1957.
(Editor) *The Comic Tradition in America: An Anthology of American Humor,* Doubleday, 1958.
Mark Twain and Southwestern Humor, Little, Brown, 1959.
(Editor) Nathaniel Hawthorne, *The Scarlet Letter: Text, Sources, Criticism,* Harcourt, 1961.
(Editor) Mark Twain, *Huckleberry Finn: Text, Sources, Criticism,* Harcourt, 1961.
(Editor) Harriet Beecher Stowe, *Uncle Tom's Cabin; or, Life among the Lowly,* Harvard University Press, 1962.
(Editor) *The American Society,* Braziller, 1963.
(Editor) *The Professions in America,* Houghton, 1965.
William Dean Howells: An American Life, Harcourt, 1971.
Visions of America: Eleven Literary Historical Essays, Greenwood Press, 1973.
A Divided People, Greenwood Press, 1977.
The Air-Line to Seattle: Studies in Literary and Historical Writing about America, University of Chicago Press, 1983.
Hemingway: The Life and the Work, Simon & Schuster, 1987.

Also editor of *World in a Glass,* 1966. Contributor to *Commentary* and other magazines. General editor, "Riverside Literature" series, Houghton, 1962—. Associate editor, *Daedalus,* 1962-68, and *New England Quarterly,* 1963-68.

SIDELIGHTS: In *Hemingway: The Life and the Work,* Kenneth S. Lynn "looks at Hemingway's early childhood more closely [than previous biographers]; he also sees in that the seeds of androgyny that shaped the writer's life," describes Patrick Hynan in the Toronto *Globe and Mail.* Lynn examines the influence of Hemingway's mother on the author's life and work, postulating that Grace Hemingway's insistence on treating her son and his older sister as twins of the same sex caused a confusion in sexual identity that lingered throughout the author's life. "By bringing to light certain key events in Hemingway's childhood," comments the *New York Times*'s Christopher Lehmann-Haupt, "[Lynn] not only deals with material his predecessors either overlooked or actively denied, he also puts his subject's life and work into perspective." In pursuing Hemingway's fascination with androgyny and sexual roles,

"Lynn traces this theme through the *oeuvre* without appearing a Freudian busybody," notes Harold Beaver in the *Times Literary Supplement*. "His interpenetration of literary text with biographical comment . . . is masterly."

Some critics have faulted Lynn for overextending his study; Richard Eder writes in the *Los Angeles Times Book Review* that the biographer "has let his theme run away with him." Chicago *Tribune Books* contributor Scott Donaldson similarly remarks that "like all biographies with a theme, Lynn's finds the evidence it is looking for, and sometimes the effect is to diminish a novel or story somewhat by transforming it into one more item on a covert agenda." The critic admits, however, that "only rarely do [Lynn's] readings invite objection, almost always he is persuasive." And Jonathan Yardley of the *Washington Post Book World* finds Lynn's biography "scrupulous about staying within the bounds presented by his evidence." Summarizes Yardley: "Lynn has much to tell us that is new, provocative and convincing. His *Hemingway* is at once a distillation of all previous scholarship—in itself no mean accomplishment—and an excursion into territory that, though not precisely unexplored, has never before been examined with such care and insight." "The book is very different from anything else on Hemingway," observes Donaldson, ". . . and the most insightful study yet of the inter-connections between the artist's life and his writing."

BIOGRAPHICAL/CRITICAL SOURCES:

PERIODICALS

Globe and Mail (Toronto), August 1, 1987.
Los Angeles Times Book Review, July 26, 1987.
New York Times, May 3, 1983, July 13, 1987.
New York Times Book Review, July 19, 1987.
Times Literary Supplement, February 10, 1984, October 30, 1987.
Tribune Books (Chicago), July 12, 1987.
Washington Post Book World, July 19, 1987.

M

MacDONALD, Margaret Read   1940-

PERSONAL: Born January 21, 1940, in Seymour, Ind.; daughter of Murray Ernest (a builder) and Mildred (Amick) Read; married Robert Burns Ruff, August, 1962 (divorced January, 1963); married James Bruce MacDonald (an employee of the Environment Protection Agency), August 20, 1965; children: Jennifer Skye, Julie Liana. *Education:* Indiana University, A.B., 1962, Ph.D., 1979; University of Washington, Seattle, M.L.S., 1964; University of Hawaii, M.Ed.Ec., 1968.

ADDRESSES: Home—11507 Northeast 104th, Kirkland, Wash. 98033. *Office*—Bothell Public Library, 9654 Northeast 182nd, Bothell, Wash. 98011.

CAREER: King County Library System, Seattle, Wash., children's specialist, 1964-65; San Francisco Public Library, San Francisco, Calif., children's librarian, 1966; Hawaii State Library, Honolulu, Oahu Bookmobile librarian, 1966-68; storyteller, Singapore American School, 1968-69; librarian, Fairfield Methodist Girl's School (Singapore), 1969; Mountain-Valley Regional Library System, Sacramento, Calif., children's consultant, 1969-70; Montgomery County Library System, White Oak, Md., children's librarian, 1970-72; University of Washington, Seattle, visiting lecturer in librarianship, 1975-79; King County Library System, children's specialist at Bothell Public Library, 1977—. Occasional adjunct professor of storytelling to Seattle Pacific University, Western Washington University, Pennisula College, and other northwestern U.S. colleges, 1983—.

MEMBER: American Library Association, American Folklore Society, Children's Literature Association, Association for Library Service to Children, National Association for the Preservation and Perpetuation of Storytelling, Oral History Association, Washington Library Association, Washington State Folklife Council (vice-chairman, 1986-87), Youth Theatre Northwest (member of board, 1988—).

AWARDS, HONORS: The Storyteller's Sourcebook: A Subject, Title, and Motif Index to Folklore Collections for Children was named one of the outstanding reference sources of 1982 by American Library Association.

WRITINGS:

The Storyteller's Sourcebook: A Subject, Title, and Motif Index to Folklore Collections for Children, Gale, 1982.

Twenty Tellable Tales: Audience Participation Folktales for the Beginning Storyteller, H. W. Wilson, 1986.
When the Lights Go Out: 20 Scary Tales to Tell, H. W. Wilson, 1988.
Booksharing: 101 Programs for Preschoolers, Shoe String, 1988.
Scipio, Indiana: Threads from the Past, Ye Galleon, 1988.
The Skit Book, Neal-Schuman, 1989.

WORK IN PROGRESS: Spiv's Scipio, "one man's view of a small Indiana town," based on recorded interviews; a collection of twenty moral tales for storytellers, to be published in 1990 for H. W. Wilson.

SIDELIGHTS: Margaret Read MacDonald commented to *CA* on *The Storyteller's Sourcebook:* "As a library storyteller, I frequently consulted Stith Thompson's *Motif-Index of Folk-Literature* to locate tale variants for stories I was learning. I needed a reference tool that would index children's folktale collections with this same kind of detail. So I made one. It took ten years to read and index the 556 collections and 389 picture books."

MacDonald added: "My storytelling collections, *Twenty Tellable Tales* and *When the Lights Go Out,* grew from my own needs as a children's librarian and professor of storytelling. The tales were not 'written' but were 'told into shape.' Once they reached a solid form through repeated tellings I taped my performance and edited such tellings into the collections of tellable tales.

"Meanwhile, part of my attention is focused on a small town in southern Indiana. Using participant observation techniques and tape-recorded interviews, I am trying to assemble a portrait of this town. As a folklorist, I am particularly interested in the oral narrative style of one resident, 'Spiv' Helt."

*   *   *

MALMGREN, Harald B(ernard)   1935-

PERSONAL: Born July 13, 1935, in Boston, Mass.; son of Berndt B. and Magda H. (Nilsson) Malmgren; married Patricia A. Nelson, June 26, 1959 (divorced); married Linda V. Einberg, October 3, 1987; children: Karen P., Britt P., Erika N. *Education:* Studied at Rensselaer Polytechnic Institute, 1953-

54; Yale University, B.A., 1957; Oxford University, D.Phil., 1961; also studied at Harvard University.

ADDRESSES: Home—Summerfield Farm, Rte. 1, Box 318, Warrenton, Va. 22186. *Office*—2001 L St. N.W., Washington, D.C. 20036.

CAREER: Cornell University, Ithaca, N.Y., Justine S. Evans Assistant Professor of Economics, 1961-62; Institute for Defense Analyses, Washington, D.C., head of economics group, 1962-64; Office of Special Representative for Trade Negotiations, Washington, D.C., assistant special representative, 1964-69; Overseas Development Council, Washington, D.C., senior fellow, 1969-71; Malmgren, Inc., Washington, D.C., president, 1971-72; Office of Special Representative for Trade Negotiations, deputy special representative and ambassador, 1972-75; president of Malmgren, Inc., 1976—; Malmgren, Golt, Kingston & Co., Ltd., London, England, chairman, 1979—. Consultant to President's Advisory Council on Executive Organization, 1969-71, and President's Commission on International Trade and Investment Policy, 1971; director of Overseas Development Council, Center for Strategic and International Studies, Institute for International Economics, and Trade Policy Research Centre, London. Has lectured at Georgetown University, 1964-66, School of Advanced International Studies at Johns Hopkins University, 1966-71, and George Washington University, 1975-76.

MEMBER: American Economic Association, Royal Economic Society, Institute for Strategic Studies (London), Council on Foreign Relations.

AWARDS, HONORS: Social Science Research Council fellowship, 1958-60; Woodrow Wilson International Center for Scholars fellowship, 1975-76.

WRITINGS:

Trade for Development, Overseas Development Council, 1971.
International Economic Peacekeeping, Quadrangle, 1972.
(With Charles R. Frank and others) *Assisting Developing Countries: Problems of Debts, Burden-Sharing, Jobs, and Trade,* Praeger, 1972.
Pacific Basin Development, Heath, 1972.
International Order for Public Subsidies, Trade Policy Research Centre, 1977.
(With William Turner) *Summit Meetings and Collective Leadership in the 1980's,* Atlantic Council of the United States, 1980.
Changing Forms of World Competition and World Trade Rules, foreword by John Heinz, Center for Strategic and International Studies, Georgetown University, 1981.
(With Jack Baranson) *Technology and Trade Policy: Issues and an Agenda for Action,* U.S. Department of Labor, 1981.

Also contributor to books of collected papers and to festschrifts. Contributor to *New Republic* and to professional journals. Editor of *World Economy, Washington Quarterly,* and *International Economy.*

*   *   *

MAMALAKIS, Markos J(ohn) 1932-

PERSONAL: Born October 30, 1932, in Salonica, Greece; son of Ioannis P. (a historian) and Renate (Rocha) Mamalakis; married Angelica Athanasiou, January 31, 1960; children: Anna, Katja, Marina, John, Andreas, Philip, Irene, Peter, Joanna,

Alexandra, Emmanuel, Thomas. *Education:* University of Salonica, LL.D. (summa cum laude), 1955; attended University of Munich, 1955-57; University of California, Berkeley, M.A., 1959, Ph.D., 1962. *Religion:* Greek Orthodox.

ADDRESSES: Home—2977 North Shepard Ave., Milwaukee, Wis. 53211. *Office*—Bolton 804, University of Wisconsin, Milwaukee, Wis. 53201.

CAREER: University of Western Ontario, London, instructor, 1961-62, assistant professor of economics, 1962-63; Yale University, New Haven, Conn., assistant professor of economics, 1963-67; University of Wisconsin—Milwaukee, associate professor, 1967-69, professor of economics, 1969—, director of Center for Latin American Studies, 1967-72. Visiting professor, Universidad de Chile, 1964-66; Ford Foundation visiting professor, summer, 1966; visiting professor, University of Goettingen, 1975-76. Has also lectured at University of London, University of Chicago, University of Kansas, Getulio Vargas Foundation, Oxford University, University of Sussex, and numerous other universities; has appeared on radio and television programs. Member of Institute for Economic Research, Queen's University, Kingston, Ontario, summer, 1962-63.

MEMBER: International Association for Income and Wealth, American Economic Association, Latin American Studies Association, Canadian Economic Association.

AWARDS, HONORS: Fulbright Smith-Mundt exchange program scholarship, University of California, Berkeley, 1957-58, 1958-61; Social Science Research Council grant to analyze the service sector in Latin America, 1960-65, 1969; Canada Council research grants, 1962, 1963; Ford Foundation fellow, 1963; Fulbright-Hays faculty research grant to examine role of services in the economic development of the Iberian Peninsula, 1971; German Research Foundation grant to analyze role of minerals in economic development, 1975-76; Tinker Foundation grants to write four volumes of *Historical Statistics of Chile,* 1978, 1979.

WRITINGS:

(With Clark Reynolds) *Essays on Chilean Economy,* Irwin, 1965.
La teoria de los choques entre sectores (title means "The Theory of Sectoral Clashes"), Instituto de Economia, Universidad de Chile, 1966.
The Role of the Government in the Resource Transfer and Resource Allocation Process: The Chilean Nitrate Sector, 1880-1930, Latin American Center, University of Wisconsin, 1968.
(Contributor) Raymond Mikesell and others, editors, *Foreign Investment in Minerals and Petroleum,* Johns Hopkins Press for Resources for the Future, 1971.
(Contributor) Gustav Ranis, editor, *Government and Economic Development,* Yale University Press, 1971.
The Growth and Structure of the Chilean Economy: 1840-1972, Yale University Press, 1976.
(Compiler) *Historical Statistics of Chile,* Greenwood Press, Volume 1: *National Accounts,* 1978, Volume 2: *Demography and Labor Force,* 1980, Volume 3: *Forestry and Related Activities,* 1982, Volume 4: *Money, Prices, and Credit Services,* 1983, Volume 5: *Banking and Financial Services,* 1985.

Also author of *From Independence to Allende,* 1976. Contributor of articles and reviews to professional journals, including

Latin American Research Review, Journal of Development Studies, Journal of Interamerican Studies, and *Economia.*

WORK IN PROGRESS: "Working of topics of economic development in an effort to assist in the formulation of policies alleviating poverty in all areas and forms."

BIOGRAPHICAL/CRITICAL SOURCES:

PERIODICALS

American Reference Books Annual, Volume 11, 1980, Volume 12, 1981, Volume 17, 1986.
Hispanic American Historical Review, February, 1980, August, 1981, August, 1983, August, 1984.
Journal of Economic History, June, 1979, December, 1985.

* * *

MANLEY, Michael Norman   1924-

PERSONAL: Born December 10, 1924, in Kingston, Jamaica; son of Norman W. (premier of Jamaica) and Edna (a sculptress and painter; maiden name, Swithenbank) Manley; married Beverly Anderson, 1972; children: Rachel Manley Ennevor, Joseph, Sarah, Natasha, David. *Education:* London School of Economics and Political Science, London, B.Sc., 1949.

ADDRESSES: Office—P.N.P. Headquarters, 89 Old Hope Rd., Kingston 6, Jamaica.

CAREER: Journalist and broadcaster on "Caribbean News," British Broadcasting Corp., 1949-51; associate editor, *Public Opinion,* 1952; National Workers Union, Kingston, Jamaica, sugar supervisor, 1953-55; island supervisor and first vice-president, 1955-62; Government of Jamaica, Kingston, member of Senate, 1962-67, member of House of Representatives from central Kingston, 1967-72, prime minister, 1972-80, minister of external affairs, 1972-75, minister of economic affairs, 1972-75, minister of defense, 1972—, minister of youth and community development, 1974-75, and minister of national mobilization and human resources develoment, 1977—, leader of opposition party, 1980—. Jamaican representative to executive council of Caribbean Congress of Labour. President of People's National Party, 1969—. President of Caribbean Bauxite Mineworkers and Metal Workers Federation, 1964-74; vice president of Socialist International, 1979—; president of National Workers Union, 1984—. *Military service:* Royal Canadian Air Force, 1942-45.

AWARDS, HONORS: Order of the Liberator (Venezuela), 1973; LL.D. from Morehouse College, 1973; Order of Jose Marti (Cuba), 1975; gold medal from United Nations, 1978, for work against apartheid.

WRITINGS:

The Politics of Change: A Jamaican Testament, Deutsch, 1974.
A Voice at the Workplace, Deutsch, 1975.
The Search for Solutions, Maple House Publishing, 1976.
Jamaica: Struggle in the Periphery, Writers and Readers, 1982.
Up the Down Escalator: Development and the International Economy, a Jamaican Case Study, Deutsch, 1987, Howard University Press, 1988.
A History of West Indies Cricket, Deutsch, 1988.

AVOCATIONAL INTERESTS: Reading, music, gardening, boxing, tennis, cricket.

MANN, Peggy

PERSONAL: Born in New York, N.Y.; daughter of Harvey T. (a lawyer) and Edna (a psychologist; maiden name, Brand) Mann; married William Houlton (a public relations executive); children: Jenny, Betsy. *Education:* University of Wisconsin, B.A.; graduate study at Columbia University, New School for Social Research, and University of Birmingham, Birmingham, England. *Politics:* Democrat. *Religion:* Jewish.

ADDRESSES: Agent—Curtis Brown Ltd., 10 Astor Place, New York, N.Y. 10022.

CAREER: Former scriptwriter, Columbia Broadcasting System, New York City, and radio-television copywriter, Mc-Cann-Erickson, New York City; former staff writer, *Reader's Digest;* former chief of book club copy, Doubleday & Company, Inc., New York City; currently free-lance writer.

MEMBER: PEN, Dramatists Guild, Authors League of America, Authors Guild, American Society of Journalists and Authors.

AWARDS, HONORS: "*Gizelle, Save the Children!*" was selected by the American Library Association as one of the eight nonfiction books on their young adult best of the year list, 1981; *Twelve Is Too Old* was recommended in the Columbia Broadcasting System/Library of Congress "Read More About It" program on drug abuse.

WRITINGS:

FOR ADULTS

A Room in Paris, Doubleday, 1959.
Golda: The Life of Israel's Prime Minister, McCann, 1971.
(With R. Kluger) *The Last Escape: The Launching of the Largest Secret Rescue Movement of All Time* (Literary Guild alternate selection), Doubleday, 1973.
Ralph Bunche: UN Peacemaker, McCann, 1975.
The Tell-tale Line: The Secrets of Handwriting Analysis, Macmillan, 1976.
Luis Munoz Marin: The Man Who Remade Puerto Rico, Coward, 1976.
Easter Island: Land of Mysteries, Holt, 1976.
"*Gizelle, Save the Children!,*" Dodd, 1981.
Marijuana Alert!, McGraw, 1984.
Arrive Alive: How to Keep Drunk and Drugged Drivers off the Road, McGraw, 1985.

FOR CHILDREN

The Street of the Flower Boxes, Coward, 1966.
That New Baby, Coward, 1967.
The Boy with the Billion Pets, Coward, 1968.
Clara Barton: Battlefield Nurse, Coward, 1969.
When Carlos Closed the Street, Coward, 1969.
The Clubhouse, Coward, 1969.
Amelia Earhart: Pioneer of the Skies, Coward, 1970.
The Twenty-five-Cent Friend, Coward, 1970.
How Juan Got Home, Coward, 1972.
The Lost Doll, Random House, 1972.
William the Watchcat, Rand McNally, 1972.
Whitney Young, Jr.: Crusader for Freedom, Garrard, 1972.
The Secret Dog of Little Luis, Coward, 1973.
My Dad Lives in a Downtown Hotel, Doubleday, 1973.
Now Is Now, Scholastic Book Services, 1974.
Last Road to Safety, Macmillan, 1975.
(With J. Houlton) *Ghost Boy,* Macmillan, 1975.
Handwriting: A Secret Way to Look Inside, Macmillan, 1975.

(With V. Siegal) *The Man Who Bought Himself: The Story of Peter Still*, Macmillan, 1975.

A Present for Yanya, Random House, 1975.

There Are Two Kinds of Terrible, Doubleday, 1976.

Lonely Girl, Scholastic Book Services, 1976.

The Secret Ship, Doubleday, 1977.

Twelve Is Too Old, Doubleday, 1981.

Pot Safari: A Visit to the Top Marijuana Researcher in the United States, Woodmere Press, 1988.

The Sad Story of Mary Wanna; or, How Marijuana Harms You, Woodmere Press, 1988.

OTHER

Contributor to magazines, including *McCall's, Harper's Bazaar, Seventeen, Saturday Evening Post, Holiday, Cosmopolitan, Glamour, Mademoiselle, Ladies Home Journal, Family Circle,* and *Woman's Day*.

WORK IN PROGRESS: Adapting *A Room in Paris* as a play.

SIDELIGHTS: Peggy Mann told *CA:* "Until July 1978, I was a 'regular writer.' Aside from several books on the Holocaust (*The Last Escape, "Gizelle, Save the Children!," The Secret Ship*) I had no particular speciality. That summer I covered a conference for the *Washington Post* on the health hazards of marijuana held in Reims, France. I knew virtually nothing about marijuana—except that I assumed it was a relatively harmless drug. I was stunned to learn at this conference that it was, in fact, an extremely harmful drug.

"My *Washington Post* article on the subject, detailing new scientific findings on marijuana, was the first long article to reach the general public on this subject. I have been writing about the physical and psychological health hazards of marijuana ever since—and have undoubtedly written more on the subject than any other writer. One of my *Reader's Digest* articles on the health hazards of marijuana drew more requests for reprints in a shorter space of time than articles on any other subject ever in the *Digest:* over three million in eleven months. This attests to the need for more information on the subject of this widely used drug.

"I have also written about the hazards of marijuana and driving, marijuana plus alcohol and driving, kids and drugs, the parent movement for drug-free youth, and about cocaine."

MEDIA ADAPTATIONS: The Last Escape has been optioned to a motion picture company and *"Gizelle, Save the Children!"* has been optioned for production as a television mini series. Three of Mann's books have been adapted for national television programs: *My Dad Lives in a Downtown Hotel*, ABC-TV, *The Street of the Flower Boxes*, NBC-TV, and *There Are Two Kinds of Terrible*, CBS-TV, which appeared on television as "Two Kinds of Love."

*   *   *

MARMOR, T(heodore) R(ichard) 1939-

PERSONAL: Born February 24, 1939, in New York, N.Y.; son of James and Mira (Karpf) Marmor; married Jan Schmidt, October 20, 1961; children: Laura Carleton, Sarah Rogers. *Education:* Harvard University, B.A., 1960, Ph.D., 1965; attended Wadham College, Oxford, 1961-62. *Politics:* Democrat.

ADDRESSES: Home—139 Armory St., Hamden, Conn. 06511. *Office*—Institution for Social and Policy Studies, 111 Prospect St., Box 16A Yale Station, New Haven, Conn. 06520.

CAREER: Harvard University, Cambridge, Mass., instructor, 1965-66; research fellow at University of Essex, Colchester, England, and Nuffield College, Oxford University, Oxford, England, 1966-67; University of Wisconsin—Madison, 1967-69, began as assistant professor, became associate professor of political science; fellow at Adlai Stevenson Institute, Chicago, Ill., 1969, and John F. Kennedy Institute, Cambridge, 1970; University of Minnesota, Minneapolis, associate professor of political science, 1970-73; University of Chicago, Chicago, associate professor of political science, 1973-78; Yale University, New Haven, Conn., professor of public health and political science and chairman of Center for Health Studies, 1979-83, professor of public management and political science, 1983—. Visiting fellow, Russell Sage Foundation, 1987-88; fellow, Canadian Institute for Advanced Research, 1987-92. Member of board of directors, Center for the Study of Drug Development. Senior advisor on health and social security, Mondale/Ferraro campaign, 1984. Consultant to U.S. Department of Health, Education, and Welfare, Senator Ribacoff (Conn.), and state of Illinois governor's office.

MEMBER: National Academy for Social Insurance, Association for Public Policy and Management, American Political Science Association.

WRITINGS:

(With wife, Jan S. Marmor) *The Politics of Medicare*, Humanities, 1970.

(Editor and contributor) *Poverty Policy*, Aldine-Atherton, 1971.

(With William D. White) *Paraprofessionals and Issues of Public Regulation*, Professional Organizations Committee (Toronto), 1979.

(Editor with Judith Feder and John Holahan) *National Health Insurance: Conflicting Goals and Policy Choices*, Urban Institute, 1980.

(With Stephen M. Davidson) *The Cost of Living Longer*, Lexington Books, 1980.

(With John B. Christianson) *Health Care Policy: A Political Economy Approach*, Sage Publications, 1982.

Political Analysis and American Medical Care: Essays, Cambridge University Press, 1983.

(Contributor) J. Doig and E. Hargrove, editors, *Leadership and Innovation: A Biographical Perspective on Entrepreneurs in Government*, Johns Hopkins University Press, 1987.

(Editor with Jerry Mashaw) *Social Security: Beyond the Rhetoric of Crisis*, Princeton University Press, 1988.

The Career of John C. Calhoun, Garland Publishing, 1988.

Contributor to periodicals, including *American Political Science Review* and *Political Quarterly*. Editor, *Journal of Health Policy, Politics and Law*, 1980-84.

WORK IN PROGRESS: A book on the politics of American social welfare policy, with J. Mashaw.

SIDELIGHTS: T. R. Marmor told *CA:* "[I am] interested in the American version of the welfare state, which means learning about what non-America has done. I am concerned about the attacks on the major institutions of America's welfare state and the failure to make the protections of these social insurance programs, particularly in the area of health care, available to all Americans."

BIOGRAPHICAL/CRITICAL SOURCES:

PERIODICALS

American Political Science Review, September, 1986.

Annals of the American Academy of Political Social Sciences,
    May, 1984.
Economist, September 12, 1970.
Ethics, January, 1987.
Journal of Political Economy, August, 1983.
Journal of Politics, February, 1986.

*   *   *

MARS-JONES, Adam   1954-

PERSONAL: Born October 26, 1954, in London, England; son
of William Lloyd (a judge) and Sheila (an attorney; maiden
name, Cobon) Mars-Jones. *Education:* Cambridge University,
B.A., 1976, M.A., 1978.

ADDRESSES: Home—3 Gray's Inn Square, London WC1R
5AH, England. *Agent*—Pat Kavanagh, A. D. Peters & Co.,
10 Buckingham St., London WC2N 6BU, England.

CAREER: Writer; film critic, *The Independent,* London, England.

AWARDS, HONORS: Benjamin C. Moomaw Prize for Oratory, University of Virginia; Somerset Maugham Award, 1982,
for *Lantern Lecture.*

WRITINGS:

Fabrications (stories; contains "Hoosh-Mi" and "Bathpool
    Park"), Knopf, 1981 (published in England with an ad-
    ditional title story as *Lantern Lecture,* Faber, 1981).
(Editor) *Mae West Is Dead: Recent Lesbian and Gay Fiction,*
    Faber, 1983.
(With Edmund White) *The Darker Proof: Stories from a Cri-
    sis,* Faber, 1987, New American Library, 1988.

SIDELIGHTS: Fiction writer Adam Mars-Jones first caught
critical attention with his 1981 story collection *Fabrications,*
hailed as a triumphant debut by Galen Strawson, a *Times Literary Supplement* reviewer. In an article assessing the English
version of the book, called *Lantern Lecture,* Strawson found
that "there is something punk, in the modern sense of the
word, about this extremely clever and original collection of
stories. It's to do with the emotionally deadpanned style of
delivery, the technical impassivity of the allusive, *cloisonne*
construction."

More recently, in response to the social emergency surrounding the disease AIDS, Mars-Jones has collaborated with Edmund White to produce *The Darker Proof: Stories from the
Crisis.* This collection deals "less with the disease and its
case-histories than with the effect it has had on the consciousness of people who are living in close proximity to it," according to Anne Billson in a London *Times* interview with
Mars-Jones. As the interview relates, Mars-Jones has maintained a personal interest in the subject matter by acting as
"buddy"—someone readily available to provide physical and
moral support—to a pair of AIDS victims. While he tells Billson that he never before considered writing about the disease
from the standpoint of a buddy, he saw that "the book wouldn't
have been written if I hadn't buddied, because I wouldn't have
had a sense of knowing the reality [of AIDS], rather than just
the culture of it."

Calling Mars-Jones's work in *The Darker Proof* "an important
discovery," *Washington Post* critic Richard McCann adds that
the writer "devotes his considerable intelligence and compassion to the exploration of smaller moments in which characters
renegotiate their daily lives." While the Mars-Jones style is

"highly discursive," says McCann, it still "allows him to
build toward powerfully dramatic realizations, particularly when
he writes, as he often does, of the guilty and grief-stricken
transactions between the sick and the (still) well."

BIOGRAPHICAL/CRITICAL SOURCES:

PERIODICALS

Los Angeles Times Book Review, November 1, 1981.
Times (London), February 23, 1983, June 29, 1987, August
    9, 1987.
Times Literary Supplement, October 9, 1981.
Washington Post, May 30, 1988.
Washington Post Book World, November 1, 1981.

*   *   *

MARTIN, David (Lozell)   1946-

PERSONAL: Born March 13, 1946, in Granite City, Ill.; son
of Curtis C. (a steelworker) and Marjorie (Morris) Martin;
married Gretchen Bayon (a teacher), June 15, 1968 (divorced,
1987); married Arabel Allfrey (a farmer), May 23, 1988; children: (first marriage) Matthew David, Joshua Robert. *Education:* University of Illinois, B.S., 1969.

ADDRESSES: Home—Blue Goose Farm, H.C. 73, Box 9,
Alderson, W.Va. 24910. *Agent*—Robert Datilla, Phoenix Literary Agency, 315 South F. St., Livingston, Mont. 59047.

CAREER: American School Board Journal, Evanston, Ill.,
managing editor, 1971-76; *Learning,* Palo Alto, Calif., managing editor, 1976-78; *American School Board Journal* and
Executive Educator, Washington D.C., editor and assistant
publisher, 1978-82; Association of Governing Boards of Universities and Colleges, Washington, D.C., vice-president, beginning 1984; currently writing and farming full-time. *Military
service:* U.S. Air Force, 1969.

AWARDS, HONORS: Eight All-America awards from Educational Press Association for excellence in education journalism, including Laurence B. Johnson Award for Editorial
Writing, 1975; Bread Loaf Writers Conference fellow, 1980;
The Crying Heart Tattoo was named a *New York Times* notable
novel of 1982; Aspen Institute fellow, 1983.

WRITINGS:

NOVELS

Tethered, Holt, 1979.
The Crying Heart Tattoo, Holt, 1982.
Final Harbor, Holt, 1984.
The Beginning of Sorrows, Weidenfeld & Nicolson, 1987.

SIDELIGHTS: "David Martin's underlying concern as a novelist might be baldly stated as contemporary man-woman relationships (and what goes wrong)," notes Charles Champlin
of the *Los Angeles Times Book Review.* But what sets Martin
apart from other writers "is the striking and even strident
individuality of his men, women and relationships," explains
Champlin. In his first novel, *Tethered,* Martin explores the
strained ties between a wife, husband, and son living on a
farm in Illinois. Although the novel's premise is fairly simple,
Martin includes a larger element to enhance the work. A *Kirkus Reviews* writer, for example, asserts that *Tethered* "en-
dows the most familiar homespun materials with form and
flair," calling it "a fine first novel." The critic elaborates by
observing that the narrative is "all done with interwoven attention to a few farm-life symbols that deftly take the novel

beyond a mere rural-boyhood narrative." Similarly, *The Crying Heart Tattoo,* Martin's next novel, contains a story within the plot which parallels the action of the protagonists. The novel recounts the thirty-year affair between Sonny and Felicity, a woman twenty years his senior; throughout the course of their relationship, Felicity tells her lover the story of Graveda, an Indian woman journeying to rejoin her tribe. The novel alternates between the two stories, providing the reader with opportunity to draw comparisons between Felicity and Graveda.

Critics disagree as to the effectiveness of this parallel story. While *New York Times Book Review* contributor Johanna Kaplan remarks that "the beginning sections [of the novel] spring buoyantly to life in fresh, crisp, spontaneous language," she believes that the Graveda sections "do not serve to sharpen the novel's narrative thrust; they are arch, constricted and leaden with symbols." Even more critical is Jonathan Yardley, who writes in the *Washington Post* that the author's "attempt to give a mythic dimension to the story . . . accomplishes nothing except to give us two silly stories when one was more than enough." But Champlin finds that Graveda's tale, "richly eventful and enchanting in its own bizarre way, is not so much an escapist fantasy as it is a parable in parallel. . . . The reverberations from tale to story and back are clever and amusing," adds the critic, ". . . but not *too* clever. Not the least of Martin's success with 'The Crying Heart Tattoo' is how he navigates so skillfully along a tightrope of dangerous choices," details Champlin. And *Detroit News* contributor Bud Foote, although he has some reservations, "appreciate[s] Martin's attempt to try something both unusual and unusually difficult." The critic concludes that "if I have found fault with it, it has been only in order to say that *The Crying Heart Tattoo* is not the masterpiece it is trying to be. And that is high praise indeed."

Martin's later novels display some of the same elements that characterize his first two. *Final Harbor,* his third, "is another essay in unorthodoxy, a testing set piece, again funny, again moving, despite its bizarre and raucous events," states Champlin. The novel takes place in Harper's Ferry, where a number of different fanatics, religious and otherwise, are assembling; a focus for many of these people is Colleen, a "professional virgin" who inspires them. "The month-long gathering of these characters provides Mr. Martin with a perfect vehicle for satire," writes Nancy Ramsey in the *New York Times Book Review,* giving the seeming "tall tale" a sharp edge. The result is a book that "deserves a place within the vernacular tradition of American fiction," comments Ramsey. Similarly, *The Beginning of Sorrows,* according to *Tribune Books* contributor James Park Sloan, "is the kind of novel they used to write when novels were the journalism of the soul." Martin returns to rural Illinois for the setting, relating the suffering of the townspeople of Breaker's Bride, whom the critic compares to an "extended family." The sum of this "tragic universe," comments Sloan, is "half pastoral and half Gothic." Thus the novel contains "no redemption, no moral vision, no great tragedy—just a final stunning despair," notes Michael Carroll in the *Los Angeles Times Book Review.* Yet the story is interesting and relevant, for as Sloan reports, "David Martin is the rare contemporary writer who can reasonably be described as having insight into the human heart. With a technique rarely used in modern storytelling, Martin provides brief excursions into the intimate thoughts of all his characters." The effect, explains the critic, is that "we watch transfixed as the novel builds piece by piece . . . to a shattering Gothic finale that neither storyteller nor reader can evade."

BIOGRAPHICAL/CRITICAL SOURCES:

PERIODICALS

Chicago Tribune Book World, October 10, 1982.
Detroit News, March 14, 1982.
Kirkus Reviews, September 15, 1979.
Los Angeles Times Book Review, March 14, 1982, September 9, 1984, August 16, 1987.
Ms., December, 1982.
New York Times, March 19, 1982.
New York Times Book Review, April 18, 1982, October 7, 1984.
Times Literary Supplement, June 24, 1983.
Tribune Books (Chicago), July 26, 1987,
Village Voice, May 18, 1982.
Washington Post, March 17, 1982.
West Coast Review of Books, January, 1980, November, 1984.

*   *   *

MARTIN, Emily   1944-
(Emily M. Ahern)

PERSONAL: Born November 7, 1944, in Birmingham, Ala.; daughter of Henry W. and Zoe (Martin) Godschalk; married Dennis Ahern (a professor), May 11, 1966. *Education:* University of Michigan, B.A., 1966; Cornell University, Ph.D., 1971.

ADDRESSES: Office—Department of Anthropology, Johns Hopkins University, 34th and Charles Sts., Baltimore, Md. 21218.

CAREER: Yale University, New Haven, Conn., assistant professor of anthropology, 1972-76; Johns Hopkins University, Baltimore, Md., associate professor, 1976-78, professor, 1978—, chair of department, 1984—.

WRITINGS:

The Cult of the Dead in a Chinese Village, Stanford University Press, 1973.
(Contributor) Arthur P. Wolf, editor, *Studies in Chinese Society,* Stanford University Press, 1978.
(Editor with Hill Gates, and contributor) *The Anthropology of Taiwanese Society,* Stanford University Press, 1981.
Chinese Ritual and Politics, Cambridge University Press, 1982.
The Woman in the Body: A Cultural Analysis of Reproduction, Beacon Press, 1987.

*   *   *

MARTIN, Herbert Woodward   1933-

PERSONAL: Born October 4, 1933, in Birmingham, Ala.; son of David Nathaniel and Willie Mae (Woodward) Martin. *Education:* University of Toledo, B.A., 1964; State University of New York at Buffalo, M.A., 1967; Middlebury College, M.Litt., 1972; Carnegie-Mellon University, D.A., 1979. *Religion:* Lutheran.

ADDRESSES: Home—715 Turner St., Toledo, Ohio 43607. *Office*—Department of English, 300 College Park, Dayton, Ohio 45469-0001.

CAREER: State University of New York at Buffalo, instructor, summer, 1966; Aquinas College, Grand Rapids, Mich., 1967-70, began as instructor, became assistant professor and poet-in-residence; University of Dayton, Dayton, Ohio, 1970—, began as assistant professor, became professor of English and poet-in-residence. Visiting distinguished professor of poetry at Central Michigan University, fall, 1973. Consultant for contemporary black writers collection at University of Toledo, 1974—.

WRITINGS:

"Dialogue" (one-act play), produced in New York City at Hardware Poets Playhouse, 1963.
"Three Garbage Cans," first produced in Grand Rapids, Michigan, fall, 1968.
New York: The Nine Million and Other Poems, Abracadabra Press, 1969.
The Shit-Storm Poems, Pilot Press, 1972.
The Persistence of the Flesh (poems), Lotus Press, 1976.
Paul Laurence Dunbar: A Singer of Songs (booklet), State Library of Ohio, 1979.
The Forms of Silence, Lotus Press, 1980.

Also author of *Letters from the World.* Work represented in anthologies, including *The Poetry of Black America, Introduction to Black Literature, Urban Reader, 10 Michigan Poets,* and *Face the Whirlwind.* Contributor of poetry to journals, including *Obsidian, Poetry Australia, Nimrod, Nexus, Wisconsin Review, Images,* and *Beloit Poetry Journal.* Editor, *Great Lakes Review,* 1978—; guest editor, *University of Dayton Review,* 1988.

WORK IN PROGRESS: Revision of *The Shit-Storm Poems; Arias and Silences: Poems Edited for Ezra Pound; The Log of the Vigilante,* a long poem; *Chasing the Wind; Presiding; Private Poems; Public Portraits.*

SIDELIGHTS: When asked to comment on his work and other interests, Herbert Woodward Martin remarked, "I have said so many foolish things in the past, that I think I will sit this one out."

Martin has studied with John Ciardi, Karl Shapiro, W. D. Snodgrass, John Frederick Nims, Miller Williams, Judson Jerome, Donald Hall, John Logan, Robert Creely, and Edward Albee.

In addition to having given poetry readings at several universities, Martin has performed as narrator for orchestral presentations including Aaron Copeland's "A Lincoln Portrait," Sir William Walton's "Facade," Vincent Persichetti's "Second Lincoln Inaugural," and Robert Borneman's "Reformation 69/ 70." He has also collaborated with composer Joseph Fennimore on settings for song cycles.

*   *   *

MATTHEWS, Kathy   1949-

PERSONAL: Born July 1, 1949, in New York, N.Y.; daughter of James Ignatious and Loretta (Foohs) Matthews; married Frederic W. Hills (an editor), March 24, 1980. *Education:* Johns Hopkins University, B.A., 1971.

ADDRESSES: Home and office—380 Clinton St., Brooklyn, N.Y. 11231.

CAREER: McGraw-Hill Book Co., New York City, editor, 1974-76; Viking Press, Inc., New York City, editor, 1976-77; Random House, Inc., New York City, editor, 1977-80; writer, 1980—.

WRITINGS:

On Your Own: Ninety-Nine Alternatives to a Nine-to-Five Job, Random House, 1976.
Take a Letter Yourself, Ballantine, 1982.
(With Sophia Loren) *On Women and Beauty,* Morrow, 1985.
(With Sally Haddock) *The Making of a Woman Vet,* Simon & Schuster, 1985.
Medical Makeover, Morrow, 1986.
Ballet Is the Best Exercise, Simon & Schuster, 1986.
(With Dr. Rober Giller) *Maximum Metabolism,* Putnam, 1989.

SIDELIGHTS: Kathy Matthews told *CA:* "*Take a Letter Yourself* is a funny book about the life of the American secretary. No one pays secretaries much attention, yet they run America. Most offices function just fine without the boss, but when the secretary is out, bedlam is the result. I also thought it was about time that some general office myths be exploded. *Take a Letter* was my revenge on all the terrible bosses I worked for in the past.

"Right now my main occupation is with the mechanics of getting words into a workable form. I have two electronic typewriters: one has been in a repair shop for two months, the other was designed by the people who brought us the Ferrari and is beautiful to look at but not worth a damn when it comes to actually performing its function. I also have a word processor which I am frightened of and a daisy wheel printer which I haven't even managed to get out of its carton. I'm reading up on fountain pens."

BIOGRAPHICAL/CRITICAL SOURCES:

PERIODICALS

New York Times Book Review, February 6, 1977.

*   *   *

MAXMEN, Jerrold S(amuel)   1942-

PERSONAL: Born June 27, 1942, in Detroit, Mich.; son of Harold A. (a dentist) and Ethel (Tucker) Maxmen; married Mary Elizabeth Berman (a costume designer), December 18, 1966. *Education:* Wayne State University, B.A., 1963, M.D., 1967. *Politics:* Liberal. *Religion:* Jewish.

ADDRESSES: Home and office—30 Fifth Ave., No. 6E, New York, N.Y. 10011. *Agent*—Carl Brandt, Brandt & Brandt Literary Agents, Inc., 1501 Broadway, New York, N.Y. 10036.

CAREER: Mount Zion Hospital, San Francisco, Calif., intern, 1967-68; Yale University, New Haven, Conn., resident in psychiatry, 1968-71; Dartmouth College, Hanover, N.H., assistant professor of psychiatry, 1971-74; Albert Einstein College of Medicine, Bronx, N.Y., assistant professor of psychiatry, 1974-77; Columbia University, New York, N.Y., associate professor of clinical psychiatry, 1977—, director of medical student training in psychiatry at College of Physicians and Surgeons, 1977-80. Private practice of psychiatry, 1980—. Director of inpatient unit at Dartmouth-Hitchcock Mental Health Center, 1971-74; director of hospital services at Soundview Throgs-Neck Community Mental Health Center, 1975.

MEMBER: American Civil Liberties Union, American Psychiatric Association, Amnesty International.

AWARDS, HONORS: Fellow of National Fund for Medical Education, 1973-74; distinguished psychiatrist lecturer of American Psychiatric Association, 1979.

WRITINGS:

(With G. J. Tucker and M. D. LeBow) *Rational Hospital Psychiatry,* Brunner, 1974.
The Post-Physician Era: Medicine in the Twenty-first Century, Wiley, 1976.
A Good Night's Sleep, Norton, 1981.
The New Psychiatry: How Modern Psychiatrists Think about Their Patients, Theories, Diagnoses, Drugs, Psychotherapies, Power, Training, Families, and Private Lives, Morrow, 1985.
Essential Psychopathology, Norton, 1986.

Contributor of more than thirty articles to medical journals and to periodicals, including *Social Policy* and *Self.*

WORK IN PROGRESS: One nonfiction book.

SIDELIGHTS: While many people believe that traditional psychological analysis is no longer effective, according to Laurence Miller in *Psychology Today,* Jerrold Maxmen's book *The New Psychiatry* gives quite a different impression. Maxmen, says Miller, "stresses the importance of an integrated approach to biology and psychology, and . . . he refrains from the kind of biological crusading that characterizes other works in this field." Maxmen points out that "while biology may be responsible for the types of symptoms that appear in a mental disorder, psychology determines the content and meaning of those symptoms," Miller continues. The reviewer concludes that the book is valuable not only for its integration of biological and psychological approaches to curing mental illness, but also for its investigation into the practice of psychiatry itself: "It is in this type of intradisciplinary self-analysis that *The New Psychiatry* is at its best."

BIOGRAPHICAL/CRITICAL SOURCES:

PERIODICALS

Psychology Today, October, 1985.

*   *   *

MAYFIELD, Marlys   1931-
(Marlys Frey)

PERSONAL: Born May 15, 1931, in Atlanta, Ga.; daughter of Robert B. (a Red Cross field director) and Gladys (Greene) Mayfield; married Walter Frey, 1952 (divorced, 1971); children: Walter, Mark, Martine. *Education:* Attended University of London, University of Graz, University of Vienna, and University of Zurich, 1949-53; Trinity University, B.A., 1955; University of California, Berkeley, M.A., 1958.

ADDRESSES: Office—81 Alvarado Rd., Berkeley, Calif. 94705.

CAREER: Merritt College, Oakland, Calif., instructor in English, 1966-70; College of Alameda, Alameda, Calif., instructor in English and humanities, 1970-86; currently editor and publisher of Hobbit House Press. Consultant in the teaching of critical thinking.

WRITINGS:

(With Dorr Bothwell) *Notan: The Dark-Light Principle of Design,* Reinhold, 1968.
(Under name Marlys Frey) *Naked Life Poems,* Hobbit House Press, 1978.
(Under name Marlys Frey) *Poems from Some Acupuncture Points of the Earth,* Hobbit House Press, 1979.
Thinking for Yourself: Developing Critical Thinking Skills through Writing, Wadsworth, 1987.

WORK IN PROGRESS: Dorr Bothwell: The Samoan Years and *Doing Your Own Thinking: A Practical Handbook.*

SIDELIGHTS: Marlys Mayfield described her work to *CA* this way: "In poetry my purpose is to write truthfully about my own life, to write accurately about my perception of both ordinary and nonordinary reality, and to use forms and language that are easy for the reader to understand. In my textbooks I want to help others develop clarity of understanding about their own perceptions and thinking."

AVOCATIONAL INTERESTS: "My children and grandchildren, the arts, massage; learning all I can to increase my consciousness and give what I can towards the healing of our planet."

*   *   *

McDONOUGH, Jerome   1946-
(Jerry McDonough)

PERSONAL: Surname is pronounced Mick-*dunn*-a; born November 26, 1946, in Seguin, Tex.; son of Jerome Charles (a professor) and Dorothy (a draftsperson; maiden name, Munson) McDonough; married Raenell Roberts (a musician), December 21, 1978; children: Brian Christopher. *Education:* West Texas State University, B.S., 1968, M.A., 1972. *Politics:* Democrat. *Religion:* Catholic.

ADDRESSES: Home—6106 Dartmouth, Amarillo, Tex. 79109. *Agent*— I. E. Clark, P.O. Box 246, Schulenburg, Tex. 78956.

CAREER: Pioneer Corp., Amarillo, Tex., editor and writer for corporate magazine *The Jet,* 1969-70; Caprock School, Amarillo, Tex., theatre director, 1970—; playwright. Part-time instructor in creative writing at Amarillo College, 1970-81. Guest artist, International Thespian Society National Convention, Muncie, Ind., 1988. *Military service:* U.S. Army Reserve, 1968-74.

MEMBER: Dramatists Guild, Authors League of America.

AWARDS, HONORS: First place awards from Texas Educational Theatre Association Playwriting Contest, 1975, for "Asylum," and 1978, for "Eden"; "Juvie" was included in *The Best Short Plays of 1984* and named the most produced play of 1986 by *Dramatists* magazine.

WRITINGS:

PLAYS

(Author of book and lyrics) "A Stretch at the Galluses" (musical; also see below), music by John Gibson, first produced in Amarillo, Texas, at Theater 66, summer, 1970.
The Betrothed (one-act), Samuel French, 1972.
Filiation (one-act), I. E. Clark, 1973.
Fables (five scenes; first produced at West Texas State University, fall, 1973), I. E. Clark, 1974.
Tranceiver (one-act), Samuel French, 1974.
A Short Sketch at the Galluses, (one-act; adapted from the musical "A Stretch at the Galluses"), Eldridge Publishing, 1974.
"The Old Oak Encounter" (one-act), published in *A Pocketful of Wry,* edited by I. E. Clark, I. E. Clark, 1974.
Asylum (five scenes), I. E. Clark, 1975.
Dirge (one-act), Baker's Plays, 1975.
The Noble's Reward (one-act), Eldridge Publishing, 1975.
A Christmas Carol (one-act; adapted from the novella by Charles Dickens), I. E. Clark, 1976.

Requiem (one-act), I. E. Clark, 1977.
Eden (one-act), I. E. Clark, 1978.
O, Little Town (one-act), I. E. Clark, 1978.
Stages (one-act), I. E. Clark, 1979.
It's Sad, So Sad When an Elf Goes Bad (one-act), I. E. Clark, 1979.
Plots (five scenes), I. E. Clark, 1981.
The Nearest Star (one-act), I. E. Clark, 1981.
Juvie (one hour), I. E. Clark, 1982.
Limbo (one-act), I. E. Clark, 1983.
Roomers (one-act), I. E. Clark, 1984.
Not Even A Mouse (one-act), I. E. Clark, 1984.
Addict (one hour), I. E. Clark, 1985.
The Least of These (one-act), Pioneer Drama Service, 1985.
Hark, Harold the Angel Sings (one-act), Pioneer Drama Service, 1986.
Faugh (one-act), I. E. Clark, 1986.
I'll Be Cloned for Christmas (one-act), Pioneer Drama Service, 1987.
Mirrors (one-act), I. E. Clark, 1987.

OTHER

Contributor to periodicals, sometimes under name Jerry McDonough, including *Writer's Digest, Dramatists Guild Quarterly, Texas Poetry,* and *Prolog.*

WORK IN PROGRESS: Three plays, "B.A.T.S.," "Blues," and "Stations," all for I. E. Clark; three other plays, "Dolls," "B. J.'s Power and Light Company," "Children's"; a play "on the possibilities of some impossible relationships"; a musical; contemporary and religious songs.

SIDELIGHTS: Jerome McDonough told *CA:* "I am sometimes asked why my plays have one word titles. The way that this system evolved escapes me, but at some point I decided that my titles should by limited to one word and that the word must mean at least two things, both of which tie it to the play. The only exceptions to the one word rule are my Christmas plays which serve an admittedly limited audience, but one for which I have a great affection. The miracle of Christ's birth deserves endless celebration. Another observation that is often made is that my plays are frequently ritualistic. This probably traces mostly to my Catholicism, but it also reflects my admiration of the presentational style of many nontraditional forms such as street theatre and the work of Peter Schumann's Bread and Puppets Theater.

"My writings usually attack mindlessness, whatever its form. Personal freedom, a humanely responsible personal freedom, has been a dominant theme of mine. My fondest hope is that my son, Brian, may always be happy, and my writings have tried to point the way to a world in which such happiness is possible—or away from worlds where it is not. A sense of and a demand for caring and love have become even more central in my plays in the last decade. My son, Brian, taught me about nurturing and warmth from the moment of his birth in 1978.

"The impetus for the gritty sociological pieces ('Juvie' and 'Addict' and the forthcoming 'Dolls' and 'Blues' and 'Children's') was my rising horror of the world into which Brian was growing. I was aware of excellent material on my target subjects, but it was inaccessible to many young people due to the brutal frankness of its language. There had to be a way to deal with these subjects powerfully and honestly and yet retain performability for this audience. The popularity of 'Juvie' and 'Addict' attests to the success of these experiments (This also underlines my long-held conviction that simply knowing a word is insufficient justification for using it).

"I find that *having written* is a great joy. The prospect of writing, however, is chilling and the process itself is abhorrent. A solid writing regimen is the best thing for a writer. I wish I had one. The best impetus for me is happening upon something so frightening that I cannot *not* write about it. Whether the work begins immediately or gestates over a period of time, the work will happen. I must try to help. Perhaps the most treasured cliche in writing goes: 'Write what you know about.' That advice is nearly correct for me. Simply alter it to read: 'Write what you want to know about.'"

AVOCATIONAL INTERESTS: Computers, composing music, travel.

*   *   *

McDONOUGH, Jerry
    See McDONOUGH, Jerome

*   *   *

McFEELY, Mary Drake   1932-

PERSONAL: Born June 30, 1932, in New York, N.Y.; daughter of Joseph W. (a lawyer) and Mae (McClave) Drake; married William S. McFeely (a historian); children: William Drake, Eliza, Jennifer. *Education:* Smith College, B.A., 1953; Southern Connecticut State College, M.S.L.S., 1970.

ADDRESSES: Home—126 Dearing St., Athens, Ga. 30605.

CAREER: New Haven Free Public Library, New Haven, Conn., branch librarian, 1966-69; New Haven Colony Historical Society, New Haven, librarian, 1969-70; Amherst College, Amherst, Mass., assistant reference librarian, 1971-74; Smith College, Northampton, Mass., reference librarian, 1974-86; freelance editor, 1986—. Member of American Book Award selection committee for biography and autobiography, 1980.

MEMBER: American Library Association, Association of College and Research Libraries.

AWARDS, HONORS: Fellow of Council on Library Resources, 1978-79.

WRITINGS:

Women's Work in Britain and America, G. K. Hall, 1982.
(Editor) *Women's Annual 1984-1985,* G. K. Hall, 1985.
Lady Inspectors: The Campaign for a Better Workplace 1893-1921, Basil Blackwell, 1988.

*   *   *

McINTOSH, Kinn Hamilton
    (Catherine Aird)

PERSONAL: Born in England; daughter of Robert Aeneas Cameron (a physician) and V. J. (Kinnis) McIntosh. *Education:* Attended school in Huddersfield, England.

ADDRESSES: Agent—Hughes, Lassie Ltd., 31 Southampton Row, London WC1B 5HL, England.

CAREER: Writer.

AWARDS, HONORS: A Most Contagious Game was selected by Anthony Boucher as one of the thirteen outstanding mystery novels of 1967.

WRITINGS:

UNDER PSEUDONYM CATHERINE AIRD

The Religious Body, Doubleday, 1966.
A Most Contagious Game (Mystery Guild selection), Doubleday, 1967.
Henrietta Who? (Mystery Guild selection), Doubleday, 1968.
The Complete Steel, MacDonald & Co., 1969, published as *The Stately Home Murder,* Doubleday, 1970.
A Late Phoenix, Doubleday, 1971.
His Burial Too, Doubleday, 1973.
Slight Mourning, Collins, 1975, Doubleday, 1976.
Parting Break, Doubleday, 1977.
Some Die Elegant, Doubleday, 1979.
Passing Strange, Doubleday, 1980.
Last Respects, Doubleday, 1982.
Harm's Way, Doubleday, 1984.

OTHER

Also editor, under name Kinn Hamilton McIntosh, of *Sturry—The Changing Scene,* 1972, *Fordwich—The Lost Port,* 1975, and *Villages of the Stone Lathe,* 1979.

WORK IN PROGRESS: Biographies of Gordon Daviot and Josephine Tey; a novel; a book of local history.

SIDELIGHTS: Kinn Hamilton McIntosh, writing under the pseudonym Catherine Aird, has been grouped "among the more civilized practitioners of fictional homicide" by *Washington Post Book World* critic Jean M. White. McIntosh's forte is constructing murder stories set in small English villages. In one novel, *His Burial Too,* the action hinges around a church belfry "whose only door is blocked by heavy fragments of a marble statuary group that fell, crunching a luckless chap beneath it," as Charles Champlin describes it in a *Los Angeles Times* review. The critic adds that McIntosh's "is a lively and intelligent voice, finding her own place in a familiar but not yet exhausted tradition."

BIOGRAPHICAL/CRITICAL SOURCES:

PERIODICALS

Los Angeles Times, February 27, 1981.
Washington Post Book World, March 15, 1981.

*   *   *

McKENNA, Patricia
    See GOEDICKE, Patricia (McKenna)

*   *   *

McLAREN, Colin Andrew   1940-

PERSONAL: Born December 14, 1940, in Eastcote, Middlesex, England; son of Kenneth George (a meteorologist) and Elizabeth Maxwell (a teacher; maiden name, Raisbeck) McLaren; married Janice Patricia Foale (a medical sociologist), March 25, 1964; children: Judith Rebecca, Justin Benedict. *Education:* University of London, B.A., 1963, M.Phil., 1973.

ADDRESSES: Home—Aberdeen, Scotland. *Office*—The Library, King's College, University of Aberdeen, Aberdeen, Scotland.

CAREER: London County Council, London, England, assistant archivist, 1963-65; University of London, London, re-

search assistant, 1965-67; London Borough of Hammersmith, London, archivist, 1967-69; University of Aberdeen, Aberdeen, Scotland, archivist and keeper of manuscripts, 1969—.

AWARDS, HONORS: Festival Fringe First Award from Edinburgh Festival, 1976; Sony/Society of authors Award for best adaptation for radio, 1986, for "Munchausen."

WRITINGS:

FICTION

Rattus Rex, Rex Collins, 1978.
Crows in a Winter Landscape, Rex Collins, 1979.
Mother of the Free, Rex Collins, 1980.
A Twister Over the Thames, Rex Collins, 1981.
The Warriors Under the Stone, Rex Collins, 1982.

PLAYS; FIRST PRODUCED IN EDINBURGH, SCOTLAND, AT EDINBURGH FESTIVAL

(With W. J. S. Kirton) "STG 75" (revue), 1975.
"An Exotic in Edinburgh" (one-man), 1976.
(With Kirton) "STG 76" (revue), 1976.
"The Anatomy Lesson" (one-man), 1977.
(With Kirton) "ARC 1" (revue), 1977.

RADIO PROGRAMS; FIRST BROADCAST BY BRITISH BROADCASTING CORP. (BBC-RADIO)

"An Exotic in Edinburgh" (based on own one-man play), 1977.
"Round Tower Tales," 1980.
"Thirty-nine and Counting," 1981.
"Six From South Kensington," 1982.
"Camerarities," 1983.
"Storytellers," 1984.
"Broomhouse Reach," 1984.
"Collectors' Items," 1985.
"Romances and Picaresques," 1985.
"Munchausen," 1985.
"Reflections of a Nation," 1986.
"Embracing the Eccentric," 1987.
"The Star, the Light and the Flame," 1987.

OTHER

Contributor of stories and articles to *Look and Listen.*

SIDELIGHTS: Colin Andrew McLaren told *CA:* "When I was young I quickly picked up my parents' enthusiasm for historical fiction and cannot now remember a time when I did not intend to write it. By the age of ten, however, I realized that a writer's life was a lot more comfortable if he had a profession to support him and discovered, to my astonishment, that if I became an archivist, people would actually pay me a salary for doing what I most enjoyed—reading and deciphering historical documents. I therefore did what was necessary at school and university to enter that profession. Once I was established in it, I served the usual apprenticeship of writing for magazines and the stage and published my first novel when I was thirty-seven, two years later than I had intended. I have no other interests or occupations beyond reading the London *Times,* watching a decent game of rugby or cricket, and keeping up with the latest productions at the National Theatre and the R.S.C."

*   *   *

McLEAVE, Hugh George   1923-

PERSONAL: Born July 28, 1923, in Kilwinning, Scotland;

son of Nathaniel and Letitia (Johnstone) McLeave; married December 19, 1956. *Education:* University of Glasgow, M.A., 1949. *Religion:* Church of Scotland.

ADDRESSES: Home—36, Cours Gambetta, 13000 Aix-en-Provence, France. *Agent*—Harold Ober Associates, 40 East 49th St., New York, N.Y. 10017.

CAREER: Journalist in London, England, 1950-67, served as science correspondent for *News Chronicle* and *Daily Mail,* 1954-67, and as editor of *Stethoscope* (medical journal); full-time writer, 1967—. *Military service:* British Army, more than five years in World War II, with service in the Far East most of that time; became captain.

MEMBER: Savage Club.

AWARDS, HONORS: The Risk Takers was chosen by the American Heart Association as one of the best medical books of 1963; *The Damned Die Hard* was chosen by the Military Book Club as its book of 1973.

WRITINGS:

NONFICTION

Chesney: The Fabulous Murderer, W. H. Allen, 1954.
McIndoe: Plastic Surgeon, Muller, 1961.
The Risk Takers, Muller, 1962, Holt, 1963.
A Time to Heal: The Life of Ian Aird, Heinemann, 1964.
The Last Pharaoh: Farouk of Egypt, M. Joseph, 1969, McCall, 1970.
The Damned Die Hard (Playboy Book Club and Literary Guild selection), Saturday Review Press, 1973.
A Man and His Mountain (biography of Paul Cezanne), Macmillan, 1977.
Rogues in the Gallery, David R. Godine, 1981.

FICTION

The Steel Balloon, Muller, 1964.
The Sword and the Scales, Harcourt, 1968.
Vodka on Ice, Harcourt, 1969.
A Question of Negligence, Harcourt, 1970.
Only Gentlemen Can Play, Harcourt, 1974.
A Borderline Case, Scribner, 1979.
Double Exposure, Scribner, 1979.
No Face in the Mirror, Macmillan, 1980.
Second Time Around, Walker & Co., 1981.
The Icarus Threat, Gollancz, 1984.
The Life and Death of Liam Faulds, St. Martin's, 1984.
Death Masque, Hale, 1985, Walker & Co., 1986.

SIDELIGHTS: Hugh George McLeave told *CA:* "For me, writing is a compulsive activity. I like to think creative writing is really holding a dialogue with the subconscious mind and allowing the reader to eavesdrop on the result."

McLeave's books have been translated into several languages, including German, Dutch, French, and Danish.

AVOCATIONAL INTERESTS: Travel, music, golf, swimming, chess, languages (speaks French, Spanish, and German).

*   *   *

McMAHON, Pat
   See HOCH, Edward D(entinger)

MELONE, Albert P(hilip)   1942-

PERSONAL: Born April 25, 1942, in Chicago, Ill.; son of Dominic A. (an electronics technician) and Catherine (Bongeorno) Melone; married Peggy Harles, August 26, 1971; children: Dominic, Ann, Peter. *Education:* Mount San Antonio College, A.A., 1962; California State University, Los Angeles, B.A., 1964, M.A., 1967; attended Loyola Marymount University, 1964-65; University of Iowa, Ph.D., 1972.

ADDRESSES: Home—109 North Rod Lane, Carbondale, Ill. 62901. *Office*—Department of Political Science, Southern Illinois University, Carbondale, Ill. 62901.

CAREER: Idaho State University, Pocatello, lecturer, 1966, instructor in government, 1967; California State University, Los Angeles, instructor in political science, 1968; North Dakota State University, Fargo, assistant professor, 1970-75, associate professor of political science, 1975-80, chairperson of department, 1973-76; Southern Illinois University, Carbondale, visiting associate professor, 1979-80, associate professor, 1980-85, professor of political science, 1985—. Manuscript referee for Southern Illinois University Press, Brooks/Cole Publishing Co., North Dakota Institute for Regional Studies, and Minnesota Academy of Science. Consultant to North Dakota Supreme Court and Professional Market Research Audits and Surveys, New York.

MEMBER: American Political Science Association, Law and Society Association, American Judicature Society, Midwest Political Science Association, Western Political Science Association, Pi Sigma Alpha.

WRITINGS:

Lawyers, Public Policy, and Interest Group Politics, University Press of America, 1977.
(With Carl Kalvelage) *Primer on Constitutional Law,* Palisades, 1982.
(Contributor) Stuart S. Nagel, Erika Fairchild, and Anthony Champagne, editors, *The Political Science of Criminal Justice,* C. C Thomas, 1982.
Administrative Law Primer, Palisades, 1983.
Primer in Political Science, Palisades, 1983.
(Contributor) Bruce Leone, editor, *Criminal Justice: Opposing Viewpoints,* Greenhaven Press, 1983.
(With H. B. Jacobini and Kalvelage) *Research Essentials of Administrative Law,* Palisades, 1983.
Bridges to Knowledge in Political Science: A Handbook for Research, Palisades, 1984.
(Contributor) Fairchild and Vincent Webb, editors, *The Politics of Crime and Criminal Justice,* Sage Publications, 1985.
(Contributor) Walter F. Murphy and C. Hermon Pritchett, editors, *Courts, Judges, and Politics,* 4th edition, Random House, 1986.
Judicial Review and American Democracy, Iowa State University Press, 1988.

Also contributor to *Encyclopedia of the American Judicial System,* Volume II. Contributor of articles and reviews to law and political science journals, including *Policy Studies Journal, Journal of Politics, Judicature, Western Political Quarterly,* and *North Dakota Law Review.* Manuscript referee for *Journal of Politics, American Politics Quarterly,* and *Western Politics Quarterly.*

SIDELIGHTS: Albert P. Melone told *CA:* "My writing entails an attempt to explain the puzzle which is American politics.

While others find the study of the poor and powerless a significant avenue for investigation, I prefer to focus upon the rich and the powerful. My earliest and recurrent writings reflect that commitment. The greatest problem I face is deciding what not to research and publish. It is important to press forward with the original idea, tolerating occasional diversions but returning to those themes which remain truly important.''

*   *   *

MENESES, Enrique 1929-
(Ricardo Carvajal, Jeff Crain)

PERSONAL: Surname is pronounced Me-*ness*-es; born October 21, 1929, in Madrid, Spain; son of Enrique (a writer) and Carmen (Miniaty) Meneses; married Barbara Montgomery (a journalist), July 26, 1963; children: Barbara. *Education:* Received primary and secondary education at schools in France, Portugal, and Spain; Instituto San Isidro, Madrid, Bachillerato, 1949; studied law at University of Salamanca, 1949-50, and law and journalism at University of Madrid, 1950-51. *Politics:* Independent. *Religion:* ''Non-practicing Roman Catholic.''

ADDRESSES: Home—Calle Ginzo de Limia 53, Madrid-34, Spain. *Office*— Television Espanola, Prado del Rey, Madrid-24, Spain.

CAREER: Reader's Digest, circulation manager for Iberian Edition, 1951-53; Prensa Intercontinental, Paris, France, correspondent in Madrid, Spain, 1954; *Informaciones* (daily newspaper), Madrid, correspondent in Cairo, Egypt, 1955; *Paris-Match* (magazine), and Europe Number One (radio station), Paris, correspondent in Cairo, 1956-57, Havana, Cuba, 1957-58, Cairo, 1958-59, and New Delhi, India, 1959-60; Delta Press, Paris, managing editor, 1961-62; correspondent in New York City for *Blanco y Negro* (Madrid weekly magazine), Rex Features (London agency), and Dalmas (Paris news agency), 1962-63; Life Editorial Services, New York City, representative in Madrid, 1964—; Spanish National Television Network, Madrid, editor-in-chief of monthly news hour, ''A Toda Plana,'' 1964-65; Fotopress (feature agency), Madrid, editor, 1964—; Lumefa Publishing Co., Madrid, general manager, 1966-72; *Cosmopolis* (monthly news magazine), Madrid, managing editor, 1968—. Staff journalist of ''Los Reporteros,'' Spanish weekly television news program, 1973-77; affiliated with television consumer's program, 1981, and ''Robinson in Africa,'' an adventure series, 1982; also affiliated with radio series ''Los Adventureros,'' 1982. Chairman, Adventurers Ltd. (London), 1988. *Military service:* Spanish Army, 1950-51.

MEMBER: Overseas Press Club of America, Real Automobile Club of Spain.

WRITINGS:

Fidel Castro, A. Aguado, 1966, Taplinger, 1968.
Nasser: El Ultimo faraon (title means ''Nasser, the Last of the Pharoahs''), Prensa Espanola, 1968.
(With others) *How I Got That Story,* Dutton, 1968.
Seso y Sexo (title means ''Sex and Brains''), Campus, 1979.
Escrito en Carne (title means ''Written on Flesh''), Planeta, 1979.
Robinson in Africa: A Human Experience, Planeta, 1985.

Also author of *Naked Witch,* 1975. Author of magazine articles under pseudonyms Ricardo Carvajal and Jeff Crain. Editor

of Spanish editions of *Lui* (Paris), 1977, *Playboy,* 1980, and *Los Adventureros,* a monthly travel and adventure magazine.

WORK IN PROGRESS: Escrito en Aire (title means ''Written on the Air''), a second part to *Escrito en Carne.*

SIDELIGHTS: Enrique Meneses spent a year with Fidel Castro and his handful of rebels in the days before Batista was ousted. The author states that his biographies are not traditional, explaining that he has ''placed less emphasis on chronological detail than on the place occupied by Castro and Nasser within the political, historical, socio-economic and moral circumstances affecting their lives.'' He is convinced that ''man is a Product of his Environment and his own personal drive.'' *Fidel Castro* was also published in England and in German and Japanese translations.

In 1956, Meneses organized and took part in an overland expedition through Africa from Cairo to Capetown, and in 1960 formed a second expedition to the region of Bankatti on the Indian-Nepal frontier. In 1983 Meneses embarked with a film crew on a three-month trip from Madrid to Zaire and Cairo, for a television series on Africa. Meneses told *CA* about his interest in ''promoting the spirit of adventure among youngsters'' and added, ''Adventure is the best drug you can find.''

BIOGRAPHICAL/CRITICAL SOURCES:

PERIODICALS

America, October 12, 1968.
Library Journal, October 1, 1968.
Observer Review, June 30, 1968.

*   *   *

MERRILL, Dean 1943-

PERSONAL: Born December 17, 1943, in Los Angeles, Calif.; son of D. Raymond (a minister) and Mary Lucille (Frantz) Merrill; married Grace LaVonne Danielson, June 25, 1966; children: Nathan, Rhonda, Tricia. *Education:* Chicago Bible College, Th.B., 1964; Syracuse University, M.A., 1970. *Religion:* Christian.

ADDRESSES: Office—*Christian Herald,* 40 Overlook Dr., Chappaqua, N.Y. 10514.

CAREER: Campus Life (magazine), Carol Stream, Ill., various editorial postitions, 1965-69, 1971-73; Oral Roberts University, Tulsa, Okla., director of university information, 1970-71; Creation House, Inc. (publishers), Carol Stream, executive editor, 1973-74; David C. Cook Publishing Co., Elgin, Ill., various editorial positions, 1974-81; *Leadership* (magazine), Carol Stream, senior editor, 1981-85; *Christian Herald,* Chappaqua, N.Y., editor/vice-president, 1985—. Visiting lecturer in communications, Wheaton College, 1973-75.

MEMBER: Evangelical Press Association (president, 1985-87).

WRITINGS:

(With Ken Taylor) *The Jesus Book,* Tyndale, 1971.
(With Taylor) *The Way,* Tyndale, 1972.
(With Harold Myra) *Rock, Bach, and Superschlock,* A. J. Holman, 1972.
(With Janet Lynn) *Peace and Love,* Creation House, 1973.
(Editor with Clayton Baumann) *125 Crowdbreakers,* Regal Books, 1974.
The Husband Book, Zondervan, 1977, published as *How to Really Love Your Wife,* 1980.

(With Bonnie Thielmann) *The Broken God*, David Cook, 1979.
Another Chance, Zondervan, 1981.
Clergy Couples in Crisis, Word Books, 1985.
(With wife, Grace Merrill) *Together at Home*, Thomas Nelson, 1985.

Contributor to religious periodicals, including *Eternity, Christianity Today, Today's Christian Woman, Decision,* and *Christian Reader.*

* * *

MILES, (Mary) Patricia 1930-

PERSONAL: Born September 8, 1930, in Lancashire, England; daughter of Robert (a businessman) and Bridget (a teacher and writer; maiden name, Clancy) Storey; married Francis George Miles (a company executive), October 17, 1953; children: Patrick, Siobhan, Hugh. *Education:* Somerville College, Oxford, B.A. (with honors), 1953, M.A., 1956. *Politics:* "Conservative, with some reservations."

ADDRESSES: Home—Windrush, Rabley Heath, Welwyn, Hertfordshire AL6 9UF, England. *Agent*—Curtis Brown Group Ltd., 162-168 Regent St., London W1R 5TA, England; and Harold Ober Associates, Inc., 40 East 49th St., New York, N.Y. 10017.

CAREER: Writer. Oxford University Press, London, England, reader of Latin and Greek books, 1953-54; Latin teacher in girls' schools in Kent, England, 1958-60, and 1963-65; Nobel Comprehensive School, Stevenage, England, teacher of French, English, and Latin, 1967-76.

AWARDS, HONORS: The Gods in Winter was chosen for the Hans Christian Andersen list, 1980.

WRITINGS:

Nobody's Child (for children and adults), Dutton, 1975.
If I Survive (for children and adults), Hamish Hamilton, 1976.
The Gods in Winter (juvenile humor/fantasy), Dutton, 1978.
A Disturbing Influence (for adolescents), Lothrop, 1978.
Louther Hall (for adolescents), Hamish Hamilton, 1981.
(Contributor) Jean Russell, editor, *The Methuen Book of Sinister Stories,* illustrations by Tony Ross, Methuen, 1982.
The Mind Pirates (juvenile science fiction), Hamish Hamilton, 1983.
Beloved Enemy, Dragon Books, 1987.
Sweet Peril, Dragon Books, 1988.

Work is represented in several anthologies and has been translated into Swedish, Spanish, German, and Dutch.

WORK IN PROGRESS: Stone of Talorcan, a juvenile Celtic-based fantasy.

SIDELIGHTS: Patricia Miles told *CA:* "I still teach occasionally in a creative writing program for schoolchildren, and my personal aim is still to provide satisfying entertainment. More precisely: to make the past come alive for children, with humor if possible, and to use language with vigor.

"I really believe in the power for good of the imagination—by encouraging the natural sympathy and insight of the reader. We still live in the same unspoiled stretch of countryside twenty miles north of London and I still work sometimes as a guide in our local manorhouse (1492 A.D.), chiefly for the interest of meeting people, and for the historical background."

"In 1978, I accompanied my husband on a year's business assignment in Tokyo, Japan. On the way there and back we managed to visit Bangkok, Hong Kong, Hawaii, Mexico City, and also San Francisco, Washington, New York, and Swarthmore, Pa. . . . What a very great pleasure!"

AVOCATIONAL INTERESTS: Gardening, travel in France, Scandinavia, and Italy.

* * *

MILHOUSE, Paul W(illiam) 1910-

PERSONAL: Born August 31, 1910, in St. Francisville, Ill.; son of Willis Cleveland (a merchant) and Carrie (Pence) Milhouse; married Mary Frances Noblitt, June 29, 1932; children: Mary Catherine (Mrs. Ronald L. Hauswald), Pauline Joyce (Mrs. Arthur Vermillion), David. *Education:* Indiana Central College (now University of Indianapolis), A.B., 1932; American Theological Seminary (no longer in existence), B.D., 1937, Th.D., 1945.

ADDRESSES: Home—2213 Northwest 56th Ter., Oklahoma City, Okla. 73112. *Office*—Oklahoma City University, Oklahoma City, Okla. 73106.

CAREER: Pastor in Birds, Ill., 1928-29; ordained to ministry of United Brethren Church, 1931; pastor in Elliott, Ill., 1932-37, Olney, Ill., 1937-41, and Decatur, Ill., 1941-51; *Telescope-Messenger*, Harrisburg, Pa., associate editor, 1951-59; Evangelical United Brethren Church, executive secretary of Council of Administration, Dayton, Ohio, 1959-60, bishop of Kansas City, Mo., 1960-68; United Methodist Church (formed by union of Evangelical United Brethren Church and the Methodist Church, 1968), bishop of Oklahoma City, Okla., 1968-80; Oklahoma City University, Oklahoma City, bishop-in-residence, 1980—. Former member of General Assembly of World Council of Churches and National Council of Churches.

AWARDS, HONORS: D.D. from Indiana Central College, 1950, and Southern Methodist University, 1969; H.L.D., Westmar College, 1965; S.T.D., Oklahoma City University, 1969; Distinguished Alumnus Award, University of Indianapolis, 1978; Top-Hand Award for distinguished service, Oklahoma City Chamber of Commerce, 1980; Distinguished Service Award, Oklahoma City University, 1980.

WRITINGS:

Enlisting and Developing Church Leaders, Warner Press, 1945.
Come unto Me, Otterbein Press, 1946.
Except the Lord Build the House, Evangelical Press (Harrisburg), 1949.
Doorways to Spiritual Living, Otterbein Press, 1950.
Christian Worship in Symbol and Ritual, Evangelical Press, 1953.
Lift up Your Eyes, Otterbein Press, 1956.
Laymen in the Church, Warner Press, 1957.
At Life's Crossroads, Warner Press, 1959.
(Editor) *Facing Frontiers*, Otterbein Press, 1960.
Philip William Otterbein, Upper Room, 1968.
Nineteen Bishops of the Evangelical United Brethren Church, Parthenon Press, 1974.
History and Theological Roots of United Methodists, Cowan, 1980.
Organizing for Effective Ministry, Cowan, 1980.
Oklahoma City University: Miracle at 23rd and Blackwelder, Oklahoma Heritage Association, 1984.
Detours into Yesterday, Oklahoma United Methodist Church, 1984.
Turning Dollars into Service, Cowan, 1987.

Also author of a series of historical articles for *United Methodist Church Paper*. Contributor to church periodicals.

WORK IN PROGRESS: St. Luke's of Oklahoma City.

*   *   *

MILLER, Barbara S(toler) 1940-

PERSONAL: Born August 8, 1940, in New York, N.Y.; daughter of Louis O. (a business executive) and Sara (Cracken) Stoler; children: Gwenn, Alison. *Education:* Barnard College, A.B. (magna cum laude), 1962; Columbia University, M.A., 1964; University of Pennsylvania, Ph.D. (with distinction), 1968.

ADDRESSES: Office—Department of Oriental Studies, Barnard College, Columbia University, New York, N.Y. 10027.

CAREER: Columbia University, Barnard College, New York, N.Y., assistant professor, 1968-72, associate professor, 1972-77, professor of Oriental studies, 1977—, Samuel R. Milbank Professor, 1987—, chairman of department, 1972-74, 1979-87.

Member of Joint Committee on South Asia, American Council of Learned Societies-Social Science Research Council, 1982-85. Director of a summer seminar for college teachers, National Endowment for the Humanities, 1981. Member of publication board, Columbia University Press, 1973-79; faculty representative, Barnard College Board of Trustees, 1976-79; Columbia University Society of Fellows in the Humanities, member of governing board, 1978—, chairman, 1986-88; cochairperson, Barnard Studies in the Humanities, 1978—; member of executive committee, Southern Asia Institute, Columbia, 1979—; board member, American Council of Learned Societies, 1988. Member of advisory committee, Princeton University Press, 1980-86; member of advisory council on archaeology, anthropology, and related disciplines, Smithsonian Institution, 1983-85.

MEMBER: PEN (member of translation committee), American Oriental Society (director-at-large), Association for Asian Studies, American Numismatic Society, Phi Beta Kappa.

AWARDS, HONORS: Avery and Jule Hopwood Award for writing, University of Michigan, 1959; Institute of Indian Studies, senior fellow, 1974-75, 1981-82, travel grant, summer, 1977; Guggenheim fellow, 1974-75; Mellon fellow, 1976; National Council of Women award, 1979, for work in higher education; Social Science Research Council, South Asia fellow, 1981-82. Also recipient of a number of grants or stipends from American Association of University Women, 1965-66, National Endowment for the Humanities, summer, 1971, American Philosophical Society, summer, 1971, American Council of Learned Societies, 1973 and 1978, Smithsonian Institution, 1981, and National Endowment for the Humanities, 1986-88.

WRITINGS:

(Translator from the Sanskrit) D. D. Kosambi, editor, *Bhartrihari: Poems,* Columbia University Press, 1967.
(Editor and translator from the Sanskrit) *Phantasies of a Love-Thief: The Caurapancasika Attributed to Bilhana,* Columbia University Press, 1970.
(With Leonard Gordan) *A Syllabus of Indian Civilization,* Columbia University Press, 1971.

(Contributor) Jaroslav Prusek, editor, *The Dictionary of Oriental Literatures,* Basic Books, 1973.
(Editor and translator from the Sanskrit) *Love Song of the Dark Lord: Jayedeva's Gitagovinda,* Oxford University Press, 1977.
The Hermit and the Horse-Thief: Sanskrit Poems of Bhartrihari and Bilhana, Columbia University Press, 1978.
(Translator from the Spanish) Agueda Pizzaro, *Sombraventadora/Shadowinnower,* Columbia University Press, 1979.
(Editor and author of biographical essay) *Exploring India's Sacred Art: Selected Papers of Stella Kramrisch,* University of Pennsylvania Press, 1983.
(Contributor) *Essays in Gupta Culture,* Motilal Banarsidass (Delhi, India), 1983.
(Editor and translator from the Sanskrit) *Theatre of Memory: The Plays of Kalidasa,* Columbia University Press, 1984.
(Editor with Mildred Archer) William G. Archer, *Songs for the Bride: Wedding Rites of Rural India,* Brooklyn College Press, 1985.
The Bhagavad Gita: Krishna's Counsel in Time of War, Columbia University Press, 1986.

Also editor of *The Powers of Art: Patronage in Indian Culture, 1000 B.C.-1900 A.D.* Also contributor to *The Divine Consort,* 1982. Contributor to numerous journals. Guest editor, *Journal of South Asian Literature,* 1971. Member of editorial board, *Translations from the Oriental Classics,* Columbia University Press, 1975—.

WORK IN PROGRESS: The Buddha: His Way to Enlightenment, a translation and study of Asvagosha's *Buddhacarita; Yoga: Discipline of Body and Spirit,* a translation and study of the Yogasutras attributed to Patanjali; a novel; studies of text and image in Indian art, focusing on coins, painting, and poetry.

SIDELIGHTS: Barbara S. Miller told *CA:* "My close rereading of works of American and European literature in the context of Asian works has stimulated me to return to a major preoccupation of my student years: the writing of poetry and fiction. I am currently at work on a novel, tentatively entitled *A Nest of Mothers.* In it I am examining the relationships among an orphaned young Russian woman, her brother (an air force pilot 'lost' in the Himalayan foothills while flying a transport plane from India to China in 1944), her two aunts (one a poet, the other a physician), and her foster mother (an eccentric collector of Oriental art). The characters are modeled on various members of my family, partly based on diaries, poems, and other documents that have recently come into my possession.

"I feel that the novel is the most appropriate form in which to express the range of my ideas about the 'encounter' with Asia. Rather than conflicting with my scholarly work, the long and highly disciplined sessions of analyzing my fictional characters are helping me to 'flesh out' the personalities of the elusive kings, priests, and poets of ancient India."

Miller is competent in French, Spanish, Hindi, Sanskrit, Pali, and Prakrits. She has traveled extensively in India and also in other parts of Asia, Europe, South America, and Africa.

BIOGRAPHICAL/CRITICAL SOURCES:

PERIODICALS

Antioch Review, spring, 1980.
Times Literary Supplement, December 23, 1983.

MILLER, John P(earse, Jr.) 1943-

PERSONAL: Born July 27, 1943, in Kansas City, Mo.; son of John Pearse (a businessman) and Joy (Vencill) Miller; married Jean Foley, December 30, 1967; children: Patrick, Nancy. *Education:* Attended University of Vienna, 1963-64; University of Missouri, B.A. (honors), 1965; Harvard University, M.A.T., 1967; University of Toronto, Ph.D., 1971.

CAREER: High school teacher of history in Scarsdale, N.Y., 1965-66; University of Missouri, Kansas City, instructor in education, 1968-69; Ontario Institute for Studies in Education, Thunder Bay, assistant professor of curriculum, beginning 1972. Has conducted workshops, seminars, and evaluation projects.

MEMBER: Association of Humanistic Psychology, Association of Transpersonal Psychology, Ontario History and Social Science Teachers Association, Phi Beta Kappa.

WRITINGS:

Humanizing the Classroom: Models of Teaching in Affective Education, Praeger, 1976.
(With Richard Hersh) *Values Education: Alternative Models,* McKay, 1978.
(With Hersh and Glen D. Fielding) *Models of Moral Education: An Appraisal,* Longman, 1980.
The Compassionate Teacher: How to Teach and Learn with Your Whole Self, Prentice-Hall, 1981.
The Educational Spectrum: Orientations to Curriculum, Longman, 1983.
(With Wayne Seller) *Curriculum, Perspectives and Practice,* Longman, 1985.

Contributor of articles and reviews to American and Canadian journals.

SIDELIGHTS: John P. Miller once wrote *CA:* "My writing in education is influenced by recent developments in humanistic psychology and transpersonal psychology. I am particularly interested in research on meditation, states of consciousness, and the brain, and its implications for education."

BIOGRAPHICAL/CRITICAL SOURCES:

PERIODICALS

Educational Studies, summer, 1977.*

*   *   *

MILLER, Zane L. 1934-

PERSONAL: Born May 19, 1934, in Lima, Ohio; son of Paul Jennings (a railroadman) and Beryl (Dutton) Miller; married Janet Smith, December 27, 1955. *Education:* Miami University, Oxford, Ohio, B.S., 1956, M.A., 1959; University of Chicago, Ph.D., 1966. *Politics:* Democrat.

ADDRESSES: Home—812 Dunore Rd., Cincinnati, Ohio. *Office*—Department of History, University of Cincinnati, Cincinnati, Ohio 45221.

CAREER: Northwestern University, Evanston, Ill., instructor in American history, 1964-65; University of Cincinnati, Cincinnati, Ohio, assistant professor, 1965-70, associate professor, 1970-74, professor of history, 1974—, co-director of Center for Neighborhood and Community Studies, 1981—.

MEMBER: American Historical Association, Organization of American Historians, American Association of University Professors, Southern Historical Association, Ohio Academy of History.

AWARDS, HONORS: National Science Foundation grant; National Endowment for the Humanities fellow; Social Science Research Council research fellow; Newberry Library fellow; Ohio Academy of History book award, for *Suburb: Neighborhood and Community in Forest Park, Ohio, 1935-1976.*

WRITINGS:

Boss Cox's Cincinnati, Oxford University Press, 1968.
(Editor with Henry D. Shapiro) *Science and Society in the West: Selected Writings of Dr. Daniel Drake,* University Press of Kentucky, 1970.
(Contributor) Kenneth Jackson and Stanley K. Schultz, editors, *Cities in American History,* Knopf, 1972.
(Contributor) James F. Richardson, editor, *The American City: Historical Studies,* Xerox College Publishing, 1972.
The Urbanization of Modern America: A Brief History, Harcourt, 1973, revised edition, 1987.
(Contributor) Raymond Mohl and Richardson, editors, *The Urban Experience,* Wadsworth, 1973.
(Contributor) Leo Schnore, editor, *The New Urban History,* Princeton University Press, 1975.
(Contributor) Alexander Callow, editor, *The Urban Bosses,* Oxford University Press, 1976.
(With Shapiro) *Clifton: Neighborhood and Community in an Urban Setting,* Laboratory in American Civilization, University of Cincinnati, 1976.
(With George Roth) *Cincinnati's Music Hall,* Jordan & Co., 1978.
(Editor with Paula Dubeck) *Urban Professionals and the Future of the Metropolis,* Kennikat, 1980.
(Contributor) Greer, editor, *Ethnics, Machines, and the American Urban Future,* Schenkman, 1981.
Suburb: Neighborhood and Community in Forest Park, Ohio, 1935-1976, University of Tennessee Press, 1981.
(Editor with Thomas M. Jenkins) *The Planning Partnership,* Sage Publications, 1982.
(Contributor) Clive Emsley, editor, *Essays in Comparative History,* Open University Press, 1984.
(Contributor) Gary B. Nash, editor, *Retracing the Past,* Harper, 1986.
(With Howard Gillette, Jr.) *American Urbanism: A Historiographical Review,* Greenwood Press, 1987.

Co-editor of "Urban Life and Urban Landscape" series, Ohio State University Press, and of "Greater Cincinnati Bicentennial History" series, University of Illinois Press, both 1986—. Contributor to history journals.

WORK IN PROGRESS: A research project entitled *Planning and the Persisting Past: Cincinnati's Over-the-Rhine since 1984.*

*   *   *

MILLS, Claudia 1954-

PERSONAL: Born August 21, 1954, in New York, N.Y.; daughter of Charles Howard (a safety engineer) and Helen (a teacher; maiden name, Lederleitner) Mills; married Richard W. Wahl (a natural resources economist), October 19, 1985. *Education:* Wellesley College, B.A., 1976; Princeton University, M.A., 1979.

ADDRESSES: Home—7302 Birch Ave., Takoma Park, Md. 20912. *Office*—Center for Philosophy and Public Policy, University of Maryland, College Park, Md. 20742.

CAREER: Four Winds Press, New York, N.Y., editorial secretary and production assistant, 1979-80; University of Maryland, College Park, editor of *QQ: Report from the Center for Philosophy and Public Policy*, 1980—.

MEMBER: Authors Guild, Children's Book Guild of Washington, D.C., Society of Children's Book Writers, Phi Beta Kappa.

WRITINGS:

Luisa's American Dream (juvenile), Four Winds, 1981.
At the Back of the Woods (juvenile), Four Winds, 1982.
The Secret Carousel (juvenile), Four Winds, 1983.
(Editor with Douglas Maclean) *Liberalism Reconsidered*, Rowman & Littlefield, 1983.
All the Living (juvenile), Macmillan, 1983.
What about Annie? (juvenile), Walker, 1985.
Boardwalk with Hotel (juvenile), Macmillan, 1985.
The One and Only Cynthia Jane (juvenile), Macmillan, 1986.
(Editor with Robert K. Fullinwider) *The Moral Foundations of Civil Rights*, Rowman & Littlefield, 1986.
Melanie Magpie (juvenile), Bantam, 1987.
Cally's Enterprise (juvenile), Macmillan, 1988.

SIDELIGHTS: Claudia Mills told *CA:* "I have been writing books for children and teenagers since I was a child and a teenager. My autobiographical manuscript, *T Is for Tarzan*, written when I was fourteen, was widely circulated through my junior high school, as adolescent friends and foes waited turns to see how they were slandered.

"I didn't begin serious professional writing, however, until I left graduate school impulsively in mid-year to take a secretarial job at Four Winds Press. I occupied myself during the four-hour round-trip commute from Princeton by writing picturebook and novel manuscripts, which I submitted to Four Winds Press under various pseudonyms. It was very easy—but so disheartening—to slip a rejected manuscript unobtrusively into my book bag.

"Finally a manuscript proved promising enough on a first skim for the editor to hand it over to me, her secretary, for a reader's report. I took the challenge and wrote an objective, candid report on my own manuscript, including suggestions for needed revisions. The editor forwarded to the author (me) her 'excellent reader's report' and then I dutifully took my own suggestions in rewriting. I finally confessed my duplicity when the manuscript was completed. Fortunately, the editor had a keen sense of humor, and the manuscript was published as *At the Back of the Woods*."

*   *   *

MILNE, Christopher (Robin)   1920-

PERSONAL: Born August 21, 1920, in London, England; son of A(lan) A. (author of "Winnie the Pooh" series) and Dorothy (de Selincourt) Milne; married Lesley de Selincourt, July 24, 1948; children: Clare. *Education:* Trinity College, Cambridge, B.A. (with honors), 1947.

ADDRESSES: Home—Embridge Forge, Dartmouth, Devon TQ6 0LQ, England. *Agent*—Curtis Brown Ltd., 575 Madison Ave., New York, N.Y. 10022.

CAREER: Harbour Bookshop, Dartmouth, England, owner, 1951-81; writer. *Military service:* British Army, Royal Engineers, 1941-46; served in the Middle East and Italy; became lieutenant.

WRITINGS:

The Enchanted Places (autobiography), Methuen, 1974, Dutton, 1975.
The Path through the Trees (autobiography), Dutton, 1979.
The Hollow on the Hill: The Search for a Personal Philosophy, Methuen, 1982.
The Windfall (also see below), Methuen, 1985.
The Open Garden (essays; includes *The Windfall*), Methuen, 1988.

SIDELIGHTS: "Practically everybody's heard of Christopher Robin and his friend 'Winnie-the-Pooh,'" writes Nancy Mills in the *Detroit News Magazine*. "He's the little boy who was immortalized in A. A. Milne's imaginative Pooh Bear tales, first published in 1924. What most people don't know is that Christopher Robin grew up." As Christopher Milne, the author of two autobiographies and a book of philosophy, 'Christopher Robin' reflects on his public life as a literary figure of great renown, and on his private life as a bookseller, husband, and father who champions the preservation of the environment from his secluded home in Devon, England.

Milne's first book, *The Enchanted Places,* delves into his early years and his relationship, often strained, with his parents. Milne's mother, Dorothy de Selincourt (of England's distinguished de Selincourt family), made no secret of the fact that she had wanted a baby girl called Rosemary, and as a result Christopher Robin spent his first eight years with long hair and somewhat unboyish clothes. "I remained a boy," Milne remarks in the book. "But only just. I was one of her few failures." Milne told *CA* that his relationship with his celebrated father was rather closer, "with a shared love of cricket, golf, mathematics and crossword puzzles. [I] even came to share [my] father's unsuspected agnosticism—something which often surprises those who have misinterpreted [his] well known poem 'Vespers' ('Hush! Hush! Whisper who dares? Christopher Robin is saying his prayers.') And [we] both were haunted in later life by ['Christopher Robin's'] world-wide fame."

In a *Time* review of *The Enchanted Places*, Timothy Foote suggests that the book is as much about A. A. Milne as about his son. Foote states: "*Enchanted Places* is eloquent about the joys of countryside, the felicities of light verse. Milne writes with wit and humane perception about his later relationship with his father. In a space hardly larger than a Pooh book, he has, in fact, unobtrusively condensed a mini-memoir, a portrait of A. A. Milne, a bittersweet study of a literary celebrity in the '20s and something very like an annotated *Winnie-the-Pooh*. It is pure HUNNY all the way to the bottom of the jar."

The Path through the Trees, Milne's second autobiography, takes the author from age nineteen, when he yearns to be a World War II combat soldier, through adulthood and the opening of his Harbour Bookshop in the small town of Dartmouth. Roy Fuller, in a *Listener* article, notes the author's "constant inclination to chamfer off the edges of experience, more in a dreamy, self-centered manner than as a way of romanticising things." Fuller continues: "Those with special concerns—fellow-warriors, booksellers, teachers—may find their own bits, so to speak, quite absorbing. Moreover, [Milne] philosophises and observes nature, if not with great profundity, certainly in a fashion appealing to many. It cannot be said that he comes out as a particularly likeable fellow, but one must admire him. He had courage, though not constitutionally courageous." In the *New York Times Book Review*, Moira Hodgson calls *The Path through the Trees* "a sad book. It is not a book about grand passion, great ambition or even eccentric behavior. . . . [It] is not the 'success story' characteristic of most autobiographies. It is the account of the way in which a gentle, shy and kindly man survived worldwide notoriety. Mr. Milne leaves Pooh behind and takes his reader on a country walk—because it is here, in the countryside, that he can turn away from the complexities of the past to the simplicity of the present.''

Milne's great respect for nature and his questioning of Christianity have culminated in his book *The Hollow on the Hill: The Search for a Personal Philosophy*. In this work the author expounds on the need to recognize nature as a supreme life force and urges the preservation of the environment. For Milne, writes an *Economist* reviewer, ''Christianity is ultimately destructive, because its emphasis on heaven encourages its adherents to treat the world as a camp site, and because its insistence on the supremacy of man over the other animals is destroying the balance of nature.'' Brian Sibley, writing about *The Hollow on the Hill* in the *Listener*, is skeptical about Milne's personal philosophy: ''[He] can offer few credentials for speaking on such matters other than the questing curiosity of Everyman, and he is constantly trying to be fair and reasonable and inoffensive, while at the same time attempting to give his essentially after-dinner philosophies an authoritative—even scientific—tone.'' Sibley labels the author's dogma ''a kind of ecological pantheism [that is] probably the oldest religious concept in the world. When he says—and I don't doubt him for a moment—that he has 'an intense and burning love of the natural world,' . . . I can't help thinking he is closer to Adam the gardener or David the harpist than he perhaps realizes.''

Milne told *CA* that his fourth book, *The Windfall*, ''though described as a fable, is more accurately an allegory: it is the history of mankind seen through the eyes of Eve in those early chapters of Genesis. Although expressed in different ways, my theme remains the same: a pantheism that I share with Richard Jefferies and a love of a world that we seem determined to destroy. No doubt those who disagree with me will continue to dismiss what I say in patronising tones. And indeed one can argue that, since there is now so little we can do to avoid it, we might just as well continue on our comfortable way until the Flood engulfs us.''

Milne's appreciation for nature developed in Ashdown Forest, a woodland owned and preserved by the Milne family since 1925. ''It was a heavily wooded ancient forest until the eighteenth century, when the trees were chopped down during the industrial revolution,'' the author told David Langsam of the Toronto *Globe and Mail*. Consisting mostly of open heath, the forest includes about sixty trees and Gills Lap, a section of elevated land flattened at the top and covered with pines. The forest where Milne and his toys once shared the adventures now immortalized in his father's books is open to tourists who come from nearby London.

In 1987, proposed exploration for gas and oil in land adjacent to Ashdown Forest brought the otherwise quiet author into the news as an environmental advocate. He opposes the plans of British Petroleum and Margaret Thatcher's government, who have the most to gain if oil is found there. Not appeased by the company's stated intent to limit the environmental impact of future developments, Milne seeks public support against what he predicts will be the inevitable destruction of a unique and beautiful woodland. Speaking to Langsam, Milne names his fight to preserve the formerly protected site ''the key environmental issue facing Britain.'' England, he points out, has

''very few areas where the public can roam at will and enjoy the scenery. . . . Once they start going to those who wish to look underground for oil, there is very little left of the England of which we are so proud.''

As an author, Christopher Milne inevitably finds himself compared to his father. He tells Mills: ''I was very easily influenced by my father. He never wanted me to and I never dared to enter his particular field—writing—either as a competitor or even as a friendly companion of his. This was his field and he didn't want me there. I didn't ever want to measure myself alongside him, but to some extent I suppose I've had to. It's all right now [that] he's dead. It doesn't really matter whether I succeed. . . . I've now ventured onto his field briefly and I'm happy that it's worked.''

BIOGRAPHICAL/CRITICAL SOURCES:

BOOKS

Authors in the News, Volume 2, Gale, 1976.
Milne, Christopher, *The Enchanted Places*, Methuen, 1974, Dutton, 1975.
Milne, Christopher, *The Path through the Trees*, Dutton, 1979.
Milne, Christopher, *The Hollow on the Hill: The Search for a Personal Philosophy*, Methuen, 1982.

PERIODICALS

Detroit News Magazine, April 25, 1976.
Globe and Mail (Toronto), September 26, 1987.
Listener, September 27, 1979.
New Statesman, January 17, 1975.
New York Times Book Review, September 2, 1979.
Time, June 23, 1975.
Virginia Quarterly Review, winter, 1980.
Washington Post Book World, August 26, 1979.

*   *   *

MILTON, Arthur 1922-

PERSONAL: Born June 7, 1922, in New York, N.Y.; married; children: Donna Eve Conte, Robert V. Conte, Claudia Marie, Robert Laurence, Linda Sue, Patricia Ann.

ADDRESSES: Home—425 East 58th St., New York, N.Y. 10022. *Office*—255 East 49th St., New York, N.Y. 10017.

CAREER: Insurance consumerist. Feature writer for *Financial World*, 1960-65; president of Arthur Milton & Co., Inc. (brokers of life insurance company stock); registered broker for Securities and Exchange Commission; chief executive officer, Arthur Milton Organization (an independent insurance and consulting business). Broadcaster for Armed Forces Radio; guest on television and radio programs; lecturer and public speaker. Sponsor of New York State's College of Insurance; insurance and finance consultant.

MEMBER: General Insurance Brokers Association (former member of board of directors), Atlantic Alumni of the Life Insurance Agency Management Association (former member of board of directors).

AWARDS, HONORS: Named life insurance man of the year five times on an All-Star Honor Roll of industry leaders, 1950-60.

WRITINGS:

Life Insurance Stocks: The Modern Gold Rush, Citadel, 1963.

How to Get a Dollar's Value for a Dollar Spent, Citadel, 1964.

Life Insurance Stocks: An Investment Appraisal, Timely Publications Corp., 1965.

Inflation: Everyone's Problem, Citadel, 1968.

Insurance Stocks: A Fortune to Share, Information, Inc., 1969.

You Are Worth a Fortune, Citadel, 1977.

Will Inflation Destroy America?, Citadel, 1977.

How Your Insurance Policies Rob You, Citadel, 1981, revised edition, 1985.

A Nation Saved: Thank You President Reagan, Citadel, 1983.

Milton on America: Taking the Economic Pulse of the U.S.A., Citadel, 1987.

Also author of *A. L. Williams: The Life Insurance Industry's Henry Ford,* 1982, *Tell Yesterday Goodbye,* 1982, and *Why A. L. Williams Is Right for the Consumer,* 1986. Author of *Something More Can Be Done!* (public safety pamphlet). Syndicated newspaper columnist. Contributor to business magazines.

SIDELIGHTS: Arthur Milton has combined his background in insurance and his work as a registered broker of the Securities and Exchange Commission to become a successful author. He was active in the insurance industry as an agent, general agent, and general insurance broker. He came into contact with top management executives, and became convinced that management is one of the keys to proper appraisal of an insurance company. Another of his concerns is consumer protection legislation, and his views on this subject have been published in the *Congressional Record.*

Milton told *CA:* "*Milton on America: Taking the Economic Pulse of the U.S.A.* is an effort to dissuade the doomsayers as to the greatness and economic potential in our country that will go beyond the year 2000. In this era of consumer awareness it should be a constant teaching process so that all Americans can live wisely within their income, save and invest intelligently, and strive for dignity in their twilight years."

*   *   *

MINER, Caroline Eyring 1907-

PERSONAL: Born December 14, 1907, in Colonia Juarez, Mexico; daughter of Edward C. (a cattleman) and Caroline C. (Romney) Eyring; married Glen Bryant Miner (a teacher and statistician), May 20, 1931; children: Caroline (Mrs. Edward E. Morgan), Bryant Albert, Rosemary (Mrs. D. Clayton Fairbourn), Edward Glen, Henry Lee, Camilla Virginia (Mrs. George D. Smith), Joseph Kay, Steven Eyring. *Education:* Brigham Young University, A.B., 1929; Utah State University, M.S., 1943; additional summer study at University of Hawaii, University of Alaska, and University of California, Berkeley. *Religion:* Church of Jesus Christ of Latter-day Saints (Mormon).

ADDRESSES: Home—2415 St. Mary's Dr., Salt Lake City, Utah 84108.

CAREER: Teacher, primarily of English, in Pima, Ariz., 1927-28, Safford, Ariz., 1929-31, Logan, Utah, 1939-43, Salt Lake City, Utah, 1946-47, and Riverton, Utah, 1947-49; University of Utah, Salt Lake City, instructor in English, 1949-50; Salt Lake City Public Schools, teacher of English at secondary level, 1952-73. Lecturer to schools and organizations.

MEMBER: National League of American Pen Women (president of Salt Lake City chapter, 1968-70; state president, 1970-

72), League of Utah Writers (vice-president, 1974 and 1976; president, 1975), Utah Mothers Association (president, 1973-75), Reynolds Literary Club (president, 1956-66), Delta Kappa Gamma.

AWARDS, HONORS: Distinguished service award, Brigham Young University, 1962; named Kiwanis Teacher of 1963; Utah Mother of the Year, 1973; Utah Poet of the Year, 1973; American Cancer Society award, Utah division, 1983.

WRITINGS:

(Co-author) *If I Were in My Teens,* Bookcraft, 1955.

To Warm the Heart (stories and essays), Deseret, 1961.

Earthbound No Longer (poetry), Publishers Press, 1961.

Building a Home to Last Forever (religious), Deseret, 1962.

As a Great Tree (biography), Publishers Press, 1962.

Life Story of Edward Christian Eyring, Publishers Press, 1966.

Lasso the Sunrise (poetry), Publishers Press, 1976.

Facts and Fancies (biography), Deseret, 1976.

Miles Romney and Elisabeth Gaskell, Publishers Press, 1978.

Camilla, Deseret, 1980.

Joy, Deseret, 1980.

A Legacy Remembered: 1914-1970, Deseret, 1982.

To Everything a Season (poetry), Deseret, 1986.

Contributor of more than one hundred poems and essays to magazines.

SIDELIGHTS: Caroline Eyring Miner traveled around the world in 1955. Since then she has visited South and Central America, Russia (with a party of students), Alaska, the South Pacific, the Caribbean, Finland, Africa, China, Spain, Turkey, Israel, the Galapagos Islands, and Antarctica. She has also camped around the United States and in Mexico and Canada.

AVOCATIONAL INTERESTS: Reading, gardening, oil painting, genealogy.

*   *   *

MINER, Jane Claypool 1933-
(Jane Claypool; Veronica Ladd, a pseudonym)

PERSONAL: Born April 22, 1933, in McAllen, Tex.; married and widowed twice; children: Kathryn Du Vivier. *Education:* California State University, Long Beach, B.A., 1956; graduate study at University of California, Los Angeles, and California State University, Los Angeles.

ADDRESSES: Home—2883 Lone Jack Rd., Olivenhain, Calif. 92024.

CAREER: Teacher at public schools in Long Beach, Calif., 1956-58, Torrance, Calif., 1959-62 and 1964-69, Trenton, Calif., 1963-64, and Los Angeles, Calif., 1969-71; junior high school teacher in Pittsfield, Mass., 1978-81; Taconic High School, Pittsfield, teacher, ending 1981; writer, 1981—. Public speaker on several subjects, including writing, teenagers, and real estate.

MEMBER: Society of Children's Book Writers, National Arts Club, American Society of Journalists and Authors.

WRITINGS:

YOUNG ADULT FICTION; UNDER NAME JANE CLAYPOOL

Choices, Scholastic Book Services, 1978.

Why Did You Leave Me?, Scholastic Book Services, 1978.

Dreams Can Come True, Scholastic Book Services, 1981.

Senior Class, Scholastic Book Services, 1982.

No Place to Go, Scholastic Book Services, 1982.
Maggie, Scholastic Book Services, 1982.
To Pursue a Dream, Grosset, 1982.
A Day at a Time, Crestwood, 1982.
A Man's Pride, Crestwood, 1982.
Navajo Victory, Crestwood, 1982.
Split Decision, Crestwood, 1982.
A New Beginning, Crestwood, 1982.
Miracle of Time, Crestwood, 1982.
This Day Is Mine, Crestwood, 1982.
The Tough Guy, Crestwood, 1982.
A Love for Violet, Westminster, 1982.
Jasmine Finds Love, Westminster, 1982.
I'll Love You Forever, Scholastic Book Services, 1983.
Teenage Models, Scholastic Book Services, 1983.
Joanna, Scholastic Book Services, 1983.
Roxanne, Scholastic Book Services, 1985.
Veronica, Scholastic Book Services, 1986.
Jeanne, Up and Down, Scholastic Book Services, 1987.
What Will My Friends Say?, Scholastic Book Services, 1987.

YOUNG ADULT NONFICTION; UNDER NAME JANE CLAYPOOL

Alcohol and You, F. Watts, 1981, revised edition, 1987.
How to Get a Good Job, F. Watts, 1982.
Working in a Hospital, Messner, 1983.
Alcohol and Teens, Messner, 1983.
Unemployment, F. Watts, 1983.
Eating Disorders, F. Watts, 1983.
Turning Points in World War II, Hiroshima and Nagasaki, F. Watts, 1984.
Young Parents, J. Messner, 1985.

Also author of *Why Are Some People Fat?,* Creative Education.

YOUNG ADULT NOVELS; UNDER PSEUDONYM VERONICA LADD

Flowers for Lisa, Simon & Schuster, 1982.
Promised Kiss, Simon & Schuster, 1982.
For Love of Lori, Simon & Schuster, 1982.
The Look of Love, Simon & Schuster, 1983.

OTHER

Author of reading lessons and educational filmstrips. Contributor of more than one hundred stories and articles to magazines and newspapers.

BIOGRAPHICAL/CRITICAL SOURCES:

PERIODICALS

Berkshire Eagle, April 14, 1981.

*   *   *

MISTER X
See HOCH, Edward D(entinger)

*   *   *

MITCHELL, Alan   1922-

PERSONAL: Born November 4, 1922, in Ilford, Essex, England; son of Alec Duncan (a research chemist) and Marjorie (Fyson) Mitchell; married Marjorie Beryl Clark, October 5, 1946 (divorced, 1961); married Philippa Dunn, February 20, 1962; children: (second marriage) Clio, Julia. *Education:* Attended University of Liverpool, 1942-43; Trinity College, Dublin, B.A., 1951, B.A.Ag. (with first class honors), 1951.

Politics: "Socialist, tinged with anarchy and very independent." *Religion:* "Positively nil."

ADDRESSES: Home—"Rosemead" Rowledge, Farnham, Surrey, England. *Office*—Forestry Commission, Alice Holt Lodge, Wrecclesham, Farnham, Surrey, England.

CAREER: Forestry Commission, Farnham, England, assistant geneticist, 1953-63, silviculturist, 1963-70, dendrologist, 1970-84. Arboricultural consultant, 1984—. Founder and compiler of British National Tree Register. *Military service:* Royal Navy, 1941-45; became petty officer; served in Far East.

MEMBER: Royal Forestry Society, Institute of Foresters, British Trust for Ornithology, Royal Horticultural Society, National Trust, Surrey Bird Club, Surrey Naturalists.

AWARDS, HONORS: Veitch Memorial Medal, Royal Horticultural Society, 1966; Victorian Medal of Honor, Royal Horticultural Society, 1971; Gold Medal, Royal Forestry Society, 1978; M.A., University of Surrey, 1978.

WRITINGS:

Field Guide to Trees of Britain and Northern Europe, Collins, 1974.
Birds of Gardens and Woodlands, Collins, 1976.
Birds of Shore and Estuary, Collins, 1978.
Hand Guide to Trees, Collins, 1980.
The Gardener's Book of Trees, Dent, 1981.
Trees of Britain and Northern Europe, Collins, 1982.
Complete Guide to Trees of Britain and Northern Europe, Dragons World, 1985.
The Trees of North America, Facts on File, 1987.

Author of fortnightly column, "Nature Notes," in *Farnham Herald,* and of occasional tree items in *The Guardian.* Contributor to *Guinness Book of Records* and to forestry and gardening journals.

SIDELIGHTS: Alan Mitchell once told *CA* that he had "no faith whatever in mankind's 'leaders,' who are contemptible, ignorant hate-mongers ruining the world. I try to arouse interest in the delights of the natural world and show the utter evil of destroying life, people, forests, anything, for absurd temporary vague propaganda like 'the Western way of life' or any other and the lies and tortures excused by such partisan nonsense."

Mitchell more recently added that he "consider[s] that 'private enterprise,' now largely subsidised by taxpayers through arms production, is the greatest enemy of democracy, subverting and attacking it wherever it tries to arise. There is no democracy in big business, and that runs and rules the western world. I hope I have been some influence in the rise in interest in trees and 'treewatching' and I write to increase this and an appreciation of an ecological outlook in general."

AVOCATIONAL INTERESTS: Astronomy, traditional jazz, evolution, steam engines, travel in North America, gardening, politics, arguing.

*   *   *

MODESITT, L(eland) E(xton), Jr.   1943-

PERSONAL: Born October 19, 1943, in Denver, Colo.; son of Leland Exton (an attorney) and Nancy Lila (Evans) Modesitt; married Christina Alma Gribben (an educator), October 22, 1977; children: Leland Exton III, Susan Carnall, Catherine Grant, Nancy Mayo, Elizabeth Leanore, Kristen Linnea. *Ed-*

ucation: Williams College, B.A., 1965; graduate study at University of Denver, 1970-71. *Politics:* Republican. *Religion:* United Methodist.

ADDRESSES: Home—3213 Latigo Ct., Oakton, Va. 22124. *Office*—Multinational Business Services, Inc., 11 Dupont Circle, Washington, D.C. 20036.

CAREER: C. A. Norgren Co. (industrial pneumatics company), Littleton, Colo., market research analyst, 1969-70; Koebel & Co. (real estate and construction firm), Denver, Colo., sales associate, 1971-72; legislative assistant to U.S. Representative Bill Armstrong, 1973-79; administrative assistant to U.S. Representative Ken Kramer, 1979-81; U.S. Environmental Protection Agency, Washington, D.C., director of Office of Legislation, 1981-83, director of Office of External Affairs, 1984-85; Multinational Business Services, Inc., Washington, D.C., regulatory/communications consultant, 1985—. Lecturer in science fiction writing at Georgetown University, 1980-81. *Military service:* U.S. Navy, 1965-69; became lieutenant.

MEMBER: Delta Kappa Epsilon.

WRITINGS:

The Fires of Paratime (Science Fiction Book Club main selection), Timescape, 1982.
Hammer of Darkness, Avon, 1985.
The Ecologic Envoy, Tor Books, 1986.
Dawn for a Distant Earth (first book in "Forever Hero" trilogy), Tor Books, 1987.
The Silent Warrior (second book in "Forever Hero" trilogy), Tor Books, 1987.
In Endless Twilight (third book in "Forever Hero" trilogy), Tor Books, 1988.
The Ecolitan Operation, Tor Books, 1989.

Contributor to science fiction magazines, including *Analog Science Fiction-Science Fact, Galaxy,* and *Isaac Asimov's Science Fiction Magazine.*

WORK IN PROGRESS: Timedivers' Dawn, a "prequel" to *The Fires of Paratime; The Ecologic Secession,* a sequel to *The Ecolitan Operation.*

SIDELIGHTS: L. E. Modesitt, Jr., told *CA:* "Writers write. They have to, or they would not be writers. I am a writer who worked at it long enough to become an author. Virtually all of my early and formal training in writing was devoted to poetry—where I had a choice! I did not write my first science fiction story for publication until I was twenty-nine, and my first novel was published just before my thirty-ninth birthday.

"Although the various aspects of power and how it changes people and how government systems work and how they don't are themes underlying what I write, I try to concentrate on people—on heroes in the true sense of the word. A man who has no fear is not a hero. He's a damned fool. A hero is a man or woman who is shivering with fear and who conquers that fear to do what is right.

"I also believe that a writer simultaneously has to entertain, educate, and inspire. If he or she fails in any of these goals, the book will somehow fall flat."

Washington, D.C., where Modesitt once served as director of legislation for the Environmental Protection Agency and is currently employed as a consultant, represents a wellspring of ideas for his science fiction novels. According to Pam Mc-

Clintock in the *Washington Times,* "He says that the material in the Forever Hero Trilogy is, to a large extent, drawn from his time at EPA." Modesitt indicates to McClintock that he has been interested in writing for a long time and would someday like to write full-time: "I like to write, and I'm learning to write a little faster. I like words. Writing takes a lot of time, but I'm only writing one book a year, and that really only means two pages a day. There are some things I don't do. I generally don't watch television. I don't do a lot of socializing. I'll squirrel away an hour here and there, and pretty soon the pages mount up."

BIOGRAPHICAL/CRITICAL SOURCES:

PERIODICALS

Environmental Forum, October, 1982, April, 1983.
Los Angeles Times Book Review, December 19, 1982.
Washington Times, February 3, 1988.

*   *   *

MOFFAT, Gwen   1924-

PERSONAL: Born July 3, 1924, in Brighton, Sussex, England; married Gordon Moffat, 1948 (divorced); married John Lees (a mountain guide), 1956; children: (first marriage) Sheena. *Education:* Educated in English Schools.

ADDRESSES: Home—Bozeman, Mont. *Agent*—Mark Hamilton, A. M. Heath and Co., Ltd., 79 St. Martins Ln., London WC2N 4AA, England.

CAREER: Mountain guide; first woman to be granted guides' certificates of British Mountaineering Council, 1953, and Association of Scottish Climbing Clubs, 1957; specialized in English Lake District, North Wales, and Glencoe and Ben Nevis areas. Radio and television broadcaster. *Military service:* Women's Royal Army Corps, 1943-47.

MEMBER: Society of Authors, Crime Writers' Association, Sierra Club, Alpine Club, Pinnacle Club.

AWARDS, HONORS: Welsh Arts Council grant, 1973.

WRITINGS:

Space below My Feet (autobiographical), Houghton, 1961.
Two Star Red: A Book about R.A.F. Mountain Rescue, Hodder & Stoughton, 1964.
On My Home Ground, Hodder & Stoughton, 1968.
Survival Count (nonfiction), Gollancz, 1972.
Hard Option (novel), Gollancz, 1975.
Hard Road West: Alone on the California Trail (nonfiction), Viking, 1981.
The Buckskin Girl, David & Charles, 1982.
The Storm Seekers, Secker & Warburg, in press.

CRIME NOVELS

Lady with a Cool Eye, Gollancz, 1973.
Deviant Death, Gollancz, 1974.
The Corpse Road, Gollancz, 1974.
Miss Pink at the Edge of the World, Scribner, 1975.
Over the Sea to Death, Scribner, 1976.
A Short Time to Live, Gollancz, 1976.
Persons Unknown, Gollancz, 1978.
Die Like a Dog, David & Charles, 1982.
Last Chance Country, Gollancz, 1983.
Grizzly Trail, Gollancz, 1984.
Snare, Macmillan, 1987.

OTHER

Contributor to *Daily Express* and *Sunday Express* (both Scottish editions), *Glasgow Herald*, *Guardian*, *She*, *Woman*, and other newspapers and journals.

WORK IN PROGRESS: A Melinda Pink crime novel.

BIOGRAPHICAL/CRITICAL SOURCES:

PERIODICALS

Christian Science Monitor, December 6, 1961.
New York Times Book Review, January 1, 1984.

*   *   *

MONMONIER, Mark Stephen   1943-

PERSONAL: Surname is pronounced Mon-mon-ear; born February 2, 1943, in Baltimore, Md.; son of John Carroll (a railway accountant) and Martha (an elementary school teacher; maiden name, Mason) Monmonier; married Margaret Janet Kollner, September 4, 1965; children: Jo Kerry. *Education:* Johns Hopkins University, B.A., 1964; Pennsylvania State University, M.S., 1967, Ph.D., 1969. *Politics:* Independent. *Religion:* Roman Catholic.

ADDRESSES: Home—302 Waldorf Parkway, Syracuse, N.Y. 13224. *Office*—Department of Geography, Syracuse University, Syracuse, N.Y. 13224-1160.

CAREER: University of Rhode Island, Kingston, assistant professor of geography, 1969-70; State University of New York at Albany, assistant professor of geography, 1970-73; Syracuse University, Syracuse, N.Y., associate professor, 1973-79, professor of geography, 1979—. Consultant to U.S. Geological Survey.

MEMBER: American Congress on Surveying and Mapping, Association of American Geographers (chairman of cartography specialty group, 1980-81), American Cartographic Association (vice-president, 1982-83; president, 1983-84), Pi Tau Sigma, Tau Beta Pi.

AWARDS, HONORS: Guggenheim fellow, 1984-85.

WRITINGS:

Maps, Distortion, and Meaning, Association of American Geographers, 1977.
Computer-Assisted Cartography, Prentice-Hall, 1982.
(With George A. Schnell) *The Study of Population: Elements, Patterns, and Processes*, Charles A. Merrill, 1983.
Technological Transition in Cartography, University of Wisconsin Press, 1985.
(With Schnell) *Map Appreciation*, Prentice-Hall, 1988.
Maps with the News: The Development of American Journalistic Cartography, University of Chicago Press, 1989.

Contributor of more than one hundred articles to scientific journals. Associate editor of *American Cartographer*, 1977-82, editor, 1982-84.

WORK IN PROGRESS: A book tentatively entitled *How to Lie with Maps* about "the variety of ways maps are used to persuade or mislead."

SIDELIGHTS: Mark Stephen Monmonier told *CA:* "Integrating words and maps is an intriguing challenge that complements nicely my pure research on digital cartography and statistical graphics. I hope in the years ahead to turn from writing about maps to writing about geography and to integrating words with a variety of visual images—cartographic, diagrammatic, and photographic."

*   *   *

MOORE, Clayton
See HENDERSON, M(arilyn) R(uth)

*   *   *

MORAN, John C(harles)   1942-

PERSONAL: Born October 4, 1942, in Nashville, Tenn.; son of John Charles (a salesman and store owner) and Rachel Louise (a registered nurse; maiden name, Heflin) Moran; married Olga Cristina Robleda (a professor of mathematics), August 17, 1967; children: John Charles, Louis Patrick, Olga Cecilia Veronica. *Education:* George Peabody College, B.A., 1967, M.L.S., 1968. *Politics:* "Isolationist/Fortress America as espoused by Father Coughlin, Col. Lindbergh, et. al.; populist; Prohibition Party; follower of the political visions of Gen. Franco, Dr. Salazar, and Dr. Garcia Moreno." *Religion:* Holy Roman Catholic Apostolic Church.

ADDRESSES: Office—F. Marion Crawford Memorial Society, Saracinesca House, 3610 Meadowbrook Ave., Nashville, Tenn. 37205.

CAREER: Has worked as a surgical assistant, letter carrier, librarian, and editor; F. Marion Crawford Memorial Society, Nashville, Tenn., director, 1975—; currently works at other positions and ventures in Honduras.

MEMBER: Gabriel Garcia Moreno Memorial Association (member of board of directors; honorary director).

WRITINGS:

In Memoriam: Gabriel Garcia Moreno, 1875-1975, Dawn Heron Press, 1975.
(Editor) F. Marion Crawford, *Francesca da Rimini*, Worthies Library, F. Marion Crawford Memorial Society, 1980.
Seeking Refuge in Torre San Nicola: An Introduction to F. Marion Crawford, Worthies Library, F. Marion Crawford Memorial Society, 1980.
An F. Marion Crawford Companion, Greenwood Press, 1981.
(With others) *A Bibliography of the Agricultural Sector of Honduras, 1975-85*, USAID (Tegucigalpa), 1985.
A Bibliography of the Marketing of Fresh Fruits and Vegetables in Honduras (1975-1985), USAID, 1985.
(Editor) Anne Crawford, Baroness von Rabe, *A Shadow on a Wave*, Worthies Library, F. Marion Crawford Memorial Society, 1989.

Contributor of bibliographical and critical articles to various professional and literary journals. Editor, *The Romantist*, 1977—, and editor of its "Lost Crawfordiana" section.

WORK IN PROGRESS: On-going research on Francis Marion Crawford; *The Last Days and Death of Dr. and Gen. William Walker;* book-length studies on Robert Hugh Benson, Canon P. A. Sheehan, and H. Warner Munn; long articles on the Jan Garber Orchestra, 1932-42.

SIDELIGHTS: John C. Moran told *CA:* "As to the world of letters, my main interest coincides with the mission of the F. Marion Crawford Memorial Society (founded in 1975), which is to effect or at least substantially promote the re-establishment of Francis Marion Crawford as a major American author beyond the genre limitations of fantastic literature—a field where he has always been considered a master despite the post-1920 'blackout' in 'establishment' critical circles both journalistic and academic.

"The Society's labors are not limited to Crawford; its purview is modern Romanticism with emphasis on fantastic and imaginative literature. Therefore, the Society is interested in many authors (and artists and musical composers). . . . We did not launch the Crawford revival which had already begun by 1975, for it was inevitable because of the dynamics of history and literary change. The Society has, however, greatly hastened and expanded (co-ordinated) this revival. . . .

"At present I am completing a gap-filling study of the last days and death of the 'filibuster' Gen. William Walker (1860 at Trujillo, Honduras). The only full-length literary studies that I would like to complete before my end would be about Robert Hugh Benson (1871-1914) and the great Irish novelist—a cardinal figure in the Gaelic Revival and patriot whose works played a major role in rekindling the nationalism that freed most of Ireland from the bloody and hypocritical grip of perfidious Albion—the Rev. Patrick A. Sheehan, who was a *real* Irish/Celtic novelist, hence ignored for cultural reasons by the critical 'establishment' in the English-speaking world.

"Many years ago I chose not to continue with my institutional study of English literature, preferring to independently devote my attention to lesser-known and neglected-by-literary-establishments authors, especially those in the fields of fantastic and imaginative literature. Crawford is and will always be my main interest."

*   *   *

MOREHEAD, Joe
See MOREHEAD, Joseph H(yde), Jr.

*   *   *

MOREHEAD, Joseph H(yde), Jr.   1931-
(Joe Morehead)

PERSONAL: Born January 30, 1931, in New York, N.Y.; son of Joseph H. and Irma (Gray) Morehead; married Bebe Ann Behnke, September 4, 1966; children: Adam Gray. *Education:* Trinity College, Hartford, Conn., B.A., 1952; Columbia University, M.A., 1955; University of Kentucky, M.L.S., 1964; University of California, Berkeley, Ph.D., 1973.

ADDRESSES: Home—22 Michaelangelo St., Latham, N.Y. 12110. *Office*—School of Information Science and Policy, Nelson A. Rockefeller College of Public Affairs and Policy, State University of New York at Albany, Albany, N.Y. 12222.

CAREER: Orlando Junior College, Orlando, Fla., instructor in English, 1954-56; U.S. Department of the Air Force, education director in London, England, 1957-62; San Francisco Public Library, San Francisco, Calif., documents librarian, 1964-70; State University of New York at Albany, Nelson A. Rockefeller College of Public Affairs and Policy, School of Information Science and Policy, 1970—, began as assistant professor, currently associate professor of information science and policy. *Military service:* U.S. Air Force, 1952-54; became first lieutenant.

MEMBER: American Library Association, Government Documents Round Table, New York Library Association, Phi Beta Kappa (charter member of Alpha Alpha chapter).

AWARDS, HONORS: Outstanding Alumnus Award, Kentucky College of Library and Information Science, 1984.

WRITINGS—Under name Joe Morehead:

(Contributor) Bill Katz, editor, *Magazines for Libraries,* Bowker, 2nd edition (Morehead was not associated with first edition), 1972.
(Editor) *Albany Municipal Documents: A Directory of Sources* (booklet), School of Library and Information Science, State University of New York at Albany, 1974.
Introduction to United States Public Documents, Libraries Unlimited, 1975, 3rd edition, 1983.
Theory and Practice in Library Education: The Teaching-Learning Process, Libraries Unlimited, 1980.
Essays on Public Documents and Government Policies, Haworth Press, 1986.

Author of column "Into the Hopper" for *Serials Librarian.* Contributor of articles and reviews to *Synergy, Bulletin of Bibliography, Reference Quarterly, Journal of Education for Librarianship, College Student Journal, Library Journal, Government Publications Review,* and *American Reference Books Annual.*

SIDELIGHTS: Joe Morehead told *CA:* "My teaching and writing are largely concerned with the impact of public policy decisions on the production and distribution of government publications. In the present climate of less government and budgetary retrenchment, there is a real danger that access to public documents will be abridged under the guise of saving taxpayer dollars. People in my profession have an obligation to exercise vigilance in the face of that threat."

*   *   *

MORRISON, Toni   1931-

PERSONAL: Born Chloe Anthony Wofford, February 18, 1931, in Lorain, Ohio; daughter of George and Ramah (Willis) Wofford; married Harold Morrison, 1958 (divorced, 1964); children: Harold Ford, Slade Kevin. *Education:* Howard University, B.A., 1953; Cornell University, M.A., 1955.

ADDRESSES: Office—Random House, 201 East 50th St., New York, N.Y. 10022. *Agent*—Lynn Nesbit, International Creative Management, 40 West 57th St., New York, N.Y. 10019.

CAREER: Texas Southern University, Houston, instructor in English, 1955-57; Howard University, Washington, D.C., instructor in English, 1957-64; Random House, New York, N.Y., senior editor, 1965—; State University of New York at Purchase, associate professor of English, 1971-72; State University of New York at Albany, Schweitzer Professor of the Humanities, 1984-89; Princeton University, Princeton, N.J., Robert F. Goheen Professor of the Humanities, 1989—. Visiting lecturer, Yale University, 1976-77, and Bard College, 1986-88.

MEMBER: American Academy and Institute of Arts and Letters, National Council on the Arts, Authors Guild (council), Authors League of America.

AWARDS, HONORS: National Book Award nomination and Ohioana Book Award, both 1975, both for *Sula;* National Book Critics Circle Award and American Academy and Institute of Arts and Letters Award, both 1977, both for *Song of Solomon;* New York State Governor's Art Award, 1986; National Book Award nomination and National Book Critics Circle Award nomination, both 1987, and Pulitzer Prize for fiction and Robert F. Kennedy Award, both 1988, all for *Beloved;* Elizabeth Cady Stanton Award from the National Organization of Women.

WRITINGS:

The Bluest Eye (novel), Holt, 1969.
Sula (novel), Knopf, 1973.
(Editor) *The Black Book* (anthology), Random House, 1974.
Song of Solomon (novel; Book-of-the-Month Club selection), Knopf, 1977.
Tar Baby (novel), Knopf, 1981.
''Dreaming Emmett'' (play), first produced in Albany, New York, January 4, 1986.
Beloved (novel), Knopf, 1987.

Contributor of essays and reviews to numerous periodicals, including *New York Times Magazine.*

WORK IN PROGRESS: A sequel to *Beloved.*

SIDELIGHTS: Toni Morrison might best be described as the high priestess of village literature. Her award-winning novels chronicle small-town black American life, employing ''an artistic vision that encompasses both a private and a national heritage,'' to quote *Time* magazine contributor Angela Wigan. Through works such as *The Bluest Eye, Song of Solomon* and *Beloved,* Morrison has earned a reputation as a gifted story-teller whose troubled characters seek to find themselves and their cultural riches in a society that warps or impedes such essential growth. According to Charles Larson in the *Chicago Tribune Book World,* each of Morrison's novels ''is as original as anything that has appeared in our ltierature in the last 20 years. The contemporaneity that unites them—the troubling persistence of racism in America—is infused with an urgency that only a black writer can have about our society.'' Morrison's artistry has attracted critical acclaim as well as commercial success; *Dictionary of Literary Biography* contributor Susan L. Blake calls the author ''an anomaly in two respects'' because ''she is a black writer who has achieved national prominence and popularity, and she is a popular writer who is taken seriously.'' Indeed, Morrison has won two of modern literature's most prestigious citations, the 1977 National Book Critics Circle Award for *Song of Solomon* and the 1988 Pulitzer Prize for *Beloved. Atlantic* correspondent Wilfrid Sheed notes: ''Most black writers are privy, like the rest of us, to bits and pieces of the secret, the dark side of their group experience, but Toni Morrison uniquely seems to have all the keys on her chain, like a house detective. . . . She [uses] the run of the whole place, from ghetto to small town to ramshackle farmhouse, to bring back a panorama of black myth and reality that [dazzles] the senses.''

''It seems somehow both constricting and inadequate to describe Toni Morrison as the country's preeminent black novelist, since in both gifts and accomplishments she transcends categorization,'' writes Jonathan Yardley in the *Washington Post Book World,* ''yet the characterization is inescapable not merely because it is true but because the very nature of Morrison's work dictates it. Not merely has black American life been the central preoccupation of her . . . novels . . . but as she has matured she has concentrated on distilling all of black experience into her books; quite purposefully, it seems, she is striving not for the particular but for the universal.'' In her work Morrison strives to lay bare the injustice inherent in the black condition and blacks' efforts, individually and collectively, to transcend society's unjust boundaries. Blake notes that Morrison's novels explore ''the difference between black humanity and white cultural values. This opposition produces

the negative theme of the seduction and betrayal of black people by white culture . . . and the positive theme of the quest for cultural identity.'' *Newsweek* contributor Jean Strouse observes: ''Like all the best stories, [Morrison's] are driven by an abiding moral vision. Implicit in all her characters' grapplings with who they are is a large sense of human nature and love—and a reach for understanding of something larger than the moment.''

Quest for self is a motivating and organizing device in Morrison's fiction, as is the role of family and community in nurturing or challenging the individual. In the *Times Literary Supplement,* Jennifer Uglow suggests that Morrison's novels ''explore in particular the process of growing up black, female and poor. Avoiding generalities, Toni Morrison concentrates on the relation between the pressures of the community, patterns established within families, . . . and the developing sense of self.'' According to Dorothy H. Lee in *Black Women Writers (1950-1980): A Critical Evaluation,* Morrison is preoccupied ''with the effect of the community on the individual's achievement and retention of an integrated, acceptable self. In treating this subject, she draws recurrently on myth and legend for story pattern and characters, returning repeatedly to the theory of *quest.* . . . The goals her characters seek to achieve are similar in their deepest implications, and yet the degree to which they attain them varies radically because each novel is cast in unique human terms.'' In Morrison's books, blacks must confront the notion that all understanding is accompanied by pain, just as all comprehension of national history must include the humiliations of slavery. She tempers this hard lesson by preserving ''the richness of communal life against an outer world that denies its value'' and by turning to ''a heritage of folklore, not only to disclose patterns of living but also to close wounds,'' in the words of *Nation* contributor Brina Caplan.

Although Morrison herself told the *Chicago Tribune* that there is ''epiphany and triumph'' in every book she writes, some critics find her work nihilistic and her vision bleak. ''The picture given by . . . Morrison of the plight of the decent, aspiring individual in the black family and community is more painful than the gloomiest impressions encouraged by either stereotype or sociology,'' observes Diane Johnson in the *New York Review of Books.* Johnson continues, ''Undoubtedly white society is the ultimate oppressor, and not just of blacks, but, as Morrison [shows,] . . . the black person must first deal with the oppressor in the next room, or in the same bed, or no farther away than across the street.'' Morrison is a pioneer in the depiction of the hurt inflicted by blacks on blacks; for instance, her characters rarely achieve harmonious heterosexual relationships but are instead divided by futurelessness and the anguish of stifled existence. *Times Literary Supplement* reviewer Jennifer Uglow writes: ''We have become attuned to novels . . . which locate oppression in the conflicts of blacks (usually men) trying to make it in a white world. By concentrating on the sense of violation experienced within black neighborhoods, even within families, Toni Morrison deprives us of stock responses and creates a more demanding and uncomfortable literature.'' *Village Voice* correspondent Vivian Gornick contends that the world Morrison creates ''is thick with an atmosphere through which her characters move slowly, in pain, ignorance, and hunger. And to a very large degree Morrison has the compelling ability to make one believe that all of us (Morrison, the characters, the reader) are penetrating that dark and hurtful terrain—the feel of a human life—simultaneously.'' Uglow concludes that even the laughter of

Morrison's characters "disguises pain, deprivation and violation. It is laughter at a series of bad, cruel jokes. . . . Nothing is what it seems; no appearance, no relationship can be trusted to endure."

Other critics detect a deeper undercurrent to Morrison's work that contains just the sort of epiphany for which she strives. "From book to book, Morrison's larger project grows clear," declares Ann Snitow in the *Voice Literary Supplement.* "First, she insists that every character bear the weight of responsibility for his or her own life. After she's measured out each one's private pain, she adds on to that the shared burden of what the whites did. Then, at last, she tries to find the place where her stories can lighten her readers' load, lift them up from their own and others' guilt, carry them to glory. . . . Her characters suffer—from their own limitations and the world's—but their inner life miraculously expands beyond the narrow law of cause and effect." *Harvard Advocate* essayist Faith Davis writes that despite the mundane boundaries of Morrison's characters' lives, the author "illuminates the complexity of their attitudes toward life. Having reached a quiet and extensive understanding of their situation, they can endure life's calamities. . . . Morrison never allows us to become indifferent to these people. . . . Her citizens . . . jump up from the pages vital and strong because she has made us care about the pain in their lives." In *Ms.,* Margo Jefferson concludes that Morrison's books "are filled with loss—lost friendship, lost love, lost customs, lost possibilities. And yet there is so much life in the smallest acts and gestures . . . that they are as much celebrations as elegies."

Morrison sees language as an expression of black experience, and her novels are characterized by vivid narration and dialogue. *Village Voice* essayist Susan Lydon observes that the author "works her magic charm above all with a love of language. Her soaring . . . style carries you like a river, . . . sweeping doubt and disbelief away, and it is only gradually that one realizes her deadly serious intent." In the *Spectator,* Caroline Moorehead likewise notes that Morrison "writes energetically and richly, using words in a way very much her own. The effect is one of exoticism, an exciting curiousness in the language, a balanced sense of the possible that stops, always, short of the absurd." Although Morrison does not like to be called a poetic writer, critics often comment on the lyrical quality of her prose. "Morrison's style has always moved fluidly between tough-minded realism and lyric descriptiveness," notes Margo Jefferson in *Newsweek.* "Vivid dialogue, capturing the drama and extravagance of black speech, gives way to an impressionistic evocation of physical pain or an ironic, essay-like analysis of the varieties of religious hypocrisy." Uglow writes: "The word 'elegant' is often applied to Toni Morrison's writing; it employs sophisticated narrative devices, shifting perspectives and resonant images and displays an obvious delight in the potential of language." *Nation* contributor Earl Frederick concludes that Morrison, "with an ear as sharp as glass . . . has listened to the music of black talk and deftly uses it as the palette knife to create black lives and to provide some of the best fictional dialogue around today."

According to Jean Strouse, Morrison "comes from a long line of people who did what they had to do to survive. It is their stories she tells in her novels—tales of the suffering and richness, the eloquence and tragedies of the black American experience." Morrison was born Chloe Anthony Wofford in Lorain, Ohio, a small town near the shores of Lake Erie. *New York Review of Books* correspondent Darryl Pinckney describes her particular community as "close enough to the Ohio

River for the people who lived [there] to feel the torpor of the South, the nostalgia for its folkways, to sense the old Underground Railroad underfoot like a hidden stream." While never explicitly autobiographical, Morrison's fictions draw upon her youthful experiences in Ohio. In an essay for *Black Women Writers at Work* she claims: "I am from the Midwest so I have a special affection for it. My beginnings are always there. . . . No matter what I write, I begin there. . . . It's the matrix for me. . . . Ohio also offers an escape from stereotyped black settings. It is neither plantation nor ghetto."

Two important aspects of Chloe Wofford's childhood—community spirit and the supernatural—inform Toni Morrison's mature writing. In a *Publishers Weekly* interview, Morrison suggests ways in which her community influenced her. "There is this town which is both a support system and a hammer at the same time," she notes. ". . . Approval was not the acquisition of things; approval was given for the maturity and the dignity with which one handled oneself. Most black people in particular were, and still are, very fastidious about manners, very careful about behavior and the rules that operate within the community. The sense of organized activity, what I thought at that time was burdensome, turns out now to have within it a gift—which is, I never had to be taught how to hold a job, how to make it work, how to handle my time." On several levels the pariah—a unique and sometimes eccentric individual—figures in Morrison's fictional reconstruction of black community life. "There is always an elder there," she notes of her work in *Black Women Writers: A Critical Evaluation.* "And these ancestors are not just parents, they are sort of timeless people whose relationships to the characters are benevolent, instructive, and protective, and they provide a certain kind of wisdom." Sometimes this figure imparts his or her wisdom from beyond the grave; from an early age Morrison absorbed the folklore and beliefs of a culture for which the supernatural holds power and portent. Strouse notes that Morrison's world, both within and outside her fiction, is "filled with signs, visitations, ways of knowing that [reach] beyond the five senses."

Lorain, Ohio, is in fact the setting of *The Bluest Eye,* published in 1969. Morrison's first novel portrays "in poignant terms the tragic condition of blacks in a racist America," to quote Chikwenye Okonjo Ogunyemi in *Critique: Studies in Modern Fiction.* In *The Bluest Eye,* Morrison depicts the onset of black self-hatred as occasioned by white American ideals such as "Dick and Jane" primers and Shirley Temple movies. The principal character, Pecola Breedlove, is literally maddened by the disparity between her existence and the pictures of beauty and gentility disseminated by the dominant white culture. As Phyllis R. Klotman notes in the *Black American Literature Forum,* Morrison "uses the contrast between Shirley Temple and Pecola . . . to underscore the irony of black experience. Whether one learns acceptability from the formal educational experience or from cultural symbols, the effect is the same: self-hatred." Darwin T. Turner elaborates on the novel's intentions in *Black Women Writers: A Critical Evaluation.* Morrison's fictional milieu, writes Turner, is "a world of grotesques—individuals whose psyches have been deformed by their efforts to assume false identities, their failures to achieve meaningful identities, or simply their inability to retain and communicate love."

Blake characterizes *The Bluest Eye* as a novel of initiation, exploring that common theme in American literature from a minority viewpoint. Ogunyemi likewise contends that, in essence, Morrison presents "old problems in a fresh language and with a fresh perspective. A central force of the work derives from her power to draw vignettes and her ability to portray emotions, seeing the world through the eyes of adolescent girls.'' Klotman, who calls the book ''a novel of growing up, of growing up young and black and female in America,'' concludes her review with the comment that the ''rite of passage, initiating the young into womanhood at first tenuous and uncertain, is sensitively depicted.... *The Bluest Eye* is an extraordinarily passionate yet gentle work, the language lyrical yet precise—it is a novel for all seasons.''

In *Sula,* Morrison's 1973 novel, the author once again presents a pair of black women who must come to terms with their lives. Set in a Midwestern black community called The Bottom, the story follows two friends, Sula and Nel, from childhood to old age and death. Snitow claims that through *Sula,* Morrison has discovered ''a way to offer her people an insight and sense of recovered self so dignified and glowing that no worldly pain could dull the final light.'' Indeed, *Sula* is a tale of rebel and conformist in which the conformity is dictated by the solid inhabitants of The Bottom and even the rebellion gains strength from the community's disapproval. *New York Times Book Review* contributor Sara Blackburn contends, however, that the book is ''too vital and rich'' to be consigned to the category of allegory. Morrison's ''extravagantly beautiful, doomed characters are locked in a world where hope for the future is a foreign commodity, yet they are enormously, achingly alive,'' writes Blackburn. ''And this book about them—and about how their beauty is drained back and frozen—is a howl of love and rage, playful and funny as well as hard and bitter.'' In the words of *American Literature* essayist Jane S. Bakerman, Morrison ''uses the maturation story of Sula and Nel as the core of a host of other stories, but it is the chief unification device for the novel and achieves its own unity, again, through the clever manipulation of the themes of sex, race, and love. Morrison has undertaken a... difficult task in *Sula.* Unquestionably, she has succeeded.''

Other critics have echoed Bakerman's sentiments about *Sula.* Yardley declares: ''What gives this terse, imaginative novel its genuine distinction is the quality of Toni Morrison's prose. *Sula* is admirable enough as a study of its title character,... but its real strength lies in Morrison's writing, which at times has the resonance of poetry and is precise, vivid and controlled throughout.'' Turner also claims that in *Sula* ''Morrison evokes her verbal magic occasionally by lyric descriptions that carry the reader deep into the soul of the character.... Equally effective, however, is her art of narrating action in a lean prose that uses adjectives cautiously while creating memorable vivid images.'' In her review, Davis concludes that a ''beautiful and haunting atmosphere emerges out of the wreck of these folks' lives, a quality that is absolutely convincing and absolutely precise.'' *Sula* was nominated for a National Book Award in 1974.

From the insular lives she depicted in her first two novels, Morrison moved in *Song of Solomon* to a national and historical perspective on black American life. ''Here the depths of the younger work are still evident,'' contends Reynolds Price in the *New York Times Book Review,* ''but now they thrust outward, into wider fields, for longer intervals, encompassing many more lives. The result is a long prose tale that surveys nearly a century of American history as it impinges upon a single family.'' With an intermixture of the fantastic and the realistic, *Song of Solomon* relates the journey of a character named Milkman Dead into an understanding of his family heritage and hence, himself. Lee writes: ''Figuratively, [Milk-

man] travels from innocence to awareness, i.e., from ignorance of origins, heritage, identity, and communal responsibility to knowledge and acceptance. He moves from selfish and materialistic dilettantism to an understanding of brotherhood. With his release of personal ego, he is able to find a place in the whole. There is, then, a universal—indeed mythic—pattern here. He journeys from spiritual death to rebirth, a direction symbolized by his discovery of the secret power of flight. Mythically, liberation and transcendence follow the discovery of self.'' Blake suggests that the connection Milkman discovers with his family's past helps him to connect meaningfully with his contemporaries; *Song of Solomon,* Blake notes, ''dramatizes dialectical approaches to the challenges of black life.'' According to Anne Z. Mickelson in *Reaching Out: Sensitivity and Order in Recent American Fiction by Women,* history itself ''becomes a choral symphony to Milkman, in which each individual voice has a chance to speak and contribute to his growing sense of well-being.''

Mickelson also observes that *Song of Solomon* represents for blacks ''a break out of the confining life into the realm of possibility.'' Charles Larson comments on this theme in a *Washington Post Book World* review. The novel's subject matter, Larson explains, is ''the origins of black consciousness in America, and the individual's relationship to that heritage.'' However, Larson adds, ''skilled writer that she is, Morrison has transcended this theme so that the reader rarely feels that this is simply another novel about ethnic identity. So marvelously orchestrated is Morrison's narrative that it not only excels on all of its respective levels, not only works for all of its interlocking components, but also—in the end—says something about life (and death) for all of us. Milkman's epic journey... is a profound examination of the individual's understanding of, and, perhaps, even transcendence of the inevitable fate of his life.'' Gornick concludes: ''There are so many individual moments of power and beauty in *Song of Solomon* that, ultimately, one closes the book warmed through by the richness of its sympathy, and by its breathtaking feel for the nature of sexual sorrow.''

Song of Solomon won the National Book Critics Circle Award in 1977. It was also the first novel by a black writer to become a Book-of-the-Month Club selection since Richard Wright's *Native Son* was published in 1940. *World Literature Today* reviewer Richard K. Barksdale calls the work ''a book that will not only withstand the test of time but endure a second and third reading by those conscientious readers who love a well-wrought piece of fiction.'' Describing the novel as ''a stunningly beautiful book'' in her *Washington Post Book World* piece, Anne Tyler adds: ''I would call the book poetry, but that would seem to be denying its considerable power as a story. Whatever name you give it, it's full of magnificent people, each of them complex and multilayered, even the narrowest of them narrow in extravagant ways.'' Price deems *Song of Solomon* ''a long story,... and better than good. Toni Morrison has earned attention and praise. Few Americans know, and can say, more than she has in this wise and spacious novel.''

Morrison's 1981 book *Tar Baby* remained on bestseller lists for four months. A novel of ideas, the work dramatizes the fact that complexion is a far more subtle issue than the simple polarization of black and white. Set on a lush Caribbean island, *Tar Baby* explores the passionate love affair of Jadine, a Sorbonne-educated black model, and Son, a handsome knockabout with a strong aversion to white culture. According to Caplan, Morrison's concerns ''are race, class, culture and the effects of late capitalism—heavy freight for any narrative.... She is attempting to stabilize complex visions of society—that is, to examine competitive ideas.... Because the primary function of Morrison's characters is to voice representative opinions, they arrive on stage vocal and highly conscious, their histories symbolically indicated or merely sketched. Her brief sketches, however, are clearly the work of an artist who can, when she chooses, model the mind in depth and detail.'' In a *Dictionary of Literary Biography Yearbook* essay, Elizabeth B. House outlines *Tar Baby*'s major themes; namely, ''the difficulty of settling conflicting claims between one's past and present and the destruction which abuse of power can bring. As Morrison examines these problems in *Tar Baby*, she suggests no easy way to understand what one's link to a heritage should be, nor does she offer infallible methods for dealing with power. Rather, with an astonishing insight and grace, she demonstrates the pervasiveness of such dilemmas and the degree to which they affect human beings, both black and white.''

Tar Baby uncovers racial and sexual conflicts without offering solutions, but most critics agree that Morrison indicts all of her characters—black and white—for their thoughtless devaluations of others. *New York Times Book Review* correspondent John Irving claims: ''What's so powerful, and subtle, about Miss Morrison's presentation of the tension between blacks and whites is that she conveys it almost entirely through the suspicions and prejudices of her black characters.... Miss Morrison uncovers all the stereotypical racial fears felt by whites and blacks alike. Like any ambitious writer, she's unafraid to employ these stereotypes—she embraces the representative qualities of her characters without embarrassment, then proceeds to make them individuals too.'' *New Yorker* essayist Susan Lardner praises Morrison for her ''power to be absolutely persuasive against her own preferences, suspicions, and convictions, implied or plainly expressed,'' and Strouse likewise contends that the author ''has produced that rare commodity, a truly public novel about the condition of society, examining the relations between blacks and whites, men and women, civilization and nature.... It wraps its messages in a highly potent love story.'' Irving suggests that Morrison's greatest accomplishment ''is that she has raised her novel above the social realism that too many black novels and women's novels are trapped in. She has succeeded in writing about race and women symbolically.''

Reviewers have praised *Tar Baby* for its provocative themes and for its evocative narration. *Los Angeles Times* contributor Elaine Kendall calls the book ''an intricate and sophisticated novel, moving from a realistic and orderly beginning to a mystical and ambiguous end. Morrison has taken classically simple story elements and realigned them so artfully that we perceive the old pattern in a startlingly different way. Although this territory has been explored by dozens of novelists, Morrison depicts it with such vitality that it seems newly discovered.'' In the *Washington Post Book World*, Webster Schott claims: ''There is so much that is good, sometimes dazzling, about *Tar Baby*—poetic language,... arresting images, fierce intelligence—that... one becomes entranced by Toni Morrison's story. The settings are so vivid the characters must be alive. The emotions they feel are so intense they must be real people.'' Maureen Howard states in *New Republic* that the work ''is as carefully patterned as a well-written poem.... *Tar Baby* is a good American novel in which we can discern a new lightness and brilliance in Toni Morrison's enchantment with language and in her curiously polyphonic stories that echo

life.'' Schott concludes: ''One of fiction's pleasures is to have your mind scratched and your intellectual habits challenged. While *Tar Baby* has shortcomings, lack of provocation isn't one of them. Morrison owns a powerful intelligence. It's run by courage. She calls to account conventional wisdom and accepted attitude at nearly every turn.''

In addition to her own writing, Morrison has served as an editor at Random House and has helped to publish the work of other noted black Americans, including Toni Cade Bambara, Gayle Jones, Angela Davis, and Muhammed Ali. Discussing her aims as an editor in a quotation printed in the *Dictionary of Literary Biography*, Morrison said: ''I look very hard for black fiction because I want to participate in developing a canon of black work. We've had the first rush of black entertainment, where blacks were writing for whites, and whites were encouraging this kind of self-flagellation. Now we can get down to the craft of writing, where black people are talking to black people.'' One of Morrison's important projects for Random House was *The Black Book*, an anthology of items that illustrate the history of black Americans. *Ms.* magazine correspondent Dorothy Eugenia Robinson describes the work: ''*The Black Book* is the pain and pride of rediscovering the collective black experience. It is finding the essence of ourselves and holding on. *The Black Book* is a kind of scrapbook of patiently assembled samplings of black history and culture. What has evolved is a pictorial folk journey of black people, places, events, handcrafts, inventions, songs, and folklore.... *The Black Book* informs, disturbs, maybe even shocks. It unsettles complacency and demands confrontation with raw reality. It is by no means an easy book to experience, but it's a necessary one.''

While preparing *The Black Book* for publication, Morrison uncovered the true and shocking story of a runaway slave who, at the point of recapture, murdered her infant child so it would not be doomed to a lifetime of slavery. For Morrison the story encapsulated the fierce psychic cruelty of an institutionalized system that sought to destroy the basic emotional bonds between men and women, and worse, between parent and child. ''I certainly thought I knew as much about slavery as anybody,'' Morrison told the *Los Angeles Times*. ''But it was the interior life I needed to find out about.'' It is this ''interior life'' in the throes of slavery that constitutes the theme of Morrison's Pulitzer Prize-winning novel *Beloved*. Set in Reconstruction-era Cincinnati, the book centers on characters who struggle fruitlessly to keep their painful recollections of the past at bay. They are haunted, both physically and spiritually, by the legacies slavery has bequeathed to them. According to Snitow, *Beloved* ''staggers under the terror of its material— as so much holocaust writing does and must.''

In *People* magazine, V. R. Peterson describes *Beloved* as ''a brutally powerful, mesmerizing story about the inescapable, excruciating legacy of slavery. Behind each new event and each new character lies another event and another story until finally the reader meets a community of proud, daring people, inextricably bound by culture and experience.'' Through the lives of ex-slaves Sethe and her would-be lover Paul D., readers ''experience American slavery as it was lived by those who were its objects of exchange, both at its best—which wasn't very good—and at its worst, which was as bad as can be imagined,'' writes Margaret Atwood in the *New York Times Book Review*. ''Above all, it is seen as one of the most viciously antifamily institutions human beings have ever devised. The slaves are motherless, fatherless, deprived of their mates, their children, their kin. It is a world in which people suddenly vanish and are never seen again, not through accident or covert operation or terrorism, but as a matter of everyday legal policy.'' *New York Times* columnist Michiko Kakutani contends that *Beloved* ''possesses the heightened power and resonance of myth—its characters, like those in opera or Greek drama, seem larger than life and their actions, too, tend to strike us as enactments of ancient rituals and passions. To describe 'Beloved' only in these terms, however, is to diminish its immediacy, for the novel also remains precisely grounded in American reality—the reality of Black history as experienced in the wake of the Civil War.''

Acclaim for *Beloved* has come from both sides of the Atlantic. In his *Chicago Tribune* piece, Larson claims that the work ''is the context out of which all of Morrison's earlier novels were written. In her darkest and most probing novel, Toni Morrison has demonstrated once again the stunning powers that place her in the first ranks of our living novelists.'' *Los Angeles Times Book Review* contributor John Leonard likewise expresses the opinion that the novel ''belongs on the highest shelf of American literature, even if half a dozen canonized white boys have to be elbowed off. . . . Without 'Beloved' our imagination of the nation's self has a hole in it big enough to die from.'' Atwood states: ''Ms. Morrison's versatility and technical and emotional range appear to know no bounds. If there were any doubts about her stature as a pre-eminent American novelist, of her own or any other generation, 'Beloved' will put them to rest.'' London *Times* reviewer Nicholas Shakespeare concludes that *Beloved* ''is a novel propelled by the cadences of . . . songs—the first singing of a people hardened by their suffering, people who have been hanged and whipped and mortgaged at the hands of whitepeople—the men without skin. From Toni Morrison's pen it is a sound that breaks the back of words, making *Beloved* a great novel.''

Morrison is an author who labors contentedly under the labels bestowed by pigeonholing critics. She has no objection to being called a black woman writer, because, as she told the *New York Times*, ''I really think the range of emotions and perceptions I have had access to as a black person and a female person are greater than those of people who are neither. . . . My world did not shrink because I was a black female writer. It just got bigger.'' Nor does she strive for that much-vaunted universality that purports to be a hallmark of fine fiction. ''I never asked Tolstoy to write for me, a little colored girl in Lorain, Ohio,'' she told the *New Republic*. ''I never asked Joyce not to mention Catholicism or the world of Dublin. Never. And I don't know why I should be asked to explain your life to you. We have splendid writers to do that, but I am not one of them. It is that business of being universal, a word hopelessly stripped of meaning for me. Faulkner wrote what I suppose could be called regional literature and had it published all over the world. That's what I wish to do. If I tried to write a universal novel, it would be water. Behind this question is the suggestion that to write for black people is somehow to diminish the writing. From my perspective there are only black people. When I say 'people,' that's what I mean.''

Black woman writer or simply American novelist, Toni Morrison is a prominent and respected figure in modern letters. In the *Detroit News,* Larson suggests that hers has been ''among the most exciting literary careers of the last decade'' and that each of her books ''has made a quantum jump forward.'' Iron-

ically, Elizabeth House commends Morrison for the universal nature of her work. ''Unquestionably,'' House writes, ''Toni Morrison is an important novelist who continues to develop her talent. Part of her appeal, of course, lies in her extraordinary ability to create beautiful language and striking characters. However, Morrison's most important gift, the one which gives her a major author's universality, is the insight with which she writes of problems all humans face. . . . At the core of all her novels is a penetrating view of the unyielding, heartbreaking dilemmas which torment people of all races.'' Snitow notes that the author ''wants to tend the imagination, search for an expansion of the possible, nurture a spiritual richness in the black tradition even after 300 years in the white desert.'' Dorothy Lee concludes of Morrison's accomplishments: ''Though there are unifying aspects in her novels, there is not a dully repetitive sameness. Each casts the problems in specific, imaginative terms, and the exquisite, poetic language awakens our senses as she communicates an often ironic vision with moving imagery. Each novel reveals the acuity of her perception of psychological motivation—of the female especially, of the Black particularly, and of the human generally.''

''The problem I face as a writer is to make my stories mean something,'' Morrison states in *Black Women Writers at Work*. ''You can have wonderful, interesting people, a fascinating story, but it's not about anything. It has no real substance. . . . I want my books to always be about something that is important to me, and the subjects that are important in the world are the same ones that have always been important.'' In *Black Women Writers: A Critical Evaluation,* she elaborates on this idea. Fiction, she writes, ''should be beautiful, and powerful, but it should also *work*. It should have something in it that enlightens; something in it that opens the door and points the way. Something in it that suggests what the conflicts are, what the problems are. But it need not solve those problems because it is not a case study, it is not a recipe.'' The author who has said that writing ''is discovery; it's talking deep within myself'' told the *New York Times Book Review* that the essential theme in her growing body of fiction is ''how and why we learn to live this life intensely and well.''

BIOGRAPHICAL/CRITICAL SOURCES:

BOOKS

Bell, Roseann P., editor, *Sturdy Black Bridges: Visions of Black Women in Literature,* Doubleday, 1979.

Christian, Barbara, *Black Women Novelists: The Development of a Tradition, 1892-1976,* Greenwood Press, 1980.

Contemporary Literary Criticism, Gale, Volume 4, 1975, Volume 10, 1979, Volume 22, 1982.

Cooper-Clark, Diana, *Interviews with Contemporary Novelists,* St. Martin's, 1986.

Dictionary of Literary Biography, Gale, Volume 6: *American Novelists since World War II,* 1980, Volume 33: *Afro-American Fiction Writers after 1955,* 1984.

Dictionary of Literary Biography Yearbook: 1981, Gale, 1982.

Evans, Mari, editor, *Black Women Writers (1950-1980): A Critical Evaluation,* Doubleday, 1984.

Mekkawi, Mod, *Toni Morrison: A Bibliography,* Howard University Library, 1986.

Mickelson, Anne Z., *Reaching Out: Sensitivity and Order in Recent American Fiction by Women,* Scarecrow Press, 1979.

Ruas, Charles, *Conversations with American Writers,* Knopf, 1985.

Tate, Claudia, editor, *Black Women Writers at Work*, Continuum, 1986.

PERIODICALS

American Literature, January, 1981.
Atlantic, April, 1981.
Black American Literature Forum, summer, 1978, winter, 1979.
Black Scholar, March, 1978.
Black World, June, 1974.
Callaloo, October-February, 1981.
Chicago Tribune, October 27, 1987.
Chicago Tribune Books, August 30, 1988.
Chicago Tribune Book World, March 8, 1981.
CLA Journal, June, 1979, June, 1981.
Commentary, August, 1981.
Contemporary Literature, winter, 1983.
Critique: Studies in Modern Fiction, Volume XIX, number 1, 1977.
Detroit News, March 29, 1981.
Essence, July, 1981, June, 1983, October, 1987.
First World, winter, 1977.
Harper's Bazaar, March, 1983.
Harvard Advocate, Volume CVII, number 4, 1974.
Hudson Review, spring, 1978.
Los Angeles Times, March 31, 1981, October 14, 1987.
Los Angeles Times Book Review, August 30, 1987.
Massachusetts Review, autumn, 1977.
MELUS, fall, 1980.
Ms., June, 1974, December, 1974, August, 1987.
Nation, July 6, 1974, November 19, 1977, May 2, 1981.
New Republic, December 3, 1977, March 21, 1981.
Newsweek, November 30, 1970, January 7, 1974, September 12, 1977, March 30, 1981.
New York, April 13, 1981.
New Yorker, November 7, 1977, June 15, 1981.
New York Post, January 26, 1974.
New York Review of Books, November 10, 1977, April 30, 1981.
New York Times, November 13, 1970, September 6, 1977, March 21, 1981, August 26, 1987, September 2, 1987.
New York Times Book Review, November 1, 1970, December 30, 1973, June 2, 1974, September 11, 1977, March 29, 1981, September 13, 1987.
New York Times Magazine, August 22, 1971, August 11, 1974, July 4, 1976, May 20, 1979.
Obsidian, spring/summer, 1979.
People, July 29, 1974, November 30, 1987.
Philadelphia Inquirer, April 1, 1988.
Publishers Weekly, August 21, 1987.
Saturday Review, September 17, 1977.
Spectator, December 9, 1978, February 2, 1980, December 19, 1981.
Studies in Black Literature, Volume VI, 1976.
Time, September 12, 1977, March 16, 1981, September 21, 1987.
Times (London), October 15, 1987.
Times Literary Supplement, October 4, 1974, November 24, 1978, February 8, 1980, December 19, 1980, October 30, 1981, October 16-22, 1987.
U.S. News and World Report, October 19, 1987.
Village Voice, August 29, 1977, July 1-7, 1981.
Vogue, April, 1981, January, 1986.
Voice Literary Supplement, September, 1987.
Washington Post, February 3, 1974, March 6, 1974, September 30, 1977, April 8, 1981, Februrary 9, 1983, October 5, 1987.
Washington Post Book World, February 3, 1974, September 4, 1977, December 4, 1977, March 22, 1981, September 6, 1987.
World Literature Today, summer, 1978.*

—*Sketch by Anne Janette Johnson*

*   *   *

MOST, Bernard   1937-

PERSONAL: Born September 2, 1937, in New York; son of Max (a painter) and Bertha (Moskowitz) Most; married Amy Beth Pollack, February 12, 1967; children: Glenn Evan, Eric David. *Education:* Pratt Institute, B.F.A. (with honors), 1959. *Politics:* Independent.

ADDRESSES: Home—3 Ridgecrest E., Scarsdale, N.Y. 10583.

CAREER: McCann-Erickson, Inc. (advertising agency), New York City, art director, 1959-65; Benton & Bowles, Inc. (advertising agency), New York City, associate creative director, 1965-78; MCA Advertising, Inc., New York City, senior vice-president and creative director, 1978-86; Bernie & Walter, Inc. (creative consulting company), partner, 1986—.

MEMBER: Authors Guild, Authors League of America.

AWARDS, HONORS: Awards from Art Directors Club, Type Directors Club, and American Institute of Graphic Arts; Clio Award; Andy Award; *If the Dinosaurs Came Back, My Very Own Octopus, Boo!*, and *There's an Ant in Anthony* were each selected as a Children's Choice Book by the International Reading Association and Children's Book Council; *There's an Ant in Anthony* was chosen as an ALA Notable Book.

WRITINGS:

SELF-ILLUSTRATED CHILDREN'S BOOKS

If the Dinosaurs Came Back (Book-of-the-Month Club selection), Harcourt, 1978.
There's an Ant in Anthony, Morrow, 1980.
Turn Over, Prentice-Hall, 1980.
My Very Own Octopus, Harcourt, 1980.
Boo!, Prentice-Hall, 1980.
There's an Ape Behind the Drape, Morrow, 1981.
Whatever Happened to the Dinosaurs? (Book-of-the-Month Club selection), Harcourt, 1984.
Dinosaur Cousins? (Book-of-the-Month Club selection), Harcourt, 1987.
The Littlest Dinosaurs, Harcourt, 1989.

OTHER

Contributor of illustrations to national magazines.

WORK IN PROGRESS: Books for Harper and Harcourt.

SIDELIGHTS: Bernard Most commented: "My books are 'concept books' in that they get children to participate in the ideas of the books beyond the actual reading of them."

If the Dinosaurs Came Back has been translated into Chinese, Japanese, and French.

*   *   *

MUELLER, Virginia   1924-

PERSONAL: Born March 22, 1924, in Sheboygan, Wis.; daughter of Arno and Cora (Hoogstra) Kernen; married Walter A. Mueller (a teacher), July 20, 1946; children: Linda (Mrs.

Jerome Medlin), Christine (Mrs. Reed Simon), Walter David, David John. *Education:* Attended Rhinelander School of Art (University of Wisconsin Extension); additional study through Institute of Children's Literature. *Religion:* Protestant.

ADDRESSES: Home—Route 1, Glenbeulah, Wis. 53023.

CAREER: Free-lance writer, 1975—.

MEMBER: Society of Childrens Book Writers.

WRITINGS:

JUVENILES

Noises and Sounds, Columbia Broadcasting System, 1968.
The King's Invitation, illustrated by J. Roberts, Concordia, 1968.
The Secret Journey, illustrated by B. Wind, Concordia, 1968.
What Is Faith?, edited by Judith Sparks, Standard Publishing, 1969.
The Silly Skyscraper, Concordia, 1970.
Who Is Your Neighbor?, edited by Sparks, Standard Publishing, 1973.
Clem, the Clumsy Camel, Concordia, 1974.
Monster and the Baby, Albert Whitman, 1985.
A Playhouse for Monster, Albert Whitman, 1985.
A Halloween Mask for Monster, Albert Whitman, 1986.
Monster Can't Sleep, Albert Whitman, 1986.

WITH DONNA LUGG PAPE

Bible Activities for Kids, Bethany Fellowship, Books 1 and 2, illustrated by Carol Karle, 1980, Books 3 and 4, 1981, Books 5 and 6, 1982.
Think Pink Solve and Search Puzzles, Xerox Publishing, 1980.
Texas Puzzle Book, Eakin Publications, 1981.
Arkansas Puzzle Book, Rose Publishing (Little Rock, Ark.), 1983.
Louisiana Puzzle Book, Eakin Publications, 1983.
Wisconsin Puzzle Book, Bess Press, 1984.
Tennessee Puzzle Book, Winston-Derek, 1984.
Hawaii Puzzle Book, Bess Press, 1984.
California Trivia Puzzle Book, Bess Press, 1985.
Vermont Puzzle Book, Countryman Press, 1987.

Also author, with Pape, of *Country Music Puzzle Book.*

WORK IN PROGRESS: More "Monster" stories; *Jenny's Bargain,* an Americana story that deals with overcoming prejudice.

AVOCATIONAL INTERESTS: Collecting antiques, visiting historical sites, reading, classical piano.

BIOGRAPHICAL/CRITICAL SOURCES:

PERIODICALS

Booklist, September 1, 1986.
Publishers Weekly, August 22, 1986.
School Library Journal, December, 1985, December, 1986.

*   *   *

MURCHIE, Guy 1907-

PERSONAL: Born January 25, 1907, in Boston, Mass.; son of Guy and Agnes (Donald) Murchie; married Eleanor Forrester Parker, March, 1932; married Barbara Cooney, December 23, 1942; married Kathe Luise Rautenstrauch, January 17, 1949; married Marie Johanna Klees, May 6, 1987; children:

(with Cooney) Gretel, Barnaby; (with Rautenstrauch) Jed. *Education:* Harvard University, B.S., 1929. *Religion:* Baha'i Faith.

ADDRESSES: Home—333 Old Mill Rd. Apt. 215, Santa Barbara, Calif. 93110.

CAREER: Chicago Tribune, Chicago, Ill., feature writer, 1934-42, war correspondent, 1940-42; American Airlines, Air Transport Command, navigation instructor, 1942-43, navigator, 1943-44; Apple Hill Camp, Pepperell, Mass., and Nelson, N.H., founder and director, 1945-55. Instructor, Landhaven School, Camden, Maine, 1949. Navigator, Seaboard & Western Airlines, 1951-52. Pepperell, Mass., school board member, 1946-50, welfare board member, 1947-49.

MEMBER: Institute of Navigation (council member, 1956-58, 1961-63), United World Federalists, Phi Beta Kappa.

AWARDS, HONORS: John Burroughs Medal for best nature book, 1955, for *Song of the Sky: An Exploration of the Ocean of Air;* American Library Association selection as one of fifty most notable books of 1961, and Thormod Monsen Award, Society of Midland Authors, 1962, both for *Music of the Spheres: The Material Universe from Atom to Quasar, Simply Explained;* American Book Award nominee, 1982, for *The Seven Mysteries of Life: An Exploration in Science and Philosophy.*

WRITINGS:

Men on the Horizon, Houghton, 1932.
(Editor and contributor) *Mutiny of the Bounty and Other Sea Stories,* Consolidated, 1937.
(With Thomas Russell Gowenlock) *Soldiers of Darkness,* Doubleday, 1937.
(And illustrator) *Song of the Sky: An Exploration of the Ocean of Air* (Book-of-the-Month Club selection), Houghton, 1954, revised edition, Ziff-Davis Publishing, 1979, abridged edition published as *The World Aloft,* Houghton, 1960.
(And illustrator) *Music of the Spheres: The Material Universe from Atom to Quasar, Simply Explained,* Houghton, 1961, revised edition for young adults published in two volumes, Dover.
(And illustrator) *The Seven Mysteries of Life: An Exploration in Science and Philosophy* (Book-of-the-Month Club alternate selection), Houghton, 1978.

Contributor to anthologies; also contributor to annuals, including *The Old Farmer's Almanac,* and to newspapers and periodicals, including *Atlantic, Holiday, Reader's Digest,* and *Science Digest.*

WORK IN PROGRESS: Veil of Glory, a book on the Baha'i Faith; *The Soul School: Confessions of a Passenger on Planet Earth,* an autobiography.

*   *   *

MURPHY, James J(erome) 1923-

PERSONAL: Born September 9, 1923, in San Jose, Calif.; son of James Joseph (a clerk) and Marie Therese (Utzerath) Murphy; married Kathleen Woods, February 7, 1948; children: Sheila Maureen, Brian Robert. *Education:* St. Mary's College of California, B.A., 1947; Stanford University, M.A., 1950, Ph.D., 1957. *Religion:* Roman Catholic.

ADDRESSES: Home—915 Villanova Dr., Davis, Calif. 95616. *Office*—Department of Rhetoric, University of California, Davis, Calif. 95616.

CAREER: United Press International (UPI), San Francisco, Calif., newsman, 1947-48; Stanford University, Stanford, Calif., assistant professor of speech, 1954-59; Princeton University, Princeton, N.J., assistant professor of speech, 1959-65; University of California, Davis, associate professor, 1965-68, professor of rhetoric, 1968—, vice-chancellor, 1968-69, associate dean, College of Letters and Science, 1972-75, chairman, department of rhetoric, 1975-86. Acting director of Davis Humanities Institute, 1988—. *Military service:* U.S. Army Air Forces, 1943-45. U.S. Air Force Reserve, 1945-69; retired as major.

MEMBER: International Society for the History of Rhetoric (president, 1979-81), Modern Language Association of America, Speech Communication Association, Medieval Academy of America, Medieval Association of the Pacific (president, 1966-70), Pacific Philological Association.

AWARDS, HONORS: Anniversary Award for Distinguished Scholars, Speech Association of America, 1965; American Council of Learned Societies fellow, 1971-72; annual book award, Speech Communication Association, 1975, for *Rhetoric in the Middle Ages;* awarded papal medal by Pope John Paul II, 1979; Chevalier dans l'Ordre des Palmes Academiques from le Ministre de l'Education Nationale de la Republique Francaise, 1988.

WRITINGS:

(With Jon M. Ericson) *The Debater's Guide,* Bobbs-Merrill, 1961.
(Editor and author of introduction and notes) Quintilian, *On the Early Education of the Citizen-Orator* (Book I and chapters 1-10 of Book II of *Institutio oratoria*), translation by John Selby Watson, Library of Liberal Arts, 1966.
(Editor with Peter Kontos) *Teaching Urban Youth,* Wiley, 1967.
(Editor) *Demosthenes' "On the Crown": A Critical Study of a Masterpiece of Ancient Oratory,* translation by John J. Keaney, Random House, 1967.
(Editor and translator) *Three Medieval Rhetorical Arts,* University of California Press, 1971.
(Editor) *Medieval Rhetoric: A Select Bibliography,* University of Toronto Press, 1971, 2nd edition, 1989.
(Editor) *A Synoptic History of Classical Rhetoric,* Random House, 1972.
Rhetoric in the Middle Ages: A History of Rhetorical Theory from Saint Augustine to the Renaissance, University of California Press, 1974.
(Editor and contributor) *Medieval Eloquence: Studies in the Theory and Practice of Medieval Rhetoric,* University of California Press, 1977.
(Compiler) *Renaissance Rhetoric: A Short-Title Catalogue,* Garland, 1981.
(Editor and contributor) *The Rhetorical Tradition and Modern Writing,* Modern Language Association of America, 1982.
(Editor and contributor) *Renaissance Eloquence: Studies in the Theory and Practice of Renaissance Rhetoric,* University of California Press, 1983.
(With Carole Newlands) *The Attack of Peter Ramus on Quintilian: A Translation of "Rhetoricae distinctiones in Quintilianum" (1549),* Northern Illinois University Press, 1987.
Quintilian on the Teaching of Speaking and Writing, Southern Illinois University Press, 1987.

Contributor of over thirty articles to periodicals, including *Medieval Studies, Speech Monographs, Philological Quarterly,* and *Journal of the American Forensic Association.* Editor of *Rhetorica: A Journal of Rhetoric;* member of editorial boards of *Philosophy and Rhetoric, Language and Communication, Writing Communication Annual,* and *Rhetorik: Ein internationalisches Jahrbuch.*

SIDELIGHTS: James J. Murphy told *CA:* "There is an ancient Greek saying that 'he who does not know rhetoric will be a victim of it.' Since human communication has always been a dominant force in our civilization, I've long been interested in tracing its history to see how its future can be shaped. I always tell students they must study the history of rhetoric so they won't spend their time re-inventing the wheel—that is, redoing what someone else has already done. When you look at it that way, the history of rhetoric is a fascinating subject that tells us a good deal about every stage of our civilization."

*   *   *

MURRAY, Les(lie) A(llan)   1938-

PERSONAL: Born 1938, in Nabiac, New South Wales, Australia; son of Cecil Allan (a dairy farmer) and Miriam Pauline (Arnall) Murray; married Valerie Gina Maria Morelli, 1962; children: five. *Education:* Attended University of Sydney. *Politics:* "Distrust especially volunteer police, and side with the genuine, not the advertised, underdog. And be rueful *before* you're presumptuous." *Religion:* Catholic by conversion.

ADDRESSES: *Home*—Coolongolook Road, Bunyah, NSW 2429, Australia.

CAREER: Australian National University, Institute of Advanced Studies, Canberra, translator of scholarly and technical material from western European languages, 1963-67; research in folklore, history, and language in Great Britain, 1967-68; officer in Prime Minister's Department, 1970-71; free-lance writer, 1971—. Has given poetry readings, lectures, and talks in theaters, schools, and universities in Australia, Britain, Europe, and the United States. *Military service:* Royal Australian Naval Reserve, 1960-61.

MEMBER: Australian Society of Authors, Australian Translators' Association.

AWARDS, HONORS: Grace Leven Prize for best book of verse published in Australia, joint winner, 1965, sole winner, 1980; Cook Bi-Centenary Prize for Poetry, 1970; shared National Book Award, 1974; C. J. Dennis Memorial Prize, 1976; shared Mattara Prize, 1981; Australian Literature Society Gold Medal, 1984; Fellowship of Australian Writers Medal, 1984; Australia Prize, 1985; National Poetry Award, 1988; ABC Bicentennial Prize for Poetry, 1988.

WRITINGS:

POETRY

(With Geoffrey J. Lehmann) *The Ilex Tree,* Australian National University Press, 1965.
The Weatherboard Cathedral, Angus & Robertson, 1969.
Poems against Economics, Angus & Robertson, 1972.
Lunch and Counter Lunch, Angus & Robertson, 1974.
The Vernacular Republic, Angus & Robertson, 1975, published as *The Vernacular Republic: Poems, 1961-1981,* Persea Books, 1982, expanded and updated editions, Angus & Robertson, 1982 and 1987.
Ethnic Radio, Angus & Robertson, 1978.
The Boys Who Stole the Funeral (verse novel), Angus & Robertson, 1980.
The People's Otherworld, Angus & Robertson, 1984.
Selected Poems, Carcanet, 1986.

The Daylight Moon, Angus & Robertson, 1987, Posea, 1988.

OTHER

(Translator from the German) Troubetzkoy, *An Introduction to the Techniques of Phonological Description*, Nijhoff, 1967.

The Peasant Mandarin (prose articles and essays), University of Queensland Press, 1978.

Persistence in Folly (essays), Angus & Robertson, 1985.

The Australian Year (prose), photography by Peter Solness and others, Angus & Robertson, 1985.

(Editor) *New Oxford Book of Australian Verse*, Angus & Robertson, 1986.

(Editor) *Anthology of Australian Religious Verse*, Collins/Dove, 1986.

Acting editor, *Poetry Australia*, 1973-79.

SIDELIGHTS: Les A. Murray is considered one of Australia's most highly regarded poets. His verse is firmly rooted in his native landscape, and is marked by what critics commend as wit, humor, and verbal ingenuity. "Wit, imagination, clear perception, creative use of language, subtlety of tone and gentle intensity, are but some of the strengths of Murray's talent," writes Carmel Gaffney in *Quadrant*. Calling him "perhaps the most naturally gifted poet of his generation in Australia," and praising his "genuine wit, and what is rarer, genuine humor," David Malouf adds in *Poetry Australia* that in *Lunch and Counter Lunch*, "the verbal inventiveness seems almost unlimited, and one is reminded of late [W. H.] Auden in the poet's capacity to talk about almost anything and make it sizzle and twang."

"Of all the poets now writing in Australia Les A. Murray is probably the most Australian and probably also the best," claims Fleur Adcock in a *Times Literary Supplement* review of *The Vernacular Republic: Poems, 1961-1981*. Regarding Murray's techniques, Adcock observes: "He is a highly sophisticated user of language, and there is nothing archaic or limited about his stylistic range or his handling of tones and forms. He is a linguist . . . with an enthusiastic appetite for words and a joyfully profligate energy in using them." Clive James indicates in the *New York Review of Books* that in *The Vernacular Republic*, Murray is implying that "Australia is not yet fully in possession of its own culture," and that "the Australian poets of his generation have a duty to do something about this."

Describing Murray's poetry as "parochial," Blake Morrison in a *Times Literary Supplement* review of *The People's Otherworld* adds that "this parochialism gives it its strength and universality." Morrison explains: "It is pastoral and historical, concerned with 'ancestors, axemen, dairymen, horsebreakers,' but amounts to much more than a mere 'National Park of sentimental preservation.'" Murray, as Neil Corcoran suggests in a *Times Literary Supplement* review of *Selected Poems*, is creating Australia in his poetry: "What is at first impressive in Les A. Murray is the sheer sweep of his descriptiveness: Australia's atmospheres, weathers, agriculture, animals, industry, urban sprawl, large emptinesses and sudden congestions seem to be present almost exhaustively in these poems, elbowing and jostling together with fragments of anecdote, narrative and monologue." Praising Murray's "conceptual resourcefulness," and comparing him to Seamus Heaney, Corcoran finds that "the poems are immensely rich in their ability to convey a country felt, as it were, along the arteries," and concludes that the poetry has "great integrity

and verve." According to Peter Porter in a *Journal of Commonwealth Literature* essays on Murray, "Les Murray has brought pleasure and wisdom to contemporary Australian poetry."

Murray told *CA* that he has a "vital interest in giving utterance and form to hitherto unexpressed elements of Australian mind and character. Somewhat vain about technical skill. Am inclined to be celebratory in intention and baroque in method. Seek post-Galileo universes. Chief sources of inspiration: Australian landscape, folklore, history, war, technology, deserts also important. Metaphysical more often than social; I like poetry partly because it isn't exclusively tied to the human. One may write about trees, mountains, the future, the heavens, because it is understood that one is also writing about the human whatever the ostensible subject. This belief suits me."

AVOCATIONAL INTERESTS: Geography, regional studies, landscape, farming, mythology, animals, plants, fine machinery, tall tales, driving through beautiful country.

BIOGRAPHICAL/CRITICAL SOURCES:

BOOKS

Contemporary Literary Criticism, Volume 40, Gale, 1986.

PERIODICALS

Journal of Commonwealth Literature, Volume 17, number 1, 1982.

New York Review of Books, April 14, 1983.

Poetry Australia, December, 1975.

Quadrant, July/August, 1984.

Times Literary Supplement, July 30, 1982, August 9, 1985, August 22, 1986.

*　　*　　*

MYERS, Robert J(ohn)   1924-

PERSONAL: Born January 1, 1924, in Elkhart, Ind.; son of Hallet Frederick and Grace (Mattern) Myers; married Elizabeth Lauchlin Watson, September 21, 1953; children: Timothy, Holly, Lynn. *Education:* Attended DePauw University, 1942-43; University of Chicago, M.A., 1948, Ph.D., 1959.

ADDRESSES: Home—330 39th St., Apt. PHL, New York, N.Y. 10016.

CAREER: United States Army, Japan, area analyst, 1949-55, second secretary in Indonesia and Cambodia, 1956-65; *Washington*, Washington, D.C., co-founder and publisher, 1965-68; *New Republic*, Washington, D.C., publisher, 1968-79. Director and vice-president of Liveright Publishing Co., 1969-74; Madeira School, member of board, 1970—, president, 1975-78; vice-president, New Republic Books, Inc., 1975-79. President, Carnegie Council on Ethics and International Affairs, 1980—. *Military service:* U.S. Army, 1943-46; served in China, Burma, and India.

MEMBER: Asia Society, Phi Beta Kappa, Cosmos Club (Washington, D.C.).

WRITINGS:

Social Insurance and Allied Government Programs, Irwin, 1965.

Medicare, Irwin, 1970.

Private Pension and Profit-Sharing Plans, Industrial Relations Counselors, 1972.

The Tragedie of King Richard, the Second: The Life and Times of Richard II (1367-1400), King of England (1377-1399)

Compared to Those of Richard of America in His Second Administration (satirical drama), Acropolis Books, 1973.

The Coming Collapse of the Post Office (nonfiction), Prentice-Hall, 1975.

The Cross of Frankenstein (gothic novel), Lippincott, 1975.

The Slave of Frankenstein (gothic novel), Lippincott, 1976.

The Virgin and the Vampire, Pocket Books, 1977.

(Editor with Kenneth Thompson) *A Tribute to Hans Morgenthau,* New Republic Books, 1977, augmented edition published as *Truth and Tragedy: A Tribute to Hans Morgenthau,* Transaction Books, 1984.

Indexation of Pension and Other Benefits, Irwin, 1979.

(Editor) *Religion and the State: The Struggle for Legitimacy and Power,* Sage Publications, 1986.

(Editor) *The Political Morality of the International Monetary Fund,* Transaction Books, 1987.

(Editor) *On Love and Marriage,* Peter Pauper, 1987.

(Editor) *International Ethics in the Nuclear Age,* University Press of America and Carnegie Council on Ethics and International Affairs, 1987.

(Editor with Han Sung-joo) *Korea: The Year 2000,* University Press of America and Carnegie Council on Ethics and International Affairs, 1988.

SIDELIGHTS: In *The Coming Collapse of the Post Office,* Robert J. Myers details why he believes the United States postal service is in trouble. The author examines the forces that helped create the Postal Reorganization Act of 1970, ''that ill-fated act of Congress that handed over the controls of the mail service to a government-owned corporation,'' explains Russell Mokhiber in the *Washington Post Book World.* The supporters of the government-corporation idea, Mokhiber continues, had hoped for a more efficient mail service once the ''inept'' hands of government managers had been removed and ''hardnosed'' business rules had taken their place. Yet in *The Coming Collapse of the Post Office,* Myers traces the postal service's movement in the opposite direction, describing the enterprise as ''a band of quasi-business, quasi-governmental officials . . . running the Postal Service like a private fiefdom.'' Although the author suggests some ways in which the postal service might save money, he asserts that the present system cannot last and that it must return to government control or reverse a historical trend by opening up to private competition. More recently, in his *The Political Morality of the International Monetary Fund,* Myers examines ways in which the fund might be restructured. In *Choice,* G. T. Potter notes that although ''the discussion provides an interesting introduction to the issues confronting the global economy,'' it does not reach ''any final conclusions about the political morality'' of its subject.

In addition to his studies of government agencies and programs, Myers is also recognized for his fictional writings. *The Tragedie of King Richard, the Second: The Life and Times of Richard II (1367-1400), King of England (1377-1399) Compared to Those of Richard of America in His Second Administration,* for example, is a political satire that draws parallels between Richard Nixon, then president, and the tragic hero of Shakespeare's ''Richard II.'' Although Joseph McClellan suggests in the *Washington Post Book World* that the satire has ''a political meaning underlined with a most heavy hand,'' a *Publishers Weekly* contributor observes, ''Using Elizabethan rhetoric, flourishes and stage conventions to witty effect, Myers has created a work that parallels the moral thrust of Shakespeare's 'Richard II.' '' And in a very different work, *The Cross of Frankenstein,* Myers presents a pastiche of Mary Shelley's *Frankenstein.* The author supposes that Dr. Frankenstein has a son, endowed with the same scientific abilities as his father. The younger Frankenstein becomes enmeshed in a bizarre adventure that includes a kidnapping, a deceitful butler, a resurrection of the dead, poison, treachery, and pursuit. ''The book is removed from the ordinary run of mock-Gothic daftness,'' a reviewer comments in the *Times Literary Supplement.* ''The style . . . rises to a majesty of awfulness. . . . Right on, Mr. Myers, write on.''

BIOGRAPHICAL/CRITICAL SOURCES:

BOOKS

Myers, Robert J., *The Coming Collapse of the Post Office,* Prentice-Hall, 1975.

PERIODICALS

Choice, October, 1987.

Publishers Weekly, September 3, 1973.

Times Literary Supplement, November 7, 1975.

Washington Post Book World, September 30, 1973, July 13, 1975.

* * *

MYRSIADES, Kostas J.   1940-

PERSONAL: Born May 21, 1940, in Vourliotes, Samos, Greece; came to the United States in 1948, naturalized citizen, 1957; son of John (a vintner) and Mary (Laghos) Myrsiades; married Linda Suny (an assistant professor of management communications), 1965; children: Yani, Leni. *Education:* University of Iowa, B.A., 1963; Indiana University, M.A., 1965, Ph.D., 1972; University of Athens, Certificate in Classical and Modern Greek, 1966.

ADDRESSES: Home—370 North Malin Rd., Newtown Square, Pa. 19073. *Office*—Department of English, West Chester University, Main Hall, West Chester, Pa., 19380.

CAREER: Homer English Institute, Athens, Greece, instructor in English, 1965-66, 1969; West Chester University, West Chester, Pa., assistant professor of English, 1969-73; Deree College, Athens, assistant professor of modern Greek literature and director of Center for Hellenic Studies, 1973-74; West Chester University, associate professor, 1974-77, professor of English, 1977—, assistant dean of College of Arts and Sciences, 1982-83, director of comparative literature studies, 1983—, director of graduate English studies, 1983-85, chairperson of English department, 1985—.

MEMBER: Modern Language Association of America, Modern Greek Studies Association, American Literary Translators Association, American Comparative Literature Association, Association for Computers and the Humanities, Association for the Departments of English, English Association of Pennsylvania State College and University Faculty, Greek-Turkish University Alliance.

AWARDS, HONORS: West Chester University grants, 1980, 1982, 1986, and 1987; Lilly fellow at University of Pennsylvania, 1981; Philadelphia Council of the Humanities grant, 1983; Delaware Valley Faculty Exchange grant, 1984; Faculty Merit Awards for Scholarship and Service, 1984 and 1987; University Scholars grant, 1988.

WRITINGS:

Takis Papatsonia, G. K. Hall, 1974.

(Contributor) Kostas E. Tsiropoulos, editor, *Timi ston T. K. Papatsoni* (title means "In Honor of Takis K. Papatsonis"), Tetradhia Eythinis, 1976.

(Contributor) G. Valetas, editor, *Afieroma ston Yanni Ritso* (title means "Festschrift for Yannis Ritsos"), Aiolika Ghramata, 1976.

(Editor and translator, with Kimon Friar) Yannis Ritsos, *Scripture of the Blind,* Ohio State University Press, 1979.

(Contributor) Athina Kallaianesi, editor, *Afieroma ston Yanni Ritso* (title means "Festschrift for Yannis Ritsos"), Kedhros, 1981.

(Editor and author of introduction) *Approaches to Teaching Homer's Iliad and Odyssey,* Modern Language Association of America, 1987.

(Editor and translator, with Friar) Ritsos, *Monovasia and The Women of Monemvasia,* Nostos Press, 1987.

(Author and translator, with wife, Linda S. Myrsiades) *The Karagiozis Heroic Performance in Greek Shadow Theater,* University Press of New England, 1988.

Ursa Minor and Other Poems, Nostos Press, in press.

Contributor to *Encyclopedia of World Literature in the Twentieth Century, Dictionary of Literary Biography,* and *European Writers.* Contributor of more than one hundred articles, poems, translations, and reviews to language and literature journals in the United States and Greece. Guest editor of *College Literature,* 1976, 1978, 1988, *Falcon,* 1978, *Grove: Contemporary Poetry and Translation,* 1979, and *Durak: An International Magazine of Poetry,* 1980.

WORK IN PROGRESS: The Karagiozis Comic Performance in the Modern Greek Oral Tradition, with Linda S. Myrsiades; *Nota Bene for Literary Study and Research;* and *Greek Resistance Literature of the Forties.*

SIDELIGHTS: Kostas J. Myrsiades told *CA:* "My interest lies in the poetry of the Western world's longest continuous literary tradition from Homer to the poetry of twentieth-century Greece. I am especially interested in modern Greek poets who, like Kazantzakis, Cavafy, Seferis, Papatsonis, and Ritsos, use Homeric myths to speak of man and the human condition in new and contemporary ways. Moving from Homer to the contemporary arts of Greece (art, film, literature) allows me to study both the alpha and the omega of Greek culture. Translating modern Greek poetry provides me with an opportunity to explode both the richness and the Greekness (*romiosini*) of these poets into an equally rich language—English. Moreover, dealing with separate languages (classical, Byzantine, modern) permits me to emphasize the Hellenic (that which is universally Greek without regard to specific locality) rather than the Greek (the purely local). In translating from the modern Greek oral tradition (Karagiozis), I am interested in experimenting with new translation theories and in new ways of applying these to the Greek oral texts. My present approach to these texts takes its point of departure from performance theory which is itself influenced by Kenneth Burke. Performance focuses on the act, the performer, and the audience, subject to the same rules that govern all human behavior, but most particularly as a communicative behavior with a focus on understanding verbal art as doing, that is as a performed way of speaking."

N

NABOKOV, Peter (Francis) 1940-
(Peter Towne)

PERSONAL: Born October 11, 1940, in Auburn, N.Y.; son of Nicolas (a writer and composer) and Constance (Holladay) Nabokov. *Education:* Attended St. Johns College; Columbia University, B.S., 1965; Goddard College, M.S., 1973.

ADDRESSES: Home—820 Riley Dr., 8S, Albany, Calif. 94706.

CAREER: Worked on Navaho, Sioux, and Crow reservations in Montana, 1962, and later sailed with the Merchant Marine; *New Mexican,* Santa Fe, N.M., staff reporter, 1967-68; Monterey Peninsula College, Monterey, Calif., instructor in American Indian studies, 1970-73, 1977-78; Human Resources Research Organization, Carmel, Calif., research associate, 1972-75; University of California, Berkeley, instructor, 1979-82, 1984-85; D'Arcy McNickle Center for the History of the American Indian, Newberry Library, Chicago, Ill., resident fellow, 1986-87; Native American Educational Services College, Chicago, Ill., co-instructor, 1987; University of California, Santa Cruz, lecturer, 1987-88. Research associate, Museum of the American Indian, Heye Foundation, 1962-82, and Santa Barbara Museum of Natural History, 1978-82. Lecturer at Center for the Study of Indian History, Haskell Indian Junior College, University of California, Santa Barbara, College of the Virgin Islands, Colorado College, University of North Dakota, University of Montana, and University of Colorado.

MEMBER: Society for the Prevention of Cruelty to Children.

AWARDS, HONORS: Albuquerque Press Club awards, two first prizes, and New Mexico Press Association, first prize in editorial writing, all 1967; American Library Association Best Book for Young Adults citation, *Library School Journal* Best Book citation, and Carter G. Woodson Book Award from National Council for the Social Studies, all 1978, all for *Native American Testimony: An Anthology of Indian and White Relations,* Volume I: *First Encounter to Dispossession.*

WRITINGS:

Two Leggings: The Making of a Crow Warrior, Crowell, 1967.
Tijerina and the Courthouse Raid, University of New Mexico Press, 1970, revised edition, Ramparts, 1971.
(Under pseudonym Peter Towne) *George Washington Carver,* Crowell, 1975.

(Editor) *Native American Testimony: An Anthology of Indian and White Relations,* Crowell, Volume I: *First Encounter to Dispossession,* 1978, Volume II: *Reservation to Resurgence,* 1988.
Indian Running, Capra, 1981, published as *Indian Running: Native American History and Tradition,* Ancient City Press, 1987.
Architecture of Acoma Pueblo: The 1934 Historic American Buildings Survey Project, Ancient City Press, 1986.
(With Robert Easton) *Dwellings at the Source: Architecture of the American Indian,* Oxford University Press, 1989.
Sacred Geography: Reflections and Sources on Environment/Religion, Harper, 1989.
Bibliography of the Crow, Scarecrow Press, 1989.

CONTRIBUTOR

Murray L. Wax and Robert Buchanan, editors, *Solving "The Indian Problem": The White Man's Burdensome Business,* New York Times, 1975.
Chester Klevens, editor, *Methods and Materials of Continuing Education,* Klevens Publishing, 1976.
Shelter II, Shelter Publications, 1978.
Calvin Martin, editor, *The American Indian and the Problem of History,* Oxford University Press, 1987.
Dell Upton, editor, *Roots: America's Vernacular Heritage,* American Heritage Press, 1987.

Also contributor to *Our Indian Heritage,* Reader's Digest.

OTHER

(With Wayne Olts) "Peoples of the Earthlodge" (film), North Dakota Council for the Humanities and Public Issues, 1987.

Contributor to numerous periodicals, including *Nation, Co-Evolution Quarterly, New Scholar, East West Journal, Camera Arts, American West, Parabola, Progressive, Washington Post,* and *New York Times Book Review.*

SIDELIGHTS: In his books about the American Indian, Peter Nabokov presents a sympathetic and compelling view of their history and traditions. His *Two Leggings: The Making of a Crow Warrior* is "a crisp, unexaggerated re-creation of the life of a nineteenth-century Plains Indian warrior," as Meredith Brown of *Saturday Review* states. A detailed biography that also examines Indian society of the time, it is "a unique record of a vanished culture," writes Hardin E. Smith in *Li-*

brary Journal. Similarly, Brown assesses it "a handbook to the values and patterns of leadership in a culture that flourished less than 100 years ago."

Calling Nabokov's *Tijerina and the Courthouse Raid* "centrally the history of a social movement," Edgar Z. Friedenberg explains in the *New York Review of Books* that it chronicles "the formation and development, under [Reies Lopes] Tijerina's leadership, of the Alianzo Federal de los Pueblos Libres—the Federation of Free City States—and of the remarkable events in which the Alianzo has been involved in its organizing of so called 'Mexican-Americans' in the state of New Mexico." Friedenberg maintains that the book is "even more valuable as sociology than as history, because it shows so clearly how things work, and on the basis of such carefully and quite literally painfully gathered evidence, both by observation and documentation." Similarly, the value of *First Encounter to Dispossession,* Volume I of *Native American Testimony: An Anthology of Indian and White Relations,* according to N. Scott Momaday of the *New York Times Book Review,* is its "keen insight into the mind and spirit of the American Indian. In these many utterances, there emerges one voice, and it is one of great poignancy and power, often one of great beauty."

In *Indian Running,* Nabokov studies Indian ceremonial running through an account of the six-day run from Taos, New Mexico, to Second Mesa, Hopi, Arizona, to commemorate the three-hundredth anniversary of the Pueblo Indian revolt. "Nabokov has assembled an amazing array of written knowledge on Native Americans running," writes Kenneth Funston in the *Los Angeles Times Book Review.* And although Funston faults its "bookishness" and Nabokov's reluctance in "poking around the present world, the living people," he believes that "ironically, in the dust of his retiring journalism, Nabokov opens a whole system of Native American etiquette, a way of being—and a way of letting others be."

BIOGRAPHICAL/CRITICAL SOURCES:

PERIODICALS

Commonweal, November 10, 1978.
Library Journal, June 15, 1967.
Los Angeles Times Book Review, November 29, 1981.
Nation, June 1, 1970.
New Leader, February 16, 1970.
New York Review of Books, December 18, 1969.
New York Times Book Review, January 11, 1970, April 30, 1978.
Saturday Review, September 9, 1967.
Yale Review, June, 1970.

*   *   *

NAGEL, James (Edward)   1940-

PERSONAL: Born May 20, 1940; son of Ray (a farmer) and May (Fjeldseth) Nagel; married Gwen Lindberg (an English instructor). *Education:* Moorhead State College (now University), B.A., 1962; Pennsylvania State University, M.A., 1964, Ph.D., 1971.

ADDRESSES: Home—15 Northgate Rd., Wellesley, Mass. 02181. *Office*—Department of English, Northeastern University, 360 Huntington Ave., Boston, Mass. 02115.

CAREER: Moorhead State College, Moorhead, Minn., instructor in English, 1965-68; Northeastern University, Boston, Mass., assistant professor, 1971-74, associate professor, 1974-

80, professor of English, 1980—. Fulbright lecturer in New Zealand, 1977; lecturer on worldwide tour, 1977.

MEMBER: Modern Language Association of America, Conference of Editors of Learned Journals (secretary, 1974-77; vice president, 1978-82), Hemingway Society (president, 1983-86), Hemingway Foundation, Northeast Modern Language Association.

WRITINGS:

(Compiler) *Vision and Value: A Thematic Introduction to the Short Story* (text edition), Dickenson, 1970.
(Editor) *Critical Essays on "Catch 22,"* Dickenson, 1974.
(With wife, Gwen L. Nagel) *Sarah Orne Jewett: A Reference Guide,* G. K. Hall, 1977.
(Editor) *American Fiction: Historical and Critical Essays,* Northeastern University Press, 1977.
Stephen Crane and Literary Impressionism, Pennsylvania State University Press, 1980.
(Editor with Richard Astro) *American Literature: The New England Heritage,* Garland Publishing, 1981.
(Compiler) *Critical Essays on Hamlin Garland,* G. K. Hall, 1982.
(Editor) *Ernest Hemingway: The Writer in Context,* University of Wisconsin Press, 1984.
(Editor) *Critical Essays on Joseph Heller,* G. K. Hall, 1984.

Contributor of articles to literary journals. Bibliographer for *MLA International Bibliography,* 1970-74; editor, *Studies in American Fiction,* 1973—; general editor, "Critical Essays on American Literature" series, 1978.

WORK IN PROGRESS: A book on Hemingway and Agnes Von Kurowsky; a study of Hemingway's narrative methods; a book on the contemporary short story cycle.

AVOCATIONAL INTERESTS: Tennis, swimming, hiking, raising rare cats.

*   *   *

NAMIOKA, Lensey   1929-

PERSONAL: Born June 14, 1929, in Peking, China; daughter of Yuen Ren (a linguist) and Buwei (a physician and writer; maiden name, Yang) Chao; married Isaac Namioka (a mathematician), September 9, 1957; children: Aki, Michi (daughters). *Education:* Attended Radcliffe College, 1947-49; University of California, Berkeley, B.A., 1951, M.A., 1952.

ADDRESSES: Home—2047 23rd Ave. E., Seattle, Wash. 98112. *Agent*—Ruth Cohen, Box 7626, Menlo Park, Calif. 94025.

CAREER: Wells College, Aurora, N.Y., instructor in mathematics, 1957-58; Cornell University, Ithaca, N.Y., instructor in mathematics, 1958-61; broadcasting monitor, Japan Broadcasting Corp., 1969—. Translator for American Mathematical Society, 1958-66.

MEMBER: Seattle Free Lances.

WRITINGS:

(Translator) Buwei Y. Chao, *How to Order and Eat in Chinese,* Vintage, 1974.
The Samurai and the Long-Nosed Devils (juvenile), McKay, 1976.
White Serpent Castle (juvenile), McKay, 1976.
Japan: A Traveler's Companion, Vanguard, 1979.

Valley of Broken Cherry Trees (juvenile), Delacorte, 1980.
Village of the Vampire Cat (juvenile), Delacorte, 1981.
Who's Hu? (juvenile), Vanguard, 1981.
China: A Traveler's Companion, Vanguard, 1985.
Phantom of Tiger Mountain (juvenile), Vanguard, 1986.
Island of Ogres, Harper, 1989.

Contributor of travel and humor articles to magazines and newspapers.

WORK IN PROGRESS: Wormholes: Life with Chaos.

SIDELIGHTS: Lensey Namioka writes: "For my writings I draw heavily on my Chinese cultural heritage and on my husband's Japanese cultural heritage. My involvement with Japan started before my marriage, since my mother spent many years in Japan. My long years of training in mathematics had little influence on my writing, except for an urge to economy."

AVOCATIONAL INTERESTS: Music ("prefer to make it myself badly than to hear it performed superbly").

BIOGRAPHICAL/CRITICAL SOURCES:

PERIODICALS

Chicago Tribune Book World, July 5, 1981.

*   *   *

NAYLOR, Gloria   1950-

PERSONAL: Born January 25, 1950, in New York, N.Y.; daughter of Roosevelt (a transit worker) and Alberta (a telephone operator; maiden name, McAlpin) Naylor. *Education:* Brooklyn College of the City University of New York, B.A., 1981; Yale University, M.A., 1983.

ADDRESSES: Office—c/o Ticknor & Fields, 52 Vanderbilt Ave., New York, N.Y. 10016. *Agent*—Sterling Lord, One Madison Ave., New York, N.Y. 10010.

CAREER: Missionary for Jehovah's Witnesses in New York, North Carolina, and Florida, 1968-75; worked for various hotels in New York, N.Y., including Sheraton City Squire, as telephone operator, 1975-81; writer, 1981—. Writer in residence, Cummington Community of the Arts, 1983; visiting lecturer, George Washington University, 1983-84, and Princeton University, 1986-87; cultural exchange lecturer, United States Information Agency, India, 1985; scholar in residence, University of Pennsylvania, 1986; visiting professor, New York University, 1986, and Boston University, 1987; Fannie Hurst Visiting Professor, Brandeis University, 1988. Senior fellow, Society for the Humanities, Cornell University, 1988.

AWARDS, HONORS: American Book Award for best first novel, 1983, for *The Women of Brewster Place;* Distinguished Writer Award, Mid-Atlantic Writers Association, 1983; National Endowment for the Arts fellowship, 1985; Candace Award, National Coalition of 100 Black Women, 1986; Guggenheim fellowship, 1988.

WRITINGS:

FICTION

The Women of Brewster Place, Viking, 1982.
Linden Hills, Ticknor & Fields, 1985.
Mama Day, Ticknor & Fields, 1988.

NONFICTION

Centennial, Pindar Press, 1986.

OTHER

Also author of unproduced screenplay adaptation of *The Women of Brewster Place,* for American Playhouse, 1984, and of an unproduced original screenplay for Public Broadcasting System's "In Our Own Words," 1985. Contributor of essays and articles to periodicals, including *Southern Review, Essence, Ms., Life, Ontario Review,* and *People.* Contributing editor, *Callaloo,* 1984—; "Hers" columnist for *New York Times,* 1986.

WORK IN PROGRESS: A novel dealing with "whores, language, and music"; a screenplay for Zenith Productions, London.

SIDELIGHTS: "I wanted to become a writer because I felt that my presence as a black woman and my perspective as a woman in general had been underrepresented in American literature," Gloria Naylor commented. Her first novel, *The Women of Brewster Place,* which features a cast of seven strong-willed black women, won the American Book Award for best first fiction in 1983. Naylor has continued her exploration of the black female experience in two subsequent novels that remain focused on women while also expanding her fictional realm. In *Linden Hills,* for example, Naylor uses the structure of Dante's *Inferno* to create a contemporary allegory about the perils of black materialism and the ways in which denying one's heritage can endanger the soul. Naylor's third novel, *Mama Day,* draws on another literary masterpiece—Shakespeare's *Tempest*—and artfully combines Shakespearean elements with black folkloric strains. By drawing on traditional western sources, Naylor places herself firmly in the literary mainstream, broadening her base from ethnic to American writing. Unhappy with what she calls the "historical tendency to look upon the output of black writers as not really American literature," Naylor told *Publishers Weekly* interviewer William Goldstein that her work attempts to "articulate experiences that want articulating—for those readers who reflect the subject matter, black readers, and for those who don't—basically white middle class readers."

Naylor's first novel grew out of a desire to reflect the diversity of the black experience—a diversity that she feels neither the black nor the white critical establishment has recognized. "There has been a tendency on the part of both," she commented, "to assume that a black writer's work should be 'definitive' of black experience. This type of critical stance denies the vast complexity of black existence, even if we were to limit that existence solely to America. While *The Women of Brewster Place* is about the black woman's condition in America, I had to deal with the fact that one composite picture couldn't do justice to the complexity of the black female experience. So I tried to solve this problem by creating a microcosm on a dead-end street and devoting each chapter to a different woman's life. These women vary in age, personal background, political consciousness, and sexual preference. What they do share is a common oppression and, more importantly, a spiritual strength and sense of female communion that I believe all women have employed historically for their psychic health and survival."

Reviewing *The Women of Brewster Place* in the *Washington Post,* Deirdre Donahue writes: "Naylor is not afraid to grapple with life's big subjects: sex, birth, love, death, grief. Her women feel deeply, and she unflinchingly transcribes their emotions.... Naylor's potency wells up from her language. With prose as rich as poetry, a passage will suddenly take off and sing like a spiritual.... Vibrating with undisguised emotion, 'The Women of Brewster Place' springs from the same roots that produced the blues. Like them, her book sings of sorrows proudly borne by black women in America.''

To date, Naylor has linked her novels by carrying over characters from one narrative to another. In *The Women of Brewster Place,* one of the young residents is a refugee from Linden Hills, an exclusive black suburb. Naylor's second novel spotlights that affluent community, revealing the material corruption and moral decay that would prompt an idealistic young woman to abandon her home for a derelict urban neighborhood. Though *Linden Hills,* as the book is called, approaches the Afro-American experience from the upper end of the socioeconomic spectrum, it is also a black microcosm. This book ''forms the second panel of that picture of contemporary urban black life which Naylor started with in *Women of Brewster Place,*'' writes *Times Literary Supplement* contributor Roz Kaveney. ''Where that book described the faults, passions, and culture of the good poor, this shows the nullity of black lives that are led in imitation of suburban whites.''

In addition to shifting her focus, Naylor has also raised her literary sights in her second novel. *Linden Hills,* which has been described as a contemporary allegory with gothic overtones, is an ambitious undertaking structurally modeled after Dante Alighiere's *Inferno.* Among its many accomplishments, Dante's Italian masterpiece describes the nine circles of hell, Satan's imprisonment in their depths, and the lost souls condemned to suffer with him. In Naylor's modern version, ''souls are damned not because they have offended God or have violated a religious system but because they have offended themselves. In their single-minded pursuit of upward mobility, the inhabitants of Linden Hill, a black, middle-class suburb, have turned away from their past and from their deepest sense of who they are,'' writes Catherine C. Ward in *Contemporary Literature.* To correspond to Dante's circles, Naylor uses a series of crescent-shaped drives that ring the suburban development. Her heroes are two young street poets—outsiders from a neighboring community who hire themselves out to do odd jobs so they can earn Christmas money. ''As they move down the hill, what they encounter are people who have 'moved up' in American society . . . until eventually they will hit the center of their community and the home of my equivalent of Satan,'' Naylor told Goldstein. Naylor's Satan is one Luther Needed, a combination mortician and real estate tycoon, who preys on the residents' baser ambitions to keep them in his sway.

Though *Women's Review of Books* contributor Jewelle Gomez argues that ''the Inferno motif . . . often feels like a literary exercise rather than a groundbreaking adaptation,'' most critics commend Naylor's bold experiment. *San Francisco Review of Books* contributor Claudia Tate, for instance, praises ''Naylor's skill in linking together complicated stories in a highly structured but unobtrusive narrative form. In combining elements of realism and fantasy with a sequence of ironic reversals, she sets into motion a series of symbols which become interlinked, producing complex social commentary. For example, the single ambition for residents of Linden Hills is to advance economically, but in order to achieve this end they must sacrifice the possibility of emotional and personal fulfillment. When the goal is attained, they measure their success by reversing the expected movement in social climbing.''

Even those who find the execution flawed endorse Naylor's daring. Says *New York Times Book Review* contributor Mel Watkins: ''Although Miss Naylor has not been completely successful in adapting the 'Inferno' to the world of the black middle class, in 'Linden Hills' she has shown a willingness to expand her fictional realm and to take risks. Its flaws notwithstanding, the novel's ominous atmosphere and inspired set pieces . . . make it a fascinating departure for Miss Naylor, as well as a provocative, iconoclastic novel about a seldom-addressed subject.'' Concludes the *Ms.* reviewer, ''In this second novel, Naylor serves notice that she is a mature literary talent of formidable skill.''

Naylor's third novel, *Mama Day,* is named for its main character—a wise old woman with magical powers whose name is Miranda Day, but whom everyone refers to as Mama Day. This ninety-year-old conjurer made a walk-on appearance in *Linden Hills* as the illiterate, toothless aunt who hauls about cheap cardboard suitcases and leaky jars of preserves. But it is in *Mama Day* that this ''caster of hoodoo spells . . . comes into her own,'' according to *New York Times Book Review* contributor Bharati Mukherjee. ''The portrait of Mama Day is magnificent,'' she declares.

Mama Day lives on Willow Springs, a wondrous island off the coast of Georgia and South Carolina that has been owned by her family since before the Civil War. The fact that slaves are portrayed as property owners demonstrates one of the ways that Naylor turns the world upside down, according to Rita Mae Brown. Another, continues Brown in her *Los Angeles Times Book Review,* is ''that the women possess the real power, and are acknowledged as having it.'' When Mama Day's grand niece Cocoa brings George, her citified new husband, to Willow Springs, he learns the importance of accepting mystery. ''George is the linchpin of 'Mama Day,''' Brown says. ''His rational mind allows the reader to experience the island as George experiences it. Mama Day and Cocoa are of the island and therefore less immediately accessible to the reader. The turning point comes when George is asked not only to believe in Mama Day's power but to act on it. Cocoa is desperately ill. A hurricane has washed out the bridge so that no mainland doctor can be summoned.'' Only Mama Day has the power to help George save her life. She gives him a task, which he bungles because he is still limited by purely rational thinking. Ultimately, George is able to save Cocoa, but only by great personal sacrifice.

The plot twists and thematic concerns of *Mama Day* have led several reviewers to compare the work to Shakespeare. ''Whereas 'Linden Hills' was Dantesque, 'Mama Day' is Shakespearean, with allusions, however oblique and tangential, to 'Hamlet,' 'King Lear,' and, especially, 'The Tempest,''' writes Chicago *Tribune Books* critic John Blades. ''Like Shakespeare's fantasy, Naylor's book takes place on an enchanted island. . . . Naylor reinforces her Shakespearean connection by naming her heroine Miranda.'' Mukherjee also believes that *Mama Day* ''has its roots in 'The Tempest.' The theme is reconciliation, the title character is Miranda (also the name of Prospero's daughter), and Willow Springs is an isolated island where, as on Prospero's isle, magical and mysterious events come to pass.''

Naylor's ambitious attempt to elevate a modern love story to Shakespearean heights ''is more bewildering than bewitching,'' according to Blades. ''Naylor has populated her magic kingdom with some appealingly offbeat characters, Mama Day foremost among them. But she's failed to give them anything very original or interesting to do.'' Mukherjee also acknowledges the shortcomings of Naylor's mythical love story, but asserts ''I'd rather dwell on *Mama Day*'s strengths. Gloria Naylor has written a big, strong, dense, admirable novel; spacious, sometimes a little drafty like all public monuments, designed to last and intended for many levels of use.''

BIOGRAPHICAL/CRITICAL SOURCES:

BOOKS

Contemporary Literary Criticism, Volume 28, Gale, 1984.

PERIODICALS

Chicago Tribune Book World, February 23, 1983.
Christian Science Monitor, March 1, 1985.
Commonweal, May 3, 1985.
Contemporary Literature, Volume XXVIII, number 1, 1987.
Detroit News, March 3, 1985, February 21, 1988.
Los Angeles Times, December 2, 1982.
Los Angeles Times Book Review, February 24, 1985, March 6, 1988.
London Review of Books, August 1, 1985.
Ms., June, 1985.
New Republic, September 6, 1982.
New York Times, February 9, 1985.
New York Times Book Review, August 22, 1982, March 3, 1985, February 21, 1988.
Publishers Weekly, September 9, 1983.
San Francisco Review of Books, May, 1985.
Times (London), April 21, 1983.
Times Literary Supplement, May 24, 1985.
Tribune Books (Chicago), January 31, 1988.
Washington Post, October 21, 1983.
Washington Post Book World, March 24, 1985, February 28, 1988.
Women's Review of Books, August, 1985.

—*Sketch by Donna Olendorf*

*   *   *

NEILSON, Andrew 1946-

PERSONAL: Born November 15, 1946, in Ordsall, England; son of Edward (a naval officer) and Traudi (Hayek) Neilson; married Sally Davies, July 19, 1980; children: Lucy, Richard. *Education:* University of Liverpool, B.A., 1968.

ADDRESSES: Home—Las Nayas, Partida Lluca, Javea (Alicante), Spain. *Agent*—Blake Friedmann, 37-41 Gower St., London WC1E 6HH, England.

CAREER: Seating International (contract furniture company), London, England, founder and operator, 1973-76; founder and operator of Aaronite Ltd. (fire protection company), 1976-81; writer, 1981—.

WRITINGS:

Braking Point (suspense novel), W. H. Allen, 1983.
Dead Straight (suspense novel), W. H. Allen, 1983.
The Monza Protest (suspense novel), W. H. Allen, 1985.
Bloody Business (suspense novel), Sphere, 1989.

WORK IN PROGRESS: Sand Dollars, a novel ''set on a Caribbean Island, with the Communist Revolution and American Rescue as background.''

SIDELIGHTS: Andrew Neilson told *CA:* ''My brother was a mechanic for a Formula I and for an endurance sportscar racing team, but I had no interest in motor racing until he invited me to a meeting at Oulton Park (Cheshire, England) in 1968. From then on I was totally hooked. The start of a motor race is the

most exciting sporting activity imaginable, especially from the driver's seat!

''I started competing in Ireland in 1970 with a modified sportscar, winning my class in the championship. From then on I was mainly involved in amateur sportscar racing, occasionally winning, and breaking the lap record at Snetterton (Norfolk, England). Then in 1979 I managed my best friend's attempt on the British Formula Atlantic Championship—which he won. The next season we moved up to the British Formula I Championship, but this resulted in a horrific accident—my best friend was nearly burned to death.

''Later that year I married, sold my business (which specialized in fire protection for oil fields in England, the North Sea, and Norway), and started writing—a long-standing ambition. My first publishers billed me as 'the Dick Francis of motor racing.' I love the tautness and tension of the thriller framework, and within it I wanted to explain motor racing to my readers, particularly what motivates people to take part in such an incredibly dangerous activity.''

Regarding *Braking Point,* a reviewer for the *Manchester Evening News* wrote that he had ''never come across a better novel on the subject [motor racing] than Andrew Neilson's.'' The critic added: ''The author knows his subject, but doesn't labour it, and he does let his readers live the life of a top driver, learning a lot of his secrets. . . without making a lesson of it.''

BIOGRAPHICAL/CRITICAL SOURCES:

PERIODICALS

Manchester Evening News, July 1, 1983.
Motor Sport, December, 1985.

*   *   *

NEMEROV, Howard (Stanley) 1920-

PERSONAL: Born March 1, 1920, in New York, N.Y.; son of David and Gertrude (Russek) Nemerov; married Margaret Russell, January 26, 1944; children: David, Alexander Michael, Jeremy Seth. *Education:* Harvard University, A.B., 1941.

ADDRESSES: Home—6970 Cornell Ave., St. Louis, Mo. 63130.

CAREER: Hamilton College, Clinton, N.Y., instructor, 1946-48; Bennington College, Bennington, Vt., member of faculty in literature, 1948-66; Brandeis University, Waltham, Mass., professor of English, 1966-68; Washington University, St. Louis, Mo., visiting Hurst Professor of English, 1969-70, professor of English, 1970-76, Edward Mallinckrodt Distinguished University Professor of English, 1976—. Visiting lecturer in English, University of Minnesota, 1958-59; writer-in-residence, Hollins College, 1962-63. Consultant in poetry, Library of Congress, 1963-64; chancellor, American Academy of Poets, beginning 1976. *Military service:* Royal Canadian Air Force, 1942-44; became flying officer; U.S. Army Air Forces, 1944-45; became first lieutenant.

MEMBER: National Institute of Arts and Letters, American Academy of Arts and Letters, American Academy of Arts and Sciences (fellow), Phi Beta Kappa (honorary member), Alpha of Massachusetts.

AWARDS, HONORS: Bowdoin Prize, Harvard University, 1940; *Kenyon Review* fellowship in fiction, 1955; Oscar Blumenthal Prize, 1958, Harriet Monroe Memorial Prize, 1959, Frank O'Hara Memorial Prize, 1971, Levinson Prize, 1975, all from

Poetry magazine; second prize, *Virginia Quarterly Review* short story competition, 1958; National Institute of Arts and Letters Grant, 1961; Golden Rose Trophy, New England Poetry Club, 1962; Brandeis Creative Arts Award, 1963; D.L., Lawrence University, 1964, and Tufts University, 1969; National Endowment for the Arts Grant, 1966-67; First Theodore Roethke Memorial Award, 1968, for *The Blue Swallows;* St. Botolph's Club (Boston) Prize for Poetry, 1968; Guggenheim fellow, 1968-69; Academy of American Poets fellowship, 1970; Pulitzer Prize and National Book award, 1978, and Bollingen Prize, 1981, Yale University, all for *The Collected Poems of Howard Nemerov;* the first Aiken Taylor Award for Modern Poetry, 1987, from *Sewanee Review* and University of the South; National Medal of Art, 1987, for promoting "excellence, growth, support and availability of the arts in the United States"; honorary degree from Washington and Lee University.

WRITINGS:

The Melodramatists (novel), Random House, 1949.
Federigo: Or the Power of Love (novel), Little, Brown, 1954.
The Homecoming Game (novel), Simon & Schuster, 1957.
A Commodity of Dreams and Other Stories, Simon & Schuster, 1959.
(Editor and author of introduction) Henry Wadsworth Longfellow, *Longfellow: Selected Poetry,* Dell, 1959.
Poetry and Fiction: Essays, Rutgers University Press, 1963.
(Author of foreword) Miller Williams, *A Circle of Stones,* Louisiana State University, 1964.
(Author of introduction) Owen Barfield, *Poetic Diction: A Study in Meaning,* McGraw-Hill, 1964.
(Author of commentary) William Shakespeare, *Two Gentlemen of Verona,* Dell, 1964.
Journal of the Fictive Life (autobiography), Rutgers University Press, 1965, reprinted with a new preface, University of Chicago Press, 1981.
(Editor and contributor) *Poets on Poetry,* Basic Books, 1965.
(Editor) Marianne Moore, *Poetry and Criticism,* Adams House & Lowell House Printers, 1965.
(Contributor) Sheldon Norman Grebstein, editor, *Perspectives in Contemporary Criticism,* Harper, 1968.
(Contributor) A. Cheuse and R. Koffler, editors, *The Rarer Action: Essays in Honor of Francis Fergusson,* Rutgers University Press, 1971.
Stories, Fables and Other Diversions, David R. Godine, 1971.
Reflexions on Poetry and Poetics, Rutgers University Press, 1972.
(Contributor) Robert Boyers, editor, *Contemporary Poetry in America: Essays and Interviews,* Schocken, 1975.
(Contributor) Shirley Sugarman, editor, *Evolution of Consciousness: Studies in Polarity,* Wesleyan University Press, 1976.
Figures of Thought: Speculations on the Meaning of Poetry and Other Essays, David R. Godine, 1978.
(Contributor) Arthur Edelstein, editor, *Images and Ideas in American Culture: The Functions of Criticism, Essays in Memory of Philip Rahv,* Brandeis University Press, 1979.
New and Selected Essays, with foreword by Kenneth Burke, Southern Illinois University Press, 1985.
The Oak in the Acorn: On Remembrance of Things Past and on Teaching Proust, Who Will Never Learn, Louisiana State University Press, 1987.

POETRY

The Image and the Law, Holt, 1947.

Guide to the Ruins, Random House, 1950.
The Salt Garden, Little, Brown, 1955.
Small Moment, Ward Ritchie Press, 1957.
Mirrors and Windows, University of Chicago Press, 1958.
New and Selected Poems, University of Chicago Press, 1960.
Endor: Drama in One Act (verse play; also see below), Abingdon, 1961.
The Next Room of the Dream: Poems and Two Plays (includes the verse plays "Endor" and "Cain"), University of Chicago Press, 1962.
(Contributor) Ted Hughes and Thom Gunn, editors, *Five American Poets,* Faber, 1963.
The Blue Swallows, University of Chicago Press, 1967.
A Sequence of Seven with a Drawing by Ron Slaughter, Tinker Press, 1967.
The Winter Lightning: Selected Poems, Rapp & Whiting, 1968.
The Painter Dreaming in the Scholar's House (limited edition), Phoenix Book Shop, 1968.
Gnomes and Occasions, University of Chicago Press, 1973.
The Western Approaches: Poems, 1973-75, University of Chicago Press, 1975.
The Collected Poems of Howard Nemerov, University of Chicago Press, 1977.
Sentences, University of Chicago Press, 1980.
Inside the Onion, University of Chicago Press, 1984.

OTHER

"The Poetry of Howard Nemerov" (two audio cassettes), Jeffrey Norton, 1962.
"Howard Nemerov" (sound recording), Tapes for Readers, 1978.
"Howard Nemerov" (sound recording), Tapes for Readers, 1979.

Contributor of poems to numerous periodicals, including *Harvard Advocate, Kenyon Review, Poetry, New Yorker, Nation* and *Polemic.* Contributor of essays, articles and reviews to literary journals, including *Hudson Review, Poetry, Atlantic, Partisan Review* and *Virginia Quarterly Review.* Contributor of short fiction to *Harvard Advocate, Story, Esquire, Carleton Miscellany, Reporter* and *Virginia Quarterly Review.*

SIDELIGHTS: Howard Nemerov is a highly acclaimed poet appreciated for the range of his capabilities and subject matter, "from the profound to the poignant to the comic," James Billington remarked in his frequently quoted announcement of Nemerov's appointment to the post of United States poet laureate. A distinguished professor at Washington University in St. Louis since 1969, Nemerov writes poetry and fiction that engage the reader's mind without becoming academic, many reviewers report. Though his works show a consistent emphasis on thought—the process of thinking and ideas themselves—his poems relate a broad spectrum of emotion and a variety of concerns. As Joyce Carol Oates remarks in the *New Republic,* "Romantic, realist, comedian, satirist, relentless and indefatigable brooder upon the most ancient mysteries—Nemerov is not to be classified." Writing in the study *Howard Nemerov,* Peter Meinke states that these contrasting qualities are due to Nemerov's "deeply divided personality." Meinke points out that Nemerov himself has spoken of a duality in his nature in *Journal of the Fictive Life* in which he says that "it has seemed to me that I must attempt to bring together the opposed elements of my character represented by poetry and fiction." Comments Meinke, "These 'opposed elements' in Howard Nemerov's character are reflected in his life and work:

in the tensions between his romantic and realistic visions, his belief and unbelief, his heart and mind."

If Nemerov harbors impulses toward both poetry and fiction, he expresses them as opposites suspended in balanced co-existence rather than dissonance. A direct expression of this equilibrium is his poem "Because You Asked about the Line between Prose and Poetry." Writes *Poetry* contributor Mary Kinzie, "It is about rain gradually turning into snow, but still acting like rain (only somehow lighter and thicker), until— there is suddenly snow flying instead of rain falling." As the poem states, "There came a moment that you couldn't tell. / And then they clearly flew instead of fell." Kinzie continues, "What clearly flew? Clearly, the pieces of snow, now soft and crowded flakes," but these words also leave room to suggest the sudden upward flight of some dark swallows Nemerov had mentioned earlier in the poem. These birds, Kinzie says, are "the suggestive warrant for any kind of flight. . . . So is the poem launched. Not going straight to its goal—not falling like rain—a poem imperceptibly thickens itself out of the visible stream of prose." The choice—the crossing of the line that separates opposing impulses—is not consciously traceable, Nemerov told Melinda Miller of the *Washington Post:* "It's like a fairy tale. You're allowed to do it as long as you don't know too much about it."

The Harvard graduate's first book of poems, *The Image and the Law*, characteristically is based on opposed elements, on a duality of vision. As F. C. Golffing explains in *Poetry,* "Mr. Nemerov tells us that he dichotomizes the 'poetry of the eye' and the 'poetry of the mind,' and that he attempts to exhibit in his verse the 'ever-present dispute between two ways of looking at the world.'" Some reviewers find that this dichotomy leads to a lack of coherence in the verse. *New York Times* writer Milton Crane, for example, feels that the poems "unfortunately show no unity of conception such as their author attributes to them." The book was also criticized for being derivative of earlier modern poets such as T. S. Eliot, W. H. Auden, W. B. Yeats, and Wallace Stevens.

After reading *Guide to the Ruins,* Nemerov's second book of verse, *Saturday Review* contributor I. L. Salomon asserts that Nemerov "suffers from a dichotomy of personality." Within Nemerov, Salomon claims, an "instinct for perfection" and unity contends with a modern "carelessness in expression." Yet Crane notices not so much modern "carelessness" as praiseworthy modern sensibility; he believes that *Ruins* is "the work of an original and sensitive mind, alive to the thousand anxieties and agonies of our age." And Meinke contends that it is Nemerov's "modern awareness of contemporary man's alienation and fragmentation" combined with a breadth of wit in the eighteenth century sense of the word" which "sets Nemerov's writing apart from other modern writers."

Like *Image and the Law* and *Guide to the Ruins, The Salt Garden,* when it first came out, drew criticism for being derivative. "The accents of Auden and [John Crowe] Ransom," observed Louis Untermeyer in the *Saturday Review,* "occasionally twist his utterance into a curious poetic patois." Similarly, in the *Yale Review,* Randall Jarrell found that "you can see where he found out how to do some of the things he does— he isn't, as yet, a very individual poet." Years later, when asked if his work had changed in character or style, he replied in *Poets on Poetry,* "In style, . . . for I began and for a long time remained imitative, and poems in my first books . . . show more than traces of admired modern masters—Eliot, Auden, Stevens, [E. E.] Cummings, Yeats." Meinke, too, maintains that Nemerov in his early work was "writing Eliot, Yeats, and Stevens out of his system." Yet at the same time that Untermeyer and Jarrell faulted Nemerov for his imitation, like other readers, they were impressed by his growth as a poet. Jarrell commented that "as you read *The Salt Garden* you are impressed with how much the poet has learned, how well he has developed," while Hayden Carruth remarked in *Poetry,* "Nemerov's new book is his third . . . and his best; steady improvement, I take it, is one sign of formidable ability."

The Salt Garden, many critics feel, marks the beginning of other changes in Nemerov's work, as well. Meinke observes that in this volume "Nemerov has found his most characteristic voice: a quiet intelligent voice brooding lyrically on the strange beauty and tragic loneliness of life." In a *Salmagundi* review of *The Collected Poems of Howard Nemerov,* Willard Spiegelman, like Meinke, discovers in the poems from *The Salt Garden* "Nemerov's characteristic manner and tone." Spiegelman still finds opposed elements, but in balance; Nemerov's manner is "genuinely Horatian according to Auden's marvelous definition of looking at 'this world with a happy eye / but from a sober perspective.' Nemerov's *aurea mediocritas* [golden mean] sails between philosophical skepticism . . . and social satire on one side, and, on the other, an open-eyed, child-like appreciation of the world's miracles."

Another change which began with *Salt Garden* and continues in *Mirrors and Windows, The Next Room of the Dream,* and *The Blue Swallows* is Nemerov's growing concern with nature. In 1966, Nemerov wrote in *Poets on Poetry* of the impact of the natural world on his work: "During the war and since, I have lived in the country, chiefly in Vermont, and while my relation to the landscape has been contemplative rather than practical, the landscape nevertheless has in large part taken over my poetry." This interest in the landscape has led Chad Walsh to say in *Book World* of *Swallows* that "in its quiet lyricism and sensitivity to nature it suggests Robert Frost." The comparison to Frost, suggested by many other critics, is also made on the grounds that Nemerov, like Frost, brings philosophical issues into his poetry. As he says in *Poets on Poetry,* he is not so much an observer of nature as its medium, bringing into speech "an unknowably large part of a material world whose independent existence might be likened to that of the human unconscious, a sleep of causes, a chaos of the possible-impossible." Phrasing it differently in the poem "A Spell before Winter," Nemerov writes, "And I speak to you now with the land's voice, / It is the cold, wild land that says to you / A knowledge glimmers in the sleep of things: / The old hills hunch before the north wind blows."

A feature of the poems more frequently pointed out by critics is a witty, ironic manner and a serious, perhaps pessimistic, philosophy. James Dickey observes the seriousness that underlies Nemerov's wit. Nemerov, Dickey maintains in *Babel to Byzantium,* "is one of the wittiest and funniest poets we have. . . . But the enveloping emotion that arises from his writing is helplessness: the helplessness we all feel in the face of the events of our time, and of life itself. . . . And beneath even this feeling is a sort of hopelessly involved acceptance and resignation which has in it more of the truly tragic than most poetry which deliberately sets out in quest of tragedy." At the same time, Julia A. Bartholomay detects a somewhat different dichotomy. She contends in *The Shield of Perseus: The Vision and Imagination of Howard Nemerov* that in Nemerov's poetry there is a basic dualism that "underlies the two different . . . attitudes which appear consistently in the poet's work. On the one hand, he is very much the witty, sophisticated man of his time. . . . Nemerov often views life with a humorous but bitter irony. . . . On the other hand, the poet perceives the world ontologically. His experience may be philosophical, subjective, lyrical, or even mystical.'' Bartholomay argues that Nemerov's double view is expressed in his poetry through the use of paradox. The paradoxes reflect the ''divisiveness, fragmentation, complexity, and absurdity of modern existence.''

Not all critics applaud the tragic irony which Dickey and many others find in Nemerov's poetry. Carruth, for example, comments in the *New York Times Book Review*: ''No one would deny that famous and marvelous poems have been written in the manner of poetic irony. . . . But today this manner is an exceedingly tired manner, betraying an exceedingly tired poetic attitude. . . . And Nemerov's tired attitude is revealed in tired poetry: spent meters, predictable rhymes, and metaphors haggard with use.'' *New York Times* critic Thomas Lask also objects to Nemerov's irony. He believes that in *Blue Swallows* it has turned bitter, expressing ''loathing and contempt for man and his work.'' In contrast, Laurence Lieberman, writing in the *Yale Review,* feels that ''Howard Nemerov has perfected the poem as an instrument for exercising brilliance of wit. Searching, discursive, clear-sighted, he has learned to make the poem serve his relaxed manner and humane insights so expertly, I can only admire the clean purposefulness of his statements, his thoughtful care, the measure and grace of his lines.''

However strong his ironic voice, Nemerov has mellowed with age, according to many reviewers. Meinke claims that ''Nemerov has progressed steadily in his poetry to a broader, more tolerant view, less bitter and more sad.'' Likewise, Harvey Gilman finds in a *Chicago Review* assessment of *Gnomes and Occasions* that ''Nemerov's tone modulates as saving wit gives way to wistful contemplation, reminiscence, and prayer. The mask of irony is lowered and Nemerov writes a more sustained elegiac verse. . . . True, the epigrammatic manner remains in evidence . . . but the wit is here tinged with whimsy and warmth.'' Similarly, Spiegelman observes: ''Nemerov, growing old, becomes younger as he adopts the manner of an ancient sage. Cynicism barely touches his voice; the occasional sardonic moments are offset by feeling and sympathy. . . . In the 40's and 50's Nemerov was rabbinically fixated on sin and redemption. What was, early on, a source of prophetic despair . . . , becomes in the poems of his middle age the cause of poetic variety and energy, metaphysical delight, and emotional equilibrium.'' And Helen Vendler discerns in a critique of *Collected Poems* in *Part of Nature, Part of Us: Modern American Poets* that as ''the echoes of the *grand maitres* fade, the poems get steadily better. The severity of attitude is itself chastened by a growing humanity, and the forms of the earth grow ever more distinct.''

Gnomes and Occasions indulges Nemerov's penchant for short, aphoristic verses in which the images carry the burden of persuasion. In these ''gnomes,'' Nemerov achieves a ''Biblical resonance,'' says Kenneth Burke in a *Sewanee Review* essay designed to be an introduction to Nemerov's early poems, which are still ranked with the best postwar American poetry. More than one critic has referred to Nemerov's writings as wisdom literature. For example, Vendler reports that Nemerov's ''mind plays with epigram, gnome, riddle, rune, advice, meditation, notes, dialectic, prophecy, reflection, views, knowledge, questions, speculation—all the forms of thought. His wishes go homing to origins and ends.'' Scholars link this stylistic tendency to the poet's Jewish heritage. Meinke describes the early Nemerov as a ''non-practicing Jew engaged

in a continual dialogue with Christianity . . . testing its relevance in the modern world.'' In addition to the influence of Dante and St. Augustine, that of W. B. Yeats leaves its mark on the poems, says *Dictionary of Literary Biography* contributor Robert W. Hill, ''not so much in form or style as in subject matter and in a decidedly religious quality of the language.'' For instance, one of Nemerov's definitions of poetry given in ''Thirteen Ways of Looking at a Skylark'' in *Poetry* states: ''In the highest range the theory of poetry would be the theory of the Incarnation, which seeks to explain how the Word became Flesh.''

Nemerov, however, does not reconstruct the world with imagination as other poets have done. Explains Hill, ''While Yeats went about his way inventing new religion and culling the cabala for hints and signs, Nemerov's poems show him to be a critic of the secularizers: coming from the Jewish tradition, his sense of the decline of religion is not so easily pacified by new contrivances as Yeats's was. But the connections Nemerov feels with the seers of the past are clearly modern, clearly attached with the threads of the naturalistic modes, the beliefs in touchable things rather than in the untouchable.'' Thus Nemerov uses acts of the imagination not to alter the world but to make it known. To the extent that this process is magical, ''Our proper magic is the magic of language,'' claims the poet, according to *Contemporary Authors Bibiliography Series* contributor Gloria Young.

Poetry as a link between the material and spiritual worlds emerges as the theme of *Sentences*. In this volume, Nemerov achieves thematic coherence by organizing the poems into three sections, ''Beneath,'' ''Above,'' and ''Beyond.'' Bonnie Costello, writing in *Parnassus: Poetry in Review*, relates that the sections ''mark off, respectively, poems of low diction and subject (our social sphere of sex and power), poems of higher diction and subject (metaphysics and poetry), and those of middle diction and subject (our origin and fate).'' Critics approve the last two sections more than the first, which they claim is beneath the level of quality they have come to expect from Nemerov. The section castigates the purveyors of low artistic, social and political values, relates Ronald Baughman in the *Dictionary of Literary Biography Yearbook: 1983*. ''The reviewers damn the writer for accomplishing the goal which he has set for himself—the portrayal of man acting beneath dignity.'' Looking over the entire book, Baughman offers, ''*Sentences* contains a wide range of poems, extending from the mocking, bitter verse of section one to the interesting but restrained appraisals of section two to the deeply moving contemplations of section three. The volume's theme—the order art gives to the randomness of life—develops with this movement from beginning to end. Nemerov's title is reminiscent of Stephen Spender's poem 'Subject: Object: Sentence,' in which Spender states, 'A sentence is condemned to stay as stated— / As in *life-sentence, death-sentence,* for example.' As Howard Nemerov dramatizes his life and death sentences, he reveals his attempts to connect, through the power of his art, with the world below, nature above, and the spirit beyond.''

The *Collected Poems* presents verse from all of the earlier volumes. Its publication in 1977 spurred a re-evaluation of Nemerov's works as a whole. Phoebe Pettingell notes in the *New Leader* that the book shows ''a gradual intensifying of a unified perspective,'' the poet's obsession with the theme of ''man's sometimes tragic, sometimes ludicrous relation to history, death and the universe.'' Robert B. Shaw, writing in the *Nation*, relates, ''To what extent, he repeatedly wonders, is the world we see our own creation? . . . Is the poem a mirror reflecting the appearances of the world in responsible detail, or is it a window, a transparent medium through which we may see . . . ? Or might it begin in one and with care and luck become the other? Nemerov never fully unravels these aesthetic and metaphysical knots. They provide him the material for endless reflection." Tom Johnson offers this assessment in the *Sewanee Review:* "Nemerov has written more incisively of science and its place in our imaginations than anyone else has yet managed to do in good (or even readable) poems. . . . The breadth of accomplishment and depth of insight are one's most striking impressions from first readings of the *Collected Poems,* enriched later by the humor, in intricacy, the grace." Shaw recommends *Collected Poems* to readers whose interest in poetry stems more from curiosity than from experience with the genre. "Such readers," Shaw says, "can expect to be charmed by the easy flow of Nemerov's reasoned discourse, and moved by those fine moments in his poems in which reason is overcome by awe."

Nemerov's prose has also been commended, especially for displaying an irony and wit similar to that of his poems. His novels, as Meinke remarks, "like his poems, . . . are basically pessimistic. The condition of man is not an enviable one: we act foolishly and understand imperfectly. Nemerov's dark viewpoint, which in his poetry is redeemed by beauty . . . , in his fiction is redeemed by humor." Meinke terms *The Melodramatists* "a highly successful first novel," and in the *Nation* Diana Trilling seconds him, commenting that after a slow start, it is "a considerable first novel—literate and entertaining, with a nice satiric barb." *Federigo: Or the Power of Love* and *The Homecoming Game* were also well received. For example, in the *New York Times,* Richard Sullivan calls the latter book a "beautifully controlled satire" with characters "rendered with authentic irony," and *Atlantic* reviewer C. J. Rolo finds that it has "wit, dash, and point."

Through the characters in these novels, Nemerov explores "the consequences of the overactive imagination," writes Carl Rapp in the *Dictionary of Literary Biography: Novelists since World War II.* Characters with romantic expectations of finding meaningful action and self-realization amid the social pressures of their times instead realize that they are the victims of their own fantasies. Thus, the novels, like the poetry, comment on the relationship between imagination and reality. Nemerov published his last novel *The Homecoming Game* (about a professor who discovers his limits when faced with opposing groups on campus) in 1957. Rapp suggests, "Nemerov has perhaps come to feel that the novelist himself, with his own incorrigible tendency to fantasize melodramatic scenes and situations, presents a spectacle as ridiculous as that of his own characters. In recent poems such as 'Novelists' and 'Reflexions of a Novelist,' he observes that it is, of course, the novelist who is preeminently the man with the overactive imagination, the egomaniac, the voyeur." Nemerov told Robert Boyers in a *Salmagundi* interview that he left off being a novelist when Bennington College chose to retain him as its poet and hired Bernard Malamud to be its novelist.

Though through with the novel form, Nemerov continues to work with prose in short stories and literary criticism. Like his poetry and fiction, Nemerov's essays have won for him the respect of many well-known writers and critics. To *Figures of Thought: Speculations on the Meaning of Poetry and Other Essays,* Benjamin DeMott responds in the *New York Times Book Review:* "Taken as a whole . . . these 'speculations' are uncommonly stimulating and persuasive. . . . [This book] communicates throughout a vivid sense of the possibility of a

richer kind of knowing in all areas than we're in the process of settling for . . . ; like the high art it salutes, it brims with the life of things." Moreover, Joyce Carol Oates adds: "The book is a marvelous one, rewarding not only for what it tells us about poetry in general . . . , but for what it tells us about the processes of the imagination. Nemerov is, quite simply, a brilliant mind."

New and Selected Essays, a more recent collection of essays spanning thirty years of Nemerov's criticism, is also considered valuable. "It is the *texture* of [Nemerov's] thinking that is exhilarating, and not the Grand Propositions—though one of the latter (his favorite) is sturdy indeed: 'Poetry is getting something right in language.'. . . The theoretical essays and the studies of particular writers are the ones most wealthy in serviceable lore," offers Richard Wertime in the *Yale Review.* Deborah S. Murphy and Young state in the *Contemporary Authors Bibliography Series* that since "Nemerov is a poet who is continually changing and growing, becoming more complex in subject matter and apparently simpler in style," the body of his work has only begun to receive the serious critical attention it merits.

Nemerov's books have brought him every major award for poetry, including the National Book Award, the Pulitzer Prize, the Bollingen Prize, and the National Medal of Art. Regarding his fame, he told Jake Thompson of the *Chicago Tribune,* "You do the best you can and really don't worry about immortality all that much, especially as you have to be dead to achieve it. . . . Oh, you want praise and recognition and above all money. But if that was your true motive, you would have done something else. All this fame and honor is a very nice thing, as long as you don't believe it."

MEDIA ADAPTATIONS: The Homecoming Game was adapted as a play entitled "Tall Story" and filmed by Warner Bros. in 1959.

CA INTERVIEW

CA interviewed Howard Nemerov by telephone on December 2, 1987, at his home in St. Louis, Missouri.

CA: In Journal of the Fictive Life *you analyzed dreams in their relationship to real life and to the creation of fiction. Do dreams figure for you in the making of poetry?*

NEMEROV: In some very indirect way they probably do. I have never, to my knowledge, made a poem directly out of a dream, because mostly dreams don't make much sense.

CA: Do the dreams ever provide inspiration for a poem, or ideas, or lines, as poems seem to come to you?

NEMEROV: Once in a great while my dreams give me my character with an epigrammatic incision that I don't altogether like, like being told that you're going to play Prospero without any time to get up the lines, but the play is *King Lear.*

CA: The Image and the Law, your first book of poems, was published in 1947; your first novel, The Melodramatists, *came out two years later. Were you equally interested in the beginning in writing poetry and fiction?*

NEMEROV: I think so. I remember two publishers, at least, saying that if I would write a novel, they would publish the poems. That went into it too, though it was not a primary motive.

CA: You stopped writing fiction some years ago. Do you ever think of doing it again?

NEMEROV: No. I'm far too lazy. You discover you can write about your friends the novelists in fourteen lines, and you don't need a word processor because you process so few words.

CA: Your poems begin, you've said, not with ideas but with single lines that come to you somehow. Are there things you can do to invite those beginnings, to create a mental atmosphere for them?

NEMEROV: Well, if you find out, I hope you'll let me know. It would be something you could sell, wouldn't it?

CA: You've mentioned somewhere, I believe, that walking might be a good thing to do.

NEMEROV: Walking helps. That's why poetry comes in feet. There are some times when everything helps, and some times when nothing will. When I do write, I do my best, such as it is, very rapidly. I do have technical ability. But when the voice is not there, it doesn't matter. You can do something and it will turn out flat and stupid, as if you were writing an editorial. So, for maybe six months I write, and maybe two years thereafter I am pretty silent. I don't mean silent altogether, but specifically about verse.

CA: Does it bother you when you're not writing?

NEMEROV: Yes, it does. Although, after two dozen books, it's not quite as serious as after two or three. It will either return or it won't. I've already done a fair bit, you know. It's just that it's such a pleasure doing it; the results don't matter that much anymore.

CA: Does reading seem to stimulate your poetic imagination in any way?

NEMEROV: It stimulates my thievish instincts. I've plagiarized—or, as a friend of mine, Albert Lebowitz, says, we must now say *Bidenized*—most everything.

CA: How much of a poem seems to be given in that first bit that comes to you? Is it merely the first brick in the construction, or does it somehow contain the rest?

NEMEROV: It must do the latter, but I don't know how. You're given a little something, and then you suddenly see what follows. Or you see that there's something illusionist about all that. For months, or even years, when I'm not able to write, I take down everything, just put down the disconnected thoughts. And mostly they stay there, but once in a while, long after, you find a way to knit them up together.

CA: How early in the writing of a poem, usually, can you tell what its structure is going to be?

NEMEROV: With the little ones that I make up while walking, like two and four and six lines, there's no problem. They just come. If they're longer than that, as they usually are, listening and working it out is part of the fun. It's amazing that one thought should seem to follow another.

CA: Is the form itself ever contained in the original line that comes to you?

NEMEROV: Sometimes you know immediately if the thing wants to be a sonnet, which is convenient, or if it wants to be a sestina, which happens only very rarely.

CA: Do you say it aloud as you write so that you can hear the sounds and the cadences?

NEMEROV: No. Like the deaf Beethoven, I can hear it without saying it aloud. Once in a while, in a fit of vanity and self-indulgence, I mouth the lines as I write, but not often.

CA: That doesn't sound terribly self-indulgent.

NEMEROV: When you get some gorgeous thing going, it's fun to do.

CA: Do you do a lot of public readings?

NEMEROV: Yes. My books are constantly on the top of the worst-seller charts, so it's the only way I have of making extra money.

CA: You've said that poetry is getting something right in language. Have the technical aspects of getting it right become much easier with the years of doing it?

NEMEROV: Yes, I think so. I'm much more aware of them— that is, not of the discipline, but of the opportunities.

CA: Then you can work at that part of it less consciously now than, say, twenty or thirty years ago?

NEMEROV: I don't know that there's that much difference. I've always done things easily or it's been impossible. I invented our family motto, which says, "If at first you don't succeed, give up."

CA: You've written a great deal of criticism. What kind of role do you think criticism should ideally play in letters?

NEMEROV: That's a very hard question. There's all sorts of criticism. There is snippish reviewing to begin with, which I suffer from some, but I'm pretty indurated now. Once in a while—not very often—a critic can tell you something you can use and didn't see before.

CA: But as far as writing your criticism goes, what do you want it to do? What sort of audience do you want for it?

NEMEROV: I've never written for an audience, because I don't know what an audience looks like. I usually, at least earlier in my career, have written criticism because I was asked to review books by an editor or was asked for an essay. That's pretty much still true, except for the things I do for class and later work up into essays.

CA: Some of your essays read as if they were done just for the sheer pleasure of the doing.

NEMEROV: How nice. That would be ideal, wouldn't it?

CA: Do you think criticism should be accessible on some level to all readers who are culturally literate, to borrow E. D. Hirsch's term?

NEMEROV: Yes, I do. I've had to be put through a lot of structuralism and deconstruction just from being on committees that give awards for scholarly books, and an awful lot of it is in that giant vocabulary for milling around confusedly.

CA: Are there changes you would like to see in the critical treatment and reviewing of poetry?

NEMEROV: Well, it would be nice if I got reviewed once in a while. On the other hand, when I used to get reviewed, I didn't always like the results. You take your lumps. I never interfere, as far as possible, in the muse's administration.

CA: Do you think criticism of poetry is generally done well?

NEMEROV: I've seen it done well in such quarterlies as the *Sewanee Review,* the *Southern Review,* and the *Kenyon Review,* where people do say intelligent and considered and decent things, mannerly things. Whereas in the *New York Times Book Review,* for example, they go all overboard, and then they make the mistake of quoting a few lines and you see they're talking about junk.

CA: Do you discuss writing much with other writers?

NEMEROV: Practically not at all. We have a good few writers here—the poets John Morris, Donald Finkel, Constance Urdang, Mona Van Duyn; the novelists Stanley Elkin, Charles Newman, and Bill Gass. As far as I can remember, we never talk about writing.

CA: You've been a teacher for many years . . .

NEMEROV: Over forty. I was saying to the secretary this morning, ''I don't see *how* I did it.''

CA: How do you feel about the teaching, and in particular how well do you think the combination of teaching and writing has worked for you?

NEMEROV: It's been the best thing that could have happened to me. I think, as Wallace Stevens said, that ''poetry is the scholar's art.'' So it has been my education. I like to read books, and to get paid for that—or even underpaid, which is no longer the case—is a very pleasant thing. You work hard, but you don't need to sit in an office from nine to five, and you're working at your bidding, not somebody else's.

CA: What do you feel is the teacher's proper role?

NEMEROV: Well, there are all sorts of us, you know. I think I'm allowed to get by as the exception in the patch: I'm not a scholar; I do it my way, which is very freewheeling. As I said in a book recently, my style is amble and bumble.

CA: Do you teach writing?

NEMEROV: Rarely. I'm going to teach the graduates in the writers' program the next term, but that's an exception for the last fifteen years. I used to do it on a more regular basis, but when I got to be fifty without ever having made a poet, I thought I could leave it to somebody else.

CA: I wonder how many poets are made, really, in classes. How do you think the writing schools and workshops are affecting poetry?

NEMEROV: Often very badly. People are encouraged to think by their teachers and their confreres that anything is all right. I've just read two anthologies of younger poets—and of course I'm an old gent now and very narrow-minded to begin with—but they do seem a lot of the time to just drool down the page until nothing happens and they stop. They write too long, very self-indulgently, very often without point. But of course I'm talking about a lot of poets, and that doesn't obviously include the exceptions, who will be few at any time.

On the other hand, I think it's very nice that people should be given a little bit of training in something they want to do. Most of them won't go on doing it, and they shouldn't. As I explain to my pupils, this is a democracy, and that's very good; everyone should have a chance at doing this if this is what they want to do. But they should be warned that, later on, this is elitist in the extreme. If they're going to continue, they've got a long, hard way to go. Not everybody is going to agree with you—in fact, very few people will.

CA: In Journal of the Fictive Life *you called poetry a ''ruined temple'' and said that ''someday it will be much in demand as an antique, or classic of our literature.'' That book was published in 1965. Has anything been written that would change your mind at all?*

NEMEROV: I don't know how my mind would change on that subject.

CA: Would you talk about how you feel about poetry now? What's good? What's bad?

NEMEROV: I mostly don't think about it. If you are sent three books and three manuscripts a week out of the blue, you tend to think less and less about it. You try to be polite and honor the correspondents in the sense of manners, and nothing more. It's not for me to decide those things.

CA: When you take a critical look back at the body of your work . . .

NEMEROV: Oh, I'd be the last person in the world to do that. I look back, but not critically, in the spirit of admiration. I think, That young fellow had talent. Where did it go?

CA: There must be many things you're proud of.

NEMEROV: Yes, there are many things. They're all my children, even the squat, ugly ones.

CA: Are there things you started that seem unfinished to you?

NEMEROV: Many, many things.

CA: Anything that you'll continue to work on?

NEMEROV: No. There's one poem I nearly finished and then I couldn't figure out how to end it. I lost the manuscript for five years in a mess of other papers. When it turned up one Sunday while I was looking through all this junk, I suddenly knew how to finish it. And that was very fortunate, because it was, I think, one of my very luckiest poems. It's called ''The Makers.'' It's in *Sentences.*

CA: Does any of the work you've done point to any directions you'd like the work to go in the future?

NEMEROV: Nope. These are not terms in which I think, mostly. In fact, when you're writing poetry, you're doing something that's related to thought but a little bit different. It is nothing like automatic writing, but it goes as if something other than yourself were telling you what came next. And that's also a great pleasure.

CA: Is there anything at all you can say about what may be next for you?

NEMEROV: I've never known what I was going to write until the day I sat down and wrote it, usually after a period of mild melancholy and sterility, like *Journal of the Fictive Life.* I remember I was talking with the poet Ben Belitt about how I was through, I had nothing to write. Then the next morning I began writing that book. I had no inkling it was coming.

CA: Would you like to go on teaching and writing?

NEMEROV: Yes. I'm reaching the sixth or seventh adolescence now with the usual turmoils about how to put up with becoming old. I'm doing all right, but I think you require a certain amount of new personality to go with it. Something magisterial, I think, ought to look good on me. I'm shopping around, but I haven't found it.

BIOGRAPHICAL/CRITICAL SOURCES:

BOOKS

Bartholomay, Julia A., *The Shield of Perseus: The Vision and Imagination of Howard Nemerov,* University of Florida Press, 1972.

Boyers, Robert, editor, *Contemporary Poetry in America: Essays and Interviews,* Schocken, 1974.

Boyers, Robert, editor, *Excursions: Selected Literary Essays,* Kennikat Press, 1975.

Contemporary Authors Bibliography Series, Volume 2, Gale, 1986.

Contemporary Literary Criticism, Gale, Volume 2, 1974, Volume 6, 1976, Volume 9, 1978, Volume 36, 1986.

DeMott, Robert J. and Sanford E. Marovits, editors, *Artful Thunder: Versions of the Romantic Tradition in American Literature in Honor of Howard P. Vincent,* Kent State University Press, 1975.

Dickey, James, *Babel to Byzantium,* Farrar, Straus, 1968.

Dictionary of Literary Biography, Gale, Volume 5: *American Poets since World War II,* 1980, Volume 6: *American Novelists since World War II, Second Series,* 1980.

Dictionary of Literary Biography Yearbook: 1983, Gale, 1984.

Donoghue, Denis, editor, *Seven American Poets from Mac-Leish to Nemerov,* University of Minnesota Press, 1975.

Duncan, Bowie, editor, *The Critical Reception of Howard Nemerov: A Selection of Essays and a Bibliography,* Scarecrow Press, 1971.

Howard, Richard, editor, *Preferences,* Viking, 1974.

Hungerford, Edward, editor, *Poets in Progress: Critical Prefaces to Ten Contemporary Americans,* Northwestern University Press, 1962.

Hutton, Charles, editor, *Imagination and the Spirit: Essays in Literature and the Christian Faith Presented to Clyde S. Kilby,* Eerdmans, 1971.

Kumin, Maxine, *To Make a Prairie: Essays on Poets, Poetry and Country Living,* University of Michigan Press, 1979.

Labrie, Ross, *Howard Nemerov,* Twayne, 1980.

Lieberman, Laurence, editor, *Unassigned Frequencies: American Poetry in Review, 1964-77,* University of Illinois Press, 1977.

Maxfield, Melinda R., editor, *Images and Innovations: Update 1970's,* Center for the Humanities, Converse College, 1979.

Meinke, Peter, *Howard Nemerov,* University of Minnesota Press, 1968.

Mills, William, *The Stillness in Moving Things: The World of Howard Nemerov,* Memphis State University Press, 1975.

Nemerov, Howard, *The Next Room of the Dream: Poems and Two Plays,* University of Chicago Press, 1962.

Nemerov, Howard, *Poets on Poetry,* Basic Books, 1966.

Nemerov, Howard, *Journal of the Fictive Life* (autobiography), Rutgers University Press, 1965, reprinted with a new preface, University of Chicago Press, 1981.

Nemerov, Howard, *New and Selected Essays,* Southern Illinois University Press, 1985.

Nemerov, Howard, *Sentences,* University of Chicago Press, 1980.

Rosenthal, M. L., *The Modern Poets: A Critical Introduction,* Oxford University Press, 1961.

Vendler, Helen, *Part of Nature, Part of Us: Modern American Poets,* Howard University Press, 1980.

Waggoner, Hyatt, *American Poets from the Puritans to the Present,* Houghton, 1968.

Wyllie, Diana E., *Elizabeth Bishop and Howard Nemerov: A Reference Guide,* Hall, 1983.

PERIODICALS

America, October 5, 1974, April 8, 1978, February 1, 1986, May 7, 1988.

American Book Review, March, 1979.

American Poetry Review, May/June, 1975, January, 1976.

American Scholar, summer, 1959, summer, 1968.

Antioch Review, spring, 1963, summer, 1987.

Atlantic, November, 1954, May, 1957, November, 1961, February, 1968.

Book World, December 24, 1967.

Chicago Review, Volume XXV, number 1, 1973.

Chicago Tribune, July 4, 1988.

Chicago Tribune Book World, March 29, 1981.

Christian Science Monitor, January 29, 1964.

Commonweal, February 13, 1959.

Encounter, February, 1969.

Georgia Review, winter, 1976, fall, 1985.

Harper's, September, 1963.

Hudson Review, summer, 1963, spring, 1964, spring, 1976, autumn, 1984.

Island, fall, 1966.

Journal of Aesthetics and Art Criticism, spring, 1979.

Kenyon Review, winter, 1952.

London Review of Books, February 21-27, 1985.

Los Angeles Times, June 19, 1987.

Massachusetts Review, spring, 1981.

Modern Language Notes, December, 1978.

Nation, July 13, 1963, November 8, 1975, February 25, 1978, November 11, 1978.

New Leader, December 5, 1977, April 30, 1984.

New Republic, June 23, 1958, April 28, 1973, April 8, 1978.

New Yorker, March 14, 1959, April 1, 1961.

New York Herald Tribune Book Review, March 1, 1959, July 30, 1961.

New York Times, August 10, 1947, May 21, 1950, March 3, 1957, March 30, 1968, April 28, 1968, December 26, 1978, June 5, 1987, June 11, 1987, May 18, 1988.

New York Times Book Review, April 3, 1949, May 21, 1950, July 17, 1955, February 8, 1959, March 1, 1959, January 8, 1961, July 21, 1963, April 28, 1968, November 8, 1975, December 18, 1977, April 16, 1978.

Parnassus: Poetry in Review, fall/winter, 1973, spring/summer, 1975, spring/summer, 1976, fall/winter, 1977, fall/winter, 1981.

Partisan Review, winter, 1961, winter, 1965.

Poet and Critic, Number 11, 1979.

Poetry, November, 1947, June, 1955, December, 1958, September, 1963, March, 1965, February, 1967, August, 1975, December, 1976, September, 1978, September, 1981, February, 1988.

Poets and Writers, May/June, 1987.

Prairie Schooner, spring, 1965.

Reporter, September 12, 1963.

Salmagundi, fall/winter, 1975, summer/fall, 1978.

San Francisco Review of Books, July, 1984.

Saturday Review, July 1, 1950, May 21, 1955, September 27, 1958, February 21, 1959, February 11, 1961, July 6, 1963.

Sewanee Review, winter, 1952, spring, 1961, fall, 1968, summer, 1978, October, 1985, January, 1988.

Southern Review, winter, 1974, summer, 1975, fall, 1976, summer, 1979, winter, 1979.

Thought, summer, 1979.

Times Literary Supplement, February 19, 1960, June 11, 1976, October 6, 1978.

University of Windsor Review, spring, 1969.

Virginia Quarterly Review, spring, 1978, autumn, 1984, spring, 1988.

Washington Post, January 15, 1981, March 31, 1987, June 11, 1987.

Washington Post Book World, December 25, 1977, June 11, 1987, May 18, 1988.

Webster Review, spring, 1974, fall, 1980.

World Literature Today, summer, 1981, autumn, 1984, winter, 1986.

Yale Review, autumn, 1954, autumn, 1955, summer, 1961, summer, 1964, autumn, 1968, spring, 1976, summer, 1985.

OTHER

''One on One'' (filmed interview), Kent State University Television Center, October 5, 1979.

—Interview by Jean W. Ross

*   *   *

NEUSTADT, Richard E(lliott) 1919-

PERSONAL: Born June 26, 1919, in New York, N.Y.; son of Richard Mitchells (a U.S. Social Security official; also a U.S. presidential advisor) and Elizabeth (a social worker; maiden name, Neufeld) Neustadt; married Bertha Frances Cummings (an educator), December 21, 1945 (died May 5, 1984); married Shirley Williams (a founder of the Social Democratic Party of Great Britain), December, 1987; children: (first marriage) Richard Mitchells, Elizabeth Ann. *Education:* University of California, Berkeley, A.B., 1939; Harvard University, M.A., 1941, Ph.D., 1951. *Politics:* Democrat.

ADDRESSES: Home—1010 Memorial Dr., Cambridge, Mass. 02138. *Office*—John Fitzgerald Kennedy School of Government, Harvard University, Cambridge, Mass. 02138.

CAREER: U.S. Office of Price Administration, Washington, D.C., assistant economist, 1942; U.S. Bureau of the Budget, Washington, D.C., assistant to the director, 1946-49; White House, Washington, D.C., special assistant, 1950-53; Cornell University, Ithaca, N.Y., assistant professor of public administration, 1953-54; Columbia University, New York, N.Y., 1954-64, began as associate professor, became professor of government and head of department; Harvard University, John Fitzgerald Kennedy School of Government, Cambridge, Mass., professor of government, 1965-78, associate dean, 1965-75, director of Institute of Politics, 1966-71, Lucius N. Littauer Professor of Public Administration, 1978—. Visiting professor at Princeton University, 1957; Nuffield College, Oxford University, visiting scholar, 1960-61, associate member, 1965-67; trustee of Radcliffe College, 1977-80. Consultant to U.S. Presidents Harry S. Truman, beginning in 1950, John F. Kennedy, 1960-63, and Lyndon B. Johnson, 1964-66. Special consultant to U.S. Senate Subcommittee on National Policy Machinery, 1959-61, U.S. Bureau of Budget, 1961-71, U.S. Senate Subcommittee on National Security Staffing and Operations, 1962-67, U.S. Atomic Energy Commission, 1962-68, and U.S. Department of State, 1962-69; consultant to Rand Corp., 1964-78. Member of advisory board, U.S. Commission on Money and Credit, 1960-61. *Military service:* U.S. Naval Reserve, 1942-46; became lieutenant senior grade.

MEMBER: American Academy of Arts and Sciences (fellow), Council on Foreign Relations, Institute of Strategic Studies, American Philosophical Society, American Political Science Association, American Association of University Professors, National Capital Democratic Club, Cosmos Club (Washington).

AWARDS, HONORS: Woodrow Wilson Foundation Award, American Political Science Association, 1961; Grawemeyer Award (with Ernest R. May), 1988.

WRITINGS:

The Presidency at Mid-Century, Bobbs-Merrill, 1956.

Presidential Power: The Politics of Leadership, Wiley, 1960, updated edition with an afterword on John F. Kennedy, 1968, subsequent updated editions published as *Presidential Power: The Politics of Leadership, with Reflections on Johnson and Nixon,* 1976, and *Presidential Power: The Politics of Leadership from FDR to Carter,* 1980.

The Presidency and Legislation: The Growth of Central Clearance (originally published in *American Political Science Review*), Bobbs-Merrill, 1962.

(Contributor) *The Secretary of State and the Ambassador,* Praeger, 1964.

(Contributor) David B. Truman, editor, *The Congress and America's Future,* Prentice-Hall, 1965.

Alliance Politics, Columbia University Press, 1970.

(Co-author of afterword) Robert F. Kennedy, *Thirteen Days: A Memoir of the Cuban Missile Crisis,* Norton, 1971.

(With Harvey V. Fineberg) *The Swine Flu Affair: Decision-Making on a Slippery Disease* (introduction by Joseph A. Califano, Jr.), U.S. Department of Health, Education, and Welfare, 1978, revised edition published as *The Epidemic That Never Was: Policy-Making and the Swine Flu Scare* (introduction by David A. Hamburg), Vintage Books, 1982.

(With Ernest R. May) *Thinking in Time: The Uses of History for Decision-Makers,* Free Press, 1986.

Contributor to *Harper's, U.S. News and World Report, Reporter, American Political Science Review, Political Science*

Review, Political Science Quarterly, and *Law and Contemporary Problems.*

SIDELIGHTS: In their book *Thinking in Time: The Uses of History for Decision-Makers,* Harvard University professors Richard E. Neustadt and Ernest R. May "advocate[e] more and better use of history by those charged with making decisions," Bernard Gwertzman writes in the *New York Times.* The authors, who teach a course entitled "Uses of History," intend *Thinking in Time* "as a blinking yellow light for those who are in public life, such as policy makers, staff aides and reporters, so that before they burst forth with some historical analogy they give some thought to whether it is accurate, pertinent or apt," continues Gwertzman. Ronald Steel elaborates in the *New York Review of Books:* "Through a series of examples, or case studies, Neustadt and May try to demonstrate how history can be used to illuminate the choices facing decision makers: how it can clarify the alternatives available and separate the salient issues from the irrelevant or misleading ones." Steel adds: "What [Neustadt and May] propose is not simply that students read more history. . . . Rather, they suggest a particular way of learning from history to frame sharper questions and avoid disastrous decisions."

A former consultant to U.S. Presidents Harry S Truman, John F. Kennedy, and Lyndon B. Johnson, Neustadt is also the author of *Presidential Power: The Politics of Leadership,* a book reported to have been influential to Kennedy during his administration. First published in 1960, *Presidential Power* offers Neustadt's insights into the executive branch of government, especially in areas of decision-making. The latest edition of *Presidential Power,* covering the presidency from Franklin D. Roosevelt to Jimmy Carter, continues to "spell out clearly" Neustadt's pervading theme of "presidential weakness," comments Esmond Wright in *Encounter.* Neustadt's work remains "a sophisticated . . . inside view, vivid and original and with some admirable case studies of the President in action."

BIOGRAPHICAL/CRITICAL SOURCES:

PERIODICALS

Encounter, December, 1980.
New Republic, July 7, 1986.
Newsweek, March 6, 1961.
New York Herald Tribune, March 21, 1965.
New York Review of Books, February 11, 1971, November 6, 1986.
New York Times, January 12, 1965, May 24, 1970, March 13, 1986.
New York Times Book Review, November 30, 1980, March 27, 1983, March 16, 1986.
Time, January 22, 1965, February 3, 1967.
Washington Post, July 22, 1965.
Washington Post Book World, March 30, 1986.*

*   *   *

NEUSTADT, Richard M(itchells)   1948-

PERSONAL: Born February 4, 1948, in Washington, D.C.; son of Richard Elliot (a professor) and Bertha (an educator; maiden name, Cummings) Neustadt. *Education:* Harvard University, A.B. (magna cum laude), 1969, J.D. (cum laude), 1974. *Politics:* Democrat.

CAREER: Associate of Wald, Horhrader and Ross (law firm), 1974-76; White House, Washington, D.C., assistant director

of domestic policy staff, beginning in 1977. *Military service:* U.S. Naval Reserve, active duty, 1970-72; became lieutenant, junior grade.

WRITINGS:

(With Ken Jost, Robert Luskin, and Laurence Eichel) *The Harvard Strike,* Houghton, 1970.
On Television Network News, John F. Kennedy School of Government, Harvard University, 1974.
(Editor with Nancy Jesuale and Nicholas P. Miller) *CTIC Cablebooks,* Volume 2: *A Guide for Local Policy,* Cable Television Information Center, 1982.
The Birth of Electronic Publishing: Legal and Economic Issues in Telephone, Cable, and Over-the-Air Teletext and Videotext, Knowledge Industry Publications, 1982.

BIOGRAPHICAL/CRITICAL SOURCES:

PERIODICALS

Washington Post, May 27, 1970.*

*   *   *

NGUGI, James T(hiong'o)
See NGUGI wa Thiong'o

*   *   *

NGUGI wa Thiong'o   1938-
(James T[hiong'o] Ngugi)

PERSONAL: Original name, James Thiong'o Ngugi; born January 5, 1938, in Limuru, Kenya; married; children: five. *Education:* Makerere University, B.A., 1963; University of Leeds, B.A., 1964.

ADDRESSES: c/o William Heinemann Ltd., 15 Queen St., London W1X 8BE, England.

CAREER: Teacher in East African schools, 1964-70; Northwestern University, Evanston, Ill., visiting lecturer, 1970-71; senior lecturer and chairman of department of literature at University of Nairobi, Kenya.

AWARDS, HONORS: Recipient of awards from the 1965 Dakar Festival of Negro Arts and the East African Literature Bureau, both for *Weep Not, Child.*

WRITINGS:

Homecoming: Essays on African and Caribbean Literature, Culture, and Politics, Heinemann, 1972, Lawrence Hill, 1973.
Secret Lives, and Other Stories, Heinemann Educational, 1974, Lawrence Hill, 1975.
Petals of Blood (novel), Heinemann Educational, 1977.
(With Micere Githae Mugo) *The Trial of Dedan Kimathi,* Heinemann Educational, 1977, Swahili translation by the authors published as *Mzalendo kimathi,* c. 1978.
Mtawa Mweusi, Heinemann, 1978.
Caitaani mutharaba-ini, Heinemann Educational, 1980, translation by the author published as *Devil on the Cross,* Zimbabwe Publishing, 1983.
Writers in Politics: Essays, Heinemann, 1981.
Detained: A Writer's Prison Diary, Heinemann, 1981.
Njamba Nene na mbaathi i mathagu, Heinemann Educational, 1982.
(Co-author and translator with Ngugi wa Mirii) *I Will Marry When I Want* (play), Heinemann, 1982.

Barrel of a Pen: Resistance to Repression in Neo-Colonial Kenya, New Beacon, 1983.
Decolonising the Mind: The Politics of Language in African Literature, Heinemann, 1986.

UNDER NAME JAMES T. NGUGI

The Black Hermit (play; first produced in Nairobi in 1962), Mekerere University Press, 1963, Humanities, 1968.
Weep Not, Child (novel), introduction and notes by Ime Ikeddeh, Heinemann, 1964, P. Collier, 1969.
The River Between (novel), Humanities, 1965.
A Grain of Wheat (novel), Heinemann, 1967, 2nd edition, Humanities, 1968.
This Time Tomorrow (play; includes ''The Reels'' and ''The Wound in the Heart''; produced and broadcast in 1966), East African Literature Bureau, 1970.

CONTRIBUTOR TO ANTHOLOGIES

E. A. Komey and Ezekiel Mphahlele, editors, *Modern African Short Stories*, Faber, 1964.
W. H. Whiteley, editor, *A Selection of African Prose*, Oxford University Press, 1964.
Neville Denny, editor, *Pan African Short Stories*, Nelson, 1965.
Oscar Ronald Dathorne and Willfried Feuser, editors, *Africa in Prose*, Penguin, 1969.

OTHER

Contributor of stories to *Transition* and *Kenya Weekly News*. Editor of *Zuka* and *Sunday Nation* (Nairobi).

SIDELIGHTS: Novelist, dramatist, essayist, and literary critic Ngugi wa Thiong'o is East Africa's most prominent writer. Known to many simply as Ngugi, he has been described by Shatto Arthur Gakwandi in *The Novel and Contemporary Experience in Africa* as a ''novelist of the people,'' for his works show his concern for the inhabitants of his native country, Kenya, who have been oppressed and exploited by colonialism, Christianity, and in recent years, by black politicians and businessmen. As *Africa Today* contributor D. Salituma Wamalwa observes: ''Ngugi's approach to literature is one firmly rooted in the historical experience of the writer and his or her people, in an understanding of society as it is and a vision of society as it might be.''

Throughout his career as a writer and professor, Ngugi has worked to free himself and his compatriots from the effects of colonialism, Christianity, and other non-African influences. In the late 1960s, for example, Ngugi and several colleagues at the University of Nairobi successfully convinced school officials to transform the English Department into the Department of African Languages and Literature. Shortly thereafter Ngugi renounced his Christian name, James, citing Christianity's ties to colonialism. He took in its place his name in Gikuyu (or Kikuyu), the dominant language of Kenya. Ngugi strengthened his commitment to the Kenyan culture in 1977, when he declared his intention to write only in Gikuyu or Swahili, not English. In response to a query posed in an interview for *Journal of Commonwealth Literature* concerning this decision, Ngugi stated: ''Language is a carrier of a people's culture, culture is a carrier of a people's values; values are the basis of a people's self-definition—the basis of their consciousness. And when you destroy a people's language, you are destroying that very important aspect of their heritage . . . you are in fact destroying that which helps them to define themselves . . . that which embodies their collective memory as a people.''

Ngugi's determination to write in Gikuyu, combined with his outspoken criticisms of both British and Kenyan rule, have posed threats to his security. In 1977 Ngugi's home was searched by Kenyan police, who confiscated nearly one hundred books, then arrested and imprisoned Ngugi without a trial. At the time of his arrest, Ngugi's play *Ngaahika Ndena* (''I Will Marry When I Want''), co-authored with Ngugi wa Mirii, had recently been banned on the grounds of being ''too provocative,'' according to *American Book Review* contributor Henry Indangasi; in addition, his novel *Petals of Blood*, a searing indictment of the Kenyan government, had just been published in England. Although Ngugi was released from prison a year later, his imprisonment cost him his professorship at the University of Nairobi. When his theatre group was banned by Kenyan officials in 1982, Ngugi, fearing further reprisals, left his country for a self-imposed exile in London.

Ngugi chronicles his prison experience in *Detained: A Writer's Prison Diary*, and expresses his political views in other nonfiction works such as *Barrel of a Pen: Resistance to Repression in Neo-Colonial Kenya*. He has received the most critical attention, however, for his fiction, particularly his novels. Ngugi's first novel *Weep Not, Child* deals with the Mau Mau rebellion against the British administration in the 1950s, and his third novel *A Grain of Wheat* concerns the aftermath of the war and its effects on Kenya's people. Although critics describe the first novel as somewhat stylistically immature, many comment favorably on the universality of its theme of the reactions of people to the stresses and horrors of war and to the inevitable changes brought to bear on their lives.

In contrast, several reviewers believe that *A Grain of Wheat* fulfills the promise of Ngugi's first novel. *A Grain of Wheat* portrays four characters who reflect upon the events of the Mau Mau rebellion and its consequences as they await the day of Kenyan independence, December 12, 1963. G. D. Killam explains in his book *An Introduction to the Writings of Ngugi:* ''Uhuru Day, the day when independence from the colonial power is achieved, has been the dream of each of these figures from their schooldays. But there is little joyousness in their lives as they recall over the four days their experiences of the war and its aftermath.''

In their book *Ngugi wa Thiong'o: An Exploration of His Writings*, David Cook and Michael Okenimkpe praise the ''almost perfectly controlled form and texture'' of *A Grain of Wheat*. Killam comments: ''*A Grain of Wheat* is the work of a writer more mature than when he wrote his first two books. . . . In *A Grain of Wheat* [Ngugi] takes us into the minds of his characters, sensibilities resonant with ambiguities and contradictions, and causes us to feel what they feel, to share in significant measure their hopes and fears and pain.'' Shatto Arthur Gakwandi similarly observes in *The Novel and Contemporary Experience in Africa:* ''The general tone of *A Grain of Wheat* is one of bitterness and anger. The painful memories of Mau Mau violence still overhang the Kikuyu villages as the attainment of independence fails to bring the cherished social dreams.'' Gakwandi adds: ''While the novel speaks against the harshness of colonial oppression, it is equally bitter against the new leaders of Kenya who are neglecting the interests of the peasant masses who were the people who made the greatest sacrifices during the war of liberation. Ngugi speaks on behalf of those who, in his view, have been neglected by the new government.''

Petals of Blood, Ngugi's fourth novel, is considered his most ambitious and representative work. Like *A Grain of Wheat*,

Petals of Blood describes the disillusionment of the common people in post-independence Kenya. Killam notes, however, that in *Petals of Blood* Ngugi "widens and deepens his treatment of themes which he has narrated and dramatized before—themes related to education, both formal and informal; religion, both Christian and customary; the alienation of the land viewed from the historical point of view and as a process which continues in the present; the struggle for independence and the price paid to achieve it." *Petals of Blood* is also described as Ngugi's most overtly political novel. A *West Africa* contributor notes an ideological shift in the novel "from the earlier emphasis on nationalism and race questions to a class analysis of society." Critics cite in particular the influence of both Karl Marx and Frantz Fanon, the latter of whom, according to Killam, "places the thinking of Marx in the African context." In *World Literature Written in English* Govind Narian Sharma comments: "Whereas traditional religious and moral thought has attributed exploitation and injustice in the world to human wickedness and folly, Ngugi, analyzing the situation in Marxist terms, explains these as 'the effect of laws of social development which make it inevitable that at a certain stage of history one class, pursuing its interests with varying degrees of rationality, should dispossess and exploit another.'"

Petals of Blood concerns four principle characters, all being held on suspicion of murder: Karega, a teacher and labor organizer; Munira, headmaster of a public school in the town of Ilmorog; Abdulla, a half-Indian shopkeeper who was once a guerrilla fighter during the war for independence; and Wanja, a barmaid and former prostitute. "Through these four [characters]," writes Civia Tamarkin in the *Chicago Tribune Book World,* "Ngugi tells a haunting tale of lost hopes and soured dreams, raising the simple voice of humanity against the perversity of its condition." *American Book Review* contributor Henry Indangasi describes *Petals of Blood* this way: "Through numerous flashbacks, and flashbacks within flashbacks, and lengthy confessions, a psychologically credible picture of the characters, and a vast canvas of Kenya's history is unfolded."

Several reviewers note that Ngugi's emphasis on the economic and political conditions in Kenya at times overshadows his narrative. The *West Africa* contributor explains: "*Petals of Blood* is not so much a novel as an attempt to think aloud about the problems of modern Kenya: the sharp contrast between the city and the countryside, between the 'ill-gotten' wealth of the new African middle-class and the worsening plight of the unemployed workers and peasants." Charles R. Larson expresses a like opinion in *World Literature Today:* "*Petals of Blood* is not so much about these four characters (as fascinating and as skillfully drawn as they are) as it is about political unrest in post-independence Kenya, and what Ngugi considers the failures of the new black elite (politicians and businessmen) to live up to the pre-independence expectations." Foreshadowing Ngugi's 1977 arrest, Larson concludes, "In this sense *Petals of Blood* is a bold venture—perhaps a risky one—since it is obvious that the author's criticisms of his country's new ruling class will not go unnoticed."

Critics also maintain that this emphasis lends a didactic tone to the novel. Larson, for instance, comments in the *New York Times Book Review:* "The weakness of Ngugi's novel as a work of the creative imagination ultimately lies in the author's somewhat dated Marxism: revolt of the masses, elimination of the black bourgeois; capitalism to be replaced with African socialism. The author's didacticism weakens what would otherwise have been his finest work." *New Yorker* contributor

John Updike similarly observes that "the characters . . . stagger and sink under the politico-symbolical message they are made to carry." *World Literature Today* contributor Andrew Salkey, on the other hand, offers this view: "It's a willfully diagrammatic and didactic novel which also succeeds artistically because of its resonant characterization and deadly irony. It satisfies both the novelist's political intent and the obligation I know he feels toward his art."

Despite these reservations, the majority of critics concur that *Petals of Blood* is an important literary contribution. Sharma, for example, writes that "Ngugi's *Petals of Blood* is a complex and powerful work. It is a statement of his social and political philosophy and an embodiment of his prophetic vision. Ngugi provides a masterly analysis of the social and economic situation in modern Kenya, a scene of unprincipled and ruthless exploitation of man by man, and gives us a picture of the social and moral consequences of this exploitation." Cook and Ikenimkpe state that *Petals of Blood* "stands as a rare literary achievement: with all its faults upon it, [it is still] a skillfully articulated work which in no degree compromises the author's fully fledged radical political viewpoint." Indangasis concludes: "In many senses, literary and nonliterary, *Petals of Blood* will remain a major but controversial contribution to African literature, and the literature of colonised peoples."

BIOGRAPHICAL/CRITICAL SOURCES:

BOOKS

Bailey, Diana, *Ngugi wa Thiong'o: The River Between, a Critical View,* edited by Yolande Cantu, Collins, 1986.
Contemporary Literary Criticism, Gale, Volume 3, 1975, Volume 7, 1977, Volume 13, 1980, Volume 36, 1986.
Cook, David and Michael Okenimkpe, *Ngugi wa Thiong'o: An Exploration of His Writings,* Heinemann, 1983.
Gakwandi, Shatto Arthur, *The Novel and Contemporary Experience in Africa,* Africana Publishing, 1977.
Killam, G. D., *An Introduction to the Writings of Ngugi,* Heinemann, 1980.
Ngugi wa Thiong'o, *Detained: A Writer's Prison Diary,* Heinemann, 1981.
Larson, Charles R., *The Emergence of African Fiction,* Indiana University Press, 1972.
Palmer, Eustace, *An Introduction to the African Novel,* Africana Publishing, 1972.
Palmer, Eustace, *The Growth of the African Novel,* Heinemann, 1979.
Robson, Clifford B., *Ngugi wa Thiong'o,* Macmillan (London), 1979.
Roscoe, Adrian, *Uhuru's Fire: African Literature East to South,* Cambridge University Press, 1977.
Tibble, Ann, *African/English Literature,* Peter Owen (London), 1965.
Tucker, Martin, *Africa in Modern Literature: A Survey of Contemporary Writing in English,* Ungar, 1967.

PERIODICALS

African Literature Today, Number 5, 1971, Number 10, 1979.
Africa Today, Volume 33, number 1, 1986.
American Book Review, summer, 1979.
Books Abroad, autumn, 1967, spring, 1968.
Books in Canada, October, 1982.
Chicago Tribune Book World, October 22, 1978.
Christian Science Monitor, October 11, 1978, September 5, 1986.
Iowa Review, spring/summer, 1976.

Journal of Commonwealth Literature, September, 1965, Number 1, 1986.

Listener, August 26, 1982.

Michigan Quarterly Review, fall, 1970.

New Republic, January 20, 1979.

New Statesman, October 20, 1972, July 24, 1981, June 18, 1982, August 8, 1986.

New Yorker, July 2, 1979.

New York Times, May 10, 1978, November 9, 1986.

New York Times Book Review, February 19, 1978.

Observer, June 20, 1982.

Times Literary Supplement, January 28, 1965, November 3, 1972, August 12, 1977, October 16, 1981, June 18, 1982, May 8, 1987.

Washington Post, October 9, 1978.

West Africa, February 20, 1978.

World Literature Today, spring, 1978, fall, 1978, spring, 1981, autumn, 1982, summer, 1983, winter, 1984, fall, 1987.

World Literature Written in English, November, 1979, autumn, 1982.*

—*Sketch by Melissa Gaiownik*

*   *   *

NISSENSON, Hugh   1933-

PERSONAL: Born March 10, 1933, in Brooklyn, N.Y.; son of Charles Arthur and Harriette (Dolch) Nissenson; married Marilyn Claster (a television writer and producer), November 10, 1962; children: Katherine, Kore Johanna. *Education:* Swarthmore College, B.A., 1955. *Politics:* Registered Democrat. *Religion:* Jewish.

ADDRESSES: Home—411 West End Ave., New York, N.Y. 10024.

CAREER: Full-time free-lance writer, 1958—.

AWARDS, HONORS: Wallace Stegner literary fellow at Stanford University, 1961-62; Edward Lewis Wallant Memorial Award for fiction, 1965, for *A Pile of Stones;* PEN/Faulkner Award nomination, 1985, American Book Award nomination, fiction, 1985, and Ohioana Books Award, fiction, Ohioana Library Association, 1986, all for *The Tree of Life.*

WRITINGS:

A Pile of Stones (short stories), Scribner, 1965.
Notes from the Frontier (nonfiction), Dial, 1968.
In the Reign of Peace (short stories), Farrar, Straus, 1972.
My Own Ground (novel), Farrar, Straus, 1976.
The Tree of Life (novel), Harper, 1985.
The Elephant and My Jewish Problem: Selected Stories and Journals, 1957-1987, Harper, 1988.

Stories included in anthologies. Stories and articles published in *The New Yorker, Harper's, Commentary, Holiday, Esquire, Playboy, London Magazine,* and other magazines.

WORK IN PROGRESS: A science fiction novel.

SIDELIGHTS: Hugh Nissenson has long been acclaimed for his short stories, many of which explore contemporary perspectives on Jewish history and myth. The 1972 collection *In the Reign of Peace,* for example, contains "meticulous stories, perfected, polished, as a result often radiant," notes Cynthia Ozick in the *New York Times Book Review.* "The strength of Nissenson's prose is not in what he puts in . . . but how he omits," adds Ozick. Similarly, *New York Times* contributor

Thomas Lask observes that Nissenson "never writes in abstractions. The frame around his stories is firm and four-square. The settings are solid and easily followed." Lask also praises the author for creating "a group of superbly crafted tales that always mean what they say." But for all Nissenson's success with his stories, "what he wanted eventually to write," relates John F. Baker in a *Publishers Weekly* interview, "was a work in which the arts of narrative, poetry, and painting are combined—and that is what he has finally achieved in *The Tree of Life.*"

The 1811 diary of widower Thomas Keene, who has settled in frontier Ohio, *The Tree of Life* "dramatizes, sometimes with almost unbearable intensity, the American dream and its attendant nightmare," describes Paul Gray in *Time.* Keene catalogues his daily life in the journal, listing possessions, reporting events, recording feelings. The effect, as Elaine Kendall of the *Los Angeles Times Book Review* recounts, is that "this small novel works like a laser beam, penetrating the American experience with searing and concentrated intensity. Hugh Nissenson has created a complete world—inhabitants, artifacts, dwellings, customs and behavior, always working with an archaeologist's precision." In order to recreate frontier Ohio with accuracy, Nissenson acquainted himself with many of the objects Keene would have used. "As the work progressed," reports *Los Angeles Times* writer Garry Abrams, "so would Nissenson's collection of artifacts and other aids that would transport his imagination—[including] a Harper's Ferry musket, a tomahawk, . . . and a set of buckskins such as Keene might have worn." The latter item, Nissenson told Abrams, was most helpful: "The first time I put on my buckskin in my New York apartment, I looked in the mirror and it was a wonderful experience because suddenly I was transformed, it was real."

This transformation is illustrated by the verisimilitude of Keene's mixed media journal; Tom LeClair finds that "the novel itself is . . . artfully and authentically compressed," as he writes in the *Washington Post Book World.* "The account is a novelistic 'Waste Land'—a collage, like [T. S.] Eliot's poem, of precise and representative fragments." Expressing a similar opinion, Kendall comments that the line drawings and woodcuts make "our vision of Keene's vanished world even more complete and explicit than the plain straightforward prose could do alone." The critic adds that *The Tree of Life* "reverberates with a power far out of proportion to its modest length, cutting to the invisible roots of realism where all fiction begins."

In addition to the realism evident in *The Tree of Life,* critics have remarked on the complex levels of meaning in the novel. "Giving narrative momentum to Nissenson's researched inventory is a dual plot, where the personal and the historical, love and war, intersect," notes LeClair. *Village Voice* contributor Eliot Fremont-Smith also sees an intricacy in the novel's plotting: "Part of the book's eeriness derives from the certain if not quite conscious knowledge of what is to come—expansion for the whites, doom for the Indians—the sense of the inevitable, and so early." "Finally, with the shock of a trapdoor falling beneath one's feet," writes the *New York Times*'s Christopher Lehmann-Haupt, "one realizes that 'The Tree of Life' isn't an artifact at all, but instead a poem in the form of a diary, whose every image performs a complex set of duties. One can pick out almost any word or phrase, and an extensive web of associations seems to stretch away in every direction." Concludes the critic: "On first reading, [*The Tree of Life*] possesses us as a vital documentary of 19th-century frontier life. On second reading, it confronts us where our deepest and most disturbing fantasies intersect with our sense of history. . . . It is a book that plants deep seeds.''

Recounting his working methods, Nissenson told Baker: ''I write and rewrite, and that's why it takes me so long. For the novel to survive, it has to do what the movie can't—which means you have to assert the primacy of the word. It's no good going in for long descriptions as they did in the 19th century; the camera can do that. You have to trim away the fat, achieve more with less.'' The author continued: ''I want above all, as [Joseph] Conrad said, to make people *see* and *feel*. And to do that, you must have some sort of a narrative, to make people follow you. Nobody ever tires of a story.''

BIOGRAPHICAL/CRITICAL SOURCES:

BOOKS

Contemporary Literary Criticism, Gale, Volume 4, 1975, Volume 9, 1978.
Dictionary of Literary Biography, Volume 28: *Twentieth Century American-Jewish Fiction Writers*, Gale, 1984.
Nissenson, Hugh, *The Elephant and My Jewish Problem: Selected Stories and Journals, 1957-1987*, Harper, 1988.

PERIODICALS

Chicago Tribune Book World, October 27, 1985.
Los Angeles Times, January 22, 1986.
Los Angeles Times Book Review, November 3, 1985.
New Yorker, December 23, 1985.
New York Times, March 18, 1972, March 30, 1976, October 14, 1985.
New York Times Book Review, July 11, 1965, April 28, 1968, March 19, 1972, April 4, 1976, October 27, 1985.
Publishers Weekly, November 1, 1985.
Saturday Review, July 3, 1965, April 13, 1968.
Time, October 21, 1985.
Village Voice, October 22, 1985.
Washington Post Book World, November 3, 1985.

*   *   *

NKOSI, Lewis   1936-

PERSONAL: Born December 5, 1936, in Natal, South Africa; son of Samson and Christine Margaret (Makathini) Nkosi; married Bronwyn Ollernshaw; children: Louise, Joy (twins). *Education:* Attended M. L. Sultan Technical College, 1954-55, and Harvard University, 1961-62; University of London, diploma in English literature, 1974; University of Sussex, 1977.

ADDRESSES: Home—Flat 4, Burgess Park Mansions, Fortune Green Rd., London NW6, England. *Agent*—Deborah Rogers Ltd., 29 Goodge St., London WC1, England.

CAREER: Ilanga lase Natal (title means ''Natal Sun,'' Zulu-English weekly newspaper), staff member, 1955; *Drum* (magazine), chief reporter, Johannesburg, South Africa, 1956-60, *Golden City Post* (*Drum* Sunday newspaper), chief reporter, 1956-60; *South African Information Bulletin*, staff member, 1962-68; *The New African*, London, England, literary editor, 1965-68. Editor of journal in Dar es Salaam, Tanzania, during 1960s. Correspondent in southern United States, *Observer* (London). Producer of British Broadcasting Company (BBC) radio series ''Africa Abroad,'' 1962-65, interviewer of leading African writers for National Education Television (NET) series ''African Writers of Today,'' 1963. Visiting Regents Professor of African Literature, University of California, Irvine, 1970.

AWARDS, HONORS: Nieman fellowship in journalism, Harvard University, 1961-62; Dakar World Festival of Negro Arts prize, 1966, for *Home and Exile and Other Selections*.

WRITINGS:

The Rhythm of Violence (also see below; play; first produced in London, 1963), Oxford University Press, 1964.
Home and Exile and Other Selections (essays), Longmans, Green, 1965, expanded edition, Longman, 1983.
(Contributor) *African Writing Today*, edited by Ezekiel Mphalele, Penguin, 1967.
(Contributor) *Plays from Black Africa* (includes ''The Rhythm of Violence''), edited by Frederic N. Litto, Hill & Wang, 1968.
''We Can't All Be Martin Luther King'' (radio play), BBC, 1971.
''The Chameleon and the Lizard'' (libretto), first produced in London at Queen Elizabeth Hall, 1971.
''Malcolm'' (play), first produced in London, 1972.
The Transplanted Heart: Essays on South Africa, Ethiope Publishing, 1975.
Tasks and Masks: Themes and Styles of African Literature, Longman (London), 1981, published as *Tasks and Masks: An Introduction to African Literature*, Longman, 1982.
Mating Birds, East African Publishing House, 1983, Harper, 1987.

Also author of screenplay, ''Come Back Africa,'' 1959. Author of television play, ''Malcolm,'' produced in England and Sweden in 1967. Author of radio play, ''The Trial,'' 1969. Contributor to periodicals and journals, including *Guardian, New Statesman, Observer, Transition, Black Orpheus, Spectator, West Africa, African Report, African Today*, and *New Yorker*.

WORK IN PROGRESS: A libretto for the King's Singers.

SIDELIGHTS: Exiled after leaving South Africa to study at Harvard University, Lewis Nkosi has written short stories, plays, and criticism from his adopted home in England. Much of his work, however, deals with African literature and social concerns. ''As a playwright and short-story writer, he is also the most subtly experimental of the black South African writers, many of whom are caught in the immediacy of the struggle against apartheid,'' comments Henry Louis Gates, Jr. in the *New York Times Book Review*. According to Alistair Niven in *British Book News* Nkosi is ''one of the architects of the contemporary black consciousness in South Africa.''

Mating Birds, Nkosi's first novel, brought him wide critical attention. The book focuses on South Africa's response to miscegenation through the story of a young man, Ndi Sibiya, a rural chief's son, who ''meets'' a white stripper named Veronica, on a segregated beach. Although the rules of apartheid keeps them from speaking to each other, a wordless flirtation commences. Sibiya becomes pulled into an obsessive relationship with Veronica and ends up following her everywhere. Eventually, Veronica seems to invite her suitor back to her bungalow, where Sibiya believes he is seduced. Veronica, however, calls the police and accuses Sibiya of rape, for which he is arrested. According to South African law, if he is found guilty, he can be executed.

Many critics see the novel as a comment on apartheid. According to *Nation* contributor George Packer, ''*Mating Birds* feels like the work of a superb critic. Heavy with symbolism, analytical rather than dramatic, it attempts nothing less than an allegory of colonialism and apartheid, one that dares to linger in complexity.'' Gates writes that *Mating Birds* ''confronts boldly and imaginatively the strange interplay of bondage, desire and torture inherent in interracial sexual relationships within the South African prison house of apartheid.''

Critics have also praised Nkosi's portrayal of Sibiya's feelings for Veronica. Margaret Walters claims in the *Observer*, ''the most remarkable thing in this short novel is the account of the obsession that grips Sibiya.'' Gates says that summarzing the plot ''does not capture the book's lyrical intensity or its compelling narrative power. Mr. Nkosi has managed to re-create for his readers all the tortures of an illicit obsession, especially the ambiguities and interdeterminacy of motivation and responsibility.'' And *Washington Post Book World* contributor Alan Ryan writes, ''*Mating Birds* is very possibly the finest novel by a South African, black or white, about the terrible distortion of love in South Africa since Alan Paton's *Too Late the Phalarope*.''

But some readers dislike even the possibility of rape to convey Sibiya's response to white society. ''Nkosi's handling of the sexual themes complicates the distribution of our sympathies, which he means to be uniequivocally with the accused man,'' points out Rob Nixon in the *Village Voice*. ''For in rebutting the prevalent white South African fantasy of the black male as a sex-crazed rapist, Nkosi edges unnecessarily close to reinforcing the myth of the raped woman as someone who deep down was asking for it.'' For Gates, however, the question of whether Sibiya rapes Veronica remains unclear. This causes problems for the reader, as ''we are never certain who did what to whom or why.'' He quotes Sibiya's reflections on his trial: ''But how could I make the judges or anyone else believe me when I no longer *knew* what to believe myself? . . . Had I raped the girl or not?'' Gates continues, ''We cannot say. Accordingly, this novel's great literary achievement—its vivid depiction of obsession—leads inevitably to its great flaw.'' Sara Maitland in the *New Statesman* objects to Nkosi's portrayal of Veronica: ''Surely there must be another way for Nkosi's commitment, passion and beautiful writing to describe the violence and injustice of how things are than this stock image of the pale evil seductress, the eternally corrupting female?''

Despite the novel's shortcomings, says Michiko Kakutani in the *New York Times*, *Mating Birds* ''nonetheless attests to the emergence of . . . a writer whose vision of South Africa remains fiercely his own.'' *West Coast Review of Books* contributor Sherman W. Smith believes that ''Lewis Nkosi certainly must be one of the best writers out of Africa in our time.'' And Ryan suggests that ''Nkosi's quiet voice is likely to linger in the ear long after the shouts and cries have faded away.''

BIOGRAPHICAL/CRITICAL SOURCES:

BOOKS

Contemporary Literary Criticism, Volume 45, Gale, 1987.
Nkosi, Lewis, *Mating Birds*, East African Publishing House, 1983, Harper, 1987.

PERIODICALS

Best Sellers, July, 1986.
Books and Bookmen, October, 1986.
British Book News, March, 1987.
Choice, June, 1982.
Listener, August 28, 1986.
London Review of Books, August 7, 1986.

Nation, November 22, 1986.
New Statesman, August 29, 1986.
New Yorker, May 26, 1986.
New York Times, March 22, 1986.
New York Times Book Review, May 18, 1986.
Observer, July 27, 1986.
Spectator, August 16, 1986.
Times Literary Supplement, February 3, 1966, August 27, 1982.
Village Voice, July 29, 1986.
West Coast Review of Books, September, 1986.
World Literature Today, spring, 1983, summer, 1984.*

*　　　*　　　*

NOLL, Roger G(ordon) 1940-

PERSONAL: Born March 13, 1940, in Monterey Park, Calif.; son of Cecil Ray (a broadcaster and lawyer) and Hjordis A. (a realtor; maiden name, Westover) Noll; married Robyn R. Schreiber, August 25, 1962; children: Kimberlee Elizabeth. *Education:* California Institute of Technology, B.S. (with honors), 1962; Harvard University, A.M., 1965, Ph.D., 1967.

ADDRESSES: Office—Department of Economics, Stanford University, Stanford, Calif. 94305.

CAREER: California Institute of Technology, Pasadena, instructor, 1965-67, assistant professor, 1967-69, associate professor, 1969-71, professor of economics, 1973-84, chairman of the Division of Humanities and Social Sciences, 1978-82; Stanford University, Stanford, Calif., professor of economics, 1984—, director of public policy program, 1986—. Visiting professor, Graduate School of Business, Stanford University, 1976-77. Fellow, Center for Advanced Study in the Behavioral Sciences, 1983-84. Senior staff economist for President's Council of Economic Advisors, 1967-68; member of committee, National Council on Marine Resources and Engineering, 1968, Office of Science and Technology, 1970-71, National Research Council, 1970-73, and National Academy of Sciences, 1975-76; secretary, President's Interagency Task Force on Income Maintenance, 1968; member, Federal Interagency Committee on Education, 1968, and President's Commission for a National Agenda for the Eighties, 1980; senior fellow and co-director of Studies in the Regulation of Economic Activity, Brookings Institution, 1970-73; chairman, Fourth Annual Conference on Telecommunications Policy Research, 1975-76, and Los Angeles School Monitoring Committee, 1978-79. Has testified on professional sports, drug regulation, airline regulation, and regulatory reform before several Congressional committees. Member, Commerce Technical Advisory Board Panel on Venture Capital, 1968-69; member of advisory council, Jet Propulsion Laboratory, 1976-81, National Aeronautics and Space Administration, 1978-81, National Science Foundation, 1978—, Committee for Economic Development, 1979-82, Commission on Behavioral and Social Sciences and Education, National Research Council, 1984—, and Department of Energy Research Advisory Board, 1986-88. Consultant to numerous corporations and governmental agencies and commissions, including U.S. Department of Justice, 1974-77 and 1979-81, Federal Communications Commission, 1977-81, and Department of Energy, 1979.

MEMBER: American Economic Association.

AWARDS, HONORS: National Science Foundation fellow, 1963-64; book award, National Association of Educational Broadcasters, 1974, for *Economic Aspects of Television Regulation;* Guggenheim fellow, 1983-84.

WRITINGS:

Reforming Regulation: An Evaluation of the Ash Council Report, Brookings Institution, 1971.

(With Merton J. Peck and John J. McGowan) *Economic Aspects of Television Regulation*, Brookings Institution, 1973.

(Editor and contributor) *Government and the Sports Business*, Brookings Institution, 1974.

(With Bruce Owen) *The Political Economy of Deregulation*, American Enterprise Institute, 1983.

(Editor) *Regulatory Policy and the Social Sciences*, University of California Press, 1985.

CONTRIBUTOR

Increasing Understanding of Public Problems and Policies, Farm Foundation, 1969.

John P. Crecine, editor, *Financing the Metropolis: Public Policy in Urban Economics, the Urban Affairs Annual Reviews IV*, Sage Publications, 1970.

(With Peck and McGowan) *On the Cable: Report of the Sloan Commission on Cable Communications*, McGraw, 1971.

(With William Capron) Capron, editor, *Technological Change in Regulated Industries*, Brookings Institution, 1971.

Compendium on Price and Wage Controls: Now and the Outlook for 1973, Joint Economic Committee, U.S. Congress, 1972.

Rolla Edward Park, editor, *The Role of Analysis in Regulatory Decisionmaking: The Case of Cable Television*, Heath, 1973.

The Changing Role of the Public and Private Sectors in Health Care, National Health Council, 1973.

Government Policies and Technological Innovation, Volumes I and II, National Technical Information Service, 1974.

The Economics of Federal Subsidy Programs, Part VIII: *Selected Subsidies*, U.S. Government Printing Office, 1974.

William G. Shepard, editor, *Public Policies toward Business: Readings and Cases*, Irwin, 1975.

Neil H. Jacoby, editor, *The Business-Government Relationship in American Society: A Reassessment*, University of California Press, 1975.

Controls on Health Care, National Academy of Sciences, 1975.

W. B. Littrell and G. Sjoberg, editors, *Current Issues in Social Policy*, Sage Publications, 1976.

Henry Owen and Charles L. Schultze, editors, *Setting National Priorities: The Next Ten Years*, Brookings Institution, 1976.

(With Paul A. Thomas) *Research with Recombinant DNA*, National Academy of Sciences, 1977.

(With others) Paul W. MacAvoy, editor, *Deregulation of Cable Television*, American Enterprise Institute, 1977.

W. S. Moore, editor, *Regulatory Reform*, American Enterprise Institute, 1978.

Robert F. Lanzillotti, editor, *Economic Effects of Government-Mandated Costs*, Public Policy Center, University of Florida, 1978.

(With John A. Ferejohn and Robert E. Forsythe) Vernon L. Smith, editor, *Research in Experimental Economics*, JAI Press, Volume I, 1979, (with Ferejohn, Forsythe, and Thomas R. Palfrey) Volume II, 1982.

Michael L. Dertouzos and Joel Moses, editors, *The Future Impact of Computers on Information Processing*, MIT Press, 1979.

(With Ferejohn and Forsythe) Clifford S. Russell, editor, *Collective Decisionmaking*, Resources for the Future (Washington, D.C.), 1979.

(With Alain Enthoven) Stuart H. Altman and Robert Blendon, editors, *Medical Technology: The Culprit behind Health Care Costs*, Sun Valley Forum on National Health, U.S. Department of Health, Education, and Welfare, 1979.

Richard S. Gordon, editor, *Issues in Health Care Regulation*, McGraw, 1980.

Stephen L. Feldman and Robert M. Wirtshafter, editors, *On the Economics of Solar Energy*, Heath, 1980.

(With Paul L. Joskow) Gary Fromm, editor, *Studies in Public Regulation*, MIT Press, 1981.

Walter Adams, editor, *The Structure of American Industry*, 6th edition, Macmillan, 1982.

(With Robert W. Hahn) Wesley Magat, editor, *Reform of Environmental Regulation*, Lexington Books, 1982.

(With Hahn) Leroy Graymer and Frederick Thompson, editors, *Reforming Social Regulation*, Sage Publications, 1982.

Jorg Finsinger, editor, *Public Sector Economics*, Macmillan, 1983.

Eli Noam, editor, *Telecommunications Today and Tomorrow*, Harcourt, 1983.

(With Forrest Nelson) Franklin M. Fisher, editor, *Antitrust and Regulation: Essays in Memory of John J. McGowan*, MIT Press, 1985.

Ronald E. Grieson, editor, *Antitrust and Regulation*, Lexington Books, 1986.

Marcellus S. Snow, editor, *Marketplace for Telecommunications*, Longman, 1986.

OTHER

Author of reports for the President and Attorney General of the United States, 1979; author of research reports for organizations, including Brookings Institutiton, National Science Foundation, Federal Communications Commission, Exxon Research Foundation, and Department of Energy. Contributor to numerous congressional reports and hearings; contributor to proceedings of Conference on Communications Policy Research, 1973, Conference on the Economics of Professional Sports, 1974, Future Planning Conference, 1976, and Symposium on Media Concentration, 1978. Contributor of articles to professional journals, including *Administrative Law Reform, American Economic Review, Review of Social Economics, Yale Law Journal, American Behavioral Scientist,* and *American Political Science Review;* contributor of reviews to *Engineering and Science, Journal of Economic Literature, Science, Issues in Science and Technology, Journal of Institutional and Theoretical Economics, Public Policy, Review of Economics and Statistics, Journal of Politics,* and *Journal of Law, Economics and Organization.* Also contributor of articles to *Pasadena Star-News, Los Angeles Times,* and *San Francisco Chronicle.*

WORK IN PROGRESS: The Technology of the Pork Barrel; Deregulating Telecommunications.

SIDELIGHTS: "Like many applied economists, I try to keep one foot in the professional literature and the other in communicating with non-economists," Roger G. Noll told *CA.* "Economic analysis provides a fascinating perspective from which to analyze how people and organizations behave in certain kinds of settings, and how our economic institutions can be made to produce better results. And, because so much of what government does amounts to allocating economic resources, economics also has something to say about political institutions. The old, nineteenth-century discipline of political economy—a marriage of politics and economics—is making a comeback, and I am lucky to witness the renaissance."

BIOGRAPHICAL/CRITICAL SOURCES:

PERIODICALS

Washington Post, September 26, 1971.

*   *   *

NORMAN, Edward (Robert)   1938-

PERSONAL: Born November 22, 1938, in London, England; son of Ernest Edward (an accountant) and Yvonne (Bush) Norman. *Education:* Selwyn College, Cambridge, B. A., 1961, M. A. and Ph. D., 1964, D. D., 1978.

ADDRESSES: Home—Christ Church College, Canterbury, Kent CT1 1QU, England.

CAREER: Cambridge University, Cambridge, England, fellow in history, Selwyn College, 1961-64, fellow and assistant lecturer in history, Jesus College, 1964-72, dean of Peterhouse, 1972-88; Christ Church College of Higher Education, Canterbury, England, dean, 1988—. B.B.C. Reith Lecturer, 1978; Wilkinson Professor, Wycliffe College, University of Toronto, 1981.

WRITINGS:

The Catholic Church and Ireland in the Age of Rebellion, 1859-1863, Longmans, Green, 1965.
The Catholic Church and Irish Politics in the Eighteen Sixties, Dundalgan Press, 1965.
Anti-Catholicism in Victorian England, Unwin, 1968.
The Conscience of the State in North America, Cambridge University Press, 1968.
(With F. K. S. St. Joseph) *The Early Development of Irish Society,* Cambridge University Press, 1969.
A History of Modern Ireland, Allen Lane, 1971.
Church and Society in Modern England, Clarendon, 1976.
Christianity and the World Order, Oxford University Press, 1979.

Christianity in the Southern Hemisphere, Oxford University Press, 1981.
The English Catholic Church in the Nineteenth Century, Oxford University Press, 1983.
Roman Catholicism in England: From the Elizabethan Settlement to the Second Vatican Council, Oxford University Press, 1985.
The Victorian Christian Socialists, Cambridge University Press, 1987.

Editor, *Cambridge Review,* 1963-64.

SIDELIGHTS: Historian Edward Norman specializes in researching the Christian Church in the British Isles. In *Roman Catholicism in England,* Norman "has written a brilliantly objective account of Roman Catholicism in England from the Elizabethan Settlement to the Second Vatican Council," states Frank Longford in *Contemporary Review.* Only one hundred pages long, "the book is a miracle of compression, and it is all most elegantly turned," praises A. N. Wilson in the *Spectator.* But Wilson also objects to what he considers the book's overtly congenial tone: "The author is extremely polite about everyone, a fact which, given his previous publications, I found mildly eery. . . . He is judicious to the point of dullness." *Listener* contributor John Bossy, however, praises Norman's handling of his subject: "If you want a grasp of this particular English tradition, economically and dispassionately conveyed, this is the book." And Longford believes that the author "has written about English Catholicism in a manner for which English Catholics can be grateful and of which he can be proud."

BIOGRAPHICAL/CRITICAL SOURCES:

PERIODICALS

Contemporary Review, May, 1985.
Listener, February 14, 1985.
Spectator, February 23, 1985.

O

OAKESHOTT, Michael (Joseph)   1901-

PERSONAL: Born December 11, 1901, in Kent, England; son of Joseph Francis and Frances Maude (Hellicar) Oakeshott. *Education:* Gonville and Caius College, Cambridge, B.A., 1923, M.A., 1927.

ADDRESSES: Home—Victoria Cottage, Acton, Swanage, Dorset, England.

CAREER: Cambridge University, Cambridge, England, fellow of Gonville and Caius College, 1924—, university lecturer in history, 1932-49; Oxford University, Nuffield College, Oxford, England, professorial fellow, 1949-50; University of London, London School of Economics and Political Science, London, England, professor of political science, 1951-69. Muirhead Lecturer, University of Birmingham, 1953; visiting professor, Harvard University, 1958; Mond Lecturer, University of Manchester, 1959. *Military service:* Royal Artillery, 1940-45; became captain.

AWARDS, HONORS: Fellow of British Academy, 1966.

WRITINGS:

Experience and Its Modes, Cambridge University Press, 1933, reprinted, 1986.
(With G. T. Griffith) *A Guide to the Classics; or, How to Pick the Derby Winner,* Faber, 1936, revised edition published as *New Guide to the Derby: How to Pick the Winner,* Faber, 1947.
The Social Political Doctrines of Contemporary Europe, forward by Ernest Barker, Cambridge University Press, 1939, Macmillan, 1942, reprinted, Darby, 1980.
(Editor and author of introduction) Thomas Hobbes, *Leviathan; or, The Matter, Forme, and Power of a Commonwealth, Ecclesiasticall and Civil,* Basil Blackwell, 1946, Collier, 1962.
The Voice of Poetry in the Conversation of Mankind, Bowes, 1959.
Rationalism in Politics, and Other Essays, Methuen, 1962.
Hobbes on Civil Association, Basil Blackwell, 1975, revised edition, 1980.
On Human Conduct, Oxford University Press, 1975.
On History and Other Essays, Basil Blackwell, 1983.

Editor of the *Cambridge Journal,* 1947-53.

BIOGRAPHICAL/CRITICAL SOURCES:

PERIODICALS

Times Literary Supplement, October 21, 1983.

*   *   *

O'DONNELL, James H(owlett) III   1937-

PERSONAL: Born October 11, 1937, in Memphis, Tenn.; son of James Howlett, Jr. (a salesman) and Cornelia (Tant) O'Donnell; married second wife, Mabry Miller (a professor of speech), December 30, 1972; children: John Moore, Anne Elizabeth, Susan Margaret. *Education:* Lambuth College, B.A., 1959; Duke University, M.A., 1961, Ph.D., 1963. *Politics:* Democrat. *Religion:* Methodist.

ADDRESSES: Home—118 Meadow Lane, Marietta, Ohio 45750. *Office*—Department of History, Marietta College, Marietta, Ohio 45750.

CAREER: Radford College, Radford, Va., associate professor, 1963-66, professor of history, 1966-69; Marietta College, Marietta, Ohio, associate professor, 1969-73, professor of history, 1973—. Visiting professor, University of Tennessee. Media and environmental consultant.

MEMBER: Organization of American Historians, Southern Historical Association, Phi Alpha Theta.

AWARDS, HONORS: Research grants from American Philosophical Society, 1972 and 1976, Colonial Williamsburg, 1973, and Huntington Library, 1974; American Council of Learned Societies fellow, 1975-76; National Endowment for the Humanities summer seminar, 1983; Edwin A. Harness fellow, 1988.

WRITINGS:

Southern Indians in the American Revolution, University of Tennessee Press, 1973.
The Cherokees of North Carolina in the American Revolution (pamphlet), Department of Cultural Resources, Division of Archives and History (Raleigh), 1976.
Southeastern Frontiers: Europeans, Africans, and American Indians, 1513-1840; a Critical Bibliography, Indiana University Press for the Newberry Library, 1982.

Contributor to historical journals.

WORK IN PROGRESS: Northern Indians in the American Revolution; Joseph Brant.

* * *

O'NEILL, Olivia
See BARSTOW, Phyllida

* * *

OOSTHUIZEN, G(erhardus) C(ornelis) 1922-

PERSONAL: Born June 18, 1922, in Alexandria District, South Africa; son of Carel Adam (a farmer) and Anna Johanna (Potgieter) Oosthuizen; married Anna Cornelia Opperman (a medical practitioner); children: Carel, Rudolf, Gerhardus. *Education:* University of Stellenbosch, B.A., 1941, M.Th., 1953; University of South Africa, M.A., 1946, Ph.D., 1955; Free University, Amsterdam, Netherlands, Th.D., 1958.

ADDRESSES: Home—2 Jamieson Dr., Westville, Durban, South Africa. *Office*—University of Durban-Westville, Private Bag X54001, Durban, South Africa.

CAREER: Ordained minister of Dutch Reformed Church, 1944; pastor of church in Bulawayo, Rhodesia, 1950-56, and Queenstown, South Africa, 1956-59; University of Fort Hare, Alice, Cape Province, South Africa, professor of missiology, 1969-71, professor of religious studies, 1972—. Visiting professor in West Berlin, 1966-67, and the Netherlands, 1970-71. Director of research unit for New Religions and Independent Indigenous Churches in South Africa. Former mayor of Alice, Cape Province. *Military service:* South African Air Force, chaplain, 1944-46; became captain.

MEMBER: International Association for Missiological Studies, International Association for the History of Religions, International Association for the Study of Prehistoric Religions and Ethnology, South African Academy for Arts and Science, Missiological-Anthropological Research Association.

WRITINGS:

Theological Discussions and Confessional Developments in the Churches of Asia and Africa, Wever (Netherlands), 1958.
Delayed Action, Gollancz, 1961.
Die kerk in gisterde Asie en Afrika, Lovedale Press (South Africa), 1962.
The Theology of a South African Messiah, E. J. Brill, 1967.
Post-Christianity in Africa: A Theological and Anthropological Study, Eerdmans, 1968.
Shepherd of Lovedale: A Life for Southern Africa, Keartlands, 1970.
(Contributor) *World Mission Handbook,* Lutterworth, 1970.
Theological Battleground in Asia and Africa: The Issues Facing the Churches and the Efforts to Overcome Western Division, Humanities, 1972.
(Editor) *The Ethics of Tissue Transplantation,* Howard Timmons (Cape Town), 1972.
(Co-editor) *The Great Debate: Abortion in the South African Context,* Howard Timmins, 1974.
Pentecostal Penetration into the Indian Community in Metropolitan Durban, Human Sciences Research Council (Pretoria), 1975.
Moving to the Waters: Fifty Years of Pentecostal Revival in Bethešda, 1925-1975, Bethesda Publications, 1975.
(Editor with H. A. Shapiro and S. A. Strauss) *Euthanasia,* Oxford University Press, 1977.

Iconography of Afro-Christian Religions, E. J. Brill, 1979.
(With J. H. Hofmeyr) *Socio-religious Survey of Chatsworth,* Institute for Economic and Social Research, University of Durban-Westville, 1979.
(Editor with Shapiro and Strauss) *Genetics and Society,* Oxford University Press, 1980.
(Editor with A. A. Clifford-Vaughan, A. L. Behr, and G. A. Rauche) *Challenge to a South African University,* Oxford University Press, 1981.
Succession Conflict Within the Church of the Nazarites, Institute for Social and Economic Research, University of Durban-Westville, 1981.
(With Hofmeyr) *Religion in a South African Community,* Institute for Social and Economic Research, University of Durban-Westville, 1981.
(Editor with Shapiro and Strauss) *Professional Secrecy in South Africa,* Oxford University Press, 1983.
(Editor with Shapiro and Strauss) *Clinical Experimentation in South Africa,* Hodder & Stoughton, 1985.
(Editor) *Religion Alive: The New Movements and Indigenous Churches in South Africa,* Hodder & Stoughton, 1986.
(With others) *Religion, Social Change, and Intergroup Relations in South Africa,* Greenwood Press, 1986.
The Healing Prophet in the African Independent Churches, C. Hurst, in press.

Contributor of articles to journals in the Netherlands, Germany, Switzerland, South Africa, South East Asia, and the United States.

* * *

OPTIC, Oliver
See STRATEMEYER, Edward L.

* * *

OZ, Amos 1939-

PERSONAL: Given name Amos Klausner; born May 4, 1939, in Jerusalem, Israel; son of Yehuda Arieh (a writer) and Fania (Mussman) Klausner; married Nily Zuckerman, April 5, 1960; children: Fania, Gallia, Daniel. *Education:* Hebrew University of Jerusalem, B.A., 1963; St. Cross College, Oxford, M.A., 1970.

ADDRESSES: Home—Israel. *Agent*—Mrs. D. Owen, 28 Narrow St., London E. 14, England.

CAREER: Writer, 1962—. Has worked as tractor driver, youth instructor, school teacher, and agricultural worker at Kibbutz Hulda, Israel. Visiting fellow, St. Cross College, Oxford University, 1969-70. Writer in residence, Hebrew University of Jerusalem, 1975, and Colorado College, 1985. *Military service:* Israeli Army, 1957-60; also fought as reserve soldier in the tank corps in Sinai, 1967, and in the Golan Heights, 1973.

MEMBER: P.E.N. International, Hebrew Writers Association.

AWARDS, HONORS: Holon Prize for Literature, 1965; Israel-American Cultural Foundation award, 1968; B'nai B'rith annual literary award, 1973; Brehner Prize, 1978.

WRITINGS:

Artzot ha'tan (short stories), Massada [Tel Aviv], 1965, translation by Nicholas de Lange and Philip Simpson published as *Where the Jackals Howl, and Other Stories,* Harcourt, 1981.

Makom acher (novel), Sifriat Po'alim [Tel Aviv], 1966, translation by de Lange published as *Elsewhere, Perhaps*, Harcourt, 1973.

Michael sheli (novel), Am Oved [Tel Aviv], 1968, translation by de Lange in collaboration with Oz published as *My Michael*, Knopf, 1972.

Ad mavet (two novellas), Sifriat Po'alim, 1971, translation by de Lange in collaboration with Oz published as *Unto Death*, Harcourt, 1975.

Laga'at ba'mayim, laga'at ba'ruach (novel), Am Oved, 1973, translation by de Lange in collaboration with Oz published as *Touch the Water, Touch the Wind*, Harcourt, 1974.

Anashim acherim (anthology; title means "Different People"), Ha'Kibbutz Ha'Meuchad [Tel Aviv], 1974.

Har he'etza ha'raah (three novellas), Am Oved, 1976, translation by de Lange in collaboration with Oz published as *The Hill of Evil Counsel*, Harcourt, 1978.

Soumchi (juvenile), Am Oved, 1978, translation by Oz and Penelope Farmer published as *Soumchi*, Harper, 1980.

Be'or ha'tchelet he'azah (essays; title means "Under This Blazing Light"), Sifriat Po'alim, 1979.

Menucha nechonah (novel), Am Oved, 1982, translation by Hillel Halkin published as *A Perfect Peace*, Harcourt, 1985.

Po ve'sham b'eretz Yisra'el bistav 1982 (nonfiction), Am Oved, 1983, translation by Maurie Goldberg-Bartura published as *In the Land of Israel*, Harcourt, 1983.

(Editor with Richard Flantz and author of introduction) *Until Daybreak: Stories from the Kibbutz*, Institute for the Translation of Hebrew Literature, 1984.

Also editor of *Siach lochamium* (title means "The Seventh Day"). Contributor of essays and fiction to periodicals in Israel, including *Davar*.

SIDELIGHTS: Author Amos Oz has spent his career examining the experience of the Jewish people in Israel. Through fiction and nonfiction alike, he describes a populace under emotional and physical siege and a society threatened by internal contradictions and contention. Himself a native-born Israeli (a *sabra*), Oz writes books that are "indispensible reading for anyone who wishes to understand . . . life in Israel, the ideology that sustains it, and the passions that drive its people," according to Judith Chernaik in the *Times Literary Supplement*. Immensely popular in his own country, Oz has also established an international reputation; translations of his books have appeared in more than fifteen languages, including Japanese, Dutch, Norwegian, and Rumanian. In a *New Republic* assessment of the author's talents, Ian Sanders notes: "Amos Oz is an extraordinarily gifted Israeli novelist who delights his readers with both verbal brilliance and the depiction of eternal struggles—between flesh and spirit, fantasy and reality, Jew and Gentile. . . . His carefully reconstructed worlds are invariably transformed into symbolic landscapes, vast arenas where primeval forces clash." *Times Literary Supplement* contributor A. S. Byatt observes that in his works on Israel, Oz "can write with delicate realism about small lives, or tell fables about large issues, but his writing, even in translation, gains vitality simply from his subject matter." *New York Review of Books* correspondent D. J. Enright calls Oz "his country's most persuasive spokesman to the outside world, the literary part of it at least."

"In a sense Amos Oz has no alternative in his novels but to tell us what it means to be an Israeli," writes John Bayley in the *New York Review of Books*. A *sabra* who grew up along with the young nation, Oz has seen military service in two armed conflicts—the Six Day War and the Yom Kippur War—and he has lived most of his adult life as a member of Kibbutz Hulda, one of Israel's collective communities. His fictional themes arise from these experiences and are considered controversial for their presentations of individuals who rebel against the society's ideals. *New York Times Book Review* contributor Robert Alter contends that Oz's work is "symptomatic of the troubled connection Israeli writers increasingly feel with the realities of the Jewish state." Chernaik elaborates on this submerged "interior wilderness" that Oz seems compelled to explore: "He hears and sees more acutely than most, and has an uncanny gift for recording the distinctive features of his world, juxtaposing the socialist dreams and apocalyptic visions of the early Zionists, the naive arrogance of the young, and the nightmares of the mad and embittered. The overwhelming impression left by his fiction is of the precariousness of individual and collective human effort, a common truth made especially poignant by a physical landscape thoroughly inhospitable to human settlement, and given tragic dimensions by the modern history of the Jews and its analogues in Biblical history." Oz himself told the *New Republic* that he tries to tap his own turmoil in order to write. His characters, he said, "actually want two different things: peace and excitement, excitement and peace. These two things don't get along very easily, so when people have peace, they hate it and long for excitement, and when they have excitement, they want peace."

A central concern of Oz's fiction is the conflict between idealistic Zionism and the realities of life in a pluralistic society. As a corollary to this, many of his *sabra* characters have decidedly ambivalent feelings towards the Arab population, especially Palestinians. *Commentary* essayist Ruth R. Wisse writes that in book after book, "Oz has taken the great myths with which modern Israel is associated—the noble experiment of the kibbutz, the reclamation of the soil, the wars against the British and the Arabs, the phoenix-like rise of the Jewish spirit out of the ashes of the Holocaust—and shown us their underside: bruised, dazed, and straying characters who move in an atmosphere of almost unalleviated depression. . . . Oz in his fiction specializes in exposing the darker motives and disturbed dreams of those who must sustain these structures on which the country stands." Nehama Aschkenasy offers a similar assessment in *Midstream*: "The collective voice is suspiciously optimistic, over-anxious to ascertain the normalcy and sanity of the community and the therapeutic effect of the collective body on its tormented member. But the voice of the individual is imbued with a bitter sense of entrapment, of existential boredom and nausea, coupled with a destructive surrender to the irrational and the antinomian." Needless to say, this theme is one of Oz's most controversial. *New York Times Book Review* correspondent Morris Dickstein notes that the author often "takes the viewpoint of the detached participant, the good citizen who does his duty, shares his family's ideals but remains a little apart, wryly skeptical, unable to lose himself in the communal spirit. . . . Oz is intrigued by the tension between community and offbeat individuality."

The kibbutz provides Oz with a common background and inspiration. Its lifestyle serves as a powerful symbol of the nation's aspirations, as well as a microcosm of the larger Jewish family in Israel, suffocatingly intimate and inescapable, yet united in defense against the hostile forces besieging its borders. Alter declares that nearly all of Oz's fiction "is informed by the same symbolic world picture: a hemmed-in cluster of fragile human habitations (the kibbutz, the state of Israel itself) surrounded by dark, menacing mountains where jackals howl and hostile aliens lurk. . . . This symbolic opposition is the vehicle for a series of troubled narrative meditations on the rationalist-idealist enterprise of socialist Zionism and, beyond that, on civilization and its discontents, for the jackals out there often find an answering voice in the jackal beneath the skin of those who dwell within the perimeter of civilization.'' According to *Jewish Quarterly* contributor Jacob Sonntag, the people of Oz's fiction ''are part of the landscape, and the landscape is part of the reality from which there is no escape.'' If the landscape is inescapable, the bonds of family also offer little relief. Dickstein writes: ''The core of feeling in Oz's work is always some sort of family, often a family being torn apart.'' *Los Angeles Times* correspondent Elaine Kendall similarly observes that Oz's fiction ''confronts the generational conflicts troubling Israel today; emotional rifts intensified by pressure and privation. In that anguished country, the usual forms of family tension seem reversed; the young coldly realistic; the elders desperately struggling to maintain their belief in a receding ideal.''

''Daytime Israel makes a tremendous effort to create the impression of the determined, tough, simple, uncomplicated society ready to fight back, ready to hit back twice as hard, courageous and so on,'' Oz told *Partisan Review*. ''Nocturnal Israel is a refugee camp with more nightmares per square mile I guess than any other place in the world. Almost everyone has seen the devil.'' The obsessions of ''nocturnal Israel'' fuel Oz's work, as Mark Shechner notes in *Nation*. ''In [Oz's] fiction,'' Shechner writes, ''the great storms that periodically descend on the Jews stir up strange and possessed characters who ride the gusts as if in a dream: raging Zionists, religious fanatics poised to take the future by force, theoreticians of the millennium, strategists of the end game, connoisseurs of bitterness and curators of injustice, artists of prophecy and poets of doctrine.'' This is not to suggest, however, that Oz's work is unrelentingly somber or polemical. According to Dickstein, the ''glow of Oz's writing comes from the spare and unsentimental warmth of his own voice, his feeling for atmosphere and his gallery of colorful misfits and individualists caught in communal enterprises.'' Bayley likewise concludes: ''One of the admirable things about Oz's novels is the humor in them, a humor which formulates itself in having taken, and accepted, the narrow measure of the Israeli scene. Unlike much ethnic writing his does not seek to masquerade as *Weltliterature*. It is Jewish literature acquiescing amusedly in its new militantly provincial status.''

Oz's accounts of his own childhood illustrate the stresses placed upon the young in modern Israel. He was born Amos Klausner in Jerusalem in 1939 and grew up ''in a right-wing Zionist family, in a house filled with books,'' to quote the author from a *New Republic* interview. Oz's father was a librarian and expert on comparative literature, well versed in a dozen languages, but Oz grew up speaking only Hebrew. in *Partisan Review* he described his early years. ''My father wanted me to become the archetype of the new Israeli: simple, blond, cleansed of Jewish neurosis, tough, gentile-looking,'' he said. ''. . . I was meant to be a new leaf altogether: a sabra, tough, simple, unambivalent.'' And yet, he told *New Republic,* he was also expected to ''carry the Jewish genius, and bring honor to the family.'' At fifteen he rebelled against the scholarly atmosphere and his parents' bourgeois values. He joined Kibbutz Hulda, changed his name to Amos Oz, and undertook menial labor in the fields. A childhood yearning to be a writer could not be so easily expelled, however. Eventually Oz returned to Jerusalem to study at the Hebrew University; on holidays he returned to the kibbutz, where he was allowed to schedule time for writing among his other community duties. As his stories and novels began to sell, he was granted more and more days away from the fields in order to pursue his craft. He told *New Republic:* ''In the end, when I look at myself, I am doing exactly what my father wanted me to do. In the kibbutz I look like one of the members, and yet I follow my forefathers. I deal with words. My escape was a full circle.''

Oz is an unusual Israeli writer in that he has chosen to stay at the kibbutz throughout his career, even though the income from his royalties is substantial. As a member of the collective, he signs his paychecks over to the kibbutz treasurer, not keeping any fraction of them himself. Far from complaining, however, Oz feels that the system works to his benefit. ''I don't have to live on advances,'' he told the *New York Times Book Review,* ''I don't fill out income tax forms, I have no mortgage, I don't have to write book reviews or lecture, and the only essays I do are for rage. . . . It means a very modest standard of living, but I much prefer this life to existence in a literary aquarium.'' Nor does Oz overlook the opportunity the kibbutz offers him to study many personalities at close range. ''I know a hell of a lot about the people in Hulda— their family history, secret pains, loves and ambitions,'' he told *Publishers Weekly*. ''In this respect I am living in the middle of a rushing stream.'' Even when he was younger, he said in *Partisan Review*, the kibbutz ''evoked and fed my curiosity about the strange phenomenon of flawed, tormented human beings dreaming about perfection, aching for the Messiah, aspiring to change human nature. This perpetual paradox of magnanimous dream and unhappy reality is indeed one of the main threads in my writing.'' Furthermore, he told the *Washington Post,* his fellow kibbutzniks react to his works in fascinating ways: ''It's a great advantage, you know, to have a passionate, immediate milieu and not a literary milieu—a milieu of real people who tell me straight in my face what they think of my writing.''

My Michael, a novel about the psychological disintegration of a young Israeli housewife, was Oz's first work translated and published in English. *New Republic* contributor Lesley Hazleton calls the book ''a brilliant and evocative portrait of a woman slowly giving way to schizoid withdrawal'' and ''. . . a superb achievement, . . . the best novel to come out of Israel to date.'' In *Modern Fiction Studies,* Hana Wirth-Nesher expresses the view that Oz uses his alienated protagonist ''to depict the isolation and fear that many Israelis feel partially as a country in a state of siege and partially as a small enclave of Western culture in a vast area of cultures and landscapes unlike what they have known. . . . Both the social and spatial aspects of Jerusalem in this novel express symbolically the awe and insecurity of its inhabitants.'' Alter praises *My Michael* for managing ''to remain so private, so fundamentally apolitical in its concerns, even as it puts to use the most portentous political materials.'' Indeed, *Washington Post Book World* reviewer Audrey C. Foote finds the work's message to be ''a caustic repudiation of the cherished conception of the young *sabra* as invariably vigorous, dedicated, and brave.'' Paul Zweig claims in the *New York Times Book Review* that when *My Michael* was published in Israel shortly after the Six Day War, it proved ''extremely disturbing to Israelis. At a time when their country had asserted control over its destiny as never before, Oz spoke of an interior life which Israel had not had time for, which it had paid no heed to, an interior life that contained a secret bond to the Asiatic world beyond its border.'' Controversial though it was, *My Michael* was a bestseller in Israel; it established Oz's reputation among his countrymen and gave him entree into the international world of letters.

Oz's first novel, *Elsewhere, Perhaps,* was his second work to be translated and published abroad. Most critics feel that the book is the best fictional representation of kibbutz life to emerge from Israel; for instance, *Jewish Quarterly* reviewer Jacob Sonntag writes: ''I know of no other book that depicts life in the Kibbutz more vividly, more realistically or with greater insight.'' In *The Nation,* William Novak notes that the story of sudden violent events in the lives of three kibbutz families ''engages our sympathies because of the compelling sincerity and moral concerns of the characters, and because of the extent to which this is really the story of an entire society.'' *New York Times Book Review* correspondent A. G. Mojtabai stresses the realistic sense of conflict between military and civilian values portrayed in *Elsewhere, Perhaps.* According to Mojtabai, two perceptions of ''elsewhere'' are active in the story: ''elsewhere, perhaps, the laws of gravity obtain—not here; elsewhere, perhaps in some kingdom by the sea exists the model which our kibbutz imperfectly reflects, a society harmonious, healthful, joyful, loving—not here, not yet.'' Novak concludes that the novel's publication in the United States ''should help to stimulate American appreciation of contemporary Israeli literature and society.''

''As a seamstress who takes different pieces of cloth and sews them into a quilt, Amos Oz writes short pieces of fiction which together form a quilt in the reader's consciousness,'' notes J. Justin Gustainis in *Best Sellers.* ''Just as the quilt may be of many colors but still one garment, Oz's stories speak of many things but still pay homage to one central idea: universal redemption through suffering.'' Oz began his literary career as an author of short fiction; he has since published several volumes of stories and novellas, including *Where the Jackals Howl, Unto Death,* and *The Hill of Evil Counsel.* Aschkenasy suggests that the stories in *Where the Jackals Howl* ''are unified by an overall pattern that juxtaposes an individual permeated by a sense of existential estrangement and subterranean chaos with a self-deceiving community collectively intent upon putting up a facade of sanity and buoyancy in order to deny— or perhaps to exorcise—the demons from without and within.'' Chernaik notes of the same book that the reader coming to Oz for the first time ''is likely to find his perception of Israel permanently altered and shaped by these tales.'' The novellas in *Unto Death* ''take as their theme the hatred that surrounds Jews and that destroys the hated and the haters alike,'' to quote Joseph McElroy in the *New York Times Book Review.* *Midstream* contributor Warren Bargad finds this theme one manner of expressing ''the breakdown of the myth of normalcy which has been at the center of Zionist longing for decades: the envisioned State of Israel, with its promise of autoemancipation, which would make of the Jewish people a nation among nations. For Oz it is still an impossible dream.''

In an assessment of Oz's nonfiction, Shechner describes what he calls the 'two Amos Ozes.'' One, Shechner writes, is ''a fiction writer with an international audience, the other an Israeli journalist of more or less hometown credentials. . . . Oz's journalism would seem to have little in common with the crepuscular world of his fiction. A blend of portraits and polemics, it is straightforward advocacy journalism, bristling with editorials and belonging to the world of opinions, ideologies and campaigns.'' Despite his sometimes bleak portrayal of his homeland in his fiction, Oz believes in Israel and expresses strong opinions on how it should be run. Alter notes: ''In contrast to the inclination some writers may feel to withdraw into the fastness of language, the Oz articles reflect a strenuous effort to go out into Israeli society and sound its depth.'' Furthermore, according to Roger Rosenblatt in the *New York Times Book Review,* as a journalist, Oz establishes ''that he is no ordinary self-effacing reporter on a quest, but a public figure who for years has participated in major national controversies and who regularly gives his views of things to the international press, 'ratting' on his homeland.'' *Washington Post Book World* contributor Grace Schulman suggests that Oz's journalism ''may be the way to an esthetic stance in which he can reconcile the conflicting demands of artistic concern and political turbulence.''

In the Land of Israel, a series of interviews Oz conducted with a wide variety of Israelis, is his best known work of nonfiction. Shechner claims that the book ''provoked an outcry in Israel, where many saw the portraits of Jews as exaggerated and tailored to suit Oz's politics.'' The study does indeed present a vision of a pluralistic, creatively contentious society, ''threatened as much by the xenophobia and self-righteous tribalism within as by enemies without,'' according to Gene Lyons in *Newsweek.* Christopher Lehmann-Haupt offers a similar opinion in the *New York Times.* ''All together,'' he writes, ''the voices of 'In the Land of Israel' serve to elucidate the country's complex ideological cross-currents. And conducted as they are by Mr. Oz, they sing an eloquent defense of what he considers a centrist position, though some of his critics might call it somewhat left-of-center. Mr. Oz has distilled his country's dilemma to the tragic realization that every human being faces, which is, as one old pioneer put it: 'To be without power is both a sin and a catastrophe. On the other hand, to live by force is no less a catastrophe, and maybe a sin, too.''' The book has disturbed American critics as much as their Israeli counterparts. Schulman notes: ''Amos Oz writes of a country in turmoil. . . . Like a journey through the circles of Dante's Inferno, Oz's travels take him from despair to agony.'' *Atlantic* reviewer Irving Howe likewise contends that *In the Land of Israel* ''sets one's mind reeling with speculations and anxieties.'' Lyons feels that the work is most valuable for what it shows the reader about Oz and his positions *vis a vis* his country's future. Lyons concludes: ''Eloquent, humane, even religious in the deepest sense, [Oz] emerges here—and I can think of no higher praise—as a kind of Zionist Orwell: a complex man obsessed with simple decency and determined above all to tell the truth, regardless of whom it offends.''

Oz's novel *A Perfect Peace,* published in Israel in 1982 and the United States in 1985, returns to the modern kibbutz for its setting. The story revolves around two young kibbutzniks— one rebellious after a lifetime in the environment, the other an enthusiastic newcomer—and an aging politician, founder of the collective. According to Alter, the novel is ''a hybrid of social realism and metaphysical brooding, and it gains its peculiar power of assertion by setting social institutions and political issues in a larger metaphysical context. There is a vivid, persuasive sense of place here . . . but local place is quietly evoked against a cosmic backdrop.'' *Times Literary Supplement* reviewer S. S. Prawer observes that the work holds the reader's attention by providing a ''variety of boldly drawn characters who reveal themselves to us in and through their speech. . . . Oz's storytelling, with its reliance on journals and inner monologues, is pleasantly old-fashioned; he conscientiously underpins his construction with recurrent motifs and personal tics in the approved manner; and he conjures up the kibbutz environment in the sober prose that makes much of typical smells, sounds and sights.'' in a *New York Times Book Review* piece, Schulman contends that it is ''on a level other than the documentary that this novel succeeds so well. It is concerned with inner wholeness, and with a more profound peace than respect between generations and among countries. . . . The impact of this novel lies in the writer's creation of characters who are outwardly ordinary but inwardly bizarre, and at times fantastic.'' ''This is Oz's strangest, riskiest and richest novel to date,'' Rita Kashner notes in the *Washington Post Book World*. ''He writes in his usual clean, blunt prose, his characters' voices ring true, and he creates a world which makes perfect sense, except that at its core is a series of impenetrable mysteries. . . . Oz has spent craftsman's years developing a tender, ironic humor and an accuracy of voice that serve him brilliantly here.''

Critics find much to praise in Oz's portraits of the struggling nation of Israel. ''Mr. Oz's words, his sensuous prose and indelible imagery, the people he flings living onto his pages, evoke a cauldron of sentiments at the boil; yet his human vision is capacious enough to contain the destruction and hope for peace,'' writes Richard R. Lingeman in the *New York Times*. ''He has caught a welter of fears, curses and dreams at a watershed moment in history, when an uneasy, restless waiting gave way to an upsurge of violence, of fearsome consequences. The power of his art fuses historical fact and symbol; he makes the ancient stones of Jerusalem speak, and the desert beyond a place of jackals and miracles.'' Kendall concludes: ''This land of Oz is harsh and unfamiliar, resisting interpretation, defying easy solutions. His Israel is a place few tourists ever see and visiting dignitaries rarely describe. There, tension is the only constant and the howling of the jackals ceases only to begin again each night. Oz writes about that tension and that sound: how it feels, what it does.'' In the *Saturday Review*, Alfred Kazin states that Oz's effect on him is always to make him realize ''how little we know about what goes on inside the Israeli head. . . . To the unusually sensitive and humorous mind of Amos Oz, the real theme of Jewish history—especially in Israel—is unreality. When, and how can a Jew attain reality in the Promised Land, actually touch the water, touch the wind?'' Chernaik feels that Oz is ''without doubt a voice for sanity, for the powers of imagination and love, and for understanding. He is also a writer of marvellous comic and lyric gifts, which somehow communicate themselves as naturally in English as in Hebrew.''

Hebrew is the language in which Oz chooses to write; he calls it a ''volcano in action,'' still evolving rapidly into new forms. Oz likes to call himself the ''tribal storyteller,'' as he explained in the *New York Times:* ''I bring up the evil spirits and record the traumas, fantasies, the lunacies of Israeli Jews, natives and those from Central Europe. I deal with their ambitions and the powderbox of self-denial and self-hatred.'' In a *Washington Post* interview, he maintained that Israel would always be the source from which his inspiration would spring. ''I'm fascinated,'' he said of his homeland. ''Yes, indeed, I'm disgusted, appalled, sick and tired sometimes. Even when I'm sick and tired, I'm there. . . . It's my thing, if you will, in the same sense that William Faulkner belonged in the Deep South. It's my thing and my place—and my addiction.'' Married and the father of three children, Oz continues to live and work at Kibbutz Hulda. He also speaks and travels frequently bringing his personal thoughts to television and lecture audiences in Israel and abroad. Describing his creative impulses, Oz told the *New York Times:* ''Whenever I find myself in total agreement with myself, then I write an article—usually in rage—telling the government what to do. But when I detect hesitation, more than one inner voice, I discover in me the embryo of characters, the seeds of a novel.''

MEDIA ADAPTATIONS: My Michael was adapted as a film under the same title in Israel.

BIOGRAPHICAL/CRITICAL SOURCES:

BOOKS

Contemporary Literary Criticism, Gale, Volume V, 1976, Volume VIII, 1978, Volume IX, 1979, Volume XXVII, 1981, Volume XXXIII, 1985.

PERIODICALS

Atlantic, December, 1983.
Best Sellers, October, 1978.
Commentary, July, 1974, April, 1984.
Jewish Quarterly, spring-summer, 1974.
Los Angeles Times, May 21, 1981, June 24, 1985.
Los Angeles Times Book Review, December 11, 1983.
Midstream, November, 1976, January, 1983.
Modern Fiction Studies, spring, 1978.
Nation, September 7, 1974, June 8, 1985.
National Review, April 20, 1984.
New Leader, January 6, 1975.
New Republic, November 29, 1975, October 14, 1978, June 27, 1981, July 29, 1985.
Newsweek, November 21, 1983, July 29, 1985.
New Yorker, November 18, 1974, August 7, 1978, August 19, 1985.
New York Review of Books, February 7, 1974, January 23, 1975, July 20, 1978, September 26, 1985.
New York Times, May 19, 1978, July 18, 1978, May 22, 1981, October 31, 1983.
New York Times Book Review, May 21, 1972, November 18, 1973, November 24, 1974, October 26, 1975, May 28, 1978, April 26, 1981, March 27, 1983, November 6, 1983, June 2, 1985.
Partisan Review, Number 3, 1982, Number 3, 1986.
Publishers Weekly, May 21, 1973.
Saturday Review, June 24, 1972, November 2, 1974, May 13, 1978.
Spectator, January 9, 1982, December 17, 1983, August 10, 1985.
Studies in Short Fiction, winter, 1982.
Time, January 27, 1986.
Times (London), August 1, 1985.
Times Literary Supplement, July 21, 1972, February 22, 1974, March 21, 1975, October 6, 1978, September 25, 1981, July 27, 1984, August 9, 1985.
Village Voice, February 14, 1984.
Washington Post, December 1, 1983.
Washington Post Book World, May 28, 1972, May 31, 1981, June 14, 1981, November 13, 1983, July 14, 1985.
World Literature Today, spring, 1982, spring, 1983, summer, 1984, autumn, 1986.

—*Sketch by Anne Janette Johnson*

P

P. L. K.
    See KIRK-GREENE, Anthony (Hamilton Millard)

*   *   *

PAD, Peter
    See STRATEMEYER, Edward L.

*   *   *

PARKINSON, Michael   1944-

PERSONAL: Born August 11, 1944; son of John (a bus driver) and Margaret (Corrin) Parkinson; married Frances Anderson (a secondary school teacher), July 9, 1966. *Education:* University of Liverpool, B.S. (with honors), 1965; University of Manchester, M.A. (with distinction), 1968. *Politics:* Radical. *Religion:* None.

ADDRESSES: Office—Department of Political Theory, Social Studies Building, University of Liverpool, Liverpool L69 3BX, England.

CAREER: University of Liverpool, Liverpool, England, resident fellow, 1967-70, lecturer in political theory and institutions, 1970—. Visiting associate professor, Washington University, 1972-73.

WRITINGS:

The Labour Party and the Organization of Secondary Education, 1918-65, Routledge & Kegan Paul, 1970.
Politics of Urban Education: Research Report on an SSRC Project into the Formation of an Education Policy in an Urban Setting, University of Liverpool, 1973.
(With Edgar Litt) *U.S. and U.K. Educational Policy: A Decade of Reform,* Praeger, 1979.
Liverpool on the Brink: One City's Struggle against Government Cuts, Policy Journals, 1985.

Contributor of articles to *Political Studies.*

WORK IN PROGRESS: A study of English local political parties.

BIOGRAPHICAL/CRITICAL SOURCES:

PERIODICALS

Times Literary Supplement, August 7, 1970.*

PATTERSON, Edwin W(ilhite)   1889-1965

PERSONAL: Born January 1, 1889, in Kansas City, Mo.; December 23, 1965, of cancer in Charlottesville, Va.; Louis Lee Patterson (a salesman) and Roberta (Wilh... terson; married Dorothy Madison Thomson, December... children: Clifton Connell (deceased), Edwin W., Jr... (Mrs. Howard A. Ideson). *Education:* Univer... souri—Columbia, A.B., 1909, LL.B., 1911; ...versity Law School, S.J.D., 1920. *Politics:* D...

ADDRESSES: Home—1652 Brandywine D5; ... Va. *Office*—Clark Hall, University of Texas ... ville, Va. ...rsity of ...

CAREER: Admitted to Missouri St...essor, be... State Bar, 1921; practice of law, K... Iowa City, University of Texas, Main Univer... New York, at Austin), adjunct professor of, 1924-45, Car... Colorado, Boulder, 1917-20, ...Cardozo Professor came professor of law; Stat...nia, Charlottesville, professor of law, 1920-22;...ting professor of law, N.Y., associate professor...visiting professor of law dozo Professor of Juris...University of Southern California Emeritus, 1957-65; ...orial Lecturer, University of visiting scholar, be... Stanford Universit... at University of T... ...Association (chairman of committee iformia, 1958-5...gulation of insurance costs, 1935-40), Missouri, 195... Political and Legal Philosophy, Acade...

MEMBER: ... Jurisprudencia, Phi Beta Kappa, Phi Delta on qualif... Americ... ...mia C... Phi...

HONORS: LL.D., University of Missouri—Co... ...96; Outstanding Civilian Service Award from U.S. A for teaching of jurisprudence at Judge Advocate Gen... s School.

WRITINGS:

The Insurance Commissioner in the United States, Harvard University Press, 1927, reprinted, Johnson Reprint, 1968.

Essentials of Insurance Law, McGraw, 1935, 2nd edition, 1957.
(With Noel T. Dowling and Richard R. Powell) *Materials for Legal Method,* [New York], 1946.
Jurisprudence: Men and Ideas of the Law, Foundation Press, 1953.
Sources Readings in Jurisprudence, Judge Advocate General's School, 1960.
Legal Protection of Private Pension Expectations, Irwin, 1960.
Law in a Scientific Age, Columbia University Press, 1963.

EDITOR

Cases and Materials on the Law of Insurance, Commerce Clearing House, 1932, 4th edition (with William F. Young, Jr.), Foundation Press, 1961, 5th edition, 1971.
Cases on Contracts, Foundation Press, 1935, 4th edition (with George W. Gable and Harry W. Jones) published as *Cases [and] Materials on Contracts,* 1957.

[...] of *An Introduction of Jurisprudence.* Author of [...] contributor of numerous articles to law journals [...] ates and Europe.

[...]win W. Patterson once told *CA:* "I enjoy [...] know it is going to be hard work. Aside [...] themes and cultural heritage, the most im- [...] to [...] er to do is to discipline himself in habits [...] books [...] d writing style is important in even [...] as law or legal philosophy. Yet I [...] gerations used by some writers in [...] their partisan views. If I had it all [...] ve more of my energy to whole [...] ticles."

BIOGRAPH[...]

PERIODICAL[...]

Columbia Law [...]

OBITUARIES: [...] URCES:

PERIODICALS

New York Times, Dece[...]

*

PATTERSON, (Horace) Or[...] 1940-

PERSONAL: Born June 5, 1940, [...] came to the U.S., 1970, domiciled, [...] and Almina (Morris) Patterson; marrie[...] September 5, 1965; children: Rhiannon[...] University of the West Indies, B.Sc., 19[...] of Economics, Ph.D., 1965.

ADDRESSES: Office—520 James Hall, Harv[...] Cambridge, Mass. 02138.

CAREER: University of London, London School of [...] ics and Political Science, London, England, assistant l[...] 1965-67; University of the West Indies, Kingsto[...], lecturer, 1967-70; Harvard University, Cambridge, Ma[...] visiting lecturer, 1970-71, Allston Burr senior tutor, 1971-73[...] professor of sociology, 1971—; Institute for Advanced Study, Princeton, N.J., visiting member, 1975-76. Member of tech- nical advisory committee to prime minister and government of Jamaica, 1972-74, special adviser to prime minister for social policy and development, 1973-80. Visiting fellow,

Wolfson College, Cambridge University, 1978-79; Phi Beta Kappa visiting scholar, 1988-89.

MEMBER: American Sociological Association.

AWARDS, HONORS: Jamaica Government Exhibition scholar, 1959-62; Commonwealth scholar, Great Britain, 1962-65; first prize, Dakar Festival of Negro Arts, 1966, for *Children of Sisyphus;* M.A., Harvard University, 1971; Guggenheim fellow, 1978-79; distinguished contribution to scholarship award, American Sociological Association, 1983, for *Slavery and Social Death: A Comparative Study;* Ralph Bunch Award, American Political Science Association, 1983.

WRITINGS:

The Children of Sisyphus (novel), Hutchinson, 1964, Houghton, 1965, reprinted, Longman, 1982, published as *Dinah,* Pyramid Books, 1968.
(Contributor) Andrew Salkey, editor, *Stories from the Caribbean,* Elek, 1965, published as *Island Voices,* Liveright, 1970.
The Sociology of Slavery: An Analysis of the Origins, Development, and Structure of Negro Slave Society in Jamaica, MacGibbon & Kee, 1967, Farleigh Dickinson University Press, 1969.
An Absence of Ruins (novel), Hutchinson, 1967.
Die the Long Day (novel), Morrow, 1972.
Ethnic Chauvinism: The Reactionary Impulse, Stein & Day, 1977.
Slavery and Social Death: A Comparative Study, Harvard University Press, 1982.

Contributor of articles and short fiction to periodicals. Member of editorial board, *New Left Review,* 1965-66.

WORK IN PROGRESS: The Dark Side of Freedom: An Historical Sociology of the Western Mind (working title), for Basic Books.

SIDELIGHTS: Orlando Patterson's novels and scholarly work both reflect his West Indian background. Born in Jamaica, Patterson brings new insights to his subjects, whether they be the slave societies of his sociological studies or the Caribbean characters of his novels. His first novel, *The Children of Sisyphus,* is recognized as "a Jamaican landmark" by Richard Deveson in the *Times Literary Supplement.* Another novel, *Die the Long Day,* "once again looks at West Indian society through the anguish of its indomitable women," describes Jan Carew in the *New York Times Book Review.* Set on a colonial Jamaican sugar plantation, the work focuses on the attempts of a slave, Quasheba, to save her daughter from the syphilitic advances of a plantation owner. By focusing his story on Quasheba's struggle with the plantation system, Patterson "throws new light on this unstable situation and on the subtleties of the master-slave relationship," observes Carew. "In so doing, he gives a better understanding on contemporary West Indian society."

Patterson's focus on slave societies in his fiction is reflected in his sociological studies of slavery and ethnic issues. Although Patterson is dealing with social issues in his scholarly works, he uses historical research and techniques as his basis. [...] *The Sociology of Slavery: An Analysis of the Origins, Development, and Structure of Negro Slave Society in Jamaica,* [...] thor has used "the critical techniques of the historian in [...] rang[...]g information and deriving conclusions from his wide- [...] writer [...] cumentation," relates a *Times Literary Supplement* [...] ugh the critic remarks that some of Patterson's assumptions are questionable, overall he finds that ''Dr. Patterson has asked new questions and elicited some new answers.... [He] has much to say that is comparatively new and stimulating.''

Slavery and Social Death: A Comparative Study takes the historical emphasis of Patterson's earlier work on Jamaica and extends it through several centuries and cultures. Studying slave societies from Ancient Rome to Civil War America, *Slavery and Social Death* ''seeks a definition of slavery which is independent of [property] idioms and which provides a basis for considering the relations between the slave and the society into which he has, somehow, to be incorporated,'' summarizes Michael Banton in the *Times Literary Supplement*. In order to redefine the concept of slavery, Patterson uses sources from various fields, including history and economics, to support his theory. Remarks David Brion Davis in the *New York Review of Books:* ''No previous scholar I know of has gained such a mastery of secondary sources in all the Western European languages.''

Because of the broad base for Patterson's study, some critics find discrepancies and errors in the work. Davis finds that several points are unclear, and criticizes the author's ''inconsistency in portraying the fundamental contradiction of human bondage.'' Banton also notes several specific errors; he does admit, however, that for a specialist colleague in ancient history, ''Patterson's analytical model allows him to grasp the nature of slavery in the ancient Mediterranean world more securely than many professional classicists.''

For whatever shortcomings *Slavery and Social Death* may contain, its value lies in Patterson's ability ''to offer a coherent theory that challenges deeply rooted assumptions and presents new points of departure for further research,'' comments Davis. ''Patterson has helped to set out the direction for the next decades of interdisciplinary scholarship.'' Banton's assessment of the work reflects what other critics have said about Patterson's writing overall, his fiction included: ''Because it deals with fundamental issues both of past human life and of our attempts to understand it, *Slavery and Social Death* throws a questioning ray upon the present as well.''

BIOGRAPHICAL/CRITICAL SOURCES:

PERIODICALS

New Republic, February 11, 1978.
New York Review of Books, February 17, 1983.
New York Times Book Review, September 10, 1972.
Times Literary Supplement, April 13, 1967, July 13, 1967, September 9, 1983, October 24, 1986.
Voice Literary Supplement, December, 1982.

*   *   *

PEARY, Dannis   1949-
(Danny Peary)

PERSONAL: Born August 8, 1949, in Philippi, W.Va.; son of Joseph Y. (a professor) and Laura (Chaitan) Peary; married Suzanne Rafer (an editor), June 21, 1980; children: Zoe. *Education:* University of Wisconsin-Madison, B.A., 1971; University of Southern California, M.A. (with honors), 1975.

ADDRESSES: Home—New York, N.Y. *Office*—15 Stuyvesant Oval 9B, New York, N.Y. 10009. *Agent*—Christine Tomasino, Robert L. Rosen Associates, 7 West 51st St., New York, N.Y. 10019.

CAREER: Writer, 1971—. Script reader for Brut Productions, 1975. Sports editor for *Los Angeles Panorama*, 1976. Photo researcher for Workman Publishing, 1977. Writer for syndicated radio program, ''The Tim McCarver Show,'' 1986.

WRITINGS:

UNDER NAME DANNY PEARY

Close-Ups: The Movie Star Book, Workman, 1978.
(Editor with brother, Gerald Peary) *The American Animated Cartoon: A Critical Anthology*, Dutton, 1980.
Cult Movies: The Classics, the Sleepers, the Weird and the Wonderful, Dell, 1981.
Cult Movies II, Dell, 1983.
(Editor) *Omni's Screen Flights/Screen Fantasies: The Future according to the Science Fiction Cinema*, introduction by Harlan Ellison, Doubleday, 1984.
Guide for the Film Fanatic, Simon & Schuster, 1986.
Cult Movies III, Simon & Schuster, 1988.
(Editor) *Cult Baseball Players*, Simon & Schuster, 1989.

Contributor to anthologies. Contributor of articles to newspapers and magazines, including *Philadelphia Bulletin*, *TV Guide* (Canada and America), *Bijou*, *Focus on Films*, *Take One*, *The Velvet Light Trap*, *Boston Globe*, *Newsday*, and *Films and Filming*. Contributing editor for *Video Times*, 1985.

SIDELIGHTS: The American Animated Cartoon: A Critical Anthology, edited by Danny Peary, is a collection of articles by animators and others involved in the animation industry. Selections include Art Babbit's explanation of the drawing techniques used in Goofy cartoons, and Richard Thompson's comments on his Road Runner-versus-Coyote film shorts and Bugs Bunny and Daffy Duck cartoons. Winsor McCay, R. Bray, and Vlad Tytla are among the other animators represented. Walt Disney's testimony before the House Un-American Activities Committee is reproduced in *The American Animated Cartoon*, as are John Canemaker's articles about several of the early developers of animation.

According to *Los Angeles Times Book Review* critic Charles Solomon, the book is ''valuable for the amount of information compressed in readily accessible form.'' He adds, ''the fact that enough serious criticism exists to fill a book like 'The American Animated Cartoon' is indeed a hopeful sign; this medium is finally receiving its due respect and attention.''

Peary told *CA:* ''I treat film as a pop culture: part art, part mass entertainment. I write for no specific audience, but my intention is to make the serious film student more of a fan and the fan more of a student. I choose projects that require research because I am very enthusiastic about film and want to learn as much as I want to enlighten the reader.''

BIOGRAPHICAL/CRITICAL SOURCES:

PERIODICALS

Los Angeles Times Book Review, February 11, 1979, October 12, 1980, September 9, 1984.
Philadelphia Inquirer, November 4, 1983.
Seattle Times, January 2, 1987.
Telegram-Post (Bridgeport, Conn.), October 1, 1983.

*   *   *

PEARY, Danny
See PEARY, Dannis

PENROSE, Margaret
[Collective pseudonym]

WRITINGS:

"DOROTHY DALE" SERIES

Dorothy Dale, a Girl of Today, Cupples & Leon, 1908.
. . . at Glenwood School, Cupples & Leon, 1908.
Dorothy Dale's Great Secret, Cupples & Leon, 1909.
. . . and Her Chums, Cupples & Leon, 1909.
Dorothy Dale's Queer Holidays, Cupples & Leon, 1910.
Dorothy Dale's Camping Days, Cupples & Leon, 1911.
Dorothy Dale's School Rivals, Cupples & Leon, 1912.
. . . in the City, Cupples & Leon, 1913.
Dorothy Dale's Promise, Cupples & Leon, 1914.
. . . in the West, Cupples & Leon, 1915.
Dorothy Dale's Strange Discovery, Cupples & Leon, 1916.
Dorothy Dale's Engagement, Cupples & Leon, 1917.
. . . to the Rescue, Cupples & Leon, 1924.

"MOTOR GIRLS" SERIES

The Motor Girls; or, A Mystery of the Road, Cupples & Leon, 1910.
. . . on a Tour; or, Keeping a Strange Promise, Cupples & Leon, 1910.
. . . at Lookout Beach; or, In Quest of the Runaways, Cupples & Leon, 1911.
. . . through New England; or, Held by the Gypsies, Cupples & Leon, 1911.
. . . on Cedar Lake; or, The Hermit of Fern Island, Cupples & Leon, 1912.
. . . on the Coast; or, The Waif from the Sea, Cupples & Leon, 1913.
. . . on Crystal Bay; or, The Secret of the Red Oar, Cupples & Leon, 1914.
. . . on Waters Blue; or, The Strange Cruise of the Tartar, Cupples & Leon, 1915.
. . . at Camp Surprise; or, The Cave in the Mountains, Cupples & Leon, 1916.
. . . in the Mountains; or, The Gypsy Girl's Secret, Cupples & Leon, 1917.

"RADIO GIRLS" SERIES

The Radio Girls of Roselawn; or, A Strange Message from the Air (also see below), Cupples & Leon, 1922.
The Radio Girls on the Program; or, Singing and Reciting at the Sending Station (also see below), Cupples & Leon, 1922.
The Radio Girls on Station Island; or, The Wireless from the Steam Yacht (also see below), Cupples & Leon, 1922.
The Radio Girls at Forest Lodge; or, The Strange Hut in the Swamp (also see below), Cupples & Leon, 1924.

"CAMPFIRE GIRLS" SERIES

The Campfire Girls of Roselawn; or, A Strange Message from the Air (originally published as *The Radio Girls of Roselawn; or, A Strange Message from the Air*), Goldsmith, 1930.
. . . on the Program; or, Singing and Reciting at the Sending Station (originally published as *The Radio Girls on the Program; or, Singing and Reciting at the Sending Station*), Goldsmith, 1930.
. . . on Station Island; or, The Wireless from the Steam Yacht (originally published as *The Radio Girls on Station Is-*

land; or, The Wireless from the Steam Yacht), Goldsmith, 1930.
. . . at Forest Lodge; or, The Strange Hut in the Swamp (originally published as *The Radio Girls at Forest Lodge; or, The Strange Hut in the Swamp*), Goldsmith, 1930.

SIDELIGHTS: Margaret Penrose was the pseudonym used to produce some of the earliest series fiction intended especially for girls. Dorothy Dale was the daughter of a Civil War veteran turned newspaper editor and publisher, living in a small eastern town; the series chronicled her adventures in school and out. The "Radio Girls" and the "Motor Girls" books were both attempts to create series for girls which would be as popular as the "Radio Boys" and "Motor Boys." Both these latter series, says Carol Billman in her *The Secret of the Stratemeyer Syndicate,* "depict protagonists who travel to seacoasts and mountains, confront hermits and gypsies, and untangle minor mysteries—in short, they do the things that would become staple activities for adventure series heroines."

Both Howard and Lilian Garis contributed to volumes under this pseudonym. For further information see the entries in this volume under Harriet S. Adams, Howard R. Garis, Edward L. Stratemeyer, and Andrew E. Svenson.

BIOGRAPHICAL/CRITICAL SOURCES:

BOOKS

Billman, Carol, *The Secret of the Stratemeyer Syndicate: Nancy Drew, the Hardy Boys, and the Million Dollar Fiction Factory,* Ungar, 1986.
Garis, Roger, *My Father Was Uncle Wiggily,* McGraw-Hill, 1966.
Johnson, Deidre, editor and compiler, *Stratemeyer Pseudonyms and Series Books: An Annotated Checklist of Stratemeyer and Stratemeyer Syndicate Publications,* Greenwood Press, 1982.
Prager, Arthur, *Rascals at Large; or, The Clue in the Old Nostalgia,* Doubleday, 1971.

*   *   *

PETER
See STRATEMEYER, Edward L.

*   *   *

PEVSNER, Stella

PERSONAL: Born in Lincoln, Ill.; married; children: four. *Education:* Attended Illinois University and Northwestern University.

ADDRESSES: Home—Palantine, Ill.

CAREER: Writer. Has worked as a teacher; has written advertising copy for a drugstore chain and for various advertising agencies; former promotion director, Dana Perfumes; free-lance writer of articles, commercial film strips, and reading texts.

MEMBER: Authors Guild.

AWARDS, HONORS: Chicago Women in Publishing first annual award for children's literature, 1973, for *Call Me Heller, That's My Name;* Dorothy Canfield Fisher Award, Vermont Congress of Parents and Teachers, 1977, and Junior Literary Guild outstanding book, both for *A Smart Kid Like You;* Golden Kite Award, Society of Children's Book Writers, and Clara Ingram Judson Award, Society of Midland Authors, both 1978, both for *And You Give Me a Pain, Elaine;* Carl Sandburg Award, Friends of the Chicago Public Library, 1980, for *Cute Is a Four-Letter Word.*

WRITINGS:

JUVENILES

The Young Brontes (one-act play), Baker, 1967.
Break a Leg!, Crown, 1969, published as *New Girl,* Scholastic, Inc., 1983.
Footsteps on the Stairs, Crown, 1970.
Call Me Heller, That's My Name, Seabury, 1973.
A Smart Kid Like You, Seabury, 1975.
Keep Stompin' Till the Music Stops, Seabury, 1977.
And You Give Me a Pain, Elaine, Seabury, 1978.
Cute Is a Four-Letter Word, Houghton, 1980.
I'll Always Remember You. . .Maybe, Houghton, 1981.
Lindsay, Lindsay, Fly Away Home, Houghton, 1983.
Me, My Goat, and My Sister's Wedding, Houghton, 1985.
Sister of the Quints (Junior Literary Guild selection), Ticknor & Fields, 1987.

SIDELIGHTS: Stella Pevsner wrote *CA:* "One of the reasons I find writing for children so satisfying is I know in advance my potential audience. Not *personally,* of course! Yet I'm reasonably aware of what will amuse, intrigue, delight or create recognition in readers of a certain age range.

"Having four children of my own has kept me in touch with young emotions, and the many friends who have trooped through the house have given me not only ideas for characters, but little quirky details that help spark a story.

"Recently, a writer of adult novels said to me, 'It must be great to get letters from kids. They're so candid.' True. Sometimes a child will ask, 'Did the things in the book really happen to you?' Of course they didn't. Things were different in my youth. Still, I'm pleased to think they seemed so real. Incidentally, there must be many *Elaines* around, because since that book was published several girls have written to ask, 'Do you know my sister?' One of my favorite letters is from a girl who said, 'Your book is like a movie in my mind.'

"Perhaps because of a life-long fascination with plays (and plays appear in several of my books) I do picture a story in scenes. While I tend to keep description brief, I see the people, what they're wearing, what they're doing, and where they are as they speak their lines.

"Besides being interested in theatre, ballet, art fairs and antique doll collecting I'm really tuned in to travel. Even as a child I couldn't imagine living my life without seeing the places I was reading about. In the past few years, between books, I've taken off for foreign countries. Once, in a Tokyo airport, a group of Japanese children singled me out to ask about life in the United States. My daughter, who was with me, said later, 'But how did they know you like kids so much?' Once, in India, some boys started out trying to sell me spices and ended up talking about. . .books! (Sure, I bought some spices, too.)

"All of this is to say that I really do enjoy young people, no matter where. Although the lives of children today are a great deal different from earlier eras, emotions and feeling remain the same. Kids still hurt, they still struggle, and they still triumph.

"I hope my books help by saying, 'Yes, life is like this sometimes. It's not always easy. But you can make it if you just keep trying. . .and keep remembering how to laugh.' Humor, I believe, is important in a book, for books and enjoyment go together.''

MEDIA ADAPTATIONS: A Smart Kid Like You was made into an ABC Afterschool Special in 1976, under the title "Me and Dad's New Wife."

BIOGRAPHICAL/CRITICAL SOURCES:

PERIODICALS

Language Arts, April, 1979.

*   *   *

PHARR, Robert Deane   1916-

PERSONAL: Born July 5, 1916, in Richmond, Va.; son of John Benjamin (a minister) and Lucie (a teacher; maiden name, Deane) Pharr; married Nellie Ellis, February 14, 1937; children: Lorelle (Mrs. Donald Jones). *Education:* Attended St. Paul's Normal and Industrial School (now St. Paul's College), Lawrenceville, Va., 1933, and Lincoln University, Lincoln University, Pa., 1934; Virginia Union University, B.A., 1939; Fisk University, graduate study. *Politics:* None. *Religion:* None.

CAREER: Employed chiefly as a waiter at exclusive resort hotels and private clubs, including a period at Columbia University's faculty club; novelist.

MEMBER: Omega Psi Psi.

AWARDS, HONORS: Grants from the Rockefeller Foundation, the New York State Council on the Arts, and other funding agencies.

WRITINGS:

The Book of Numbers, Doubleday, 1969.
S.R.O., Doubleday, 1971.
(Contributor) Abraham Chapman, editor, *New Black Voices,* New American Library, 1972.
The Welfare Bitch, Doubleday, 1973.
The Soul Murder Case: A Confession of the Victim, Avon, 1975.
Giveadamn Brown, Doubleday, 1978.

SIDELIGHTS: "Both a persistent social critic and a perceptive student of the human condition," Robert Dean Pharr "is committed to depicting the inevitable and often unpredictable tragedies of life," observes Richard Yarborough in a *Dictionary of Literary Biography* essay. Inspired by the example of Sinclair Lewis's novel *Babbitt,* Pharr writes novels that provide realistic insights into the life of black Americans. According to Yarborough, Pharr's first novel, *The Book of Numbers,* "confronts one of the most painful questions surrounding the Afro-American experience: How can ambitious, intelligent, energetic blacks . . . achieve the capitalist American Dream when the conventional roads to power and financial security are unjustly closed to them?"

The Book of Numbers relates the story of Dave Greene, a young black man who arrives in a small Southern town and begins making his fortune by running a numbers game. Many critics praise the novel for its lifelike portrayal of the community; a *Times Literary Supplement* critic writes that the novel has "a convincing sense of engulfment in that time and place of being *properly* there, rather than there because it is a bit like here." *New York Times Book Review* contributor Martin Levin echoes this assessment, commenting that "fortifying the novel's supple style is its inescapable vitality; it surges through The Block, bringing to life every major and minor invention.'' Pharr achieves this effect by creating ''vividly rendered characters who represent a large cross section of Afro-America in the 1930s,'' remarks Yarborough.

While Pharr's subsequent novels have not been as successful as *The Book of Numbers,* they still demonstrate the author's gift for creating realistic characters and places. *S.R.O.,* which takes place entirely within the walls of a Harlem single-room-occupancy hotel, follows the lives of various drunks, junkies, homosexuals, and prostitutes, both black and white, who live on the edge of society. ''Pharr's writing at the beginning is flawless,'' observes Jan Carew in the *New York Times Book Review.* ''His description of narrator Sid Bailey's alcoholic fantasies is so vivid that one is almost forced to look away from the page to avoid the smell of his putrid breath and the bite of his terror.'' Although Jerry Bryant thinks that Pharr romanticizes the ghetto and its inhabitants, ''there is an outrageous irony and an effective good-humored bitterness in his best writing,'' the critic comments in *Nation.* ''He has an acute eye for detail and an instinct for shaping a sentence.'' Because of the extreme length of the novel (almost 600 pages), however, Yarborough finds that the novel loses some of its impact as it proceeds. Nevertheless, he admits that ''at its best, *S.R.O.* is an alternately humorous and harrowing picaresque novel about a man desperately in search of a foundation, a rock upon which he might rest as he confronts a lifetime of failure, frustration, and emptiness.''

Pharr's next novels were passed over by most critics, but in his 1978 novel *Giveadamn Brown,* Pharr once again demonstrated his ability to create a ''knowing, surrealistically honest vision of life in Harlem,'' describes Garrett Epps in *Washington Post Book World.* Although a *New Yorker* critic finds the plot, dealing with an underground narcotics operation, ''contrived,'' the critic also remarks that ''the tough, emotion-laden dialogue and the scores of scarred lives the author describes ring absolutely true.'' Reflecting this opinion, Epps writes that when the plot of the novel seems tailor-made for a movie adaptation, ''no movie could capture the haunted, painful narrative voice which has always been Pharr's chief strength.'' ''If only through the sheer, relentless energy of his language,'' says Yarborough, ''his fiction consistently carries the existential message that while life is often a hell, it can not only be survived but lived to the fullest.'' The critic concludes: ''Chapters in an ongoing tale of physical and psychological endurance, Pharr's novels testify to the strength and resilience of the human spirit.''

MEDIA ADAPTATIONS: The Book of Numbers was made into a movie entitled ''Book of Numbers,'' released by Avco Embassy in 1973.

BIOGRAPHICAL/CRITICAL SOURCES:

BOOKS

Dictionary of Literary Biography, Volume 33: *Afro-American Fiction Writers After 1955,* Gale, 1984.

PERIODICALS

Nation, November 22, 1971.
Newsweek, June 16, 1969.
New Yorker, April 24, 1978.
New York Times, April 4, 1969.
New York Times Book Review, April 27, 1969, October 31, 1971, September 28, 1975.

Time, June 6, 1969.
Times Literary Supplement, October 30, 1970.
Washington Post Book World, April 9, 1978.*

*   *   *

PICANO, Felice   1944-

PERSONAL: Born February 22, 1944, in New York, N.Y.; son of Phillip (a grocer) and Ann (Del Santo) Picano. *Education:* Queens College of the City University of New York, B.A., 1964.

ADDRESSES: Home—307 West 11th St., New York, N.Y. 10014. *Agent*—Jane Berkey, Jane Rotrosen Agency, 226 East 32nd St., New York, N.Y. 10016.

CAREER: New York City Department of Welfare, New York City, social worker, 1964-66; *Art Direction,* New York City, assistant editor, 1966-68; Doubleday Bookstore, New York City, assistant manager, 1969-70; free-lance writer, 1970-72; Rizzoli's Bookstore, New York City, assistant manager and buyer, 1972-74; free-lance writer, 1974—; founder and publisher of the Sea Horse Press Ltd., 1977—; co-founder and co-publisher of the Gay Presses of New York, 1980—. Instructor of fiction writing classes, YMCA West Side Y Writers Voice Workshop, 1982—.

WRITINGS:

The Deformity Lover and Other Poems, Sea Horse Press, 1978.
(Editor) *A True Likeness: An Anthology of Lesbian and Gay Writing Today,* Sea Horse Press, 1980.
An Asian Minor: The True Story of Ganymede (novella), Sea Horse Press, 1981.
Slashed to Ribbons in Defense of Love and Other Stories, Gay Presses of New York, 1983.
Ambidextrous: The Secret Lives of Children (memoir), Volume 1, Gay Presses of New York, 1985.
Window Elegies (poetry), Close Grip Press, 1986.
''Immortal'' (play with music; based on Picano's novella *An Asian Minor: The True Story of Ganymede*), produced Off-Off Broadway, 1986.
''One o'Clock'' (one-act play), produced Off-Off Broadway, 1986.

NOVELS

Smart as the Devil, Arbor House, 1975.
Eyes, Arbor House, 1976.
The Mesmerist, Delacorte, 1977.
The Lure, Delacorte, 1979.
Late in the Season, Delacorte, 1981.
House of Cards, Delacorte, 1984.

CONTRIBUTOR TO ANTHOLOGIES

Campbell, editor, *New Terrors, Number Two,* Pan Books (England), 1978.
Leland, editor, *Orgasms of Light,* Gay Sunshine, 1979.
Denneny, editor, *Aphrodisiac: Fiction from Christopher Street,* Coward, 1980.
Coffey, editor, *Masters of Modern Horror,* Coward, 1981.
Young, editor, *On the Line,* Crossing Press, 1982.
F. Grossman, editor, *Getting from Here to There: Writing and Reading Poetry,* Boynton/Cook, 1982.
Ortleb and Denneny, editors, *The Christopher Street Reader,* Coward, 1983.
Stephen Coote, editor, *The Penguin Book of Homosexual Verse,* Penguin, 1983.

Young, editor, *The Male Muse, Number Two,* Crossing Press, 1983.

Martin Humphries, editor, *Not Love Alone,* Gay Mens Press (London), 1985.

George Stambolian, editor, *Men on Men,* New American Library, 1986.

OTHER

Also author of the screenplay "Eyes," based on Picano's novel *Eyes,* 1986.

Contributor of articles, poems, stories, and reviews to periodicals, including *OUT, Mouth of the Dragon, Islander, Cumberland Review, Connecticut Poetry Review, Cream City Review,* and *Soho Weekly News.* Book editor, *New York Native,* 1980-83.

WORK IN PROGRESS: A novel, *Shadow Master;* second volume of memoir, *Men Who Loved Me.*

SIDELIGHTS: Several of Felice Picano's works have been translated into French, Japanese, Spanish, and Portuguese. He describes his writing to *CA:* "In my poetry I am keeping a sort of notebook of fragmentary experiences and understandings. In the past, this meant a polarization of subject matter: poems dealing either with perceptions gathered from the world of nature as revealed in Big Sur or Fire Island; or poems dealing with contemporary aspects of urban life and characters—portraits of epileptics, deformity lovers, obscene phone callers, etc. Of late, however, my poetry has become more autobiographical—though not at all confessional—integrating interior and exterior worlds. And forms have changed from lyric and monologic to more experimental structures such as self-interviews, imaginary dialogues, and letters to unknown persons.

"In fiction I write about the possible rather than the actual, and so, I suppose, 'Romances' in Hawthorne's sense of the word, even with 'realistic' settings, characters, and actions. My novels, novellas, and short stories deal with ordinary individuals who are suddenly thrust into extraordinary situations and relationships which test their very existence. Unusual perceptions and abilities, extrasensory powers, and psychological aberrations become tools and weapons in conflicts of mental and emotional control. Previous behavioral patterns are inadequate for such situations and must be changed to enable evolved awareness and survival, or they destroy their possessor. Thus, perspective is of the utmost importance in my fiction, both for structure and meaning. I am dedicated to experimenting with new and old points of view, which seem to have progressed very little since the pioneering work of Henry James and James Joyce."

Picano adds that more recently he has begun to work in film and theater, starting with adaptations of previously written works: "These intensely collaborative efforts—apparently so very different than other solitary writing—have proven to be fascinating not only because I've learned the strengths and weaknesses in collaboration, but also because through experienced theater and film director's views of what the public requires, I've learned how completely idiosyncratic I and my perspective has been, is, and will probably continue to be. Few writing experiences can equal the intensity of theater rehearsals leading to opening night, and nothing can equal the simultaneous frustration and elation of having others speak the works you've written."

BIOGRAPHICAL/CRITICAL SOURCES:

PERIODICALS

New York Times Book Review, December 2, 1979.
Village Voice, December 24, 1979.

*   *   *

PILCHER, Rosamunde   1924-
(Jane Fraser)

PERSONAL: Born September 22, 1924, in Lelant, Cornwall, England; daughter of Charles (a commander in the Royal Navy) and Helen (Harvey) Scott; married Graham Hope Pilcher (a company director), December 7, 1946; children: Fiona, Robin, Philippa, Mark. *Education:* Educated at public schools in England and Wales. *Politics:* Conservative. *Religion:* Church of Scotland.

ADDRESSES: Home—Over Pilmore, Invergowrie, by Dundee DD2 5EL, Scotland. *Agent*—Curtis Brown, 162-168 Regent St., London W1, England.

CAREER: Writer. *Military service:* Women's Royal Naval Service, 1942-46.

WRITINGS:

The Blue Bedroom and Other Stories, St. Martin's, 1985.
The Shell Seekers (novel), St. Martin's, 1988.

ROMANCE NOVELS

A Secret to Tell, Collins, 1955.
April, Collins, 1957.
On My Own, Collins, 1965.
Sleeping Tiger, Collins, 1967, St. Martin's, 1974.
Another View, Collins, 1969, St. Martin's, 1974.
The End of the Summer, Collins, 1971, St. Martin's, 1975.
Snow in April, St. Martin's, 1972.
The Empty House, Collins, 1973, St. Martin's, 1975.
The Day of the Storm, Collins, 1975.
Under Gemini, Collins, 1976.
Wild Mountain Thyme, St. Martin's, 1979.
The Carousel, St. Martin's, 1982.
Voices in Summer, St. Martin's, 1982.

ROMANCE NOVELS; UNDER PSEUDONYM JANE FRASER

Halfway to the Moon, Mills & Boon, 1949.
The Brown Fields, Mills & Boon, 1951.
Dangerous Intruder, Mills & Boon, 1951.
Young Bar, Mills & Boon, 1952.
A Day like Spring, Mills & Boon, 1953.
Dear Tom, Mills & Boon, 1954.
Bridge of Corvie, Mills & Boon, 1956.
A Family Affair, Mills & Boon, 1958.
A Long Way from Home, Mills & Boon, 1963.
The Keeper's House, Mills & Boon, 1963.

PLAYS

(With Charles C. Gairdner) *The Dashing White Sergeant* (three-act; first produced in London, 1955), Evans, 1955.
"The Tulip Major," first produced in Dundee, Scotland, 1957.

Also author of *The Piper of Ordre,* with Gairdner, published by Evans.

OTHER

Also contributor of many short stories to magazines in the

United States and Great Britain, including *Good Housekeeping*, *McCall's*, *Redbook*, *Woman and Home*, *Woman*, and *Woman's Own*.

SIDELIGHTS: British author Rosamunde Pilcher specializes in "light reading for intelligent ladies," as she states in a *Publishers Weekly* interview with Amanda Smith. Pilcher has written over twenty novels, primarily in the romance genre, and in the past ten years has sold more short stories to *Good Housekeeping* magazine than any other writer. She began her career writing what she describes in the *Publishers Weekly* interview as "sort of mimsy little love stories for Mills and Boon" under the pseudonym Jane Fraser. In search of a new image, Pilcher moved from Mills & Boon to Collins, and from there to the American publisher St. Martin's, who published her bestselling novel *The Shell Seekers* in 1988.

The Shell Seekers, Pilcher's longest and most complex work, focuses on Penelope Keeling, an independent, offbeat British woman. Through flashbacks to the World War II era and the recent past, the reader learns of Penelope's idyllic childhood in Cornwall, England, her hasty wartime marriage, her troubled relationship with two of her three children, and the unexpected deaths of her mother and her one true love. Now comfortably settled in a country cottage filled with items from this rich but tragic past, Penelope draws strength and comfort from these cherished possessions—particularly *The Shell Seekers*, a masterpiece painted by her father, Lawrence Stern—and from the simple pleasures of gardening, letter writing, and sharing meals with friends and family.

Although *The Shell Seekers* is not autobiographical, the novel loosely parallels Pilcher's life in several ways. For instance, Pilcher grew up near the artistic community of Cornwall, and like Penelope, served in the Women's Royal Naval Service during World War II. She also is related by marriage to Victorian painter Thomas Millie Dow, who, as Laurel Graeber observes in the *New York Times Book Review*, "could have been a contemporary of the fictional Lawrence Stern." As Pilcher comments to Graeber: "I did feel that I had put a lot of myself down on paper. . . . I feel that if I had died the next day after writing [*The Shell Seekers*], everyone would know exactly what happened."

The Shell Seekers was warmly received by critics. *Washington Post* contributor Susan Dooley writes: "Pilcher's book is a story about all the steps of love, from the first flush of gratitude at finding a winter aconite specking the snow to the awe of discovering another person whose life fits into your own. There are no complex ideas or complicated events. And there are no trapezes set up in the bedroom so the characters can astound the reader with high-flying feats. *The Shell Seekers* is about ordinary people doing ordinary things, and Pilcher has made that seem every bit as important as it really is." *The Shell Seekers*, remarks a *Publishers Weekly* contributor, "is a satisfying and savory family novel, in which rich layers of description and engagingly flawed characters more than make up for the occasional cliche." *New York Times Book Review* contributor Maeve Binchy comments that the flashbacks "are done with the ease and charm of a kindly friend showing you a photograph album: not a mammoth session to glaze the eyes, but a gentle journey telling you these longed-for facts about people you already know." She concludes: "It is a measure of this story's strength and success that a reader can be carried for more than 500 pages in total involvement with Penelope, her children, her past and the painting that hangs in her country cottage. *The Shell Seekers* is a deeply satisfying story, written with love and confidence."

As a romance writer, Pilcher hasn't always received the respect she feels she deserves, but she hopes that the warm critical response and wide readership that *The Shell Seekers* has received will enhance her reputation. She explains in *Publishers Weekly*: "All my life I've had people coming up and saying, 'Sat under the hair dryer and read one of your little stories, dear. So clever of you. Wish I had the time to do it myself.' I just say, 'Yeah, fine, pity you don't'. I've been beavering away. And now I'm hoping that nobody will ever, ever say that again."

CA INTERVIEW

CA interviewed Rosamunde Pilcher by telephone on July 18, 1988, at her home near Dundee, Scotland.

CA: Your immensely popular new novel, The Shell Seekers, *is a bigger book, a larger and more complex story, than your earlier ones. It's also great fun to read. Does it seem to be bringing new readers to your work?*

PILCHER: It's hard to know. I've had such wonderful crits from all over the United States. I think in England they're inclined to be a little more what I would call literary; they don't review books unless they think they're fairly obscure, or very literary. Some magazines do, but those haven't come through yet. On the whole, though, the reception's been very good. It's in most of the bestseller lists in one form or another—not at the top, but there, in the first ten.

CA: The book came out later there, didn't it?

PILCHER: Yes, in June, and the booksellers did a big push for summer reading. The cover of the English edition is a reproduction of the painting in the book, the children on the beach. It makes a rather nice summery cover. I think that's been an added attraction.

CA: The United States edition, by St. Martin's, is beautiful, especially the flowered dustjacket.

PILCHER: I think it's a very handsome book, and I love the endpapers. They did very well, and I'm delighted with it.

CA: As you told Amanda Smith for Publishers Weekly, *the kind of people you wrote about in* The Shell Seekers *were familiar to you from your growing-up years. What was unfamiliar in the book? What did you have to do research on?*

PILCHER: I had to do a lot of research on paintings. I have a great friend who is the Scottish representative for Christie's, the fine arts dealers. He was enormously helpful. And funnily enough, I also had to do quite a lot of research back into the war. You think you remember, but you forget. With the part about Whale Island, which is the Royal Navy Gunnery School, where my character Penelope was being trained as a WREN, I got an old friend of mine who'd been the captain of Whale Island to read that chapter, just to make sure I hadn't got anything wrong. With the bit about the Americans being trained for combat, I took a little literary license, but not enough to offend anybody. And I had to do medical research. It was just small things like that, but it all took a bit of time.

CA: There are many threads to the plot of The Shell Seekers, *a lot of individual stories that intertwine. How did you keep track of them in the writing?*

PILCHER: I had it fairly carefully plotted before I started. The only thing that was difficult was knowing exactly when to slip the flashbacks in. I knew I was going to write a particular chunk, but sometimes I had to feel my way, to decide just exactly when it was going to come in. Apart from that, it was all plotted right from the beginning to the last page, practically.

CA: You manage to go beyond the ordinary tensions of plot and create real mysteries in your work. In The Shell Seekers, *for example, there was the question of where the sketches for Lawrence Stern's work were, if indeed they still existed, and who would get them; there was the mystery about the Scottish character Danus Muirfield.*

PILCHER: I think that everybody has mysteries in their lives, really—things that they don't tell other people about, that people find out about later. I think we all have bits of ourselves that we keep secret. The young Scotsman I found quite difficult to write. Halfway through the characterization, he became rather negative. I wanted him to be this rather secretive person, and yet he seemed to have had such a happy life, I couldn't quite think why he *was* so secretive. Then I hit upon the idea of the older brother who had died of meningitis, which slotted it much more into place. It gave Danus a much stronger motive for being rather secretive. He was, funnily enough, my most difficult character to draw, although he wasn't a very important one. But once I'd got that part settled, he fell into place and became a real person.

CA: Reading the portions of the book set in St. Ives, your fictional Porthkerris, I felt I was there, you made it so clear.

PILCHER: I was born and brought up in a little village only three miles away from St. Ives. St. Ives was our shopping town. We used to catch the little chuffer train that goes round the cliffs; that was how my mother took us shopping, because we didn't have a car. We went to school in St. Ives. We went to dancing class and to the beach there. So I did know it very well indeed. And I still go back, because my son's been living there and my husband's family are all there as well.

CA: Penelope Keeling is one of the nicest characters I've come across in recent fiction. She's also a very plucky lady, as are most of the female characters in your work. Is there a bit of you in most of them?

PILCHER: I suppose a little bit. But I'm not Penelope. I'm younger than she is. I made her older because I wanted her to be grown-up and to have experienced those few years before the war as a grown-up person. I'm not a manic gardener or anything like that. And I've got four children, who are all very nice, and a husband. I don't think Penelope was me. We were all so desperately conventional and closeted and well-behaved. I like to think that she was a free person, which none of us were. Because of her upbringing, she was much more liberal in her attitudes and much more grown-up. We were all terribly stupid girls; we were brought up in such a rigid pre-war society, and so many girls got married because they just couldn't think of anything else to do. It was tragic. Nobody was ever encouraged to go out and do their own thing or have flats in London or have careers. The whole thing was to think about

what "people would *say*." I suppose in writing about Penelope I wanted to imagine having had a life like hers, which I would really have loved. Maybe it was a bit of wish-fulfillment. And people in St. Ives, friends of mine who had artists or writers for parents, *did* live that way. There was a lot of tremendous creativity going on down there then—potters and painters and sculptors. They all had families, and we knew all the children. I always thought it was a lovely life.

CA: Houses are very important in your books. Do you imagine and create them in much the same way as you do your characters?

PILCHER: No. In a way, they're all real houses. Penelope's little house in Gloucestershire, Podmore's Thatch, was a real house, but it wasn't in Gloucestershire—I just put it there. The house in London was a real house, but not nearly so beautiful as the one I put in the book; it was rather a shabby old house. The cottage in Cornwall was just any little Cornish house, really; they're all like that. But again, it was put in a place where I'd known a big house. I just sort of changed them all around, but they're all based on fact. I love houses, and I love gardens. And I love the atmosphere different women create in them. I think it's very interesting.

CA: There's also the nice little London house in Voices in Summer.

PILCHER: My daughter lived in that one. Now she lives in Long Island, and the house is sold. It *was* a little house, very tall and thin. She lived there for about seven years.

CA: There's a strong emphasis on family in your writing. Would you comment on the importance of family to you?

PILCHER: I think it's terribly important. It's the most important thing of all. My children are now all grown up; the eldest is forty and the youngest is thirty. And they all live totally different lives, in different places. They all have different friends. But when they all come together, it's as though they'd never been away. They hug and kiss each other and scream with laughter and have a good time. But then they go, and that's it: they're all back in their own worlds again, doing their own jobs and bringing up their own children. But they're very close to each other.

CA: You knew at the age of seven that you wanted to be a writer, and, with encouragement from your father, started right in doing it. What kinds of things did you write when you were so young?

PILCHER: I wrote plays and I wrote terrible stories in an exercise book. I think I was lucky in that I was a solitary child. My older sister was five years older than I was and never wanted to do anything except read books; she never wanted to play with me. So I was very much cast on my own. Living as we did, you could go wandering off down to the beach and nobody bothered about you. It was very nice. I started then living inside my own head, and it was always a great comfort to me because I could disappear and escape into my own imagination. I was never short of something to do.

The writing grew from there. I suppose I was about sixteen when I wrote a little short story and sent it to Winnifred Johnson, an elderly lady who edited three women's magazines in London. She wrote back and said, "It's not right yet, but you'll get it.'' She was a tremendous help to me. She was like a very nice headmistress, a great lucky break in my life. Because of her, from the very beginning, I had a market to send things to, and knew I was going to get some sort of a comment. Finally she bought one of my stories, and that was the beginning.

CA: You also said in the Publishers Weekly *interview that, though you'd been writing successfully since you were eighteen, things had "really started working" by the time you were fifty. What do you think of as the turning point at that time?*

PILCHER: My agent, Felicity Bryan, had worked a lot in the States, and she went over for Curtis Brown and had lunch with Tom McCormick, who's the president of St. Martin's. He said to her, "Have you got a light romantic writer we could publish for women?" And she said, "Yes, I have." It all started from there. One of the books they published was called *Sleeping Tiger,* and I got a terribly good crit on it from the *New York Times.* Then people began to be interested. And then *Good Housekeeping* started reading and buying my work, which was terrific. It snowballed from there.

CA: And through the years you've sold a lot of stories to Good Housekeeping.

PILCHER: Yes, apparently I have. I hadn't realized how many, funnily enough, until someone said that they'd published more of mine in the last ten years than anyone else's. It's quite difficult, because they pay very well, and when it started I thought, I mustn't get greedy; I mustn't try and write for *Good Housekeeping.* I don't know why they're buying these particular stories, but whatever it is, I can't go out and find it. I've just got to keep writing for myself, the way I always have done. If they want it, it's a lucky chance. I usually sold the work in this country first. I never sat down and said, Now I'm going to write a story for the American market.

CA: How do you feel about the label "romantic fiction"?

PILCHER: I don't really like it much. I don't mind being called a writer of light fiction. But on the other hand, this is what I've written all my life, romantic fiction, because this is what sold, and I wasn't in it for the fun. I was in it for a job, to make some money for myself. I had so many other things to do, bringing up four little children. And I'm not brilliantly intelligent and well educated, so I had to do something I could cope with. And obviously romantic fiction at that time was the thing that was selling. The magazines couldn't get enough of it.

CA: You've said you write on an "old steam typewriter." Have you been at all tempted to try a computer?

PILCHER: Not in the very least. I bought an electric typewriter, just an ordinary portable one, about five years ago. I worked and worked at it, and at the end of about six weeks, I burst into tears and gave it to my son. I just couldn't work it. I know I wouldn't be able to work a computer if I couldn't even work an electric typewriter! I went back to my old one. One of the girls came up from Hodder & Stoughton, the London publishers, the other day, and she asked, "Where do you write your books?" I said, "I'll show you." We went along to this extremely small bedroom, which looked very neat—I had the bed made up for someone who might come and stay. There was this little typewriter sitting on the table, and she

simply couldn't believe it. There were no books, no dictionary or anything, because it was a bedroom. Very unprofessional.

CA: Can you write short stories while you're working on a book?

PILCHER: I have got out of the way of writing short stories. After I finished *The Shell Seekers,* I didn't want to look at a typewriter. It had taken me two years. It's a bit of a habit writing short stories; if you get out of the habit, it's quite difficult to start again. You have to be so very brief, and I'd been writing a wordy book. It's such a different technique. I did write one short story while I wrote *The Shell Seekers,* but that was a long time ago. I think I could go back to them, but it's quite a change of gear between writing a very full novel and then just reeling off a little short story.

CA: What kinds of people do you get letters from about the stories and books?

PILCHER: I don't quite know. I would think half of the letters I've had on *The Shell Seekers* from the United States have been from older people who've related to Penelope, women in their sixties. I got one wonderful letter from an old gentleman who is a retired doctor living in Florida. I could just imagine him. He said, "Somebody gave me your book to read, and I never take any notice of what they say: I think they're stupid anyway. But after a week, I thought I'd read it." It was terribly funny. He was obviously a bad-tempered old gentleman, but he was actually writing to say he'd enjoyed it! I've had one or two letters from quite young people. And a lot from men—about a third of them. It's nice to think an intelligent man can read something you've written without being bored or offended.

CA: Do you make publicity tours?

PILCHER: I've just done a little one over here for the first time in my life. I did some television interviews and radio interviews and went to book shops. I'm going down to Exeter on Thursday, where there's a big new book shop being opened. But that's the end of it, I hope.

CA: Has there been talk of making a television series or a movie from The Shell Seekers?

PILCHER: Not so far.

CA: How would you feel about that?

PILCHER: Well, it would be great. The locations would be pretty if nothing else. And it wouldn't be too difficult. They did one called *Paradise Postponed,* by John Mortimer. *The Shell Seekers* is slightly the same sort of story as *Paradise Postponed,* with a legacy and a lot of people all wondering "why?" I think perhaps it might be a little bit too soon after that one for them to want it for television.

CA: You referred in an earlier interview to a big Scottish novel. Is that still just a thought at this point?

PILCHER: It is just a thought. I'm not really committing myself; I haven't decided yet. I can't do very much in the summer, because everybody comes to stay and the grass grows and everything. When the fall comes, I'll get my brain back into gear again. There's been such a lot to do with this book coming out, and I haven't had time to think. But I think the next obvious progression would be a Scottish one, one that would appeal to everybody!

BIOGRAPHICAL/CRITICAL SOURCES:

PERIODICALS

Library Journal, January, 1988.
New York Times Book Review, February 7, 1988.
Publishers Weekly, March 30, 1984, June 14, 1985, November 23, 1987, January 29, 1988.
Washington Post, January 12, 1988.

—Interview by Jean W. Ross

*   *   *

PINKUS, Oscar   1927-

PERSONAL: Born June 10, 1927, in Losice, Poland; son of Abraham (a teacher) and Chaja (Perelmuter) Pinkus; married Ilse Strasser, November 24, 1956; children: Dena, Michael. *Education:* Attended University of Rome and Polytechnic of Torino, 1945-47; Iowa State University, B.S., 1950; Rensselaer Polytechnic Institute, M.S., 1951; Harvard University, postgraduate study, 1953.

ADDRESSES: Home—25 Knightsbridge, Guilderland, N.Y. 12084; and 68 Segal St., Ashkelon, Israel. *Office*—c/o Mechanical Technology, Inc., 968 Albany-Shaker Rd., Latham, N.Y. 12110.

CAREER: General Electric Co., Lynn, Mass., research engineer; Republic Aviation, Farmingdale, N.Y., researcher in gas dynamics; Israel Institute of Technology, Haifa, Israel, aeronautics professor; Mechanical Technology, Inc., Latham, N.Y., senior consultant in fluid dynamics.

MEMBER: American Society of Mechanical Engineers.

WRITINGS:

(With B. Sternlicht) *Theory of Hydrodynamic Lubrication,* McGraw, 1961.
Friends and Lovers (novel), World Publishing, 1963.
The House of Ashes (autobiography), World Publishing, 1964.
A Choice of Masks (autobiography), Prentice-Hall, 1970.
(With D. F. Wilcock) *Strategy for Energy Conservation through Tribology,* American Society of Mechanical Engineers, 1977, 2nd edition, 1982.
Embers (poems), Poets' and Painters' Press (London), 1979.
The Son of Zelman (novel), Schenkman, 1982.

WORK IN PROGRESS: Victor, a novel; *A Second Birth,* a novel; *The Black Crusade: Hitler's Aims and Strategy in the Second World War; Thermal Aspects of Fluid Film Tribology.*

SIDELIGHTS: Besides his native country of Poland, Oscar Pinkus has lived in Italy, Israel, Spain, and England; he speaks and writes Italian, Hebrew, and German.

BIOGRAPHICAL/CRITICAL SOURCES:

BOOKS

Pinkus, Oscar, *The House of Ashes* (autobiography), World Publishing, 1964.
Pinkus, Oscar, *A Choice of Masks* (autobiography), Prentice-Hall, 1970.

PERIODICALS

New Yorker, September 21, 1963, April 10, 1970.

New York Review of Books, April 8, 1965.
New York Times Book Review, May 19, 1963, October 25, 1964.

*   *   *

PISAR, Samuel   1929-

PERSONAL: Born March 18, 1929, in Bialystok, Poland; came to the United States in 1953; naturalized by special act of Congress in 1961; son of David (a businessman) and Helaina (Suchowolski) Pisar; married Norma Marmorston, December 30, 1955 (divorced, 1971); married Judith Frehm (an art expert), September 2, 1971; children: (first marriage) Helaina, Alexandra; (second marriage) Leah. *Education:* Queens College, University of Melbourne, LL.B. (with honors), 1953; Harvard University, LL.M., 1955, S.J.D., 1959; University of Paris, Doctor of Law, 1969.

ADDRESSES: Home—23 Square de l'Avenue Foch, 75016 Paris, France. *Office*—575 Madison Ave., New York, N.Y. 10022; and 68 Boulevard de Courcelles, 75017 Paris, France.

CAREER: Admitted to Bars of Washington, D.C., New York, California, and London, England; UNESCO, Paris, France, legal counselor, 1956-59; member of President Kennedy's Task Force on Foreign Economic Policy and adviser to Senate Committee on Foreign Commerce and Joint Economic Committee of Congress, Washington, D.C., 1961-62; Kaplan, Livingston, Goodwin, Berkowitz & Selvin (law firm), Beverly Hills, Calif., and Paris, partner, 1962-72; Law Offices of Samuel Pisar, New York, Washington, D.C., and Paris, senior partner, 1972—. Barrister-at-law at Gray's Inn, London, and at Conseil Juridique, Paris.

MEMBER: World Center for Computer Science and Human Resources (vice-chairman, 1981—), American Bar Association, American Society of International Law, Association Nationale des Conseils Juridiques.

AWARDS, HONORS: Citizen of Honor, Aix-en-Provence, 1979; Kenneth B. Smilen *Present Tense* Literary Award, 1981, for *Of Blood and Hope;* Doctor of Humane Letters, Dropsie University, 1982; fellow, Carnegie-Mellon University, 1983; Medaille de la Sorbonne, 1983; Doctor of Law, Pepperdine University, 1984.

WRITINGS:

Coexistence and Commerce: Guidelines for Transactions between East and West, McGraw, 1970.
Les Armes de la Paix, Denoel (Paris), 1971.
Le sang de l'espoir, R. Laffont, 1979, translation published as *Of Blood and Hope,* Little, Brown, 1980.
La ressource humaine, Lattes (Paris), 1983.

Contributor of numerous articles on economic, financial and legal subjects to *Harvard Law Review* and other American, British, and French periodicals.

SIDELIGHTS: When Samuel Pisar was a young boy, the 1941 German invasion of his hometown in Poland changed the course of his life. Because of the event, Pisar was never to see his parents, sister, or grandmother again. He spent four years in and out of concentration camps, including Auschwitz, "the crown jewel of the star-studded Nazi archipelago of concentration camps," as Pisar labels it in his memoir *Of Blood and Hope.* As a result of what reviewers call cunning and good luck, Pisar survived the Holocaust and has since established himself as an international lawyer, with law degrees from Harvard University and the University of Paris. He has worked for the United Nations Educational, Scientific, and Cultural Organization (UNESCO), for the Kennedy administration as a member of the task force on foreign and economic policy, and he has represented several Hollywood stars, such as Elizabeth Taylor and Richard Burton. In 1972, Pisar set up his own international practice, the Law Offices of Samuel Pisar, in New York, Washington, D.C., and Paris, France. *Of Blood and Hope* is a record of Pisar's life events and his testimony of the power of hope. "Hope is never lost in life. I'm entitled to say that," remarked Pisar to *Publishers Weekly* interviewer Genevieve Stuttaford.

According to Nancy C. Hargrove in the *Dictionary of Literary Biography Yearbook: 1983,* Pisar presents "three distinct but inseparable subjects" in *Of Blood and Hope:* "On one level the book is an account of [Pisar's] experiences in the Nazi concentration camps of World War II and of the ways in which those experiences informed and influenced the entirety of his life; thus it falls into the category of 'Holocaust literature'.... On another level, *Of Blood and Hope* is an autobiography of a man who, against tremendous odds, achieved great success on an international scale, and in this sense it is an inspiring and hopeful work suggesting humanity's ability to endure and to prevail. Finally, it is a treatise on international politics and economics, with special emphasis on the need for coexistence between capitalist and communist countries, especially the United States and the U.S.S.R. It both suggests ways in which coexistence can be attained and warns of the horrifying dangers of 'a global Auschwitz' if this goal is not reached."

As an account of his Holocaust experience and of one man's ability to succeed in spite of his past, Pisar's memoir is viewed favorably. Although *Books of the Times* contributor Richard F. Shepard claims the reader might come to Pisar's memoir with mixed feelings, "as you read, you find this is an extraordinary case, a case that is more the material for a novel than one rooted in fact.... It is an autobiography filled with anecdote, yet it is more than mere recollection. It is about the emergence of a personality who is trying to find, out of his own experience, a path to the future." In addition, *Times Literary Supplement* critic George Theiner believes "the circumstances under which [Pisar] actually grew up, and his later 'reincarnation,' make this an extraordinary tale indeed.... Pisar brings to his story a narrative skill and a sharpness of intellect which lifts the book above the general run of concentration-camp literature.... This story of one man's moral and spiritual redemption makes inspiring reading."

If there is a controversy surrounding *Of Blood and Hope,* it has to do with Pisar's warning regarding future holocausts. Stuttaford records Pisar's feelings: "My book is a kind of confessional poem, a Homeric vision of things. I wanted to convey how in just 40 years I saw the world destroyed, then redeemed.... The next Holocaust will be the definitive one, a global gas chamber. Our capacity for evil is as great as our capacity for genius. Everything is possible.... But we can prevent future tragedies and doomsday itself. I hope my book inspires people to think in those terms." As *New York Review of Books* commentator Neal Ascherson sees it, Pisar has turned "the appalling experience of his youth into a prologue for prophecy.... He interprets his survival and his memories as involving his responsibility to the world rather than as an indictment against himself.... Pisar should be read, not only for what he suffered and saw but for what that suffering allows him to see today." In a very different vein, *Washington Post* contributor Allan A. Ryan, Jr., believes Pisar provides a lot

of "dead-end generalities[,] ...the result of Pisar's attempt to fuse the lessons of the Holocaust with the lessons of the power struggle between East and West that developed after the war and is with us still. It is not at all evident that there is much in common there, however much Pisar's own life may have spanned the two phenomena. The prospect of nuclear confrontation, frightening as it is, stands apart from the stupefying attempt at genocide that enabled ordinary men to slaughter their neighbors' wives and children." With a different viewpoint, Dorothy Rabinowitz senses "the ring of enlightened liberal opinion" in Pisar's memoir: "It is that opinion, not the lessons learned as a young boy in Auschwitz, that is reflected in Mr. Pisar's indictment of America's 'costly and far-flung military establishment.' Auschwitz taught its victims many lessons, but a distrust of the efficacy of arms was not one of them." These latter opinions notwithstanding, *Of Blood and Hope* is a work valued for its complex, multi-faceted themes, and as a treatise of hope.

AVOCATIONAL INTERESTS: Tennis, chess, photography.

BIOGRAPHICAL/CRITICAL SOURCES:

BOOKS

Dictionary of Literary Biography Yearbook: 1983, Gale, 1983.
Pisar, Samuel, *Of Blood and Hope,* Little, Brown, 1980.

PERIODICALS

Books of the Times, September, 1980.
Chicago Tribune, September 20, 1970.
New York Review of Books, June 12, 1980.
New York Times, November 15, 1970.
New York Times Book Review, September 27, 1970, June 29, 1980.
People, August 25, 1980.
Publishers Weekly, May 23, 1980.
Saturday Review, September 19, 1970, August, 1980.
Times (London), October 23, 1980.
Times Literary Supplement, October 31, 1980.
Wall Street Journal, April 28, 1971.
Washington Post, May 20, 1980.

—*Sketch by Cheryl Gottler*

*　　　*　　　*

POHL, Frederick Julius 1889-

PERSONAL: Born August 18, 1889, in Durham, N.Y.; son of Frederick Joseph (a clergyman) and Adelaide (Von Nardroff) Pohl; married Josephine McIlvain Pollitt (an author), May 14, 1926 (died, 1978); married Loretta C. Baker (an organ and piano teacher), 1980. *Education:* Amherst College, B.A., 1911; Columbia University, M.A., 1914, graduate study, 1914-15.

ADDRESSES: Home—83 Lindburgh Blvd., Westfield, Mass. 01085.

CAREER: Ohio Wesleyan University, Delaware, Ohio, instructor in English, 1911-14; State College of Delaware (now Delaware State College), Dover, instructor in English, 1915-17; Boys High School, Brooklyn, N.Y., teacher, 1917-51. Pohl has exhibited his paintings at the Atheneum Museum, Westfield, Mass. *Military service:* U.S. Army, Medical Corps, 1918-19; became sergeant.

MEMBER: American Revolution Round Table, Long Island Historical Society Club, Andiron Club (president) and Ship Lore Club (both New York).

AWARDS, HONORS: Distinguished achievement award, New York chapter of the Boys High School Alumni Association, 1986.

WRITINGS:

When Things Were New (nine plays), [Brooklyn, N.Y.], 1925.
(With Vincent York) *Brittle Heaven,* Broadway, 1934.
Amerigo Vespucci: Pilot Major, Columbia University Press, 1944, revised edition, Octagon, 1966.
Sinclair Expedition to Nova Scotia in 1398, privately printed, 1950.
The Lost Discovery, Norton, 1952.
The Vikings on Cape Cod, privately printed, 1957.
Atlantic Crossings before Columbus, Norton, 1961.
The Viking Explorers, Crowell, 1966.
The Viking Settlements of North America, C. N. Potter, 1972.
Like to the Lark, C. N. Potter, 1972.
Prince Henry Sinclair, C. N. Potter, 1974.
William Shakespeare: A Biography, Security Dupont, 1983.
The New Columbus, Security Dupont, 1986.
"Edward Bancroft: Undetected Patriot" (ninety-minute television play), Cable Vision, Inc., 1988.

WORK IN PROGRESS: An autobiography.

SIDELIGHTS: Frederick Pohl told *CA:* "No definitive or even critical biography of Shakespeare was possible previous to the publication of my *Like to the Lark,* because you cannot trace a poet's or playwright's growth in his art unless you know the sequential order of composition of his works in his formative years. Shakespeare scholars, arguing against each other, gave seven different years for the writing of Shakespeare's earliest comedy, and more than seven for [his commencement of] his autobiographical sonnets. They did not know when he went to London, what he may have written before he went there, or when he wrote the plays that appeared during his first few years in London."

Pohl considers his most important achievement to be his breaking of this "impasse by finding three corroborating statistical studies of stylistic propensities in Shakespeare's poetry which establish the sequential order of its composition. Now for the first time in four centuries a biography of Shakespeare" has been published. O. B. Hardison, former director of the Folger Shakespeare Library in Washington, D.C., calls the author's statistical research in *Like to the Lark* "unimpeachable, so far as I know, and I expect [it] will remain so."

Concerning his book, *The New Columbus,* Pohl told *CA:* "The Columbus biography is new in every detail. For example, Columbus came [from] a book-loving family. His father had a library in seven languages, and the title and cost of each book in it is in the history books. And his son assembled the largest private library of his century—20,000 volumes. *The New Columbus* has in it the recent findings of scholars in Europe, my own findings, and a hold-over of much material gathered when I was writing the biography of Vespucci."

*   *   *

POOTS-BOOBY, Edna
   See LARSEN, Carl

*   *   *

POPENOE, Paul (Bowman) 1888-

PERSONAL: Born October 16, 1888, in Topeka, Kan.; son of Fred Oliver (a businessman) and Marion Amanda (Bowman) Popenoe; married Betty Lee Stankovitch, August 23, 1920; children: Paul, Jr., Oliver, John, David. *Education:* Attended Occidental College, 1905-07, and Stanford University, 1907-08. *Politics:* Republican. *Religion:* Protestant.

ADDRESSES: Home—2503 North Marengo Ave., Altadena, Calif. 91001. *Office*—5287 Sunset Blvd., Los Angeles, Calif. 90027.

CAREER: Pasadena Star, Pasadena, Calif., city editor, 1908-11; West India Gardens, Altadena, Calif., agricultural explorer in Iraq, North Africa, India, and Europe, 1911-13; American Genetic Association, Washington, D.C., editor of *Journal of Heredity,* 1913-18; American Social Hygiene Association, New York, N.Y., executive secretary, 1919-20; date grower in Coachella Valley, Calif., writer and researcher, 1920-26; Human Betterment Foundation, Pasadena, secretary, 1926-34; University of Southern California, Los Angeles, lecturer in biology, 1933-47. American Institute of Family Relations, Los Angeles, Calif., 1930—, founder and general director, 1930-60, president, 1960-63, currently chairman of board of directors. Summer instructor at colleges and universities, including five years at Teachers College, Columbia University; lecturer at nearly two hundred colleges and universities. *Military service:* U.S. Army, Sanitary Corps, 1917-19; served on surgeon general's staff as director of control of infectious disease, 1917-18; director of section on vice and liquor control, War Department Committee on Training Camp Activities, 1918-19; became captain.

MEMBER: American Genetic Association, American Social Health Association, American Society of Human Genetics, Society for the Study of Evolution, American Eugenics Society, National Council for Family Relations, Human Betterment Association of America, Population Society of America, Sociedad Mexicana de Eugenesia (honorary member), Sociedad Argentina de Eugenesia (honorary member), Instituto Argentino de la Poblacion (honorary member), Cosmos Club (Washington, D.C.).

AWARDS, HONORS: D.Sc., Occidental College, 1929; Distinguished Service Award, Washburn University Alumni Association, 1955.

WRITINGS:

Date Growing in the Old World and the New, West India Gardens (Altadena, Calif.), 1913.
(With Roswell Hill Johnson) *Applied Eugenics,* Macmillan, 1918, revised edition, 1933.
Modern Marriage: A Handbook, Macmillan, 1925, 2nd edition published as *Modern Marriage: A Handbook for Men,* 1940.
The Child's Heredity, Williams & Wilkins, 1926.
The Conservation of the Family, Williams & Wilkins, 1926, reprinted, Garland Publishing, 1985.
Problems of Human Reproduction, Williams & Wilkins, 1926.
Practical Applications of Heredity, Williams & Wilkins, 1930.
(With Ezra Seymour Gosney) *Twenty-eight Years of Sterilization,* Human Betterment Foundation, 1930, published as *Sterilization for Human Betterment,* Arno Press, 1980.
Preparing for Marriage, Institute of Family Relations (Los Angeles), 1938.
Social Life for High School Girls and Boys, American Social Hygiene Association, 1941.
Marriage, Before and After, Wilfred Funk, 1943, reprinted, 1982.

Sexual Inadequacy of the Male: A Manual for Counselors,
American Institute of Family Relations (Los Angeles),
1946.
Marriage Is What You Make It, Macmillan, 1950, reprinted,
Abbey Press, 1970.
Divorce—17 Ways to Avoid It!, Trend Books, 1959.
(With Dorothy Cameron Disney) *Can This Marriage Be Saved?,*
Macmillan, 1960.
Sex, Love, and Marriage, Belmont Books, 1963.
(With Evelyn Millis Duvall and David R. Mace) *The Church
Looks at Family Life,* Broadman, 1964.
Techniques of Marriage and Family Counseling, Volume 1,
American Institute of Family Relations, 1972.
The Date Palm, edited by Henry Field, Field Research Proj-
ects, 1973.

Author of numerous pamphlets published by American Institute of Family Relations; also author of syndicated newspaper
column, ''Your Family and You,'' 1947—. Contributor to
scientific journals and popular magazines. Member of editorial
board, *Parents Magazine,* 1928—, and *Senior Citizen,* 1952—.
Editor, *Family Life* (monthly publication of American Institute
of Family Relations), 1940—.

WORK IN PROGRESS: Continuous research on techniques of
marriage counseling, and on sex differences among human
beings.

SIDELIGHTS: The American Institute of Family Relations,
founded by Paul Popenoe in 1930, has been called ''the first
organized attempt to bring all the resources of science to bear
on the promotion of successful family life.'' Popenoe prefers
to think of the institute as being devoted, not to the problem
of divorce, but ''to making marriages happy—which naturally
prevents divorce.'' In his writings and through the institute,
Popenoe expresses his conviction that ''almost any two normal
persons can make a success of marriage if they want to and if
they know how,'' and that ''a majority of all divorces are not
only unnecessary but undesirable for all concerned. . . . A very
moderate amount of effort before marriage, and in many instances even after difficulties become serious, would prevent
most of the broken homes'' which come into being every year.
Popenoe asserts that ''romance should be expected to flourish
better in an atmosphere of health, knowledge, and efficiency,
than in an atmosphere of ignorance, inefficiency, and disease,'' but he adds that ''most people do not seem to agree,
because they persist in marrying without any preparation.''

In his days as an agricultural explorer, Popenoe developed a
special interest in the cultivation of the date palm, and his
Date Growing in the Old World and the New, unique when it
was published, is still possibly the most complete treatment
of the subject. He collected and brought to America sixteen
thousand offshoots of famous varieties of date palms, which
formed one of the major foundations of the Southwest's present date industry.

Popenoe speaks French, Spanish, German, some Italian and
Arabic. Many of his books have been translated into German,
French, Dutch, Italian, and Japanese.

AVOCATIONAL INTERESTS: Gardening.

BIOGRAPHICAL/CRITICAL SOURCES:

PERIODICALS

Ladies' Home Journal, September, 1960.*

POWLEDGE, Fred   1935-

PERSONAL: Born February 23, 1935, in Nash County, N.C.;
son of Arlius Raymond (an auditor) and Pauline (Stearns)
Powledge; married Tabitha Morrison (an editor), December
21, 1957; children: Pauline Stearns. *Education:* University of
North Carolina, B.A., 1957.

ADDRESSES: Home and office—Route 3, Box 549, Hollywood, Md. 20636. *Agent*—F. Joseph Spieler, 410 West 24th
St., New York, N.Y. 10011.

CAREER: Associated Press, editor-writer in New Haven, Conn.,
1958-60; *Atlanta Journal,* Atlanta, Ga., reporter, 1960-63;
New York Times, New York, N.Y., reporter, 1963-66; free-
lance writer, 1966—. Lecturer, New School for Social Research, 1968-69. Consultant for a project on the nation's social
welfare system, Ford Foundation. *Military service:* U.S. Army
Reserve, 1957-63.

AWARDS, HONORS: Russell Sage fellowship in journalism
and the behavioral sciences, Columbia University.

WRITINGS:

Black Power—White Resistance: Notes on the New Civil War,
World Publishing, 1967.
To Change a Child, Quadrangle, 1968.
*Model City, A Test of American Liberalism: One Town's Ef-
forts to Rebuild Itself,* Simon & Schuster, 1970.
Mud Show: A Circus Season, Harcourt, 1975.
Born on the Circus, Harcourt, 1976.
The Backpacker's Budget Food Book, McKay, 1977.
Journeys through the South, Vanguard Press, 1979.
*So You're Adopted: A Book about the Experience of Being
Adopted,* Scribner, 1982.
*Water: The Nature, Uses, and Future of Our Most Precious
and Abused Resource,* Farrar, Straus, 1982.
A Forgiving Wind: On Becoming a Sailor, Sierra Books, 1983.
Fat of the Land, Simon & Schuster, 1984.
Adoption Maze: And How to Get Through It, Mosby, 1985.
You'll Survive, Scribner, 1986.

Contributor to periodicals, including *New Yorker, Esquire,
Penthouse,* and *Nation.*

WORK IN PROGRESS: A book on the history of the civil
rights movement, to be published by Little, Brown.

SIDELIGHTS: Fred Powledge's interest in race relations and
social upheaval stems, he says, from being a white Southerner
exposed to the ideas of both democracy and racism. A more
recent interest in environmental matters grew out of the realization that ''air, water, and earth need recognition of their
rights, just as people do.'' Bayard Webster of the *New York
Times* calls the author's *Water: The Nature, Uses, and Future
of Our Most Precious and Abused Resource* ''an invaluable
guide'' for ''those who want or need to know the intricacies,
significance, and genesis of our water problems.''

The environmentally-related issue of the healthfulness of today's food is addressed in Powledge's *Fat of the Land.* In this
book he is not, as *Los Angeles Times* contributor Carolyn See
notes, ''a ranting moralist exhorting us to go back to whole
grains and carrot juice.'' Instead, he ''does a thorough and
sometimes entertaining job of telling us how the food system
works, why it works the way it does, and what consumers
could do to change it if they really wanted to,'' according to
Molly Sinclair of the *Washington Post.*

BIOGRAPHICAL/CRITICAL SOURCES:

PERIODICALS

Los Angeles Times, May 7, 1984.
New York Review of Books, February 29, 1968.
New York Times, November 23, 1982.
New York Times Book Review, August 12, 1979.
Washington Post, July 25, 1984.
Washington Post Book World, January 9, 1983, August 14, 1983.

* * *

PRADO, C(arlos) G(onzalez) 1937-

PERSONAL: Born June 19, 1937, in Guatemala City, Guatemala; son of Carlos Gonzalez (an attorney) and Concha Prado; married Catherine Buchanan, August 26, l962. *Education:* University of California, Berkeley, B.A. (with honors), 1961, M.A., 1965; Queen's University, Kingston, Ontario, Ph.D., 1970.

ADDRESSES: Home—P.O. Box 105, Kingston, Ontario, Canada K7L 4V6. *Office*—Department of Philosophy, Queen's University, Kingston, Ontario, Canada K7L 3N6.

CAREER: Chaminade University, Honolulu, Hawaii, instructor in philosophy, 1965-66; Queen's University, Kingston, Ontario, lecturer, 1968-70, assistant professor, 1970-75, associate professor, 1975-83, professor of philosophy, 1983—. Visiting fellow at Princeton University, 1981-82, 1988-89; lecturer at colleges and universities.

MEMBER: Canadian Philosophical Association.

AWARDS, HONORS: Canada Council grant, 1972; fellow of Social Sciences and Humanities Research Council, 1981-82.

WRITINGS:

(Contributor) John King-Farlow, editor, *The Challenge of Religion Today*, Neale Watson, 1976.
Illusions of Faith: A Critique of Noncredal Religion, Kendall/Hunt, 1980.
Making Believe: Philosophical Reflections on Fiction, Greenwood Press, 1984.
Rethinking How We Age, Greenwood Press, l986.
The Limits of Pragmatism, Humanities, 1987.

Contributor of about thirty-five articles and reviews to philosophy journals. Member of board of referees of *Dialogue*, 1983.

WORK IN PROGRESS: A book on the rationality of suicide in advanced age.

SIDELIGHTS: C. G. Prado told *CA:* "My first book was a philosophical critique of contemporary trends in religion, my second a more interdisciplinary proposal about the role of fiction in conceptualization. In my third book I applied philosophical techniques to misperception of aging. My most recent book was a study of the limitations of pragmatic construals of science. In my new project I look at the issue of suicide as an alternative to serious mental deterioration."

* * *

PRESTON, James J(ohn) 1941-

PERSONAL: Born January 12, 1941, in Hollywood, Calif.; son of Louis (a painter) and Hazel (Lathrop) Preston; married Carolyn Pastore (a teacher), February 11, 1967; children: Christina Marie, Thomas Carey, Jeremy Winslow. *Education:* San Francisco State University, B.A., 1967; University of Vermont, M.Ed., 1970; Hartford Seminary Foundation, Ph.D., 1974. *Politics:* Democrat. *Religion:* Episcopalian.

ADDRESSES: Home—R.D. 3, Box 414, Glenn Dr., Oneonta, N.Y. 13820. *Office*—Department of Anthropology, State University College, Oneonta, N.Y. 13820.

CAREER: Principal of school for children with learning disabilities, Burlington, Vt., 1967-70; Utkal University, Orissa, India, research affiliate, 1972-73; Northwestern Connecticut Community College, Winsted, instructor in anthropology, 1973-74; State University College at Oneonta, Oneonta, N.Y., assistant professor, 1974-79, associate professor, 1979-84, professor of anthropology, 1984—, chairman of department, 1975-78. Visiting scholar at University of North Carolina, 1977; visiting lecturer at State University College at Plattsburgh, 1979. Public speaker. Manuscript reviewer for Burgess Publishing Co., 1978, and Indiana University Press, 1987. Director of local community program on coping with death, 1978; life member of N. K. Bose Foundation. Consultant, St. Anthony's Relic Shrine, 1986, and National Conference of Catholic Bishops. *Military service:* U.S. Army, 1962-63.

MEMBER: American Anthropological Association, American Academy of Religion, Association for Asian Studies, Society for the Scientific Study of Religion, Tantric Society.

AWARDS, HONORS: National Endowment for the Humanities fellowship, 1977; grants from American Council of Learned Societies for India, 1978, and New York State Office for the Aging, 1978; Walter B. Ford professional development grant from State University College of Oneonta, 1982, 1984; Dewar Fund grant, St. James Episcopal Church, 1985; experienced faculty travel award, New York State/U.U.P. Joint Labor Management Commission, 1985, 1987; research grant, Bureau of Catholic Indian Missions, 1986, 1987.

WRITINGS:

(Editor with Bhahagrahi Misra, and contributor) *Community, Self, and Identity: Styles of Communal Living in World Cultures*, Mouton, 1978.
Cult of the Goddess: Religious Change in a Hindu Temple, Vikas Publishers, 1980.
(Editor and contributor) *Mother Worship: Theme and Variations*, University of North Carolina Press, 1982.
(Editor and author of preface) *The Oneonta Faculty Convivium: Collected Essays I (1983-1984)*, State University of New York, 1985.
Sacred Centers: Development of a Classificatory Scheme, Mayur Publications, 1987.

CONTRIBUTOR

John Morgan, editor, *Critical Essays in Religion and Culture*, University Press of America, 1979.
Susan Seymour, editor, *Transformation of a Sacred City: Bhubaneswar, India*, Westview, 1980.
J. S. Yadava and Vinayshil Gautam, editors, *The Communication of Ideas*, Concept Publishing, 1980.
Giri Raj Gupta, editor, *Religion in Modern India*, Vikas Publishers, 1983.
Joanne Punzo Waghorne and Norman Cutler, editors, *Gods of Flesh, Gods of Stone: The Embodiment of Divinity in India*, Anima Press, 1985.
Alan Morinis, editor, *Journeys to Sacred Places: The Anthropology of Pilgrimage*, Cambridge University Press, in press.

H. C. Das, editor, *Folk Culture of India*, [Bhubaneswar, India], in press.

Iain Prattis, editor, *Anthropological Poetics*, University of Chicago Press, in press.

Also contributor to *Encyclopedia of Religion*, Volumes 5, 6, 12.

OTHER

Contributor of articles and reviews to anthropology journals, including *Science News, International Review of Cross-Cultural Studies*, and *Cultural Futures Research*. Anthropology editor of *Intellect*, 1977; reviewer of anthropology manuscripts for *Human Organization: Journal of the Society for Applied Anthropology*, 1980, and *Anthropological Quarterly*, 1983; associate book review editor of *Mentalities*, 1982-1983; associate reviewer for *Choice*, 1982—.

WORK IN PROGRESS: The Anthropology of Imaginative Experience and *The Making of a Saint: A Study of the Devotion to the Blessed Kateri Tekakwitha*.

SIDELIGHTS: James J. Preston wrote: "All of my work is devoted to a deeper understanding of the role of the human imagination in the development of our concepts of the universe. This is particularly true of my writings on religion. My forthcoming book on imaginative experience is an attempt to probe into the fundamental principles operative in the human imagination. Unfortunately, the social and behavioral sciences have neglected this vital aspect of human nature. Religion represents a powerful exercise of imagination in order to understand the many invisible forces believed to impinge upon our lives.

"My interest in Indian religions (particularly Hinduism) has included studies of temples as cultural institutions, the elaborate use of iconography, and the great variety of sacred imagery available for Indians to express their conception of the sacred."

*   *   *

PRICE, Richard   1941-

PERSONAL: Born November 30, 1941, in New York, N.Y.; son of George and Gertrude (Swee) Price; married Sally Hamlin (an anthropologist and writer), June 22, 1963; children: Niko, Leah. *Education:* Harvard University, A.B. (magna cum laude), 1963, Ph.D., 1970; attended Ecole Pratique des Hautes Etudes, 1963-64.

ADDRESSES: Home—Anse Chaudiere, 97217 Anses d'Arlet, Martinique.

CAREER: Yale University, New Haven, Conn., lecturer, 1969, assistant professor, 1970-73, associate professor of anthropology, 1973-74; Johns Hopkins University, Baltimore, Md., professor of anthropology, 1974-87, chairman of department, 1974-77, 1979-85. Guest curator of Museum of Cultural History, University of California, Los Angeles, and of Walters Art Gallery, Baltimore, 1978-81; visiting professor, University of Paris, 1985-87, and University of Minnesota, 1987-88. Has conducted field research in Peru, 1961, Martinique, 1962-63, 1983, 1986, 1988, Andalusia, 1964, Mexico, 1965-66, and Suriname, 1966-68, 1974, 1975, 1976, 1978, 1979.

MEMBER: American Anthropological Association, American Ethnological Society, African Studies Association, Royal Anthropological Institute (Great Britain), Koninklijk Instituut voor Taal, Landed Volkenkunde, Phi Beta Kappa, Sigma Xi.

AWARDS, HONORS: Social Science Research Council and American Council of Learned Societies for Latin America fellowship, 1972-73; African Studies Association grant, 1972-73; Sigma Xi grant, 1974; National Science Foundation grant, 1976-78; fellowship in residence, Netherlands Institute for Advanced Study, 1977-78; American Council of Learned Societies fellowship, 1978; senior Fulbright fellowship for University of Leiden and University of Utrecht, 1981-82; National Endowment for the Humanities research grant, 1981-83; Elsie Clews Parsons Prize, American Folklore Society, 1984, for *First-Time: The Historical Vision of an Afro-American People;* Centre National de la Reserche Scientifique Research fellowship, 1986-87.

WRITINGS:

(Editor and author of introduction) *Maroon Societies: Rebel Slave Communities in the Americas*, Doubleday, 1973, revised edition, Johns Hopkins Press, 1979.

Saramaka Social Structure: Analysis of a Maroon Society in Surinam (monograph), Institute of Caribbean Studies, University of Puerto Rico, 1975.

(With Sidney W. Mintz) *An Anthropological Approach to the Afro-American Past*, ISHI Publications, 1976.

The Guiana Maroons: A Historical and Bibliographical Introduction, Johns Hopkins University Press, 1976.

(With wife, Sally Price) *Music from Saramaka: A Dynamic Afro-American Tradition* (sound recording), Folkways Records, 1977.

(With S. Price) *Afro-American Arts of the Suriname Rain Forest*, University of California Press, 1980.

First-Time: The Historical Vision of an Afro-American People, Johns Hopkins University Press, 1983.

To Slay the Hydra: Dutch Colonial Perspectives of the Saramaka Wars, Karoma, 1983.

(With S. Price, editor and author of introduction and notes) John Gabriel Stedman, *Narrative of a Five Years Expedition against the Revolted Negroes of Surinam*, Johns Hopkins University Press, 1988.

Representations of Slavery: John Gabriel Stedman's "Minnesota" Manuscripts, James Ford Bell Library, 1989.

Alabi's World: Conversion, Colonialism, and Resistance on an Afro-American Frontier, Johns Hopkins University Press, 1989.

CONTRIBUTOR

Evon Z. Vogt, editor, *Aerial Photography in Anthropological Field Work*, Harvard University Press, 1974.

(With S. Price) Barbara Kirshenblatt-Gimblett, editor, *Speech Play*, University of Pennsylvania Press, 1976.

(Author of foreword) Roger Bastide, *The African Regions of Brazil*, Johns Hopkins Press, 1978.

Mintz, editor, *Esclave—facteur de production*, Dunod, 1981.

Mircea Eliade, editor, *The Encyclopedia of Religion*, Free Press, 1987.

(With S. Price) David Dabydeen, editor, *The Black Presence in English Art*, Manchester University Press, 1988.

Pierre Bonte, Michel Izard, and others, editors, *Dictionnaire de l'ethnologie et de l'anthropologie*, Presses Universitaires de France, 1988.

(With S. Price) Norman E. Whitten and Dorothea Whitten, editors, *Imagery and Creativity*, University of Illinois Press, 1989.

Gary H. Gossen and J. Klor de Alva, editors, *In Word and Deed: Death and Creation in the New World*, University of Texas Press, 1989.

Ira Berlin and Philip Morgan, editors, *Cultivation and Culture: Labor and the Shaping of Slave Life*, Cambridge University Press, in press.

OTHER

Contributor of about eighty articles and reviews to scholarly journals. Editor of "Studies in Atlantic History and Culture" series, Johns Hopkins University Press, 1974—; general editor of "Studies on the Non-Western Arts," G. K. Hall, 1980—.

WORK IN PROGRESS: Two Evenings in Saramaka: Afro-American Tale-Telling from the Suriname Rain Forest, with Sally Price; editing and annotating, with S. Price, *Stedman's "Surinam": Life in an Eighteenth-Century Slave Society*, for Johns Hopkins University Press; *Ensayos sobre arte afroamericana*, with S. Price; *Medard, or the Seine of History*.

BIOGRAPHICAL/CRITICAL SOURCES:

PERIODICALS

Times Literary Supplement, January 15, 1982.

*　　*　　*

PRICE, Sally 1943-

PERSONAL: Born September 16, 1943, in Boston, Mass.; daughter of Arthur T. (a librarian) and Pauline (director of a college scholarship foundation; maiden name, Randolph) Hamlin; married Richard Price (an anthropologist), June 22, 1963; children: Niko, Leah. *Education:* Radcliffe College, A.B. (cum laude), 1965; Johns Hopkins University, Ph.D., 1981; attended Sorbonne, University of Paris, 1963-64.

ADDRESSES: Home—Anse Chaudiere, 97217 Anses d'Arlet, Martinique.

CAREER: University of California, Los Angeles, Museum of Cultural History, senior museum scientist, 1979-80; University of Utrecht, Utrecht, Netherlands, postdoctoral fellow, 1981-82; Johns Hopkins University, Baltimore, Md., postdoctoral fellow, 1982-84, assistant professor of anthropology, 1984-85, assistant professor of anthropology and art history, 1985-86; Laboratoire d'Anthropologie Sociale, Paris, France, chercheur associe, 1985-87; visiting associate professor, University of Minnesota, 1987-88. Has conducted field research in Martinique, 1963, 1983, 1986, Andalusia, 1964, Mexico, 1965, 1966, and Suriname, 1966, 1967-68, 1975, 1976, 1978, 1979, 1987.

AWARDS, HONORS: Johns Hopkins University fellowship, 1974-75; Danforth Foundation Graduate fellowship, 1975-76; Atlantic History and Culture Program field grants, Johns Hopkins University, 1975, 1976; National Science Foundation Graduate fellowships, 1975-77, 1978-79; second prize, Elsie Clews Parsons Essay Competition, American Ethnological Society, 1977; Fulbright-Hays fellowship, 1977-78; Tropical South American Program grant, University of Florida, 1978; NATO Postdoctoral fellowship in science, 1981-82; Alice and Edith Hamilton Prize, University of Michigan, 1982; Wenner-Gren Foundation grants, 1984-85, 1985-86; American Council of Learned Societies fellowship, 1985-86; National Endowment for the Humanities grant, 1985-88.

WRITINGS:

(With husband, Richard Price) *Music from Saramaka: A Dynamic Afro-American Tradition* (sound recording), Folkways Records, 1977.

(With R. Price) *Afro-American Arts of the Suriname Rain Forest*, University of California Press, 1980.
Co-Wives and Calabashes, University of Michigan Press, 1984.
(Editor with Sidney W. Mintz) *Caribbean Contours*, Johns Hopkins University Press, 1985.
(With R. Price, editor and author of introduction and notes) John Gabriel Stedman, *Narrative of a Five Years Expedition against the Revolted Negroes of Surinam*, Johns Hopkins University Press, 1988.
Primitive Art in Civilized Places, Rutgers University Press, 1989.

CONTRIBUTOR

(With R. Price) Barbara Kirshenblatt-Gimblett, editor, *Speech Play*, University of Pennsylvania Press, 1976.
Johnnetta B. Cole, editor, *Anthropology for the Nineties*, Free Press, 1988.
(With R. Price) David Dabydeen, editor, *The Black Presence in English Art*, Manchester University Press, 1988.
Pierre Bonte, Michel Izard, and others, editors, *Dictionnaire de l'ethnologie et de l'anthropologie*, Presses Universitaires de France, 1988.
(With R. Price) Norman E. Whitten, Jr., and Dorothea S. Whitten, editors, *Imagery and Creativity*, University of Illinois Press, 1989.

OTHER

Contributor of articles and reviews to periodicals. *New West Indian Guide/Nieuwe West-Indische Gids*, book review editor, 1982-86, member of editorial board, 1982—; member of national advisory board, "Women and Culture" Series, University of Michigan Press, 1983—; member of editorial advisory board, *Hemisphere*, 1988—.

WORK IN PROGRESS: Two Evenings in Saramaka: Afro-American Tale-Telling from the Suriname Rain Forest, with Richard Price; editing and annotating, with R. Price, *Stedman's "Surinam": Life in an Eighteenth-Century Slave Society*, for Johns Hopkins University Press; *Ensayos sobre arte afroamericana*, with R. Price.

SIDELIGHTS: Sally and Richard Price's *Afro-American Arts of the Suriname Rain Forest* catalogues an exhibition of artifacts made by the Maroons (Bush Negroes) of Suriname that was presented by the Museum of Cultural History at the University of California, Los Angeles in 1980. "The Prices describe the cultural background of [the Maroons's] daily lives, and the many kinds of ritual which order their matrilineal society," describes Philip J. C. Dark in the *Times Literary Supplement*. "They go on to consider the nature and role of art in Maroon life." The critic concludes by calling the Prices's book "an outstanding study in the relatively new field of 'ethnoaesthetics.'" Sally Price's *Co-Wives and Calabashes* uses a similar approach, exploring Maroon art from a different angle; *New York Times Book Review* contributor Alice Schlegel calls Price "the first person to devote an entire book to the lives and arts of the women living in northern South America." Besides being "a case study in art," *Co-Wives and Calabashes* "raises questions about neglected issues and is an interesting case study in the social context of tribal art."

BIOGRAPHICAL/CRITICAL SOURCES:

PERIODICALS

New York Times Book Review, June 17, 1984.
Times Literary Supplement, January 15, 1982.

PRINGLE, Peter 1940-

PERSONAL: Born June 28, 1940, in England; son of Herbert John (an air force officer) and Leslie (White) Pringle. *Education:* Oxford University, B.A. (with honors), 1962.

CAREER: London Sunday Times, London, England, reporter, 1968-75, New York City bureau chief, beginning 1975. Washington correspondent for London *Observer.*

WRITINGS:

(With others) *Insight on Middle East War,* Viking, 1974.
(With others) *Insight on Portugal,* Deutsch, 1974.
(With Peter Cole) *Can You Positively Identify This Man?: George Ince and the Barn Murder,* Deutsch, 1975.
(With James Spigelman) *The Nuclear Barons,* Holt, 1981.
(With William Arkin) *S.T.O.P.: The Secret U.S. Plan for Nuclear War,* Norton, 1983.
(With Nigel Hawkes, Geoffrey Lean, David Leigh, Robin McKie, and Andrew Wilson) *The Worst Accident in the World: Chernobyl—The End of the Nuclear Dream,* William Collins, 1986.

SIDELIGHTS: The Nuclear Barons by Peter Pringle and James Spigelman provides a complete history of nuclear energy in terms of both its military and commercial development. According to *Nation* reviewer Jessica Mitford, Pringle and Spigelman's ''valiant effort'' has succeeded: ''For the general reader, *The Nuclear Barons* is an excellent overview; for those who want to probe deeper, a valuable research tool with meticulous notes and bibliography. A felicitous collaboration.'' Mitford feels Pringle and Spigelman are at their best when describing the expansion of nuclear power from weaponry into the commercial arena, a description which also includes the authors's recollection of ''the extravagant hopes once held out for this source of energy . . . [and] the Machiavellian attempts to suppress data pointing to its dangers,'' writes Mitford. In the *Washington Post Book World,* commentator Gregg Easterbrook directs his attention to Pringle and Spigelman's argument that ''making electricity from atoms never made much sense, either economically or technologically. Yet utility executives and government officials the world over have longed for it, like boys dreaming of hot rods. They've sunk hundreds of billions of dollars into it, then often looked the other way when their dream machines produced more grief than power. . . . [Pringle and Spigelman] attribute most of nuclear power's appeal to the lure of 'Big Science'. . . . It is here that Pringle and Spigelman are most convincing, where so many critiques of the nuclear industry falter. They understand that human foibles and well-intentioned blunders, not sinister conspiracies, lie at the heart of the nuclear mess.'' Impressed with *The Nuclear Barons* on the whole, Mitford is disturbed by what she calls its ironic conclusion, the fact that Pringle and Spigelman feel there may be no alternatives to nuclear power. Writes Mitford: ''Would that [Pringle and Spigelman] would turn their exceptional talent for intelligible exposition of difficult subjects to a cogent discussion of alternative sources of energy! I should be first in line to buy such a book by these authors.''

AVOCATIONAL INTERESTS: Cooking, walking, sailing, flying, collecting fossils.

BIOGRAPHICAL/CRITICAL SOURCES:

PERIODICALS

Globe and Mail (Toronto), August 9, 1986.

Nation, May 8, 1982.
New York Times Book Review, January 31, 1982.
Spectator, February 20, 1982.
Washington Post Book World, September 20, 1981.*

*   *   *

PRITIKIN, Nathan 1915-1985

PERSONAL: Born August 29, 1915, in Chicago Ill.; committed suicide, February 21, 1985, in Albany, N.Y.; son of Jacob I. (in advertising) and Esther (Leavitt) Pritikin; married Ilene Robbins (a nutritional consultant); children: Jack, Janet, Robert, Ralph, Kenneth. *Education:* Attended University of Chicago, 1933-35.

ADDRESSES: Office—Pritikin Programs, 1910 Ocean Front Walk, Santa Monica, Calif. 90405.

CAREER: Self-employed in Chicago area, 1935-57, and in Santa Barbara area, 1957-76; Pritikin Research Foundation, Santa Barbara, Calif., chairman of the board, 1976-85. Director of Longevity Centers in Santa Barbara and Santa Monica, Calif., 1976-85. Inventor, with U.S. and foreign patents in chemistry, physics, and electronics; researcher of nutrition, exercise, and degenerative disease.

AWARDS, HONORS: D.Sc., Kirksville College of Osteopathic Medicine, 1982.

WRITINGS:

(With Jon Leonard and Jack Hofer) *Live Longer Now,* Grosset, 1974.
(With Patrick McGrady, Jr.) *The Pritikin Program for Diet and Exercise,* Grosset, 1979.
The Pritikin Permanent Weight-Loss Manual, illustrated by Joann T. Rounds, Bantam, 1982.
The Pritikin Promise: 28 Days to a Longer, Healthier Life, Simon & Schuster, 1983.
(With wife, Ilene Pritikin) *The Official Pritikin Guide to Restaurant Eating,* Bobbs-Merrill, 1984.
Diet for Runners, drawings by Nell Taylor, Simon & Schuster, 1985.

Contributor to nutrition and medical communications journals.

SIDELIGHTS: In the late 1950s, Nathan Pritikin was diagnosed as having heart disease. At the time, his doctors recommended rest and dairy products, advice which Pritikin said only made matters worse. After researching the topic for two years, Pritikin was convinced that his diet was the cause of his clogged arteries and, as a consequence, developed a strict diet and exercise regimen. As its main emphasis, the Pritikin regimen calls for a drastic reduction in the intake of fats and cholesterol, increased consumption of complex carbohydrates and high-fiber foods, and frequent exercise. According to Martil Weil in his *Washington Post* obituary notice for Pritikin, ''besides cutting back on the meat, milk and eggs dear to the diets of many Americans, Mr. Pritikin urged those who heard and read him to all but ban from their dishes and glasses such common ingredients as salt and sugar, caffeine and alcohol.'' Pritikin held fast to his regimen for almost thirty years, convinced that the right diet could add decades to a person's fruitful existence by not only preventing heart disease but by reversing the process in those already affected by degeneration. Pritikin took his program to the public by lecturing nationwide, by establishing three Longevity Centers within the United States, and by writing a handful of books, including his best-selling

The Pritikin Program for Diet and Exercise and *The Pritikin Promise: 28 Days to a Longer, Healthier Life*.

It was in 1976 that Pritikin opened his first Longevity Center in Santa Barbara, California. It was later moved to Santa Monica, California, and others were opened in Downingstown, Pennsylvania, and Surfside, Florida. For a fee of a few thousand dollars or more, individuals are guided through the Pritikin program, eating mainly fresh and cooked fruits and vegetables, whole grain foods, and minimal amounts of fish and poultry. In addition, participants regularly walk and jog. In 1985, *Los Angeles Times* writer Jack Jones interviewed Eugenia Killoran, spokesperson at the Santa Monica Longevity Center. According to Jones, "Killoran said 18,000 people have gone through the program. She maintained that the average participant shows a cholesterol decrease of 25% and a similar drop in body fat. She said 85% of those who enter the program with high blood pressure are off medication by the time they leave and that 50% of the diabetics depart no longer needing insulin injections."

At the same time that Pritikin was told he had heart disease, he was also diagnosed positive for leukemia. Although he was in remission for nearly thirty years, the disease resurfaced in 1984. The various cancer treatments Pritikin underwent caused dangerous side effects, including anemia, kidney failure, and impending liver failure. Suffering intensely, Pritikin took his own life in February, 1985. In that same year, results of Pritikin's autopsy were published in the *New England Journal of Medicine*. As Alan Parachini wrote in the *Detroit News:* "Pritikin . . . met his death by suicide with arteries like [those] of a young man. . . . The extraordinary condition of the vessels supplying blood to the 69-year-old Pritikin's heart is being hailed by advocates of the dietary regimen Pritikin pioneered as proof that his eating habits can reverse hardening of the arteries." Criticism of Pritikin's program has mainly revolved around three points: lack of long-term monitoring of individuals on the regimen; that the diet is needlessly restrictive and therefore too difficult to adhere to; and Pritikin's claim that the program could reverse heart disease. Despite the challenges to the program, in Killoran's opinion, "[Pritikin] touched a lot of people because of his commitment and drive. He was this little man who said, 'I'm going to wipe out heart disease,' and he did. No matter who attacked him, he kept standing and arguing and now . . . everyone is agreeing," recorded Jones.

Pritikin had previously written to *CA:* "The study of degenerative diseases has been my avocation, and since I have never had an employer to control my time, I have spent one quarter of all my working hours reading medical literature. The low incidence of atherosclerotic disease (such as cardiovascular disease, diabetes, hypertension, angina) in populations on low fat diets has been widely observed by many investigators. From this observation, I decided to see if putting people on a low fat, high complex carbohydrates diet would reverse these disease conditions.

"My first study of consequence, which I financed, was a twelve-month trial, very ambitious both in number of participants and in geographic extent. The study was done in 1974 with sixty physicians in twenty-two states and Canada who put two thousand patients on a diet that I designed. Later, I did a study in Long Beach, Calif., far more important because it was a controlled study. After a five-month trial, the results achieved on our diet were dramatic compared with the results on the American Heart Association diet. In addition to all the clinical improvements, the angiographic results indicated reversal of artery closure.

"I presented a paper at the 52nd Annual Session of the American Congress of Rehabilitation Medicine and the 37th Annual Assembly of the American Academy of Physical Medicine and Rehabilitation, in Atlanta. Ga., on November 19, 1975. Because of the very impressive results I reported, the local paper and the wire services gave it national coverage.

"In January, 1976, I opened the Longevity Center with nine patients and six spouses. Since then, because of our dramatic health improvements, such as saving people from bypass surgery, getting them back to health and taking them off medications, more and more patients over the months have come to the Center for our four-week therapy program of diet and exercise. By 1979, almost four thousand patients have been treated in our center, and the results continue to be better than any conventional medical therapy for degenerative diseases.

"In 1978, over six hundred physicians and health professionals attended our scientific meeting and were able to receive ten units of Class I Continuing Medical Education Credit, the same as a physician would receive if he attended an American Heart Association Conference.

"To widely disseminate our findings, I have spoken before many medical schools, hospital staffs, universities, the American Heart Association, and the American College of Cardiology. If I could have four hours of prime-time television, I could change the diet habits of half the people in the United States."

BIOGRAPHICAL/CRITICAL SOURCES:

PERIODICALS

Detroit News, July 4, 1985.
Executive, June, 1979.
Health, July-August, 1981.
New York Review of Books, February 21, 1980.
New York Times Book Review, July 1, 1979.
People, August 13, 1979, December 3, 1979.
Runner's World, December, 1984.
Us, June 28, 1977, May 15, 1979.

OBITUARIES:

PERIODICALS

Chicago Times, February 23, 1985.
Chicago Tribune, February 24, 1985.
Los Angeles Times, February 23, 1985.
Newsweek, March 4, 1985.
New York Times, February 23, 1985.
Time, March 4, 1985.
Washington Post, February 23, 1985.

[Sketch reviewed by wife, Ilene Pritikin]

Q

QUIGLEY, Carroll 1910-1977

PERSONAL: Born November 9, 1910, in Boston, Mass.; died January 3, 1977, in Washington, D.C.; son of William Francis and Mary F. (Carroll) Quigley; married Lillian Fox (a writer), May 22, 1937; children: Denis Carroll, Thomas Fox. *Education:* Harvard University, A.B. (with high honors), 1933, A.M., 1934, Ph.D., 1938. *Politics:* Independent. *Religion:* Roman Catholic.

CAREER: Princeton University, Princeton, N.J., instructor in history, 1935-37; Harvard University, Cambridge, Mass., instructor and tutor in history, government, and economics, 1938-41; Georgetown University, School of Foreign Service, Washington, D.C., lecturer, 1941-47, professor of history, 1947-76. Lecturer at Brookings Institution, 1961-77, U.S. Department of State Foreign Service Institute, 1961-77, and U.S. Department of Agriculture Graduate School, 1967-77; scholar in residence, Fairfax County Schools, Va. Member, U.S. Civil Service Commission, 1967-69. Industrial College of the Armed Forces, consultant and lecturer, beginning 1951, honorary member of faculty, 1968-77; Smithsonian Institution, consultant, 1957-60, collaborator, 1957-62; consultant to U.S. House of Representatives Committee on Astronautics and Space Exploration, 1958, U.S. Navy, 1964, and U.S. Air Force, 1966; consultant on social science curriculum to Montgomery County, Md., Public Schools, 1967-77.

MEMBER: International Society for the Comparative Study of Civilizations (council member, beginning 1971), American Historical Association, American Anthropological Association, American Association for the Advancement of Science, Academy of Political Science, American Economic Association, Society for General Systems Research, Conference on British Studies, English-Speaking Union of the Commonwealth (London; life), Royal Commonwealth Society (London), Anthropological Society of Washington, Harvard Club of Washington.

AWARDS, HONORS: Harvard traveling fellowship to archives of Paris and Milan, 1937-38; Georgetown University Vicennial gold medal, 1962, and 175th Anniversary medal of merit, 1964.

WRITINGS:

Evolution of Civilizations: An Introduction to Historical Anal-ysis, Macmillan, 1961, 2nd edition, Liberty Press (Indianapolis, Ind.), 1979.

Tragedy and Hope: A History of the World in Our Time, Macmillan, 1966, reprinted, Revisionist Press, 1984.

The World since 1939: A History, Collier, 1968.

The Anglo-American Establishment, Books in Focus, 1981.

Weapons Systems and Political Stability: A History, University Press of America, 1983.

Contributor of numerous articles to scholarly publications. Member of board of editors, *Current History,* 1961-77; book reviewer, *Washington Post Sunday Star,* 1965-72.

BIOGRAPHICAL/CRITICAL SOURCES:

BOOKS

Melko, Matthew, *The Nature of Civilizations,* Porter Sargent, 1970.

PERIODICALS

New York Times, December 9, 1965.*

* * *

QUINN, Sally 1941-

PERSONAL: Born July 1, 1941, in Savannah, Ga.; daughter of William Wilson (an army officer) and Bette (Williams) Quinn; married Benjamin C. Bradlee (executive editor of the *Washington Post*), October 20, 1978; children: Josiah Quinn Crowninshield. *Education:* Smith College, B.A., 1963. *Religion:* None.

ADDRESSES: Home—3014 N St. N.W., Washington, D.C. 20007. *Agent*—Sterling Lord Agency, Inc., 660 Madison Ave., New York, N.Y. 10021.

CAREER: Journalist and novelist. Worked as translator, librarian, secretary, public relations agent, actress, and dancer; *Washington Post,* Washington, D.C., profile writer, 1969-73; Columbia Broadcasting System (CBS) News, New York, N.Y., anchorwoman on "CBS Morning News," 1972-73; *Washington Post,* general assignments writer, 1974-80. Notable journalism assignments include political conventions and presidential campaigns in 1968, 1972, and 1976, Iran's [Persia]

2,500th anniversary celebration, and profiles of many famous personalities. Lecturer.

WRITINGS:

We're Going to Make You a Star, Simon & Schuster, 1975.
Regrets Only (novel; Literary Guild selection), Simon & Schuster, 1986.

Contributor of articles to *Esquire, Redbook, Family Circle, Cosmopolitan, New York, Vogue*, and *Harper's Bazaar*.

WORK IN PROGRESS: A sequel to *Regrets Only*.

SIDELIGHTS: Sally Quinn had no previous writing experience when she went directly to *Washington Post* executive editor Ben Bradlee to ask for a job. Bradlee agreed to give Quinn a chance and hired her as a reporter for the paper's "Style" section. In a relatively short period of time, Quinn's coverage of Washington's elite became the talk of the town, and Quinn herself quickly emerged as a well-known and frequently controversial reporter. With her talent for interviewing and her ability to zero in on the heart of an issue, Quinn was assigned to cover such events as political conventions and presidential campaigns.

In 1972 CBS courted Quinn to fill the co-anchor spot on their "CBS Morning News" program. Quinn was placed in front of the camera with no training, guidance, or previous television experience. Television critics and network executives criticized Quinn's on-air performance. Frustrated, Quinn left the program in January of 1973, after several months of what she describes to Jim Scott in *Editor and Publisher* as "a bitter, back-biting career. The worst part of it [was] I had to get up at 1:30 a.m. to do the show." She goes on to explain: "I didn't like the job for it was largely just reading the news. On interviewing for the *Post*, I often take two hours. This takes skill to draw out your subject. Anybody can read the news."

Quinn's experience during these months and her treatment by network executives is the basis of her first literary work, *We're Going to Make You a Star*. While some reviewers dismissed the book as "a get revenge" type book, other critics viewed *We're Going to Make You a Star* as an informative and entertaining look at one person's entanglement with network big business.

"I enjoyed this book immensely," states Eliot Fremont-Smith in the *Village Voice*. "Horrendous in scabby detail, and punctuated just often enough with hints of serious thought or at least of serious reporting . . . the book is, first and last, a jazzy entertainment. Oh, no, someone may say, it's about failure. . . . No, no, say I, it's about a fabulous success. Its own, her own. Tongues are wagging. Eyes are winking. Sally Quinn is back at the *Post* . . . famous once more, about to be rich, and felt sorry for."

After reading *We're Going to Make You a Star*, Anne Chamberlin describes Quinn in a *Washington Post Book World* review as "a golden creature of a new generation, with no time for faltering or doubt, or the other fuzzy obstacles strewn in life's path." Chamberlin continues writing that in *We're Going to Make You a Star* Quinn's "purpose is to show how she was misquoted and misunderstood and to shift the blame for her television disasters to the vulgar, inept, fear-ridden, sexist CBS producers and executives, who never prepared her for her job, ignored her suggestions, wrecked her self-confidence, and damaged her health." Similarly a *Publishers Weekly* reviewer

remarks that "while there's no question that the inexperienced Ms. Quinn was thrown into a sink-or-swim situation on TV, one can't help wondering why this supposedly savvy journalist didn't take on some responsibility for learning her new craft."

Eden Ross Lipson states in the *New York Times Book Review:* "[Quinn] took the job at CBS for the money, the fame, the potential of power and because 'it never occurred to me that I would be anything but terrific.' She has written an apologia for the same reasons. . . . *We're Going to Make You a Star* is [Quinn's] account of the nationally publicized meteoric fall of Sally Quinn, and it is a sad tale indeed."

Quinn's second book, *Regrets Only*, is a novel of power, influence, and relationships set in Washington, D.C. Jim Field of Toronto's *Globe and Mail* writes that most of *Regrets Only* is "a big, juicy gossip-laden tale, filled to bursting with wall-to-wall dialogue and an insider's knowledge of her subject." Christopher Lehmann-Haupt comments in the *New York Times* that Quinn "has achieved something enviable through her knowledge of the capital social scene. She has created the possibility of high drama, if not something approaching classical tragedy." Disappointed with the novel, however, Lehmann-Haupt believes that "out of her mountains of prose comes a mole hill."

But other reviewers see the book differently. In the *Washington Post*, Richard Cohen points out that "in its own way, [*Regrets Only*] takes apart and shows you how a certain segment of Washington works. It's very good on social Washington and on journalism, the stresses and strains and ethical problems." And Alessandra Stanley remarks in *Time* that *Regrets Only* "highlights a growing Washington phenomenon: reporters are no longer just ink stained hacks who cover the capital's celebrities; they have become, in fiction and fact, stars in their own right. In a town where power and glory are as ephemeral as the jobs that confer them, top reporters who stay put can become the most enduring part of the celebrity elite. It is a theme of Sally Quinn's novel—and of her life." Susan Isaacs concludes in the *Washington Post Book World* that Quinn's *Regrets Only* is "intelligent and absorbing. . . . A bright, flashy and occasionally amusing work of fiction that provides Washington with the same sort of glamour treatment Jackie Collins gave Hollywood and Judith Krantz offered Manhattan, Paris, and Beverly Hills. . . . In her first novel, Sally Quinn . . . has done a bang-up job of describing the glittery surface of life in the capital."

MEDIA ADAPTATIONS: The movie rights to *Regrets Only* have been purchased by American Broadcasting Co. and Warner Bros.

CA INTERVIEW

CA interviewed Sally Quinn by telephone on November 11, 1987, at her home in Washington, D.C.

CA: Regrets Only, published in 1986, marked not only your debut as a novelist, but also a change from daily journalism to a long spell of the solitary kind of writing. Were there some tough hurdles involved in making that leap?

QUINN: The worst! It was really, really hard. To me, having that sort of daily hit that you get in journalism was always exhilarating. You go out and do a story, and there's your name in the paper the next day. You get a kind of high from that

that you get used to. I've never had cocaine, but it must be like cocaine—an instant rush. In Washington it's even compounded, because the things you're writing about have national and international significance and consequences. You're writing about the most powerful people in the world, the people who *run* the world, and they all read your stuff. The paper runs your story, and the next day you go out and everybody's saying, "My God, I loved your story!" or "That was a great piece" or "How *could* you?" There's a furor—and I did write things that were very controversial, which makes it even more of a high.

Washington doesn't support writers; it supports journalists, and you're only as good as yesterday's story. If you're not writing about what's going on where the action is, forget it. We have people here like Larry McMurtry and Herman Wouk and Susan Shreve, a number of really fine writers. You would think that they'd be central characters, but they're not writing about what's going on, they're not involved in the daily power grind. Writers are not necessarily considered important unless they're writing about what's going on.

CA: Very different from New York, where they are centerstage.

QUINN: Yes. Different from any other place. Writers are usually the most revered, the most sought-after people, but not in Washington. But in journalism you have the rush, the high of having your name in the paper every day and having everybody see you, and then suddenly you're *not* in the paper every day. Then people will come up—if they make any effort at all—and say, "How's the book going?" And you say, "Fine," and that's it. When you're writing a book, there's nothing to talk about, whereas if people come up and say, "I liked your piece on Cap Weinberger," you have a whole conversation about Cap Weinberger. They don't care. It's not an introspective city at all.

The energy level in journalism is different too. There's more energy in a newsroom, probably, than any other room anywhere—except maybe the stock market. It's not like going to a private office to work, where you have colleagues nearby; everybody's in one big place. To come from that environment to a tiny room in your house where's there's nobody and no action and no nothing is extremely difficult. I actually did try it about two years before I took a leave of absence. I was gone six weeks and I cried every day. Finally Ben said, "I can't stand this anymore. You're going to have to go back to work." It took me two more years before I got the paper out of my system and was really ready to get to that solitary kind of writing. And I think that it was a very grown-up thing for me to do.

CA: People's perceptions of you change remarkably when you're not in an office. They tend to think you're not doing anything.

QUINN: That's right. When my book came out, and when it got on the bestseller list, I think everybody in the city was stunned. I don't think anybody really thought I was writing a book except my close friends.

CA: Some of the characters in Regrets Only *provided Washingtonians a great guessing game when the book was published. Given their similarities to real people, which you've acknowledged in your own comments about the book, were they hard to develop as fictional figures?*

QUINN: Well, I didn't take them from real people. It wasn't ever a case of taking real people and just changing the names and faces. I made them up. After I'd finished, I'd go back and read over the copy and think, "Oh, that person reminds me of someone." It has to come from somewhere, from some experience. But it wasn't a deliberate kind of thing. Most writers say that they write along without making an effort to copy a certain real person, but it just happens that your experiences come out on the page.

CA: You've always been able to deal with failure or inexperience in a positive way. You talked about that in "Failing with Style," published in Harper's Bazaar, *September, 1986, and to some extent in your book* We're Going to Make You a Star. *Do you feel that your lack of writing experience when you started out with the* Washington Post *was actually an advantage in some ways?*

QUINN: I do, because I never learned how to write like a journalist. I hadn't gone to journalism school; I hadn't started out on a small paper or in a Metro section where they tell you the five w's—who, what, where, why, and when—that have to be in the lead. The first time I went out to do a piece, I had covered a party. I called my boyfriend, who was a journalist at the time, and said, "I can't do this." It was 9:30 and my deadline was 11:00. I went into total panic. He said, "Don't write it like a newspaper story. Just pretend you're calling up a friend and telling her about the party, and do it that way." I think the lead of the story was something like "You wouldn't believe who was at. . . ." It just sort of fell into the piece. It was very chatty, very conversational. It was very revolutionary and it worked. The way I write is the way I talk; it's simple. I'm facile in the sense that I can write very fast, but I don't use eloquent language because I don't talk that way. I talk the way people talk, and that's the way I write, too, both in fiction and in journalism.

CA: Writing the book about your bad experience with CBS must have been great therapy. Did you start it immediately after you left television, or was it necessary to wait a while and distance yourself from it a bit?

QUINN: I started it almost right after I left. A friend of mine, Michael Janeway, was then at the *Atlantic.* He called me up and asked me if I would do a piece about it for the magazine, and I thought it was a good idea. So I sat down and it just came pouring out. It was so therapeutic. And after 13,000 words—he had asked for 3,000 or 4,000—I called him. He said, "Keep going. You've got a book." He really encouraged me. He said Little, Brown, which was then connected with *Atlantic,* would publish the book. So I kept writing. I wrote it in three months.

CA: You named names in We're Going to Make You a Star, *some for shamefully sexist and insulting behavior toward you, some for incredible mismanagement. Were there any repercussions from the book?*

QUINN: People were upset and angry, but nobody denied anything I wrote. The book is being reissued by Ballantine because of the continuing problems the "CBS Morning News" is having. Since my paperback came out and was successful, they thought it would be a good thing to do. I'm now a little worried about it, because some of the people I had problems with then and wrote about are now friends of mine. I hate to dredge the whole thing up. I didn't know that they were even publishing it until they had it in print. I've written a foreword and afterword for the new publication. In doing those I went back and glanced over certain parts of the book, and I was really shocked at how forthright I had been. I don't think I would do that today. I don't think I would be able to write that book today, because I'm a different person. I was a lot younger and angrier then than I am now, and I would handle it differently. I think I'm more understanding of people's mistakes and failures now than I was then.

CA: Do you think women have an easier time in television today than when you were at CBS in the early '70s?

QUINN: I have a lot of close friends in television, and I don't think women have a tough time today. I think the only thing that matters is ratings. But I want to make it clear that my situation certainly was not all due to the fact that I was a woman. They did the same thing to Robert Hughes several years later on ''20/20''—threw him in front of the camera with no experience. Here was an incredibly intelligent, witty, talented, attractive man, and the same thing happened to him. The public determines what works on television and what doesn't. I don't think an Oprah Winfrey could have survived ten years ago because she's black. The American public's receptivity is what determines what goes over on television. If the producers thought a woman would get the highest ratings on the evening news, you'd have a woman anchor. They don't care about anything but ratings. On the ''CBS Morning News'' with Diane Sawyer and Charles Kuralt, when the ratings started going down, they got rid of Kuralt, not Diane. I don't think it really matters one way or the other whether you're a man or a woman on television.

CA: As a reporter for the ''Style'' section of the Washington Post, *you gained a reputation for eliciting amazing revelations from people, even when they knew you'd be writing about them. Were there tricks to that?*

QUINN: I don't think there were any tricks, but it does seem to me that a lot of interviewers don't know how to go about interviewing people. A lot of reporters come on to a subject as adversaries; they're hostile or confrontational. If I'm being interviewed, that will close me up faster than anything else. I won't play. They'll get *yes, no,* very terse answers. If I'm doing the interviewing, my goal is to make the subject feel comfortable and open up, so I'm sympathetic, I'm friendly. And it works. Then people relax; they feel that you like them and they can confide in you. I don't think that's a trick; it's just common sense.

CA: In the course of your career you've done some interviews that most people would consider intimidating. Who was the hardest?

QUINN: The person who was the hardest to get anything out of was Warren Beatty. He is a master at giving an interview and saying nothing. You take all these notes, and then you go home and open your notebook and find that there's nothing to write; he hasn't said anything at all. But I don't think I've

ever really been intimidated by anyone I've interviewed. I've interviewed all the presidents since I've been working, but I don't find presidents very intimidating.

CA: Who was the most fun?

QUINN: Alice Roosevelt Longworth. I had a wonderful time with her. She had promised me an interview on her ninetieth birthday, and she had saved up a lot of things to say. So when I went to have tea with her, I spent about four hours and she really unloaded on me. I took a bucket with me and came home and dumped it out in my typewriter. That was really fun. And Big Ruby, the mother-in-law of Alabama ex-governor George Wallace. Characters are fun.

CA: What kind of advice would you give aspiring journalists on the Washington scene?

QUINN: It depends on what your talents are. I would never say to a young Bob Woodward, ''Make your name by going out and doing profiles.'' That's not what he does; he's the best investigative reporter in the history of the world. If you told me to be an investigative reporter, it would be a disaster. I don't have the patience for it. You have to go with your talents, do what you do best. I do think that one of the things people like to know about in Washington is what people are really like, the people who are in power. Who are these people making life-and-death decisions that have impact on all our lives? What are they really like?

I think there's a lot of mistrust of journalism and journalists around the country. People just don't like the press very much. Some young journalists who are hungry and want to make a name for themselves make the mistake of trying to emulate some of the older ones by being overly tough, trying to be hatchet people. That's not the way the best journalists operate. The best journalists think their mission is to provide information to the public and to tell the truth—to get at the truth, but not to get people. There's a big difference there, and a lot of young journalists lose sight of that. Their goal is to make a name for themselves. That will come if you do your work well, if you do good reporting and good writing. But it's not going to come the way you want it to if you just go out to get people in order to make a name for yourself.

CA: You told Time, *''All of a sudden, I didn't have an identity of my own. On the place card I was Mrs. Ben Bradlee.'' If this was a reference to getting married and becoming half of a couple, it's a problem that women have everywhere. How did you deal with it?*

QUINN: That wasn't when we got married; it was when I left the paper. I think there are not that many women who are married to men with as high a profile as Ben has. The fact that I have one too makes it easier. I also love Ben's success. I love the fact that he is who he is, so I'm never upset about that. A lot of women get angry about the fact that their husbands are the ones everybody wants to talk to. And in Washington, if you're not in power, you're nothing, so people treat the wives as if they were invisible—or occasionally the husbands, if they happen to be spouses of important women. I think you've got to have an enormous amount of self-confidence. What doesn't work is to get angry at your spouse, which a lot of people do. That's what I see happening more and more, especially in this day of women's emancipation. In the old days it was just assumed that women would be happy to have their husbands in the spotlight, but now women want that kind of attention too. If they don't have it, they get angry at their husbands, not at the world or other people, where the blame really lies.

CA: In the process of finding and reading articles about you, I had the pleasure of seeing a piece in House and Garden *on your Washington home, and one in* Architectural Digest *on the house in East Hampton. You're a terrific decorator. Is that a special pleasure for you?*

QUINN: I think the word my husband used last night was obsession. I'm doing two friends' houses—I don't do it for money, just for fun—and I lay awake all last night trying to work out a problem with one of the living rooms. I love it, but what I don't like is the hassle—dealing with the upholsterers, ordering the fabric, doing the paperwork. If I could do it as a profession, if I could walk in with a trail of minions behind me and assign the details to them, I would be a decorator in a minute.

CA: Washington has a lot of good writers of all kinds. In addition to friends at the Post, *do you enjoy the company of many other writers?*

QUINN: We see almost nobody but journalists and writers; we have very few friends who are politicians. We see a few lawyers, but almost all of them are connected with journalism, like First Amendment lawyers.

CA: Is Regrets Only *going to become a movie?*

QUINN: It's been bought by ABC and Warner Brothers. The script is in the second rewrite. Lee Remick wants to play the part of Sadie, but they're having problems with the script because they want to make it a one-woman thing for her sake. I don't know what they're going to do with Allison, and it's such a two-woman book, I don't know what's going to happen. You just can't care, or you'll go crazy.

CA: Is the sequel well under way? I've read that there was going to be one, and the book was really set up for a sequel.

QUINN: It is under way. But, you know, I didn't set it up for a sequel. I had no intention of doing one; in fact, I was going to do a nonfiction book after *Regrets Only,* I just didn't know what happened in the end. I had to end it on an uncertain note—I didn't know what else to do. It took me a year after I finished the book before I finally woke up one morning and realized what had happened in the story. My editor tried to talk me out of doing a sequel; she said they're very tricky. My publisher wasn't very enthusiastic. But I finally said, "I have to write this. It's the rest of the story!" So they finally agreed.

BIOGRAPHICAL/CRITICAL SOURCES:

BOOKS

Authors in the News, Volume 2, Gale, 1976.

PERIODICALS

Chicago Tribune, July 27, 1986, August 10, 1986.
Editor and Publisher, July 6, 1974.

Globe and Mail (Toronto), October 25, 1986.
Harper's Bazaar, September, 1986.
Los Angeles Times Book Review, August 24, 1986.
Newsweek, August 11, 1986.
New York Times, August 7, 1986.
New York Times Book Review, August 17, 1975.
People, August 18, 1986.
Publishers Weekly, June 9, 1975.
Time, August 11, 1986.
Village Voice, July 28, 1975.
Washington Post, October 18, 1986.
Washington Post Book World, August 10, 1975, July 27, 1986, September 6, 1987.*

—*Sketch by Margaret Mazurkiewicz*

—*Interview by Jean W. Ross*

*   *   *

QUINT, Jeanne
See BENOLIEL, Jeanne Quint

*   *   *

QUIRK, Lawrence J.   1923-

PERSONAL: Born September 9, 1923, in Lynn, Mass.; son of Andrew Lawrence and Margaret Louise (Connery) Quirk. *Education:* Suffolk University, B.A. (cum laude), 1949; graduate study at Boston University, 1949-50.

ADDRESSES: Home—74 Charles St., New York, N.Y. 10014.

CAREER: Writer for film magazines, and former editor of *Screen Life, Screen Parade, Screen Stars, Movie World,* and *Hollywood Stars;* editor and publisher, *Quirk's Reviews,* 1972—. Has also worked for *Lynn Item,* Lynn, Mass., *Boston Record-American,* Boston, Mass., *New York World-Telegram and Sun,* and as film critic for *Motion Picture Herald, Motion Picture Daily,* and other periodicals. *Military service:* U.S. Army, 1950-53; public relations assignments, 1951-53; became sergeant.

AWARDS, HONORS: Walt Whitman Award, 1979, for *Some Lovely Image.*

WRITINGS:

Robert Francis Kennedy, Holloway, 1968.
The Films of Joan Crawford, Citadel, 1968.
The Films and Career of Ingrid Bergman, Citadel, 1970, revised edition published as *The Complete Films of Ingrid Bergman,* 1989.
The Films of Paul Newman, Citadel, 1971, revised edition, 1981.
The Films of Fredric March, Citadel, 1971.
(Author of introduction) *Anthology of Photoplay Magazine, 1928-1940,* Dover, 1971.
The Films of William Holden, Citadel, 1973.
The Great Romantic Films, Citadel, 1974.
The Films of Robert Taylor, Citadel, 1975.
Some Lovely Image (novel), Quirk Publishing, 1976.
The Films of Ronald Colman, Citadel, 1977.
The Films of Warren Beatty, Citadel, 1979.
The Films of Myrna Loy, Citadel, 1980.
The Films of Gloria Swanson, Citadel, 1984.
Claudette Colbert: An Illustrated Biography, Crown, 1985.
Bette Davis: Her Films and Career, revised edition, Citadel, 1985.

Lauren Bacall: Her Films and Career, Citadel, 1986.
The Complete Films of William Powell, Citadel, 1986.
Jane Wyman: The Actress and the Woman, Norton, 1986.
Margaret Sullavan: Child of Fate, St. Martin's, 1987.
Norma: The Story of Norma Shearer, St. Martin's, 1988.

Contributor to *Variety, Photoplay, Modern Screen, New York Times, Films in Review,* and *Theatre.*

WORK IN PROGRESS: A major comprehensive biography of Bette Davis; a biography of James R. Quirk of *Photoplay.*

SIDELIGHTS: One of the country's leading film authorities, Lawrence J. Quirk is the nephew of James R. Quirk, founder of *Photoplay* and editor and publisher of the magazine during its glory days of the 1920s. Lawrence J. Quirk established the James R. Quirk Awards in 1973, for meritorious achievements in film-related fields. The award has been given to over twenty-two people, including Lillian Gish, Joan Crawford, and Blanche Sweet.

BIOGRAPHICAL/CRITICAL SOURCES:

PERIODICALS

Los Angeles Times, August 1, 1988.

R

RABINOWITZ, Alan 1927-

PERSONAL: Born January 18, 1927, in New York, N.Y.; son of Aaron (in real estate) and Clara (Greenhut) Rabinowitz; married Andrea Wolf (a psychiatric social worker), December 2, 1951; children: Eric W., Peter MacG., Martha L., Katherine W. *Education:* Yale University, A.B., 1948; Harvard University, M.B.A., 1950; Massachusetts Institute of Technology, Ph.D., 1969. *Politics:* Democrat.

ADDRESSES: Home—3400 East Laurelhurst Dr., Seattle, Wash. 98105.

CAREER: Affiliated with Fred F. French Investing Co., 1950-59; Regional Plan Association, New York, N.Y., member of staff, 1956-57; Arthur D. Little, Inc., Cambridge, Mass., member of staff, 1959-63; Urban Survey Corp., Cambridge, president, 1963-69; Boston Redevelopment Authority, Boston, Mass., administrator of program planning and finance, 1969-71; University of Washington, Seattle, professor of urban planning and chairman of department, 1971-86. Fellow, Harvard-M.I.T. Joint Center for Urban Studies, 1969. *Military service:* U.S. Naval Reserve, active duty, 1945-46, 1952-54.

MEMBER: American Institute of Certified Planners.

WRITINGS:

Municipal Bond Finance and Administration, Interscience, 1969.
Industrial Zoning in Seattle, [Seattle], c. 1973.
Development of the Real Estate Investment Industry, 1972-75, privately printed, 1978.
The Real Estate Gamble: Lessons from 50 Years of Boom and Bust, AMACOM, 1980.
Land Investment and the Predevelopment Process: A Guide for Finance and Real Estate Professionals, Quorum/Greenwood Press, 1988.

Contributor to planning journals.

* * *

RAND, Ayn 1905-1982

PERSONAL: First name rhymes with "pine"; original name Alice Rosenbaum; born February 2, 1905, in St. Petersburg, Russia (now Leningrad, U.S.S.R.); came to United States, 1926, naturalized, 1931; died March 6, 1982, in New York, N.Y.; buried in Kensico Cemetery, Valhalla, N.Y.; daughter of Fronz (a chemist) and Anna Rosenbaum; married Charles Francis "Frank" O'Connor (an artist), April 15, 1929. *Education:* University of Petrograd (now University of Leningrad), graduated with highest honors in history, 1924. *Politics:* Radical for capitalism. *Religion:* Atheist.

ADDRESSES: Office—The Ayn Rand Letter, P.O. Box 177, Murray Hill Station, New York, N.Y. 10016. *Agent*—Curtis Brown Ltd., 10 Astor Place, New York, N.Y. 10003.

CAREER: Worked as tour guide at Peter and Paul Fortress; Cecil B. DeMille Studio, Hollywood, Calif., movie extra and junior screenwriter, 1926-32, began as filing clerk, became office head in wardrobe department; worked as screenwriter for Universal Pictures, Paramount Pictures, and Metro-Goldwyn-Mayer, 1932-34; worked as free-lance script reader for RKO Pictures, then for Metro-Goldwyn-Mayer, both New York City, 1934-35; worked without pay as a typist for Eli Jacques Kahn, an architect in New York City, doing research work for *The Fountainhead,* 1937; Paramount Pictures, New York City, script reader, 1941-43; Hal Wallis Productions, Hollywood, Calif., screenwriter (worked under special contract which committed her to work only six months of each year; during the other six months she pursued her own writing), 1944-49; full-time writer and lecturer, 1951-82.

Visiting lecturer at Yale University, 1960, Princeton University, 1960, Columbia University, 1960 and 1962, University of Wisconsin, 1961, Johns Hopkins University, 1961, Harvard University, 1962, Massachusetts Institute of Technology, 1962. Presenter of annual Ford Hall Forum, Boston, Mass., beginning 1963.

AWARDS,HONORS: Doctor of Humane Letters, Lewis and Clark College, 1963.

WRITINGS:

NOVELS

We the Living (also see below), Macmillan, 1936, reprinted, Random House, 1959.
Anthem, Cassell, 1938, revised edition, Pamphleteers, Inc., 1946.
The Fountainhead (also see below), Bobbs-Merrill, 1943, reprinted with special introduction by Rand, 1968.
Atlas Shrugged, Random House, 1957.

NONFICTION

For the New Intellectual: The Philosophy of Ayn Rand, Random House, 1961.
The Virtue of Selfishness: A New Concept of Egoism, with additional articles by Nathaniel Branden, New American Library, 1964.
Capitalism: The Unknown Ideal, with additional articles by Branden and others, New American Library, 1966.
Introduction to Objectivist Epistemology, Objectivist, 1967.
The Romantic Manifesto: A Philosophy of Literature, World Publishing, 1969.
The New Left: The Anti-Industrial Revolution, New American Library, 1982.
Philosophy: Who Needs It, with introduction by Leonard Peikoff, Bobbs-Merrill, 1971.
The Ayn Rand Lexicon: Objectivism from A to Z, with introduction and notes by Peikoff, New American Library, 1984.

PLAYS

Night of January 16th (produced as ''Woman on Trial'' at Hollywood Playhouse, October, 1934, first produced on Broadway under the title ''Night of January 16th,'' at Ambassador Theater, September 16, 1935; produced under the title ''Penthouse Legend,'' 1973), Longmans, Green, 1936, reprinted, New American Library, 1971.
''The Unconquered'' (adaptation by Rand of *We the Living*), first produced on Broadway, February 14, 1940.

OTHER

''Love Letters'' (screenplay; adapted from the novel of the same title by Chris Massie), Paramount, 1945.
''You Came Along'' (screenplay), Paramount, 1945.
''The Fountainhead'' (filmscript; adaptation by Rand of the novel), Warner Bros., 1949.
The Early Ayn Rand: A Selection from Her Unpublished Fiction, with introduction and notes by Peikoff, New American Library, 1984.

Co-editor and contributor, *The Objectivist Newsletter,* 1962-65, and its successor, *The Objectivist* (monthly journal), 1966-71; writer and publisher, *The Ayn Rand Letter,* 1971-76. Columnist for *Los Angeles Times.*

SIDELIGHTS: ''Ayn Rand is dead. So, incidentally, is the philosophy she sought to launch dead; it was in fact stillborn.'' William F. Buckley's derogatory obituary in the *National Review* sounded a note of wishful thinking on the part of Ayn Rand's persistent critics. More objective observers of the contemporary political and publishing scenes, however, might be moved to remark, as Mark Twain did upon hearing rumors of his own demise, that the news of that death was greatly exaggerated. Rather than quelling interest in her or her philosophy, Rand's death, in March of 1982, initiated a new era of academic interest and fueled the continued promotion of her philosophies by her followers. In the five years following her death there were as many books published about Rand as there were during all the years of her life. Some of her writing is also being published posthumously: *Philosophy: Who Needs It,* a volume of essays she had planned but did not complete, came out the year of her death; and *The Early Ayn Rand: A Selection from Her Unpublished Fiction,* was issued in 1984. Her novels continue to sell well as do some of her nonfiction works, and further publishing ventures are planned by her literary executor, Leonard Peikoff.

Ayn Rand, born Alice Rosenbaum in St. Petersburg, Russia, in 1905, occupies a unique position in the history of American literature. In many ways she was a paradox: a writer of popular romances whose ideas were taken seriously, a fierce individualist who collected many followers. Politically and aesthetically, she defied the cultural currents of her times.

Rand's lifelong enmity to collectivist political systems was engendered by her personal experiences growing up in Russia and living through the Bolshevik revolution and the beginnings of the Soviet system. In 1979 when Phil Donahue asked her about her feelings for Russia, Rand described them as ''complete loathing.'' Russia, she said, is ''the ugliest, and incidentally, most mystical country on earth.'' She was an American patriot in the manner that only one who has emigrated from a totalitarian regime can be.

Capitalism was the system she championed; one of her best-known novels, *Atlas Shrugged,* is described as, among other things, a theodicy of capitalism. A rugged individualist and a believer in rational self-interest, Rand was a proponent of laissez-faire capitalism, a system she defined as the only social system based on the recognition of individual rights, the only system that bans force from social relationship, and the only system that fundamentally opposes war. Rand's defense of capitalism on moral grounds is unique. She based this defense on her view that only capitalism is consonant with man's rational nature, protective of his survival as man, and fundamentally just.

Rand's championing of individual rights and minimal government is part of her appeal to the Libertarian political movement, although she herself denounced Libertarians, calling them hippies of the right and advocates of anarchism. Neither, however, would she ally herself with most Conservatives because of what she called their mysticism, their staunch support of religion. Among her most persistent concerns about America was her belief that capitalism was being sold out by the very people who should be its strongest advocates. Rand felt that rather than supporting capitalism for the morality of its central vision, most capitalists defended it only on practical bases.

In ''Global Balkanization'' Rand pointed out the following paradoxes: ''Capitalism has been called a system of greed—yet it is the system that raised the standard of living of its poorest citizens to heights no collectivist system has ever begun to equal, and no tribal gang can conceive of. Capitalism has been called nationalistic—yet it is the only system that banished ethnicity, and made it possible, in the United States, for men of various, formerly antagonistic nationalities to live together in peace. Capitalism has been called cruel—yet it brought such hope, progress and general good will that the young people of today, who have not seen it, find it hard to believe. As to pride, dignity, self-confidence, self-esteem—these are characteristics that mark a man for martyrdom in a tribal society and under any social system except capitalism.''

Tibor Machan explained in the *Occasional Review* that ''for Rand, as for Aristotle, the question How should a human community be organized? can only be answered after the question How should I, a human being, live my life? has been answered. Rand follows the Greek tradition of regarding politics as a subfield of ethics.''

Rand's firsthand experience of Communism determined her politics for life. Her family lived through the privations of World War I and then struggled to adapt themselves to the new Communist regime. For her, life in Russia at that time was dreary, and the future held little hope, particularly for one who rejected the system in power. Rand wanted to write about a world as it could be, to show life as she felt it was meant to be lived. As a young girl, she had decided to become a writer. Still, she chose to major in history at the University of Petrograd (now the University of Leningrad). She dismissed literature and philosophy, the fields in which she would later make her mark, because she had rejected the majority of what the academic world valued in both of those fields. Aristotle is the only philosopher to whom she acknowledges any intellectual debt; early in her life, she had been attracted to the theories of Friedrich Wilhelm Nietzsche, but she discarded his writing when she encountered his *The Birth of Tragedy* with its antirational stance. Barbara Branden notes in *The Passion of Ayn Rand* that Nietzsche, according to Rand, "said that reason is an inferior faculty, that drunken-orgy emotions were superior. That finished him as a spiritual ally." Her favorite novelists were Victor Hugo and Fyodor Dostoevsky, her favorite playwrights, Friedrich Schiller and Edmond Rostand.

After graduating with highest honors from the university, Alice Rosenbaum found work as a tour guide in the Peter and Paul Fortress. Dreadfully unhappy in Soviet Russia, she was rescued from her dead-end job by a letter from relatives in America. An invitation from the Portnoy family to visit them in Chicago was her passage to freedom. She left Russia in 1926 and never saw members of her immediate family again, except for a sister with whom she was reunited briefly in the early 1970s.

In the United States Alice Rosenbaum became Ayn Rand. Her unique personality and insistent individuality are reflected in her name choice. Her first name, which should be pronounced to sound like the German number one, "ein," rhymes with "pine." The last name she adopted from the Remington-Rand typewriter she used to write her first movie scenarios in America.

Despite her raw language skills, Rand left Chicago after a brief stay and headed for Hollywood where she hoped to make her living writing for the movies. On her second day in town she was befriended by her favorite American director, Cecil B. DeMille, who took her to watch the shooting of "The King of Kings" and then gave her work first as an extra and then as a junior writer. Rand's April 15, 1929, marriage to Charles Francis "Frank" O'Connor, also an extra in "The King of Kings," insured that she would be allowed to stay in America.

Shortly after her marriage, Rand got a job in the wardrobe department of RKO. She hated the work, but it provided sustenance while she improved her English and perfected her craft. Her progress was remarkable, and she was one of a very few writers—Joseph Conrad and Vladimir Nabokov come to mind—to attain artistic success in a language nonnative to them. It is possible that one of Ayn Rand's few childhood friends was Nabokov's sister. Barbara Branden tells of the relationship, based on common intellectual interests, in her biography of Rand.

Rand's first novel was written in response to a promise she had made to a friend of her family at a farewell party given for her before she left Russia. Her friend had implored her to tell Americans that Russia was a huge cemetery and that its citizens were slowly dying; and in *We the Living* Rand details the deterioration of spirit and body under the Communist system. In particular, she wanted to show that Communism wreaks havoc not only on average people but particularly on the best and the brightest. All three of the major characters are de-

stroyed. The heroine loses her life; the anti-Communist hero loses his spirit; and the Communist hero's faith and life are so undermined by the excesses he sees in the system that he takes his own life. By making one of her major characters a hero of the revolution, one who had believed fervently in the Communist cause, Rand was able to communicate basic flaws in the system. In the foreword to the 1959 edition, Rand warned her readers not to dismiss the story of Russia of the 1920s as inapplicable to the Russia of their own day: "*We the Living* is not a story about Soviet Russia in 1925. It is a story about Dictatorship, any dictatorship, anywhere, at any time, whether it be Soviet Russia, Nazi Germany, or—which this novel might do its share in helping to prevent—a socialist America." Rand continually emphasized that her opposition to Communism was based on the evil of its essential principle, that Man should exist for the sake of the state. She warned Americans against accepting the myth that the Communist ideal was noble, although its methods might be evil.

The publishing world was not taken with Rand's accomplishments in *We the Living,* which was rejected by many publishing houses as either too intellectual or too anti-Soviet. It was not until after Rand had achieved some success as a playwright that *We the Living* finally appeared in 1936. Macmillan, the publisher, had so little faith in the novel that they did little promotion and issued only one edition of three thousand copies. The reviews were not enthusiastic. Although Lee E. Cannon in the *Christian Century* called it "vigorous" and emotionally intense, Ben Belitt in the *Nation* questioned the accuracy of Rand's depiction of the U.S.S.R., claiming that she was out "to puncture a bubble—with a bludgeon." Rand was often subsequently accused of overkill.

Though neither her publisher nor her reviewers expected much from the book, *We the Living* earned word-of-mouth recommendation and sold more copies in its second year than just after publication. However, Macmillan had destroyed the type and *We the Living* was not published again in the United States until it was reissued by Random House in 1959. It has since sold more than two million copies.

Rand's primary reputation is as a novelist, but her first professional success was as a playwright. In all, Rand wrote four plays, two of which were produced on Broadway. She originally called her first play "Penthouse Legend," but its title was changed twice. Under the title "Woman on Trial" it opened in October, 1934, at the Hollywood Playhouse under the direction of E. E. Clive. Al Woods then purchased the rights, and under the title "Night of January 16th" it began a seven-month run on Broadway in September of 1935. A 1973 revival bearing Rand's original title "Penthouse Legend" was not so successful.

Night of January 16th is significant for dramatic ingenuity as well as for historical sidelights. Rand developed the innovative theatrical device of using audience members at each performance to serve as the jury in this courtroom drama. (A number of celebrities acted as jurors for the play: Jack Dempsey served on the opening night jury; Helen Keller was foreman for an all-blind jury.) Rand wrote alternative endings for the cast to use in response to either the guilty or the not guilty verdict. Moreover, the Broadway production provided actor Walter Pidgeon in the role of "Guts" Regan with a vehicle to revive his flagging career. The play also inspired Gertrude M. Moffat, Chair of the New York League of Women Voters, to write to the *New York Times* to complain of the all-male juries who were initially selected to judge Karen Andre, the defendant in the play. Moffat used the play to question a New York law that specified ''male'' jurors; women should be judged by their peers, which include women, she argued. The New York law was subsequently changed.

Anthem, a novella, first published in England in 1938, is Rand's shortest work. A parable-like dystopian tale, it portrays a totally collectivized world after some great war or holocaust. Originally titled ''Ego,'' the work illustrates the negative effects on society of the suppression of individual ego and talent for the supposed good of all: When, in the name of all, no individual is allowed to stand above the others, then all stand in darkness. *Anthem* was republished in 1946 and 1953, and in 1961 the New American Library issued a paperback edition that continues to go through new printings. In a 1966 issue of the *New York Times Book Review* Gerald Raftery called the work ''a surprising favorite among high-school taste-makers.'' Larry M. Arnoldson reported in the *Journal of Reading* that his reading of *Anthem* to his high school class created a log jam for the school librarian who had only one copy of each of Rand's novels and over fifty students on a waiting list for the books.

The Fountainhead might not have been published at all were it not for the faith of Archibald G. Ogden, who was at that time a new young editor for Bobbs-Merrill. He wired the head of the company, who had told him to reject it, ''If this is not the book for you, then I am not the editor for you.'' At that point it had already been refused by some dozen other publishers.

Rand had done extensive research before she began writing *The Fountainhead,* which was originally titled ''Secondhand Lives.'' Although she worked for some time in the office of Eli Jacques Kahn, a famous New York architect, Rand's main purpose was not to extol the profession of architecture. The central theme in this novel, as in the ones before it, is individualism versus collectivism, the difference being that in *The Fountainhead* the focus is not on the political system, as it was in *We the Living,* but on what Rand called collectivism in the soul. *The Fountainhead* is a defense of egoism, a positive rational egoism. Protagonist Howard Roark explains to Dominique Fracon at one point in the book, ''To say 'I love you' one must know first how to say the 'I.''' The egoism Rand defined in this novel is an integral part of the individualism she championed, just as the selfishness she described is a virtue as opposed to the selflessness she abhorred.

In *The Fountainhead* Rand moved closer to her goal of creating the ideal man. Because of the resemblance in their professions and architectural styles, it was generally assumed that Howard Roark was modeled after Frank Lloyd Wright. Barbara Branden asserted in *Who Is Ayn Rand?: An Analysis of the Novels of Ayn Rand,* however, that Rand insisted, ''The only resemblance is in their basic architectural principles and in the fact that Wright was an innovator fighting for modern architecture against tradition. There is no similarity in their respective characters, nor in their philosophical convictions, nor in the events in their lives.'' Rand had tried unsuccessfully to interview Wright while she was writing her novel. It was only after the success of *The Fountainhead* that they established an amicable relationship. Eventually he designed a home for her; it was never built.

Asked about the models for her other main characters, Rand remarked that Wynand could have been William Randolph Hearst or Henry Luce or Joseph Pulitzer. Harold Laski, the British Socialist, was the main model for Ellsworth Toohey.

Other lesser sources for Toohey were Heywood Broun, Lewis Mumford, and Clifton Fadiman, although when Rand met Fadiman some years later, they liked each other. A young woman Rand had met in Hollywood, whose main goal was not to have things because she wanted them but only so that she would have more than her neighbors, was the inspiration for Peter Keating. Ayn Rand characterized the book's heroine, Dominique Francon, as herself in a bad mood.

In *The Fountainhead* Rand declares that Howard Roark's success progresses ''as if an underground stream flowed through the country and broke out in sudden springs that shot to the surface at random, in unpredictable places.'' She might have been discussing the publishing history of her novel. Although D.L. Chambers, the head of Bobbs-Merrill, had ultimately supported his editor Archie Ogden's dedication to the book, he did not give *The Fountainhead* his wholehearted support once it was published. Rather than print significant numbers of new editions as the book gained popularity, he kept issuing small editions that quickly went out of print. When Bobbs-Merrill decided to produce a twenty-fifth anniversary deluxe edition in 1968, Nora Ephron, not an admirer of Rand's theories or writing abilities, noted in the *New York Times Book Review* that *The Fountainhead* was ''one of the most astonishing phenomena in publishing history.'' At that date it had sold over two and one-half million copies. By the 1980s the number of copies sold was closer to four and one-half million.

Positive reviewers appreciated the powerful writing, intensity, and dramatic plot of *The Fountainhead*. Rand's favorite review was by Lorine Pruette in a May, 1943, *New York Times Book Review*. Pruette correctly identified *The Fountainhead* as a novel of ideas, pointing out that a novel of ideas by an American woman was a rarity. She lauded the quality of Rand's intellect, calling her ''a writer of great power'' with ''a subtle and ingenious mind and the capacity of writing brilliantly, beautifully, bitterly.''

The success of *The Fountainhead* brought Rand to the attention of her kind of reader, individuals who shared her perception of life. It also precipitated a lucrative movie sale, which necessitated a move back to Hollywood from New York, where Rand and her husband had moved for the Broadway production of ''Night of January 16th.'' In California they bought a house of steel and glass in very modern design, a house which might have been designed by Howard Roark. There Rand wrote the screenplay for *The Fountainhead* and major parts of *Atlas Shrugged.*

In 1950 Nathaniel Branden (born Nathaniel Blumenthal) wrote a fan letter to Rand which so impressed her that she did something quite uncharacteristic: she answered his letter. Their meeting set in motion a series of events that would profoundly affect many lives. By the time Rand's next book was published, Branden had joined Frank O'Connor on the dedication page. Her afterword describes Branden as her ''ideal reader'' and ''intellectual heir.'' Nathaniel Branden and his wife, Barbara Weidman Branden, became more than fans and students; they became close friends and intellectual allies. The Brandens' move to New York was followed shortly by a similar move by Rand and Frank O'Connor.

The Brandens introduced many of their friends and relatives to Rand and these people formed a close group called by Rand ''the class of '43'' because of their shared interest in *The Fountainhead*, which had been published in that year. She also called them ''the children,'' by which she meant that they were the children of her brain. Members of this group included Alan

Greenspan, who became head of the Federal Reserve System and economic advisor to three presidents; Leonard Peikoff, Barbara Branden's cousin and Rand's literary executor; Nathaniel Branden's sister, Elayne Kalberman, the circulation manager for *The Objectivist Newsletter*, and her husband, Harry Kalberman; Allan Blumenthal; Edith Efron; Mary Ann Rukavina; and Robert and Beatrice Hessen. They were privy to prepublication reading of *Atlas Shrugged*, and from their ranks the philosophical movement that Rand called Objectivism was born.

Atlas Shrugged was to be Rand's last novel, but it initiated her career as a well-known philosopher and public figure. She became a popular campus speaker in the 1960s, a regular at the Ford Hall Forum, and a columnist for the *Los Angeles Times*. She was interviewed by Johnny Carson, Tom Snyder, Phil Donahue, and *Playboy*. Nathaniel Branden began teaching her basic philosophical principles through a twenty-lecture course of study offered by Nathaniel Branden Lectures. Nathaniel Branden Lectures developed into the Nathaniel Branden Institute, which began to offer taped courses on Objectivism in cities throughout the United States. A publication branch of the Institute printed essays and monographs; a book service sold approved books. The first issue of *The Objectivist Newsletter*, which was published from 1962-65, contained articles by Rand, both Brandens, and Greenspan. *The Objectivist Newsletter* was replaced in 1966 by *The Objectivist*. In 1971 the format was changed to a simple typewritten letter called *The Ayn Rand Letter*. Rand continued issuing numbers of this letter until February of 1976.

In *Atlas Shrugged* Ayn Rand accomplished her goal of creating the ideal man. His name is John Galt, and he and a number of like-minded followers succeed in stopping the motor of the world by removing themselves and their productive capacities from exploitation by those forces they regard as looters and leeches. All of Rand's novels dramatize the primacy of the individual. The unique and precious individual human life is the standard by which good is judged. If something nourishes and sustains life, it is good; if it negates or impoverishes the individual's pursuit of happiness, then it is evil. The secondary themes in Rand's fiction unfold as the logical consequence of her major theme, but it was not until *Atlas Shrugged*, the fullest explication in fiction of her philosophy, that Rand worked out all the political, economic, and metaphysical implications of that theme.

Critical calumny greeted the publication of *Atlas Shrugged*, especially from the battlements of the conservative establishment. Whittaker Chambers in the *National Review* called it "remarkably silly," "bumptious," and "preposterous." He remarked, "Out of a lifetime of reading, I can recall no other book in which a tone of overriding arrogance was so implacably sustained. Its shrillness is without reprieve. Its dogmatism is without appeal." *Catholic World*'s Riley Hughes called it a "shrill diatribe against 'non-productive' people." Hughes claimed that though Rand decried mysticism, her book is full of parallels to Christianity: "Her John Galt is offered as a secular savior (Dagny is his Magdalene); and his disciples find him at his place of torture." In the *Saturday Review*, Helen Beal Woodward, who conceded that "Ayn Rand is a writer of dazzling virtuosity," reacted negatively to the "stylized vice-and-virtue characters" and "prolixity." Woodward found *Atlas Shrugged* a book "shot through with hatred." Such critical attacks had no effect on the reading public who have made *Atlas Shrugged* a multi-million selling phenomenon. *Atlas Shrugged*, like *Uncle Tom's Cabin*, is a book that fueled a

movement. Its publication established Rand as a thinker whose influence extended to such diverse locales as Parliament (Margaret Thatcher is an admirer); tennis courts (Billie Jean King acknowledges Rand's effect on her); the Federal Reserve System (Alan Greenspan calls her instrumental in forming his thinking); and the Alaskan legislature (it issued a citation in memoriam of Rand at the request of Dick Randolph, a Libertarian legislator).

Rand was fifty-two when she published her last novel, but the end of her career as a fiction writer launched the beginning of her career as a public philosopher, speaker, and cult figure. The publication of *For the New Intellectual: The Philosophy of Ayn Rand* in 1961 began a series of nonfiction books that anthologized her essays on such diverse subjects as the American public school system, Romanticism, and racism. In her nonfiction writings as well as in her fiction, she characterized the main areas of conflict in the field of human rights: (1) individualism versus collectivism, (2) egoism versus altruism, (3) reason versus mysticism. In Rand's philosophy all of these areas are interconnected. Reason is the tool by which the individual discerns that which is life-sustaining and ego-nourishing. Collectivism, altruism, and mysticism work against individual freedom, a healthy ego, and rationality.

Rand's career as the leader of an intellectual movement had two phases. Until 1968 Nathaniel Branden was her chief spokesperson and teacher of her philosophies. In that year Rand broke with both Brandens, who had separated by then. The rupture, with its public response, established divisions between friends and relatives that never healed. It also established divisions among her other admirers: some remained purists, continuing to call themselves Objectivists and publishing only that which was sanctioned by Rand or which did not deviate from her dictums; others acknowledged influence, but moved from the letter of Rand's philosophy to other interpretations and permutations. Leonard Peikoff became Rand's associate editor for *The Objectivist*.

To the end of her life, Rand's appearance on a television program or at a Ford Hall Forum would create controversy and inordinate audience response. She possessed great charisma and an intense intellectuality that affected both admirers and detractors. Her last years were clouded by ill health (she lost a lung to cancer) and grief (her husband, who she called her greatest value, died in 1979). Yet she made an appearance on a Phil Donahue show in 1979, affirming her love of life and her belief that there is no hereafter. If she believed in a hereafter, she explained, her desire to be with her husband would necessitate her committing suicide so as to join him. Some four months before her death, she delivered a speech at the conference of the National Committee for Monetary Reform. Thus until her death alone in her apartment on March 6, 1982, Ayn Rand's unquenchable spirit continued to assert itself.

MEDIA ADAPTATIONS: Night of January 16th was filmed by Paramount and released in 1941. A year later, *We the Living* was filmed in Italy; a revised and abridged version of the Italian film was released in the United States in 1988.

BIOGRAPHICAL/CRITICAL SOURCES:

BOOKS

Baker, James T., *Ayn Rand*, Twayne, 1987.
Barnes, Hazel Estella, *An Existential Ethics*, Knopf, 1967.
Branden, Barbara, *The Passion of Ayn Rand*, Doubleday, 1986.

Branden, Nathaniel, *Who Is Ayn Rand?: An Analysis of the Novels of Ayn Rand,* with biographical essay by Barbara Branden, Random House, 1977.

Cerf, Bennett, *At Random,* Random House, 1977.

Contempory Literary Criticism, Gale, Volume 3, 1975, Volume 30, 1984, Volume 44, 1987.

Den Uyl, Douglas and Douglas Rasmussen, editors, *The Philosophical Thought of Ayn Rand,* University of Illinois Press, 1984.

Ellis, Albert, *Is Objectivism a Religion?,* Lyle Stuart, 1968.

Gladstein, Mimi Reisel, *The Ayn Rand Companion,* Greenwood Press, 1984.

Haydn, Hiram, *Words and Faces,* Harcourt, 1974.

O'Neill, William, *With Charity Toward None: An Analysis of Ayn Rand's Philosophy,* Philosophical Library, 1971.

Peary, Gerald and Roget Shatzkin, editors, *The Modern American Novel and the Movies,* Unger, 1978.

Rand, Ayn, *We the Living,* Random House, 1959.

Rand, Ayn, *The Fountainhead,* Bobbs-Merrill, 1968.

Schwartz, Peter, editor, *The Battle for Laissez-Faire Capitalism,* Intellectual Activist, 1983.

Slusser, George E., Eric S. Rabkin, and Robert Scholes, editors, *Coordinates: Placing Science Fiction and Fantasy, Alternative Series,* Southern Illinois University Press, 1984.

Tuccille, Jerome, *It Usually Begins with Ayn Rand,* Stein & Day, 1972.

PERIODICALS

Atlantic, November, 1957.
Boston Review, December, 1984.
Catholic World, January, 1958.
Chicago Sunday Tribune, October 13, 1957.
Christian Century, July 1, 1936, December 13, 1961.
Christian Science Monitor, October 10, 1957.
Christianity Today, July 18, 1982.
College English, February, 1978.
Commonweal, November 8, 1957.
English Journal, February, 1983.
House and Garden, August, 1949.
Journal of Reading, March, 1982.
Journal of Thought, January, 1969.
Life, April 7, 1967.
Los Angeles Times, November 12, 1988.
Los Angeles Times Book Review, September 2, 1984.
Ms., September, 1978.
Nation, April 22, 1936.
National Review, December 28, 1957, October 3, 1967, April 2, 1982.
New Republic, April 24, 1961, December 10, 1966, February 21, 1970.
New Statesman, March 11, 1966.
Newsweek, March 27, 1961.
New Yorker, October 26, 1957.
New York Herald Tribune Book Review, October 6, 1957.
New York Herald Tribune Books, April 19, 1936.
New York Times, April 19, 1936, May 16, 1943, October 13, 1957, March 9, 1966, March 10, 1982, September 13, 1987.
New York Times Book Review, May 16, 1943, April 9, 1961, February 27, 1966, December 22, 1967, May 5, 1968.
Objectivist Forum, June, 1982, August, 1982, October, 1982, December, 1982.
Occasional Review, winter, 1976.
Personalist, spring, 1971.
Playboy, March, 1964.

Rampart Journal of Individualist Thought, spring, 1968.
Reason, November, 1973, May, 1978, December, 1982.
Religious Humanism, winter, 1970.
San Francisco Chronicle, April 9, 1961.
Saturday Evening Post, November 11, 1961.
Saturday Review, October 12, 1957.
Saturday Review of Literature, April 18, 1936.
Time, October 14, 1957, September 30, 1974.
Washington Post Book World, December 12, 1982.
West Coast Review of Books, November, 1984.

OTHER

''Donahue,'' WGN-TV, Chicago, Illinois, April 29, 1979.

OBITUARIES:

PERIODICALS

AB Bookman's Weekly, March 29, 1982.
Detroit Free Press, March 7, 1982.
Los Angeles Times, March 7, 1982.
Newsweek, March 15, 1982.
New York Times, March 8, 1982.
Publishers Weekly, March 19, 1982.
Time, March 15, 1982.
Times (London), March 8, 1982.*

—*Sidelights by Mimi Reisel Gladstein*

*   *   *

RAVENEL, Shannon   1938-

PERSONAL: Born August 13, 1938, in Charlotte, N.C.; daughter of Elias Prioleau (a stockbroker) and Harriet (an insurance salesperson; maiden name, Steedman) Ravenel; married Dale Purves (a physician and professor of physiology), May 25, 1968; children: Sara Blake Purves, Harriet Ravenel Purves. *Education:* Hollins College, B.A., 1960.

ADDRESSES: Office—P.O. Box 3176, University City, Mo. 63130.

CAREER: Houghton Mifflin Co., Boston, Mass., editor of trade books, 1961-71; Algonquin Books, Inc., Chapel Hill, N.C., 1982—, began as fiction editor and member of board of directors, currently senior editor and vice-president. Lecturer in creative writing, Washington University, St. Louis, Mo., 1983-85.

WRITINGS:

''THE BEST AMERICAN SHORT STORIES'' SERIES; EDITOR

The Best American Short Stories 1977, Houghton, 1977.
(With Ted Solotaroff) . . . *1978,* Houghton, 1978.
(With Joyce Carol Oates) . . . *1979,* Houghton, 1979.
(With Stanley Elkin) . . . *1980,* Houghton, 1980.
(With Hortense Calisher) . . . *1981,* Houghton, 1981.
(With John Gardner) . . . *1982,* Houghton, 1982.
(With Anne Tyler) . . . *1983,* Houghton, 1983.
(With John Updike) . . . *1984,* Houghton, 1984.
(With Gail Godwin) . . . *1985,* Houghton, 1985.
(With Raymond Carver) . . . *1986,* Houghton, 1986.
(With Ann Beattie) . . . *1987,* Houghton, 1987.
(With Mark Helprin) . . . *1988,* Houghton, 1988.

''NEW STORIES FROM THE SOUTH: THE YEAR'S BEST'' SERIES; EDITOR

New Stories from the South: The Year's Best 1986, Algonquin Books, 1986.

. . . 1987, Algonquin Books, 1987.
. . . 1988, Algonquin Books, 1988.

SIDELIGHTS: The Best American Short Stories, issued annually, is a collection of approximately twenty stories chosen from a field of more than one thousand which Shannon Ravenel and other editors gather from over 185 periodicals. The more recent annual publication known as *New Stories from the South: The Year's Best* is similarly compiled but representation is restricted to authors from the American South.

Ravenel told *CA:* "I am not an author, but an editor, following in the footsteps of the late Martha Foley, who edited thirty-seven volumes of *The Best American Short Stories.* In selecting 120 stories each year, from which the guest editor chooses twenty to be reprinted, I read all eligible work published first serially in the calendar year. We do not consider stories by foreign authors—only those by residents of the United States and Canada. Excerpts from novels are not eligible, nor are translations. The magazines I consult are made available to me by their editors, all of whom supply the collection with complementary subscriptions. After several years of this reading, I am still unable to define my personal criteria beyond saying that I simply choose those stories I cannot forget. I continue to be impressed—amazed—by the enormous number of highly talented writers publishing short fiction in North America. There is never a shortage of fine stories from which to choose the 'best.'"

BIOGRAPHICAL/CRITICAL SOURCES:

PERIODICALS

Los Angeles Times Book Review, September 27, 1981, December 5, 1982.
New York Times Book Review, November 26, 1978, November 4, 1979, November 21, 1982.
Poets and Writers, November-December, 1987.

*   *   *

REED, E.
See EVANS, Mari

*   *   *

REED, Rex (Taylor) 1938-

PERSONAL: Born October 2, 1938, in Fort Worth, Tex.; son of J. M. (an oil company supervisor) and Jewell (Smith) Reed. *Education:* Louisiana State University, B.A., 1960.

ADDRESSES: Home—Roxbury, Conn. *Office*—c/o Macmillan Inc., 866 Third Ave., New York, N.Y. 10022.

CAREER: Worked variously as a jazz singer, television performer, pancake cook, record salesman, and actor, 1960-65; film critic for *Women's Wear Daily,* 1965-69, *Cosmopolitan, Status,* and *Holiday,* beginning 1965; music critic for *Stereo Review,* 1968-75; affiliated with Daily News syndicate, 1971—; former film critic for *Vogue, New York Daily News, Gentleman's Quarterly,* and the *New York Post;* currently co-host of syndicated television series "At the Movies." Columnist for Chicago Tribune syndicate. Member of jury at Berlin, Venice, Atlanta, and U.S.A. Film Festivals; lecturer. Actor in 1970 film "Myra Breckinridge"; cameo appearance in "Superman," 1978.

WRITINGS:

Do You Sleep in the Nude?, New American Library, 1968.

Conversations in the Raw, World Publishing, 1970.
Big Screen, Little Screen, Macmillan, 1971.
People Are Crazy Here, Delacorte, 1974.
Valentines and Vitriol, Delacorte, 1977.
Travolta to Keaton, Morrow, 1979.
Personal Effects (novel), Arbor House, 1986.

Contributor to numerous magazines, including *Ladies Home Journal, Esquire, Harper's Bazaar, New York Times, Playboy,* and *Vogue.*

SIDELIGHTS: As much a celebrity as many of the entertainers he writes about, critic and journalist Rex Reed is best known for interviews that strip the glamour from Hollywood stars. His incisive writing has earned him a reputation as the "hatchet man" of show business journalism, but Reed asserts that he never goes to interviews with preconceived ideas. "I give people the benefit of the doubt, and if they hang themselves that's their problem," he told a reporter from *Newsweek.* Nonetheless, according to John Simon writing in *National Review,* "clever bitchiness" is a hallmark of Reed's style.

The only child of an oil company supervisor whose work required extensive travel, Reed grew up in a succession of small Southern towns. By the time he graduated from Natchitoches High School in Louisiana, he had attended no less than thirteen public schools. He was, as he told the *Newsweek* reporter, "always the new kid," an experience that he found traumatic: "It was a terrible thing. I withdrew from it all and went to the movies every afternoon. Now when I go to interview movie people they say, 'But when did you see that?'" In college he became a columnist, critic and editorial writer for the campus newspaper and it was there he first established the reputation for controversy that would characterize his career. After attacking segregation in an editorial entitled "The Prince of Prejudice," he was burned in effigy by the Ku Klux Klan.

From the Baton Rouge, Louisiana, campus where he graduated with a degree in journalism, Reed moved to New York City. There he perfected his skills as a free-lance writer while working at a number of odd jobs. His first big break came in 1965 when two celebrity interviews he conducted were published in the *New York Times* and *New York* magazine. Since that time, both his film criticism and his interviews have been in national demand.

In 1968, some of Reed's early *New York Times, Esquire* and *Cosmopolitan* articles were compiled in a provocatively entitled best-seller, *Do You Sleep in the Nude?* The publication was so successful that Reed has compiled his better celebrity interviews into book form ever since. Among those whom Reed has singled out for attention are Paul Newman, Jack Nicholson, Lucille Ball, Barbra Streisand, and such normally reticent stars as Walter Matthau and Geraldine Page. In fact, he is so renowned that "the Rex Reed treatment" has become "one of the hallmarks of success for an actor or director," according to Henry Flowers writing in the *New York Times Book Review.*

Despite the popularity of his books, many critics disparage Reed's style. "There is panic and fearful insecurity behind this frantic compulsion to mix with the famous and sniff the hem of power. But Rex sees neither the humor nor the mediocrity in a system that elevates his brand of witless ballyhoo to stardom," writes John Lahr in the *New York Times Book Review.* Of Reed's 1977 book, Lahr concludes, "*Valentines and Vitriol* is superficial even in its shallowness. Rex calls himself a 'critic,' as much a misnomer as 'sanitary engineer.'" While Flowers agrees that "Reed's is a severely limited talent," he tempers his assessment by acknowledging that "within his limitations he is excellent."

Reed's first novel, *Personal Effects*, stays true to the author's showbiz leanings. The story of how a Hollywood journalist, Billy Buck, involves himself in the investigation of a famous actress's murder didn't win Reed many fans among reviewers. Karen Stabiner, for one, writing in the *Los Angeles Times Book Review*, sees *Personal Effects* as "a big candy box of a Hollywood novel—good for a quick sugary rush when ingested in small doses, but guaranteed to give you a bad case of mental bloat by the time you're through." Stabiner adds the dubious praise that *Personal Effects* "is a hoot, in the grand tradition of trashy Hollywood fiction, the kind of novel that keeps the word 'sprawling' in the top-10 of book-reviewing adjectives."

BIOGRAPHICAL/CRITICAL SOURCES:

BOOKS

Authors in the News, Volume 1, Gale, 1976.

PERIODICALS

Globe and Mail (Toronto), May 10, 1986.
Los Angeles Times Book Review, February 26, 1986.
National Review, July 5, 1974.
Newsweek, January 8, 1968.
New York Times Book Review, July 21, 1968, November 9, 1969, May 22, 1977.

*　　*　　*

REYNOLDS, Clark G(ilbert)　1939-

PERSONAL: Born December 11, 1939, in Pasadena, Calif.; son of William Gilbert (a golf professional) and Alma (Clark) Reynolds; married Constance Caine, August 3, 1963; children: Dwight Dale, Ward William, Colleen Elizabeth. *Education:* University of California, Santa Barbara, B.A., 1961; Duke University, M.A., 1963, Ph.D., 1964.

ADDRESSES: Office—Department of History, College of Charleston, Charleston, S.C. 29464.

CAREER: U.S. Naval Academy, Annapolis, Md., assistant professor of history, 1964-68; University of Maine, Orono, associate professor, 1968-74, professor of history, 1974-76; U.S. Merchant Marine Academy, professor of humanities, 1976-78, chairman of department, 1976-78; curator, Patriots Point Naval and Maritime Museum, 1978-87; College of Charleston, S.C., professor of history, 1988—, chairman of department, 1988—.

MEMBER: North American Society for Oceanic History, American Historical Association, American Military Institute, U.S. Naval Institute.

WRITINGS:

(With J. J. Clark) *Carrier Admiral*, McKay, 1967.
The Fast Carriers: The Forging of an Air Navy, McGraw, 1968.
Command of the Sea: The History and Strategy of Maritime Empires, Morrow, 1974, revised edition published in two volumes, 1983.
Famous American Admirals, Van Nostrand, 1978.
The Carrier War, Time-Life, 1982.
The Fighting Lady, Pictorial Histories, 1986.
History and the Sea, University of South Carolina Press, 1989.

Towers: The Air Admiral, Naval Institute Press, 1989.

Contributor to journals, including *American Neptune, Military Affairs*, and *Naval History*.

WORK IN PROGRESS: This Island America.

BIOGRAPHICAL/CRITICAL SOURCES:

PERIODICALS

Naval History, winter, 1989.
New York Times Book Review, January 12, 1969.
U.S. Naval Institute Proceedings, October, 1973.

*　　*　　*

REZMERSKI, John Calvin　1942-

PERSONAL: Surname is pronounced Rez-*mer*-ski; born January 15, 1942, in Kane, Pa.; son of John James and Augusta (Dickinson) Rezmerski; married Mary K. Naegle, January 22, 1966 (divorced, 1982); married Lorna J. Johnson, October 4, 1987; children: (first marriage) Marysia, Nicholas, Peter. *Education:* Gannon College, B.A., 1963; John Carroll University, M.A., 1965; further graduate study at University of Kansas, 1965-67. *Politics:* "Utopian." *Religion:* "Animist."

ADDRESSES: Home—P.O. Box 202, Eagle Lake, Minn. 56024. *Office*—Department of English, Gustavus Adolphus College, St. Peter, Minn. 56082.

CAREER: Gustavus Adolphus College, St. Peter, Minn., associate professor of English, 1967—.

AWARDS, HONORS: Devins Memorial Award, Kansas City Poetry Contest, 1969, for *Held for Questioning: Poems;* National Endowment for the Arts creative writing fellowship, 1973; Rhysling Award, 1987.

WRITINGS:

Held for Questioning: Poems, University of Missouri Press, 1969.
An American Gallery (poems), Three Rivers Press, 1977.
Dreams of Bela Lugosi (poetry chapbook), Knife River Press, 1977.
(With Gregory Mason) *The Sandman* (screenplay), Westerheim Press, 1981.
Growing Down (poems), Minnesota Writers Publishing House, 1982.

CONTRIBUTOR TO POETRY ANTHOLOGIES

25 Minnesota Poets, Nodin Press, 1975.
Heartland II, Northern Illinois University Press, 1976.
25 Minnesota Poets #2, Nodin Press, 1977.
Blood of Their Blood, New Rivers Press, 1980.
The Not Like Any Other Children's Book, Book, Smith & Smith, 1982.
Minnesota Writes: Poetry, Nodin Press, 1987.
Time Gum, Rune Press, 1988.

OTHER

Also contributor to other poetry anthologies. Contributor to literary magazines, including *Poetry Now, Dacotah Territory, Three Rivers Poetry Journal, New Letters, Poetry Northwest*, and *Jam To-Day*. Contributor of articles to magazines, including *Twin Cities, Corporate Report*, and *Theatrework*.

WORK IN PROGRESS: Chin Music and Dirty Sermons (poems); *Solipsism Is a Way of Life* (epigrams); *Awra Skies* (novel); "Over the Hill" (play).

BIOGRAPHICAL/CRITICAL SOURCES:

PERIODICALS

Chelsea Review, December, 1969.

*   *   *

RICE, Allan Lake   1905-1984

PERSONAL: Born March 1, 1905, in Philadelphia, Pa.; died April 11, 1984, in Florida; son of Earle C. and Georgene (Smith) Rice; married Rigmor Hallqvist, November 6, 1943; children: Deborah, Suzanne (Mrs. Lawrence Henry), Christopher. *Education:* University of Pennsylvania, A.B., 1927, M.A., 1928, Ph.D., 1932.

ADDRESSES: Home—P.O. Box 492, Kimberton, Pa. 19442.

CAREER: Princeton University, Princeton, N.J., instructor in German, 1930-36; University of Pennsylvania, Philadelphia, assistant professor of German and Swedish, 1936-47; Ursinus College, Collegeville, Pa., professor of German and Swedish, 1947-75, professor emeritus, 1975-84; free-lance translator in ten languages, 1975-84. Professor of Swedish, Augustana College, summers, 1948 and 1950. *Military service:* U.S. Naval Reserve, assistant naval attache, active duty, 1942-45; served in Sweden and Finland; became commander.

MEMBER: Society for the Advancement of Scandinavian Study, Phi Beta Kappa.

AWARDS, HONORS: Decorated by King of Sweden, 1970; Nordstjaarnan (Sweden), 1971.

WRITINGS:

Gothic Prepositional Compounds in Their Relation to the Greek Originals, Kraus Reprint, 1932.
Swedish: A Practical Grammar, Fortress Press, 1958, 3rd edition, 1968.
German: A Practical Grammar, Ursinus College Supply Store, 5th edition, 1972.
(Translator from the German) Harald Mellerowicz, *Ergometry: Basics of Medical Exercise Testing*, edited by Vojin N. Smodlaka, Urban & Schwarzenberg, 1981.

Contributor to periodicals of articles on model railroading.

WORK IN PROGRESS: *The New Approach to Swedish Grammar.*

AVOCATIONAL INTERESTS: Model railroading (trolley-car era).*

[Death date provided by wife, Rigmor Rice]

*   *   *

RICE, Otis K(ermit)   1919-

PERSONAL: Born June 6, 1919, in Hugheston, W.Va.; son of Charles Orion (a timberman) and Mary Catherine (Belcher) Rice. *Education:* Attended West Virginia Institute of Technology, 1935-40; Morris Harvey College, B.S., 1943, A.B. (magna cum laude), 1944; West Virginia University, M.A., 1945; University of Kentucky, Ph.D., 1960. *Politics:* Democrat.

ADDRESSES: Home—P.O. Box 147, Hugheston, W.Va. 25110. *Office*—Department of History, West Virginia Institute of Technology, Montgomery, W.Va. 25136.

CAREER: Teacher and principal in public schools, Kanawha County, W.Va., 1938-57; West Virginia Institute of Technology, Montgomery, assistant professor, 1957-59, associate professor, 1959-60, professor of history, beginning 1960, professor emeritus, 1987—, chairman of department of history and social sciences, 1962—, director of Division of Humanities and Sciences, 1968—, acting dean, summer, 1969, chairman of humanities divisions, 1972-84, dean of School of Human Studies, 1984-87. Visiting summer professor at Morris Harvey College, 1961 and 1968, and Marshall University, 1963, 1964, 1966, and 1967. Danforth associate, 1968—. Member, West Virginia Antiquities Commission, 1968-70, West Virginia Historic Road Markers Advisory Board, 1970, West Virginia Historical Records Advisory Board, 1977—, and Kanawha County Bicentennial Commission, 1982-88.

MEMBER: Organization of American Historians, Southern Historical Association, Western Historical Association, West Virginia Historical Association (president, 1955-56; treasurer, 1959-69), West Virginia Historical Association of Professional Historians (president, 1970-71), Kentucky Historical Society, Greenbrier Historical Society, Phi Alpha Theta, Kappa Delta Pi.

AWARDS, HONORS: Summer research grants, American Association for State and Local History, 1961 and 1965; recipient of first annual award presented by Humanities Foundation of West Virginia, 1987.

WRITINGS:

The Allegheny Frontier: West Virginia Beginnings, 1730-1830, University Press of Kentucky, 1970.
West Virginia: The State and Its People, McClain Printing Co., 1972.
Frontier Kentucky, University Press of Kentucky, 1975.
The Hatfields and the McCoys, University Press of Kentucky, 1978.
Charleston and the Kanawha Valley, Windsor Publications, 1981.
A History of Greenbrier County, West Virginia, McClain Printing Co., 1985.
Lewisburg, West Virginia, United Methodist Church: A Bicentennial History, McClain Printing Co., 1988.

AUTHOR OF INTRODUCTION TO REPRINT EDITIONS

John Stuart, *Narrative of the Indian Wars and Other Occurrences*, McClain Printing Co., 1971.
John J. Jacob, *A Biographical Sketch of the Life of the Late Captain Michael Cresan*, McClain Printing Co., 1971.
Joseph Doddridge, *Logan: The Last of the Race of Shikellemus, Chief of the Cayuga Nation*, McClain Printing Co., 1971.

OTHER

Contributor of articles on West Virginia to *Dictionary of American History, Encyclopedia of Southern History, Book of Knowledge, Collier's Encyclopedia, Merit Students Encyclopedia,* and *Encyclopedia of American Forest and Conservation History*. Contributor of nearly eighty articles and reviews to historical journals. *West Virginia History*, book review editor, 1971-80, member of editorial board, 1980—.

SIDELIGHTS: Otis K. Rice told *CA* that he "is convinced that regional and local history, carefully researched, analyzed and synthesized, can illuminate and inform our national experience." He believes "that while history may contribute to our understanding of contemporary issues and problems it enables us to view and appreciate those who lived in different times and contexts and thus to gain a greater understanding of man, his aspirations, and achievements.''

*   *   *

RICHARDS, Audrey I(sabel)   1899-1984

PERSONAL: Born July 8, 1899, in London, England; died June 29, 1984; daughter of Henry Erle (a barrister) and Isabel (Butler) Richards. *Education:* Newnham College, Cambridge, M.A., 1922; London School of Economics and Political Science, Ph.D., 1929. *Religion:* Church of England.

ADDRESSES: Home—11 Highsett, Hills Rd., Cambridge CB2, England.

CAREER: University of London, London School of Economics and Political Science, London, England, lecturer in social anthropology, 1931-33 and 1935-37; University of the Witwatersrand, Johannesburg, South Africa, lecturer in social anthropology, 1938-40; British Colonial Office, London, staff member, 1940-44; University of London, reader in social anthropology, 1946-50; Makerere University College, Kampala, Uganda, director of East African Institute of Social Research, 1950-56; Cambridge University, Cambridge, England, fellow of Newnham College, 1956-57, Smuts Reader in Anthropology, 1961-67, director, Centre for African Studies, 1964-66, honorary fellow of Newnham College, 1967-84. Did anthropological field work in Northern Rhodesia (now Zimbabwe), 1930-31, 1933-34, and 1957, in Northern Transvaal, 1939-40, in Uganda, 1950-55. Director of Anglia Television Co., 1958-63. Visiting lecturer or professor at Northwestern University, University of Ghana, University of Chicago, and McGill University.

MEMBER: Royal Anthropological Institute (president, 1960-62), African Studies Association (United Kingdom; president, 1963-66), Association of Social Anthropologists, American Academy of Arts and Sciences (overseas fellow).

AWARDS, HONORS: Wellcome Medal for applied anthropology; Rivers Memorial Medal for field work; Commander, Order of the British Empire, 1955; fellow of British Academy, 1967.

WRITINGS:

Hunger and Work in a Savage Tribe: A Functional Study of Nutrition among the Southern Bantu, Routledge & Sons, 1932, World Publishing, 1964.
Land, Labour and Diet in Northern Rhodesia: An Economic Study of the Bemba Tribe, Oxford University Press, for International Institute of African Languages and Cultures, 1939, 2nd edition, 1962.
Bemba Marriage and Present Economic Conditions, Rhodes-Livingstone Institute, 1940.
(Editor) *Economic Development and Tribal Change: A Study of Immigrant Labour in Buganda,* Heffer, for East African Institute of Social Research, 1952, revised edition, Oxford University Press, 1975.
(Contributor) Frank Lorimer, editor, *Culture and Human Fertility: A Study of the Relation of Cultural Conditions to Fertility in Non-Industrial and Transitional Societies,* UNESCO, 1954.
Chisungu: A Girl's Initiation Ceremony among the Bemba of Northern Rhodesia, Grove, 1956.

(Editor) *East African Chiefs: A Study of Political Development in Some Uganda and Tanganyika Tribes,* Faber & Faber, 1960.
(Reviser of translation with Beatrice Hooke) *Conversations with Ogotemmeli: An Introduction to Dogon Religious Ideas,* translated from the French by Ralph Butler, Oxford University Press, for International African Institute, 1965.
The Changing Structure of a Ganda Village: Kizozi, 1892-1952, East African Publishing House (Nairobi), 1966.
The Multicultural States of East Africa, McGill-Queens University Press, 1969.
(Editor with Adam Kuper) *Councils in Action,* Cambridge University Press, 1971.
(Editor with Ford Sturrock and Jean M. Fortt) *Subsistence to Commercial Farming in Present-Day Buganda: An Economic and Anthropological Survey,* Cambridge University Press, 1973.
(With Jean Robin) *Some Elmdon Families,* Cambridge University Press, 1974.

WORK IN PROGRESS: Preparing anthropological material from Uganda.

AVOCATIONAL INTERESTS: Walking, gardening.

BIOGRAPHICAL/CRITICAL SOURCES:

BOOKS

La Fontaine, Jean Sybil, editor, *The Interpretation of Ritual: Essays in Honour of A. I. Richards,* Tavistock Publications, 1972.

OBITUARIES:

PERIODICALS

Times (London), July 3, 1974.*

*   *   *

RICHARDSON, Harry W(ard)   1938-

PERSONAL: Born December 8, 1938, in Batley, Yorkshire, England; son of George (a builder) and Lena (Wright) Richardson; married Margaret Gatiss, August 22, 1960; children: Paul Antony, Clare Francesca, Matthew Philip. *Education:* University of Manchester, B.A. (first class honors), 1959, M.A., 1961.

ADDRESSES: Office—Department of Economics, State University of New York at Albany, Albany, N.Y. 12222.

CAREER: University of Aberdeen, Aberdeen, Scotland, assistant lecturer in economics, 1960-62; University of Newcastle upon Tyne, Newcastle upon Tyne, England, lecturer in economics, 1962-64; University of Strathclyde, Glasgow, Scotland, lecturer in economics, 1964-65; University of Aberdeen, senior lecturer in economics, 1966-68; University of Kent at Canterbury, England, director of Centre for Research in the Social Sciences, beginning 1969; currently affiliated with State University of New York at Albany. Visiting professor, University of Pittsburgh, 1971, 1973.

WRITINGS:

Economic Recovery in Britain, 1932-39, Weidenfeld & Nicolson, 1967.
(With Derek Howard Aldcroft) *Building in the British Economy between the Wars,* Allen & Unwin, 1968.
Regional Economics: Location Theory, Urban Structure and Regional Change, Praeger, 1969.

Elements of Regional Economics, Penguin, 1969.
(With Aldcroft) *The British Economy, 1870-1939,* Macmillan (London), 1969, Humanities, 1970.
(Editor) *Regional Economics: A Reader,* St. Martin's, 1970.
Urban Economics, Penguin, 1971.
Input-Output and Regional Economics, Wiley, 1972.
Regional Growth Theory, Wiley, 1973.
The Economics of Urban Size, Lexington Books, 1973.
Economic Aspects of the Energy Crisis, Lexington Books, 1975.
Regional Development Policy and Planning in Spain, Lexington Books, 1975.
(With others) *Housing and Urban Spatial Structure: A Case Study,* Lexington Books, 1975.
The New Urban Economics, and Alternatives, Academic Press, 1977.
City Size and National Spatial Strategies in Developing Countries, International Bank for Reconstruction and Development, 1977.
Regional Economics, University of Illinois Press, 1979.
National Urban Development Strategies, Department of Geography, University of Reading, 1981.
(Editor with Joseph H. Turek) *Economic Prospects for the Northeast,* Temple University Press, 1985.

Contributor to business and history journals.

WORK IN PROGRESS: Research in urban and regional economics and in quantitative economic theory.

BIOGRAPHICAL/CRITICAL SOURCES:

PERIODICALS

Listener, June 29, 1967.
Observer Review, April 4, 1967.
Times Literary Supplement, July 9, 1970.*

*   *   *

RICHARDSON, Jeremy John   1942-

PERSONAL: Born June 15, 1942, in Bridgnorth, England; son of Samuel Radcliffe (an insurance broker) and Sarah (Hill) Richardson; married Anne Philippsen (a librarian), April 15, 1967. *Education:* University of Keele, B.A. (honors), 1964; University of Manchester, M.A., 1965, Ph.D., 1970. *Politics:* Conservative. *Religion:* Church of England.

ADDRESSES: Home—1 Duchess Park, Helensburgh, Scotland. *Office*—Department of Politics, University of Strathclyde, McCance Bldg., 16 Richmond St., Glasgow G1 1XQ, Scotland.

CAREER: University of Keele, Keele, Staffordshire, England, lecturer in politics, 1966-82; University of Strathclyde, Glasgow, Scotland, professor of politics and head of department, 1982—.

MEMBER: Political Studies Association, Association of University Teachers.

WRITINGS:

The Policy Making Process, Routledge & Kegan Paul, 1969, Humanities, 1970.
(Editor with Richard Kimber) *Campaigning for the Environment,* Routledge & Kegan Paul, 1974.
Pressure Groups in Britain, Rowman & Littlefield, 1974.
(Editor) *Policy Styles in Western Europe,* Allen & Unwin, 1982.

(Editor with R. Henning) *Policy Responses to Unemployment in Western Democracies,* Sage Publications, 1984.
(With Jeremy W. Moon) *Unemployment in the United Kingdom: Politics and Policies,* Gower, 1985.
(With A. G. Jordan) *British Politics and the Policy Process,* Allen & Unwin, 1987.

Also author, with Jordan, of *Pressure Groups in Britain,* 1987. Contributor to journals on political affairs.

WORK IN PROGRESS: New Technology Policies in Western Europe; Local Responses to Unemployment in the United Kingdom; Policy Responses to Economic Crisis in Western Europe.

AVOCATIONAL INTERESTS: Mountain walking, sailing.

*   *   *

RIVE, Richard (Moore)   1931-

PERSONAL: Surname rhymes with "leave"; born March 1, 1931, in Cape Town, South Africa; son of Nancy (Ward) Rive. *Education:* Hewat Training College (now Hewat College of Education), Cape Town, Teacher's Diploma, 1951; University of Cape Town, B.A., 1962, B.Ed., 1968; Columbia University, M.A., 1966; Oxford University, D.Phil., 1974.

ADDRESSES: Home—31 Windsor Park Ave., Heathfield 7800, Cape Town, South Africa.

CAREER: Former teacher of English and Latin at South Peninsula High School, Cape Town, South Africa; affiliated with Harvard University, Cambridge, Mass., 1987; Hewat College of Education, Cape Town, formerly lecturer in English, head of Department of English, 1988—.

AWARDS, HONORS: Farfield Foundation fellowship to travel and study contemporary African literature in English and French, 1963; Fulbright scholar and Heft scholar, 1965-66; named Writer of the Year for South Africa, 1970, for "The Visits"; African Theatre Competition Prize, British Broadcasting Corp., 1972, for "Make Like Slaves."

WRITINGS:

African Songs (short stories), Seven Seas, 1963.
(Editor and contributor) *Quartet: New Voices from South Africa,* Crown, 1963.
Emergency (novel), introduction by Ezekiel Mphahlele, Faber, 1964, Collier Books, 1970.
(Compiler) *Modern African Prose,* Heinemann, 1964, reprinted, 1982.
Selected Writings: Stories, Essays, and Plays, Ad Donker (Johannesburg), 1977.
Writing Black (autobiography), D. Philip (Cape Town), 1982.
Advance, Retreat: Selected Short Stories, D. Philip, 1983.
"Buckingham Palace," *District Six,* D. Philip, 1986, Ballantine, 1987.

CONTRIBUTOR TO ANTHOLOGIES

Peggy Rutherford, editor, *Darkness and Light: An Anthology of African Writing,* Drum Publications (Johannesburg), 1958, published as *African Voices,* Grosset, 1959.
Langston Hughes, editor, *An African Treasury: Articles, Essays, Stories, Poems by Black Africans,* Crown, 1960.
Hughes, editor, *Poems from Black Africa,* Indiana University Press, 1963.
Ellis Ayitey and Mphahlele, editors, *Modern African Stories,* Faber, 1964.

Neville Denny, editor, *Pan African Short Stories,* Thomas Nelson, 1965.

Mphahlele, editor, *African Writing Today,* Penguin, 1967.

Leonard Sainville, editor, *Anthologie de la litterature negro-africaine: Romanciers et conteurs negro-africains,* Volume II, Presence Africaine, 1968.

Austin J. Shelton, Jr., editor, *The African Assertion: A Critical Anthology of African Literature,* Odyssey Press, 1968.

OTHER

Also author of "Make Like Slaves" (play), 1972. Contributor to periodicals in Africa, Europe, Asia, New Zealand, and the United States. Assistant editor, *Contrast* (literary quarterly).

WORK IN PROGRESS: A South African Abroad.

SIDELIGHTS: Raised in Cape Town, the son of a black American father and "colored" South African mother, Richard Rive often writes of the injustices of apartheid with "delightful humor where one would expect bitterness and anger," describes Kofi Anyidoho in *World Literature Today.* Although much of Rive's work can be characterized as "strong stuff," his specialty lies in "the ironies inherent in racial relationships," notes Robert L. Berner in a *World Literature Today* review of *Selected Writings: Stories, Essays, and Plays. Writing Black,* for example, an autobiographical series of sketches and essays, "is a stream of countless little episodes spiced with brief, often devastating sketches of unforgettable characters" says Anyidoho. "Rive's design rarely abandons us to the singular beauty or horror of the individual episode or sketch," comments the critic. Instead of focusing on the meaning of each separate instance, in *Writing Black* Rive demonstrates the "larger patterns of converging significance."

Rive also uses multiple images and themes to unify his fiction writing. In the *Journal of the New African Literature and the Arts,* Bernth Lindfors describes Rive's style as "characterized by strong rhythms, daring images, brisk dialogue, and leitmotifs (recurring words, phrases, images) which function as unifying devices." In *Emergency,* a novel describing the declaration of a state of emergency in Cape Town, Lindfors finds that this style "stumbles along in fits and starts and spurts," hampering the flow of the novel. The critic thinks that for Rive to "write a successful novel he must learn to use his talent in a new way."

Like *Emergency,* Rive's *"Buckingham Palace," District Six* dramatizes the oppressive actions of the apartheid government in Cape Town. In relating the story of the inhabitants of District Six, a "colored" slum slated for demolition by the government, Rive "brilliantly intensifies their tragedy by homing in on their humorous humanity rather than on their eventual dispersal," comments a *Publishers Weekly* reviewer. Rive's talent, according to William Walsh in the *Times Educational Supplement,* allows him to "keep in productive balance irony bordering on despair" and characters that demonstrate the humor and strangeness of the human condition. William Finnegan, in the *New York Times Book Review,* criticizes some of these characters and situations, remarking that those based on "worn-smooth issues . . . sink nearly to the level of a television sitcom." Nevertheless, Finnegan finds that the novel "gains sudden, almost headlong momentum and a genuine power" when describing the "war" of the government against District Six. Like most of Rive's writing, *"Buckingham Palace," District Six* "is not writing from the revolution's front lines," comments Finnegan. "But it is good, affecting melodrama. And it does help explain" the effects of apartheid in Cape

Town. "The novelist in the South African setting has to handle material that has become by now a huge cliche," comments Ezekiel Mphahlele in the introduction to Rive's *Emergency,* "violence, its aftermath, and the response it elicits. In this he travels a path that has many pitfalls." By focusing on the humanity of his characters so they are neither "tiny" nor "poetic," Mphahlele feels that Rive "has avoided these pitfalls."

Rive's work has been translated into twelve languages, including Russian.

AVOCATIONAL INTERESTS: Mountain climbing, coaching track athletics.

BIOGRAPHICAL/CRITICAL SOURCES:

BOOKS

Rive, Richard, *Emergency,* introduction by Ezekiel Mphahlele, Collier Books, 1970.

Rive, Richard, *Writing Black* (autobiography), D. Philip (Cape Town), 1982.

PERIODICALS

Journal of the New African Literature and the Arts, fall, 1966.
New York Times Book Review, October 4, 1987.
Publishers Weekly, June 12, 1987.
Times Educational Supplement, August 21, 1987.
Times Literary Supplement, April 1, 1965.
Transition, February, 1966.
World Literature Today, spring, 1978, summer, 1982.

*   *   *

ROBINSON, Patricia
See GOEDICKE, Patricia (McKenna)

*   *   *

ROBSON, Lucia St. Clair   1942-

PERSONAL: Surname is pronounced *Rob*-son; born September 24, 1942, in Baltimore, Md.; daughter of Robert McCombs and Jeanne (Savage) Robson. *Education:* Palm Beach Junior College, A.A., 1962; University of Florida, B.A., 1964; Florida State University, M.L.S., 1974.

ADDRESSES: Home and office—Arnold, Md. *Agent*—Virginia Barber Literary Agency, Inc., 353 West 21st St., New York, N.Y. 10011.

CAREER: U.S. Peace Corps, volunteer worker in Caripito, Venezuela, 1964-66; teacher at public school in Brooklyn, N.Y., 1966-68; Hialeah Public Library, Hialeah, Fla., librarian, 1968-69; teacher of English in Japan, 1969-71; Fort Jackson Library, Columbia, S.C., librarian, 1971-72; Anne Arundel County Public Library, Annapolis, Md., librarian, 1975-82; writer, 1981—.

MEMBER: Western Writers of America.

AWARDS, HONORS: America Golden Spur Award for best historical novel, Western Writers of America, 1982, for *Ride the Wind.*

WRITINGS:

HISTORICAL NOVELS

Ride the Wind, Ballantine, 1982.
Walk in My Soul, Ballantine, 1985.
Light a Distant Fire, Ballantine, 1988.

WORK IN PROGRESS: A historical novel set in feudal Japan, to be published by Ballantine.

SIDELIGHTS: Lucia St. Clair Robson told *CA:* "Creating historical fiction can have an unforeseen effect on a writer. Time-tripping becomes an addiction, a necessity as basic as corn dogs and cable TV. Research trips become forays into the past." She continued: "On research trips one finds tracks of the past in the asphalt of the present. On the back roads it's easier for me to understand the lives my characters led, than it would be for them to understand mine. Sharing the car with their ghosts and a companionable solitude, there is time for remembering events that happened over a hundred years before I was born." In 1985 she remarked to *CA:* "Writing historical fiction is as close as I can come to the career I really would like to pursue—being a time travel agent."

BIOGRAPHICAL/CRITICAL SOURCES:

PERIODICALS

Library Journal, September 15, 1982.
Washington Post, July 15, 1985.

*   *   *

ROCKLEY, L(awrence) E(dwin)   1916-

PERSONAL: Born August 11, 1916, in Leicester, England; son of Arthur Edwin (an electrical engineer) and Laura (Norman) Rockley; married Margaret Joan Gray, February 10, 1940; children: Anne Cathryn (Mrs. Nigel R. Hopkins), Richard David. *Education:* Attended University College, Leicester (now University of Leicester) and Leicester College of Technology, 1933-38; B.Com. (London), 1948; Warwick University, M.Phil. *Religion:* Methodist.

ADDRESSES: Home—Charnwood, 121 Windy Arbour, Kenilworth, Warwickshire CV8 2BJ, England.

CAREER: Leicester Electricity Undertaking, Leicester, England, senior assistant, 1946-47; City Treasurer's Office, Leicester, principal assistant and deputy chief internal auditor, 1947-56; National Coal Board, Warwickshire, England, area chief auditor, 1957-60; Lanchester Polytechnic, Coventry, England, beginning 1960, began as lecturer, principal lecturer in business finance, 1965-80. Principal, Rockley-Evans Associates, 1966—; managing director, Cailvale Ltd., 1973—. Lecturer, British Productivity Council; consultant to business firms. *Military service:* British Army, 1940-46; became major.

MEMBER: Institute of Municipal Treasurers and Accountants (associate), British Institute of Management (associate).

AWARDS, HONORS: Annual "Book of the Year" Award, Society of Commercial Accountants, 1971, for *Finance for the Non-Accountant;* Social Science Research Council grant to do research for Ph.D. dissertation.

WRITINGS:

Production Control Information, Kynoch Press, 1965.
Capital Investment Decisions, Business Books Ltd., 1968.
Finance for the Non-Accountant, Business Books Ltd., 1970, 4th edition, 1984.
Non-Accountant's Guide to Finance, Business Books Ltd., 1972.
Investment for Profitability, Business Books Ltd., 1972.
Non-Accountant's Guide to the Balance Sheet, Business Books Ltd., 1973.

Public and Local Authority Accounts, Heinemann, 1975, 2nd edition, 1975.
The Meaning of Balance Sheets and Company Reports, Business Books Ltd., 1975, 2nd edition, 1983.
Finance for the Purchasing Executive, Brookfield Publishing, 1978.
A Policy for Disclosure, Associated Business Press, 1980.
Security: Its Management and Control, Brookfield Publishing, 1981.

Contributor to business journals.*

*   *   *

ROCKWOOD, Roy
[Collective pseudonym]

WRITINGS:

A Schoolboy's Pluck; or, The Career of a Nobody (originally serialized in *Young People of America,* 1895-96, under title "A Nobody Schoolboy; or, Backbone against the World" by Philip A. Alyer), Mershon, 1900.
The Wizard of the Sea; or, A Trip under the Ocean (originally serialized in *Young Sports of America,* 1895, under title "The Wizard of the Deep; or, Over and under the Ocean in Search of the $1,000,000 Pearl" by Theodore Edison), Mershon, 1900.
The Cruise of the Treasure Ship; or, The Castaways of Floating Island (also see below), Mershon, 1906.
Jack North's Treasure Hunt; or, Daring Adventures in South America (also see below), Chatterton-Peck, 1907.
(Contributor) *Popular Stories for Boys,* Cupples & Leon, 1934.

"BOMBA THE JUNGLE BOY" SERIES

Bomba the Jungle Boy; or, The Old Naturalist's Secret, Cupples & Leon, 1926, reprinted, Grosset & Dunlap, 1953, published as *Bomba the Jungle Boy,* 1978.
. . . at the Moving Mountain; or, The Mystery of the Caves of Fire, Cupples & Leon, 1926, reprinted, Grosset & Dunlap, 1953, published as *Bomba the Jungle Boy: The Moving Mountain,* 1978.
. . . at the Giant Cataract; or, Chief Nascanora and His Captives, Cupples & Leon, 1926, reprinted, Grosset & Dunlap, 1953.
. . . on Jaguar Island; or, Adrift on the River of Mystery, Cupples & Leon, 1927, reprinted, Grosset & Dunlap, 1953.
. . . in the Abandoned City; or, A Treasure 10,000 Years Old, Cupples & Leon, 1927, reprinted, Grosset & Dunlap, 1953.
. . . on Terror Trail; or, The Mysterious Men from the Sky, Cupples & Leon, 1928, reprinted, Grosset & Dunlap, 1953.
. . . in the Swamp of Death; or, The Sacred Alligators of Abarago, Cupples & Leon, 1929, reprinted, Grosset & Dunlap, 1953.
. . . among the Slaves; or, Daring Adventures in the Valley of Skulls, Cupples & Leon, 1929, reprinted, Grosset & Dunlap, 1953.
. . . on the Underground River; or, The Cave of Bottomless Pits, Cupples & Leon, 1930, reprinted, Grosset & Dunlap, 1953.
. . . and the Lost Explorers; or, A Wonderful Revelation, Cupples & Leon, 1930, reprinted, Grosset & Dunlap, 1953.
. . . in a Strange Land; or, Facing the Unknown, Cupples & Leon, 1931.
. . . among the Pygmies; or, Battling with Stealthy Foes, Cupples & Leon, 1931.

. . . and the Cannibals; or, Winning against Native Dangers, Cupples & Leon, 1932.

. . . and the Painted Hunters; or, A Long Search Rewarded, Cupples & Leon, 1932.

. . . and the River Demons; or, Outwitting the Savage Medicine Man, Cupples & Leon, 1933.

. . . and the Hostile Chieftain; or, A Hazardous Trek to the Sea, Cupples & Leon, 1934.

. . . Trapped by the Cyclone; or, Shipwrecked on the Swirling Seas, Cupples & Leon, 1935.

. . . in the Land of Burning Lava; or, Outwitting Superstitious Natives, Cupples & Leon, 1936.

. . . in the Perilous Kingdom; or, Braving Strange Hazards, Cupples & Leon, 1937.

. . . in the Steaming Grotto; or, Victorious through Flame and Fury, Cupples & Leon, 1938.

"DAVE DASHAWAY" SERIES

Dave Dashaway, the Young Aviator; or, In the Clouds for Fame and Fortune, Cupples & Leon, 1913.

. . . and His Hydroplane; or, Daring Adventures over the Great Lakes, Cupples & Leon, 1913.

. . . and His Giant Airship; or, A Marvelous Trip across the Atlantic, Cupples & Leon, 1913.

. . . around the World; or, A Young Yankee Aviator among Many Nations, Cupples & Leon, 1913.

. . ., Air Champion; or, Wizard Work in the Clouds, Cupples & Leon, 1915.

"DAVE FEARLESS" SERIES

Dave Fearless after a Sunken Treasure; or, The Rival Ocean Divers (originally published as *The Rival Ocean Divers; or, The Search for a Sunken Treasure;* also see below), G. Sully, 1918.

. . . on a Floating Island; or, The Cruise of the Treasure Ship (originally published as *The Cruise of the Treasure Ship; or, The Castaways of Floating Island;* also see below), G. Sully, 1918.

. . . and the Cave of Mystery; or, Adrift on the Pacific (originally published as *Adrift on the Pacific; or, The Secret of the Island Cave;* also see below), G. Sully, 1918.

. . . among the Icebergs; or, The Secret of the Eskimo Igloo, Garden City, 1926.

. . . Wrecked among Savages; or, The Captives of the Headhunters, Garden City, 1926.

. . . and His Big Raft; or, Alone on the Broad Pacific, Garden City, 1926.

. . . on Volcano Island; or, The Magic Cave of Blue Fire, Garden City, 1926.

. . . Captured by Apes; or, In Gorilla Land, Garden City, 1926.

. . . and the Mutineers; or, Prisoners on the Ship of Death, Garden City, 1926.

. . . under the Ocean; or, The Treasure of the Lost Submarine, Garden City, 1926.

. . . in the Black Jungle; or, Lost among the Cannibals, Garden City, 1926.

. . . near the South Pole; or, The Giant Whales of Snow Island, Garden City, 1926.

. . . Caught by Malay Pirates; or, The Secret of Bamboo Island, Garden City, 1926.

. . . on the Ship of Mystery; or, The Strange Hermit of Shark Cove, Garden City, 1927.

. . . on the Lost Brig; or, Abandoned in the Big Hurricane, Garden City, 1927.

. . . at Whirlpool Point; or, The Mystery of the Water Cave, Garden City, 1927.

. . . among the Cannibals; or, The Defense of the Hut in the Swamp, Garden City, 1927.

"DEEP SEA" SERIES

The Rival Ocean Divers; or, The Search for a Sunken Treasure (originally serialized in *Golden Hours,* 1901, under title "The Rival Ocean Divers; or, A Boy's Daring Search for Sunken Treasure"), Stitt, 1905.

The Cruise of the Treasure Ship; or, The Castaways of Floating Island, Stitt, 1907.

Adrift on the Pacific; or, The Secret of the Island Cave, Grosset & Dunlap, 1908.

Jack North's Treasure Hunt; or, Daring Adventures in South America, Grosset & Dunlap, 1908.

"GREAT MARVEL" SERIES

Through the Air to the North Pole; or, The Wonderful Cruise of the Electric Monarch, Cupples & Leon, 1906.

Under the Ocean to the South Pole; or, The Strange Cruise of the Submarine Wonder, Cupples & Leon, 1907.

Five Thousand Miles Underground; or, The Mystery of the Center of the Earth, Cupples & Leon, 1908.

Through Space to Mars; or, The Most Wonderful Trip on Record, Cupples & Leon, 1910.

Lost on the Moon; or, In Quest of the Field of Diamonds, Cupples & Leon, 1911.

On a Torn-Away World; or, Captives of the Great Earthquake, Cupples & Leon, 1913.

The City beyond the Clouds; or, Captured by the Red Dwarfs, Cupples & Leon, 1925.

By Air Express to Venus; or, Captives of a Strange People, Cupples & Leon, 1929.

By Space Ship to Saturn; or, Exploring the Ringed Planet, Cupples & Leon, 1935.

"SEA TREASURE" SERIES

Adrift on the Pacific; or, The Secret of the Island Cave, Grosset & Dunlap, 1908.

The Cruise of the Treasure Ship; or, The Castaways of Floating Island, Grosset & Dunlap, 1908.

The Rival Ocean Divers; or, The Search for a Sunken Treasure, Grosset & Dunlap, 1908.

Jack North's Treasure Hunt; or, Daring Adventures in South America, Grosset & Dunlap, 1908.

"SPEEDWELL BOYS" SERIES

The Speedwell Boys on Motorcycles; or, The Mystery of a Great Conflagration, Cupples & Leon, 1913.

. . . and Their Racing Auto; or, A Run for the Golden Cup, Cupples & Leon, 1913.

. . . and Their Power Launch; or, To the Rescue of the Castaways, Cupples & Leon, 1913.

. . . in a Submarine; or, The Treasure of Rocky Cove, Cupples & Leon, 1913.

. . . and Their Ice Racer; or, Lost in the Great Blizzard, Cupples & Leon, 1915.

OTHER

Also author of *Flyer Fred, the Cyclist Ferret; or, Running Down the Rough and Ready Rascals* (originally serialized in *Banner Weekly,* 1896), for the dime novel series Half-Dime Library. Contributor to periodicals, including *Golden Hours, Banner Weekly, Young Sports of America,* and *Bright Days.*

SIDELIGHTS: Roy Rockwood was the pseudonym used by the Stratemeyer Syndicate for some of its most popular boys' series. Edward Stratemeyer, Howard R. Garis, and Leslie McFarlane are known to have used this pseudonym to produce stories in various genres ranging from jungle and racing adventure to science fiction.

The most prominent of these adventure series was "Bomba the Jungle Boy," "whose adventures in many volumes provided an endless survival course for thousands of youngsters who were never likely to find themselves within miles of a jungle," remembers Leslie McFarlane in his autobiography *Ghost of the Hardy Boys.* Bomba was described by Arthur Prager in *Rascals at Large: or, The Clue in the Old Nostalgia* as "Stratemeyer's answer to Tarzan." Like Tarzan, Bomba was a foundling, raised from childhood in the jungles of the upper Amazon basin by the half-demented naturalist Cody Casson. The resemblances were not exact; Prager states that while Tarzan "spoke like a true English gentleman, and conversed easily in French as well," the Jungle Boy "usually referred to himself in the third person." Also, while Tarzan's exploits explore themes of sex and violence, Bomba's adventures center around his search for his parents, Andrew and Laura Bartow. Prager points out that a strain of racism ran through both series, but indicates that Bomba's was more overt "until the jungle lad got to civilization and found that all men are vile and only the virgin jungle is pure. By the end of the series he had found out that you can't trust anybody, regardless of color."

The Rockwood pseudonym was also used for the "Speedwell Boys" series, which Prager compares to the later "Hardy Boys" novels, and for the "Dave Fearless" diving adventures. Dan and Billy Speedwell "were mechanically inclined, and could break down an automobile engine and repair it in no time at all," reports Prager. The brothers and their girl friends, Mildred and Lettie, built racing machines that they crashed periodically. Leslie McFarlane, who contributed at least three volumes to Dave Fearless's adventures, recalls that Dave "was no novice in the diving business"; at the age of twenty-one, he was a fully qualified diver. With his friend Bob Vilett, a marine engineer, he braved dangers below and above the ocean waves.

One of the best remembered of all series produced under this pseudonym, however, was the "Great Marvel" series, described by Prager as "a mixture of Jules Verne and Edgar Rice Burroughs (in his science fiction period), toned [down] to subteen level." In some ways, the series was very innovative; Prager remarks that in one volume of the series Stratemeyer "invented jet propulsion." He concludes that the series "was fun to read, and omitted much of the corn that was chronic in similar series of the pre-war era."

MEDIA ADAPTATIONS: Twelve black-and-white films loosely based on the "Bomba the Jungle Boy" series were made between 1949 and 1955. All were directed by Ford Beebe and starred Johnny Sheffield (who also played "Boy" in the Tarzan films) as Bomba: "Bomba, the Jungle Boy," Allied Artists, 1949; "Bomba on Panther Island," Allied Artists, 1949; "Bomba and the Hidden City," Allied Artists, 1950; "The Lost Volcano," Allied Artists, 1950; "Elephant Stampede," Allied Artists, 1951; "The Lion Hunters," Allied Artists, 1951; "African Treasure," Allied Artists, 1952; "Bomba and the Jungle Girl," Allied Artists, 1952; "Safari Drums," Allied Artists, 1953; "The Golden Idol," Allied Artists, 1954; "Killer

Leopard," Allied Artists, 1954; and "Lord of the Jungle," Allied Artists, 1955.

BIOGRAPHICAL/CRITICAL SOURCES:

BOOKS

Dizer, John T., Jr., *Tom Swift & Company: "Boys' Books" by Stratemeyer and Others*, McFarland & Co., 1982.
Garis, Roger, *My Father Was Uncle Wiggly*, McGraw-Hill, 1966.
Johnson, Deidre, editor and compiler, *Stratemeyer Pseudonyms and Series Books: An Annotated Checklist of Stratemeyer and Stratemeyer Syndicate Publications*, Greenwood Press, 1982.
McFarlane, Leslie, *Ghost of the Hardy Boys*, Two Continents, 1976.
Prager, Arthur, *Rascals at Large; or, The Clue in the Old Nostalgia*, Doubleday, 1971.

PERIODICALS

Journal of Popular Culture, winter, 1974.

*   *   *

RODGERS, Carolyn M(arie)   1945-

PERSONAL: Born December 14, 1945, in Chicago, Ill.; daughter of Clarence and Bazella (Colding) Rodgers. *Education:* Attended University of Illinois, 1960-61; Roosevelt University, B.A., 1965; University of Chicago, M.A., 1983. *Religion:* African Methodist Episcopal.

CAREER: Y.M.C.A., Chicago, Ill., social worker, 1963-68; Columbia College, Chicago, lecturer in Afro-American literature, 1968-69; University of Washington, Seattle, instructor in Afro-American literature, summer, 1970; Albany State College, Albany, Ga., writer in residence, 1972; Malcolm X College, Chicago, writer in residence, 1972; Indiana University, Bloomington, instructor in Afro-American literature, summer, 1973.

MEMBER: Organization of Black American Culture Writers Workshop, Gwendolyn Brooks Writers Workshop, Delta Sigma Theta.

AWARDS, HONORS: First Conrad Kent Rivers Memorial Fund Award, 1968; National Endowment for the Arts grant, 1970; Poet Laureate Award, Society of Midland Authors, 1970; National Book Award nomination, 1976, for *how i got ovah: New and Selected Poems;* Carnegie Award, 1979, PEN awards.

WRITINGS:

POETRY

Paper Soul, Third World Press, 1968.
Songs of a Blackbird, Third World Press, 1969.
2 Love Raps, Third World Press, 1969.
Now Ain't That Love, Broadside Press, 1970.
For H. W. Fuller, Broadside Press, 1970.
For Flip Wilson, Broadside Press, 1971.
Long Rap/Commonly Known as a Poetic Essay, Broadside Press, 1971.
how i got ovah: New and Selected Poems, Doubleday/Anchor, 1975.
The Heart as Ever Green: Poems, Doubleday/Anchor, 1978.
Translation: Poems, Eden Press, 1980.
Finite Forms: Poems, Eden Press, 1985.

CONTRIBUTOR TO ANTHOLOGIES

Ahmed Alhamsi and Harun K. Wangara, editors, *Black Arts,* Broadside Press, 1969.

Arnold Adoff, editor, *Brothers and Sisters,* Macmillan, 1970.

Orde Coombs, editor, *We Speak as Liberators,* Dodd, 1970.

Ted Wilentz and Tom Weatherley, editors, *Natural Process,* Hill & Wang, 1970.

Gwendolyn Brooks, editor, *Jump Bad,* Broadside Press, 1971.

Dudley Randall, editor, *The Black Poets,* Bantam, 1971.

Woodie King, editor, *Blackspirits,* Random House, 1972.

Richard A. Long and Eugenia W. Collier, editors, *Afro-American Writing,* New York University Press, 1972.

William R. Robinson, editor, *Nommo,* Macmillan, 1972.

Adoff, editor, *The Poetry of Black America,* Harper, 1973.

Stephen Henderson, editor, *Understanding the New Black Poetry,* Morrow, 1973.

Black Sister, Indiana University Press, 1983.

Amiri Baraka, editor, *Confirmation Anthology,* Morrow, 1984.

Mari Evans, editor, *Black Women Writers (1950-1980): A Critical Evaluation,* Doubleday/Anchor, 1984.

Also contributor to *No Crystal Stairs,* 1984.

OTHER

(Editor) *Roots* (anthology), Indiana University Press, 1973.

A Little Lower Than Angels (novel), Eden Press, 1984.

Former reviewer for *Chicago Daily News* and columnist for *Milwaukee Courier.*

WORK IN PROGRESS: Rain, short stories; *Arise,* a novel.

SIDELIGHTS: "Carolyn Marie Rodgers is best known as one of the new black poets to emerge from the Chicago Organization of Black American Culture during the 1960s," writes Jean Davis in a *Dictionary of Literary Biography* essay. Calling her "one of the most sensitive and complex poets to emerge from this movement and struggle with its contradictions," Bettye J. Parker-Smith suggests in Mari Evans's *Black Women Writers (1950-1980): A Critical Evaluation* that Rogers has been "instrumental in helping create, and give a new definition or receptive power to, poetry as a Black art form." Although Rodgers's poetry has always concerned the search for self, it has evolved from a militant, sociological perspective to a more introspective one. Davis indicates that while Rodgers has spent most of her career as a poet in her native Chicago, she has gained national recognition for "her thematic concerns with feminist issues, particularly those affecting the black woman in a changing society." Angelene Jamison asserts in her essay, also in *Black Women Writers (1950-1980),* that like "most of the Black women poets of the last twenty years [who] are casually referred to only as by-products of the New Black Arts Movement," Rodgers still awaits both the attention her work deserves, as well as her "appropriate place in literature."

Rodgers began writing "quasi seriously" as an outlet for the frustrations of her first year at college, as she recalls in an interview with Evans in her *Black Women Writers (1950-1980);* she later participated in the Organization of Black American Culture's Writers Workshop and soon became part of the prolific black arts movement of the 1960s. Rodgers's "theological and philosophical approach to the ills that plague Black people . . . and her attempts to master an appropriate language to comunicate with the masses of Black people" suggest to Parker-Smith that she is "an exemplar of the 'revolutionary poet.'" Rodgers, who considers her work both art as well as polemic, tells Evans that she has no distinctly defined political

stance and that she feels literature "functions as a type of catharsis or amen arena" in the lives of people: "I think it speaks not only to the political sensibility but to the heart, the mind, the spirit, and the soul of every man, woman, and child."

Noting that Rodgers's poetry voices varied concerns, including "revolution, love, Black male-female relationships, religion, and the complexities of Black womanhood," Jamison declares that "through a skilfully uncluttered use of several literary devices, she convincingly reinterprets the love, pain, longings, struggles, victories, the day-to-day routines of Black people from the point of view of the Black woman. Gracefully courageous enough to explore long-hidden truths, about Black women particularly, her poetry shows honesty, warmth, and love for Black people." Commenting about the "intensely personal" aspect of Rodger's poetry, Parker-Smith believes that this autobiographical element helps one to more easily comprehend her work. Rodgers "struggles to affirm her womanliness," but hasn't the strength to "move beyond those obstacles that threaten the full development of Black womanhood," Parker-Smith explains. "For her, there are three major dilemmas: the fear of assimilating the value system of her mother, which interferes with claiming an independent lifestyle of her own; the attempt to define her 'self' by the standards of the social system responsible for creating her own and her mother's condition; and the search for love (a man) that will simultaneously electrify and save her."

Rogers's first volume of poetry, *Paper Soul,* "reflects the duality of an individual struggling to reconcile complex realities, dilemmas, and contradictions," says Davis, who recognizes a thematic shift in her second volume of poetry, *Songs of a Blackbird.* Davis suggests that the former addresses "identity, religion, revolution, and love, or more accurately a woman's need for love," whereas the latter deals with "survival, street life, mother-daughter conflict, and love." Indicating that these poems are increasingly concerned with "the black woman poet as a major theme," Davis states that "questions of identity for the poet remain connected with relationships between black men and women but become more centrally located in the woman's ability to express herself."

While finding Rodgers's poetry from the late 1960s "vivid and forceful," Davis notes that these first two volumes were not unanimously praised: "Nor did the young poet win unqualified acceptance as a significant new voice among black poets." She states, for instance, that Dudley Randall and Haki Madhubuti had "reservations about her language and her rendering of black speech." Davis posits, however, that Rodgers's "use of speech patterns and of lengthened prose-like lines was an attempt at breaking away from the restrictions of conventional forms and modes, and most especially from those considered appropriate for women poets." Inasmuch as "theme and language" were the general hallmarks of the black art movement from this period, Parker-Smith believes that "the use of obscenities and Black speech patterns" was especially courageous for female artists. Although acknowledging a certain inconsistency in the language of her early poetry, Davis believes that "Rodgers nonetheless had an eye for the contradictions of black experience, particularly the revolutionary or militant experience of the 1960s." And, despite their initial objections to her work, says Davis, poets and critics such as Madhubuti, Randall, and Gwendolyn Brooks, "nonetheless . . . recognized her genuine talent and remarked her development."

In Rodgers's *how i got ovah: New and Selected Poems,* written in the mid-1970s, though, she exhibits "a clarity of expression and a respect for well-crafted language," states Davis, who perceives "humor, sincerity, and love" in the autobiographical poems about "black revolution, feminism, religion, God, the black church, and the black family, especially the mother." Similarly, Hilda Njoki McElroy writes in *Black World:* "It is obvious that Carolyn Rodgers loves her craft and her people. *How I got Ovah* is a result of this love match. It is an important literary contribution containing many aspects of human frailty/achievement, love/hate, positive/negative, funny/sad, beautiful/ugly which makes it deeeeep, very deeeeeep." Suggesting that these poems "reveal Rodgers's transformation from a . . . militant Black woman to a woman intensely concerned with God, traditional values, and her private self," Davis adds that "although her messages often explore social conflict, they usually conclude with a sense of peace, hope, and a desire to search for life's real treasure—inner beauty."

Parker-Smith describes what she refers to as the "two distinct and clear baptisms" that Rodgers's work has experienced: "The first can be viewed as being rough-hewn, folk-spirited, and held 'down at the river' amid water moccasins in the face of a glaring midday sun; the climax of a 'swing-lo-sweet-chariot' revival." Parker-Smith indicates that Rodgers's early work, which is "characterized by a potpourri of themes," exemplifies this period and "demonstrates her impudence, through the use of her wit, obscenities, the argumentation in her love and revolution poems, and the pain and presence of her mother." Parker-Smith points out that Rodgers "questions the relevance of the Vietnam War, declares war on the cities, laments Malcolm X, and criticizes the contradictory life-style of Blacks. And she glances at God." Although this was a time when Rodgers "whipped with a lean switch, often bringing down her wrath with stinging, sharp, and sometimes excruciating pain," Parker-Smith suggests that "the ribald outcry, the incongruity and cynicism that characterize the first period are links in Rodgers' chain of personal judgments—her attempts to come to grips with 'self'—and with the Black Arts Movement as a whole."

"The second baptism takes place just before Carolyn Rodgers is able to shake herself dry from the first river," Parker-Smith continues: "This one can perhaps be classified as a sprinkling and is protected by the blessings of a very fine headcloth. It is more sophisticated. It is cooler; lacks the fire and brimstone of the first period. But it is nonetheless penetrating." During this time, Rodgers moved from Third World Press to a larger commercial publishing house; and, according to Parker-Smith, having broken with the Organization of Black American Culture as well, Rodgers "moved back inside her once lone and timid world." Considering *how i got ovah* and *The Heart as Ever Green: Poems* to exemplify this second phase, Parker-Smith finds that Rodgers closely examines "the revolution, its contradictions, and her relationship to it." Rodgers also "listens to her mother's whispers" and "embraces God," says Parker-Smith, who concludes that "it is impossible to separate the poet's new attitude toward religion from her attitude toward revolution (the one seems to have evoked the other), they have converged to assist her in her continuous search for 'self.'" And although Parker-Smith suggests Rodgers did not take her craft seriously enough in the early poetry, she believes that "a more developed talent" emerges in the second period, revealing "growth and strength and a higher level of clarity, with a new level of sophistication."

Identity and potentiality are central themes in Rodgers's work; and according to Davis, "the evolving feminism" in her poetry is but "a natural extension of her reflections on herself and her world." "I see myself as becoming," Rodgers calls Evans. "I am a has-been, would perhaps, going to be. Underneath, I'm a dot. With no i's." Davis suggests that "determination to grow and to be is the most prevalent idea" in Rodgers's *The Heart As Ever Green,* where "the themes of human dignity, feminism, love, black consciousness, and Christianity are repeated throughout." Rodgers expresses to Evans that "honesty in vision and aspect" are most important to her in her work; and suggesting that the "level of honesty in her work [is] indicative of her own freedom," Jamison believes that "in a variety of idioms ranging from the street to the church, she writes about Black women with a kind of sensitivity and warmth that brings them out of the poems and into our own lives." Jamison adds that "clearly, her artistry brings these women to life, but it is her love for them that gives them their rightful place in literature. The love, the skill, indeed the vision, which she brings to her poetry must certainly help Black women rediscover and better understand themselves."

"It is impossible to assess the actual merit of Carolyn Rodgers' achievements at this point," says Parker-Smith. "And it is difficult to see where she will go from here. She has changed from a rebel to a religious loyalist, but a religious loyalist of a peculiarly different state was present from the start. . . . Her frantic search for love, the constant battle with her mother, the ambiguity about religion, are factors that run wild in her soul." Davis remarks that Rodgers has witnessed changes both in herself and her work: "In the beginning of her career, she reveals, 'I was just a writer out here just writing. Then I went to an orientation of Black (Negro) work and then I wrote with a message, a sociological orientation. Actually, I've come full circle to a certain extent. I don't write the same message.'" Although survival represents a dominant theme in her stories and poetry, Davis adds that Rodgers "interweaves the idea of adaptability and conveys the concomitant message of life's ever-changing avenues for black people whom she sees as her special audience." Davis relates Rodgers's statement about her writing being "for whoever wants to read it . . . one poem doesn't do that. But I try to put as many as I can in a book. A poem for somebody young, religious people, the church people. Just people. Specifically, Black people. I would like for them to like me." Rodgers acknowledges to Evans that the direction of her writing has "indeed" changed in the last decade: "My focus is on life, love, eternity, pain, and joy. These matters are cared about by Brown people, aren't they?"

BIOGRAPHICAL/CRITICAL SOURCES:

BOOK

Dictionary of Literary Biography, Volume 41: *Afro-American Poets since 1955,* Gale, 1985.
Evans, Mari, editor, *Black Women Writers (1950-1980): A Critical Evaluation,* Doubleday-Anchor, 1984.

PERIODICALS

Black Scholar, March, 1981.
Black World, August, 1970, February, 1976.
Chicago Tribune, November 19, 1978.
Negro Digest, September, 1968.
Washington Post Book World, May 18, 1975.†

—*Sketch by Sharon Malinowski*

ROSE, Richard 1933-

PERSONAL: Born April 9, 1933, in St. Louis, Mo.; son of Charles I. (a merchant) and Mary (Conely) Rose; married Rosemary J. Kenny, April 14, 1956; children: Clare, Charles, Lincoln. *Education:* Johns Hopkins University, B.A., 1953; London School of Economics and Political Science, graduate study, 1953-54; Oxford University, D.Phil., 1959. *Politics:* "Border-state democrat." *Religion:* "Lapsed Southern Presbyterian."

ADDRESSES: Home—1 East Abercromby St., Helensburgh, Dunbartonshire G84 7SP, Scotland. *Office*—Centre for the Study of Public Policy, University of Strathclyde, Glasgow G1 1XH, Scotland.

CAREER: St. Louis Post-Dispatch, St. Louis, Mo., reporter, 1955-57; University of Manchester, Manchester, England, lecturer in politics, 1961-66; University of Strathclyde, Glasgow, Scotland, professor of politics, 1966-81, professor of public policy, 1982—, director of Centre for the Study of Public Policy, 1976—. Visiting scholar at Brookings Institution, 1976; visiting professor at European University Institute, Florence, Italy, 1977 and 1978; visiting fellow at American Enterprise Institute, 1980; Hinkley Distinguished Professor, Johns Hopkins University, 1987; lecturer at universities in Europe, North America, and Australia. Member of United States-United Kingdom Fulbright Education Commission, 1971-75. Consultant to Northern Ireland Constitutional Convention, 1975-76, and to Organization for Economic Cooperation and Development. Member of International Monetary Fund, 1984.

MEMBER: International Political Science Association (member of council, 1976-82), International Sociological Association, European Consortium for Political Research (co-founder), American Political Science Association, Political Studies Association (United Kingdom, honorary vice president), American Civil Liberties Union, British Politics Group (co-founder), United Kingdom Politics Work Group (chairman, 1978—), Phi Beta Kappa, Reform Club (London), Cosmos Club (Washington, D.C.).

AWARDS, HONORS: Guggenheim fellow at Woodrow Wilson Center, 1974; Japan Foundation fellow, 1984.

WRITINGS:

(With D. E. Butler) *The British General Election of 1959,* St. Martin's, 1960.
(With Mark Abrams) *Must Labour Lose?,* Penguin, 1960.
Politics in England: An Interpretation, Little, Brown, 1964, 2nd edition, 1974 (published in England as *Politics in England Today: An Interpretation,* Faber, 1974), 3rd edition published as *Politics in England: An Interpretation for the 1980s,* 4th edition published as *Politics in England: Resistance and Change,* 1985.
Influencing Voters, St. Martin's, 1967.
People in Politics, Basic Books, 1970.
Governing without Consensus: An Irish Perspective, Beacon Press, 1971.
The Problem of Party Government, Macmillan (London), 1974, Free Press, 1975.
(With T. Mackie) *International Almanac of Electoral History,* Macmillan, 1974, 2nd edition, 1982.
(With D. W. Urwin) *Regional Differentiation and Political Unity in Western Nations,* Sage, 1975.

Northern Ireland: A Time of Choice, American Enterprise Institute, 1976.
Managing Presidential Objectives, Free Press, 1976.
What Is Governing?: Purpose and Policy in Washington, Prentice-Hall, 1978.
(With B. Guy Peters) *Can Government Go Bankrupt?,* Basic Books, 1978.
Do Parties Make a Difference?, Chatham House, 1980, 2nd edition, 1984.
(With Ian McAllister) *United Kingdom Facts,* Holmes & Meier, 1982.
The Territorial Dimension in Government: Understanding the United Kingdom, Chatham House, 1982.
Understanding Big Government, Sage, 1984.
(With McAllister) *The Nationwide Competition for Votes,* Frances Pinter, 1984.
Public Employment in Western Nations, Cambridge University Press, 1985.
(With McAllister) *Voters Begin to Choose,* Sage, 1986.
(With D. Van Mechelen) *Patterns of Parliamentary Legislation,* Gower, 1986.
Ministers and Ministries, Oxford University Press, 1987.
(With T. Karran) *Taxation by Political Inertia,* Allen & Unwin, 1987.
The Post-Modern Presidency, Chatham House, 1988.

EDITOR

Studies in British Politics: A Reader in Political Sociology, St. Martin's, 1966, 3rd edition, 1976.
Policy-Making in Britain, Free Press, 1969.
(With M. Dugan) *European Politics,* Little, Brown, 1974.
Electoral Behavior: A Comparative Handbook, Free Press, 1974.
Lessons from America: An Exploration, Wiley, 1974.
The Management of Urban Change in Britain and Germany, Sage, 1974.
The Dynamics of Public Policies, Sage, 1976.
Comparing Public Policies, Ossolineum, 1977.
(With Dennis Kavanagh) *New Trends in British Politics,* Sage, 1977.
(With G. Hermet and Alain Rouquie) *Elections without Choice,* Macmillan, 1978.
(With Ezra Suleiman) *Residents and Prime Ministers,* American Enterprise Institute, 1980.
Challenge to Governance, Sage, 1980.
(With William B. Gwyn) *Britain: Progress and Decline,* Tulane University, 1980.
Electoral Participation: A Comparative Analysis, Sage, 1980.
(With P. Madgwick) *The Territorial Dimension in United Kingdom Politics,* Academic Press, 1982.
(With E. Page) *Fiscal Stress in Cities,* Cambridge University Press, 1982.
(With R. Shiratori) *The Welfare State East and West,* Oxford University Press (New York), 1986.

OTHER

Election correspondent, London *Times,* 1964, and *Daily Telegraph,* 1979—. Contributor to London *Times, New Society,* and journals in Great Britain, United States, and Europe, and to television networks, including British Broadcasting Corp.

WORK IN PROGRESS: Comparative policy studies; Washington in international perspective.

SIDELIGHTS: Richard Rose's work has been translated into French, German, Italian, Spanish, Norwegian, Swedish, Hebrew, Chinese, and Japanese.

AVOCATIONAL INTERESTS: Architecture, music, travel.

BIOGRAPHICAL/CRITICAL SOURCES:

PERIODICALS

Times (London), February 17, 1981.

*　*　*

ROSENTHAL, A(braham) M(ichael) 1922-

PERSONAL: Born May 2, 1922, in Sault Ste. Marie, Ontario, Canada; brought to United States in 1926, naturalized in 1951; son of Harry and Sarah Marie (Dickstein) Rosenthal; married Ann Marie Burke, March 12, 1949 (divorced); married Shirley Lord Anderson, June 10, 1987; children: (first marriage) Jonathan Harry, Daniel Michael, Andrew Mark. *Education:* City College (now City College of the City University of New York), B.S., 1944.

ADDRESSES: Home—262 Central Park W., New York, N.Y. 10024. *Office*—*New York Times,* 229 West 43rd St., New York, N.Y. 10036.

CAREER: New York Times, New York, N.Y., staff member, 1944—, United Nations correspondent, 1946-54, foreign correspondent in India, 1954-58, in Warsaw, Poland, 1958-59, in Geneva, Switzerland, 1960-61, and in Tokyo, Japan, 1961-63, metropolitan editor, 1963-67, assistant managing editor, 1967-68, associate managing editor, 1968-69, managing editor, 1969-77, executive editor, 1977-86, associate editor, 1986—.

MEMBER: Council on Foreign Relations, Overseas Press Club, Players.

AWARDS, HONORS: Overseas Press Club citation for work in India, 1956, for work in Poland, 1960, and for magazine writing, 1965; Pulitzer Prize for international reporting, 1960; Page One Award of New York Newspaper Guild, 1960, 1965; George Polk Memorial Award, 1960, 1965; LL.D., City College of the City University of New York, 1974; Honor Award of the Association of Indians in America, 1974, for contribution to arts and letters and to better understanding between the peoples of India and the United States; Carr Van Anda Award, Ohio University, 1976, for enduring contributions to journalism; New York County Bar Association Award, 1978; Elijah Parish Lovejoy Award, Colby College, 1981, for journalistic achievement; John H. Finley Medal, City College of the City University of New York, 1981, for distinguished service to the City of New York; honorary degree, State University of New York, 1984.

WRITINGS:

Thirty-eight Witnesses, McGraw, 1964.
(With Arthur Gelb) *The Night the Lights Went Out,* Signet Books, 1965.
(With Gelb) *The Pope's Journey,* Bantam, 1965.
(With Gelb) *One More Victim,* New American Library, 1967.
(Editor with Gelb) *The New York Times of New York: An Uncommon Guide to the City of Fantasies,* Times Books, 1986.

EDITOR WITH ARTHUR GELB; "THE SOPHISTICATED TRAVELLER" SERIES

The Sophisticated Traveller: Beloved Cities; Europe, Villard Books, 1984.
. . . Winter; Love It or Leave It, Villard Books, 1984.

. . . Great Tours and Detours, Villard Books, 1985.
. . . Enchanting Places and How to Find Them; From Pleasant Hill to Katmandu, Villard Books, 1986.

OTHER

Author of column "On My Mind" for the *New York Times.* Contributor to *New York Times Magazine, Saturday Evening Post, Collier's,* and *Foreign Affairs.**

*　*　*

ROSENTHAL, Shirley Lord 1934-
(Shirley Lord)

PERSONAL: Born August 28, 1934, in London, England; came to the United States in 1971; daughter of Francis James (a company director) and Mabel (Williamson) Stringer; married Cyril Lord, January 17, 1960 (divorced, December, 1973); married David Jean Anderson (a business consultant), August 3, 1974 (died, January, 1985); married A. M. Rosenthal (an editor), June 10, 1987. *Education:* Attended South West Essex Technical College, Essex, England. *Politics:* Conservative. *Religion:* Roman Catholic.

ADDRESSES: Home—262 Central Park West, New York, N.Y., 10024. *Office*—*Vogue* Magazine, 350 Madison Ave., New York, N.Y. 10017.

CAREER: London Star, London, England, woman's editor, 1960-61; *Evening Standard,* London, woman's editor, 1961-63; *London Evening News,* woman's editor, 1963-67; *Harper's Bazaar,* London and New York City, beauty and health editor, 1963-73; *Vogue,* New York City, beauty and health editor, 1973-75; Helena Rubinstein, New York City, vice-president for public relations, 1975-80; *Vogue,* director of special projects, 1980—. Professional tours in England and the United States include "Shirley Lord Show" and "Shirley Lord Beauty Breakfast." City commissioner for Craigavon, Northern Ireland.

WRITINGS—Under name Shirley Lord:

Small Beer at Claridge's (autobiography), M. Joseph, 1968.
The Easy Way to Good Looks, Crowell, 1976.
Golden Hill (novel), Crown, 1982.
One of My Very Best Friends (novel), Crown, 1985.

Author of syndicated column, "Be Beautiful," Field Syndicate, 1975—.

WORK IN PROGRESS: A series of twelve books on beauty, health, and psyche; a radio series on teenage beauty; a novel.

BIOGRAPHICAL/CRITICAL SOURCES:

PERIODICALS

New York Times, October 21, 1982.
New York Times Book Review, October 24, 1982, October 27, 1985, June 11, 1987.
Washington Post Book World, December 5, 1982.

*　*　*

ROSENTHAL, Sylvia 1911-

PERSONAL: Born April 24, 1911, in Schenectady, N.Y.; daughter of Abram (a merchant) and Bessie (in business; maiden name, Siegel) Dworsky; married Theodore Rosenthal (a physician), January 29, 1930 (deceased); children: Anne Rosenthal Satin, Michael. *Education:* Attended Emerson College, 1937-39; New York University, B.A., 1943.

ADDRESSES: Home—180 East End Ave, New York, N.Y. 10128.

CAREER: Grolier, Inc., New York City, senior editor, 1961-72, managing editor of *New Book of Knowledge,* 1972-76; free-lance writer, 1976—. Former talk show host on WHN-Radio; instructor in radio production and scriptwriting for children's programs, Hunter College Extension, producing children's programs for WNYC-Radio and national radio during the 1940s.

MEMBER: Authors Guild.

WRITINGS:

Live High on Low Fat, Lippincott, 1962, 3rd edition, 1975.
Cosmetic Surgery: A Consumer's Guide, Lippincott, 1977.
(Editor) *Fresh Food,* Dutton, 1978.
(With Fran Shinagel) *How Cooking Works: An Indispensable Kitchen Handbook,* Macmillan, 1981.
(With Gene Hovis) *Gene Hovis's Uptown Down Home Cookbook,* Little, Brown, 1987.
(Adaptor) Rudolf Sodamin, *The Cruise Cookbook* (first published in West Germany), Little, Brown, 1988.

Cosmetic Surgery: A Consumer's Guide has been translated into French and Dutch. Also author of children's radio scripts and records, including "The City Sings for Michael," 1946.

SIDELIGHTS: Sylvia Rosenthal commented: "My first book grew out of my need to follow doctor's orders after my husband had a heart attack. It catapulted me into the subject of food, for which I had always had great enthusiasm and interest, and made me a pioneer in the field of low-cholesterol, low-fat cooking.

"A low-fat diet can be exciting. People think we have great eats in our home—it's possible to produce fine cream soups, flaming crepes, great meat dishes with fine sauces, lavish-looking desserts, and all manner of goodies without sending your cholesterol soaring. *Live High on Low Fat* has been around since 1962 and mail still comes trickling in from all over the United States and abroad from satisfied customers."

In addition to her cooking-related books, Rosenthal is the author of *Cosmetic Surgery: A Consumer's Guide,* of which she commented: "While I've had no personal experience with cosmetic surgery (which doesn't mean I couldn't use it), my research gave me great respect for the process. For *Cosmetic Surgery* I interviewed dozens of plastic surgeons and patients, and I would not discourage anyone with the guts for elective surgery. It's made a lot of people feel better about themselves and, in many cases, brought about great improvement."

BIOGRAPHICAL/CRITICAL SOURCES:

PERIODICALS

Christian Science Monitor, December 3, 1981.
New York Times Book Review, April 2, 1978.
Washington Post Book World, December 13, 1981.

*   *   *

ROSS, Raymond S(amuel)   1925-

PERSONAL: Born April 14, 1925, in Milwaukee, Wis.; son of Samuel and Agnes (Thorkildsen) Ross; married Jean Joy Reichmann, June 19, 1948; children: Mark, Scott. *Education:* Attended University of Illinois, 1943; Marquette University, Ph.B., 1949, M.A., 1950; Purdue University, Ph.D., 1954.

ADDRESSES: Home—12745 Avondale Lane, Traverse City, Mich. 49684. *Office*—Department of Speech Communication and Theatre, Wayne State University, Detroit, Mich. 48202.

CAREER: Marquette University, Milwaukee, Wis., instructor, 1950-51; Ohio State University, Columbus, 1954-58, began as instructor, became assistant professor of speech; Wayne State University, Detroit, Mich., 1958—, began as assistant professor, professor of speech, 1965-85, professor emeritus, 1985—. Distinguished visiting professor, Pepperdine University, 1986. Coordinator, University of Michigan-Wayne State University Institute of Industrial Relations, 1959—. *Military service:* U.S. Army, 1943-45.

MEMBER: International Communication Association, American Psychological Association, American Speech and Hearing Association, Speech Communication Association.

AWARDS, HONORS: Foundation for Economic Education (U.S. Steel Corp.) postdoctoral fellowship, 1955; distinguished alumni award of Marquette University School of Speech, 1963.

WRITINGS:

(Co-author) *The Air Force Staff Officer,* U.S. Government Printing Office, 1961.
Speech Communication Fundamentals and Practice, Prentice-Hall, 1965, 7th edition, 1986.
(Contributor) *The Communicative Arts and Sciences of Speech,* C. E. Merrill, 1967.
Persuasion: Communication and Interpersonal Relations, Prentice-Hall, 1974.
Essentials of Speech Communication, Prentice-Hall, 1979, 2nd edition, 1984.
(With son, Mark G. Ross) *Understanding Persuasion,* Prentice-Hall, 1981.
(With M. G. Ross) *Relating and Interacting: An Introduction to Interpersonal Communication,* Prentice-Hall, 1982.
Understanding Persuasion: Foundations and Practice, Prentice-Hall, 1985.

Associate editor, *Speech Monographs* and *Communication Quarterly.*

WORK IN PROGRESS: Small Groups in Organizational Settings, for Prentice-Hall; 8th edition of *Speech Communication Fundamentals and Practice.*

*   *   *

RUDMAN, Masha Kabakow   1933-

PERSONAL: Born January 16, 1933, in New York, N.Y.; daughter of Benedict and Rose (Wolf) Kabakow; married Seymour L. Rudman (a clinical psychologist), June 14, 1953; children: Rachel, Reva, Deborah. *Education:* Hunter College (now Hunter College of the City University of New York), B.A. (cum laude), 1953, M.S., 1956; University of Massachusetts, Ed.D., 1970. *Religion:* Jewish.

ADDRESSES: Home—83 Stony Hill Rd., Amherst, Mass. 01002. *Office*—School of Education, University of Massachusetts, Amherst, Mass. 01003.

CAREER: Teacher at public schools in New York City, 1953-59; Hunter College of the City University of New York, New York City, lecturer in education, 1964-65; University of Massachusetts, Amherst, instructor, 1965-70, assistant professor, 1978—. Consultant.

MEMBER: International Reading Association, National Council of Teachers of English, Association for Supervision and Curriculum Development, Society of Children's Book Writers, Massachusetts Reading Council, Phi Delta Kappa.

WRITINGS:

Children's Literature: An Issues Approach, Heath, 1976, 2nd edition, Longman, 1984.
(With Barbara Lee) *Mind Over Media: New Ways to Improve Your Child's Reading and Writing Skills,* Seaview, 1982, revised edition with a preface by Bill Cosby published as *Leading to Reading: New Ways You Can Make Reading Fun for Children,* Berkley, 1983.
For Love of Reading, Consumer Reports Books, 1988.
(With Joanne E. Bernstein) *Books to Help Children Cope with Separation and Loss,* Bowker, 1989.

WORK IN PROGRESS: A book tentatively entitled *Children's Literature: Resources for the Classroom* for Christopher Gordon.

SIDELIGHTS: Masha Kabakow Rudman once told *CA:* "I view my writing as an extension of my teaching. My message to parents and teachers is that it's important to take advantage of all our resources, and to respect our own ideas and feelings. I try to contribute as many strategies as possible for doing just that."

Rudman recently added: "The field of children's literature has come to be appreciated more and more over the past ten years. Parents, teachers and librarians now can take advantage of the wealth of wonderful books available for children. My work helps adults to access appropriate and compelling juvenile literature so that children will gain the best advantage from their reading."

*   *   *

RUFFIN, C(aulbert) Bernard III 1947-

PERSONAL: Born November 22, 1947, in Washington, D.C.; son of C. Bernard, Jr. (a police officer), and Lillian (a personnel officer; maiden name, Jones) Ruffin. *Education:* Bowdoin College, A.B., 1969; Yale University, M.Div., 1972. *Politics:* Republican.

ADDRESSES: Home and office—1666 Valencia Way, Reston, Va. 22090.

CAREER: Ordained Lutheran minister, 1974; intern pastor of Lutheran church in Loganton, Pa., 1972-73; pastor of Lutheran church in Alexandria, Va., 1974-76; Holy Comforter Lutheran Church, Washington, D.C., assistant pastor, 1976—; South Lakes High School, Reston, Va., social studies teacher, 1982—. Substitute teacher at public schools in Fairfax County, Va., 1976-82; member of board of directors of Capital Lutheran High School, 1979-82.

MEMBER: Hymn Society of America (member of executive committee, 1980-82), Afro-American Historical and Genealogical Society, Phi Beta Kappa.

WRITINGS:

Fanny Crosby, United Church Press, 1976.
(With Stella M. Fries and Janet Z. Gabler) *Some Chambersburg Roots: A Black Perspective,* privately printed, 1980.
Padre Pio: The True Story, Our Sunday Visitor, 1982.
The Twelve, Our Sunday Visitor, 1984.
The Days of the Martyrs, Our Sunday Visitor, 1985.

The Ancestors and Descendants of Martin and Margaret Greenwood (1470-1985), Minuteman Press, 1986.
The Life of Brother Andre, Our Sunday Visitor, 1988.

SIDELIGHTS: C. Bernard Ruffin III told *CA:* "I am a Christian traditionalist who believes in the inerrancy of the Scriptures and am interested in writing church history from a traditional, non-sectarian point of view. I am also interested in American history and the history of Western civilization."

AVOCATIONAL INTERESTS: Classical music (especially opera), weight lifting, genealogy.

*   *   *

RUFFRIDGE, Frank(lin James) 1931-

PERSONAL: Born February 23, 1931, in Jamesville, Mich.; son of Franklin (a critic) and Constance (Trouncer) Ruffridge; married Helena Ima Freech (a psychiatrist), February 23, 1955; children: Franklin III, Constance. *Education:* Westport College, A.B., 1958; graduate study at various universities. *Politics:* "Responsible freedom."

ADDRESSES: Home—9568 Columbia, Redford, Mich. 48239.

CAREER: Writer. Ran away from home at fourteen and tried in vain to join the Marines by lying about his age; worked at many odd jobs, 1945-54, including water boy at a zoo, errand boy for a team of oil-well drillers, assistant to a government chicken inspector, and "travelling bartender" for a large caterer; while in college, worked as a bartender and as a distributor of leaflets. Director, annual community Arts and Oddities Carnival, 1971-76. Consultant, Midwest Wildlife Preserve Foundation, 1986-87.

MEMBER: American Club, Time and Truth Society, Zoo Society (general secretary, 1985—).

AWARDS, HONORS: Zoo Society grant, 1959, for work on a manuscript concerning alligator preservation (never completed); Time and Truth Society best book award, 1971, for *Everything You Never Needed to Know;* Gregor N. Maloris Award for nonfiction, Bell and Hammer Society, 1988, for *Omnia mutantor—sic transit gloria mundi.*

WRITINGS:

Zoos I Have Known, Zoo Society, 1959.
My Most Unforgettable Zoo, Zoo Society, 1960.
What's in a Dictionary Besides Words?, privately printed, 1962.
My Life as an Inspector of Chickens, Including an Entirely New Method of Chicken-Sexing, privately printed, 1963.
Time Doesn't Really Fly!, Reps Publishing, 1965.
Dictionary Reading for Fun and Profit, Reps Publishing, 1967.
(Translator from the English with Everett S. Tuffnell) Bernard Owill, *Je lis seulement a la nuit* (title means "I Read Only at Night"), privately printed, 1969.
Everything You Never Needed to Know, Demo Publishing, 1971.
Many's the Time. . ., Bore Press, 1972.
Who Invited You?, Demo Publishing, 1974.
I've Been Meaning to Tell You: All the Things Not to Say to a Crazy Person, Bore Press, 1976.
(Editor) *Nonsense, My Dear* (anthology of light verse), Bore Press, 1978.
Natural Nemeses: Tales of Gales, Gophers, and Grubs, Reps Publishing, 1978.

The Wear of Where: Appropriate Apparel, How-To Handbooks, 1980.

Mens sana in corpore sano, Ursidae Books, 1982.

Cabin Fever!, Canadian Knights Press, 1984.

Who's Running This Zoo, Anyway? (Oh, I am), Finnegan & Wade, 1986.

Omnia mutantor—sic transit gloria mundi, Ursidae Books, 1988.

Contributor of light verse, reviews, and articles to periodicals, including *Bore Quarterly* and several animal behavior journals.

SIDELIGHTS: Frank Ruffridge told *CA:* "I've *done* a lot of weird things in my life, and now I'm trying to *write* about them. People are too complacent. They should be *jolted*. (My wife thinks I'm crazy, but she may be right—she's a psychiatrist!) What we need to think about is Time and Nature and Animals, instead of war and money and status. I believe thinking should be a *passionate* process. My thoughts tend to run to the wild—bears, wilderness, and the parallels between human and nonhuman animal behavior in uncivilized surroundings, for example."

He later added: "A little while back, I began to re-evaluate my life and work (I felt I was entitled, now that I've hit the big 5-0, and passed it!). I noticed all the frivolity in it which has caused some critics to sneer. But I think it's wonderful! People take their lives and their very existence far too seriously. They should take a lesson from the wild (or even John Lennon) once in a while and just let things be. That's why I wrote my latest book. Even the title is a satire on the gravity of those who bow to Schopenhauer, as well as those who revere the Pursuit of Knowledge without knowing where it is leading them. For the most part, *Omnia mutantor* et cetera *is* frivolous, but it does have a message in it, too."

AVOCATIONAL INTERESTS: Making drinks, telling jokes in the mirror, walking, philosophizing.

S

SABATO, Larry (J.)   1952-

PERSONAL: Born August 7, 1952, in Norfolk, Va.; son of N. J. (a civil servant) and Margaret (a secretary; maiden name, Simmons) Sabato. *Education:* University of Virginia, B.A., 1974; graduate study at Princeton University, 1974-75; Queen's College, Oxford, D.Phil., 1977.

ADDRESSES: Office—Woodrow Wilson Department of Government and Foreign Affairs, 240 Cabell Hall, University of Virginia, Charlottesville, Va. 22901.

CAREER: New College, Oxford University, Oxford, England, lecturer in politics, 1977-78; University of Virginia, Charlottesville, assistant professor, 1978-83, associate professor of government and foreign affairs, 1983—, member of faculty senate, 1982—. Visiting lecturer in politics at New College, Oxford, 1980; guest scholar at the Brookings Institution, Washington, D.C., 1980; Thomas Jefferson Visiting Fellow at Downing College, Cambridge, 1982. Senior fellow at Duke University's Center for the Study of the Governorship, 1982—. Director of Virginia public opinion poll, 1980—.

MEMBER: American Political Science Association, American Association of Political Consultants, Southern Political Science Association (member of executive council, 1987—), Phi Beta Kappa.

AWARDS, HONORS: Danforth fellowship from Danforth Foundation, 1974-76; Rhodes Scholarship from Rhodes Foundation, 1975-78; best book citation from *Choice,* 1979, for *Goodbye to Goodtime Charlie: The American Governor Transformed, 1950-75;* American Philosophical Association grants, 1979, 1983, and 1986; National Endowment for the Humanities fellowship, 1980; Moody grant from Lyndon Baines Johnson Foundation, 1980; University of Virginia Research Policy Council grants, 1980, 1983, and 1986; Outstanding Young Teacher Award from University of Virginia, 1981; Kellogg National fellowship, 1983-86; Earhart Foundation grants, 1983 and 1986; Gerald R. Ford Foundation grant, 1987; Sesquicentennial fellow from University of Virginia, 1988.

WRITINGS:

Aftermath of Armageddon: An Analysis of the 1973 Virginia Gubernatorial Election, Institute of Government, University of Virginia, 1975.

Virginia Votes: 1969-1974, Institute of Government, University of Virginia, 1976.
The Democratic Party Primary in Virginia: Tantamount to Election No Longer, University Press of Virginia, 1977.
Virginia Votes: 1975-1978, Institute of Government, University of Virginia, 1979.
Goodbye to Good-Time Charlie: The American Governor Transformed, 1950-1975, D. C. Heath, 1978, revised edition published as *The American Governorship Transformed,* Congressional Quarterly Press, 1983.
The Rise of Political Consultants: New Ways of Winning Elections, Basic Books, 1981.
Virginia Votes: 1979-1982, Institute of Government, University of Virginia, 1983.
PAC Power: Inside the World of Political Action Committees, Norton, 1984.
(Editor with Thomas R. Morris) *Virginian Government and Politics,* 2nd edition, Institute of Government, University of Virginia, 1984.
The Party's Just Begun: Shaping Political Parties for America's Future, Little, Brown, 1987.
Virginia Votes: 1983-1986, Institute of Government, University of Virginia, 1987.

CONTRIBUTOR

Weldon Cooper and Morris, editors, *Virginia Government and Politics,* University Press of Virginia, 1976.
John V. Moeser, editor, *A Virginia Profile: 1960-2000,* Commonwealth Books, 1981.
Allan Cigler and Burdett Loomis, editors, *The Changing Nature of Interest Groups,* Congressional Quarterly Press, 1983.
Thomas E. Mann and Norman Ornstein, editors, *The American Election of 1982,* American Enterprise Institute for Public Policy Research, 1983.
Vernon Bogdanor, editor, *Parties and Democracy in Britain and America,* Praeger, 1984.
Robert P. Steed and others, editors, *The 1984 Presidential Election in the South: Patterns of Southern Party Politics,* Praeger, 1985.
L. Patrick Devlin, editor, *Political Persuasion in Presidential Campaigns,* Transaction Books, 1987.
Joseph L. Fisher, editor, *Virginia Alternatives for the 1990s: Selected Issues in Public Policy,* George Mason University Press, 1987.

James Reichley, editor, *Elections American Style*, Brookings Institution, 1987.
James F. Lea, editor, *Contemporary Southern Politics: Continuity and Change*, Louisiana State University Press, 1988.
Dictionary of Political Institutions, Basil Blackwell, 1988.

OTHER

Also contributor of more than seventy-five articles and book reviews to newspapers and periodicals, including *Virginia Quarterly Review, Economist, National Civic Review, State Government, New York Times, Washington Post, Baltimore Sun, Miami Herald, Richmond Times-Dispatch, Virginian Pilot, Roanoke Times*, and *Campaigning Reports*. Editor of the *State Opinion Report* (publication of the National Governors' Association), 1981—; member of board of contributing editors, *Encyclopedia of American Political Parties*, Garland Press, 1988.

SIDELIGHTS: Larry Sabato's *The Rise of Political Consultants: New Ways of Winning Elections* is a study of the role of consultants in political campaigns. It includes a historical overview of the profession and a detailed analysis of the effects of press, polls, advertising, and direct mail on the outcome of an election. Sabato maintains that the political consultant "rarely sees his responsibilities as extending beyond those he has to his client," contending that "closer association with the political parties, whether voluntary or forced, may help to harness consultant's considerable talents for a higher and more constructive purpose than the election of individual candidates."

David S. Broder of the *Washington Post* recommends *The Rise of Political Consultants* "if you want to understand what is happening in the world of campaign consultants." Robert Sherrill expresses a similar opinion in the *New York Times Book Review:* "There is absolutely no better guide through their world, nor is there likely to be soon, than Mr. Sabato's 'The Rise of Political Consultants'. . . . Perhaps the best thing about Mr. Sabato is his reasonable skepticism," Sherrill continues. "He is convinced the consultants are important mainly because they are *perceived* as important. . . . Reform, says Mr. Sabato, is up to the press, which must 'stop treating consultants as the gods of the political wars,' 'examine the damaging effects they and their new campaign technologies are having on the American political system,' and 'publicize the shockingly unethical practices that are so pervasive.'"

Sabato told *CA:* "Up to this time I have concentrated my research on three general subjects in American politics and government: campaigns and elections, state government and politics in the fifty states, and Virginia politics and government. My immediate research plans are extensions of earlier projects.

"As a consequence of my initial work on campaign technology, which resulted in the publication of *The Rise of Political Consultants: New Ways of Winning Elections,* I am conducting additional studies on three campaign techniques: media advertising, polling, and direct mail. In each case I am collecting hundreds of campaign products (television and radio ads, polls, and fund-raising letters), in an attempt to assess more precisely both the techniques used in campaigns and the effectiveness of those techniques. I also hope that these items of campaign hardware will eventually serve as the core of a 'library of new campaign technology.'

"Beyond the new campaign technologies, I am closely following the explosive growth of political action committees (PACs) and the independent single-issue groups."

BIOGRAPHICAL/CRITICAL SOURCES:

PERIODICALS

New York Times Book Review, December 27, 1981.
Washington Post, November 8, 1981.
Washington Post Book World, October 28, 1984.

* * *

SABERHAGEN, Fred(erick Thomas) 1930-

PERSONAL: Born May 18, 1930, in Chicago, Ill.; son of Frederick Augustus and Julia (Moynihan) Saberhagen; married Joan Dorothy Spicci, June 29, 1968; children: Jill, Eric, Thomas. *Education:* Attended Wright Junior College, 1956-57.

ADDRESSES: Home—Albuquerque, N.M. *Agent*—Eleanor Wood, Spectrum Literary Agency, 432 Park Ave. S., Suite 1205, New York, N.Y. 10016.

CAREER: Motorola, Inc., Chicago, Ill., electronics technician, 1956-62; free-lance writer, 1962-67; *Encyclopaedia Britannica*, Chicago, assistant editor, 1967-73; free-lance writer, 1973—. *Military service:* Electrical technician, U.S. Air Force, 1951-55.

MEMBER: Science Fiction Writers of America.

WRITINGS:

The Golden People, Ace Books, 1964.
Water of Thought, Ace Books, 1965, reprinted, Pinnacle Books, 1981.
The Broken Lands (also see below), Ace Books, 1967.
The Black Mountains (also see below), Ace Books, 1970.
Changeling Earth (also see below), DAW Books, 1973.
The Book of Saberhagen (short stories), DAW Books, 1975.
Specimens, Popular Library, 1975.
Love Conquers All (first published in *Galaxy* magazine, 1974-75), Ace Books, 1978.
Mask of the Sun, Ace Books, 1978.
The Veils of Azlaroc, Ace Books, 1978.
The Ultimate Enemy (short stories), Ace Books, 1979.
The Empire of the East (contains *The Broken Lands, The Black Mountains*, and *Changeling Earth*), Ace Books, 1979.
(Editor) *A Spadeful of Spacetime* (anthology), Ace Books, 1980.
(With Roger Zelazny) *Coils*, Tor Books, 1980.
Octagon, Ace Books, 1981.
Earth Descended (short stories), Tor Books, 1981.
A Century of Progress, Tor Books, 1982.
(Editor with wife, Joan Saberhagen) *Pawn to Infinity* (science fiction anthology), Ace Books, 1982.
The Frankenstein Papers, Baen Books, 1986.

"BERSERKER" SERIES

Berserker (short stories), Ballantine, 1967.
Brother Assassin, Ballantine, 1969 (published in England as *Brother Berserker*, Macdonald & Co., 1969).
Berserker's Planet, DAW Books, 1975.
Berserker Man, Ace Books, 1979.
The Berserker Wars (short stories), Tor Books, 1981.
The Berserker Throne, Simon & Schuster, 1985.
(With Poul Anderson, Ed Bryant, Stephen R. Donaldson, Larry Niven, Connie Willis, and Zelazny) *Berserker Base*, Tor Books, 1985.

"DRACULA" SERIES

The Dracula Tape, Warner Paperback, 1975.
Holmes-Dracula File, Ace Books, 1978.
An Old Friend of the Family, Ace Books, 1979.
Thorn, Ace Books, 1980.
Dominion, Tor Books, 1981.

"SWORDS" TRILOGY

The First Book of Swords (also see below), Tor Books, 1984.
The Second Book of Swords (also see below), Tor Books, 1985.
The Third Book of Swords (also see below), Tor Books, 1985.
The Complete Book of Swords: Comprising the First, Second, and Third Books, Doubleday, 1985.

"LOST SWORDS" SERIES

The First Book of Lost Swords: The Woundhealer's Story, T. Doherty, 1986.
The Second Book of Lost Swords: Sightblinder's Story, Tor Books, 1987.

WORK IN PROGRESS: A science fiction work entitled *After the Fact.*

BIOGRAPHICAL/CRITICAL SOURCES:

BOOKS

Dictionary of Literary Biography, Volume 8: *Twentieth-Century American Science Fiction Writers*, Gale, 1981.

PERIODICALS

Extrapolation, December, 1976.

*   *   *

St. MEYER, Ned
    See STRATEMEYER, Edward L.

*   *   *

SALKEY, (Felix) Andrew (Alexander) 1928-

PERSONAL: Born January 30, 1928, in Colon, Panama; son of Andrew Alexander and Linda (Marshall) Salkey; married Patricia Verden, February 22, 1957; children: Eliot Andrew, Jason Alexander. *Education:* Attended St. George's College, Kingston, Jamaica, and Munro College, St. Elizabeth, Jamaica; University of London, B.A., 1955.

ADDRESSES: Home—8 Windsor Court, Moscow Rd., London W2, England. *Office*—School of Humanities and Arts, Hampshire College, Amherst, Mass.

CAREER: Writer and broadcast journalist. British Broadcasting Corp. (BBC-Radio), London, England, interviewer, scriptwriter, and editor of literary program, 1952-56; Comprehensive School, London, assistant master of English literature and language, 1957-59; free-lance writer and general reviewer of books and plays, 1956-76; Hampshire College, Amherst, Mass., professor of writing, 1976—. Narrator in film "Reggae," 1978.

AWARDS, HONORS: Thomas Helmore poetry prize, 1955, for long poem, "Jamaica Symphony"; Guggenheim fellowship, 1960, for novel *A Quality of Violence*, and for folklore project; Casa de las Americas Poetry Prize, 1979, for *In the Hills Where Her Dreams Live: Poems for Chile, 1973-1978.*

WRITINGS:

A Quality of Violence (novel), Hutchinson, 1959, reprinted, New Beacon Books, 1979.
Escape to an Autumn Pavement, Hutchinson, 1960.
(Editor) *West Indian Stories*, Faber, 1960.
Hurricane (juvenile), Oxford University Press, 1964, reprinted, Arden Library, 1986.
(Editor of Caribbean section) *Young Commonwealth Poets '65*, Heinemann, 1965.
(Editor and author of introduction) *Stories from the Caribbean*, Elek, 1965, published as *Island Voices: Stories from the West Indies*, Liveright, 1970.
Earthquake (juvenile), Oxford University Press, 1965, reprinted, 1980.
The Shark Hunters, Nelson, 1966.
Drought, Oxford University Press, 1966.
Riot (juvenile), Oxford University Press, 1967.
(Compiler) *Caribbean Prose: An Anthology for Secondary Schools*, Evans, 1967.
The Late Emancipation of Jerry Stover, Hutchinson, 1968, reprinted, Longman, 1983.
Jonah Simpson (juvenile), Oxford University Press, 1969.
The Adventures of Catullus Kelly, Hutchinson, 1969.
(Editor and author of introduction) *Breaklight: An Anthology of Caribbean Poetry*, Hamish Hamilton, 1971, published as *Breaklight: The Poetry of the Caribbean*, Doubleday, 1972.
Havana Journal, Penguin, 1971.
Anancy's Score (short stories), Bogle-L'Ouverture, 1973.
Caribbean Essays: An Anthology, Evans Brothers, 1973.
Georgetown Journal: A Caribbean Writer's Journey from London via Port of Spain to Georgetown, Guayana, 1970, New Beacon Books, 1973.
Jamaica (poetry), Hutchinson, 1973, 2nd edition, 1983.
Joey Tyson (juvenile), Bogle-L'Ouverture, 1974.
Come Home, Malcolm Heartland, Hutchinson, 1976.
(Editor and author of introduction) *Writing in Cuba since the Revolution: An Anthology of Poems, Short Stories, and Essays*, Bogle-L'Ouverture, 1977.
In the Hills Where Her Dreams Live: Poems for Chile, 1973-1978, Casa de las Americas (Havana), 1979, published as *In the Hills Where Her Dreams Live: Poems for Chile, 1973-1980*, Black Scholar Press, 1981.
The River That Disappeared (juvenile), Bogle-L'Ouverture, 1979.
Away (poetry), Allison & Busby, 1980.
(Editor) *Caribbean Folk Tales and Legends*, Bogle-L'Ouverture, 1983.
Danny Jones (juvenile), Bogle-L'Ouverture, 1983.
One: The Story of How the People of Guyana Avenge the Murder of Their Pasero with Help from Anancy and Sister Buxton (novel), Bogle L'Ouverture, 1985.

Contributor of over thirty radio plays and features to British Broadcasting Corp., over twelve radio plays and features to radio stations in Belgium, Germany, and Switzerland, and many short stories, essays, features, and articles for newspapers and magazines in England, Europe, and Africa.

SIDELIGHTS: Although Andrew Salkey has written a collection of short stories, several volumes of poetry, and has edited a number of anthologies, he is perhaps more known for his adult novels and books for young people. Described by Peter Nazareth in *World Literature Today* as a "Third World storyteller extraordinaire in the Afro-Caribbean mold," Andrew Salkey writes books that contain significant themes, vivid imagery, lively dialogue, and spirited characterization. A reviewer for the *Times Literary Supplement* notes that a reader can recognize Salkey's fiction "by the importance of the themes he treats and sometimes by the sheer exhilaration and inventiveness of his dialogue and the exuberance of his characterization."

Salkey once expressed his thoughts on writing fiction in this manner: "I tend to write in a fairly straight line, from beginning to middle to end, although in fits and starts, and I don't mind going back over certain parts of the composition, rewriting and re-casting them, again and again, until they fit together with the other parts and help the whole story to shape up nicely. I like my writing to entertain me, if I can manage it; I like it to turn me on to write more and more, and to write well. Finally, I suppose the most important feature of my work as a writer is the matter of the central place I always give to persons and personal relationships in my storytelling. I simply couldn't make a narrative move without them."

Salkey's success as a storyteller may be due to the fact that Salkey himself has always loved folktales, myths, and legends. He explained in his introduction to *Caribbean Folk Tales and Legends* that these types of books "often conceal more than they tell; it's our business, as either listeners or readers, to winkle out the hidden meanings, associations and suggestions."

AVOCATIONAL INTERESTS: Collecting contemporary paintings by unestablished painters and classical and contemporary editions of novels, books of poetry, and literary criticism.

BIOGRAPHICAL/CRITICAL SOURCES:

BOOKS

Salkey, Andrew, *Caribbean Folk Tale and Legends*, Bogle-L'Ouverture, 1983.

PERIODICALS

Library Journal, March 15, 1970.
Los Angeles Times, January 9, 1981.
Times Literary Supplement, February 20, 1969, October 16, 1969, July 20, 1973, January 9, 1981.
World Literature Today, summer, 1979, autumn, 1980, spring, 1981, summer, 1981, summer, 1983.

*   *   *

SALMON, Nathan Ucuzoglu   1951-

PERSONAL: Original name, Nathan Salmon Ucuzoglu; name legally changed in 1978; born January 2, 1951, in Los Angeles, Calif.; son of Mair (a factory worker) and Rebecca (a medical clerk; maiden name, Sene) Ucuzoglu; married Eileen Conrad (a communications director), August 28, 1980. *Education:* University of California, Los Angeles, B.A., 1973, M.A., 1974, C.Phil., 1977, Ph.D., 1979. *Religion:* Atheist.

ADDRESSES: Home—463 San Marino Dr., Santa Barbara, Calif. 93111. *Office*—Department of Philosophy, University of California, Santa Barbara, Calif. 93106.

CAREER: California State University, Northridge, lecturer, 1977-78; Princeton University, Princeton, N.J., assistant professor, 1978-82; University of California, Riverside, associate professor, 1982-84; University of California, Santa Barbara, associate professor, 1984-85, professor of philosophy and de-

partment vice-chairman, 1985—. Visiting senior research philosopher, Princeton University, 1982. Fulbright lecturer in Yugoslavia, 1986. Speaker at universities and philosophical associations worldwide.

MEMBER: American Philosophical Association, Royal Institute of Philosophy, Phi Beta Kappa.

AWARDS, HONORS: Research grants from Princeton University, 1979-80, University of California, Riverside, 1982-84, and University of California, Santa Barbara, 1984-87; Gustave O. Arlt Award in the Humanities, Council of Graduate Schools in the United States, 1984, for *Reference and Essence.*

WRITINGS:

Reference and Essence, Princeton University Press, 1981.
(Contributor) Peter A. French and others, editors, *Midwest Studies in Philosophy XI: Studies in Essentialism*, University of Minnesota Press, 1986.
Frege's Puzzle, MIT Press, 1986.
(Contributor) J. Tomberlin, editor, *Philosophical Perspectives 1: Metaphysics*, Ridgeview Publishing (Atascadero, Calif.), 1987.
(Editor with Scott Soames, author of introduction and contributor) *Propositions and Attitudes*, Oxford University Press, 1988.
(Contributor) J. Almog, J. Perry, and H. Wettstein, editors, *Themes from Kaplan*, Oxford University Press, 1988.
(Contributor) D. Gabbay and F. Guenthner, editors, *Handbook of Philosophical Logic IV: Topics in the Philosophy of Language*, Reidel Publishing (Dordrecht, Netherlands), 1988.
(Contributor) J. Tomberlin, editor, *Philosophical Perspectives 3: Philosophy of Mind and Action Theory*, Ridgeview Publishing, 1989.

Also contributor to *Handbuch Sprachphilosophie*, edited by M. Dascal, D. Gerhardus, K. Lorenz, and G. Meggle, published by Walter De Gruyter. Contributor of articles to *Analysis, Journal of Philosophy, Philosophical Studies, Philosophia*, and *Philosophical Review.*

SIDELIGHTS: Nathan Ucuzoglu Salmon told *CA* he writes "on analytical metaphysics and the philosophy of language." In *Reference and Essence*, Salmon presents recent linguistic and philosophical questions supporting his argument that current theories of reference are distinctly independent of theories about the essence of objects. According to Christopher Peacocke in his *Times Literary Supplement* review, "this is a valuable and reliable critical survey of the American literature [on the theory of reference] of the past ten years, one that should be of much help to students. . . . The organization and layout of *Reference and Essence* are exemplary; the seams between the English and the formulae are invisible. . . . the book as a whole leaves one eager to learn the results of Salmon's future development—however expansive—of these themes." A *Choice* reviewer warns, however, "readers who find the original works hard going will not find this book any simpler." Salmon's following book, *Frege's Puzzle*, examines "the degree of informativeness of certain sentences," explains *Times Literary Supplement* contributor David Freedman. While Freedman finds Salmon's vocabulary "inordinately technical" when it deals with current semantic theories, and thinks the work unsuitable for students, he adds, "Salmon gives a superior analysis of the puzzle, and . . . his book deserves the attention of any professional philosopher of language."

BIOGRAPHICAL/CRITICAL SOURCES:

PERIODICALS

Choice, May, 1982, November, 1986.
Times Literary Supplement, October 8, 1982, December 19, 1986.

*   *   *

SARNA, Jonathan D(aniel) 1955-

PERSONAL: Born January 10, 1955, in Philadelphia, Pa.; son of Nahum Mattathias (a professor) and Helen Horowitz (an assistant librarian) Sarna; married Ruth Langer (a rabbi), 1986; children: Aaron Yehvda. *Education:* Hebrew College, Boston, Mass., B.H.L. (with honors), 1974; Brandeis University, B.A. (summa cum laude), 1975, M.A. (Judaic studies), 1975; Yale University, M.A. (history), 1976, M.Phil., 1978, Ph.D., 1979.

ADDRESSES: Home—2480 Twigwood Rd., Cincinnati, Ohio 45237. *Office*—Department of History, Hebrew Union College-Jewish Institute of Religion, 3101 Clifton Ave., Cincinnati, Ohio 45220.

CAREER: American Jewish Historical Society, Waltham, Mass., archivist, 1973-75, acting assistant librarian, 1976; America-Holy Land Project of American Jewish Historical Society and Institute for Contemporary Jewry, Waltham, researcher, 1975-77; Hebrew Union College-Jewish Institute of Religion, Cincinnati, Ohio, visiting lecturer, 1979-80, assistant professor, 1980-84, associate professor of American Jewish history, 1984—, academic adviser at Center for the Study of the American Jewish Experience, 1981-84, academic director, 1984-86, director, 1986—. Visiting assistant professor at University of Cincinnati, 1983-84; visiting associate professor at Hebrew University, 1986-87. Loewenstein-Weiner Fellow, American Jewish Archives, 1977. Lecturer at universities and to organizations. Director of applied research for Survivors of Hitler's Germany in Cincinnati Oral History Project, sponsored by American Jewish Archives and National Council of Jewish Women, 1980. Member of leadership council and Jewish education committee of Cincinnati Jewish Federation; member of board of directors of American Jewish Committee; co-director of Kehilla: A Jewish Community Think Tank.

MEMBER: American Historical Association, Organization of American Historians, American Jewish Historical Society (member of academic council; archivist, 1973-75; librarian, 1976), Immigration History Society, Association for Jewish Studies, Society for Historians of the Early American Republic, Canadian Jewish Historical Society, Cincinnati Historical Society, Phi Beta Kappa.

AWARDS, HONORS: Seltzer-Brodsky Essay Prize from YIVO Institute, 1977, for "The American Jewish Response to Nineteenth Century Christian Missions"; National Foundation for Jewish Culture fellowship, 1977-79; Memorial Foundation for Jewish Culture fellowship, 1977-79, 1982-83; Bernard and Audre Rapoport fellow at American Jewish Archives, 1979-80; National Jewish Book Award nomination, 1981, for *Jacksonian Jew: The Two Worlds of Mordecai Noah;* American Council of Learned Societies fellow, 1982; Lady Davis Endowment, 1986-87.

WRITINGS:

(Editor) *Jews in New Haven,* Jewish Historical Society of New Haven, 1978.

Jacksonian Jew: The Two Worlds of Mordecai Noah, Holmes & Meier, 1981.
(Editor and translator) *"People Walk on Their Heads": Moses Weinberger's Jews and Judaism in New York,* Holmes & Meier, 1982.
(Co-editor) *Jews and the Founding of the Republic,* Markus Wiener, 1985.
The American Jewish Experience: A Reader, Holmes & Meier, 1986.
The Americanization of Jewish Culture: A History of the Jewish Publication Society, 1888-1988, Jewish Publication Society, in press.

CONTRIBUTOR

Nathan W. Kaganoff, editor, *Guide to America-Holy Land Studies,* Volume I, Arno, 1980, Volume II, Praeger, 1982.
David Gerber, editor, *The Encounter of Jew and Gentile in America: New Historical Perspectives,* University of Illinois Press, 1984.

OTHER

General editor of "Masterworks of Modern Jewish Writing," six volumes, Markus Wiener/Schocken. Editor of North American Judaism section, *Religious Studies Review,* 1984—; member of editorial committee, *Queen City Heritage,* 1985—. Contributor of over eighty articles and reviews to journals, including *Journal of American History, Spectator, Commentary, Midstream, Nation, Jewish Digest, Ethnicity,* and *Tradition;* also contributor to numerous newspapers.

WORK IN PROGRESS: Jewish-Christian Relations in the United States; American Synagogue History: A Bibliography; Yahadut Amerika—Pirsumim Belvrit: A Bibliography of Hebrew Writings in American Jewish History.

SIDELIGHTS: Jonathan D. Sarna once told *CA:* "My interest in American Jewish history dates back to high school. Before then, I had already become fascinated by America's past (not surprising, considering that I am the first in my family to be born here), and I had been introduced to Jewish history which I learned from my father beginning when I was old enough to listen to stories.

"American Jewish history, which I discovered on my own as a teenager, synthesized these two interests and promised to explain something of the world which I was struggling to understand. Later, I realized that the field was still in its formative stages of development: filled with searching questions waiting to be asked and answered. Here was a frontier worth conquering, and I plunged in head first. As a high school senior I tried to write the history of American anti-Semitism.

"Being at Brandeis University as an undergraduate permitted me to work at the American Jewish Historical Society, located on the Brandeis campus. There I discovered the endless joys of grappling with primary sources, the raw materials of history, and I began to get a grasp of the history field as a whole. By the time I entered Yale, I had learned enough to know that I wanted to explore what seemed to me to be a central theme in American Jewish history: the effort to be American and Jewish at the same time. My study of Mordecai Noah, one of the first American Jews to be prominent in both the secular and Jewish communities, followed naturally, and the title summarizes the thesis: 'Jacksonian Jew' shows attempted synthesis, 'the *two* worlds of Mordecai Noah' demonstrates that tensions remained.

"My work on Mordecai Noah brought me into contact with early nineteenth-century sources of American Jewish history (by contrast, most recent work in the field dates to the post-1881 period), and this remains one important focus of my research. But I also discovered, while working on Noah, that no serious study of the interactions between Jews and non-Jews in this country had ever been written. This seemed to me to be a great challenge, and I have consequently been gathering material and formulating a conceptual scheme, which I hope one day will result in my writing a full-scale historical analysis of Jewish-Christian relations in the United States. In the meantime, I am focusing more narrowly on three issues: the relationship between Christian missionaries and American Jews, the nature of American anti-Semitism, and the culture of American Jews in its non-Jewish context.

"My approach to American Jewish history generally and to Jewish-Christian relations in particular has been heavily influenced by contemporary writings in history, religion, and social science, particularly those dealing with structural tensions, ambivalences, and historical complexity. American Jewish history must, in my opinion, be informed by the latest findings in American history and Jewish history. At the same time, the field must also be making creative strides of its own, from which others should be able to learn. Too often, American Jews have viewed themselves—and been viewed—only narrowly and in the present. One of my challenges as an American Jewish historian is to change this: to forge a field that speaks to current concerns while putting them in broader historical perspective, thereby shedding light on past and present at once."

*   *   *

SARNO, Ronald A(nthony) 1941-

PERSONAL: Born September 26, 1941, in Jersey City, N.J.; son of Anthony Vincent and Philomena (Pilla) Sarno; married Una McGinley, July 26, 1975; children: Niamh (daughter). *Education:* Attended Bellarmine College, Plattsburgh, N.Y., 1959-63, and Weston College, 1963-66; Boston College, A.B., 1965, M.A., 1966; Woodstock College, M.Div., 1972; New York University, Ph.D., 1984; Fordham Law School, J.D. candidate. *Politics:* Democrat. *Religion:* Catholic.

ADDRESSES: Home—145 North Maple St., Ridgewood, N.J. 07450. *Office*—22 Prospect St., 1st Floor, Ridgewood, N.J. 07450.

CAREER: Parochial high school teacher of English and religion, New York City, 1966-69; facilitator, high school human relations workshops, National Conference of Christians and Jews, 1968-71; U.S. Christian Life Communities, national college moderator, 1970-75, east region representative, 1975-79; St. Joseph's Hospital and Medical Center, Paterson, N.J., administrative assistant in department of pediatrics, 1976-79; Mountainview Medical Associates, P.C., Nyack, N.Y., administrator, 1980-82; Caldwell College, Caldwell, N.J., chief development officer, 1982-83; Family Dynamics, Inc., New York City, director of development and public relations, 1983-86; Memorial Sloan-Kettering Cancer Center, New York City, administrative manager, 1986-88. Associate director, St. Ignatius Retreat House, Manhasset, N.Y., 1972-75. Lecturer on mass media, St. Peter's College, 1970; lecturer on New Testament, St. John's University, 1975.

MEMBER: Society of Research Administrators, National Federation of Fund Raising Executives, Federation of Christian Ministries, Lions Club of Little Ferry (secretary, 1983-84;

president, 1984-85; vice-president, 1985-86; deputy district governor of District 16A International Lions, 1986-87).

AWARDS, HONORS: Certificate of appreciation, National Fellowship of Christian Ministries, 1982; award from International Lions, 1983.

WRITINGS:

Achieving Sexual Maturity, Paulist/Newman, 1969.
Let Us Proclaim the Mystery of Faith, Dimension, 1970.
The People of Hope, Liguorian, 1971.
The Cruel Caesars: Their Impact on the Early Church, Alba House, 1976.
(With Len Badia) *Morality: How to Live It Today,* Alba House, 1979.
Using Media in Religious Education, Religious Education Press, 1987.

Also author of *Prayers for Modern, Urban, Uptight Man;* also editor of *Liturgical Handbook for Christian Life Communities,* 1974. Contributor to *Jesuit Yearbook.* Contributor of about twenty-five articles to periodicals, including *America* and *Chicago Studies.* Assistant editor, *Sacred Heart Messenger,* 1967; contributing editor, *National Jesuit News,* 1971-72; staff member, *Entertainment and Mass Media Law Journal.*

WORK IN PROGRESS: Research on legal questions of liability and privacy, and private and public communications for law review journal articles.

SIDELIGHTS: Ronald A. Sarno told *CA:* "I always feel slightly outdated when writing because I really believe that media have far more influence on people today than print. However, I have also found that my writing has always received an appreciative, if limited audience. I am in the unusual position of telling print-oriented readers how much influence the non-print media have on their lives, especially on religious and philosophical opinions."

*   *   *

SAXON, Van
See HENDERSON, M(arilyn) R(uth)

*   *   *

SCHERMAN, Katharine 1915-

PERSONAL: Born October 7, 1915, in New York, N.Y.; daughter of Harry and Bernardine (Kielty) Scherman; married Axel G. Rosin (associated with Book-of-the-Month Club), April 10, 1943; children: Karen, Susanna. *Education:* Swarthmore College, B.A., 1938.

ADDRESSES: Home—90 Riverside Dr., New York, N.Y. 10024. *Agent*—Harold Ober Associates, Inc., 40 East 49th St., New York, N.Y. 10017.

CAREER: Author. *Saturday Review of Literature,* New York City, secretary, 1938-40; J. B. Lippincott Co., New York City, editor, 1940-41; *Life,* New York City, researcher and writer, 1941-44; Book-of-the-Month Club, New York City, writer and editor, 1944-49.

WRITINGS:

The Slave Who Freed Haiti: The Story of Toussaint Louverture (juvenile), Random House, 1954.
Spring on an Arctic Island, Little, Brown, 1956.
Catherine the Great (juvenile), Random House, 1957.

The Sword of Siegfried (juvenile), Random House, 1959.
William Tell (juvenile), Random House, 1961.
The Long White Night, Little, Brown, 1964.
Two Islands: Grand Manan and Sanibel, Little, Brown, 1971.
Daughter of Fire: A Portrait of Iceland, Little, Brown, 1976.
The Flowering of Ireland, Little, Brown, 1981.
The Birth of France: Warriors, Bishops, and Long-Haired Kings, Random House, 1987.

SIDELIGHTS: In an *Atlantic* review of Katharine Scherman's book *Daughter of Fire: A Portrait of Iceland,* P. L. Adams explains that the reader is introduced to a country that is "strange and beautiful" with "a violent past, a volcanically dangerous present, [and] a superb literature." Additionally, a reviewer for *Choice* finds this "a travel book in the old style: readable, leisurely, detailed, and intelligent. . . . Scherman's account evokes the atmosphere of Iceland in a uniquely imaginative way."

Another of Scherman's books, *The Flowering of Ireland,* recounts the history of Ireland between the fifth and twelfth centuries, before that country's conversion to Christianity. Michiko Kakutani writes in the *New York Times* that Scherman's *The Flowering of Ireland* is a "fine and decorous portrait of a country and its faith." R. E. Dunbar explains in the *Christian Science Monitor* that while researching this book Scherman "visited many, if not all, of the places about which she has written, and her vivid, firsthand accounts make her readers feel they are right beside her."

Scherman wrote to *CA* that *The Birth of France: Warriors, Bishops, and Long-Haired Kings* "is the history of the earliest kings of France, the Teutonic warrior chieftains who were the bridge between the collapse of the Roman Empire in Europe and the rise of the empire of Charlemagne. Along with the tale of these savage kings and queens is the companion story of the rise of Christianity in this raw world: the spiritual catalyst through which Gallo-Roman Christianity merged with the tough vitality of the pagan Franks to produce the race and the nation of France."

AVOCATIONAL INTERESTS: Ornithology, mountain climbing, music (plays both piano and cello in chamber music ensembles).

BIOGRAPHICAL/CRITICAL SOURCES:

PERIODICALS

Atlantic, April, 1976.
Choice, June, 1976.
Christian Science Monitor, September 2, 1981.
Library Journal, March 15, 1976, May 15, 1981.
Los Angeles Times Book Review, September 6, 1987.
New York Times, July 21, 1980.
Tribune Books (Chicago), September 22, 1987.

*   *   *

SCHEUERMAN, Richard D(ean) 1951-

PERSONAL: Born April 18, 1951, in Colfax, Wash.; son of Donovon Clair (a farmer) and Mary Gertrude (Johns) Scheuerman; married Lois Jean Morasch (a receptionist), June 16, 1973. *Education:* Washington State University, B.A., 1973; Defense Language Institute, diploma in Russian, 1974; graduate study at Pacific Lutheran University. *Religion:* Christian.

CAREER: Cashmere Public Schools, Cashmere, Wash., teacher of history, English, and Russian, beginning 1974. *Military service:* U.S. Air Force, 1973-74.

MEMBER: American Historical Society of Germans from Russia, Smithsonian Institute (associate member), Farm House Fraternity, Phi Alpha Theta.

AWARDS, HONORS: Governor's Award for best nonfiction on Northwest history, State of Washington, 1986, for *Renegade Tribe: The Palouse Indians and the Invasion of the Inland Pacific Northwest.*

WRITINGS:

Pilgrims on the Earth: A German-Russian Chronicle, Ye Galleon Press, 1974, 2nd edition, 1976.
(With Clifford E. Trafzer) *The Volga Germans: Pioneers of the Northwest,* University Press of Idaho, 1981.
The Wenatchi Indians: Guardians of the Valley, Ye Galleon Press, 1983.
(With Trafzer) *Renegade Tribe: The Palouse Indians and the Invasion of the Inland Pacific Northwest,* Washington State University Press, 1986.
(With Trafzer) *Chief Joseph's Allies: The Palouse Indians and the Nez Perce War of 1877,* Sierra Oaks, 1987.
Northwestern Indian Images: A Photographic Look at Plateau Indians, Sierra Oaks, 1987.

*   *   *

SCHIFFER, Michael B(rian) 1947-

PERSONAL: Born October 4, 1947, in Winnipeg, Manitoba, Canada; came to United States in 1953, naturalized in 1962; son of Louie (a salesman) and Frances-Fera (Ludmer) Schiffer; married Annette Leve, December 22, 1968; children: Adam Joseph, Jeremy Alan. *Education:* University of California, Los Angeles, B.A. (summa cum laude), 1969; University of Arizona, M.A., 1972, Ph.D., 1973.

ADDRESSES: Office—Department of Anthropology, University of Arizona, Tucson, Ariz. 85721.

CAREER: University of Arkansas, Fayetteville, assistant professor of anthropology, 1973-75; University of Arizona, Tucson, assistant professor, 1975-79, associate professor, 1979-82, professor of anthropology, 1982—, assistant director of Archaeological Field School in Grasshopper, Ariz., summer, 1973, director of Laboratory of Traditional Technology, 1984—. Visiting distinguished archaeologist at University of South Carolina, summer, 1977; visiting associate professor at University of Washington, summer, 1979; distinguished visiting professor at Arizona State University, autumn, 1982. Member of staff of Southwest Expedition of Field Museum of Natural History, summer, 1969, research assistant, summer, 1970, research associate, summer, 1971, co-director of excavations, 1970-71; director of Cache River Archeological Project in northeastern Arkansas, 1973-74, Big Running Water Ditch Project and Village Creek Project, both spring, 1974, and Arkansas Eastman Archeological Project, 1974-75; methodologist with Corduroy Creek Archaeological Project in east central Arizona, 1978-79, and with Tudor Alden Project in Chile, summer, 1985; archaeologist with Phoenix District of U.S. Bureau of Land Management, summers, 1980-81; microstratigrapher for Kourion Project in Crete, summer, 1985.

MEMBER: American Anthropological Association (fellow), Society for American Archaeology, American Association for the Advancement of Science (fellow), Society for Historical Archaeology, Phi Beta Kappa, Phi Eta Sigma, Pi Gamma Mu.

AWARDS, HONORS: Woodrow Wilson fellowship, 1969-70.

WRITINGS:

Behavioral Archeology, Academic Press (New York, N.Y.), 1976.

(Editor with George J. Gumerman, and contributor) *Conservation Archaeology: A Guide for Cultural Resource Management Studies*, Academic Press (New York, N.Y.), 1977.

(Editor with Richard A Gould, and contributor) *Modern Material Culture: The Archaeology of Us*, Academic Press (New York, N.Y.), 1981.

(Editor with Randall H. McGuire, and contributor) *Hohokam and Patayan: Prehistory of Southwestern Arizona*, Academic Press (New York, N.Y.), 1982.

(With William J. Rathje) *Archaeology*, Harcourt, 1982.

Formation Processes of the Archaeological Record, University of New Mexico Press, 1987.

(Editor) *Archaeological Method and Theory*, Volume 1, University of Arizona Press, in press.

CONTRIBUTOR

Charles L. Redman, editor, *Research and Theory in Current Archeology*, Wiley, 1973.

James Mueller, editor, *Sampling in Archaeology*, University of Arizona Press, 1975.

Stanley South, editor, *Research Strategies in Historical Archeology*, Academic Press (New York, N.Y.), 1977.

Charles R. McGimsey III and Hester A. Davis, editors, *The Management of Archeological Resources: The Airlie House Report*, Society for American Archaeology, 1977.

Gould, editor, *Explorations in Ethnoarchaeology*, University of New Mexico Press, 1978.

Paul F. Grebinger, editor, *Discovering Past Behavior: Experiments in the Archaeology of the American Southwest*, Gordon & Breach, 1978.

Gumerman and Robert C. Euler, editors, *Investigations of the Southwestern Anthropological Research Group*, Museum of Northern Arizona, 1978.

Alice W. Portnoy, editor, *Scholars as Managers*, Heritage Conservation and Recreation Service, Interagency Archeological Services, 1978.

Brian Hayden, editor, *Lithic Use-Wear Analysis*, Academic Press (New York, N.Y.), 1979.

Colin Renfrew and Kenneth Cooke, editors, *Transformations: Mathematical Approaches to Culture Change*, Academic Press (New York, N.Y.), 1979.

J. R. McKinlay and K. L. Jones, editors, *Archaeological Resource Management in Australia and Oceania*, New Zealand Historic Places Trust, 1979.

Susan Kent, editor, *Method and Theory for Activity Area Research: An Ethnoarchaeological Approach*, Columbia University Press, 1987.

R. D. Leonard and G. T. Jones, editors, *The Concept and Measurement of Archaeological Diversity*, Cambridge University Press, in press.

Gordon Bronitsky, editor, *Pottery Technology: Ideas and Approaches*, Westview, in press.

OTHER

Editor of series "Advances in Archaeological Method and Theory," Academic Press (New York, N.Y.), 1976-84, Academic Press (Orlando, Fla.), 1985-87. Contributor of more than twenty-five articles and reviews to anthropology and archaeology journals, such as *American Antiquity, Kiva, American Anthropologist,* and *Science and Archaeology.* Assistant editor of *Kiva,* 1970.

WORK IN PROGRESS: Research on archaeological epistemology, theory and methodology, experimental archaeology, ceramic technology, and modern material culture.

SIDELIGHTS: Michael B. Schiffer told *CA:* "One theme of my work has been the need to relate the past and present through artifacts. That's why I have used archaeological methods to study modern artifacts, and why I am using modern analytical approaches to unlock the secrets of ancient technologies. I hope in the years ahead to find new ways to apply archaeology to the benefit of modern society."

*   *   *

SCHNELL, George A(dam) 1931-

PERSONAL: Born July 13, 1931, in Philadelphia, Pa.; son of Earl Blackwood and Emily (Bernheimer) Schnell; married Mary Lou Williams (in real estate sales), June 21, 1958. *Education:* Pennsylvania State University, M.S., 1960, Ph.D., 1965. *Politics:* Democrat. *Religion:* Reformed Church.

ADDRESSES: Home—4 Joalyn Rd., New Paltz, N.Y. 12561. *Office*—Department of Geography, Hamner House 1, State University of New York College at New Paltz, N.Y. 12561.

CAREER: State University of New York College at New Paltz, assistant professor, 1962-65, associate professor, 1965-68, professor of geography, 1968—, chairman of department, 1969—, founding board member of Institute for Development, Planning, and Land Use Studies. Visiting professor, University of Hawaii, summer, 1966; adjunct professor, Empire State College of the State University of New York, 1974—. *Military service:* U.S. Army, 1952-54.

MEMBER: Association of American Geographers, National Council on Geographical Education, Pennsylvania Academy of Science, Pennsylvania Geographic Society.

AWARDS, HONORS: National Science Foundation summer fellow, 1965.

WRITINGS:

(Contributor of maps) John M. Scherwig, *Guineas and Gunpowder*, Harvard University, 1969.

(Editor with George J. Demko and Harold M. Rose) *Population Geography: A Reader*, McGraw, 1970.

(With Kenneth Corey and others) *The Local Community: A Handbook for Teachers*, Macmillan, 1971.

(Contributor of maps) Lewis Brownstein, *Education and Rural Development in Kenya: A Case Study of Primary School Graduates*, Praeger, 1972.

(Contributor) Q. H. Stanford, editor, *The World's Population: Problems of Growth*, Oxford University Press (Canada), 1972.

(Contributor) *Readings on West Virginia and Appalachia*, Kendall-Hunt, 1976.

(With Mark Stephen Monmonier) *The Study of Population: Elements, Patterns, Processes*, C. E. Merrill, 1983.

(Contributor with Monmonier) S. K. Majumdar and E. W. Miller, editors, *Pennsylvania Coal: Resources, Technology, and Utilization*, Pennsylvania Academy of Science, 1983.

(Contributor with Monmonier) Majumdar and Miller, editors, *Hazardous and Toxic Wastes: Technology, Management, and Health Effects*, Pennsylvania Academy of Science, 1984.

(Co-editor and contributor) *Proceedings of a Conference on Economic Development and the Quality of Life,* Mid-Hudson Regional Development Council, 1986.

(With Monmonier) *Map Appreciation,* Prentice-Hall, 1988.

(With Peter Fairweather) *The Shawangunk Mountains: A Critical Environmental Region,* Institute for Development, Planning, and Land Use Studies, 1988.

Also author of audio units, ''Weather, Climate, and Man,'' Learning Systems, Inc., 1971. Contributor to proceedings; contributor to geography and other professional journals. Member of editorial board, Pennsylvania Academy of Science, 1968-88; member of editorial and advisory board, Pennsylvania Coal Project; guest editor, *Pennsylvania Geographer,* 1973. Associate editor, *Journal of the Pennsylvania Academy of Sciences,* 1988—.

WORK IN PROGRESS: A research project, ''The Reciprocity between Growth of a College and its Service Area.''

SIDELIGHTS: George A. Schnell told *CA:* ''I enjoy teaching very much, especially undergraduates, and am especially gratified to see them go on to succeed in graduate and professional schools and gain positions of responsibility. This success is very much based upon their ability to communicate—to write—and I hope that helping them to learn to write has become an important part of my role in their academic lives.''

*   *   *

SCHYDLOWSKY, Daniel M(oses)   1940-

PERSONAL: Surname is pronounced Sheed-lov-skee; born April 20, 1940, in Lima, Peru; came to United States, 1962; son of Luis (a businessman) and Gertrud (Rosenberg) Schydlowsky; married Beverly H. Minker (a psychiatric social worker), August 2, 1970; children: Andrew, Jonathan. *Education:* University of San Marcos, B.A., LL.B., M.A., all 1961; Harvard University, M.A., 1964, Ph.D., 1966. *Religion:* Jewish.

ADDRESSES: Home—23 Philbrick Rd., Brookline, Mass. 02146. *Office*—745 Commonwealth Ave., Boston, Mass. 02215.

CAREER: Harvard University, Cambridge, Mass., instructor, 1966-67, assistant professor of economics, 1967-72, research associate, Center for International Affairs, 1966-72; Boston University, Boston, Mass., professor of economics, 1972—, senior research associate, Center for Latin American Development Studies, 1972—, and Center for Asian Development Studies, 1977—. Consultant to Organization of American States, United Nations, International Bank for Reconstruction and Development, and Inter-American Development Bank.

MEMBER: American Economic Association, Econometric Society, Colegio de Economistas del Peru, Instituto de Desarrollo Economico y Social (Buenos Aires).

WRITINGS:

(Contributor) M. S. Brodersohn, editor, *Estrategias de industrializacion para la Argentina,* DiTella (Buenos Aires), 1969.

(With Gustav Fritz Papanek and J. J. Stern) *Decision Making for Economic Development,* Houghton, 1971.

(Contributor) Herbert S. Grubel and Harry G. Johnson, editors, *Effective Tariff Protection,* Unipub, 1971.

(Contributor) Stephen E. Guisinger, editor, *Trade and Investment Policies in the Americas,* Southern Methodist University Press, 1973.

(Contributor) Sidney Robbins and Robert B. Stobaugh, Jr., editors, *Money in the Multinational Enterprise: A Study of Financial Policy,* Basic Books, 1973.

International Trade Policy in the Economic Growth of Latin America, Center for Latin American Development Studies, Boston University, 1973.

Methodology for the Empirical Estimation of Shadow Prices, Center for Latin American Development Studies, Boston University, 1973.

Project Evaluation in Economies in General Disequilibrium: An Application of Second Best Analysis, Center for Latin American Development Studies, Boston University, 1973.

Price and Scale Obstacles to Export Expansion in LDC's, Center for Latin American Development Studies, Boston University, 1975.

Capital Utilization, Growth, Employment, and BOP and Price Stabilization, Center for Latin American Development Studies, Boston University, 1976.

The Design of Benefit-Cost Analysis of Investment Projects in Peru: A Country-Specific View, Center for Latin American Development Studies, Boston University, 1977.

Containing the Costs of Stabilization in Semi-Industrialized LDC's: A Marshallian Approach, Center for Latin American Development Studies, Boston University, 1979.

(With Juan J. Wicht) *Anatomia de un fracaso economico: Peru, 1968-1978,* 2nd edition, Centro de Investigacion, Universidad del Pacifico, 1979.

The Short Run Potential for Employment Generation on Installed Capacity in Latin America, Center for Latin American Development Studies, Boston University, 1980.

(With I. Gonzales and Abusada) *Propuestas para el desarrollo Peruano, 1980-1985,* Asociacion de Exportadores del Peru (Lima), 1980.

Comentarios sobre la politica economia, Centro de Investigacion, Universidad del Pacifico, 1982.

La promocion de exportaciones no tradicionales en el Peru, Asociacion de Exportadores del Peru, 1983.

Contributor to reports of Center for International Affairs, Harvard University, and to journals published in the United States, Peru, Argentina, and Colombia.

WORK IN PROGRESS: Research on Latin American economic development, centered on employment created through use of multiple shift work in industry; research on commercial policy; research on investment criteria.

SIDELIGHTS: Daniel M. Schydlowsky has lived at intervals in Argentina, Colombia, and Indonesia. Besides his native Spanish and English, he speaks French and German, and has some ability in Hebrew, Italian, and Portuguese.*

*   *   *

SCOTT, Dan
[Collective pseudonym]

WRITINGS:

''BRET KING'' MYSTERY STORIES

The Mystery of Ghost Canyon, Grosset & Dunlap, 1960.
The Secret of Hermit's Peak, Grosset & Dunlap, 1960.
The Range Rodeo Mystery, Grosset & Dunlap, 1960.
The Mystery of Rawhide Gap, Grosset & Dunlap, 1960.
The Mystery at Blizzard Mesa, Grosset & Dunlap, 1961.
The Secret of Fort Pioneer, Grosset & Dunlap, 1961.
The Mystery of the Comanche Caves, Grosset & Dunlap, 1962.

The Phantom of Wolf Creek, Grosset & Dunlap, 1963.
The Mystery at Bandit Gulch, Grosset & Dunlap, 1964.

SIDELIGHTS: Bret King is a modern cowboy who lives on Rimrock Ranch in New Mexico. The ranch is provided with modern equipment, and the young cowhand often has to combat enemies who use the latest scientific apparatus. Andrew E. Svenson wrote some of the volumes in this mystery series. For more information, see the entries in this volume for Harriet S. Adams, Edward L. Stratemeyer, and Andrew E. Svenson.

BIOGRAPHICAL/CRITICAL SOURCES:

BOOKS

Johnson, Deidre, editor and compiler, *Stratemeyer Pseudonyms and Series Books: An Annotated Checklist of Stratemeyer and Stratemeyer Syndicate Publications*, Greenwood Press, 1982.

* * *

SERVENTY, Vincent (Noel)

PERSONAL: Born in Armadale, Western Australia; son of Victor Vincent (a wine grower) and Annie (Gabelish) Serventy; married Caroline Darbyshire (a writer under name Carol Serventy), September 1, 1955; children: Karen, Cathy, Matthew. *Education:* University of West Australia, B.Sc., 1945, B.Ed., 1950.

ADDRESSES: Home—8 Reiby Rd., Hunters Hill, New South Wales 2110, Australia.

CAREER: Senior lecturer in science and mathematics at Claremont Teachers College, 1955-57; Education Department of Western Australia, Nature Advisory Service, Perth, instructor in science and head of department, 1958-61; writer and lecturer. Writer and producer of television series, including "Nature Walkabout," twenty-six half-hour films on Australian natural history, beginning 1967, "Around the Bush," six quarter-hour films, "Rolf's Walkabout," and "Shell's Australia"; advisor and co-producer of "The Australian Ark," thirteen one-hour films, 1972; featured on nature shows on Australian Broadcasting Corporation television. Chairman, Nature Conservation Council of New South Wales, 1970-73, 1976—; member, National Parks and Wildlife Advisory Council of New South Wales, 1966—; trustee, National Photographic Index of Birds, Australian Museum, 1974—; councillor and founder, Gould League of New South Wales, 1966—; founder of Western Australia National Trust. Zoologist member of the Australian Geographical Society expedition to the islands of the Recherche Archipelago, 1952; leader of the first natural history expedition into the Great Victoria Desert of Australia, 1960; member of the first party to make a crossing of Lake Eyre by boat, 1975.

MEMBER: World Wildlife Fund (trustee; past president and founder of Australian branch), Society of Authors, Wildlife Preservation Society of Australia (president), Australian Heritage Commission (past commissioner), Western Australian Naturalists Society (honorary life member), Western Australia Tree Society (founder), Strehlow Foundation (fellow).

AWARDS, HONORS: Natural History Medallion, 1974; member, Order of Australia, 1976; Ridder (knight), Order of the Golden Ark, Netherlands, 1985.

WRITINGS:

Australia's Great Barrier Reef: A Handbook on the Corals, Shells, Crabs, Larger Animals, and Birds, with Some Re- marks on the Reef's Place in History, Georgian House, 1955, 2nd edition, 1966.
The Australian Nature Trail, Georgian House, 1965.
A Continent in Danger, Reynal, 1966.
Nature Walkabout, A.H. & A.W. Reed, 1967.
Landforms of Australia, Angus & Robertson, 1967, American Elsevier Publishing Co., 1968.
Australian Wildlife Conservation, illustrated by Faye Owner, Angus & Robertson, 1968.
Wildlife of Australia, Nelson, 1968, Taplinger, 1972, abridged edition, Nelson, 1972, revised edition, 1977, new enlarged edition, Hamish Hamilton, 1977.
Australia's National Parks: Landforms, Plants, Animals Revealed through Nature Reserves, Angus & Robertson, 1969.
Southern Walkabout, A.H. & A.W. Reed, 1969.
Turtle Bay Adventure, illustrated by Faye Owner, Andre Deutsch, 1969.
Around the Bush with Vincent Serventy, Australian Broadcasting Commission, 1970.
The Great Barrier Reef, Golden Press, 1970.
Dryandra, the Story of an Australian Forest, A.H. & A.W. Reed, 1970.
(Co-photographer with Rolf Harris) Carol Serventy and Alwen Harris, *Rolf's Walkabout*, Bailey & Swinfen, 1971.
(With John Warham and brother, D. L. Serventy *The Handbook of Australian Sea-Birds*, A.H. & A.W. Reed, 1971.
The Singing Land: 22 Natural Environments of Australia from Surging Ocean to Arid Desert, Angus & Robertson, 1972, Scribner, 1974.
Desert Walkabout, Collins, 1973, Taplinger, 1977.
(Editor and annotator with A. H. Chisholm) John Gould, *The Birds of Australia*, Lansdowne Press, 1973.
(With wife, Carol Serventy) *The Koala*, Dutton, 1975.
In Praise of Australian Trees, Rigby, 1979.
Zoo Walkabout, Collins, 1979.
(With Robert Raymond) *Lakes and Rivers of Australia*, Summit Books, 1980.
(With Raymond) *Rainforests of Australia*, Summit Books, 1980.
(With C. Serventy) *Australian Birds*, Rigby, 1981.
Plantlife of Australia, Cassell, 1981.
(Editor-in-chief) *Australian Warblers*, Angus & Robertson, 1982.
Coral Reefs (juvenile), Hodder & Stoughton, 1982.
Deserts (juvenile), Hodder & Stoughton, 1982.
Australian Native Trees, A.H. & A.W. Reed, 1984.
Australia's Natural Wonders, Lansdowne Press, 1984.
(With J. Olsen, M. Durack, G. Dutton, and A. Bortignon) *Land beyond Time*, Macmillan, 1984.
Waterbirds of Australia, Angus & Robertson, 1985.
The Desert Sea, Macmillan, 1985.
Australia's World Heritage Sites, Macmillan, 1986.

"ANIMALS IN THE WILD" SERIES; JUVENILES

Shark and Ray, Raintree Publishers, 1985.
Crocodile and Alligator, Raintree Publishers, 1985.
Turtle and Tortoise, Raintree Publishers, 1985.
Whale and Dolphin, Raintree Publishers, 1985.
Kangaroo, Raintree Publishers, 1985.
Koala, Raintree Publishers, 1985.
Kookaburra, Raintree Publishers, 1985.
Penguin, Raintree Publishers, 1985.
Lizard, Raintree Publishers, 1986.
Parrot, Raintree Publishers, 1986.

OTHER

Also author of *Australia's Wildlife Heritage*, five volumes,

1975, *Glovebox Guide to Australian Nature,* 1980, *Australian Landforms,* four volumes, 1981, *Australian Trees,* 1984. Contributor to *Emu* and *Western Australian Naturalist.* Editor, *Wildlife in Australia,* 1966-82; editor-in-chief and contributor, *Australia's Wildlife Heritage,* 1973-76; member of editorial board, Collins Publishers' Australian Naturalist series, 1972—.

SIDELIGHTS: Vincent Serventy is one of the foremost conservationists working in Australia today. His family has a long history in conservation—an island off the west coast Australia has been named Serventy Island in their honor. He writes, "I hope to achieve a better world environment," and cites Henry David Thoreau and Gilbert White as his mentors.

One of Serventy's books, *Dryandra, the Story of an Australian Forest,* was included in a list of great books of Australian literature. Many others have received favorable reviews. He told *CA:* "I think I like best one from a little girl who wrote, 'When I go over sea and water, I just go over sea and water. But when I go with Vincent Serventy I see the wonder of it.'"

BIOGRAPHICAL/CRITICAL SOURCES:

PERIODICALS

New Age News, November, 1987.
Times Literary Supplement, January 5, 1967.

*   *   *

SHANGE, Ntozake   1948-

PERSONAL: Original name Paulette Williams; name changed in 1971; name pronounced En-to-zaki Shong-gay; born October 18, 1948, in Trenton, N.J.; daughter of Paul T. (a surgeon) and Eloise (a psychiatric social worker and educator) Williams; married second husband, David Murray (a musician), July, 1977 (divorced). *Education:* Barnard College, B.A. (with honors), 1970; University of Southern California, Los Angeles, M.A., 1973; graduate study, University of Southern California.

ADDRESSES: Office—Department of Drama, University of Houston—University Park, 4800 Calhoun Rd., Houston, Tex. 77004.

CAREER: Writer and performer. Faculty member in women's studies, California State College, Sonoma Mills College, and the University of California Extension, 1972-75; artist in residence, New Jersey State Council on the Arts; creative writing instructor, City College of New York; currently associate professor of drama, University of Houston. Lecturer at Douglass College, 1978, and at many other institutions, such as Yale University, Howard University, Detroit Art Institute, and New York University. Dancer with Third World Collective, Raymond Sawyer's Afro-American Dance Company, Sounds in Motion, West Coast Dance Works, and For Colored Girls Who Have Considered Suicide (her own dance company); has appeared in Broadway and Off-Broadway productions of her own plays, including "For Colored Girls Who Have Considered Suicide/When the Rainbow Is Enuf," and "Where the Mississippi Meets the Amazon." Director of several productions, including "The Mighty Gents," produced by the New York Shakespeare Festival's Mobile Theatre, 1979, "A Photograph: A Study in Cruelty," produced in Houston's Equinox Theatre, 1979, and June Jordan's "The Issue" and "The Spirit of Sojourner Truth," 1979. Has given poetry readings.

MEMBER: Actors Equity, National Academy of Television Arts and Sciences, Dramatists Guild, PEN American Center, Academy of American Poets, Poets & Writers, Inc., Women's Institute for Freedom of the Press, New York Feminist Arts Guild.

AWARDS, HONORS: Obie Award, Outer Critics Circle Award, Audelco Award, Mademoiselle Award, and Tony, Grammy, and Emmy award nominations, 1977, all for "For Colored Girls Who Have Considered Suicide/When the Rainbow Is Enuf"; Frank Silvera Writers' Workshop Award, 1978; *Los Angeles Times* Book Prize for Poetry, 1981, for *Three Pieces;* Guggenheim fellowship, 1981; Medal of Excellence, Columbia University, 1981; Obie Award, 1981, for "Mother Courage and Her Children"; Pushcart Prize.

WRITINGS:

For Colored Girls Who Have Considered Suicide/When the Rainbow Is Enuf: A Choreopoem (first produced in New York City at Studio Rivbea, July 7, 1975; produced Off-Broadway at Anspacher Public Theatre, 1976; produced on Broadway at Booth Theatre, September 15, 1976), Shameless Hussy Press (San Lorenzo, Calif.), 1975, revised version, Macmillan, 1976.
Sassafrass (novella), Shameless Hussy Press, 1976.
Melissa & Smith, Bookslinger Editions, 1976.
"A Photograph: A Study of Cruelty" (poem-play), first produced Off-Broadway at Public Theatre, December 21, 1977, revised version, "A Photograph: Lovers in Motion" (also see below), produced in Houston, Texas, at the Equinox Theatre, November, 1979.
(With Thulani Nkabinde and Jessica Hagedorn) "Where the Mississippi Meets the Amazon," first produced in New York City at Public Theatre Cabaret, December 18, 1977.
Natural Disasters and Other Festive Occasions (prose and poems), Heirs, 1977.
Nappy Edges (poems), St. Martin's, 1978.
Boogie Woogie Landscapes (play; also see below; first produced in New York City at Frank Silvera Writers' Workshop, June, 1979, produced on Broadway at the Symphony Space Theatre, produced in Washington D.C. at the Kennedy Center), St. Martin's, 1978.
"Spell #7: A Geechee Quick Magic Trance Manual" (play; also see below), produced on Broadway at Joseph Papp's New York Shakespeare Festival Public Theater, July 15, 1979.
"Black and White Two Dimensional Planes" (play), first produced in New York City at Sounds in Motion Studio Works, February, 1979.
"Mother Courage and Her Children" (an adapted version of Bertolt Brecht's play, *Mother Courage and Her Children*), first produced Off-Broadway at the Public Theatre, April, 1980.
Three Pieces: Spell #7; A Photograph: Lovers in Motion; Boogie Woogie Landscapes (plays), St. Martin's, 1981.
A Photograph: Lovers in Motion, Samuel French, 1981.
Spell #7: A Theatre Piece in Two Acts, Samuel French, 1981.
Sassafrass, Cypress & Indigo: A Novel, St. Martin's, 1982.
"Three for a Full Moon" and "Bocas," first produced in Los Angeles, Calif., at the Mark Taper Forum Lab, Center Theatre, April 28, 1982.
(Adapter) Willy Russell, "Educating Rita" (play), first produced in Atlanta, Georgia, by Alliance Theatre Company, 1982.
A Daughter's Geography (poems), St. Martin's, 1983.
See No Evil: Prefaces, Essays and Accounts, 1976-1983, Momo's Press, 1984.
From Okra to Greens: Poems, Coffee House Press, 1984.

From Okra to Greens: A Different Kinda Love Story; A Play with Music & Dance (first produced in New York City at Barnard College, November, 1978), Samuel French, 1985.

Betsey Brown: A Novel, St. Martin's, 1985.

"Three Views of Mt. Fuji" (play), first produced at the Lorraine Hansberry Theatre, June, 1987, produced in New York City at the New Dramatists, October, 1987.

Ridin' the Moon in Texas: Word Paintings (responses to art in prose and poetry), St. Martin's, 1987.

Also author of *Some Men* (poems in a pamphlet that resembles a dance card), 1981. Author of the play "Mouths" and the operetta "Carrie," both produced in 1981. Has also written for a television special starring Diana Ross, and appears in a documentary about her own work for WGBH TV. Contributor to periodicals, including *Black Scholar, Third World Women, Ms.,* and *Yardbird Reader.*

WORK IN PROGRESS: "In the Middle of a Flower," a play; a film adaptation of her novella, *Sassafrass;* a third novel.

SIDELIGHTS: Born to a surgeon and an educator, Ntozake Shange—originally named Paulette Williams—was raised with the advantages available to the black middle class. But one by one, the roles she chose for herself—war correspondent, and jazz musician, to name a few—were dismissed as "'no good for a woman,'" she told Stella Dong in a *Publishers Weekly* interview. She chose to become a writer because "there was nothing left." Frustrated and hurt after separating from her first husband, Shange attempted suicide several times before focusing her rage against the limitations society imposes on black women. While earning a master's degree in American Studies from the University of Southern California, she reaffirmed her personal strength based on a self-determined identity and took her African name, which means "she who comes with her own things" and she "who walks like a lion." Since then she has sustained a triple career as an educator, a performer/director in New York and Houston, and a writer whose works draw heavily on her experiences and the frustrations of being a black female in America. "I am a war correspondent after all," she told Dong, "because I'm involved in a war of cultural and esthetic aggression. The front lines aren't always what you think they are."

Though she is an accomplished poet and an acclaimed novelist, Shange became famous for her play, "For Colored Girls Who Have Considered Suicide/When the Rainbow Is Enuf." A unique blend of poetry, music, dance and drama called a "choreopoem," it is still being produced around the country more than ten years after it "took the theater world by storm" in 1975. Before it won international acclaim, "For Colored Girls," notes Jacqueline Trescott in the *Washington Post,* "became an electrifying Broadway hit and provoked heated exchanges about the relationships between black men and women. . . . When [it] debuted, [it] became the talk of literary circles. Its form—seven women on the stage dramatizing poetry—was a refreshing slap at the traditional, one-two-three-act structures." Whereas plays combining poetry and dance had already been staged by Adrienne Kennedy, Mel Gussow of the *New York Times* states that "Miss Shange was a pioneer in terms of her subject matter: the fury of black women at their double subjugation in white male America."

Shange's anger wasn't always so evident. "I was always what you call a nice child," she told *Time* magazine contributor Jean Vallely. "I did everything nice. I was the nicest and most correct. I did my homework. I was always on time. I never got into fights. People now ask me, 'Where did all this rage come from?' And I just smile and say it's been there all the time, but I was just trying to be nice."

Shange's childhood was filled with music, literature, and art. Dizzy Gillespie, Miles Davis, Chuck Berry, and W.E.B. Du Bois were among the frequent guests at her parents' house. On Sunday afternoons Shange's family held variety shows. She recalled them in a self-interview published in *Ms.:* "my mama wd read from dunbar, shakespeare, countee cullen, t. s. eliot. my dad wd play congas & do magic tricks. my two sisters & my brother & i wd do a soft-shoe & then pick up the instruments for a quartet of some sort: a violin, a cello, flute & saxophone. we all read constantly. anything. anywhere. we also tore the prints outta art books to carry around with us. sounds/images, any explorations of personal visions waz the focus of my world."

However privileged her childhood might have seemed, Shange felt that she was "living a lie." As she explained to *Newsday* reviewer Allan Wallach: "[I was] living in a world that defied reality as most black people, or most white people, understood it—in other words, feeling that there was something that I could do, and then realizing that nobody was expecting me to do anything because I was colored and I was also female, which was not very easy to deal with."

Writing dramatic poetry became a means of expressing her dissatisfaction with the role of black women in society. She and a group of friends, including various musicians and the choreographer-dancer Paula Moss, would create improvisational works comprised of poetry, music, and dance, and would frequently perform them in bars in San Francisco and New York. When Moss and Shange moved to New York City, they presented "For Colored Girls" at a Soho jazz loft, the Studio Rivbea. Director Oz Scott saw the show and helped develop the production as it was performed in bars on the Lower East Side. Impressed by one of these, black producer Woodie King, Jr., joined Scott to stage the choreopoem Off-Broadway at the New Federal Theatre, where it ran successfully from November, 1975 to the following June. Then Joseph Papp became the show's producer at the New York Shakespeare Festival's Anspacher Public Theatre. From there, it moved to the Booth Theatre uptown. "The final production at the Booth is as close to distilled as any of us in all our art forms can make it," Shange says of that production in the introduction to *For Colored Girls,* published in 1976. "The cast is enveloping almost 6,000 people a week in the words of a young black girl's growing up, her triumphs and errors, [her] struggle to be all that is forbidden by our environment, all that is forfeited by our gender, all that we have forgotten."

In "For Colored Girls," poems dramatized by the women dancers recall encounters with their classmates, lovers, rapists, abortionists, and latent killers. The women survive the abuses and disappointments put upon them by the men in their lives and come to recognize in each other, dressed in the colors of Shange's personal rainbow, the promise of a better future. As one voice, at the end, they declare, "i found god in myself / and i loved her / . . . fiercely." To say this, remarks Carol P. Christ in *Diving Deep and Surfacing: Women Writers on Spiritual Quest,* is "to say . . . that it is all right to be a woman, that the Black woman does not have to imitate whiteness or depend on men for her power of being." "The poetry," says Marilyn Stasio in *Cue,* "touches some very tender nerve endings. Although roughly structured and stylistically unrefined, this fierce and passionate poetry has the power to move a body to tears, to rage, and to an ultimate rush of love."

While some reviewers are enthusiastic in their praise for the play, others are emphatically negative. ''Some Black people, notably men, said that . . . Shange broke a taboo when her 'For Colored Girls . . .' took the theater world by storm,'' Connie Lauerman reports in the *Chicago Tribune.* ''[Shange] was accused of racism, of 'lynching' the black male.'' But the playwright does not feel that she was bringing any black family secrets to light. She told Lauerman, ''Half of what we discussed in 'For Colored Girls' about the dissipation of the family, rape, wife-battering and all that sort of thing, the U.S. Census Bureau already had. . . . We could have gone to the Library of Congress and read the Census reports and the crime statistics every month and we would know that more black women are raped than anyone else. We would know at this point that they think 48 per cent of our households are headed by single females. . . . My job as an artist is to say what I see.''

If these conditions are unknown to some, she feels it is all the more important to talk about them openly. Defending her portrayal of the acquaintance who turned out to be a rapist, she told interviewer Claudia Tate that men who deal with the issues by saying they have never raped anyone trouble her: ''Maybe we should have a Congressional hearing to find out if it's the UFOs who are raping women. . . . After all, that is a denial of reality. It does *not* matter if you did or did not do something. . . . When is someone going to take responsibility for what goes on where we live?'' In the same interview, printed in *Black Women Writers at Work,* Shange explained that she wrote about Beau Willie Brown, a war veteran who is on drugs when he drops two small children off a high-rise balcony, because she ''refuse[s] to be a part of this conspiracy of silence'' regarding crimes that hurt black women.

Some feminist responses to the play were negative, reports *Village Voice* critic Michele Wallace, who suspects ''that some black women are angry because 'For Colored Girls' exposes their fear of rejection as well as their anger at being rejected. They don't want to deal with that so they talk about how Shange is persecuting the black man.'' Sandra Hollin Flowers, author of the *Black American Literature Forum* article '''Colored Girls': Textbook for the Eighties,'' finds most inappropriate the charges that Shange portrays black men as stupidly crude and brutal. ''Quite the contrary, Shange demonstrates a compassionate vision of black men—compassionate because though the work is not without anger, it has a certain integrity which could not exist if the author lacked a perceptive understanding of the crisis between black men and women. And there is definitely a crisis. . . . This, then is what makes *Colored Girls* an important work which ranks with [Ralph] Ellison's *Invisible Man,* [Richard] Wright's *Native Son,* and the handful of other black classics—it is an artistically successful female perspective on a long-standing issue among black people.''

''Shange's poems aren't war cries,'' Jack Kroll writes in a *Newsweek* review of the Public Theatre production of ''For Colored Girls.'' ''They're outcries filled with a controlled passion against the brutality that blasts the lives of 'colored girls'—a phrase that in her hands vibrates with social irony and poetic beauty. These poems are political in the deepest sense, but there's no dogma, no sentimentality, no grinding of false mythic axes.'' Critic Edith Oliver of the *New Yorker* remarks: ''The evening grows in dramatic power, encompassing, it seems, every feeling and experience a woman has ever had; strong and funny, it is entirely free of the rasping earnestness of most projects of this sort. The verses and monologues that constitute the program have been very well chosen—contrasting in mood yet always subtly building.''

While Wallace was not completely satisfied with ''For Colored Girls,'' and complained of the occasional ''worn-out feminist cliches,'' she was still able to commend Shange. She wrote: ''There is so much about black women that needs retelling; one has to start somewhere, and Shange's exploration of this aspect of our experience, admittedly the most primitive (but we were all there at some time and, if the truth be told, most of us still are) is as good a place as any. All I'm saying is that Shange's 'For Colored Girls' should not be viewed as the definitive statement on black women, but as a very good beginning.'' She continued: ''Very few have written with such clarity and honesty about the black woman's vulnerability and no one has ever brought Shange's brand of tough humor and realism to it.''

Reviews of Shange's next production, ''A Photograph: A Study of Cruelty,'' are less positive, although critics are generally impressed with the poetic quality of her writing. ''Miss Shange is something besides a poet but she is not—at least not at this stage—a dramatist,'' Richard Eder declares in a *New York Times* review. ''More than anything else, she is a troubadour. She declares her fertile vision of the love and pain between black women and black men in outbursts full of old malice and young cheerfulness. They are short outbursts, song-length; her characters are perceived in flashes, in illuminating vignettes.''

Shange's next play, ''Spell #7: A Geechee Quick Magic Trance Manual,'' more like ''For Colored Girls'' in structure, elicits a higher recommendation from Eder. Its nine characters in a New York bar discuss the racism black artists contend with in the entertainment world. At one point, the all-black cast appears in overalls and minstrel-show blackface to address the pressure placed on the black artist to fit a stereotype in order to succeed. ''That's what happens to black people in the arts no matter how famous we become. . . . Black Theater is not moving forward the way people like to think it is. We're not free of our paint yet,'' Shange told Tate. ''On another level, Spell #7 deals with the image of the black woman as a neutered workhorse, who is unwanted, unloved, and unattended by anyone,'' notes Elizabeth Brown in the *Dictionary of Literary Biography.* ''The emphasis is still on the experiences of the black woman but it is broadened and deepened, and it ventures more boldly across the sexual divide,'' Eder writes in the *New York Times.* Don Nelson, writing in the *New York Daily News,* deems the show ''black magic. . . . The word that best describes Shange's works, which are not plays in the traditional sense, is power.''

To critics and producers who have complained that Shange's theater pieces do not present an easily marketable issue or point, Shange responds that a work's emotional impact should be enough. As she told Tate, ''Our society allows people to be absolutely neurotic and totally out of touch with their feelings and everyone else's feelings, and yet be very respectable. This, to me, is a travesty. So I write to get at the part of people's emotional lives that they don't have control over, the part that can and will respond. . . . *For Colored Girls* for me is not an issue play. . . . There are just some people who are interesting. There's something there to make you feel intensely. Black writers have a right to do this,'' she said, although such works are not often rewarded with financial success. She names a number of successful plays that don't have a point except to celebrate being alive, and claims, ''Black and Latin writers have to start demanding that the fact we're alive is point enough!'' Furthermore, works which rely on emotional appeal reach a larger audience, she maintains in the same interview: ''The kind of esteem that's given to bright-ness/smartness obliterates average people or slow learners from participating fully in human life. . . . But you cannot exclude any human being from emotional participation.''

Shange writes to fulfill a number of deeply felt responsibilities. Describing the genesis of *For Colored Girls,* for instance, Shange told Tate that she wrote its poems because she wanted young black women ''to have information that I did not have. I wanted them to know what it was truthfully like to be a grown woman. . . . I don't want them to grow up in a void of misogynist lies.'' It is her commitment to break the silence of mothers who know, but don't tell their daughters, that ''it's a dreadful proposition to lose oneself in the process of tending and caring for others,'' she said. The play ''calls attention to how male-oriented black women . . . [and] women in general are,'' and how their self-esteem erodes when they allow them-selves to be exploited, writes Tate. Says Shange, ''When I die, I will not be guilty of having left a generation of girls behind thinking that anyone can tend to their emotional health other than themselves.''

Speaking of her works in general, she said, ''I think it was Adrienne Rich or Susan Griffin who said that one of our re-sponsibilities as women writers is to discover the causes for our pain and to respect them. I think that much of the suffering that women and black people endure is not respected. I was also trained not to respect it. For instance, we're taught not to respect women who can't get their lives together by them-selves. They have three children and a salary check for $200. The house is a mess; they're sort of hair-brained. We're taught not to respect their suffering. So I write about things that I know have never been given their full due. . . . I want people to at least understand or have the chance to see that *this* is a person whose life is not only valid but whose life is valiant. My responsibility is to be as honest as I can and to use what-ever technical skills I may possess to make these experiences even clearer, or sharper, or more devastating or more beauti-ful.'' Women writers should also demand more respect for writing love poems, for seeing ''the world in a way that allows us to care more about people than about military power. The power we see is the power to feed, the power to nourish and to educate. . . . It's part of our responsibility as writers to make these things important,'' Shange said.

Shange's poetry books, like her theater pieces, are distinc-tively original. *Nappy Edges,* containing fifty poems, is too long, says Harriet Gilbert in the *Washington Post Book World;* however, she claims, ''nothing that Shange writes is ever en-tirely unreadable, springing, as it does, from such an intense honesty, from so fresh an awareness of the beauty of sound and of vision, from such mastery of words, from such com-passion, humor and intelligence.'' Alice H. G. Phillips relates in the *Times Literary Supplement,* ''Comparing herself to a jazzman 'takin a solo', she lets go with verbal runs and trills, mixes in syncopations, spins out evocative hanging phrases, variations on themes and refrains. Rarely does she come to a full stop, relying instead on line breaks, extra space breaking up a line, and/or oblique strokes. . . . She constantly tries to push things to their limit, and consequently risks seeming

overenthusiastic, oversimplistic or merely undisciplined. . . . But at its best, her method can achieve both serious humour and deep seriousness.''

In her poetry, Shange takes many liberties with the conven-tions of written English, using nonstandard spellings and punc-tuation. Some reviewers feel that these innovations present unnecessary obstacles to the interested readers of *Nappy Edges, A Daughter's Geography,* and *From Okra to Greens: Poems.* Explaining her ''lower-case letters, slashes, and spelling'' to Tate, she said that ''poems where all the first letters are cap-italized'' bore her; ''also, I like the idea that letters dance. . . . I need some visual stimulation, so that reading becomes not just a passive act and more than an intellectual activity, but demands rigorous participation.'' Her idiosyncraitc punctua-tion assures her ''that the reader is not in control of the pro-cess.'' She wants her words in print to engage the reader in a kind of struggle, and not be ''whatever you can just ignore.'' The spellings, she said, ''reflect language as I hear it. . . . The structure is connected to the music I hear beneath the words.''

Shange's rejection of standard English serves deeper emotional and political purposes as well. In a *Los Angeles Times Book Review* article on Shange's *See No Evil: Prefaces, Essays and Accounts, 1976-1983,* Karl Keller relates, ''[Shange] feels that as a black female performer/playwright/poet, she has wanted 'to attack deform n maim the language that i was taught to hate myself in. I have to take it apart to the bone.' '' Speaking to Tate, she declared, ''We do not have to refer continually to European art as the standard. That's absolutely absurd and racist, and I won't participate in that utter lie. My work is one of the few ways I can preserve the elements of our culture that need to be remembered and absolutely revered.''

Shange takes liberties with the conventions of fiction writing with her first full-length novel, *Sassafrass, Cypress & Indigo.* ''The novel is unusual in its form—a tapestry of narrative, poetry, magic spells, recipes and letters. Lyrical yet real, it also celebrates female stuff—weaving, cooking, birthing ba-bies,'' relates Lauerman. Its title characters are sisters who find different ways to cope with their love relationships. Sas-safrass attaches herself to Mitch, a musician who uses hard drugs and beats her; she leaves him twice, but goes back to him for another try. To male readers who called Mitch a ''weak'' male character, she replied to Lauerman, ''[He] had some faults, but there's no way in the world you can say [he wasn't] strong. . . . I think you should love people with their faults. That's what love's about.'' Cypress, a dancer in feminist pro-ductions, at first refuses to become romantically involved with any of her male friends. Indigo, the youngest sister, retreats into her imagination, befriending her childhood dolls, seeing only the poetry and magic of the world. The music she plays on her violin becomes a rejuvenating source for her mother and sisters. ''Probably there is a little bit of all three sisters in Shange,'' Lauerman suggests, ''though she says that her novel is not autobiographical but historical, culled from the experiences of blacks and from the 'information of my feel-ings.' ''

Critics agree that Shange's poetry is more masterfully wrought than her fiction, yet they find much in the novel to applaud. Writes Doris Grumbach in the *Washington Post Book World,* ''Shange is primarily a poet, with a blood-red sympathy for and love of her people, their folk as well as their sophisticated ways, their innocent, loving goodness as much as their lack of immunity to powerful evil. . . . But her voice in this novel is entirely her own, an original, spare and primary-colored sound that will remind readers of Jean Toomer's *Cane*.'' In Grumbach's opinion, ''Whatever Shange turns her hand to she does well, even to potions and recipes. A white reader feels the exhilarating shock of discovery at being permitted entry into this world she couldn't have known''' apart from the novel.

''There is poetry in . . . *Sassafrass, Cypress & Indigo:* the poetry of rich lyrical language, of women you want to know because they're so original even their names conjure up visions,'' comments Joyce Howe in the *Village Voice. Betsey Brown: A Novel,* ''lacks those fantastical qualities, yet perhaps because this semiautobiographical second novel is not as easy to love, it is the truer book.'' Betsey is thirteen, growing into young womanhood in St. Louis during the 1950s. ''An awakening sense of racial responsibility is as important to Betsey as her first kiss,'' relates Patchy Wheatley, a *Times Literary Supplement* reviewer. As one of the first students to be bused to a hostile white school, Betsey learns about racism and how to overcome it with a sense of personal pride. Says the reviewer, ''By interweaving Betsey's story with those of the various generations of her family and community, Shange has also produced something of wider significance: a skilful exploration of the Southern black community at a decisive moment in its history.''

''Black life has always been more various than the literature has been at liberty to show,'' comments Sherley Anne Williams in a *Ms.* review. Though she is not impressed with *Betsey Brown* ''as a literary achievement,'' she welcomes this important-because-rare look at the black middle class. In a *Washington Post* review, Tate concurs, and notes the differences between *Betsey Brown* and Shange's previous works: ''Shange's style is distinctively lyrical; her monologues and dialogues provide a panorama of Afro-American diversity. Most of Shange's characteristic elliptical spelling, innovative syntax and punctuation is absent from 'Betsey Brown.' Missing also is the caustic social criticism about racial and sexual victimization. . . . 'Betsey Brown' seems also to mark Shange's movement from explicit to subtle expressions of rage, from repudiating her girlhood past to embracing it, and from flip candor to more serious commentary.'' Shange told Dong that she is as angry and subversive as ever, but doesn't feel as powerless, she said, ''because I know where to put my anger, and I don't feel alone in it anymore.''

MEDIA ADAPTATIONS: A musical-operetta version of Shange's novel *Betsey Brown* was produced by Joseph Papp's Public Theater in 1986.

AVOCATIONAL INTERESTS: Playing the violin.

BIOGRAPHICAL/CRITICAL SOURCES:

BOOKS

Betsko, Kathleen and Rachel Koenig, editors, *Interviews with Contemporary Women Playwrights,* Beech Tree Books, 1987.

Christ, Carol P., *Diving Deep and Surfacing: Women Writers on Spiritual Quest,* Beacon Press, 1980.

Contemporary Literary Criticism, Gale, Volume 8, 1978, Volume 25, 1983, Volume 38, 1986.

Dictionary of Literary Biography, Volume 38: *Afro-American Writers after 1955: Dramatists and Prose Writers,* Gale, 1985.

Shange, Ntozake, *For Colored Girls Who Have Considered Suicide/When the Rainbow Is Enuf,* Shameless Hussy Press, 1975, Macmillan, 1976.

Shange, Ntozake, *See No Evil: Prefaces, Essays and Accounts, 1976-1983,* Momo's Press, 1984.

Squier, Susan Merrill, editor, *Women Writers and the City: Essays in Feminist Literary Criticism,* University of Tennessee Press, 1984.

Tate, Claudia, editor, *Black Women Writers at Work,* Continuum, 1983.

PERIODICALS

American Book Review, September, 1983, March, 1986.

Black American Literature Forum, summer, 1981.

Black Scholar, March, 1979, March, 1981, December, 1982, July, 1985.

Chicago Tribune, October 21, 1982.

Chicago Tribune Book World, July 1, 1979, September 8, 1985.

Christian Science Monitor, September 9, 1976, October 8, 1982, May 2, 1986.

Cue, June 26, 1976.

Daily News, July 16, 1979.

Detroit Free Press, October 30, 1978.

Ebony, August, 1977.

Essence, November, 1976, May, 1985, June, 1985.

Freedomways, Third Quarter, 1976.

Horizon, September, 1977.

Los Angeles Times, October 20, 1982, June 11, 1985, July 28, 1987.

Los Angeles Times Book Review, August 22, 1982, October 20, 1982, January 8, 1984, July 29, 1984, June 11, 1985, July 19, 1987.

Mademoiselle, September, 1976.

Ms., September, 1976, December, 1977, June, 1985, June, 1987.

New Leader, July 5, 1976.

Newsday, August 22, 1976.

New Statesman, October 4, 1985.

Newsweek, June 14, 1976, July 30, 1979.

New York Amsterdam News, October 9, 1976.

New Yorker, June 14, 1976, August 2, 1976, January 2, 1978.

New York Post, June 12, 1976, September 16, 1976, July 16, 1979.

New York Theatre Critics' Reviews, Volume XXXVII, number 16, September 13, 1976.

New York Times, June 16, 1976, December 22, 1977, June 4, 1979, June 8, 1979, July 16, 1979, July 22, 1979, May 14, 1980, June 15, 1980.

New York Times Book Review, June 25, 1979, July 16, 1979, October 21, 1979, September 12, 1982, May 12, 1985, April 6, 1986.

New York Times Magazine, May 1, 1983.

Plays & Players, Volume 27, number 3, December, 1979.

Publishers Weekly, May 3, 1985.

Saturday Review, February 18, 1978, May/June, 1985.

Time, June 14, 1976, July 19, 1976, November 1, 1976.

Times (London), April 21, 1983.

Times Literary Supplement, December 6, 1985, April 15-21, 1988.

Washington Post, June 12, 1976, June 29, 1976, February 23, 1982, June 17, 1985.

Washington Post Book World, October 15, 1978, July 19, 1981, August 22, 1982, August 5, 1984.

Variety, July 25, 1979.

Village Voice, August 16, 1976, July 23, 1979, June 18, 1985.*

SHELDON, Ann
[Collective pseudonym]

WRITINGS:

"LINDA CRAIG" SERIES

Linda Craig and the Palomino Mystery, Doubleday, 1962, reprinted under title *Linda Craig: The Palomino Mystery,* Wanderer, 1981.

. . . and the Clue on the Desert Trail, Doubleday, 1962, reprinted under title *Linda Craig: The Clue on the Desert Trail,* Wanderer, 1981.

. . . and the Secret of Rancho del Sol, Doubleday, 1963, reprinted under title *Linda Craig: The Secret of Rancho del Sol,* Wanderer, 1981.

. . . and the Mystery of Horseshoe Canyon, Doubleday, 1963, reprinted under title *Linda Craig: The Mystery of Horseshoe Canyon,* Wanderer, 1981.

. . . and the Ghost Town Treasure, Doubleday, 1964, reprinted under title *Linda Craig: The Ghost Town Treasure,* Wanderer, 1982.

. . . and the Mystery in Mexico, Doubleday, 1964, reprinted under title *Linda Craig: The Mystery in Mexico,* Wanderer, 1981.

Linda Craig: The Haunted Valley, Wanderer, 1982.
Linda Craig: The Secret of the Old Sleigh, Wanderer, 1983.
Linda Craig: The Emperor's Pony, Wanderer, 1983.
Linda Craig: The Phantom of Dark Oaks, Wanderer, 1984.

"LINDA CRAIG ADVENTURES" SERIES

The Golden Secret, Minstrel, 1988.
A Star for Linda, Minstrel, 1988.
The Silver Stallion, Minstrel, 1988.
The Crystal Trail, Minstrel, 1988.
The Glimmering Ghost, Minstrel, 1989.
The Ride to Gold Canyon, Minstrel, 1989.
A Horse for Jackie, Minstrel, 1989.

SIDELIGHTS: This series featured Linda Craig and her prize-winning palomino Chica d'Oro. Linda and her brother Bob were orphans, having lost their parents—a military officer and his wife—in an accident in Hawaii. They lived on their grandparents' ranch, Rancho del Sol, in the San Quinto valley of southern California. With the help of their friends they solved mysteries, an association Arthur Prager described in *Rascals at Large; or, The Clue in the Old Nostalgia* as "Nancy Drew on horseback."

Carol Billman, in her *The Secret of the Stratemeyer Syndicate,* echoes Prager's assessment. She points out that the many Gothic elements which characterize Nancy Drew's adventures are present in the Linda Craig stories: *The Phantom of Dark Oaks,* for instance, is "a story full of spiral staircases, a stately plantation, supernatural noises, and the threat of ghosts—Nancy Drew in western drag." In 1988 a new series of "Linda Craig" adventures appeared. Among other changes, Linda's horse was renamed Amber. Harriet Adams initiated the Linda Craig series. For more information see the entries in this volume for Harriet S. Adams, Edward L. Stratemeyer, and Andrew E. Svenson.

MEDIA ADAPTATIONS: "The Tom Swift and Linda Craig Mystery Hour" was produced by Paramount and aired by ABC-TV on July 3, 1983. It starred Willie Aames as Tom and Lori Loughlin as Linda.

BIOGRAPHICAL/CRITICAL SOURCES:

BOOKS

Billman, Carol, *The Secret of the Stratemeyer Syndicate: Nancy Drew, the Hardy Boys, and the Million Dollar Fiction Factory,* Ungar, 1986.

Johnson, Deidre, editor and compiler, *Stratemeyer Pseudonyms and Series Books: An Annotated Checklist of Stratemeyer and Stratemeyer Syndicate Publications,* Greenwood Press, 1982.

Prager, Arthur, *Rascals at Large; or, The Clue in the Old Nostalgia,* Doubleday, 1971.

*　　*　　*　　*

SHIRE, Helena (Mary) Mennie　1912-

PERSONAL: Born June 21, 1912, in Aberdeen, Scotland; daughter of John Henderson and Jane (Rae) Mennie; married Edward S. Shire (a reader in physics at Cambridge University and fellow of King's College), March 31, 1936; children: Alisoun (Mrs. David Gardner-Medwin), John, Christine (Mrs. Brian Bromwich). *Education:* University of Aberdeen, M.A. (first class honors), 1933; Newnham College, Cambridge, B.A., 1935; London School of Economics and Political Science, additional study, 1941-43. *Religion:* Church of Scotland.

ADDRESSES: Home—2 Bulstrode Gardens, Cambridge CB3 0EN, England. *Office*—Robinson College, Cambridge University, Cambridge CB2 1ST, England.

CAREER: University of London, London, England, lecturer in medieval literature at Queen Mary College, 1941-44, lecturer in English for foreigners at London School of Economics and Political Science, 1941-44; Cambridge University, Cambridge, England, member of faculty of English, 1951—, associate college lecturer in English at King's College, 1954-75, fellow of Robinson College, 1975—.

MEMBER: Scottish Text Society (member of council), Saltire Society (president of Cambridge branch).

AWARDS, HONORS: Carnegie Trust for Universities of Scotland senior research fellow in arts, 1961-63; grant for travel in America, 1971; LL.D., University of Aberdeen, 1988.

WRITINGS:

(Editor with Kenneth Elliott) *Musica Britannica,* Volume XV, *Music of Scotland, 1500-1700,* Royal Music Association, 1957.

(Editor) *Alexander Montgomerie: A Selection from His Songs and Poems,* Oliver & Boyd, for Saltire Society, 1960, reprinted, State Mutual Book, 1985.

Song, Dance, and Poetry of the Court of Scotland under King James VI, Cambridge University Press, 1969.

(Editor with Marion Stewart) *King Orphius, Sir Colling, The Brother's Lament,* [and] *Litel Musgray,* Ninth of May, 1973.

A Preface to Spenser, Longman, 1978.

(Editor) Olive Fraser, *The Pure Account: Poems,* Aberdeen University Press, 1981.

(Editor) *The Poems of Olive Fraser,* Canongate Publishing, 1989.

Also editor of small volumes issued in limited editions under the imprint Ninth of May: *Poems from Panmure House* (three poems transcribed from *The Commonplace-book,* compiled from about 1630 onwards), 1960; *Sir Robert Ayton: A Choice of*

Poems and Songs, 1961; *The Thrissil, the Rois, and the Flour-de-lys* (unpublished poems of sixteenth-century Scotland), 1962; and *The Sheath and the Knife or Leesome Brand,* 1974.

Translator of songs and plays from Polish. Contributor to *Literature and Western Civilization* and *Etudes Econaisis.* Also contributor to *Saltire Review, Les Fetes de la Renaissance, Music and Letters,* and other journals.

WORK IN PROGRESS: A sequel to *Song, Dance and Poetry of the Court of Scotland under King James VI,* on music and poetry of pre-Reformation Scotland and contemporary Europe; translating Polish folk-songs and twentieth-century Polish drama into Scots or English.

SIDELIGHTS: Helena Mennie Shire was instigator in 1950 of the research project Musica Scotica, to discover and collate all manuscripts and early printed records of art-song of Scotland. She has made research trips to France, Portugal, and Poland to observe folk and religious festivals, and has done library research in the United States.

*   *   *

SHIVERS, Jay S(anford) 1930-

PERSONAL: Born July 7, 1930, in New York, N.Y.; son of Ted M. and Mabel (Sinkoff) Shivers; married Rhoda Goldstein (a teacher), February 14, 1951; children: Jed Mark. *Education:* Indiana University, B.S., 1952; New York University, M.A., 1953, additional study, 1953-55; University of Wisconsin, Ph.D., 1958. *Politics:* Independent.

ADDRESSES: Home—South Eagleville Rd., Storrs, Conn. 06268. *Office*—U-34, University of Connecticut, Storrs, Conn. 06268.

CAREER: Hillside Psychiatric Hospital, Glen Oaks, N.Y., recreational leader, 1952-53; Goldwater Memorial Hospital, Welfare Island, N.Y., director of recreational rehabilitation, 1953; University of Wisconsin—Madison, instructor in education, 1955-57; U.S. Veterans Administration Hospital, Madison, recreational supervisor, 1957-58; Mississippi Southern College (now University of Southern Mississippi), Hattiesburg, professor of recreational service education and chairman of department, 1958-62; University of Connecticut, Storrs, assistant professor, 1962-66, associate professor, 1967-69, professor of recreational service education, 1970—. Visiting summer professor at Eastern Washington State College (now Eastern Washington University), 1963, and California State College at Hayward (now California State University, Hayward), 1967. Chairman of Mansfield (Conn.) Park Planning Committee, 1962—. Mansfield Recreational Services, 1965—, and Connecticut Older Worker Employee Network, 1982—. Member of scientific committee, Van Cle Foundation, 1976. *Military service:* U.S. Army, Counter-Intelligence Corps, special agent, 1953-55.

MEMBER: International Recreation Association, World Leisure and Recreation Association, International Playground Association, International Rehabilitation Association, National Recreation and Park Association, Society of Professional Recreation Educators, National Therapeutic Recreational Society, American Association for Health, Physical Education and Recreation, American Academy of Leisure Science (founding fellow, 1980), American Association of University Professors, United World Federalists, Connecticut Recreation and Park Association, Sierra Club, Phi Delta Kappa.

AWARDS, HONORS: Certificate of Achievement from Hospital Section, American Recreation Society, 1965; honor award from Connecticut Recreation Society, 1968; National Literary Award of National Recreation and Park Association, 1979; distinguished service award of National Therapeutic Recreational Society, 1983.

WRITINGS:

Horizons Unlimited: The Organization of Recreational Services in the State of Mississippi, Mississippi Recreation Association, 1959.
(With George Hjelte) *Public Administration of Park and Recreational Services,* Macmillan, 1962.
Leadership in Recreational Service, Macmillan, 1963.
Principles and Practices of Recreational Service, Macmillan, 1967.
Camping: Management, Counselling Program, Appleton, 1971.
Planning Recreational Places, A. S. Barnes, 1971.
(With Hjelte) *Public Administration of Recreational Services,* Lea & Febiger, 1972, 2nd edition, 1978.
(With C. R. Calder) *Recreational Crafts for School and Community,* McGraw, 1974.
(With Hollis F. Fait) *Therapeutic Recreational Service,* Lea & Febiger, 1975.
Essentials of Recreational Service, Lea & Febiger, 1978.
Perceptions of Recreation and Leisure, Holbrook, 1978.
(With H. Ibrahim) *Leisure: Emergence and Expansion,* Hwong Publishing, 1979.
Recreational Leadership: Group Dynamics and Interpersonal Relations, Princeton Publishing, 1980, 2nd edition, 1985.
(With Fait) *Recreational Service for the Aging,* Lea & Febiger, 1980.
(With Joseph W. Halper) *The Crisis in Urban Recreational Service,* Fairleigh Dickenson University Press, 1981.
Special Recreational Service: Therapeutic and Adapted, Lea & Febiger, 1984.
(With Charles Bucher) *Recreation for Today's Society,* 2nd edition (Shivers was not associated with previous edition), Prentice-Hall, 1984.
Recreational Safety: The Standard of Care, Associated University Presses, 1985.
Introduction to Recreational Service Administration, Lea & Febiger, 1987.
Camping: Organization and Operation, Prentice-Hall, 1988.
Advanced Management for Recreational Service, Prentice-Hall, 1988.

Also author of master plans for recreational service in various towns. Contributor of more than fifty articles to recreation and rehabilitation journals. *Recreation in Treatment Centers,* member of editorial board, 1962-69, editor, 1964-66.

WORK IN PROGRESS: Recreational Crafts for Everyone, for W. C. Brown.

*   *   *

SNOW, Donald M(erritt) 1943-

PERSONAL: Born June 22, 1943, in Fort Wayne, Ind.; son of Clarence A. and Dorothea (a writer; maiden name, Johnston) Snow; married Donna Bock (an administrator), May 30, 1969; children: Eric DeVries. *Education:* University of Colorado, B.A., 1965, M.A., 1967; Indiana University, Ph.D., 1969.

ADDRESSES: Home—2935 Juniper Lane, Tuscaloosa, Ala. 35405. *Office*—Department of Political Science, University of Alabama, Box I, Tuscaloosa, Ala. 35487.

CAREER: University of Alabama, Tuscaloosa, assistant professor, 1969-77, associate professor, 1977-82, professor of political science, 1982—, director of international studies, 1972—. Professor at Air Command and Staff College, 1980; guest lecturer at Air War College, Army War College, Naval War College, and U.S. Military Academy. Secretary of the Navy Senior Research Fellow, Naval War College, 1985-86.

MEMBER: International Studies Association (chairman of section on military studies, 1983-85), Academy of Political Science, Air Force Association, Inter-University Seminar on the Armed Forces and Society.

WRITINGS:

Introduction to Game Theory, Consortium for International Studies Education, 1978.
Nuclear Strategy in a Dynamic World: American Policy in the Nineteen Eighties, University of Alabama Press, 1981.
(Editor) *Introduction to World Politics: A Conceptual and Developmental Perspective,* University Press of America, 1981.
(With Dennis M. Drew) *Introduction to Strategy,* Air Command and Staff College, 1981.
The Nuclear Future: Toward a Strategy of Uncertainty, University of Alabama Press, 1983.
(With Gary L. Guertner) *The Last Frontier: An Analysis of the Strategic Defense Initiative,* Lexington Books, 1986.
National Security: Enduring Problems of U.S. Defense Policy, St. Martin's, 1986.
The Necessary Peace: Nuclear Weapons and Superpower Relations, Lexington Books, 1987.
(With Dennis M. Drew) *Making Strategy,* Air University Press, 1987.
(Editor) *Fencers: U.S.-Soviet Relations Face the 1990s,* Lexington Books, 1988.
(With Dennis M. Drew) *The Eagle's Talons: War, Politics, and the American Experience,* Air University Press, 1988.

Contributor to political science and military journals.

WORK IN PROGRESS: A manuscript on the evolving impact of the communications revolution on the conduct of international relations and national security affairs.

SIDELIGHTS: Donald M. Snow commented to *CA:* "In a world of thermo-nuclear weaponry, an understanding of the dynamics of military force is a matter of national and international survival in a way more fundamental than at any previous time in history. Trying to make some contribution to that knowledge is my primary motivation. This endeavor, it seems to me, is of particular importance at a time when, in the wake of the Vietnam War, Americans remain uncertain about the continuing relevance and uses of military force. At the same time, the awesome destructive power of modern weapons makes a clear insight absolutely crucial."

AVOCATIONAL INTERESTS: Racquetball, squash, coaching, refereeing youth soccer, running.

* * *

SNOW, Dorothea J(ohnston)   1909-

PERSONAL: Born April 17, 1909, in McMinnville, Tenn.; daughter of Fred Russell and Theresa Ella (Mosher) Johnston; married Clarence A. Snow, 1929; children: Donald M. *Education:* Attended art school in Fort Wayne, Ind., two years. *Religion:* Methodist.

ADDRESSES: Home—3 Idlewild, Tuscaloosa, Ala. 35405.

CAREER: Art teacher in public schools in Tampa, Fla., 1927-28, and Des Moines, Iowa, 1928-29; Art Publishing Co., Chicago, Ill., art director, 1933-36; writer of children's books and illustrator for children's magazines.

MEMBER: Women's National Book Association, Society of Midland Authors.

AWARDS, HONORS: Friends of American Writers Top Juvenile Award, 1961, for *Sequoyah: Young Cherokee Guide;* Indiana University Hoosier Author Award, 1968, for *Tomahawk Claim.*

WRITINGS:

JUVENILES

No-Good, the Dancing Donkey, illustrations by Esther Friend, Rand McNally, 1944.
(And illustrator) *Puddlejumper,* Rand McNally, 1948.
Eli Whitney: Boy Mechanic, illustrations by Charles V. John, Bobbs-Merrill, 1948, 2nd edition, illustrations by Al Fiorentino, 1962.
(And illustrator) *Goofy,* John Martin, 1948.
(And illustrator) *Peter, the Lonesome Hermit,* Whitman Publishing, 1948.
John Paul Jones: Salt-Water Boy, illustrations by Paul Laune, Bobbs-Merrill, 1950, 2nd edition, illustrations by William Moyers, 1962.
Raphael Semmes: Tidewater Boy, illustrations by P. Laune, Bobbs-Merrill, 1952, 2nd edition, illustrations by James Ponter, 1962.
Come, Chucky, Come, illustrations by Joshua Tolford, Houghton, 1952.
The Whistling Mountain Mystery, illustrations by Robert Todd, Bobbs-Merrill, 1954.
Jeb and the Flying Jenny, illustrations by J. Tolford, Houghton, 1954.
Samuel Morse: Inquisitive Boy, illustrations by Dorothy Bayley Morse, Bobbs-Merrill, 1955, 2nd edition, illustrations by Walt Reed, 1960.
Roy Rogers' Favorite Western Stories, Whitman Publishing, 1956.
Lassie and the Mystery at Blackberry Bog, Whitman Publishing, 1956.
Circus Boy under the Big Top, illustrations by Tony Sgroi, Whitman Publishing, 1957.
Circus Boy and Captain Jack, Whitman Publishing, 1957.
Circus Boy and War on Wheels, Whitman Publishing, 1958.
Lassie and the Secret of the Summer, Whitman Publishing, 1958.
Indian Chiefs (short stories), illustrations by E. Joseph Dreany, Whitman Publishing, 1959.
The Secret of the Stone Frog, illustrations by Raymond Burns, Bobbs-Merrill, 1959.
Sequoyah: Young Cherokee Guide, illustrations by Frank Giacoia, Bobbs-Merrill, 1960.
Bugs Bunny's Birthday Surprise, Whitman Publishing, 1960.
Donald Duck on Tom Sawyer's Island, Whitman Publishing, 1960.
A Doll for Lily Belle, illustrations by Nedda Walker, Houghton, 1960.

Henry Hudson: Explorer of the North, illustrations by John C. Wonsetler, Houghton, 1962.
The Mystery of Ghost Burro Canyon, illustrations by David Stone, Bobbs-Merrill, 1967.
A Sight of Everything, illustrations by Vee Guthrie, Houghton, 1963.
Benjamin West: Gifted Young Painter, illustrations by George Buctel, Bobbs-Merrill, 1967.
Tomahawk Claim, Bobbs-Merrill, 1968.
Billy's Secret, Rand McNally, 1972.

TEEN NOVELS

The Charmed Circle, Whitman Publishing, 1962.
That Certain Girl, Whitman Publishing, 1964.
Listen to Your Heart, Bouregy, 1977.
Love's Dream Remembered, Bouregy, 1979.
Silver Bird, Bouregy, 1980.
Love's Wondrous Ways, Bouregy, 1981.
By Love Bewitched, Bouregy, 1981.
Gardens of Love, Bouregy, 1982.
Golden Summer, Bouregy, 1983.
Love's Bright Torch, Bouregy, 1984.

OTHER

Also contributor to *Children's Activities, Child Life, Wee Wisdom,* and other children's magazines.

WORK IN PROGRESS: Once in a Blue Moon, a young adult novel, for Bouregy.

SIDELIGHTS: While Dorothea J. Snow once told *CA* that she adhered to an inflexible writing schedule, she now adds that she alternates between writing and painting. She is no advocate of the tryout method of perfecting manuscripts and finds her family's reactions to her unpublished work confusing. Snow was brought up in the South, and uses southern mountain backgrounds for much of her writing.

*   *   *

SOLOMON, Neil   1932-

PERSONAL: Born February 27, 1932, in Pittsburgh, Pa.; son of Max Maurice and Clara (Eisenstein) Solomon; married Frema Rose Sindell, June 26, 1955; children: Theodore, Scott, Clifford. *Education:* Western Reserve University (now Case Western Reserve University), A.B., 1954, M.D. and M.S. (both with honors), both 1961; University of Maryland, Ph.D. (with honors), 1965. *Religion:* Jewish.

ADDRESSES: Office—1726 Reisterstown Rd., Suite 213, Baltimore, Md., 21208.

CAREER: U.S. Public Health Service, Cleveland, Ohio, trainee in physiology at School of Medicine, Case Western Reserve University, 1955-61; Johns Hopkins Hospital, Baltimore, Md., intern, 1961-62, assistant resident, 1962-63, instructor in medicine, 1964-69, assistant professor of psychiatry and behavioral sciences, 1969-78; University of Miami, School of Medicine, Miami, Fla., associate professor, 1978-79, professor of pharmacology, 1979-81.

Medical practice specializing in endocrinology, metabolism, and gerontology, Baltimore, 1965—. Diplomate of National Board of Medical Examiners; licensed to practice medicine in Maryland and Ohio. Secretary of health and mental hygiene for the State of Maryland, 1969-79; adviser to U.S. Secretary of Health, Education and Welfare. Assistant professor of med-

icine at University of Maryland, 1965-69, associate professor of physiology, 1965-69. Visiting physician at Baltimore City Hospital and assistant chief of medicine, 1963-68; senior assistant surgeon for U.S. Public Health Service, 1963-64, and National Institutes of Health, 1964-65; visiting physician at University of Maryland Hospital, 1965-68. Member of national advisory committee for the State of Maryland to the Selective Service System, 1970, Maryland governor's Commission on Environmental Pollution, 1970, and Environmental Council for Maryland, 1972; commissioner for Food and Drug Administration, 1975; member of board of trustees of Non-Profit Housing for Elderly People, 1965, and Homewood School, 1968; member of medical advisory board of American Joint Distribution Committee, 1972; member of board of advisers of Maryland Acupuncture Foundation, 1973, and St. Jude Volunteers, 1973.

MEMBER: American Federation for Clinical Research, American Heart Association, American Medical Association, American Physiological Society, American Public Health Association, American Association for the Advancement of Science, American College of Allergists, Federation of American Societies for Experimental Biology, American Association of University Professors, Association of Mental Health Administrators (honorary member), Authors Guild, Authors League of America, American Federation of Television and Radio Artists, Southern Medical Association, New York Academy of Science, Maryland Public Health Association, Maryland Society for Medical Research, Medical and Chirurgical Faculty of Maryland, Baltimore City Medical Society, Johns Hopkins Medical Society, Johns Hopkins Medical and Surgical Association, University of Maryland Alumni Association, Case Western Reserve University Alumni Association, Ohio Society of Washington, D.C., Phi Delta Epsilon, Alpha Omega Alpha.

AWARDS, HONORS: Lederle Award from American Geriatric Society, 1962; Schwentker Award from Johns Hopkins Hospital, 1963; American Heart Association fellowship, 1965-67; conservation communications award from National Wildlife Federation, 1971; Myrtle Wreath Award from Hadassah, 1973; Leader in Life Saving award from Safety First Club of Maryland, 1973; public health award from Maryland Optometric Association, 1973; award of honor for environmental improvements from American Institute of Architects, Potomac Valley chapter, 1973; first honor roll award from Izaak Walton League of America, 1974; presidential award from Maryland Public Health Association, 1974.

WRITINGS:

(With Sally Sheppard) *The Truth about Weight Control: How to Lose Excess Pounds Permanently,* Stein & Day, 1972.
(With Mary Knudson) *Dr. Solomon's Easy, No-Risk Diet,* Coward, 1974.
(With Evalee Harrison) *Dr. Solomon's Proven Master Plan for Total Body Fitness and Maintenance,* Putnam, 1976.
Dr. Solomon's High Health Diet and Exercise Plan: How to Make Cholesterol Work for You, Putnam, 1980.
Stop Smoking, Lose Weight, Putnam, 1981.

CONTRIBUTOR

The Biology of Aging, C. C Thomas, 1970.
Disorders of Metabolism: Obesity, Saunders, 1971.

OTHER

Syndicated columnist for *Los Angeles Times,* 1974—. Contributor of about fifty articles to professional journals.

SOYINKA, Wole 1934-

PERSONAL: First name is pronounced *woh*-leh; surname is pronounced shaw-*yin*-ka; given name, Akinwande Oluwole; born July 13, 1934, in Isara, Nigeria; son of Ayo (a headmaster) and Eniola Soyinka. *Education:* Attended University of Ibadan; University of Leeds, B.A. (with honors), 1959. *Religion:* "Human liberty."

ADDRESSES: Office—Department of Dramatic Arts, University of Ife, Ile-Ife, Oyo, Nigeria. *Agent*—Greenbaum, Wolff & Ernst, 437 Madison Ave., New York, N.Y. 10022.

CAREER: Playwright, poet, and novelist. University of Ibadan, Nigeria, research fellow in drama, 1960-61, chairman of department of theatre arts, 1967-71; University of Ife, professor of drama, 1972; Cambridge University, Cambridge, England, fellow of Churchill College, 1973-74; University of Ife, chairman of department of dramatic arts, 1975—. Director of own theatre groups, Orisun Players and 1960 Masks, in Lagos and Ibadan, Nigeria. Visiting professor at University of Sheffield, 1974, University of Ghana, 1975, and Cornell University, 1986.

MEMBER: International Theatre Institute (president), Union of Writers of the African Peoples (secretary-general).

AWARDS, HONORS: Rockefeller Foundation grant, 1960; John Whiting Drama Prize, 1966; Dakar Negro Arts Festival award, 1966; *New Statesman* Jock Campbell Award, 1968, for *The Interpreters;* Nobel Prize in Literature, 1986; named Commander of the Federal Republic of Nigeria by General Ibrahim Babangida, 1986; D.Litt., Yale University and University of Leeds; Prisoner of Conscience Prize, Amnesty International.

WRITINGS:

The Man Died: Prison Notes of Wole Soyinka, Harper, 1972, 2nd edition, Rex Collings, 1973.
Myth, Literature and the African World (essays), Cambridge University Press, 1976.
Ake: The Years of Childhood (autobiography), Random House, 1981.
Isara, Random House, 1988.

NOVELS

The Interpreters, Deutsch, 1965.
(Translator) D. O. Fagunwa, *The Forest of a Thousand Daemons: A Hunter's Saga,* Nelson, 1967, Humanities, 1969.
Season of Anomy, Rex Collings, 1973.

POETRY

Idanre and Other Poems, Methuen, 1967, Hill & Wang, 1969.
Poems from Prison, Rex Collings, 1969, expanded edition published as *A Shuttle in the Crypt,* Hill & Wang, 1972.
(Editor and author of introduction) *Poems of Black Africa,* Hill & Wang, 1975.
Ogun Abibiman, Rex Collings, 1976.

CONTRIBUTOR

D. W. Jefferson, editor, *The Morality of Art,* Routledge & Kegan Paul, 1969.
O. R. Dathorne and Wilfried Feuser, editors, *African Prose,* Penguin, 1969.

PLAYS

"The Invention," first produced in London at Royal Court Theatre, 1955.
A Dance of the Forests (also see below; first produced in London, 1960), Oxford University Press, 1962.
The Lion and the Jewel (also see below; first produced at Royal Court Theatre, 1966), Oxford University Press, 1962.
Three Plays (includes "The Trials of Brother Jero" [also see below], one-act, produced Off-Broadway at Greenwich Mews Playhouse, November 9, 1967; "The Strong Breed" [also see below], one-act, produced at Greenwich Mews Playhouse, November 9, 1967; and "The Swamp Dwellers" [also see below]), Mbari Publications, 1962, Northwestern University Press, 1963.
Five Plays (includes "The Lion and the Jewel," "The Swamp Dwellers," "The Trials of Brother Jero," "The Strong Breed" and "A Dance of the Forests"), Oxford University Press, 1964.
The Road (produced in Stratford, England, at Theatre Royal, 1965), Oxford University Press, 1965.
Kongi's Harvest (also see below; produced Off-Broadway at St. Mark's Playhouse, April 14, 1968), Oxford University Press, 1966.
Three Short Plays, Oxford University Press, 1969.
The Trials of Brother Jero, Oxford University Press, 1969, published with "The Strong Breed" as *The Trials of Brother Jero and The Strong Breed: Two Plays,* Dramatists Play Service, 1969.
"Kongi's Harvest" (screenplay), produced by Calpenny-Nigerian Films, 1970.
Madmen and Specialists (two-act; produced in Waterford, Conn. at Eugene O'Neill Memorial Theatre, August 1, 1970), Methuen, 1971, Hill & Wang, 1972.
(Contributor) *Palaver: Three Dramatic Discussion Starters* (includes "The Lion and the Jewel"), Friendship Press, 1971.
Before the Blackout (revue sketches; also see below), Orisun Acting Editions, 1971.
(Editor) *Plays from the Third World: An Anthology,* Doubleday, 1971.
The Jero Plays (includes "The Trials of Brother Jero" and "Jero's Metamorphosis"), Methuen, 1973.
(Contributor) *African Theatre: Eight Prize Winning Plays for Radio,* Heinemann, 1973.
Camwood on the Leaves, Methuen, 1973, published with "Before the Blackout" as *Camwood on the Leaves and Before the Blackout,* Third Press, 1974.
(Adapter) *The Bacchae of Euripides: A Communion Rite* (first produced in London at Old Vic Theatre, August 2, 1973), Methuen, 1973, Norton, 1974.
Collected Plays, Oxford University Press, Volume 1, 1973, Volume 2, 1974.
Death and the King's Horseman (produced at University of Ife, 1976; produced in Chicago at Goodman Theatre, 1979; produced in New York at Vivian Beaumont Theatre, March, 1987), Norton, 1975.
Opera Wonyosi (light opera), Indiana University Press, 1981.
A Play of Giants, Methuen, 1984.
Six Plays, Methuen, 1984.
Requiem for a Futurologist, Rex Collings, 1985.

Also author of television script, "Culture in Transition."

OTHER

Co-editor, *Black Orpheus,* 1961-64; editor, *Transition* (now *Ch'Indaba*), 1974-76.

SIDELIGHTS: Many critics consider Wole Soyinka as Africa's finest writer. The Nigerian playwright's unique style blends traditional Yoruban folk-drama with European dramatic form to provide both spectacle and penetrating satire. Soyinka told *New York Times Magazine* writer Jason Berry that in the African cultural tradition, the artist "has always functioned as the record of the mores and experience of his society." His plays, novels and poetry all reflect that philosophy, serving as a record of twentieth-century Africa's political turmoil and its struggle to reconcile tradition with modernization. Eldred Jones states in his book *Wole Soyinka* that the author's work touches on universal themes as well as addressing specifically African concerns: "The essential ideas which emerge from a reading of Soyinka's work are not specially African ideas, although his characters and their mannerisms are African. His concern is with man on earth. Man is dressed for the nonce in African dress and lives in the sun and tropical forest, but he represents the whole race."

As a young child, Soyinka was comfortable with the conflicting cultures in his world, but as he grew older he became increasingly aware of the pull between African tradition and Western modernization. Ake, his village, was mainly populated wth people from the Yoruba tribe, and was presided over by the *ogboni*, or trial elders. Soyinka's grandfather introduced him to the pantheon of Yoruba gods and to other tribal folklore. His parents were key representatives of colonial influences, however: his mother was a devout Christian convert and his father acted as headmaster for the village school established by the British. When Soyinka's father began urging Wole to leave Ake to attend the government school in Ibadan, the boy was spirited away by his grandfather, who administered a scarification rite of manhood. Soyinka was also consecrated to the god Ogun, ruler of metal, roads, and both the creative and destructive essence. Ogun is a recurring figure in Soyinka's work and has been named by the author as his muse.

Ake: The Years of Childhood is Soyinka's account of his first ten years, and stands as "a classic of childhood memoirs wherever and whenever produced," states *New York Times Book Review* contributor James Olney. Numerous critics have singled out Soyinka's ability to recapture the changing perspective of a child as the book's outstanding feature; it begins in a light tone but grows increasingly serious as the boy matures and becomes aware of the problems faced by the adults around him. The book concludes with an account of a tax revolt organized by Soyinka's mother, and the beginnings of Nigerian independence. "Most of 'Ake' charms; that was Mr. Soyinka's intention," writes John Leonard of the *New York Times*. "The last 50 pages, however, inspire and confound; they are transcendent." Olney agrees that "the lyricism, grace, humor and charm of 'Ake' . . . are in the service of a profoundly serious viewpoint that attempts to show us how things should be in the community of men and how they should not be. Mr. Soyinka, however, does this dramatically, not discursively. Through recollection, restoration and re-creation, he conveys a personal vision that was formed by the childhood world that he now returns to evoke and exalt in his autobiography. This is the ideal circle of autobiography at its best. It is what makes 'Ake,' in addition to its other great virtues, the best introduction available to the work of one of the liveliest, most exciting writers in the world today."

Soyinka published some poems and short stories in *Black Orpheus,* a highly-regarded Nigerian literary magazine, before leaving Africa to attend the University of Leeds in England. There his first play was produced. "The Invention" is a comic satire based on a sudden loss of pigment by South Africa's black population. Unable to distinguish blacks from whites and thus enforce its apartheid policies, the government is thrown into chaos. "The play is Soyinka's sole direct treatment of the political situation in Africa," notes Thomas Hayes in the *Dictionary of Literary Biography Yearbook: 1986*. Soyinka returned to Nigeria in 1960, shortly after independence from colonial rule had been declared. He began to research Yoruba folklore and drama in depth and incorporated elements of both into his play *A Dance of the Forests*.

A Dance of the Forests was commissioned as part of Nigeria's independence celebrations. In his play, Soyinka warned the newly independent Nigerians that the end of colonial rule did not mean an end to their country's problems. It shows a bickering group of mortals who summon up the *egungun* (spirits of the dead, revered by the Yoruba people) for a festival. They have presumed the *egungun* to be noble and wise, but they discover that their ancestors are as petty and spiteful as any living people. "The whole concept ridicules the African viewpoint that glorifies the past at the expense of the present," suggests John F. Povey in *Tri-Quarterly*. "The sentimentalized glamor of the past is exposed so that the same absurdities may not be reenacted in the future. This constitutes a bold assertion to an audience awaiting an easy appeal to racial heroics." Povey also praises Soyinka's skill in using dancing, drumming and singing to reinforce his theme: "The dramatic power of the surging forest dance [in the play] carries its own visual conviction. It is this that shows Soyinka to be a man of the theatre, not simply a writer."

After warning against living in nostalgia for Africa's past in *A Dance of the Forests,* Soyinka lampooned the indiscriminate embrace of Western modernization in *The Lion and the Jewel*. A *Times Literary Supplement* reviewer calls this play a "richly ribald comedy," which combines poetry and prose "with a marvellous lightness in the treatment of both." The plot revolves around Sidi, the village beauty, and the rivalry between her two suitors. Baroka is the village chief, an old man with many wives; Lakunle is the enthusiastically Westernized schoolteacher who dreams of molding Sidi into a "civilized" woman. In *Introduction to Nigerian Literature,* Eldred Jones comments that *The Lion and the Jewel* is "a play which is so easily (and erroneously) interpreted as a clash between progress and reaction, with the play coming down surprisingly in favour of reaction. The real clash is not between old and new, or between real progress and reaction. It is a clash between the genuine and the false; between the well-done and the half-baked. Lakunle the school teacher would have been a poor symbol of any desirable kind of progress. . . . He is a man of totally confused values. [Baroka's worth lies in] the traditional values of which he is so confident and in which he so completely outmaneouvres Lakunle who really has no values at all." Bruce King, editor of *Introduction to Nigerian Literature,* names *The Lion and the Jewel* "the best literary work to come out of Africa."

Soyinka was well established as Nigeria's premier playwright when in 1965 he published his first novel, *The Interpreters*. The novel allowed him to expand on themes already expressed in his stage dramas, and to present a sweeping view of Nigerian life in the years immediately following independence. Essentially plotless, *The Interpreters* is loosely structured around the informal discussions between five young Nigerian intellectuals. Each has been educated in a foreign country and returned hoping to shape Nigeria's destiny. They are hampered by their own confused values, however, as well as the corruption they encounter everywhere. Some reviewers liken Soyinka's writing style in *The Interpreters* to that of James Joyce and William Faulkner. Others take exception to the formless quality of the novel, but Eustace Palmer asserts in *The Growth of the African Novel:* "If there are reservations about the novel's structure, there can be none about the thoroughness of the satire at society's expense. Soyinka's wide-ranging wit takes in all sections of a corrupt society—the brutal masses, the aimless intellecutals, the affected and hypocritical university dons, the vulgar and corrupt businessmen, the mediocre civil servants, the illiterate politicians and the incompetent journalists. [The five main characters are all] talented intellectuals who have retained their African consciousness although they were largely educated in the western world. Yet their western education enables them to look at their changing society with a certain amount of detachment. They are therefore uniquely qualified to be interpreters of this society. The reader is impressed by their honesty, sincerity, moral idealism, concern for truth and justice and aversion to corruption, snobbery and hypocrisy; but anyone who assumes that Soyinka presents all the interpreters as models of behaviour will be completely misreading the novel. He is careful to expose their selfishness, egoism, cynicism and aimlessness. Indeed the conduct of the intellectuals both in and out of the university is a major preoccupation of Soyinka's in this novel. The aimlessness and superficiality of the lives of most of the interpreters is patent."

Neil McEwan points out in *Africa and the Novel* that for all its seriousness, *The Interpreters* is also "among the liveliest of recent novels in English. It is bright satire full of good sense and good humour which are African and contemporary: the highest spirits of its author's early work.... Behind the jokes of his novel is a theme that he has developed angrily elsewhere: that whatever progress may mean for Africa it is not a lesson to be learned from outside, however much of 'modernity' Africans may share with others." McEwan further observes that although *The Interpreters* does not have a rigidly structured plot, "there is unity in the warmth and sharpness of its comic vision. There are moments which sadden or anger; but they do not diminish the fun." Palmer notes that *The Interpreters* notably influenced the African fiction that followed it, shifting the focus "from historical, cultural and sociological analysis to penetrating social comment and social satire."

1965 also marked Soyinka's first arrest by the Nigerian police. He was accused of using a gun to force a radio announcer to broadcast incorrect election results. No evidence was ever produced, however, and the PEN writers' organization launched a protest campaign, headed by William Styron and Norman Mailer. Soyinka was released after three months. He was next arrested two years later, during Nigeria's civil war. Soyinka was completely opposed to the conflict, and especially to the Nigerian government's brutal policies toward the Ibo people who were attempting to form their own country, Biafra. He traveled to Biafra to establish a peace commission composed of leading intellectuals from both sides; when he returned, the Nigerian police accused him of helping the Biafrans to buy jet fighters. Once again he was imprisoned. This time Soyinka was held for more than two years, although he was never formally charged with any crime. Most of that time he was kept in solitary confinement. When all of his fellow prisoners were vaccinated against meningitis, Soyinka was passed by; when he developed serious vision problems, they were ignored by his jailers. He was denied reading and writing materials, but he manufactured his own ink and began to keep a prison

diary, written on toilet paper, cigarette packages and in between the lines of the few books he secretly obtained. Each poem or fragment of journal he managed to smuggle to the outside world became a literary event and a reassurance to his supporters that Soyinka still lived, despite rumors to the contrary. He was released in 1969 and left Nigeria soon after, not returning until a change of power took place in 1975.

Published as *The Man Died: Prison Notes of Wole Soyinka,* the author's diary constitutes "the most important work that has been written about the Biafran war," believes Charles R. Larson, contributor to *Nation.* "'The Man Died' is not so much the story of Wole Soyinka's own temporary death during the Nigerian Civil War but a personified account of Nigeria's fall from sanity, documented by one of the country's leading intellectuals." Gerald Weales's *New York Times Book Review* article suggests that the political content of *The Man Died* is less fascinating than "the notes that deal with prison life, the observation of everything from a warder's catarrh to the predatory life of insects after a rain. Of course, these are not simply reportorial. They are vehicles to carry the author's shifting states of mind, to convey the real subject matter of the book; the author's attempt to survive as a man, and as a mind. The notes are both a means to that survival and a record to it." Larson underlines the book's political impact, however, noting that ironically, "while other Nigerian writers were emotionally castrated by the war, Soyinka, who was placed in solitary confinement so that he wouldn't embarrass the government, was writing work after work, books that will no doubt embarrass the Nigerian Government more than anything the Ibo writers may ever publish." A *Times Literary Supplement* reviewer concurs, characterizing *The Man Died* as "a damning indictment of what Mr. Soyinka sees as the iniquities of wartime Nigeria and the criminal tyranny of its administration in peacetime."

Many literary commentators feel that Soyinka's work changed profoundly after his prison term, darkening in tone and focusing on the war and its aftermath. In the *Dictionary of Literary Biography Yearbook: 1986,* Thomas Hayes quotes Soyinka on his concerns after the war: "I have one abiding religion—human liberty ... conditioned to the truth that life is meaningless, insulting, without this fullest liberty, and in spite of the despairing knowledge that words alone seem unable to guarantee its possession, my writing grows more and more preoccupied with the theme of the oppressive boot, the irrelevance of the color of the foot that wears it and the struggle for individuality."

In spite of its satire, most critics had found *The Interpreters* to be ultimately an optimistic book. In contrast, Soyinka's second novel expresses almost no hope for Africa's future, says John Mellors in *London Magazine:* "Wole Soyinka appears to have written much of *Season of Anomy* in a blazing fury, angry beyond complete control of words at the abuses of power and the outbreaks of both considered and spontaneous violence.... The plot charges along, dragging the reader (not because he doesn't want to go, but because he finds it hard to keep up) through forest, mortuary and prison camp in nightmare visions of tyranny, torture, slaughter and putrefaction. The book reeks of pain.... Soyinka hammers at the point that the liberal has to deal with violence in the world however much he would wish he could ignore it; the scenes of murder and mutilation, while sickeningly explicit, are justifed by ... the author's anger and compassion and insistence that bad will not become better by our refusal to examine it."

Like *Season of Anomy*, Soyinka's postwar plays are considered more brooding than his earlier work. *Madmen and Specialist* is called "grim" by Martin Banham and Clive Wake in *African Theatre Today*. In the play, a doctor returns from the war trained as a specialist in torture and uses his new skills on his father. The play's major themes are "the loss of faith and rituals" and "the break-up of the family unit which traditionally in Africa has been the foundation of society," according to Charles Larson in the *New York Times Book Review*. Names and events in the play are fictionalized to avoid censorship, but Soyinka has clearly "leveled a wholesale criticism of life in Nigeria since the Civil War: a police state in which only madmen and spies can survive, in which the losers are mad and the winners are paranoid about the possibility of another rebellion. The prewar corruption and crime have returned, supported by the more sophisticated acts of terrorism and espionage introduced during the war." Larson summarizes: "In large part 'Madmen and Specialists' is a product of those months Soyinka spent in prison, in solitary confinement, as a political prisoner. It is, not surprisingly, the most brutal piece of social criticism he has published." In a similar tone, *A Play of Giants* presents four African leaders—thinly disguised versions of Jean Bedel Bokassa, Sese Seko Mobutu, Macias Ngeuma, and Idi Amin—meeting at the United Nations building, where "their conversation reflects the corruption and cruelty of their regimes and the casual, brutal flavor of their rule," discloses Hayes. In Hayes's opinion, *A Play of Giants* demonstrates that "as Soyinka has matured he has hardened his criticism of all that restricts the individual's ability to choose, think, and act free from external oppression. . . . . [It is] his harshest attack against modern Africa, a blunt, venomous assault on . . . African leaders and the powers who support them."

Soyinka's work is frequently described as demanding but rewarding reading. Although his plays are widely praised, they are seldom performed, especially outside of Africa. The dancing and choric speech often found in them are unfamiliar and difficult for non-African actors to master, a problem Holly Hill notes in her London *Times* review of the Lincoln Center Theatre production of *Death and the King's Horseman*. She awards high praise to the play, however, saying it "has the stateliness and mystery of Greek tragedy." When the Swedish Academy awarded Soyinka the Nobel Prize in Literature in 1986, its members singled out *Death and the King's Horseman* and *A Dance of the Forests* as "evidence that Soyinka is 'one of the finest poetical playwrights that have written in English,'" reports Stanley Meisler of the *Los Angeles Times*. Hayes summarizes Wole Soyinka's importance: "His drama and fiction have challenged the West to broaden its aesthetic and accept African standards of art and literature. His personal and political life have challenged Africa to embrace the truly democratic values of the African tribe and reject the tyranny of power practiced on the continent by its colonizers and by many of its modern rulers."

BIOGRAPHICAL/CRITICAL SOURCES:

BOOKS

Banham, Martin and Clive Wake, *African Theatre Today*, Pitman Publishing, 1976.

Banham, Martin, *Wole Soyinka's "The Lion and the Jewel,"* Rex Collings, 1981.

Contemporary Literary Criticism, Gale, Volume 3, 1975, Volume 5, 1976, Volume 14, 1980, Volume 36, 1986, Volume 44, 1987.

Dictionary of Literary Biography Yearbook: 1986, Gale, 1987.

Dunton, C. P., *Notes on "Three Short Plays,"* Longman, 1982.

Gakwandi, Shatto Arthur, *The Novel and Contemporary Experience in America*, Heinemann, 1977.

Gibbs, James, editor, *Study Aid to "Kongi's Harvest,"* Rex Collings, 1973.

Gibbs, James, editor, *Critical Perspectives on Wole Soyinka*, Three Continents, 1980.

Gibbs, James, editor, *Notes on "The Lion and the Jewel,"* Longman, 1982.

Gibbs, James, *Wole Soyinka*, Macmillan, 1986.

Gibbs, James, Ketu Katrak and Henry Gates, Jr., editors, *Wole Soyinka: A Bibliography of Primary and Secondary Sources*, Greenwood Press, 1986.

Goodwin, K. L., *Understanding African Poetry*, Heinemann, 1979.

Jones, Eldred, editor, *African Literature Today, Number 5: The Novel in Africa*, Heinemann, 1971.

Jones, Eldred, editor, *African Literature Today, Number 6: Poetry in Africa*, Heinemann, 1973.

Jones, Eldred, *Wole Soyinka*, Twayne, 1973 (published in England as *The Writings of Wole Soyinka*, Heinemann, 1973).

Katrak, Ketu, *Wole Soyinka and Modern Tragedy: A Study of Dramatic Theory and Practice*, Greenwood Press, 1986.

King, Bruce, editor, *Introduction to Nigerian Literature*, Africana Publishing, 1972.

Larson, Charles R., *The Emergence of African Fiction*, revised edition, Indiana University Press, 1972.

Laurence, Margaret, *Long Drums and Cannons: Nigerian Dramatists and Novelists*, Praeger, 1968.

McEwan, Neil, *Africa and the Novel*, Humanities Press, 1983.

Moore, Gerald, *Wole Soyinka*, Africana Publishing, 1971.

Morell, Karen L., editor, *In Person—Achebe, Awoonor, and Soyinka at the University of Washington*, African Studies Program, Institute for Comparative and Foreign Area Studies, University of Washington, 1975.

Ogunba, Oyin, *The Movement of Transition: A Study of the Plays of Wole Soyinka*, Ibadan University Press, 1975.

Ogunba, Oyin, and others, editors, *Theatre in Africa*, Ibadan University Press, 1978.

Palmer, Eustace, *The Growth of the African Novel*, Heinemann, 1979.

Parsons, E. M., editor, *Notes on Wole Soyinka's "The Jero Plays,"* Methuen, 1982.

Pieterse, Cosmo, and Dennis Duerden, editors, *African Writers Talking: A Collection of Radio Interviews*, Africana Publishing, 1972.

Probyn, editor, *Notes on "The Road,"* Longman, 1981.

Ricard, Alain, *Theatre et Nationalisme: Wole Soyinka et LeRoi Jones*, Presence Africaine, 1972.

Roscoe, Adrian A., *Mother Is Gold: A Study in West African Literature*, Cambridge University Press, 1971.

Soyinka, Wole, *The Man Died: Prison Notes of Wole Soyinka*, Harper, 1972.

Soyinka, Wole, *Myth, Literature and the African World*, Cambridge University Press, 1976.

Soyinka, Wole, *Ake: The Years of Childhood*, Random House, 1981.

Tucker, Martin, *Africa in Modern Literature: A Survey of Contemporary Writing in English*, Ungar, 1967.

PERIODICALS

America, February 12, 1983.

Ariel, July, 1981.

Black Orpheus, March, 1966.
Book Forum, Volume III, number 1, 1977.
Books Abroad, summer, 1972, spring, 1973.
British Book News, December, 1984, April, 1986.
Chicago Tribune Book World, October 7, 1979.
Christian Science Monitor, July 31, 1970, August 15, 1970.
Commonweal, February 8, 1985.
Detroit Free Press, March 20, 1983, October 17, 1986.
Detroit News, November 21, 1982.
Globe & Mail (Toronto), June 7, 1986.
London Magazine, April/May, 1974.
Los Angeles Times, October 17, 1986.
Nation, October 11, 1965, April 29, 1968, September 15, 1969, November 10, 1969, October 2, 1972, November 5, 1973.
New Republic, October 12, 1974, May 9, 1983.
New Statesman, December 20, 1968.
Newsweek, November 1, 1982.
New Yorker, May 16, 1977.
New York Review of Books, July 31, 1969, October 21, 1982.
New York Times, November 11, 1965, April 19, 1970, August 11, 1972, September 23, 1982, May 29, 1986, May 31, 1986, June 15, 1986, October 17, 1986, November 9, 1986, March 1, 1987, March 2, 1987.
New York Times Book Review, July 29, 1973, December 24, 1973, October 10, 1982, January 15, 1984.
New York Times Magazine, September 18, 1983.
Research in African Literatures, spring, 1983.
Saturday Review/World, October 19, 1974.
Spectator, November 6, 1959, December 15, 1973, November 24, 1981.
Time, October 27, 1986.
Times (London), October 17, 1986, April 6, 1987.
Times Literary Supplement, April 1, 1965, June 10, 1965, January 18, 1968, December 31, 1971, March 2, 1973, December 14, 1973, February 8, 1974, March 1, 1974, October 17, 1975, August 5, 1977, February 26, 1982.
Tri-Quarterly, fall, 1966.
Village Voice, August 31, 1982.
Washington Post, October 30, 1979, October 17, 1986.
World, February 13, 1973.
World Literature Today, winter, 1977, autumn, 1981, summer, 1982.

—*Sketch by Joan Goldsworthy*

*   *   *

SPEED, Eric
[Collective pseudonym]

WRITINGS:

"WYNN AND LONNY" RACING SERIES

The Mexicali 1000, Grosset & Dunlap, 1975.
Road Race of Champions, Grosset & Dunlap, 1975.
GT Challenge, Grosset & Dunlap, 1976.
Gold Cup Rookies, Grosset & Dunlap, 1976.
Dead Heat at Le Mans, Grosset & Dunlap, 1977.
The Midnight Rally, Grosset & Dunlap, 1978.

SIDELIGHTS: Andrew E. Svenson and Sylvia Wilkerson worked together on this series about car racing. For more information see the entries in this volume for Harriet S. Adams, Edward L. Stratemeyer, and Andrew E. Svenson.

BIOGRAPHICAL/CRITICAL SOURCES:

BOOKS

Johnson, Deidre, editor and compiler, *Stratemeyer Pseudonyms and Series Books: An Annotated Checklist of Stratemeyer and Stratemeyer Syndicate Publications,* Greenwood Press, 1982.

*   *   *

SPERRY, Raymond
See GARIS, Howard R(oger)

*   *   *

SRAFFA, Piero   1898-1983

PERSONAL: Born August 5, 1898, in Turin, Italy; died September 3, 1983, in Cambridge, England; son of Angelo (a law professor) and Irma (Tivoli) Sraffa. *Education:* University of Turin, LL.D., 1920.

ADDRESSES: Office—Department of Economics, Trinity College, Cambridge University, Cambridge, England.

CAREER: University of Cagliari, Sardinia, Italy, professor of political economy, 1926-27; Cambridge University, Trinity College, Cambridge, England, lecturer in economics, 1927-65, life fellow, 1938-83. *Military service:* Italian Army, 1917-18.

WRITINGS:

(Editor) *The Works and Correspondence of David Ricardo,* twelve volumes, Cambridge University Press, 1951-73.
Production of Commodities by Means of Commodities: A Prelude to a Critique of Economic Theory, Cambridge University Press, 1960, new edition, 1975.
(Editor) David Ricardo, *Principles of Political Economy,* Volume 1, Cambridge University Press, 1981.

Contributor to the *Manchester Guardian Reconstruction Supplements.*

SIDELIGHTS: Piero Sraffa's work has been translated into French, German, Italian, and Polish.

OBITUARIES:

PERIODICALS

Times (London), September 6, 1983.*

*   *   *

STEVENS, R. L.
See HOCH, Edward D(entinger)

*   *   *

STONE, Alan
See SVENSON, Andrew E(dward)

STRATEMEYER, Edward L. 1862-1930

(Manager Henry Abbott, Horatio Alger, Jr., Philip A. Alyer, P. T. Barnum, Jr., Theodore Barnum, Emerson Bell, Captain Ralph Bonehill, Jim Bowie, Jim Daly, Theodore Edison, Albert Lee Ford, Ralph Hamilton, Captain Lew James, Oliver Optic, Peter Pad, Peter, Ned St. Meyer, E. Ward Strayer, Ed Ward, Tom Ward, Arthur M. Winfield, Edna Winfield, Zimmy; joint pseudonyms: Louis Charles, Nat Woods; house pseudonyms: Nick Carter, Julia Edwards, Hal Harkaway, Harvey Hicks)

PERSONAL: Born October 4, 1862, in Elizabeth, N.J.; died of lobar pneumonia, May 10, 1930, in Newark, N.J.; son of Henry Julius (a tobacconist and dry goods dealer) and Anna (Siegal) Stratemeyer; married Magdalene Baker Van Camp, March 25, 1891; children: Harriet Stratemeyer Adams, Edna Camilla Stratemeyer Squier. *Education:* Attended public schools in Elizabeth, N.J.

CAREER: Worked in family's tobacco shop in Elizabeth, N.J., until 1889; briefly owned and managed a stationery store; freelance writer, 1889-1930. Founder and chief executive of Stratemeyer Literary Syndicate, New York, N.Y., ca. 1906-30.

WRITINGS:

The Minute Boys of Lexington, Estes & Lauriat, 1898.
(With William Taylor Adams, under pseudonym Oliver Optic) *An Undivided Union,* Lee & Shepard, 1899.
The Minute Boys of Bunker Hill, Estes & Lauriat, 1899.
(Under pseudonym Captain Ralph Bonehill) *Young Hunters in Puerto Rico; or, The Search for a Lost Treasure,* Donohue, 1900.
Between Boer and Briton; or, Two Boys' Adventures in South Africa, Lee & Shepard, 1900, published as Volume 13 of "Stratemeyer Popular Series," Lothrop, Lee & Shepard, published as *The Young Ranchman; or, Between Boer and Briton,* Street & Smith, 1920.
(With brother, Louis Stratemeyer, under joint pseudonym Louis Charles) *Fortune Hunters of the Philippines; or, The Treasure of the Burning Mountain,* Mershon, 1900.
(With L. Stratemeyer, under joint pseudonym Louis Charles) *The Land of Fire; or, Adventures in Underground Africa* (originally serialized in *Bright Days,* 1896, under title "The Land of Fire; or, A Long Journey for Fortune"), Mershon, 1900.
American Boys' Life of William McKinley, Lee & Shepard, 1901.
(Under pseudonym Captain Ralph Bonehill) *Three Young Ranchmen; or, Daring Adventures in the Great West* (originally serialized in *Young People of America,* 1895-96, under title "Three Ranch Boys; or, The Great Winthrop Claim" by Edward Stratemeyer), Saalfield, 1901.
(Under pseudonym Arthur M. Winfield) *Larry Barlow's Ambition; or, The Adventures of a Young Fireman* (originally serialized in *Golden Hours,* 1902, under title "Brave Larry Barlow; or, The Fire Fighters of New York" by Roy Rockwood), Saalfield, 1902.
(Under pseudonym Captain Ralph Bonehill) *The Boy Land Boomer; or, Dick Arbuckle's Adventures in Oklahoma,* Saalfield, 1902.
(Under pseudonym Captain Ralph Bonehill) *Bob the Photographer; or, A Hero in Spite of Himself* (originally serialized in *Good News,* 1893-94, under title "Camera Bob; or,

The Thrilling Adventures of a Travelling Photographer'' by Edward Stratemeyer), Wessels, 1902.
(Under pseudonym Captain Ralph Bonehill) *The Young Naval Captain; or, The War of All Nations* (originally serialized in *Golden Hours,* 1900-01, under title "Holland, the Destroyer; or, America against the World" by Hal Harkaway), Thompson & Thomas, 1902, published as *Oscar, the Naval Cadet; or, Under the Sea,* Donohue.
(Under pseudonym Arthur M. Winfield) *Mark Dale's Stage Adventure; or, Bound to Be an Actor* (originally serialized in *Good News,* 1895, under title "A Footlight Favorite; or, Born to Be an Actor" by Manager Henry Abbott), McKay, 1902.
(Under pseudonym Captain Ralph Bonehill) *Neka, the Boy Conjurer; or, A Mystery of the Stage* (originally serialized in *Good News,* 1895-96, under title "Neka, King of Fire; or, A Mystery of the Variety Stage" by Manager Henry Abbott), McKay, 1902.
(Under pseudonym Arthur M. Winfield) *The Young Bank Clerk; or, Mark Vincent's Strange Discovery* (originally serialized in *Good News,* 1893-94, under title "Missing Money; or, The Young Bank Messenger's Discovery"), McKay, 1902.
(Under pseudonym Captain Ralph Bonehill) *Lost in the Land of Ice; or, Daring Adventures around the South Pole* (originally serialized in *Golden Hours,* 1900-01, under title "Lost in the Land of Ice; or, Bob Baxter at the South Pole" by Roy Rockwood), Wessels, 1902.
(Under pseudonym Arthur M. Winfield) *The Young Bridge-Tender; or, Ralph Nelson's Upward Struggle* (originally serialized in *Good News,* 1895, under title "By Pluck Alone; or, Ralph Nelson's Upward Struggle" by Harvey Hicks), McKay, 1902.
(Under pseudonym Captain Ralph Bonehill) *The Tour of the Zero Club; or, Adventures amid Ice and Snow* (originally serialized in *Good News,* 1894-95, under title "The Tour of the Zero Club; or, Perils by Ice and Snow" by Harvey Hicks), Street & Smith, 1902.
(Under pseudonym Arthur M. Winfield) *A Young Inventor's Pluck; or, The Mystery of the Wellington Legacy* (originally serialized in *The Holiday,* 1891, under title "Jack the Inventor; or, The Trials and Triumphs of a Young Machinist" by Edward Stratemeyer), Saalfield, 1902.
Two Young Lumbermen; or, From Maine to Oregon for Fortune, Lee & Shepard, 1903, published as Volume 14 of "Stratemeyer Popular Series," Lothrop, Lee & Shepard.
Joe the Surveyor; or, The Value of a Lost Claim (originally serialized in *Good News,* 1894), Lee & Shepard, 1903, published as Volume 11 of "Stratemeyer Popular Series," Lothrop, Lee & Shepard.
Larry the Wanderer; or, The Rise of a Nobody (originally serialized in *Good News,* 1894, under title "Larry the Wanderer; or, The Ups and Downs of a Knockabout"), Lee & Shepard, 1904, published as Volume 12 of "Stratemeyer Popular Series," Lothrop, Lee & Shepard.
(Under pseudonym Captain Ralph Bonehill) *The Island Camp; or, The Young Hunters of Lakeport* (originally serialized in *The Popular Magazine,* 1903-04, under title "Snow Lodge''; also see below), A. S. Barnes, 1904.
American Boys' Life of Theodore Roosevelt, Lee & Shepard, 1904.
(Under pseudonym Captain Ralph Bonehill) *The Winning Run; or, The Baseball Boys of Lakeport* (also see below), A. S. Barnes, 1905.

(Under pseudonym Horatio Alger, Jr.) *Joe the Hotel Boy; or, Winning out by Pluck* (also see below), Cupples & Leon, 1906.

Defending His Flag; or, A Boy in Blue and a Boy in Gray (originally serialized in *The American Boy*, 1906-07, under title "In Defense of His Flag"), Lothrop, Lee & Shepard, 1907.

(Under pseudonym Horatio Alger, Jr.) *Ben Logan's Triumph; or, The Boys of Boxwood Academy* (also see below), Cupples & Leon, 1908.

First at the North Pole; or, Two Boys in the Arctic Circle, Lothrop, Lee & Shepard, 1909, published as Volume 15 of "Stratemeyer Popular Series," published as *The Young Explorers; or, Adventures above the Arctic Circle*, Street & Smith, 1920.

(Under pseudonym E. Ward Strayer) *Making Good with Margaret*, G. Sully, 1918.

"SHIP AND SHORE" SERIES

The Last Cruise of the Spitfire; or, Luke Foster's Strange Voyage (originally serialized in *Argosy*, 1892, under title "Luke Foster's Grit; or, The Last Cruise of the Spitfire"), Merriam, 1894, published as Volume 1 of "Stratemeyer Popular Series," Lothrop, Lee & Shepard.

Reuben Stone's Discovery; or, The Young Miller of Torrent Bend (originally serialized in *Argosy*, 1892), Merriam, 1895, published as Volume 2 of "Stratemeyer Popular Series," Lothrop, Lee & Shepard.

True to Himself; or, Roger Strong's Struggle for Place (originally serialized in *Argosy*, 1891-92), Lee & Shepard, 1900, published as Volume 3 of "Stratemeyer Popular Series," Lothrop, Lee & Shepard.

"BOUND TO SUCCEED" SERIES

Richard Dare's Venture; or, Striking out for Himself (originally serialized in *Argosy*, 1891; also see below), Merriam, 1894, revised edition, Lee & Shepard, 1899.

Oliver Bright's Search; or, The Mystery of a Mine (originally serialized in *Argosy*, 1892-93, under title "One Boy in a Thousand; or, The Mystery of the Aurora Mine" by Arthur M. Winfield; also see below), Merriam, 1895, revised edition, Lee & Shepard, 1899.

To Alaska for Gold; or, The Fortune Hunters of the Yukon, Lee & Shepard, 1899, published as Volume 6 of "Stratemeyer Popular Series," Lothrop, Lee & Shepard.

"BOUND TO WIN" SERIES

Bound to Be an Electrician; or, Franklin Bell's Road to Success (originally serialized in *Bright Days*, 1896, under title "Bound to Be an Electrician; or, A Clear Head and a Stout Heart" by Arthur M. Winfield; also see below), Allison, 1897.

(Under pseudonym Arthur M. Winfield) *The Schooldays of Fred Harley; or, Rivals for All Honors* (originally serialized in *Good News*, 1894; also see below), Allison, 1897.

(Under pseudonym Captain Ralph Bonehill) *Gun and Sled; or, The Young Hunters of Snow-Top Island* (originally serialized in *Young People of America*, 1895-96), Allison, 1897.

Shorthand Tom; or, The Exploits of a Young Reporter (originally serialized in *Good News*, 1894; also see below), Allison, 1897.

(Under pseudonym Arthur M. Winfield) *The Missing Tin Box; or, The Stolen Railroad Bonds* (originally serialized in

Good News, 1893, under title "The Tin Box Mystery; or, The Stolen Railroad Bonds" by Edward Stratemeyer; also see below), Allison, 1897.

(Under pseudonym Captain Ralph Bonehill) *Young Oarsmen of Lakeview; or, The Mystery of Hermit Island* (originally serialized in *Young People of America*, 1895, under title "Single Shell Jerry; or, The Rival Oarsmen of Lakeview"), Allison, 1897.

The Young Auctioneers; or, The Polishing of a Rolling Stone (originally serialized in *Good News*, 1894-95; also see below), Allison, 1897.

(Under pseudonym Arthur M. Winfield) *Poor but Plucky; or, The Mystery of a Flood* (originally serialized in *Young People of America*, 1895, under pseudonym Albert Lee Ford; also see below), Allison, 1897.

(Under pseudonym Captain Ralph Bonehill) *The Rival Bicyclists; or, Fun and Adventures on the Wheel* (originally serialized in *Young Sports of America*, 1895, under title "Joe Johnson, the Bicycle Wonder; or, Riding for the Championship of the World" by Roy Rockwood), Donohue, 1897, reprinted as part of the "Boys' Liberty" series under title *Rival Cyclists* by Donohue.

Fighting for His Own; or, The Fortunes of a Young Artist (originally serialized in *Argosy*, 1892, under pseudonym Arthur M. Winfield; also see below), Allison, 1897.

(Under pseudonym Arthur M. Winfield) *By Pluck, not Luck; or, Dan Granbury's Struggle to Rise* (originally serialized in *Young Sports of America* [first installment] and *Young People of America* [remaining installments], 1895, under title "Quarterback Dan, the Football Champion; or, Kicking for Fame and Fortune" by Captain Young of Yale [first installment] and Clarence Young [remaining installments]; also see below), Allison, 1897.

(Under pseudonym Captain Ralph Bonehill) *Leo the Circus Boy; or, Life under the Great White Canvas* (originally serialized in *Young Sports of America*, 1895, under title "Limber Leo, Clown and Gymnast; or, With the Greatest Show on Earth" by P. T. Barnum, Jr.; serialized in *Young Sports of America*, 1896, under title "Leo, the Circus Boy; or, Life under the Great White Canvas" by Theodore Barnum), Allison, 1897.

"OLD GLORY" SERIES

Under Dewey at Manila; or, The War Fortunes of a Castaway, Lee & Shepard, 1898.

A Young Volunteer in Cuba; or, Fighting for the Single Star, Lee & Shepard, 1898.

Fighting in Cuban Waters; or, Under Schley on the Brooklyn, Lee & Shepard, 1899.

Under Otis in the Philippines; or, A Young Officer in the Tropics, Lee & Shepard, 1899.

The Campaign of the Jungle; or, Under Lawton through Luzon, Lee & Shepard, 1900.

Under MacArthur in Luzon; or, Last Battles in the Philippines, Lee & Shepard, 1901.

"ROVER BOYS SERIES FOR YOUNG AMERICANS"; UNDER PSEUDONYM ARTHUR M. WINFIELD

The Rover Boys at School; or, The Cadets of Putnam Hall, Mershon, 1899.

. . . on the Ocean; or, A Chase for Fortune, Mershon, 1899.

. . . in the Jungle; or, Stirring Adventures in Africa, Mershon, 1899.

. . . out West; or, The Search for a Lost Mine, Mershon, 1900.

. . . *on the Great Lakes; or, The Secret of the Island Cave,* Mershon, 1901.

. . . *in the Mountains; or, A Hunt for Fun and Fortune,* Mershon, 1902.

. . . *on Land and Sea; or, The Crusoes of Seven Islands,* Mershon, 1903.

. . . *in Camp; or, The Rivals of Pine Island,* Mershon, 1904.

. . . *on the River; or, The Search for the Missing Houseboat,* Stitt, 1905.

. . . *on the Plains; or, The Mystery of Red Rock,* Mershon, 1906.

. . . *in Southern Waters; or, The Deserted Steam Yacht,* Mershon, 1907.

. . . *on the Farm; or, Last Days at Putnam Hall,* Grosset & Dunlap, 1908.

. . . *on Treasure Isle; or, The Strange Cruise of the Steam Yacht,* Grosset & Dunlap, 1909.

. . . *at College; or, The Right Road and the Wrong,* Grosset & Dunlap, 1910.

. . . *Down East; or, The Struggle for the Stanhope Fortune,* Grosset & Dunlap, 1911.

. . . *in the Air; or, From College Campus to Clouds,* Grosset & Dunlap, 1912.

. . . *in New York; or, Saving Their Father's Honor,* Grosset & Dunlap, 1913.

. . . *in Alaska; or, Lost in the Fields of Ice,* Grosset & Dunlap, 1914.

. . . *in Business; or, The Search for the Missing Bonds,* Grosset & Dunlap, 1915.

. . . *on a Tour; or, Last Days at Brill College,* Grosset & Dunlap, 1916.

"FLAG OF FREEDOM" SERIES; UNDER PSEUDONYM CAPTAIN RALPH BONEHILL

When Santiago Fell; or, The War Adventures of Two Chums (also see below), Mershon, 1899, published as *For His Country; or, The Adventures of Two Chums* by Edward Stratemeyer, Street & Smith, 1920.

A Sailor Boy with Dewey; or, Afloat in the Philippines (also see below), Mershon, 1899, published as *Comrades in Peril; or, Afloat on a Battleship* by Edward Stratemeyer, Street & Smith, 1920.

Off for Hawaii; or, The Mystery of a Great Volcano (also see below), Mershon, 1899, published as *The Young Pearl Hunters; or, In Hawaiian Waters* by Edward Stratemeyer, Street & Smith, 1920.

The Young Bandmaster; or, Concert, Stage, and Battlefield (originally serialized in *Golden Hours,* 1899, under title "The Young Bandmaster; or, Solving a Mystery of the Past"; also see below), Mershon, 1900.

Boys of the Fort; or, A Young Captain's Pluck (also see below), Mershon, 1901, published as *Boys of the Fort; or, True Courage Wins* by Edward Stratemeyer, Street & Smith, 1920.

With Custer in the Black Hills; or, A Young Scout among the Indians (also see below), Mershon, 1902, published as *On Fortune's Trail; or, The Heroes of the Black Hills* by Edward Stratemeyer, Street & Smith, 1920.

"MEXICAN WAR" SERIES; UNDER PSEUDONYM CAPTAIN RALPH BONEHILL

For the Liberty of Texas, Estes, 1900, reprinted under name Edward Stratemeyer, Lothrop, Lee & Shepard, 1909, reprinted, 1930.

With Taylor on the Rio Grande, Estes, 1901, reprinted under name Edward Stratemeyer, Lothrop, Lee & Shepard, 1909, reprinted, 1930.

Under Scott in Mexico, Estes, 1902, reprinted under name Edward Stratemeyer, Lothrop, Lee & Shepard, 1909, reprinted, 1930.

"SOLDIERS OF FORTUNE" SERIES

On to Pekin; or, Old Glory in China, Lee & Shepard, 1900.

Under the Mikado's Flag; or, Young Soldiers of Fortune, Lee & Shepard, 1904.

At the Fall of Port Arthur; or, A Young American in the Japanese Navy, Lothrop, Lee & Shepard, 1905.

Under Togo for Japan; or, Three Young Americans on Land and Sea, Lothrop, Lee & Shepard, 1906.

"RISE IN LIFE" SERIES; UNDER PSEUDONYM HORATIO ALGER, JR.

Out for Business; or, Robert Frost's Strange Career, Mershon, 1900.

Falling in with Fortune; or, The Experiences of a Young Secretary, Mershon, 1900.

Young Captain Jack; or, The Son of a Soldier (originally serialized in *Golden Hours,* 1901), Mershon, 1901.

Nelson the Newsboy; or, Afloat in New York, Mershon, 1901.

Jerry the Backwoods Boy; or, The Parkhurst Treasure, Mershon, 1904.

Lost at Sea; or, Robert Roscoe's Strange Cruise, Mershon, 1904.

From Farm to Fortune; or, Nat Nason's Strange Experience, Stitt, 1905.

The Young Book Agent; or, Frank Hardy's Road to Success, Stitt, 1905.

Randy of the River; or, The Adventures of a Young Deck Hand, Chatterton-Peck, 1906.

Joe, the Hotel Boy; or, Winning out by Pluck, Grosset & Dunlap, 1912.

Ben Logan's Triumph; or, The Boys of Boxwood Academy, Grosset & Dunlap, 1912.

"COLONIAL" SERIES

With Washington in the West; or, A Soldier Boy's Battles in the Wilderness, Lee & Shepard, 1901.

Marching on Niagara; or, The Soldier Boys of the Old Frontier, Lee & Shepard, 1902.

At the Fall of Montreal; or, A Soldier Boy's Final Victory, Lee & Shepard, 1903.

On the Trail of Pontiac; or, The Pioneer Boys of the Ohio, Lee & Shepard, 1904.

The Fort in the Wilderness; or, The Soldier Boys of the Indian Trails, Lee & Shepard, 1905.

Trail and Trading Post; or, The Young Hunters of the Ohio, Lothrop, Lee & Shepard, 1906.

"PUTNAM HALL" SERIES; UNDER PSEUDONYM ARTHUR M. WINFIELD

The Putnam Hall Cadets; or, Good Times in School and Out, Mershon, 1901, reprinted as Volume 5 of series under title *The Cadets of Putnam Hall; or, Good Times in School and Out,* Grosset & Dunlap, 1921.

. . . *Rivals; or, Fun and Sport Afloat and Ashore,* Mershon, 1906, reprinted as Volume 6 of series under title *The Rivals of Putnam Hall; or, Fun and Sport Afloat and Ashore,* Grosset & Dunlap, 1921.

. . . Champions; or, Bound to Win Out, Grosset & Dunlap, 1908, reprinted as Volume 4 of series under title *The Champions of Putnam Hall; or, Bound to Win Out*, 1921.

. . . Rebellion; or, The Rival Runaways, Grosset & Dunlap, 1909, reprinted as Volume 3 of series under title *The Rebellion at Putnam Hall; or, The Rival Runaways*, 1921.

. . . Encampment; or, The Secret of the Old Mill, Grosset & Dunlap, 1910, reprinted as Volume 2 of series under title *Camping Out Days at Putnam Hall; or, The Secret of the Old Mill*, 1921.

. . . Mystery; or, The School Chums' Strange Discovery, Grosset & Dunlap, 1911, reprinted as Volume 1 of series under title *The Mystery at Putnam Hall; or, The School Chums' Strange Discovery*, 1921.

"PAN-AMERICAN" SERIES

Lost on the Orinoco; or, American Boys in Venezuela, Lee & Shepard, 1902.

The Young Volcano Explorers; or, American Boys in the West Indies, Lee & Shepard, 1902.

Young Explorers of the Isthmus; or, American Boys in Central America, Lee & Shepard, 1903.

Young Explorers of the Amazon; or, American Boys in Brazil, Lee & Shepard, 1904.

Treasure Seekers of the Andes; or, American Boys in Peru, Lothrop, Lee & Shepard, 1907.

Chased across the Pampas; or, American Boys in Argentina and Homeward Bound, Lothrop, Lee & Shepard, 1911.

"WORKING UPWARD" SERIES

The Young Auctioneers; or, The Polishing of a Rolling Stone, Lee & Shepard, 1903, published as Volume 7 of "Stratemeyer Popular Series," Lothrop, Lee & Shepard.

Bound to Be an Electrician; or, Franklin Bell's Road to Success, Lee & Shepard, 1903, published as Volume 8 of "Stratemeyer Popular Series," Lothrop, Lee & Shepard.

Shorthand Tom, the Reporter; or, The Exploits of a Bright Boy (originally published as *Shorthand Tom; or, The Exploits of a Young Reporter*), Lee & Shepard, 1903, published as Volume 9 of "Stratemeyer Popular Series," Lothrop, Lee & Shepard.

Fighting for His Own; or, The Fortunes of a Young Artist, Lee & Shepard, 1903, published as Volume 10 of "Stratemeyer Popular Series," Lothrop, Lee & Shepard.

Oliver Bright's Search; or, The Mystery of a Mine, Lee & Shepard, 1903, published as Volume 5 of "Stratemeyer Popular Series," Lothrop, Lee & Shepard.

Richard Dare's Venture; or, Striking out for Himself, Lee & Shepard, 1903, published as Volume 4 of "Stratemeyer Popular Series," Lothrop, Lee & Shepard.

"FRONTIER" SERIES; UNDER PSEUDONYM CAPTAIN RALPH BONEHILL

With Boone on the Frontier; or, The Pioneer Boys of Old Kentucky (also see below), Mershon, 1903, published as *Boys of the Wilderness; or, Down in Old Kentucky* by Edward Stratemeyer, Street & Smith, 1932.

Pioneer Boys of the Great Northwest; or, With Lewis and Clark across the Rockies (also see below), Mershon, 1904, published as *Boys of the Great Northwest; or, Across the Rockies* by Edward Stratemeyer, Street & Smith, 1932.

Pioneer Boys of the Gold Fields; or, The Nugget Hunters of '49 (also see below), Stitt, 1906, published as *Boys of the Gold Fields; or, The Nugget Hunters* by Edward Stratemeyer, Street & Smith, 1932.

"BRIGHT AND BOLD" SERIES; UNDER PSEUDONYM ARTHUR M. WINFIELD

Poor but Plucky; or, The Mystery of a Flood, Donohue, 1905.

The Schooldays of Fred Harley; or, Rivals for All Honors, Donohue, 1905.

By Pluck, not Luck; or, Dan Granbury's Struggle to Rise, Donohue, 1905.

The Missing Tin Box; or, The Stolen Railroad Bonds, Donohue, 1905.

"DAVE PORTER" SERIES

Dave Porter at Oak Hall; or, The Schooldays of an American Boy, Lee & Shepard, 1905.

. . . in the South Seas; or, The Strange Cruise of the Stormy Petrel, Lothrop, Lee & Shepard, 1906.

Dave Porter's Return to School; or, Winning the Medal of Honor, Lothrop, Lee & Shepard, 1907.

. . . in the Far North; or, The Pluck of an American Schoolboy, Lothrop, Lee & Shepard, 1908.

. . . and His Classmates; or, For the Honor of Oak Hall, Lothrop, Lee & Shepard, 1909.

. . . at Star Ranch; or, The Cowboy's Secret, Lothrop, Lee & Shepard, 1910.

. . . and His Rivals; or, The Chums and Foes of Oak Hall, Lothrop, Lee & Shepard, 1911.

. . . on Cave Island; or, A Schoolboy's Mysterious Mission, Lothrop, Lee & Shepard, 1912.

. . . and the Runaways; or, Last Days at Oak Hall, Lothrop, Lee & Shepard, 1913.

. . . in the Gold Fields; or, The Search for the Landslide Mine, Lothrop, Lee & Shepard, 1914.

. . . at Bear Camp; or, The Wild Man of Mirror Lake, Lothrop, Lee & Shepard, 1915.

. . . and His Double; or, The Disappearance of the Basswood Fortune, Lothrop, Lee & Shepard, 1916.

Dave Porter's Great Search; or, The Perils of a Young Civil Engineer, Lothrop, Lee & Shepard, 1917.

. . . under Fire; or, A Young Army Engineer in France, Lothrop, Lee & Shepard, 1918.

Dave Porter's War Honors; or, At the Front with the Flying Engineers, Lothrop, Lee & Shepard, 1919.

"BOY HUNTERS" SERIES; UNDER PSEUDONYM CAPTAIN RALPH BONEHILL

Four Boy Hunters; or, The Outing of the Gun Club, Cupples & Leon, 1906.

Guns and Snowshoes; or, The Winter Outing of the Young Hunters, Cupples & Leon, 1907.

Young Hunters of the Lake; or, Out with Rod and Gun, Cupples & Leon, 1908.

Out with Gun and Camera; or, The Boy Hunters in the Mountains, Cupples & Leon, 1910.

"LAKEPORT" SERIES

The Gun Club Boys of Lakeport; or, The Island Camp, (originally published as *The Island Camp; or, The Young Hunters of Lakeport* by Captain Ralph Bonehill), Lothrop, Lee & Shepard, 1908.

The Baseball Boys of Lakeport; or, The Winning Run (originally published as *The Winning Run; or, The Baseball Boys of Lakeport* by Captain Ralph Bonehill), Lothrop, Lee & Shepard, 1908.

The Boat Club Boys of Lakeport; or, The Water Champions, Lothrop, Lee & Shepard, 1908.

The Football Boys of Lakeport; or, More Goals Than One, Lothrop, Lee & Shepard, 1909.

The Automobile Boys of Lakeport; or, A Run for Fun and Fame, Lothrop, Lee & Shepard, 1910.

The Aircraft Boys of Lakeport; or, Rivals of the Clouds, Lothrop, Lee & Shepard, 1912.

"FLAG AND FRONTIER" SERIES; UNDER PSEUDONYM CAPTAIN RALPH BONEHILL

With Boone on the Frontier; or, The Pioneer Boys of Old Kentucky, Grosset & Dunlap, 1912.

Pioneer Boys of the Great Northwest; or, With Lewis and Clark across the Rockies, Grosset & Dunlap, 1912.

Pioneer Boys of the Gold Fields; or, The Nugget Hunters of '49, Grosset & Dunlap, 1912.

With Custer in the Black Hills; or, A Young Scout among the Indians, Grosset & Dunlap, 1912.

Boys of the Fort; or, A Young Captain's Pluck, Grosset & Dunlap, 1912.

The Young Bandmaster; or, Concert, Stage, and Battlefield, Grosset & Dunlap, 1912.

Off for Hawaii; or, The Mystery of a Great Volcano, Grosset & Dunlap, 1912.

A Sailor Boy with Dewey; or, Afloat in the Philippines, Grosset & Dunlap, 1912.

When Santiago Fell; or, The War Adventures of Two Chums, Grosset & Dunlap, 1912.

"SECOND ROVER BOYS SERIES FOR YOUNG AMERICANS"; UNDER PSEUDONYM ARTHUR M. WINFIELD

The Rover Boys at Colby Hall; or, The Struggles of the Young Cadets, Grosset & Dunlap, 1917.

. . . on Snowshoe Island; or, The Old Lumberman's Treasure Box, Grosset & Dunlap, 1918.

. . . under Canvas; or, The Mystery of the Wrecked Submarine, Grosset & Dunlap, 1919.

. . . on a Hunt; or, The Mysterious House in the Woods, Grosset & Dunlap, 1920.

. . . in the Land of Luck; or, Stirring Adventures in the Oilfields, Grosset & Dunlap, 1921.

. . . at Big Horn Ranch; or, The Cowboys' Double Roundup, Grosset & Dunlap, 1922.

. . . at Big Bear Lake; or, The Camps of the Rival Cadets, Grosset & Dunlap, 1923.

. . . Shipwrecked; or, A Thrilling Hunt for Pirates' Gold, Grosset & Dunlap, 1924.

. . . on Sunset Trail; or, The Old Miner's Mysterious Message, Grosset & Dunlap, 1925.

. . . Winning a Fortune; or, Strenuous Days Afloat and Ashore, Grosset & Dunlap, 1926.

OTHER

Also author of *Dave Porter on the Atlantic; or, The Castaways of the Menagerie Ship.* Contributor of stories to magazines, including *Golden Days, Argosy, Good News, Boys of America, Bright Days, Young Sports of America,* and *Young People of America,* under a variety of pseudonyms, including Manager Henry Abbott, Horatio Alger, Jr., Philip A. Alyer, P. T. Barnum, Jr., Theodore Barnum, Emerson Bell, Captain Ralph Bonehill, Allen Chapman, Louis Charles, Theodore Edison, Julia Edwards, Albert Lee Ford, Ralph Hamilton, Hal Harkaway, Harvey Hicks, Peter, Roy Rockwood, Ned St. Meyer, Ed Ward, Arthur M. Winfield, Edna Winfield, Captain Young of Yale, and Clarence Young; contributor of stories to dime novel series, under a variety of pseudonyms, including Man-

ager Henry Abbott, Horatio Alger, Jr., Jim Bowie, Nick Carter, Jim Daly, Julia Edwards, Captain Lew James, Peter Pad, Ned St. Meyer, Tom Ward, Edna Winfield, Nat Woods, and Zimmy. Plotter and editor of books for Stratemeyer Literary Syndicate. Editor, *Good News;* founder and editor, *Bright Days.*

SIDELIGHTS: "If anyone ever deserved a bronze statue in Central Park, somewhere between Hans Christian Anderson and Alice in Wonderland," declares Arthur Prager in *Saturday Review,* "it is Edward Stratemeyer, incomparable king of juveniles." Between 1886, when he wrote his first story on wrapping paper in his family's tobacco shop, and his death in 1930, Stratemeyer wrote, outlined, and edited more than 800 books under sixty-five pseudonyms, plus myriad short stories. His beloved creations include Dick, Tom, and Sam Rover (the Rover Boys), Bert, Nan, Freddie, and Flossie Bobbsey (the Bobbsey Twins), Tom Swift, Bomba the Jungle Boy, Frank and Joe Hardy, and Nancy Drew. John T. Dizer, writing in *Tom Swift & Company: "Boys' Books" by Stratemeyer and Others,* calls the literary syndicate that he founded "the most important single influence in American juvenile literature." "As oil had its Rockefeller, literature had its Stratemeyer," eulogized *Fortune* magazine shortly after his death.

"The bulk of Stratemeyer's literary apprenticeship was served in writing and editing for periodicals," explains *Dictionary of Literary Biography* contributor Mary-Agnes Taylor. His initial success—his first story sold to *Golden Days,* a Philadelphia weekly paper for boys, for $75—encouraged the young author to write more stories. He soon became a regular contributor to Frank Munsey's periodical *Golden Argosy* and, in 1893, the magazine and dime novel publishers Street & Smith offered him the editorship of their journal *Good News.* By 1896 he was also editing the Street & Smith periodicals *Young Sports of America* (which became *Young People of America*) and *Bright Days,* as well as contributing women's serials to the *New York Weekly* under the pseudonym Julia Edwards, and dime novels under the pseudonyms Captain Ralph Bonehill and Allen Chapman, as well as under his own name. "Perhaps the greatest advantage of his association with Street and Smith, however," continues Taylor, "was his exposure to the literary idols of his time," including Frederic Van Rensselaer Dey, "creator of dime novel detective hero Nick Carter; Upton Sinclair, who wrote the True Blue series as Ensign Clark Fitch, USN; prolific dime novelist Edward S. Ellis; William Taylor Adams; and Horatio Alger himself." After the deaths of Adams and Alger, Stratemeyer was chosen to complete some of their unfinished manuscripts, using the pseudonyms Oliver Optic and Horatio Alger, Jr.

Stratemeyer's success as a novelist came in 1898, during the Spanish-American War. "War was glamour in those days. Uniforms were splendid, and battles were glorious," explains Prager. The author had recently submitted a novel about several young men serving on a battleship to Lothrop, Lee & Shepard, a publishing house in Boston, when news of Admiral Dewey's victory over the Spanish fleet at Manila Bay reached the U.S. The publishers wrote the author, inquiring if he could revise his story to reflect Dewey's victory. Stratemeyer did, and *Under Dewey at Manila; or, The War Fortunes of a Castaway,* featuring Larry and Ben Russell and their chum Gilbert Pennington, became "the financial hit of the juvenile publishing industry in 1899," according to Prager. Popular demand brought the boys back for many more adventures in the "Old Glory" and the "Soldiers of Fortune" series, and Stratemeyer further exploited the market for war stories with books featuring boys in the French and Indian War, the American Revolution, and the Mexican War. Many were well-received by critics, including parents, teachers, and churchmen as well as the readers themselves.

"These early books are important in two respects," declares Taylor. "They are crammed with well-researched facts and they make use of some literary techniques that mark virtually all of the author's later works." Stratemeyer directly addressed the reader in the introductions of his books, and his voice often interrupted the text. Frequently the story's action paused near the beginning of the volume to allow the narrator to recap the hero's previous adventures, and each account included an advertisement for the next volume in the series. Stratemeyer's prose was also rather stilted, reflecting his early association with Alger and Adams at Street & Smith, and he often relied on stereotyped views of various ethnic groups. "Except for Alger himself," declares Russel B. Nye in *The Unembarrassed Muse: The Popular Arts in America*, "no writer of juvenile fiction had a more unerring sense of the hackneyed."

Whatever the drawbacks of Stratemeyer's prose, his work became highly popular with young readers. Late in 1899, realizing that the attraction of contemporary war stories was likely to be temporary, he introduced the "Rover Boys Series for Young Americans" under the pen name Arthur M. Winfield. These books chronicled the adventures of three brothers—Dick, Tom, and Sam Rover—at Putnam Hall, a military boarding school, and later at midwestern Brill College, and they captured the imaginations of turn-of-the-century adolescent Americans in a way no other series heroes had before. "Between the publication of the first three volumes late in 1899 and the publication of the last volume in 1926," reports Taylor, "sales ran somewhere between five and six millions of copies." The brothers, described as "lively, wide-awake American boys" by the author, were supported by a memorable cast of characters, including Dora Stanhope, and Grace and Nellie Laning, their sweethearts, their chums John "Songbird" Powell and William Philander Tubbs, and assorted bullies and other villains: Josiah Crabtree, Tad Sobber, Jesse Pelter, and Dan Baxter, among others.

Stratemeyer originally conceived the "Rover Boys" series in the vein of *Tom Brown's Schooldays*, depicting youthful adventures, games and hijinks, but he also featured elements of melodrama and detective fiction, claims Carol Billman in *The Secret of the Stratemeyer Syndicate: Nancy Drew, the Hardy Boys, and the Million Dollar Fiction Factory*. Many volumes featured searches for missing people or buried treasure; *The Rover Boys in the Jungle*, for instance, took our heroes to Africa in search of their father. The Rovers and their friends "faced unprecedented dangers," explains the *Literary Digest*. "As the fun-loving Tom expressed it, on the historic occasion when an avalanche was rolling down on them from above, their cabin was in flames, Dan Baxter and his cronies were taking pot-shots at them from across the canyon, Dora Stanhope was clinging to the edge of the cliff, and the battle-ship *Oregon* was still ten miles away, 'Well, we're in a pretty pickle, and no mistake!'" "But always, to our immense surprise," the *Digest* concludes, "they would emerge unscathed, restore the missing fortune, and be rewarded by three rousing cheers and—a sop to the feminine trade—an arch look from Dora and Nellie and Grace; while the discomfited bullies, outwitted again, began plotting at once their future conspiracies, to be related in the next volume of the Rover Boys Series for Young Americans."

Eventually Stratemeyer permitted Dick, Tom and Sam to graduate and to start a business together, pooling their resources to form the Rover Company. They married their girls and settled down to raise families in adjoining houses on New York's Riverside Drive. Stratemeyer went on to chronicle their children's adventures in the "Second Rover Boys Series for Young Americans," which lasted for ten volumes. However, the younger Rovers never achieved the success their fathers had, explains Prager, writing in *Rascals at Large; or, The Clue in the Old Nostalgia*. "The generation that had loved the Rover Boys moved on to new things. Did the Crash wipe out the Rover Company? Did their Riverside Drive houses succumb to high taxes and urban blight? We never found out."

The Rover's success encouraged Stratemeyer to create other series. "Almost as soon as the first sales figures came in," reports Prager in *Saturday Review*, "he was designing a dozen similar series and concocting pseudonyms. He took his basic Rover figures, changed the names, associated them with some kind of speedy vehicle or popular scientific device, and slipped them into his formula." Stratemeyer soon found that his ideas outstripped his writing capacity and began to hire independent writers to fill in his outlines. Working with "Uncle Wiggily" creator Howard R. Garis under the pseudonym Clarence Young, Stratemeyer created the "Motor Boys" series; as Allen Chapman, he devised the adventures of the "Radio Boys" and "Ralph of the Railroad" series; as Victor Appleton, the "Motion Picture Boys" and "Tom Swift" series; as Franklin W. Dixon, the "Hardy Boys" and "Ted Scott Flying Stories" series, and many others. For sports enthusiasts he produced the "Baseball Joe" books under the pseudonym Lester Chadwick, and as Roy Rockwood he created Bomba the Jungle Boy, a teen-aged Tarzan. For girls and younger readers, he introduced the "Moving Picture Girls," the "Outdoor Girls," and the "Bobbsey Twins" series, using the pseudonym Laura Lee Hope; as Alice B. Emerson he developed the "Betty Gordon" and "Ruth Fielding" series, and as Carolyn Keene he invented Nancy Drew.

Stratemeyer engaged in innovative publishing strategies in order to get his many series published. "Using the kind of reasoning that would later make Henry Ford a billionaire," Prager declares in *Saturday Review*, "he talked his publishers into slashing the prices of the 'Rover' and 'Motor Boys' series from a dollar to 50 cents, relying on volume sales to make up and exceed lost profit. The plan was a smashing success. At half a dollar, kids could buy the books without going through the parent-middleman." By around 1906 demand had increased so much that Stratemeyer had to systematize his production by setting up the Stratemeyer Syndicate, "a kind of literary assembly line," Prager calls it, resembling in some ways the syndicate devised by the French writer Alexandre Dumas half a century before. Stratemeyer created plot outlines for series titles and sent to contract writers, who wrote the actual stories. They then returned the manuscript to Stratemeyer, who edited it and had it put on electrotype plates, which were then leased to the publishers. Stratemeyer retained all rights to the stories, paying his contract writers an average of one hundred dollars a book. "The whole process," Prager explains, "took a month to six weeks."

Stratemeyer's success and his factory-like writing process made enemies among those who considered themselves guardians of the juvenile mind. A few years after the Boy Scouts of America were established Franklin K. Mathiews, the Chief Scout Librarian, and James E. West, the Chief Scout Executive, contacted Grosset & Dunlap, one of Stratemeyer's chief publishers, and proposed a mass reprinting of a list of Boy Scouts Approved Books in inexpensive editions. Somewhat later, Mathiews published an article in *Outlook* magazine savagely denouncing juvenile fiction that did not meet his standards, although he never mentioned the Stratemeyer Syndicate by name. "Mathiews began by noting that in most surveys of children's reading, inferior books, (defined as those not found in libraries), were widely read and probably as influential as the better books," reports Ken Donelson in *Children's Literature*. Mathiews suggested that the poor quality of Syndicate-type fiction, revealed in the lack of moral purpose and uncontrolled excitement of the stories, could cripple a young reader's imagination "as though by some material explosion they had lost a hand or foot." "I wish I could label each one of these books: 'Explosives! Guaranteed to Blow Your Boy's Brains Out,'" he declared. The Chief Scout Librarian backed up his accusations with statements from other librarians testifying to the poor quality of series books and encouraged other authors, especially Percy Keese Fitzhugh, to write series fiction, but Stratemeyer's sales remained high. He had, however, learned something from the encounter: future Syndicate series "toned down danger, thrills, and violence in favor of well-researched instruction," says Prager in *Saturday Review*.

One measure of Stratemeyer's success lies in the fact that now, more than half a century after his death, new volumes are added yearly to series he created. The "Bobbsey Twins," "Hardy Boys" and "Nancy Drew" books continue to captivate readers, and sales are as high as ever. Despite critics' misgivings, states Prager in *Rascals at Large,* the books "are well worth a reappraisal in the light of current taste, and like most items handcrafted in those days, they wear like iron and last for years." "Stratemeyer's legacy—respectable or not—is read on," declares Billman, "night after night, reader after reader, generation after generation."

Upon Stratemeyer's death in 1930, the Syndicate was administered by his daughters, Harriet Adams and Edna Squier. Adams remained in control of the Syndicate until her death in 1982. For more information on Stratemeyer, his Syndicate and its pseudonyms, see the entries in this volume for Harriet S. Adams, Howard R. Garis, and Andrew E. Svenson, and for the following pseudonyms: Victor Appleton, Lester Chadwick, Allen Chapman, Elmer A. Dawson, Franklin W. Dixon, Julia K. Duncan, Alice B. Emerson, James Cody Ferris, Graham B. Forbes, Laura Lee Hope, Francis K. Judd, Carolyn Keene, Margaret Penrose, Roy Rockwood, Helen Louise Thorndyke, Frank V. Webster, and Clarence Young.

BIOGRAPHICAL/CRITICAL SOURCES:

BOOKS

Billman, Carol, *The Secret of the Stratemeyer Syndicate: Nancy Drew, the Hardy Boys, and the Million Dollar Fiction Factory,* Ungar, 1986.
Dictionary of Literary Biography, Volume 42: *American Writers for Children before 1900,* Gale, 1985.
Dizer, John T., *Tom Swift & Company: "Boys' Books" by Stratemeyer and Others,* McFarland & Co., 1982.
Garis, Roger, *My Father Was Uncle Wiggily,* McGraw-Hill, 1966.
Johnson, Deidre, editor and compiler, *Stratemeyer Pseudonyms and Series Books: An Annotated Checklist of Stratemeyer and Stratemeyer Syndicate Publications,* Greenwood Press, 1982.
McFarlane, Leslie, *Ghost of the Hardy Boys,* Two Continents, 1976.

Nye, Russel B., *The Unembarrassed Muse: The Popular Arts in America,* Dial, 1970.
Prager, Arthur, *Rascals at Large; or, The Clue in the Old Nostalgia,* Doubleday, 1971.
Reynolds, Quentin, *The Fiction Factory; or, From Pulp Row to Quality Street,* Random House, 1955.

PERIODICALS

American Heritage, December, 1976.
Children's Literature, Volume 7, 1978.
Fortune, April, 1934.
Journal of Popular Culture, spring, 1974.
Literary Digest, April 21, 1928.
Midwest Quarterly, October, 1972.
Outlook, November 18, 1914.
Saturday Review, January 25, 1969, July 10, 1975.

OBITUARIES:

PERIODICALS

New York Times, May 13, 1930.*

—*Sketch by Kenneth R. Shepherd*

*   *   *

STRAYER, E. Ward
See STRATEMEYER, Edward L.

*   *   *

STREET, Pamela 1921-

PERSONAL: Born March 3, 1921, in Wilton, Wiltshire, England; daughter of Arthur George (an author, broadcaster, and farmer) and Vera Florence (Foyle) Street; married David Francis Hamilton McCormick, July 3, 1945 (divorced, 1971); children: Miranda. *Education:* Godolphin School, England. *Politics:* Conservative. *Religion:* Church of England.

ADDRESSES: Home—47 South St., Flat 5, London W1Y 5PD, England.

CAREER: Writer. Secretary and researcher for Sir Arthur Bryant (a historian), beginning 1971. *Wartime service:* British Auxiliary Territorial Service, 1942-45; became second lieutenant.

WRITINGS:

My Father, A. G. Street, R. Hale, 1969, 2nd edition, 1984.
Portrait of Wiltshire, International Publications Service, 1971, 3rd revised edition published as *Illustrated Portrait of Wiltshire,* R. Hale, 1986.
Arthur Bryant: Portrait of a Historian, Collins, 1979.

NOVELS

Light of Evening, R. Hale, 1981.
Morning Glory, R. Hale, 1982.
The Stepsisters, R. Hale, 1982.
The Mill-Race (also see below), R. Hale, 1983.
The Way of the River (also see below), R. Hale, 1984.
Many Waters (also see below), R. Hale, 1985.
Unto the Fourth Generation (also see below), R. Hale, 1985.
Portrait of Rose, R. Hale, 1986.
Personal Relations, R. Hale, 1987.
The Mill-Race Quartet (contains *The Mill-Race, The Way of the River, Many Waters,* and *Unto the Fourth Generation*), Pan Books, 1988.
The Timeless Moment, R. Hale, 1988.

The Beneficiaries, R. Hale, 1989.

OTHER

Also author of the radio short story "Mr. Brown and Prudence" for British Broadcasting Corp. (BBC-Radio), 1988.

BIOGRAPHICAL/CRITICAL SOURCES:

PERIODICALS

Times Literary Supplement, January 18, 1980.

*　　*　　*

STRENG, Frederick J(ohn)   1933-

PERSONAL: Born September 30, 1933, in Seguin, Tex.; son of Adolph Carl (a teacher) and Elizabeth (Hein) Streng; married Ruth Helen Billnitzer, June 6, 1955 (divorced); married Bette Sue Blossom, May 23, 1981; children: (first marriage) Elizabeth Ann, Mark Andrew. *Education:* Texas Lutheran College, B.A., 1955; Southern Methodist University, M.A., 1956; additional study at Wartburg Theological Seminary, 1956-57; University of Chicago, B.D., 1960, Ph.D., 1963; additional study at Benares Hindu University, 1961-62. *Politics:* Independent. *Religion:* "Liberal Christian."

ADDRESSES: Office—Department of Religious Studies, Southern Methodist University, Dallas, Tex. 75275.

CAREER: University of Dubuque, Dubuque, Iowa, instructor in English, 1957; University of Southern California, Los Angeles, assistant professor of history of religions, 1963-66; Southern Methodist University, Dallas, Tex., associate professor of history of religions, 1966-73, professor of religious studies, 1974—. Carnegie Fellow in the Civilization of India, University of Chicago, 1962-63; visiting associate professor, University of California, Berkeley, spring, 1973; visiting professor, Harvard University Divinity School, fall, 1973; visiting professor of humanities, Gakuin University, 1986-87.

MEMBER: American Academy of Religion, American Society for the Study of Religion, Society for Asian and Comparative Philosophy (president, 1970-72), Society for Buddhist-Christian Studies.

AWARDS, HONORS: Fulbright grant to India, 1961-62.

WRITINGS:

Emptiness: A Study in Religious Meaning, Abingdon, 1967.
Understanding Religious Life, Dickenson, 1969.
(Editor with others) *Ways of Being Religious: Readings for a New Approach to Religion*, Prentice-Hall, 1973.
(Editor with Paul Ingram) *Buddhist-Christian Dialogue: Possibilities for Mutual Transformation*, University of Hawaii Press, 1986.

CONTRIBUTOR

G. M. C. Sprung, editor, *The Problem of Two Truths in Buddhism and Vedanta*, Reidel, 1973.
S. K. Lee and K. Y. Rhi, editors, *Buddhism and the Modern World*, Dongguk University, 1977.
S. T. Katz, editor, *Mysticism and Philosophical Analysis*, Society for Promoting Christian Knowledge, 1978.
P. Slater and D. Wieber, editors, *Traditions in Contact and Change*, Wilfred Laurier University Press, 1983.
M. Eliade, editor, *Encyclopedia of Religion*, Macmillan, 1987.
J. G. Larson and E. Deutsch, editors, *Interpreting across Boundaries: New Essays in Comparative Philosophy*, Princeton University Press, 1988.

M. A. Jazayery and W. Winter, editors, *Languages and Cultures*, Mouton, 1988.

OTHER

Contributor to professional journals.

WORK IN PROGRESS: Development of a method for studying religion combining elements of "structuralism" and phenomenology; research in the significance of the history of religions for Christian theology.

AVOCATIONAL INTERESTS: Music, the plastic arts, creative literature, photography.

*　　*　　*

SVENSON, Andrew E(dward)   1910-1975
(Alan Stone, Jerry West)

PERSONAL: Born May 8, 1910, in Belleville, N.J.; died August 21, 1975, in Livingston, N.J.; son of Andrew and Laura (Soleau) Svenson; married Marian Stewart, August 31, 1932; children: Laura S. Schnell, Andrew E., Jr., Jane S. Kossman, Eric, Eileen C. de Zayes, Ingrid S. Herdman. *Education:* Attended Carnegie Institute of Technology; University of Pittsburgh, B.A., 1932; Montclair State Teachers College (now Montclair State College), teaching certificate, 1933. *Religion:* Episcopalian.

CAREER: Newark Star-Eagle, Newark, N.J., feature writer, 1933-34; *Newark Evening News*, Newark, reporter, writer, and editor, 1934-48; Stratemeyer Syndicate, Maplewood, N.J., and East Orange, N.J., writer and editor, 1948-75, partner, 1961-75. Instructor in writing, Rutgers University, 1945-54, and Upsala College, 1948-54.

MEMBER: American Association of University Professors, American Professors of Journalism, Mystery Writers of America, Western Writers Association, Sigma Nu, Phi Delta Epsilon, Players Club and Dutch Treat Club (both New York), Rotary Club International (president of East Orange, N.J., chapter, 1970-71), Masonic Order (Bloomfield, N.J., Lodge No. 40), Shriners.

WRITINGS:

UNDER PSEUDONYM ALAN STONE; "TOLLIVER ADVENTURE" SERIES

The Tollivers and the Mystery of the Lost Pony, World Publishing, 1967.
. . . and the Mystery of Pirate Island, World Publishing, 1967.
. . . and the Mystery of the Old Jalopy, World Publishing, 1967.

UNDER PSEUDONYM JERRY WEST; "HAPPY HOLLISTERS" SERIES

The Happy Hollisters, Doubleday, 1953, reprinted, Grosset & Dunlap, 1979.
. . . on a River Trip, Doubleday, 1953, reprinted, Grosset & Dunlap, 1979.
. . . at Sea Gull Beach, Doubleday, 1953, reprinted, Grosset & Dunlap, 1979.
. . . and the Indian Treasure, Doubleday, 1953.
. . . at Mystery Mountain, Doubleday, 1954.
. . . at Snowflake Camp, Doubleday, 1954.
. . . and the Trading Post Mystery, Doubleday, 1954.
. . . at Circus Island, Doubleday, 1955.
. . . and the Secret Fort, Doubleday, 1955.
. . . and the Merry-Go-Round Mystery, Doubleday, 1955.

. . . at Pony Hill Farm, Doubleday, 1956.
. . . and the Old Clipper Ship, Doubleday, 1956.
. . . at Lizard Cove, Doubleday, 1957.
. . . and the Scarecrow Mystery, Doubleday, 1957.
. . . and the Mystery of the Totem Faces, Doubleday, 1958.
. . . and the Ice Carnival Mystery, Doubleday, 1958, reprinted, Grosset & Dunlap, 1979.
. . . and the Mystery in Skyscraper City, Doubleday, 1959.
. . . and the Mystery of the Little Mermaid, Doubleday, 1960.
. . . and the Mystery at Missile Town, Doubleday, 1961.
. . . and the Cowboy Mystery, Doubleday, 1961.
. . . and the Haunted House Mystery, Doubleday, 1962.
. . . and the Secret of the Lucky Coins, Doubleday, 1962.
. . . and the Castle Rock Mystery, Doubleday, 1963.
. . . and the Cuckoo Clock Mystery, Doubleday, 1963.
. . . and the Swiss Echo Mystery, Doubleday, 1963.
. . . and the Sea Turtle Mystery, Doubleday, 1964.
. . . and the Punch and Judy Mystery, Doubleday, 1964.
. . . and the Whistle-Pig Mystery, Doubleday, 1964.
. . . and the Ghost Horse Mystery, Doubleday, 1965.
. . . and the Mystery of the Golden Witch, Doubleday, 1966.
. . . and the Mystery of the Mexican Idol, Doubleday, 1967.
. . . and the Monster Mystery, Doubleday, 1969.
. . . and the Mystery of the Midnight Trolls, Doubleday, 1970.

OTHER

Also involved in creating, plotting, and editing other Stratemeyer Syndicate series, including the "Tom Swift Jr." series (as Victor Appleton II), the "Mel Martin Baseball Stories" series (as John R. Cooper), the "Hardy Boys" series (as Franklin W. Dixon), the "Bobbsey Twins" series (as Laura Lee Hope), the "Christopher Cool—TEEN Agent" series (as Jack Lancer), the "Bret King" series (as Dan Scott), the "Linda Craig" series (as Ann Sheldon), the "Wynn and Lonny Racing Series" (as Eric Speed), and the "Honey Bunch and Norman" series (as Helen Louise Thorndyke).

Andrew E. Svenson's manuscripts and related works are held at the Western History Research Center of the University of Wyoming, Laramie, Colo., and in the de Grummond Collection of the William David McCain Graduate Library, University of Southern Mississippi, Hattiesburg, Miss.

SIDELIGHTS: "Andy Svenson loves getting people into trouble," declared James V. O'Connor in the September 1973 issue of *Rotary International Magazine,* "but only for the fun of getting them out of it." For many years the former Newark newspaperman and college English professor entertained young readers with the adventures of the "Hardy Boys," "Bobbsey Twins," and "Happy Hollisters." His widow, Marian Svenson, told *CA* that he started writing for the Stratemeyer Syndicate in 1948 at the suggestion of Howard R. Garis of "Uncle Wiggily" fame, himself a long-time Syndicate staffer. Svenson first worked on volumes in the "Mel Martin Baseball Stories" series under the pseudonym John R. Cooper, moved on to write and edit volumes in the "Hardy Boys" and "Bobbsey Twins" series, and eventually rose to partnership in the Syndicate, designing, writing, and editing his own series books.

Svenson often articulated the Syndicate's philosophy behind its stories. "All of the books produced by the Stratemeyer Syndicate are packed with action, excitement, danger, and suspense, with the forces of good overcoming evil," explained O'Connor. "The trick in writing children's books is to set up danger, mystery and excitement on page one," Svenson told the *Wall Street Journal's* Roger B. May. "Force the kid to turn the page. I've written page one as many as 20 times.

Then in the middle of each chapter there's a dramatic point of excitement, and at chapter's end, a cliffhanger." He elaborated on the Syndicate's techniques to the *New Yorker,* explaining that "whether we do yarns about *Ubermenschen* or pig-tailed Philo Vances, we subscribe to the Stratemeyer formula. . . . A low death rate but plenty of plot. Verbs of action, and polka-dotted with exclamation points and provocative questions. No use of guns by the hero. No smooching. The main character introduced on page one and a slam-bang mystery or peril set up." "It's an age-old formula of action and of just punishment for the 'bad guys,'" O'Connor continued, "but Andy knows this pleases young readers. He considers himself an entertainer of children, 'filling a need in their lives when they are learning that books can be fun and can open up the vistas of their imagination.'"

Of the series that Svenson created and wrote himself, the most successful was the "Happy Hollisters." This series chronicles the adventures of the five Hollister children: Pete (age twelve), Pam (age ten), Ricky (age seven), Holly (age six), and Sue (age four). The stories are very family-oriented; the children often solve their mysteries on family vacations, and occasionally John and Elaine Hollister, their parents, play a part in the solution. This may explain part of the attraction the series has for readers. Carol Billman points out in *The Secret of the Stratemeyer Syndicate: Nancy Drew, the Hardy Boys, and the Million Dollar Fiction Factory* that the Hollisters "represent a kind of dream family for many readers of the series, who project themselves as members of this big, active, and harmonious group." O'Connor suggests that Svenson based many of the Hollisters's escapades on his own family's experience, and Marian Svenson told *CA* that "plots and ideas for story material were often gleaned from newspaper clippings, conversations with all kinds of persons from every walk of life and his own personal observations."

Svenson "gave many talks and lectures before various groups" in connection with his role as a Syndicate partner, Marian Svenson told *CA,* "capturing the rapt attention of both adults and children alike. He particularly enjoyed his encounter with children who often inspired him in his work. . . . He was a man of keen observation," she concluded, "with bright, sparkling humor, and at the same time, kind and sympathetic to everyone." Svenson's "Happy Hollisters" books were translated, published and sold in France, Spain, Germany, Norway, Japan and Catalonia.

Svenson also created and wrote the "Tolliver Adventure" series, which featured a black family much like the Hollisters, but it was not as successful. For more information see the sketches in this volume for Harriet S. Adams, Howard R. Garis, James Duncan Lawrence, and Edward L. Stratemeyer, and for the following pseudonyms: Victor Appleton II, John R. Cooper, Franklin W. Dixon, Laura Lee Hope, Jack Lancer, Dan Scott, Ann Sheldon, Eric Speed, and Helen Louise Thorndyke.

AVOCATIONAL INTERESTS: Photography, travel, gardening, hiking.

BIOGRAPHICAL/CRITICAL SOURCES:

BOOKS

Billman, Carol, *The Secret of the Stratemeyer Syndicate: Nancy Drew, the Hardy Boys, and the Million Dollar Fiction Factory,* Ungar, 1986.

PERIODICALS

Journal of Popular Culture, spring, 1974.
New Yorker, March 20, 1954.
Rotary International Magazine, September, 1973.
Wall Street Journal, January 15, 1975.
Yellowback Library, January/February, 1986.

OBITUARIES:

PERIODICALS

AB Bookman's Weekly, October 13, 1975.
New York Times, August 23, 1975.
Publishers Weekly, September 29, 1975.

[Sketch reviewed by wife, Marian Svenson]

*　　　*　　　*

SZIRTES, George   1948-

PERSONAL: Born November 29, 1948, in Budapest, Hungary; son of Laszlo (an engineer) and Magdalena (a photographer; maiden name, Nussbacher) Szirtes; married Clarissa Upchurch (an artist), July 11, 1970; children: Thomas Andrew, Helen Magdalena. *Education:* Leeds College of Art, B.A., 1972; University of London, A.T.C., 1973.

ADDRESSES: Home—20 Old Pard Rd., Hitchin, Hertfordshire SG5 2JR, England.

CAREER: Writer. Instructor in writing at schools and colleges in England, 1975-81; St. Christopher School, Letchworth, England, director of art, 1981—. Etchings exhibited at Victoria and Albert Museum. Member of literature panel of Eastern Arts Association, 1981—.

MEMBER: International PEN, Royal Society of Literature (fellow).

AWARDS, HONORS: Co-recipient of Geoffrey Faber Memorial Prize from Faber & Faber Ltd. Arts Council, 1980, for *The Slant Door;* Arts Council fellowship, 1984; Poetry Book Society choices and recommendations, 1984, 1986, 1988; British Council fellowship, 1985; Cholmondely Prize for poetry, awarded by the Marchioness of Cholmondely, 1987.

WRITINGS:

The Iron Clouds (poems), Dodman Press, 1975.
An Illustrated Alphabet (poems), Mandeville Press, 1978.
(With Alistair Elliott, Craig Raine, Alan Hollinghurst, Cal Clothier, and Anne Cluysenaar) *Poetry Introduction 4,* Faber, 1978.
The Slant Door (poems), Secker & Warburg, 1979.
Homage to Cheval, Priapus Press, 1981.
November and May (poems), Secker & Warburg, 1981.
The Kissing Place (poems), Starwheel Press, 1982.
Short Wave (poems), Secker & Warburg, 1984.
The Photographer in Winter (poems), Secker & Warburg, 1986.
Metro (poems), Oxford University Press, 1988.
Selected Poems (English translation of Hungarian poems), Europa, 1988.
(Translator from the Hungarian) Imre Madach, *The Tragedy of Man,* Corvina, 1988.

CONTRIBUTOR

Writers of East Anglia, edited by Angus Wilson, Secker & Warburg, 1977.
New Poems, 1977/78, edited by Gavin Ewart, Hutchinson, 1978.

Poems for Shakespeare, edited by Patricia Beer, Shakespeare Trust, 1979.
Poetry Book Society Anthology, edited by Peter Porter, Poetry Book Society, 1980.
The Music of What Happens, edited by Derwent May, BBC Publications, 1981.
Between Comets, edited by William Scammell, Taxus, 1984.
British Poetry since 1945, edited by Edward Lucie-Smith, Penguin, 1985.
Slipping Glimpses, edited by Carol Rumens, Poetry Book Society, 1985.
The Words Book, 1985-86, edited by Philip Vine, Words Publications, 1986.
With a Poet's Eye, edited by Pat Adams, Tate Gallery, 1986.

Also contributor to *New Poetry,* Volumes 1-5, Arts Council/Hutchinson.

OTHER

Contributor to periodicals, including *Times Literary Supplement, New Statesman, Listener, Encounter,* and *Quarto.*

WORK IN PROGRESS: Several translations from the Hungarian; an opera libretto based on D. H. Lawrence's short story, "The Rocking Horse Winner."

SIDELIGHTS: From his earlier surrealistic and painterly style of poetry to his growing interest in themes dealing with his native Hungary, George Szirtes has gained critical recognition as an important poet in the literary world. "People find Szirtes's poetry attractive because they recognise in it a basic understanding of human feeling and a proverbial sense of language," comments *Observer* contributor Peter Porter. This appeal may in part be due to the influence of Szirtes's background and experience upon his poetry. "I arrived in England as a refugee in 1956," he told *CA.* "My early education was science based, but I began writing and painting at school. I studied fine art and travelled in Europe on a scholarship, the longest stay being in Italy. I was exhibiting pictures at this time, but probably the most important influence on my writing was the poet Martin Bell, who was one of my tutors. After marriage to the artist Clarissa Upchurch, and a brief but intense religious period during which I was baptised, we settled at my present address, and I taught full- and part-time in various institutions." Armed with these diverse credentials, Szirtes has slowly made a place for himself among English poets.

The poet's work first appeared in magazines in 1973, the influence of his training as a painter making his writing saliently visual. "Szirtes chooses words like pigments," Peter Porter writes, "as though they could be modified in their mixing." However, some critics like Alan Brownjohn of *Encounter* feel that Szirtes's work is at its best when he gets away "from some habits of using the painter's eye for intriguing detail to get poems off the ground and employing a rather garish, surrealistic fantasy." *The Slant Door,* Szirtes's first volume of poetry, contains much of this surrealism, but it also marks the point where the poet "moves very steadily towards a greater confidence, clarity, and originality of outlook," as Alan Brownjohn further remarks. Overall, the critical reaction to *The Slant Door* has been positive. William Palmer of *Poetry Review* sums up the author's effort as being "one of the best first books of poetry in the past few years, that is if we judge by successful poems and not by promise or critically adduced intentions."

November and May, Szirtes's second collection of poems, was, for him, a transitional book. He told *CA:* "If I had to summarize my aims at the time [I wrote *November and May*], I would [say] that I felt my task was to preserve as fresh whatever was delightful and miraculous.'' A number of critics have found the poems in the book grimmer and more morose than his earlier work. ''Szirtes is more interested in evoking the sadness involved in attempting to explain than in offering explanations,'' says *Times Literary Supplement* contributor Tim Dooley. His focus turns from the clearer, starker style for which *The Slant Door* was lauded to the '''mundane apparition,' the unattended moment of mystery or menace; to look out, too, for the words and rhythms that will evoke this malady of the quotidian with oblique forcefulness, deadened, remote decorum of manner,'' as Alan Jenkins of *Encounter* describes it. This predilection for expressing disturbing ideas while maintaining a somber tone has been compared to that of Irish poet Louis MacNeice, while Szirtes's love for the tangible has caused him to be compared to Geoffrey Grigson, the British poet. By such a contrast of the philosophical with the visually real, *November and May* and *The Slant Door* complement each other well.

With Szirtes's two visits to his native Hungary in 1984 and 1985, the poet rediscovered a personal subject to write about. *Short Wave,* a book that contains more than Szirtes's usual number of love poems, was his first to begin to ''explore the idea and feel of Europe,'' explained the poet to *CA*. Peter Porter writes about this work: ''*Short Wave* is a book of considerable accomplishment. Szirtes's voice is now completely his own.'' Though some critics like Andrew Motion of *Poetry Review* feel that this book creates a ''sense of blandness when . . . considered as a whole,'' others like John Lucas of *New Statesman* believe that ''*Short Wave* is a truly original volume of poems. It is witty but in no superficial sense.'' However, where *Short Wave* is the first poetry collection in which the author expresses an original voice by exploring his homeland, his next two books do this in even greater depth.

The Photographer in Winter deals largely with the Hungary of the 1940s and 1950s. It ''offers a powerful epigraph and model of ancestral allusion,'' explains *Books and Bookmen* contributor Barbara Hardy. This collection covers almost ev-

erything that Szirtes associates with the Hungary of the past, from the title poem, which is about the poet's mother, to descriptions of Hungarian architecture and satires on politics and propaganda. Simon Rae comments in *London Magazine*: ''Szirtes tends to see the past frozen into stone, petrified into a photographic image that cannot develop or be changed, but only assimilated—by art—into some sort of pattern.''

When Szirtes writes about Hungary, he does it from the point of view of someone looking back in time. *Metro* deals with themes of the past similar to those in *The Photographer in Winter*, the central element of the work investigating, as Szirtes explained to *CA*, ''the life of my mother before I was born (the time she spent in the Budapest ghetto and in the concentration camp) and relates this to the unhappy devotion she bore for her brother who failed to respond to her affection.'' Such themes, though personal, are written from a standpoint ''unsettlingly poised between commitment and detachment,'' observes Lachlan Mackinnon of *Times Literary Supplement* about *The Photographer in Winter*. Perhaps this is due to Szirtes's largely English viewpoint which prevents him from being in complete contact with his Hungarian past. Mackinnon continues by saying that *The Photographer in Winter* ''contains an implicit criticism of much English poetry for its inwardness, its political isolation.'' But other critics such as Barbara Hardy do not see anything negative about Szirtes's dual identity. ''He belongs with [his compatriots],'' says Hardy, ''but he lends a strong voice to English poetry.''

BIOGRAPHICAL/CRITICAL SOURCES:

PERIODICALS

Books and Bookmen, April, 1986.
Encounter, November, 1979, August, 1982.
London Magazine, August-September, 1986.
New Statesman, January 13, 1984.
Observer, August 19, 1979.
Poetry Review, December, 1980, April, 1984.
Times Literary Supplement, July 2, 1982, November 28, 1986.

—Sketch by Kevin S. Hile

T

TAYLOR, Andrew (McDonald) 1940-

PERSONAL: Born March 19, 1940, in Warrnambool, Victoria, Australia; son of John McDonald (a lawyer) and Margaret (Fraser) Taylor; married Jill Burriss, January 31, 1965 (divorced); married Beate Josephi, 1980; children: Travis, Sarah. *Education:* University of Melbourne, B.A, (with first class honors), 1961, M.A. (with first class honors), 1970; State University of New York at Buffalo, additional graduate study, 1970-71. *Politics:* "Unattached Left."

ADDRESSES: Home—334 Halifax St., Adelaide, South Australia 5000, Australia. *Office*—Department of English, University of Adelaide, Adelaide, South Australia 5001, Australia.

CAREER: British Institute, Rome, Italy, English teacher, 1964-65; University of Melbourne, Melbourne, Australia, Lockie Fellow in Australia Literature, 1965-69; University of Adelaide, Adelaide, Australia, lecturer, 1971-74, senior lecturer in English, 1974—. Member of the literature board of the Australian Council, 1978-81. Helped to organize Adelaide's "Friendly Street" poetry readings; chairman of Writers' Week committee of Adelaide Festival of Arts, 1980 and 1982.

MEMBER: Australian and New Zealand American Studies Association, Association for the Study of Australian Literature, Australian Society of Authors.

AWARDS, HONORS: American Council of Learned Societies fellowship, 1970-71; regional winner of Commonwealth Poetry Prize, 1986, for *Travelling.*

WRITINGS:

(Editor) *Byron, Selected Poems,* Cassell, 1971.
The Cool Change (poems), University of Queensland Press, 1971.
Ice Fishing (poems), University of Queensland Press, 1973.
The Invention of Fire (poems), University of Queensland Press, 1976.
The Cat's Chin and Ears: A Bestiary, Angus & Robertson, 1976.
Parabolas: Prose Poems, Makar Press, 1976.
The Crystal Absences, the Trout (poems), Island Press, 1978.
(Editor) *Number Two Friendly Street,* Adelaide University Union Press, 1978.
Selected Poems, University of Queensland Press, 1982.

Bernie the Midnight Owl (juvenile), Penguin Books, 1984.
(Translator from German with wife, Beate Josephi) *Miracles of Disbelief,* Leros Press, 1985.
(Editor) *Unsettled Areas* (fiction), Wakefield Press, 1986.
Travelling (poems), University of Queensland Press, 1986.
Reading Australian Poetry (essays), University of Queensland Press, 1987.
Selected Poems: 1960-1985, University of Queensland Press, 1988.

Also author of opera libretti, "The Letters of Amalie Dietrich" and "Borossa," both first produced in 1988. Author of radio scripts on poetry for Australian Broadcasting Commission. Contributor to magazines and newspapers.

WORK IN PROGRESS: A book of poems; stories; libretti and essays.

SIDELIGHTS: Andrew Taylor writes: "Several years living in Europe and several in the U.S.A., Canada, and Mexico have counteracted Australia's isolation (my involvement with Adelaide Festival of Arts is another attempt at this). But I also like watching plants grow slowly and resolutely in one place. . . ."

AVOCATIONAL INTERESTS: Travel, gardening, animals, children.

BIOGRAPHICAL/CRITICAL SOURCES:

PERIODICALS

Parnassus: Poetry in Review, Vol. 11, no. 2.
World Literature Today, winter, 1983.

*   *   *

TAYLOR, Charles 1931-

PERSONAL: Born November 5, 1931, in Montreal, Quebec, Canada; son of Walter Margrave (an industrialist) and Simone (a fashion designer; maiden name, Beaubien) Taylor; married Alba Romer (an artist), April 2, 1956; children: Karen, Miriam, Wanda, Gabriella, Gretta. *Education:* McGill University, B.A., 1952; Oxford University, B.A., 1955, M.A., 1960, D.Phil., 1961. *Politics:* New Democratic Party (social democrat). *Religion:* Roman Catholic.

ADDRESSES: Home—344 Metcalfe Ave., Montreal, Quebec, Canada H3Z 2T3. *Office*—Department of Philosophy, McGill University, Box 6070, Station A, Montreal, Quebec, Canada H3C 3G1.

CAREER: McGill University, Montreal, Quebec, 1961—, began as assistant professor, currently professor of philosophy and political science. Professor of philosophy, University of Montreal, 1962-71. Chichele Professor of Social and Political Theory, Oxford University, 1976—. Vice-president of New Democratic Party of Canada, 1965-73.

MEMBER: Canadian Philosophical Association, Canadian Political Science Association, Royal Society of Canada, Ligue des Droits de l'Homme.

WRITINGS:

The Explanation of Behaviour, Humanities, 1964.
Pattern of Politics, McClelland & Stewart, 1970.
Hegel, Cambridge University Press, 1975.
Erklaerung und Interpretation in den Wissenschaften vom Menschen, Suhrkamp, 1975.
Hegel and Modern Society, Cambridge University Press, 1979.
Human Agency and Language, Cambridge University Press, 1985.
Philosophy and the Human Sciences, Cambridge University Press, 1985.
Negotive Freiheit, Suhrkamp, 1988.

Contributor of articles to political and philosophical journals. Founder and former editor, *New Left Review.*

WORK IN PROGRESS: "Working on philosophy of language, nature of subjectivity, social philosophy, and the problem of growth."

SIDELIGHTS: Charles Taylor wrote *CA:* "I am interested in philosophical anthropology, the theory of human nature; I am dissatisfied with widespread mechanistic accounts, more drawn to views defended in other philosophical traditions, e.g., Hegel, Humboldt, Heidegger; but believe these must be reformulated. No one philosophical school has the resources for this reformulation alone.

"I am very interested in French and German, as well as Anglo-Saxon philosophy. Being from Montreal, I grew up bi-lingual; and have since also learned German, Spanish, some Italian and Polish, and of course, Latin and Greek."

BIOGRAPHICAL/CRITICAL SOURCES:

PERIODICALS

Globe and Mail (Toronto), May 16, 1987.

*   *   *

THAYER, H(orace) S(tandish) 1923-

PERSONAL: Born May 6, 1923, in New York, N.Y.; son of Vivian Trow (an educator and author) and Florence (Adams) Thayer; married Elizabeth B. Hewitt, February 28, 1958; children: Hewitt Standish, Alexandrea Adams, Jonathan Trow. *Education:* Bard College, B.A., 1945; Columbia University, M.A., 1947, Ph.D., 1949.

ADDRESSES: Home—Oak Tree Rd., Palisades, N.Y. 10964. *Office*—Department of Philosophy, City College of the City University of New York, Convent Ave. and 138th St., New York, N.Y. 10031.

CAREER: Bard College, Annandale-on-Hudson, N.Y., instructor in philosophy, 1947-49; Columbia University, New York City, instructor, 1949-54, assistant professor of philosophy, 1954-60, concurrently assistant professor at Barnard College, 1954-59; City College of the City University of New York, New York City, assistant professor, 1961-65, associate professor, 1965-68, professor of philosophy, 1968—, chairman of the department, 1965-68. Visiting professor at New York State School of Psychiatry, 1959-65. Member of the Institute for Advanced Study, Princeton, N.J., 1974-75, 1982-83. Member of advisory committee, American Council of Learned Societies, 1973—; member of board of advisors, Cousteau Society, 1975—.

MEMBER: American Philosophical Association, Association for Symbolic Logic, Mind Association, Century Association (New York).

AWARDS, HONORS: Humanities Research Council Award, Columbia University, 1961; Guggenheim fellowship, 1970; National Endowment for the Humanities fellowships, 1974-75, 1982-83.

WRITINGS:

The Logic of Pragmatism: An Examination of John Dewey's Logic, Humanities, 1952.
(Editor) *Newton's Philosophy of Nature,* Hafner, 1953.
Meaning and Action: A Critical History of Pragmatism, Bobbs-Merrill, 1968, abridged edition published as *Meaning and Action: A Study of American Pragmatism,* 1972, 2nd edition of original title, Hackett, 1981.
(Editor and author of introduction and commentary) *Pragmatism: The Classic Writings,* New American Library, 1970.
(Author of introduction) Jo Ann Boydston, editor, *The Middle Works of John Dewey, 1899-1924,* Volume 7: *1912-1914,* Southern Illinois University Press, 1979.
(Editor with Irving L. Horowitz) *Eithics, Science, and Democracy: The Philosophical Work of Abraham Edel,* Transaction Books, 1986.

Contributor to *Encyclopedia of Philosophy, Encyclopaedia Britannica,* and to philosophy journals.

WORK IN PROGRESS: A study of William James's philosophy; research in aspects of Greek philosophy and history of science.

BIOGRAPHICAL/CRITICAL SOURCES:

PERIODICALS

American Historical Review, October, 1969.
Political Science Quarterly, September, 1971.
Yale Review, October, 1969.

*   *   *

THEINER, George (Fredric) 1927-1988
(Jonathan George, a joint pseudonym)

PERSONAL: Surname is pronounced "Tiner"; born November 4, 1927, in Prague, Czechoslovakia; died July 17, 1988; son of Jan (a printing works executive) and Hermina (Mueller) Theiner; married Anna Helis, March 6, 1954; married Shirley Harris, October 25, 1975; children: (first marriage) Anna, Paul. *Education:* Attended Leamington College, England, 1940-44, and London College of Printing, 1944-45.

ADDRESSES: Home—154 Barry Rd., Dulwich, London SE22 0JW, England. *Office*—Index on Censorship, 39C Highbury

Pl., London N5 1QP, England. *Agent*—David Higham Associates, Ltd., 5-8 Lower John St., Golden Square, London W1R 4HA, England.

CAREER: Czechoslovak News Agency, Prague, Czechoslovakia, editor, 1946-50; began translating Czech and Slovak literature as a spare-time hobby, 1950; Pedagogical Publishing House, Prague, production assistant, 1954-56; Artia Publishing House, Prague, English literary editor, 1956-62; free-lance writer and translator in Prague, 1962-68; George Weidenfeld & Nicolson, Ltd. (publishers), London, England, administrative editor, 1969-72; Index on Censorship (publishers), London, assistant editor, 1973-82, editor, beginning 1982. *Military service:* Czechoslovak Army, 1950-53; served in Silesian coal mines as "enemy of the State."

MEMBER: English PEN Center (chairman of writers in prison committee).

AWARDS, HONORS: Czechoslovak Writers Union prize for translations of Czech literature, 1968.

WRITINGS:

(With John Burke, under joint pseudonym Jonathan George) *The Kill Dog,* Doubleday, 1970.
The Secret Vysocany Congress: Proceedings and Documents of the Extraordinary Fourteenth Congress of the Communist Party of Czechoslovakia, 22 August 1968, Allen Lane, 1971.
(Editor) *They Shoot Writers, Don't They?,* Faber & Faber, 1984.

TRANSLATOR FROM CZECH OR SLOVAK

Jan Vladislav, *Persian Fables* (retold), Spring Books, 1960.
Death Is Called Engelchen, Artia Publishing House (Prague), 1961.
A Dog's Life, Artia Publishing House, 1962.
Arnost Lustig, *Night and Hope,* Dutton, 1962.
Vaclav Jan Stanek, *Introducing Birds,* Golden Pleasure Books (London), 1963.
Stanek, *Pictorial Encyclopedia of the Animal Kingdom,* Crown, 1963.
(And editor) *The Monkey King,* Hamlyn, 1964.
That Particular Fault . . . , Artia Publishing House, 1964.
Vladimir Hulpach, *American Indian Tales and Legends,* Hamlyn, 1965.
Seven Short Stories, Orbis Publishing House (Prague), 1966.
Lustig, *Dita Sax,* Hutchinson, 1966.
Modern Fairy Tales, Hamlyn, 1967.
(With Ian Milner) Miroslav Holub, *Selected Poems,* Penguin, 1967.
Karel Jalovec, *German and Austrian Violin Makers,* edited by Patrick Hanks, Tudor, 1967.
Klara Jarunkova, *Don't Cry for Me,* Four Winds, 1968.
Slovak Short Stories, Orbis Publishing House, 1969.
(And compiler) *New Writing in Czechoslovakia* (fiction), Penguin, 1969.
Frantisek Tichy, *The Drawings of Frantisek Tichy,* notes by Vojtech Volauka, Hamlyn, 1969.
Hulpach, Emanuel Frynta, and Vaclav Cibula, *Heroes of Folk Tale and Legend,* Hamlyn, 1970.
European Tales and Legends, Hamlyn, 1970.
Diary of a Counter-Revolutionary, McGraw, 1970.
Vladislav, *Italian Fairy Tales,* Hamlyn, 1971.
(With Ewald Osers) *Three Czech Poets: Vitezslav Nezval, Antonin Bartusek, Josef Hanslik,* Penguin, 1971.
Ivan Klima, *My Merry Mornings,* Readers International, 1985.

Ludvik Vaculik, *A Cup of Coffee with My Interrogator: The Prague Chronicles of Ludvik Vaculik,* Readers International, 1987.
(With Rosemary Kavan and Kaca Polackova) Josef Skvorecky, *The Mournful Demeanor of Lieutenant Boruvka,* Norton, 1987.

OTHER

Also author of several original children's stories and translator from the Czech and Slovak of several art books, children's books, film scripts, radio plays, short stories, and poems. Translations of poems have appeared in *Modern Poetry in Translation, Art and Literature, City Lights Journal, Stand,* and other English and American periodicals.

SIDELIGHTS: George Theiner once told *CA:* "I have wanted to write ever since I was at school, literature and languages being my favorite subjects. On returning to Prague from England after the war I became a journalist, running an English news service for CTK and giving this up when decent journalism became impossible owing to the changed political circumstances. . . . I have always wanted to travel, but in pre-Dubcek Czechoslovakia this was virtually impossible for a non-Party man known to have liberal and pro-Western views. It was a great achievement when, in 1962 through the good offices of the Writers Union, I was able to come to England for the first time since the war for the publication of Arnost Lustig's collection of short stories about the Terezin ghetto, *Night and Hope,* which I translated. . . . I left Czechoslovakia with my family after the Russian invasion [in 1968] and have settled in London. . . . I am also interested in the theatre and films."

[Sketch reviewed by wife, Shirley Theiner]

*   *   *

THORNDYKE, Helen Louise [Collective pseudonym]

WRITINGS:

"HONEY BUNCH" SERIES

Honey Bunch: Just a Little Girl, Grosset & Dunlap, 1923.
. . . *Her First Visit to the City,* Grosset & Dunlap, 1923.
. . . *Her First Days on the Farm,* Grosset & Dunlap, 1923.
. . . *Her First Visit to the Seashore,* Grosset & Dunlap, 1924.
. . . *Her First Little Garden,* Grosset & Dunlap, 1924.
. . . *Her First Days in Camp,* Grosset & Dunlap, 1925.
. . . *Her First Auto Tour,* Grosset & Dunlap, 1926.
. . . *Her First Trip on the Ocean,* Grosset & Dunlap, 1927.
. . . *Her First Trip West,* Grosset & Dunlap, 1928.
. . . *Her First Summer on an Island,* Grosset & Dunlap, 1929.
. . . *Her First Trip on the Great Lakes,* Grosset & Dunlap, 1930.
. . . *Her First Trip in an Airplane,* Grosset & Dunlap, 1931.
. . . *Her First Visit to the Zoo,* Grosset & Dunlap, 1932.
. . . *Her First Big Adventure,* Grosset & Dunlap, 1933.
. . . *Her First Big Parade,* Grosset & Dunlap, 1934.
. . . *Her First Little Mystery,* Grosset & Dunlap, 1935.
. . . *Her First Little Circus,* Grosset & Dunlap, 1936.
. . . *Her First Little Treasure Hunt,* Grosset & Dunlap, 1937.
. . . *Her First Little Club,* Grosset & Dunlap, 1938.
. . . *Her First Trip in a Trailer,* Grosset & Dunlap, 1939.
. . . *Her First Trip to a Big Fair,* Grosset & Dunlap, 1940.
. . . *Her First Twin Playmates,* Grosset & Dunlap, 1941.

. . . Her First Costume Party, Grosset & Dunlap, 1943.
. . . Her First Trip on a Houseboat, Grosset & Dunlap, 1945.
. . . Her First Winter at Snowtop, Grosset & Dunlap, 1946.
. . . Her First Trip to the Big Woods, Grosset & Dunlap, 1947.
. . . Her First Little Pet Show, Grosset & Dunlap, 1948.
. . . Her First Trip to a Lighthouse (also see below), Grosset & Dunlap, 1949.
. . . Her First Visit to a Pony Ranch, Grosset & Dunlap, 1950.
. . . Her First Tour of Toy Town (also see below), Grosset & Dunlap, 1951.
. . . Her First Visit to Puppyland, Grosset & Dunlap, 1952.
. . . Her First Trip to Reindeer Farm (also see below), Grosset & Dunlap, 1953.
. . . and Norman Ride with the Sky Mailman (also see below), Grosset & Dunlap, 1954.
. . . and Norman Visit Beaver Lodge (also see below), Grosset & Dunlap, 1955.

"HONEY BUNCH AND NORMAN" SERIES

Honey Bunch and Norman, Grosset & Dunlap, 1957.
. . . on Lighthouse Island (originally published as part of the "Honey Bunch" series under title *Honey Bunch: Her First Trip to a Lighthouse*), Grosset & Dunlap, 1957.
. . . Tour Toy Town (originally published as part of the "Honey Bunch" series under title *Honey Bunch: Her First Tour of Toy Town*), Grosset & Dunlap, 1957.
. . . Play Detective at Niagara Falls, Grosset & Dunlap, 1957.
. . . Ride with the Sky Mailman (originally published as part of the "Honey Bunch" series), Grosset & Dunlap, 1958.
. . . Visit Beaver Lodge (originally published as part of the "Honey Bunch" series), Grosset & Dunlap, 1958.
. . . Visit Reindeer Farm (originally published as part of the "Honey Bunch" series under title *Honey Bunch: Her First Trip to Reindeer Farm*), Grosset & Dunlap, 1958.
. . . in the Castle of Magic, Grosset & Dunlap, 1959.
. . . Solve the Pine Cone Mystery, Grosset & Dunlap, 1960.
. . . and the Paper Lantern Mystery, Grosset & Dunlap, 1961.
. . . and the Painted Pony, Grosset & Dunlap, 1962.
. . . and the Walnut Tree Mystery, Grosset & Dunlap, 1963.

SIDELIGHTS: Grosset & Dunlap's advertisements for these series, which were intended for children ages four to eight, described Honey Bunch Morton as "a dainty, thoughtful little girl who keeps one wondering what she is going to do next." She was occasionally joined in her escapades by her friend Norman who, as the series progressed, became a more active participant in her adventures. Eventually, the Stratemeyer Syndicate began a new series co-starring Norman with Honey Bunch.

Bobbie Ann Mason, in her book *The Girl Sleuth: A Feminist Guide,* calls Honey Bunch Morton "Shirley Temple's literary precursor, portrayed and illustrated as a dainty stereotype—clean, obedient, cute, talented." While Norman and Stub, Honey Bunch's tomboy friend, occasionally indulged in mischief, Honey Bunch herself was always well-behaved, says Mason: "She learned to be, in fact, a juvenile Victorian matron." The stories themselves, the reviewer continues, focus on comfortable home-centered values; Honey Bunch's world is cozy, and her favorite spot is the "kitty corner," a "perfect world in miniature, a little elf nook, a playhouse, a gingerbread cottage, an English garden in a terrarium, a hideaway in an attic."

Harriet S. Adams and Andrew E. Svenson both worked on these series; Adams produced at least seven volumes herself. Another five volumes in the "Honey Bunch" series are credited to Mildred Augustine Wirt Benson. For additional information on this pseudonym, see the entries in this volume for Harriet S. Adams, Edward L. Stratemeyer, and Andrew E. Svenson.

BIOGRAPHICAL/CRITICAL SOURCES:

BOOKS

Johnson, Deidre, editor and compiler, *Stratemeyer Pseudonyms and Series Books: An Annotated Checklist of Stratemeyer and Stratemeyer Syndicate Publications,* Greenwood Press, 1982.
Mason, Bobbie Ann, *The Girl Sleuth: A Feminist Guide,* Feminist Press, 1975.
Paluka, Frank, *Iowa Authors: A Bio-Bibliography of Sixty Native Writers,* Friends of the University of Iowa Libraries, 1967.

* * *

TIMMINS, Lois Fahs   1914-

PERSONAL: Born July 3, 1914, in New York, N.Y.; daughter of Charles Harvey (a librarian, editor, and author) and Sophia (an author; maiden name, Lyon) Fahs; married James W. Timmins, August 12, 1942 (divorced, 1957); children: Nancy Timmins Kirk, Kathy. *Education:* Northwestern University, B.S. (magna cum laude), 1935; Columbia University, M.A., 1936, Ed.D., 1941, postdoctoral study, 1952. *Religion:* Unitarian.

ADDRESSES: Home—6145 Anita St., Dallas, Tex. 75214-2612.

CAREER: Mount Allison University, Sackville, New Brunswick, instructor in physical education, 1936-39; Willimantic State Teachers College, Willimantic, Conn., assistant professor of physical education, 1941-43; Danbury State Teachers College, Danbury, Conn., instructor in Adult Education Service, 1948-52; Texas Woman's University, Denton, assistant professor of recreation, 1953-57; Timberlawn Psychiatric Hospital, Dallas, Tex., director of recreation therapy, 1957-72, director of Halfway House, 1972-77, assistant to the administrator, director of publicity, 1977-80; Communication Studies (publisher), Dallas, director, 1980—. Professional speaker, workshop leader.

MEMBER: International Association of Independent Publishers.

AWARDS, HONORS: Citation from National Therapeutic Recreation Society, 1976, in recognition of exceptional contributions to the field; awarded top rating for professional showcase, International Platform Association, 1982.

WRITINGS:

Swing Your Partner: Old Time Dances of New Brunswick and Nova Scotia, privately printed, 1939.
Games and Dances for Community Schools, MacDonald College (St. Anne de Bellevue, Quebec), 1941.
(Contributor) Sophia Lyon Fahs and Elizabeth M. Manwell, *Consider the Children: How They Grow,* revised edition (Timmins was not contributor to earlier edition), Beacon Press, 1951.
Understanding through Communication, C. C Thomas, 1972.
Life-Time Chart, Communication Studies, 1978.
Finding Words for Your Feelings, Communication Studies, 1985.

Also author of cassettes, *Making Friends with All Your Feelings,* 1984, *The Mirrors Inside You,* 1984, *Ambivalence,* 1985, and *Our Secret World of Feelings: Anger, Fear, Distress, Shame, Guilt, Joy,* 1986. Author of a guide for *Finding Words for Your Feelings.* Contributor of about seventeen articles, principally on recreation, to journals.

WORK IN PROGRESS: A selective bibliography of books on feelings and how to cope with them.

SIDELIGHTS: Lois Fahs Timmins told *CA:* "[My] book on communication arose out of ten years of teaching patients at Timberlawn. The book outlines the theory and practice which were utilized in the course of those ten years, with eighty-four sessions described in detail. *Life-Time Chart* is a significant concept, an invention to demonstrate it, and a means of 'putting it all together.' At about age sixty it dawned on me that you only go around once in life, and that it would be an insightful experience to attempt to record major events in chronological sequence."

AVOCATIONAL INTERESTS: Magic (semi-professional magician for about fifteen years), swimming (set national record in 100-yard backstroke in 1935), real estate, sailing.

* * *

TIPPETT, Michael (Kemp) 1905-

PERSONAL: Born January 2, 1905, in London, England; son of Henry William and Isabel (Kemp) Tippett. *Education:* Attended Royal College of Music, 1923-28, 1930.

ADDRESSES: Agent—c/o Schott & Co., 48 Great Marlborough St., London W1V 2BN, England.

CAREER: Writer and composer. Teacher of French and music; Morley College, London, England, music director, 1940-51; Bath Festival, Bath, England, artistic director, 1969-74; Kent Opera, Kent, England, president, 1978—. Ran Choral and Orchestral Society, Oxted, England, until 1931; Adult education work in music, Labour Coordinating Committee and Royal Arsenal Cooperative Society Educational Departments, England, 1932.

MEMBER: London College of Music (president), Royal College of Music (fellow), Worshipful Company of Musicians (honorary liveryman), Guildhall School of Music and Drama (honorary member), Royal Northern College of Music (honorary fellow), Academie der Kuenste (Berlin; extraordinary member), American Academy of Arts and Letters (honorary member), Peace Pledge Union (president), Campaign for Nuclear Disarmament (Bath, England; honorary president).

AWARDS, HONORS: Cobbett Medal for Chamber Music, 1948; Companion of the Order of the British Empire, 1959; Knight of the British Empire, 1966; Gold Medal, Royal Philharmonic Society, 1976; Order of the Companions of Honour, United Kingdom, 1979; Incorporated Society of Musicians Distinguished Musician Award, 1982; Order of Merit, United Kingdom, 1983; Prix de Composition Musicale of the Fondation Prince de Monaco, 1984; D.Mus. from sixteen colleges and universities, including Cambridge University, 1964, Oxford University, 1967, University of London, 1975, and the Royal College of Music, 1982; D.Univ., University of York, 1966; D.Litt. from University of Bath, 1972, and University of Warwick, 1974.

WRITINGS:

Moving into Aquarius (essays), Routledge & Kegan Paul, 1959, expanded edition, Paladin, 1974.
Music of the Angels: Essays and Sketchbooks of Michael Tippett, edited by Meirion Bowen, Eulenburg, 1980.

OPERAS

The Midsummer Marriage (first produced in Coventry, England, at the Royal Opera House, January, 1955), Schott & Co., 1952.
King Priam (first produced in Coventry at the Coventry Cathedral Festival, May, 1962), Schott & Co., 1961.
The Knot Garden (first produced in Coventry at the Royal Opera House, December, 1970), Schott & Co., 1970.
The Ice Break (first performed in Coventry at the Royal Opera House, July, 1977), Schott & Co., 1976.

OTHER

Composer of orchestral works, including "Concerto for Double String Orchestra," 1939, "Symphony Number 1," 1945, "Suite for the Birthday of Prince Charles (Suite in D)," 1948, "Fantasia Concertante on a Theme of Corelli," 1953, "Symphony Number 2," 1957, "Concerto for Orchestra," 1963; "Symphony Number 3," 1972, "Symphony Number 4," 1977, and "Triple Concerto," 1979. Also composer of chamber music, works for brass, piano and organ works, choral works, and vocal works.

SIDELIGHTS: Michael Tippett also wrote music during the late 1920s and early 1930s. However, all of these early works have been withdrawn from publication by the composer.

AVOCATIONAL INTERESTS: Walking.

* * *

TOWNE, Peter
See NABOKOV, Peter (Francis)

* * *

TREFIL, James S. 1938-

PERSONAL: Born September 10, 1938, in Chicago, Ill.; son of Stanley (a personnel manager) and Sylvia (a social worker; maiden name, Mestek) Trefil; married Elinor Pletka, September 2, 1960 (divorced, January, 1972); married Jeanne Waples, October 20, 1973; children: James Karel, Stefan James, Dominique Katherine, Flora Jeanne, Tomas. *Education:* University of Illinois, B.A., 1960; Oxford University, B.A., 1962, M.A., 1962; Stanford University, M.S., 1964, Ph.D., 1966.

ADDRESSES: Home—8514 Canterbury Dr., Annandale, Va. 22003. *Office*—Department of Physics, George Mason University, Fairfax, Va. 22030.

CAREER: Stanford Linear Accelerator Center, Stanford, Calif., fellow, 1966; European Center for Nuclear Research, Geneva, Switzerland, fellow, 1966-67; Massachusetts Institute of Technology, Cambridge, fellow at Laboratory for Nuclear Science, 1967-68; University of Illinois, Urbana, assistant professor of physics, 1968-70; University of Virginia, Charlottesville, fellow, Center for Advanced Studies, and associate professor, 1970-75, professor of physics, 1975-88; George Mason University, Fairfax, Va., Clarence J. Robinson Professor of Physics, 1988—.

MEMBER: American Physical Society (fellow), Cell Kinetics Society, Society for Scientific Exploration (vice-president and founding member).

AWARDS, HONORS: Marshall Scholar, 1960-62; Air Force Office of Scientific Research postdoctoral fellow, 1966-67; President and Visitor's Research Prize, University of Virginia, 1979; American Association for the Advancement of Science/ Westinghouse Science Journalism Award, 1983.

WRITINGS:

Introduction to the Physics of Fluids and Solids, Pergamon, 1975.

Physics as a Liberal Art, Pergamon, 1978.

From Atoms to Quarks: The Strange World of Particle Physics, Scribner, 1980.

(With Robert T. Rood) *Are We Alone?,* Scribner, 1981.

Living in Space, Scribner, 1981.

The Unexpected Vista: A Physicist's View of Nature, Scribner, 1983.

The Moment of Creation: Big Bang Physics from before the First Millisecond to the Present Universe, Scribner, 1983.

A Scientist at the Seashore, Scribner, 1984.

Space, Time, Infinity: The Smithsonian Views the Universe, Pantheon/Smithsonian Books, 1985.

Meditations at Ten Thousand Feet: A Scientist in the Mountains, Scribner, 1986.

Meditations at Sunset: A Scientist Looks at the Sky, Scribner, 1987.

(Contributor and co-author of appendix) E. D. Hirsch, Jr., *Cultural Literacy: What Every American Needs to Know,* Houghton, 1987.

WORK IN PROGRESS: Research on science books for general audiences; a "dictionary" of cultural literacy, with E. D. Hirsch, Jr., and Joseph Kett.

SIDELIGHTS: Clarence J. Robinson Professor of Physics at George Mason University, James S. Trefil in one respect "surpasses almost all other scientists writing about science for the public," notes Alan P. Lightman in the *New York Times Book Review.* He elaborates: "As in his previous books and articles, we feel a real person talking to us about the physical world. . . . Such immediacy must be treasured in science communication." Through his books and articles, Trefil has clarified such subjects as atomic theory and the big bang for popular audiences; in his self-described "Natural Philosopher" trilogy Trefil explores everyday questions about man's surroundings and applies physical theory in obtaining their answers. In *A Scientist at the Seashore,* the first book in the series, Trefil begins at a beach and investigates the influence of physics on tides, waves, sailing, skipping stones, and other topics. Similarly, *Meditations at Ten Thousand Feet: A Scientist in the Mountains* includes examinations of geology, such as the formation of mountains and glaciers, plate tectonics, and the age of the earth. And a theoretical approach to topics such as the color of light, clouds, and thunderstorms characterizes *Meditations at Sunset: A Scientist Looks at the Sky.* All three of these books have been praised for explanations that are comprehensible without being condescending or oversimplified.

One reason for the success of Trefil's trilogy is that his essays "are lucidly written in a style that is personal and discursive rather than technical," comments Gerald Feinberg in the *New York Times Book Review.* "Whether he is writing about the oceans, the cosmos or the Earth itself," observes Lee Dembart of the *Los Angeles Times,* "he exudes awe and wonder that things are as they are. He is the best kind of teacher," continues the critic. "His knowledge of the subject is expert, but he conveys it with the enthusiasm of a beginner." Jonathan Weiner similarly remarks upon the author's approach: "Trefil . . . seems to be an ideal physics teacher: clear, affable and as pleased by the beauty of natural laws as most people are by sunsets," the critic writes in the *New York Times Book Review.* "He holds your attention without begging for it, and he almost always knows when a point has been made or when an analogy is needed. I enjoyed reading even stories I already knew well . . . because of the superb clarity of the explanations," adds Weiner.

Analyzing the proficiency of Trefil's explanations, Ellen W. Chu states in the *New York Times Book Review* that they "omit nothing crucial and, most important, engage our active participation. Without patronizing," continues Chu, "he makes the 'scientific method' a real step-by-step process of discovery he invites us to share with him, not a rigid intellectual exercise performed only by fully registered scientists." Part of this process includes connecting the various elements of his analyses so that they form a coherent whole. "This is science writing at its best," comments Dembart, "a broad sweep over many disciplines that helps make the outlines of the jigsaw puzzle of the universe clearer." Chu similarly observes that "no matter how far afield [Trefil] takes us, he ties everything back to something familiar; his direct, unpretentious style makes the book painless and enjoyable reading." "Taken as a whole," writes Feinberg, "I found 'Meditations at 10,000 Feet' an impressive achievement in science writing for the general public." The critic concludes that Trefil's readers "will learn a good deal about science. They will also have a chance to see something that is much less common in science writing than clear exposition—how a scientist can use his training to understand his everyday experience."

Trefil told *CA:* "I regard my writing as an outgrowth of my work as a teacher. Both involve explaining concepts clearly. I write about physical science, which is the area of my research, and about energy, a subject which I teach. I am particularly interested in wood heating, as I have used it myself for a number of years.

"I feel that science has come to play such a large role in our lives that it is absolutely crucial that the general public know what is happening. Unfortunately, very few scientists involve themselves in this sort of work. The situation may be changing, but not fast enough."

BIOGRAPHICAL/CRITICAL SOURCES:

PERIODICALS

Los Angeles Times, April 16, 1986.
Los Angeles Times Book Review, July 5, 1987.
New York Times Book Review, April 24, 1983, September 25, 1983, February 24, 1985, November 17, 1985, May 11, 1986, July 12, 1987.
Times Literary Supplement, February 20, 1981.
Washington Post, July 14, 1987.
Washington Post Book World, July 24, 1983, March 17, 1985, April 20, 1986.

*   *   *

TUCHMAN, Maurice   1936-

PERSONAL: Born November 30, 1936, in Jacksonville, Fla.; son of Henry and Pearl (Warman) Tuchman. *Education:* Studied at University of Mexico, 1956; City College (now City College of the City University of New York), B.A., 1957; Columbia University, M.A., 1959.

ADDRESSES: Office—Los Angeles County Museum of Art, 5909 Wilshire Blvd., Los Angeles, Calif. 90036.

CAREER: Curator. Solomon R. Guggenheim Museum, New York City, member of curatorial and lecture staff, 1962-64; Los Angeles County Museum of Art, Los Angeles, Calif., senior curator of twentieth-century art, 1964—. Organizer of ''Van Gogh and Expressionism'' exhibition and author of accompanying catalogue, Solomon R. Guggenheim Museum, summer, 1964; organizer of over sixty exhibitions and author of accompanying catalogues, Los Angeles County Museum of Art, beginning in 1965; director of ''New Art'' exhibition of U.S. pavilion, ''Expo 70,'' Osaka, Japan, 1970. Lecturer throughout the United States, and in England and Australia, on *The Spiritual in Art: Abstract Painting 1890-1985,* 1987. Member of advisory committees to Archives of American Art, Skowhegan School of Painting, and Museum of Art, Carnegie Institute; member of art advisory panel to commissioner of Internal Revenue Service, 1975-78. Participant in ''Works of Art in Public Places,'' National Endowment for the Arts, 1977-79. Nominator for MacArthur Foundation, 1981-83.

MEMBER: American Association of Museums (member of board of directors, International Council of Museums Committee, 1979-83), American Arts Alliance (member of board of directors, 1977-80), American Federation of Arts (member of National Exhibitions Committee), Los Angeles Design Alliance (member of board of governors, 1984).

AWARDS, HONORS: Fulbright scholar at Freie Universitaet, Berlin, 1960-61.

WRITINGS:

EXHIBITION CATALOGUES

Van Gogh and Expressionism: Commentary, Solomon R. Guggenheim Museum, 1964.
New York School, the First Generation: Paintings of the 1940s and 1950s, [Los Angeles], 1965, revised edition, New York Graphic Society, 1971 (published in England as *The New York School: Abstract Expressionism in the 40s and 50s,* Thames & Hudson, 1971).
R. B. Kitaj: A Retrospective, Los Angeles County Museum of Art, 1965.
Edward Kienholz: A Retrospective, Los Angeles County Museum of Art, 1966.
(Editor) *American Sculpture of the Sixties,* New York Graphic Society, 1967.
Chaim Soutine, 1893-1943, Los Angeles County Museum of Art, 1968.
11 Los Angeles Artists, Hayward Gallery, Arts Council of Great Britain, 1971.
Fifty Tantric Mystical Diagrams, Los Angeles County Museum of Art, 1971.
(Author of introduction) *European Painting in the Seventies: New Work by Sixteen Artists,* Los Angeles County Museum of Art, 1975.
California: Five Footnotes to Modern Art History, Los Angeles County Museum of Art, 1977.
Private Images: Photographs by Artists, two volumes, Los Angeles County Museum of Art, 1977.
Richard Diebenkorn: Paintings and Drawings, 1943-1976, Albright-Knox Gallery, 1977.

Richard Diebenkorn: The Early Years, 1943-1955, Rizzoli, 1977.
Ken Price: Happy's Curios, Los Angeles County Museum of Art, 1978.
(With Stephanie Barron) *Seven Artists in Israel, 1948-1978* (also see below), Los Angeles County Museum of Art, 1978.
Sven Lukin: New Work, Los Angeles County Museum of Art, 1978.
(With Barron) *The Avant-garde in Russia, 1910-1930: New Perspectives,* Los Angeles County Museum of Art, 1980.
(Editor) *Art in Los Angeles: Seventeen Artists in the Sixties,* Los Angeles County Museum of Art, 1981.
Gallery Six: Robert Graham; Five Statues, Los Angeles County Museum of Art, 1981.
(With Anne Carnegie Edgerton) *The Michael and Dorothy Blankfort Collection* (introduction by Michael Blankfort), Los Angeles County Museum of Art, 1982.
Gallery Six: Italo Scanga, Los Angeles County Museum of Art, 1983.
Gallery Six: Jim Dine in Los Angeles, Los Angeles County Museum of Art, 1983.
Gallery Six: Susan Rothenberg, Los Angeles County Museum of Art, 1983.
(With Edgerton) *The Modern and Contemporary Art Council Young Talent Awards, 1963-1983: Essay and Catalogue,* Los Angeles County Museum of Art, 1983.
The Spiritual in Art: Abstract Painting 1890-1985, Los Angeles County Museum of Art/Abbeville Press, 1986.
David Hockney: A Retrospective, Los Angeles County Museum of Art, 1988.

Also author of forty other catalogues for exhibitions at Los Angeles County Museum of Art.

OTHER

Art and Technology: A Report on the Art and Technology Program of the Los Angeles County Museum of Art, 1968-1971, also published as *A Report on the Art and Technology Program of the Los Angeles County Museum of Art, 1967-1971,* both Los Angeles County Museum of Art, 1971.

Contributor, *Columbia Encyclopedia,* 3rd edition, 1962; contributor and member of advisory committee, ''Random House Library of Painting and Sculpture,'' four volumes, 1981. Contributor to various art periodicals. Has worked on film and video documentaries, including consultant and writer, ''American Sculpture of the Sixties,'' 1967, consultant and narrator, ''Chaim Soutine,'' 1968, associate producer, ''Richard Diebenkorn,'' 1976, and producer, ''Seven Artists in Israel,'' 1978; writer, co-producer, and on-camera host, ''Olympic Arts'' feature segments, 1984 Summer Olympics broadcast, ABC-TV.

BIOGRAPHICAL/CRITICAL SOURCES:

PERIODICALS

Los Angeles Times Book Review, February 22, 1987.
Saturday Review, November 25, 1968.
Times Literary Supplement, May 15, 1981.

*   *   *

TURNER, Philip (William) 1925-
(Stephen Chance)

PERSONAL: Born December 3, 1925, in Rossland, British

Columbia, Canada; son of Christopher Edward (a clergyman) and Emma (Johnston) Turner; married Margaret Diana Samson, September 23, 1950; children: Simon, Stephen, Jane. *Education:* Worcester College, Oxford, B.A., 1950, M.A., 1962.

ADDRESSES: Home—St. Francis, 1 West Malvern Rd., Malvern, Worcestershire, England. *Agent*—Watson, Little Ltd., Suite 8, 26 Charing Cross Rd., London WC2H 0DG, England.

CAREER: Ordained priest of Church of England, 1951; curate in Leeds, 1951-56; priest-in-charge, Crawley, Sussex, 1956-62; vicar of St. Matthews, Northampton, 1962-66; British Broadcasting Corp., Midland Region, Birmingham, religious broadcasting organizer, 1966-70; Briar Mill High School, Droitwich, England, teacher of English and divinity, 1971-73; Eton College, Windsor, England, chaplain, 1973-75; writer. Part-time instructor of history, Malvern College, beginning 1975. *Military service:* Royal Naval Volunteer Reserve, 1943-46; became sub-lieutenant.

MEMBER: Society of Authors.

AWARDS, HONORS: Carnegie Medal for best children's book published in United Kingdom, Library Association, 1965, for *The Grange at High Force.*

WRITINGS:

"DARNLEY MILLS" SERIES; JUVENILE FICTION

Colonel Sheperton's Clock, Oxford University Press, 1964, World Publishing, 1966, published as *The Mystery of the Colonel's Clock,* Goodchild, 1984.
The Grange at High Force, Oxford University Press, 1965, World Publishing, 1967, published as *The Adventure at High Force,* Goodchild, 1984.
Sea Peril, Oxford University Press, 1966, World Publishing, 1968, reprinted, Goodchild, 1984.
Steam on the Line, World Publishing, 1968.
War on the Darnel, World Publishing, 1969, reprinted, Goodchild, 1986.
Devil's Nob, Hamish Hamilton, 1970, Thomas Nelson, 1973.
Powder Quay, Hamish Hamilton, 1971.
Dunkirk Summer, Hamish Hamilton, 1973.
Skull Island, Dent, 1977.

UNDER PSEUDONYM STEPHEN CHANCE; JUVENILE FICTION

Septimus and the Danedyke Mystery, Bodley Head, 1971, Thomas Nelson, 1973.
... and the Minster Ghost, Bodley Head, 1972, published as *Septimus and the Minster Ghost Mystery,* Thomas Nelson, 1974.
... and the Stone of Offering, Bodley Head, 1976, published as *The Stone of Offering,* Thomas Nelson, 1977.
... and the Spy Ring, Bodley Head, 1979.

PLAYS

"Mann's End" (also see below), first produced in Armley, Yorkshire, England, 1953.
"Passion in Paradise Street" (also see below), first produced in Armley, Yorkshire, England, 1954.
Christ in the Concrete City (first produced in Hinckley, Yorkshire, England, 1953), S.P.C.K., 1956, revised edition, 1960, Baker's Plays, 1965, revised edition, 1983.

(Contributor) *Three One-Act Plays* (includes *How Many Miles to Bethlehem?;* also see below), British Council of Churches, 1957.
(With Jack Windross) *Tell It with Trumpets: Three Experiments in Drama and Evangelism* (includes "Mann's End," "Passion in Paradise Street," and "Six-Fifteen to Eternity"), S.P.C.K., 1959.
Cry Dawn in Dark Babylon: A Dramatic Meditation (first produced under title "Benny Death and His Old Bones" in Durham, England, 1957), S.P.C.K., 1959.
This Is the Word, and Word Made Flesh, S.P.C.K., 1962.
Casey: A Dramatic Meditation on the Passion (first produced in Crawley, Sussex, England, 1961), S.P.C.K., 1962.
Men in Stone (also see below), Baker's Plays, 1966.
Sex Morality: Two Plays —So Long at the Fair and Men in Stone, Joint Board of Christian Education of Australia and New Zealand, 1966.
Cantata for Derelicts, United Church Publishing House (Canada), 1967.
Madonna in Concrete, S.P.C.K., 1971.
Watch at the World's End, Baker's Plays, 1980.
How Many Miles to Bethlehem?, Baker's Plays, 1986.

Also author of a Passion play, "The Price of a Slave," and a farce based on Victorian melodrama, produced in Chichester, 1950.

OTHER

The Christmas Story: A Carol Service for Children, Church Information Office, 1964.
Peter Was His Nickname, Waltham Forest Books, 1965.
The Bible Story, Oxford University Press, 1968, published as *Brian Wildsmith's Illustrated Bible Stories,* F. Watts, 1969.
Wigwig and Homer (juvenile fiction), Oxford University Press, 1969, World Publishing, 1970.
Decision in the Dark: Tales of Mystery (short stories), Dent, 1978.
Rookoo and Bree (juvenile fiction), Dent, 1979.
(Adaptor) *The Good Shepherd,* Dent, 1986.
The Candlemass Treasure (juvenile fiction), Lutterworth, 1988.

SIDELIGHTS: Philip Turner, an Anglican priest, is noted for his writing of both ecclesiastical plays and children's novels. He first began to write plays, he says in his *Something about the Author Autobiography Series* entry, as a means to bring the church to those who could not attend regular services. He remembered the tradition of early English drama: "In the past the Church had taken the Faith into the streets; plays performed on horse-drawn stages called 'pageant waggons.' Why not do that in the twentieth century?" He continues, "Of course there were no suitable plays, so I had to write them."

Turner began writing children's books somewhat later, "partly as a relaxation from the task of interpreting Christianity," he says. Perhaps his most famous books are found in the series focusing on the inhabitants of Darnley Mills —an English village near an old Benedictine abbey. Unlike many series, Turner's works are not linked to a specific character or characters. Although many of the books describe the adventures of three modern boys —David, Arthur, and Peter —in the town and the area surrounding it, others relate tales of the First World War and Victorian times in the same setting. Turner's writing skill, reports a reviewer for *Horn Book* magazine, is reflected in his "ability to use an ecclesiastical setting for an interesting adventure story for boys."

Turner told *CA:* "I think my motivation —both in plays and children's books —has been ultimately religious. Not in an ecclesiastical sense, but as part of the unending search for the truth about Man's condition. Sounds extraordinarily pompous, but it is as near the truth as I can get. I am also moved by a strong sense of 'place,' and by the comedy of being human at all. As I get older, I find myself more and more preoccupied by the sheer wonder of creation, its preciousness and fragility."

Several of Turner's book have been translated into other languages, including Japanese and German.

MEDIA ADAPTATIONS: Septimus and the Danedyke Mystery was produced on British television as "Danedyke."

BIOGRAPHICAL/CRITICAL SOURCES:

BOOKS

Something about the Author Autobiography Series, Volume 6, Gale, 1988.

PERIODICALS

Books and Bookmen, May, 1968.
Commonweal, May 23, 1969, November 21, 1969.
Horn Book, February, 1967, August, 1967.
New Statesman, May 24, 1968, March 5, 1971.
New York Times Book Review, March 30, 1969, November 9, 1969.
Observer, November 30, 1969, December 6, 1970, April 4, 1971, July 29, 1973, February 9, 1975, August 5, 1979.
Saturday Review, June 17, 1967, May 11, 1968, May 10, 1969, February 21, 1970.
Times Educational Supplement, February 10, 1978, July 7, 1978.
Times Literary Supplement, June 17, 1965, March 14, 1968, October 30, 1970, April 2, 1971.
Washington Post Book World, February 2, 1969, May 4, 1969.

*   *   *

TUTUOLA, Amos   1920-

PERSONAL: Born 1920, in Abeokuta, Nigeria; son of Charles (a cocoa farmer) and Esther (Aina) Tutuola; married Alake Victoria, 1947; children: Olubunmi, Oluyinka, Erinola. *Education:* Attended schools in Nigeria. *Religion:* Christian.

ADDRESSES: P.O. Box 2251, Ibadan, Nigeria. *Home*—Ago-Odo, West Nigeria. *Office*—Nigerian Broadcasting Corp., Ibadan, Nigeria, West Africa.

CAREER: Worked on father's farm; trained as a coppersmith; employed by Nigerian Government Labor Department, Lagos, and by Nigerian Broadcasting Corp., Ibadan, Nigeria. Freelance writer. Visiting research fellow, University of Ife, 1979; associate, international writing program at University of Iowa, 1983. *Military service:* Royal Air Force, 1943-45; served as metal worker in Nigeria.

MEMBER: Mbari Club (Nigerian authors; founder).

AWARDS, HONORS: Named honorary citizen of New Orleans, 1983; *The Palm-Wine Drinkard and His Dead Palm-Wine Tapster in the Dead's Town* and *My Life in the Bush of Ghosts* received second place awards in a contest held in Turin, Italy, 1985.

WRITINGS:

The Palm-Wine Drinkard and His Dead Palm-Wine Tapster in the Dead's Town, Faber, 1952, Grove, 1953.
My Life in the Bush of Ghosts, Grove, 1954, reprinted, Faber, 1978.
Simbi and the Satyr of the Dark Jungle, Faber, 1955.
The Brave African Huntress, illustrated by Ben Enwonwu, Grove, 1958.
The Feather Woman of the Jungle, Faber, 1962.
Ajaiyi and His Inherited Poverty, Faber, 1967.
(Contributor) *Winds of Change: Modern Short Stories from Black Africa,* Longman, 1977.
The Witch-Herbalist of the Remote Town, Faber, 1981.
The Wild Hunter in the Bush of the Ghosts (facsimile of manuscript), edited with an introduction and a postscript by Bernth Lindfors, Three Continents Press, 1982.
Pauper, Brawler, and Slanderer, Faber, 1987.

WORK REPRESENTED IN ANTHOLOGIES

Rutherford, Peggy, editor, *Darkness and Light: An Anthology of African Writing,* Drum Publications, 1958.
Hughes, Langston, editor, *An African Treasury: Articles, Essays, Stories, Poems by Black Africans,* Crown, 1960.
Hughes, Langston, and Christiane Reynault, editors, *Anthologie africaine et malgache,* Seghers, 1962.
Ademola, Frances, editor, *Reflections,* African Universities Press, 1962, new edition, 1965.
Sainville, Leonard, editor, *Anthologie de la litterature negro-africaine: Romanciers et conteurs negro africains,* two volumes, Presence Africaine, 1963.
Whiteley, W. H., compiler, *A Selection of African Prose,* two volumes, Oxford University Press, 1964.
Rive, Richard, editor, *Modern African Prose,* Heinemann Educational, 1964.
Komey, Ellis Ayitey and Ezekiel Mphahlele, editors, *Modern African Stories,* Faber, 1964.
Tibble, Anne, editor, *African-English Literature: A Survey and Anthology,* Peter Owen, 1965.
Edwards, Paul, compiler, *Through African Eyes,* two volumes, Cambridge University Press, 1966.
Mphahlele, Ezekiel, editor, *African Writing Today,* Penguin, 1967.
Beier, Ulli, editor, *Political Spider: An Anthology of Stories from "Black Orpheus,"* Heinemann Educational, 1969.
Larson, Charles, editor, *African Short Stories: A Collection of Contemporary African Writing,* Macmillan, 1970.

SIDELIGHTS: With the publication of his novel *The Palm-Wine Drinkard and His Dead Palm-Wine Tapster in the Dead's Town* in 1952, Amos Tutuola became the first internationally recognized Nigerian writer. Since that time, Tutuola's works, in particular *The Palm-Wine Drinkard,* have been the subject of much critical debate. *The Palm-Wine Drinkard* was praised by critics outside of Nigeria for its unconventional use of the English language, its adherence to the oral tradition, and its unique, fantastic characters and plot. Nigerian critics, on the other hand, described the work as ungrammatical and unoriginal. Discussing the first criticism in his book *The Growth of the African Novel,* Eustace Palmer writes: "Tutuola's English is demonstrably poor; this is due partly to his ignorance of the more complicated rules of English syntax and partly to interference from Yoruba." The second criticism, concerning Tutuola's lack of originality, is based on similarities between Tutuola's works and those of his predecessor, O. B. Fagunwa, who writes in the Yoruba language.

The influence of Fagunwa's writings on Tutuola's work has been noted by several critics, including Abiola Irele, who writes in *The African Experience in Literature and Ideology:* "It is clear that much of the praise and acclaim that have been lavished upon Tutuola belong more properly to Fagunwa who provided not only the original inspiration but indeed a good measure of material for Tutuola's novels. The echoes of Fagunwa in Tutuola's works are numerous enough to indicate that the latter was consciously creating from a model provided by the former." Irele adds, however, "that despite its derivation from the work of Fagunwa, Tutuola's work achieves an independent status that it owes essentially to the force of his individual genius."

Tutuola's genius is described by reviewers as an ability to refashion the traditional Yoruba myths and folktales that are the foundation of his work. Eustace Palmer notes, for instance, in *The Growth of the African Novel:* "Taking his stories direct from his people's traditional lore, he uses his inexhaustible imagination and inventive power to embellish them, to add to them or alter them, and generally transform them into his own stories conveying his own message." O. R. Dathorne comments in an essay published in *Introduction to Nigerian Literature:* "Tutuola is a literary paradox; he is completely part of the folklore traditions of the Yorubas and yet he is able to modernize these traditions in an imaginative way. It is on this level that his books can best be approached. . . . Tutuola deserves to be considered seriously because his work represents an intentional attempt to fuse folklore with modern life."

In *The Palm-Wine Drinkard,* for example, the Drinkard's quest for his tapster leads him into many perilous situations, including an encounter with the Red Fish, a monster Tutuola describes as having thirty horns "spread out as an umbrella," and numerous eyes that "were closing and opening at the same time as if a man was pressing a switch on and off." Tutuola also amends a traditional tale concerning a Skull who borrows appendages belonging to other persons in order to look like a "complete gentleman" to include referencesto modern warfare. Tutuola writes: "If this gentleman went to the battle field, surely, enemy would not kill him or capture him and if bombers saw him in a town which was to be bombed, they would not throw bombs on his presence, and if they did throw it, the bomb itself would not explode until this gentleman would leave that town, because of his beauty." Gerald Moore observes in *Seven African Writers* that these descriptions are evidence "of Tutuola's easy use of the paraphernalia of modern life to give sharpness and immediacy to his imagery."

The Palm-Wine Drinkard was hailed by critics such as V. S. Pritchett and Dylan Thomas, the latter of whom describes the work in the *Observer* as a "brief, thronged, grisly and bewitching story." Thomas concludes: "The writing is nearly always terse and direct, strong, wry, flat and savoury. . . . Nothing is too prodigious or too trivial put down in this tall, devilish story." The work also has been favorably compared to such classics as *The Odyssey, Pilgrim's Progress,* and *Gulliver's Travels.* Some critics, however, expressed reservations about Tutuola's ability to repeat his success. According to Charles R. Larson's *The Emergence of African Fiction,* critic Anthony West stated, "*The Palm-Wine Drinkard* must be valued for its own freakish sake, and as an unrepeatable happy hit."

Despite the reservations of critics like West, Tutuola went on to publish seven additional works, and while critics are, as Larson observes in *The Emergence of African Fiction,* "a little

less awed now than they were in the early 1950's," Tutuola's works continue to merit critical attention. Among the more widely reviewed of these books is *The Witch-Herbalist of the Remote Town.* Published thirty years after *The Palm-Wine Drinkard,* this book involves a quest initiated by the protagonist, a hunter, to find a cure for his wife's barrenness. The journey to the Remote Town takes six years; along the way the hunter encounters bizarre and sometimes frightening places and people, including the Town of the Born-and-Die Baby and the Abnormal Squatting Man of the Jungle, who can paralyze opponents with a gust of frigid air by piercing his abdomen. The hunter eventually reaches the Remote Town, and the witch-herbalist gives him a broth guaranteed to make his wife fertile. The plot is complicated though, when the hunter, weak from hunger, sips some of the broth.

As with *The Palm-Wine Drinkard,* critical commentary of *The Witch-Herbalist of the Remote Town* focuses in particular on Tutuola's use of the English language. Edward Blishen, for instance, comments in the *Times Educational Supplement:* "The language is wonderfully stirring and odd: a mixture of straight translation from Yoruba, and everyday modern Nigerian idiom, and grand epical English. The imagination at work is always astonishing. . . . And this, not the bargain, is folklore not resurrected, but being created fresh and true in the white heat of a tradition still undestroyed." *Voice Literary Supplement* critic Jon Parales writes: "His direct, apparently simple language creates an anything-can-happen universe, more whacky and amoral than the most determinedly modern lit." *Washington Post Book World* contributor Judith Chettle offers this view: "Tutuola writes with an appealing vigor and his idiosyncratic use of the English idiom gives the story a fresh and African perspective, though at times the clumsiness of some phrasing does detract from the thrust of the narrative. No eye-dabbing sentimentalist, Tutuola's commentary is clear-eyed if not acerbic, but underlying the tale is a quiet and persistent lament for the simpler, unsophisticated and happier past of his people."

An *Africa Today* contributor, Nancy J. Schmidt, observes that Tutuola's language has become increasingly more like that of standard English over the years. She cites other differences between this work and earlier ones as well. "Tutuola's presence is very evident in *Witch-Herbalist,* but the strength of his presence and his imagination are not as strong as they once were," writes Schmidt, who adds that "neither Tutuola nor his hero seem to be able to take a consistent moral stand, a characteristic that is distinctly different from Tutuola's other narratives." Commenting on the reasons for these differences, Schmidt writes: "They may reflect contemporary Yoruba culture, Tutuola's changing attitude toward Yoruba and Nigerian cultures as well as his changing position in Yoruba and Nigerian cultures, the difficulties of writing an oral narrative for an audience to whom oral narratives are becoming less familiar and less related to daily behavior, and the editorial policies for publishing African fictional narratives in the 1980s."

In the *New York Times Book Review* Charles Larson likewise notes Tutuola's use of standard English, but maintains that "the outstanding quality of Mr. Tutuola's work—the brilliance of the oral tradition—still remains." Larson concludes: "'The Witch-Herbalist of the Remote Town' is Mr. Tutuola at his imaginative best. Every incident in the narrative breathes with the life of the oral tradition; every episode in the journey startles with a kind of indigenous surrealism. Amos Tutuola is still his continent's most fantastic storyteller."

MEDIA ADAPTATIONS: Kola Ogunmola has written a play in Yoruba entitled *Omuti,* based on *The Palm-Wine Drinkard,* published by West African Book Publishers.

BIOGRAPHICAL/CRITICAL SOURCES:

BOOKS

Collins, Harold R., *Amos Tutuola,* Twayne, 1969.
Contemporary Literary Criticism, Gale, Volume 5, 1976, Volume 14, 1980, Volume 29, 1984.
Herskovits, Melville J. and Francis S. Herskovits, *Dahomean Narrative: A Cross-Cultural Analysis,* Northwestern University Press, 1958.
Irele, Abiola, *The African Experience in Literature and Ideology,* Heinemann, 1981.
King, Bruce, editor, *Introduction to Nigerian Literature,* Evans Brothers, 1971.
Larson, Charles R., *The Emergence of African Fiction,* revised edition, Indiana University Press, 1972.
Laurence, Margaret, *Long Drums and Cannons: Nigerian Dramatists,* Praeger, 1969.
Lindfors, Bernth, editor, *Critical Perspectives on Amos Tutuola,* Three Continents Press, 1975.
Lindfors, Bernth, *Early Nigerian Literature,* Africana Publishing, 1982.
Moore, Gerald, *Seven African Writers,* Oxford University Press, 1962.
Palmer, Eustace, *The Growth of the African Novel,* Heinemann, 1979.
Tucker, Martin, *Africa in Modern Literature: A Survey of Contemporary Writing in English,* Ungar, 1967.

Tutuola, Amos, *The Palm-Wine Drinkard and His Dead Palm-Wine Tapster in the Dead's Town,* Faber, 1952, Grove, 1953.

PERIODICALS

Africa Today, Volume 29, number 3, 1982.
Ariel, April, 1977.
Books Abroad, summer, 1968.
Critique, fall/winter, 1960-61, fall/winter, 1967-68.
Journal of Canandian Fiction, Volume 3, number 4, 1975.
Journal of Commonwealth Literature, August, 1974, August, 1981, Volume 17, number 1, 1982.
Listener, December 14, 1967.
London Review of Books, April 2, 1987.
Los Angeles Times Book Review, August 15, 1982.
Nation, September 25, 1954.
New Statesman, December 8, 1967.
New Yorker, April 23, 1984.
New York Times Book Review, July 4, 1982.
Observer, July 6, 1952, November 22, 1981.
Okikie, September, 1978.
Presence Africaine, 3rd trimestre, 1967.
Spectator, October 24, 1981.
Times Educational Supplement, February 26, 1982.
Times Literary Supplement, January 18, 1968, February 26, 1982, August 28, 1987.
Voice Literary Supplement, June, 1982.
Washington Post, July 13, 1987.
Washington Post Book World, August 15, 1982.

—*Sketch by Melissa Gaiownik*

U

UPCHURCH, Boyd (Bradfield) 1919-
(John Boyd)

PERSONAL: Born October 3, 1919, in Atlanta, Ga.; son of Ivie Doss (a railroad man) and Margaret Blake (Barnes) Upchurch; married Fern Gillaspy (a real estate broker), January 26, 1944 (died, 1984); married Mary Coe (an administrator in education), 1986. *Education:* Attended Atlanta Junior College, 1938-40; University of Southern California, A. B., 1947. *Politics:* Democrat. *Religion:* Methodist.

ADDRESSES: Home—1151 Aviemore Terrace, Costa Mesa, Calif. 92627.

CAREER: Star Engraving Company, Los Angeles, Calif., staff member, 1947-71, worked as salesman and production manager; full-time writer, 1971-79. *Military service:* U. S. Naval Reserve, active duty, 1940-46; became lieutenant commander; mentioned in dispatches of Royal Navy (England).

WRITINGS:

The Slave Stealer, Weybright & Talley, 1968.
Scarborough Hall, Berkley, 1975.
(With Richard H. Ichord) *Behind Every Bush: Treason or Patriotism* (nonfiction), Seville, 1979.

SCIENCE FICTION; UNDER PSEUDONYM JOHN BOYD

The Last Starship from Earth, Weybright & Talley, 1968.
The Pollinators of Eden, Weybright & Talley, 1969.
The Rakehells of Heaven, Weybright & Talley, 1969.
Sex and the High Command, Weybright & Talley, 1970.
The Organ Bank Farm, Weybright & Talley, 1970.
The Gorgon Festival, Weybright & Talley, 1972.
The I. Q. Merchant, Weybright & Talley, 1972.
The Doomsday Gene, Weybright & Talley, 1973.
Andromeda Gun, Berkley, 1974.
Barnard's Planet, Berkley, 1975.
The Girl with the Jade Green Eyes, Viking, 1978.
(Contributor) Roy Torgeson, editor, *Other Worlds 2,* Zebra Books, 1980.

Contributor to *Galaxy.*

WORK IN PROGRESS: "A Southern Gentleman."

SIDELIGHTS: "As well as employing an element of humor—often satiric—and demonstrating a fondness for literary allusion," Boyd Upchurch's science fiction, written under the pseudonym John Boyd, "explores the dangers of man's inability to keep morally and emotionally abreast of his exploding technology," asserts Tyler Smith in a *Dictionary of Literary Biography* essay. Upchurch has based some of his science fiction novels on classical stories, such as those of Phaedra, Prometheus, and Dante's *Inferno.* In *Sex and the High Command,* Upchurch updates Aristophenes's classic play "Lysistrata," speculating about the results of a female secession from society after the discovery of a drug that makes men obsolete. The author, "who is able to keep a cool head in the face of such imminent horrors," notes *New York Times Book Review* contributor Martin Levin, "squeezes all possible shades of gray and black humor from them." *The Girl with the Jade Green Eyes* reports the government's reaction to another extraordinary event: the appearance of superior alien forms on Earth. The creatures, including the beautiful green-eyed girl of the title, inspire the suspicion of several government and military agencies who compete among each other for information. In producing this satiric account, Upchurch uses the alien's viewpoint, "which turns out to be just right for observing the involuted, absurd, nightmare-logic world of international espionage and power politics,"comments Gerald Jonas of the *New York Times Book Review.* Calling the novel "a sophisticated variant on an old theme," the critic adds that the author "is a cool customer. He is in complete control throughout this novel."

AVOCATIONAL INTERESTS: Civil War history.

BIOGRAPHICAL/CRITICAL SOURCES:

BOOKS

Dictionary of Literary Biography, Volume 8: *Twentieth-Century American Science Fiction Writers,* Gale, 1981.

PERIODICALS

New York Times Book Review, June 16, 1968, February 1, 1970, February 26, 1978.
Times Literary Supplement, April 16, 1971.

*   *   *

URY, William L(anger) 1953-

PERSONAL: Born September 12, 1953, in Harvey, Ill.; son

of Melvin C. (an attorney and businessman) and Janice (a businesswoman; maiden name, Gray) Ury. *Education:* Yale University, B.A. (magna cum laude), 1975; Harvard University, M.A., 1977, Ph.D., 1980.

ADDRESSES: Home—Lincoln, Mass. *Office*—Harvard Law School, Cambridge, Mass. 02138.

CAREER: Harvard University, Cambridge, Mass., director of Harvard Nuclear Negotiation Project, Harvard Law School, 1980—, assistant professor at Harvard Business School, Boston, Mass., 1982-84, associate director, Program on Negotiation, Harvard Law School, 1984—. Lecturer and consultant on negotiation and mediation at Harvard University.

WRITINGS:

(With Roger Fisher) *International Mediation: A Working Guide,* International Peace Academy, 1978.
(With Fisher) *Getting to Yes: Reaching Agreement without Giving In,* Houghton, 1981.
Beyond the Hotline: How Crisis Control Can Prevent Nuclear War, Houghton, 1985.
(With Jeanne Brett and Stephen Goldberg) *Designing Dispute Resolution Solutions,* Jossey-Bass, 1988.

Also author of unpublished manuscripts, (with Annette Hochstein) *The Jerusalem Question: Problems, Procedures, and Options,* 1980, and *Talk Out or Walk Out: Controlling Conflict in a Kentucky Coal Mine,* 1982. Also contributor of articles to *International Journal of the Sociology of Language* and *Harvard International Review.*

SIDELIGHTS: In *Getting to Yes: Reaching Agreement without Giving In,* co-authors William L. Ury and Roger Fisher advocate a concise, step-by-step method for successful negotiations. They suggest that parties not be dogmatic about their positions, but focus instead on the underlying needs of both sides. Don't allow personality differences to interfere with problems solving, the authors advise, and don't think of each other as adversaries, but as parties working together for mutual gain. *Washington Post* writer Joseph McLellan lauded Fisher and Ury for their common sense approach to negotiations, and noted that *Getting to Yes* ''is a joy to read for those who delight in concise, lucid, logical exposition.''

BIOGRAPHICAL/CRITICAL SOURCES:

PERIODICALS

Times Literary Supplement, August 27, 1982.
Washington Post, December 26, 1981, May 20, 1985.

V

VAJDA, Stephan 1926-1987

PERSONAL: Born March 19, 1926, in Budapest, Hungary; died March 18, 1987, in Vienna, Austria; son of Ferenc and Maria (Oesterreicher) Vajda; married Eva Szana (a translator), 1949. *Education:* Attended University of Budapest. *Religion:* Roman Catholic.

ADDRESSES: Home and office—9 Bergler Strasse, 21, Vienna, Austria.

CAREER: Abandoned law studies to become a journalist in Hungary; worked for Schoenbrunn Film, Vienna, Austria, as art director for television and film; also worked as free-lance writer.

MEMBER: Oesterreichische Gesellschaft fuer Literatur.

AWARDS, HONORS: Georg Mackensen Preis, 1963, for best short story published in Germany; awards from Austrian Ministry of Education, 1963 and 1964.

WRITINGS:

L'Accident (novel), Stock (Paris), 1961.
Budapest AA 338 (novel), Doubleday, 1963.
Modellfall Bartholomaeusnacht, J. Lanz (Vienna), 1972.
"Mir san vom k.u.k.": Die kuriose Geschichte des oesterreichische Militaermusik, Ueberreuter (Vienna), 1977.
Felix Austria: Eine Geschichte Oesterreichs, Ueberreuter, 1980.
Reisen anno 1900: Ein Fuehrer durch die Laender der k.u.k. Monarchie, Ueberreuter, 1981.
Die Belagerung: Bericht ueber das Tuerkenjahr 1683, two volumes, Orac (Vienna), 1983.

Also author of plays in German for screen, television, and the stage.*

[Death date provided by wife, Eva Vajda]

*   *   *

Van PEEBLES, Melvin 1932-

PERSONAL: Born August 21, 1932, in Chicago, Ill.; children: Mario, Meggan, Melvin. *Education:* Graduated from Ohio Wesleyan University.

CAREER: Writer, actor, producer of plays, director, and composer. Worked as operator of cable cars in San Francisco,

Calif., and as a floor trader for the American Stock Exchange. Director of motion pictures, including "Watermelon Man," 1970. *Military service:* U.S. Air Force; served as navigator-bombardier.

MEMBER: Directors Guild of America, French Directors Guild.

AWARDS, HONORS: First Prize from Belgian Festival for "Don't Play Us Cheap."

WRITINGS:

Un ours pour le F.B.I. (novel), Buchet-Chastel, 1964, translation published as *A Bear for the F.B.I.,* Trident, 1968.
Un Americain en enfer (novel), Editions Denoel, 1965, translation published as *The True American: A Folk Fable,* Doubleday, 1976.
Le Chinois du XIV (short stories), Le Gadenet, 1966.
La Fete a Harlem [and] *La Permission* (two novels; former adapted from the play by Van Peebles, "Harlem Party"; also see below), J. Martineau, 1967, translation of *La Fete a Harlem* published as *Don't Play Us Cheap: A Harlem Party,* Bantam, 1973.
Sweet Sweetback's Baadasssss Song (adapted from the screenplay by Van Peebles; also see below), Lancer Books, 1971.
The Making of Sweet Sweetback's Baadasssss Song (nonfiction), Lancer Books, 1972.
Aint Supposed to Die a Natural Death (play; directed by the author and produced in New York City at the Ethel Barrymore Theatre, 1971; adapted from the recordings by Van Peebles, "Brer Soul" and "Ain't Supposed to Die a Natural Death"), Bantam, 1973.
Just an Old Sweet Song, Ballantine, 1976.
(With Kenneth Vose, Leon Capetanos, and Lawrence Du Kose) *Greased Lightning* (screenplay; produced by Warner Bros., 1977), Yeah, 1976.
Bold Money: A New Way to Play the Options Market, Warner Books, 1986.
Bold Money: How to Get Rich in the Options Market, Warner Books, 1987.

OTHER

"Harlem Party" (play), produced in Belgium, 1964, produced as "Don't Play Us Cheap," directed by the author and produced in New York City at the Ethel Barrymore Theatre, 1972.

(And director) "The Story of a Three Day Pass" (screenplay), Sigma III, 1968.

(And director) "Sweet Sweetback's Baadasssss Song" (screenplay), Cinemation Industries, 1971.

"Sophisticated Gents" (television screenplay; adapted from *The Junior Bachelor Society* by John A. Williams), produced as a four hour miniseries and broadcast on NBC-TV, September, 1981.

"Waltz of the Stork" (play), directed by author and produced in New York City at the Century Theatre, 1982.

"Champeeen!" (play), directed by author and produced in New York City at the New Federal Theatre, 1983.

Also author and director of "Don't Play Us Cheap" (adapted from the play by Van Peebles). Also creator of short films, including "Sunlight," Cinema 16, and "Three Pick Up Men for Herrick," Cinema 16.

Composer for recordings, including "Brer Soul," "Aint Supposed to Die a Natural Death," "Watermelon Man" (soundtrack for the motion picture), "Serious as a Heart Attack," "Sweet Sweetback's Baadasssss Song" (soundtrack for the motion picture), and "Don't Play Us Cheap" (soundtrack for the motion picture).

SIDELIGHTS: Melvin Van Peebles began his career as an artist by creating short films. He had hoped that his first film efforts would lead to a filmmaking opportunity in Hollywood but moguls there were unimpressed. Instead of obtaining a position as a director or even assistant director, he was offered a job as an elevator operator. Seemingly at a dead end, Van Peebles suddenly received word from Henri Langlois, an associate of the French Cinematheque film depository who'd been impressed with Van Peebles's films. Langlois invited Van Peebles to come to Paris. There, Van Peebles enjoyed brief celebrity as an avant-garde filmmaker. But he had no opportunities to pursue filmmaking.

Van Peebles worked for some time as an entertainer in cafes until he discovered a means by which he could once again take up filmmaking. In France, one could gain entry into the Directors Guild if he wished to adapt his own French writings. So Van Peebles, in self-taught French, began writing novels. His first work, *A Bear for the F.B.I.*, concerned events in the life of an American middle-class black. Critical response was favorable, with Martin Levin remarking in the *New York Times Book Review* that "Van Peebles crystallizes the racial problem with rare subtlety." However, Van Peebles noted that the subtlety of the novel hindered his chances of being published in the United States. "I wrote the first work and my 'calling card,' to establish my reputation so I could get my 'black' novels published," Van Peebles claimed. "But the publishers aren't interested unless you either lacerate whites or apologize to them."

American publishers displayed a similar lack of interest toward Van Peebles's next novel, *The True American*, which was written in 1965 but not published in the United States until 1976. It is the story of George Abraham Carver, a black prisoner who is accidentally killed by falling rocks. Carver arrives in Hell and learns that blacks are treated well there. This is because the majority of Hell's residents are white and, supposedly, the preferential attention the blacks receive causes the white residents more grief. Despite the "promising" premise, the novel was reviewed unfavorably in *New Yorker*. "Unfortunately," wrote the critic, "the book never really lives up

to its promise, largely because of its pasteboard characters, its meandering plot, and its author's tendency to use a two-ton sledgehammer to drive home every point he makes about racist America."

Van Peebles continued to write, though, and produced in rapid succession a collection of short stories, *Le Chinois du XIV*, and two short novels, *La Fete a Harlem* and *La Permission*. At the same time, he was also arranging another film project. With the financial assistance of the French Ministry of Cultural Affairs and a private citizen, Van Peebles made "The Story of a Three Day Pass," a film about a black soldier's encounter with a French woman. "The Story of a Three Day Pass" attracted substantial audiences in France and, upon its release in the United States, Van Peebles was in demand in Hollywood.

In 1969, after returning to the United States, Van Peebles agreed to direct a film written by Herman Raucher entitled "Watermelon Man." This film deals with a white insurance agent who awakens one morning to discover that he's turned into a black man. "It's authentic stuff," related Van Peebles, "that laughs *with*, not at people." Later, he insisted, "I thought I had to make 'Watermelon Man' in order to do the films I really wanted to do.

Van Peebles's next film, "Sweet Sweetback's Baadasssss Song," is probably his best known work to date. He made the film in three weeks, using nonunion crews while keeping union officials disinterested by spreading rumors that he was making a pornographic film, something unworthy of their attention. Hollywood had refused to finance the film after a reading of the screenplay failed to impress studio officials. Fortunately, Van Peebles received a sizeable loan from Bill Cosby which enabled him to complete the film. There was also difficulty promoting the film. Distributors declined to present it, theatres refused to book it, and talk shows refused to host Van Peebles. Eventually, he resorted to promoting it himself by passing out leaflets on street corners. Such determination ultimately paid off for Van Peebles. As a writer for *Time* noted, Van Peebles's "fast talk, plus audience word of mouth, made it a limited success. But that was enough." After the initial success of the film, it was mass-released to more than one hundred theatres and enjoyed brief status as the top money-makng film in *Variety*.

The film elicited a variety of critical responses. The story of a black sex-show performer who avenges a youth's beating at the hands of two policemen by murdering them and eventually escapes to Mexico enraged some reviewers. Robert Hatch accused him in *Nation* of relying "on rather irresponsible contemporary emotionalism to revitalize stock films he must have seen in his childhood." In the *New York Times* Vincent Canby claimed, "instead of dramatizing injustice, Van Peebles merchandizes it." He also declared that "the militancy of 'Sweet Sweetback' is of a dull order, seemingly designed only to reinforce the prejudices of black audiences without in any way disturbing those prejudices." Clayton Riley conceded in the *New York Times*, "The film is an outrage," but then observed that it was "designed to blow minds." He wrote, "Through the lens of the Van Peebles camera comes a very basic Black America, unadorned by faith, and seething with an eternal violence." In the same review, Riley contended, "It is a terrifying vision, the Blood's nightmare journey through Watts, and it is a vision Black people alone will really understand in all of its profane and abrasive substance." In his study of black filmmakers published in the 1979 book, *American Film Now:*

The People, the Power, the Money, the Movies, James Monaco takes a new look at Van Peebles's 1971 screenplay. "['Sweet Sweetback's Baadasssss Song'] situates itself squarely in a long and important tradition in Black American narrative art," Monaco writes. "The Sweetback character has been mimicked and repeated a number of times since, but never with such purity of purpose and such *elan.* Van Peebles bent the medium of film to his will. No one else has bent it so far or so well since."

Van Peebles told a *Time* reporter that the film was not just for black audiences. "If films are good," he expressed, "the universality of the human experience will transcend the race and creed and crap frontiers." But he also noted that the film does have some specific messages for blacks. "Of all the ways we've been exploited by the Man, the most damaging is the way he destroyed our self-image," he asserted. "The message of 'Sweetback' is that if you can get it together and stand up to the Man, you can win." In a *New York Times* interview, Van Peebles asked a writer, "When's the last time you saw a film in which the black man won in the end?" He then declared, "In my film, the black audience finally gets a chance to see some of their own fantasies acted out—about rising out of the mud and kicking ass."

After the success of "Sweet Sweetback," Van Peebles was inundated with filmmaking offers from Hollywood studios. However, he insisted that he maintain his independence. "I'll only work with them on my terms," he stated. "I've whipped the man's ass on his own turf. I'm number one at the box office—which is the way America measures things—and I did it on my own. Now they want me, but I'm in no hurry."

Much of Van Peebles's most recent work has been as a playwright. "Aint Supposed to Die a Natural Death," his first play to be produced in the United States, proved to be a popular one with Broadway audiences. In *Cue* Marilyn Stasio called it a "tremendously vital musical with a dynamic new form all its own." She also wrote, "The show is an electrifying piece of theatre without having songs, a book, a story line, choreography, or even standard production numbers—and yet all these elements are on the stage, skillfully integrated into a jolting new experience." And Peter Bailey commented in *Black World* that "Aint Supposed to Die a Natural Death" "presented us with an effective and moving evening in the theater. Broadway has never seen anything like it. Van Peebles' characters come alive and make us deal with them on their own terms."

A writer for *Variety* was impressed with the U.S. production of another Van Peebles play, "Don't Play Us Cheap." The reviewer noted that "this new show does not seem to be infused with hate, and it offers what appears to [be] a racial attitude without foul language, deliberate squalor or snarling ugliness." The same critic observed that "points are made with humor rather than rage and are probably more palatable for general audiences." "'Don't Play Us Cheap' is a somewhat special show," concluded the writer for *Variety,* "probably with greater meaning and appeal for black audiences than for whites." Van Peebles later adapted the play for film.

In 1986, Van Peebles published *Bold Money: A New Way to Play the Options Market* adding another twist to his variety of writing talents. As a result of losing an interesting wager with a friend, Van Peebles was obliged to take the examination to become an options trader. After failing the exam, Van Peebles became a clerk on the floor of the American Stock Exchange in order to learn enough to pass the exam. As Van Peebles told Laurie Cohen and Fred Marc Biddle in the *Chicago Tribune,* "If I had to find one characteristic that is most symbolic of me, I think I am tenacious."

After trading options for three years and passing the examination, Van Peebles was asked by Warner Books to write a how-to-book on making money in the options market. A critic for *Kirkus Reviews* writes of *Bold Money: A New Way to Play the Options Market* that Van Peebles's "often impudent but prudent text is an excellent choice for rookies seeking a like-it-is introduction to a fast game." A year after his first money book was published he wrote *Bold Money: How to Get Rich in the Option Market.*

BIOGRAPHICAL/CRITICAL SOURCES:

BOOKS

Contemporary Literary Criticism, Gale, Volume 2, 1974, Volume 20, 1982.
Monaco, James, *American Films Now: The People, the Power, the Money, the Movies,* Oxford University Press, 1979.

PERIODICALS

Best Sellers, October 15, 1968.
Black World, April, 1972.
Chicago Tribune, March 24, 1986.
Cue, October 30, 1971, May 27, 1972.
Kirkus Reviews, December 1, 1985.
Nation, May 24, 1971.
Newsweek, June 6, 1969, June 21, 1971.
New Yorker, March 1, 1976.
New York Times, May 18, 1969, April 24, 1971, May 9, 1971, September 29, 1981, January 6, 1982.
New York Times Book Review, October 6, 1968.
Saturday Review, August 3, 1968.
Time, August 16, 1971.
Variety, May 24, 1971.*

*   *   *

VOGT, Evon Zartman, Jr.   1918-

PERSONAL: Born August 20, 1918, in Gallup, N.M.; son of Evon and Shirley (Bergman) Vogt; married Catherine Christine Hiller, September 4, 1941; children: Shirley Naneen (Mrs. Geza Teleki), Evon Zartman III, Eric Edwards, Charles Anthony. *Education:* University of Chicago, A.B., 1941, M.A., 1946, Ph.D., 1948.

ADDRESSES: Home—14 Chauncy St., Cambridge, Mass. 02138. *Office*—Peabody Museum of American Archaeology and Ethnology, Harvard University, Cambridge, Mass. 02138.

CAREER: Harvard University, Cambridge, Mass., instructor, 1948-50, assistant professor, 1950-55, associate professor, 1955-59, professor of anthropology, 1959—, chairperson of department, 1969-73, master of Kirkland House, 1974-82, assistant curator of American ethnology at Peabody Museum of American Archaeology and Ethnology, 1950-59, curator of Middle American ethnology, 1960—, member of expeditions to New Mexico, 1947-53, and Mexico, 1954—, director of Chiapas project, 1957—. Visiting professor, University of Hawaii, 1972. Fellow of Center for Advanced Study in the Behavioral Sciences, 1956-57. Member of Division of Anthropology and Psychology for National Research Council, 1955-

57; member of advisory panel in anthropology for National Science Foundation, 1964-66. *Military service:* U.S. Naval Reserve, active duty, 1942-46; became lieutenant.

MEMBER: American Academy of Arts and Sciences (fellow; councillor, 1974-78), National Academy of Sciences (chairman, anthropology section, 1981-84), American Anthropological Association (fellow; member of executive board, 1958-60), Society of American Archaeology, American Folklore Society, Royal Anthropological Society of Great Britain and Ireland, Harvard Club (Boston), Tavern Club (Boston).

AWARDS, HONORS: Bernard de Sahagun Prize, Republic of Mexico, and Harvard Press Faculty Prize, both 1969, for *Zinacantan: A Maya Community in the Highlands of the Chiapas;* Commander, Order of the Aztec Eagle, Republic of Mexico, 1978.

WRITINGS:

(With Clyde Kluckhohn) *Navaho Means People,* Harvard University Press, 1951.
Navaho Veterans: A Study of Changing Values, Peabody Museum of American Archaeology and Ethnology, Harvard University, 1951.
Modern Homesteaders: The Life of a Twentieth-Century Frontier Community, Belknap Press, 1955.
(Editor with William Armand Lessa) *Reader in Comparative Religion: An Anthropological Approach,* Row, Peterson, 1958, 4th edition, Harper, 1979.
(With Ray Hyman) *Water Witching, U.S.A.,* University of Chicago Press, 1959, 2nd edition, 1979.
(Editor with Alberto Ruz L.) *Conference on "The Cultural Development of the Maya," Burg Wartenstein, Austria, 1962,* Department of Philosophy and Letters, Universidad Nacional Autonoma de Mexico, 1964.
(With Gordon R. Wiley) *Seminar on the Maya,* Department of Anthropology, Harvard University, Volume I: *1964-1965,* 1965, Volume III: *1969-1970,* 1969.
(Editor with Ethel M. Albert) *People of Rimrock: A Study of Values in Five Cultures,* Harvard University Press, 1966.
(Editor) *Handbook of Middle American Indians,* Volume VII: *Ethnology, Part 1,* Volume VIII: *Ethnology, Part 2,* University of Texas Press, 1969.
Zinacantan: A Maya Community in the Highlands of Chiapas, Belknap Press, 1969.
The Zinacantecos of Mexico: A Modern Maya Way of Life, Holt, 1970.
(Editor) *Harvard Chiapas Project, 1957-71,* Harvard University, 1971.
(Editor with Walter W. Taylor and John L. Fischer, and contributor) *Culture and Life: Essays in Memory of Clyde Kluckhohn,* Southern Illinois University Press, 1973.
(Editor) *Aerial Photography in Anthropological Research,* Harvard University Press, 1974.
Tortillas for the Gods: A Symbolic Analysis of Zinacanteco Rituals, Harvard University Press, 1976.
Bibliography of the Harvard Chiapas Project: The First Twenty Years, 1957-1977, Peabody Museum of Archaeology and Ethnology, Harvard University, 1978.
(Editor with Richard M. Leventhal) *Prehistoric Settlement Patterns: Essays in Honor of Gordon R. Wiley,* University of New Mexico Press, 1983.

Also editor of *Los Zinacantecos,* 1966. Contributor to professional journals.

SIDELIGHTS: In 1957 Evon Zartman Vogt, Jr., established the Harvard Chiapas project, designed to study the contemporary Mayan Indians of Chiapas, Mexico. The project has continued for over thirty years, and has produced numerous books, articles, and theses; Vogt has published a seventy-five page bibliography covering the first twenty years alone. *Zinacantan: A Maya Community in the Highlands of the Chiapas,* published in 1969, "is based upon the twenty months Vogt has personally spent in research and upon the findings of his students and associates," describes *Saturday Review* contributor Robert F. Murphy. "[But] whereas the latter have published on certain delimited aspects of Zinacantecan society, Vogt has set himself the task of producing a general ethnography of the community." Although the book also considers theoretical issues and cultural change, remarks the critic, "above all the book is splendid ethnography." Assessing the author's work directing the Chiapas project, Murphy concludes that "Vogt is clearly one of those rare academicians who combine scholarly talent with administrative ability and dedication to teaching."

BIOGRAPHICAL/CRITICAL SOURCES:

PERIODICALS

Saturday Review, August 23, 1969.
Times Literary Supplement, February 4, 1977.

*   *   *

VRETTOS, Theodore   1919-

PERSONAL: Surname is accented on first syllable; born November 23, 1919, in Peabody, Mass.; son of Leonidas and Zacharoula (Karabelas) Vrettos; married Vassille Parianos, September 15, 1946. *Education:* Attended Holy Cross Greek Seminary, 1941-45; graduate study at Tufts College and Harvard University. *Religion:* Greek Orthodox.

ADDRESSES: Home—75 Prospect St., Peabody, Mass. 01960.

CAREER: Northeastern University, Boston, Mass., instructor of English, 1965; Endicott College, Beverly, Mass., writer in residence, 1966-70; Salem State College, Salem, Mass., director of creative writing program, 1970-80; Simmons College, Boston, writer in residence, 1980—.

WRITINGS:

Hammer on the Sea (novel), Little, Brown, 1965.
A Shadow of Magnitude (nonfiction), Putnam, 1974.
Origin (novel), Caratzas, 1978.
Birds of Winter (novel), Houghton, 1980.
Lord Elgin's Lady (novel), Houghton, 1982.

Contributor to magazines, including *Literary Review, Audience, Catholic Digest,* and *Yankee.*

WORK IN PROGRESS: Two novels, *Snow Red* and *Days of Games.*

SIDELIGHTS: Many of Theodore Vrettos's novels combine a contemporary Greek setting and situation with parallels to classical mythology and history. For example, one level of his "powerful and compelling novel," *Birds of Winter,* "concerns Greece on the eve of Mussolini's invasion," relates *Boston Globe* writer Robert Taylor. "Another level concerns the spiritual quest of the story's aptly named youthful hero, Jason." "Like Greece itself," summarizes a *New Yorker* critic, "this spare story has a deceptively simple surface; every passage is permeated with allusions to the heroes of ancient history and mythology.'' Taylor adds that the author's talents keep the story from becoming a simple imitation: ''It is the distinguished achievement of the author to merge the atmospheric element, how Greece looks, the odors and sounds of a time and place, with the pilgrimage theme, into a story of gathering narrative force.''

BIOGRAPHICAL/CRITICAL SOURCES:

PERIODICALS

Boston Globe, August 20, 1980.
Los Angeles Times Book Review, August 29, 1982.
New Yorker, August 25, 1980.
New York Times Book Review, October 26, 1980.
Washington Post, September 26, 1980.
Washington Post Book World, June 6, 1982.

W

WALKER, Alice (Malsenior) 1944-

PERSONAL: Born February 9, 1944, in Eatonton, Ga.; daughter of Willie Lee and Minnie Tallulah (Grant) Walker; married Melvyn Rosenman Leventhal (a civil rights lawyer), March 17, 1967 (divorced, 1976); children: Rebecca Grant. *Education:* Attended Spelman College, 1961-63; Sarah Lawrence College, B.A., 1965.

ADDRESSES: Home—San Francisco, Calif.

CAREER: Writer. Wild Trees Press, Navarro, Calif., co-founder and publisher, 1984-88. Has been a voter registration worker in Georgia, a worker in Head Start program in Mississippi, and on staff of New York City welfare department. Writer-in-residence and teacher of black studies at Jackson State College, 1968-69, and Tougaloo College, 1970-71; lecturer in literature, Wellesley College and University of Massachusetts—Boston, both 1972-73; distinguished writer in Afro-American studies department, University of California, Berkeley, spring, 1982; Fannie Hurst Professor of Literature, Brandeis University, Waltham, Mass., fall, 1982. Lecturer and reader of own poetry at universities and conferences. Member of board of trustees of Sarah Lawrence College. Consultant on black history to Friends of the Children of Mississippi, 1967.

AWARDS, HONORS: Bread Loaf Writer's Conference, scholar, 1966; first prize, *American Scholar* essay contest, 1967; Merrill writing fellowship, 1967; McDowell Colony fellowship, 1967, 1977-78; National Endowment for the Arts grant, 1969, 1977; Radcliffe Institute fellowship, 1971-73; Ph.D., Russell Sage College, 1972; National Book Award nomination, 1973, for *Revolutionary Petunias and Other Poems;* Lillian Smith Award, Southern Regional Council, 1973, for *Revolutionary Petunias;* Richard and Hinda Rosenthal Foundation Award, American Academy and Institute of Arts and Letters, 1974, for *In Love and Trouble;* Guggenheim Award, 1977-78; National Book Critics Circle Award nomination, 1982, Pulitzer Prize, 1983, and American Book Award, 1983, all for *The Color Purple;* D.H.L., University of Massachusetts, 1983; O. Henry Award, 1986, for "Kindred Spirits."

WRITINGS:

POETRY

Once: Poems (also see below), Harcourt, 1968, reprinted, Women's Press, 1988.

Five Poems, Broadside Press, 1972.

Revolutionary Petunias and Other Poems (also see below), Harcourt, 1973.

Goodnight, Willie Lee, I'll See You in the Morning (also see below), Dial, 1979.

Horses Make a Landscape Look More Beautiful, Harcourt, 1984.

Alice Walker Boxed Set—Poetry: Good Night, Willie Lee, I'll See You in the Morning; Revolutionary Petunias and Other Poems; Once, Poems, Harcourt, 1985.

FICTION

The Third Life of Grange Copeland (novel; also see below), Harcourt, 1970.

In Love and Trouble: Stories of Black Women (also see below), Harcourt, 1973.

Meridian (novel), Harcourt, 1976.

You Can't Keep a Good Woman Down (short stories; also see below), Harcourt, 1981.

The Color Purple (novel), Harcourt, 1982.

Alice Walker Boxed Set—Fiction: The Third Life of Grange Copeland, You Can't Keep a Good Woman Down, and In Love and Trouble, Harcourt, 1985.

To Hell with Dying (juvenile), illustrations by Catherine Deeter, Harcourt, 1988.

The Temple of My Familiar (novel), Harcourt, 1989.

CONTRIBUTOR TO ANTHOLOGIES

Helen Haynes, editor, *Voices of the Revolution,* E. & J. Kaplan (Philadelphia), 1967.

Langston Hughes, editor, *The Best Short Stories by Negro Writers from 1899 to the Present: An Anthology,* Little, Brown, 1967.

Robert Hayden, David J. Burrows, and Frederick R. Lapides, compilers, *Afro-American Literature: An Introduction,* Harcourt, 1971.

Toni Cade Bambara, compiler, *Tales and Stories for Black Folks,* Zenith Books, 1971.

Woodie King, compiler, *Black Short Story Anthology,* New American Library, 1972.

Arnold Adoff, compiler, *The Poetry of Black America: An Anthology of the Twentieth Century,* Harper, 1973.

Lindsay Patterson, editor, *A Rock against the Wind: Black Love Poems,* Dodd, 1973.

Sonia Sanchez, editor, *We Be Word Sorcerers: Twenty-five Stories by Black Americans*, Bantam, 1973.

Mary Anne Ferguson, compiler, *Images of Women in Literature*, Houghton, 1973.

Margaret Foley, editor, *Best American Short Stories: 1973*, Hart-Davis, 1973.

Foley, editor, *Best American Short Stories, 1974*, Houghton, 1974.

Michael S. Harper and Robert B. Stepto, editors, *Chants of Saints: A Gathering of Afro-American Literature, Art and Scholarship*, University of Illinois Press, 1980.

Mary Helen Washington, editor, *Midnight Birds: Stories of Contemporary Black Women Authors*, Anchor Press, 1980.

Dexter Fisher, editor, *The Third Woman: Minority Women Writers of the United States*, 1980.

OTHER

Langston Hughes: American Poet (children's biography), Crowell, 1973.

(Editor) *I Love Myself When I'm Laughing . . . and Then Again When I Am Looking Mean and Impressive: A Zora Neale Hurston Reader*, introduction by Mary Helen Washington, Feminist Press, 1979.

In Search of Our Mothers' Gardens: Womanist Prose, Harcourt, 1983.

Living by the Word: Selected Writings, 1973-1987, Harcourt, 1988.

Contributor to periodicals, including *Negro Digest*, *Denver Quarterly*, *Harper's*, *Black World*, and *Essence*. Contributing editor, *Southern Voices*, *Freedomways*, and *Ms.*

WORK IN PROGRESS: Finding the Green Stone, "a fable," with Catherine Deeter.

SIDELIGHTS: "*The Color Purple*, Alice Walker's third [novel,] could be the kind of popular and literary event that transforms an intense reputation into a national one," according to Gloria Steinem of *Ms*. Judging from the critical enthusiasm for *The Color Purple*, Steinem's words have proved prophetic. Walker "has succeeded," as Andrea Ford notes in the *Detroit Free Press*, "in creating a jewel of a novel." Peter S. Prescott presents a similar opinion in a *Newsweek* review. "I want to say," he comments, "that *The Color Purple* is an American novel of permanent importance, that rare sort of book which (in Norman Mailer's felicitous phrase) amounts to 'a diversion in the fields of dread.'"

Although Walker's other books—novels, volumes of short stories, and poems—have not been completely ignored, they have not received the amount of attention that many critics feel they deserve. For example, William Peden, writing about *In Love and Trouble: Stories of Black Women* in *The American Short Story: Continuity and Change, 1940-75*, calls the collection of stories "a remarkable book that deserves to be much better known and more widely read." And while Steinem points out that *Meridian*, Walker's second novel, "is often cited as the best novel of the civil rights movement, and is taught as part of some American history as well as literature courses," Steinem maintains that Walker's "visibility as a major American talent has been obscured by a familiar bias that assumes white male writers, and the literature they create, to be the norm. That puts black women (and all women of color) at a double remove."

Jeanne Fox-Alston and Mel Watkins both feel that the appeal of *The Color Purple* is that the novel, as a synthesis of characters and themes found in Walker's earlier works, brings together the best of the author's literary production in one volume. Fox-Alston, in the *Chicago Tribune Book World*, remarks: "Celie, the main character in Walker's third . . . novel, *The Color Purple*, is an amalgam of all those women [characters in Walker's previous books]; she embodies both their desperation and, later, their faith." Watkins states in the *New York Times Book Review*: "Her previous books . . . have elicited praise for Miss Walker as a lavishly gifted writer. *The Color Purple*, while easily satisfying that claim, brings into sharper focus many of the diverse themes that threaded their way through her past work."

Walker's central characters are almost always black women; the themes of sexism and racism are predominant in her work, but her impact is felt across both racial and sexual boundaries. Walker, according to Steinem, "comes at universality through the path of an American black woman's experience. . . . She speaks the female experience more powerfully for being able to pursue it across boundaries of race and class." This universality is also noted by Fox-Alston, who remarks that Walker has a "reputation as a provocative writer who writes about blacks in particular, but all humanity in general."

However, many critics see a definite black and female focus in Walker's writings. For example, in her review of *The Color Purple*, Ford suggests that the novel transcends "culture and gender" lines but also refers to Walker's "unabashedly feminist viewpoint" and the novel's "black . . . texture." Walker does not deny this dual bias; the task of revealing the condition of the black woman is particularly important to her. Thadious M. Davis, in his *Dictionary of Literary Biography* essay, comments: "Walker writes best of the social and personal drama in the lives of familiar people who struggle for survival of self in hostile environments. She has expressed a special concern with 'exploring the oppressions, the insanities, the loyalties and the triumph of black women.'" Walker explains in a *Publishers Weekly* interview: "The black woman is one of America's greatest heroes. . . . Not enough credit has been given to the black woman who has been oppressed beyond recognition."

Critics reviewing Walker's first collection of short stories, *In Love and Trouble: Stories of Black Women*, respond favorably to the author's rendering of the black experience. In *Ms.* Barbara Smith observes: "This collection would be an extraordinary literary work, if its only virtue were the fact that the author sets out consciously to explore with honesty the textures and terror of black women's lives. Attempts to penetrate the myths surrounding black women's experiences are so pitifully rare in black, feminist, or American writing that each shred of truth about these experiences constitutes a breakthrough. The fact that Walker's perceptions, style, and artistry are also consistently high makes her work a treasure." Mary Helen Washington remarks in a *Black World* review: "The stories in *In Love and Trouble* . . . constitute a painfully honest, searching examination of the experiences of thirteen Black women." The critic continues: "The broad range of these characters is indication of the depth and complexity with which Alice Walker treats a much-abused subject: the Black woman."

Walker bases her description of black women on what Washington refers to as her "unique vision and philosophy of the Black woman." According to Barbara A. Bannon of *Publishers Weekly*, this philosophy stems from the "theme of the poor black man's oppression of his family and the unconscious reasons for it." Walker, in her interview with the same magazine, asserts: "The cruelty of the black man to his wife and family

is one of the greatest [American] tragedies. It has mutilated the spirit and body of the black family and of most black mothers.'' Through her fiction, Walker describes this tragedy. For instance, Smith notes: ''Even as a black woman, I found the cumulative impact of these stories [contained *In Love and Trouble*] devastating. . . . Women love their men, but are neither loved nor understood in return. The affective relationships are [only] between mother and child or between black woman and black woman.'' David Guy's commentary on *The Color Purple* in the *Washington Post Book World* includes this evaluation: ''Accepting themselves for what they are, the women [in the novel] are able to extricate themselves from oppression; they leave their men, find useful work to support themselves.'' Watkins further explains: ''In *The Color Purple* the role of male domination in the frustration of black women's struggle for independence is clearly the focus.''

Some reviewers criticize Walker's fiction for portraying an overly negative view of black men. Katha Pollitt, for example, in the *New York Times Book Review*, calls the stories in *You Can't Keep a Good Woman Down* ''too partisan.'' The critic adds: ''The black woman is *always* the most sympathetic character.'' Guy notes: ''Some readers . . . will object to her overall perspective. Men in [*The Color Purple*] are generally pathetic, weak and stupid, when they are not heartlessly cruel, and the white race is universally bumbling and inept.'' Charles Larson, in his *Detroit News* review of *The Color Purple*, points out: ''I wouldn't go as far as to say that all the male characters [in the novel] are villains, but the truth is fairly close to that.'' However, neither Guy nor Larson feel that this emphasis on women is a major fault in the novel. Guy, for example, while conceding that ''white men . . . are invisible in Celie's world,'' observes: ''This really is Celie's perspective, however—it is psychologically accurate to her—and Alice Walker might argue that it is only a neat inversion of the view that has prevailed in western culture for centuries.'' Larson also notes that by the end of the novel, ''several of [Walker's] masculine characters have reformed.''

This idea of reformation, this sense of hope even in despair, is at the core of Walker's vision, even though, as John F. Callahan states in *New Republic*, ''There is often nothing but pain, violence, and death for black women [in her fiction].'' In spite of the brutal effects of sexism and racism suffered by the characters of her short stories and novels, critics note what Art Seidenbaum of the *Los Angeles Times* calls Walker's sense of ''affirmation . . . [that] overcomes her anger.'' This is particularly evident in *The Color Purple*, according to reviewers. Ford, for example, asserts that the author's ''polemics on . . . political and economic issues finally give way to what can only be described as a joyful celebration of human spirit— exulting, uplifting and eminently universal.'' Prescott discovers a similar progression in the novel. He writes: ''[Walker's] story begins at about the point that most Greek tragedies reserve for the climax, then . . . by immeasurable small steps . . . works its way toward acceptance, serenity and joy.'' Walker, according to Ray Anello, who quotes the author in *Newsweek*, agrees with this evaluation. Questioned about the novel's importance, Walker explains: ''Let's hope people can hear Celie's voice. There are so many people like Celie who make it, who come out of nothing. People who triumph.''

Davis refers to this idea as Walker's ''vision of survival'' and offers a summary of its significance in Walker's work. ''At whatever cost, human beings have the capacity to live in spiritual health and beauty; they may be poor, black, and uneducated, but their inner selves can blossom.'' This vision, extended to all humanity, is evident in Walker's collection *Living by the Word: Selected Writings 1973-1987*. Although ''her original interests centered on black women, and especially on the ways they were abused or underrated,'' *New York Times Book Review* contributor Noel Perrin believes that ''now those interests encompass all creation.'' Judith Paterson similarly observes in Chicago *Tribune Books* that in *Living by the Word*, ''Walker casts her abiding obsession with the oneness of the universe in a question: Do creativity, love and spiritual wholeness still have a chance of winning the human heart amid political forces bent on destroying the universe with poisonous chemicals and nuclear weapons?'' Walker explores this question through journal entries and essays that deal with Native Americans, racism in China, a lonely horse, smoking, and response to the criticism leveled against both the novel and film version of *The Color Purple*. Many of these treatments are personal in approach, and Jill Nelson finds many of them trivial. Writing in the *Washington Post Book World*, Nelson comments that ''*Living by the Word* is fraught with . . . reaches for commonality, analogy and universality. Most of the time all Walker achieves is banality.'' But Derrick Bell differs, noting in his *Los Angeles Times Book Review* critique that Walker ''uses carefully crafted images that provide a universality to unique events.'' The critic further asserts that *Living by the Word* ''is not only vintage Alice Walker: passionate, political, personal, and poetic, it also provides a panoramic view of a fine human being saving her soul through good deeds and extraordinary writing.''

MEDIA ADAPTATIONS: The Color Purple was made into a feature film by Warner Brothers in 1985; the film was directed by Steven Spielberg, and received several Academy Award nominations.

CA INTERVIEW

CA interviewed Alice Walker by telephone on June 6, 1988, at her home in California.

CA: Before The Color Purple, *which won you both the Pulitzer and the American Book Award and was made into a very popular movie, you had to your credit two earlier novels, two short story collections, four volumes of poetry, and a respectable body of essays and critical writing. Has* The Color Purple *brought a large general readership to your other writings?*

WALKER: Yes. I would say that I now reach many more people.

CA: You've described the way the characters of The Color Purple *came to you, demanding first that you move from Brooklyn to a quieter place and finally that you give up just about everything else to listen to their voices. Were any of them difficult to capture once you had settled into the conditions they seemed to require?*

WALKER: I wasn't trying to capture them; it was really just the opposite, more a matter of being in a place where they could be free, where they wouldn't *feel* captured, they wouldn't feel pressed, they wouldn't feel anything but just at home. Partly that is because they are all parts of myself, composites and memories and reconstructions, with lots of help from the intangibles.

CA: Did the characters go away completely after you finished the book?

WALKER: I have to explain that describing them as voices and spirits coming to me is a way of making it easier for people who don't write to understand what it feels like actually to create something. I do feel visited; all of my characters are absolutely right there in the house with me, and I often think about what one or the other one would say about something, or how something would look to them, or what would make them laugh and what would make them cry. I think of how they would say things. In a sense, then, they're always with me. They have lives, so they're still talking and commenting; they're still company for me. But they're not necessarily saying things that I will write. They're just free.

CA: How early did you know the story would take the epistolary form?

WALKER: I think almost from the beginning, just because that is so organic. It was the only thing I could use to keep Nettie and Celie connected, since Nettie was in Africa and Celie was in Georgia. There was no telephone; Celie would not have been able to use a telegraph machine. They had letters, and that was it. So the decision about the form was fairly simple.

CA: There has been some very vocal resentment of the way you've portrayed your men. In the essay "In the Closet of the Soul," collected in your new book, Living by the Word, *you responded to that. Do you see the resentment as positive in some ways?*

WALKER: Yes, I think it has been wonderful. It has given a lot of people an insight into the art, if you can call it an art, of criticism itself, because many people who never thought about it before, many people who have actually read my work and who had a very different response to all of it than the critics had, now have an understanding of some of the things that critics do in criticizing work—things that have nothing to do with the work or the writer, but have to do with whatever subject matter the critics are themselves interested in projecting. Sometimes they're just capitalizing on the publicity of somebody else's work; they inject themselves and use it as a platform.

CA: How much of a hand did you have in the movie?

WALKER: I was a consultant; I was available to them for questions, and I advised them on as many things as they could think of and as I could think of. They used a lot of my suggestions from the script I had written. I spent as much time on the set as I could, which turned out to be about half the time.

CA: In your interview with John O'Brien that was originally published in Interviews with Black Writers, *you said that not a single line of the first draft for* The Third Life of Grange Copeland, *your first novel, ended up in the book. Has your other writing been revised anywhere near so heavily?*

WALKER: It's been a totally different experience each time. In fact, *The Color Purple* was written originally almost entirely the way it appears in the book. There was an article in the *New York Times Magazine* for which they photographed some of the manuscript pages, and they're really identical in most cases with the final book. I think it had to do with the kind of solitude I wrote it in.

I wrote *The Third Life of Grange Copeland* while living in Mississippi in the middle of incredible racial turmoil, and sometimes terror and silence and craziness. That was also the time of giving birth—I finished the book three days before my daughter was born. And I moved several times while I was writing that book. It was a very different kind of writing. I was trying to capture something—then I *was* trying to capture something: partly the slipping away of a way of life. That was what I was trying to capture for myself, to remember a way of life that was changing and at the same time write this book which looks at, among other things, a lot of violence now in families and a lot of love in families and intergenerational relationships. It was very different. They're all very different.

CA: Reviewing your second novel, Meridian, *for* Newsweek, *Margot Jefferson noted that you have "a Southern writer's love for storytelling." You have written about your mother's stories and what they've meant to you. Do you feel that your roots as a writer go back to that tradition?*

WALKER: Yes, I do. And beyond my own mother, I think the South has always been a place where the oral tradition has been given credit. It's been respected. Before television, the storyteller was it. The storyteller and the musician were deeply loved. When you saw them coming down the road, you knew that you had a good evening ahead of you. This is true in so many parts of the world today. We go to Bali a good bit (we've been twice and hope to go again), and it's like coming back to the same culture that I grew up in. They tell stories, and the storyteller is respected. They present shadow puppets and little plays and dramas. Their culture is still very folk-oriented.

CA: Your poetry was the first thing published. Had you been writing poetry since the injury to your eye when you were eight, which you've said paradoxically enabled you "really to see people and things"?

WALKER: I think the poetry that I actually *call* poetry didn't start coming until I was a teenager. Then at Spelman College I started writing poetry in a more conscious way and actually published some poems in the college magazine. I started writing fiction when I transferred to Sarah Lawrence.

*CA: In "How Poems Are Made/A Discredited View" (*Horses Make a Landscape Look More Beautiful*) there's the verse "Letting go / in order to hold on / I gradually understand / how poems are made." Has the process of making poetry, or your feelings about it, changed over the years you've been doing it?*

WALKER: I think so. I haven't actually considered how the process has changed, but I think that my poems today are more about the world outside myself. It is more definitely a poetry of reclaiming ancient, global connections that I wasn't aware of when I was younger. I love writing poetry—it must be the next best thing to singing beautifully.

CA: How well do you think black women are doing in terms of self-image and of actually having a strong voice in society?

WALKER: I think they're doing well. Obviously there are so many black women and white women and Native American women who aren't doing well, who are having more children than they can take care of and bad relationships and no money and no jobs. But, given where we are in the United States, the racism and the sexism and the economy and the predominant culture, which is not affirming of us, I think black women do remarkably well and manage to have very strong voices

and very positive hearts. In my life, I tend to see a lot of these women.

CA: You're a champion and master of black folk speech. Would you comment on the problems involved in preserving that heritage while needing to deal on most levels in standard English? What sort of mix seems ideal to you?

WALKER: I use them both naturally. In speaking to you, I speak in the language we both understand, and it's perfectly easy to do. But when I'm speaking to my mother it's in black folk English; and if my grandmother and grandfather were alive and I were speaking to them, I'd do the same. It's the language they spoke, and we'd understand that. Sometimes in speaking to people who are my peers but would have parents and grandparents like mine and would therefore understand the old language, I use the language of my grandparents. It's very cozy; it immediately creates a world. We know immediately where we're from, who our people are. It's like having your own country.

For me, speaking the old language is a matter of loving it. There's almost no other way that I can see my grandmother's face. I have no clear photograph of her; and even if I did, it wouldn't work as well as using her language. When I use her language, I can see her face, I can smell her kitchen, and I can feel her hands. All of that is in the language.

CA: In teaching black literature, there's a similar problem, which is to retain the feeling for its special qualities while presenting it as a real part of the larger body of literature. What thoughts do you have on teaching it?

WALKER: The ideal is to have a teacher who loves it and really understands its value. I think it's always fairly useless for people to try to teach something that they don't care about or that they think is not what they should be teaching. In a way, I wonder if it could ever be taught really well in schools by just anyone; I tend to think not. I think that our literature, like Native American literature, should be taught by people who love it. That is the way it will have a life. I say that partly because I sometimes run into teachers who teach my work and who obviously resent it. They resent the work, they resent my point of view, they resent having to teach women, they resent having to teach black people. In that case, it would be just as well not to have them try to do it, but to have people who really love it, and really understand it, do it.

CA: Do you find the growing body of critical writing on black literature cogent and useful, by and large?

WALKER: I don't read much of the awful criticism, where the intention of the critic is to wound or maim. I think a lot of criticism has become very debased, that it's not helpful. It's not helpful to the writer, it's not helpful to the reader, and it's not even helpful to the critic, because there's so much meanness, often, and a real inability to get into the heart of the writer and try to see the world through the heart of the writer. But of course there's some really astonishingly wonderful criticism being written and published. I recently received an amazing book called *Conjuring: Black Women, Fiction, and Literary Tradition*, edited by Marjorie Pryse and Hortense Spillers. I also see on my desk Mary Helen Washington's latest book, *Invented Lives: Narratives of Black Women 1860-1960*. And there are many other excellent critics doing exemplary work: critics who are as interested in nurturing and healing the reader

as the writer is. I think of Sherley Anne Williams, Deborah McDowell, Barbara Christian, Lorraine Bethel (a superb critic from whom not enough is heard). I thank the Goddess for these scholars!

CA: You wrote in the 1970 essay "Duties of a Black Revolutionary Artist," now collected in In Search of Our Mother's Gardens, *"My major advice to young black artists would be that they should shut themselves up somewhere away from all debates about who they are and what color they are and just turn out paintings and poems and stories and novels." Would you revise that at all eighteen years later?*

WALKER: No, because in that it is assumed that the rest of the time they are right in the middle of life, of struggle, of everything else that's happening in the world. I know from my own experience that it's very hard to create something whole in the midst of a society in which everything is fragmented. You do have to get away and take those long walks and sit by the water and let your self come to you. One of the great dangers in a society that is so fragmented, so chaotic, is the loss of the self and the filling in of what would have been the self with TV. What you often have is a society full of people who are empty of themselves but full of television. This will never create art; this will only create more Big Macs to munch.

CA: Tell me about your publishing venture Wild Trees Press, and how it's going.

WALKER: It's going well, but I think we're going to be shifting to something else. We've published six books now, and it's very difficult because we're only three people. My partner and I are both writers, and we're both working on books—actually we've just finished two books of our own. We have just published a book by a Balinese painter. He came here from Bali last night and is downstairs now. We're going to launch his book over the next couple of weeks. But it takes an awful lot of energy, and a lot of money; it takes a lot of our time. So I think we're going to rest from it for a bit and maybe do something else or just concentrate on our own work. We haven't decided. It's been great, though. It's been a wonderful experience to publish beautiful books and be on the other side of the publishing process; we're now learning what publishers are up against in dealing with writers.

CA: Gloria Steinem, in her Ms. *article on you in June, 1982, testified to the closeness your readers feel to you. Do you hear a great deal from them?*

WALKER: I do. I get lots and lots of letters, and generally I just *feel* them. They write, and when I see them in this part of the world, Northern California, I'm always aware of my community, the people who support me and the people who tell me that they've been moved or touched by reading something that I've written, or that some aspect of their lives has been changed by it. This is very good. In fact, during the critical attacks that people made on me and *The Color Purple*—especially the movie, when that came out—I was aware of the presence of those people who support me. The negative criticism was more than balanced by the hundreds of letters that came from people who testified out of their own lives to say, This happened to me when I was five, or, I was so happy to have something I could look at that was outside of myself, and yet I could see myself in it; that made it easier for me to

deal with stuff that I hadn't wanted to look at for thirty years. And so on.

CA: It's obvious from what you've written about them that your mother's gardens have served you well as both inspiration and metaphor. Do you tend a garden of your own now, a literal garden?

WALKER: I do, yes—a literal garden. In fact, just last week I planted a hundred more onions, my first batch of corn, my tomatoes, my beans, my eggplant, my artichokes, everything. I do garden, and it's lovely.

CA: Is the quiet place still the environment you need to do your thinking and writing in?

WALKER: Yes. The first thing I did, even before I could afford it, was find some acreage up in the northern part of the state with a little shack on it. It was literally a shack, actually sliding down the hill, it was so shacky. But I knew that I had to have a place that I could retire to, in the sense of getting away: *repair* to, as people used to say. It's been good; it's been the best thing I've ever done, next to having my daughter.

CA: Besides Living by the Word, *there's the new children's book made from your earlier short story "To Hell with Dying" and, I believe, another children's book in the works.*

WALKER: Yes. The next children's book is *Finding the Green Stone,* and it will be illustrated by the same wonderful illustrator who collaborated with me on the last one, Catherine Deeter.

CA: What's beyond that that you can talk about—or is it still and always a matter of waiting for the voices?

WALKER: My new novel. I can't talk about it, but I've finished it, and it's called *The Temple of My Familiar.* It's about the last five hundred thousand years. Beyond that there are several other things planned. But I can't ever talk about work that's ahead; that seems to curtail my sense of freedom. And it doesn't really involve voices; it just involves more time.

BIOGRAPHICAL/CRITICAL SOURCES:

BOOKS

Contemporary Literary Criticism, Gale, Volume 5, 1976, Volume 6, 1976, Volume 9, 1978, Volume 19, 1981, Volume 27, 1984, Volume 46, 1988.
Dictionary of Literary Biography, Gale, Volume 6: *American Novelists since World War II,* 2nd series, 1980, Volume 33: *Afro-American Fiction Writers after 1955,* 1984.
Evans, Mari, editor, *Black Women Writers (1950-1980): A Critical Evaluation,* Anchor, 1984.
O'Brien, John, *Interviews with Black Writers,* Liveright, 1973.
Peden, William, *The American Short Story: Continuity and Change, 1940-1975,* 2nd edition, revised and enlarged, Houghton, 1975.
Prenshaw, Peggy W., editor, *Women Writers of the Contemporary South,* University Press of Mississippi, 1984.

PERIODICALS

American Scholar, winter, 1970-71, summer, 1973.
Ann Arbor News, October 3, 1982.
Atlantic, June, 1976.
Black Scholar, April, 1976.

Black World, September, 1973, October, 1974.
Chicago Tribune, December 20, 1985.
Chicago Tribune Book World, August 1, 1982, September 15, 1985.
Commonweal, April 29, 1977.
Detroit Free Press, August 8, 1982, July 10, 1988, January 4, 1989.
Detroit News, September 15, 1982, October 23, 1983, March 31, 1985.
Freedomways, winter, 1973.
Globe and Mail (Toronto), December 21, 1985.
Jet, February 10, 1986.
Los Angeles Times, April 29, 1981, June 8, 1983.
Los Angeles Times Book Review, August 8, 1982, May 29, 1988.
Ms., February, 1974, July, 1977, July, 1978, June, 1982, September, 1986.
Nation, November 12, 1973, December 17, 1983.
Negro Digest, September-October, 1968.
New Leader, January 25, 1971.
New Republic, September 14, 1974, December 21, 1974.
Newsweek, May 31, 1976, June 21, 1982.
New Yorker, February 27, 1971, June 7, 1976.
New York Review of Books, January 29, 1987.
New York Times, December 18, 1985, January 5, 1986.
New York Times Book Review, March 17, 1974, May 23, 1976, May 29, 1977, December 30, 1979, May 24, 1981, July 25, 1982, April 7, 1985, June 5, 1988.
New York Times Magazine, January 8, 1984.
Oakland Tribune, November 11, 1984.
Parnassus: Poetry in Review, spring-summer, 1976.
Poetry, February, 1971, March, 1980.
Publishers Weekly, August 31, 1970, February 26, 1988.
Saturday Review, August 22, 1970.
Southern Review, spring, 1973.
Times Literary Supplement, August 19, 1977, June 18, 1982, July 20, 1984, September 27, 1985, April 15, 1988.
Tribune Books (Chicago), July 17, 1988
Washington Post, October 15, 1982, April 15, 1983, October 17, 1983.
Washington Post Book World, November 18, 1973, October 30, 1979, December 30, 1979, May 31, 1981, July 25, 1982, December 30, 1984, May 29, 1988.
World Literature Today, winter, 1985, winter, 1986.
Yale Review, autumn, 1976.

—*Interview by Jean W. Ross*

*   *   *

WALLACE, Amy 1955-

PERSONAL: Born July 3, 1955, in Los Angeles, Calif.; daughter of Irving (a writer) and Sylvia (a writer; maiden name, Kahn) Wallace. *Education:* Graduated from Berkeley Psychic Institute. *Politics:* "Changes all the time." *Religion:* "Ecstatic."

ADDRESSES: Office—P.O. Box 4507, Berkeley, Calif. 94704. *Agent*—Arthur Pine Associates, Inc., 1780 Broadway, New York, N.Y. 10019.

CAREER: Psychic reader; writer.

WRITINGS:

(Editor with father, Irving Wallace, and brother, David Wallechinsky) *The People's Almanac Presents the Book of Lists* (Book-of-the-Month Club special selection), Morrow, 1977.

(With I. Wallace) *The Two: A Biography* (Literary Guild special selection), Simon & Schuster, 1978.

(With William Henkin) *The Psychic Healing Book,* Delacorte, 1978.

(Editor with I. Wallace, mother, Sylvia Wallace, and D. Wallechinsky) *The People's Almanac Presents the Book of Lists #2* (Literary Guild special selection), Morrow, 1980.

(Editor with I. Wallace and D. Wallechinsky) *The People's Almanac Presents the Book of Predictions,* Morrow, 1980.

(Editor with I. Wallace, S. Wallace, and D. Wallechinsky) *The Intimate Sex Lives of Famous People,* Delacorte, 1981.

(Editor with I. Wallace and D. Wallechinsky) *The People's Almanac Presents the Book of Lists #3,* Morrow, 1983.

(Editor with I. Wallace and D. Wallechinsky) *Significa,* Dutton, 1983.

(Contributor) Fred A. Bernstein, *The Jewish Mothers' Hall of Fame,* Doubleday, 1986.

The Prodigy: A Biography of William Sidis, Dutton, 1986.

SIDELIGHTS: As a member of the writing Wallace family, which includes parents Irving and Sylvia Wallace and brother David Wallechinsky, Amy Wallace has had a hand in some of the clan's more successful collaborative projects, like *The People's Almanac Presents the Book of Lists* and *The Intimate Sex Lives of Famous People.* But Amy Wallace has also seen her name on the cover of a solo effort, *The Prodigy: A Biography of William Sidis.* That work caught critical attention for its subject matter, the story of a little-remembered figure from the early part of this century. William James Sidis was born in 1898 to parents who believed that an infant's mind was a virtually bottomless receptacle waiting to be filled with knowledge. Under their tutelage, Billy Sidis was speaking before age one, had mastered spelling, reading and counting by two, and had taught himself Greek and Latin by three.

When Billy turned nine, his father, a Harvard University professor, tried to enroll the boy in the mathematics program there, but Billy was not admitted until age eleven. As *Times Literary Supplement* critic Stuart Sutherland relates, the elder Sidis "claims to have taught [the boy] to reason, not to master facts, and he was largely self-taught. He lectured to the Harvard Mathematical Club at the age of twelve with such originality that according to the *New York Times* 'he made the professors gasp.' He graduated from Harvard with an undistinguished degree, merely *cum laude,* not *magna cum laude* let alone *summa cum laude.* This failure disgusted his mother, but it probably did not worry William, for he regarded universities with disdain."

While Sidis' intellectual prowess seemed beyond criticism, the youth's personal life suffered terribly by comparison. Because his parents had neglected teaching him social graces, Sidis was awkward among peers, unwashed, badly dressed, and increasingly eccentric. "At Harvard, William was ostracized and made the butt of practical jokes," reports John Gross in a *New York Times* article on *The Prodigy.* "At the Rice Institute (later Rice University) in Houston, where he was appointed professor of mathematics at the age of 17, [Sidis] proved almost as much of a misfit, and he soon left. Returning to Boston, he threw himself into radical politics. . . . When he was 23 he finally broke with [his overpossessive parents] and headed for New York."

Sidis spent the rest of his days working in computational jobs, never employing his mental gifts to their fullest. He died at age 46. In *The Prodigy,* Wallace argues "that [father] Boris Sidis' educational methods were not the sources of Billy Sidis'

neuroses. Rather, it was the parents' failure to provide Billy with emotional protection from a hostile and jealous society. She offers instructive comparisons with two other child prodigies—the 19th century philosopher John Stuart Mill and Billy Sidis' Harvard classmate Norbert Wiener, the founder of cybernetics—who were helped by some supportive others through dazzling careers," says *Washington Post Book World* critic Wray Herbert. He adds that the author "makes a good case, and one can only wonder what contributions Billy Sidis might have made had he not been scared into hiding at such an early age."

To *Chicago Tribune Book World* reviewer Alden Whitman, however, Wallace "has not done justice to [Billy Sidis' life]. Her book is merely a Sunday supplement chronicle, . . . whereas it might have been an insightful biography, one that explained what made him tick." And while Gross shares the opinion that "some of the writing in 'The Prodigy' is rather scrappy," he ultimately finds that the book "does justice to an often sad, often grotesque but always fascinating story."

In a *Chicago Tribune* interview, Wallace, when asked if modern-day parents could take any lesson from Billy Sidis' parents on child-rearing, responded that "Sidis' parents did some things right: They made learning seem like a game, and they answered all his questions. But they also made mistakes, such as disdaining sports and physical activity; bodily coordination was always a problem for Sidis. It's fine to encourage your children, but you get into trouble when you start expecting specific things from them. Sidis was expected to be a great scientist, but he refused to go along and died in the obscurity he sought for himself."

MEDIA ADAPTATIONS: Twentieth Century-Fox has purchased the film rights to *The Intimate Sex Lives of Famous People.*

BIOGRAPHICAL/CRITICAL SOURCES:

BOOKS

Bernstein, Fred A., *The Jewish Mothers' Hall of Fame,* Doubleday, 1986.

PERIODICALS

Chicago Tribune, September 28, 1986.
Chicago Tribune Book World, July 13, 1986.
Los Angeles Times, June 4, 1981.
Los Angeles Times Book Review, March 9, 1980.
New York Times, December 25, 1981, June 13, 1986.
New York Times Book Review, March 19, 1978.
Time, June 1, 1981.
Times Literary Supplement, October 24, 1986.
Washington Post, February 28, 1980.
Washington Post Book World, July 27, 1986.*

*   *   *

WALLACE, Irving   1916-

PERSONAL: Born March 19, 1916, in Chicago, Ill.; son of Alexander and Bessie (Liss) Wallace; married Sylvia Kahn (a writer), June 3, 1941; children: David Wallechinsky, Amy Wallace. *Education:* Attended Williams Institute, Berkeley, Calif., and Los Angeles City College.

ADDRESSES: Home and office—P.O. Box 49328, Los Angeles, Calif. 90049.

CAREER: Free-lance magazine writer and interviewer, 1931-53; screenwriter, 1949-58, for Columbia, Warner Bros., Twentieth Century-Fox, Universal, RKO, Metro-Goldwyn-Mayer, and Paramount. Reporter for the Chicago Daily News/Sun Times Wire Service at the Democratic and Republican national conventions, 1972. *Military service:* U.S. Army Air Forces, writer in the First Motion Picture Unit and Signal Corps Photographic Center, 1942-46; became staff sergeant.

MEMBER: Authors Guild, Authors League of America, PEN, Writers Guild of America, Manuscript Society, Society of Authors (London).

AWARDS, HONORS: Supreme Award of Merit and honorary fellowship from George Washington Carver Memorial Institute, 1964, for writing *The Man* and for contributing "to the betterment of race relations and human welfare"; Commonwealth Club silver medal, 1965; *Best Sellers* magazine award, 1965, for *The Man;* Paperback of the Year citation, National Best Sellers Institute, 1970, for *The Seven Minutes;* Popular Culture Association award of excellence, 1974, for distinguished achievements in the popular arts; Venice Rosa d'Oro Award, 1975, for contributions to American letters.

WRITINGS:

The Fabulous Originals: Lives of Extraordinary People Who Inspired Memorable Characters in Fiction, Knopf, 1955, reprinted, Kraus, 1972.
The Square Pegs, Knopf, 1957.
The Fabulous Showman: The Life and Times of P. T. Barnum (Literary Guild selection), Knopf, 1959.
The Sins of Philip Fleming (novel), Fell, 1959, reprinted, New American Library, 1985.
The Chapman Report (novel), Simon & Schuster, 1960, reprinted, New American Library, 1985.
The Twenty-seventh Wife (biography), Simon & Schuster, 1960, reprinted, New American Library, 1985.
The Prize (novel; Book-of-the-Month Club special selection), Simon & Schuster, 1962, reprinted, New American Library, 1985.
The Three Sirens (novel; Mid-Century Book Club selection), Simon & Schuster, 1963.
The Man (novel; Reader's Digest Book Club selection; Book-of-the-Month Club alternate selection), Simon & Schuster, 1964.
The Sunday Gentleman (collected writings), Simon & Schuster, 1965.
The Plot (novel; Book-of-the-Month Club alternate selection), Simon & Schuster, 1967, reprinted, Pocket Books, 1984.
The Writing of One Novel (nonfiction), Simon & Schuster, 1968, reprinted, Dutton, 1986.
The Seven Minutes (novel; Literary Guild alternate selection), Simon & Schuster, 1969, reprinted, Pocket Books, 1983.
The Nympho and Other Maniacs (Literary Guild alternate selection), Simon & Schuster, 1971.
The Word (novel; Book-of-the-Month Club selection), Simon & Schuster, 1972.
The Fan Club (novel; Literary Guild alternate selection), Simon & Schuster, 1974.
(Editor with son, David Wallechinsky) *The People's Almanac* (Literary Guild special selection), Doubleday, 1975.
The R Document (novel; Reader's Digest Book Club selection; Literary Guild alternate selection), Simon & Schuster, 1976.
(Editor with D. Wallechinsky and daughter, Amy Wallace) *The People's Almanac Presents the Book of Lists* (Book-of-the-Month Club special selection), Morrow, 1977.

(Editor with D. Wallechinsky) *The People's Almanac #2* (Literary Guild special selection), Morrow, 1978.
(With A. Wallace) *The Two: A Biography* (Literary Guild special selection), Simon & Schuster, 1978.
The Pigeon Project (novel; Literary Guild selection), Simon & Schuster, 1979.
(Editor with wife, Sylvia Wallace, A. Wallace, and D. Wallechinsky) *The People's Almanac Presents the Book of Lists #2* (Literary Guild special selection), Morrow, 1980.
The Second Lady (novel), New American Library, 1980.
(Editor with A. Wallace and D. Wallechinsky) *The People's Almanac Presents the Book of Predictions,* Morrow, 1980.
(Editor with A. Wallace, S. Wallace, and D. Wallechinsky) *The Intimate Sex Lives of Famous People,* Delacorte, 1981.
(Editor with D. Wallechinsky) *The People's Almanac #3,* Morrow, 1981.
The Almighty (novel), Doubleday, 1982.
(Editor with A. Wallace and D. Wallechinsky) *The People's Almanac Presents the Book of Lists #3,* Morrow, 1983.
(Editor with A. Wallace and D. Wallechinsky) *Significa,* Dutton, 1983.
The Miracle (novel), Dutton, 1984.
The Seventh Secret (novel), Dutton, 1986.
The Celestial Bed (novel), Delacorte, 1987.
The Guest of Honor (novel), Delacorte, 1989.

SCREENPLAYS

(With John Monks, Jr., and Charles Hoffman) "The West Point Story," Warner Bros., 1950.
"Meet Me at the Fair," Universal, 1953.
(With Lewis Meltzer) "Desert Legion," Universal, 1953.
(With William Bowers) "Split Second," RKO, 1953.
(With Roy Huggins) "Gun Fury," Columbia, 1953.
(With Horace McCoy) "Bad for Each Other," Columbia, 1954.
(With Gerald Adams) "The Gambler from Natchez," Twentieth Century-Fox, 1954.
"Jump into Hell," Warner Bros., 1955.
"Sincerely Yours," Warner Bros., 1955.
"The Burning Hills," United Artists, 1956.
"Bombers B-52," Warner Bros., 1957.
(With Irwin Allen and Charles Bennett) "The Big Circus," Allied Artists, 1959.

OTHER

Author of plays "And Then Goodnight," "Because of Sex," "Hotel Behemoth," "Speak of the Devil," "Murder by Morning," and, with Jerome Weidman, "Pantheon." Also author of biographies for *Collier's Encyclopedia,* 1960, *American Oxford Encyclopedia,* and *Encyclopaedia Britannica.* Contributor of over 500 articles and short stories to magazines, including *Saturday Evening Post, Reader's Digest, Esquire, Parade,* and *Cosmopolitan.*

SIDELIGHTS: One of America's most popular writers (and one of its chief literary exports with volumes printed in 31 languages worldwide), Irving Wallace began his career while still in his teens, contributing stories and articles to magazines. He reports that he was amazed when, at that young age, he discovered that the periodicals actually paid people to write for them, and from that moment on, he knew how he would spend his life. Romance combined with career when Wallace married fellow writer Sylvia Kahn in 1941; they would collaborate on two books and two children. The Wallaces saw their writing dynasty continue when their offspring, Amy Wallace and David Wallechinsky (the latter having adopted his paternal grandfather's original surname), became successful authors on their own.

Best known for his novels, Wallace has through the years developed an unusual forte in his fiction. He takes a highly complicated subject—a Kinsey-type survey or the Nobel Prize selection, for instance—and weaves it into a plot designed to hook readers with characters who have much at stake. In this way, Wallace's novels are notable for the amount of research that goes into them. As the author elaborates in John Leverence's study *Irving Wallace: A Writer's Profile,* when he begins a book he's "always curious to investigate what psychological motives bring a certain person into his field or profession. Why is a surgeon a surgeon? Why does he enjoy cutting flesh? Why does he like to tune in on patients' private lives? Why does that woman like to teach, and why does this man like to dig into the earth?"

Among Wallace's early fiction, *The Chapman Report* and *The Prize* (all of the author's novels begin with "The," a trait he attributes to superstition), dealing respectively with the Kinsey studies of human sexual behavior and the Nobel Prize story, are the most popular. Both works, according to *New York Times Book Review* critic Lawrence Lafore, "skillfully combine the most alluring features of the headline, the expose, the editorial and the mystery story." *The Chapman Report* in particular proved a highly controversial book when it first appeared in 1960, mainly because its sexual *roman a clef* elements were based on discussions Wallace had conducted with his actual neighbors at the time.

"Let me tell you how [*The Chapman Report*] came about," says Wallace in his *Contemporary Authors Autobiography Series* piece. "For years I had wanted to write a novel about the married or once-married young women who lived in my community. . . . I had a friendly face, and I was a good listener, and often at parties other men's wives confided their marital difficulties and sexual problems to me. Yet, my author's instinct told me to refrain from writing a novel about unhappy and restless young wives." One day during research for an article, he continues, "I came across [a study] about some sociologists who were taking a survey of women, on college campuses, I think. . . . I asked myself—what if a team of male sociologists arrived in my community to make a sex survey and interviewed the women I knew? How would these personal interviews affect the women? And how would the interviews affect members of the sex survey team?"

Controversy and the ensuing publicity combined to help make *The Chapman Report* a bestseller, and such fictions are rarely greeted with critical hosannas. But no one could deny that the author could reach an audience that might not otherwise investigate such subject matter. In Lafore's article, the critic remarks that a reader might learn almost nothing about the novel's main characters "except their sexual maladjustments. While a unique fascination with mass rape may create problems, it does not in itself create a personality." Yet at the same time, notes Lafore, Wallace "is refreshingly free of the pedantries and complexities to which novelists are too often prey. He uses few words (aside from anatomical ones), and introduces few ideas, that would be unfamiliar to a high-school sophomore."

On the heels of *The Chapman Report* came *The Prize,* a novel born of the fact that no fictional work had ever been published about the Nobel Prize. After extensive research that included trips to Stockholm and unprecedented interviews with subjects involved in the Nobel selection committee, Wallace released

the book to praise for its unique theme and pans for what some saw as stylistic faults. In the Leverence work, Ray B. Browne includes *The Prize* in his critique of Wallace's sense of continuity. While the author's plots "are rich and complex," and each contains an important message, writes Browne, "once this message has been developed, . . . and after the puzzle has been solved, Wallace seems to lose most of his interest in the book. [He] is actually mostly gripped by the themes themselves. Little wonder then that after the questions and answers have been demonstrated and worked out, the author rushes to close the book, apparently content to erase the characters once they have illustrated his point." Still, finds Browne, Wallace, with his "direct, carefully chosen and clear" style, has produced in *The Prize* "a kind of high-water mark in subject and accomplishment. Since that novel Wallace has continued to explore new areas of investigation and to provide rich entertainment."

Such rich entertainment came in the form of two subsequent novels, *The Man* and *The Word,* another pair of bestsellers. Each contains a provocative theme. In *The Man,* the author speculates on what might happen should a black man, alone in the white bastion of American politics, suddenly find himself appointed president. Protagonist Douglass Dilman, a midlevel congressman who becomes chief of state when circumstances eliminate those ahead of him, came about as a Wallace-style reaction to the controversy then brewing over the integration of public schools. As the author himself reveals in his *Contemporary Authors Autobiography Series* article, *The Man* "was an immediate success, . . . [drawing] heavy mail, much of it from readers who admitted it had changed their attitude toward blacks completely."

In a *Best Sellers* review, Eugene J. Linehan sees merit in Wallace's presentation of an emotional theme: "The test of a novel is its people. You will find the men and women of these events singularly real. It is not easy to write well of current events; to walk us around the White House and maintain balance and sense. The danger is that such a choice of subject may lead the author into gross sentimentality or sensationalism. It seems to me that Irving Wallace has succeeded [in *The Man*] in bringing a thrilling story to the end of his book and kept his people alive and real."

Wallace tackled no less a subject than the Bible in *The Word.* Fabricating the discovery of a new set of New Testaments written by James, brother of Jesus, was challenging scholarship, the author acknowledges. But the sense of realism he developed in *The Word* resulted in "endless letters . . . asking me if The Gospel According to James, which I had invented, really had been dug up by archeologists, translated, and where copies might be purchased," as Wallace notes in the Leverence book. "While creating my gospel," he adds, "I drew upon the best research, archeological discoveries, theories and speculations of the finest Biblical scholars."

The Word, published in 1972, quickly attained international bestseller status. Its commercial acceptance, however, didn't stop some reviewers from accusing the author of concocting a potboiler. "The Irving Wallace formula for a best seller seems to be: put everything in, make a goulash," as a *New Republic* critic states, adding that besides the biblical plot, the novel traffics in "spies, international police, two miracles (one gets tentatively canceled out) and a proposed Protestant Vatican. . . . It also has doses of sex, drugs, tragic irony, [and] scholarly hokum."

To Steven Kroll, in a *New York Times Book Review* piece, *The Word* presents an uncomfortable attitude toward women. "Even well-educated women end up as assistants and secretaries," he says. "If they're not capable of real love, they tend to go in for 'geisha acrobatics.' No doubt about it. Wallace women serve." But Kroll further goes on to say that whatever reservations he has about the author's tone, Wallace does have "a flair for controversial, topical subjects and a good liberal's serious respect for honesty, justice and nonconformity. He's also very adept at those unlikely coincidences that keep a reader wondering. But when you've been made to wonder, you feel cheated if you don't get answers, and 'The Word' bypasses those answers for a sweeping message of faith."

Not all Wallace novels center on lofty themes of sexual research, Nobel Prizes, integration, or religion. Many of his other fictional works fall into the category of hard-driving entertainments. Chief among them is *The Fan Club*, a suspense tale in which a Marilyn Monroe-type movie star is kidnapped by a group of men who have made her the object of their long-running fantasies. "The group hassles about how they deserve the actress, since 'the fat cats' get everything in life, including tax write-offs," *New York Times Book Review* writer Joe Flaherty finds. Flaherty, while pointing out that *The Fan Club*'s implicit appeal "is not sexual but [in] our passion to consummate with consumerism," sees in this point that Wallace's "genius comes to the fore. Every brand name is right; and the jet set life style, as decadent as it may be, is the stuff that makes a closet queen of every straphanger."

The 1980s brought a steady stream of fiction from Wallace, including *The Almighty*, *The Miracle*, *The Seventh Secret*, and *The Celestial Bed*. None of these novels was hailed as a masterpiece, though in Anatole Broyard's opinion, "a novel like 'The Miracle' is beyond criticism because it has no literary pretensions." As Broyard continues in a *New York Times* feature, this tale of a purported series of healing miracles in Lourdes, where the Virgin Mary was said to have appeared on several occasions in the past, employs "a timely theme that will interest a wide readership." Further, "There is a kind of crossword-puzzle suspense in reading 'The Miracle,' what might be called a mechanical curiosity. The main trouble with the book is not that it has renounced literary ambition in favor of a more ordinary appeal, but that it doesn't do justice to the ordinary. The language, for example, is not conversational, but a strange dialect of pidgin English used by some popular novelists."

One such popular novelist, the Catholic priest Andrew M. Greeley, reviewed *The Miracle* for *Washington Post Book World* and pronounced himself "frankly envious" of Wallace's ability to tell a religious story that is "witty, ingenious, brilliant" and, "with its irony within ironies, . . . persuasive and even true on a number of different levels." The novel, Greeley concludes, is not "profound [like] *Song of Bernadette* from so long ago. It is, however, a marvelously told tale which, oddly enough, may, for all its slick, quick-flowing style, tell us more about the meaning of Lourdes than did Franz Werfel's classic."

"Across the years the plots and themes of Wallace's numerous books have varied widely, but the body of his work is traceable largely to a characteristic he identifies as 'my desire to listen, to let the imagination run wild, and then to write,'" as *Los Angeles Times* reporter Marshall Berges states. Still quoting Wallace, the article concludes, "I love to tell stories, to create people and worlds half real, half imaginary. Even if I could

not earn a penny from my writing, I would earn my livelihood at something else and continue to write at night."

Nonfiction readers can find the Wallace name on a number of volumes he characterizes in *Contemporary Authors Autobiography Series* as "our family books." These include *The People's Almanac* series and its popular spinoff, *The People's Almanac Presents the Book of Lists*. "It all began with my son," Wallace remarks in the autobiographical essay. "From the age of eight, David had always been an almanac buff. . . . Then, one day in 1971, he began to question the infallibility of the almanacs and other reference books he had been reading. He began to see that a good deal of history and current events was distorted by reference books—not necessarily deliberately, but for various reasons." And worst of all, adds Wallace, "most [almanacs] were unforgivably dull."

And so it was David Wallechinsky who embarked on a new sort of reference work, with the enthusiastic input of his father and the assistance of 169 free-lance writers, among them Charles Schulz, "who wrote the definitive biography of Snoopy for us," continues Wallace. As for working alongside his son, the author finds that "David's ego was strong enough to accept me, and we became collaborators—and before it was over we became friends."

The People's Almanac debuted in 1975 to warm reviews and high-ranking bestseller status. Critics and public alike seemed to respond to a reference work that covered topics of history and trivia that no one had ever studied. When research showed that readers especially enjoyed the various lists contained within the series, the result was *The People's Almanac Presents the Book of Lists* (known popularly as just *The Book of Lists*), which would join its predecessor in multiple volumes throughout the 1970s and 1980s. Eventually, each member of the Wallace family would have a hand in the browser's delights. "We aren't a conglomerate," the patriarch tells Joseph McLellan in a *Washington Post* interview. "We're four very autonomous individuals having fun together. We enjoy sitting around and talking about book ideas and it's good for me. Writing fiction is a lonely kind of work. These [nonfictions] are more relaxing than a novel, and your research isn't far from your writing."

MEDIA ADAPTATIONS: Feature-film productions—Columbia Pictures bought *The Fabulous Showman* and *The Fan Club;* Warner Bros. filmed *The Chapman Report* in 1962; Metro-Goldwyn-Mayer filmed *The Prize* in 1963; Brenco Pictures and Stanley Meyer bought *The Three Sirens;* ABC Circle Films bought and filmed *The Man*, which was released by Paramount in 1972; Twentieth Century-Fox bought *The Plot*, and filmed *The Seven Minutes* in 1971, then bought film rights to *The Intimate Sex Lives of Famous People;* United Artists bought *The R Document*. Television productions—Columbia Broadcasting System (CBS) bought *The Word* and broadcast an eight-hour miniseries in 1978; Lindsay Wagner's independent production company bought rights to *The Second Lady*.

AVOCATIONAL INTERESTS: Travel, collecting autographed letters, inscribed first-edition books, and impressionist paintings.

CA INTERVIEW

CA interviewed Irving Wallace by telephone on July 27, 1987, at his home in Los Angeles, California.

CA: Your stories have gotten you named one of the five most popular living writers in English by Saturday Review *and have attracted, at best estimate, something like a billion readers. What does a story have to have in the first place to attract you as a writer?*

WALLACE: I get a lot of ideas. I make notes on them and put them in a drawer, and perhaps one keeps lingering in my head. It has to be something that sticks in my mind, usually for a few years. It should have conflict—that's the key to writing a novel: conflict with another person, with nature, with yourself. It should be a good story, one that interests me, that I don't necessarily know a lot about. I prefer that a subject be different from anything I've done before. I can research the background. I remember when I did *The Seven Minutes*. It was about an obscenity case, and I didn't really know much about law in terms of obscenity cases. I was able to borrow and Xerox some obscenity cases that ran in Los Angeles under California law to study how it was done.

CA: Thorough research is one of the hallmarks of your writing and seems to be something you especially enjoy. Perhaps one of the most unusual instances of research was for The Man, *when you spent ten days in and out of the Kennedy White House finding out what it's like to be President. What stands out in your mind as particularly difficult or rewarding or interesting among the research jobs?*

WALLACE: The most difficult was for *The Word*. That was in the works perhaps twelve years—not that I worked on it for twelve years, but I had it in my mind for that long. It was about the discovery of a new bible, and throughout Europe and the United States I kept interviewing theologians, archaeologists, all kinds of people, to find out whether it was believable, whether it was possible, and if so, what would a new bible, a new gospel, be like? That was very, very difficult. With *The Prize*, I went to Stockholm twice and talked to Nobel Prize judges. Once you've made the breakthrough, it's possible to get the material. But *The Word* was by far the most exacting book to research.

CA: Simply listening to what other people say has given you the ideas for such books as The Prize *and* The Chapman Report. *Did you learn very early how to listen so fruitfully?*

WALLACE: I don't know how that happened. I have a lot of writer friends, and their big problem is that they don't listen; they just want to talk—they're lonely. If they listened a little more, they'd hear an awful lot of things. Everybody wants to talk. If you're prepared to listen, you're going to hear things about other people's lives and environment. I was always interested in hearing what was going on with other people; that was no problem.

CA: Specifically, The Prize *had its beginnings in your talk with Nobel Prize judge Sven Hedin, which revealed some shockingly narrow and discriminatory views and led to this book that was banned in Sweden, Norway, and Denmark. Has the status of the book changed in those countries?*

WALLACE: I wrote an update on this in *The Writing of One Novel*, which was originally published in 1969, six years after *The Prize*. I went back to Stockholm about three years ago and had a press conference, and they were very nice to me. It was a whole new generation of people. But *The Prize* was still banned; it had not been published in any Scandinavian country. And for the movie, with Paul Newman, they cancelled the sound stage rentals and everything else that was going to be

used by MGM. As one Danish paper said, they have so little in Scandinavia that's world-famous, and when somebody picks on the one thing they do have, the Nobel Prize, it affects all of them and they don't like it. Copies of the book may have gotten into Denmark, Norway, and Sweden by some means; but according to what I heard from the press at the conference, it didn't exist. When you write something that's banned, everybody says, Oh, great; you get a lot of attention. Well, what good is the attention if nobody has the book available to read?

CA: You've done some interviews with very interesting people, such as the artist Diego Rivera and Japanese Foreign Minister Yosuke Matsuoka fourteen months before the bombing of Pearl Harbor. What interviews were most exciting?

WALLACE: One was the Matsuoka interview. That was thrilling because he said the Japanese might attack the United States. It was unbelievable to get such information from the second biggest man in the country. Another was Pablo Picasso. I spent an afternoon with him in Paris, and he took me around his studio and had his secretary with him to translate. That was very interesting. And there was an interview I had with Mitsuru Toyama, the ninety-nine-year-old head of the Black Dragon Society in Japan. They were assassins, and people were afraid to see him. His Black Dragon Society had murdered a lot of people to get things straight in Japan before Pearl Harbor. But I was too dumb to be afraid. I asked for an interview and got it, and then I couldn't get anybody to interpret for me, because they were all afraid of him! I finally got some storekeeper who knew English; he trembled through the whole interview.

CA: Your first book sale, The Fabulous Originals, *was a collective biography based on real-life people who inspired literary characters, and since then you've written other collective biographies. What did you find especially appealing about that form?*

WALLACE: For one thing, it's like writing short stories; it's a short form and you get a lot of variety. If you write a novel, or a biography of one person, that's a very long process. For *The Nympho and Other Maniacs*, which, despite the title, was a very serious book on independent women, I knew a lot about Byron and I was able to take three of the most important women in his life and write separate stories about them, yet they were interconnected. It's a good form because you don't have to devote years to doing research. I did a book called *The Twenty-seventh Wife*, the story of Ann Eliza Webb, the last wife of Mormon leader Brigham Young. I never quite finished that: I never found out when she died or where she was buried. Obviously the Mormons had hidden that information because she was a disgrace to him. I went up to Salt Lake City and found it very difficult to get people to talk to me, but some people did, and that's what opened it up.

CA: The Chapman Report *brought about the enmity of Alfred Knopf, legal action by the Kinsey Institute for Sex Research, praise from Margaret Mead, an obscenity trial for its Italian publisher, and tremendous sales and popularity all round. Does the book continue to attract new readers almost thirty years after its original publication?*

WALLACE: Yes. That was the first big one, and it's still popular. All my novels are in print. What happens is that every time I get a new novel out in hardback, almost all the paperback companies reissue my old novels. Then a lot of people will go out and buy the paperbacks of the others. So the books go on and on, and that's very exciting.

CA: What books remain the most popular?

WALLACE: I'd say the most popular are *The Chapman Report* and *The Word*. To the best of my knowledge, they've sold the most copies. Probably seven million copies in American paperbacks alone.

CA: You have collaborated on books with your wife Sylvia, daughter Amy, and son David Wallechinsky—all authors in their own right as well. How do you work together on such projects as The Book of Lists *and its sequels? Is there a lot of brainstorming?*

WALLACE: Yes, that's what we do. We're night people, all of us, and we usually meet around midnight or one in the morning, which is wonderful if you sleep late. We sit around my desk and talk. Amy might say, "I heard Marat was killed in the bathtub by Corday. I wonder what other great events have happened in the bathtub?" So we'd all contribute what we know from our research and reading, and then we'd try to dig out more to fill out the list. *The Book of Lists* was great fun, and it really was mostly from brainstorming.

CA: Some of the list ideas are fun themselves.

WALLACE: Yes. It was fun to do—but very difficult, especially since we were trying to do a good job, not a hasty, sloppy job. We had people working for us whom we'd send to find out more details about Marat and Corday, or Archimedes sitting in the bathtub, while we'd go on to other things. We did have that kind of help.

CA: How did you put together The Intimate Sex Lives of Famous People, *another collaboration?*

WALLACE: That was also very difficult until we caught on to it. We found material by going first to autobiographies and then to letters. Letters were great. James Joyce wrote fantastic letters to Nora, for example. Sometimes biographies had good information on the topic, but not as much as what we could dig up from the really intimate stuff people wrote about themselves. For some people we just couldn't find anything. We worked very, very hard on that book to make it accurate, because of the sensationalism of the subject. I think we got it pretty accurate.

CA: Travel has almost always been an important part of your life. Does most of it revolve around research for books?

WALLACE: It's half and half. I go abroad every year. In fact, I'll be going in two or three weeks. I have some ideas for future books that I want to talk to people about and look up things for. And part of it is just to relax a little, to get away between books.

CA: You've said that while you're gathering material for a specific book, you're also getting ideas for other books. Obviously you're dealing with many facts and impressions at the same time. Do you have a highly sophisticated system for keeping track of all your material in various stages?

WALLACE: No, it's very unsophisticated, and I only work on one book at a time, really. When I get ideas, I usually write them down with a pencil; if I'm traveling, I go to my room at the hotel and type up something that struck me as interesting. When I get back home, I put these ideas in a file cabinet, and then, as I said earlier, an idea keeps niggling at me, and one day I say, Wouldn't it be good to do a book about Venice? Then I'll drag out all my notes—usually they're in folders under the subject I have in mind—spread them out, line them up, and see if the idea still interests me as much as I thought it would. If it does, I look at my notes to get other ideas and start making more notes.

Eventually I make a very crude, rough outline. A lot of writers write without an outline. They just sit down with a blank sheet of paper and see what happens. But I don't. I devote a lot of time trying to think out an idea. For example, a black man becoming president. How is that possible? That starts me developing the story and the character. Soon, lo and behold, I have the line of the book. And at least I know where it's going. The trouble with a lot of books is that you get the idea, but you don't know how to resolve it. With *The Second Lady*, I had an ending but I knew it was no good. I couldn't finish the book, because I didn't have the right ending. So I said to myself, What would happen to these characters? Finally one day while I was walking around, it struck me—a great idea, a brilliant ending. It meant I had to change some of the book in order to make it work, but I did. I got so many letters on that ending that I had to prepare photocopies of an explanation of why I did it that way.

CA: While you can counter the bad reviews you get with as many good ones, do you ever find the negative ones useful in any way?

WALLACE: Not really. If somebody says I don't have enough characterization or the plot's weak, what good does that do me? That's the best I could do. Nobody can tell me how to write; I can only write. Actually, I don't read the reviews fully anymore. I glance at the big ones. In the *New York Times*, for example, five of my last six reviews have been very good. In the *Los Angeles Times*, six out of my last six have been very bad. There's nothing you can do about it. You have to keep remembering that the person reviewing you is only a person— not a team, and not the population. It's just somebody who has an opinion, and may have a prejudiced opinion, because if you've been a best-seller or sold your books to movies, they feel you might not be honest. Academics frown on writers who are very popular. They feel you wouldn't be popular unless you were writing deliberately for popularity, and better you should live in an attic and suffer a little—then you might be *honest*. Well, that's all nonsense. There's a chance that, as a writer, you may be much more dishonest if you're broke, because you need money so badly. If you have enough money and it doesn't soften you up and make you want to repeat yourself, you may be much better off. You can write as you please; you don't care.

CA: Do you ever find it hard to keep a balance between the listening time, the association with other people, and the solitary work of putting words on paper?

WALLACE: Not really, because they come separately. I'm listening to people long before I'm writing the book. Usually listening is an accident at a party, or somewhere like that, unless I'm specifically doing interviews to find out about something. But when I sit down by myself to write the book, there's very little listening. That's the period when you take things out of your head and put them on paper. And unless you're a person who can be alone a lot, you'd better not be a writer.

CA: You were associated with some very fine writers and movie people in military service during World War II and later when you wrote for a while for Hollywood. Is there ever any temptation to go back and do more screenwriting?

WALLACE: No. When I quit, I quit forever. Movie writing generally has been, and still is, writing by committee. The director gets in, and the producer, and the star. You find yourself hardly being a writer at all, but more a kind of secretary taking down their notes. I don't like to write that way. I like to write as I please, and I don't want anybody to tell me how. Every time I've sold a book to the movies—and I've sold a lot—they ask me if I want to write the screenplay, and I say no. If I needed the money, I'd do it, but since I don't need the money, I've refused. I remember I sold *The Chapman Report*, after about nine offers, to Richard and Darryl Zanuck. I went off on one of my first big vacations in years to Venice, Italy, where I often go now. The phone rang one night when I was coming back from dinner, and it was Richard Zanuck calling from Burbank, where the project had moved from Twentieth Century-Fox to Warner Brothers. He said, "Irving, we have George Cukor here to direct the movie. He's read all the scripts and doesn't like them. He said the best thing to do would be to have the fellow who wrote the book do it. We'll pay you a lot of money if you'll come back right now and get to work with Mr. Cukor." I said, "No, thank you very much. I don't want to come back to dusty Burbank from beautiful Venice, Italy." One of the most important things to me, after I was able to make a living at writing, was to be independent, not to have a boss, to be a free-lancer all my life. This has affected my children, David and Amy. I've often heard them say the main thing is that they don't want to have a boss. They don't want to have hours, they just want to work for themselves. I consider that one of the most important things of all in being a writer.

CA: You've been in the forefront of various moves to get a better deal for writers, such as when you sold paperback rights to The Chapman Report *before the hardcover rights were sold. And you were the first American writer to be offered one hundred percent of the paperback advance. Are there still improvements you'd like to see between writers and publishers?*

WALLACE: One of the big things I'd like to see would be to make it part of the deal when you sign the contract for a new book that you are guaranteed information on your book. I find that most of my writer friends don't know their first-print order, how many copies of the book have been sold—they know literally nothing. The publisher believes that once he has the book, it's *his* book, and he doesn't tell the writer anything. There may be some exceptional cases, of course. But basically a writer is absolutely left out of the whole process of the selling of the book, which is, after all, part of the writing of the book. It's one thing we haven't been able to lick. It's very, very difficult to get a publisher to keep you informed. I know they're busy, and once they have a book they're looking for new books, and so on. But the fact is, it's very miserable for the writer to spend a couple of years on a book and not know a thing about it after the publisher gets it.

CA: When you were very young, you said, you were startled to learn from The Writer's Yearbook *that people actually got paid for writing magazine stories, which to you was just fun. . .*

WALLACE: What a day that was!

CA: Has getting paid handsomely for writing diminished your fun much, or is it still the joy it was when you first started?

WALLACE: It's different now. In those days it was such a reward to get five dollars or twenty dollars or a hundred dollars, you were out of your mind. Now you can get a million dollars or two million or whatever it is, and all that tells you is that somebody out there loves you and respects what you do and thinks what you do may make money for them. It's a different kind of satisfaction. It's not that you need the money; it's that you have approval.

BIOGRAPHICAL/CRITICAL SOURCES:

BOOKS

Authors in the News, Volume 1, Gale, 1976.
Cawelti, John G., *Adventure, Mystery, and Romance,* University of Chicago Press, 1976.
Contemporary Authors Autobiography Series, Volume 1, Gale, 1984.
Contemporary Literary Criticism, Gale, Volume 7, 1977, Volume 13, 1980.
Leverence, John, *Irving Wallace: A Writer's Profile,* Popular Press, 1974.
Newquist, Roy, *Conversations,* Rand McNally, 1967.
Wallace, Irving, *The Sunday Gentleman,* Simon & Schuster, 1965.
Wallace, Irving, *The Writing of One Novel,* Simon & Schuster, 1968, reprinted, Dutton, 1986.

PERIODICALS

Best Sellers, September 15, 1964.
Chicago Tribune, January 17, 1988.
Chicago Tribune Book World, April 29, 1977.
Detroit News, September 23, 1984.
Journal of Popular Culture, summer, 1973.
Los Angeles Times, June 4, 1981, December 19, 1982, January 27, 1985, April 27, 1987.
Los Angeles Times Book Review, May 15, 1977, September 23, 1984, March 2, 1986.
New Republic, March 25, 1972.
Newsweek, November 1, 1982.
New York, April 1, 1974.
New York Times, August 31, 1984.
New York Times Book Review, September 22, 1963, December 12, 1965, October 2, 1969, March 21, 1971, March 19, 1972, June 16, 1974, March 14, 1976, March 19, 1978, October 12, 1980, October 31, 1982, September 13, 1984.
Philadelphia Bulletin, April 28, 1974.
Saturday Review, March 18, 1978.
Time, April 15, 1974.
Times (London), August 23, 1974, April 30, 1987.
Times Literary Supplement, May 13, 1965, September 10, 1971, October 25, 1974.
Washington Post, April 11, 1976, February 28, 1980, September 23, 1980, October 22, 1980, November 17, 1982.
Washington Post Book World, March 19, 1978, August 12, 1984.

Writer, January, 1965, November, 1968.

—Sketch by Susan Salter
—Interview by Jean W. Ross

*   *   *

WALLACE, Sylvia

PERSONAL: Born in New York, N.Y.; daughter of Harry (a shopkeeper) and Rose (a shopkeeper; maiden name, Reisman) Kahn; married Irving Wallace (a writer), June 3, 1941; children: David Wallechinsky, Amy Wallace. *Education:* Attended Columbia University. *Politics:* Liberal. *Religion:* Jewish.

ADDRESSES: Home and office—P.O. Box 49328, Los Angeles, Calif. 90049. *Agent*—Arthur Pine Associates, Inc., 1780 Broadway, New York, N.Y. 10019.

CAREER: Copywriter and editor for Dell Publishing Co., New York City, 1944-48, and McFadden Publishing Co., New York City, 1952-57; free-lance writer and ghostwriter, 1947—.

WRITINGS:

The Fountain (novel), Morrow, 1976.
(Contributor) Irving Wallace, Amy Wallace, and David Wallechinsky, editors, *The People's Almanac Presents the Book of Lists* (Book-of-the-Month Club special selection), Morrow, 1977.
Empress (novel), Morrow, 1980.
(Editor with husband, I. Wallace, and children, A. Wallace and D. Wallechinsky) *The People's Almanac Presents the Book of Lists #2* (Literary Guild special selection), Morrow, 1980.
(Editor with I. Wallace, A. Wallace, and D. Wallechinsky) *The Intimate Sex Lives of Famous People,* Delacorte, 1981.
(Contributor) Fred A. Bernstein, *The Jewish Mothers' Hall of Fame,* Doubleday, 1986.

SIDELIGHTS: When Sylvia Wallace was growing up in the Bronx, her parents owned a small candy store located in the front of the family's accommodations. "Now," she once told *CA,* "I dwell in a 17-room sprawling French country house . . . in Brentwood, a suburb of Los Angeles. Half of the house is given over to offices for self, husband, children. I find it ironic that after all these years, and so much success, I once again find myself living in the back of the store."

The success she refers to centers on the Wallace clan's familial knack for turning out books, many of them bestsellers. Sylvia Wallace's contribution to the library includes two novels, *The Fountain* and *Empress,* and contributions to the widely popular compilations *The People's Almanac Presents the Book of Lists* and one of its sequels. In 1981 the Wallaces brought forth a compilation that had nothing to do with such fare as "12 Famous Cat Lovers" and "15 Pieces of Trash and When They Will Disintegrate." Instead, a provocative volume called *The Intimate Sex Lives of Famous People* proved a virtual "encyclopedia of what our celebrated betters, lessers, do between the sheets," as *Time*'s Gerald Clarke puts it. For those interested in the romantic idiosyncrasies of such figures as Albert Einstein, Leo Tolstoy, and Marilyn Monroe, the authors and their assistants, "with the patience of prospectors," continues Clarke, "have unearthed revealing passages from [some] 1,500 biographies, autobiographies and manuscripts. They are shy only about naming their sources, and wise readers will approach some of their 206 case histories with the same skepticism they would a Pulitzer prizewinning newspaper story.

Most of their tales, however, have been confirmed elsewhere, and the Wallaces know at least one fact absolutely: percales are threaded with gold."

MEDIA ADAPTATIONS: Twentieth Century-Fox has purchased the film rights to *The Intimate Sex Lives of Famous People.*

AVOCATIONAL INTERESTS: Politics, skiing, "beach haunting," European travel, the family farmhouse on the island of Menorca.

BIOGRAPHICAL/CRITICAL SOURCES:

BOOKS

Bernstein, Fred A., *The Jewish Mothers' Hall of Fame,* Doubleday, 1986.

PERIODICALS

Los Angeles Times, June 4, 1981.
Los Angeles Times Book Review, March 9, 1980.
Time, June 1, 1981.
Washington Post, February 28, 1980.*

*   *   *

WALLECHINSKY, David 1948-

PERSONAL: Wallechinsky is original family surname; the surname Wallace was bestowed on the author's grandfather by a U.S. Immigration agent at Ellis Island; born February 5, 1948, in Los Angeles, Calif.; son of Irving (a writer) and Sylvia (a writer; maiden name, Kahn) Wallace; married Flora Chavez; children: Elijah, Aaron. *Education:* Attended University of California at Los Angeles, Santa Monica College, and San Francisco State College (now University).

ADDRESSES: Office—P.O. Box 49699, Los Angeles, Calif. 90049.

CAREER: Filmmaker and writer. Co-writer of "Significa" column for *Parade,* 1981-84; writer, "Column of Lists," syndicated to 40 newspapers. Commentator for National Broadcasting Corp. (NBC) radio during 1988 Summer Olympics.

AWARDS, HONORS: The film "Gas" was selected as a U.S. entry to the Venice Film Festival in 1971.

WRITINGS:

(With Frank "Chico" Bucaro) *Chico's Organic Gardening and Natural Living,* Lippincott, 1972.
(Editor with Michael Shedlin) *Laughing Gas,* And/Or Press, 1973.
(Editor with father, Irving Wallace) *The People's Almanac* (Literary Guild special selection), Doubleday, 1975.
(With Michael Medved) *What Really Happened to the Class of '65?,* Random House, 1976.
(Editor with I. Wallace and sister, Amy Wallace) *The People's Almanac Presents the Book of Lists* (Book-of-the-Month Club special selection), Morrow, 1977.
(Editor with I. Wallace) *The People's Almanac #2* (Literary Guild special selection), Morrow, 1978.
(Editor with I. Wallace, mother, Sylvia Wallace, and A. Wallace) *The People's Almanac Presents the Book of Lists #2* (Literary Guild special selection), Morrow, 1980.
(Editor with I. Wallace and A. Wallace) *The People's Almanac Presents the Book of Predictions,* Morrow, 1980.
(Editor with I. Wallace) *The People's Almanac #3,* Morrow, 1981.

(Editor with I. Wallace, S. Wallace, and A. Wallace) *The Intimate Sex Lives of Famous People*, Delacorte, 1981.

(Editor with I. Wallace and A. Wallace) *The People's Almanac Presents the Book of Lists #3*, Morrow, 1983.

(Editor with I. Wallace and A. Wallace) *Significa*, Dutton, 1983.

The Complete Book of the Olympics, Viking, 1984, revised edition, 1988.

Midterm Report: The Class of '65; Chronicles of an American Generation, Viking, 1987, published in paperback as *Class Reunion '65: Tales of an American Generation*, Penguin, 1988.

Author and director of feature film "Gas," 1969, and of short comedy films. Contributor of articles and poems to magazines.

WORK IN PROGRESS: The Fortune, a novel, for Bantam.

SIDELIGHTS: Although born David Wallace to the authorial family that includes parents Irving and Sylvia Wallace, and sister Amy Wallace, David Wallechinsky changed his surname to match that of his grandfather, whose own name was shortened to Wallace when he arrived at U.S. Immigration on Ellis Island. Wallechinsky followed his parents' lead in becoming a professional writer early in life, and since then has collaborated with various members of his family on several highly popular works, books usually centering around various lists, almanacs, predictions, and other significa. But Wallechinsky is also the author of two books that examine the lives of his former high-school classmates. In the first, *What Really Happened to the Class of '65?*, written with school chum turned film critic Michael Medved, Wallechinsky presents an oral history of his group of Los Angeles high-school alumni, ten years after their graduation.

The authors received praise for their project, which revealed how youthful expectations can be fulfilled or dashed, depending on twists of fate and personal choices. The book also proved a commercial success, selling in high numbers and inspiring a television series. A subsequent ten-years-after volume seemed inevitable, and Wallechinsky, working alone this time, delivered on the concept in 1987, when he published *Midterm Report: The Class of '65; Chronicles of an American Generation*. In this edition, the author broadened his scope beyond Los Angeles to include a cross-section of Americans who all had the "class of '65" experience in common. As the former hippies, jocks, and flower children approached middle age, *Midterm Report* showed how the acquisitive values of the 1980s had influenced the youth of the 1960s.

Those critics who compared the two books generally found *What Really Happened to the Class of '65?* more rewarding. *Washington Post Book World* reviewer Jonathan Yardley, for instance, sees *Midterm Report* in a mixed way. On the one hand, he wonders if Wallechinsky's selection of participants doesn't reveal some of his own sympathies: "Though a number of [the interviewees] are interesting and appealing, they are anything but representative of a generation that is large, diverse, and uncategorizable. With only a few exceptions, they are the people whose experience and opinions conform rather conveniently to [the author's] own Berkleyesque *Weltanschauung*, which is to say that *Midterm Report* portrays only a rather narrow percentage of the class of '65."

But on the other hand, Yardley finds that "some of the people come quite fully to life: a woman who underwent divorce and then the death of her eldest child, yet has managed to maintain a positive outlook on life that is genuinely affecting; an un-

reconstructed hippie who walked across the United States, just for the hell of it; an Army major and his wife who fear that their daughter's severe intestinal difficulties may have been caused by his exposure to Agent Orange; a musician who composes songs that take amusing advantage of the new sexual license. If one is willing to read *Midterm Report* solely for the stories they tell, then it is an interesting piece of oral history." And to a *Chicago Tribune* critic, "even the most mundane [of these histories] are fascinating and worthy of the reader's respect."

In another Wallechinsky solo effort, *The Complete Book of the Olympics*, the author employs his list-making skills to chronicle "the first eight finishers for every single Olympic event since 1896, along with their times and distances—as well as the world's record at the time," according to Erich Segal, writing in the *New York Times Book Review*. "But the bare statistics are fleshed out by anecdotes that add a human and often humorous dimension." Noting that the only important element missing from the book is an index, Segal remarks that "nothing can diminish the fact that this is an extremely meticulous—one may even say Olympian—piece of scholarship. . . . This is a volume that will be of service for many Olympiads to come."

Wallechinsky tells *Los Angeles Times* reporter Richard Hoffer that *The Complete Book of the Olympics* holds a special place in his life. The work Wallechinsky at first considered a "fun obsession" turned out to be a project that consumed the author's life for "seven months . . . , seven days a week, 12 hours a day." What he found in his vast research, continues Wallechinsky, is that "everybody had a story. These were everyday people, but diverse. There are only two places in the world where people get together—the United Nations and the Olympics. In the United Nations, you have an elite; in the Olympic village you have real people."

MEDIA ADAPTATIONS: What Really Happened to the Class of '65? was adapted into a television series for NBC in 1977. Twentieth Century-Fox has purchased the film rights to *The Intimate Sex Lives of Famous People*.

BIOGRAPHICAL/CRITICAL SOURCES:

BOOKS

Wallechinsky, David, *Midterm Report: The Class of '65; Chronicles of an American Generation*, Viking, 1987, published in paperback as *Class Reunion '65: Tales of an American Generation*, Penguin, 1988.

Wallechinsky, David, and Michael Medved, *What Really Happened to the Class of '65?*, Random House, 1976.

PERIODICALS

Chicago Tribune, July 30, 1980, January 24, 1988.

Los Angeles Times, June 4, 1981, January 28, 1984.

Los Angeles Times Book Review, March 9, 1980, September 28, 1986.

New Republic, February 24, 1980.

New York Times, December 25, 1980.

New York Times Book Review, December 14, 1975, June 19, 1977, January 28, 1979, June 3, 1984, August 31, 1986.

Time, March 15, 1976, May 2, 1977, June 1, 1981.

Washington Post, February 28, 1980, January 1, 1981.

Washington Post Book World, October 1, 1978, August 17, 1986.

WARD, Douglas Turner 1930-

PERSONAL: Born May 5, 1930, in Burnside, La.; son of Roosevelt (co-owner of a tailoring business) and Dorothy (seamstress and co-owner of a tailoring business; maiden name, Short) Ward; married Diana Hoyt Powell (an editor), 1966; children: two. *Education:* Attended Wilberforce University, 1946-47, University of Michigan, 1947-48, and Paul Mann's Actors' Workshop, 1955-58.

ADDRESSES: Home—222 East 11th St., New York, N.Y. 10003. *Office*—Negro Ensemble Co., 424 West 55th St., New York, N.Y. 10019. *Agent*—Gilbert Parker, Curtis Brown Ltd., 575 Madison Ave., New York, N.Y. 10022.

CAREER: Playwright, actor, producer, and director; worked as a journalist in New York City, 1948-51; Negro Ensemble Company (NEC), New York City, co-founder, 1965, artistic director, 1967—. Appeared in productions of "The Iceman Cometh," 1956, 1959, and 1960-61, "Lost in the Stars," 1958, "A Raisin in the Sun," 1959, 1960-61, "The Blacks," 1961, "Pullman Car Hiawatha," 1962, "The Blood Knot," 1963, "Rich Little Rich Girl" and "One Flew Over the Cuckoo's Nest," 1964, "Coriolanus," "Happy Ending," and "Day of Absence," 1965, "Kongi's Harvest" and "Summer of the Seventeenth Doll," 1968, "The Reckoning" and "Ceremonies in Dark Old Men," 1969, and "Frederick Douglass in His Own Words," 1972; appeared as actor on television, including "Ceremonies in Dark Old Men," January 6, 1975, "Studio One," and "The Edge of Night"; appeared in film "Man and Boy," 1971. Producer or director of and actor in plays, including "Daddy Goodness," 1968, "Man Better Man," 1969, "Ododo," 1970, "The River Niger," 1972, and "First Breeze of Summer," 1975. Director of plays, including "Contribution," 1969, "Brotherhood" and "Day of Absence," 1970, "Ride a Black Horse," 1971, "Perry's Mission," 1971, "A Ballet Behind the Bridge," 1972, "The Great MacDaddy," "Black Sunlight," "Nowhere to Run, Nowhere to Hide," 1974, "Waiting for Mongo," 1975, "Livin' Fat," 1976, and "A Soldier's Play," 1982-83.

AWARDS, HONORS: Vernon Rice Drama Desk Award, 1966, Obie Award, 1966, Lambda Kappa Nu citation, 1968, special Tony award, League of American Theatres and Producers, Inc., 1969, Brandeis University creative arts award, 1969, all for "Happy Ending" and "Day of Absence"; Vernon Rice Drama Desk Award, 1969, for role in "Ceremonies in Dark Old Men"; Obie Award, *Village Voice,* 1970, for role in "The Reckoning"; Margo Jones Award, 1973, to Ward and NEC for producing new plays; Tony award nomination, 1974, best supporting actor.

WRITINGS:

Happy Ending and Day of Absence: Two Plays (comedies; first produced Off-Broadway at St. Mark's Playhouse, November 15, 1965), published with introduction by Sheila A. Rush, Dramatists Play Service, 1966, published as *Two Plays,* Third Press, 1971.

(Contributor) William Couch, Jr., editor, *New Black Playwrights,* Louisiana State University Press, 1968.

(Contributor) William Brasmer and Dominick Consolo, editors, *Black Drama,* Merrill, 1970.

The Reckoning: A Surreal Southern Fable (first produced Off-Broadway at St. Mark's Playhouse, September 2, 1969), Dramatists Play Service, 1970.

Brotherhood (first produced Off-Broadway with "Day of Absence" at St. Mark's Playhouse, April 26, 1970), Dramatists Play Service, 1970.

(Contributor) Clinton Oliver and Stephanie Sills, editors, *Contemporary Black Drama,* Scribner, 1971.

(Contributor) Robert Hayden, David Burrows, and Frederick Lapides, editors, *Afro-American Literature,* Harcourt, 1971.

(Contributor) Ruth Miller, editor, *Blackamerican Literature,* Free Press, 1971.

"The Redeemer," first produced in Louisville at Actors' Theatre, January 26, 1979.

SIDELIGHTS: Throughout his theatrical career, playwright and actor Douglas Turner Ward has shown great versatility both on and off the stage. "Whatever role the versatile Mr. Ward plays—as actor, playwright, journalist, director, artistic director of the Negro Ensemble Company—he is a man of great force, dedication, and verbosity," writes Mel Gussow in the *New York Times.* Through the Negro Ensemble Company, or NEC, which he co-founded in 1965 with Robert Hooks and Off-Broadway producer Gerald A. Krone, Ward has helped shape contemporary black theatre. "Ward was one of the first writers to approach theater from a modern black perspective using humor," points out Stephen M. Vallillo in the *Dictionary of Literary Biography.* "Comic, not militant or angry, his plays tend to be extended jokes, ironic situations that he develops into short dramatic pieces. Underneath the humor, however, is a biting satire that examines the relations and interdependence between blacks and whites." Vallillo adds that Ward's "work, and that of his theater, explores the wide range of black experience—its politics, its home life, its humor, and its drama. Ward's contribution to black theater is immense."

An article Ward wrote for the *New York Times* gave birth to the NEC. Entitled "American Theatre: For Whites Only?" the article defined American theater, from off-off-Broadway to Broadway, as "a Theater of Diversion—a diversionary theater, whose main problem is not that it's too safe, but that it is surpassingly irrelevant." Ward emphasized the need for "the development of a permanent Negro repertory company of at least off-Broadway size and dimension. . . . A theater concentrating primarily on themes of Negro life, but also resilient enough to incorporate and interpret the best of world drama— whatever the source." He continued that "this is not a plea for either a segregated theater, or a separatist one. Negroes constitute a numerical minority, but Negro experience, from slavery to civil rights, has always been of crucial importance to America's existence." Shortly after the article was published, Ward received a Ford foundation grant to start his theater. Two years after the founding of the NEC, John G. O'Connor noted in the *Wall Street Journal* that "from the beginning, the NEC's productions have been notable for their excellent acting, intelligent direction, and imaginative presentation." He also felt that the company was "already perhaps the finest acting-producing company in the United States."

While the NEC produces the work of many playwrights, it has served Ward well as a vehicle for his own writing and acting skills. Two of Ward's early plays, "Happy Ending" and "Day of Absence" ran on a double bill at the NEC, and Ward took major roles in both productions. Critics have praised the two works' originality. "Both plays are comedy satires, with sharp, jagged teeth, drawing their substance and their thrust from the bitter-sweet reality of race relations as seen from the bottom side of the coin," notes William Barrow in *Negro Digest.*

"Happy Ending" relates the plight of two black servants who despairingly face their employers' imminent divorce. When the women's proud nephew upbraids them for weeping, his aunts reveal that everything he owns, including his suits, have come from the white couple. The breakup of their home will mean the destruction of his lifestyle. At hearing this, the nephew starts to cry himself; part of the play's ironic humor comes from his change in attitude regarding his social status. According to Howard Taubman in the *New York Times*, "increasingly the Negro is using sardonic laughter to express his resentment at years of forced inferiority and to articulate his passion for change." Wilfrid Sheed in *Commonweal* comments on Ward's ability to portray the situation without racism: "Mr. Ward's message that the servant is finally corrupted as much as the master might not come so gracefully from a white playwright. But these are not raceplays in the usual sense; race is treated mainly as a local aspect of universal institution."

In "Day of Absence," white residents of a Southern town panic when the black labor force disappears for one day. Whites find themselves completely unable to function, and the Mayor ends up begging Washington to ship in more "Nigras." The play shows the dependence of all whites, but especially the middle and upper-classes, on blacks. "Day of Absence" was performed as a "reverse minstrel show." "The comedy is broad and heavy," writes Barrow. "The Negro actors wear white faces, and a few of them are wildly ingenuous." Writing in *Negro Digest*, Helen Armstead Johnson brings up the play's more serious aspects: "As funny as the images and memories are, the bitter truths and ironies are all too apparent.... It dramatizes a secret wish, which, no doubt, every Black person has had at one time or another." Barrow agrees, saying that both "Happy Ending" and "Day of Absence" "speak to black people with the resonance of experience."

In a discussion between playwrights and critics sponsored by the Modern Language Association, *New York Times* contributor Michael T. Kaufman reports that George Wellwarth objected to "outdated" relationships in "Happy Ending" and "Day of Absence." According to Wellwarth, Ward "writes about the master-servant relationship as if it still existed and presents us with the ironic paradox of the servant superior to the master." To this, Ward responded: "Stereotypes have changed—from Stepin Fetchit to a menacing black militant hiding behind every lamppost—but they are still stereotypes. As for the servant-master relationship, it exists, you can see it on the street corners in the Bronx where women shape up for jobs as domestics." Gail Stewart in the *Dictionary of Literary Biography* notes that Ward modified the cunning servant character found in Greek and Roman comedy to create his own servants; yet despite its association with the classical theater, Stewart finds that "'Day of Absence' is one of the most revolutionary plays written by an American black, for Ward depicts the enormity of the contribution of blacks to American life and in the same stroke the enormity of the exploitation that blacks have historically suffered."

Ward subsequently wrote a play called "The Reckoning." On a grimmer note than his two previous works, this picture of a Southern governor blackmailed by a pimp and his girlfriend still falls within the realm of comedy. But critics have responded to "The Reckoning" with more ambivalence, partially because the black pimp who forces the governor to publicly welcome a black march on the state capitol becomes the hero. According to Theophilus Lewis in *America*, "the author substitutes social justice for moral principle." A *Variety* con-

tributor claims that the conflict between the governor and Scar, the pimp, "is resolved not on the basis of right and wrong, or logic, but as a test of unscrupulous force." However, Edith Oliver states in the *New Yorker* that Ward was probably not concerned over whether audiences feel comfortable with his play: "Liking or not liking the play does not seem especially pertinent.... Mr. Ward is not out to attract or enchant or lightly amuse us, but his play's passion is alive."

Despite critics' feelings about Ward's presentation of justice and morality in "The Reckoning," they continue to praise his writing. The *Variety* essayist also states that "as a playwright, Ward has admirable capacities. He has an instinct for provocative situation, and dramatic conflict." And in *Cue*, Lawrence Wunderlich writes that "Ward's concept and language soar well beyond the keyhole-and-tape-recorder school of playwriting into careening flights of blank verse, simile, metaphor, alliteration, and, in the final analysis, a perfectly viable poetry for the theatre."

In "Brotherhood," which ran on a double bill with a restaging of "Day of Absence," Ward mocks the idea of facile relationships between blacks and whites. The plot concerns a white man and woman who invite a black couple into their home for the evening. The living room set appears strange from the beginning, as objects are draped with sheets and left covered through the play. When the black man and woman arrive, they are well-dressed and polite, which seems to disconcert their hosts. The white couple behaves oddly throughout the visit, and when the guests leave, the coverings are removed, and the objects revealed represent the couple's true feelings. But the black couple has also been hiding hatred behind smiles. "'Brotherhood' is probably more of a dramatic metaphor than a play," writes Clive Barnes in the *New York Times*. "It is a stark and startling accusation of racism against white and black alike." While some critics dislike the play, finding it less satisfying than earlier works, Barnes praises Ward's objectivity. He continues, "Ward plays no sides. He looks at our two nations with an unvarying yet compassionate eye."

BIOGRAPHICAL/CRITICAL SOURCES:

BOOKS

Contemporary Literary Criticism, Volume 19, Gale, 1981.
Dictionary of Literary Biography, Volume 7: *Twentieth-Century American Dramatists*, 1981, Volume 38: *Afro-American Writers after 1955*, 1984.
Mitchell, Loften, *Black Drama: The Story of the American Negro Theatre*, Hawthorn, 1967.

PERIODICALS

Cue, April 5, 1969, September 13, 1969, March 28, 1970.
Negro Digest, March, 1967, December, 1967, April, 1970.
New Leader, September 29, 1969.
New Yorker, September 13, 1969, March 28, 1970.
New York Times, November 16, 1965, August 14, 1966, September 5, 1969, September 14, 1969, March 18, 1970, December 30, 1970.
Show Business, September 20, 1969, November 29, 1969.
Variety, September 10, 1969.
Village Voice, September 11, 1969, January 22, 1970, March 26, 1970.
Wall Street Journal, February 19, 1969.
Washington Post, January 31, 1970.*

—Sketch by Jani Prescott

WARD, Ed
See STRATEMEYER, Edward L.

*　　*　　*

WARD, J(ohn) P(owell)　1937-

PERSONAL: Born November 28, 1937, in Felixstowe, England; son of Ronald Arthur (a theologian) and Evelyn Annie (a teacher and writer; maiden name, Powell) Ward; married Sarah Woodfull Rogers (a farmer), January 31, 1965; children: John Ralph Tristan, Thomas James. *Education:* University of Toronto, B.A., 1959; Peterhouse, Cambridge, B.A., 1961, M.A., 1969; University of Wales, M.Sc.(Econ), 1969.

ADDRESSES: Home—Court Lodge, Horton Kirby, Near Dartford, Kent DA4 9BN, England. *Office*—University College of Swansea, Singleton Park, Swansea SA2 8PP, Wales.

CAREER: University of Wales, University College of Swansea, senior lecturer in English, 1963—.

MEMBER: Welsh Academy.

AWARDS, HONORS: Literature award from Welsh Arts Council, 1982, for *Poetry and the Sociological Idea;* poetry award for *The Clearing.*

WRITINGS:

The Other Man (poems), Christopher Davies, 1969.
The Line of Knowledge (poems), Christopher Davies, 1972.
From Alphabet to Logos (experimental poems), Second Aeon, 1973.
Things (poems), Bran's Head Books, 1981.
To Get Clear (poems), Poetry Wales Press, 1981.
Poetry and the Sociological Idea, Harvester Press, 1981.
Raymond Williams (criticism), University of Wales Press, 1981.
Wordsworth's Language of Men, Harvester Press, 1984.
The Clearing (poems), Poetry Wales Press, 1984.
The Poetry of R. S. Thomas, Poetry Wales Press, 1987.

Editor of *Poetry Wales,* 1975-80.

SIDELIGHTS: A noted modern British poet, J. P. Ward has issued several volumes of verse, including *To Get Clear,* a collection of largely metaphysical poems that inspired *Times Literary Supplement* reviewer Anne Stevenson to write: "At his best Ward has a way with narrative which carries a poem through from beginning to end in an irresistible sweep of language. The reader boards a poem as if he were getting on a bus; before he knows it he has arrived at a destination well past anything he expected." Stevenson continued: "Ward . . . manages brilliantly, combining an uncompromising integrity with a contemporary flair for understatement."

Ward also elicited praise from a *Times Literary Supplement* critic for his book *Poetry and the Sociological Idea,* a look at poetry before and after the "sociological idea" which began in the nineteenth century. Charles Madge wrote: "I can say from practical experience that sociology and poetry do not sit easily together. J. P. Ward has written brilliantly about their incompatibility. . . . This is a brilliant and original book."

Ward once told *CA:* "By the 'sociological idea' I mean the idea that permeates most contemporary people's minds (including my own) that there is an entity named 'society' within which we live, which has considerable claims on us and considerably forms us. All nations, countries, tribes, and regions are not unique or individual, for they exemplify this overall 'society' notion and can be shown to possess its characteris-

tics. It is the most pervading conception of our era. Because of it, language is seen not as a set of terms matching and evoking realities, but as a means by which we stay in touch with each other—a means by which 'society' exists.

"My book argues that this belief, if dominant, is not compatible with the view and use of language held by poets. I show by close reading of Spenser, Donne, Milton, Pope, and Wordsworth that their use of language is not compatible with even those sociological positions each poet might have been thought most likely to hold. I then show from close readings of Baudelaire, Mallarme, Yeats, Stevens, William Carlos Williams, Eliot, Pound, Hardy, and Berryman, that in the era of the sociological idea (roughly the late nineteenth and twentieth centuries) the poets actually respond to the sociological idea explicitly, finding themselves in enormous tension against it."

Commenting on books he wrote in the 1980s, Ward added, "I see in hindsight that I have been magnetized toward the conception of getting clear, which in my life surrounds the activities of writing poetry on the one hand and scholarship and intellectual work on the other. I am always very sorry that, after 2,500 years, the academic and scholar still get a bad press, when the search for clarity of fact and idea are fundamentals in civilization. The poet, on the other hand (though not in contradiction), writes the more brilliantly for not knowing what he is writing. He sees with his eyes shut—the blind seer. And she does, too."

BIOGRAPHICAL/CRITICAL SOURCES:

PERIODICALS

Review of English Studies, August, 1984.
Times Literary Supplement, November 27, 1981, May 7, 1982, September 20, 1985.

*　　*　　*

WARD, Tom
See STRATEMEYER, Edward L.

*　　*　　*

WARREN, Mary Bondurant　1930-

PERSONAL: Born February 5, 1930, in Athens, Ga.; daughter of John Parnell (a lumber dealer) and Mary Caire (a personnel director; maiden name, Brannon) Bondurant; married James Randolph Warren (a farm equipment dealer), November 27, 1953; children: Eve Bondurant (Mrs. James Corbin Weeks), Mark Standard, Amy Moss (Mrs. Edward Victor Sanders), Stuart Heard, Lisa Brannon David. *Education:* University of Georgia, B.S., 1951; Oak Ridge Institute of Nuclear Studies, D.R.I.P., 1952.

ADDRESSES: Home—Pocataligo, Route 3, Box 3120, Danielsville, Ga. 30633. *Office*—Heritage Papers, Danielsville, Ga. 30633.

CAREER: Union Carbide, Oak Ridge, Tenn., staff member, 1950-51; Oak Ridge Institute of Nuclear Studies, Medical Division, Oak Ridge, conducted radio biophysics research, 1951-52; Emory University, School of Medicine, Atlanta, Ga., conducted radioisotope research, 1952-53; Georgia Institute of Technology, Atlanta, technical editor for engineering experiment station, 1954; Veterans Administration Hospital, Atlanta, radioassay consultant, 1956-57; Heritage Papers, Danielsville, Ga., owner, 1964—. Chairman of Clarke County (Ga.) Civil War Centennial Commission, 1961-65.

MEMBER: South Caroliniana Society (life member), Georgia Genealogical Society, Athens Historical Society (charter member; member of board of directors; president, 1962-63).

WRITINGS:

(Contributor) John Stegeman, *These Men She Gave*, University of Georgia Press, 1964.

Jackson Street Cemetery, Athens, Ga., Heritage Papers, 1966.

Mars Hill Baptist Church, Oconee County, Ga., Heritage Papers, 1966.

Marriage Book "A", Clarke County, Ga., Heritage Papers, 1966.

Georgia Genealogical Bibliography, 1963-67, Heritage Papers, 1968.

Marriages and Deaths, 1763 to 1820: Abstracted from Extant Georgia Newspapers, Heritage Papers, 1968.

Family Puzzlers, 1964-1967, Heritage Papers, 1969.

Family Puzzlers, 1969, Heritage Papers, 1970.

(Editor and author of revisions) L. M. Hill, *Hills of Wilkes County, Ga., and Allied Families*, Heritage Papers, 1972, 2nd edition, 1987.

Marriages and Deaths, 1820 to 1830: Abstracted from Extant Georgia Newspapers, Heritage Papers, 1972.

South Carolina Jury Lists: 1718 Through 1783, Heritage Papers, 1977.

Citizens and Immigrants: South Carolina, 1768, Heritage Papers, 1978.

(Editor) Bowen, *Chronicles of Wilke's County, Georgia*, Heritage Papers, 1978.

(Editor) A. L. Hull, *Annals of Athens, Georgia* (Warren was not associated with the previous edition), Heritage Papers, 1978.

South Carolina Wills, Heritage Papers, 1981.

(Editor) A. B. Stroud, *The Strouds*, 2nd edition (Warren was not associated with previous edition), Heritage Papers, 1983.

(Compiler) *Georgia Marriages, 1811-1820*, Heritage Papers, 1984.

(Compiler) *Georgia Memorials, 1755-1775*, Heritage Papers, 1984.

(Annotator and indexer) Reverend Morgan Edwards, *Materials toward a Baptist History, 1770-1772*, Heritage Papers, Volume I: *Pennsylvania, Rhode Island, New Jersey, Delaware*, 1984, Volume II: *Maryland, Virginia, North Carolina, South Carolina, Georgia*, 1984.

(Co-author) *Whites Among the Cherokee, Georgia, 1828-1838*, Heritage Papers, 1987.

(Compiler) *Georgia Land Owners' Memorials, 1758-1776*, Heritage Papers, 1988.

(Co-author) *South Carolina Newspapers, 1760: The South Carolina Gazette*, Heritage Papers, 1988.

Also author of "Athens Lives and Legends," a column published in *Athens Daily News*, and "Family Puzzlers," a column published in *Athens Banner Herald, Oglethorpe Echo*, and *Athens Daily News*, 1964-67. Editor of *Family Puzzlers*, 1964—, *Carolina Genealogist*, 1970-85, and *Georgia Genealogist*, 1970-85.

SIDELIGHTS: Mary Bondurant Warren writes *CA:* "My interest is research—discovering, codifying, and publishing records of historical and genealogical value in a useful form. With computers and microfilms to assist, we now explore obscure documents and voluminous collections avoided in the past!"

Warren goes on to write, "*Family Puzzlers*, our weekly genealogical magazine, strives to enhance the research skills of its readers by bringing to light just such sources."

WARUK, Kona
See HARRIS, (Theodore) Wilson

* * *

WASSERMAN, Harvey 1945-

PERSONAL: Born December 31, 1945, in Boston, Mass.; son of Sigmund J. (a businessman) and Phyllis (Shapiro) Wasserman. *Education:* University of Michigan, B.A., 1967; graduate study at University of Chicago, 1967-68, and New York University, 1968.

CAREER: Writer for United Press International and *Time*, 1966-67, and for Liberation News Service, 1967-68; elementary school teacher in New York, N.Y., 1968-69; Hampshire College, Amherst, Mass., instructor in history, 1973—.

MEMBER: Phi Beta Kappa, Phi Kappa Phi.

AWARDS, HONORS: Detroit Press Club Award, 1967, for editorials in *Michigan Daily;* Woodrow Wilson fellowship, 1967-68.

WRITINGS:

Harvey Wasserman's History of the United States, Harper, 1972, reprinted, Four Walls Eight Windows, 1988.

(Editor) *Energy War: Reports from the Front*, Lawrence Hill, 1979.

(With Norman Solomon, Robert Alvarez, and Eleanor Walters) *Killing Our Own: The Disaster of America's Experience with Atomic Radiation*, Delacorte, 1982.

America Born and Reborn: The Cycles of U.S. History, Macmillan, 1984.

Contributor to *Sundance, Win*, and other periodicals. Editorial director, *Michigan Daily*, 1966-67.*

* * *

WATERS, Michael 1949-

PERSONAL: Born November 23, 1949, in New York, N.Y.; son of Raymond G. (a detective) and Dorothy (a professional tennis player; maiden name, Smith) Waters; married Robin Irwin (a dancer), May 13, 1972. *Education:* State University of New York College at Brockport, B.A., 1971, M.A., 1972; attended University of Nottingham, 1970-71; University of Iowa, M.F.A., 1974; Ohio University, Ph.D., 1977.

ADDRESSES: Office—Department of English, Salisbury State College, Salisbury, Md. 21801.

CAREER: Poet. Ohio University, Athens, teaching fellow, 1975-77, instructor, 1977-78; Salisbury State College, Salisbury, Md., instructor, 1978-79, assistant professor, 1979-84, associate professor, 1984—. Poet-in-the-schools, New York State Arts Council, 1974-75, and Ohio Arts Council, 1975-78; poet-in-residence, South Carolina Arts Commission, 1974-75; visiting professor in American literature, University of Athens, Greece, 1981-82; Margaret Banister Writer-in-Residence, Sweet Briar College, 1987-89. Has given over forty poetry readings.

AWARDS, HONORS: National Young Poets award from London Poetry Society (England), 1971; award for excellence in poetry from Winthrop College, 1975, for *Fish Light;* Yaddo fellowship, 1978, 1980, 1983, 1984, 1987; National Endowment for the Arts residencies for writers grants, 1979, 1981,

1983, creative writing fellowship, 1984; Salisbury State College Foundation grant, 1982; Maryland Arts Council work-in-progress grant, 1983, 1985; Pushcart Prize, 1984; Towson State University Prize for Literature, 1985, for *Anniversary of the Air*.

WRITINGS:

POEMS

A Rare Breed of Antelope, Byron Press (London), 1972.
Fish Light, Ithaca House, 1975.
In Memory of Smoke, Rook Press, 1977.
The Scent of Apples, Croissant & Co., 1977.
Instinct, Croissant & Co., 1978.
Not Just Any Death, Boa Editions, 1979.
Among Blackberries, Service-berry Press, 1979.
Air Touched by the Axe, Inland Boat, 1980.
Dogs in the Storm, Breakwater Press, 1981.
The Stories in the Light, Thunder City Press, 1983.
The Faithful, Ion Books, 1984.
Anniversary of the Air, Carnegie-Mellon University Press, 1985.
The Barn in the Air, Livingston University Press, 1987.
The Burden Lifters, Carnegie-Mellon University Press, 1988.

EDITOR

Dissolve to Island: On the Poetry of John Logan, Ford-Brown & Co., 1984.

CONTRIBUTOR TO ANTHOLOGIES

The Ardis Anthology of New American Poetry, Ardis, 1976.
George Garrett, editor, *Intro 8: The Liar's Craft*, Doubleday, 1977.
Paul Feroe, editor, *Silent Voices: Recent American Poems on Nature*, Ally Press, 1978.
Gerald Costanzo, editor, *Three Rivers Ten Years*, Carnegie-Mellon University Press, 1983.
Wayne Dodd, editor, *The Ohio Review: Ten Year Retrospective*, The Ohio Review, 1983.
Alan F. Pater, editor, *Anthology of Magazine Verse and Yearbook of American Poetry* (annual), Monitor Book, 1984, 1985, 1987.
Bill Henderson, editor, *The Pushcart Prize, IX: Best of the Small Presses*, Pushcart Press/Avon, 1984.
William Heyer, editor, *The Generation of 2000: Contemporary American Poets*, Ontario Review Press, 1984.
Jack Myers and Roger Weingarten, editors, *New American Poets of the 80's*, Wampeter, 1984.
Dave Smith and David Bottoms, editors, *The Morrow Anthology of Younger American Poets*, Morrow, 1985.
Stanley W. Lindberg and Stephen Corey, editors, *Keener Sounds: Selected Poems from the Georgia Review*, University of Georgia Press, 1987.

OTHER

Contributing editor, *The Pushcart Prize*, 1984—. Reviewer, *Choice: Current Reviews for College Libraries*, 1986—. Contributor to journals, including *American Poetry Review*, *Poetry*, *Rolling Stone*, *Yale Review*, *Georgia Review*, and *Antioch Review*. *Ohio Review*, editorial assistant, 1976-77, associate editor, 1977-78; associate editor, *Raccoon*, 1982—.

WORK IN PROGRESS: Bountiful, a book of poems.

SIDELIGHTS: Works by Michael Waters have been translated into Russian and Arabic. His book, *Not Just Any Death*, was included in the United States National Book Exhibition in the People's Republic of China in 1981.

WEBSTER, Frank V.
[Collective pseudonym]

WRITINGS:

Only a Farm Boy; or, Dan Hardy's Rise in Life, Cupples & Leon, 1909.
Tom, the Telephone Boy; or, The Mystery of a Message, Cupples & Leon, 1909.
The Boy from the Ranch; or, Roy Bradner's City Experiences, Cupples & Leon, 1909.
The Young Treasure Hunter; or, Fred Stanley's Trip to Alaska, Cupples & Leon, 1909, reprinted, Saalfield, 1938.
Bob, the Castaway; or, The Wreck of the Eagle, Cupples & Leon, 1909, reprinted, Saalfield, 1938.
The Young Firemen of Lakeville; or, Herbert Dare's Pluck, Cupples & Leon, 1909, reprinted, Saalfield, 1938.
The Newsboy Partners; or, Who Was Dick Box?, Cupples & Leon, 1909.
The Boy Pilot of the Lakes; or, Nat Morton's Perils, Cupples & Leon, 1909.
Two Boy Gold Miners; or, Lost in the Mountains, Cupples & Leon, 1909, reprinted, Saalfield, 1938.
Jack, the Runaway; or, On the Road with a Circus, Cupples & Leon, 1909, reprinted, Saalfield, 1938.
Comrades of the Saddle; or, The Young Rough Riders of the Plains, Cupples & Leon, 1910, reprinted, Saalfield, 1938.
The Boys of Bellwood School; or, Frank Jordan's Triumph, Cupples & Leon, 1910, reprinted, Saalfield, 1938.
Bob Chester's Grit; or, From Ranch to Riches, Cupples & Leon, 1911, reprinted, Saalfield, 1938.
Airship Andy; or, The Luck of a Brave Boy, Cupples & Leon, 1911.
The High School Rivals; or, Fred Markham's Struggles, Cupples & Leon, 1911.
Darry, the Life Saver; or, The Heroes of the Coast, Cupples & Leon, 1911, reprinted, Saalfield, 1938.
Dick, the Bank Boy; or, The Missing Fortune, Cupples & Leon, 1911.
Ben Hardy's Flying Machine; or, Making a Record for Himself, Cupples & Leon, 1911.
The Boys of the Wireless; or, A Stirring Rescue from the Deep, Cupples & Leon, 1912, reprinted, Saalfield, 1938.
Harry Watson's High School Days; or, The Rivals of Rivertown, Cupples & Leon, 1912.
The Boy Scouts of Lenox; or, Hiking over Big Bear Mountain, Cupples & Leon, 1915.
Tom Taylor at West Point; or, The Old Army Officer's Secret, Cupples & Leon, 1915.
Cowboy Dave; or, The Round Up at Rolling River, Cupples & Leon, 1915, reprinted, Saalfield, 1938.
Two Boys of the Battleship; or, For the Honor of Uncle Sam, Cupples & Leon, 1915.
Jack of the Pony Express; or, The Young Rider of the Mountain Trails, Cupples & Leon, 1915, reprinted, Saalfield, 1938.

SIDELIGHTS: Some sources group all the books published under the pseudonym Frank V. Webster as a single series even though they did not share the same characters, themes, or settings. Cupples & Leon's advertisements described the books as very much like those "of the boys' favorite author, the late lamented Horatio Alger, Jr." For additional information on this pseudonym, see the entries in this volume for Harriet S. Adams, Edward L. Stratemeyer, and Andrew E. Svenson.

BIOGRAPHICAL/CRITICAL SOURCES:

BOOKS

Johnson, Deidre, editor and compiler, *Stratemeyer Pseud-onyms and Series Books: An Annotated Checklist of Stra-temeyer and Stratemeyer Syndicate Publications*, Green-wood Press, 1982.

*   *   *

WEINER, Irving B(ernard)   1933-

PERSONAL: Born August 16, 1933, in Grand Rapids, Mich.; son of Jacob H. (a businessman) and Mollie Jean (Laevin) Weiner; married Frances Shair, June 9, 1963; children: Jeremy Harris, Seth Howard. *Education:* University of Michigan, A.B., 1955, M.A., 1957, Ph.D., 1959.

ADDRESSES: Home—1286 River Rd., Teaneck, N.J. 07666. *Office*—Office of Academic Affairs, Fairleigh Dickinson University, Teaneck, N.J. 07070.

CAREER: U.S. Veterans Administration, clinical trainee, 1956-58; University of Michigan, Ann Arbor, Bureau of Psychological Service, counselor, 1957-59; University of Rochester, Rochester, N.Y., instructor in psychiatry, 1959-62, senior instructor, 1962-64, assistant professor, 1964-67, associate professor, 1967-69, professor of psychiatry, pediatrics, and psychology, 1969-72, head of Division of Psychology, University Medical Center, 1968-72; Case Western Reserve University, Cleveland, Ohio, professor of psychology and chairman of department, 1972-77, dean of graduate studies, 1976-79; University of Denver, Denver, Colo., vice-chancellor for academic affairs, 1979-83, professor of psychology, 1979-85; Fairleigh Dickinson University, Teaneck, N.J., vice-president for academic affairs and professor of psychology, 1985—. Diplomate, American Board of Professional Psychology.

MEMBER: American Association for the Advancement of Science, American Psychological Association (fellow), Society for Personality Assessment (president, 1976-78), Society for Adolescent Medicine, Association of Internship Centers (member of executive committee, 1971-76), Eastern Psychological Association, New York Academy of Sciences, Phi Beta Kappa, Sigma Xi, Phi Kappa Phi.

AWARDS, HONORS: Distinguished professional achievement award from Genesee Psychological Association, 1974; distinguished contribution award from Society for Personal Assessment, 1983.

WRITINGS:

Psychodiagnosis in Schizophrenia, Wiley, 1966.
Psychological Disturbance in Adolescence, Wiley, 1970.
(With Marvin Goldfried and George Stricker) *Rorschach Handbook of Clinical and Research Applications*, Prentice-Hall, 1971.
(Compiler with David Elkind) *Child Development*, Wiley, 1972, reprinted as *Readings in Child Development*, R. E. Krieger, 1980.
Psychopathology of Schizophrenia (sound recording), Jeffrey Norton, 1974.
Principles of Psychotherapy, Wiley, 1975.
Clinical Methods in Psychology, Wiley, 1976, 2nd edition, 1983.
(With Elkind) *Development of the Child*, Wiley, 1978.
Child and Adolescent Psychopathology, Wiley, 1982.

(With John E. Exner, Jr.) *The Rorschach: A Comprehensive System*, Volume 3: *Assessment of Children and Adolescents*, Wiley, 1982.
(With Douglas C. Kimmel) *Adolescence: A Developmental Transition*, Lawrence Erlbaum, 1985.
(Editor with Allen K. Hess) *Handbook of Forensic Psychology*, Wiley, 1987.

Editor, ''Wiley Series on Psychological Disorders'' and ''Wiley Series on Personality Processes.'' Editor, *Journal of Personality Assessment*, 1985—; member of editorial board, *Professional Psychology*, 1971-76, *Journal of Adolescent Health Care*, 1979—, *Children and Youth Services Review*, 1979—, *Journal of Pediatric Psychology*, 1983—, *Developmental and Behavioral Pediatrics*, 1985—, *Studi Rorschachiaxi*, 1985—, and *Evaluacion Psicologica*, 1985—.

*   *   *

WEISS, Edna
See BARTH, Edna

*   *   *

WELCH, Liliane   1937-

PERSONAL: Born October 20, 1937, in Esch-Alzette, Luxembourg; daughter of Jean-Pierre (an ''employe prive'') and Claire (a nurse; maiden name, Bravy) Meyer; married Cyril Welch (a professor); children: Colette. *Education:* University of Montana, B.A., 1960, M.A., 1961; Pennsylvania State University, Ph.D., 1964.

ADDRESSES: Home—10 Dominican Dr., Sackville, New Brunswick, Canada E0A 3C0. *Office*—Department of French and Spanish, Mount Allison University, Sackville, New Brunswick, Canada E0A 3C0.

CAREER: East Carolina University, Greenville, N.C., assistant professor of French, 1965-66; Antioch College, Yellow Springs, Ohio, assistant professor of French, 1966-67; Mount Allison University, Sackville, New Brunswick, assistant professor, 1967-71, associate professor, 1971-77, professor of French, 1977.

MEMBER: League of Canadian Poets, Humanities Association of Canada, Federation of New Brunswick Writers, New Brunswick Faculty Association (president 1972-73), Sackville Humanities Association (president, 1977-78), Mount Allison University Faculty Association (president, 1971-72), Union of Canadian Writers, Union of Luxembourg Writers.

WRITINGS:

(With husband, Cyril Welch) *Emergence: Baudelaire, Mallarme, Rimbaud*, Bald Eagle Press, 1973.
Winter Songs (poems), Killaly Press, 1977.
(With C. Welch) *Address: Rimbaud, Mallarme, Butor*, Sono Nis Press, 1979.
Syntax of Ferment (poems), Fiddlehead, 1979.
Assailing Beats (poems), Borealis Press, 1979.
October Winds (poems), Fiddlehead, 1980.
Brush and Trunks (poems), Fiddlehead, 1981.
From the Songs of the Artisans (poems), Fiddlehead, 1983.
Manstorna (poems), Ragweed, 1985.
Word-House of a Grandchild (poems), Ragweed, 1987.
Seismographs (prose), Ragweed, 1988.

WORK IN PROGRESS: Poetry collections on women.

WESLEY, Richard (Errol) 1945-

PERSONAL: Born July 11, 1945, in Newark, N.J.; son of George Richard (a laborer) and Gertrude (Thomas) Wesley; married Valerie Wilson, May 22, 1972; children: Thembi, Nandi (daughters). *Education:* Howard University, B.F.A., 1967.

ADDRESSES: Office—Elegba Productions, P.O. Box 43091, Upper Montclair, N.J. 07043; and Jay D. Kramer, 36 East 61st St., New York, N.Y. 10021. *Agent*—Phil Gersh Agency, 130 West 42nd St., New York, N.Y. 10036.

CAREER: Playwright and screenwriter. United Airlines, Newark, N.J., passenger service agent, 1967-69; currently president of Elegba Productions, Upper Montclair, N.J. Member and playwright in residence with Ed Bullins and J. E. Gaines, New Lafayette Theatre, 1969-73. Guest lecturer in black theatre and film, Manhattanville College, 1975; guest lecturer in black art and creative writing, Manhattan Community College, 1980-81 and 1982-83. Member of board of directors, Theatre of Universal Images (Newark), and of Frank Silvera Writer's Workshop (New York), 1974-82. Member of selection committee for Black Film Festival, Newark, 1982—.

MEMBER: Writers Guild of America East.

AWARDS, HONORS: Outstanding Playwright Award, Samuel French, 1965, for ''Put My Dignity on 307''; Drama Desk Award for Outstanding Playwrighting, 1972, for ''The Black Terror''; Rockefeller grant, 1973; Image Award, NAACP, 1974, for *The Sirens,* ''The Past Is the Past,'' and ''Goin' thru Changes,'' and 1977, for *The Mighty Gents.*

WRITINGS:

PLAYS

''Put My Dignity on 307,'' first produced in Washington, D.C., at Howard University, 1967.
''The Streetcorner,'' first produced in Seattle, Wash., at Black Arts/West, 1970, produced in New York at Lincoln Center Plaza, summer, 1972.
''Headline News,'' first produced in New York at the Black Theatre Workshop, 1970.
''Knock Knock, Who Dat,'' first produced in New York at Theatre Black, University of the Streets, October 1, 1970.
''The Black Terror,'' (first produced at Howard University, February, 1971; produced in New York at the Public Theatre, November, 1971), published in *New Lafayette Theatre Presents the Complete Plays and Aesthetic Comments by Six Black Playwrights,* edited by Ed Bullins, Doubleday, 1974.
''Gettin' It Together'' (one act; also see below; first produced in Roxbury, Mass., at the Elma Lewis School of Fine Arts, May 13, 1971; produced in New York at the Public Theatre, 1972), published in *The Best Short Plays 1980,* edited by Stanley Richards, Chilton, 1980.
''Strike Heaven on the Face,'' first produced in New York at the Lyceum Theatre, January 15, 1973.
''Goin' thru Changes'' (one-act), first produced in Waterford, Conn., at the Eugene O'Neill Memorial Theatre Center, 1974; produced in New York at the Billie Holliday Theatre, 1974.
The Sirens (first produced in New York at the Manhattan Theatre Club, 1974), Dramatists Play Service, 1975.
''The Past Is the Past'' (one-act; also see below; first produced in Waterford, Conn. at the Eugene O'Neill Memorial Theatre Center, August 1, 1974; produced in New York at the Billie Holliday Theatre, 1974), published in *The Best Short Plays of 1975,* edited by Stanley Richards, Chilton, 1975.
The Mighty Gents (first produced in Waterford, Conn., at the Eugene O'Neill Memorial Theatre Center, 1974; produced as ''The Last Street Play'' in New York at the Urban Art Corps and the Manhattan Theatre Club, 1977; restaged under original title on Broadway at the Ambassador Theatre, April 16, 1978), Dramatists Play Service, 1979.
''The Past Is the Past'' and ''Gettin' It Together'': Two Plays, Dramatists Play Service, 1979.
''The Dream Team,'' first produced in Chester, Ct., at the Goodspeed Opera House, 1984.

Also author of unproduced plays, ''Springtime High,'' 1968, and ''Another Way,'' 1969.

SCREENPLAYS AND TELEPLAYS

''Uptown Saturday Night,'' First Artists Corp., 1974.
''Let's Do it Again'' (sequel to ''Uptown Saturday Night''), First Artists Corp., 1975.
''The House of Digs Drear'' (teleplay), Public Broadcasting Service, 1984.
''Fast Forward'' (based on story by Timothy March), Columbia Pictures, 1985.
''Native Son'' (based on novel of same title by Richard Wright), Cinecom, 1986.

OTHER

(Author of book) ''On the Road to Babylon'' (musical), first produced in Milwaukee, Wis., at the Todd Wehr Theatre, December 14, 1979.

Contributor to *Black World* and *Black Creation.* Managing editor, *Black Theatre Magazine,* 1969-73.

SIDELIGHTS: Richard Wesley once remarked that his writings are ''inspired primarily by social and political conditions in the United States.'' Steven R. Carter observes in the *Dictionary of Literary Biography* that Wesley bridges ''the two forms of black theater in the 1960s and 1970s, the militant theater and the theater of experience,'' adding that he ''has made significant contributions to both.'' Recognizing most of Wesley's plays to be ''sensitive, emphatic depictions of blacks who have either escaped from or remained fixed in various self-imprisoning and self-mutilating patterns of behavior arising from oppression,'' Carter notes that Wesley also expresses his talent in screenwriting. ''All in all,'' says Carter, ''Wesley is among the most versatile and perceptive Afro-American dramatists and scriptwriters.''

''The Black Terror,'' first produced in 1971, brought Wesley recognition and earned him a Drama Desk Award. The play is about a black revolutionary group committed to violence. The protagonist, who has been trained in guerrilla warfare in Vietnam by the army, joins the group and becomes its assassin, but ''begins to question their eagerness to die to demonstrate their revolutionary fervor,'' writes Carter. Troubled by the necessity of violence, his conflict is compounded when he is ordered to kill a black political moderate. Carter considers it ''a powerful political statement urging black revolutionaries to abandon the rhetoric and practice of revolutionary suicide and to pay more attention to the concrete realities of black life in the United States in shaping their tactics.'' Calling it ''grim and gripping'' and ''a thoughtful play that will annoy many people,'' Clive Barnes praises its objectivity and continues in the *New York Times:* "This is a remarkable and provocative play—the kind of political play that needs to be written and demands to be seen by black and white alike." Carter finds that the play "amply demonstrated Wesley's skill in dramatizing ideas, giving them an urgency, appeal, and impact that audiences cannot easily leave behind."

Wesley's "The Past Is the Past," which Carter deems his "finest short play," is about a father who coincidentally meets the illegitimate son he had abandoned twenty years earlier. He is "acutely aware of his son's identity and provides painful, honest answers to the boy's questions while striving to keep an emotional distance from him," says Carter. The critic adds that it is apparent that the answers reveal that the father "has reflected a great deal about the past without being able to overcome its effects and that he regards his own experience as typical of black men of his generation." In *Nation,* Harold Clurman states that "without recrimination there is a fiber of understanding between the two." And Edith Oliver, who feels the play may become a classic on the theme of mutual recognition and acceptance between father and son, declares that "the play is entirely about feelings, and it is written with a combination of strength and delicacy and craftsmanship that adds up to perfection."

Wesley's *The Mighty Gents* is about "the adult, drifting survivors of a youth gang in Newark's black ghetto," writes Richard Eder in the *New York Times,* adding that "ten years later they are trapped in poverty and lethargy; they spend their time sitting around aimlessly, drinking and engaging in ritualized horseplay." Carter observes that "they are all losers with only the memory of past 'wins' in gang fights to sustain their self-respect." And the protagonist, says Carter, believes that he and the other gang members can regain their past glory by "beating up and robbing a small-time gangster... who had once belonged to a rival gang." Although Eder thinks that the play "has some diffuseness and some uninspired and commonplace passages," he nonetheless finds it "moving and impressive." And Carter, who considers it "Wesley's finest work," explains that it is "filled with complex, intriguing characterizations, intricate, haunting symbolism, powerful poetic language, and searing, unforgettable insights." Describing the play as "poignant" and "truthful," Mel Gussow maintains in the *New York Times* that "Wesley is a natural playwright, with a great gift for creating character, evoking atmosphere and using dialogue and gestures as motifs."

Wesley debuted as a screenwriter with the comedy "Uptown Saturday Night" featuring Sidney Poitier, Bill Cosby, Harry Belafonte, Flip Wilson, and Richard Pryor. The film follows the adventures of two men who "sneak off from their wives for the first time and, during their one and only visit to an after-hours gambling club, are robbed of a $50,000 winning lottery ticket," writes Carter. The film's success led to a sequel, "Let's Do It Again," which Wesley also wrote. More recently, Wesley has written the screenplay for Richard Wright's classic novel, *Native Son,* about a poor black youth who accidentally murders the daughter of his white employer. Some critics believe that the film version, which features Victor Love and Oprah Winfrey, does not capture the novel's moral complexity. Richard Harrington, for instance, suggests in the *Washington Post* that Wesley fails to overcome "the central challenge posed by Wright's book, in which Bigger's complexity—and the context for the controversy raging around him—is contained outside the dialogue." According to Harrington, "Wesley's script is simply too literal." On the other

hand, critics also acknowledge the difficulties inherent in the task of distilling such a classic into a two-hour film. While calling it a "magnanimous, modestly budgeted, morally medicinal adaptation," Rita Kempley concludes in the *Washington Post* that the film "is as worthy as it is self-righteous."

In addition to his screenwork, says Megan Rosenfeld in the *Washington Post,* Wesley "continues to work on several plays exploring his generation of middle-class black college graduates." Wesley refers to this generation, says Rosenfeld, as "the most spoiled of the 20th century." The deprivation and upheaval endured by the parents of this generation during the Great Depression and the war that followed resulted in a material wealth provided the children that had been denied the parents. Calling him a "thoughtful and serious man, always curious about how people think," Rosenfeld observes that Wesley "wants his plays to lead audiences to make their own choices, and believes that art must have a purpose to justify itself." Wesley strives to project in his work the idea that success is achieved through discipline: "Sometimes I meet people who are still stuck in 'black is beautiful.' The thing is, like, so what? So we're beautiful, now what? You can't use racism as an excuse any more for not doing anything. It's been like that for 400 years, so what? It's a racist society, and you have two alternatives: You can move ahead or you die."

BIOGRAPHICAL/CRITICAL SOURCES:

BOOKS

Contemporary Literary Criticism, Volume 7, Gale, 1977.
Dictionary of Literary Biography, Volume 38: *Afro-American Writers after 1955: Dramatists and Prose Writers,* Gale, 1985.
Fabre, Genevieve, *Drumbeats, Masks and Metaphor: Contemporary Afro-American Theater,* Harvard University Press, 1983.
Hughes, Catherine, *Plays, Politics and Polemics,* Drama Book Specialists, 1973.

PERIODICALS

Black Creation, winter, 1973.
Black World, April, 1972, July, 1973.
Los Angeles Times, November 13, 1978, January 26, 1983.
Nation, May 17, 1975.
New Yorker, January 28, 1974.
New York Times, November 11, 1971, November 21, 1971, April 25, 1977, April 18, 1978, February 15, 1985, December 23, 1986.
Show Business, May 23, 1974.
Variety, April 26, 1972.
Washington Post, November 16, 1982, November 19, 1982, January 16, 1987.

—*Sketch by Sharon Malinowski*

*   *   *

WEST, Jerry
   See SVENSON, Andrew E(dward)

*   *   *

WEST, (Mary) Jessamyn   1902-1984

PERSONAL: Born July 18, 1902, in Jennings County, Ind.; died of a stroke February 23 (some sources say February 22), 1984 in Napa, Calif.; daughter of Eldo Ray (a citrus farmer) and Grace Anna (Milhous) West; married Harry Maxwell

McPherson (a school superintendent) August 16, 1923; children: Ann Cash (adopted daughter). *Education:* Whittier College, A.B., 1923; attended University of California at Berkeley; studied at Oxford University, 1929. *Religion:* Society of Friends (Quaker).

ADDRESSES: Home and office—2480 3rd Ave., Napa, Calif. 94558.

CAREER: Writer, 1935-84. Taught at writers' conferences at Breadloaf, Indiana University, University of Notre Dame, University of Colorado, Squaw Valley University of Utah, University of Washington, Stanford University, University of Montana, Portland University, University of Kentucky, and Loyola Marymount University. Visiting professor at Wellesley College, University of California at Irvine, Mills College, and Whittier College. Visiting lecturer at numerous colleges.

MEMBER: American Civil Liberties Union, National Association for the Advancement of Colored People.

AWARDS, HONORS: Indiana Authors' Day Award, 1956, for *Love, Death, and the Ladies' Drill Team;* Thermod Monsen Award, 1958, for *To See the Dream;* California Commonwealth Club award, 1970, and California Literature Medal, 1971, both for *Crimson Ramblers of the World, Farewell;* Janet Kafke prize for fiction, 1976; Indiana Arts Commission Award for Literature, 1977, for body of work. Honorary doctorates from Whittier College, Mills College, Swarthmore College, Indiana University, University of Indiana—Terre Haute, Western College for Women, Wheaton College, Juniata College, and Wilmington College.

WRITINGS:

FICTION

The Friendly Persuasion (short stories), Harcourt, 1945, reprinted, Buccaneer Books. 1982.
The Witch Diggers (novel), Harcourt, 1951.
Cress Delahanty (short stories; Book-of-the-Month Club selection), Harcourt, 1953.
Little Men (novel), Ballantine, 1954, republished as *The Chile Kings,* 1967.
Love, Death, and the Ladies' Drill Team (short stories), Harcourt, 1955 (published in England as *Learn To Say Goodbye,* Hodder & Stoughton, 1960).
South of the Angels (novel), Harcourt, 1960.
A Matter of Time (novel), Harcourt, 1966.
Leafy Rivers (novel), Harcourt, 1967.
Except for Me and Thee: A Companion to "The Friendly Persuasion," (short stories), Harcourt, 1969.
Crimson Ramblers of the World, Farewell (short stories), Harcourt, 1970.
The Massacre at Fall Creek (novel; Literary Guild main selection), Harcourt, 1975.
The Life I Really Lived (novel), Harcourt, 1979.
The State of Stony Lonesome (novel), Harcourt, 1984.
The Collected Stories of Jessamyn West, Harcourt, 1987.

NONFICTION

To See the Dream, Harcourt, 1957.
Love Is Not What You Think, Harcourt, 1959 (published in England as *A Woman's Love,* Hodder & Stoughton, 1960).
Hide and Seek: A Continuing Journey, Harcourt, 1973.
The Woman Said Yes: Encounters with Death and Life (Book-of-the-Month Club alternate selection), Harcourt, 1976 (published in England as *Encounters with Death and Life: Memoirs,* Gollancz, 1978).

Double Discovery: A Journey, Harcourt, 1980.

PLAYS

A Mirror for the Sky (opera libretto; first performed at the University of Oregon at Eugene, May 24, 1957), Harcourt, 1948.
''The Friendly Persuasion'' (screenplay; based on story collection of same title), produced by Allied Artists, 1956.
''The Big Country'' (screenplay), produced by United Artists, 1958.
''Stolen Hours'' (screenplay), produced by United Artists, 1963.

OTHER

(Contributor) *Cross Section 1948: A Collection of New American Writing,* Simon & Schuster, 1948.
(Editor) *A Quaker Reader,* Viking, 1962.
The Secret Look: Poems, Harcourt, 1974.

Contributor to *O. Henry Memorial Award Prize Stories of 1946,* and to *The Living Novel,* 1957. Also contributor of fiction and nonfiction articles to numerous periodicals, including *Town and Country, Mademoiselle, Collier's, Ladies' Home Journal, New Mexico Quarterly, Yale Review, Kenyon Review, Good Housekeeping, McCall's, Harper's, New Yorker, Redbook,* and *Saturday Evening Post.*

WORK IN PROGRESS: ''I am constantly writing—with more in mind to do than time will ever permit—novels, stories, articles.''

SIDELIGHTS: The late Jessamyn West was a prolific and varied writer whose works include fiction, nonfiction, poetry, screenplays, and even an opera libretto. She is remembered, however, for her numerous short stories that plumb rural American life without sentiment or oversimplicity. Much of West's fiction reflects her involvement with the Society of Friends (Quakers), the religion of her ancestors who farmed in southern Indiana. Her popular story collections *The Friendly Persuasion* and *Except for Me and Thee: A Companion to "The Friendly Persuasion"* recreate Quaker lives in a nineteenth century farming community; these and her tales of adolescence, *Cress Delahanty* and *The State of Stony Lonesome,* remain her best known works. *New York Times Book Review* contributor Nancy Hale called West's stories ''homespun but with an exceedingly subtle warp and woof,'' and explained that West used ''small-town life to convey human events that warm the heart and evoke instant sympathy.'' According to Bill Crider in the *Dictionary of Literary Biography,* West's many volumes were ''well-received, even acclaimed, by reviewers'' for their ''vivid, vigorous, and eloquent style and the compassion and humanity with which she treats . . . serious themes.'' In his book-length study entitled *Jessamyn West,* Alfred S. Shivers concluded that the author's work retains its ''high merit with respect to sensitivity of characterizations, restraint, genuineness of feeling, psychology, and delightful humor.''

Los Angeles Times correspondent Kay Mills noted that West wrote ''from memory. Her own. Her mother's. That of her Quaker religion and of the two regions she [called] home— southern Indiana, where she was born, and Southern California, where she was raised.'' Both regions from which West drew her inspiration were rugged and sparsely populated when she first encountered them, so her focus of concern was almost always the country. ''Much of Jessamyn West's better writing ignores the ugliness and artificiality of mid-twentieth-century urban life and ensconces itself amid the bucolic back country

America of previous eras,'' Shivers commented. ''Her personal love for solitude as a housewife among her chores; her unusual predilection for the writings of [Henry David] Thoreau; her girlhood spent on ranches without (it seems) any important regrets; her dislike of, or at least uneasiness with, highway commercialism—all are consistent with the withdrawal and the idyllic tone found in [her work].'' Most critics agreed that West used local color to great effect in her fiction. John T. Flanagan claimed in the *Indiana Magazine of History* that West's success in realizing scenes derived from ''her cntrol of the physical locale and her use of authentic and specific colors and objects.... Nor is this local color obtrusive. The Indiana and California backgrounds fit naturally into the story, providing both a backdrop and a proscenium for the narrative action.''

West's chronicles of rural life are hardly mere idyllic tales of simpler times, however. She strove to create realistic characters, especially teenagers and women, with personalities well-grounded in human nature. Flanagan found West's people ''a constant delight, freshly conceived, individual, even a bit eccentric.... Generally commonsensical but often endowed with a quirky humor or an ironical point of view, her characters enter the reader's presence in full stature and linger there like old acquaintances.'' Her Quaker background notwithstanding, West tackled the subject of sexual passion, generally but not always celebrating the stability of marriage over the momentary attraction of a liason. According to *New York Times Book Review* contributor Webster Schott, West dominated among women novelists as ''an advocate of human respect, reason over emotions, and a tough, all-purpose femininity that can face and solve most situations on its own terms.'' Shivers similarly observed that the author made ''no claim that fiction should be morally improving'' even though many of her books ''exude a subtle moral atmosphere.'' Within the parameters of domestic drama, West explored universal themes such as values, sexuality, and maturity; to quote *Dictionary of Literary Biography Yearbook* essayist Ann Dahlstrom Farmer, her characters ''are complex, not because they represent several ideas but because they are realistic, many-faceted individuals.''

Critics also cited West's work for a consistency and quality of style. *Washington Post* reviewer Suzanne Fields maintained that the author wrote ''gracefully, occasionally poetically, in a voice both innocent and brave.'' Flanagan called West's prose ''vivid and original . . . often exemplified by surprising similes taken from ordinary life and observation.'' In the *New York Herald Tribune Book Review,* Virgilia Peterson related style to substance, explaining that West was ''not tuned to the high-strung, nervous, angry pitch that, perhaps more than any other, characterizes the writing of our time. Nor [was] she afraid of sentiment. So much tenderness [welled] up and [spilled] out of her that some would say she [was] not leery enough of it. But none of her tenderness [was] blind.... What [established] her certainly as one of the most trustworthy and endearing among current American novelists is that, knowing the evil, she [persisted] in countervailing it with the good.'' Likewise, *New York Times Book Review* correspondent Laurence Lafore found West's work to be grounded ''in a classic tradition that imposes a discipline almost as rigid, and as fecund, as the sonnet form. And her ideas [were] as consistent as her methods. Some readers may feel a want of variety; more will welcome the cumulative, and coherent, revelation of her view of the world and of art.''

West was born in Indiana on July 18, 1902, to a farming family of modest circumstances. She was related to Richard Nixon through her mother's family, and she became a close and lifelong friend of his, sometimes even travelling with the presidential entourage. When West was still young, her father decided to seek his fortune in California. Eventually the family moved to an undeveloped wilderness area near Yorba Linda, where they began a successful citrus orchard. West and her brother and sister were allowed to roam freely through the arid Orange County lands, and the young girl was able to cultivate her solitary, observant nature. Adolescence brought an interest in reading as well as a fascination with the life and work of Thoreau. Dahlstrom Farmer observed that Thoreau's writings prized two things that West herself prized, namely ''solitude and journal-keeping as enhancers of observation and introspection.'' Although she admired many writers, West quelled her own authorial ambitions and studied to become a school teacher. After graduating from Whittier College, she married Harry Maxwell McPherson and set to work in a one-room school. She soon discovered a great desire to further her education, however, and in 1929 she embarked for a summer session at Oxford University. Upon her return to the United States, she enrolled in a graduate program at the University of California at Berkeley.

Just before taking her doctoral orals, West suffered a severe lung hemorrhage and was diagnosed as having an advanced case of tuberculosis. She was placed in the terminal ward of a Los Angeles sanitorium, and her doctors gave her little hope of survival. After two years in the hospital, West was sent home so that she could ''die amongst her loved ones.'' West's mother refused to accept the inevitability of her daughter's untimely death, however. She went to great lengths to provide favorite foods, and just as important for the depressed patient, entertainment. Reaching into her own past, West's mother recalled her Quaker forebears and told West about them. According to Angela Wigan in *Time* magazine, the elder West recounted ''stories about courtship and farming, blizzards and Quaker meetings.'' As West slowly recovered, she ''turned her mother's gift into her own response to extinction—her writing.'' While still an invalid she bagan to create sketches about an Indiana Quaker farm couple raising a family during the Civil War era. Her husband encouraged her to submit the stories to magazines, and by the time she had regained her health—early in 1940—her work was being accepted by such publications as the *Atlantic Monthly, Harper's,* and the *Ladies' Home Journal.* In retrospect, West was quoted in *Women Writers of the West Coast* as crediting her near-fatal illness with giving her the courage to begin writing. ''I thought my life was over,'' she said of those hopeless days. ''Instead, for me, it was the beginning of my life.''

The Friendly Persuasion, published in 1945, collects a number of West's stories about Jess and Eliza Birdwell, the Quaker farmers in rural Indiana. Crider described the book thus: ''The stories carry the family from the ten years preceding the Civil War to Jess's old age, around the turn of the century. A remarkable feeling of familial love and understanding permeates the book, which is also notable for its warmth and humor.'' Crider added that the collection ''was an immediate success,'' with critics and general readers alike. *Saturday Review* commentator William Hogan called *The Friendly Persuasion* ''a warm, winning tale'' that established West's reputation for ''style, characterization, humor, and impetuosity.'' In *Book Week,* Flora Henderson wrote that the work ''makes a delightful addition to American literature. There is poetry here, but so subtly woven into the fabric of story and character that it never intrudes.'' Ernestine Evans made similar observations in the *New York Herald Tribune Book Review*. ''Miss West's style is full of surprises, vivid metaphors, odd turns of plot, yet she is never disconcerting, over-ingenious or repetitive,'' Evans contended. ''Though distilled from family legends of the Irish Quaker community into which she was born, the tales are less nostalgic than provocative. One feels not that loveliness used to be and is no more but that life could be . . . even quieter and funnier than currently advertised.''

According to Shivers, West was able to reconcile her religious tradition with the demands of artistic truth in *The Friendly Persuasion* and its sequel, *Except for Me and Thee*. West ''resisted the moralizing impulse,'' Shivers noted, even though her stories revolve around characters with traditional values. In the *Saturday Review,* Nathan L. Rothman commented: ''If we do not get any definitive sense of the world outside [West's Quaker community,] we do get something at least as precious, an intimate knowledge of their inner life. . . . While the tales are slight . . . each of them permits Miss West the full expression of her central theme, the lovely, gentle, ethical esence of the . . . Quaker. The mood is nostalgic, primitive, like a dream of vanished innocence.'' Another *Saturday Review* critic pointed out that although West was writing of a pioneer family, she depicted them ''with loving sympathy rather than sentimentality.'' Flanagan concluded in the *Great Lakes Review* that both story collections reveal ''a fine understanding of the operations of the folk mind.'' West wrote a screenplay based on *The Friendly Persuasion,* and it was produced as a feature film in 1956. The movie won the Golden Palm Award at the Cannes Film Festival and was nominated for an Academy Award for best picture of the year.

Some of West's early short stories explore the life of a young girl growing up on the California desert. These were collected in a volume entitled *Cress Delahanty,* published in 1953. Acclaimed as a work for teens and adults alike, *Cress Delahanty* follows the heroine of the title through the years of her adolescence, showing moments that advance her maturity. *English Journal* essayist Frederic I. Carpenter called Cress ''the typical adolescent American girl,'' portrayed with ''complete success.'' *New York Times* reviewer Frances Gaither likewise described the character as ''no guileless sprite, but a warm-blooded morsel of humanity.'' In a *Commonweal* review, T. E. Cassidy wrote: ''Anyone who knows adolescence, and especially that of young girls, will love [*Cress Delahanty*.] It is beautifully written, with the most extraordinary insight and delicacy.'' West continued to be fascinated by the transitional years between youth and womanhood; her books *The Witch Diggers, Leafy Rivers, Crimson Ramblers of the World, Farewell,* and *The State of Stony Lonesome* all contain one or more young characters who are determined to establish their identities through a positive affirmation of maturity. Flanagan noted: ''Miss West's most engaging portraits . . . are the adolescent girls, the young women reaching out for emotional and economic security, whose lives are strange juxtapositions of embarrassment, humiliation, surprise, and minor triumph.'' Addressing his comments to the adult audience, Shivers concluded: ''In Miss West's detailed sketches of pert, intelligent, and nearly always engaging little people, she attains a success enviable in any literature and in any period.''

West was always conscious of death due to her own ill health, but her involvement with the theme of mortality intensified when her sister was stricken with a painful—and fatal—form of cancer. West wrote about her sister's ordeal in two contro-versial books, the novel *A Matter of Time* and the nonfiction memoir *The Woman Said Yes: Encounters with Death and Life*. The latter volume revealed that West cooperated with her sister and helped her commit suicide when her pain became unendurable. Some reviewers objected to both works on ethical grounds; others, including Crider, saw a deeper point to the author's confession. In his assessment of *The Woman Said Yes,* Crider wrote: ''Though for many readers West's complicity in her sister's suicide will seem the center of the story, the life enhancement theme should not be ignored; and though many readers may doubt the morality of the sister's final decision for euthanasia, it is an unforgettable statement.'' Dahlstrom Farmer also observed that, true to West's belief in the individual, ''she considered both the fictional and the factual accounting [of her sister's death] to be about personal choice, not about a general recommendation.'' Dahlstrom Farmer further explained that West felt ''the most important search anyone could make is the search for self, to learn what 'feelings, beliefs, and convictions' he holds, and once having found them, to have the courage and integrity to be true to them.'' This, Dahlstrom Farmer concluded, is the abiding message of West's writings on euthanasia—the individual's perogative to act on conviction.

In 1975 West published *The Massacre at Fall Creek,* a historical novel based on the first American trial of white men for the slaying of Indians. Most critics praised the work for its sensitive delineation of complex issues such as the difference between murder and an act of war and the definition of basic humanity. *Newsweek* reviewer Peter S. Prescott called *The Massacre at Fall Creek* ''an honorable, affecting piece of work that grapples plainly with what I take to be the principal concerns of good fiction: who we are and why, how we live and what we think of our condition.'' Elizabeth Fisher offered even more favorable comments in the *New York Times Book Review,* writing that West took ''a little-known incident . . . and fashioned from it a rousing adventure story solidly informed with philosophical and moral content. . . . Working at the height of her powers, with wisdom and maturity, ofttimes a quiet irony, close observation and well-researched detail, West has written a novel of character and incident. Believable women and men are caught in a train of events that make the reader turn the pages. . . . This is a fine piece of work, effective fiction and entertainment, and more besides.''

Jessamyn West died in 1984, the same year her final novel, *The State of Stony Lonesome,* was published. By the time she died, West had documented her long life in several nonfiction memoirs, spanning all her years save her infancy. The earliest of these biographies is *To See the Dream,* the 1957 chronicle of her adventures during the filming of ''The Friendly Persuasion'' in Hollywood. The 1973 title *Hide and Seek: A Continuing Journey* contains reminiscences about her childhood in California as well as some philosophical reflections that form the basis for her fiction. *The Woman Said Yes* explores her mother's courageous decision to nurse her back to health when she was tubercular and then details her decision to aid her sister in suicide. *Double Discovery,* released in 1980, is composed of both her youthful letters and journals from her first trip abroad in 1929 and her mature reflections on the rediscovery of that long-lost youthful self. In a *Dictionary of Literary Biography Yearbook* eulogy, Jacqueline Koenig concluded that West ''accomplished things when she'd never actually known anyone else who did them. She must have been fearless. In her life and her work, she perfected a combination of intelligence, toughness, determination, compassion, talent, beauty, kindness, and love that is inspirational. She truly lived the life she really wanted.'' That life ended suddenly, in a massive stroke.

''The works of Jessamyn West provide the literary record of a remarkable career,'' Crider maintained in his essay. Indeed, West's reputation for realistic character studies and careful use of local detail has attracted the attention of regional scholars in the Midwest as well as in California. Crider noted, however, that West's ''talents as a storyteller'' have accounted for her ''large popular success.'' Shivers also observed that West wove ''some stories of incomparable beauty; and she has made richer the imagination of millions of now loyal readers throughout the world.'' Flanagan offered the most cogent praise of West's contribution to national letters in his *Indiana Magazine of History* retrospective on her work. ''Certainly few contemporary writers evince the ability to create people with the idiosyncracies, homeliness, honesty, wit and simple humanity of those in whose portraiture Jessamyn West [excelled],'' Flanagan wrote. ''A reader must be grateful for her precision, her authenticity, and her charm. She is a writer to be treasured.''

West once told *CA* that the four cornerstones of her life were ''family, words on paper (this means books and writing), the world of nature (weeds, wind, buzzards, clouds), and privacy.''

BIOGRAPHICAL/CRITICAL SOURCES:

BOOKS

Contemporary Literary Criticism, Gale, Volume 7, 1977, Volume 17, 1981.
Dictionary of Literary Biography, Volume 6: *American Novelists since World War II, Second Series,* Gale, 1980.
Dictionary of Literary Biography Yearbook 1984, Gale, 1985.
Gleasner, Diana, *Breakthrough: Women in Writing,* Dodd, 1959.
Muir, Jane, *Famous Modern American Women Writers,* Dodd, 1959.
Shivers, Alfred S., *Jessamyn West,* Twayne, 1972.
West, Jessamyn, *To See the Dream,* Harcourt, 1957.
West, Jessamyn, *Hide and Seek: A Continuing Journey,* Harcourt, 1973.
West, Jessamyn, *The Woman Said Yes: Encounters with Death and Life,* Harcourt, 1976.
West, Jessamyn, *Double Discovery: A Journey,* Harcourt, 1980.
Women Writers of the West Coast, Capra, 1983.

PERIODICALS

Atlantic, January, 1954, December, 1955, May, 1975.
Book Week, November 18, 1945.
Chicago Sun Tribune, January 14, 1951, January 3, 1954.
Chicago Tribune Book Week, November 6, 1966.
Christian Science Monitor, January 13, 1951.
Commonweal, February 16, 1951, January 15, 1954, March 8, 1957.
Critic, winter, 1976.
English Journal, September, 1957.
Explicator, December, 1964.
Great Lakes Review, winter, 1975.
Harper's, July, 1969.
Indiana Magazine of History, December, 1971.
Los Angeles Times, July 24, 1983, February 26, 1987.
Los Angeles Times Book Review, December 23, 1984.
Nation, March, 1957.
Newsweek, April 14, 1975, November 12, 1979.

New York Herald Tribune Book Review, November 25, 1945, January 14, 1951, January 3, 1954, October 16, 1955, February 10, 1957, April 24, 1960.
New York Post, October 5, 1970.
New York Times, November 25, 1945, January 14, 1951, October 17, 1963, October 27, 1966, October 5, 1967, November 2, 1980.
New York Times Book Review, January 14, 1951, January 3, 1954, October 16, 1955, February 10, 1957, April 24, 1960, October 1, 1967, May 11, 1969, January 10, 1971, May 13, 1973, April 27, 1975, May 2, 1976, December 16, 1979, October 19, 1980, January 6, 1985.
Publishers Weekly, April 28, 1969.
San Francisco Chronicle, January 15, 1951, January 10, 1954, April 28, 1960.
Saturday Review, November 17, 1945, January 9, 1954, December 3, 1955, February 23, 1957, September 21, 1957, April 23, 1960, October 7, 1967, May 10, 1969, September 26, 1980.
Time, May 24, 1976.
Times Literary Supplement, April 8, 1977.
Washington Post, January 5, 1980.
Washington Post Book World, April 1, 1973, May 18, 1975, January 6, 1985.
Weekly Book Review, November 25, 1945.
Writer's Digest, May, 1967, January, 1976.

OTHER

West's collected papers are stored at Whittier College.

OBITUARIES:

PERIODICALS

Newsweek, March 5, 1984.
New York Times, February 24, 1984.
Publishers Weekly, March 9, 1984.
Time, March 5, 1984.
Variety, February 29, 1984.*

—*Sketch by Anne Janette Johnson*

*   *   *

WHETTEN, Lawrence L.   1932-

PERSONAL: Born June 12, 1932, in Provo, Utah. *Education:* Brigham Young University, B. A., 1954, M. A., 1955; graduate study, Rutgers University, 1955-56; graduate study as exchange student to U. S. S. R., 1958; New York University, Ph. D. (with honors), 1963.

ADDRESSES: Home—Widenmayerstrasse 41, D-8000 Munich 22, West Germany.

CAREER: U. S. Air Force, 10th Tactical Reconnaisance Wing, Europe, operations intelligence officer, 1960-63, Headquarters USAF Europe, Wiesbaden, West Germany, senior political analyst, 1963-70; University of Oklahoma European Program, Munich, West Germany, guest professor of political science, 1970-71; University of Southern California Graduate Program in International Relations, Munich, resident professor and director, 1971-78, director, 1978-86; professor in overseas program, Boston University, 1987; Erich Voegelin Gastprofessur, Munich University, 1987-88. Part-time guest professor, University of Maryland European Programs, Heidelberg, various periods between 1961-73. Guest lecturer at more than one hundred and fifty universities and at Ministries of Defense and Ministries of Foreign Affairs in thiry-five countries throughout Europe, Africa, and Asia, including the Soviet Academies of Science and the Foreign Service Institute. Staff consultant, Foreign Policy Research Institute, Philadelphia, 1969-70, 1971-72; consultant to U. S. Army Russian Institut (USARI), Garmisch, 1975-77, to Stiftung fuer Wissenschaft und Politik, 1976-79, and Research and Development Associates, 1977-79.

MEMBER: International Institute for Strategic Studies, Gesellschaft fuer Auslandskunde, United States Strategic Institute, American Academy of Political and Social Science, American Association for the Advancement of Soviet Studies, Royal Institute of International Affairs (London), International Institute for Strategic Studies.

AWARDS, HONORS: Research grants from Foreign Policy Research Institute, 1969, 1970, Royal Institute for International Affairs, 1970, Ford Foundation, 1970, University of Southern California, 1975, 1976, and 1983, Stiftung fuer Wissenschaft und Politik, 1975, 1977, 1978, Thyssen Foundation, 1979-82, 1983, and Volkswagen Foundation, 1980-82.

WRITINGS:

Germany's Ostpolitik: Relations between the Federal Republic and the Warsaw Pact Countries, Oxford University Press for Royal Institute of International Affairs, 1971.
The Soviet Presence in the Eastern Mediterranean (monograph), National Strategy Information Agency, 1971.
Contemporary American Foreign Policy: Minimal Diplomacy, Defensive Strategy and Detente Management, Heath, 1974.
The Canal War: Four Power Conflict in the Middle East, MIT Press, 1974.
(Editor and contributor) *The Future of Soviet Military Power,* Crane, Russak, 1976.
Current Research in Comparative Communism: An Analysis and Bibliographic Guide to the Soviet System, Praeger, 1976.
(Editor and contributor) *Political Implications of Soviet Military Power,* Crane, Russak, 1976.
Great Power Behavior in the Arab-Israeli Conflict, International Institute for Strategic Studies, 1976.
The Political Implications of Nuclear Terrorism in Europe, Research and Development Associates, 1977.
Management of Soviet Scientific Research and Technological Development: Some Military Aspects, Stiftung Wissenschaft und Politik, 1977.
Germany East and West: Conflicts, Collaboration and Confrontation, New York University Press, 1981.
Scientific Establishment in Relation to the Soviet Military-Industrial Complex, Delft University, 1981.
New International Communism: The Foreign and Defense Policies of the Latin European Communist Parties, Lexington Books, 1982.
(Editor) *Future Courses in International Communism,* Lexington Books, 1982.
(With Sabri Sayari) *Analysis of Turkish Foreign Policy and Its Domestic Origins,* Lexington Books, 1982.
(Editor) *The Present State of Communist Internationalism,* Lexington Books, 1983.

CONTRIBUTOR

William Kinter, editor, *European Security for the 19702,* Foreign Policy Research Institute, 1971.
Robert Pfaltzgraff, editor, *Alliance Problems in the 1970s,* Foreign Policy Research Institute, 1972.

Phillip A. Richardson, editor, *American Strategy at the Crossroads,* U. S. Government Printing Office, 1973.
Robert R. King and Robert W. Dean, editors, *East European Perspectives on European Security and Cooperation,* Praeger, 1974.
Strategic Appraisals of the Middle East, Air War College, 1976.
Se-Jin Kim, editor, *International Peace and Inter-System Relations in Divided Countries,* Research Center for Peace and Unification (Seoul), 1977.
P. E. Haley and Lewis Snider, editors, *In the Lion's Ned: The Lebanese War and the Limits of Conflict and Power in the Middle East,* Syracuse University Press, 1978.
Arlene Broadhurst, editor, *The Future of NATO and the Warsaw Pact,* Westview, 1982.
Klaas G. Smedan, editor, *Bewapening,* Stichting Studium Generale aan de Technische Hogeschool te Delft, 1982.

OTHER

Contributor of numerous articles to international relations and military journals in the United States, Switzerland, England, and Argentina. Member of editorial board, *Studies in Comparative Communism* and *Afro-Asian Studies.*

WORK IN PROGRESS: Turkey's Relations between the Super Powers; The Gorbachavean Phenomena: Political, Economic and Social Reforms in the USSR and Eastern Europe.

*   *   *

WHITE, Curtis   1951-

PERSONAL: Born January 24, 1951, in Oakland, Calif.; son of Earl and Wilma White. *Education:* University of San Francisco, B.A. (cum laude), 1973; Johns Hopkins University, M.A., 1974; University of Iowa, Ph.D., 1979.

ADDRESSES: Home—317 East Chestnut, No. 3, Bloomington, Ill. 61701.

CAREER: Illinois State University, Normal, associate professor of English, 1979—.

WRITINGS:

Heretical Songs (stories), Fiction Collective, 1981.
(Editor with Mark Leyner and Thomas Glynn) *American Made* (stories), Fiction Collective, 1986.
Metaphysics in the Midwest (stories), Sun and Moon, 1988.

Contributor to magazines, including *San Francisco Quarterly, Southwest Review, Cimarron Review, Fiction International,* and *Epoch.*

WORK IN PROGRESS: A collection of stories entitled *Burb.*

*   *   *

WHITE, Edgar (B.)   1947-

PERSONAL: Born April 4, 1947, in Montserrat, British West Indies; came to United States, 1952; son of Charles and Phyllis White. *Education:* Attended City College of the City University of New York, 1964-65; New York University, B.A., 1968; additional study at Yale University, 1971-73. *Politics:* "Rastafarian." *Religion:* "Rastafarian."

ADDRESSES: Home—6 Baalbee Rd., London N.5, England. *Office*—24 Bond St., New York, N.Y. 10003.

CAREER: Musician, playwright, and novelist. Playwright-in-residence at Yale University Drama School, 1971-72, and at

New York Shakespeare Festival Public Theatre. Artistic director of acting company, Yardbird Players Co., 1974-77; member of Black Theatre Alliance.

MEMBER: Authors Guild.

AWARDS, HONORS: O'Neill playwright award; grants from Rockefeller Foundation, 1974, New York State Council on the Arts, 1975, Creative Artists Public Service, and National Endowment for the Arts.

WRITINGS:

PLAYS

"The Figures at Chartres," first produced Off-Broadway at the New York Shakespeare Festival Public Theatre, January 24, 1969.

Underground: Four Plays (contains "The Burghers of Calais" [first produced in Boston at Theatre Company of Boston, March 24, 1971; produced in Brooklyn at Billie Holiday Theatre, 1972], "Fun in Lethe; or, The Feast of Misrule," "The Mummer's Play" [first produced Off-Broadway at the New York Shakespeare Festival Public Theatre, 1965], and "The Wonderful Yeare" [first produced in New York at Other Stage Theatre, October 24, 1969]), Morrow, 1970.

"Seigismundo's Tricycle: A Dialogue of Self and Soul," first produced Off-Broadway at the New York Shakespeare Festival Public Theatre, April, 1971.

"Transformations: A Church Ritual," first produced Off-Broadway at the New York Shakespeare Festival Public Theatre, April 23, 1972.

The Crucificado: Two Plays (contains "The Crucificado" [first produced in New Haven, Conn. at Yale Repertory Theatre, January, 1972; produced in New York City at Vinnette Carroll's Urban Art Corps, June 13, 1972], and "The Life and Times of J. Walter Smintheus" [first produced Off-Broadway at Theatre DeLys, December 7, 1970]), Morrow, 1973.

"La Gente," first produced at the New York Shakespeare Festival, July 18, 1973.

"Ode to Charlie Parker," first produced in New York City at Studio Rivbea, September, 1973.

"Offering for Nightworld," first produced in Brooklyn at Brooklyn Academy of Music, 1973.

"Les Femmes Noires," first produced Off-Broadway at the New York Shakespeare Festival Public Theatre, February 21, 1974.

"The Pygmies and the Pyramid," first produced in New York City at Yardbird Theatre Co., August, 1976.

"The Defense," first produced in New York City at New Federal Theatre, November 11, 1976.

Lament for Rastafari and Other Plays (contains "Lament for Rastafari" [first produced in Brooklyn at Billie Holiday Theatre, 1971], "Trinity—The Long and Cheerful Road to Slavery" [first produced in London at Riverside Studio, February 25, 1982; produced Off-Broadway at Henry Street Playhouse, 1987], and "Like Them That Dream" [first produced in Albany, N.Y. at Market Theater, 1987; produced Off-Broadway at Theater Four, 1988]), Marion Boyars, 1983.

Nine Night and Ritual by Water, Methuen, 1984.

Redemption Song, Marion Boyars, 1985.

NOVELS

Sati, the Rastifarian, Lothrop, 1973.

Omar at Christmas, Lothrop, 1973.

Children of Night, Lothrop, 1974.

The Rising, Marion Boyars, 1988.

CONTRIBUTOR TO ANTHOLOGIES

What We Must See: Young Black Storytellers, edited by Orde Coombs, Dodd, 1971.

Black Review No. 1, edited by Mel Watkins, Morrow, 1971.

Black Short Story Anthology, edited by Woodie King, Jr., Columbia University Press, 1972.

Yardbird Lives!, edited by Ishmael Reed and Al Young, Grove, 1978.

OTHER

The Yardbird Reader, privately printed, 1973.

Also contributor to journals, including *Liberator* and *Scripts*.

SIDELIGHTS: Edgar White began his writing career at an early age. At sixteen White wrote his first drama, "The Mummer's Play." This work was produced at the Shakespeare Festival Public Theatre in 1965 when White was just eighteen. Since that time White has written numerous books and many plays. Over sixteen of these plays have been produced.

Steven Carter writes in the *Dictionary of Literary Biography* that White's work "abounds in irony, literary allusions, wit, and techniques inspired by an impressive knowledge of European, Oriental, African, and American drama. [White] has come to stress, coolly and symbolically, the importance of his black roots and the need to strike down white supremacy, even if it is only one absurdity in an absurd world."

BIOGRAPHICAL/CRITICAL SOURCES:

BOOKS

Dictionary of Literary Biography, Gale, Volume 38: *Afro-American Writers after 1955: Dramatists and Prose Writers*, 1985.

Fabre, Genevieve, *Drumbeats, Masks and Metaphors: Contemporary Afro-American Theatre*, Harvard University Press, 1983.

Harrison, Paul Carter, *The Drama of Nommo*, Grove, 1972.

PERIODICALS

New York Times, December 3, 1986, April 6, 1988.

Times (London), April 15, 1983, October 16, 1985.

* * *

WHITMAN, Cedric H(ubbell) 1916-1979

PERSONAL: Born December 1, 1916, in Providence, R.I.; died June 5, 1979, in Cambridge, Mass.; son of George Alfred and Muriel (Hubbell) Whitman; married Ruth A. Bashein, October 13, 1941 (divorced, 1958); married Anne Miller (in research and editorial work), June 7, 1959 (deceased); children: (first marriage) Rachel Claudia, Leda Miriam. *Education:* Harvard University, A.B., 1943, Ph.D., 1947.

ADDRESSES: Home—3 Shady Hill Square, Cambridge, Mass. 02138.

CAREER: Educator and author. Harvard University, Cambridge, Mass., instructor, 1947-50, assistant professor, 1950-55, associate professor, 1955-59, professor, 1959-66, Francis R. Jones Professor of Classical Greek Literature, 1966-74, Eliot Professor of Greek Literature, beginning 1974, chairman of classics department, 1960-66. Charles Beebe Martin class lecturer, Oberlin College, 1961. *Military service:* U.S. Army, 1942.

MEMBER: American Philological Association, American Academy of Arts and Sciences, Archaeological Institute of America.

AWARDS, HONORS: American Philological Association Award of Merit, 1952, for *Sophocles: A Study in Heroic Humanism;* Christian Gauss Award for best book of literary scholarship published in the United States, Phi Beta Kappa, 1958, for *Homer and the Heroic Tradition;* Guggenheim fellowship to Greece, 1961-62.

WRITINGS:

Orpheus and the Moon Craters (poems), Middlebury College Press, 1941.
Sophocles: A Study in Heroic Humanism, Harvard University Press, 1951.
Homer and the Heroic Tradition, Harvard University Press, 1958.
Aristophanes and the Comic Hero, Harvard University Press, 1964.
Abelard (narrative poem), Harvard University Press, 1965.
Euripides and the Full Circle of Myth, Harvard University Press, 1974.
(Translator) Musaeus, *Hero and Leander,* Harvard University Press, 1975.
The Heroic Paradox: Essays on Homer, Sophocles, and Aristophanes, edited and introduced by Charles Segal, Cornell University Press, 1982.
(Under name Cedric Whitman) *Chocorus and Other Poems,* introduced by Robert Fitzgerald, William Bauhan, 1983.

Also translator of *Fifteen Odes of Horace,* Stinehour.

SIDELIGHTS: Cedric H. Whitman's interests included modern Greek language and literature, an interest stimulated by trips to Greece in 1951, 1953, and a year's stay there in 1961-62.

BIOGRAPHICAL/CRITICAL SOURCES:

PERIODICALS

Times Literary Supplement, June 17, 1983.*

*   *   *

WIER, Dara 1949-

PERSONAL: Surname is pronounced like "wire"; born December 30, 1949, in New Orleans, La.; daughter of Arthur Joseph (a director of vocational rehabilitation services) and Grace (a teacher; maiden name, Barrois) Dixon; married Allen Wier (a writer and teacher), April 2, 1969 (divorced, 1983); married Michael Pettit (a poet), September 1, 1983; children: (second marriage) Emily Caitlin Pettit. *Education:* Attended Louisiana State University, 1967-70; Longwood College, B.S., 1971; Bowling Green State University, M.F.A., 1974.

ADDRESSES: Home—504 Montague Rd., Amherst, Mass. 01002. *Office*—Department of English, University of Massachusetts, Amherst, Mass. 01003.

CAREER: University of Pittsburgh, Pittsburgh, Pa., instructor in English, 1974-75; Hollins College, Hollins, Va., instructor, 1975-76, assistant professor of English, 1977-80; University of Alabama, Tuscaloosa, associate professor, 1980-85, director of graduate studies, 1980-82, director of writing program,

1983-84; University of Massachusetts, Amherst, associate professor, 1984—. Visiting poet at several universities, including University of Texas, 1983, University of Idaho, 1985. Has given poetry readings.

MEMBER: Authors Guild, Authors League of America, PEN, Poetry Society of America, Associated Writing Programs (member of board of directors, 1979-83; president, 1981-82).

AWARDS, HONORS: National Endowment for the Arts fellowship, 1980.

WRITINGS:

Blood, Hook, & Eye (poems), University of Texas Press, 1977.
The 8-Step Grapevine (poems), Carnegie-Mellon University Press, 1981.
All You Have in Common (poems), Carnegie-Mellon University Press, 1984.

Work anthologized in *A Circle Is the Perfect Line,* 1974; *Intro Six,* Doubleday, 1974; *Fiction and Poetry by Texas Women,* 1975; *Mothers and Daughters,* 1978; *Morrow Anthology of Younger American Poets,* 1984. Contributor of more than one hundred poems, stories, and reviews to literary magazines and popular journals, including *Southern Review, New Republic, North American Review,* and *American Poetry Review.*

WORK IN PROGRESS: The Book of Knowledge, a collection of poems; short stories.

SIDELIGHTS: Dara Wier writes: "Because I think the best poetry embodies mystery which evokes contemplation, I wish my own work to be acts of and instigators of meditation."

*   *   *

WILDER-SMITH, A(rthur) E(rnest) 1915-

PERSONAL: Born December 22, 1915, in Reading, England; son of Arthur William (a farmer) and Elfrida Minne (Wilder) Smith; married Beate Gottwaldt, September 17, 1950; children: Oliver, Petra, Clive, Einar. *Education:* University of Reading, B.Sc. (general), 1937, B.Sc. (chemistry; with honors), 1938, Ph.D., 1941; Geneva University, P.D., 1955, Dr. es sciences, 1964; Eidgenoessische Technische Hochschule Zuerich, D.Sc., 1964. *Politics:* None. *Religion:* Evangelical (Anglican).

ADDRESSES: Home and office—Roggern, Einigen CH 3646, Switzerland.

CAREER: Imperial Chemical Industries, Billingham, England, technical assistant on senior staff, 1940-45; University of London, British Empire Cancer Campaign, London, England, Countess of Lisburne Memorial Fellow in Cancer Research, 1945-49; Geistlich Soehne Ltd. (pharmaceuticals firm), Lucerne, Switzerland, chief of research, 1951-55; University of Geneva, Ecole de Medecine, Geneva, Switzerland, privat docent, 1956-64; University of Illinois, Medical Center, Chicago, professor of pharmacology and member of College of Nursing faculty, 1964-71; lecturer at university seminars throughout Europe and North America, 1971—. Visiting assistant professor, University of Illinois, 1957-58; visiting professor, University of Bergen, 1960-62, Hacetepe University, 1969-71. Has appeared on television shows. Consultant to North Atlantic Treaty Organization (NATO) on drug abuse, 1969-74, and to European and U.S. pharmaceutical firms.

MEMBER: Chemical Society (London), Royal Society of Chemistry (fellow), Sigma Psi, Rho Chi.

AWARDS, HONORS: Ridley research fellow, 1939-40; University of Illinois, senior class instructor of the year, 1966, 1967, 1968, and 1969, Golden Apple award, 1966, 1967, and 1969.

WRITINGS:

(With wife, Beate Wilder-Smith) *Die Ehe* (title means "Marriage"), Haenssler, 1957.

Why Does God Allow It? and Other Essays, Victory Press, 1960 (published in German as *Warum laesst Gott es zu?,* Haenssler, 1973), reprinted, C. L. P. Master Books, 1981.

Herkunft und Zukunft des Menschen: Ein kritischer Ueberblick der dem Darwinismus und Christentum zugrunde liegenden naturwissenschaftlichen und geistlichen Prinzipien, Brunnen (Basel), 1966, translation published as *Man's Origin, Man's Destiny: A Critical Survey of the Principles of Evolution and Christianity,* H. Shaw, 1968.

The Drug Users: The Psychopharmacology of Turning On, H. Shaw, 1969.

Die Erschaffung des Lebens, Haenssler, 1970, translation published as *The Creation of Life: A Cybernetic Approach to Evolution,* H. Shaw, 1970.

The Paradox of Pain, H. Shaw, 1971.

Ist das ein Gott der Liebe? (title means "Is This a God of Love?"), Haenssler, 1971.

Tauferkenntnis und Liebe zu Jesus Christus (title means "Baptismal Doctrine and Christian Devotion"), Haenssler, 1973.

Gott: Sein oder Nichtsein?, Haenssler, 1973, translation published as *God: To Be or Not To Be?,* 1975.

Grundlage zu einer neuen Biologie, Haenssler, 1974, translation published as *A Basis for a New Biology,* 1976.

Ursache und Behandlung der Drogenepidemie, Haenssler, 1974, translation published as *Causes and Cures of the Drug Epidemic,* 1974.

Ergriffen? Ergreife! (title means "Won? Then Win!"), Haenssler, 1975.

Die Demission des wissenschaftlichen Materialismus, Haenssler, 1976.

Der Mensch im Stress (title means "Man under Stress"), Haenssler, 1977.

(With B. Wilder-Smith) *Kunst und Wissenschaft der Ehe,* Haenssler, 1977.

Die Zuverlaessigkeit der Bibel und christliche Vollmacht, Schulte & Gerth (Germany), 1978.

Greift der Christ zur Waffe, Schulte & Gerth, 1978.

Die Naturwissenschaften Kennen Keine Evolution, Schwabe-Verlag, 1978, translation by Petra Wilder-Smith published as *The Natural Sciences Know Nothing of Evolution,* C.L.P. Master Books, 1981.

Der Mensch: Ein sprechender Computer, Schulte & Gerth, 1979.

Terrorismus: Das kriminelle Gehirn, Schulte & Gerth, 1980.

Wer denkt, muss glauben, Haenssler, 1980, translation published as *He Who Thinks Has to Believe,* C.L.P. Master Books, 1981.

Also author of *Christsein: Warum und Wie* and *Allversoehnung: Ausweg oder Irrweg,* both Prodromos-Serie, *The Scientific Alternative to Neo-Darwinian Theory,* T.W.F.T. (Costa Mesa, Calif.), and *Inflation,* Schwengler Verlag (Switzerland). Author of video film scripts, all produced by Evangelische Omroep, including "How the World Came to Be" (seven-part television series), 1980-81, "Drug Abuse" (film), 1981, "Dimension Theory, Black Holes, and Flatland," 1981, "Thermodynamics and Origins" (film), 1988, and "Information Theory and Origins" (film), 1988. Also author of ed-

ucational series of videocassettes for schools and universities on evolution and creation.

SIDELIGHTS: A. E. Wilder-Smith told *CA:* "In my writings it has been and still is my aim to try to correct some of the ravages of scientific materialism in the personal lives of my readers. A few years ago anything appearing under the title of science was automatically regarded as sacrosanct. In recent years this form of 'scienticism' is being corrected, though we have a long way to go.

"Some of my works are concerned with the direct consequences of scientific materialism on the 'man in the street.' A poll taken recently in some main cities in Germany asked two questions: 1) Do you believe in a personal God? and 2) If not, why? 52% of the questioned answered with 'no,' they were atheists. Of these 52% some 85% justified their 'no' with, 'Because Evolution has proved that there is no God, Chance did it all.' The clearest proof that Evolution has never delivered such a proof lies in the nature of the genetic code itself, which can be considered as containing three separate aspects: a) The reduced entropy system used as a carrier for the genetic information, b) The language or code system which rides on the reduced entropy system and which is very nearly universal for all types of biology, c) The bytes of genetic information which ride on a) and b). Neither a), b), nor c) can, according to recent developments in information theory, ever be considered for a moment to be products of chance or random molecular movements. They are all results of programming, and if programming arises by pure NeoDarwinian randomness, then all information theory becomes valueless. But all programmes always demand a programmer somewhere down the line.

"The first part of my writings deals with this aspect of modern science and the arising of creation as we know it. The second part deals with the more philosophical aspects of the problems of life. If a good Programmer programmed the elements and biology, why did He allow all the terrible things which happen daily in the world around us to happen with impunity? In fact, 'Why does God allow it?' This title has been on sale for some fifteen years in Germany, Austria, and Switzerland (German-speaking) and deals with a very live issue in these countries indeed. Europe has seen war as America has not, so that this question is by no means academic. My book dealing with this question of 'Warum laesst Gott es zu?' ('Why does God allow it?') has been sold on the German-speaking market to the tune of some one million copies in past years. It appears on the U.S. market as *Why Does God Allow It?*

"Europe, and particularly German-speaking Europe, prides itself on being philosophically minded. They boast, rightly, of their Goethes and their Immanuel Kants. Many of these philosophically proud people think that if they use their brains and thought processes they cannot be so naive as to believe in a Creator, be He good or bad or indifferent. With this audience in mind I wrote the short book entitled *Wer denkt, muss glauben* (*He Who Thinks Has to Believe*), which has in a few years sold in the German-speaking world to the tune of some 200,000 [copies]. The small book has just appeared on the U.S. market. The question is whether the American approaches his problems as does the European. I somehow think that in his heart of hearts he does."

Wilder-Smith's work has been translated into English, French, Norwegian, Finnish, Rumanian, Czechoslovakian, Dutch, Russian, Korean, and Hebrew.

WINFIELD, Arthur M.
See STRATEMEYER, Edward L.

*   *   *

WINFIELD, Edna
See STRATEMEYER, Edward L.

*   *   *

WOODS, Nat
See STRATEMEYER, Edward L.

*   *   *

WURMBRAND, Heinrich Richard   1909-

PERSONAL: Born March 24, 1909, in Bucharest, Romania; came to United States in 1966, naturalized in 1971; son of Henry (a dentist) and Amalia (Eckstein) Wurmbrand; married Sabine Oster (a writer), October 26, 1936; children: Mihai. *Education:* Attended a Protestant university in Cluj, Romania, 1956.

ADDRESSES: Home—P.O. Box 11, Glendale, Calif. 91209.

CAREER: Ordained Lutheran minister, 1956. Prior to ordination, worked as secretary to Anglican Church Mission to the Jews, beginning 1939; member, Swedish Israel Mission, Bucharest, Romania, 1941-44; member, Norwegian Israel Mission, 1944-48. Imprisoned in Romania, 1948-56, 1959-64. Teacher at seminary in Bucharest. Founder, general director, and honorary president, Jesus to the Communist World, Glendale, Calif., 1967—; founder and president, International Christian Mission to the Communist World, Geneva, Switzerland. Testified before the United States International Security Subcommittee, 1966, and the United States House Committee on Un-American Activities, 1967.

AWARDS, HONORS: D.D., Indiana Christian University, 1972.

WRITINGS:

The Wurmbrand Letters, Cross Publications, 1967, published as *Wurmbrand's Letters,* Diane Publishing, 1971.
Today's Martyred Church: Tortured for Christ, Hayfield Publishing, 1967, published as *Tortured for Christ,* Revell, 1968, Good News, 1987.
Charles Foley, editor, *Christ in the Communist Prisons,* Coward-McCann, 1968, published as *In God's Underground,* Fawcett, 1968.
(Editor) *The Underground Saints,* Revell, 1968 (published in England as *The Soviet Saints,* Hodder & Stoughton, 1968).
Why Am I a Revolutionist? (booklet), [Glendale, Calif.], c. 1969.
If That Were Christ, Would You Give Him Your Blanket? (sequel to *Tortured for Christ*), Word Publications, 1969, revised edition published in England as *The Church in Chains,* Hodder & Stoughton, 1974.
With God in Solitary Confinement, Hodder & Stoughton, 1969, Diane Books, 1979.
Stronger than Prison Walls, Fleming Revell, 1969 (published in England as *Sermons in Solitary Confinement,* Hodder & Stoughton, 1969).

If Prison Walls Could Speak, Hodder & Stoughton, 1970.
Christ on the Jewish Road, Hodder & Stoughton, 1970, Diane Books, 1973.
(Author of introduction) *Russian Christians on Trial: Eye Witness Report from a Soviet Courtroom* (booklet), Diane, 1971.
Victorious Faith (meditations), Harper, 1974 (published in England as *Little Notes which Like Each Other,* Hodder & Stoughton, 1974).
The Answer to Moscow's Bible, Hodder & Stoughton, 1975, published as *My Answer to the Moscow Atheists,* Arlington House, 1975.
Was Marx a Satanist?, Diane Books, 1975, revised and enlarged edition, 1976, 3rd edition, 1977.
Reaching toward the Heights: Book of Daily Devotions, Zondervan, 1977.
Where Christ Is Still Tortured, Diane Books, 1982, published as *Where Christ Still Suffers,* Bridge Publishing, 1984.
One Hundred Prison Meditations: Cries of Truth from behind the Iron Curtain, Bridge Publishing, 1984.
Marx and Satan, Good News, 1986.

Also author of books and sermons on cassettes. Contributor to Christian magazines in the United States and abroad.

WORK IN PROGRESS: Answer to Half a Million Letters.

SIDELIGHTS: Pastor Richard Heinrich Wurmbrand told *CA:* "I have lived under Communism, worked in the underground church in Romania under Nazism and Communism, have been in prison under both regimes (under the Communists, fourteen years). I share with the readers my experiences in the underground church and in prison. I tell the activity of the underground church today, my whole life being dedicated now to helping the persecuted Christians in Communist countries." A *Times Literary Supplement* contributor describes Wurmbrand as "a man who, lifting his soul towards God, never underrated the harsh reality of the world that had imprisoned him."

Wurmbrand was born Jewish, became an atheist, and then converted to Christianity. His subsequent underground ministry to captive Romanians and to Soviet soldiers led to his kidnapping and incarceration in 1948. In the Communist prison where he was held, as he later told the United States International Security Subcommittee, he underwent medieval torture. After Wurmbrand's 1957 release, he resumed his former work, only to be arrested again in 1959. Released five years later during a general amnesty but still in danger from the government, Wurmbrand left his country when a group of Norwegian Christians paid $10,000 to the Romanian Communists.

The Lutheran pastor's prison experiences appear in many of his books, including *Christ in the Communist Prisons.* According to a *Kirkus Reviews* contributor, "the reader is fascinated by the account of a somewhat naive faith that was strong enough to withstand years of torture, both mental and physical." Joseph Sobran states in the *National Review* that "Wurmbrand writes with a relentless passion that never falls into simple emotionalism but is always thoughtful and informative. He describes the harrowing tortures, explains his own strategy and tactics, draws Scriptural analogies, philosophizes, tells uplifting anecdotes, reminisces, and gives practical advice. His book is so engrossing because it is so nearly unbearable." And Paul Kiniery observes in *Best Sellers* that "it is an amazing story." While he finds Wurmbrand's account of prisoners in solitary confinement communicating through tapping on the walls somewhat far-fetched, Kiniery adds, "This seems to be the story of an honest man. . . . Perhaps I am merely quibbling. If only one-tenth of the book were factual it would be a devastating indictment of everything communistic.''

Pastor Wurmbrand's books have been translated into fifty-two languages.

BIOGRAPHICAL/CRITICAL SOURCES:

BOOKS

Drewer, Mary, *Richard Wurmbrand: The Man Who Came Back,* Hodder & Stoughton, 1974.
Moise, Anutza, *A Ransom for Wurmbrand,* Zondervan, 1973.

PERIODICALS

Best Sellers, February 15, 1968, May, 1977.
Kirkus Reviews, December 1, 1967.
National Review, August 15, 1986.
Times Literary Supplement, March 20, 1969.

*   *   *

WYNAR, Bohdan S(tephen)   1926-

PERSONAL: Born September 7, 1926, in Lviv, Ukraine; came to United States in 1950, naturalized in 1957; son of John O. and Euphrosina (Doryk) Wynar; married Tatianna Gajecky, August 23, 1980; children: Taras (son), Michael, Roxolana. *Education:* University of Munich, Diplom-Volkswirt, 1949, Ph.D., 1950; University of Denver, M.A. in L.S., 1958.

ADDRESSES: Home—6008 South Lakeview, Littleton, Colo. 80120. *Office*—Ukrainian Academic Press, Libraries Unlimited, Inc., P.O. Box 263, Littleton, Colo. 80120.

CAREER: Tramco Corp., Cleveland, Ohio, methods analyst and statistician, 1951-53; free-lance journalist in Cleveland, 1954-56; University of Denver, Denver, Colo., assistant to director of university libraries, 1958-59, head of Technical Services Division of university libraries, 1959-62, associate professor of library science in Graduate School of Librarianship, 1962-66; State University College at Geneseo, Geneseo, N.Y., director of Division of Library Education, 1966-69, professor of library science and dean of School of Library Science, 1967-69; Libraries Unlimited, Inc., and Ukrainian Academic Press, both Littleton, Colo., president and editor-in-chief, 1969—. President, Ukrainian Research Foundation, 1974—. Member of board of directors and executive board, ZAREVO, Inc., president of Denver branch, Ukrainian Congress Committee, 1964-66.

MEMBER: American Library Association, American Association for the Advancement of Slavic Studies, American Association of University Professors, Ukrainian Academy of Arts and Sciences, Sevcenko Societe Scientifique (Paris; secretary of economics section, 1957—), Colorado Library Association, New York Library Association.

AWARDS, HONORS: Isadore Gilbert Mudge Citation from American Library Association, 1977, for distinguished contributions to reference librarianship.

WRITINGS:

Growth of Soviet Light Industry, New Pathway (Winnipeg), 1955.
Rozvytok Ukrain'skoi Lehkoi Promyslovosty, Ukrainian Economic Commission, 1955.
Soviet Colonialism in Ukraine, La Parole (Paris), 1957.
(Editor with H. W. Axford) *Inkynabula,* Graduate School of Librarianship, University of Denver, 1958.
(Director of preparation) *Manual for Catalog Department, Division of Technical Services,* Division of Technical Services, University of Denver Library, 1961.
Syllabus for Research Methods in Librarianship, Graduate School of Librarianship, University of Denver, 1962.
Syllabus for Technical Processes in Libraries, [Denver], 1962.
Introduction to Bibliography and Reference Books: A Guide to Materials and Bibliographical Sources, Graduate School of Librarianship, University of Denver, 1963, 2nd edition, published as *Introduction to Bibliography and Reference Work: A Guide to Materials and Sources,* Colorado Bibliographic Institute, 1964, 4th edition, Libraries Unlimited, 1967.
Ukrains'ka Promyslovist', Sevcenko Societe Scientifique (Paris), 1964.
(With Earl Tannenbaum) *Introduction to Cataloging and Classification,* Colorado Bibliographic Institute, 1964, 3rd edition (sole author), Libraries Unlimited, 1967, 7th edition, 1985.
(Editor) *Dr. Malcolm Glenn Wyer: A Bio-Bibliography,* Graduate School of Librarianship, University of Denver, 1966.
Historiography of Economic Writings on Ukraine, [Munich], 1967.
Library Acquisitions: A Classified Bibliographic Guide to the Literature and Reference Tools, Libraries Unlimited, 1968, 2nd edition, 1971.
(Editor) *American Reference Books Annual,* Libraries Unlimited, 1970—.
Research Methods in Library Science: A Bibliographic Guide with Topical Outlines, Libraries Unlimited, 1971.
Reference Books in Paperback: An Annotated Guide, Libraries Unlimited, 1972, 2nd edition, 1976.
Best Reference Books, 1970-1976: Titles of Lasting Value Selected from American Reference Books Annual, Libraries Unlimited, 1976, new edition (with Susan Holte) published as *Best Reference Books, 1970-1980: Titles of Lasting Value Selected from American Reference Books Annual,* 1980, 3rd edition published as *Best Reference Books, 1980-85,* 1986.
(Editor with Jesse Shera and George Bobinski) *Dictionary of American Library Biography,* Libraries Unlimited, 1978.
(Editor) *Colorado Bibliography,* Libraries Unlimited, 1980.
(Editor) *Recommended Reference Books for Small and Medium-Sized Libraries and Media Centers,* Libraries Unlimited, 1981, 8th edition, 1988.
(Editor) *Library Science Annual,* Libraries Unlimited, 1985—.
(Editor) *ARBA Guide to Biographical Dictionaries,* Libraries Unlimited, 1986.
(Editor) *ARBA Guide to Subject Encyclopedias and Dictionaries,* Libraries Unlimited, 1986.

Also author of *Economic Colonialism in Ukraine,* 1958, *Ukrainian Economic Studies Abroad: Historical Materials and Sources,* 1965, *Major Writings on Soviet Economy,* 1966, *Economic Thought in Kievan Rus',* 1974, *Social and Economic History of Ukraine,* and *Ukraine: A Retrospective Bibliographic Guide;* co-author of *Comprehensive Bibliography of*

Cataloging and Classification, two volumes, 1973. Editor of *Preliminary Checklist of Colorado Bibliography,* 1963, *Recommended Reference Books,* 1980—, and *Biographical Reference Sources,* 1986. Translator of D. Chyzhevsky's *A History of Ukrainian Literature.* Editor, "Studies in Librarianship" series, Graduate School of Librarianship, University of Denver, 1963-66, and "Research Studies in Library Science" series, Libraries Unlimited, 1970—. Co-editor and contributor, *Encyclopedia of Ukraine* (English and Ukrainian editions), University of Toronto Press, 1955—. Contributor of over 200 articles to professional publications. Editor, *Rozbudova Derzhavy* (Ukrainian quarterly), 1953-57.

WORK IN PROGRESS: Supplements to *Dictionary of American Library Biography, Social and Economic History of Ukraine,* and *Ukraine: A Retrospective Bibliographic Guide.*

Y

YIANNOPOULOS, A(thanassios) N(ikolaos) 1928-

PERSONAL: Born March 13, 1928, in Thessaloniki, Greece; came to United States, 1953, naturalized, 1963; son of Nikolaos Athanassios and Areti T. (Alvanos) Yiannopoulos; married Mirta Valdes, May 9, 1982; children: Maria, Nicholas, Alexander. *Education:* University of Thessaloniki, LL.B., 1950; University of Chicago, M.C.L., 1953; University of California, Berkeley, LL.M., 1954, J.S.D., 1956; University of Cologne, J.D., 1961. *Religion:* Greek Orthodox.

ADDRESSES: Home—3625 St. Charles Ave., New Orleans, La. 70115. *Office*—301 Joseph Jones Hall, Tulane University, 6823 St. Charles Ave., New Orleans, La. 70118.

CAREER: Admitted to Greek bar, 1958; Louisiana State University Law School, Baton Rouge, research associate professor, 1958-62, professor of law and coordinator of Law Institute program and research, 1962-79; Tulane University Law School, New Orleans, La., W. R. Irby Professor of Law, 1979—. Visiting associate professor, Ohio State University Law School, 1959. Director in charge of revision of Louisiana Civil Code, Law Institute, 1962—. Member of board of directors, Music Society, 1961-79; president, Baton Rouge Symphony Association, 1972-73. *Military Service:* Greek Army, 1950-53; became second lieutenant.

MEMBER: Phi Alpha Delta.

AWARDS, HONORS: Order of the Phoenix.

WRITINGS:

(Co-author) *American, Greek Private International Law,* Oceana, 1957.

Negligence Clauses in Ocean Bills of Lading: Conflict of Laws and the Brussels Convention of 1924, a Comparative Study, Louisiana State University Press, 1962.

(Translator) Aubry and Rau, *Obligations,* West Publishing, 1965.

(Editor) *Civil Law in the Modern World,* Louisiana State University Press, 1965.

Civil Law Property: The Law of Things, Real Rights, and Real Actions, West Publishing, 1966, published as *Property: The Law of Things, Real Rights, Real Actions,* 1967, 2nd edition, 1980.

Personal Servitudes: Usufruct, Habitation, and Rights of Use, West Publishing, 1968, 3rd edition, 1989.

Civil Law Property Coursebook: Louisiana Legislation, Jurisprudence, and Doctrine, Claitor's, 1975, 4th edition, 1988.

Louisiana Civil Law System (course outlines), Claitor's, 1977.

(Editor) *Louisiana Civil Code,* annual editions, West Publishing, 1980—.

Predial Servitudes, West Publishing, 1983.

(Editor with James M. Klebba and Thomas Schoenbaum) *Legal and Institutional Analysis of Louisiana's Water Laws with Relationship to the Water Laws of Other States and the Federal Government,* six volumes, Louisiana Department of Transportation and Development, Office of Public Works, 1983.

(With Schoenbaum) *Admiralty and Maritime Law: Cases and Materials,* Michie Co., 1984.

Contributor of articles to legal journals and to *Encyclopaedia Britannica.* Editor in chief, *Encyclopaedia of Cooperative Law,* Volume G-Property, Max Planck Institute, Hamburg.

* * *

YOLA, Yerima
See KIRK-GREENE, Anthony (Hamilton Millard)

* * *

YOUNG, Clarence
[Collective pseudonym]

WRITINGS:

''JACK RANGER'' SERIES

Jack Ranger's Schooldays; or, The Rivals of Washington Hall, Cupples & Leon, 1907.

. . . Western Trip; or, From Boarding School to Ranch and Range, Cupples & Leon, 1908.

. . . School Victories; or, Track, Gridiron and Diamond, Cupples & Leon, 1908.

. . . Ocean Cruise; or, The Wreck of the Polly Ann, Cupples & Leon, 1909.

. . . Gun Club; or, From Schoolroom to Camp and Trail, Cupples & Leon, 1910.

. . . Treasure Box; or, The Outing of the Schoolboy Yachtsmen, Cupples & Leon, 1911.

"MOTOR BOYS" SERIES

The Motor Boys; or, Chums through Thick and Thin, Cupples & Leon, 1906.

. . . Overland; or, A Long Trip for Fun and Fortune, Cupples & Leon, 1906.

. . . in Mexico; or, The Secret of the Buried City, Cupples & Leon, 1906.

. . . across the Plains; or, The Hermit of Lost Lake, Cupples & Leon, 1907.

. . . Afloat; or, The Stirring Cruise of the Dartaway, Cupples & Leon, 1908.

. . . on the Atlantic; or, The Mystery of the Lighthouse, Cupples & Leon, 1908.

. . . in Strange Waters; or, Lost in a Floating Forest, Cupples & Leon, 1909.

. . . on the Pacific; or, The Young Derelict Hunters, Cupples & Leon, 1909.

. . . in the Clouds; or, A Trip for Fame and Fortune, Cupples & Leon, 1910.

. . . over the Rockies; or, A Mystery of the Air, Cupples & Leon, 1911.

. . . over the Ocean; or, A Marvelous Rescue in Mid-Air, Cupples & Leon, 1911.

. . . on the Wing; or, Seeking the Airship Treasure, Cupples & Leon, 1912.

. . . after a Fortune; or, The Hut on Snake Island, Cupples & Leon, 1912.

. . . on the Border; or, Sixty Nuggets of Gold, Cupples & Leon, 1913.

. . . under the Sea; or, From Airship to Submarine, Cupples & Leon, 1914.

. . . on Road and River; or, Racing to Save a Life, Cupples & Leon, 1915.

Ned, Bob and Jerry at Boxwood Hall; or, The Motor Boys as Freshmen, Cupples & Leon, 1916, reprinted as *The Motor Boys at Boxwood Hall; or, Ned, Bob and Jerry as Freshmen,* 1916.

Ned, Bob and Jerry on a Ranch; or, The Motor Boys among the Cowboys, Cupples & Leon, 1917, reprinted as *The Motor Boys on a Ranch; or, Ned, Bob and Jerry among the Cowboys,* 1917.

Ned, Bob and Jerry in the Army; or, The Motor Boys as Volunteers, Cupples & Leon, 1918, reprinted as *The Motor Boys in the Army; or, Ned, Bob and Jerry as Volunteers,* 1918.

Ned, Bob and Jerry on the Firing Line; or, The Motor Boys Fighting for Uncle Sam, Cupples & Leon, 1919, reprinted as *The Motor Boys on the Firing Line; or, Ned, Bob and Jerry Fighting for Uncle Sam,* 1919.

Ned, Bob and Jerry Bound for Home; or, The Motor Boys on the Wrecked Troopship, Cupples & Leon, 1920, reprinted as *The Motor Boys Bound for Home; or, Ned, Bob, and Jerry on the Wrecked Troopship,* 1920.

. . . on Thunder Mountain; or, The Treasure Chest of Blue Rock, Cupples & Leon, 1924.

"RACER BOYS" SERIES

The Racer Boys; or, The Mystery of the Wreck, Cupples & Leon, 1912, reprinted under pseudonym Vance Barnum as *Frank and Andy Afloat; or, The Cave on the Island,* G. Sully, 1921.

. . . at Boarding School; or, Striving for the Championship, Cupples & Leon, 1912, reprinted under pseudonym Vance

Barnum as *Frank and Andy at Boarding School; or, Rivals for Many Honors,* G. Sully, 1921.

. . . to the Rescue; or, Stirring Days in a Winter Camp, Cupples & Leon, 1912, reprinted under pseudonym Vance Barnum as *Frank and Andy in a Winter Camp; or, The Young Hunters' Strange Discovery,* G. Sully, 1921.

. . . on the Prairies; or, The Treasure of Golden Peak, Cupples & Leon, 1913.

. . . on Guard; or, The Rebellion at Riverview Hall, Cupples & Leon, 1913.

. . . Forging Ahead; or, The Rivals of the School League, Cupples & Leon, 1914.

OTHER

Also contributor of short stories to periodicals *Bright Days* and *Young Sports of America* (which became *Young People of America*), replacing earlier pseudonym Captain Young of Yale.

SIDELIGHTS: The "Motor Boys" series, published under the pseudonym Clarence Young, was the first Stratemeyer Syndicate series produced by Edward L. Stratemeyer and Howard R. Garis working together. Garis, best known as the author of the "Uncle Wiggily" stories, did much of the writing for the series while Stratemeyer provided detailed plot outlines.

Roger Garis, in *My Father Was Uncle Wiggily,* an account of his family's adventures in writing, says that the Motor Boys were enormously popular, and explains why: "To visualize a series based on travels in an auto would, today, be rather difficult. But at the time my father wrote [the Motor Boys series] the automobile, while not exactly a rarity, was nevertheless a symbol of adventure. Anyone who set forth for an extended trip in an auto had to consider the possibility of motor breakdowns, punctures, explosions, fire, accidents with other cars or with horse-drawn wagons, and in general hazards which, while present to a degree today, were then more or less expected. So the very idea of The Motor Boys—boys who were courageous enough to speed over mountains and through valleys and across dangerous terrain in one of those newfangled horseless carriages—was one to create excitement."

The "Motor Boys" were also popular for reasons other than their story lines. In an innovative publishing move, Stratemeyer and Cupples & Leon priced them at fifty cents each, considerably lower than any other hardback books on the market. The low price enabled young readers to buy the books themselves without having to turn to their parents. Leslie McFarlane, in his autobiography *Ghost of the Hardy Boys,* describes the buyers' reaction to the series: "'The Motor Boys' took off like Barney Oldfield. The magic of the internal combustion engine had a good deal to do with it, of course, but the fifty cent price actually did the trick! Over the next few years 'The Motor Boys' added nineteen new titles, went through thirty-five editions and sold five million copies before they ran out of gas." For more information see the entries in this volume for Harriet S. Adams, Howard R. Garis, Edward L. Stratemeyer, and Andrew E. Svenson.

BIOGRAPHICAL/CRITICAL SOURCES:

BOOKS

Garis, Roger, *My Father Was Uncle Wiggily,* McGraw-Hill, 1966.

Johnson, Deidre, editor and compiler, *Stratemeyer Pseudonyms and Series Books: An Annotated Checklist of Stra-*

temeyer and Stratemeyer Syndicate Publications, Greenwood Press, 1982.

McFarlane, Leslie, *Ghost of the Hardy Boys*, Two Continents, 1976.

Prager, Arthur, *Rascals at Large; or, The Clue in the Old Nostalgia*, Doubleday, 1971.

*   *   *

YOUNG, Ian (George)   1945-

PERSONAL: Born January 5, 1945, in London, England; son of George Roland and Joan (Morris) Young. *Education:* Attended Malvern Collegiate Institute, 1957-63, and University of Toronto, 1964-67. *Politics:* Libertarian.

ADDRESSES: Home and office—2483 Gerrard St. East, Scarborough, Ontario, Canada M1N 1W7.

CAREER: Writer, editor, and publisher. Director of Catalyst Press, 1969-81.

MEMBER: Hermetic Order of the Silver Sword, Mackay Society.

AWARDS, HONORS: Various Canada Council and Ontario Arts Council awards.

WRITINGS:

POEMS

White Garland: 9 Poems for Richard, Cyclops, 1969.
Year of the Quiet Sun, Anansi, 1969.
Double Exposure, New Books, 1970, new edition, Crossing Press, 1974.
(With Richard Phelan) *Cool Fire: 10 Poems by Ian Young and Richard Phelan*, Catalyst, 1970.
(With Phelan) *Lions in the Stream*, Catalyst, 1971.
Some Green Months, Catalyst, 1972.
Autumn Angels, Village Bookstore, 1973.
Yuletide Story, Catalyst, 1973.
Don, Catalyst, 1973.
Invisible Worlds, Missing Link, 1974.
Common-Or-Garden Gods, Catalyst, 1976.
Alamo, Dreadnaught Co-operative, 1976.
Whatever Turns You On in the New Year, Catalyst, 1976.
Sex Magick, Stubblejumper Press, 1986.

EDITOR

The Male Muse: A Gay Anthology, Crossing Press, 1973.
On the Line: New Gay Fiction, Crossing Press, 1981.
Overlooked and Underrated (essays), Little Caesar Press, 1982.
The Son of the Male Muse, Crossing Press, 1983.

CONTRIBUTOR TO ANTHOLOGIES

T.O. Now: The Young Toronto Poets, Anansi, 1968.
Poets of Canada 1969, Rae-Art, 1969.
Fifteen Winds, edited by Alfred W. Purdy, Ryerson, 1969.
Notes for a Native Land: A New Encounter with Canada, edited by Andy Wainwright, Oberon Press, 1969.
Printed Matter: An Anthology of Black Moss, edited by Robert Hawkins, Sun Parlor Advertising, 1970.
Storm Warning, edited by Al Purdy, McClelland & Stewart, 1971.

The Book Cellar Anthology, edited by Randall Ware, Peter Martin, 1971.
New American and Canadian Poetry, edited by John Gill, Beacon Press, 1971.
Contemporaries: Twenty-eight New American Poets, edited by Jean Malley and Hale Tokay, Viking, 1972.
Voice and Vision, edited by Jack Hodgins and William H. New, McClelland & Stewart, 1972.
The Speaking Earth, edited by John Metcalf, Van Nostrand, 1973.
Angels of the Lyre, edited by Winston Leyland, Panjandrum Books/Gay Sunshine, 1975.
Mirrors, edited by Jon Pearce, Gage, 1975.
This Is My Best, Coach House, 1976.
Orgasms of Light, edited by Leyland, Gay Sunshine, 1977.
End of the World Speshul, edited by bill bissett, blewointmentpress, 1977.
Larkspur and Lad's Love, edited by Clare MacCulloch, Brandstead Press, 1977.
Gay Source: A Catalog for Men, edited by Dennis Sanders, Coward, 1977.
The Poets of Canada, edited by John Robert Colombo, Hurtig, 1978.
Lavender Culture, edited by Karla Jay and Allen Young, Jove, 1978.
Fire, edited by Peter Carver, Peter Martin, 1978.
Tributaries, edited by Barry Dempster, Mosaic Press/Valley Editions, 1978.
To Say the Least: Canadian Poets from A to Z, edited by P. K. Page, Press Porcepic, 1979.
The New Gay Liberation Book, edited by Len Richmond and Gary Noguera, Ramparts Press, 1979.
A True Likeness: Lesbian and Gay Writing Today, edited by Felice Picano, Sea Horse Press, 1980.
Flaunting It!: A Decade of Gay Journalism from the Body Politic, edited by Ed Jackson and Stan Persky, New Star Books/Pink Triangle Press, 1982.
Structure and Meaning, Houghton, 1983.
The World of the Novel: The Stone Angel, edited by Lillian Perigoe and Beverley Copping, Prentice-Hall, 1983.
The Penguin Book of Homosexual Verse, edited by Stephen Coote, Penguin, 1983.

OTHER

(Translator) Count Jacques d'Adelsward Fersen, *Curieux d'Amour*, Timothy d'Arch Smith, 1970.
The Male Homosexual in Literature (bibliography), Scarecrow, 1975, 2nd edition, 1982.
Gay Resistance: Homosexuals in the Anti-Nazi Underground (essays), Stubblejumper Press, 1985.

Contributor to *Body Politic*, *Gay News*, *Magasin Gai* (Sweden), and other publications.

WORK IN PROGRESS: An anthology of dissident opinions on AIDS.

SIDELIGHTS: Ian Young once told *CA:* "I write what I call an objectivist poetry (that is, poetry which has as its prime reference an objective reality, an object or event in the material world). What is often referred to as 'irony' in this sort of writing is in fact an unexpected but appropriate and revealing relationship or juxtaposition of things, images, events or states of being, in a taut and meaningful way to illuminate, to bring a subtle and perhaps hidden aspect of a situation or condition, into awareness. This is why I write: to bring into consciousness, to make connections, and thus to gain better control of my reality and to help others gain better control of theirs. When someone tells me a poem of mine has brought something into focus or shown him something that he *almost* knew but couldn't quite 'put his finger on,' I know the poem has been successful for that person: it has caused that personal metamorphosis which art should create.

''Much of my writing and publishing activity has reflected my involvement in the gay liberation and anarchist movements and in ceremonial magic. For some years I have been a member of the Hermetic Order of the Silver Sword, a nondenominational brotherhood of gay men practicing ceremonial magic in the service of understanding, healing, and enlightenment. At present the Order is revising the rituals of the Order of the Golden Dawn, preserving the beauty and symbolism and updating the Victorian language. My book publishing company, Catalyst, is especially interested in the work of gay writers and Canadian writers, and we are eager to read manuscripts of all sorts, particularly fiction and poetry.''

BIOGRAPHICAL/CRITICAL SOURCES:

BOOKS

Ian Young: A Bibliography, 1962-1980, Canadian Gay Archives, 1981.

PERIODICALS

Advocate, April 25, 1973.
Books in Canada, May, 1976.
Carleton, February 6, 1970.
Christopher Street, Volume 1, number 6, 1976.
Gay Books Bulletin, fall/winter, 1982.
Gay News, September 3-16, 1982.
Gay Sunshine, January/February, 1973.
Margins, March, 1976.
Quill and Quire, July, 1976.
Saturday Night, February, 1970.
Vancouver Province, February 7, 1969.
Varsity, February 6, 1970.

Z

ZACHARIAS, Lee
See ZACHARIAS, Lela Ann

* * *

ZACHARIAS, Lela Ann 1944-
(Lee Zacharias)

PERSONAL: Born December 1, 1944, in Chicago, Ill; daughter of Joseph Ryan (an oil worker) and Dorothine (a cafeteria manager; maiden name, Hurley) Ives; married Richard Kirk Zacharias, October 29, 1966 (divorced, 1976); married Michael George Gaspeny, August 15, 1982; children: (second marriage) Max Nathan. *Education:* Indiana University, A.B., 1966; Hollins College, M.A., 1973; University of Arkansas, M.F.A., 1975.

ADDRESSES: Home—Greensboro, N.C. *Office*—Department of English, University of North Carolina, Greensboro, N.C. 27412. *Agent*—Rhoda Weyr Agency, 216 Vance St., Chapel Hill, N.C. 27514.

CAREER: Indiana University, Research Center of Language Sciences, Bloomington, assistant director of publications, 1967-70; University of North Carolina, Greensboro, lecturer, 1975-76, assistant professor, 1976-81, associate professor of English, 1981—, coordinator of writing program, 1977—. Visiting lecturer, Princeton University, 1980-81. Has taught photography to children.

MEMBER: Poets and Writers, PEN, Associated Writing Programs (vice-president, 1980-81; president, 1981-82; historian, 1982-83).

AWARDS, HONORS: National Endowment for the Arts fellowship, 1980; Sir Walter Raleigh Award, State of North Carolina, 1982, for *Lessons;* North Carolina Arts Council fellowship, 1985; recipient of writing and photography awards from Virginia Commonwealth University, University of Arkansas, Indiana University, and Virginia Museum.

WRITINGS—Under name Lee Zacharias:

Helping Muriel Make It through the Night (short stories), Louisiana State University Press, 1976.
Lessons (novel), Houghton, 1981.

Contributor to academic journals, literary journals, and popular magazines, including *Redbook, Kansas Quarterly,* and *New England Review.* Editor of *Greensboro Review,* 1977—.

WORK IN PROGRESS: Infrared, a novel.

SIDELIGHTS: Lee Zacharias's first novel, *Lessons,* "is a lively, often wise, novel that goes down easy but reaches for and sometimes achieves a more substantial seriousness," remarks Rosellen Brown in the *Chicago Tribune Book World.* The novel follows the story of Jane Hurdle, a young woman whose career as a professional musician is interrupted by various personal troubles, including a difficult marriage to a man twenty-two years her senior. "To think of this book as merely another tale of a woman's search for self-discovery, however, would be a mistake," asserts Susan Bolotin in the *New York Times Book Review.* "It has more in common with any one of the hundreds of picaresque novels about young men who long to sail the sea or make their fortunes in Londontown." "Zacharias preserves and clarifies the past through the voice of her heroine," notes Meredith Marsh in the *New Republic,* "... and it is a remarkable voice—funny, insightful, able to range comfortably from a teenager's easy slang to an adult's rhapsody and elegy." As the author relates in a *Library Journal* interview, "I invented a student. And made the wonderful mistake of giving her my voice." *Lessons,* Zacharias adds, "was the discovery every writer makes when he finds an image he can marry with his voice."

Although they comment favorably on the novel's style and voice, some critics find Jane's predicament unconvincing. Although Brown calls the portrait of Jane's husband, Ben, "one of the book's triumphs," she still finds it "very difficult to believe [Jane would] have stayed married to this petty tyrant for 14 years." The critic adds that Jane's "motivation is never sufficiently colored by self-hate to account for so long a trance at the hands of a troll." This idea "that Jane has married Ben to punish herself ... is difficult to dramatize at length," remarks Marsh; the result is that "too often Jane stops seeing the victim of her own warring strengths and needs and instead dwindles into the victim of poor plump lascivious Ben." This flaw, according to Bolotin, makes Jane seem "in the end, a cold fish. In literature, as in life, it is possible to like a difficult character, as long as she accepts her faults as her own." But the critic thinks Jane falls short in this respect, for "one suspects that all her mental and verbal self-criticism is only rationalization.'' And *Washington Post Book World* editor Brigitte Weeks similarly observes that Jane ''defies sympathy [and] seems intent on self-defeat.''

Despite this criticism, Weeks calls the novel an ''ambitious work of fiction,'' explaining that ''the handling of time in *Lessons* is sophisticated and successful. We follow Jane intimately for two decades from the high school band to the promise of Philharmonic.'' The critic adds that ''the story builds in apparently random sequence but every flashback or memory fills in a part of the puzzle.'' ''Though written with an intentional jumpiness, the book is constructed with a technical tautness that invites analysis,'' states Bolotin. ''Divided into one short prologue and four parts, it is symphonic in structure.'' The critic explains that ''this sounds contrived, but except for a few passages in which Miss Zacharias gets carried away, . . . it works.'' Marsh concludes that despite ''problems of focus,'' *Lessons* is ''a book that is always a great pleasure to read and is often superb. Jane's wry view of her stepdaughter is amusing, her flirtations are vivid, her tender relationship with her brother, his death, and her own long depression are very moving.'' ''Limitations notwithstanding,'' maintains Brown, ''[this is] a very well-written, large-hearted, often delightful novel.'' Although Zacharias has been noted for her short fiction, adds the critic, *Lessons* ''bodes well for her future as a novelist.''

Zacharias told *CA:* ''I remain interested in photography, but it plays almost no role in my writing. I find fiction a far more flexible compromise with reality, though the 90-second process of watching a print come up in the developer is infinitely more exciting than the half-decade it takes for a novel to get born. Carrying the print out to good light and rereading one's words can be equally rewarding, though all too often they are equally disappointing. Writing is hard work.''

BIOGRAPHICAL/CRITICAL SOURCES:

PERIODICALS

Chicago Tribune Book World, November 22, 1981.
Library Journal, June 15, 1981.
Listener, July 15, 1982.
New Republic, October 21, 1981.
New York Times Book Review, October 18, 1981.
Times Literary Supplement, July 23, 1982.
Washington Post Book World, September 27, 1981.

*   *   *

ZIMMER, Paul J.   1934-

PERSONAL: Born September 18, 1934, in Canton, Ohio; son of Jerome F. (a shoe salesman) and Louise (Surmont) Zimmer; married Suzanne Koklauner, April 4, 1959; children: Erik Jerome, Justine Mary. *Education:* Attended Kent State University, 1952-53, 1956-59, B.A., 1968. *Politics:* Democrat. *Religion:* None.

ADDRESSES: Home—204 Lexington Ave., Iowa City, Iowa 52242. *Office*—University of Iowa Press, 214 Graphic Services Building, Iowa City, Iowa 52242.

CAREER: Macy's Department Store, San Francisco, Calif., manager of book departments, 1961-63; San Francisco News Co., San Francisco, manager, 1963-64; University of California, Los Angeles, manager of bookstore, 1964-66; University of Pittsburgh Press, Pittsburgh, Pa., assistant director, 1967-78; University of Georgia Press, Athens, director, 1978-84; University of Iowa Press, Iowa City, director, 1984—. Poet in residence, Chico State College (now California State University, Chico), 1970. *Military service:* U.S. Army, 1954-55.

AWARDS, HONORS: Borestone Mountain Award, 1971; National Endowment for the Arts fellowship, 1974-75, and 1982-83; Helen Bullis Memorial Award, *Poetry Northwest,* 1975; Pushcart Prize, 1977, 1981; American Academy and Institute of Arts and Letters Award in Literature, 1985; National Poetry Series selection, 1988.

WRITINGS:

POETRY

A Seed on the Wind, privately printed, 1960.
The Ribs of Death, October House, 1967.
The Republic of Many Voices, October House, 1969.
(Contributor) William Heyen, editor, *American Poets in 1976,* Bobbs-Merrill, 1976.
The Zimmer Poems, Dryad, 1976.
With Wanda: Town and Country Poems, Dryad, 1980.
The Ancient Wars, Slow Loris Press, 1981.
Earthbound Zimmer, Chowder Press, 1983.
Family Reunion: Selected and New Poems, University of Pittsburgh Press, 1983.
The American Zimmer, Nightowl Press, 1984.
The Great Bird of Love, University of Illinois Press, 1989.

Editor, ''Pitt Poetry'' series, 1967-78.

WORK IN PROGRESS: A book of poems; a short novel.

SIDELIGHTS: Poet Paul J. Zimmer ''is forever creating characters to inhabit the home of his poetry,'' notes Thomas Goldstein in a *Dictionary of Literary Biography* essay. Much of Zimmer's work is peopled with historical as well as fictional characters; in collections such as *The Zimmer Poems,* a semiautobiographical character ''Zimmer'' is the primary persona. The poet frequently uses an anecdotal approach in his work; as Goldstein comments, ''The reader watches Zimmer's characters struggle with their personal problems and dilemmas real or imagined, and experiences a certain affection for them whether he laughs or cries.''

BIOGRAPHICAL/CRITICAL SOURCES:

BOOKS

Dictionary of Literary Biography, Volume 5: *American Poets since World War II,* Gale 1980.

*   *   *

ZIMMY
See STRATEMEYER, Edward L.

Indexing note: All *Contemporary Authors New Revision Series* entries are indexed in the *Contemporary Authors* cumulative index, which is bound into the back of even-numbered *Contemporary Authors* original volumes (blue and black cover with orange bands) and available separately as an offprint.